THE
JAPANESE
EXPERIENCE

THE
JAPANESE
EXPERIENCE

A Short History of Japan

W.G. Beasley

University of California Press

BERKELEY   LOS ANGELES   LONDON

University of California Press
Berkeley and Los Angeles, California

University of California Press, Ltd.
London, England

Published by arrangement with Weidenfeld & Nicolson

© 1999 W.G. Beasley

ISBN 0-520-22050-1

Filmset by Selwood Systems, Midsomer Norton
Printed in Great Britain by
Butler & Tanner Ltd
Frome and London

9 8 7 6 5 4 3 2 1

CONTENTS

List of maps ix
List of illustrations xi
Japanese words, names and dates xiii
Introduction: Patterns and Periods xv

1 *Origins* 1
   Myths 2
   Archaeology 7
   The Yamato state 11
   Primitive religion 16

2 *The Making of a Monarchy* 19
   Chinese-style government 20
   Capital cities 30
   The Fujiwara regents 34

3 *Buddhism and Chinese Culture* 41
   Buddhism and Shinto 42
   Tribute missions and Chinese learning 48
   Literature, art and music 54

4 *The Ebbing of the Chinese Tide* 61
   Public land, private land 62
   The rise of a warrior class after 800 66
   Heian culture 69

5 *Japanese Feudalism* 78
   The Kamakura Bakufu (1185–1333) 80
   Feudalism in the Muromachi period (1336–1460) 89

6 *Medieval Culture 1200–1450* *98*

Buddhism   100
Prose literature and drama   104
Chinese influence on the arts   110

7 *The Unifiers* *116*

Warfare and warlords (1460–1560)   117
Nobunaga and Hideyoshi (1560–1598)   122
The Tokugawa settlement (1600–1650)   128

8 *Relations with Asia and Europe 1500–1700* *134*

The China trade   135
Korea and Ryukyu   141
Christianity and seclusion   147

9 *Edo Society* *152*

The ruling class   153
The village and the town   161

10 *Edo Culture* *171*

Chinese thought, Japanese thought   172
Literature and the arts   178

11 *The Coming of the West 1840–1873* *188*

Unequal treaties   189
Nationalism and politics   196
Study of the West   203

12 *The Modern State* *210*

Political institutions   211
Social change   219
Tradition and modernity   225

13 *Fifty Years of Foreign Wars 1894–1945* *230*

Industry and empire   231
The struggle for Greater East Asia   241

Contents

14 *Postwar Japan*   *251*

Glossary   *269*
Bibliography   *275*
Index   *287*

MAPS

1 Japan and the Asian mainland in early periods   282
2 Western Japan: ancient and medieval   283
3 Japan: from feudal to modern   284
4 Japan and East Asia: 1840–1945   285

ILLUSTRATIONS

Between pages 110 and 111

Statue of Maitreya Buddha (*Kōryūji Temple, Kyoto*)

Buddhist temple of Hōryūji (*Ronald Sautebin, Fribourg*)

A memorial statue of Ganjin (*Tōshō-daiji Temple, Nara/Shogakukan Inc., Tokyo*)

The Phoenix Pavilion of the Byōdōin at Uji (*author's photo*)

A scene from the Tale of Genji picture-scroll (*Tokugawa Museum, Nagoya*)

The Heiji incident: the emperor escapes from the palace (*Tokyo National Museum*)

Portrait of Minamoto Yoritomo (*Jingo-ji Temple, Kyoto*)

The itinerant preacher Kūya Shōnin (*Rokuharamitsu-ji Temple, Kyoto*)

Feudal lord on horseback (*Kyoto National Museum*)

A Nō mask (*Tokyo National Museum*)

A memorial statue of Toyotomi Hideyoshi (*Osaka City*)

Himeji Castle (*author's photo*)

Between pages 206 and 207

A daimyo with his escort enters the outskirts of Edo (*Historiographical Institute, Tokyo University*)

The Shogun's apartments, Nijō Castle (*Nijō Castle, Kyoto*)

Kabuki theatre (*British Museum/Bridgeman Art Library*)

Geisha writing letters (*National Gallery, Prague/Werner Forman Archive*)

Sumō wrestlers, nineteenth century (*author's collection*)

A British squadron in Nagasaki harbour, 1855 (*author's collection*)

Japanese soldiers leave for Manchuria, 1936 (*Weidenfeld Archives*)

Japanese sign the surrender agreement, 1945 (*Weidenfeld Archives*)

Prewar education: homage to the emperor (*Weidenfeld Archives*)
Postwar education: cramming schools (*Camera Press*)
Economic summit in Tokyo, 1986 (*Camera Press*)
The Asakusa district of Tokyo (*Hulton Getty*)

JAPANESE WORDS, NAMES
AND DATES

Both Chinese and Japanese words are written by means of ideo-graphs, which can be transcribed into western alphabets in several different ways. Those chosen for use in this book are the ones most often found in works about Japanese history published in English. Macrons to indicate long vowel sounds are given in personal names and in Japanese words printed in italics, but not in place names (e.g. Tokyo is used, not Tōkyō) or Japanese words that are usually anglicised (e.g. Shogun, not Shōgun). Japanese personal names appear in the traditional order, i.e. family name, followed by given name.

Japan adopted the Chinese lunar calendar in the seventh century and used it, subject to some variation over time, until the western (Gregorian) calendar replaced it in 1873. Dates in this book are given throughout in the Gregorian form, wherever specific information exists to make this possible. Similarly, centuries are numbered in accordance with western practice, since Japan did not possess a serial chronology until modern times.

Introduction:
Patterns and Periods

The history of Japan, like that of China, has a high degree of
continuity from ancient times to the twentieth century. The
Japanese have always occupied part or all of the same territory, its
borders defined by the sea. They have spoken and written a
common language, once it had taken firm shape in about the
tenth century. Their population has been largely homogenous,
little touched by immigration except in very early periods. Awareness of this has given them a sense of being racially distinct. 'We
Japanese', *ware-ware Nihonjin*, is a phrase that constantly recurs.

Yet Japanese society and culture have changed more through
time than these statements might seem to imply. At both the
beginning and the end of the story – so far as the end can yet be
told – developments within Japan have been greatly influenced
by ideas and institutions, art and literature, imported from elsewhere. To talk of 'Japanese civilisation', therefore, begs a question.
What is it about the history of Japan that is specifically Japanese,
apart from the land and the people? It is hoped that this book
might suggest some answers.

When the Christian era began in Europe, the Japanese islands
were a remote and little-known part of China's 'barbarian' periphery. They acquired the rudiments of an organised state quite
late in time – somewhere between the fall of the Han in China

(AD 220) and the sack of Rome by the Goths (AD 410) – and long remained thereafter a fairly primitive kingdom, ruled by ancestors, or so it is claimed, of the present imperial line. It was the arrival of Buddhism from Korea in the sixth and seventh centuries, bringing with it a wider knowledge of things Chinese, that raised them to a higher level of development. Under Buddhist tutelage, Japan became substantially Chinese, not only in religion, but also in political institutions, writing system and the lifestyle of the ruling class. The experience left a mark that was to prove indelible.

Chineseness was nevertheless confined to an urban, largely aristocratic segment of the population. Outside the capital its influence was shallow; and eventually the political and social structures that supported it began to crumble. There was no such upheaval, caused by attack from outside, as prompted the transition in Europe from ancient to medieval, but the results of decay were similar, if slower. By the eleventh century, Japan was sufficiently 'ungoverned' to begin to move from a nominally centralised and aristocratic-bureacratic state towards one that was increasingly feudal. By 1450 the process was complete: Japan was a feudal monarchy, much as France and England were in the Middle Ages. There were two main differences. One was that feudal Japan was Buddhist, not Christian. The other was that the country had two rulers, both of whom held hereditary office: an emperor of ancient lineage, who possessed influence rather than power; and a feudal overlord, the Shogun, claiming kingly privilege that rested on military force.

It is at this point that parallels between Japan and China break down. Chinese emperors in and after the fourteenth century were autocrats, served by appointed ministers who acknowledged Confucian thought as the proper guide for political behaviour. Feudal Japan, by contrast, remained predominantly Buddhist and governed by the equivalent of barons. The latter, it is true, like the older court aristocracy, turned to Chinese culture for both prestige and pleasure, but it was not until society had endured another long spell of civil war that they looked to China again for political example. Even then they did so only in limited degree.

The structure that eventually emerged under the Tokugawa (1600–1868) did not closely correspond to anything found in Europe or China. The emperor remained powerless. The Shogun grew in authority, using his personal vassals as bureaucrats and exercising tighter control over feudal lords. Neo-Confucian ideology became orthodox within the ruling class, much as in China, but without detracting from the claims of vassalage and birth as determinants of status. Chinese culture enjoyed a renaissance. Alongside it, however, there was a popular culture, patronised by 'commoners', that owed more to Japanese urban taste and urban wealth than it did to China or the traditions of the country's upper class. This was a complex pattern, not quite feudal, not quite Chinese, hinting at developments that in Europe could be labelled 'early modern', but never fully satisfying any definition of it.

Such was the Japan into which an expanding, capitalist West intruded in the middle of the nineteenth century. For China the same threat came earlier and in more aggressive guise. Chinese resistance to it, which was both traditionalist and ineffective, began a period of a hundred years of Chinese weakness and political disunity, ending in a revolution that swept away the heritage of the past. Japan's response took a different path. This was in part because her ruling class was a military one, which had methods and priorities that were not the same as those of China's mandarins. It was partly, perhaps, because her society had an institutional and cultural ambiguity that made for great flexibility. Whatever the explanation, Japan's revolution came more rapidly and served different ends. The Meiji Restoration, as it is called, not only overthrew the Tokugawa, as China's revolutionaries overthrew the Manchus nearly fifty years later, but also brought to power a group of men who were dedicated to the aim of expanding the country's wealth and strength. What they meant by this was to combine government and military structures in the western manner with modern industry, traditional ideology and a minimum of social change. It proved to be a durable formula.

In the short term, the policy brought notable success. Japan

became a world power, an exporter of industrial products on a considerable scale, a name to be conjured with. A bid for empire in the twentieth century proved a step too far and ended in disaster, bringing a change of course; but by then the foundation of modern skills and social cohesion had been firmly laid, with the result that the years after 1945 saw an 'economic miracle'. Japan became wealthy, both as a country and as a place to live.

So great a transformation as that which occurred after 1868 has inevitably carried with it many unintended results. In matters that might be called 'consumer choice', they have left Japan more 'western' now than it ever was Chinese. One difference, indeed, between the ancient and the modern is that what was alien in the distant past was for the few, what is alien in the present is almost universal. Only feudalism, which dominates the centuries in between, seems in retrospect – not in all respects justifiably – to be thoroughly Japanese. Perhaps that is why its influence lingers.

CHAPTER I

Origins

The Japanese islands – four major ones, plus several hundred smaller ones round their coasts – are part of a series of island chains looped down the east coast of Asia from Kamchatka in the north to the Philippines in the south. They approach the mainland closely at two points. The straits in the north, where access to the continent is through Hokkaido and Sakhalin, has not had a prominent place in Japanese history, at least until modern times. By contrast, the Tsushima Straits, which separate western Japan from the southern coast of Korea, has been the principal route, commercial, cultural and military, between Japan and the older centres of civilisation on the mainland. These straits are about 100 miles wide. Since two islands, Tsushima and Iki, serve as staging points, it was possible for even quite primitive craft to effect a crossing, but the length of the voyage, plus frequent bad weather, made the passage difficult. The Mongols discovered this to their cost when they tried to invade Japan in 1274 and 1281.

The sea was less of a barrier to foreign culture than to foreign armies. From the seventh century onwards, if not earlier, the religion and philosophy, the art and literature, the economic skills and governmental institutions of China found their way to Japan, at first via Korea and the Tsushima Straits, then more directly across the East China Sea. In much the same manner, though

twelve centuries later, the ideas, institutions and technology of Europe and America began to arrive on a comparable scale, this time by the 'ocean' route. These are central themes in Japanese history.

Because cultural imports were not preceded or accompanied by political control, they established themselves in Japan by virtue of their utility or prestige. This enabled other cultural elements, themselves indigenous, to retain a significant role in Japanese life. Shinto, for example, which was the country's primitive religion, served to promote the myth of imperial divine descent at one end of the time-span and helped shape modern nationalism at the other; feudalism, much akin to Europe's, but in origin and character entirely Japanese, dominated the long middle period of Japanese history, both socially and politically; while the Japanese language, for all that it was written from earliest times in the Chinese script, survived as the preferred mode of expression for popular literature, whether poetry or prose. Japanese, not Chinese, was always the language of romance, humour, tales of war.

Myths

Some aspects of native culture go back to lifetimes well before the written record, which makes their origins difficult to disentangle or explain. Writing is said to have been introduced to Japan by a scholar from Korea in AD 405, but the first accounts of the country's earliest history and legends, compiled in Japan, were set down very much later than that. They appear in two chronicles dating from the eighth century, the *Kojiki*, completed in 712, and the *Nihon Shoki*, also known as the *Nihongi*, completed in 720. Both belong to a period when Chinese ideas were taking hold among Japan's élite; both use the Chinese script (indeed, the *Nihon Shoki* is written entirely in Chinese); and both look to Chinese models of historical writing for their methods of dating and compilation. They sometimes transpose selected incidents

and speeches, plagiarised from Chinese texts, into a Japanese context. When reading them, therefore, it is hard at times to distinguish Japanese fact from Chinese style.

It is remarkable in these circumstances that what the chronicles have to say about national origins has come to be regarded as quintessentially Japanese. After all, there is evidence of Chinese concepts in the way in which the supposedly 'Japanese' heavenly deities are described; some of the legends are similar to those of other parts of Asia, notably Korea and Manchuria; and there are distortions of fact and chronology, designed to glorify Japan's imperial line for the sake of reinforcing the authority of the rulers under whom the books were written. Despite all this, the narrative, as the chronicles set it down, has in substance been an object of respect for many millions of Japanese almost ever since. It is a part of the national heritage. For this reason, a summary of it is a necessary starting-point for the discussion of Japanese history.

The *Kojiki* begins, in the words of Chamberlain's translation of 1882, 'when chaos had begun to condense, but force and form were not yet manifest'. Thereafter, as the High Plain of Heaven separated out from the mass, deities emerged, from whom were descended Izanagi and Izanami, male and female procreators of the islands of Japan. They were also the progenitors of a further generation of gods and goddesses, among whom were the sun-goddess Amaterasu, the moon-god Tsukiyomi (who plays very little part in the rest of the story) and the storm-god Susa-no-o. In the most famous version – the chronicles provide alternative 'traditions' at a number of points – we are told that Izanami, while giving birth to the fire-god, dies of her burns. Greatly distraught, Izanagi follows her to the Nether World and insists on seeing her, only to discover that she is already in a state of putrefaction. Since this makes her a source of contamination and therefore taboo, he takes to flight, seeking to purify himself by lustration; and as he bathes himself, Amaterasu is born from his left eye, Tsukiyomi from his right eye, Susa-no-o from his nose (so observing the left-right-centre order of precedence that Japan derived from China).

Of these three deities, Amaterasu is sent to rule the High Plain

3

of Heaven, assisted by Tsukiyomi, while Susa-no-o, a fierce and cruel figure, is dispatched to the Nether World. Before going, however, his visits his sister. They quarrel. Thereupon Susa-no-o engages in a number of outrageous acts, breaking down the barriers between the rice-fields, and flaying a piebald colt, which he casts into the hall where his sister is weaving. The incident, clearly an attack on the norms of 'civilisation', as transmitted to Japan from the Asian mainland, gives deep offence. Amaterasu withdraws into a cave, leaving the world in darkness. The 'eighty myriads of gods' thereupon seek to lure her back, setting out offerings of jewels (comma-shaped stones called *magatama*) and a large bronze mirror, in which she can see herself. One of them also performs a dance outside her cave. When these attractions succeed in drawing her out, the other gods restrain her from concealing herself again.

Having so nearly deprived the world of light by his behaviour, Susa-no-o is punished. He is fined, his hair is plucked out – his toenails and fingernails, too, in one version – and he is once more ordered to the Nether World. He takes his time about the journey. First he goes to southern Korea. Then he crosses to the coast of Japan again at Izumo, where he kills a man-eating serpent, in the tail of which he finds a sword, called Kusanagi, 'the grass-cutter'. He presents it to his sister, presumably as a symbol of submission and atonement. Together with the jewels and the mirror used to lure Amaterasu from the cave, it becomes one of the three imperial regalia of Japan.

In the course of these events, several children are born to Amaterasu. One of them becomes the father to a son, Ninigi, whom Amaterasu – or the boy's grandfather, if one prefers an alternative text, more in keeping with Japan's subsequent social history – decides to send down as ruler to Japan. Preceded by envoys, whose task it was to pacify or subdue the evil deities living there, including descendants of Susa-no-o, Ninigi eventually descends 'with an awful path-cleaving ... through the eightfold clouds of Heaven' to Mount Takachiho, in what was later to be the 'sun-facing' province of Hyuga in southern Kyushu. He takes

with him the jewels, the mirror and the sword as evidence of the authority with which he has been invested.

Ninigi is held to be the first divine ruler of Japan. In the fullness of time his descendant, Jimmu, became the first human ruler. Setting out from Hyuga to conquer his kingdom, we are told, Jimmu chose to go by ship up the east coast of Kyushu to the north of the island, then eastward through the Inland Sea, a voyage of many months, during which he made several lengthy pauses along the way. At the end of it, his first attempt to land in central Japan was repulsed by the local inhabitants. Jimmu, therefore, recognising – belatedly, it must be said – that it was wrong for a descendant of the sun-goddess to advance against the rising sun, led his men round the coast of the Ise peninsula to launch a fresh attack from the opposite direction. This time he was successful. Fighting his way into the Yamato plain to the south of Nara, he built a palace there; and on the eleventh day of the second lunar month of the following year, which corresponds to 660 BC in the western calendar, he assumed the imperial dignity.

If such a series of events occurred at all, which is doubtful, it could not have been as early as the chronicles imply. The nature of the Japanese record itself suggests as much. The date chosen by the scribes for Jimmu's enthronement was an auspicious one by Chinese standards, but it had the disadvantage of leaving the historian with many more years to fill than he had facts to fill them with before arriving at better-authenticated periods. As a result, the next eight reigns of the dynasty, as officially recorded, contain little more than genealogical information, padded out chronologically to meet editorial needs. Jimmu's reign is said to have lasted eighty years, that of the sixth emperor over a hundred. Reigns of sixty years or more are common. This seems improbable. In fact, modern scholars tend to dismiss as legendary all emperors before the tenth, Sujin, who can be dated to the second half of the third century AD. Even he remains too shadowy a figure to be wholly convincing as the founder of a dynasty, so a case is sometimes made for starting 'history' with the fifteenth emperor, Ōjin, a little more than a century later.

Some light is thrown on these earliest periods by what is said about Japan in the Chinese dynastic histories, but since it takes the form of intermittent travellers' tales, it does not help us much in making out a chronology. The most useful Chinese account is found in the *Wei chih*, part of a history compiled sometime before AD 297. It describes the arrival in the middle years of that century of envoys from the rulers of Wo (Japanese: Wa), which is usually taken to be a state in Kyushu. The Chinese court sent a return mission to Wo in AD 240, bearing gifts of swords and mirrors, and its members came back with information about the Japanese which is duly recorded. It is entirely believable: that they cultivated grains, including rice, as well as the mulberry; that they could spin and weave, but did not keep horses, oxen or sheep; that they were fond of liquor; that they showed respect for persons of importance by squatting or kneeling at the roadside with both hands on the ground. The text also described the use by Japanese of tattoos on faces and painted designs on bodies to signify rank, an assertion borne out by archaeological findings.

On politics the Chinese record, through explicit, is less convincing. The evidence suggests that the Chinese envoys did not travel beyond the coastal fringe of northern Kyushu, which left them to rely on hearsay for what they said about other parts of Japan. Their statement that Kyushu was divided into small kingdoms under local rulers is probably to be trusted. On the other hand, they were going well beyond what they had seen in person when they reported that these states were subject in some unspecified manner to a more distant land, Yamatai, ruled by a queen. It has always been taken for granted that Chinese Yamatai equals Japanese Yamato. It does not necessarily follow, however, that the 'queen's country' was the kingdom that Jimmu is said to have founded in the Nara plain, historically known as the province of Yamato. The argument that it does is strengthened by the *Wei chih*'s reference to a great burial mound, raised over the queen's tomb when she died. Such burial mounds (*kofun*) did appear in the Nara region from about the mid third century. Against that, the instructions given in the *Wei chih* for reaching Yamatai from

Kyushu – they are specified in compass directions and days of travel – would, if obeyed exactly, bring the traveller to a point in the Pacific Ocean off the southeast coast of Kyushu. Some Japanese scholars, accepting the compass bearings, but using a lower estimate for the distance travelled in a single day, have preferred to believe that Yamatai was somewhere in Kyushu. Recent archaeological finds have hinted at a site no further away than Saga prefecture. Others, accepting longer distances, but adjusting the directions, place Yamatai in the Nara plain. The case remains unproven. We cannot be sure that such a state existed there at that time.

Archaeology

Archaeology does little to solve such problems of political chronology. The Japanese were not given to erecting monuments, bearing inscriptions that named and dated their rulers. Those inscriptions that have been found are on portable articles, like swords, usually so damaged by exposure as to be illegible, or nearly so. It is only a partial compensation that the study of objects from excavated sites, especially during the past fifty years, together with improvements in the scientific means of dating them, has enabled scholars to put together a persuasive account of the phases in the prehistoric society of Japan.

The earliest evidence of human settlement appears to date from 30,000 years ago or more. In successive ice ages, the fall in sea levels led for a time to the creation of land bridges between Japan and the Asian continent: that is, to what is now Manchuria in the north, to the Korean peninsula in the west, and down the Ryukyu chain towards central and southern China. Not very much is known about the peoples who entered by these routes, but the variety of their points of departure helps to account for the existence of several different strains of primitive culture in Japan. Starting about 10,000 BC, one of these advanced to the stage of

producing a rope-pattern pottery, known as Jōmon. The people who made it used tools and weapons of stone, and lived by hunting, fishing and gathering shellfish; but in later millenniums they began to supplement their diet by the addition of plants and nuts, which some scholars believe were cultivated. There are even signs of rice culture – though not in paddy fields – by the first millennium BC, as well as the grouping of pit-dwellings into small communities.

The next major change occurred about 300 BC with the emergence in southwest Japan of what is called Yayoi culture, named after an excavation site in the Tokyo region. The feature that most distinguished it from Jōmon was wet rice cultivation, carried on at first in low-lying land, subject to natural flooding. It used a type of rice that comes from the lower Yangtse basin in China, brought to Japan, it appears, through Shantung and Korea, or perhaps via the Ryukyu islands. This indication of continental influence is supported by the Yayoi culture's use of bronze for weapons and ceremonial objects. Since copper seems not to have been discovered in Japan until the early eighth century, the ore used to make these objects there – the manufacturing techniques themselves were known, perhaps brought by immigrants – must have come from China and Korea, or been obtained by melting down imported pieces. The oldest bronze mirrors, found in Kyushu, were undoubtedly imported, but from about the beginning of the Christian era craftsmen in Japan were making similar and sometimes nearly identical ones in substantial numbers. They were also making bronze bells, spears and halberds, whose size and appearance suggest that their purpose was ritual, rather than practical. The geographical distribution of these – bronze weapons in Kyushu, bells in central Japan, meeting and to some extent overlapping in the Inland Sea – suggests the existence of two distinct, and possibly rival, centres of culture, but we do not known enough to work out the significance of this.

Iron was introduced from the mainland at very much the same time as bronze, but was put to use mainly for the making of swords and agricultural implements. One result was to make the

agrarian economy more productive: it is thought to have supported a population of as many as 600,000 in the early centuries
of the Christian era. Yayoi culture also spread northeastward at
this stage, reaching the plain round modern Tokyo by the third
century AD. Paddy fields had come into existence, fed in some
cases by river water through simple irrigation systems; mortars
and pestles were used for milling grain; and fragments of hempen
cloth have been found in some of the settlements. The use of
ritual bronzes indicates a degree of social and religious differ-
entiation. Given such evidence of a society much less primitive than that of the Jōmon period, it is reasonable to conclude
that Japan was ready for a more elaborate form of political
structure.

When it came, it was characterised by the appearance of burial
mounds (*kofun*). The earliest group of these in the southern part
of the Nara plain can be dated to AD 250–350: that is, the first
century of what is known as the Yamato kingdom. The next were
located on the western slopes above the modern city of Nara, at
a time when Yamato power was spreading to more distant regions,
in both the west and the northeast. In the fifth century, the focus
shifted more towards the eastern shores of the Inland Sea (the
starting-point of the sea routes to Kyushu and Korea). The tumuli
also grew larger with the passage of time, marking, no doubt, an
increase in the manpower and resources available to Japanese
rulers. The largest of all, said to be the tomb of the sixteenth
emperor, Nintoku, who reigned early in the fifth century, had a
keyhole-shaped mound nearly 500 metres in length, surrounded
by three moats. It has never been excavated.

Standing in rings around the tombs were pottery cylinders,
called *haniwa*, which were surmounted by models and figurines
of various kinds. These tell us a good deal about the nature of the
society producing them. There are models of boats, much like
those which are still to be found in fishing villages along the coast
of Japan; models of buildings, similar to early Shinto shrines;
figures of men in Chinese-style armour; models of horses, complete with saddles, stirrups and bridles. No one point of origin

would satisfactorily explain the nature, dress and decoration of all that is reproduced in these objects, though the Korean peninsula seems likely to be the route by which the horses, armour, weapons and other equipment reached Japan. The *kofun* themselves resemble the burial mounds of southern Korea. The nearest equivalents to *haniwa* the present writer has ever seen are small figures and models deriving from Inner Mongolia at the time of the Northern Wei dynasty (386–535), but it would be by no means difficult to trace points of similarity between *haniwa* and the terracotta pieces found in earlier Chinese tombs.

The grave goods found in the stone chambers within the tumuli differ in some degree according to date. In the early period they included comma-shaped jewels (*magatama*), mirrors and other Yayoi-type bronzes, but from the fifth century onwards there is a prevalence of iron weapons, armour and horse-trappings, appropriate to a horse-riding warrior class, together with an increasing number of objects imported from Korea, or made by Korean immigrants, such as gilt-bronze crowns and other personal ornaments, as well as items of pottery. One of the recently excavated (but late-dated) tombs, that at Takamatsuzuka in the south of the Nara plain, was found to have well-preserved wall paintings, executed wholly in the Korean style.

In 1948 Egami Namio put forward what has become known as the 'horse-rider' theory to account for the objects associated with the tombs. Not convinced that they were satisfactorily explained by closer diplomatic relations with Korean kingdoms, though these undoubtedly existed in the fifth and sixth centuries, he argued that there had been a conquest of Yamato by mounted invaders, coming from outside. Their ultimate place of origin, he said, was one of the semi-agricultural, semi-nomadic kingdoms established by 'barbarians' along the northern frontier of China during the Han dynasty. At the end of the third century, when that area was still in turmoil following the fall of the Han, some of its people established themselves in Korea, then spilt over into Kyushu, whence Ōjin, Nintoku's father, led them against Yamato (in a manner reminiscent of Jimmu).

Egami's theory, which offends so many national and dynastic sensibilities, has not found ready acceptance among Japanese historians. They point out a number of technical weaknesses in it, not least on the matter of dating. For the non-specialist this is slippery ground. What can be accepted without undue controversy, however, is that from the fifth century onwards the development of a more powerful Yamato monarchy was accompanied, for whatever reasons, by a significant increase in the 'Korean' component in Japanese life. The horse, whose absence the *Wei chih* remarked upon, is first mentioned in the chronicles in the reign of Nintoku. It almost certainly entered Japan from Korea. Iron-working was a skill for which Koreans were famous in East Asia. It was apparently brought to Japan, like irrigation, sericulture and weaving, by the many Korean immigrants to whom the chronicles refer. Parts of the Japanese creation myth have affinities with those of Korea, which may have had an influence on the compilers of the *Kojiki* and *Nihon Shoki*. All these things, moreover, are related directly or indirectly to the power of the imperial house.

The Yamato state

In considering the influence that Korea had on the political development of Japan after the building of burial mounds began, it is convenient to start with the fifteenth emperor, Ōjin, whose reign spanned the years on either side of AD 400. His predecessors appear to have extended the control of the Yamato kings from their base in the Nara plain, first to the neighbouring regions of Japan, then to the north and west. That is about all we know of them. Of Ōjin we know more: that his accession marks a possible break in the ruling line; that he and his successors were much involved in the affairs of Korea; and that they used this connection to strengthen their authority at home. The chronicles describe Ōjin and his son, Nintoku, in much the same clichés, both of

incident and language, that Chinese historians use of founders of a dynasty.

Towards the end of his life, the fourteenth emperor, Chūai, was told by his consort, the empress Jingū, that the gods had revealed to her in a shamanistic trance their wish that he should send an expedition against Korea. Chūai dismissed the command as coming from 'lying deities' – after all, there was nothing to be seen, he said, in the quarter where Korea was supposed to lie – and insisted that he must concentrate on suppressing rebels at home. At this the gods declared, once more to Jingū, that by disobedience he had sacrificed his right to rule. Nevertheless, they promised, the child she was already bearing in her womb would be emperor if she herself obeyed their wishes. Chūai died soon after. Jingū thereupon launched and led an expedition to Korea, binding a stone in her loins to delay the birth of her child until the fighting should be over. The venture was successful; the child, Ōjin, was born on Jingū's return to Japan; in due course he succeeded as emperor.

One might be inclined to disregard this story as nothing more than the echo of a palace scandal, were it not for the references to involvement in Korea. For two centuries and more after Ōjin came to the throne, Korea was to be of the first importance to Japan, both as a scene of military adventure and as a key to cultural development. In this respect the reign of Ōjin marks a new departure.

Under the Han dynasty (202 BC–AD 220) China had established two military colonies in north Korea. It was not until the early fourth century, a hundred years after the fall of the Han in China, that these finally succumbed to local attacks, but once they did so, three Korean kingdoms came into existence and engaged in a struggle for power in the peninsula: Koguryŏ in the north, incorporating semi-sinicised peoples from southern Manchuria, who had close relations – sometimes friendly, often not – with Chinese states across the frontier; Paekche in the southwest, which developed contacts with parts of China across the Yellow Sea; and Silla in the southeast, which proved in the end to be the most

powerful, despite being more remote from China. Japan became involved in the struggles between them as the result of an appeal for help from Paekche soon after the middle of the fourth century. This led to a series of occasional military expeditions, Jingū's among them, which gave Japan booty, prisoners and opportunities for learning about Chinese civilisation. According to the chronicles, there was even a Japanese enclave on the south Korean coast, known as Mimana (Kaya), though modern scholars have expressed some doubts about it. By courtesy of Paekche's maritime skills and diplomatic connections, a direct link was also made with mainland China from time to time. In 425 and 478 envoys from Yamato reached the court of the Liu Sung dynasty in what is now Nanking. Another eleven missions went to China between then and 502. Paekche, too, contributed to Japanese culture, sending visitors and immigrants with a knowledge of Chinese writing and the Buddhist faith.

The prestige attaching to Japanese involvement in Korea accrued mostly to the imperial house, though there is little to show that emperors in person did much to earn it. Missions from foreign monarchs, seeking alliance, enhanced the imperial prestige. So did Buddhism in some degree. There were also more material benefits. Military loot was a form of portable wealth; trade followed in the footsteps of diplomacy; prisoners of war were a cheap form of labour, often possessing exploitable skills. Immigrants and visitors were another by-product of the connection. Those with a knowledge of Chinese writing could help with the keeping of records and accounts, enhancing the efficiency of government and the management of imperial estates, while others brought with them an expertise in metalworking or irrigation. Enjoying the lion's share of these advantages, the throne expanded its wealth and power at a greater rate than its potential rivals in Japan. When the emperor Yūryaku sent envoys to China in 478, for example, they claimed on his behalf that his forebears had already conquered 'fifty-five countries of hairy men' to the east, 'sixty-five countries of various barbarians' to the west, and ninety-five countries 'crossing the sea to the north' (*Sung shu*).

The degree of unity within this kingdom was almost certainly not very great. The most important units in fifth-century social structure were clans, or kinship groups, called *uji*. These had originated as agricultural communities, engaged in wet rice cultivation, whose hereditary heads had a duty to propitiate the gods on behalf of the *uji*'s members as a whole. Groups of *uji* were eventually consolidated into federations, forming small 'countries' (*kuni*), such as were described in the Chinese records. Their 'kings' and 'queens' had similar functions to the heads of *uji*. Yamato's 'imperial' clan had no doubt begun as one of these, but by the time of Ōjin and Nintoku it was powerful enough to claim the leadership of what one might call a federation of federations, first in the Nara plain, then more widely. The heads of other clans became attached to it as part of the ruler's entourage, among them the Mononobe, whose role was military, and the Nakatomi, court liturgists, whose ritual functions concerned the cult of the sun-goddess Amaterasu. A later addition to the court was the Soga clan, said to be of Korean immigrant descent, which owed its influence to the part it played in managing royal estates.

Subordinate to the *uji* in some cases, merely lower in the social scale in others, were organisations called *be* and *tomo*. The words are sometimes translated into English as 'guilds', but this is misleading. It is true that they existed to perform specialist functions: fishing and the gathering of mountain products; household duties at court and the conduct of religious rituals; service as palace guards; crafts such as weaving or ironworking and the making of weapons; irrigation and the care of horses. A few consisted of immigrants, for whom this was a means of integration into Japanese society. Almost all, however, cultivated land, in order to support the specialists among their number. Fictive kinship links existed between their members. In these respects the *be* and *tomo* overlapped in some degree with *uji*.

There was no administrative machinery to bind such elements into anything like a state, at least in the early days, but after the accession of Ōjin this gap began to be filled. One step was the bestowal of hereditary titles (*kabane*) on the leaders of *uji*, *be* and

tomo. Those most influential at court were made *omi* and *muraji*: that is, ministers. Others, lower down in the scheme of things, together with local dignitaries in the provinces, were given lesser titles. There appears to have been competition for these titles: the nineteenth emperor, Ingyō, felt the need to proclaim a series of ordeals by boiling water to identify those whose claims were valid.

The growing dominance of the imperial clan, reflected in these arrangements, enabled the twenty-fifth emperor, Muretsu, to behave in ways that showed little respect for the feelings of his subjects. He 'prepared strange diversions and gave licence to lewd voices'; he drank alcohol to excess 'in the company of the women of the palace'; he diverted himself by making men climb trees, then killing them, either by cutting down the trees, or by using the men as living targets for his arrows (*Nihon Shoki*). Compare this with the same book's account of Nintoku's behaviour less than a hundred years earlier. Seeing that the people were poor because of his demands for forced labour, Nintoku had suspended the system for three years, so ensuring that 'the wind and the rain came in due season, the five grains produced in abundance ... [and] the people had plenty'.

If this were a Chinese history, rather than a Japanese one written in Chinese, the pattern would be recognisable: Nintoku was an emperor at the beginning of a dynasty, Muretsu one at the end. Historiographical convention required the attribution of virtue to the one, tyranny and corruption to the other. In the eyes of the scribes, in fact, the monarchy was on the eve of significant change. They were right. Muretsu died without an heir towards the end of the fifth century. His successor, an obscure and distant relative, perhaps not even that, was chosen by senior members of the court.

Primitive religion

Before turning our attention to the subsequent history of the monarchy, we should consider briefly the early religious beliefs and practices of Japan, which were of some relevance to it. Our knowledge of what is now called Shinto, the Way of the Gods (*kami*), rests heavily on the *Kojiki* and *Nihon Shoki*. Because these were compiled at a time when Japan was coming under increasing Chinese cultural influence (Chapter 3), it is difficult to be sure how far the account they give of pre-Buddhist religion is distorted by the assumptions and prejudices of the scribes, who were chosen for their work because they were 'experts' in things Chinese, or even immigrants. There are, for example, traces of Chinese influence in what is said about the creation. One or two of the *kami* identified in the texts appear to be Chinese or Korean in origin, perhaps because they were deities of immigrant communities, who called them *kami* in deference to local custom. More pervasively, some concepts and vocabulary – the veneration of swords and mirrors, words like *jingū* (shrine) and *tennō* (emperor) – are found in Chinese Taoism. This may mean nothing more than that historians, writing in Chinese, used what seemed to them to be the appropriate terms for what they had to record, but it nevertheless makes it difficult to be sure that the phenomena themselves were distinctive and indigenous, or to decide what their original nature was. For instance, there has long been controversy about whether ancestor worship, to which there is reference in the chronicles, was a custom native to Japan, or part of the mind-set of the historians.

The term *kami*, not surprisingly, poses problems of translation into languages other than Japanese. To call them 'gods and goddesses', or simply 'deities', though convenient, is potentially misleading, unless one intends to make comparison with ancient Greece and Rome. The *kami* were superior beings, to whom humans might attribute supernatural powers, but they were neither omniscient nor omnipotent. They were, moreover,

diverse, as well as numerous. Some, especially those named in the story of the creation and the imperial myth, were thought of as anthropomorphic, both male and female. With these one might include the tutelary and ancestral *kami* of the most powerful clans (*uji*) existing in the Nara state at the time the chronicles were compiled: that is, their *uji-gami*. Amaterasu, after all, was not only the sun-goddess, but also the *uji-gami* of the imperial house. It was natural that tradition, as stated in the chronicles, should accord a similar character and place, if at a less elevated level, to the *uji-gami* of those clan heads who served the emperor in a senior capacity.

A second category, older than the first, comprised the *kami* of the countryside: those to whom appeal was made for fertility and good harvests, or the spirits of storm and earthquake, of lakes and rivers, of mountains and forest, even particular trees and stones, from which harm might threaten. These were not as a rule anthropomorphic, though they might be demonic, or appear occasionally in human form, or take possession of humans. Some of them had links with *uji-gami*, as deities of the locality to which an *uji* traced its origin. As pressure increased to reshape the received tradition of primitive times for the benefit of an emerging monarchy, notably in the sixth and seventh centuries, most of this group of *kami* became of secondary importance. The chronicles reflect this. Throughout history, however, they retained a much greater popularity among the rural population than they did at the emperor's court.

Shinto shrines were simple in form, as were the acts of worship performed at them. It was not until the Yamato monarchy was well established that shrine building became common, starting with those at Ise and Izumo, which had political importance. Even in the modern period, many lesser shrines are no more than roadside huts or even roped-off 'spaces'. For the most part, the worshipper was expected to do no more than bow, clap the hands and provide a small offering. Priests, who were described as officials in the more notable shrines – there was originally no clear distinction between ritual (*matsuri*) and government (*matsurigoto*),

whether for the emperor or for minor functionaries – would recite prayers, usually to offer thanks for favours received, or to turn away the *kami*'s wrath. The latter was most likely to be occasioned by pollution and uncleanliness, though it might be triggered by any action that disturbed the natural order. It was not in particular a response to offences against ethics or criminal misdemeanours. Shinto subscribed to no regular code of moral behaviour. Contamination by death, the physical manifestations of sickness, menstruation and childbirth, or behaviour that threatened the crop and other sources of food, such as Susa-no-o had committed – these were the things that humans had above all to avoid.

For individuals who offended, the most common ritual response was ablution or lustration, for which water and salt were provided at shrines. Exorcists could be used to intercede with the *kami* in serious cases. Ritual abstainers ensured the purity of major observances, especially at court; diviners, interpreting the cracks in heated tortoiseshells, discovered the reasons for a *kami*'s anger and sought ways to avert it; shamans, usually women, did the same by means of dreams and trances.

What is conspicuously lacking from this list is any doctrine of transcendent faith, or universal system of values, which might have given intellectual cohesion to the whole. Japanese were to find these things in Buddhism. Indeed, it may well have been their absence from Shinto that enabled the two religions to co-exist, even to establish a symbiotic relationship, for most of Japanese history.

CHAPTER 2

The Making of a Monarchy

Unlike China, Japan, at least officially, has had only one dynasty since the beginning of time. This fact has done much to determine the monarchy's nature and political role. There is a pattern to Chinese dynasties. Each begins with a phase of state building by men of vigour and ability, who bring an infusion of new blood; next comes one of 'power and glory', as their descendants enjoy the fruits of this beginning; and finally the dynasty goes into a decline, marked by a growth of luxury and incompetence at the centre, which make the country's rulers – not only the emperor – too weak to govern effectively. At this point comes chaos and confusion, preparing the way for the cycle to start again.

The pattern does not translate exactly to Japan. In Japan, it could be said, a single dynasty has gone through a single cycle, which is by definition incomplete. The first two stages, those of state building and apogee, have been comparable with China's, but the third, that of decline, has been both long drawn out and different in character. From about the tenth century onwards, Japanese emperors lost the greater part of their temporal power, as did the later rulers of dynasties in China; but they retained their thrones, as well as a measure of influence, by virtue of a quasi-religious function, rooted in the distant past. Their claim to divine descent made them the source of all legitimate authority, still

wielded in their name when they themselves lacked power. In reality, it passed, sometimes by force, sometimes by more devious means, to successive houses of hereditary office-holders, initially within the court, later outside it; and since each survived at least as long as the average Chinese dynasty, these in turn could be described in the language of rise, apogee and decline. The first of them, the Fujiwara, were regents to the emperor from 966 until the nineteenth century, though for the greater part of that time they, too, were virtually powerless.

Chinese-style government

Events on the mainland of Asia during the second half of the sixth century provided a powerful motive for changes in the nature of Japanese monarchy. Of the Korean kingdoms, Silla was strong enough by 562 to engulf the Japanese foothold on the southern coast. More ominously, the Sui dynasty, having reunited China in 589, began to show signs of restoring Chinese influence in the Korean peninsula. Koguryŏ and Paekche in the north and west were the first to feel the pressure, but it soon extended to Silla, too, with the result that by 594 all three Korean states had entered into tribute relations with China, accepting nominal Chinese suzerainty in return for a promise of security and trade. It seemed likely that Japan would soon find it wise to follow suit. In these circumstances, both Japanese and Korean rulers came to recognise the advantage of having a home base that was centralised in the Chinese manner, hence better able to defend itself. The most straightforward way of creating it was to adopt a Chinese form of monarchy and government.

Buddhism had already brought about in Japan a climate of opinion that was receptive to a decision of this kind. The religion had reached Japan – or, more precisely, the Japanese court – through a mission from Paekche in the middle of the century. It did not at first make a great deal of headway, since it was opposed

by clans like the Nakatomi, which had a vested interest in the worship of the *kami*. The Soga took up its cause, however, and their victory in a civil war in 587 gave Buddhism greater influence. This in turn reinforced the political motives for a close relationship with China. The Soga's principal ally within the imperial clan, Prince Shōtoku, was a devout Buddhist. As regent to the empress Suiko, an office to which he was appointed in 593 at the age of twenty, he devoted himself for nearly thirty years to promoting the growth of Chinese thought and institutions in Japan.

In medieval and modern times Shōtoku, both as Buddhist and as siniciser, has been a cult figure. The imperial collection contains an imaginary portrait of him, dating from about 700, which shows him with his two young sons, all three very Chinese in dress and hairstyle; in the Hōryūji temple at Nara, close to the site of Shōtoku's palace, there is an illustrated biography, originally painted on sliding panels in 1069; the Kōryūji in Kyoto has a statue, attributed by reason of its style to the Kamakura period (1185–1333), showing him, supposedly at the age of sixteen, seated on a chair (a Chinese habit that he did *not* succeed in making popular in Japan). Shōtoku, in fact, is traditionally held to have lived very much in the Chinese manner.

His main political achievement – though because of the nature of the records we cannot be sure how far it was indeed a personal one – was to make a start on the task of giving Japan a framework of institutions, modelled on those of China, which would turn an association of clans under the emperor's military command into something more like a centralised state. He introduced cap ranks at court in 604, in order to relate the status of office-holders more clearly to that of the monarch and each other; he began the compilation of chronicles – an activity designed to assert the legitimacy of a dynasty, as Chinese historians saw it – though the text, if completed, has not survived; and he sent embassies to the Sui, starting in 600, partly to establish his country's place in a China-centred international system, partly to carry laymen and priests to study China's society and religion. The practice was to continue intermittently until 838.

The most important political document with which his name is linked – both its date and attribution have been questioned, but there is not much doubt that it reflects Shōtoku's own ideas – is the so-called Seventeen Article Constitution of 604, more accurately described as the Seventeen Injunctions. It begins with a quotation from the Confucian Analects, asserting that 'Harmony is to be valued'. It then enjoins reverence for 'the three treasures': that is, the Buddha, the Buddhist Law and the Buddhist priesthood. Finally, it turns to the behaviour deemed appropriate at the Japanese court, whose officials it addressed. The first of these, respect for the emperor's will, is expounded in wholly Chinese terms. 'The lord is Heaven, the vassal is Earth. Heaven overspreads and Earth upbears. When this is so the four seasons follow their due course.' At a less elevated level, officials are enjoined to make 'decorous' thought their guiding principle, dealing impartially with the suits that are brought before them. They should attend at court early in the morning and retire late. They must not seek to treat the emperor's lands or subjects as their own: 'in a country there are not two lords, the people have not two masters'.

Not very much of this was put into practice in Shōtoku's lifetime. Some of it, after all, was contrary to the interests of his Soga allies, whose power rested on their efficiency and victory in civil war, not imperial autocracy. Nevertheless, what he did was significant in two respects. He set out aspirations that eventually were to be orthodox in Japanese court politics; and by sending students to China, he made it possible for his successors to proceed on the basis of a much more thorough understanding of Chinese government. Some of the students remained in China for twenty or thirty years, so witnessing both the fall of the Sui and the succession in 618 of the T'ang, a much more prestigious dynasty. The T'ang, indeed, were to become Japan's model. The first mission was sent to their capital in 630.

By the time the last of Shōtoku's students came back to Japan at the end of that decade, opposition had developed to the power and pretensions of the Soga. They were even accused of seeking to usurp the imperial dignity for themselves. A conspiracy took

shape, led by a clan head, Nakatomi no Kamatari, later to found the Fujiwara house, and Prince Naka-no-Ōe, son of the reigning empress, Kyōgoku. In 645 these men carried out a *coup d'état*. As an immediate result, the two principal leaders of the Soga were killed, the empress abdicated in favour of Naka-no-Ōe's uncle, Kōtoku, and Naka-no-Ōe became nominal head of government, much as Shōtoku had been a generation earlier. Kamatari took a senior post in the new regime. Scholars recently returned from China became its advisers.

Although this event is called a 'reform' by historians, there is no convincing evidence that the purpose of the conspirators went in the first place beyond removal of the Soga. What followed, however, was a series of steps clearly designed to transfer power from clan leaders to the throne and its immediate servants. A system of administration was set out, both at the centre and in newly defined provinces, and put under the supervision of officials appointed by the court; a revised system of ranks was introduced, modelled on that of the T'ang; heads of *uji* were deprived of lands and people said to have been improperly granted in previous reigns; and although some landholders at the district level, who were thought to be of unblemished character, were made eligible for local office, the emperor's subjects were in general warned that both land and people were the ruler's – that is, not simply under the sway of their hereditary chiefs. Registers of population were to be kept. Standardised measures were introduced for the assessment of tax on rice-land. Land surveys were carried out, making use of them. New rates of tax and labour dues were announced, payable to the court and its representatives.

A further innovation, as much symbolic as practical, was a change in the Japanese calendar. Use of the Chinese calendar was always a condition of belonging to China's tribute system. Its adoption in Japan in 645 was therefore a claim to international status. From that time on, irregularly in the seventh century, but constantly thereafter until the present day, Japanese were to designate years in the way the Chinese did, according to their place in a series of named periods of time, each of which bore an

era-name (*nengō*) chosen for its auspicious meaning. The *nengō* that started the series was Taika, 'Great Reform'. The first year of Taika was AD 645 by western reckoning, the second was 646, and so on. Taika was replaced by Hakuchi in 650 – the decision was the ruler's prerogative – though there was then a gap from 655 to 672, when no such label was in use. In fact, the next one of any moment was Taihō, 'Great Law', introduced in 701, when it marked the issue of administrative codes.

As was implied by the failure to use *nengō* between 655 and 672, the reform movement lost impetus after its first few years. The setback was temporary, however, since the need for reform had by no means come to an end. Almost as soon as Naka-no-Ōe became emperor under the reign-title Tenji in 661, he was confronted with a crisis over Korea. Paekche, hard pressed by the forces of Silla and the T'ang, appealed for Japanese help, as it had done before, but the expedition sent in response to the appeal was roundly defeated. Japan was once again on the defensive. When Koguryŏ asked for assistance in 668, it was refused. The result was to leave the whole of the Korean peninsula under the domination of Silla and the T'ang. Japan for its part, conscious of continued unrest at home, set out to erect defence works in Tsushima, along the northern coast of Kyushu and in the Inland Sea. This could hardly have seemed the time to abandon the task of building a stronger monarchy.

Our knowledge of Japanese state building during the second half of the seventh century is by no means complete, though it is clear that Temmu, Tenji's successor and younger brother, played a major part in it. New administrative codes, said to have been drafted under both Tenji and Temmu, have not survived. Nor is there an extant text of the Taihō Code of 701, which was to serve as the basis of Japanese government for the next 200 years. An account of political institutions in the Nara period (710–84) must therefore rest on what is known as the Yōrō Code, drawn up in 718, but not put into force until 757. It embodied the so-called *ritsuryō* system – *ritsu* is penal law, *ryō* are administrative statutes – laying it down that emperors ruled through a central bureaucracy,

the structure and functions of which were described in detail. The very concept was novel, as the highly personal nature of earlier Japanese government implies.

The highest decision-making body under the *ritsuryō* system was the Daijōkan, or Council of State, founded in 689. The Council was small: three ministers, the Daijō-daijin (Great Minister of State, or Chancellor), Sadaijin (Minister of the Left) and Udaijin (Minister of the Right); four senior councillors; a few junior ones; a small secretariat. The office of Daijō-daijin was rarely filled, perhaps because its extensive powers made it a threat to the throne. On both occasions when appointments were made during the eighth century, the incumbents were subsequently dismissed for seeking to usurp the emperor's authority. This left the overall supervision of government for the most part to the Council's other senior members, amounting to half a dozen men. On major questions they made recommendations to the emperor, who was expected to approve or disapprove, but not revise them. On lesser ones they acted on their own.

Under the control of the Daijōkan there were eight executive ministries. One, the Imperial Household Ministry (Kunaishō), responsible for the management of the emperor's household and the revenue from imperial estates, stood a little apart from the rest. The others included Finance, which dealt mostly with tax receipts; People's Affairs (land and population registers); and Military Affairs (administering conscription). Three more were required to manage the huge amount of paperwork that the bureaucracy produced: drafts of laws and decrees; lists of rituals and ceremonials; records of rank, genealogy and succession among the nobility, and of appointments and promotions for officials; the texts of recommendations and petitions, together with the decisions taken about them. There was no Ministry of Foreign Affairs. A Justice Ministry presided over the legal aspects of government business. There was no system of courts, since all officials were required to administer the law in their different spheres, conducting investigations in response to complaints and petitions. They possessed no detailed list of offences that might

warrant punishment, except for the 'eight outrages' of crimes against the public interest. These included treason and rebellion, serious cases of murder (those involving assault within the family, killing by dismemberment, or witchcraft) and violations of Confucian morality.

Apart from the ministries, there were several subordinate or semi-independent bureaux, one of which investigated cases of official misconduct and maintained order in the capital. Others were concerned with the imperial library, calendars, divination, court music and ceremonial dancing. Outside the capital there was a governor-general at Dazaifu in northern Kyushu, whose high rank – he was often a imperial prince – marked the importance of relations with China and Korea. The province of Settsu, which guarded the sea approaches to the capital, was also under an official of more than ordinary rank. Elsewhere there were governors in each province, appointed on rotation by the court from among the central cohort of officials, and responsible for all matters of civil and military government in their area (though they did not always go there in person). Each had a small staff, including specialists in medicine and Chinese studies. A detachment of conscripts was put under the governor's command. At the next level down were district officials, chosen from local notables and appointed for life.

While the provincial administration looks remarkably simple for what were in theory very wide-ranging duties, that of the capital seems to have been overmanned. It has been estimated that in 718 it employed about 330 officials in its upper levels, another 6,000 in lesser posts. This seems excessive for a country with a total population of perhaps 5 million. What is more, the members of this bureaucracy were enmeshed in a maze of regulations, setting out their responsibilities and their office-hours, the precedents to be followed (Chinese as well as Japanese), and the arrangements for appointment and promotion. As early as 678 Temmu had ordered that officers of both central and provincial government should report each year on the abilities of their subordinates, in order that they might be considered for

advancement. In 701 the emperor Mommu instructed those of the fifth rank and above to record each month the number of days on which they had been present at their place of duty.

By the time the legal commentary *Ryō no Gige* was issued in 834, these requirements had become an elaborate reporting system, applicable to officials of almost every grade. It was based on two criteria. A man acquired 'merit' for his diligence and probity in office. He was credited with 'excellence' in accordance with his success in meeting the demands it made upon him. These demands were defined in a fairly rudimentary way. A lesser councillor had to act in strict conformity with the instructions he received; a guards officer must maintain rigid discipline; a chamberlain had to be in constant attendance at court; and so on down a long list, covering official historians, court musicians, diviners and even barrier guards in similar manner. The combination of 'merit' and 'excellence' made it possible to allocate all these people to one of nine classes, ranging from Superior, First Class, for the very best to Inferior, Third Class, for those who were said to flatter and lie, or showed themselves avaricious and dishonest.

That this structure as a whole was more appropriate to a country of the size and complexity of China than it was to one as 'backward' as Japan is obvious enough. Yet it was not just a blind copy of the T'ang model. Apart from a number of technical differences, which need not detain us here, the *ritsuryō* system departed from Chinese practice in two major respects, which are important to an understanding of the Japanese monarchy. One concerns the role of inherited rank. The other was a product of the theory underlying the emperor's own authority.

Eighth-century Japan was not a meritocracy, however much its reports on officials might make it seem so. Parallel to the hierarchy of office, and at least equally significant, was a scale of numbered ranks, subdivided into sections. Only those who held ranks one to three could be chosen as minister in the Council of State. Ranks four and five gave entry to other senior posts, filled by direct imperial appointment, while ranks six to eight were for

more humdrum members of officialdom. Below those again were unnumbered ranks for minor functionaries. Such ranks were a qualification for office, not a reward for filling it successfully. What is more, at the very highest levels they were reserved in practice for descendants of former clan heads and other senior members of the court aristocracy, together with offshoots of the imperial house. The children and even grandchildren of such persons could enter the structure as of right at one of its higher points.

As a result, posts that carried the greatest influence became the preserve of a circle of families, which mere bureaucratic efficiency did not enable others to penetrate. For example, between 701 and 764 the offices of Minister of the Left and Minister of the Right were shared by men from only five of these. Nor did the narrowing of opportunity end there. Of the eleven senior officials of the Council of State in 772, no fewer than eight were from the Fujiwara house, founded by Nakatomi no Kamatari; two more were relatives of the Fujiwara; and the other was descended from the Mononobe. In other words, those branches of the old clan aristocracy that had committed themselves to the new Chinese-style governmental institutions had found in 'careers' a substitute for the private control of land and people on which their ancestors had relied. Those in the Council of State possessed real power, for the emperor could take no executive action without them. In addition, they enjoyed valuable emoluments, as did many of their associates. Men of the eighth rank and above were exempt from labour service and regular state taxes on land. Both rank and office carried financial advantages, either in the form of allocations of revenue from stated groups of tax-paying households, or as periodical grants of tax goods from the treasury. These benefits, which were substantial for those of the fifth rank and above, had a tendency to become customary, even though they were in theory official emoluments. One is bound to conclude that emperors like Tenji and Temmu had succeeded in their aim of breaking down the independence of the clans only by converting one segment of the clan leadership into privileged, hereditary

members of what on the face of it was an appointive bureaucracy. In the long run, this was to undermine the power of the monarchy itself.

Despite this institutional weakness, Japanese emperors had a theoretical source of authority that made them in principle more secure in their position than those of China were. In China the emperor, as Son of Heaven, ruled as mediator between Heaven and Earth. His tenure was sanctioned by Heaven's will, expressed in what was called the Mandate of Heaven (*t'ien-ming*); but it was widely believed that this could be withdrawn if he failed to provide just and stable government, or behave in accordance with the Confucian ethic. Were he so to fail, the divine displeasure would be revealed for all to witness in heavenly portents, or natural calamities, or popular unrest. All these were signals that the emperor had lost the right to rule. There was no such doctrine in Japan. An emperor who reigned by virtue of divine descent could not be subject to a conditional mandate of this kind, even though his relationship to the sun-goddess, Amaterasu, could be likened in some ways to the Chinese emperor's claim to be Son of Heaven.

Japanese emperors had no objection to preaching from a Chinese text when it suited their purpose. In 683 Temmu issued a decree stating that 'auspicious signs' had been observed, confirming that government was 'in harmony with the laws of Heaven' (*Nihon Shoki*). Yet in the same document he described himself as 'a God Incarnate'. The second of these concepts, moreover, seems to have had a practical impact on his policy. He reinstated the practice of installing an imperial princess at the Ise shrines to worship Amaterasu on the emperor's behalf. When he ordered the compilation of the *Kojiki*, he required it to show that the bonds between the emperor and the *kami* were 'the foundations of imperial rule'. The *ritsuryō* system, of which he was one of the architects, placed the ceremonies of enthronement and succession, conceived within the tradition of imperial divine descent, under the supervision of the Jingikan. This was a body responsible for matters concerning the worship of *kami*, which

technically outranked the Council of State. In a court where other forms of protocol and ritual were overwhelmingly Chinese, these exceptions mattered.

Capital cities

Rulers whose court was in so many respects Chinese aspired to have a palace and a capital that were equally so. During much of the sixth and seventh centuries, the two concepts of palace and capital had been almost synonymous. They moved for each new reign, because death caused ritual pollution. Still, from the time the Soga came to power in 587, the moves were small enough to make the Asuka district in the south of the Nara plain the dynasty's political heartland, giving its name to a century's history. It was there that the earliest Buddhist temples were established. It was also there that Japan's first real capital city was built. This was Fujiwara, conceived by the emperor Temmu, but completed by his widow and successor, who moved the court to the new site in 694. Modelled on Loyang, which was then China's capital, the city measured some 3 kilometres by 2 in size; had a Chinese-style grid of streets, divided into eastern and western halves by a central north–south avenue; and included a large palace enclosure, placed at the northern end.

Fujiwara was destroyed by fire in 711, one year after the court had left it for a city known historically as Nara, though more accurately called Heijō (the name given to China's prototype for the great T'ang capital, Ch'ang-an). Heijō had a river route to the Inland Sea, which may be why the place was chosen, but in other respects it was similar to Fujiwara, if a good deal larger (5 kilometres by 4). Unlike Chinese cities it had no walls, but it had two gates, Suzakumon in the north and Rashōmon in the south, a pattern that was to be repeated more famously in the next capital, called Heian.

There was a great deal of open space within the city, despite its

urban ground-plan: wide avenues; two large enclosures forming the palace precinct, its buildings surrounded by open corridors; extensive grounds for temples and aristocratic mansions. The palace itself comprised buildings of two different kinds. The ceremonial ones were recognisably Chinese in style. Though a little modified by later rebuilding, an example of them – a long, low wooden structure with white plaster walls and a curved roof of tiles, set on a raised stone plinth – can still be seen in modern Nara at the Tōshōdaiji, a Buddhist temple to which it was transferred as a lecture hall. Other buildings within the precinct, used mainly for living accommodation, were more 'Japanese' in appearance, as were those of the aristocracy, who were allotted plots in the city in accordance with their rank. Lacking the stone plinth, the plaster walls and the tiled roof, these usually had planked floors, supported on pillars set directly in the ground, and were roofed in thatch or shingles. A report by the Council of State in 724 complained that too many of the city's dwellings lacked dignity. Nobles of the fifth rank and above were urged to build more impressive ones, painted in red and white, and give them roofs of tiles: that is, to adopt the Chinese style.

Not even temple buildings always passed this test: the Tōdaiji's great treasure house, the Shōsōin, which still survives, has something of the look of an oversized log cabin. This serves to remind us that Japan did not at this early date adopt the Chinese practice of building in stone or brick, whether because of the lack of appropriate materials and skills, or because of the risk from earthquakes. One result was a high degree of impermanence. Fire was a constant hazard. In fact, our knowledge of the architecture of the period owes less to surviving examples in the ordinary sense than it does to replicas, created by centuries of rebuilding, which disaster or decay occasioned from time to time. Rebuilding, no matter how carefully carried out, may not always have been exact. Nor can we be completely sure about original locations. Buildings like these were remarkably easy to move, given sufficient manpower. When we read that the Yakushiji was removed from Asuka to Nara, this is likely to be the literal truth.

Though we have no contemporary pictures of it, eighth-century Nara almost certainly lacked visual grandeur, despite the desire to impress that was evident in its planning. It was not until they built castles in the sixteenth century that Japanese architects created buildings with as great an impact on the observer as that produced by Europe's classical monuments or medieval churches. With the exception of pagodas – constructed in wood they look strangely un-Chinese – even palaces and temples were mostly single-storey, their roof spans restricted by lack of engineering knowledge. Wooden walls, left unpainted, helped to render them unobtrusive, while dispersal over level, often wooded sites denied them a dominating presence. Restraint in this sense was to be a lasting feature of Japanese art, but it meant that Nara, unlike Ch'ang-an, impressed more by its acreage than its splendour.

The city comprised people, as well as buildings, of course, and these were much more colourful, at least if they were members of the aristocracy. Costume, also Chinese in manner, was much less sober than it was later to become. Leaving aside the princes of the imperial house, there were over a hundred nobles of the fifth rank and above, wearing, at least on formal occasions, robes of some opulence. Hundreds more held lesser ranks. A surprisingly large proportion of these persons were immigrants. A list of noble families compiled in 815 (by which time the total had risen slightly from its Nara levels) showed that about one family in three of those included in it came originally from China or Korea: more than 170 out of nearly 1,200 came from China, some 240 from different parts of Korea. To the nobility one must add several thousand non-noble government servants, plus a considerable number of priests and other residents of religious establishments, comprising a substantial upper class. Then there were the artisans and craftsmen. Many of these, too, were immigrants, engaged in silk weaving, metalworking or one of the other kinds of technical expertise needed, for example, to build and decorate palaces, shrines and temples. In addition, there was a large floating population of temporary inhabitants, including militia on duty in the capital, and men and women performing labour

service there. Estimates of the total have varied widely, but Nara may well have contained 100,000 persons in the early eighth century, rising to as many as 200,000 by the time the court departed in 784. Thereafter it declined rapidly in size and population as Heian took its place as the centre of government.

The transfer to Heian took place in two stages. Early in Kammu's reign (781–806) the decision was taken to move north again, this time to Nagaoka on the Yodo river. The step was taken in 784; but in the next year or two a high-profile assassination there, followed by natural calamities, which were blamed on malignant spirits, brought second thoughts. Another site was chosen, farther north still, in a mountain bowl between the rivers Kamogawa and Katsuragawa. In 794 it was made the capital and named Heian, the city of Peace and Tranquillity (no doubt in the hope that this is what it would prove to be).

To students of history the event is momentous. Heian is not just a place but also a label, marking the apogee of classical, aristocratic culture in Japan. Contemporaries, lacking foresight, presumably found the occasion more routine, the latest in a series of such decisions. It was not even thought to warrant the introduction of a new era-name (*nengō*). Enryaku, the name chosen when Kammu came to the throne in 781, remained in force until he died in 806.

The new city was a little larger than Nara, but in other respects the two were very similar: a grid of avenues and streets, divided into eastern and western quarters by a central avenue, which linked the northern palace precinct to the southern gate; no walls, except those which separated districts; a population largely employed in government. Both were modelled on Ch'ang-an, the capital of the T'ang, though on a smaller scale. Heian's buildings showed the same contrast between those in the Chinese style for the conduct of public business, their roofs green-tiled and supported on crimson pillars, and those for residential purposes, built of unpainted wood, thatched, or roofed in cryptomeria bark. There was a pleasure park south of the palace for the exclusive use of the court. Aristocratic residences, repeating

the motif, had landscape gardens to the south of their open courtyards. Indeed, the most striking difference between the old and the new was the ban on Buddhist temples in Heian's centre, designed to reduce the religion's influence at court. It seems difficult to believe, if one looks at the city now.

Heian was to remain the emperor's home for over a thousand years. During that time many things changed. A number of 'detached' palaces were added, as refuges from fire and ritual pollution, or for the use of abdicated monarchs. Large commercial quarters developed, as artisans and tradesmen multiplied. Settlement spilt eastward across the initial boundaries along the banks of the Kamogawa, distorting the pattern of the grid. Even the name changed: long known informally as Kyoto, 'the capital city', this became its regular description from the eleventh century. All the same, for the first hundred years and more of its existence, Heian provided a familiar setting for the forms of government and culture that Japan had evolved in Nara. It was not until the tenth century, when the connection with China weakened, that they were seriously undermined.

The Fujiwara regents

During the first part of the Heian period (894–1185), power at court fell more and more into the hands of the Fujiwara house. The foundation of its political fortunes had been laid by Nakatomi no Kamatari. The part he played in the *coup d'état* that overthrew the Soga in 645, then in the reforms designed to strengthen the throne in the next two decades, ensured for his descendants the rank and imperial patronage that gave them access to high office. His son, Fubito, was the first to bear the name of Fujiwara. Fubito's sons, in turn, founded the family's four main branches, of which the northern house was to prove the most powerful. Fubito also married a daughter to the emperor Mommu. This both reinforced his own prestige and began a custom that was to

last for centuries. Generation after generation of Fujiwara daughters were married into the imperial line, until a young emperor or heir to the throne was more likely than not to have one Fujiwara as father-in-law, another as maternal grandfather. While the court was still in Nara, the Fujiwara had begun to exploit these advantages to build up a network of 'clients' at various levels in the bureaucracy, making use of their access to the emperor through marriage ties to influence appointments. In addition, they established for themselves a strong position in the Council of State, through which they were able on most occasions to dominate the central government machine.

After the move to Heian, the emphasis changed. Early in the ninth century, the emperor Saga set up a private office within the palace to handle paperwork under his own supervision, following the example of several great noble houses, including the Fujiwara, who had developed such a machinery to deal with the complex affairs of their estates. A substantial amount of government business, concerning land rights and taxation, was diverted to these offices and thereby removed in part from the jurisdiction of the regular ministries. The Fujiwara were in a better position to profit from the device than either the emperor or the rest of the nobility. The emperor's actions were severely circumscribed by protocol. The Fujiwara, on the other hand, were not only the greatest of the noble houses, wealthier and more influential than their peers in rank, but also had 'family' standing in the affairs of the palace. Their position was formalised in 866, when Fujiwara Yoshifusa was made regent (Sesshō) to his grandson, the emperor Seiwa. This was the first time the post had been filled by someone not of royal blood. In 887 Yoshifusa's nephew and adopted son, Mototsune, completed this structure of familial control by creating a new office, that of Kampaku, to extend the powers of the regent into an emperor's adult life. Mototsune himself, having been Sesshō until then, became Kampaku. His descendants monopolised both posts until the Kamakura period (1185–1333), when they passed to other branches of the Fujiwara house.

Because they bypassed formal government institutions in this

way, the Fujiwara had no need to replace the monarchy. Their example was later followed by feudal rulers, using different offices. Yet the regents did not rely exclusively on matrimonial influence and their undoubted skill in bureaucratic manipulation. They were ruthless, both in removing stubborn opponents – including emperors, if need be – and in persuading Fujiwara daughters into suitable marriages. They were ready to use force to gain their ends, though usually through bands of armed retainers, rather than private armies. It would be misleading, therefore, to treat them as no more than subtle and successful courtiers.

The most magnificent of them was Fujiwara Michinaga (966–1028), the story of whose life and times is told in an eleventh-century chronicle entitled *Eiga monogatari*, or The Tale of Splendour. Michinaga had luck: several senior nobles who might have challenged him for office died in an epidemic in 995, leaving him regent at the age of thirty. He also had four daughters, three of whom he married to emperors, one to a crown prince. At the zenith of his career, just after he took Buddhist holy orders in 1019, the retired emperor was his son-in-law, the reigning emperor was his grandson, the crown prince was both son-in-law and grandson. One of his Fujiwara sons succeeded him, first as Sesshō, then as Kampaku. Yet there is little in the chronicle about what he did with the power this eminence gave him, other than build a Buddhist monastery. Its dedication was a famous spectacle, recorded in detail. There was a performance of the lion dance and a procession of carefully chosen monks; spectators attended from the court in a veritable traffic jam of ox-drawn carriages; commoners, afraid of not getting near enough to see, went in even greater numbers on the day of rehearsal.

It was not to be expected that dignities of this kind could be won without opposition. Some of it stemmed from rivalries between branches of the Fujiwara house itself. Some – intermittently – marked attempts by the imperial family to resume a measure of control. One of these came under the emperors Uda and Daigo, following the death of Fujiwara Mototsune in 991. It centred on Sugawara Michizane, one of the few outstanding

scholar-statesmen to emerge from Heian's education system, a man whose immediate ancestors, starting with only modest rank, had risen to a place of some distinction by dint of scholarly reputation and ability in office. So, at first, did Michizane himself. He held several minor posts after graduation from the university, all requiring a superior knowledge of Chinese; became professor of Chinese literature in 877; and was made governor of a province in 886. This was a bureaucratic career pattern, very Chinese in character, more than an aristocratic one. What changed it was that on his return to the capital he was chosen by the emperor Uda as a suitable recruit – able, and from a background likely to guarantee his loyalty to the throne – to take part in a move against the Fujiwara. Promoted well beyond his expectations, he was made Minister of the Right in 899, hence a member of the Council of State, an advancement almost unheard of for one of his birth. Yet it was not enough to make sure of victory over the Fujiwara. After Uda abdicated in 897, Michizane lost the certainty of royal support. In 901 he was accused of plotting against the new emperor, was stripped of office, and was sent to a post in Kyushu. This was tantamount to exile. Fujiwara pre-eminence was restored.

Michizane himself died in Kyushu in 903, an event followed by storms and earthquakes in the capital, which were blamed on his angry ghost. To appease it he was posthumously pardoned and advanced in rank. Forty years later a Shinto shrine was erected in his honour at Kitano in Kyoto. This most Confucian of senior ministers was therefore transformed into a *kami*, in which capacity he is now the patron to whom examination candidates appeal.

Later efforts to counter the influence of the Fujiwara were to carry greater weight, because they involved the emperor and his family more directly. The emperor was still central to the political system, after all, since it was in his name that government was carried on. Even the Fujiwara recognised the need to treat him with due ceremony and respect, at least in public. They found it convenient nevertheless to ensure that reigns were short, for once a ruler reached years of discretion he might well become less

biddable. Abdication at an early age became the rule. Ten emperors had reigns that spanned the years from 858 to 986. Their average age when their reigns came to an end, whether by death or abdication, was a little less than thirty years. Their average age at death was forty-seven years. The interval between the two, where it occurred, was spent as a rule in Buddhist monasteries. Not all the abdications were voluntary. Some, indeed, are mysterious. The emperor Kazan, according to one account, simply disappeared from the palace one night in 986, to be discovered next day in a monastery (though a different version claims that he went there under Fujiwara escort).

Abdication was nevertheless a double-edged weapon for the regents, since it provided ex-emperors, if they had a mind to do so, with an opportunity to exploit the filial piety of their sons and successors. The first to make a significant move in that direction was Go-Sanjō* (r.1068–73), a rare non-Fujiwara monarch, who had reached the throne because of a lack of suitable Fujiwara candidates. As emperor, he began by taking steps to amass 'private' land rights for the imperial house itself, seeking to make it more independent of state revenue. He then abdicated, leaving his son, Shirakawa, to continue the process under his own supervision. Shirakawa abdicated in his turn in 1087 and lived until 1129. Both men remained politically active after abdication, building up a private administrative structure, known as the In-no-Chō, which was much like the house organs of the Fujiwara and other great families. It ran the family estates, handled the paperwork of land rights and tax exemption in consultation with the state bureaucracy, and created a body of officials of its own, some of whom also held posts in the formal government structure. In other words, the emperor's father, through the device of abdication, acquired a power base of much the same kind as the Fujiwara already possessed.

---

* The prefix Go- in Japanese reign-titles means 'the later'; thus Go-Sanjō is 'the later Sanjō'. Sanjō II would be the western equivalent. The same applies to some other famous emperors, such Go-Toba and Go-Daigo (Chapter 5).

There were thus two networks of 'private' authority in the capital during the later Heian years, one headed by an ex-emperor, the other by a Fujiwara regent or Kampaku. Both were backed by other elements within the aristocracy, both were engaged in constant rivalries, centring on the succession, or land rights, or appointments to office. Force was sometimes involved, used even against the emperor's person. In 1160, for example, in the course of the so-called Heiji disturbance, which became the subject of a well-known picture scroll, both the ex-emperor Go-Shirakawa and the emperor Nijō were seized by armed insurgents, acting for rival contestants, who were trying to bring about changes in senior appointments.

It is difficult to judge how far these political developments affected the capital's ruling class as a whole. Perhaps it was not a great deal. The lives of most of its members, after all, revolved around the regular bureaucracy. They were concerned with administration, not with policy or high politics; and since the established structure of government had been only bypassed under the Fujiwara, not abolished, there were still things for them to do. This was in any case a society in which 'place' counted for more than function. Both in and out of the workplace, human relations were wrapped in a web of etiquette, based on rigid distinctions of rank. A man's reputation, if one can trust the picture drawn by contemporary literature, depended less on competence in office than on the composition of graceful poetry, or skill in music and dancing. Poetry contests were taken very seriously. So were other polite accomplishments, like board games (*go* is one which has retained its popularity) and incense guessing. Outdoor pursuits – not for women, who were rarely expected to venture out of doors, except to visit temples and festivals – included highly ritualised forms of sport, like *kemari* (a kind of handball played with the feet) and mounted archery (*yabusame*). *Sumō* wrestling was a popular spectator sport, as it still is.

These have the appearance of occupations for a wealthy, leisured élite whose members had little by way of demanding duties to perform. The judgement may be a little harsh – the most vivid

39

descriptions of Heian life were written by ladies of the court, who may well have ignored those parts of their menfolk's daily round from which they were themselves excluded – but one is certainly left with the impression of a world that was frivolous as well as status-bound. The capital had some of the characteristics of an aristocratic village: a limited human and geographical base, which made people and places familiar to almost everyone; strict codes of acceptable behaviour; a wealth of shared superstitions. Over it all presided an emperor, who was usually young, surrounded by respectful courtiers, but much overborne in matters of politics by both his father and his father-in-law. The atmosphere was exceedingly metropolitan. Provincial offices carried a rank one degree lower than their equivalents in central government. Being sent to one of them, even as governor, was to be sentenced to the wilderness. Indeed, to most of its inhabitants the very outskirts of Heian itself seemed distant and forbidding.

CHAPTER 3

Buddhism and Chinese Culture

Buddhism – as it evolved in India, before moving north and east – offered its believers in its simplest form a prospect of personal salvation: that is, an escape from the cycle of birth and rebirth in a world of suffering, to be achieved through prayer, scriptures and meditation. The immediate purpose was to free the individual from preoccupation with the self. This could most easily be pursued by abandoning the life of everyday temptation, in order to follow a better one in poverty, asceticism and monastic calm.

By the time the religion reached Japan from China, it had become a good deal more elaborate than this. Sects had developed, each emphasising particular forms of devotion, or certain parts of the Buddhist scriptures (sutras), or both. It had incorporated into its pantheon a multiplicity of figures, varied in type and origins: several manifestations of the Buddha, both historical and conceptual, which were credited with a range of different powers and qualities; bodhisattvas, who had reached the brink of Buddhahood themselves, but refrained from entering it in order to bring salvation to others; guardian devas and attendant demons, sometimes recruited from other religions. The motives for adopting it had also changed, at least for China's northern neighbours. To them, Buddhism had become a part of Chinese culture. It was therefore a symbol of civilisation and a passport to membership

of an international élite of which China was the acknowledged focus. Beyond that, it was a powerful supernatural force – more so than gods of local origin – which could be called on to protect both rulers and their subjects from foreign attack, pestilence or natural disasters.

Buddhism and Shinto

In 552, or possibly 538, depending on which set of records one believes, the ruler of Paekche sent a Buddhist monk to Japan, bearing an image of Buddha and copies of sutras, to urge that the religion be adopted there. The proposal, when put to senior members of the court, precipitated conflict. The immigrant Soga clan, persuaded that the introduction of a Chinese religion would serve to gain favour with both China and its deities, urged acceptance, pointing out that Buddha was everywhere worshipped in the 'frontier lands', save only Japan. The Mononobe and Nakatomi, as spokesmen for the traditional religious values of Japan's agricultural community, objected that such action would offend the *kami*. The emperor, too, inclined to this view, since his own position as priest-king depended on the indigenous beliefs. He therefore ruled that the Soga be allowed to worship Buddha by way of trial, but only privately. The decision produced a battle of omens. A pestilence gave the Mononobe and Nakatomi grounds for having the Soga temple destroyed; a fire at the palace cast immediate doubt on the wisdom of this step; an epidemic swung the pendulum back again; imperial illness brought further consideration. The contest finally became involved in a succession dispute in 587, in which the Soga were victorious. Putting their own candidate on the throne, they were able thereafter to ensure that Buddhism had the patronage of the court.

Under Prince Shōtoku (Chapter 2) the spread of Buddhism was coupled with Chinese-style reforms of political institutions, designed to strengthen the central authority. There was much

building of Buddhist temples and monasteries, employing Korean architects, Korean artists, and Korean and Chinese priests. Most of these establishments were placed close to the centres of power, and much official favour was shown to them. All this contributed to the monarchy's prestige. The Soga duly profited. Apparently aware of this advantage, the conspirators of 645, although they overthrew the Soga, did not attack the religion they had favoured. The emperor Kōtoku (r.645–54) was said in the chronicles to have 'honoured the religion of Buddha and despised the way of the *kami*' (*Nihon Shoki*). In 651 Buddhist ceremonies were held in his palace. In 652 lectures on Buddhism began there. Government supervision over priests, nuns, and their lands and buildings, instituted in 623, was scrupulously maintained. In the following century, the Yōrō Code made clerics subject to the civil law, not only for lay offences – bribery, drunkenness, brawling – but also for religious ones, such as the propagation of false doctrines. The only evident concession to their otherworldly status was that the penalties they suffered when convicted were less severe than those imposed on laymen.

By 741, when orders were given that at each provincial capital there must be a Buddhist temple, able to offer up prayers for the country's safety, Buddhism had the standing of a state religion in Japan, though it still shared that role with Shinto. One stated motive for the 741 decree was to give thanks for the protection that Buddha had afforded during a smallpox epidemic. In 743 the emperor gave further evidence of his gratitude in another decree, announcing that a great bronze statue of the Buddha Vairocana was to be built and installed at Nara. In 749, accompanied by ministers and senior court officials, he attended a ceremony at the newly completed Tōdaiji there, which was to house it, in order to celebrate the discovery of gold deposits in northern Japan, which were enough for the statue's gilding. The emperor expressed humility, describing himself as Buddha's 'servant', even his 'slave'; but almost immediately afterwards he addressed a rescript to the court, announcing rewards and honours to mark the event, in which he attributed Japan's good fortune with respect to gold,

not only to Buddha, but also to 'the guidance and grace of the gods that dwell in Heaven and the gods that dwell on Earth': that is, to the two principal categories of *kami*. His own function as priest-king, it appears, could not be held to rely exclusively on an alien religion.

Buddhism, after all, remained essentially Chinese. Most of its senior figures, both men and women, had come to Japan from China or Korea. Its scriptures were written in Chinese. Its priests, if they were to be given proper ordination, had to receive it from these new arrivals, or go to China to the centres of their faith. The sects established in Japan were all Chinese in origin. The Hossō sect, which possessed two of Nara's most famous temples, the Kōfukuji, endowed in honour of Nakatomi Kamatari, and the Hōryūji, founded by Prince Shōtoku, had been introduced from China by a Japanese monk who had studied there in the seventh century. The Ritsu sect had invited a well-known Chinese monk, Ganjin (Chien-chen), to come to Japan to establish a seat of ordination in 753. It was many years and many adventures before he got there – he arrived in Kyushu at his sixth attempt – but he eventually practised ordination in Nara at Tōdaiji, before transferring to Tōshōdaiji, where his Chinese disciples succeeded him as abbots.

Tōdaiji was the headquarters of the Kegon sect, so named after the Kegon Sutra, the basic tenet of which is that the historical Buddha (Sakyamuni, known in Japanese as Shaka) is a manifestation of the supreme and universal Buddha, Vairocana, and is himself manifested in lesser Buddhas in a myriad worlds. The concept is represented visually in many statues and paintings, showing Vairocana seated on a lotus flower with a thousand petals, each petal a universe, on each petal a Buddha. Perhaps because one could see in this imagery a parallel with the temporal power, Kegon received special favour from the Japanese court. The great bronze Buddha at Tōdaiji, known throughout Japan as the Nara Daibutsu, became one of the country's principal Buddhist monuments.

All the sects established at Nara were courtly and scholastic,

doing little to attract those members of the population who lacked Chinese linguistic skills. With the move to Heian, from which these sects were largely excluded, something of broader appeal began to emerge. In 804 the monk Saichō (767–822) was given permission to travel to China with one of Japan's official missions, in order to complete his studies of the Tendai (T'ien-t'ai) sect and secure accreditation from it. He returned in 805 to found a sect of that name in Japan. Its senior temple, Enryakuji, was built on Mount Hiei, dominating Heian's northern outskirts. From there it could protect the capital from evil spirits (and intervene on occasions in the city's politics, as later events were to show). Tendai doctrines were based on the Lotus Sutra (*Hokke-kyō*), which taught the central importance of a single universal Buddha; but it also recognised the need for faith in the bodhisattva, Kannon, and endorsed the practice of meditation, as well as giving heed to various forms of esoteric Buddhism. As a result, Tendai became an eclectic core from which other major sects were eventually to break away.

No less influential was Saichō's contemporary, Kūkai (774–835). He, too, went to China in 804, but he stayed until 806, studying the Shingon (True Word) teachings, which had been recently introduced into China from southern India. They focused on the universal Buddha, Mahavairocana (Dainichi in Japanese), rather than on Sakyamuni; but the sect's most notable characteristic was its concern with magic and esoteric rituals, using mantras (secret verbal formulae) and mandalas (diagrams setting out concepts of the Buddhist world) for purposes of worship and exposition. On his return to Japan, Kūkai established himself and his followers on Mount Koya to the south of the Nara plain. From there he exercised a distant but significant influence on the court. This was partly because courtiers had already acquired a taste for ritual and magic in other contexts, but it was not unrelated, perhaps, to the fact that they looked on Kūkai as one of themselves. He was of aristocratic birth, wealthy enough to have given a feast for 500 monks when ordained in China. He was also a scholar and poet of some reputation. Among his

writings there is a wide-ranging survey of Chinese and Indian religious thought, as well as a detailed and systematic account of the rules for composing Chinese verse.

It is clear, therefore, that China exercised as much of an influence on Japanese religion as it did on the country's political institutions. For many centuries, in fact, the *kami* were reduced in the national context to secondary standing. Buddhism had had ample experience of coming to terms with the worship of local gods in the course of its passage through Central and Southeast Asia. *Kami*, which were multifarious but inchoate, posed no new problem; and since the two religions were concerned for the most part with different areas of religious and human experience, a form of co-existence was soon established between them. Within the palace, emperors had a Buddhist chapel for their personal use, but took part in Shinto ceremonials at their enthronement and on other suitable occasions, such as rice planting and harvest. Both kinds of priest were expected to invoke the help of their respective gods in times of trouble.

The first public sign of a more far-reaching relationship came with the inauguration of the Nara Tōdaiji in 749. In 747 the court had appealed for intercession with the *kami* on behalf of the work being carried out there. The priests of the Usa shrine in northern Kyushu, which was dedicated to Hachiman, a *kami* linked by tradition with the emperor Ōjin, not only responded promptly to this appeal, but also carried the symbolic presence of their deity in procession to Nara, in order that he might become the temple's guardian when it was complete. The practice was extended in later years to many other temples and monasteries, which received *kami* to protect their precincts and *torii* (shrine gates) to mark their entrances. More immediately, it brought material benefits to the Usa Hachimangu. The shrine was raised to high court rank, a device used previously to bestow state subsidy and tax advantages on certain Buddhist houses. Hachiman himself was later recognised as a bodhisattva.

These initiatives opened the way for Buddhist priests to take part in Shinto rites, a practice that was given official approval in

759. From this it was only a short step to asserting that the *kami* were manifestations of Buddhas or bodhisattvas, a claim of the kind that had been advanced in China to link Confucius with Vairocana. The first such reference to *kami* was made in general terms in a document of 859. In 937 the doctrine was applied for the first time to a specific *kami* (Hachiman). By the Middle Ages there are references to Hachiman as an avatar of Amida (Amitabha) and to Amaterasu as an avatar of Dainichi (Mahavairocana, whose Sanskrit name means Great Sun).

The relationship between Buddhism and Shinto outside the metropolitan area developed differently. As Buddhism slowly penetrated the countryside, the belief spread that *kami*, like humans, were unenlightened beings, condemned to their present state because of their actions in other lives: that is, by karma. They sought enlightenment in the Buddhist manner, but their sufferings and frustrations on the path towards it were given vent meanwhile in malevolent uses of miraculous powers – in earthquakes, floods, pestilence and crop failures – to the evident discomfort of their human neighbours. Instead, therefore, of setting the shrines of *kami* as guardians at the gates of Buddhist houses, it was better to establish Buddhist temples at or near Shinto shrines, so as to help both the *kami* and the local inhabitants in this situation. The Hachimangu at Usa was one of the first to benefit from this arrangement, but eventually such *jingū-ji*, or 'shrine-temples', as they were called, numbered many thousands.

In this way, Buddhism emerged as the senior partner in something like a symbiosis between the two religions. In the legal codes (*ritsuryō*) each had a separate section, but in less formal contexts the distinction between them was anything but clear. Like Shinto, Buddhism acquired shamans, healers and diviners, despite some official disapproval. Shinto for its part contributed a range of rites and gestures to ward off evil or misfortune that seem to have been common to both. Ennin, a distinguished Buddhist monk, who was later to be abbot of Tendai's Enryakuji, when seeking to ensure a safe voyage home from China in 839, engaged the services of a Shinto diviner and himself made offerings to two

kami, the god of Sumiyoshi, who was the patron of seafarers, and the Dragon King of the Sea. If even learned clerics behaved like this, treating Buddhas, bodhisattvas and *kami* as members of a single pantheon, it is easy to see why others made little distinction between them.

Tribute missions and Chinese learning

The urge to acquire a greater knowledge of both Buddhism and Chinese political institutions was a principal motive for the missions that Japan sent to China between 607 and 838–9. There were nineteen of these, an average of one every twelve years, though the intervals were in fact irregular. They were of considerable size: two ships carrying 250 men in the early years, rising to twice that many in the eighth century. Activity on this scale shows how highly they were valued by the state. So does the fact that the voyages were carried on despite considerable dangers. Japanese ships, flat-bottomed and depending largely on oars, were not entirely suitable for long and often stormy passages across the East China Sea (the route that had to be followed once the coast of Korea was made politically inhospitable by the rise of Silla). Nor were their commanders well informed about the conditions they would encounter. Many ships were wrecked; others had to turn back; nearly a third of the travellers who set out from Japan in the Nara period seem never to have returned. In 752 the senior envoy, having reached China, chose not to face the voyage home. In 838 several senior members of the mission, having twice tried without success to reach the China coast, pleaded illness to avoid another attempt. They were punished.

The majority of those who made up the members of one of these expeditions were seamen, guards and attendants, who were not in a position to contribute greatly to Japan's knowledge of the Chinese world. They were not permitted as a rule to go beyond their port of arrival. At the other end of the social scale

were the envoy and his deputy, men of high rank, chosen for their literary reputation, who were accompanied by several other senior officials as councillors, plus interpreters in Chinese and Korean, diviners, doctors, a painter and scribes. A troupe of musicians completed the party, no doubt to add to its dignity. The ambassador and his entourage were entertained at China's expense once they reached the Yangtse region, travelling to the capital, Ch'ang-an, where they were housed in the state lodgings set aside for foreign envoys. While there they presented formal greetings from their emperor, together with suitable 'tribute' gifts; took part in various ceremonies at the court; then set out for home bearing Chinese gifts – more valuable than those they had brought – together with the books, paintings, images and other objects they had been able to collect.

These elements of the mission can be described as diplomatic relations, rather than personal study, though some of the envoys pursued what enquiries they could into the procedures of the Chinese court or the nature of Buddhist and Confucian doctrine. More detailed investigations were left to their staff. The painter was expected to copy pictures and sketch images. The doctor took the opportunity to enhance his understanding of Chinese medicine. One member of the mission of 838–9 paid what appears to have been a staggering amount (in gold) for lessons in the playing of the lute (*biwa*) from a famous Chinese teacher.

There were also Japanese students and student-priests, who were not part of the envoy's diplomatic entourage, but whose studies had official sponsorship. Their numbers were fairly small, but as they often stayed in China for a number of years, receiving a stipend from the Chinese government if what they proposed to do had its approval, they added much greater depth to their country's knowledge of China and its culture. Their careers, too, were likely to benefit, more so, as far as one can judge, than those of the officials. Two such students who went with the mission of 608, one layman and one priest, having remained in China for thirty years, returned to become advisers on reform to those who carried out the *coup d'état* of 645. Another, Kibi no

Mabiki, who went in 717, stayed for seventeen years; became head of Nara university and lecturer to the court on the Chinese classics; went to China again as vice-ambassador in 752; and ended by becoming a senior minister. Among the clerics, we have already had occasion to mention Saichō and Kūkai, who came back to Japan to found two major Buddhist sects in the early ninth century. All these are exceptional cases, of course, which is why they are well known, but there are many more who became technical experts or respected scholars at a rather more modest level of achievement.

A smaller contribution to Japanese knowledge was made by Chinese and other foreign missions coming to Kyushu, or even to Nara and Heian. The Chinese ones were a formal recognition of tribute status, valued for the gifts they brought, but not particularly educational. Those from Korea and other nearby states, described in the Japanese chronicles as bringing tribute from their rulers, were chiefly an excuse for trade. Trade, in fact, once established, was to continue in the hands of Chinese and Korean merchants long after the tribute missions came to an end. It was principally in goods for which the missions had created a demand: medicines, perfumes, silks, damasks and brocades from China, plus some books and paintings; metalwork, cosmetics, honey and ginseng from Korea; skins, including those of bears and a kind of tiger, from Parhae, a kingdom on the Manchurian border. The returns were silk floss and the simpler textiles: that is, the same items that were sent by Japan as 'tribute' to China.

The impact of these relationships on Japan was very varied. A report by a returning ambassador in 719 prompted a revision of Japanese court dress in the most recent Chinese style; another a century later led to reforms in protocol. Since many of the imports were luxury goods, the first choice of which went to the imperial house and members of its court, they served to make the atmosphere of the capital more Chinese and contribute to a more 'civilised' way of life. In 756 the empress Kōmyō donated to the Tōdaiji the treasures collected by her late husband, the emperor Shōmu. They became the nucleus of a famous collection, housed

in the Shōsōin. Among them were a Chinese New Year card, an ivory foot-rule, several mirrors, musical instruments, medicines and medicine jars, weapons, personal ornaments, combs, a Korean ink-stick, a glass bowl and cup, carpets, clothing, Chinese shoes, trays, spoons, even an iron ceremonial plough. All were of mainland origin, demonstrating, it has been said, that Japan was by this time the Silk Road's eastern terminal.

For Japanese who stayed at home, an understanding of China and its institutions rested more on the books the envoys brought home than on the kind of objects to be found in the Shōsōin. A catalogue of Chinese texts available in Japan in 891 lists over 1,700 titles, their subject-matter ranging from the Confucian classics, legal codes, ceremonial and protocol to medicine, divination and calendars, history and poetry. With the help of explanations from officials, doctors, priests and scholars who had been to China, plus Koreans and Chinese settled in Japan, these were to be the basis for a massive adoption of Chinese culture.

Not all of it was directly related to Buddhism and the power of the state, though these were central to it. Buddhist monks, like western missionaries of a later era, brought with them much more than the tenets of their faith. As scholars they expounded Confucian philosophy. When Japan's first state university was established in 647, it was a Korean priest who was made head of it. As men of education, priests also had some understanding of mathematics (for temple building and land measurement), of irrigation (for the management of estates) and of medicine. They painted pictures and wrote poems. Their religion itself was highly literate, so teaching Chinese was almost a pastoral duty.

It is difficult to be sure how widely Confucianism spread in Japan in these early centuries, but there can be little doubt that conformity with its ethical code, at least outwardly, was expected of officials in Nara and Heian, as it was in Ch'ang-an. Confucian doctrine held that human society mirrored the relationship between Heaven and Earth; that right behaviour was required to ensure a proper balance between the two; and that behaviour in turn was a product of self-cultivation, disciplined by education.

The sons of Japanese officials were trained in these ideas, together with some relevant skills, at the Nara university. After preliminary study of the Chinese language, they were expected to acquire a thorough knowledge of the Confucian classics and an acquaintance with the kind of practical mathematics that they might have to use in keeping tax records or supervising public works. In 728 the syllabus was expanded to include Chinese literature and law, which quickly became the most popular of its courses.

Students from families holding the fifth court rank and above, who qualified for admittance to the university at the age of thirteen, were guaranteed entry to an official career without the need to pass examinations. Those below that rank needed permission to enrol, followed by success in one of the four grades of examination, in order to obtain a post in the bureaucracy. We have some idea of what these tests required, since one of the imperial anthologies of Chinese poetry, published in 827, includes, rather surprisingly, a number of specimen examination papers, together with typical answers. The questions were philosophical, calling for essays comparing Buddhism and Confucianism, or commenting on the relative weight that should be attached to the virtues of loyalty and filial piety, if the two conflicted (a standard Confucian dilemma). The answers, equally abstract, were stereotyped statements of Confucian truths, exhibiting rhetoric more than logic. A Chinese examiner would have found them wholly familiar.

By the tenth century, the influence of the university was on the wane. Undermined by the creation of private academies for the sons of the high-born, its reputation declined still further as its professorships became hereditary and its graduates found their way into nothing more than routine posts. The Chinese ideal, in fact, was proving weaker than Japan's devotion to the privileges of birth.

Problems also arose in another field of state-supported learning, that of calendrical astronomy. In China, because the idea was accepted that heavenly portents were an indication of the monarch's virtue, and hence his right to rule, the study of calendars

and the movements of the heavenly bodies was entrusted to a well-staffed and highly regarded department of officialdom. In Japan a supposedly similar body was established in the *ritsuryō* structure, but its achievements were not strictly comparable. In the first place, its name, the Yin–Yang Bureau, implied that astrology and fortune telling were an important part of its duties. In addition, its staff seem never to have acquired a sufficient grasp of the necessary mathematics to be able to make their own corrections to the lunar calendar, especially its adjustment to solar time. The Chinese calendars that had come into use during the Nara and early Heian periods continued in force without amendment once official relations with China came to an end after 839, becoming more and more inaccurate with the passage of time; the headship of the bureau, like similar posts in the university, became hereditary; and the bureau's principal task in its later years was the preparation of an annual almanac, setting out such information as the dates of spring and autumn equinoxes, summer and winter solstices, and solar and lunar eclipses, together with the times of sunrise and sunset. All these had ritual or magical importance. To them were added personal fortune telling for each day, plus notes about lucky and unlucky directions and taboos, drawn variously from Buddhist, Taoist and Yin–Yang sources. This was something less dignified than the office in Ch'ang-an would have thought appropriate.

Another institute in the *ritsuryō* system dealt with the teaching and practice of Chinese medicine, primarily for the benefit of the court. Both treatment and pharmacopoeia were based on knowledge first brought to Japan by Korean and Chinese doctors, who were invited there in and after the mid-sixth century, but this was later supplemented by the studies of two Japanese Buddhist priests, who went to China with the mission of 608, as well as by what the doctors attached to subsequent missions learnt. Acupuncture, moxibustion (cauterisation of the skin), massage and exorcism all found their way into Japanese medical treatment in this way, as did various forms of tantric magic. Drugs were imported from both China and Korea, though substitutes for

some of them were eventually found in Japan and listed in Japanese publications on *materia medica*. By contrast, Japanese doctors do not seem to have acquired a full understanding of Chinese pathological theory until much later in history.

There is a parallel here with the failure to grasp the underlying principles of astronomy and mathematics for use in calendar making, which suggests a greater concern with the practical aspects of Chinese science and technology than with its fundamentals. One is reminded of the attitude of a group of Japanese students, sent to London in 1867, who complained at being given a general western-style education, when what they had come for was a technical training. They wanted to master 'particular arts and sciences', they said, not 'to be called an educated man'. For them, as, perhaps, for Japanese going to China earlier, more 'useful' and less time-consuming studies had advantages.

Literature, art, music

Japan's adoption of the Chinese script as a means of writing texts in Japanese, which happened at a very early date, greatly complicated the language. Japanese is polysyllabic and highly inflected. Chinese is monosyllabic and tonal. To combine the two was inherently clumsy. By the tenth century, the situation had been a little improved by the development in Japan of a phonetic syllabary (*kana*) from the cursive forms of certain Chinese ideographs, which could be used instead of ideographs to indicate such things as tenses or the positive and negative forms of verbs; but even so, Chinese loan-words and phrases remained embedded here and there in Japanese sentences, pronounced either in an approximation to that of the Chinese original, or as if they were the Japanese polysyllabic words of similar meaning. As many generations of students can testify, the result is not a language of the utmost clarity. Perhaps for that reason it has been most successfully employed in producing poetry, religious exhortations

or popular literature. Other kinds of written statement – laws, histories, scriptures, commentaries, land records – have until modern times been made for preference in Chinese, still the country's classical language. There were, for example, six 'national histories' in Chinese, starting with the *Nihon Shoki*, all organised as chronicles in the Chinese manner and providing a continuous record down to 887. Japanese also showed a taste for massive documentary collections in Chinese, covering a range of subjects from history, law and politics to Buddhist exegesis. The tradition has continued, though not always in Chinese.

As men of culture, Japan's government officials for many centuries followed the example of their Chinese counterparts in writing poetry in Chinese. Po Chü-i became their favourite model, once a knowledge of his works was brought back by the mission of 838–9, but as early as 751, the date of a volume entitled *Kaifūsō*, the court began to publish anthologies of Chinese poems, written chiefly by its members. Most of the contributions were formal, sometimes elegant, comments on 'serious' themes like Buddhism and philosophy, or occasional poems for banquets and other such celebrations. They were not highly regarded by those Chinese who came to know of them. A collection made by a Chinese merchant in Japan at the beginning of the eleventh century, taken back to China and presented at an imperial audience, was described, according to the *Sung shu*, as polished, but 'shallow and of no merit'.

In the ninth century, the writing of Chinese verse seems for a time to have stifled an earlier and more vigorous tradition of poetry in Japanese. Ballads and folk-songs are to be found scattered throughout the *Kojiki* and similar texts, written down in the Chinese script, but otherwise entirely Japanese in language. They set the pattern for two enduring habits. One was that of inserting verse into prose narratives, both historical and fictional. The other was the writing of poems in a 'pure' form of Japanese, rarely using Chinese loan-words.

The habit of writing court poetry in Japanese is best represented in the first and most famous of Japanese anthologies, *Manyōshū*, a

collection deriving mostly from the seventh and early eighth centuries, which contained more than 4,500 poems. The great majority of these were 'short' poems (*tanka*) of thirty-one syllables, arranged in lines of 5–7–5–7–7, a format which became so universally popular as to be called *waka*, 'Japanese poems'. There were also a number of longer compositions (*chōka*), as well as some in Chinese. *Tanka* were already by this date a highly developed poetic tradition, graceful, perceptive, focused on human relationships, though too brief to sustain extended themes. The imagery is sharp, often brilliantly evocative. The subject-matter, unlike that of most contemporary Chinese verse in Japan, dwelt much on personal experience, ranging from sexual love to the pains of parting and separation and death. A modern scholar has pointed out that of 145 poems written by Japanese envoys sent to Silla, two-thirds are devoted to thoughts of home and the families they left behind.

There is a freshness about the poems in the *Manyōshū* that one does not always find in later compilations. In the latter, emotion is not infrequently reduced to sentimentality, or else appears as a mannered melancholia. Long poems, too, became rare, reducing the variety and diluting the emotion. The *chōka* in *Manyōshū* – there is one on poverty and another on the death of a child which particularly come to mind – conveyed a much greater depth of feeling than is commonly found in *tanka*.

The sharp distinction between a Chinese and a Japanese style that is manifest in poetry does not occur in visual art at this early date. Shinto, though the simplicity of line and colour that characterised its shrines had a lasting effect on Japanese architecture, did not favour at first the representation of gods and priests, whether in paintings or statues. As a result, depiction of the human figure was overwhelmingly Buddhist, or else Chinese and derivative. It had a degree of variety, because there were a number of Buddhist styles of different geographical origin, but since orthodoxy claimed the right to make rules for the visual image as well as religious faith, there was little room for something distinctively Japanese.

Much of the earliest Buddhist art, especially statuary, was the work of immigrants or their immediate descendants. This makes it difficult at times to distinguish between pieces made in Japan and those that came from abroad, except by reference to their materials. Many of the bronzes made by the new arrivals show clear Korean influence, as one would expect; but since Korea owed much to China, as China did in turn to other parts of Asia, even indirectly to Greece, what entered Japan was already diverse in origin. It also required a mastery of the technology of casting, which was not easily won. By 749 it had been sufficiently acquired to make possible the casting – after several unsuccessful attempts – of the Tōdaiji's Buddha, 16 metres high and using 400 tons of bronze, but on a smaller scale artists often worked in wood and dry lacquer. This was not only cheaper, but also more likely to produce a graceful line. The pieces they produced, especially those in which lacquer was applied over a frame of hollow wood or cloth, then sometimes coloured, were much more naturalistic than the early bronzes. They were also more 'contemporary' by the standards of the T'ang, whose artists had largely abandoned the archaic styles that Japan had first derived from the mainland. Many of those now working in Japan, after all, came directly from China. The Tōshōdaiji has both wood and lacquer statues of Buddhas and their guardians, made by Chinese disciples of the founder, Ganjin (Chien-chen). There is also a notable one of Ganjin himself, said to date from 763.

Once the capital moved to Heian, the Nara artists had to rely more on the patronage of Buddhist houses than of the imperial court. This encouraged them to produce statues in wood in the manner of the Tōshōdaiji studio, rather than the more expensive (and pretentious) bronze. Much of their work consisted of standing figures, carved from single tree trunks, hollowed at the back to prevent the material from splitting, and touched with paint to colour the eyes, lips and hair. An innovation was the occasional appearance of statues of *kami*, perhaps reflecting the growing assimilation of Japan's two main religions. For example, in the guardian shrine attached to the Yakushiji there is a figure of

Hachiman, dressed as a Buddhist monk and accompanied by a very matronly empress Jingū.

The paintings of these centuries have proved less durable than the statues, but enough survives to show that they, too, were very continental in manner and inspiration. The Hōryūji temple complex provides some of the best examples. After its main hall was burnt down in 670, it was rebuilt and decorated with murals, apparently by artists of Korean or Chinese origin, using imported pigments. These murals were themselves destroyed by fire in 1949, except for a small section that had been removed for repair, but by that time the paintings had been well enough recorded and reproduced for it still to be possible to study them. They consisted of four main panels, depicting the paradises associated, respectively, with the Buddhas Shaka, Amida, Miroku and Yakushi, plus portraits of bodhisattvas and heavenly guardians. The Hōryūji also has a portable shrine, dating from the middle of the seventh century, on which Buddhist scenes in several Chinese styles are painted in oils on lacquered cypress panels.

Another Buddhist theme, stimulated by the paintings that Kūkai brought back from China in 806, was the mandala. Typically, this depicted the Buddhist pantheon, in an arrangement showing the Buddha Dainichi at the centre, surrounded by other Buddhas and bodhisattvas in concentric circles or ordered rows. The design was intended to emphasise Dainichi's centrality to the faith; and because the preparation of such a painting was conceived to be a religious act – the imagery was held to embody the deities themselves – it was carried out by monks trained in painting, not by the lay craftsmen employed by religious houses for other kinds of work. An outstanding example is the interior decoration of the five-storey pagoda of the Shingon sect's Daigoji, erected in 952 on the southwest outskirts of Heian.

There must have been a great deal of painting in Nara of which we now have no record at all. Apart from what was being done in temples and monasteries, there was a Painters' Bureau, established by the state in 728 to supervise and execute the decoration of public buildings, which had a staff of four master painters and

sixty assistants, plus others who were recruited to carry out particular commissions. Each man seems to have pursued his own task, either working on outline or filling in colour; but as the buildings on which these skills were exercised have since been rebuilt or destroyed, we have no identifiable examples by which to judge the method's effectiveness. Indeed, what pictures we do have from this period we owe almost entirely to their preservation by the great religious establishments. The inventory of items in Tōdaiji's Shōsōin, for example, includes twenty-one screens, showing landscapes and scenes of palace life, or depicting birds and plants, all in the Chinese manner. Only one is now extant, a painting of a group of Chinese ladies. Yakushiji has a picture of a Buddhist goddess, dating from 771–2, which from its appearance could easily be the portrait of a T'ang court lady, while four parts survive of an eighth-century picture scroll (*e-maki*) of the Sutra of Causes and Effects (*E-ingakyō*). This is a Japanese copy of a Chinese original, telling the life of the historical Buddha, Sakyamuni (Shaka). Landscape, buildings and costume are all very Chinese, but there are traces of Japaneseness in the faces and attitudes of the human figures in part of one scroll.

Music, which was closely linked to dance, was equally Chinese. Musicians are recorded as having arrived in Japan from the mainland as early as the fifth century, bringing with them a variety of instruments, but we know little of what they performed. In the seventh century a type of dance-drama, called *gigaku*, said to have originated in southern China, was introduced into Japan from Paekche. The dancers wore masks, some of which, preserved in the Hōryūji and Shōsōin, are thought to represent non-Chinese Asians as seen by the Chinese: they have long noses and the kind of facial expressions given to Buddhist demons in statues and paintings. Their dancing was accompanied by flute, cymbal and drums, but as there have been no performances of *gigaku* since the seventeenth century, not enough is known of either the dance or the music to reconstruct them with confidence.

Fortunately, this is not true of *gagaku*, the music that accompanies another kind of dance, *bugaku*. Both are still per-

formed by court musicians and dancers in the imperial palace and at certain festivals. There are two styles, one associated with Korea, the other with China and Southeast Asia, as well as some elements attributed to Shinto ritual music of very early date. The corpus, which was assembled by the state's Office of Music in the Heian period, is therefore eclectic, like so much else in the ancient culture of Japan. The dancers are men, wearing rich costumes, predominantly in red (China) and green (Korea); the orchestra includes a wider range of percussion, wind and string instruments than are used in *gigaku* (it includes the *biwa*, thought to be of Persian origin); and the tempo is slow, though it may well have been faster in Nara and early Heian.

Enough has been said in this chapter to show how extensive was the influence of China and Korea on Japanese art and culture in the seventh, eighth and ninth centuries. Together they created the country's 'classical' tradition, which proved to be both pervasive and enduring. Even so, as contacts with China became unofficial and less frequent in and after the tenth century, so Chinese ideas and Chinese styles became less powerful in Japan, making room for others, notionally 'Japanese', to take their place beside them. It was in this phase that the country developed a distinctive Sino-Japanese culture of its own.

CHAPTER 4

The Ebbing of the Chinese Tide

The T'ang dynasty was overthrown in 907. For the next fifty years China was divided into several competing states, which were not brought together under a single ruler until the first Sung emperor came to power in 960. That event was the start of a new phase in Chinese history. The capital was moved to Kaifeng. Thereafter, government came to rely much less on landowning aristocrats than in the past, its principal officials recruited from less affluent – and less independent – 'gentry'. Commerce grew rapidly, towns became larger and more wealthy. Against that background there developed an age of cultural brilliance, in which the importance of Buddhism declined, but philosophy, painting and the making of porcelain flourished.

The tenth century was also a turning-point for Japan, though for the most part in a contrary direction. The spectacle of China in disarray did nothing to reinforce the country's Chinese-style monarchy and political institutions, faced by an aristocratic challenge from the Fujiwara and their allies (Chapter 2). In addition, the Nara land allocation system, designed to bolster the imperial authority, fell more and more into decay. Public land gave way to private land, greatly to the advantage of the nobility and the main religious houses, a process carried out chiefly through the creation of a number of large, amorphous private estates (*shōen*). At the

local level these sustained a class of landed warriors, who in time were to pose a threat, not only to the monarchy, but also to the civilian aristocracy of the court.

As the influence of China grew weaker in political life, so it did in culture. The end of tribute missions to the mainland in the closing years of the T'ang, itself a symptom of changing circumstance, reduced the flow of knowledge to Japan (Chapter 3). Though trade continued, and Buddhism itself stayed strong, Japanese literature and art no longer looked to China with the same deference as before. The loosening of the bond, in turn, enabled cultural skills and preferences of indigenous origin to emerge, or in some cases re-emerge, with the result that by the twelfth century there was, if not a reaction against things Chinese, at least a detectable change of direction in cultural development. What had once been overwhelmingly Chinese was becoming Sino-Japanese, a hybrid.

Public land, private land

Under the Nara codes, all land belonged in theory to the emperor, to be distributed and taxed by officials acting in his name. Some was granted to the state's own servants in the ruling class in accordance with their rank and office. Some was earmarked for the support of shrines and temples. All other irrigated rice-land was allotted to the cultivators on the basis of household size, men receiving more than women, free persons more than slaves. These allocations were to be reviewed every six years, that is, two years after each population census; and in the interval between revisions the fields, known as *kubunden*, could not be transferred by sale or inheritance. They were subject to tax. So was all rank-land, as well as the office-land of local officials, though the office-land of provincial and central officials remained tax-free. Shrines and temples were not required to pay tax on their holdings.

Land tax, amounting to about 3 or 4 per cent of the crop, was

not in itself a very heavy burden, but cultivators also faced other imposts. They were required when called upon to serve as conscripts (one man per household), equipped at their household's expense. They had to provide labour for public works on sixty days a year. In periods of distress they qualified for loans of seed-rice from the authorities, but as these were repayable at harvest time at rates of interest between 30 and 50 per cent, they were not an unmixed blessing. The poorest, in fact, especially in the provinces closest to the capital, where official supervision was more strict, were tempted in times of hardship to abandon their holdings and seek alternative means of livelihood, either by farming in remoter regions or as hired labourers in the capital. This was held to be against the interests of the state. A decree of 893 ordered the capture and return of peasants escaping to the northern provinces, but measures such as this did not prevent a shortage of labour on many of the labour-intensive irrigated fields. It was made worse from time to time by epidemics of measles and smallpox – a by-product, it appears, of relations with the mainland – which produced sharp fluctuations of population in affected areas.

In an attempt to maintain the country's tax base, the Council of State sought inducements to keep farmers on the land. In 723 it ruled that land reclaimed by restoring an abandoned irrigation system could be held without reallocation for a single generation, while land brought under cultivation for the first time could be kept for three generations. By this provision farmers were offered some hope of gain from efforts to improve their land. It was not enough, however. Another decree in 743 provided that newly reclaimed land could be held in perpetuity: that is, could be passed to the developer's heirs. This in effect created a right of private property in land.

The principle of public ownership was also being undermined in other ways. The majority of households, being of fairly stable size and composition, were entitled to much the same amount of land at each reallocation. This being so, officials found it simpler to let them have the same fields, which eventually came to

be considered theirs by custom. Moreover, as the bureaucracy struggled with the system's manifold complexities, reallocation was often carried out late, or took place at more extended intervals, possibly not at all. After about 800 the redistribution of land required by the law became infrequent and irregular. At the same time, tax officials were becoming lax about forwarding revenue to the central government.

It was in these circumstances that there emerged private landed estates. The regulations under which it was permitted to bring new land into production, then retain it outside the *kubunden*, favoured developers who had status and resources: religious houses, both national and regional; members of the nobility, usually acting through agents; and men of substance in the locality, who might themselves be minor officials. After all, it was necessary first to acquire land for development, often by purchase. This done, the land had to be cleared and an irrigation system built, a task requiring a substantial labour force (usually recruited by hiring peasants from nearby areas, who might become cultivators on the new estate when the operation was completed). The final step was to register the land as privately held. This involved lodging documents with the relevant local and central offices – a task, like the rest, which would not be easy for smallholders, acting alone.

It is usual to translate the word *shōen*, the name given to these estates, as 'manor', but this suggests a greater unity of landholding and ownership than was in fact the case. The nature of *shōen* depended a good deal on local conditions, but there was usually some kind of tax-free nucleus, deriving either from the status of the nominal developer (a senior court official, a shrine or temple, perhaps) or from a specific permit issued by the government. To obtain the latter would in any case require the intervention of a powerful court family or religious order as a rule. The nucleus was likely then to be expanded by commendation: other local landholders, in the hope of sharing the tax-free privilege, or of receiving comparable benefits, such as office within the *shōen*, would join their own parcels of land to the estate, though not all

these would be made tax-free. In this way, a number of different people came to have a variety of interlocking rights in the land. These were known as *shiki*, which usually comprised a percentage of the crop. The cultivator had a customary share, which his descendants could inherit. So did the first developer of the new land, usually called the proprietor (*ryōke*), who might not be resident, if he had other holdings of any size. Further shares went to estate officials, often agents of the proprietor, or men of some standing who had commended their land to him. Finally there was a 'patron' (*honke*): that is, a noble or religious house with influence in the capital, whose function it was to provide political protection. The patron, too, was entitled to a share.

By the end of the Heian period, a *shōen* typically had at its centre a house and land held personally by the senior estate official. Its cultivators owed him both dues and labour. The rest of the land, larger in area, was that of the proprietor. The cultivators resident on it were divided into the relatively well-to-do, part of whose land was worked for them by others, possibly transients, and the smallholders, dependent on family labour. The more affluent households were likely to include a number of menials (*genin*), who were virtually slaves.

The rice paddies, which were the most highly prized part of the complex, depended on natural water supplies – possibly enhanced by storage ponds – distributed through a system of irrigation channels. Most of this irrigated land was held by the proprietor, estate officials or the better-provided local inhabitants, who would furnish seeds for the crop, perhaps also oxen for ploughing. The poor peasants had to make do with dry fields, or non-irrigated rice plots, created by burning off the ground cover. They could not afford to eat rice, which they grew to pay as tax and dues, living instead on millet, supplemented by roots and wild grasses, plus the fish, birds or animals they could catch. Their clothing was made mostly from hempen cloth, hemp being a dry-field crop. So were most of the cereals they ate – barley and millet – as well as soya beans, vegetables and mulberry (for silk), which went to their social superiors. An estate, both for its

residents and its absentee proprietors, was therefore largely self-sufficient. Only items like salt, iron agricultural tools and pottery had to be provided from outside.

As *shōen* increased in size and number, the financial effects became far-reaching. Aristocrats like the Fujiwara, who were powerful enough to be patrons many times over, grew wealthier by virtue of their income from land, and hence relied less on the emoluments of office. State revenue, by contrast – and it was this that sustained the emperor's own expenditure, as well as the government machine – became less dependable. In the ninth and tenth centuries, an attempt was made to overcome the problem by requiring tax payments to central government to be made in the form of fixed quotas, which provincial and local officials had a duty to meet (though they were allowed to retain any surplus they collected). In the eleventh century, the court turned also to the scrutiny of land rights, especially those of *shōen*. The results were fiscally disappointing. From the time of Go-Sanjō a different approach was tried: land confiscated after an investigation of title found its way, not back into the pool of *kubunden*, but into new *shōen*, registered in the name of ex-emperors, or imperial ladies, or one of the religious houses under imperial patronage. In other words, the emperor set out to solve his own financial problems by recognising in principle the legitimacy of *shōen*. By the end of the Heian period, the imperial house had acquired rights in something like a thousand such estates, spread through sixty provinces, more than any other family or institution in Japan. By doing so it increased its wealth, but further undermined the finances and the authority of the central government that acted in its name.

The rise of a warrior class after 800

Further evidence of the decay of Nara institutions had come in 792, when the conscript system was abandoned. Provincial officials relied thereafter on forces recruited locally, usually from

members of leading families in the countryside, who could afford to mount and arm themselves. At times the units so formed had police powers entrusted to them by the court, thereby becoming semi-official. Other men of similar background entered the service of local proprietors (*ryōke*) who had developed private estates. More found employment in the capital, perhaps as imperial guards, enjoying minor court rank, or in the entourage of Heian nobles. In other words, there was now a profession of arms, which could be followed in either the public or the private context.

After the middle years of Heian, warriors of this kind were to be found in all parts of Japan, but it was in the Kanto plain, Japan's largest single area of arable, bounded by the sea on one side, by the mountains from Hakone to Nikko on the other, that they were at their most numerous. The Kanto was the main supply base and recruiting ground for armies sent against the Emishi, the primitive tribes in the north. Because of the experience that the campaigns gave them, Kanto fighting men were better versed in the skills of warfare than the rest. They also took the lead in developing a warrior code, distinct from the rules of behaviour that bound the aristocracy. It emphasised courage in battle, as one would expect, but also personal loyalty to those who were deemed to be lords. In this were the seeds of vassalage. There was also a fierce pride in status and reputation. It became common for a man, when a skirmish or a battle was about to begin, to ride out in front of his fellows to announce his name and lineage, together with his previous feats of bravery, in order to find an opponent worthy of his steel, one who would meet him in single combat. To support such boasts, prowess in battle had to be proved, preferably by the taking of heads.

These warriors were becoming known as samurai, armed 'retainers', though not yet in the sense of an ordered status that the term acquired in the Edo period. Some Heian samurai might hold high rank, if they served the emperor or a Fujiwara lord. Others were little more than bodyguards, or provincials with modest land rights of their own. These found men to whom to pledge their loyalty among provincials of higher social standing

than themselves. Although the high-born of the capital were reluctant to take provincial posts, because they carried lower rank and less prestige than those at court, they were well aware that service in distant regions promised private gain. A provincial governor, like his subordinates, could manipulate tax collection to his own advantage. He could also use his office as a means of acquiring land rights in his own name. Some who profited in this way thought so highly of the benefits that they chose to stay in the province when their appointment came to an end, enlarging their landed interests, establishing family and supporters in nearby holdings, forming marriage ties with influential neighbours. By the tenth century there had come into existence in this way an upper layer of provincial society, whose members still had links with the court, but no longer wholly depended on it for favour. They acquired a following among local warriors; and with their support they undertook military adventures, sometimes against provincial rivals, sometimes against 'rebels' in the emperor's name, sometimes against the Emishi in the north. Out of the shared experience there grew a relationship that had the character of vassalage.

Two families, the Taira and the Minamoto – one might better call them clans, for they had many branches – stood out from the rest. Both were of imperial descent. Both acquired extensive land rights in the Kanto in the tenth and eleventh centuries, becoming in the process what the court had reason to consider 'overmighty subjects'. In 940 one of them, Taira Masakado, seeking to extend his influence in the provinces where he had estates, went so far as to give himself the title of 'New Emperor' and nominate provincial governors of his own. It took an alliance of regional magnates like himself, acting for the emperor in Heian, to bring him to heel. Fifty years later, Minamoto Yoshiie (1041–1108) acquired so great a reputation by victorious campaigns in the north that men flocked to declare their allegiance and commend their lands to him. This so alarmed the court that a decree was issued, prohibiting the practice. Yoshiie submitted. He remained none the less a figure of importance in the capital.

Taira and Minamoto were not mere provincials, after all. From the time of Fujiwara Michinaga (966–1028), the Minamoto had acted as the military arm of Fujiwara power, winning senior court office for their pains and a reputation as the regents' 'running dogs'. Yoshiie returned to Heian after 1091 to contribute to this role. Meanwhile the Taira, led by the Ise branch of the house, were pushing their lands into central and western Japan, becoming in the process patrons of the famous shrine at Miyajima on the shores of the Inland Sea. Once established in that region, they, too, took up a career in Kyoto, serving the retired emperors in their contests with the Fujiwara. In this way they set the stage for a struggle for power between the two great warrior clans, the outcome of which was Japan's first feudal government (Chapter 5).

Heian culture

The move away from Chinese models in Heian culture did not become evident until the middle of the period. During the first hundred years of Heian, Chinese learning was still the norm among the members of the aristocracy and officialdom. The court continued to publish collections of their Chinese verse (three of which were arranged in accordance with the rank of the contributors). Most of the poems themselves were serious in theme and no more than graceful in achievement, like those produced in Nara. They were also overwhelmingly masculine in authorship, since Chinese studies were not believed to be a proper accomplishment for women. With the passage of time, however, the prestige of things Chinese declined. Even Sugawara Michizane, who was a better Chinese poet than most, contributed to the change: his refusal to go to China as envoy in 894 marked the end of Japanese missions to Ch'ang-an. Thereafter, although Chinese remained the country's classical language, giving access to Chinese culture through books, there was no longer the stimu-

lus of occasional personal contact with the artistic and intellectual world of the Chinese capital.

Buddhism, too, though still indebted to China in matters of doctrine, adjusted to its Japanese surroundings in other respects. Buddhist houses, whose highest ranks were filled from the aristocracy, gave a lead in the development of private estates (*shōen*). Some acquired their own military force, composed of lay mercenaries or priests bearing arms. The most powerful increased their wealth and influence through branch temples, becoming larger in the process. By late Heian the Enryakuji, headquarters of the Tendai sect, supervised something approaching 400 branches and had over 3,000 buildings in its complex on Mount Hiei.

From the tenth century, however, there came a change of religious mood, as Heian society became more and more a prey to melancholy and disillusion. Men and women, faced by weak emperors, extravagant (and notoriously immoral) nobles, luxury-loving clergy and poverty-stricken peasants, began to seek a more satisfying religious experience than was afforded by the scholastic, scripture-based Buddhism of the past. They found it, as often as not, in the cult of Amida. Japan was approaching, it was said, the long-predicted onset of the Latter Days of the Law (*mappō*), when the faith would enter a phase of decline, in which it would be hard for believers to secure salvation by their own unaided efforts. They would need the help of those with greater spiritual standing than themselves – that is, of bodhisattvas – if they were to escape the sufferings of this mortal life. Amida (Amitabha) was the one to whom they chiefly turned.

In 985 the Tendai monk Genshin wrote a book that set out the argument for this in powerful terms. It began with a graphic description of the Buddhist hells, to which those who failed would be consigned. He contrasted this with an account of the Pure Land of the Western paradise, entry to which could be secured by those who sincerely invoked the name of Amida. The book was enormously popular, partly, perhaps, because so much of it was gruesome. Unlike some of his predecessors, however, Genshin did not use his popularity to found a new sect. Instead,

his ideas spread widely within both Tendai and Shingon. They also contributed to a similar movement focused on Jizō (Ksitigarbha), a bodhisattva whose powers were thought to be more efficacious in saving men from hell than in leading them to paradise.

The new religious attitudes had an important impact on Japanese literature and art in the second half of the Heian period, when the preoccupations of both became more human and this-worldly, their context more recognisable as Japanese. Their idioms of expression were also more Japanese, exemplified in prose tales (*monogatari*) and narrative picture-scrolls (*e-maki*). One step in this direction was a resumption of the publication of court collections of poetry in Japanese, a practice abandoned for many years. The first to appear, early in the tenth century, was entitled *Kokinshū*. Compared with the eighth-century *Manyōshū*, it contains hardly any long poems, a good many anonymous ones, more by women, fewer by the highest-ranking members of society. Sentiments are more refined – one is tempted to use the word pejoratively – and love poems less carnal. There are many references to the seasons, conveyed in detailed observations of birds and flowers, of wind and snow and rain. It is not difficult to believe that poems such as this were a part of aristocratic social intercourse, contributions to poetry contests on set themes. Slight, mannered, yet sharp in their imagery, they were to lay down the standards for Japanese verse for hundreds of years.

One of the contributors to *Kokinshū* was Ki no Tsurayuki, a noble who served as governor of Tosa, a province in Shikoku, between 931 and 934. After his tour of duty he travelled back to the capital, gratefully, one suspects, and mostly by sea, a 55-day journey that seemed full of peril and discomfort to a lifelong resident of Heian. He wrote an account of the voyage (in Japanese, not Chinese), which is known as *Tosa Nikki*. It contains many poems, interwoven with the prose by way of greetings and fare-wells, or as comments on the scenery. This gives his writing something of the air of a literary exercise. It is nevertheless about real people doing real things, hence a forerunner of later works that go by the name of history. There is a touch of the everyday

about it, missing from much of Japan's early writing: the pilot who interrupts a farewell party because wind and tide are right for departure, only to be dubbed 'a man of no sensibility' for his pains; alarms about the risk of storms or attack by pirates, bringing urgent appeals for help to both Buddha and the *kami*; the discovery, when the travellers reach Heian, that the governor's house and garden have suffered from neglect, despite being entrusted to the care of a neighbour.

The *Tosa Nikki* has a quite different range of subject-matter from that of other diaries in the middle years of the period. Most of these, written by court ladies, were accounts of personal experience within the narrow social circle of the palace and aristocracy: problems of marriage, the behaviour of lovers, visits to temples and festivals (ostensibly, at least, for the purpose of writing poems), the choice of clothes for such occasions, comments on the people encountered in the daily round. It is all very charming and delicately expressed, sometimes witty, occasionally acid-tongued, but contains hardly a hint of how life is lived in the capital at large, let alone the rest of Japan.

Much the same is true of Japan's first major novel, The Tale of Genji (*Genji monogatari*), written early in the eleventh century. The author was in all probability Murasaki Shikibu, a court lady whose diary was also published. Her novel, however, is a much more considerable piece of work. It tells the story of the life and loves of Prince Genji, son of an emperor, but not in the line of succession, whose birth and social graces make him well-nigh irresistible to the ladies he encounters (starting with one whom the emperor married after Genji's mother died). The plot is diffuse, its broader themes, where they exist, only lightly sketched, its characterisation subtle. This makes for a closely observed but unexciting narrative, appropriate to the way of life that it describes. There is some reference to intrigues for office and their great importance to the aristocracy, but not in other respects very much about the practice of politics and government. Genji's brief and voluntary exile, when he is out of favour, is a gentlemanly affair, taking him to the coast a mere 50 miles away, where he has

estates to support him. Later, we are told, he rises to a position of considerable influence, but this, too, impinges very little on the story. The book, in fact, is much more about its women than its men, despite Genji's central place in it.

All these works were written by aristocrats and read by aristocrats, accessible to many because they were in Japanese, popular in the world that they described. They were not regarded as 'serious' literature, which by Chinese standards excluded fiction in any case. Other tales had even less claim to dignity. Among the earliest was The Tales of Ise (*Ise monogatari*), a collection of stories, mostly about the amatory adventures of a single character, which may have been the inspiration for parts of *Genji*. Each story provided the theme for a poem. By contrast, The Bamboo-cutter's Tale (*Taketori monogatari*), which also dates, like *Ise*, from the early tenth century, is a folk-story. It tells how a tiny girl, found by the bamboo-cutter in a bamboo plant, quickly grows into a beautiful princess. Many men court her; each is set a test, which he fails; and in the end she is claimed again by her own people, the Moon-people, who had imprisoned her in the bamboo by way of punishment.

Tales of a Time Now Past (*Konjaku monogatari*) was a book on an altogether larger scale. It brought together more than a thousand stories, most of them very short, some from India and China, others from Japan, telling of men and women who are described as being real people, identified as to period, rank, office, village or temple, as the case may be. Many of the tales are about popular Buddhism, especially the doctrine of karma, setting out the influence, good and bad, which human actions can have on one's fate, either in this life or in a future one. Others take up ethical themes, such as filial piety. At the opposite end of the spectrum are tales which are sexual, even pornographic. In general, the contents are grouped by theme, whether religious or secular: daring, skill and ingenuity, the prowess and ideals of warriors, malevolent and supernatural creatures. One of the best known is the story of the Dōjōji bell and the widow who becomes a snake to secure revenge on a faithless lover-monk. This was later a famous play. Another is

'Rashōmon', of which Akutagawa Ryūnosuke wrote a twentieth-century version, made into a film by Kurosawa Akira. It describes how a man goes into the forests round Kyoto with his wife. They meet a robber, who first persuades the man to exchange his bow for a sword, then uses the bow to force him to submit. Tying the man to a tree, the robber rapes his wife. (The film version, it should be said, is less straightforward than this.)

The enormous variety of material to be found in the prose fiction of late Heian, set against backgrounds that range from the court to village life, was the beginning of a literary tradition lasting well into the nineteenth century. The main addition to it during the middle ages was a category of war tales (*gunki monogatari*), appropriate to the tastes of a warrior ruling class. The Edo era (1600–1867) added novels of urban life. In both periods there also existed a new kind of historical writing, the 'historical' tales (*rekishi monogatari*), written in Japanese, which also had their forerunners in Heian. To one of these, The Tale of Splendour (*Eiga monogatari*), we have already referred when discussing the rise of the Fujiwara. It was compiled at various dates during the eleventh century, probably by women, though this has not been established with any certainty; and it took up the narrative of Japanese history from the point at which the official chronicles in Chinese had come to an end (the year 887). The last date recorded in it is 1028. Another such work, The Great Mirror (*Ōkagami*), dating from the late eleventh or early twelfth century, covers much the same period (*c.* 850–1025). Both works are anonymous.

These histories are in one respect traditional in format, being chronicles centred on the affairs of the court, especially its politics. In *Eiga monogatari*, anecdotes are interpolated into the chronological framework: items about the family history of the Fujiwara and the imperial house, together with descriptions of ceremonial occasions. They provide more colour and human detail than were ever to be found in the official histories. *Ōkagami* does more. It elaborates the format, first, by adding separate sections of biographical and other supplementary information in the manner of China's dynastic histories, and second, by setting out its text as

if it were an exchange of reminiscence and opinion between two very old men, who had lived through the events that were being described. This contrives a place for incidents – not always disinterested, one suspects – to illustrate the kind of self-seeking, pettiness and drunken violence that were often part of the struggles for power at court. There is a tone of criticism about it that is absent from the very much blander pages of *Eiga monogatari*. There is even an attempt to identify causation in a rudimentary way, mostly in the form of references to karma.

If Heian histories were about the court, Buddhism long remained the chosen subject of art. During the ninth and tenth centuries, statuary continued to be religious, hence Chinese or Indian in appearance, though some of the later examples became more Japanese in dress and features. Painting, also religious in subject, grew more elaborate as it tried to express ideas about Amida and Jizō: that is, to depict bodhisattvas and some of the more ferocious deities. In the Phoenix Hall of the Byōdōin near Uji, commissioned in 1053, door panels and murals show several versions of Amida's descent, escorted by a large retinue of saints and guardians, to welcome the soul of a dying believer into paradise. There is a similar work on hanging scrolls at Mount Koya, the headquarters of Shingon. In both cases the main figures are traditionally Buddhist in style, but they are set in a clearly Japanese landscape.

This kind of work marks the emergence of what are called 'Japanese' paintings (Yamato-e), to distinguish them from those in the Chinese style (Kara-e). Subjects became more obviously Japanese and not necessarily Buddhist. There are murals in the Hōryūji, dating from 1069, which tell the life of Prince Shōtoku. By the twelfth century, Japan had a portrait painter, Fujiwara Takanobu, recording contemporary personalities at the court. His subjects, supposedly sketched from life, astonished his contemporaries by their fidelity to the originals, while his style was to become the norm in portraits of the great in the Kamakura, Muromachi and Edo periods.

The process of moving away from Chinese models can be

seen most clearly in the history of picture-scrolls (*e-maki*). These originated in China, where they were produced in very large numbers before and during the T'ang. The earliest recorded in Japan – hardly any are extant – were imports, copies or imitations in typically Chinese format. That is to say, the scroll was divided into panels from right to left, the top half of each panel being an illustration, the bottom half the text. There are literary references to later scrolls of this kind in the ninth century, though none survive. Nor do those from the tenth and eleventh centuries, when there is evidence that the technique was frequently in use, either to illustrate the diaries and *monogatari* of the period, or to keep a record of ceremonies and festivals. Scrolls, like poetry, had a place in courtly parlour games.

It was not until the twelfth century that the picture-scroll became established as a major art form in Japan. There are four outstanding examples from that time. The first, belonging to the early part of the century, comprised a series of scenes from the novel *Genji monogatari*, each scene taking up the full height of a panel (21.8 cm) and preceded by the relevant section of the novel's text. Paper and calligraphy are both part of the design. Colours are rich and thickly applied; the viewpoint is obliquely from above; roofs are omitted to afford a view of interiors; and faces are represented conventionally (a hook for the nose, two slits for the eyes, a red dot for the lips). Most of these conventions are to be found in subsequent Japanese art, especially Edo prints and book illustrations.

A quite different kind of work, produced some decades later, was the *Shigisan-engi*. Its subject is a folk-tale about a miracle involving a Buddhist priest and a flying ricebowl. Nearly all the scenes are set out of doors, unlike *Genji*, and include large numbers of peasants, assembled in crowds and depicted in lightly coloured line drawings of dramatic movement. Facial expressions, individually drawn, are lively, almost caricatures, having a strong resemblance to those to be found in some nineteenth-century Hiroshige prints. The scroll itself is a continuous whole, not broken up into separate panels. This was a new technique, which

was to be the norm in later *e-maki*.

Ban Dainagon e-kotoba, unlike the first two works, describes a real event, taken from the ninth century: a fire at one of the Heian palace gates, started in the course of a dispute between two courtiers. Here both types of treatment are combined. Interiors are in the manner of *Genji*, except that the faces of the nobles are given more expression; exteriors are more like *Shigisan*, especially where there are crowd scenes of guards and firefighters. The colour is often vivid, the details of dress and weaponry are drawn with care.

The fourth of this group, *Chōjū-giga*, is not at all like any of the rest. It is the work of painter-monks, not court artists; it has no written text; and it consists of black line drawings without any colouring. The first (and most famous) of its four scrolls shows animals engaged in human-type activities: swimming, wrestling, archery, conducting Buddhist ceremonial. It is often taken to be social satire. The second scroll consists of realistic drawings of animals, real and legendary. Both these are attributed to a Buddhist monk called Kakuyu, painting in the mid twelfth century. The remaining two scrolls are by a different hand, probably in the following century. One shows monks and laymen at play, the other, which is sometimes distinctly heavy-handed in its humour, various animals in parodies of human action.

The new trends in literature and art that belong to the second half of the Heian period, principally its final hundred years, manifest, one must suppose, the effect of upper-class patronage and prevailing human attitudes on the work of writers and artists. In other words, they reflect changes in society. At the same time, both *e-maki* and *monogatari* established criteria in subject-matter and style that are now taken to be inherently 'Japanese'. They were to last until Edo, or even beyond. Culturally, therefore, the later part of Heian was not only a break with the past, helping to confirm the influence of Chinese civilisation in Japan as an aspect of the 'classical', but also a bridge to the next – predominantly feudal – phase of Japanese history.

CHAPTER 5

Japanese Feudalism

The terrain has not made Japan easy to govern as a single unit. Sea passage between the four main islands depends on weather conditions. Interiors are mountainous. In Honshu and Kyushu, which have been the heartland of history, a mountain spine, high and rugged in places, runs from northeast to southwest, dividing the Pacific and Japan Sea coasts. From it spurs lead down to narrow coastal plains, enclosing steep valleys, which are the principal means of access to the interior. Rivers are short, fast running after summer rains, dwindling in the drier winter. They cannot be used for transport, except near the sea and in the small number of more extensive plains surrounding the modern cities of Sendai, Tokyo, Nagoya, Kyoto-Osaka and Fukuoka.

The geographical obstacles to centralised rule were overcome in early centuries, if at all, by virtue of the emperor's prestige, reinforced by claims of divine descent and the adoption of an imported culture in the capital. In modern times, better transport and communications have served the same end. Between the two, Japan had a more loose-knit political structure, akin to that of feudalism in medieval Europe. It was slow to develop. One essential ingredient, vassalage, by which vertical relationships within a landholding military class were governed, was already present to some degree in the eleventh century (Chapter 4). Another,

serfdom, defining the peasant's subordination to lord, did not exist in Japan in its European form, because the two land systems differed; but the fact of subordination was never in doubt, while the institutions that embodied it became more like those of Europe in and after the fifteenth century.

It must also be said that samurai were not in all respects equivalent to European knights, if only because the nature of warfare was not the same. In a land of steep, terraced hillsides and flat valley floors, laid out in flooded rice-fields and crossed by irrigation channels, one cannot easily picture heavily armoured knights, lances levelled, charging on horseback against their enemies. For most of history, samurai had lighter and more flexible armour than their European counterparts. Their chosen weapons were the bow-and-arrow when mounted, the sword for hand-to-hand fighting on foot. They were therefore cheaper to arm. Samurai needed smaller fiefs than knights, which made them more numerous, if less affluent.

Warriors, vassalage and landholding were first brought together in what might be called a feudal state as the result of Minamoto victory over the Taira between 1180 and 1185. By choosing to exercise his power thereafter from Kamakura, not Heian, Minamoto Yoritomo made a clear distinction between himself and previous 'advisers' to the emperor. He also provided historians with the first of a series of non-imperial labels for Japanese history. These were the places from which Shogun, or feudal overlords, ruled – Kamakura (1185–1333), Muromachi (1336–1573), Edo (1603–1868) – or the family names of lines of Shogun (Ashikaga, Tokugawa). The periods these identify were not equally 'feudal'. During Kamakura there was still a balance of sorts between the court, representing the vestiges of imperial rule, and the Bakufu, through which the Shogun exercised his power. In Muromachi, despite the fact that emperor and Shogun shared a capital city, Japan moved much closer to a truly feudal type of government and society. In Edo the transition to a modern state began, though vassalage remained the key to status and authority. All three stages were preceded by periods of civil war.

The Kamakura Bakufu (1185–1333)

In the twelfth-century struggles between the Taira and the Minamoto (see Chapter 4), the Taira were at first the more successful
of the two. Eventually, victory in a series of clashes between 1156
and 1160 enabled them to expel the Minamoto leaders from the
capital, leaving it under their own control. Taira Kiyomori (c.
1118–81) promptly took a leaf from the Fujiwara book. He had
himself appointed Daijō-daijin (Great Minister of State); put Taira
kinsmen into a range of other key posts in central government;
and married a daughter into the imperial line. In 1190 the emperor
Takakura was forced to abdicate, making way for his half-Taira
heir, Antoku, who was Kiyomori's grandson.

The headship of the Minamoto house had meanwhile passed
to Minamoto Yoritomo (1147–99), sent into exile in Izu province
at the edge of the Kanto plain. The years he spent there laid the
foundations for a Minamoto revival. In 1177, by marrying the
daughter of Hōjō Tokimasa, a local official of Taira descent, he
acquired Tokimasa as ally, then as vassal. He also became aware of
how important land rights were to the Kanto's fighting men, a
lesson he never forgot. When the opportunity came to seek
another trial of strength with the Taira leadership, he accordingly
offered all who would follow him written guarantees of title to
their land, whatever their lineage. This won local Taira warriors
to his cause, as well as Minamoto.

In the summer of 1180, having had indications of support
from members of the imperial family, who were jealous of Taira
Kiyomori's pretensions, Yoritomo raised the standard of revolt.
His first moves ended in defeat. From a refuge in the Hakone
mountains he then put together another force and tried again,
this time with success. By the end of the year, his opponents
were in retreat towards the capital, while Yoritomo settled down
to consolidate his hold on the Kanto plain from a base established
at Kamakura.

In 1183 Yoritomo's cousin, Yoshinaka, led a Minamoto advance

on Kyoto. He soon captured the city, but the victory was less than complete, since the Taira fled, seeking safety in their lands to the west and taking with them the child-emperor, Antoku, together with the symbols of his authority. At this point Yoritomo sent his young half-brother, Yoshitsune – a hot-head, in the estimation of his fellow commanders – to conduct the rest of the campaign. In the spring of 1184 his forces won a resounding victory at Ichi-notani, near modern Kobe, a battle, as the chronicles tell the tale, in which the turning-point came when Yoshitsune himself led a headlong mounted charge down a steep escarpment to fall on the Taira flank and rear. His bravado made him a legend.

The final confrontation came in a naval battle – or, more precisely, an engagement fought by samurai in ships – at Dannoura in the Shimonoseki Straits. This was in April of the following year. Despite the greater maritime experience of those who fought for the Taira, the weakness of their leadership – Kiyomori was dead, his surviving sons lacked resolution – plus the fighting qualities of battle-hardened Minamoto troops, once more gave Yoshitsune the advantage. When all seemed lost, a Taira court lady seized the boy-emperor and jumped with him into the sea. Both drowned. So, too, did Kiyomori's widow. With them went the sword from the imperial regalia, never to be recovered (though it was eventually replaced). Many Taira warriors committed suicide, preferring to drown rather than face capture. Local tradition says that their ghosts still haunt the scene.

These events not only confirmed Yoritomo's power, they furnished an abundant crop of war tales for Japanese literature. Some of them are true (as far as one can tell). Others are the product of fertile imaginations, not always well informed. There is, for example, a fog of uncertainty about Yoshitsune's fate after Dannoura. It seems clear that Yoritomo came to think of him as a potential rival; that he nevertheless contrived to escape to a refuge in the north; and that he was betrayed and killed there, his head sent to Kamakura. Yet the details of the story have been so embroidered over time as to become more fiction than fact, its hero, at least in Edo drama, was Yoshitsune's loyal retainer, Benkei.

One nineteenth-century version even claims that Yoshitsune survived and made his way to the Asian mainland, where he emerged again as the Mongol leader, Genghis Khan.

More soberly, the campaigns and the stories they engendered had a vital place in shaping the warrior code. Courage and loyalty remained its central themes, as they had always been. Taking part in set-piece battles, however, instead of local skirmishes or urban quarrels, provided a wider audience for the incidents in which these qualities were displayed. In such a situation, warriors became more aware of the good opinion of their fellows. Loyalty, a manly sentiment, began to take precedence over other, less urgent ties, like duty to wives and family. Indeed, those who took part in these events acquired a greater sense of being an élite, marked out from lesser men, not only by pride in bearing arms, but also by the dignity of vassalage. They began to see themselves collectively as potential rulers, no longer simply as 'retainers'. Minamoto Yoritomo was able to make use of them.

The Taira had chosen to control Japan by controlling the court, as the Fujiwara had done. Yoritomo took a different view. Content to impose his will on Kyoto from outside, he concerned himself with the day-to-day management of the sources of his strength, the land and warriors of the Kanto, creating what was to become the Bakufu. The first steps were taken during the civil war. To muster an army, Yoritomo had won over warrior-landholders to his cause by promises to guarantee their land rights. In return he required pledges of fealty and service, enrolling samurai of Taira as well as Minamoto blood to his vassals, or 'house-men' (*gokenin*). After 1183, when the fighting moved to the west, their numbers were increased by recruitment from the provinces through which the Minamoto armies passed, producing a total of over 2,000 men by the time hostilities ended. Many of these were men of substance, leading warrior bands of their own.

To regulate his dealings with this large following, Yoritomo had founded the Retainers' Office (Samurai-dokoro) in 1180, named after a Fujiwara house-organ of similar function. As his power grew, however, so did the needs of his administration.

Towards the end of 1184, two further offices were added: a General Office, later called the Mandokoro – another Fujiwara label – to handle Yoritomo's 'governmental' functions and the record keeping they required; and a feudal court, the Monchūjo, to adjudicate on disputes over land rights, boundaries and questions of vassalage. Although the latter's jurisdiction was in theory only over *gokenin*, it inevitably had to deal as well with complaints that were brought against them by non-vassals. This brought the greater part of the landed class within its purview.

There was little chance that a concentration of power as great as this could exist without reference to imperial authority. Late in 1183, when his troops were in occupation of Kyoto, Yoritomo's actions in the Kanto were given the emperor's blessing. A few months later the court gave its approval for an advance against the Taira in the west. Even so, it was December 1190 before Yoritomo himself set foot in the capital again; and although in 1192 he accepted the title of Sei-i-tai-Shōgun (abbreviated as a rule to Shogun), there is little indication that he saw this step as needed to confer legality on what he had achieved. The title made him nominally commander-in-chief in the north, giving a welcome measure of authority over samurai who were not his vassals, but beyond that he does not appear to have valued it unduly. He relinquished it before he died. In practice, indeed, it was his thirteenth-century successors who made the Shogun into *de facto* ruler of Japan. Yoritomo himself was content to rely on preponderant force, together with the co-operation of a Fujiwara ally at court, Kujō Kanezane, who became regent in 1186.

In devising the institutions through which to exercise his power, Yoritomo had as adviser another court noble, a bureaucrat named Ōe Hiromoto, who was invited to Kamakura in 1184. In 1185, when the civil war came to an end, Ōe recommended the extension to regions previously held by the Taira of two wartime offices, that of *shugo* (the military governor of a province) and *jitō* (a steward attached to a private estate, or *shōen*, representing Kamakura's tax-related interests). Both were to be chosen from Kamakura vassals. One object was to increase the Minamoto's reach, of

course. Another was to reward the *gokenin* for their services. The outcome was the creation in many parts of Japan of a network of officials, owing their first loyalty to Kamakura, who existed side by side with those appointed by Kyoto. The military governor was responsible for peacekeeping in his province. Stewards were to supervise the payment of dues from the estates on which they served, separating the part that was payable as tax from that which was owed to the various holders of land rights (*shiki*). Since these were issues about which disputes frequently arose, the *jitō*, like the *shugo*, was part of a general system of law and order. Thus Minamoto *gokenin* were spread widely through Japan, able to enrich themselves at no cost to their lord, either from tax revenue – a well-established practice among local officials of all kinds – or by the receipt of *shiki* of their own in the relevant estates. Their income, in other words, derived not from the Shogun, but either from the local population, or from the religious institutions and civil dignitaries who already held rights in *shōen*. As events were to show, this was not a formula for lasting peace in the countryside.

After Yoritomo's death in 1199, there were disturbances at the highest levels in Kamakura. His eldest son, Yoriie, was stripped of power in 1203, murdered in 1204; the next head of the house, Sanetomo, Yoriie's younger brother, was murdered in 1219. Sanetomo proved to be the last of Yoritomo's line. This left power in the hands of the most influential of the Minamoto vassals. Hōjō Tokimasa, Yoritomo's father-in-law, had been appointed regent (Shikken) to Yoriie in 1203 and had arranged Yoriie's murder in 1204. His son, Yoshitoki, replaced his father in 1205. Together they made the Hōjō regency a permanent feature of the Kamakura Bakufu.

Encouraged by what he believed to be the resulting weakness in Kamakura, the ex-emperor Go-Toba set out to restore the authority of the court. He rallied support among the warriors of central and west Japan, then sent an army against the Kanto in 1221, only to see it soundly defeated by Hōjō Yoshitoki. The victory was a signal for increasing Hōjō control of the Bakufu. The Minamoto were succeeded as Shogun by Hōjō nominees, at

first Fujiwara nobles, later princes of the royal blood. All were chosen as boys, then sent back to Kyoto on reaching manhood. In this way the Shogun, like the emperor, became a figurehead, subject to the same constraints – except the marital ones – that the Fujiwara had for centuries used to control the imperial line. There was also a new level of Bakufu dominance in Kyoto. Many of the ex-emperor's own *shōen* were confiscated, some soon to be restored under the supervision of *gokenin* as stewards, others to be distributed to the Hōjō and their allies. The powers and emoluments of *jitō* were more clearly spelt out, an implicit threat to the revenues of both emperor and courtiers. Yoshitoki's heir, Yasutoki, was installed in Kyoto as resident governor with the title of Rokuhara Tandai. Go-Toba was sent into exile, the reigning emperor replaced by another of Kamakura's choice.

The Hōjō remained effectively rulers of Japan under these arrangements until 1333. In 1232 they introduced a legal code of their own: a 'house law', defining the duties of *shugo* and *jitō*, setting out the penalties to be imposed on vassals who offended against the rules of discipline and behaviour, and laying down the principles on which disputes over landholding and succession were to be resolved. Their courts, although feudal, in the sense that they claimed jurisdiction only over *gokenin*, soon acquired an enviable reputation for evenhandedness in cases that court nobles, religious establishments and others aggrieved over land rights brought before them. Documents were carefully scrutinised, witnesses examined both in person and in writing, great efforts made to ensure that the court and its friends were not unjustly treated. All this bolstered the Bakufu's authority.

The judicial policy was part of a sharing of power between two separate political systems. Despite the military force at his disposal and the wide powers exercised on his behalf by *shugo* and *jitō*, the Shogun was not in a position to be despotic. Nor were the Hōjō. Formally, the latter, as a fourteenth-century court historian described them, were mere 'rear vassals': that is, a vassal's vassals. The Shogun himself was not a feudal overlord in the usual sense. He was a symbolic figure, recruited from Kyoto, not even a

warrior. The bonds of loyalty to him were inevitably weak. At the same time, the emperor, though his claims to absolute power were clearly unrealistic, was not devoid of political function. He continued to preside, at least in name, over a Chinese-style bureaucracy; issued laws that were binding on all but the Shogun's *gokenin*; named civil governors to provinces; received the taxes they collected. He had the means, moreover, to muster a sufficient body of armed support to challenge Kamakura in the field. This had happened in 1221, and was to happen again in 1333.

Nor can the lower levels of Japanese society be described as wholly feudal at this time. Small cultivators, living in earth-floored two-room huts, still suffered from a heavy burden of imperial taxes if they were on 'public' land. Immediately above them a mixed stratum of more substantial local residents included farmers with larger holdings, part of which was likely to be taxable by the state; local government officials appointed by the court, who also held land; officials of private estates (*shōen*); and Kamakura vassals, serving as *jitō*. More affluent, these had houses with wooden floors, outbuildings for their servants and cattle, perhaps a surrounding earth embankment to protect them against casual violence. They might all possess rights (*shiki*) in one or more of the district's *shōen*, but this did not guarantee unity of allegiances. Local officials were part of a structure stretching upwards to Kyoto's ministries. *Jitō*, as *gokenin*, had obligations to the Shogun's council. Estate officials acted on behalf of absentee patrons and proprietors, most of whom would be court nobles, or nominees of the imperial family, or the heads of religious institutions, though some might belong to powerful warrior houses. It is hard to disentangle the feudal from the non-feudal in such a situation.

The pattern was not a stable one, moreover. Despite Kamakura's efforts to restrain them, *jitō* did not remain content with the modest share of the crop – 11 per cent at best – that they were allotted as recompense for their services. There were many devices by which they could enlarge it. In particular, since their duties placed them between the cultivators and the estate officials on the one side, and the patrons and proprietors on the other, it was easy

for them to hinder, or even block, the distribution of dues from the former to the latter. They could therefore set a price for their co-operation. One 'compromise' that emerged quite frequently was for percentage dues to be made fixed annual payments, leaving the *jitō* to pocket any excess he might be able to collect. Another was division of the land itself, part of it handed to the *jitō* in private title, in return for a promise that dues on the rest would be delivered without fail.

Given that *jitō* were the Shogun's vassals, who were assumed to enjoy official favour, many patrons and proprietors accepted such terms, or even offered them. Those who did not, especially if they were confident of their own political backing, sought justice in the Bakufu's courts. By doing so, they presented Kamakura with a difficult choice. To support the *gokenin* would offend influential plaintiffs, most of them linked with the court or with major shrines and temples. This would run counter to partnership with Kyoto, which the Bakufu still valued. To find against the vassals, on the other hand, would risk undermining their loyalty. It is not surprising that an attempt was therefore made to hold a middle line. Inevitably, it satisfied neither party.

Refusal to support their more extreme demands with respect to land aroused a sense of grievance among *gokenin*. It was made more severe by the results of Mongol attacks on Japan in the second half of the thirteenth century. When Khubilai Khan became emperor of China in 1260, he set about restoring that country's international dignity, as expressed in the tribute system. Japan in Chinese eyes had in the past been part of it. He therefore sent a letter to the 'king' of Japan, demanding that envoys be sent to pay him proper homage. Though not exactly threatening – neither side, it said, 'would wish to appeal to arms to settle this question' – the messengers from Korea by whom it was delivered to the Shogun in 1268 were clear that it should be taken seriously. Hōjō Tokimune, then regent in Kamakura, ignored it. Khubilai's response took time to materialise, because he wished first to be sure of his position on the mainland, but in November 1274 a fleet carrying 40,000 troops appeared off Hakata in northern

Kyushu. Landings were made; but although the Mongols proved better organised for fighting than the Japanese, they failed to establish a satisfactory bridgehead. Facing problems of supply, they finally withdrew. Storms scattered their ships as they made for home.

There followed an uneasy interval of preparation for another trial of strength. Fresh Mongol envoys arrived in Japan in 1275 and 1279, demanding submission. They were executed. The *gokenin* in Kyushu were ordered to make ready for a new attack; reinforcements were mustered; a defensive wall was built along the north Kyushu coast. Then in June 1281 the expected enemy appeared: two fleets this time, one from Korea, one from south China, bringing no fewer than 140,000 men. For several weeks fierce fighting raged along the Kyushu beaches, neither side gaining the upper hand, but in August the weather intervened in the shape of a typhoon, dispersing the Mongol ships with heavy losses. To many Japanese, notably Buddhist and Shinto priests, it was the 'divine wind' (*kamikaze*), sent by the gods in answer to their prayers.

The Shogun's vassals, especially those in west Japan, saw things differently. They had stood for several years awaiting the second attack; were to remain on military alert, expecting more (this situation lasted until Khubilai's death in 1294); and despite having borne much of the cost of the conflict, had almost nothing to show for it, whether by way of booty or additional land grants. Where rewards were made to those who had excelled, they involved, as often as not, confiscation from those who had failed. Both blamed the Bakufu for ingratitude. Yet there was less now that they could do to make their discontents felt. The Hōjō had responded to the foreign threat by tightening their hold on the conduct of affairs: more family appointments made to Kamakura offices; many extra posts – lucrative ones – acquired throughout the country. By 1333, when at last they were overthrown, members of the Hōjō house were military governors (*shugo*) in more than half Japan's provinces, stewards (*jitō*) in an enormous number of estates.

What proved to be the catalyst in bringing about their fall was a crisis in relations with the court. Ever since 1221 Kamakura had intervened actively in Kyoto, choosing emperors, insisting on the appointment of particular officials. It assumed still more authority because of the Mongol wars. In 1275, when a fresh succession dispute arose, involving rival claims on behalf of two sons of the emperor Go-Saga, who had failed to choose between them before he died, the Bakufu stepped in to arbitrate. They and their successors, it ruled, were to constitute two imperial lines, reigning alternately. The result was to involve the Hōjō in much recrimination. Eventually, in 1326 Go-Daigo, emperor of what was called the junior line, refused to accede to a Hōjō request to abdicate in favour of a candidate from the senior one. After a further five years of acrimonious dispute, he was threatened with armed attack unless he complied. Go-Daigo fled from the capital. Captured and formally banished in 1332, he escaped in 1333. Once again troops were sent against him, led on this occasion by Ashikaga Takauji, a man who could claim descent from Minamoto Yoritomo. Go-Daigo won him over with lavish promises of reward. With Ashikaga help, an 'imperial' army, consisting mostly of disaffected samurai, was sent against Kamakura. In July the city was captured and burnt, and the last of the Hōjō committed suicide.

Feudalism in the Muromachi period (1336–1460)

Go-Daigo proved to be better at intrigue than government. His object, it soon appeared, was to restore the kind of institutions that had existed before the emperors lost their power, ignoring the changes that had taken place meanwhile. To this end, he chose court nobles as his principal officers, serving in Nara-style posts; refused to appoint a Fujiwara as Kampaku; refused — much more dangerously — to make Ashikaga Takauji Shogun. A programme was launched to restore to the aristocracy the land rights that had

fallen into warrior hands. Since the only effective military force at his disposal was composed of samurai, this, too, was folly.

For his part, Ashikaga Takauji appears in later histories as Japan's traitor *par excellence*. When he transferred his allegiance to Go-Daigo in 1333, he had abandoned his wife and sons in Kamakura, where they were likely to be held, he knew, as hostages for his loyalty. His wife, he argued, being a Hōjō, would come to no harm, his sons could be smuggled out by the guards he left behind for that purpose. In any case, 'in great undertakings one does not consider trivial things'. Following this principle, in 1335 he turned his coat again. Capturing what was left of Kamakura, he led his army against the emperor's capital, which he seized in 1336. Go-Daigo fled again, taking with him the imperial regalia, without which, he claimed, no ruler was legitimate. Disregarding this tradition, Takauji installed his own chosen candidate as emperor. The new man promptly made him Shogun.

Once Japan had acquired a warrior class, there were two avenues of power that were open to a prospective overlord. One was control of the court, which offered the prospect of legitimate authority and an opportunity to exploit the imperial prestige. The other was to depend more openly on the loyalty of warriors, secured, as it had to be, by confirmation of their lands. The Taira had opted for the first. The Minamoto, followed by the Hōjō, chose the second. Ashikaga Takauji, backed already by an army in the field, but faced – unusually – by a hostile emperor, or ex-emperor, ready to resort to force, decided that Kyoto was more critical to his success. He established himself in Muromachi, a district of the capital. To it he transferred the Bakufu's central institutions, inherited from Kamakura.

The decision proved to be a mistake. Although members of the Ashikaga house were to hold the office of Shogun until 1573, for a century and a half of the time the country was engaged in intermittent civil war. The first phase of it, known as the war between the northern and southern courts (Namboku-chō), was so named because the two sides declared allegiance to rival imperial lines, one ruling in Kyoto, protected by the Ashikaga,

the other, headed by Go-Daigo and his heirs, in exile in the Yoshino mountains to the south of the Nara plain. The latter had no army of any size, but attracted to their cause some notable 'loyalist' warriors – the most famous was Kusunoki Masashige – who kept their hopes of success alive in a series of guerrilla skirmishes. To this contest in the central provinces were added a number of smaller quarrels throughout the country, prompted by greed for land or family ambition, but carried on in the name of the northern and southern courts. As a result, all Japan was kept in ferment until 1392, when the third Ashikaga Shogun, Yoshimitsu, abandoning his former protégés, persuaded the southern line to come back to Kyoto.

Disorder, it proved, was fertile soil for the growth of warrior landed interests. The Ashikaga, unlike the Hōjō, were unwilling to act against their provincial followers, who were therefore left to seek compensation for the costs of war wherever they could find it. Inevitably, most did so at the expense of the proprietors and patrons of *shōen*. This led in time to a widespread reallocation, not only of land rights (*shiki*), but also of the land itself. In 1368 Muromachi announced that, where disputes arose, the division of land between claimants would be the norm in reaching a settlement, except where the land in question had as its patron the imperial house, or one of the branches of the Fujiwara qualified to fill the office of Regent, or a religious establishment. The exceptions were large, but the decision meant that *shōen* were now more likely to be broken up into smaller parcels, each under single ownership. Japan was moving towards a pattern that can be compared with the European fief.

Associated with the change was a degree of territorial con-solidation. In troubled times, land could be more easily defended than rights, the support of distant kin was less esteemed than that of well-armed neighbours. Men therefore tried to bring together scattered holdings and abandon those too distant to protect. There was also some modification of kinship structures. Family heads, reluctant to divide their holdings among several heirs, chose to name one or two to inherit the bulk of the estate, while laying

down instructions for keeping it together. Women's rights of inheritance necessarily suffered in this situation, because they were thought less likely, whether because of marriage or otherwise, to be able to hold what they were given. So did those of cultivators, who had to deal more often now with a single resident lord, able to put them under greater pressure. By the time the process was complete – and that was not until Japan's next long spell of civil war in many areas, starting late in the fifteenth century – the country was divided for the most part into estates of modest size, each more compact than those of the past and subject to unified control.

Those who benefited most from the years of turbulence in the fourteenth century were the military governors (*shugo*) appointed by the Ashikaga. In order to prosecute the civil war, they were given new powers: the collection of supplementary taxes for the Shogun's war chest, which were described as temporary, but had a way of becoming regular; and a measure of authority over local samurai, for the purpose of raising a force in case of need. With this as leverage, they were able to offer protection to their neighbours and build a private following. They also acquired fresh lands of their own. By the end of the century, the *shugo* was likely to be the largest landholder in the province to which he had been appointed. There would probably be a few others of substance, too, men much like themselves, but holding lands and office elsewhere. A high proportion of the local landholders of lower status were either vassals of these greater men, or acknowledged their influence in some less formal way. The *shugo*'s position, therefore, relied much less than it had before on Muromachi's favour.

Modern historians describe these men as *shugo-daimyō*, a hybrid term that places them at an intermediate stage between appointed military governors, as known in the Kamakura period, and the quasi-independent regional lords (daimyo) of the sixteenth century. The nature of their power implies at least the rudiments of subinfeudation. Under Kamakura, *shugo* and *jitō*, though different in function, had been equals in status, in so far as both

were direct vassals (*gokenin*) of the Shogun. Under the Ashikaga, the *shugo* were given an authority which put that equality in question; and as they acquired provincial vassals of their own, not all of whom owed a duty to the *shugo*'s overlord, they assumed a median place in the scale of vassalage. In this respect, too, Japan's feudalism was becoming more like Europe's.

Among the most powerful *shugo-daimyō* were several who were family members or senior vassals of the Ashikaga. The Hosokawa, for example, an Ashikaga branch house, holding office as deputy Shogun, were made *shugo* of no fewer than seven provinces, mostly in central Japan. By contrast, in west Japan the two outstanding names were those of Shimazu and Ōuchi, houses that rose to prominence without the help of Ashikaga connections. The Shimazu of southern Kyushu were descended from a Minamoto *gokenin* appointed as steward (*jitō*) to a former Taira estate, Shimazu-shō, from which the family subsequently took its name. In 1336 they declared allegiance to Ashikaga Takauji, who made them *shugo*. By the end of the fourteenth century their struggles against the *shōen*'s patrons, the Konoe family, had made them lords – not stewards – of an estate which included half the arable land in the three southern Kyushu provinces. The most important of these was Satsuma.

The Ōuchi had their base in the provinces of Nagato and Suō (later known in combination as Chōshū) at the western end of the Inland Sea. They were local officials in the area, recruited as *gokenin* to Minamoto Yoritomo during the wars against the Taira, then made *jitō* to a local *shōen*. In this capacity they accumulated land rights. When the Hōjō fell, they supported the Ashikaga, who made them *shugo* of Suō, an office in which they exploited their judicial and administrative powers to build up a following, both there and in neighbouring Nagato. At their peak they were dominant in the whole of the region west of Hiroshima: *shugo* of six provinces and possessors of a 'capital' at Yamaguchi, which won such fame as a centre of culture that it was known as 'the western Kyoto'.

One of the principal losers by these developments, apart from

the patrons of *shōen*, was the Shogun. By choosing to establish his base in Muromachi, Ashikaga Takauji had separated himself by some 300 miles from his lands in the Kanto, which had previously been his source of revenue and fighting men. True, he put the Kanto in the hands of a branch family, its head serving as his deputy (Kanrei) in the region; but in the long run, kinship was to prove no guarantee of loyalty, whether in the Kanto or elsewhere. His successors, therefore, could not rely on the Kanto's military force as a means of keeping overmighty lords in order. Other means of bolstering their authority had to be found.

One obvious device was to take court office, which still carried weight in the eyes of provincial lords, even those of considerable standing. In 1394, having settled the quarrel between the northern and southern dynasties, at least superficially, Yoshimitsu was made Daijō-daijin, head of the emperor's council. It was a post reserved to nobles of the very highest rank. Thereafter he took an ostentatious part in the social and ceremonial life of the capital.

More controversially, he re-opened relations with China in 1401 on the tribute basis from which Kamakura had held aloof. Describing himself in a letter to the Ming emperor Yung Lo as 'Your subject, the King of Japan' – Japanese patriots have condemned him for it ever since – he was given leave to send two ships to Ningpo every two years. The practice was to continue (with some irregularities) until China withdrew the privilege in 1549. This, too, was a step designed to give the Shogun a higher profile in his dealings with feudal lords, but there were also economic benefits. Japan had once more gained entry to the China trade on privileged terms. The ships that were sent there carried, in addition to envoys bound for the Chinese capital with tribute gifts, as many as two or three hundred merchants, who paid for their passage and the transport of their merchandise. Such payment was made to the sponsor of the voyage. This was sometimes the Shogun; but in later years the privilege might be granted (for an appropriate consideration) to a Buddhist house, a Shinto shrine or one of a handful of powerful lords. They in turn might pass the work of setting on foot the voyage to the merchants

of a favoured city, organised in guilds. At each level there were profits to be made.

Return gifts from the Ming, among which copper coins and silkstuffs were most highly prized, were of greater value than those Japan sent, as they had been at the time of the T'ang (Chapter 3), but it was now the Shogun who received them, not the emperor. In addition, the merchants brought back cargoes purchased on the Chinese open market. These included, as they had always done, silk and drugs, together with books, paintings and ceramics, all of which sold at high prices in Japan. A percentage went to the Bakufu, making up in part for the loss of income from the Shogun's Kanto lands, which were no longer fully under his control. The rest played a part in stimulating the growth of a commercial economy in Japan.

Not all was gain, however. The price Japan had to pay for China's consent to these arrangements, apart from the formalities of political subservience such as had to be observed by Japanese envoys, was co-operation in a drive against piracy. Pirates from the seas to the west and north of Japan, often based in the territories of lords like Shimazu and Ōuchi, had made large-scale attacks on the China coast in the fourteenth century. Yoshimitsu sent consignments of supposedly pirate heads to the Ming as an earnest of his readiness to suppress them. Yet it was always doubtful whether he had the means to do so. His writ did not run in Kyushu and western Honshu much of the time. His successors had even less power to intervene there, once civil war broke out again after 1467. The lords of that region usually gave the pirates a measure of protection. They also sought to trade with Ningpo on their own account, sometimes intercepting the official tribute ships and seizing the tallies (*kangō*), provided by the Ming, which showed a mission to be legitimate. The result was a level of turbulence in the trade – it was not unknown for rival Japanese missions to come to blows in Ningpo harbour – with which Ming officials at last lost patience. By the same token, the incidents bred a measure of resentment among the powerful lords of west Japan, directed against the Ashikaga.

The revenue that the Ashikaga were able to draw from the China trade was supplemented by yields from domestic commerce. Throughout the Kamakura and early Muromachi periods, agricultural production had been steadily increasing in Japan because of the introduction of double-cropping, new strains of seed, better irrigation, and more widespread use of fertilizer and farm animals. This made surpluses available, offered to purchasers in local markets and – on a more important scale – in Kyoto and other towns and cities, especially those that developed along the shores of the Inland Sea. Merchants who engaged in the manufacture of rice-wine (sake) in those centres, or in money-lending, often became rich, like those in the China trade. Coins, imported from China, were becoming more widely used.

The Bakufu found ways to tap this wealth. City merchants were brought under official patronage, their associations required to pay fees for the advantages this gave them. So were those religious houses that took part in trade and financial operations. Urban housing in the capital was taxed. The result was to make the Bakufu's finances less dependent on land and to provide a more flexible source of funds, which could be used to finance a less 'feudal' type of central administration.

Part of the money raised helped to pay for a local core of more or less full-time Bakufu officers. The regime had taken over from Kamakura a body of middle-ranking vassal-bureaucrats, men who handled most of the work of government and regarded the Shogun as their lord. In case of need, they could call on a permanent force of 2,000 or 3,000 mounted samurai, enfeoffed with lands in the neighbourhood of Kyoto, to keep order in and around the capital. This was particularly important because a number of leading *shugo-daimyō*, who were members of the councils responsible for the work of the Mandokoro and Samurai-dokoro, were required to live in the city under the Shogun's eye. It was hoped to limit their independence in this way, by separating them for much of the time from their lands. It also, however, provided opportunities for conspiracy. One Shogun, Ashikaga Yoshinori, tried in the fifteenth century to make use of his loyal officials and personal

guard to support a more autocratic form of rule in Kyoto, which would enable him to overrule his *shugo* advisers in the Bakufu councils. But the effort failed. In 1441 he was murdered by one of those whose influence he sought to undermine.

What seemed at this stage to be emerging at the centre in Japan was something like an Italian city state of late medieval Europe: a regime based on Kyoto and the nearby provinces, only partly feudal in its revenue and officialdom, and exercising little power in the remoter hinterland. By contrast, the rest of Japan was moving towards a more fully feudal pattern of lordship, fief and vassalage. The first result of this contradiction was a renewal of civil war. After 1460 succession disputes within the Ashikaga house, fanned by the ambitions of leading *shugo* lords, led to fighting in the capital, which grew in scale and scope until it embraced the whole of Japan. It eventually opened the way to a new political order, in which feudal lords acquired greater power within their lands, but became in other respects more subject to the Shogun's authority. So far-reaching was the change that it is more convenient to treat it separately (Chapter 7).

CHAPTER 6

Medieval Culture

1200–1450

The rise of feudalism eventually caused a decisive break with Chinese political institutions in Japan. It brought no such clearcut change in the nature of Japanese culture, though it contributed to a shift of emphasis. Where Chinese civilisation had struck deep roots, as it had in art and religion, it continued to flourish; and when Japan's links with China were renewed in the thirteenth, fourteenth and fifteenth centuries by the travels of Zen monks, it was given fresh impetus by the influence of Sung and Ming. In literature, by contrast, the trend that had begun at the very end of Heian, that of prose writing in Japanese for an audience wider than the court nobility, strengthened in Kamakura and Muromachi.

When court aristocrats lost their place as the country's most powerful patrons, first to the Shogun and his immediate vassals, then more and more to provincial lords, it was warrior preferences and tastes that came to determine the work of artists and authors. Samurai were to be for several hundreds of years the men who commissioned major buildings, who endowed monasteries, who were commemorated in portraits, who bought pictures, who gave employment to writers. Yet it does not follow from this that war tales became the only product of literature, or pictures of war the universal form of art. Senior samurai, following the example of

China's bureaucrats, thought themselves rulers as well as soldiers. Logically, they had to have the civil skills (*bun*), in addition to the military ones (*bu*), which the tasks of government required. For the sake of their prestige, they needed cultivated minds. This implied at least a passing acquaintance with classical literature and art.

Pre-feudal culture did not therefore wither on the bough because of neglect by an uncouth soldiery. Minamoto Yoritomo employed a Kyoto bureaucrat, Ōe Hiromoto, as adviser on civil institutions; the Hōjō wrote poetry; Ashikaga Shogun, especially Yoshimitsu and Yoshimasa, promoted a taste for Chinese painting, of which they were enthusiastic collectors. Court nobles of lower rank found in this situation a fresh source of income, to make good part of what they no longer received from land or official emoluments: they became teachers and advisers about the artistic traditions of Nara and Heian to aspirants from the military class. In this way, a knowledge of classical culture was given feudal sanction, extending its life into modern times.

Under feudal rule a certain refinement of taste, not only in terms of what had been valued by the aristocracy in the past, but applying also to novelties like Nō drama, the tea ceremony (*cha-no-yu*), flower arrangement (*ikebana*) and the cultivation of miniature trees (*bonsai*), spread more widely, if more thinly, through Japanese society. The change was of a piece with the dispersal of wealth and status that characterised the age politically. Arbiters of taste no longer belonged only at the emperor's court. Some also gathered at Kamakura. At Muromachi the Ashikaga held court in their own right. A number of provincial lords, like the Ōuchi in Yamaguchi, had highly regarded 'capitals'. In many other parts of the country were less important centres, where story-tellers could find an audience and priests convey the rudiments of art, while an expansion of farm production and domestic commerce produced, certainly by the fifteenth century, a proportion of wealthy commoners, aspiring to the style of life that samurai had chosen. They were the forerunners of the 'people's culture' of the Edo period.

Buddhism

Buddhism, though still Chinese in doctrine, became less scholastic during the feudal period, hence easier for the less educated members of society to comprehend. Two new sects, focusing on Amida as the path to human salvation, were the principal instruments in this change. One was Pure Land (Jōdo), which derived from China via the teachings of the priest Hōnen (1133–1212). A critic of the formalism and monastic preferences of the Buddhist establishment of his day, he argued that sincere invocation of Amida's name (*nembutsu*) was all that was needed to secure rebirth in the Western Paradise. A generation later, Shinran (1173–1262), who had briefly been a disciple of Hōnen, took the argument one step farther. Once there had been a single act of invocation, he proclaimed, provided it were heartfelt, salvation was assured. This belief became the distinguishing feature of True Pure Land (Jōdo Shinshū, usually known as Shinshū), which remains Japan's largest sect.

Neither man, it appears, began with the intention of founding a separate religious organisation. Shinran, indeed, went so far as to abandon his priestly vows, taking a wife and having children. Their successors, however, faced by both temporal and ecclesiastical persecution, found that they had in the end to organise in self-defence. By the Muromachi period they had created a structure of authority, locally and nationally, and could command a fighting force of substantial size. It was to be politically significant after 1460, playing a part in Japan's civil wars.

By making salvation depend on the simple invocation, 'Namu Amida Butsu' (Praise to Amida Buddha), Hōnen and Shinran made it easier to welcome into the faith many who could not read the scriptures, had no time or taste for the monastic rule, and were unwilling to commit themselves to a complex pattern of ethical rules in their daily lives. In the process, some other elements of the older religions also disappeared, including the comfort to be drawn from participation in elaborate rituals, which

reinforced belief in one's own salvation, and ways of coming to terms with the supernatural; but with the passing of time, means were found to make these deficiencies more bearable. Hōnen and Shinran became charismatic figures, even saints, who had handed down a 'doctrine'. Amida was held to be a miracle worker, invocation something like a magic formula. Ippen, a thirteenth-century Jōdo monk, went so far as to encourage chanting and dancing in his efforts to convert, issuing amulets – a quarter of a million, it is said – which were held to be a protection from disasters in this life and a promise of salvation in the next. The result of such ameliorations of the code was to make religious practice less austere than the founders might have hoped, but it won over many adherents.

Both Jōdo and Shinshū retained a strong communal base, which was an enormous advantage in troubled times. The cohesion and security it gave to villagers and urban residents in the civil wars of the fourteenth and later fifteenth centuries left Jōdo with a huge following in and around Kyoto, Shinshū equally in the Kanto and northeast. Yet it would be wrong to conclude on this account that the more traditional and outwardly 'Chinese' schools had been driven from centre-stage. By reason of their landed wealth and close relations with the court, Nara houses like the Tōdaiji and Kōfukuji long retained a provincial standing equal to that of many feudal lords, while Tendai's Enryakuji continued to intervene in Kyoto politics. Even when their temporal power began to erode, these sects remained the champions of the orthodox, whom the state could not readily ignore. Jōdo and Shinshū were by comparison outsiders, owing much of their success to the growing instability in the body politic.

Another strand in the religious history of the Kamakura period, Zen Buddhism (Ch'an in Chinese, meaning meditation), was more directly linked to samurai. There had been traces of Zen in Japan from very early times, but it was not until it won support among the Shogun's vassals in the thirteenth century – the warriors esteemed its self-discipline and disregard of book learning, their superiors welcomed Zen's detachment from the court – that

it became a factor of consequence. There were two Zen schools, Rinzai and Sōtō, both Chinese in origin, which had in common a belief that enlightenment was best achieved by contemplation under the guidance of a master. Rinzai put its emphasis on *kōan*, the study of a problem not open to logical solution (most famously, 'what is the sound of the clapping of one hand?'). Sōtō favoured *zazen*, meditation on the meaning of life while seated in the lotus posture. Both practices had by tradition been introduced to China in the early sixth century by the Indian monk Bodhidharma, known in Japan as Daruma. He, it was claimed, had sat for nine years in meditation facing a wall. As a result, the story goes, he lost the use of his arms and legs; and from the sixteenth century onwards, Japanese made dolls to commemorate this feat of endurance and concentration, small and pear-shaped figures as a rule, designed to return to the upright position when pushed over. They were believed to be amulets, giving protection against smallpox, and lucky charms, bringing the fulfilment of a wish, whether for better harvests or some more personal ambition.

The Tendai monk Eisai (1141–1215), who brought Rinzai to Japan, was attracted to it during visits to China made in 1168, then again in 1187–91. On his return, finding that his seniors at Enryakuji were reluctant to give it the standing he thought to be its due, he decamped to Kamakura in search of a warmer welcome. Sōtō's founder, Dōgen (1200–53), a court noble by birth, was in China from 1223 to 1227. He, too, was impressed by Zen's high reputation there, but preferred Sōtō to Rinzai because it was 'purer': that is, more monastic in outlook and less secular in its affiliations. He therefore refused invitations to Kamakura on his return, deciding to strike out on his own and settle in the province of Echizen (modern Fukui). So while Rinzai became the school of Zen that found greatest official favour, first in Kamakura, then in Muromachi, Sōtō recruited adherents from less politically influential regions.

Because Zen attached prime importance to the role of the teacher in preparing a disciple for enlightenment, it was much concerned with Japan's relations with China, where the most

distinguished teachers were to be found. A fifth of the Zen monks whose lives are recorded in one biographical work are said to have visited China. Musō Soseki (1275–1351), abbot of the Zen house of Nanzenji in Kyoto, is thought to have persuaded Ashikaga Takauji to seek to resume relations after the breach that the Mongol invasions caused. In the thirteenth century, Zen masters from China had been invited to Japan, or came as refugees from the Mongol conquests. Kenchōji, the leading Rinzai monastery in Kamakura, had no fewer than three Chinese abbots after 1246. Under the influence of men like this, Japan moved gradually towards the Chinese practice of giving some Zen houses, designated by the state as *gozan* ('the five mountains'), authority to regulate those of lesser standing. In Kamakura the selected institutions included the Kenchōji and Engakuji. Kyoto's Nanzenji was added at the end of the century. During the Muromachi period, the Tenryūji at Arashiyama, on the outskirts of the capital, was also named as one of them. By the middle of the fifteenth century, there were as many as 300 Rinzai establishments under the direction of the *gozan*, some of which were given a secondary supervisory role in their own provinces.

Because of their close connection with Chinese masters, Zen monks developed an expertise in Chinese studies that qualified them as intermediaries in the introduction of new strands of Chinese culture to Japan. Some monasteries were directly involved in the China trade itself. Once tribute missions were resumed under Ashikaga Yoshimitsu, their monks, as men of learning, much better versed in the Chinese language than their fellow-countrymen, went with them as interpreters, or even envoys. Back in Japan again, they became teachers of the tea ceremony, calligraphy and ink-painting (*sumi-e*), all deriving from their Chinese experience; made the poets Li Po and Tu Fu widely known; gave expositions of Sung Neo-Confucianism; laid out landscape gardens in the Chinese manner; and introduced Japan's artists and collectors to the painting and ceramics of the Sung. In short, they took over the task of cultural education that had been neglected in the capital since the eleventh century.

Before leaving the subject of Buddhism, a little needs to be said about one other sect, Nichiren. It was founded in the middle of the thirteenth century by a Tendai monk, after whom it is named (an unusual circumstance). He rejected what he conceived to be the doctrinal laxity of the Pure Land sects, insisting instead on the primacy of the classic Lotus Sutra (*Hokke-kyō*); and while he grudgingly accepted the new-fangled practice of invocation, he required that it be directed towards the Lotus Sutra, not towards Amida. There were several concomitants of this traditionalist attitude. One was an ethic comprising Shinto and Confucian elements, such as had already found a place in Tendai eclecticism. Another was belief in an emperor-centred polity. The latter proved offensive to feudal rulers; and since Nichiren argued his case for it in a highly combative manner, he came into conflict with Kamakura on a number of occasions. One of these led to a spell of exile on the island of Sado. Nevertheless, in later times his reputation for patriotic ardour, stemming not only from his loyalty to the emperor, but also from his efforts to rally Japan against the Mongol attacks, gave his successors a role in the development of Japanese nationalism.

Prose literature and drama

Before the seventeenth century, Japanese literature contains little that could be called political philosophy, apart from occasional passages in the histories. The early chronicles, taking their lead from China, were always careful to make a case for the reigning dynasty, though they did so by the use of arguments that would not have been acceptable in China itself – those of the emperor's divine descent – and they avoided direct discussion of the issues that this raised. This was politics, but not philosophy. Indeed, imperial rule was not challenged, whether by historians or by events, until the Heian period. Nor was the challenge then an

open one, since the Fujiwara chose to wrap their power in imperial authority.

Minamoto Yoritomo broke the pattern. By steadfastly refusing to live at court, while issuing orders from 300 miles away, he made it idle to pretend that he was a member of the Kyoto 'system', speaking for a ruler whose will he interpreted. Once he was dead, the measures that the Hōjō took to make the Kamakura Bakufu a separate organ of government, having a writ that ran through all Japan, made the situation more obvious still; and the Ashikaga, for all that they took up residence in part of the emperor's capital, continued this tradition of separateness. Historians of the period had therefore to decide how to accommodate their narrative to the fact that Japan had two rival centres of power, each claiming to be legitimate.

The first person to confront the problem was a Buddhist priest, Jien, who wrote a history entitled *Gukanshō* (Notes on Foolish Views) just before Go-Toba's attack on the Hōjō in 1221. Jien was brother to Kujō Kanezane, the senior court official (Sesshō) who worked closely with Yoritomo. He had himself served as chief abbot of the Tendai sect on several occasions. He was therefore a member of the Fujiwara élite, closely connected with that section of it which had recognised the need to come to terms with samurai power. His book reflected this. Its narrative was in chronicle form, set in the framework of imperial reigns, but passages of comment inserted here and there – some of them very jejune – revealed an underlying belief in cycles of historical change, shaped by the Buddhist concept of inevitable decline. This belief was softened by a recognition that decline could be checked, if no more than temporarily, by the will of Amaterasu, working through the imperial line and the Fujiwara house. The most recent example was what had been done by the Kujō, when faced by Minamoto victories.

To justify this somewhat self-seeking argument, Jien put forward his own view of imperial authority, couched in historical terms. Given the imperatives of lineage, he wrote, some emperors would necessarily prove to be incompetent or unprincipled. It

was for this reason that Amaterasu had from the beginning laid it down that good government required a sharing of power between ruler and minister (a Confucian choice of terminology). The Fujiwara had been the first to be advanced to the place of leading minister in accordance with this formula. When they had lost their grip on affairs, ex-emperors had come to take part of the responsibility, followed in turn by Taira and Minamoto. The nature and legitimacy of a regime, in other words, did not depend exclusively on the lineage of the ruler. It took account also of his capacity to govern. If he could not keep order, others must do so, in accordance with the will of Amaterasu.

A refutation of this modified version of the doctrine of the Mandate of Heaven (t'ien-ming) came a little over a century later from the pen of Kitabatake Chikafusa. He, too, was a court noble, though of the Murakami Genji house. A supporter of Go-Daigo in his contest with the Ashikaga, he went into exile with him to the Yoshino mountains, where he achieved some reputation as a soldier in the fighting that followed the events of 1336. He also wrote a book that gave him lasting fame: Jinnō Shōtōki (A Record of the True Descent of the Divine Sovereigns), completed between 1339 and 1343. Its immediate purpose was to set out the claims of Go-Daigo to be the legitimate ruler of Japan. To this end it stressed the importance of the imperial regalia (mirror, sword and jewels) that Go-Daigo had carried away from Kyoto; described Japan as uniquely 'the land of the gods' (kami), contrasting it with China, where frequent changes of dynasty had produced 'a country of notorious disorders'; and insisted that the imperial succession was ordained immutably by Amaterasu, never to be set aside by human action, or varied in the light of an emperor's virtues and defects. In this Kitabatake was speaking for a 'loyalist' view, directly opposed to the pragmatism of Jien. It has recurred again and again in later writing, notably after 1800.

When he turned to the events of his own day – they were, after all, his reason for writing – Kitabatake was forced to admit that Go-Daigo had failed in his dealings with Ashikaga Takauji. This might well have implications for the succession in the short term,

he conceded, since there was now a war between northern and southern courts, but these aberrations were secondary. In the last analysis, the precept that the succession rested on descent, not competence, was not to be denied.

The debate about the respective roles of emperor and Shogun, which was to be resumed under the Tokugawa, was an innovation in historical writing in Japan. No longer a simple record of ceremony and intrigue in an almost static set of institutions, the *Gukanshō* and *Jinnō Shōtōki* recognised the fact of revolutionary change, sought to explain it in a rudimentary way, and expressed controversial opinions about it. This was history with a political purpose extending far beyond the validation of authority. Other medieval works in the field did not so readily enter on this dangerous ground. Official histories continued to be produced. They were much the same in manner and technique as the so-called national histories of Nara and Heian, even to being written in Chinese, but were compiled by servants of the Bakufu, not the court, and embodied the changes of attitude that this made prudent. There were also less formal works, called 'historical tales' (*rekishi-monogatari*) and 'war tales' (*gunki-monogatari*), arranged in chronicle form, but designed for entertainment rather than instruction.

These, too, reflected changing times. They had narratives full of warlike action and deeds of valour or betrayal; were tinged with a mood of Buddhist melancholy, equating 'change' with 'decline'; and dwelt above all on human action or supernatural influence as the fountain-head of events. They were, in other words, more human and dramatic than what had earlier passed for history. Nor were they only meant to be read in the silence of the study. Most were modified over time to make them suitable for recitation to a less sophisticated audience than court romances such as *Genji* had enjoyed, perhaps even an illiterate one. Recitation was often accompanied by the playing of a lute (*biwa*), in order to set the mood, or illustrated by scenes from picture-scrolls (*e-maki*). The reciters, usually blind, were numerous enough by the fourteenth century to have formed a guild in Kyoto.

Three of these tales, compiled in the Kamakura period, dealt with incidents in the late-twelfth-century struggle between the Taira and the Minamoto. The most famous was *Heike monogatari* (Tale of the Taira House), which devoted the greater part of its space to the lives of Taira Kiyomori and Shigemori, plus Minamoto Yoshinaka and Yoshitsune: that is, the men who could be presented as tragic and heroic. Minamoto Yoritomo, less romantic, because he was above all the builder of a political order, was left in the shadows. On a not dissimilar theme, a later work, the inappropriately named *Taiheiki* (Record of Great Peace), tells of Go-Daigo and his efforts to overthrow the Kamakura Bakufu. The text, spanning the years from 1318 to 1367, is more narrative than chronicle; includes descriptions of fighting, poems, sentimental anecdotes and Buddhist moralising; and was often recited in later years, though not, it seems, to music. The author or authors are unknown. The fact that several variants exist makes it difficult to claim that a consistent political line was taken – this may be caution on the part of the various editors – but Ashikaga Takauji emerges as an unsympathetic character, while the loyalist, Kusunoki, is an object of admiration and respect. This suggests a leaning towards the southern court, the more romantic cause.

Subject-matter of this kind, accompanied as it was by a wealth of vivid detail, has made these books a treasure trove for later writers and dramatists in Japan. The reciters, who helped to make them popular, also drew upon collections of prose fiction in the manner of *Konjaku monogatari* (Chapter 4), which were still being put together. The choice implied a reaching out towards a different section of the population (and a source of income that did not depend on aristocratic patronage), but the result was to create a world of folk-heroes, both real and imaginary, known for the first time to a substantial part of the Japanese people. It became an element in the national heritage, familiar to those of every age group to the present day.

Drama also began to seek a wider than aristocratic audience, specifically in what became known as Nō and Kyōgen. Both derived originally from performances at Shinto shrines and fes-

tivals, Nō being a kind of dance, Kyōgen a display of acrobatic clowning. By the end of Heian, they had developed into public entertainment, but it was not until much later, when it found a patron in Ashikaga Yoshimitsu, that Nō acquired a more serious reputation. Thereafter it changed rapidly in style and complexity. By the seventeenth century, it was being performed by highly trained players, wearing masks and accompanied by chorus, flute and drums, very much as it is today. There were written texts (closely followed by *aficionados* in a modern theatre, as opera is in the West), marked with a notation designed to indicate the chant.

The men most responsible for this transformation were Kanami (1334–84) and his son Zeami (1363–1443). Kanami was above all a performer. Zeami was both dramatist and author of theoretical treatises on his art, laying stress on the need for elegance and restraint in a player's movements. The language he used was literary, not colloquial. His plots drew heavily on *Heike monogatari* and other such works, placing their action – if such it can properly be called, since physical movement is slow and stylised – in the upper reaches of society, both warrior and noble. Ghosts and wandering monks were introduced to provide explanatory comment or exchanges, and Japanese poems (*waka*) appeared in the dialogue here and there.

Nō as Zeami reshaped it was a far cry from Kyōgen, though the two were regularly staged together. Kyōgen had a good deal about it of the vaudeville sketch: a script that was little more than a synopsis, to be elaborated by the players; no masks or chorus; much mimicry and horseplay. Its plots might be described as social satire, making fun not of the very highest in the land, since that could well be dangerous, but of the samurai, monks, thieves, artisans, peasants and their various womenfolk encountered in everyday life. Favourite themes were the unimaginative dealings of a stupid master with his streetwise servant, or haggling between man and wife.

Bringing Nō and Kyōgen together in a single play-bill ensured that both the high-born and the commoners in the audience found something to their taste. The actors were men of low status,

their sponsors drawn from the Shogun's rather than the emperor's court, their customers very varied. This social mix set the drama at some remove from the aristocratic traditions of Heian, when music, dancing and the recitation of poetry had been skills for courtiers to demonstrate to each other. The theatre was becoming professional.

Chinese influence on the arts

In literature, the medieval period saw an increasing devotion to Japanese themes and style, accompanied by a modest degree of popularisation. Development in the visual arts took a different course. During Kamakura, at least, there was a great deal of continuity with late Heian. The replacement of members of the imperial court as patrons by feudal rulers and their warrior supporters certainly had an effect on choice of subject-matter, but it did not immediately bring about changes in style: members of the feudal class, seeking a reputation as men of culture, rightly entrusted with civil power, did so within the accepted canons of taste. In architecture, for example, the rebuilding of Nara's Kōfu-kuji and Tōdaiji, destroyed in the wars between Taira and Min-amoto, was carried out by the latter with a minimum of innovation, except, perhaps, in statuary, the new versions of which showed greater strength and realism than the old. The same was true of portraiture, both in sculpture and in painting. Much of it now was of lay figures, especially heads of samurai houses, com-memorated in pictures that were commissioned by their vassals or descendants. This was, no doubt, an attempt to assert a claim to dignity on behalf of rulers, many of whom lacked distinguished lineage, but the manner of it in many cases – especially pictures of Shogun – was unmistakably that of the school of Fujiwara Takanobu (Chapter 4). Most such subjects were shown in court dress, though in later years some were in armour or on horseback, as befitted men whose claim to fame was prowess in battle.

1 *(previous page)* Statue of
Maitreya (Miroku) Buddha, Kōryūji,
Kyoto. Said to be a gift from Prince
Shōtoku, it dates from the early
seventh century, when the Kōryūji
was founded by a wealthy
immigrant family (Korean or
Chinese). There is an almost
identical statue of Maitreya in a
temple in Korea.

2 Hōryūji, a Buddhist temple to the
south of Nara. Founded by Prince
Shōtoku between 601 and 607, its
oldest existing buildings date from
later in the seventh century. The
buildings are in the Chinese style
(tile-roofed and raised on stone
plinths) which became the chosen
model for the palace and other public
buildings in eighth-century Nara.

3 Ganjin (Chien-chen). A memorial statue of the Chinese priest, invited to Japan in the eighth century, who founded the Tōshō-daiji, a Buddhist temple in Nara, in 759 and became its first abbot. The statue is attributed to two of his disciples, who came with him from China.

4 *(top)* The Phoenix Pavilion of the Byōdōin at Uji, midway between Nara and Kyoto. Originally a Fujiwara villa, it was converted into a temple in 1052 and became a centre for the worship of Amida Buddha.

5 *(above)* Ladies of the Heian court. A scene from the Tale of Genji picture-scroll (*Genji monogatari e-maki*), showing court pastimes and the use of screens to break up the large open spaces of the palace rooms.

6 The Heiji incident. An incident during the twelth-century struggles between the Taira and the Minamoto in Kyoto, when the emperor was smuggled from the palace in disguise to escape from his Minamoto guards.

7 Minamoto Yoritomo in court dress. This portrait, long attributed to Fujiwara Takanobu (1142–1205), but now thought to have been painted after his death, was one of a series of studies of leading political figures of the time that set the style for later portraits of feudal overlords.

9 Feudal lord on horseback, fourteenth century. The figure wears full armour (of the kind often seen in museums) and is equiped with sword, bow and arrows. He has been identified as Ashikaga Takauji, but this is disputed.

10 *(right)* Nō mask. In Nō drama, as it developed in and after the fifteenth century, performers wore masks to indicate the nature of the character they portrayed. This one is for the *hannya*, a female demon.

8 *(left)* Kūya Shōnin (903–972). A statue, dating from the early thirteenth century, that shows him in his most famous role: as an itinerant preacher promoting the worship of Amida Buddha (hence the miniature statues of Amida projecting from his mouth).

11 Toyotomi Hideyoshi
(1537–1598).
A memorial statue
in court dress that
emphasises his
diminutive size
and unprepossessing
appearance.

12 Himeji Castle.
Held at one time by
Hideyoshi, later by
a senior Tokugawa
vassal, it was a
military stronghold
and administrative
centre that guarded
the approaches to
Kyoto from the west.

The most famous example of religious sculpture is the Daibutsu (Great Buddha) in Kamakura, a bronze figure of Amida over 11 metres high, cast in 1252. Since the building that housed it was destroyed by a tidal wave in 1495 and never replaced, the statue still stands impressively in the open. That apart, the city has little to show for a century and more of warrior rule, except a large array of shrines and temples. Of these, the Zen establishments showed signs of architectural novelty, deriving mostly from China. The Kenchōji, for example, is said to be a replica of the Ch'an headquarters at Hangchow. It had more elaborate gates – these became customary in medieval temples – and larger halls for communal contemplation than had been customary in Japan, but most of the points of difference from religious buildings of the past were to be found in the decoration and detail. Some features remained entirely familiar. In Kamakura, as in Heian, pagodas were distinctively unChinese, because the use of wood as a material, instead of brick or stone, required a modification of building techniques.

The Shogun's move to Muromachi after 1336 strengthened the link between court and warrior building styles. Across the road from the imperial palace, which had been moved to a new site in 1337 and made rather smaller, Ashikaga Yoshimitsu erected a splendid residence for himself, a symbol of his aristocratic – or conceivably monarchical – ambitions. (It may be recalled that he opened a correspondence with the Ming under the title 'King of Japan'.) As Daijō-daijin from 1394, always surrounded by court nobles of the higher ranks, he saw his palace as a suitable setting for both his official and his personal life. In 1397 he also acquired a villa on the northern outskirts of the city, known as the Gold Pavilion (Kinkakuji) from the fact that its central structure was covered in gold foil. It might be described as eclectically Chinese: the gold colour and the pond in which it is reflected have associations with Pure Land Buddhism, while the upper floor is Zen. The whole of what can now be seen is in any case a replica, for fire has wreaked its havoc several times, most recently as a result of arson in 1949.

Many find the Silver Pavilion (Ginkakuji) more attractive. It was built in 1482 by Ashikaga Yoshimasa as a retreat, lying below the city's eastern slopes, where he could escape the pervasive signs of weakness and civil war: a place of contemplation, provided with a separate tea-house, rooms for incense guessing and other courtly pursuits, and a notable landscape garden, designed by Soami, who also laid out the more famous rock-and-sand garden at the Ryoanji. Because of the Shogun's lavish spending on other projects, plus the financial depredations of civil war, the funds to provide the silver that was to cover the walls of the main pavilion never became available. Aesthetically, that was no bad thing.

Continuities of style between late Heian and Kamakura were maintained in painting, not only in portraiture, but in the picture-scroll (*e-maki*). Although Chinese in origin, this was undoubtedly a Japanese art form by the thirteenth century. The two basic styles, represented by the aristocratic interiors of *Genji monogatari* on the one hand, the crowd scenes of *Shigisan engi* on the other, were both to be found in thirteenth-century scrolls, as they had been in *Ban Dainagon* (Chapter 4). Most themes were narrative, either military or religious, while biography and accounts of con-temporary events made up a good proportion. Thus one finds scrolls that tell the story of Sugawara Michizane and of Ippen, a Jōdo monk; describe the building of the Kasuga Shrine in Nara; give a highly coloured account of the Mongol attacks on Japan (paying due attention to the exploits of the samurai who com-missioned the work); illustrate the ceremonies and processions held in the palace in the course of the year; depict in horrifying detail the range of human diseases, or the punishments inflicted in the Buddhist hells. There is even a scroll about a poetry contest.

The freshness and vigour shown in the earliest examples gave way in time to the repetitiveness of routine and occasional crude-ness of technique. Scrolls continued to be produced until modern times, often for purposes of record – there is one of a nineteenth-century reverberatory furnace, for example – but they were becoming more useful to the historian than attractive to the connoisseur. One reason is that illustrated books, block-printed

in multiple copies, proved cheaper and more convenient after the sixteenth century. Another is that it became customary in the Muromachi period to provide the houses of the well-to-do with alcoves (*tokonoma*), where single scrolls of vertical format (*kakemono*) could be hung, often above a flower arrangement. This encouraged the production of individual pictures, which could fulfil some of the purposes previously served by scrolls. In Edo times the latter's role was also taken over in part by genre painting and the woodblock print.

Zen, by reason of its contacts with China, reinvigorated Chinese influence on other kinds of painting in Japan. The *suiboku* style, in which light colour wash was combined with brush strokes made in various shades of ink, appeared in the fourteenth century in sketches of Zen and Taoist religious figures – Daruma was a popular choice – as well as bird-and-flower studies, pictures of animals, landscapes. The largest designs were used on screens and sliding panels in religious establishments and the houses of the great, where they became a substitute for murals. Their manner was impressionistic, their subjects often imaginary. One notable 'portrait', for example, was of the three great teachers of the East Asian world, Buddha, Lao-tzu and Confucius. Not only were they dead many centuries since, but there were no 'true likenesses' for the artist to copy. Similarly, landscapes, including those by Japanese, were usually of places existing only in the imagination, or of Chinese mountains that the painter had never seen. Painting, in other words, did not have to rely on observation. This was not in itself a new phenomenon. In 1207, when the emperor Go-Toba commissioned four men to produce scenes of famous places on sliding screens for a newly founded temple, only one of the four expressed a wish to go and see his subject for himself.

Nevertheless, the best and most famous of Japanese artists of this school, Sesshū (1420–1506), did in fact visit China, as well as painting landscapes of real places in Japan. Born in the Okayama region on the northern shores of the Inland Sea, he studied painting as a monk in Kyoto in his early years, but in 1464 transferred to Yamaguchi, the Ōuchi centre, apparently to escape

the growing disorder in the capital. Three years later he joined a trade mission sent to China by the Ōuchi, staying there two years. It was after his return, when he moved to Oita in Kyushu, that he painted most prolifically, producing work across the whole range of figure studies, bird-and-flower compositions, and landscapes, both imaginary and real. Some were mounted as *kakemono*. Others were painted on screens, usually designed as pairs or in larger sets, appropriate to the kind of rooms that were favoured by his patrons.

Sesshū's experience is a reminder that patronage was not only available in the capital, especially in the later medieval years, but it is none the less true that culturally, as well as politically, the Bakufu was the principal heir to the court. The Kamakura Shogun and the Hōjō regents, isolated in the Kanto, proved better friends to Zen than they were to Chinese art, though Hōjō Tokimune collected Chinese paintings, but the move to Muromachi under the Ashikaga encouraged cultural borrowing across a wider range. The Ashikaga presented themselves to the world as connoisseurs of Chinese culture in many of its forms. They resumed the official visits to the collection at the Shōsōin, abandoned by Kamakura; gathered round themselves men knowledgeable in the arts; collected paintings, ceramics, tea utensils and incense burners, mostly of Chinese origin or in the Chinese style; and acquired a flattering reputation as painters and poets. Great lords from the provinces, who were required to live in Kyoto as a matter of feudal duty, followed their example. Parties were held, at which guests vied with each other to produce linked verse (*renga*) in accordance with complex rules, or gathered to admire *objets d'art*, recently acquired.

Much of this lifestyle derived from the 'amateur' tradition of China's official class, modified to suit a Japanese environment. It called for a perceptive eye and a careful cultivation of taste, but not the day-to-day application to study and practice marking those who earned their living by the arts, nor the almost wholly leisured existence that had made elegant dancers and musicians of court nobles in the *Genji* years. The tea ceremony (*cha-no-yu*) is

perhaps the most apposite example. It had its origins in the Zen Buddhism of T'ang, which held it to be an aid to meditation. Introduced into Japan in the Kamakura period, it was at one time performed at rowdy 'tournaments' (for guessing types of tea), which had a reputation for riotous and alcoholic behaviour; but under the influence of Ashikaga Yoshimasa greater restraint was imposed, and the ceremony was transferred to special tea-houses in palace or castle grounds, where landscape gardens contributed to a more serene environment. In this context *cha-no-yu* provided an occasion for aesthetic appreciation, achieving popularity among both feudal lords and wealthy commoners. Politically, it was an opportunity to pursue discrete discussions. Socially, given the enormous prices paid for the most notable tea-bowls, whether imported from China or crafted in Japan, it made possible a carefully understated display of wealth.

Several of the 'lesser arts' that are associated with Zen, such as flower arrangement (*ikebana*), *bonsai* and landscape gardening, helped to provide the atmosphere of discipline and restraint in which the tea ceremony was expected to take place. Like the building of splendid villas, the patronage of drama and painting, and the support that was given to Zen, they played a part in making feudal rulers 'civilised', hence worthy and legitimate successors to the Fujiwara. Perhaps because of this, the Chinese influences that reached Japan in the Kamakura and Muromachi periods seem in retrospect to be less fundamental than those of Nara and early Heian. Nor is it surprising that this should be so. Japan had by then had several centuries to assimilate what it found most relevant in Chinese civilisation. The medieval phase did little more than bring its knowledge up to date by adding Sung to T'ang; and despite the importance of Zen as an instrument in this development, it did so as much in temporal as in religious terms.

CHAPTER 7

The Unifiers

The civil wars that broke out in central Japan in 1467 spread to most of the country in the next hundred years. Almost at once they destroyed what little remained of Ashikaga authority. In the longer run they also brought about a major change in feudal society. The greatest of the lords, engaged in struggles for power at a distance from their lands, all too often fell victim to rivals or ambitious vassals at home, destroyed in a recurrent pattern of *gekokujō*, 'low overthrows high'. As a result, all but a handful of those families that were great names in the land in 1450 were gone two centuries later. The Shimazu were the most notable survivors.

By 1500, in fact, a new generation of leaders had begun to emerge, men of a different stamp from those they had overthrown: able, bold, ruthless, as to be successful at such a time they had to be, but aware, too, that in order to lead large armies, better organised and equipped, they had to exploit their lands with more efficiency than those they had replaced. Many were innovators in methods of administration. Nearly all were brash and extrovert by comparison with the courtiers and Ashikaga nominees who ruled in Kyoto.

Fifty years later there were a handful, scattered through the country, who had the qualities and the ambition to aspire to rule Japan as a whole. Three stand out: Oda Nobunaga, Toyotomi

Hideyoshi and Tokugawa Ieyasu. Military leaders of a good deal more than average accomplishment, shrewd judges of what was politically feasible, they became in succession 'conquerors' of Japan. They then gave it a kind of political order that it had never possessed before. There is a Japanese saying, summing up their roles: 'Nobunaga mixed the cake, Hideyoshi baked it, Ieyasu ate it'. It was Tokugawa Ieyasu, in other words, living longer than the other two, who enjoyed to the full the fruits of their success. He took the title Shogun in 1603; passed it to his descendants, together with enormous holdings of land; and blocked out the shape of a governmental structure by which they ruled the country until the end of 1867.

Warfare and warlords (1460–1560)

The Japanese label for the period from 1467 to 1560 is Sengoku, 'the country at war'. Institutionally, the description is inadequate. The fact of warfare itself was nothing new, just as the issues that provoked it were familiar; but because its scale was greater than before, its techniques and tactics more advanced, the men who emerged as victors from it were holders of domains that are better described as princedoms than estates.

The first stage of the Sengoku wars, lasting until 1477, sprang from a quarrel between two great lords, resident in different parts of Kyoto, embroiled in a dispute over succession to the headship of the Ashikaga house. Ten years of fighting in and around the capital left the city in ruins, the Bakufu in disarray. Thereafter the war moved into the provinces, becoming a focus for every kind of political or territorial conflict at the local level, much as it had done in the struggle between north and south in the fourteenth century. Japan was plunged into chaos. The most powerful lords, little restrained by the Shogun's authority, fought each other for land, while their armies grew steadily in size, reaching 20,000 or even 50,000 men. Many of these were not samurai in the

acknowledged sense, but foot-soldiers (*ashigaru*), armed with spears and fighting as organised units, whose proper employment on the battlefield called for new skills of military leadership. To keep them supplied with arms and provisions, to ensure that they were always ready for action, to direct them in a campaign, not just a battle, called more for organising talents than for panache. Not every lord possessed them. Nor did the landholdings they had brought together since the days of Ashikaga Takauji always provide a sufficient economic base.

Those who lacked the qualities that were needed in this situation – or simply failed to watch their backs – were replaced by ambitious deputies or other rivals, by whom they were assassinated, defeated in battle, or overthrown while attending to business that took them away from the centre of their power. In consequence, some of the largest holdings were broken up into smaller units. The Shiba, for example, a branch of the Ashikaga, who held large parcels of land, plus office as military governor (*shugo*), in several provinces to the east and north of Kyoto, eventually saw their territories crumble. In 1453 Asakura Toshikage, a Shiba vassal, was sent to Echizen (Fukui) to settle a local dispute on his lord's behalf. He became the *shugo*'s resident deputy there in 1459; used the prerogatives of his office to acquire land rights of his own; and in 1471 declared his 'independence' from the Shiba, which he proved able to maintain against attack. In Owari (Nagoya) another deputy *shugo*, Oda Nobuhide (Nobunaga's father), overthrew Shiba control throughout the province in the first half of the sixteenth century.

Within the regions where they were the leading figures, both the old lords and the new faced problems in enforcing their will. The upper levels of rural society by this time consisted mostly of a landed gentry, known as *kokujin*, many of whom had pledged a nominal allegiance to the *shugo*; but they were not bound so tightly to his interests as to accept without demur his demands for greater powers and greater revenues for the prosecution of his wars. They lacked the resources to oppose him individually. What is more, they were themselves coming under pressure from below,

as the poverty and starvation that were the product of war prompted peasant revolt on a substantial scale. In some areas this led them to form leagues (*ikki*), coming together with others like themselves to defend their landed rights against rapacious lords and turbulent commoners. From such leagues several 'upstart' feudal leaders emerged. For example, when the head of the Ōuchi house was murdered by one of his vassals in 1551, it was not the latter who succeeded in taking his place. Instead, after a brief interval of fighting, victory went to Mōri Motonari, whose ancestors had come to prominence as the leaders of a *kokujin* league in the Hiroshima district. At the time of his death in 1571, Motonari was master of the ten most westerly provinces in the main island, Honshu.

Men lower in the social scale also formed *ikki*, usually as a defence against exploitation by the gentry and the religious houses who were their landlords. Since many villagers regularly carried arms, and some could claim a modicum of samurai status, they could be a formidable threat when brought together in large enough numbers. On occasion they would co-operate with *kokujin*, given sufficient cause, which made the rebellions they raised into something more than outbreaks of casual violence. One, in which *kokujin* and village samurai took a leading part, held Kyoto's own home province of Yamashiro in its grip from 1485 to 1492. Directed at first against the exactions of officials, it was brought to an end when the *ikki* itself became a symbol of oppression and a target of peasant revolt. Another, which proved to be still longer lasting, occurred in Kaga (Kanazawa) on the Japan Sea coast. Based on an alliance between peasants and *kokujin*, held together by the influence of the most influential of the local Buddhist sects, Jōdo Shinshū – known as Ikkō in this context – the *ikki* first intervened in a dispute over the choice of military governor in 1488; then grew steadily in power until the 1520s, when it dominated politics in the area; and for many years provided a structure of local administration, serving Ikkō leaders who behaved like feudal lords. Its power was not broken until Nobunaga overcame it in 1580.

One product of rural unrest was a modest growth in village autonomy. Some village elders, seeking to secure better living conditions while the attention of their lords was taken up with war against each other, won the right to handle local boundary disputes, determine the use of common lands, and draft and enforce village regulations. Something of the same kind occurred in towns. With the exception of a handful of political centres, like Kyoto, and the main ports engaged in the China trade (Sakai and Hakata), Muromachi towns were small, no more than local markets. They contained few, if any, wealthy merchants, had no impressive walls and could command no military force, even for defence. This meant they lacked the means to oppose their feudal masters openly, or even to buy them off in a majority of cases. A limited autonomy was the best they could achieve.

Sakai, just east of Osaka, is held to be the prime example of urban self-government in late medieval Japan. It had genuine wealth, plus a confusing sequence of different feudal lords. Taken together, these conditions enabled its inhabitants to set up a city council, having certain rights with respect to tax collection and the preservation of order in the market place, as well as in the organisation of festivals; but as the most important parts of its commercial business were carried on under official patronage (the China trade) or on behalf of feudal lords (the shipment of tax goods to market), it cannot be called a 'free' city in the wider European sense. When Nobunaga began to restore the country's central authority after 1568, he soon made it clear that the price of Sakai's freedom, such as it was, was submission to his will.

In setting out to discipline this increasingly insubordinate society, sixteenth-century lords, both old and new, had a number of advantages. One was the possession of overwhelming force, itself a consequence of war. Another was the fact that their potential opponents – *kokujin*, peasants, townsmen, priests – were socially divided and could be played off against each other. The lords best equipped to exploit this situation were therefore able to strengthen their hold until they had personal domains (later known as *han*) quite unlike the loose agglomerations of vassalage

and land rights found in earlier periods. They were compact, except for a few outlying fragments surviving from the past; ranged in size from something less than a district (the majority) to something more than a province (a small minority); were subject to a single lord's control; and were administered from a central stronghold. These were the units — not in all respects complete in this form until the seventeenth century — into which Japan was divided for the next 300 years.

At the head of each domain was its daimyo, whose authority was absolute and whose 'office' was hereditary. If his territory were large enough, he would have a massive castle, strategically located at the heart of his lands. There the greater part of his vassals were expected to reside, forming an army, readily on call, which could not only guard his frontiers, but also keep order within them. Former warrior-gentry of the countryside (*kokujin*), now firmly subjected to vassalage, filled its higher ranks. Samurai of lesser standing provided its junior officers and élite guard units, always in attendance on their lord. Foot-soldiers (*ashigaru*), some resident in the castle, some still in villages, made up the rank and file. Commoners beyond the walls, both townsmen and villagers, though still granted a measure of autonomy, had now to submit to the castle's orders.

A daimyo's legal powers were no longer restricted to the governance of vassals, jurisdiction over land rights and enforcement of the warrior code. When he made laws, they were designed to regulate all inhabitants of the domain and every aspect of their lives, or at least all that had a 'public' character. Those which Asakura Toshikage issued in Echizen were typical. They set out rules to be observed in selecting advisers and officials; provided for regular inspection of the province, in order to remedy 'errors in government'; prohibited the building of castles and strongholds, other than his own; and even warned his followers not to waste time in choosing 'an auspicious day or a correct direction' when preparing for battle. They also touched on what might be called the foreign relations of the domain. Expensive actors should not be brought from Kyoto, when local young men

could be trained to take their place. Confidential papers must not be entrusted to samurai from elsewhere. Agents were to be maintained in other provinces to report on conditions there. The list leaves little doubt that these were the orders of a self-styled prince, not just the possessor of large estates.

Nobunaga and Hideyoshi (1560–1598)

Although daimyo imposed unity on localities and even provinces, the effect was further to fragment Japan at large. A restoration of order in the wider sense required a rebuilding of the state, which had almost wholly slipped out of Ashikaga hands. This was the task to which Oda Nobunaga, Toyotomi Hideyoshi and Tokugawa Ieyasu turned in the second half of the sixteenth century. After nearly a hundred years of civil war there were at least half a dozen men who had the will and the capacity to undertake it, but some of them – the Shimazu in Kyushu, the Mōri in western Honshu, the Hōjō in Odawara – were too remote from Kyoto to intervene there easily. Others were distracted by local rivalries. In the event it was Imagawa Yoshimoto, lord of the coastal belt to the east of modern Nagoya, who set the process of unification in motion, but when his army departed for the capital in 1560 it was halted by a very much smaller force under Oda Nobunaga, whose domain lay across its path. The event was a turning-point, though it was only seen as such in retrospect.

Nobunaga spent the next few years consolidating his position in the region around his holding. An alliance with one of Imagawa's vassals, Tokugawa Ieyasu (who changed his family name from Matsudaira at about this time), gave him some protection from the east. Threats, or marriage alliances, persuaded other neighbours to open his route to the west. So when the emperor and Ashikaga Yoshiaki – an unsuccessful claimant to the title of Shogun – invited him to intervene in Kyoto in 1568, he acted promptly. His army was small, but well led and well equipped (he had been

among the first to realise the potential of firearms, introduced by the Portuguese in 1543 and already being manufactured by Japanese). Making the most of these advantages, he seized the capital, installed Yoshiaki as Shogun and appointed himself as deputy. Before long this made him the Bakufu's senior member in name as well as reality, for Yoshiaki was removed from office in 1573.

In the remaining years of his life, Nobunaga tightened his hold on the central provinces. One step was to remove potential dangers from other feudal lords, which sometimes required him to fight against his former allies. Another was to reduce the temporal power of Buddhism, which had grown immensely during the years of turbulence. Tendai's Enryakuji, for example, had the temerity to oppose Nobunaga's attack on Asakura in Echizen. In September 1571 he turned his army against it. The temple complex on Mount Hiei was stormed and its buildings were put to the torch with massive casualties. Farther afield, force was also employed against the Ikkō sect in Kaga and other provinces, though it was not until the sect's main stronghold, the Ishiyama Honganji in Osaka, was taken in 1580 that success was at last achieved.

Victory in the central region left Nobunaga free to turn his attention to the more powerful lords in other parts of Japan. First on the list, because strategically the greatest threat, were the Mōri, controlling western Honshu. Hideyoshi, the most able soldier among Nobunaga's vassals, was therefore sent against them. Slowly he pushed them back along the shores of the Inland Sea, but he had advanced no farther than the outskirts of Okayama when Nobunaga's death in 1582 threw Japan once more into crisis.

The event was typical of the age. In June 1582, *en route* to join Hideyoshi, Nobunaga spent the night at a Kyoto temple. One of his senior vassals, Akechi Mitsuhide, leading a contingent of reinforcements in the same direction, suddenly turned aside from his road as he passed the city – for reasons that have never been entirely clear – and attacked him. A spattering of musket fire at

dawn was the first indication of danger. Caught without a proper escort, Nobunaga fought his ground alone for a time, but at last, wounded, and seeing the temple in flames around him, he committed suicide. The news quickly reached Hideyoshi outside Okayama, 130 miles to the west. Keeping it secret, he came to terms with the Mōri, then made a forced march on Kyoto and defeated Akechi, who was killed by peasants as he fled. Within two weeks, setting aside Nobunaga's quarrelsome sons, Hideyoshi was master in the place of his former lord. It was a long step up the ladder for a man of his birth, no more than a village samurai in origin. Nobunaga, after all, had held thirty-two of the country's sixty-eight provinces when he died.

Hideyoshi's first aim was to ensure that what he had gained by speed he could hold by strength. Of possible rivals, the most dangerous was Ieyasu. The two came briefly into conflict in 1584–5, but chose to break off the confrontation before they came fully to grips, staying thereafter at arm's length. Other contenders were more brusquely treated. The settlement with the Mōri held, while a campaign in Shikoku in 1585 made the approaches safe from that direction. This gave Hideyoshi time to build political defences. A lavish residence was erected for him at Momoyama, on the outskirts of the capital (Nobunaga had preferred his castle at Azuchi, overlooking Lake Biwa); he became a Fujiwara by adoption, taking the family name of Toyotomi; and he was appointed Kampaku, then Daijō-daijin. Dressed thus in the imperial authority, he was ready to bring the rest of Japan to heel.

It took two campaigns. The first, against Shimazu of Satsuma, who refused to give up the gains he had made in northern Kyushu during recent years, was launched in the spring and summer of 1587 by an expedition of 200,000 men under Hideyoshi's personal direction. Shimazu, driven back behind his mountain barriers in the south, where he was threatened by yet another 'imperial' force approaching from the sea, reluctantly sued for peace. Hideyoshi granted him generous terms. As a precaution, however, the map of the rest of Kyushu was redrawn, placing Hideyoshi's men at strategic points.

That left the Kanto and the north to be pacified. The key to
them was the Hōjō domain,★ ruled from Odawara; and when it
refused to submit at the end of 1589, Hideyoshi set on foot
another huge expedition, part of it led by Ieyasu. The Hōjō
decided to stand siege, a choice of doubtful wisdom. Hideyoshi's
two main columns, approaching along the coast and through the
Hakone mountains, had western-style cannon, a knowledge of
which, like firearms, had been acquired from the Portuguese, and
they were well supplied by sea. By May 1590 they had enclosed
Odawara castle within a double ring of earthworks. The besiegers,
provided with comfortable quarters for themselves and their
dependents, together with shops, singers, musicians and courtesans for their entertainment, settled down to starve the stronghold
out. It did not take long. At the beginning of August the castle
surrendered, the Hōjō leaders committed suicide and their lands
were transferred to Ieyasu in exchange for his existing ones in
Mikawa (based on Shizuoka). This made him, next to Hideyoshi,
the most powerful daimyo in Japan.

Once these campaigns were over, Hideyoshi turned his military
talents to overseas expansion (Chapter 8), while seeking at home
to achieve stability. The court offices he held, it is true, helped
him to overcome the disadvantages of birth, but they were not
the instruments through which he chose to rule Japan. Instead,
he treated the country much as a sixteenth-century daimyo treated
his domain. The great lords were required to swear allegiance to
him and send hostages to live in Kyoto under his hand. Restrictions were imposed on the marriages and alliances they were
permitted to conclude; their lands were increased, reduced or
transferred as Hideyoshi decreed. He provided in this way not
only an enormous holding for himself and his followers, but also
a firm grip on those who might acquire ambitions to overthrow
him.

Such specific controls were reinforced by a calculated mag-

★ These Hōjō are sometimes known as Go-Hōjō, 'the later Hōjō'. They were not
descended from the Hōjō regents of the Kamakura period.

nificence, underlining the overlord's connections with the court. At his Kyoto residence and his nearby castle, to which nobles and feudal lords were regularly invited, he indulged in lavish ceremonial and hospitality. In 1587 he celebrated his Kyushu victory with a tea ceremony at which there were over 800 guests. In the following year he entertained the emperor to a banquet that was made the occasion for poetry contests. One purpose of such display was to emphasise his place in the scheme of things, to make it plain that his accomplishments were not confined to military ones. Another, perhaps, was to give him a public persona more impressive than his private one. To judge by the portrait statues that survive, Hideyoshi was not a prepossessing figure of a man. Nobunaga had called him Saru, 'monkey'.

Despite the nature of his public life, Hideyoshi did not treat the court as an instrument of government to be taken over as his own. To carry out his policies, where they concerned the country at large, he appointed commissioners (*bugyō*) from his own immediate entourage. One dealt with matters concerning land. Another supervised shrines and temples, plus the administration of Kyoto. Three more handled finance, trade and public works, respectively. None had a large staff. By the standards of Nara and Heian it was a skeletal and highly personal establishment.

It was used nevertheless to bring about important changes in political society. As early as 1583, Hideyoshi ordered land surveys to be carried out in the areas under his immediate control, a practice extended to the whole of Japan in the next ten years. Supervised by his own officials and using a newly standardised set of measures – they were chosen as favourable to the tax-collector – they recorded not just the area or value of the land, as in the past, but its assessed yield (*kokudaka*), measured in rice. In each case a single cultivator was identified, who would be responsible for paying tax. This destroyed the last vestiges of the fragmentation of ownership into *shiki*, which had been characteristic of *shōen*. It also made it possible to list the exact value of a lord's domain as a measure of his wealth and military resources, since yield determined the number of fighting men it could support. Uniformity

was imposed on both fief and village, to the great convenience of their overlord.

More famous was the decree by which Hideyoshi ordered a so-called Sword Hunt in 1588. By denying villagers the right to carry arms, it disarmed the peasantry, reducing the danger of peasant revolt. It also separated samurai from the land, making them more dependent on their daimyo. Those warriors whose lifestyle had previously rested on the income from parcels of cultivated fields had now to choose between their weapons and their former means of livelihood. If they remained in the village, it was as an unarmed rural élite, deprived of samurai status. If not, they became full-time servants of their lord, living in the precincts of his castle and looking to him for maintenance (in the form of stipends).

It took time for these regulations to be fully enforced. Even then there remained exceptions: a few senior samurai who were still enfeoffed, a larger number of rural samurai (*gōshi*) who in some areas took part in cultivation of the land. Nevertheless, for the most part a line had been drawn across Japan's social structure. Those above it were samurai, armed and privileged. Those below it were commoners, who were neither their social nor their political equals. By a further decree of 1591 samurai, even if they left the service of their lords, were not allowed to take up residence in villages, while farmers were forbidden to leave their fields to emigrate to towns or engage in commerce. These were fundamental concepts that Hideyoshi bequeathed to the Tokugawa rulers who succeeded him. The task that was left for them to complete was the building of an administrative structure, less personal than Hideyoshi's, by which the daimyo, too, could be brought to order.

The Tokugawa settlement (1600–1650)

It was unfortunate for Hideyoshi that a son, Hideyori, was born to him in 1593, his fifty-sixth year, since the event persuaded him to make fresh − and in the event unreliable − arrangements concerning his successor. His nephew and adopted son, Hidetsugu, about whose personal habits there were doubts, was disgraced, then ordered to commit suicide in 1595. Hideyori became heir. Five regents (Tairō) were appointed to protect his interests, all of whom were daimyo.

One was Tokugawa Ieyasu. When Hideyoshi died in 1598, Ieyasu, despite the promises he had made, sought power for himself, disregarding Hideyori's claims. A military balance emerged: on one side Ieyasu, holding the Kanto and supported by lords in the north, as well as by two of Hideyoshi's most able vassals; on the other an alliance of daimyo from Kyushu and the west, which included Mōri and Shimazu. In 1600 their armies met at Sekigahara, midway between Nagoya and Kyoto, and Ieyasu emerged as victor. This was as much because of political skills as military genius, for two of his declared opponents had already come to terms with him before the engagement started. One refused without warning to take part in the battle. The other changed sides once the fighting began, launching his men against the flank of those who thought him their ally.

Hideyori, still a child, was allowed to retain his father's mighty castle at Osaka, but as the years went by it became clear that as long as he stayed there he would be a focus for anti-Tokugawa sentiment of every kind. Ieyasu decided therefore to remove him. At the end of 1614 a pretext was found to send an army against him, but it soon transpired that his castle's defences were too strong to be taken by storm. Having no wish for a protracted siege, which might give opposition time to surface, Ieyasu offered peace terms in January of the following year; and when they were accepted, he took advantage of the terms of truce to fill in more of the moats − in what was claimed to be a 'misunderstanding' −

than had been specified in the agreement. Inevitably, when he attacked again in June, success came easily. Clemency was sought; the appeal was ignored; and Hideyori committed suicide, removing any further danger from those who still looked back nostalgically to Hideyoshi's day.

Like Minamoto Yoritomo – and unlike Hideyoshi – Ieyasu chose to remain in the Kanto, surrounded by his followers and his lands, rather than move to Kyoto. Edo was to be his capital, giving its name to a period and a culture. He followed Hideyoshi, on the other hand, in using his supremacy to redraw the political map once more. After Sekigahara, Shimazu was allowed to withdraw to southern Kyushu and keep his position there on promise of good behaviour. Elsewhere, sweeping changes were made. Nearly a third of the land in Japan, measured by yield (*kokudaka*), was confiscated and redistributed, putting Ieyasu and his men in possession of a vast central stronghold, running from the Kanto to the provinces surrounding Kyoto. Vassal lords of the Tokugawa (*fudai*), plus cadet branches of the Tokugawa house, were given strategic domains within this region: defending Ieyasu's capital from the north; protecting the approaches to Kyoto from the east (Hikone), the west (Himeji) and the south (Wakayama); and controlling key centres (Hamamatsu, Nagoya) along the Tokaido, the road that joined Japan's two capitals. Farther afield were the wealthiest of the lords, known as *tozama*, who had not hitherto been vassals of the Tokugawa. The Maeda of Kaga (Kanazawa), who had not opposed Ieyasu at Sekigahara, were treated favourably. Others, like Mōri of Choshu, who had fought on the 'wrong' side in that battle, had their lands drastically reduced in size. Lesser men, unlikely to be able to resist, lost their domains altogether. Kyushu and Shikoku were divided for the most part between Tokugawa allies.

This process of land reallocation continued under Ieyasu's son, Hidetada, and his grandson, Iemitsu, justified on grounds of maladministration, suspected treachery, moral turpitude, even the lack of an heir. This implied that domains were held in trust from the Shogun on condition of good government, not simply by

hereditary right. Indeed, the Tokugawa were well-nigh absolute. By the end of the seventeenth century, the head of the Tokugawa house, together with his enfeoffed retainers (*hatamoto*) below the rank of daimyo – the qualifying level for daimyo was a holding of 10,000 *koku* – and his numerous 'housemen' (*gokenin*), were masters of a little more than a quarter of the arable in Japan. Tokugawa relatives, plus the Shogun's vassal daimyo (*fudai*), shared another third. That left about a third to the 'outside' lords (*tozama*) and something under 2 per cent to the court and religious establishments.

Creating this overwhelming preponderance of land in the hands of the house head and his subordinates was fundamental to imposing order on Japan's feudal lords. It was bolstered by a number of institutional devices. In 1603 Ieyasu assumed the title of Shogun, signalling the end of an interregnum that had lasted since Ashikaga Yoshiaki had been deposed by Nobunaga thirty years before. Ieyasu is said to have possessed two genealogies in order to keep his options open. One showed descent from the Fujiwara, which would have qualified him for senior office at court. The other traced his line through the Nitta to the Minamoto, establishing a claim to be Shogun. It is by no means certain that either was genuine – false genealogies were a feature of sixteenth-century life – but the final choice of the second was a shrewd one, given that Hideyoshi had made a different one. It did not prevent Ieyasu from holding court rank and arranging an imperial marriage for Hidetada's daughter, but it strengthened his position *vis-à-vis* the samurai class, as it had done for Yoritomo. It provided a means, which he was quick to exploit, by which to make land grants under his own seal, to require written oaths of loyalty from daimyo, and to call for contributions from them for the building of Edo castle. They were made to attend him there. As Shogun he also took over the direction of foreign affairs, using for this purpose the title Taikun (since anglicised as Tycoon).

The prerogatives of his office were founded on custom, not law, but towards the end of his life Ieyasu committed them to paper. In August 1615, soon after Osaka fell, he announced a set

of thirteen regulations, known as the Buke Shohatto, which was read to the lords assembled at Fushimi, just south of Kyoto. The ceremony took place in the presence of Hidetada (who had succeeded as Shogun in 1605, to make sure that he was well established before Ieyasu died). Some of the regulations were of immediate political relevance. Others looked to the longer term. Daimyo must not give sanctuary to lawbreakers (refugees from Osaka, for example); castle building and daimyo marriages were to be subject to the Shogun's consent; men of ability – by implication, those who qualified as such in the Shogun's eyes – were to be chosen as advisers. Samurai must be encouraged to study both the civil and military arts and to lead 'a simple and frugal life'. Reinforcing this were rules against drunkenness, licentiousness, 'wanton revelry', extravagant and inappropriate dress, and travelling with retinues that were needlessly large.

Ten days later a comparable document, the Kuge Shohatto, set out regulations for the court and its nobility. The emperor and his courtiers were to devote themselves to scholarship and the arts (that is, not to government). Appointments to high court office were to be made in accordance with rank and ability (implicitly, after consultation with the Shogun's representatives). Ranks and titles could not be conferred on feudal lords without the Shogun's approval, nor could imperial relatives be named without it to posts in the Buddhist establishment. In all matters of substance, instructions issued by the Kampaku (now a Bakufu nominee) and the Bakufu's own officials in Kyoto were to be followed without fail. The penalty for contravening them was banishment from the capital. To these were added further rules about dress, precedence and family succession, none entirely novel, but imposed for the first time by a 'military' ruler.

As these two documents indicate, Ieyasu's first principle was to control the men who exercised authority, whether as daimyo or court nobles, rather than seek to govern directly all those parts of Japan that were not within his feudal jurisdiction. Providing they followed his wishes, as made known to them in general terms, Fujiwara, serving as Sesshō or Kampaku, still made day-to-day

decisions in the emperor's capital, while daimyo administered their domains. To represent him in Kyoto, Ieyasu sent a senior vassal lord as governor (Shoshidai), residing in the newly built Nijo castle. As a guarantee of daimyo compliance – reinforcing the ultimate threat of demotion or removal – he required lords to live for much of their time in Edo, much as the Ashikaga and Hideyoshi had done in Kyoto. Their wives and children remained as hostages when they withdrew to their domains.

Under Iemitsu these rules were spelt out in greater detail. By a revision of the Buke Shohatto in 1635, the arrangement became 'alternate attendance' (sankin-kōtai), by which daimyo spent half their time in Edo on a regular rota: that is, for six-monthly or yearly periods, depending on the location of their lands. This involved them in considerable expense, since they both lived and travelled in state. As a further restraint, a supplementary order of 1649 laid down the type and size of military force they could maintain.

It was mostly after Ieyasu's death in 1616 that clear political structures were devised .to prevent his intentions from being undermined by the passage of time. Under Hidetada the court made Ieyasu a *kami* of the highest rank. Iemitsu, who was Shogun from 1623 to 1651, built him a magnificent shrine at Nikko. 'Ancestral law' was thereby given the extra sanction of divinity. More practically, Iemitsu took up the task of giving government a more defined and durable character, which would be less dependent on the qualities of the ruler and his subordinates. A council of ministers (Rōjū) was formalised in 1634 as a board of four or five members, each a *fudai* lord of 25,000 *koku* or more. Its members served as duty senior minister in monthly rotation. The same principle of rotation, allowing for differences of detail, applied to other appointments. The Rōjū were collectively responsible for advice on general policy and for matters concerning feudal lords. Below them was a junior council, similarly composed, but with more restricted duties. A number of commissioners (*bugyō*) came next, responsible for shrines and temples. Together these three offices comprised the upper division of the

Bakufu's administration. At the next level down were offices filled by *hatamoto*, not of daimyo status, who conducted most of the daily business of government. There were commissioners who supervised Edo and its largely samurai population; others whose concern was with Tokugawa estates and Bakufu finance; and several 'inspectors' (*metsuke*) who sought out maladministration and derelictions of duty. Outside the capital were stewards (*daikan*) on Tokugawa estates, plus governors in some cities, notably Kyoto, Osaka and Nagasaki, all graded in rank according to their responsibilities. Only Tokugawa vassals could hold these posts.

Since nearly all the men who filled them had assistants and clerical staff, the bureaucracy was a good deal larger and more complex than that of previous feudal regimes. Its conciliar structure and the rules it designed to divide responsibility in various ways also made it cumbersome. From the Shogun's point of view, this reduced the risk of attempts to overthrow him from below (*gekokujō*), but it certainly introduced a greater degree of centralisation than is customary in feudal states. Although no great effort was made to legislate for what was done within a daimyo's boundaries, it was taken for granted that his obligation to provide 'good government' would lead him to adopt the practices exemplified by the Tokugawa. Similar norms existed in other walks of life. Accordingly, despite the fact that the bureaucrats were hereditary vassals, not hereditary aristocrats, there was enough correspondence between what was taking shape in Tokugawa Japan and what had existed in Nara and Heian to make China's example and political philosophy of seeming relevance once more (Chapter 10).

CHAPTER 8

Relations with Asia and Europe

1500–1700

Japan's earliest relations with China had a powerful influence on the whole history of the country's culture and institutions, as we have seen. At the other end of the historical time-span, starting in the nineteenth century, Europe and America had a comparable impact. The years from 1550 to 1650 can be considered as in some respects the first indication of this change of focus. This was when the tribute missions sent to the Sung, interrupted by Chinese policy in 1549, then briefly by war in 1592, were replaced by a more arm's-length relationship, resting on an illegal maritime trade. It was also the time at which there were the first direct contacts with Europeans.

The nature of these has led to it being called 'the Christian century'; but this is in fact a misnomer, in so far as Christianity was in the end decisively rejected. Events indicated nevertheless that Japan's new feudal rulers were beginning to work out a fresh approach to the outside world. It was a world, they were forced to recognise, that included Europe, as well as Asia, within its boundaries, a change that was seen from the start as potentially a threat to Japan's domestic order.

The China trade

By the early years of the sixteenth century, the missions that the Ashikaga sent to China were in Japanese eyes of value very largely for purposes of trade. Most of the voyages sailed from Hakata under the aegis of the Ōuchi lords. The ships that took part in them, usually three in number, were small, and more than half the passengers they carried were merchants, paying for cargo space. The tribute goods they took as gifts for the Ming court consisted of consignments of raw materials, plus Japanese craft products such as decorated fans and screens, lacquerware, swords and armour. The 'supplementary articles', which had to be offered first to the Chinese government, but could then be put on the open market if refused, included camphor, sulphur, and copper ore, the last of which had recently become an item of increasing importance. Swords were also sent in considerable quantity, but were a source of some disagreement. A century earlier they had been much in demand, but the expansion of production to satisfy this demand had brought a sharp decline in quality, which was reflected in the prices on offer. Japanese resisted the trend, Chinese refused to pay more, disputes multiplied.

Return gifts from the Ming included large amounts in copper coins, which the Japanese valued – and regularly requested – because of their importance to domestic commerce. Other welcome gifts were rich silk fabrics and cultural objects, mostly books and paintings. Merchants, too, took home some of the proceeds from their sales in the form of copper cash, but they also bought silk cloth of a more standard kind, which had a ready sale in Japan, as well as tea-ceremony utensils in porcelain and bronze. It was a trade in small bulk, high-value imports, which yielded large-percentage profits.

Not unexpectedly, the so-called 'Japanese' pirates (*wakō*) – according to Chinese records, Japanese were often in practice a minority, outnumbered by Koreans, offshore islanders, or renegade Chinese – tried to obtain as loot much the same goods as

made up return cargoes for the tribute missions. During the fifteenth century, the efforts of the Ashikaga and the Ming had succeeded to some extent in bringing their activities under control, but the Ming decision to put an end to Japanese official visits after 1549, imposing on trade with Japan the same restrictions as applied to other countries outside the tribute system, opened up new opportunities for the marauders. Large pirate fleets attacked the Yangtse region in 1553, then moved south to Fukien in 1561, seizing coastal settlements and stripping them of whatever could easily be carried away. Much of the booty went back to Japan for disposal, providing a source of supply that helped to make up for the loss of the tribute missions.

After 1560 renewed Ming efforts to build defences against the pirates began to have an effect, while removal of a longstanding Chinese ban on maritime trade in 1567 – though Japan remained a prohibited destination – made the inhabitants of China's southern coasts less willing to deal with *wakō* in an illegal commerce. More or less simultaneously, the restoration of a measure of order in Japan by Nobunaga and Hideyoshi (Chapter 7) was making Kyushu a less attractive pirate haven. In 1588, soon after his campaign against Satsuma ended, Hideyoshi prohibited piracy. He proved better able to enforce the law than his predecessors had been.

These circumstances favoured Portuguese attempts to gain a foothold in Japan. Already established in Goa and Malacca, they had first sent ships to Chinese waters in 1514, but it was almost thirty years later (1542 or 1543) that a party of Portuguese reached Tanegashima, an island just south of Kagoshima Bay. They came in a Chinese junk, escorted, it seems, by *wakō* from the China coast. Thereafter Portuguese ships themselves began to arrive in Kyushu, but it was not until China allowed Portugal to found a settlement at Macao (1557) and a Japanese feudal lord put Nagasaki under Jesuit jurisdiction (1571) that an ordered pattern of trading emerged. From that time on, these two ports became the terminals of a regular commerce between China and Japan, carried in Portuguese ships.

The *Great Ship*, as it was called, a carrack of between 600 and 1,600 tons, well armed and able to resist attack, sailed annually from China to Japan. It would reach Macao from Goa in time to load cargo in the early summer: silk floss and silk cloth, which were the staples of the trade; a quantity of gold, eagerly sought by daimyo for their war chests; rhubarb, sugar and similar items not readily available in Japan; and a few European products, chiefly firearms. Leaving for Nagasaki in June or July on the southerly monsoon, it would stay there for several months, selling to Japanese merchants. The return cargo for shipment to Macao, purchased with the proceeds of these sales, included camphor and copper, which Japanese had earlier taken to China, but above all silver bullion. During the sixteenth century, there had been a rapid development of silver mining in Japan, due to the adoption of Chinese (and later European) mining techniques. This provided a substantial surplus above domestic needs. Part of it, carried to Macao by the *Great Ship*, was invested there for the next Japan cargo. Part, representing Portuguese profit, went to Goa and Lisbon. A few other Japanese products, especially art objects, also found their way to Europe by this means.

The Portuguese were not left for long to enjoy their profits undisturbed. Spain, having captured Manila in 1571, soon began to trade to Japan. The Dutch, already challenging Portugal everywhere in Asian waters, were first brought to Japan by a ship that was wrecked on arrival in 1600, but were able to found a regular trading factory at Hirado (northwestern Kyushu) in 1609. The English, following the Dutch in the manner of a chain store determined to compete, came to Hirado in 1613. All three late arrivals found the Japanese market too deeply committed to trade with China to be easily changed. As Richard Cocks, the English East India factor, reported to his superiors in 1617, if England wished to trade successfully in Japan, 'then must we bring them commodities to their liking, as the Chinas, Portingales and Spaniards do, which is raw silk and silk stuffs, with Siam sapon [sappan wood] and skins'.

Lacking direct access to China's ports – Cocks tried to develop

a junk trade with the China coast from Japan, but with little success – Spain, Holland and England all secured Chinese goods for Japan by tapping the trading network created by Chinese merchants in Southeast Asia. Spain worked through the Chinese community in Manila, repatriating its profits in Japanese silver, much as Portugal did (that is, by sending them to Mexico in the annual Acapulco galleon). The Dutch, based in Batavia (Djakarta), used Chinese merchants in Indonesia and on the adjacent mainland. The English tried to do the same, but were largely frustrated by Dutch competition. They withdrew from Hirado in 1623, their factory a commercial failure. In all these cases the trade goods obtained for Japan were the same as those carried by the Portuguese, concentrating heavily on silk, mostly Chinese, though including some from India and Vietnam. There was also porcelain, usually procured via Manila, aromatic woods from Siam and elsewhere, some European guns and 'novelties'. The greater part by value of the Japanese exports for which these goods were exchanged consisted of silver bullion: Japan was a major contributor to the world's silver supplies in the sixteenth century. To this were added the kind of craft goods familiar in Japan's trade with China. In other words, while the Portuguese enjoyed a direct trade between China and Japan, the other Europeans had to make do with an indirect one, only lightly touched by the markets of Europe and Southeast Asia.

Eventually the Japanese joined in this trade as well. The *wakō* – at least those who were Japanese – had been deprived of much of their livelihood by the measures taken against them by Hideyoshi and the Ming. Nevertheless, like Drake and his fellow mariners in England at the time, they had always been ready to ply a trade, instead of fighting, if that seemed more to their advantage; and late in the century some of those who survived began to engage in trading voyages to the south. Hideyoshi, still concerned about controls, required them after 1592 to have a licence, franked by his vermillion seal (*shuin*), for every voyage they undertook. Tokugawa Ieyasu continued the practice when he came to power. Their ships are therefore known as 'red seal ships' (*shuin-sen*).

A study of the licences issued before Iemitsu put an end to the traffic in 1635 shows that about 10 per cent were in the names of daimyo, chiefly in Kyushu; a quarter were granted to foreigners resident in Japan, both Chinese and Europeans; and the remaining two-thirds went to Japanese merchants in the ports and cities connected with the China trade (Nagasaki, Hakata, Osaka, Kyoto). They authorised visits to places scattered all through Southeast Asia. During Ieyasu's lifetime these were mostly in Macao, Luzon, Siam and Indo-China (Annam, Cochin China, Cambodia, Tongking). Later Taiwan was added, while some of the more distant destinations (Java, Malacca) dropped out of the list.

The imports carried by these vessels were much the same as those brought in by Europeans from those areas. Exports were more varied, since Japanese merchants found it harder to get silver for export and easier to find alternatives. It has been calculated that the red seal ships brought back between 50 and 70 per cent of the silk and silk goods entering Japan, which made them serious competitors for the Europeans. To help in obtaining their cargoes, they founded Japanese communities at a number of ports overseas, the largest, the one in Manila, having something like 3,000 residents in 1606. The settlements did not long survive Iemitsu's regulations of 1635.

By contrast, there were only twenty Chinese merchants living in Nagasaki by about 1600, the port's trade having fallen to a trickle as a result of the restrictions that the Ming had imposed since 1549, followed by Hideyoshi's wars on the Asian mainland (see below). Tokugawa Ieyasu, encouraged by the Kyushu lords, who had economic interests at stake, proved willing to seek better relations; but although a letter was sent by one of his senior retainers to the Chinese governor of Fukien in 1611, by the time a reply came — it took ten years — Hidetada was Shogun and the opportunity was lost. Nor did the conquest of the Ming by the Manchus (Ch'ing) after 1644 make any formal difference. China's new rulers were as adamant on the subject of tribute relations as the old.

The atmosphere in Nagasaki had nevertheless improved enough to encourage more Chinese to go there in contempt of Chinese law. In Hidetada's time there were 2,000 or 3,000 Chinese residents in the port, while between thirty and sixty Chinese junks arrived each year. Some were from southern China, some from Southeast Asia. The numbers increased again after 1639, when Iemitsu expelled the Portuguese, but fell back towards the end of the century. The regulations issued by Japan in 1714–15 permitted thirty junks to trade, twenty from Chinese territory (Nanking, Ningpo, Amoy, Canton and Taiwan) and a further ten from Southeast Asia, where Chinese from the south were beginning to settle. They brought, as they had always done, silk, medicinal drugs and cultural items (books, paintings, porcelain). They took out silver, previously carried chiefly by the Portuguese, plus other traditional Japanese exports. This was now the only direct trade between Japan and China.

After 1639 the Dutch alone survived of the European merchants trading indirectly between the two. The English had withdrawn in 1623. The Bakufu banned Spanish ships because of a dispute in 1624, while the Portuguese had fallen victim to the proscription of Christianity (discussed below). Accused of giving support to both Jesuit priests and Japanese rebels, they were ordered to leave Nagasaki for good in 1639; and when a mission was sent from Macao in 1640, asking that the order be rescinded, its leaders were executed to make it clear that the Shogun meant to be obeyed. The Protestant Dutch – they were not 'Christian' as the Japanese understood the word – had always held aloof from religious quarrels, but they, too, suffered from Japanese suspicions. In 1641 they were moved from Hirado to the island of Deshima in Nagasaki harbour, originally intended to house the Portuguese. Only in that one port were they to be allowed to trade thereafter, their movements kept under tight supervision, the amount and nature of the goods they could buy made subject to official regulation, as was the number of ships that could come from Java each year. All commercial dealings had to be conducted through a monopoly ring of merchants under the watchful eyes of the

Bakufu's local representatives.

The restrictions were worth enduring at first because of the high returns on the trade, but economic circumstance became steadily more unfavourable with the passing of the years. Japan developed a silk industry of its own, reducing dependence on China for all but goods of the highest quality. Silver production fell as the more accessible deposits of ore became worked out: after 1668 the amount that could be taken out of Japan was officially restricted, leaving copper as the staple of Dutch export cargoes. As a result of these two changes, the Dutch found it difficult to make a profit at all by the eighteenth century. It is said that they remained at Deshima only because those who took part in the trade – the factors, supercargoes and ships' officers – could enrich themselves, if not the Dutch East India Company, by a combination of 'private' trade and smuggling. It became a popular belief in Nagasaki that all the Dutch captains were fat, because of the habit they had of carrying goods ashore concealed in their clothes.

Korea and Ryukyu

The presence of Portuguese, Spanish, Dutch and English merchants in Japan in the sixteenth and early seventeenth centuries marks the beginning of a maritime, western strand in Japanese history. Yet the trade in which they all took part was essentially a link between Japan and China. In much the same way, relations with Korea and Ryukyu in these years took place within the familiar context of a China-centred institution, the tribute system. In the fifteenth century, when the Ashikaga acknowledged the Shogun to be 'King of Japan', that is, a Chinese vassal, the decision had also opened the way to dealing with the Yi dynasty, which ruled a united Korea after 1392, on a footing of equality. The Sō, feudal lords of Tsushima, were intermediaries between the two. They sent missions to Korea in the name of Japan, just as the Bakufu and the Kyushu lords did to China, exchanging official

gifts. They also engaged in trade, exporting very much the kind of goods that went from Japan to Ningpo, importing skins, ginseng and honey, as had happened in the past, but also cotton cloth, which became more important than silk.

This trade, too, was beset by piracy. In 1443, in the hope of reducing the scale of *wakō* attacks on the Korean coast, the Yi concluded an agreement by which 200 Japanese ships could go to Pusan each year. A Japanese settlement was established there. The arrangement proved an uneasy one, however. Attempts by Japanese to expand their commercial foothold, much as they were doing on the China coast, brought about violent disputes, which led to a brief hiatus in the trade (1510–12); but peace was eventually restored and trade continued for most of the sixteenth century.

Hideyoshi did not wholly share the views of the Sō and the Tsushima merchants about what made Korea important to Japan. In 1586, when planning his Kyushu campaign (Chapter 7), he revealed to Mōri Terumoto that he had an ambition to conquer China. This was a task in which both Kyushu and Korea would have a part, the first as a base, the second as the route by which an attack would have to be made. He returned to the plan when the Shimazu and Hōjō had been defeated, believing, it appears, that an adventure overseas would give Japan's daimyo something other than civil war to occupy their minds. The Sō, convinced that their own interests lay in avoiding conflict with Korea, which would be bad for trade, did their best to head him off. They arranged a Korean mission to Japan, only for it to be bluntly told by Hideyoshi, when it appeared in Kyoto in 1590, that he intended to launch an attack on China, which would require him to move his forces through their country. Once victory was secured, he said, he would establish the Japanese emperor in Peking. More, in a letter to the Portuguese viceroy in Goa in the following year, he observed that China's conquest would also open the way to India.

Orders were given for an expedition to be prepared in April 1592. The bulk of the invading army was to be led by three of Hideyoshi's most trusted vassals, richly enfeoffed in Kyushu. One

was Katō Kiyomasa of Kumamoto. The other two were the 'Christian daimyo', Konishi Yukinaga, holding half Higo province, and Kuroda Nagamasa of Nakatsu. Another army, provided by Hideyoshi and Tokugawa Ieyasu from central and eastern Japan, would be held in reserve in northern Kyushu. A headquarters was built at Nagoya in Hizen. Naval transports and escort vessels were to be manned in large part by former *wakō*, totalling several thousand in a force of something over 150,000 men deployed.

About a third of these landed in the neighbourhood of Pusan at the end of May 1592. The contingents commanded by Konishi and Katō captured Seoul on 12 June, but thereafter the Japanese forces were divided, Konishi taking Pyongyang (23 July), Katō pushing north towards the Yalu river frontier with Manchuria, Kuroda moving northeast. Other units spread out to occupy central and southern Korea. In readiness for an advance against China, supplies were commandeered, land surveyed and registered, taxes collected.

It was after this initial push that things went wrong. The Japanese naval forces proved unable to carry out their task. Faced by a formidable opponent in the Korean admiral, Yi Sun-sin, they were just about able to keep open a sea lane to Pusan, but failed to make an entry to the Yellow Sea, where they should have given support to Katō and Konishi. On land, the harshness of the Japanese occupation policies provoked local risings and attacks on communication routes, making it difficult to supply the armies in the north. Then the Chinese came to Korea's rescue. A small Chinese force, which had crossed the Yalu in July 1592, had been quickly driven back. But a much larger one followed a few months later, defeating Konishi at Pyongyang in February 1593 and driving him back on Seoul. He concluded an armistice, pending peace talks, and withdrew to Pusan. Japanese troops remained there for the next four years, living off the land.

The negotiations undertaken during this interval were exceedingly devious. Chinese envoys met Hideyoshi in Kyushu in June 1593, having been led by Konishi to expect a settlement within the framework of the tribute system. Hideyoshi told them to their

astonishment that his terms included a resumption of the tribute trade, a marriage between Japan's emperor and a daughter of the Chinese emperor, and the cession to Japan of four provinces in southern Korea. This, they knew, was totally unacceptable to their superiors. Unhappily, no one had the courage to say so to Hideyoshi. Konishi therefore removed the talks to Korea again, seeking some form of words that would persuade the Chinese that Hideyoshi accepted vassal status, while concealing the concession from his awe-inspiring master. The process took time. It ended only when Konishi forged a letter in which Hideyoshi appeared to accept the title 'King of Japan'.

In December 1596 Chinese representatives again waited on Hideyoshi, this time at Osaka, prepared to invest him as king. Only then did Hideyoshi discover the deception that had been practised on him. He fell into a rage, expelled the Chinese from Japan, and set on foot preparations for another campaign. Large reinforcements were sent to Korea. Konishi and his fellow commanders took the offensive again (August 1597), though this time they set themselves a more modest objective, that of securing the four Korean provinces their master had demanded. The campaign even so was more difficult than that of 1592. The Koreans still had a naval advantage; their commanders were forewarned; a Chinese army was already in the field. Some progress was made towards Seoul before winter closed in, but the new year of 1598 saw the Japanese line come under increasing pressure. Konishi conducted a defensive campaign in the spring and summer to protect his base at Pusan, with little sign of achieving anything more than that. News of Hideyoshi's death (18 September 1598) finally brought his operations to a close. A truce was concluded. Japanese units, sometimes fighting their way out against heavy odds, began to leave Pusan for home.

The hardships suffered by Koreans under Japanese occupation left a legacy of lasting bitterness, but the Sō, taking up their role as intermediaries again, wanted to see the trade resumed. In 1605 they brought about a meeting between Korean envoys and Tokugawa Ieyasu at Fushimi. A more formal one with Hidetada

followed at Edo two years later. Prisoners were exchanged. In 1609 trade was restored to its sixteenth-century footing, subject to a limit of twenty ships a year; a Japanese settlement, guarded by samurai, was established on the outskirts of Pusan; Korean missions to Japan began once more.

Behind the *rapprochement* lay a manipulation of correspondence by the Sō, who had followed the example set by Konishi. The embassy to Hidetada in 1607 had been the product of a letter they forged, in which the Shogun signed himself 'King of Japan'. Later letters coming from Edo did not lend support to this misrepresentation, but in forwarding them to Korea the Sō reworded them, giving the impression that Japan was content to act within the tribute system. The deceit was successfully maintained until 1635. In that year it became known to the Bakufu as the result of a dispute within the Tsushima domain, but too much was now at stake to justify a diplomatic break. Those directly concerned in the affair were punished, though not severely. A decision was taken in Edo that the Shogun would use an entirely different title, that of Taikun (Tycoon), in his dealings with Korea, so as to avoid any imputation that he was subordinate to China. The Koreans silently concurred. A Korean mission of congratulation to Japan in 1636 marked the end of the incident.

Korean missions to Japan continued intermittently until 1811. Edo treated them as bearers of tribute to the Shogun, a practice – coupled with a good deal of public show – that gave some substance to Japanese claims that the country now had a position in East Asia to compare with that long held by China. Writing of a world with 'two centres', Japan and China, Japanese scholars implied an equality between the two. Some even called Japan Chūgoku (*Chung-kuo*), 'the middle country', the label by which China identified itself as the centre of a Confucian universe.

Japan's relationship with Ryukyu (Loochoo to the Chinese) encouraged similar pretensions, though it was not of the same order. In the fifteenth century, because of Ming restrictions on the Chinese junk trade, Ryukyu had become an entrepôt for the routes between Chinese ports and Southeast Asia. The islands

having acknowledged Chinese suzerainty, this gave them the right to send tribute missions and engage in trade with the mainland, but because of their distance from the Chinese coast they were able to ignore the ban on trading to the south. Since Satsuma also traded with Ryukyu, southern Kyushu was thereby provided with a 'secret' link, not only with China, but also with a shipping network that extended as far as Indonesia.

When Hideyoshi was planning his invasion of China, he called for help from Ryukyu as well as Korea. He was ignored. Nor did the 'king' of the islands respond to Satsuma efforts a few years later to persuade him to submit to Tokugawa Ieyasu. The result was a Japanese armed assault in 1609, authorised by the Tokugawa, but carried out by 3,000 men from Satsuma. Thereafter Kagoshima posted agents in the Ryukyu capital, exercising supervision over its ruler. They were careful not to break the link with China, since it furnished the legal cover for a profitable trade. The king, in fact, continued to receive his title from the Chinese emperor. On the other hand, Ryukyu also sent missions to Edo from time to time, smaller than those from Korea, and received with a degree less dignity, but serving the same purposes. Like those from Korea, they were treated as bearers of tribute.

In this way Japan enjoyed in both Korea and Ryukyu the commercial advantages of membership of China's tribute system, without formally belonging to it. Direct trade with China was carried on – illegally – through Chinese junks coming to Nagasaki, providing a channel through which to secure a knowledge of China's changing civilisation. Trade with Korea and Ryukyu, less valuable, left the Shogun safely removed from any shame that might be attached to vassal status. Indeed, he was able to enjoy a measure of prestige at home as the recipient of tribute on his own account.

Christianity and seclusion

Europe's trade carried no political implications of this kind. What is more, although it brought with it some pieces of useful information about the manufacture of guns, the mathematics of artillery, the practice of navigation and cartography, and the techniques of mining and fortification, while making minor contributions to Japanese painting and cuisine, it did not commit Japan in any important respect to European culture. The priests who came with the ships might have had a greater impact, had they been able to stay, but Christianity was rejected in the seventeenth century without having opened any important cultural doors.

The first Christian missionaries to arrive in Japan were three Jesuits, of whom one was Francis Xavier, brought to Kagoshima in a Chinese junk in 1549. Xavier himself left again in 1551, bound for Goa, with the intention of going to China, so he had little time to exert an influence in Japan; but by seeking access to the imperial court in Kyoto, then securing the patronage of the Ōtomo, who were emerging as powerful lords in the west of the country, he marked out a political framework for the mission. In the next thirty years his successors developed it. They were given permission to take up residence in Kyoto in 1560, which gave them access to the notional centre of authority. They won converts in the city and nearby provinces. Kyushu, where the trading ships came, nevertheless remained their main base. In 1563, in what was to prove a key event in the history of Christianity in Japan, they converted Ōmura Sumitada, daimyo of part of Hizen in the northwest of that island. He allowed them to settle in Nagasaki in 1571; ordered the compulsory conversion of the population in his domain in 1574; and put Nagasaki under Jesuit jurisdiction in 1580. The baptism of Ōtomo Sōrin and another daimyo at about this time, followed by that of those they ruled, raised the total of professing Christians in Japan to 150,000. By 1600 it was claimed to be twice that number.

This success owed as much to the religion's commercial as its doctrinal appeal. The Kyushu daimyo, anxious to protect their share of the trade with China, had taken note of the respect in which Portuguese captains held the Jesuits. It appeared to them that to tolerate Christianity, or show it favour, was a way of attracting Portuguese ships to Kyushu ports. The example of Nagasaki, which Ōmura's gesture made a regular terminal for the trade, confirmed them in this belief. In addition, the Jesuit priests were men of learning, whose expertise extended beyond religion into the fields of science and technology, including weaponry. This, too, made them men to cultivate.

The Kyushu campaign gave Hideyoshi his first personal knowledge of affairs in that region, including those relating to Christianity. As overlord, he objected to the administrative role of the Jesuits in Nagasaki, was alarmed by their interventions in local politics and was offended by tales of their intolerance to other religions; not only were their ideas alien, he believed, both in origin and in character, but their loyalties were directed to a foreign ruler, the Pope in Rome. These seemed reasons enough to bring them more closely under control. The difficulty Nobunaga had had in suppressing the Ikkō sect gave warning of what might happen if Christianity were allowed to spread.

On 24 July 1587, as soon as the Satsuma campaign ended, Hideyoshi issued a decree ordering Christian priests to leave Japan. Its text began with the time-honoured formula, 'Japan is the land of the gods (kami)'. From this it went on to accuse the priests of provoking attacks on shrines and temples, and stirring up 'the lower classes' contrary to law. Their presence was therefore a threat to civil order. In another decree the previous day, he had banned the practice of mass conversion on the order of feudal lords, which he held to be politically subversive. For the future, conversion must be individual, requiring approval either from representatives of authority (for samurai) or from household heads (for commoners).

These decrees were not apparently meant to be a prelude to suppression of the Christian faith, in that the only public anti-

Jesuit action taken in the next ten years was the seizure of Naga-saki. An official was appointed to govern the port in Hideyoshi's name in 1588. Starting in 1593, however, Dominican and Augustinian friars from Manila began to arrive in Japan. Confident of Spanish protection, they preached openly, in disregard of Hideyoshi's orders, spurning the more discrete means of propagation that the Jesuits had adopted, working through members of the ruling class. Annoyed, Hideyoshi gave the foreigners a sharp reminder of his wishes. In February 1597, twenty-six Christians, including three Jesuits and six Franciscans, were crucified in Nagasaki. It was the opening move in what was to become a full-scale persecution under the Tokugawa.

Tokugawa Ieyasu was wary, as Hideyoshi had been, of damaging foreign trade by acting too severely against the Christians, but he, too, found reasons to doubt their loyalty. After all, a good many of them rallied to Hideyori's cause at the end of 1614, fighting in defence of Osaka castle. Once the castle fell, therefore, he proscribed their religion and ordered the expulsion of the priests who had stayed in Japan in defiance of Hideyoshi's orders. All Japanese were henceforth to register as members of a Buddhist sect.

Hidetada and Iemitsu, the second and third Tokugawa Shogun, took still more drastic measures after Ieyasu's death in 1616. In the twenty years that followed, thousands of Christians, including many foreign priests, were executed, usually by crucifixion, or forced to recant by torture. Special commissioners were appointed to seek them out, taking, as it appears from missionary accounts, a sadistic pleasure in the task. Regulations, to be enforced by feudal lords as well as the Bakufu, were devised to remove all traces of the 'evil sect' among the population. True, small pockets of 'hidden Christians', preserving a form of the faith that was barely recognisable beneath its Buddhist accretions, were still to be found in Japan in the nineteenth century, but the campaign ensured that Christianity was not a force of any consequence in Japanese life while the Tokugawa ruled. When Japanese discovered different reasons for seeking a knowledge of the West, as they did

in the nineteenth century, they did so through intermediaries of another kind.

Action against Christianity was made easier for the Tokugawa to contemplate because after 1600 the religion was no longer indispensable to foreign trade. With the appearance of competitors, both European and Japanese, the Portuguese had lost their near-monopoly of imports coming from China. Spaniards, Dutch and English all had a share in providing them. So did Japan's own *shuin-sen*. Chinese junks at Nagasaki, and Japanese junks from Tsushima and Pusan, were additional sources of supply. Of them all, only Portuguese and Spanish had links with missionaries. Apparently with these considerations in mind, Hidetada and Iemitsu felt free to adopt a more restrictive stance towards foreign trade as well as Christianity. In 1616 Hidetada banned trade at ports other than Nagasaki and Hirado, cancelling the more liberal access earlier granted to the English. In 1636 Iemitsu required Chinese to come only to Nagasaki. He had already in the previous three years ended the issue of permits for Japanese voyages overseas, apart from those to Korea and Ryukyu, and forbidden Japanese to reside abroad on pain of death. He thereby put an end to the trade of the *shuin-sen*. Only Chinese, Portuguese and Dutch were left to carry on the country's foreign commerce.

In the early months of 1638 a large-scale peasant revolt broke out in the Shimabara peninsula, not far from Nagasaki. Large numbers of Christians joined it, apparently driven to desperation by years of persecution. The Portuguese, who had more enemies than friends in Japan for reasons of commercial rivalry, were accused of helping the rebels, directly with arms, indirectly by smuggling in priests; and in 1639 this became grounds for ending the link with Macao. The Dutch — who, it has been said, gave some assistance to the Bakufu in suppressing the rebellion — survived the crisis, but were transferred from Hirado to the island of Deshima in Nagasaki harbour, where they could more easily be policed.

They remained in Deshima for over 200 years, having little impact on the Japanese economy, but a more important one —

after 1700, at least – on knowledge of the outside world. This state of affairs was traditionally held to have made Tokugawa Japan a 'closed country' (*sakoku*). Recent scholarship has tended to question this, pointing out that relations continued with Korea and Ryukyu, helping to keep open a door to China, but the traditional view still has something to recommend it. Bakufu policy after 1640, reinforcing the attitudes that censorship encouraged among Japanese at large, was to be much more inward looking than outward looking for generations to come. There was no longer travel from Japan to China, except for a handful of priests. Intermittent western attempts to open trade again were treated with scant respect, either rejected out of hand as contrary to 'ancestral law', or turned away by threats of force. Japan, in fact, came to view the outside world, or at least the European world, through a screen of hostility and suspicion. When confronted in the nineteenth century by an expanding industrial West, these emotions conditioned the response of both her government and people for several critical years.

CHAPTER 9

Edo Society

The Tokugawa tried to stop the clock of history. Until the end of the sixteenth century the feudal society of Japan had been a natural growth, broadly consistent from one part of the country to another, but varying locally in detail and nomenclature. The new Bakufu set out to impose an ordered structure on it. Starting from the policies Hideyoshi had devised, which rested fundamentally on an enforced distinction between an upper class, composed mostly of samurai, and a lower class of 'commoners', it elaborated the country's social differences to provide for further status subdivisions above and below that central line. The object was to ensure political stability, partly to perpetuate Tokugawa power, by putting an end to the constant repetition of *gekokujō*, the process of 'low overthrows high', partly to prevent a return to the more general disorders of the immediate past. What was overlooked was the long-term effect of economic development. As the generations passed and the distribution of wealth changed, the 'system' was marred by inconsistencies and contradictions.

The restoration of peace in the seventeenth century after more than a hundred years of civil war gave a major stimulus to the Japanese economy. Labour went back to the land; agricultural production expanded; there was a greater variety of crops (silk, cotton and the sweet potato were all brought in from nearby

countries). The resulting surpluses spilt over into domestic commerce. Towns grew larger and more numerous, providing greater opportunities for merchants and artisans. As transport and communications improved, the products of distant regions became available in the principal population centres. Inevitably these conditions made for sharper disparities of wealth. Alongside landed wealth, on which samurai in the last resort depended, there emerged a commercial wealth in the hands of townsmen. Emulation of the lifestyle of the urban rich brought many samurai to debt, especially at the margins of the feudal class, and this in turn led to a blurring of status lines. Marriage and adoptions were arranged between samurai and well-to-do commoners, despite being frowned on by the social code. Conservatives demanded steps to check such practices.

It was not until the end of the Edo period that these problems threatened a social or political revolution, but long before that point was reached they had begun to undermine the accustomed patterns of Edo life. As rulers sought to expand their sources of revenue, while their more successful subjects looked for status recognition, those who were losers in the economic contest – debt-ridden samurai, dispossessed farmers, the urban poor – pressed for relief from their disabilities. By the end of the eighteenth century, Edo society was marked by a rising level of turbulence.

The ruling class

It was beyond all doubt that the Tokugawa ruled Japan after 1603, but in formal terms the Emperor's court outranked the Shogun's Bakufu. Among feudal leaders the Shogun alone reached Kyoto's highest dignities. His senior vassals, like other daimyo, were no more than in its middle ranks, despite their power and wealth. The respect language in official documents reflected this. By contrast, the higher-ranking courtiers had become by feudal

standards poor, since warriors had for centuries been eroding their rights in land. For appearance's sake, Edo subsidised the court on a steadily rising scale, but even in the eighteenth century its total contribution was no more than 120,000 *koku*, equivalent to the holding of a feudal lord of middle standing. About a third of it went to the imperial house. Another third was distributed as fiefs or stipends to members of the nobility. The most senior of these received between 1,500 and 3,000 *koku*: that is, something like the average stipend of a Tokugawa bannerman (*hatamoto*), serving as a Bakufu commissioner. Of the remaining 100 or more of leading families, nearly eighty had less than 200 *koku*, which in Edo would have classed them with 'housemen' (*gokenin*).

These were modest amounts, when one considers the rank of those who received them. A feudal lord, in order to be designated daimyo, had to hold land as vassal-in-chief that yielded at least 10,000 *koku*. If one accepts the traditional formula, that one *koku* of rice would support one person for a year, this made him master of a not inconsiderable body of people. The Shogun's own land amounted to over 4 million *koku*, yielding an annual revenue of about a third of that. Among the country's other daimyo, whose numbers rose from 200 in 1603 to just over 250 in 1850, there were sixteen whose domains were rated at 300,000 *koku* or more. Five were Tokugawa relatives, ten were *tozama*, or 'outside' lords, mostly in north and west Japan, and only one, Ii of Hikone, was a Tokugawa vassal (*fudai*) in the strictest sense. Daimyo of middle standing were those who had at least 100,000 *koku*, while those with less belonged to the lowest grade.

All the lords had samurai retainers, a small proportion of whom had fiefs and hence rear-vassals (*baishin*) of their own. Out of a total Japanese population of some 18 million in 1600, rising to 30 million in the nineteenth century, samurai, together with their families, accounted for 5 or 6 per cent. The head of the Tokugawa house had 22,500 samurai, plus another 60,000 *baishin*, though the numbers of the latter declined in the years of peace. The small apparent size of this armed following, compared with the Shogun's huge holding of land, reflects the result of victory in

Distinguished bureaucratic service became the grounds for an advance in rank, carrying with it possibilities of promotion. Samurai education was developed, in order to provide the ethos and the skills appropriate to an official career. Until this time most samurai, especially those of the higher ranks, had received their education at home, where they were given a knowledge of proper behaviour and a training in the use of weapons, flavoured with a dash of literacy. As a bureaucratic role in life became the norm, however, their superiors wanted something more. Like the aristocrats of Nara and Heian, they were deemed to need 'correct' moral attitudes if they were to play a part in government. This, it was held, they could acquire through the Confucian classics, so both Bakufu and domains began to establish schools at which these could be studied. Fifteen were founded by 1700, another seventeen in the next fifty years, seventy-five more by the end of the century.

In admitting students to the schools, preference was given to those of highest rank, who were likely to hold the most responsible offices. Middle and lower samurai might attend on a voluntary basis, or might even be excluded altogether, as were commoners as a rule. Teaching and organisation betrayed the same concern with status. Achievement as such was not greatly valued, except in military skills (which also formed part of the curriculum). An acquaintance with prescribed Confucian texts, acquired by rote learning, was all the philosophy that was given to most, while at the practical level an ability to read and compose official documents, perhaps with some help from those of greater literary accomplishment, plus a smattering of arithmetic, was as much as the school was ready to offer.

For some samurai, whose rank did not admit them to high office as of right, this was not enough. Society did not permit them to engage in trade or farming. Hence the pursuit of scholarship, or the possession of a more than local reputation for swordsmanship, or a recognised expertise in military science, all opening a path to employment by a lord – not necessarily their own – were among the very few ways of increasing their income with propriety. Most

to build. The Bakufu eventually banned them. An important step in that direction came at the beginning of the eighteenth century, when two lords, one of them a Bakufu official, quarrelled in the Shogun's castle. Swords were drawn. The one who was held to be the aggressor was ordered to commit ceremonial suicide (*seppuku*), since resort to force was forbidden in the castle precincts. His domain was confiscated, making his samurai into lordless men (*rōnin*). Forty-seven of them thereupon prepared to take revenge on the survivor of the dispute, who remained unpunished; but two years passed in plotting and dissimulation before they found means to attack his Edo residence. This was in 1703. Their enemy was killed and his head was taken to their dead lord's grave. The conspirators awaited the Bakufu's judgement.

It was not easy to determine. To punish the *rōnin* would contravene tradition, since they had acted out of loyalty to their lord. Not to do so would be to overlook a breach of the Shogun's laws. In the end the *rōnin*, too, were required to commit *seppuku*, incurring a punishment for breaking the 'public' law that was not thought to threaten their 'private' honour. It was a landmark ruling, which gave the incident lasting fame. On the one hand, it became the subject of the longest of Kabuki plays, *Chūshingura* (The Treasury of Loyal Retainers), which gives a much romanticised view of the affair. On the other, it marked a stage in the 'civilising' of the samurai. From this time on, they were still allowed as individuals to behave in accordance with their code of honour, known as Bushido – indeed, its classical expression is in a book entitled *Hagakure*, written about ten years later – and even to pursue revenge in certain personal matters, such as the unfaithfulness of a wife, but they were expected in other respects to find satisfaction of their pride in public service. Duty to Shogun or lord came first. A man would acquire the greatest respect, it was made clear, by performing the tasks he was called on to undertake by his station in life.

To encourage acceptance of the change, there were inducements. In the eighteenth century, additional emoluments were paid to those in office, serving as a supplement to stipends.

of these tasks became routine. Rarely did samurai need to take up arms after 1650. When they did so, it was usually to act against nothing more demanding than peasant revolt. As a result, they became more and more an unemployed soldiery, whose morale grew worse from one generation to another.

Other samurai – a minority, though a large one, tending steadily to increase – were employed in domain administration. Here a major preoccupation was finance: that is, raising the funds, whether in rice or cash, to pay stipends, to maintain an official residence in Edo, and to meet the cost of expensive journeys to and from the capital every year. Another was to administer the countryside, the domain's primary source of revenue. Since samurai were no longer resident outside the castle town, officials from the castle dealt with rural affairs through village headmen, or perhaps through a district office, manned by locally recruited staff. Occasional visits of inspection to the areas under their control, in order to keep a check on tax returns or supervise surveys, was all that was thought to be required by way of personal intervention. It was an authoritarian system, but not always an efficient one. Japanese farmers, like those elsewhere in the world, were adept at concealing and misrepresenting yields.

All this was a far cry from the medieval concept of the warlord as the leader of a warrior band, able to raise an army from his lands if the need arose. The daimyo of the Edo period held his territories from the Shogun, who required them to be governed in a manner that would bring well-being to their people: that is, in a way consistent with the peace and order of Japan at large. Not all, to be sure, lived up to this ideal, but for the most part they adopted the relevant vocabulary. Samurai, no longer simple warriors, assisted in this task, an army in waiting still, but comprising in the meantime the manpower of a government machine.

Since vassals might yet be required to fight, neither Shogun nor lords had any wish to discourage the samurai virtues of loyalty and courage, but quarrelsomeness and the pursuit of vengeance through vendetta, which were often the other side of the coin, were unwelcome in the kind of stable society that they were trying

the civil wars, which had made possible a degree of generosity when enfeoffing warriors. The case of Ikeda of Okayama is similar. A Tokugawa ally, Ikeda had 21 upper samurai, nearly 700 middle samurai and over 500 lower samurai in a domain that was rated at 315,000 *koku*. In both examples there is on average one samurai (disregarding rank) for every 200 or 250 *koku*. At the other extreme, the defeated, like Shimazu of Satsuma and Mōri of Choshu, who had lost more land than vassals – vassalage was a highly personal bond, not easily broken – were left with far more men than resources. Their samurai were numerous but poor.

Each daimyo, if his domain were large enough, governed it through a structure much like that which served the Shogun in Edo (Chapter 7), but on a smaller scale. At its head were senior officials, drawn from upper samurai families, qualified for their posts by hereditary rank. Such men had fiefs, not stipends. Some were expected always to be in attendance to their lord, whether in Edo or his castle town, others would stay behind to administer his lands when he went to Edo in accordance with the rules of 'alternate attendance' (*sankin-kōtai*). There was also a range of middle samurai officials, carrying out duties equivalent to those of *hatamoto* in the Bakufu. These were of full samurai rank – entitled to attend personally on their lord on ceremonial occasions – but lower in the economic as well as the social scale than the senior councillors (*karō*). They had stipends, but these varied greatly in value. At the top of the range they might be as much as 500 *koku*, enough to sustain a comfortable lifestyle; at the bottom, they barely sufficed to support a respectable household. Below this level again were lower samurai and *ashigaru*, serving as guards, messengers and clerks on very much less.

Samurai, whether in Edo or the castle town, might perform their feudal service in either of two ways. There were on the one hand the traditional military duties of a warrior in time of peace: to garrison the daimyo's castle, to serve as his escort on journeys to and from Edo, and to provide a force he could use to police his lands. This was for the majority, though once the Tokugawa imposed order on the country in the seventeenth century most

domains were willing to grant leave of absence for the purpose of acquiring the requisite knowledge, usually in one of the major cities.

It was because of this that private academies multiplied in and after the eighteenth century, matching the spread of official schools under feudal patronage. Most were founded by a scholar of some note, who supported himself by fees or regular gifts from students. The earliest academies, especially in Kyoto, catered for a more advanced study of the Confucian classics than was provided elsewhere. This remained their main attraction for many students, who came in time to include a sprinkling of well-to-do commoners. Some attention was also paid in them to mathematics. Separate schools were devoted to fencing (*kendō*) and various styles of swordsmanship. To these were added so-called 'western studies' (*yōgaku*) later in the period, inclining towards the practical and scientific: medicine, astronomy (which was related to cartography and surveying), western-style gunnery and the use and manufacture of explosives.

Advanced training of this kind provided outlets for ambition, but not on a sufficient scale to solve the larger economic problems of the samurai. Even feudal lords had difficulty in balancing income and expenditure. Revenue derived mostly from a percentage of the crop. It therefore remained buoyant during the seventeenth century, while production was rising, but after 1700, when population stabilised and the expansion of cultivated land was reaching its technological limits, yields no longer increased to any important degree. Growth became commercial growth. Since domains failed to devise effective ways of taxing it, they were left with little choice but to put further pressure on the farmers, in order to seek a higher return on land. Before long, tax demands exceeded capacity to pay, prompting resistance. In the second half of the Edo period, there was a rising level of peasant revolt, putting further constraints on revenue.

Expenditure, by contrast, continued to grow. Its principal component, other than the provision of samurai stipends, had always been the expense incurred in maintaining an establishment in

Edo and financing the daimyo's travels to it. Most of this commitment had to be met in cash. A proportion of tax rice was therefore sold to produce it, an undertaking that involved the domain's officials in financial dealings of which they had little previous understanding. Merchant advisers were employed to handle most of them. Since these were usually men who creamed off for themselves such profits as could be made from seasonal and annual variations in the price of rice, the domain saw little benefit. Indeed, when the treasury faced unanticipated needs, such as might arise from a Bakufu demand for contributions to the cost of public works, these 'official' merchants would furnish loans, the interest on which, invariably high, became a further burden.

The Bakufu was to some extent protected in this kind of situation by its possession of political authority. It could decree controls on prices and interest rates, even cancel debt in the last resort, though it sometimes found that meddling with the market in this way could make things worse in the longer term. Rank-and-file samurai had no such recourse. Like their lords, they were town-dwellers, whether in Edo or the provinces. Most had fixed incomes, payable notionally in rice. Since they needed cash for day-to-day expenses, and could obtain it only by marketing the rice that was due to them as stipends, the custom grew up of transferring the rice 'coupons' with which they were issued to a convenient merchant or moneylender, who would make a cash advance against them. This put the samurai in much the same position as the daimyo's treasury. Profit from selling the rice went to the financial agent. Any event for which no provision had been made − a marriage, an illness, a death − pushed the family into debt. Given that the temptations of urban life, due to the ever greater availability of expensive foods, clothes and entertainment, exercised a constant upward pressure on household budgets, the samurai's expenditure year on year exceeded income. On rare occasions there might be a moratorium on samurai debt, but much of the time the Shogun and the lords were just as likely to cut hereditary stipends in their search for economies that might

benefit themselves. Official assistance proved a slender straw at which to clutch.

In the course of time, the tension between wealth and rank arising from these changes caused an erosion of the status structure of the ruling class. Daimyo granted samurai rank to a few merchants whose services they especially valued. In larger numbers, middle and lower samurai sought financial support by entering into family ties through marriage or adoption with affluent commoners. More widely still, they used family and household labour to produce craft goods for sale, so setting up a kind of upper-class by-employment. Those in the greatest distress might even seek permission to abandon their rank, whether on a permanent or a temporary basis, in order to take up farming or trade.

The result was a decrease in the cohesion of Edo society. The changes inevitably aroused resentment, directed both at successful social climbers and at those who could in one way or another be held accountable for the problems that society faced. Lords and upper samurai were accused of not having done enough to remedy hardship among those whose loyalty to them had been tested over many lifetimes. The merchants were blamed for feudal debt, because it was thought to stem from their greed and manipulation of prices. Villagers, on whom samurai income depended, saw the root of their misfortunes in the growth of towns. Even so, the system still held together tolerably well in 1850, if less from inherent strength than for lack of an impetus to bring it down. Some new factor, it seemed, was needed to provide a shock to the structure before it would fall apart.

The village and the town

Hideyoshi's Sword Hunt (Chapter 7), reinforced by Tokugawa polices, ensured that Japan's villages were under the jurisdiction, not of local samurai, but of their lord, who controlled them through the officials of his castle town. The main exception was

to be found in the Shogun's lands, because they were too large to be governed as a unity. In them, domain-sized sections were put under the supervision of resident stewards (*daikan*), chosen from Tokugawa vassals, who served as both daimyo-substitutes and the Shogun's representatives.

Everywhere there was a form of indirect rule that left a good deal of influence in the hands of those with whom the officials had to deal: village headmen, village elders, and those of slightly higher status who held office in more than one village. All were non-samurai. One of their duties was to allocate the burden of tax within the community, since the lord assessed it on the village as a whole. Another was to adjudicate in such misdemeanours as seemed of too little consequence to call for samurai intervention. They also regulated festivals and other communal events. In return they were accorded benefits and social recognition which set them above their fellows: perhaps a small salary, privileges with respect to tax and labour dues, the right to bear a family name, to carry a sword, to wear superior clothes. They were likely, too, to possess the better fields and have a larger house than was permitted to other farmers. Given that such positions were hereditary, these were men who might be described in some respects as quasi-samurai, which is certainly how their neighbours and their superiors saw them. If officials were oppressive or inefficient, peasants expected the headman to take the lead in seeking redress. Should his protests in their turn prove too insistent or threatening, the domain would punish him, usually with severity.

With few exceptions – mostly of ex-samurai houses – peasant holdings were small enough to be worked by family labour, though there was an under-class of day-labourers, landless or with not enough land to support themselves, who found employment on the larger farms. Early in the period, village economies were nearly self-sufficient. Only enough of the crop was sold, or exchanged by barter, to secure necessities that were not produced in the locality, such as salt, iron (for tools) and cotton (for clothing). The proportion of the crop that was paid in tax varied with local custom and political conditions. On Bakufu estates it was

commonly 30 to 35 per cent, though it became a little more in the eighteenth century. On daimyo domains the average was nearer 40 per cent. Even higher figures are sometimes cited, but these, if true, seem to have been exceptional. At all events, the burden was a heavy one, leaving little margin for investment to improve the land, none at all for luxuries. Most finance for land reclamation and better irrigation came from outside the village, initially from feudal lords, who had reason to expect that revenue would rise with an increase in cultivated area, later from commercial (possibly urban) investors.

The situation changed in the course of the seventeenth century as a result of the growth of domestic commerce and the towns it bred. Farmers, especially in the vicinity of urban areas, began to produce for the market: silk, cotton, vegetables, vegetable oils, even rice, as conditions made it favourable. Some turned over all their land to this kind of production, relying on their profits for the purchase of the rice they owed in tax. Since prices were unstable, despite intermittent Bakufu efforts to control them, the process necessarily produced both winners and losers. The successful could invest more heavily in fertiliser, farm animals, better strains of seed. With higher incomes, they sought entry to the village élite, if they were not already members of it. Those who failed fell into debt, became tenants or day-labourers, perhaps moved to the towns. By the eighteenth century, the ideal of village life envisaged by early Tokugawa thinkers – a kind of equality in poverty, affording margin only for the payment of tax – had broken down.

The social disruption caused by economic change, plus the pressure of taxation, as feudal lords tried to maintain or increase their revenues, brought unrest to the countryside. Though never absent altogether, rebellions averaged fewer than two a year in the seventeenth century. In the next fifty years, the number doubled; in the hundred years after 1750, it doubled again. A few of the outbreaks were on a major scale, especially after 1800, involving large bodies of peasants from many villages. Others, though little more than protest marches, were nevertheless put down with the

same severity. At the local level, rioters usually directed their anger against the nearest targets: village headmen and other non-samurai officials, or well-to-do farmers, who had taken up money-lending as a supplementary source of income. The early nineteenth-century revolts were more likely to be prompted by wider issues, concerned in some way with feudal government, hence politically more worrying. Grievances cited by the rebels ranged from the imposition of new taxes and the use of false instruments in surveys of the land to the introduction of monopoly arrangements, in which the domain entered into partnership with urban merchants, putting its power to tax at the service of exploitation for the sake of revenue.

To understand more fully the nature of these developments, one needs to look at the growth of towns. Medieval towns, other than political centres like Kyoto and Kamakura, had been the site of markets serving a limited area. In the Edo period, the castle town became the norm. It had its origin in the need felt by emerging daimyo to establish a stronghold from which they could both defend and govern their lands; and it was therefore a garrison town, where a force of samurai was required by duty to reside (in effect, the whole of a lord's following, once Hideyoshi decreed his Sword Hunt in 1588). To provide this force with weapons and other supplies, a daimyo would offer legal and taxation privileges to artisans and merchants who settled there: the makers of weapons, the financial agents who collected and marketed tax rice, those who devised and managed transport facilities. Within the urban area, the samurai nucleus, grouped according to rank, was housed near the castle's walls. The most favoured commoners, divided by occupation, occupied the districts round the samurai perimeter.

To this military and governmental core, non-samurai of lesser standing were attracted in the course of time. A community composed of members of the ruling class, plus privileged suppliers, was a consumer market rich enough to bring together retailers, shop assistants, servants and porters in substantial numbers. To them were added the entrepreneurs and workers of the con-

struction industry, engaged in extending the urban boundaries, plus the men who fought fires (an important group where houses of wood and paper huddled together), those who collected night-soil (for sale as fertiliser to farmers in nearby villages), and enter-tainers of every kind. Many of the unskilled among them were immigrants from the surrounding countryside, 'released' from cultivation into penury or alternative livelihood by improvements in agricultural methods and techniques.

These towns quickly became district centres with an economic as well as political function, places to which farmers sent their tax rice and such items as they had for sale, from which they bought the foodstuffs, clothing and tools they could not produce them-selves. Because the lord and many of his retainers spent half their time in Edo, as required by the rules of 'alternate attendance', the castle town also had to develop links with other parts of Japan. Tax rice was shipped to Osaka for sale, if that city were reasonably accessible. A large part of the proceeds was then sent to Edo to pay for the domain's official residence there and the costs incurred by lord and samurai staying in it. All this helped to establish a national network of commercial and financial operations, in which domains were inextricably involved. The raising of loans, when revenue proved inadequate, was part of it.

In the larger domains, these conditions led to the growth of towns of significant size. By 1721, when an official census was taken, Japan had five cities with a population of over 100,000. The greatest was Edo, castle town of the Tokugawa lands and headquarters of the Bakufu. Because of 'alternate attendance', half its inhabitants – estimated to total as many as a million in the eighteenth century – were samurai. Another place with political functions, though smaller, was Kyoto. It had become for the most part a cultural and commercial centre after Hideyoshi's death, but was still the seat of the emperor's court. Next came Osaka, a wholesale market for the products of west Japan, already on its way to being the cotton textile capital of the country. The other two in this category, qualified by their size, not their national role, were the castle towns of Kaga (Kanazawa) and Owari (Nagoya).

There were a further five cities with populations of 50,000 or more: Nagasaki, the sole remaining port for foreign trade, together with the castle towns of Kii (Wakayama), Aizu (also called Wakayama), Aki (Hiroshima) and Satsuma (Kagoshima). Of the ten so far listed, four, including Edo, were in the domains of the Tokugawa and related families, three were the castle towns of *tozama* lords, the rest (Kyoto, Osaka, Nagasaki) were directly under the Bakufu's administration.

No fewer than sixteen other towns had a population of 30,000 or more. By the nineteenth century, in fact, Japan's urban population in centres of at least 10,000 people amounted to about a sixth of the national total. This is two-and-a-half times the estimate for 1600. In the Kanto and the provinces round Osaka and Kyoto, the proportion ran as high as a fifth.

Townspeople, like villagers, varied in status, though the gradations were related to housing and commercial wealth, not land. The most senior were the headmen and elders of the wards into which the towns were divided, performing duties that were much like those of their rural counterparts; but because the town was the home of the lord and most of his retainers – and in the case of Edo of high-ranking visitors – they were much more tightly supervised by samurai officials. Magistrates of middle samurai rank (higher in Edo, Kyoto and Osaka) intervened in almost every aspect of urban life. From an initial concern with the preservation of order and the prevention of fire, their jurisdiction was gradually extended to cover rules about debt and the implementation of the sumptuary laws, together with the regulation of the entertainment quarters, in which theatres, houses of prostitution and the venues for sports like *sumō* were to be found. The Confucian rationale for this was not that personal morals were the ruler's business – Edo society was anything but prudish – but that luxury, gambling and loose living of every kind attracted criminals and wrongdoers, raising issues of public order. Bakufu officials set an example of intervention in civic affairs in seventeenth-century Kyoto by banning the performances of *kabuki* plays by women. When troupes of boys replaced them, substituting male for female pros-

titution, these were required to be licensed. Their members were forced to live in designated quarters of the city, where they could more easily be supervised (towns, although they had no walls, were divided into districts by gates, which had to be shut at night). Similar restrictions were imposed in Edo as it grew, while the officials of daimyo followed suit in their castle towns. Books, plays and pictures were all subject to censorship (though this did nothing to prevent a very large output of pornography).

The punishments inflicted for breaking laws were in all cases severe, but more so for commoners than for samurai. Torture was freely used to extract confessions. Samurai who committed serious offences, especially political ones, might be beheaded, but they were more likely to suffer the 'lesser' penalty – it carried no loss of status or stipend for their family – of ceremonial suicide (*seppuku*), usually known in the West by its less formal name, *harakiri*, or 'belly cutting'. Even this type of execution was miti-gated by custom in the end. By the later years of the period, the offender was allowed to call on the services of a friend, who would cut off his head simultaneously with the first incision of the sword (sometimes even before it). Lesser crimes were remitted to the samurai's lord for punishment, which could often mean nothing more than a year or two of house arrest. The same penalty might be imposed on daimyo.

Commoners were treated more roughly. Leaders of a peasant revolt, or even a protest demonstration, could expect crucifixion. Other forms of punishment were equally gruesome. There was a case in Kanazawa in the 1660s of a woman who had robbed several employers and set fire to their houses to conceal what she had done. She was boiled to death in a cauldron (perhaps because she had committed the anti-social offence of arson). Also from Kanazawa comes an example of discrimination according to status. In 1690 four samurai were found guilty of hiring a group of prostitutes and holding wild parties. The townsmen who provided the women were beheaded, or had their ears and noses cut off before being banished from the city. The women themselves were sent to a rural district to be servants for life to local farmers. The

samurai were at first exiled to the countryside, later pardoned.

Incidents like this, coupled with evidence of poverty and hardship among the lower classes of both town and village, make it tempting to paint a dark picture of society in the Edo period. Yet to do so would not be entirely accurate. In the cities, at all events, many Japanese were able to find an escape from the oppressive hand of government in a 'floating world' (*ukiyo*) of theatres, geisha houses and restaurants. There wealth, not status, governed human relationships, except in so far as the residents evolved a status system of their own. Much of the period's art and literature describes the life they led (Chapter 10). The escape was more psychological than legal, but it may well have acted as a safety-valve, preventing urban discontents from becoming revolutionary.

Some commoners, not only in towns, were in any case better off as a result of commercial development. As the scale and complexities of domestic trade increased, bringing a growth of wholesale markets, banking facilities, money exchange, insurance, inns and post-stations along the main roads, and shipping routes that linked not only Edo to Osaka, but also both to the rest of Japan, so prosperity reached large sections of the country. Urban entrepreneurs made their way into rural areas to fund and organise production for the market, providing by-employment for farm families. Commerce spread beyond the towns. Its profits, moreover, opened up new opportunities. A few commoners were admitted to domain schools. More secured an education in the private academies, where sons of the rural élite – village headmen, doctors, priests, well-to-do farmers – joined those of merchants in the kind of studies once thought proper only for samurai. Even those of lower rank could acquire a knowledge of 'letters and numbers'. After 1800 hundreds of so-called 'temple schools' (*terakoya*) were founded by community leaders to provide a basic training in literacy and arithmetic, plus some homely moral philosophy, for those who in the past would have had no education at all. Perhaps 40 per cent of boys – though far fewer girls – had reached a modest standard of literacy by the time the Tokugawa were overthrown.

There was also a gain in standards of living. Japan's dense population and relative lack of resources had long encouraged the kind of material culture – and attitudes towards it – that emphasised simplicity and lack of waste. Because of this, it took only a minimum increase in national wealth to have an important impact. The greater range of goods from different regions of the country, available in the shops of the towns from the late seventeenth century onwards, was early evidence of it. Sumptuary laws, issued by the Bakufu in accord with Confucian doctrine, were a sign of rising consumption. So was the spread of social habits like gift giving and restaurant entertaining. Among foods, rice remained the preference for those who could afford it, but many could not. The poor still had to make do with cheaper substitutes (now including the potato). Sugar, too, was a luxury, only grown in the farthest south. On the other hand, fruit and vegetables were being commercially produced, especially near the cities, making possible a healthier diet for many; protein was available in the form of bean-curd and fish; sake (rice-wine) had a national market. The use of cotton, introduced from Korea in the sixteenth century and soon planted as a staple crop in central Japan, brought a huge improvement in the quality of clothing and bedding: silk had always been a fabric for the few. Cotton, indeed, was the first non-food item to achieve importance in the Osaka wholesale market.

In all these respects, the components of Japanese everyday life were becoming those that are now regarded as 'traditional'. Tradition in this sense is not much older than the Edo period. Housing is an example. Since the later Muromachi years, samurai and others of rank had lived in single-storey dwellings, divided into an earth-floored working space, which included the kitchen, and a living space with a raised floor made of thick straw mats (*tatami*) packed into oblong frames. There was a covered entrance (*genkan*), at which a visitor could step up onto the *tatami* floor, leaving outdoor footwear on a shelf or rack. The principal reception room would have an alcove (*tokonoma*) for the display of the owner's works of art or other treasures, set off by a flower

arrangement. The building itself had wide overhanging eaves; was divided into smaller rooms, as required, by sliding panels, decorated, or made of translucent rice-paper to provide more light; and was heated, if at all, by small quantities of charcoal, burnt in braziers (*hibachi*). It was a type of housing better designed for summer heat than for winter cold. An early (and superior) example of it is the Katsura villa on the outskirts of Kyoto.

In theory, sumptuary laws prohibited commoners from having houses of this kind, though the wealthy were often able to ignore the rule. Few farmers, other than village headmen, could afford them. Most had buildings with greater working space, earth-floored throughout, at least until the later part of the period. Merchant houses were to a quite different plan. They had a narrow frontage on the street, abutting those of their neighbours. At the front of it was space for a shop or other business; living quarters were farther back; the kitchen and storerooms were at the rear. The city poor as a rule had no street frontage at all, occupying the middle of an urban bloc, where they shared toilets and water with neighbours; but the introduction of public bath-houses, another Edo innovation, made life a little more hygienic for them.

The Edo period was the last stage of Japanese history before the country and its people came under the influence of the modern West. Since this was to bring about a far-reaching trans-formation, it is natural enough that to the present-day observer the institutions and values that are associated with the Edo past should seem to be 'typically' Japanese. Yet one needs to be wary of treating Edo Japan as an undifferentiated whole. There were, as we have seen, important differences between the beginning of the period and the end of it, touching political authority, social structure, economic achievement and lifestyle. So there were between regions in dress, custom and spoken language. Beneath a surface uniformity, in fact, there was still variety and change.

CHAPTER 10

Edo Culture

The Edo period is nowadays seen as the high-water mark of Japanese cultural tradition (except by those who have a sentimental attachment to Heian). Two centuries and more in which there was much greater movement of goods and people between different parts of the country, linked variously to commerce, 'alternate attendance', the travels of students seeking profitable expertise, and a habit of pilgrimage to famous temples and shrines, ensured that culture did not remain exclusively metropolitan or upper-class. Geographically it was becoming countrywide. Socially, on the other hand, divisions remained, corresponding for the most part with the line between samurai and commoner.

Samurai and court nobles shared a taste in philosophy, literature and painting that was essentially 'Chinese', or at least classically Sino-Japanese. It was both reinforced and modified by a growing knowledge of China under the Sung and Ming. By contrast, the non-samurai residents of the towns preferred novels, pictures and plays that owed more to the 'popular' strand in medieval life, as developed in Kamakura and Muromachi. For this reason the town-dwellers (*chōnin*) of the 'three cities' of Edo, Osaka and Kyoto added a distinctive element to Japanese culture. It was to remain characteristic of the age.

★

Chinese thought, Japanese thought

During the Kamakura and Muromachi periods, Buddhism had been a dominant influence on Japanese religion and culture. Amidist sects spread the faith to the greater part of the population; the great Buddhist houses accumulated lands, which gave them a quasi-feudal power; Zen played a major part in bringing to Japan the civilisation of China under the Sung and Ming. Medieval Japan was therefore in many respects a Buddhist society. By the time the Tokugawa were Shogun, some of this ground had been lost. Armed force, used against the most popular sects by Nobunaga and Hideyoshi, had weakened the religion's political independence, making it little more than an instrument of feudal government. True, Buddhism was still part of the fabric of daily life – many of its temples had the patronage of feudal lords; all Japanese were required to register at one, since they were instructed by the Bakufu to keep population records; most houses contained small Buddhist altars (*butsudan*) – but this gave it no more than a residual prestige. There was no doctrinal or social innovation to impart fresh vigour, no new sects, no charismatic Buddhist figures of the calibre of Hōnen and Shinran, of Eisai and Dōgen. For lack of any overriding structure of authority – there was no Buddhist 'church' with an acknowledged head – doctrines were diverse, the discipline exercised over the clergy weak.

Against this background, Japanese turned increasingly to the less other-wordly beliefs of Confucianism, a philosophy that addressed the social dimension of human life. It had a number of 'schools'. One, associated in China with the name of Wang Yang-ming (1472–1529), envisaged a cultivation of the moral self as the primary duty of the individual, designed to reinforce a code of behaviour towards one's fellow members of society in accordance with justice and benevolence. Another, which was central to what became known as Neo-Confucianism, as developed by the Sung scholar Chu Hsi (1130–1200), emphasised its 'state-ordering' role:

that is, creating and preserving a well-ordered society. Both strands became influential in Japan during the seventeenth century, though it was the second that had the greater prominence.

Chu Hsi placed emphasis, first, on the idea that human society must reflect the existence of an orderly universe. From this it followed that study of the universe – in a search for underlying principle, not merely an understanding of phenomena – must be part of the moral training of the statesman. Second, since the universe itself was hierarchical, so must social structure be: the concept of inequality sprang from the relationship of Heaven to Earth. Of the five human relationships, four (leaving aside that between friends) were necessarily unequal, those of ruler–subject, parent–child, husband–wife and elder–younger. Finally, since the fundamental wisdom of the sages, which remained universally valid, was to be found in the Classics, later men must seek guidance from their study.

Although Neo-Confucianism incorporated a number of religious elements, involving ancestor worship and a cult of Confucius himself, it was in essence a temporal creed. Humanity, righteousness and decorum all had a place in the virtues it identified. To Chu Hsi, however, loyalty and filial piety were the primary ones, defining the duties of low to high. To the feudal rulers of Japan, faced with the task of restoring order after generations of civil war, this gave the doctrine more appeal than the characteristically inward-looking ideas of Buddhism. An emphasis on the attitudes that ruler and subject should adopt towards each other – benevolence from the first, submission from the second – together with a stress on agriculture as the heart of the economy, could readily be accepted in a feudal society. Confucius had lived in one, after all. In addition, the duties that Chu Hsi ascribed to the bureaucrat could just as easily be applied to the functions of the samurai in time of peace. For both reasons, Neo-Confucianism was welcomed. This is not to say that it became an orthodoxy, officially prescribed, but it certainly attracted the favour of the country's ruling class.

Fujiwara Seika (1561–1619), a Zen priest in Kyoto, who was

drawn to it by what he learnt from Korean scholars at the time of Hideyoshi's campaigns, is given the credit for establishing Neo-Confucianism in Japan as a distinct political philosophy. He also brought it to the attention of Tokugawa Ieyasu; but it was his student, Hayashi Razan (1583–1657), Confucian tutor to Ieyasu after 1608, who entrenched it in the Edo establishment. Until the nineteenth century, successive members of his family were to have responsibility for the Bakufu's official school.

In the intervening 200 years, Confucian thought in Japan became diverse. One group of scholars, of whom the most famous was Kumazawa Banzan (1619–91), looked more to Wang Yang-ming than Chu Hsi, putting innate virtue before the needs of the state. Another, linked usually with the name of Ogyū Sorai (1666–1728), turned, as some recent Chinese philosophers had done, to the study of the ancient texts, seeking thereby to disentangle what was 'classical' from the commentaries of later times. This led to a greater concern with laws and institutions, which was a Legalist rather than a Confucian concept in ancient China, closely bound up with the development of imperial autocracy. Ogyū himself, denying that the actions of the ruler should be determined by a moralistic philosophy, conceived of the Shogun as an absolute ruler on the Chinese model, served by officials selected for their ability, not their birth. It was an argument in which Maruyama Masao has detected the seeds of modern thought.

To men like Kumazawa and Ogyū, one of their duties as advisers to the Shogun or feudal lords was to put forward programmes of reform for the times in which they lived. In practice, however, it was not always easy to apply a system of thought devised in China to the circumstances obtaining in Japan. Rationalising the role of Shogun and samurai, in particular, was a problem. Both owed their place in the order of things to the military prowess of ancestors, who had transmitted it to succeeding generations as of hereditary right. In this respect Ogyū had reason on his side when he compared the Shogun's position to that of Chinese emperors. There were nevertheless two difficulties. One was that Japan also had an emperor, supposedly of higher standing than the Shogun.

Another was that the officials of Japan's central government were samurai, chosen by the Shogun on the basis of their status. They did not depend on imperial appointment and approval. Nor did they face a Confucian test of attitudes and capability, as Chinese bureaucrats did through their country's state examination system. Hence the situation did not fit readily into Confucian categories.

In considering such matters, a good many scholars chose to ignore the claims of the emperor and treat the Shogun as a Confucian ruler in his own right. A group in the service of the Mito branch of the Tokugawa house, writing at the end of the eighteenth century, preferred what might be called a 'laddered' approach: the samurai, they argued, owed loyalty to his lord, the lord to Shogun, the Shogun to emperor. The implications of a dispute arising between these different levels were not thought through. Arai Hakuseki (1657–1725) probed a little more deeply. In a history of Japan entitled *Tokushi yoron*, which he completed in 1724, he arranged his material so as to trace the transfer of authority from emperor to Fujiwara, from Fujiwara to Taira and Minamoto, and then to succeeding houses of Shogun. This inevitably raised the question of legitimacy. Arai's response was to apply the Confucian test of good government as a touchstone, in effect adopting a modified version of the Chinese theory of rebellion, applied – as caution required – to the past, but not the present.

Yamaga Sokō (1622–85) was more concerned to reconcile the role of the samurai with Confucian doctrine. Even in time of peace, he maintained, those parts of the samurai's code that enjoined austerity, self-discipline and a readiness to sacrifice his life in performing his duty remained relevant to his functions as an official. In addition, however, he must be a moral exemplar, bringing the Confucian ethic to the lower orders. In carrying out this task, the ancient Chinese texts, introduced to Japan and endorsed by the founding emperors, were of greater value than the more recent works of Chu Hsi; but because they were difficult and required extensive study, for which farmers, merchants and artisans, occupied with the needs of daily living, were unable to

find the time, it was for samurai to act as their interpreters. The samurai, in fact, had to be Confucian scholar as well as warrior in order to fulfil his obligations to society.

In the hands of such men as this, Confucianism was capable of being politically radical, not always intentionally. They sought ways, for example, to overcome the malaise that was beginning to affect Japan as a result of economic change, especially where it influenced the life of samurai. Kumazawa urged a return of samurai to the land, in the belief that this would restore both their morals and their morale. Ogyū put his trust in sumptuary laws and controls on urban spending. Arai sought to make government more Confucian – and therefore more Chinese – conceiving of a revision of rituals and titles as the means to this end. All three, as befitted men who had risen to positions of influence because of scholarship, gave support to the essentially Confucian doctrine of 'promoting men of talent'. Taken to extremes this might have been thought to be an attack on status. It was therefore redefined in Japanese terms to mean the selection of able men for office among those who qualified by birth, much as had been done in Nara and Heian, though then with reference to the court nobility.

Confucian scholars were the intellectual leaders of Japan in the first half of the Edo period. Their influence was pervasive, filtering down to all levels of the population through official schools, private academies, even *terakoya*. It determined the substance not only of the country's political philosophy, but also of the standards approved for social and ethical behaviour. Accompanying it – as had been true of Buddhism in Japan's early centuries – were a range of ideas and activities that were not so much Confucian as Chinese: theories about medicine, mathematics and science; a view of the material world, obtained through 'the investigation of things' (geography, geology, botany, astronomy); the application of technology to irrigation, sericulture, mining, printing and the making of porcelain.

In the eighteenth century, this renewal of Chinese cultural influence prompted some Japanese to react against it. Most conspicuously, there was a revival of Shinto. That religion's long

subordination to Buddhism, which had lasted for a thousand years, had been disturbed from time to time by attempts to assert its independence, usually by doctrinal innovation, but on this occasion the impetus to change had its locus in popular sentiment. It began with efforts by Shinto priests, especially those of Ise, to encourage pilgrimages to the major shrines. Since these were carried out by organised groups of residents from villages and towns, to whom they offered congenial company and a welcome break from the disciplines of daily life – it was one of the few purposes for which farmers, for example, could obtain permission to travel – they grew rapidly in popularity. It is said that well over 3 million pilgrims from many parts of the country worshipped at Ise in the spring of 1705. In later years the enthusiasms so engendered gave rise to occasional popular outbursts of religious fervour, identified with the slogan *ee ja nai ka*, 'isn't it good?'.

The movement was given an intellectual grounding by three men, Kamo Mabuchi (1697–1769), Motoori Norinaga (1730–1801) and Hirata Atsutane (1776–1843). Kamo took as his model the work of those Confucian scholars – exemplified by Ogyū Sorai in Japan – who had turned to ancient texts in order to discover the 'true' meaning of what the sages wrote, freed from later accretions. In Shinto terms, Kamo believed, this involved a re-examination of the *Kojiki* and *Manyōshū*, in order to remove the distortions introduced by Buddhism and Confucianism, but as a preliminary there had also to be a study of the language in which these texts had been set down. He made this his special task. In addition, he set out the conclusions he reached from his reading, which became the central tenets of the so-called Shinto Revival. His work was taken a further stage by Motoori in a multi-volume commentary on the *Kojiki*, a monumental piece of scholarship that remains at the heart of Shinto thought to the present day. Hirata was the publicist who adjusted its findings to nineteenth-century circumstance.

Motoori, intellectually the most significant of the three, was a man of samurai descent who practised as a doctor in Ise province. His followers were mostly well-to-do farmers, townspeople and

Shinto priests, persons of some influence locally, but not unshake-ably committed to the interests and ideology of the ruling class. Hirata, however, aimed at a wider social base, which included samurai. In keeping with the changes of his time, he identified the 'alien' influence that had to be rejected as not only that of China in the past, but also that of the West in the present (though he excepted western military science and technology from his condemnation). In his hands, in fact, Shinto became potentially nationalist. Its scholarship came to be known as Kokugaku, or National Learning.

Central to it was the assertion that the emperor reigned by virtue of divine descent from the sun-goddess, Amaterasu. It was her decree that the imperial line would rule the nation 'until the end of time'; and Japanese must therefore owe the emperor absolute obedience, regardless of whether he be 'good' or 'bad'. An ethical sanction, as applied in China, was irrelevant. Nor did the Japanese in general need an ethical code: because, like their emperor and the land in which they lived, they, too, were in origin divine, albeit descended from lesser deities, it followed that they were innately good. The clinching evidence for all these claims was historical. Japan's unbroken ruling line, contrasting as it did with China's turbulent dynastic record, showed where virtue had invariably resided.

As long as the Tokugawa seemed unshaken in their power, it was likely to be difficult for those who held authority to take this argument seriously as a threat to their position. They were wrong. A century later it was the official doctrine of the Japanese state, embodied in a written constitution and taught in every school.

Literature and the arts

Most of the books about Confucianism in Edo Japan were written in Chinese. So were many works on history, law and Buddhism. Depending on subject, government records were kept in Chinese

or in a kind of hybrid Sino-Japanese (*sōrōbun*). There was poetry in Chinese – though less than in Japanese – while a number of volumes of prose fiction were based on Chinese models, or heavily influenced by them. There is a parallel with the place of Latin in medieval Europe.

The situation was in many ways like that which had existed in Nara and Heian, combined now with a popular literature that owed more to Kamakura and Muromachi. Most of the new readers were to be found in the cities, reaching lower in the social order than before as books became cheaper. Printing, carried out at first by movable metal type, then by the more economical, if more time-consuming method of carving page-sized wooden blocks, made multiple copies available, increasing sales. Writers, finding they could support themselves without relying on feudal patronage, began to produce a very large range of different kinds of work: manuals for use in every aspect of education, some of them specifically for women; works of fiction, making use of the simple *kana* script to attract a wider public; and reprints of the classics of the past, such as *Taiheiki* and *Heike monogatari*. By 1700 over 10,000 titles were in print and available from bookshops. Some were made available for rent to those who could not afford to buy; pedlars carried others to the villages. Nearly 300 publishers were engaged in the trade.

By the end of the seventeenth century, urban society was already large, varied and, for at least some of its members, affluent. A good many merchants had the wealth to enjoy the theatres and the houses of assignation that had multiplied in the pleasure quarters, priding themselves on their aesthetic taste, but relishing, too, the less refined entertainment that was offered in the theatre of melodrama and burlesque. Authority indulged them to a degree, despite its habits of censorship, since the things that pleased them did not fall within the bounds of the political. Authors, publishers and producers of plays regarded them as valued customers.

Three names dominate Japanese literature in these years, those of Ihara Saikaku (1642–93), Matsuo Bashō (1644–94) and Chikamatsu Monzaemon (1653–1725), respectively novelist, poet and

playwright. Saikaku was the son of an Osaka merchant, who abandoned business to become a poet and only turned to writing novels in the last years of his life, starting in 1682. He wrote about what he knew: the life of merchants, the making and spending of money, the 'passing world' (*ukiyo*) of the city pleasure quarters. His books, though presented as novels, were more like collections of short stories, centred on a single person or theme. Their prose was informed by a poet's brevity, a few vivid phrases serving as a rule in place of description and analysis. Three in particular are famous. The first, which appeared in 1682, has been translated under the title *The Life of an Amorous Man*. It told of the sexual adventures of a wealthy rake, the son of a Kyoto merchant, who in the end at the age of sixty set off to seek the fabled Island of Women. A second such book, *The Life of an Amorous Woman* (1686), purported to be the memoirs of a woman, looking back when old on a life of lovemaking, usually for pay, some of it in the pleasure houses of the city, some of it, more degradingly, outside them. It is the portrait of a human being's decline, touched with sadness. The third book is *The Japanese Family Storehouse* (1688), a collection of tales about ingenious ways of making money. The same kind of themes recur in a number of other works, including one on homosexuality, all earthy, rather than directly pornographic. Their villains almost always come to a bad end.

Bashō, by contrast, was of samurai background. He lived most of his life in Kyoto and Edo, but travelled extensively in other parts of Japan, belonging to a circle of intellectuals whom it is difficult to classify as either samurai or commoners. Unlike Saikaku, whose early reputation as a poet rested on the speed with which he composed 'linked verse' (*renga*), usually in public competitions, Bashō devoted himself to developing the *haiku*, a seventeen-syllable poem in lines of 5–7–5. In his hands it became an independent lyric form. Its brevity imposed limitations, making it more suitable to express a flash of insight than a train of thought, but he made it reflect an acute awareness of nature, as witnessed on his travels, and a consciousness of the human dimen-

sion of what he saw. In these respects it was the quintessence of the Japanese tradition in poetry.

Chikamatsu wrote principally for the puppet theatre. This had developed in the early seventeenth century from what were in effect recitals, accompanied by the *samisen*, a stringed instrument newly imported from Ryukyu. Puppets were used to illustrate the narrative. After 1650 a more rhythmic style of recitation was adopted, identified with the name of its originator, Takemoto Gidayū (1651–1714); larger puppets were devised, two-thirds human size; and plots became more dramatic. The last of these changes was largely Chikamatsu's work. Some of his plays were historical, drawing freely on books like *Heike monogatari*. Others depicted the life of his own time, often based on real-life scandals and *causes célèbres*, of which his audiences would have been aware. Where the historical pieces (*jidaimono*) were about honour and loyalty, the contemporary ones (*sewamono*) chose themes that explored the conflict between sentiment (*ninjō*) and duty (*giri*), especially in the context of love and marriage. Love suicides were a favourite subject. To a degree, therefore, such plays provided a commentary on the ruling philosophy of the day as it impinged on different social groups, though more for the purpose of entertainment than critique. In manner they were melodramatic, usually with a touch of the supernatural.

Some of Chikamatsu's plays were also performed in a new kind of drama, known as Kabuki. It had originated in performances at the Kitano shrine in Kyoto at the beginning of the Edo period, moving later to a theatre in the centre of the city, then spreading throughout the country. Travelling companies took it to provincial areas. The earliest troupes of players included women, who engaged in prostitution in addition to their duties as actresses, but the Bakufu banned them in 1629. Thereafter men-only companies became the norm, some members of which, the *onnagata*, showed immense skill in playing female roles. Male prostitution replaced female prostitution in their unofficial repertoire. Most plays – other than Chikamatsu's – consisted of a series of almost independent scenes, having a general unifying subject-matter or

character, but no integrated plot. In most cases they were written by a group of authors attached to a particular theatre, drawing their material, like the puppet theatre, from historical texts or current events. If the latter were deemed to carry political overtones, like the story of the forty-seven *rōnin*, the action might be transferred to an earlier century in the hope of escaping Bakufu censorship.

Whereas in Nō and the puppet plays the dialogue was provided by reciters or chanters of the text, in Kabuki the players spoke their own lines. For the most part these were simple, even banal, making little claim to intellectual depth or literary merit. The attraction of Kabuki lay rather in its spectacle and the opportunities it offered for actors to display their techniques, both of facial expression and of acrobatic movement in fighting or dance. In fact, the players and the production were more important than the plot. Actors were lionised, their appearances widely advertised, fan clubs formed. Portraits of them were sold in quantity to their admirers.

Nō drama still drew audiences, especially of samurai and those who followed their fashions, but in the eighteenth century literature became much more like Kabuki in tone. Novelists, taking their cue from Saikaku in their choice of subject-matter, dwelt more and more on the humour and the coarseness of urban life. The humour was anecdotal, wry rather than bitter, poking fun at human weaknesses, but not in the manner of the social critic. The canon of ideas approved by government was generally treated with respect. One can interpret this as an acceptance of society-as-it-is, or simply as a response to fear of punishment; but in either case it meant that the nature of the social system was never seriously debated outside works of Confucian scholarship.

Like literature, the visual arts appealed differently to different status groups. Painting showed more variety of style and subject-matter than that of earlier periods, some of it looking back to the aristocratic traditions of Heian, some extending the medieval interest in Chinese models, now a 'samurai' preference, some catering to the livelier tastes of the newly rich in towns or those

of their poorer neighbours. There were many more artistic schools than there had been in the past, just as there were in swordsmanship, the tea ceremony and flower arrangement. One result of such diversity was that the boundaries between what was 'Chinese' and what was 'Japanese' became more blurred. Another is that the art of Edo Japan is not easy to describe in a narrow compass.

The most striking qualities it inherited from the late sixteenth century were ostentation and display, contrasting sharply with what is thought of as the Zen tradition. The military leaders then coming to power looked to the decoration of their castles as an element of prestige, complementing the size of the buildings and the towering height of their central keeps. For functional reasons, castles had to be stone walled, heavily timbered and grim, lacking the elegance of Kyoto's palaces and villas. Their state rooms, though large, were usually gloomy. Lords tended therefore to favour bright colours and lavish decoration for them, quite different from the monochromes and restraint of Muromachi. Murals, painted on multi-leaved screens and sliding panels, were of subjects – birds and flowers, trees, animals, stylised landscapes – that lent themselves to bold designs, covering large expanses. They were enhanced by an extravagant use of gold leaf, set off by gleaming black lacquer.

Nobunaga set the fashion when he built his castle at Azuchi. It was completed in 1579 and burnt down in 1582, so not very much was known about it until a copy of the builder's plans was discovered in 1974. Nevertheless, some record exists of the paintings, which were the work of Kanō Eitoku (1543–90). Eitoku already had a reputation as a painter in Kyoto, where his grandfather and great-grandfather had been artists producing murals for Buddhist houses; but from the time he undertook the Azuchi commission he made a shift to temporal employers, working on the rooms of Osaka castle after Nobunaga died and contributing to the fashion for large-scale decorative painting. His grandson, Sadanobu, moved to Edo in 1621; and one of Sadanobu's sons, Tanyu (1602–74), became the most influential artist of his day,

introducing the Kanō style – red, blue and white paint, gold leaf, black lacquer, rich sculptural decoration – into the magnificent shrine erected to Ieyasu in Nikko. Their successors served the Shogun until the nineteenth century.

A more characteristically Chinese school, deriving from the Sung landscapes and black-and-white figure studies associated in Japan with Sesshū and his contemporaries, continued to attract Japanese artists under the Tokugawa. One who helped to establish this particular continuity was Hasegawa Tōhaku (1539–1610), a painter of murals, mostly for Buddhist temples, which had none of Kanō's rich colour. Among his portraits is one of the famous tea master, Sen no Rikyū. Later painters were more influenced by China's so-called 'literary' school, which flourished in southern China and became known in Japan through books and paintings brought by Chinese merchants to Nagasaki. Ike no Taiga (1723–76) is said to have learnt it by studying a Chinese album. For all that, some of Taiga's landscapes, like those of Sesshū, were of places in Japan. His friend, Yosa Buson (1716–83), a poet, who did not start painting until he reached middle age, showed greater interest in the kind of rural scenes in which people – unmistakably Japanese – had a more prominent place. One is tempted to wonder whether Bashō's poems had something to do with this.

Some of Buson's work has affinities with Yamato-e, 'Japanese' painting, which is known as such in large part because of the subjects it chose. It was carried forward into the Edo period by artists of the Tosa family, who continued to produce scrolls (e-maki) and album illustrations in the established manner. A seventeenth-century artist, Tawaraya Sōtatsu (d. 1643), about whose life little is known with any certainty, translated the style to the painting of large screens, using strong colours typical of Heian. Maruyama Ōkyo (1733–95), who began by studying in the Kano school, was more eclectic. In his large and varied corpus of work – it includes screens, scrolls and woodblock prints – one can trace the influence of Ming painters (in his use of ink) and of western art (in his treatment of perspective), as well as of Yamato-e. Western-style perspective also appears at about this time in paintings and prints

by several other artists, reflecting a growing interest in what was called 'Dutch studies' (Rangaku). This is a topic to which we must refer again (Chapter 11).

The subjects chosen by these painters, including Buson, were in many cases related to the popularity of genre painting in Edo Japan. Illustrating aspects of everyday life had long been an element in *e-maki* – witness the village scenes in *Shigisan engi*, the pictures of fighting against the Mongols in *Mōkō shūrai ekotoba*, and the accounts of court ceremonial and the building of temples in various other scrolls, some of them produced by members of the Tosa house – but it was not until the second half of the sixteenth century that it became more widely a concern of Japanese artists. They expressed it in a number of styles on screens, murals and hanging scrolls (*kakemono*). There were scenes of Kyoto street life (expensive souvenirs for daimyo visitors); studies of upper-class pastimes like horse racing and mounted archery; sets to illustrate different trades and accomplishments; mementoes of theatrical performances and religious festivals; pictorial records of the arrival of Portuguese ships and the people they brought to Japan. Any event that was likely to attract the interest of many, but could be seen by only a few, had a potential market. Artists from both the Kanō and Tosa schools, plus some from neither who remain anonymous, were happy to meet the demand.

In the rapidly growing urban areas of the seventeenth century, customers could also be found for works that were less expensive. Wealthy merchants could afford original paintings, like their social betters. Town-dwellers of more modest means, whatever their tastes, could not; but the development of woodblock printing soon made it possible to supply at least some of their needs at moderate cost. This was done first by the publication of illustrated books, then by that of independent prints (*hanga*), of which 200 or more could be made from a single set of blocks. Because the format did not lend itself to the treatment of large and complex genre subjects, such as were found in murals or on multi-leaf screens, the printed repertoire was narrower in its range and simpler in its style. For commercial reasons it catered necessarily

to interests that were widely shared. As a result, it focused in particular on the pleasure quarters, much as Saikaku and other writers did in their novels: lists of famous persons in the theatre and the world of courtesans, annotated as well as illustrated; guidebooks to the cities; sex manuals in the manner of contemporary Chinese publications, by some of which Japan's artists may well have been inspired. The erotic was a recurring theme. Sexually related illustrations, known as 'spring pictures' (*shunga*), were to be found among the works of even the most famous print designers of the day.

The first prints were in black and white, similar to those that had earlier been evolved to provide simple devotional pictures for the Buddhist faithful. The blocks provided black outlines, colour, if used, being added by hand. The style was made famous by Hishikawa Moronobu (*c.* 1625–95), who had studied under both Tosa and Kanō teachers. His prints, mostly for books, included portraits of actors, courtesans and legendary warriors, plus incidents from literature, but he also produced paintings in the genre tradition. A pair of sixfold screens of a theatre performance provide a notable example. Little change in technique occurred until late in the career of Okumura Masanobu (1686–1764), when the prints he designed began to appear in colour. Soon after his death came the first fully polychrome prints, known as 'brocade pictures', or *nishiki-e*. From that time on the black outline vanished, to be replaced by shapes in different colours; the artist became a member of a team in which designer, colourist and engraver worked together; and the finished product was sold in sufficient numbers to make counterfeiting a worthwhile occupation.

During the last hundred years of the Edo period, woodblock artists worked in highly divergent styles. Suzuki Harunobu (1725–70) is famous for willowy beauties, whose figures have an improbable grace; Kitagawa Utamaro (1753–1806) showed a preference for head-and-shoulder studies of courtesans, their features simply sketched in the manner of *Genji monogatari*; Sharaku, about whom almost nothing is known, appeared briefly on the scene at the

end of the eighteenth century to publish some very striking heads of actors; Utagawa Toyokuni (1769–1825) favoured historical subjects (often taken from Kabuki). In the opinion of most art historians, figure studies declined in quality after Toyokuni. On the other hand, Katsushika Hokusai (1760–1849) and Andō Hiroshige (1797–1858) brought the design of prints much closer to that of painting. Hokusai's views of Mount Fuji and Hiroshige's several sets depicting the way-stations along the Tokaido, the road linking Edo with Kyoto, were outstanding landscape prints. The two men also produced vivid prints of birds and flowers. This showed that the art of print making was still capable of development, in both subject and technique. Despite that, it remained within the boundaries of the traditional. For all the impact it was later to have on modern European art, painting in Japan had not yet cut itself off from its past.

CHAPTER 11

The Coming of the West
1840–1873

Occasionally in the history of a country there comes a time when a number of different social and political changes reach a critical stage together. This is the signal for a 'revolution', using the word in its widest sense. For Japan the middle of the nineteenth century was such a turning-point. It was marked by entry into multi-faceted relations with the West; the choice of Europe and America as institutional models, instead of China; the first steps in the introduction of capitalist industry. These developments coincided more or less with the overthrow of the Tokugawa Bakufu and its replacement by an emperor-centred form of government. As a result Japan's national life was transformed, much as it had earlier been in the Asuka and Nara periods.

The trigger for these events was the action taken by the western powers to open Japanese ports to foreign trade, itself part of a wider process of imperialist expansion in India and on the China coast. It once more bound Japan into a close political and com-mercial relationship with China, this time under the aegis of the West, acting through 'unequal treaties'. It also exposed her for at least a generation to the full weight of economic and military pressure that modern industrial states could bring to bear. Her response was to determine much of the region's modern history.

Unequal treaties

The immediate background to the western threat to Japan was the trade of the maritime powers with China. From the outset it had met with difficulties. Chinese officials, conditioned by centuries of the tribute system, took it as axiomatic that there should be an acceptance of Chinese law and methods of taxation among the foreigners coming to their country. Europeans and Americans did not always agree. There were occasions when Chinese custom seemed to them to be barbaric or unjust. There were also problems about balance of payments. By 1800 the world had acquired a taste for Chinese tea and silk to a value very much greater than that of China's demand for western products. To avoid using bullion to make good the difference, an alternative was found in selling opium to China; and when the Chinese government, denouncing opium as a danger to its people's health, banned the import of the drug, there was the making of a serious conflict. The opium trade became a smuggling enterprise. Since its proceeds found their way in large part to Canton, where they financed the legal purchases of tea and silk, western governments soon found themselves involved in its ramifications.

Crisis came in 1839. A conscientious Chinese viceroy at Canton, determined to uphold the law, chose to hold foreign merchants at the port as hostages until the smugglers, their fellow-countrymen, surrendered all opium held in ships offshore. In the short term, the move succeeded: the trade came to a halt, the opium was handed over and destroyed. The British Foreign Office, however – much the largest part of the opium traffic, as well as of the purchase of tea, was in British hands – held that the viceroy's action was no more legal than the smuggling he was trying to suppress. It therefore authorised the use of force to support the merchants' claims for compensation. Since China refused to accept the argument, the result was war. Desultory naval engagements in the Canton estuary in the winter of 1839–40 spread northwards up the China coast in the next two years; Britain

seized the islands of Hong Kong and Chusan; China sued for peace at Nanking.

The treaty signed there in 1842 was taken by Britain as an opportunity to settle not only the issues from which the war arose, but also the general management of the trade. Hong Kong became a British colony and naval base. Four more ports in southern China were opened to trade, in addition to Canton. Consuls were to be appointed to them, having access to Chinese officials of equivalent rank; foreign merchants were to reside in designated settlements, subject to their own national laws, administered through consular courts; customs duties were to be charged on a scale laid down by treaty (that is, not fixed by China of its own volition). These privileges were made available to all the powers that came to terms with China, by means of the inclusion in each agreement of a most-favoured-nation clause. Together they defined the 'treaty port system'. It was expanded in 1858 by the addition of extra ports in the north and along China's river system, plus the right of diplomatic residence in Peking.

To Japanese, when they learnt of them, the arrangements seemed ominous. One Japanese scholar, writing in 1847, after accounts of the Opium War had been brought to Nagasaki by Dutch and Chinese merchants, was moved to ask, 'how can we know whether the mist gathering over China will not come down as frost upon Japan?'. He had reason on his side. Western governments, consuls and commercial establishments, largely ignorant still of this part of the world, were easily persuaded that the structure they had devised to regulate their trade with China would serve just as well in dealings with other 'orientals'. This attitude did much to ensure that the treaty port system was eventually imposed on Japan with the minimum of adjustment.

In 1844 the Dutch, fearing for the future of their rights at Deshima in the international situation produced by the Opium War, approached the Edo Bakufu to seek a relaxation of the seclusion laws. The overture was rejected. A British plan to send an expedition to Japan from the China coast in 1845 came to nothing because an 'appropriate' naval force could not be found

to carry it out. In the next few years, occasional warships from Britain, France and the United States found occasion to call at Ryukyu (Loochoo) and Nagasaki, but none of these visits was followed up.

It was events in America that in the end brought a more determined effort to 'open' Japan. In 1848 the United States acquired California from Mexico, securing a substantial seaboard on the Pacific. There was talk of a transcontinental railroad, even, perhaps, a steamer route across the Pacific to Shanghai, where American trade was second only to that of Britain. Since the Japanese islands lay on the great circle route from San Francisco to the China coast, and were known from Dutch accounts to possess deposits of coal, they might, it was thought, serve as a staging-point for steamers, which at this stage of their development had limited range. For the first time, therefore, Japan's ports became of more than passing interest to one of the maritime powers.

By 1852 it was widely known that an American naval expedition was being prepared to undertake negotiations with Japan. In July of the following year, it anchored off Uraga at the entrance to Edo Bay. The two steamers and two sailing vessels that made it up were cleared for action. Its commanding officer, Commodore Matthew Perry, was very clear that he would admit no visitors to his presence but Japanese of suitable rank, while the letter he brought from President Millard Fillmore – it called for better treatment for shipwrecked seamen, the opening of ports of refuge where foreign ships could obtain coal and stores, plus permission to carry on trade – must be received with proper ceremony. On 14 July the elaborate boxes in which the President's letter and Perry's credentials were enclosed, escorted by a landing party from the squadron, were handed over at nearby Kurihama in the presence of 5,000 Japanese troops. The commodore added a letter of his own. If these 'very reasonable and pacific overtures' were not accepted at once, it said, he would return for a reply next spring, this time 'with a much larger force'. To underline the point, before he left for China he took part of his command

into Edo Bay to survey the approaches to the Tokugawa capital.

True to his promise, Perry returned with eight ships early in 1854. In the interval Edo's policy-makers had been consulting the country's feudal lords. The results had not been helpful. One small group, whose spokesman was Tokugawa Nariaki of Mito, head of a senior branch of the Shogun's house, held that so insulting a demand must be altogether rejected, if necessary at the cost of war. Anything less would not only impugn the national honour, he claimed, but also undermine the Bakufu's prestige at home. Another equally small minority, led by Ii Naosuke of Hikone, the most powerful of the Tokugawa vassal lords (*fudai*), took a very different view. To seek to buy time, even if it meant compromise, was in their opinion only politic in view of Japan's military weakness. The time so gained could be used to prepare for war, above all by the adoption of western weapons and technology. The great majority of the lords, however, were less forthright. Most of their replies were nothing more than reiterations of the duty that followed from 'ancestral law', or plaintive calls for peace. They did little to suggest how the one could be upheld or the other secured.

Faced by these inconsistencies, Abe Masahiro, the senior member of the Tokugawa council, decided to accept the substance of Perry's proposals, if all else failed. It did. In meetings at Yokohama under the guns of the American ships, Perry showed himself unmoving. In March 1854 a convention was signed. It opened Shimoda and Hakodate as ports of refuge, gave undertakings about the future treatment of castaways and provided for the appointment of an American consul at Shimoda. It made no specific mention of rights of trade, which was Edo's only diplomatic achievement.

Despite the disappointment over trade, the agreement prompted efforts at emulation. The Dutch obtained better terms for their commerce at Deshima. The British and Russian naval commanders in the north Pacific, engaged in desultory operations against each other – one of the remoter aspects of the Crimean War – found time to secure conventions much like Perry's. British

officials on the China coast, believing all that had been done so far to be inadequate, began to formulate plans for a 'proper' treaty with Japan. So did the new American consul at Shimoda, Townsend Harris, who arrived there in September 1856.

At this point Japan's dealings with the West became entangled once again in the affairs of China. Towards the end of 1856, when the Crimean War was over, fresh hostilities, arising from disputes over trade, broke out between China on the one side, and France and Britain on the other. Canton was captured, large Anglo-French forces were assembled for a campaign in the north. Both Dutch and American representatives in Japan made it plain to Edo that these forces, once victory set them free, would undoubtedly be used to support a demand for trade rights in the Japanese islands. The Bakufu, it was pointed out, would be able to offer no effective resistance, so its only hope of averting a catastrophe was to sign a commercial treaty first with countries whose demands would be less exacting. This could become a model for what would follow.

The Bakufu council, led now by Hotta Masayoshi, acknowledged the attractions of this argument. By October 1857 the representatives it sent to Nagasaki had concluded agreements not only with the Netherlands, but also with Russia, removing the upper limit long imposed on the value of the Nagasaki trade. High customs dues were retained, however, as were other Bakufu rights of interference. It was a formula Townsend Harris, a former businessman, was quite unwilling to accept. These treaties, he recorded in his journal, were 'disgraceful to all parties engaged in making them ... [and] not worth the paper on which they were written'. Instead, he proposed negotiations on a different text, which was more in line with the demands that France and Britain were currently making on Peking.

Getting it agreed by Edo proved uphill work. During the winter Harris was subjected to 'interminable discourses' by the Japanese, refusing 'points they subsequently grant, and meant to grant all the while', as well as 'many absurd proposals made by them without the hope, and scarcely the wish, of having them

accepted'. Nevertheless, he persisted. He also hammered home the warning, based, he said, on his correspondence with the governor of Hong Kong, that the arrival of a British fleet could be expected at any time. By the end of February 1858 a draft was ready for signature.

Apart from the omission of a most-favoured-nation clause, it reflected the West's experience in China, applied now to Japan. The ports of Nagasaki and Kanagawa (Yokohama) were to be opened to American trade in 1859, Niigata in 1860, Hyogo (Kobe) in 1863. Foreign traders were to be admitted to Edo in 1862 and Osaka in 1863. An American minister would be resident in Edo. Customs duties were to be specified by treaty, as in China, and settlements set aside at the treaty ports, where Americans would be subject to American law.

Not surprisingly, the sweeping concessions that had been made by Bakufu officials encountered opposition in Japan. When the draft was put to feudal lords for comment, the same arguments against it emerged as had been voiced in 1854. More dangerous, the issue became enmeshed in dynastic politics. One of Tokugawa Nariaki's sons, Yoshinobu (Keiki), an adult with a reputation for ability, was widely favoured as a candidate to succeed the ailing Shogun, Iesada. Ii Naosuke, who remained at odds with Nariaki over foreign affairs, preferred a different choice, a child, but closer to Iesada by blood. The rivalry quickly acquired ramifications. Both sides canvassed the imperial court; objections to the treaty, stated in private by the emperor, became publicly known, lending more support to Nariaki than Naosuke; ostentatious efforts were made to change his mind. At last, in an attempt by Edo to still the turmoil, Hotta Masayoshi was removed from office and Ii Naosuke appointed regent (Tairo). It was a post, only filled in times of crisis, that gave him powers to override the Bakufu council.

Within weeks he had to use them. Lord Elgin, Britain's special ambassador, and Baron Gros, his French colleague, having signed treaties with China at Tientsin in June, which granted all their principal demands, decided to go at once to Japan (though not in

company). The news was carried to Townsend Harris at Shimoda. Harris travelled at once to Kanagawa to warn the Shogun's representatives that the catastrophe he had predicted was about to become reality; the council of elders met; and Ii Naosuke, persuaded by Harris of the need for haste, decided to sign the American treaty, despite the fact that this would be to disregard the emperor's wishes. He also named the Shogun's heir – his own preferred candidate, Iemochi – and took steps to stifle opposition. Several great lords, including Nariaki, were sentenced to house arrest. A number of samurai, who had acted as their agents in the succession dispute, were executed or imprisoned.

The arrival of Elgin proved an anti-climax. He brought a single warship, not the fleet of which Harris had warned; made no secret of his lack of knowledge of conditions in Japan, borrowing Harris's secretary to advise him on the American treaty's terms; and generally behaved as if the whole expedition were a welcome relief from the grimmer duties he had faced in China. His entourage went shopping. Elgin himself, taking the Harris treaty as his model, but adding a most-favoured-nation clause, completed his negotiations in a mere two days. Having signed the document (26 August) and given a banquet for the Japanese representatives, at which they made their first acquaintance with the ritual of the loyal toast, he set off for China again, content, as he reported in a letter to his wife, to see 'an illumination of the forts in our honour'.

Treaties were also very soon signed with France, Russia and the Netherlands, bringing the total number of treaty powers to five. They incorporated Japan into a treaty port system 'made in China'. The first two British ministers appointed to Japan, Rutherford Alcock and Harry Parkes, had both been consuls in Shanghai. On leaving Japan they were promoted to Peking. Several of the British consuls in the newly opened Japanese ports had a similar background; the consular courts over which they presided looked to those in China as courts of appeal. Moreover, most of the foreign merchants who established themselves in the Japanese ports, not only the British ones, were representatives of

firms on the China coast, or had gained commercial experience there. Often they brought with them their Chinese compradores and household staff, who became Japan's most numerous 'foreign residents'. Even the trade took on a Chinese character. Instead of providing China with the Japanese goods that had traditionally found a market there, Japan began to export silk and tea to the West. This made her China's competitor, no longer her trading partner.

Nationalism and politics

The events of the summer of 1858 marked the beginning of modern nationalism in Japan. Among samurai, at least, there was already an incipient national consciousness, bred by dealings with the mainland in the past, but enforced acceptance of the treaties brought a new awareness of a foreign threat directed at something larger than the villages or domains that most Japanese described as 'home'. The treaties, after all, applied to everyone; and in imitation of the West, Japan acquired a national flag – the Hi no Maru, a red sun on a white ground – which for formal purposes replaced the separate banners of the Shogun and feudal lords. A recognition of political unity slowly spread, first from major centres to the provinces, then from samurai to other sections of the population. It was given focus by the call to 'honour the emperor'.

The response to the foreign crisis was highly emotive, breaking through the bounds of acceptable behaviour. Men felt anger: anger against the foreigners, who had brought dishonour to Japan by the content and the manner of the demands they made; anger against the Shogun and feudal lords, who had failed in their duty to prevent it. These attitudes did not at once become universal, but already by the opening of the ports in 1859 there were some – the *shishi*, or 'men of spirit' – who were willing to act on such beliefs. To them it was not enough to lament the country's fate.

They found a spokesman in a young Choshu samurai, Yoshida Shōin. In 1854, convinced that Japan could not be saved unless the samurai spirit were harnessed to the military science of the West, he had tried to smuggle himself aboard one of the American squadron's ships at Shimoda, his intention being to travel to the United States, in order to learn the secrets of western strength. Frustrated in this aim by Perry's refusal to flout the Bakufu's laws, he was taken into custody and sent back to his home in Hagi under house arrest. There Choshu after a time allowed him to found a school. Gathering a group of students, mostly, like himself, from the lower ranks of the samurai class – they included several who were to be famous leaders of Japan in the second half of the century – he taught them that the fate of the country rested not in the hands of those now in authority, but with 'grass-roots heroes', willing to sacrifice themselves in the emperor's name. Nor was he content with words. In 1858 he became involved in a plot to kill one of Ii Naosuke's senior colleagues, a step designed to mark a protest at the regent's action in choosing to sign the treaties. The plot was discovered and Shōin was arrested once more. He was executed in the following year.

The notes he had written in prison to justify what he had done were circulated privately by his friends and students, spreading his ideas among the young hotheads of the samurai class. Already embittered by the 'shame' of the treaties and by Ii Naosuke's 'purge', many of them, taking as their slogan *sonnō-jōi*, 'honour the emperor, repel the barbarian', turned to terrorism as the only means they had by which to demonstrate commitment to the anti-foreign cause. Violence was at first directed against individual foreigners in the newly opened treaty ports. Townsend Harris's secretary was a victim. Some ships' officers were killed. Unsuspecting Japanese who entered foreign service also found themselves at risk. A former castaway, recruited in Shanghai to be Rutherford Alcock's 'linguist', was murdered outside the gate of the British legation. Gradually the *shishi* grew more ambitious, seeking to force action from the Bakufu itself, or to precipitate a conflict with the West that might overturn the treaties. In March

1860 Ii Naosuke was cut down at one of the gates to Edo castle. In March 1861 a night attack on the British legation left two of its staff with wounds and several marauding samurai dead.

Edo's response lacked Ii's ruthlessness. To the fury of most western envoys in Japan, their protests about the attacks on foreigners were met by contrived delays and bureaucratic shuffle: since the culprits, when identified, often proved to be retainers of powerful lords, they were for all practical purposes outside the Shogun's jurisdiction. In the political context, a compromise was sought with the imperial court, in the hope that this might pacify the samurai. As evidence of it, a marriage was arranged between the emperor's sister – who showed reluctance – and the Shogun; but it came at an embarrassing price, for to win the court's consent the Bakufu had to promise to abrogate the treaties or expel the foreigners within the next ten years. In flat contradiction of this promise, Edo arranged to send a mission to Europe to persuade the powers to postpone the opening of any further ports and cities, the treaty provisions notwithstanding. Its argument that the rising tide of unrest in Japan was as much a threat to foreign trade as it was to Bakufu authority eventually proved persuasive. A protocol was signed in London in June 1862, granting a respite until 1868.

Nevertheless, the settlement broke down within a year. The arguments put forward by the anti-foreign activists struck a chord with many other samurai in Japan. Those of Satsuma and Choshu, in particular, whose domains had been defeated by the Tokugawa at Sekigahara in 1600, had been encouraged to cherish resentment ever since. The loss of land after that defeat had had the effect of keeping their stipends at a lower level than average, leaving them more subject than most to the pressures caused by economic change (Chapter 10). This left them restive. Brought up, moreover, like samurai elsewhere, to think of themselves as a political élite, responsible in some degree for the country's fate, they had become alarmed by 'the trend of the times' since the arrival of Perry. It was a dangerous situation for a regime that depended in the last resort on samurai loyalty.

Two incidents underlined its dangers in 1863 and 1864. In September 1862 Satsuma samurai, escorting the father of their lord, attacked a party of British merchants near Yokohama, claiming that they had failed to show the customary deference to his procession. One of the party, a visitor from Shanghai, was killed; others, including a woman, were wounded. The British government demanded apologies and compensation from both lord and Shogun. After a winter of bad-tempered diplomatic argument, the Bakufu paid. The lord of Satsuma did not. A British naval squadron was therefore sent against him in August 1863, its orders to enforce compliance. On arrival it seized several Satsuma ships; shore batteries opened fire on it; and in the action that followed, part of the town of Kagoshima was set ablaze. The squadron, having suffered damage, withdrew, but Satsuma came to terms in talks at Yokohama a few weeks later.

While this crisis was being worked out, Edo faced another from a different direction. During 1862–3 the *shishi* had become active on a larger scale. Hundreds of them swarmed in the streets of Kyoto, attacking Bakufu officials, fighting Bakufu guards, putting up posters that called on the emperor to lead a crusade against the foreigner. Responding to the pressure, the court called on the Shogun to take some positive action about the presence of foreigners in Japan; and the Bakufu, desperate to avoid hostilities with the West, which it could neither afford nor hope to win, attempted once again to escape through verbal compromise. It agreed to a decree in favour of 'expulsion', which was to take place in June 1863. Privately it decided that this was to mean no more than fresh negotiations to close the port of Yokohama. But the device proved unsuccessful. Choshu, whose samurai made up a large proportion of the Kyoto malcontents, chose to take the decree's wording literally. On the appointed day its steamers attacked an American vessel in the Shimonoseki Straits. In the next few weeks its shore batteries several times fired on foreign ships that were passing through. By the end of July the most direct sea route from Yokohama to Shanghai was closed.

This time the treaty powers took action jointly. Home govern-

ments were consulted, a process that took some months; then there was a further delay while the envoys awaited the result of Bakufu overtures to France; and it was only when these had proved abortive – a year or more after the original incidents – that a fleet of seventeen ships, furnished by four different countries, set out from Yokohama for Shimonoseki. It bombarded the coast batteries in the straits, landed men to dismantle them, then concluded a truce (14 September 1864), under the terms of which Choshu was to open the passage through the straits again and pay a large indemnity.

The bombardments at Kagoshima and Shimonoseki changed the character of Japanese relations with the West. Demonstrations of western naval might had proved enough to convince the majority of samurai, even the 'men of spirit', that something more than personal self-sacrifice would be required if Japan were to challenge the treaties with any expectation of success. Calls for the immediate use of force began to recede. Instead, plans were made to acquire the most up-to-date western weapons and a knowledge of how to manufacture them. Satsuma tried to order Armstrong guns of the kind the British squadron had used at Kagoshima. The Bakufu, Choshu and Satsuma all sent students abroad to acquire technological skills. In addition, Satsuma turned to Britain for diplomatic support – with equivocal results – and signed contracts with a Belgian entrepreneur to develop the trade that would pay for ships and guns, while the Bakufu strengthened its links with France for similar purposes.

There is a direct line from these events to the overthrow of the Tokugawa. The Bakufu was finding the suppression of unrest expensive. So, indeed, was the conduct of foreign relations. Coast defence had been an increasing burden since the Opium War. Opening the ports, providing facilities for trade, creating a rudimentary diplomatic service and sending missions abroad all added to the charges on regular expenditure. Those arising from the clashes with the treaty powers in 1863 and 1864, which resulted in the payment of indemnities, were larger still. The treaties therefore helped to empty government coffers. When the cost of

western-style rearmament spiralled after 1864, the financial strain became unbearable. By 1868 both Edo and a number of domains were heavily in debt to foreign creditors, who had underwritten their purchases of ships and guns.

Inflation accelerated. Since rice was still the principal unit of account for tax, as well as a staple food, public insolvency translated quickly into living costs, provoking further popular unrest. Even so, the results were not 'revolutionary' in the sense of breeding an ideology and a political movement aimed at achieving social change. Feudalism still had a grip on Japan. In fact, the struggles that were to follow between 1865 and 1867 had much in common with the sixteenth-century civil wars. The great domains of Kyushu and west Japan, led by Satsuma and Choshu, emerged once more as contenders for national power; the Shogun was accused of ineffective leadership at a time of danger, sacrificing thereby his right to office; the emperor was acclaimed as a symbol of unity. It was a view in which both lords and dissident samurai could join.

In the late summer of 1864 Edo, seizing what it saw as an opening created by the foreign attacks on Kagoshima and Shimonoseki, set out to restore its authority over emperor and domains. Armed patrols were sent out on the streets of Kyoto, and samurai loyalists arrested or driven from the city. When Choshu was persuaded by some of them to send its troops to restore their influence, these were repulsed in heavy fighting. Many of the 'men of spirit' were killed, others committed suicide. The survivors sought refuge in Choshu, reinforcing the local loyalists to the point at which their leaders were able to seize control of the domain.

The result was open confrontation. On the one side was the Bakufu, which turned increasingly to western armaments and western methods of administration in an effort to defend itself against its enemies at home. On the other, Choshu and Satsuma began to come together in a co-operation clearly directed against the Tokugawa. The Bakufu decided at last to seize the nettle. Choshu was declared rebel. When its newly established loyalist

leaders rejected the terms offered by way of settlement, a punitive expedition was announced and troops assembled in Osaka to carry it out. This forced Japan's daimyo to show their colours. Satsuma made secret alliance with Choshu. A few others, chiefly from the north, took their stand with the Shogun. Many more held aloof, guarding their frontiers.

The climax came in the summer of 1866, when an attack was launched on the Mōri lands in western Honshu. It was repulsed on all fronts. The defeat marked a critical loss of Bakufu prestige. To be fought to a standstill, not by the might of the treaty powers, but by a single domain (Satsuma's role was secretly to supply Choshu with arms), had an effect that was the reverse of what Edo had intended. A new Shogun, Yoshinobu (Keiki), Nariaki's son, the unsuccessful candidate in 1858, succeeded on Iemochi's death towards the end of the year; but although he presided over frantic measures to restore the Bakufu's strength, calling on the French minister, Léon Roches, as adviser, chaotic finance and low morale proved too much for him. In November 1867, in the hope of saving something from the wreck, he offered to resign.

His opponents were not willing to let him off so lightly. To leave a former Shogun undisturbed in possession of his lands and fighting men, they argued, would ensure that Tokugawa power continued, if in different form. Exploiting their links with friends at court, and calling on several other powerful domains to join them, the leaders of Satsuma and Choshu planned to 'seize the jewel' – that is, the emperor's person – as a decisive weapon. The young Mutsuhito (Meiji), come only recently to the throne, was persuaded to give them countenance (his maternal grandfather was one of the conspirators). This done, Satsuma forces, led by the domain's most famous samurai, Saigō Takamori, and joined by contingents that were furnished by four other lords, including two who were Tokugawa relatives, took over the gates of the imperial palace in the early morning of 3 January 1868. A council was summoned, its membership carefully chosen; a decree was approved, stripping the Shogun of his office and his lands; and the direct responsibility for national government was placed once

more in the emperor's hands. In the strict constitutional sense, this was the Meiji Restoration (*ōsei-fukko*), a reassertion of the prerogatives of the ancient ruling house.

Study of the West

To consider, not the events that led to the overthrow of the Tokugawa, but the changes that followed from it (Chapter 12), brings into focus a different aspect of Japan's relations with the outside world: namely, the country's knowledge of the West. During the seventeenth century, while memories of the persecution of Christianity were fresh, that knowledge had been very limited. After 1700, by contrast, there developed a vogue for Rangaku, 'Dutch studies', based on information provided by the Dutch at Deshima. Often it reflected no more than casual curiosity about 'concoctions from abroad', but there were also investigations of a kind that had more practical purposes. Japanese doctors, for example, began to study European medicine, especially surgery, not only because it became fashionable, therefore profitable, but also because it produced more convincing results than the Chinese methods in which they had been trained. Astronomy came into favour for its relevance to calendars, though the first clear illustrations of heliocentric theory came in fact from an artist, Shiba Kōkan. Much of what was done was in the 'amateur' tradition cherished by Chinese literati. Inō Tadataka (Chūkei), who was by trade a sake-brewer, turned in later life to the study of surveying. Using western instruments, he prepared a remarkably accurate map of the whole of Japan in the first few years of the nineteenth century. Other aspiring scientists, taking advantage of the visits made to Edo by the Dutch factors from Nagasaki, bombarded them with requests for clocks, telescopes, barometers, even Leiden jars. Colour prints of Dutch life at Deshima found a ready sale.

As news began to spread about European advances in India and

on the China coast at the time of the Napoleonic wars, the emphasis changed. A good many samurai, persuaded that their country faced a danger of attack from overseas, sought a knowledge of western military science. Navigation and gunnery were their principal interests, together with the design and siting of coastal batteries, but a number also took up the more theoretical branches of the subject, including the mathematics of ballistics and the chemistry of explosives. Some learnt, at first from Dutch books, then by experiment, how to build reverberatory furnaces and manufacture cannon made of iron, instead of bronze. When Perry arrived in 1853, bringing a variety of technological gifts, he found to his surprise that there were Japanese who appeared to understand the steam engine, at least in principle. Within a year or two the first steamships were being launched from Japanese yards.

On the face of it, the opening of the ports in 1859 increased Japan's access to information about the West by providing opportunity for travel. In practice, not many Japanese were allowed to avail themselves of it. For several years only those whom the Bakufu sent abroad on diplomatic missions or for military training, plus a handful who were willing to take the risk of travelling illegally, visited the countries of Europe and America. These continuing restrictions were not welcome to the treaty powers, who believed that the spread of knowledge would be good for trade. They therefore pressed the Bakufu to ease its rules; and in 1866, having demonstrated the superiority of their armaments in 1863 and 1864, they won their point. The revised customs treaty of that year laid down that 'all Japanese subjects may travel to any foreign country for purposes of study or trade', if provided with passports. From then on, Japanese travellers overseas multiplied, some sponsored by feudal lords or others in authority, some financed privately. The process was to continue until the end of the century, allowing many hundreds of men and women to attend schools and colleges in the countries of the West.

The Bakufu itself sent missions abroad, some with diplomatic functions, narrowly defined, others with a wider brief. The one

sent to the United States in 1860 to ratify the Harris treaty was intended to be of the more restricted kind, but in the event the lavish American hospitality it received and the round of educational visits arranged for it did a great deal to give its members an understanding of American society. Because of this, when a mission to Europe was being planned in 1862, primarily for the purpose of negotiating a delay in the opening of Hyogo, Edo and Osaka, the French and British resident ministers in Japan urged that it be instructed to seek a knowledge of Europe's wealth and strength as well, thereby redressing the international balance. The men whom Edo appointed to carry out this task included several of Japan's 'Dutch scholars', who went about it with enthusiasm. The result was a surprisingly detailed account of European society in the 1860s.

Between April and October 1862 the thirty-six members of the mission, travelling at the expense of various European governments and carrying with them a supply of soya sauce in champagne bottles, journeyed from Marseilles to Paris to London, then to the Hague, Berlin and St Petersburg. From there they returned to Paris by train and on by sea to Lisbon before sailing for Japan via the Mediterranean and Indian Ocean. In addition to their diplomatic duties, on which more time was spent in London than elsewhere, the envoys were ceremonially received and entertained by Napoleon III, the kings of Prussia and the Netherlands, and the tsar, though not by Queen Victoria (who was in mourning for Prince Albert). To these extremely formal activities were added numerous visits to military establishments, dockyards, factories, government departments, banks, hospitals, exhibitions, museums and newspaper offices, all assiduously recorded in the notes and sketches of the mission's secretariat. Little interest was shown in art or music.

The value of this information gathering was put in question once the party returned to Edo. During the weeks in the early part of 1863 when a report was being drafted, anti-foreign violence in Japan was reaching its peak. Reluctant to provoke the terrorists any further, senior officials formally received the document, then

buried it in the files. There it remained unused, as far as one can tell, until superseded by the much longer and better-informed report of the Iwakura embassy of 1871–3. Despite this, the mission was not without influence on Japanese knowledge of the West. The doctors and interpreters attached to it included men who were to be opinion-formers of significance: Terashima Munenori, Foreign Minister in the early Meiji years; Fukuzawa Yukichi, Japan's foremost writer on western civilisation during the rest of the century; Fukuchi Genichirō, editor of one of Tokyo's first daily papers.

Yet it must be said that this was not what the Bakufu itself had meant by learning about the West, which is better revealed by the reasons it gave for sending students overseas. The first group of these went to Holland in 1862. All but two of its members were to undergo naval training in specialist fields, ranging from navigation and gunnery to engineering and ship construction. One, apparently on his own initiative, became an explosives expert. The two exceptions were sent to Leiden to study law and economics, which were properly 'governmental' subjects in Confucian eyes. Later parties were sent to Russia (1865) and Britain (1867) with similar intentions, plus that of training interpreters.

It is doubtful whether the daimyo of Choshu and Satsuma, who also sent samurai to the West to study, had any very different motivation. Itō Hirobumi, one of five students from Choshu who went to England in 1863, described their purpose as being to make themselves 'living weapons of war'. Nevertheless, both they and the Satsuma men who followed them in 1865 had a quite different insight into western life from that of their fellow-countrymen under government sponsorship. Not for them the world of government receptions and military academies. With merchants as the go-betweens in making their arrangements, they were encouraged to follow courses in law, politics, economics and civil engineering, or even literature and the humanities, such as would qualify them for careers in business or the civil departments of their country's government. Most of the 'private' students who

13 A daimyo fulfils his duty of 'alternate attendance' (*sankin–kōtai*).
His escort, greeted with respect and curiosity by local residents,
enters the outskirts of Edo, en route to his residence there.

16 Geisha
writing letters,
a woodblock
print by Utamaro
(1753–1806).
The hairstyle is
a symbol of status
(as entertainer
and courtesan, not
simple prostitute).
The evidence of
literacy carries the
same implication.

14 *(opposite above)* Nijō Castle in Kyoto, the Shogun's private apartments. Though the castle was completed by Tokugawa Ieyasu to watch over his interests at the emperor's court, Ieyasu and his successors rarely left Edo to visit it. When they did, they occupied these apartments, protected by the 'nightingale' flooring of the corridors outside, which made it impossible to approach the rooms undetected. The style of the wall panels is that of the Momoyama period (late sixteenth century). Compare the Heian palace (plate 5).

15 *(opposite below)* Kabuki theatre. By the end of the seventeenth century, as Japanese cities became larger and more complex, Kabuki drama was being performed in regular theatres in Edo and Osaka. This print by Okumura Masanobu (1686–1764) shows the interior of one, together with a section of the audience. By this time (c.1740), Japanese artists had begun to use the western-style method of depicting perspective.

17 *Sumō* wrestlers in the nineteenth century. Before the
modern period *sumō* tournaments were held in the open,
like prizefighting in England.

18 *(top)* A British squadron in Nagasaki's outer harbour, 1855. It was engaged in naval operations against Russia during the Crimean War, but its presence was seen as a threat by Japanese. Reflecting the port's traditional role in foreign relations, the print is labelled in Dutch and Chinese, not in Japanese.

19 *(above)* Japan's expansion overseas. The First Division leaves Tokyo for service in Manchuria, 1936.

20 Surrender. The Japanese delegation wait to sign the surrender agreement aboard
USS *Missouri* in Tokyo Bay, 1 September 1945.

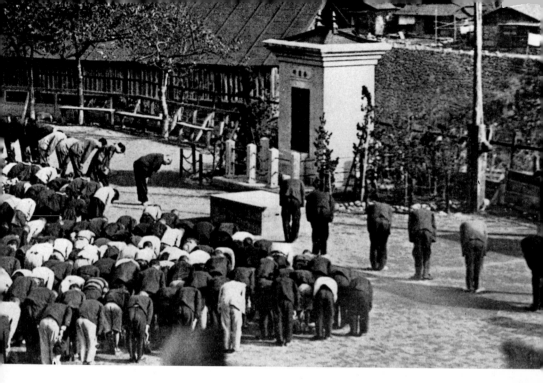

21 Prewar education. In the 1930s the school day started with a collective act of respect towards an enshrined portrait of the emperor.

22 Postwar education. To get a good start on the educational ladder, children under the age of twelve attend special 'crammer' schools (*juku*) in the school holidays.

23 (top) International recognition. One result of the postwar 'economic miracle' was Japan's membership of international bodies like the Group of Seven. Here Nakasone Yasuhiro (prime minister 1982–87) talks to the leaders of the United States (Ronald Reagan), Germany (Helmut Kohl) and France (François Mitterrand). Tokyo, 1986.

24 (above) The survival of tradition. A popular outing for the residents of Edo, later of Tokyo, was a visit to the Asakusa district of the city and its famous temple, especially during festivals. The temple was destroyed by bombing in the Pacific War, but when it was rebuilt (in ferro-concrete) such outings were resumed. The road leading to the massive gate is lined with small shops selling traditional souvenirs and crafts.

went abroad in later years did much the same, increasingly in the United States. They returned to Japan to take a vital but fairly low-profile role in the Meiji period's transformation of Japanese society: as middle-ranking bureaucrats, technical experts and managers in business and industry, translators and interpreters, and educators at every level.

The chief exceptions were those who went in the earliest groups, especially those from Choshu and Satsuma. By the intercession of the Jardine Matheson company, which arranged their travels and finances, the five from Choshu who arrived in London in 1863 found places at University College London. Three of them, together with a handful of others who joined them later, acquired a training in science and engineering. Two, Inoue Kaoru and Itō Hirobumi, went home in the spring of 1864 to play a part in the negotiations between Choshu and the treaty powers before the Shimonoseki bombardment, having little more to show for their experience than a knowledge of English and a nodding acquaintance with mid-Victorian Britain. Even so, this was enough, when added to the part they played in anti-Tokugawa politics in the next few years, to guarantee them office in the Meiji government after 1868. They rose rapidly within it to become outstanding political figures of their time, rewarded with the highest ranks.

The Satsuma students, who arrived in London in 1865 under similar auspices – those of a Scottish merchant in Nagasaki – also found their way to University College London, where they stayed for several years. Some were then called home, while others went on to America to study. These men, too, took positions of some importance in Meiji society. In addition, two of the older members of the Satsuma party, Terashima Munenori and Godai Tomoatsu, who did not enrol as students, acquired a different but equally valuable kind of knowledge. Terashima had been ordered to try to persuade the British government to give some backing to Satsuma in its growing rivalry with Edo. This led to contacts with diplomats and politicians in London, which opened the way to his own career as a Meiji diplomat. Godai's instructions were

to make arrangements with a western business firm by which the domain might raise the funds to purchase arms. He did so with a Belgian entrepreneur. The scheme was not particularly successful, but in the course of the travels and talks that led to it Godai learnt more than most Japanese about industrial society. Industry, he became convinced, was the source of western strength. After the Bakufu was overthrown he spent some time in the Meiji government's finance department, but later abandoned an official career to become an entrepreneur himself, largely in railways and mining. He was for many years President of the Osaka Chamber of Commerce. Other travellers, including some who served the Tokugawa, took a similar course. Shibusawa Ei'ichi, for example, whom the Bakufu had sent to France in 1867 as financial comptroller to the mission that represented it at the Paris Exposition, quit official life in the early Meiji period to become a highly successful banker and entrepreneur, who did much to develop the modern textile industry.

Awareness of the importance of industry to a country's ability to defend itself brought a fresh slogan into prominence in Japan: *fukoku-kyōhei*, 'enrich the country, strengthen its army', or Wealth and Strength. It was in origin a Chinese tag, dating from the time when 'wealth' was land and soldiers were farmers; but in the late Edo and early Meiji periods it came to signify instead the need for a military establishment, based on western organisation and technology, which would be paid for from the resources that commerce and industry made available. As a corollary, so at least men like Godai believed, Japan would need a change of political leadership to bring it about.

Such thinking became another strand, distinct from *sonnō-jōi*, in the ideas of those who opposed the Tokugawa. It was represented in the regime that replaced them after 1868 by a number of the younger samurai, most of whom had been abroad. This ensured that study of the West would not be neglected, despite the disappearance of those feudal patrons who had so far sponsored it. Students were still sent overseas under government auspices, or given grants if they were already there; small 'expert' missions

were dispatched to Europe and America to examine aspects of western governmental practice; a number of foreign advisers were hired; and the Iwakura embassy took over the task of the Bakufu mission of 1862, albeit on an altogether more impressive scale. Led by three senior ministers from the Council of State and taking with it a large body of attendant bureaucrats, it left Yokohama at the end of 1871 to circle the world, partly in an effort to win recognition for the imperial government, now that there was no longer a Shogun, partly, as it announced to its foreign hosts, 'to select from the various institutions prevailing among enlightened nations such as are best suited to our present condition'. In other words, it avowedly sought not only information that would be of military value, but also 'enlightenment'. Crossing the Pacific first to San Francisco, it spent several months in the United States, then visited in turn most of the capitals of western Europe before returning via the recently opened Suez canal in the spring of 1873. Along the way it carried out a programme of surveys and inspections more extensive by far than that of 1862. It was better served by its interpreters, too. As a result, the embassy's report, published in five western-style volumes a few years later, was more detailed and very much better informed than anything Japan had possessed before about the outside world, while the rank of the men responsible for it ensured that it would not be overlooked. It was, in fact, a draft for the building of an entirely remodelled Japan, reflecting the current wisdom of the West.

CHAPTER 12

The Modern State

The *coup d'état* of 3 January 1868 did not immediately settle the fate of the Tokugawa house. The Shogun Yoshinobu accepted defeat without demur. Many of his followers did not. Some fought battles against the 'imperial' army – troops from loyalist domains – on Kyoto's outskirts in the next few days. Others carried on a determined campaign in the north for several months. A squadron of Bakufu naval vessels escaped from Edo to Hokkaido, where its commanders planned to create an independent princedom for their lord. They did not surrender until the early summer of 1869.

The new rulers had therefore been in power for eighteen months before they could settle with any confidence to the business of deciding how to govern Japan. The completion of the process took them twenty years – that is, nearly half the Meiji emperor's reign (1867–1912) – and by the end of it they had turned to the West for models, believing that a modern state needed institutions appropriate to the world in which it would compete. The monarchy itself was an exception, but in other respects the government of Japan until the middle of the twentieth century was based on that of Europe in the age of Bismarck. Even after defeat in 1945 the changes that were made can be described as modifications to the pattern, not an attempt to dismantle it entirely.

The kind of centralised state that was created between 1870 and 1890 inevitably brought about a social revolution, too. Feudal privilege was destroyed; an education system was introduced, capable of training recruits to government service in the skills that were now required for it; and western-style industry was developed, providing a substantial segment of the population with novel ways to make a living, as well as a lifestyle that reflected them. Some of these changes were disruptive. With a view to preserving national unity, therefore, which was a prime consideration of its policy, the Meiji leadership brought in laws concerning censorship and the suppression of dissent. It also set out to reinforce tradition, or at least such parts of it as might contribute to good order. Meiji Japan, ideologically as well as institutionally, became a hybrid, part western, part Sino-Japanese.

Political institutions

During 1868 the emperor, still resident in Kyoto, was served, as his distant forebears had been, by a council, the Daijōkan, and several executive departments bearing Nara-period names. At the highest level they were staffed by daimyo and senior members of the court who had played a part – not necessarily an important one – in bringing the Tokugawa down. Sanjō Sanetomi and Iwakura Tomomi, nobles who had the emperor's ear, were the most distinguished. As assistants they had several samurai leaders from the loyalist domains, notably Kido Takayoshi (Kōin) of Choshu, together with Saigō Takamori and Ōkubo Toshimichi of Satsuma. These were all men with genuine power. In lesser posts there were a large number of other nobles and samurai, most of them chosen, or so it would appear, to reconcile opinion to the new regime, not for any acknowledged competence. Certainly they had little to do: the only areas directly subject to imperial rule were those surrendered by the Tokugawa; elsewhere the feudal lords retained their former rights. Indeed, had the duties

of the emperor's representatives been more onerous, the system might have broken down, for it was cumbersome and inefficient.

The central group of office-holders, who had organised the *coup d'état*, found this situation unsatisfactory. Once victory had been won in the civil war, they took steps to change it. In 1869 the court was moved to Edo, renamed Tokyo (Eastern Capital), where the Shogun's castle became the emperor's palace. Many men of undoubted dignity, whose formal rank exceeded their ability, were removed from office, clearing the way to a more effective form of imperial rule. Opinions about what would be desirable still differed widely. Some feudal lords favoured a baronial council, responsible to the emperor. Passionate loyalists, especially in the palace, urged that the emperor, despite his youth, be made in fact what he was in name, a personal autocrat. Samurai like Itō Hirobumi of Choshu and Godai Tomoatsu of Satsuma, who had been abroad and were now beginning to find a place in official-dom, set out the case for the abolition of domains and the building of a centralised state on western lines. This was also the advice that came from certain western diplomats and sympathetic foreign residents. It clearly had attractions for the ambitious.

The first step in that direction came in March 1869, when the samurai officials of Satsuma, Choshu, Tosa and Hizen persuaded their lords to submit a joint memorial, putting their lands and people at the emperor's disposal. It was an ambiguous document, leaving it open to him to confirm the state of affairs inherited from the Tokugawa, if that seemed politic; but in July the offer was accepted and the rest of the lords were ordered to follow suit. In order not to give too great a shock to feudal opinion, daimyo were then appointed 'governors' of the territories they sur-rendered, a step that seemed to leave the government with nothing more than a right to interfere. In August 1871, however, all former daimyo were summoned to an imperial audience, at which they were told – without discussion – that henceforth the domains would be replaced by prefectures (*ken*), administered from the centre in the Chinese manner. A month later all armed forces, other than those that owed allegiance to the throne, were sum-

marily dissolved. To sweeten the pill, lords were allowed to keep a tenth of the revenue from their lands as private income, while samurai retained their stipends, subject to review.

There remained the task of devising an institutional structure to replace the highly personal one that had previously bound the daimyo to the Shogun. Within a few months an imperial embassy, led by Iwakura, who was accompanied as deputies by Kido and Ōkubo, left on its travels to America and Europe (Chapter 11). One of its functions was to investigate western governmental models, in order to identify any that might be applicable to Japan. Before it left, two initial decisions about the country's government had been taken in general terms, to be put into force as soon as details were decided. A conscription law, announced in December 1872 and published in January 1873, was the first. It provided that men, regardless of social origin, were to be called to the colours at the age of twenty to serve three years, followed by four years in the reserve. This gave the regime an army of its own, replacing the feudal class. Training and organisation were to be western-style, planned and initially supervised by officers from France and Germany. An army officers' school was founded, soon followed by an arsenal, an ordnance factory and an artillery practice range. A General Staff was added in 1878. The development of a navy came more slowly, because its technical skills depended to a large extent on study overseas, but by 1894 it had a fleet of twenty-eight ships, amounting altogether to 57,000 tons.

The expense of these reforms was to be met by the introduction of a land tax, the second important measure worked out in the embassy's absence. It was announced in July 1873. The key to it was to be found in Finance Ministry recommendations, insisting that the Meiji government needed to enjoy a revenue at least as large as that which Shogun and feudal lords together had received. To achieve this, the law, as issued, prescribed that the owner of land, responsible for paying tax, was to be the former landlord or cultivator, as local enquiry might determine. He was to pay tax in cash, calculated as a percentage of capital value. The rate was initially set at 3 per cent (plus a supplement for local expenditure).

Farmers found some of these conditions harsh. There was no relief for years of bad harvest, for example, such as had sometimes been granted by feudal lords, while the need to pay in cash posed problems for those who still engaged in subsistence farming. As a consequence, rural unrest did not come to an end. By contrast, the government was broadly satisfied. It could now determine policy on the basis of a regular and predictable revenue.

Armed forces and a tax system were fundamental to the very existence of the state. Anything more elaborate by way of administrative machinery had to await the findings of the Iwakura embassy, which returned in the summer of 1873. Decision was then delayed by a serious dispute over priorities. While the embassy was away, the 'caretaker' government, led by Saigō Takamori, had become embroiled in conflict with Korea, which Saigō and his colleagues wished to resolve by force. Kido and Ōkubo strongly opposed the decision. In the first place, war, they believed, would present the powers, especially Russia, with an opportunity to interfere in the region's affairs. It would also preempt resources which, as the embassy's experience in America and Europe showed, would be better spent on institutional reform, if Japan were ever to be able to take a stand against the West.

The 'war party', as it is called, lost the subsequent argument, but the disagreement split the ruling group. Some of its members resigned in order to organise a 'consitutional' opposition. Others, including Saigō, put themselves at the head of samurai discontent, occasioned by resentment of Meiji policies that seemed designed to destroy the remaining vestiges of samurai privilege. There were a number of local rebellions in western regions in the next few years. The largest, that in Satsuma, which Saigō joined in 1877, took the whole strength of army and police to overcome it. Saigō himself committed suicide in the face of imminent defeat. In the following year, sympathisers of his cause assassinated Ōkubo, seen to be the architect of their rebellion's failure. Since Kido had died in 1877, the result was a generational change in national leadership.

Ōkubo, who as Home Minister had been the regime's strongest figure after 1873, had done much to strengthen Tokyo's control

of the country in his final years. A network of prefectural and local officials, recruited for the most part from former samurai, had been made responsible to his ministry. Their appointments and promotion were decided in the capital, their duties covered almost every aspect of provincial life. Tokyo ruled, in fact, more firmly than Edo had done for generations. The younger men who took over in the 1880s, of whom the most important were Itō Hirobumi and Yamagata Aritomo of Choshu, continued Ōkubo's work. They gave it, however, a more distinctively western flavour. Both had been abroad, Itō several times. Yamagata had studied military science in Germany. A significant number of their senior colleagues had a similar background. Such experience became a test of suitability for office.

Authoritarian regulations, issued in December 1880 and revised in 1886, were introduced to govern the workings of the central bureaucracy, echoing the Nara codes in their attention to detail. The powers and duties of ministers and their subordinates were spelt out, the limits of departmental budgets defined, a host of rules laid down concerning archives and accounts. Recruitment and promotion were made subject to examination, as in the distant past, though the tests were now in elements of 'western' learning, such as law, politics and economics, not Confucian philosophy.

The coping-stone of the structure was a western-style cabinet, established in December 1885 to replace the Council of State. Its members were departmental ministers, appointed by the emperor and responsible individually to him. The co-ordination of their work and the presentation of general recommendations on policy were duties that fell to the prime minister (replacing the Daijō-daijin). From April 1888 there was also a Privy Council, composed of senior advisers, men not currently in office, who were to be consulted by the emperor on legal and constitutional questions. The Council was specifically instructed not to 'interfere with the executive'.

Japan's legal system was also reformed. Local and regional courts, presided over by appointed judges, had been created in 1871 to replace the judicial arrangements of the Bakufu and

domains. A Supreme Court was added in 1875. In 1886 the justice minister's power to remove or dismiss judges was restricted, and from 1890 judges were appointed for life, subject to competitive examination. To this extent the judiciary was made independent of politics. The law was meanwhile being changed to bring it as far as possible into line with that of the West. A criminal code was drafted under a French adviser between 1875 and 1877, though it took another five years to get it through the processes of scrutiny. For commercial law Japan looked to Germany for advice. A draft was prepared in 1881–4, then promulgated in 1890 after review by the Justice and Foreign ministries. A new civil code took even longer to agree: the parts that touched on marriage, inheritance and other family matters proved too politically sensitive to be hurried. The first version, based on the French civil code, was rejected in 1878 as being too 'foreign'. A revision completed in 1888 met at first with similar objections; and discussion of it lasted until 1898 before there was wide enough agreement to make its promulgation possible.

The adoption of western institutions in this way brought Japan a measure of international respectability, which proved a useful adjunct to diplomacy in efforts to revise the unequal treaties (Chapter 13). It was reinforced by the introduction of a written constitution in 1889. Some of the men who had broken away from the ruling group in 1873 had made it their business to demand one, hoping thereby to weaken the power of those who had defeated them, but neither Iwakura nor Ōkubo was prepared to let authority be undermined while Japan still faced rebellion and other domestic unrest. Although Kido was more sympathetic – as the Iwakura embassy's 'constitutions' specialist, he had come to believe that representative government, cautiously framed, could contribute to national unity – ill health and early death combined to reduce his influence. Itō Hirobumi, who subsequently emerged as the senior Choshu representative in government, eventually took over his role, but with more than a touch of Ōkubo's steel. In discussions with Iwakura during 1881 he worked out an agreement on the kind of constitution that

might meet the leadership's needs, rather than those of its opponents. It should have a cabinet responsible to the emperor, they decided; a bicameral assembly with an elected lower house, though this should have no power to initiate legislation or in the last resort to deny the government funds; and an electorate defined by a property qualification. The plan remained secret, except in so far as an imperial decree, issued in October, announced that a constitution would be granted by the end of the decade. Even this was careful to state that those who campaigned for it were not to agitate for 'sudden and violent change'.

Itō himself took on the task of supervising the preparation of a draft. In 1882 he made another long visit to Europe in order to flesh out the skeleton that he and Iwakura had already outlined, spending most of his time in Vienna and Berlin. He brought back two German advisers, Alfred Mosse and Hermann Roesler. In 1886 they settled down in Itō's country residence, together with Itō and his Japanese staff, to put together detailed proposals. These were brought before the Privy Council in May 1888 and formally proclaimed by the emperor in the palace on 11 February 1889.

The text conformed to the principles agreed some eight years earlier. Central to it was the doctrine of imperial divine descent, reference to which was introduced at Itō's insistence. This would serve the purpose, he believed, of reinforcing patriotic unity, while putting those who served the emperor beyond the reach of elected representatives. The German contribution, following the Prussian example, was to try to make the monarchy strong enough to serve as a defence against the danger of social disorder. Disorder, after all, was to be expected in Japan, as it was in Europe, from the growth of an industrial economy. For this reason the emperor was given extensive powers: supreme command of the armed forces; the freedom to adjourn or prorogue the national assembly (the Diet); the right – at least in theory – to choose the cabinet and senior members of the bureaucracy. Since the constitution was his gift, he could also veto changes in it. Such provisions greatly impaired the influence that could be exercised by elected members of the lower house. Since the authorities also had at their

disposal extensive powers of censorship and law enforcement, embodied in a Press Law (1875) and a Peace Preservation Law (1887), they were confident of their ability to deal with critics. Police intervention in the election of 1892, to cite the worst example, left twenty-five dead and nearly 400 injured.

There is controversy about the long-term impact of the Meiji Constitution on Japanese politics. Defenders of the actions of Itō and his colleagues (Iwakura died in 1883) have argued that to have tried to move Japan in a single generation from feudalism to a fully representative parliament would have invited serious protest from significant elements in the population. Nor did the document itself prohibit further change, though it made it difficult. Their opponents, both at the time and since, have held that the provisions of the constitution, coupled with official measures of 'thought control', made domestic conflict inevitable in later years. By blocking or impeding full participation in policy making by social groups that were of growing importance – entrepreneurs, industrial managers, technicians, as well as trade union leaders – they undermined the standing of established institutions as a whole. They also created dangerous tensions. Political parties, no matter how law abiding, were able to make little headway. The most that Diet members could do was to create disruption, then try to exact a price for ending it. Hence the parliamentary process became mere political bargaining. Trade unions, which long remained illegal, could do no more than strike or riot, so weakening their public support. Much of Japanese opinion was accordingly unrepresented. The armed forces, by contrast, committed from an early stage to an ideology that treated 'liberals' as subversive, were able to use their special relationship with the emperor – their commander-in-chief – to free themselves more and more from civil control. This made them in the twentieth century a source of national policy distinct from that of cabinet and Diet. The consequences were disastrous, both at home and abroad. To that extent the 'emperor system', as the complex of Meiji institutions has come to be called, was at the heart of subsequent turbulence.

Social change

The abolition of domains in 1871 left Japan's former ruling class in disarray. Whereas court nobles could still find posts in the palace, or connected with culture and religion, while feudal lords at least had satisfactory incomes, most samurai found life hard. If they lacked the ability and political connections to guarantee appointments in central and local government, they were expected to live on their stipends. These had been subject to successive cuts since 1868, and were less able now to support a satisfactory lifestyle than they had been in the last years of the Tokugawa. Some tried their hand with varying success as entrepreneurs. Others farmed, or found employment in the towns, once the Edo rule forbidding them to do so was abolished in December 1871. Very few prospered. They also suffered loss of status. In 1872 the announcement of the conscription law made it clear that samurai were no longer to be treated as a military élite. 'After living a life of idleness for generations', the document said, 'the samurai have been authorised to take off their swords ... ' True, many continued to serve in army or police – they were, after all, the only men with relevant training – but it was no longer a birthright, or a guarantee of quasi-officer rank.

The final stage in their decline was the abolition of stipends. Even at their much reduced levels these had proved to be a heavy burden on government finance. From December 1873, therefore, samurai were permitted to commute their annual stipends for a capital sum, payable in interest-bearing government bonds. Not many found the offer attractive. In August 1876, as state revenue came under heavy pressure from inflation, commutation was accordingly made compulsory. For the very largest pensions, those of feudal lords, bonds were to be issued equal to the total of five years' income, bearing interest at 5 per cent. At the other end of the scale, the calculation was based on fourteen years and 7 per cent. Thus for the wealthiest, income was to be a quarter of what it had been, for the poorest as much as 98 per cent; but since the

bonds were capital, which could be held or sold at will, there was nothing to prevent the recipients from squandering it, or losing it in ill-considered ventures. Given the samurai's acknowledged lack of financial expertise, it is not surprising that many did so, ending with neither capital nor income.

For those non-samurai who lived in the countryside, the land tax brought similar opportunities and dangers. Landlords, who had won legal recognition of their holdings in the tax law, were free to use their wealth in ways more profitable than in the past. So were the richer farmers, many of whom had long engaged in moneylending and commerce. By contrast, those who were nearer subsistence level were likely to find that the burden of paying regular tax in cash to the representatives of a distant ministry left them in no better case than before. Many fell into debt, lost their lands, became tenants, much as they had done in the Edo period. Others migrated to towns.

One result was continuing armed unrest among peasants after 1873. The government suppressed it by force (another task for the modern army and police). At the same time it took steps to bind men of higher standing to its interests. New dignities were devised. In July 1884 the emperor announced his intention of honouring 'high-born descendants of illustrious ancestors', plus those who had contributed to 'the restoration of my rule'. They were to be formed into a western-style peerage. This had five ranks, ranging from prince (or duke) at the top to baron at the bottom. Of the 500 titles first bestowed, the great majority went to former members of the court and feudal nobility in what might be described as compensation for loss of perquisites. The rest – it was to be a growing proportion as time went on – were for the principal samurai leaders of the anti-Tokugawa movement and those who now held senior posts in government or armed forces.

The existence of such a peerage made it possible not only to reward the emperor's most distinguished servants, but also to include a House of Peers, well stocked with friends of the regime, as the upper chamber of the Diet. What it did not do was to make political office hereditary, or subject to inherited status, as had

been customary in the past. After Itō's civil service reforms of 1886, birth, though it might well be influential in a man's career – women did not have careers – carried no entitlement to office. In this respect the Meiji system was more 'Confucian' than that of Nara had been. In practice the keys to bureaucratic advancement, both civil and military, were family 'connections' and education: that is, education in accordance with a western-style curriculum.

Education was one of the subjects most closely studied by Japanese missions to the West both before and after 1868. In addition, several western employees (*o-yatoi*) were brought to Japan, either to teach in official schools or to advise on educational organisation, bringing with them a variety of experience from Europe and America. Their influence was evident in the Education Code of 1872. This provided for a system of primary schools to be established throughout the country, giving instruction in subjects that ranged 'from language, writing and reckoning for daily use to knowledge necessary for officials, farmers, merchants and artisans' (the four designated classes of Edo society, substituting 'officials' for 'samurai'). The schools were to be attended by children from the age of six, who would be taught for sixteen months; were to conform for the most part to a western curriculum, using translations of western texts; and were to charge fees (small ones, but sometimes more than the poorest families could pay).

From this beginning there followed a steady expansion in the number of schools, the percentage of children attending them, and the length of the compulsory course. By 1886 attendance was some 46 per cent of the relevant age group and the course had become four years. Other educational facilities also expanded. Normal schools for the training of teachers had been founded in 1872. Middle schools were added in 1881, higher middle schools in 1886 (renamed high schools in 1894). High schools for girls came in 1889. At the more advanced level, several institutions, deriving from the Tokugawa Bakufu's Confucian academy and institute of western studies, were amalgamated into a university

in 1877, then reorganised as Tokyo Imperial University in 1886. A similar body was established in Kyoto in 1903. Others later followed in Sendai, Nagoya and Fukuoka. Among private foundations, Fukuzawa Yukichi's Keiō Gijuku, dating from just before the Restoration, also acquired university status, as did Ōkuma Shigenobu's Semmon Gakkō of 1882, which was renamed Waseda. Tokyo Higher Commercial School (1887) was the nucleus from which Hitotsubashi University developed.

By the time of the Meiji Constitution of 1889, Japan provided an eight-year period of primary education, half of it compulsory, plus a middle school course of four years for those who had the ability and resources to go beyond the primary stage. Middle school graduates were likely to qualify for jobs in the lower reaches of the bureaucracy and business management. Entry to high schools was for a small minority, mostly destined to go on to university. After that, careers in senior posts in government would be open to them, or a life as members of the country's growing body of intellectuals. Tokyo University, usually through its Law Faculty, was the main source of recruits to the higher bureaucracy. Keiō and Waseda were advantageous points of entry into business, journalism and the law.

Since access to high school and university, while it did not depend on birth, required the resources to pay for modest fees and living costs, the poorest needed financial help – not provided by the state – or private patronage in order to make use of it. Even so, this was a much more open system than anything Japan had had before. It was not only the children of former samurai, but also those of landlords, well-to-do farmers and merchants who could be confident of qualifying for the most senior levels of employment in government and business, if they had the academic ability. This made education a solvent, eating away at the formal class divisions bequeathed to the Meiji period by Edo. It also spread the skills and training characteristic of bureaucracy into many other walks of life, including the largest firms.

If education was one important instrument of social change, industry was another. Since success in it – and the wealth it

brought – depended on non-traditional kinds of knowledge, together with commercial acumen, careers were likely to rest on individual achievement (reinforced, perhaps, by adoption), rather than social origin. On the other hand, the growth of Japan's industrial economy was by no means due exclusively to private enterprise. Ōkubo Toshimichi, writing as home minister in 1874, observed that manufacturing, which he considered vital to the country's future, required 'the patronage and encouragement of the government and its officials'. Few were likely to question the statement. The Bakufu and feudal lords had financed gun foundries and shipyards even before 1868; the Meiji government took over the plants they had established, then extended official initiative into railways, telegraphs and telephones. A Ministry of Public Works was established under Itō Hirobumi in 1870 to supervise the programme. It hired a large number of foreign technicians and advisers.

In an attempt to overcome inflation and an unfavourable balance of payments, the government also gave its attention to banking. The Bank of Japan (1877) was given the task of regulating the banking system, while the Yokohama Specie Bank took over control of foreign exchange. A more direct attack on balance of payments problems was made by instituting rules to standardise the quality of silk for export. Two model silk-reeling factories were established at government expense to demonstrate western machines and manufacturing methods. Import substitution in other fields was encouraged by similar action with respect to machinery (1871), cement (1875), glass (1876) and bricks (1878). In 1881, however, the Finance Ministry decided that the programme had served its purpose. It therefore set out to recover as much as possible of its capital outlay by offering the various model plants for sale. Bids proved few, prices low. As a result the successful purchasers – 'friends of government', for the most part, including Mitsui and Mitsubishi – received what was in effect a subsidy for their entry into heavy industry. The use of tax advantages and government contracts later extended subsidies into other fields, notably shipping. They became a regular part of economic policy.

Many of the entrepreneurs who took the lead in this phase of Japan's development were former samurai. Some, such as Godai Tomoatsu of Satsuma (railways and mining) and the Bakufu's Shibusawa Ei'ichi (banking and textiles), had been overseas as students or members of missions. Others had experience in running the monopolies or other commercial undertakings of their domains. Iwasaki Yatarō, for example, developed Tosa's late-Tokugawa shipping organisation into the core of what was to be the Mitsubishi company. Yet for all their importance, such individuals were a minority within the Meiji industrial leadership. After 1880, when Shibusawa's cotton-spinning factory began to show significant profits, a much wider spread of Japanese capital, much of it accumulated by merchants in the Edo period, moved into the textile industry. The number of spindles in use rose to nearly 400,000 by 1894, mostly in small, less capital-intensive firms, which used cheap labour as a substitute for the more advanced – and therefore expensive – technology available from Europe and America. Cotton thread, followed by the coarser grades of cotton cloth, soon became export goods, finding markets at first in nearby countries, then farther afield in Asia and Africa. These products became one of the two staples of foreign trade in the first half of the twentieth century. Silk for the West was the other.

Industry brought wealth to a large number of entrepreneurs, employment to managers and technicians, and job opportunities to an unskilled workforce, recruited, at least in part, from groups that had been disadvantaged by reform, or driven out of the villages by hardship. In the next generation it was to change the face of Japanese society. The change was not invariably for the good. The bourgeoisie emerged as a political force, enfranchised, but voting for parties in the lower house of the Diet whose members had limited power. The most successful businessmen tended to turn away from parliamentary politics in the search for influence. Lower in the social scale was a new kind of urban poor: the lowest-paid among industrial workers, housed increasingly in slums, and beset by unemployment and illegal strikes whenever

there was financial crisis. These were conditions – familiar enough elsewhere in the world – in which the extremes of political left and right could flourish.

Tradition and modernity

To many Japanese after the middle of the Meiji period, modernity became a cult. What they meant by it was a complex of behaviour and ideas that they associated with the contemporary West, brought home by Japanese travellers, or exemplified by foreign residents in Japan. In the provinces, especially in the countryside, life went on very much as it had in the past, but in the centre of Tokyo and one or two other cities the evidence of foreign influence was everywhere, mingled with the familiar homes and shops and kimono of tradition. Public buildings, railway stations, banks and some offices were now being built in brick or stone. There was gas lighting in the streets, telegraph wires overhead. A considerable number of Japanese were to be seen in various forms of western dress: soldiers and police in uniform; officials on their journey to or from the office, wearing frock coats and tall hats; businessmen in bowlers and suits; the wives and daughters of the rich in bonnets and long skirts. The court had adopted western ceremonial dress at the end of 1872. As early as 1873, we are told, a group of Satsuma samurai, coming to the capital in the clothes and hairstyle that had always been proper for their class, were 'stared at as foreigners had formerly been'.

There was the same mixture of old and new in literature and the arts. Western music was performed in the 1880s at the Rokumeikan, a hall built in Tokyo to provide a meeting-place for 'official' Japanese and foreigners. Lessons in ballroom dancing were given there by a German instructor. Some of the West's more serious music became a polite accomplishment in the capital. It was taught at the Tokyo School of Music, founded in 1887. In 1903 came Japan's first opera performance in Japanese, a trans-

lation of Gluck's *Orpheus*, staged with the help of a foreign conductor and pianist. Martial music had a wider appeal. After 1905 it was played by army and navy bands in turn at the bandstand in Hibiya Park, as well as in many other locations. Yet while concert halls made much of the works of Beethoven and other great names of nineteenth-century Europe, Japanese music was still studied and performed by individuals throughout the country. The two cultures also existed side by side – at arm's length from each other – in drama, attracting different audiences. The modern theatre put on translations of Shakespeare, Molière and Ibsen (though not very well). Kabuki remained popular, as it has done since. Nō plays suffered eclipse for a time, but later revived as an intellectual fashion, cultivated by theatre clubs.

In the visual arts, the division was less distinct. Japanese painters who went abroad often came back as representatives of American or European schools, rather than Japanese ones, while others, remaining at home, asserted loyalty to traditional styles; but the latter also reflected piecemeal the influence of western methods and techniques, as some of their Edo predecessors had begun to do. Woodblock prints, for example, which remained very popular, not only chose non-traditional subjects, like treaty port scenes, or the naval engagements of the Russo-Japanese War, but also drew perspective and human figures in the western manner. Despite this overlap, however, 'western' art and 'Japanese' art centred on different institutions. Traditional techniques were taught at the Tokyo Art School (Bijutsu Gakkō), directed by Okakura Kakuzō, while exhibitions of painting in the western style were organised by the Fine Arts Society (Bijutsukai). Both were founded in 1889. It was not until 1907, when the Education Ministry established an annual exhibition, that both schools presented their work together, competing for prizes.

The transition to modern taste was in some ways easier for Japanese novelists. To write in straightforward colloquial prose about the self and the individual, or about contemporary manners and society, was not too sharp a departure from what had been done by Ihara Saikaku and his followers in the Edo period. On

the other hand, the changes now taking place in Japanese life suggested a different choice of themes: nostalgia for the past, perhaps, or a zeal for social reform. Nagai Kafū (1879–1959) wrote with evident regret about the passing of the old Edo. In *Sumida-gawa* (The Sumida River, 1909) he explored the problems of a student torn between the attractions of old and new: that is, between his mother's wish that he should have a modern education for the sake of its job opportunities and his own desire to make a career in the traditional theatre. Natsume Sōseki (1867–1916), who studied for a time in England, took changing social life as his subject, drawing material from his work as a teacher and his own environment. *Waga hai wa neko de aru* (I am a cat, 1905) described his home life from the viewpoint of the household cat; *Botchan* (1906) was about a young middle school teacher. Shimazaki Tōson (1872–1943) produced similar work in his early years, but later in his life he wrote a major historical novel, *Yoakemae* (Before the Dawn, 1929–35). It was a semi-fictional account of his grandfather's village in the Restoration years.

Most of the developments in literature and the arts can be described as spontaneous: that is, were a response by individuals to changing circumstance. Their variety and appeal increased in the twentieth century, as new means were found – illustrated magazines, radio, television – to bring them to a wider audience. As a consequence, 'the culture of the masses' became predominantly western-style within a generation or two; tradition became more and more traditionalism, a conscious evocation of the past. Neither the Meiji government and its censors, nor their successors, made much attempt to check the trend, despite the grumbling of conservatives. Nevertheless, officialdom had a cultural agenda of its own, related to ideology. In the fields of religion and education it took steps to strengthen the people's loyalty to the emperor, as well as patriotism and commitment to the social order. Its principal instruments were Shinto and Confucianism.

Since the myth of imperial divine descent was a part of Shinto thought, it was logical to give Shinto a special place in the Meiji state. In 1868 the Council of Religion (Jingikan), which was

primarily concerned with Shinto ritual, was made in theory the highest organ of central government, taking precedence over the Council of State. This somewhat unrealistic arrangement did not survive the reforms that followed the abolition of domains in 1871. Despite that, the country's most important shrines remained in a special category, officially approved and subsidised. In 1882, when the popular sects of Shinto, linked with fire walking, faith healing and shamanism, were put on a private financial and organisational footing, along with other religions, the national shrines retained their separate status and finance. They continued to have a ceremonial role in festivals concerning the monarchy and the imperial family, and were served by priests appointed by the state.

Itō Hirobumi's determination to endorse the doctrine of imperial divine descent in the text of the 1889 constitution was of a piece with these decisions. To bolster them, emperor worship, together with Confucian morality, was actively promoted among the people at large. In 1872 the Bureau of Rites, the downgraded successor to the Jingikan, set out to propagate the Great Teaching (*taikyō*), an amalgam of Shinto, Confucian and Buddhist thought, by which Japanese were called on to respect the gods, revere the emperor, love their country and observe the traditional moral code. As a means of promoting habits of civic duty this proved ineffective, but it established a precedent, not least for the teaching of a compulsory ethics course (*shūshin*) in schools.

In 1879 the emperor was persuaded by some of the men about him, led by his Confucian tutor, Motoda Eifu, to issue a rescript condemning 'indiscriminate emulation of western ways' in Japan's teaching of the young. In 1890 there followed the more famous Education Rescript, insisting that loyalty and filial piety, plus respect for the constitution and the law, be put at the heart of the educational system. Thereafter the textbooks prescribed at every level — not only in the ethics course — set out to ensure that morality, patriotism and 'the spirit of reverence for the emperor' were given pride of place in the curriculum. Books used in schools were carefully scrutinised for undesirable foreign influences. A

portrait of the emperor and a copy of the Education Rescript were put in a position of honour in every educational establishment.

Outside the schools, the law permitted, and the police attempted to implement, a policy of thought control, which continued on a rising curve until 1945. All the same, one would find it hard to argue that there was total uniformity, even in matters most subject to it. There were still teachers who interpreted 'ethics' in the light of current intellectual fashion or their personal beliefs. Some remained unorthodox or uncooperative. Christians, for example, though their numbers were not large, often felt bound to challenge the official doctrine where it contradicted religious faith. Newspapers and serious magazines, available throughout Japan, canvassed or encouraged discussion of alternative ideologies, many of western provenance. It was not until much later, mostly in the years between 1930 and 1945, that the pressure to conform became so strong that the majority found it irresistible. Until then, the most that one can safely say is that Japanese left school with an awareness of their duty to the state, expressed in traditionalist phraseology, and that they were encouraged to retain it in adult life. The fact that this sat oddly with the habits and ideas they were acquiring from the West was not yet a deeply felt contradiction.

CHAPTER 13

Fifty Years of Foreign Wars
1894–1945

Japan's foreign relations in the first half of the twentieth century were in many ways conditioned by the nature of the Meiji Restoration. Ever since 1858 a prime objective of national policy had been to keep the West at bay, whether by reform at home or diplomatic action. In the first stage, lasting until 1894, institutional change and the creation of western-style armed forces were seen as a means of restoring the country's independence with respect to tariffs and legal jurisdiction: that is, revising the unequal treaties. The question had first been raised directly by the Iwakura embassy in America, though without success. Thereafter it surfaced from time to time on the diplomatic agenda, but the moment for decision never seemed right, not least because of British opposition. Japanese frustration mounted, exemplified in 1886 by a bomb thrown at the foreign minister's carriage; the Meiji reforms began to raise the country's repute abroad; and a deal was finally struck in London in 1894. Japan agreed to open the interior to foreign trade, while Britain accepted the abolition of consular courts and tariff controls. Other treaty powers followed suit.

Despite a measure of euphoria at this achievement, the change did not immediately bring equality of esteem. Nor did the world become an easier place to live in. Japanese fears and aspirations, which had supported, or even driven, the Meiji policies to this

point, therefore retained their force. They were directed now into different channels, however. Japanese soon became convinced that, if treaty revision were not enough to meet their ends, it was time to try something of another kind. Its nature emerged within the next ten years. Using methods that were sometimes military and territorial, sometimes economic, a new generation of leaders began to build for their country a position in East Asia that would, they hoped, provide lasting defence against the West. In the broadest sense, the process had public support. On the one hand it led to empire, both formal and informal. On the other it brought fifty years of intermittent war: against China (1894–5) and Russia (1904–5); within China in the context of the European struggle with Germany (1914–15), then in Siberia after the Bolshevik revolution (1918–22); and finally in a crescendo of expansion, Manchuria (1931) and the rest of China (1937) before spreading to the whole of East and Southeast Asia, as well as much of the Pacific (1941–5). Between 1894 and 1945 there was not a single decade when Japanese troops were not in action overseas.

The last and greatest of these wars, which drew in the United States and several of the European powers, ended in disaster. Outgunned, unable to match American production and technology, Japan was in the end pushed back within her older frontiers. Surrender came in 1945 after atom bombs were dropped on Hiroshima and Nagasaki. For many Japanese this meant that a dream had turned to nightmare. For most it signalled that the Meiji policies of Wealth and Strength had failed. In some respects they were wrong (Chapter 14).

Industry and empire

The weakness and disunity of China and Korea in the last part of the nineteenth century put temptation in the way of Japanese leaders. A few, in the tradition of Hideyoshi, cherished ambitions of hegemony in East Asia. The idea of a developing trade in

textiles made the prospect of political influence on the mainland attractive to many more. On the other hand, the more cautious recognised, as Kido and Ōkubo had done in 1873, that for Japan to prosper within the framework of the treaty port system, which was much too well established to be dismantled for her benefit, she would have to be circumspect. To disrupt the pattern of relations in East Asia might give the West a chance to further interests of its own.

All these considerations entered into the decisions of Itō Hirobumi's government concerning the Sino-Japanese War of 1894–5. The conflict grew out of disputes with Korea that went back as far as 1868. For twenty years or more they had been capable of settlement by diplomacy, but in 1894 a Japan grown more self-confident opted for hostilities. An army was landed in Korea. It achieved immediate success, not only against Korean forces, but also against those that China, acting within the framework of the ancient tribute system, sent to aid them. The Japanese navy established control of the seas. In less than a year Korea was occupied, and China sued for peace.

The terms Japan imposed at Shimonoseki in April 1895 were harsh. China was to renounce all claims to suzerainty over Korea; to pay a large indemnity (in bullion); to cede Taiwan (which had never been involved in the fighting); to make over to Japan a lease of the Liaotung peninsula in south Manchuria (the key to the land and sea routes between Korea and Peking); and to promise a commercial treaty, putting Japan on equal footing with the western powers in China's foreign trade. The clause concerning Liaotung proved unsustainable. Within a matter of weeks Russia, backed by Germany and France, demanded that the peninsula be restored to China, on the grounds that its retention by Japan would undermine the region's balance of power. Itō had to swallow his pride. Japan duly relinquished Liaotung.

Much of the indemnity China paid was spent by Japan in the next few years on an armament programme designed to ensure that so public a rebuff could not occur again. The Japanese navy was made more powerful. Six divisions were added to the regular

Japan asserts a degree of independence. A newspaper cartoon
(*Yorozu Chōhō*, 1894) celebrates the year in which the Japanese 'pupil'
achieved two foreign policy successes that were not wholly welcome
to his western 'teacher': treaty revision and an attack on China.

army. Taiwan was developed as a defensive outpost to the south. Economically, too, Japan became stronger. Taiwan had a valuable sugar crop; new privileges in the China trade translated into markets for Japanese goods. Against that, the international environment was becoming more threatening. Within three years of the Shimonoseki treaty, a fresh wave of western imperialism, which had begun in Africa in the previous decade, had spread to China. The powers – Britain and America reluctantly, France, Germany and Russia with appetite – set out to acquire spheres of influence, within which China was forced to grant them certain exclusive rights concerning railways, mining and loans. Germany acquired a dominant position in Shantung. Russia, having taken over the lease of Liaotung in 1898 – insult added to injury in Japanese eyes – secured mining concessions in Manchuria, together with the right to build railways connecting Vladivostock and Liaotung to the Trans-Siberian. As the final blow, when violent outbreaks, led by Boxers, spread from northern China into Manchuria in the summer of 1900, Russian troops moved into the region to protect their country's interests. They showed little disposition to withdraw.

In this company Japan was a weakling still. Her protests were ignored, and she lacked the force to make gains of her own that might serve to balance Russia's. Fortified by an alliance with Britain, signed in January 1902, she began a vigorous diplomatic campaign to reduce or limit Russian advances, but this, too, had little effect. In the winter of 1903–4, therefore, convinced that Russia posed a threat not only to the land route for her trade to China, but also to Korea and hence by extension to Japan's home islands, Tokyo decided on recourse to war. The Trans-Siberian, after all, was still only single-track in places, which would limit the reserves that Russia could bring to bear.

In February 1904 a Japanese army once more landed in Korea. Moving quickly north, it crossed the Yalu River to enter Liaotung and put Port Arthur under siege. The Japanese navy had already blockaded the port, together with Vladivostock. There then followed a year of heavy fighting, spreading as far afield as Mukden,

in which substantial casualties were suffered on both sides. Port Arthur fell in January 1905. In May of that year the Russian Baltic fleet, sent halfway round the world to relieve Vladivostock, was met and soundly defeated in the Tsushima Straits. Psychologically, the victory was decisive.

Following American mediation, peace talks were held in Portsmouth, New Hampshire, in August 1905. Once again Japan made the most of her military advantage. Her freedom of action in Korea was recognised; the lease of Liaotung was transferred to her, along with Russian mining rights in the area and the railway that linked Port Arthur to Harbin (the future South Manchurian Railway); the southern half of Sakhalin (Karafuto) was conceded to Japan again, reversing an agreement made in 1875. In this way, not only did Japan acquire a ready-made sphere of influence of her own in China and strengthen her defences to the north, but Korea was made a Japanese protectorate (late 1905), then formally taken over as a colony in 1910.

The Russo-Japanese War coincided with an important stage in Japan's economic development. Since 1895 the country's higher profile in the world, coupled with the armament programme, had led to greater government expenditure on war-related industry. This in turn had required investment in infrastructure. Increased output of iron and steel, a better supply of power from both coal and electricity, more railways and shipping – these headed the list. A need to limit dependence on imports in order to bring the balance of payments under control – the Russian war brought a rapid increase in borrowing overseas – created opportunities in the manufacture of engineering goods. The result was rapid progress in the growth of heavy industry. By 1914 Japan produced 21 million tons of coal a year, a third of the steel she required, nearly 600,000 kilowatts of electric power. She possessed 7,000 miles of railway track, much of it nationalised, six shipyards capable of building vessels of a thousand tons or more, one-and-a-half million tons of merchant shipping. In such a context Manchuria's coal and iron took on an added significance. True, Japan did not become a net importer of coal until about 1930, but she bought

70 per cent of her iron ore abroad as early as 1914. Most of it came from north China (including Manchuria) and Korea.

Taken together, the victory over Russia and industrial development at home changed the emphasis of policy towards the Asian mainland. Defence of a sphere of influence, 'bought with Japanese blood', became axiomatic for the high command and most politicians. This gave the army a stronger voice in the making of decisions. The claims of the export trade to be considered Japan's overriding economic interest overseas were weakened. There were now industrial companies, often undercapitalised by international standards, that needed protection against British and American competition, putting Japan much more in the position of France or Russia or Germany with respect to China. This meant that equality of trading opportunity there – what Britain and America called the Open Door – was no longer quite so automatically the first priority of those who spoke for Japanese business.

Despite this, the Open Door remained official policy for most of the years before 1930. It was championed by Itō Hirobumi until his assassination in 1909. Thereafter the professionals of the Foreign Ministry took up the running, supported by the financiers and large trading companies. Their critics came mostly from the services, especially the Kwantung Army, which as garrison of Liaotung had a vested interest in continued expansion on the mainland. It found backing in firms with investment in Manchuria, not least the South Manchuria Railway Company, a quasi-government concern founded in 1906, which was involved in mining as well as railways.

What might be termed the 'Manchuria party' was as a rule the weaker of the two, but it had influence enough to ensure that Japan regularly made an exception of Manchuria when framing her commitment to the Open Door. More directly, the knowledge that they could look to powerful friends in Tokyo encouraged Japan's more reckless patriots, even some army commanders, when tempted to take action on the mainland on their own initiative. In the winter of 1911–12, when China was busy over-

throwing the Manchu dynasty, Japanese army leaders sponsored attempts to organise an independent Manchuria under a Manchu figurehead. They failed because the Japanese cabinet would not back them, but they had set an example that others were to follow in later years.

One could argue that official plans for China in the aftermath of revolution were more dangerous still to the region's tranquillity. They were certainly more far-reaching. When war broke out in Europe in 1914, distracting the attention of the powers, Tokyo seized the opportunity to strengthen Japan's position in East Asia. Having declared war on Germany, ostensibly in accordance with the Anglo-Japanese alliance, the government sent troops to take over the German sphere of influence in Shantung. This done, China was presented with the bill. It took the form of what are called the Twenty-one Demands, spelling out, first, specific items relating to railway rights in Manchuria, over which Japan and China had been in dispute, then the disposal of Germany's former rights in Shantung, which Japan now claimed. To this was to be added the appointment of Japanese 'advisers' in the Chinese capital. Even more ominously, China was required 'not to cede or lease to any other power any harbour or bay or any island along the coast of China'. Along with other yet more controversial items, described as 'highly desirable' but not 'essential', this would have made the country a Japanese protectorate in all but name.

Ignoring international protest, which was muted by the exigencies of the European war, Japan embodied the substance of these demands – leaving aside the 'highly desirable' category – into treaties that China was forced to sign in May 1915. They triggered a wave of Chinese nationalist protest. To buttress the agreements, Tokyo accordingly used the leverage it had secured through its contributions to the war against Germany to win from its allies (even, if ambiguously, the United States) promises of support for its gains at the time when a postwar settlement came to be decided. Efforts were also made to find friends in China. During 1917 and 1918 a number of loans were made to the regime in Peking, supposedly to fund economic development, in reality

to bolster the power of politicians who were well disposed towards Japan, while obtaining lucrative contracts for Japanese concerns. The term 'co-prosperity' was employed to describe the relationship. As stated by Nishihara Kamezō, who arranged the loans, Japan's aim was 'to develop the limitless natural resources of China and the industry of Japan by co-ordinating the two, so as to make possible a plan for self-sufficiency under which Japan and China would become a single entity'. Prime Minister Tōjō Hideki was to use similar wording about the Co-prosperity Sphere in the early part of 1942.

Nishihara's initiative failed, largely because the Peking leaders could not deliver their side of the bargain. Other Japanese, who looked towards the more distant north, were no more successful. In the confusion that followed the Bolshevik revolution in Russia, a force of Czech volunteers, unable to continue fighting on the eastern front after Russia's separate peace with Germany, decided to make their way out of Russia along the Trans-Siberian. Their objective was Vladivostock. America, Britain, Canada and France, urged on by Japan, agreed to help the Czechs by sending an expedition to Siberia to secure the last part of their line of retreat. The force to be employed was intended to be modest, but for the Japanese army the opportunity was not one to be missed. It deployed five divisions in 1918, instead of the one that had been promised, identifying their task as being 'to maintain peace in the Far East by occupying various strategic points in Russian territory east of Lake Baikal'. This was a good deal more than saving the Czechs. Local puppet regimes were established under Japanese supervision in the area north of the Amur. Operations were later undertaken as far away as northern Sakhalin.

In the end it all came to nothing. The cost was enormous; the western powers became restive about Japanese actions; no reliable anti-communist government took shape. Meanwhile Bolshevik troops advanced steadily from Omsk. In January 1920 the United States decided to withdraw, soon followed by Britain, Canada and France. Two years later Japan reluctantly did the same. The failure seriously weakened those in Japan who had hoped for a 'forward

policy' on the mainland, backed by force. The army even lost public reputation. In the 1920s, it was said, army officers had trouble finding young women willing to marry them.

One result of the débâcle was to put China policy once again into the hands of the Foreign Ministry and its domestic allies. This brought a renewal of the emphasis on trade and the treaty port system, a kind of economic diplomacy for which Shidehara Kijūrō, foreign minister in 1924–7 and 1929–31, was the principal spokesman. He started from a position of strength. The Versailles settlement had given international recognition to Japan's wartime gains in China. As a permanent member of the League of Nations council, she had status as one of the great powers. Even the agreements made at the Washington Conference of 1921–2, which set out to restore as much as possible of the treaty port system in a China by now divided among rival warlords, had not decisively weakened her. Commitment to the Open Door and China's territorial integrity had been reaffirmed, but no attempt was made to reconcile this with the concept of spheres of influence. A four-power pact, designed to replace the Anglo-Japanese alliance, embodied promises by Britain, France, Japan and the United States to act in accordance with these platitudes, but provided no machinery of enforcement; while another treaty limiting naval armaments, for all that it was bitterly opposed by Japan's armed forces, still left her with the strongest navy in the west Pacific.

Given these advantages, Shidehara was able to play a leading role in the affairs of the treaty ports during his terms of office, promoting Japanese trade and resisting any changes in the tariff structure that might damage it. Manchuria was ring-fenced as a Japanese sphere. Nevertheless, the situation inside China was too turbulent for this state of affairs to go unchallenged for very long. Chiang Kai-shek, leading the army of the Kuomintang (Nationalist Party), had already begun the task of uniting the country by force, starting in the south. Since almost all his followers and the majority of their rivals, notably the communists, were implacably hostile to the unequal treaties, his progress

towards the north was accompanied by repeated demands for treaty revision. Britain and America were willing to consider it. Shidehara was not, or would do so only within very strict limits.

Manchuria was also a stumbling-block to international co-operation. It was not only a major source of coal and iron for Japan, but also a key strategic holding. In the view of the Army General Staff and the Kwantung Army, if China – including Manchuria – were united under Chiang Kai-shek, this would pose a threat to the whole of Japan's position on the mainland, even put the home islands in jeopardy, much as Russia had done earlier in the century. Events in China south of the Great Wall, in other words, were as much the army's business as the Foreign Ministry's. Some army officers were willing to take action on this assumption.

The result was an attempt in 1928 to force the cabinet's hand. The local warlord in Manchuria, Chang Tso-lin, whose rise was due in part to the patronage of the Kwantung Army, was proving difficult to control. In particular, he began to set himself up in the region round Peking as a rival to Chiang Kai-shek. This was unwelcome to his Japanese army sponsors, who had no wish to see Manchuria dragged into the mire of China's national politics. A plan was therefore made to remove him and find a more amenable ally. In June 1928 a bomb was detonated under the warlord's train as it was approaching Mukden. Chang died within a few hours; but before any further steps could be taken, Tokyo disavowed the plot and took steps to punish the conspirators. Shidehara – out of office at the time of the incident – was brought back to the Foreign Ministry; and the Kwantung Army was left to nurse its wounds, aware that any further action of the kind would need to be better organised.

The struggle for Greater East Asia

Japanese actions in Manchuria after 1928 took place against a very different background of politics at home. Between 1914 and 1918, while Europe was devoting itself to war production, the Japanese economy was enjoying a mushroom growth. Despite high costs and relative inefficiency, heavy industry found ready markets for its armaments, ships and machinery overseas. In the absence of European competition, Japanese consumer goods pushed into new areas. The prosperity this brought did not survive the peace, but it lasted long enough to bring about important changes in society. Commerce and industry became of greater consequence; the political parties they favoured won control of the Diet; party cabinets were formed, pursuing 'liberal' policies. Universal manhood suffrage came in 1925. The army lost several divisions, the navy's budget was cut. Shidehara was left free to engage in economic diplomacy with significant public support.

Outside politics there was a relaxation of social discipline, especially among the young, typified by the popularity of dance halls and a taste for popular entertainment of the western kind. In Europe and America these things were a response to the end of the killing. In Japan they were imported fashion, widely criticised as such by traditionalists. They branded the habits of the age – including most of the parliamentary ones – as a betrayal of the past, a descent to what Confucian moralists had always described as 'luxury'. Such moral condemnation carried over into reactionary politics, reinforced by a fear of socialism, as the postwar slump brought distress to the workers, provoking strikes and 'dangerous thoughts'. To many Japanese in the 1920s, something seemed seriously wrong with the body politic. An increasing number joined 'patriotic societies', in which disgruntled officers from the nation's forces joined hands with civilian visionaries and radicals. In this were the roots of what came to be known as 'ultra-nationalism'.

The temperature was raised to fever pitch by the world econ-

omic crisis of 1929 and 1930. As international markets collapsed and governments turned to protectionism to defend what was left of them, Japan suffered more than most. Farmers, deprived of customers for silk, their main cash crop, were reduced to penury, even starvation in some regions. Small businesses, trading in cotton textiles, were brought to ruin by foreign barriers to their exports. Larger firms survived, even grew, but only by putting pressure on their suppliers and their workforce. Inevitably there was unrest. Out of it came demands, sometimes backed by violence, for another 'restoration' to save Japan. This time it was to be a Shōwa Restoration, taking its name from the reign-title of the Meiji emperor's grandson, Hirohito, who had come to the throne in 1926. In the vanguard of the movement were the patriots, organised in private societies, mostly small, and modelling themselves on the samurai activists who had brought down the Tokugawa. In 1932 and 1936 they attacked members of the cabinet and leaders of the country's business establishment, seeking through assassination to persuade the army to seize control.

In this they were disappointed, because the generals proved unwilling in the last resort to dismantle the Meiji state. All the same, they not only created an atmosphere of terror, in which liberals knew their lives to be at risk and political parties were reduced to wary silence, but also changed the terms on which foreign policy was made. Shidehara's claim to have been acting in Japan's best interests by co-operating with the powers for the sake of trade seemed to many to be arrant nonsense in the world as it looked in 1931. The army's insistence on defending and exploiting Manchuria was much more in tune with the times. What is more, since neither the high command nor civilian governments were so ready now to restrain the hotheads, the stage was set for a situation in which military decisions emerged as often as not from below in the next few years: that is, from the 'young officers' of the General Staff – lieutenant colonels, at most – or from the independent actions of overseas commands. It was not until 1937 that Tokyo was in control again, and then not fully.

The first evidence of what this meant in practice came in 1931. As the Kwantung Army grew more and more convinced that the Chinese Nationalists were on their way to uniting China, two of its staff officers, recently appointed from the General Staff, prepared to 'insulate' Manchuria by bringing it more fully under Japanese control. In September 1931, with the collusion of colleagues in the War Ministry and General Staff, but without the authority of the cabinet or the high command, they manufactured an incident on the railway outside Mukden, which provided the pretext for a movement of Japanese troops. Southern Manchuria outside the areas that Japan already controlled was quickly occupied. Despite Tokyo's efforts in the next few weeks to limit the scope of the hostilities, the occupation was steadily pushed north on grounds of 'operational necessity'; and early in 1932 there was even a clash with Chinese forces as far south as Shanghai, followed by a naval bombardment of Nanking.

In only one respect was the central government's authority maintained. Facing criticism in the League of Nations, Tokyo vetoed army plans to make Manchuria a formal Japanese dependency. Nothing daunted, army leaders found an alternative. Pu Yi, the Manchu emperor whom the Chinese had deposed in 1912, was brought out of retirement in Tientsin in March 1932 to be made head of state in a supposedly independent Manchuria, renamed Manchukuo. The Kwantung commander-in-chief was appointed ambassador to it, responsible for defence as well as law and order; Japanese advisers filled all key posts in its administration.

One consequence was Japan's withdrawal from the League of Nations in 1933. Another was a domestic struggle for power, in which the advocates of a Shōwa Restoration were eventually defeated, but at the cost of leaving policy, especially the conduct of foreign affairs, more and more in the hands of the country's military leaders. Of the twelve prime ministers in office between May 1932 and August 1945, four were admirals and four were generals. It is within this context that one has to set the decision to mount a full-scale assault on China in the summer of 1937. A clash with Chinese troops on the outskirts of Peking, not unlike

others that preceded it, was this time allowed to escalate, reflecting a confidence within the high command that total victory would be possible. Large reserves were committed; operations were begun against Shanghai and up the Yangtse to Nanking; a naval blockade was declared for the whole of the Chinese coast. Chinese forces suffered a series of defeats, accompanied by heavy bombing of mainland cities and a number of atrocities against the civilian population, most notoriously in Nanking. Despite this, the government of Chiang Kai-shek refused to surrender. Instead, it withdrew to Chungking, whence it continued to fight a defensive campaign in the southwest. Elsewhere guerrilla forces emerged, mostly communist, to challenge what had become a piecemeal Japanese occupation of the country. By 1939 this had spread to most of China's main cities and communication routes. Though never formally declared – the hostilities were known to Japanese as the China Incident – this was war.

Meeting the cost of the campaigns, which imposed a painful burden on Japan's financial and industrial resources, required major reorganisation at home. In both Japan and Korea, steps were taken to ensure greater integration of the government machine. In areas that were in the process of becoming dependencies, puppet regimes were established under military supervision. The economy was more tightly regulated. The National Mobilisation Law of April 1938, though not at once put fully into effect, provided for the direction of manpower and investment into firms of military importance, together with control over wages and prices, and government operation of key industries, if required. In Manchukuo an Industrial Development Company was estab-lished in December 1937, designed to expand both the production of industrial raw materials for export to Japan and the provision of transport and power supply in Manchukuo itself. A year later similar companies were formed in north and central China.

This was what the prime minister, Konoe Fumimaro, described in December 1938 as the New Order in East Asia. It was to be a means of bringing together the economies of the region for the sake of common defence against the West. Japan, as the heart

of it, would furnish industrial and management skills, financial expertise and political co-ordination. Around Japan would be territories forming an inner core – Korea, Manchuria, North China – providing industrial raw materials and some supporting industries. Beyond this again was a perimeter, comprising most of China, which would be a captive market for Japanese goods, earning foreign currency to pay for vital imports from the rest of the world. Within Japan the political parties were to be combined in a single patriotic structure.

In the event, the New Order failed to deliver all that was required of it. One reason was that the China war dragged on, a constant drain on men and *matériel*. Another was that modern war required a broader spectrum of resources than East Asia on its own could offer. Self-sufficiency therefore proved elusive. Oil was the most important missing ingredient, but the list of desiderata included rubber, tin, tungsten and other rare metals as well. International trade could undoubtedly provide them, but the outbreak of war in Europe in September 1939 made supplies more difficult to get. Western countries, whose needs were much the same, had the advantage of controlling many of the areas of production. Some of these were in Southeast Asia, a largely colonial region. Others were in the Americas, available for the most part through trade with the United States. Since Japanese policies in China were deeply offensive to a sector of American opinion, and the Roosevelt administration was moving towards the support of Britain against Japan's new-found partner, Germany, this trade, too, posed major problems.

Japan's military leadership, therefore, began to consider seriously the plans long urged by some for an 'advance to the south', extending the New Order into Southeast Asia. A Tripartite Pact with Germany and Italy, signed in September 1940, following German victories in the summer campaign of that year, made resistance from the European colonies less likely to be a serious obstacle. The German invasion of Russia in 1941 was thought to remove the danger of any Russian intervention in the north. That left America's intentions as the principal question mark. American

economic pressure on Japan was growing: it escalated from an embargo on exports of scrap metal in September 1940 to a ban on oil shipments to Japan in August 1941. Deciding on a response was urgent.

The assessment in Tokyo was that without Indonesian oil the country's stocks would very soon fall too low for any large-scale military action to be conceivable. The Dutch showed no signs of making it available. This being so, an attack on Southeast Asia would have to be made no later than December 1941, if it were to be made at all. Allowing time for the disposition of men and ships, the diplomats therefore had until October to reach a settlement in Washington. After that it must be war, or confession of failure. The decision to be taken was a highly controversial one. There were many men of importance in Japan's political life, including the emperor and some of his advisers, who still held to Shidehara's view of foreign affairs. War with the United States was for them unthinkable. Equally, there were senior naval officers who believed that such a war could not be won. The debate was accordingly difficult and long drawn out. It was not until the talks in Washington were seen to have failed that the die was finally cast.

The Japanese strategy, as it then emerged, was to notify a breakdown of relations, followed at once by an attack on bases from which America and Britain might be able to counter an assault on Southeast Asia. Because of bureaucratic incompetence, however, the timing went awry. The note breaking off relations with the United States – which itself was not crystal clear – was not delivered until after carrier planes had carried out a strike against the US Pacific fleet's main base, Pearl Harbor in Hawaii. This was on the morning of Sunday, 7 December 1941. Other raids took place elsewhere: on Wake, Guam, Midway, Manila and Hong Kong. All were outstandingly successful. A few days later the battlecruiser *Repulse* and the battleship *Prince of Wales*, the most powerful British naval vessels in the region, were sunk by Japanese aircraft to the north of Singapore.

These operations opened the way to a series of Japanese con-

quests in Southeast Asia. Hong Kong surrendered on Christmas Day. Manila was taken on 2 January 1942 and occupation of the Philippines quickly followed. Japanese troops, moving down the Malay peninsula from Thailand, took Kuala Lumpur on 11 January, and Singapore, Britain's supposedly impregnable naval base, on 15 February. The Dutch in Indonesia surrendered on 9 March, and the greater part of Burma was overrun by the end of April. Japanese control had meanwhile been established in most of the smaller islands of the archipelago and western Pacific.

These victories did not immediately bring the war to an end, as many Japanese would have wished. Heavy land fighting continued: in China; along Burma's frontier with India; in the island approaches to Australia. At sea, though much of America's battle fleet had been sunk or badly damaged at Pearl Harbor, the aircraft carriers had survived. This made it possible to contest the command of the seas to the west and south of Hawaii. Nor, it transpired, was the Co-prosperity Sphere, as it was now to be called, able to bring the desired relief to Japan's hard-pressed economy. Tōjō Hideki, prime minister since October 1941, described it in January 1942 as 'an order of co-existence and co-prosperity based on ethical principles with Japan serving as its nucleus', but none of its component parts was to derive much prosperity from it. The fighting itself had caused a great deal of destruction, not least to key plants like oil installations. Administrative chaos, also a product of war, disrupted local economies and communications. The result was widespread hardship and discontent, made harder to bear by the harshness of Japanese rule in many areas. It was not only in China that guerrilla movements took up arms against the invaders.

Nor did Japan's war industry receive all the raw materials it had been led to expect. There was no effective rail route to the south through China and mainland Southeast Asia, despite attempts to complete it using local labour and prisoners of war. Shipping routes came heavily under attack, first from American submarines, later from aircraft. Three-quarters of the Japanese merchant fleet had been sunk by 1945. The shipbuilding industry lacked the steel

to replace it, even the skilled manpower by the end. Similar problems bedevilled aircraft production, despite the priority it was given.

The war, in fact, became a contest to be decided as much by industry and technology as by actual fighting; and although the campaigns in China and in Burma continued, sapping Japanese military strength, the focus shifted to the Pacific, where fighting on the ground was minimal. The American response to early Japanese successes came from two directions, starting in earnest in 1943. In the southwest Pacific, land forces under General Douglas MacArthur pushed up the island chains from Guadalcanal (February 1943) through Morotai to Leyte (December 1944). Luzon was invaded in January 1945, Manila taken in the following month. Meanwhile an 'island-hopping' advance was taking place across the central Pacific under Admiral Chester Nimitz. The technique he used was to bring together land, sea and air forces in overwhelming strength to isolate and seize small island targets, which then became bases for another similar advance. It was applied to Kwajalein in the Marshall Islands at the beginning of 1944, to Saipan in the Marianas in the following summer, then to Guam and the Palau group within a matter of weeks. The two prongs met in the Philippines in 1945. While MacArthur defeated the Japanese army there, Nimitz destroyed most of what was left of the Japanese fleet in two important naval battles.

It was by then quite clear to Japan's inner ring of leadership that the war was lost, though few were willing to admit it. A small group of diplomats and political figures close to the emperor made peace overtures secretly through Russia, but the army high command, hoping for at least a stronger bargaining position, continued to call for resistance to the death. More men, even schoolboys, were called to the colours; suicide units were formed, including pilots – known as *kamikaze* after the 'divine wind' that was said to have scattered the Mongol invading fleet in the thirteenth century – their task to crash antiquated planes, packed with explosives, on enemy ships; volunteers were organised among civilians to try to make sure that any landing on the

Japanese islands would face unsustainable casualties. A declaration by the allied leaders, meeting at Potsdam in July 1945, that Japan must submit to unconditional surrender, followed by military occupation, did not weaken this show of public resolve. The war would have to be ended by military action, it appeared.

Once the forces under MacArthur and Nimitz had joined, they carried out landings on Okinawa in April 1945, the first on actual Japanese soil. The invasion was bitterly contested, a warning of what might be encountered elsewhere. The same had been true at Iwojima in the Bonins a few weeks earlier. Nevertheless, these two events brought all Japan within easy flying range of American bombers, so making possible a massive aerial bombardment, directed at both industry and morale. All Japan's largest cities, except Kyoto, came under attack; damage and casualties were extensive, not least in Tokyo. The next step was to be an invasion of Kyushu. Before it could begin, however, a new weapon, the atom bomb, entirely changed the pattern of events. Dropped first on Hiroshima on 6 August, then on Nagasaki three days later, it caused casualties on a horrifying scale and forced even the imperial council to contemplate surrender. Reinforcing the effect, Russia declared war on Japan on 8 August, moving troops into Manchuria. Even so, the war minister and the service chiefs of staff resisted calls for peace until the emperor personally intervened. His vote left no option.

There were attempts by junior officers to overturn the decision – they set fire to the prime minister's residence and broke into the palace to find and if possible destroy the recording of the emperor's surrender speech, without success – but despite their action, plus several military suicides, an announcement of unconditional surrender was made public on 15 August. In a radio broadcast, received in silence for the most part by shocked and often unbelieving crowds, not all of whom could understand the language that was used, Hirohito broke the news for which wartime propaganda had never prepared his people. The war, he said, had developed 'not necessarily to Japan's advantage'. The country must therefore 'endure the unendurable and suffer what

is insufferable'. On 2 September members of an interim cabinet, led by the foreign minister and army chief of staff, signed the instrument of surrender aboard the American flagship in Tokyo Bay.

CHAPTER 14

Postwar Japan

It is tempting to end a history of Japan with the events of 1945. By any standard they were cataclysmic. Yet from the perspective of half a century later they seem to mark a change of direction, not a new beginning. The same emperor continued to reign, using the same reign-title. The Shōwa emperor (Hirohito) did not die until January 1989. The institutions of government, though much reformed, remained almost wholly western in their inspiration. Industry, when it revived, did so under much the same leadership as before the war, building on familiar foundations. Many elements of traditional religion survived – with less official support and in competition with new variants – and the Japanese people remained wedded to a culture that was part western, part Sino-Japanese.

It is nevertheless undeniable that defeat had a major impact on their lives. Political parties, dependent – in theory, at least – on the popular vote, became enormously more influential. So did the business interests that provided them with funds. Industry's success took on a different character from that of the early twentieth century, resting now on the production of high-tech goods for sale to the world's most advanced economies. It also spread affluence more widely through the population at home. In a wider context, external influences on Japan, political, economic

and cultural, came much more from America than Europe, contributing to a national *weltanschauung* that was more concerned with trade, the United Nations, the Cold War and the Pacific Rim than empire in Asia. Simultaneously, lifestyles and social attitudes became more and more like those of other industrial countries: less respectful to authority, more consumer-led, temporal-minded, culturally brash by the standards of an older generation.

The main source of this shift of emphasis in the postwar years was American military occupation, lasting from 1945 to 1951. Its first task, determined before surrender, was to disarm Japan and remove the country's wartime leadership. This involved both war crimes trials and an extensive 'purge', banning many thousands of Japanese from posts in government, politics, education and the media. Once this was accomplished, the focus shifted to reform. The scope of reform was founded on the belief that Japanese aggression between 1931 and 1945 had derived from fundamental faults in the body politic – not, as many Japanese asserted, from a temporary aberration, distorting the course that had been set in Meiji – and that these must be corrected in order to make the country welcome as a member of world society. 'Democratisation', in fact, became the head-word for what was being done. It embraced a multiplicity of changes to institutions and the law, enforced, ironically, by an alien military authority.

The first steps were negative ones. The emperor, under pressure from General Douglas MacArthur, Supreme Commander for the Allied Powers (SCAP), denied his own divinity in his New Year rescript for 1946. The greatest of the Shinto shrines, which had been closely linked with the imperial myth, lost their official funding and special status. A ban on 'militaristic and ultra-nationalist' ideology in schools was introduced in October 1945, soon followed by suspension of the course in 'ethics' (*shūshin*). The peerage was abolished, as were the army and navy. The huge business agglomerates (*zaibatsu*), accused of being co-conspirators of those who took Japan into war, as well as obstacles to free business competition in time of peace, were ordered to be broken

up into their component parts. An anti-monopoly law was passed in April 1947 to prevent the emergence of comparable successors.

The 'positive' measures, introduced in large part during 1946 and 1947, included the substitution of a more liberal constitution for that of 1889. The preparation of a draft was at first entrusted to the Japanese authorities, but the result was so at odds with American expectations that GHQ took over the work itself. Its version was made public in March 1946, promulgated in the emperor's name in the following November, and came into force in May 1947. The Diet, it stated, was to remain bicameral, but both houses were to be elected by universal adult suffrage: the upper house partly by prefectures, partly by a national constituency, the lower house by multi-member electoral districts. Half the members of the upper house were to stand for election every three years, much like the US Senate. The lower house was elected for a four-year term, but could be dissolved if the government fell, like the British House of Commons. Dissolution was to be the signal for a general election. The lower house had the right of final decision on all key issues, including the budget; the prime minister was elected by it; his cabinet was responsible to the Diet, not the emperor.

Two provisions of the constitution were particularly objectionable to Japanese conservatives. One was its description of the emperor as 'the symbol of the state ... deriving his position from the will of the people'. The other was the statement (Article IX) that 'the Japanese people forever renounce war as a sovereign right of the nation' and would therefore maintain no land, sea or air forces. American governments were to find this clause an embarrassment when they later looked to Japan as a Cold War ally.

Some changes were made in order to reduce the power of the central bureaucracy. A Local Autonomy Law (April 1947) gave some of its functions to prefectural and city administrations, whose governors and mayors were to be elected. The Home Ministry was to be abolished, and police forces put under regional or local control. Responsibility for schools was entrusted to boards of

education, elected locally; the authority of the Ministry of Education with respect to textbooks and curricula was watered down. Supervision of the judicial system was transferred from the Justice Ministry to a newly established Supreme Court, which had the power to rule on the constitutionality of laws. A revised Civil Code spelt out the constitution's more general references to civil rights, including the legal and political equality of women.

The declared purpose was to give Japan a form of government that would be subject to the will of the people, though for several years American GHQ was to remain the principal guardian of their liberties. It performed that function long enough, in fact, to ensure that a different generation of leadership was firmly installed in power. Once this was done, the pressures grew to bring the occupation to an end. In Washington, voices were raised to say that it was now an unnecessary drain on American resources. In Tokyo, the staff of GHQ considered that they had already done what they had been instructed to do. Consequently, peace talks started. In September 1951 a treaty was signed in San Francisco by all the countries that had been engaged in war with Japan, except Russia, China and India. It came into force when ratifications had been exchanged in 1952. This relieved the United States of its responsibility for Japanese government, but it left unresolved the question of American strategic interests in the region, where Cold War conflict was still a real possibility. To safeguard these interests, an American-Japanese security pact was also signed, extending to Japan a promise of nuclear protection in return for the lease of American bases in the Japanese islands. Arrangements were included for legal jurisdiction over American servicemen there, similar to those in Meiji period treaty ports.

Insofar as this made Japan independent, it began a testing time for 'democracy'. Out of the bewildering array of political parties that had been formed in the winter of 1945–6, four had by this time emerged as of greatest consequence. Two were broadly conservative: the Liberals and the Democrats. The others were of the left: the Socialists and the Communists, each divided into 'hardline' and 'parliamentary' factions. The Liberals, led by a

former diplomat, Yoshida Shigeru, were at first the strongest. As a principal architect of the peace treaty and the security pact, Yoshida used the American patronage this gave him to chip away at the postwar reforms that conservatives found distasteful. Some measures of decentralisation were rescinded; men who had been 'purged' were brought back into public life; action was taken to remove communists and others of the extreme left wing instead, including a number of trade union leaders. The first moves were also made towards giving Japan – in practice, if not in name – an army and navy again. They began with a quasi-military National Police Reserve, reorganised in 1954 as the Self Defence Force. Its constitutionality was justified, though not to all Japanese by any means, by the claim that it would not be made available for service overseas. It eventually became large, efficient, well equipped, complete with land, sea and air arms; and it won in following years a measure of public acceptance, though never, since the constitution was not revised, the standing of a regular army and navy.

Yoshida's policies encountered a good deal of opposition in Japan, enough to bring his resignation at the end of 1954. Almost all on the left considered his 'reverse course', as the retreat from occupation policies was called, to be wholly unacceptable. They could expect support in this from a considerable body of the general public, who were enjoying their newfound liberties. Against that, socialism was still regarded as dangerous by a majority. This influenced the view that people took of the Cold War, to which Japan was irretrievably committed, it seemed, by the defence agreement with America. As was to be expected in the only country that had suffered nuclear attack, there was a widespread sentiment opposed to any kind of international action that might lead to war. It could readily be exploited by those who took a hostile stance towards the rights and wrongs of American policy. Both Russia and China had active spokesmen on the left. The neutralist bloc, largely Asian, also had political friends.

Yoshida's resignation left the conservatives weaker in the face of this discord. It also alarmed Japan's business interests, which

saw the country's prospects of economic recovery endangered by political instability. Business leaders, therefore, acting collectively through management associations, of which the most powerful was Keidanren, proposed a plan to bring together the Liberals and the Democrats to form an all-embracing conservative party, able to check the rise of the Socialists. They offered generous finance to such an organisation. The result was the Liberal Democrat Party (LDP), founded in 1955. It was to provide Japan with cabinets for more than thirty years.

The first serious test of this realignment came in 1960, when the security pact was due for renewal. The revised agreement, presented to the Diet for approval, was denounced as contrary to the peace clause of the constitution. There was disorder in the lower house, large-scale demonstrations on the streets outside, threats of a general strike. Riot police were used on a massive scale to restore order in the capital. The treaty survived, as did the Liberal Democrats (minus their prime minister, who resigned), but the issue remained the most sensitive one in Japanese politics for many years. It was always likely to surface again whenever there was fear that nuclear weapons might be brought to Japan, or a dispute arose about the legal status of American servicemen.

Having survived this crisis, the LDP was able to devote itself to rounding out a structure that would keep it safely in office. This rested on a tripod of power. One leg of it was provided by the upper levels of the central bureaucracy, serving as experts, advisers and executive. Members of it, especially in the early years, were likely to be recruited into the party and the cabinet on retirement (a translation known as *amakudari*, or 'descent from heaven'). The second leg was business, providing money in enormous quantities for party funds, on the understanding that those who used it to get themselves elected would adopt a range of policies designed to favour economic growth. The third was the Liberal Democrat Party itself, providing an electoral and parliamentary machine. It depended not on a broad membership base, but on the careful cultivation in every constituency of persons of influence, able to deliver votes. The system was expens-

ive to run. Money was at the heart not only of electoral success, but also of party unity, since the LDP consisted of a number of rival factions, united only in their hostility to those who challenged them for office. Contributions from the party's central funds helped to reinforce co-operation.

After 1990 there were signs that this successful system was breaking down. Corruption, an almost inevitable result of the way in which the parties were financed, began to undermine public support. The end of the Cold War and the disintegration of Soviet Russia reduced the voters' suspicions of socialism. It also made unity easier on the left. Most disturbing, the 'economic miracle', for which the Liberal Democrats had always claimed the greater part of the credit, appeared to be coming to an end. Faced by a growing rigidity in its business structure, major miscalculations in financial decisions, and fierce competition from Asia's 'tiger' economies, Japan relapsed into a sharp recession that proved resistant to government efforts to bring about recovery. Many blamed the LDP. Some of its factions broke away as splinter parties, making new political alliances. Coalition cabinets were formed, in one of which a largely Liberal Democrat cabinet even had a Socialist prime minister. The situation, it seemed, was reverting to that existing before 1955. It is not yet clear when, or whether, a stable pattern will re-emerge.

Disillusion, prompted by defeat, left a lasting mark on Japanese attitudes, not only in the widespread hostility that existed to nuclear weapons and any hints of national rearmament, but also with respect to economic growth. If the Meiji search for Strength had been discredited, Wealth had not. A belief that it should now become Japan's principal aim underpinned the government's efforts to craft recovery in the early postwar years, then prompted national pride in rising performance figures, as recovery was transformed into prosperity. Industrial achievement was not only a contribution to political stability; it was also a source of international prestige. For both reasons it was held in high regard.

The end of the war left the Japanese economy in ruins. War factories had fallen idle. Those producing for the domestic consumer market had long since been deprived of much of their manpower and materials. Millions were unemployed, their numbers swollen by demobilised servicemen. Farms could not produce enough to feed the population, despite strict rationing, while much of what food there was found its way into urban black markets, or was bartered by farmers in return for household goods to the city-dwellers who crowded the trains to the country-side. Road transport was minimal for lack of vehicles; electric power supplies were frequently interrupted; coal was scarce; the population was hungry, confused, demoralised. Recovery was therefore an immediate priority, not only for Japanese governments, but also for American GHQ, which saw in these conditions a constant threat of unrest.

The chances of achieving it were better than they might have seemed to the superficial observer. There was still a good deal of undamaged industrial plant – the devastation caused by bombing is rarely as complete as it looks in aerial photographs – and skilled labour able to put it to use. There was a corps of efficient managers, most of whom escaped the 'purge'. Bureaucrats, who had learnt the techniques of controlling the allocation of capital and raw materials for the benefit of the munitions industry, were able to apply them to reviving peacetime factories and distribution networks. And crucially, the occupation proved to be a benevolent one. Food was shipped from America (prompting changes in diet and eating habits). American technology was made available to Japanese firms, often in partnership arrangements. Demands from the war-torn countries of Southeast Asia, that they be given Japanese plant by way of reparations, were rejected or ignored.

By the time war broke out between North and South Korea in 1950, recovery had proceeded far enough in Japan to enable her industry to provide a good deal of the equipment, other than arms, needed by the United Nations army that moved into the war zone. This was itself a major stimulus to production, accounting for currency earnings of nearly $600 million in 1951.

The peace treaty then made another stage of development possible by removing most constraints on Japanese export trade. The timing was fortunate. The world economy, it transpired, was on the eve of a period of rapid expansion. Japan, which possessed a growing domestic market, a government ready to make capital available and a population with a high propensity to save (a response to years of hardship), was in a position to profit by it. In 1960 the country's real growth rate was 13.2 per cent. Something like it was maintained for the whole of the succeeding decade.

The Ministry of International Trade and Industry (MITI) played a vital role in this achievement. It did so not only by the use of its familiar methods of control, but also by ensuring that the greatest benefits of growth were channelled to businesses that seemed likely to make best use of them. Some were old-established concerns: both Mitsui and Mitsubishi, whose trading companies had been dissolved in the occupation's early years, were back in large-scale operation by 1955. Others – in steel production, for example – were newly formed cartels, conceived and then approved by MITI. The anti-monopoly law was revised to make them legal.

The most successful companies in the export trade were those engaged in shipbuilding and the manufacture of high-technology items like cameras, electrical consumer goods and automobiles. All these depended on heavy capital investment. A few, especially the makers of automobiles, had long been famous names, often important in war production, but others were of recent origin, exploiting what were in effect new markets both at home and overseas. By contrast, the textile industry languished, except those sectors of it that depended on artificial fibres. Since these were petrochemical products, while most other firms that contributed largely to supply Japan's export markets were large-scale users of energy, the development once again increased Japan's dependence on imported oil, as war had done. Most of it, however, came now from the Middle East; and when Arab oil producers sharply raised their prices in 1973, then again in 1979–80, the 'oil shocks', as they were called, made the first serious dent in Japanese prosperity.

The larger import bill brought a general price rise, driving annual growth rates down to 5 per cent. Though adjustment and recovery came more quickly in Japan than in many countries, growth never in fact regained the annual levels of the 1960s.

At this point a different problem came into prominence. The drive to expand export sales as a contribution to prosperity had already produced a favourable balance of trade before 1973. Thereafter rising oil costs set it back for a time, but after 1980 it began to grow again, as government efforts to reduce the country's oil consumption achieved success. By 1990 the favourable balance reached an annual level of $90 billion. This caused alarm among the country's trading partners, especially the United States and the European Community, who threatened a variety of restrictions to counter what they saw as undesirable exploitation of their open markets. Negotiations on the subject quickly became acrimonious. They were not made easier when Japan began to use the surpluses she earned by trade to finance direct investment overseas, whether by buying bonds and real estate, or by establishing factories under Japanese ownership. The latter, it was clear, were in part intended as a way to bypass any restrictions that might be imposed on imports coming directly from Japan.

One result of higher foreign earnings was to strengthen the yen in the world's financial centres. This proved in the long run to have disadvantages for Japan. By raising the price of export goods, it not only made it easier for local manufacturers to compete with them in places where Japan had hitherto been able to dominate the market – Korea, Taiwan, Hong Kong and Singapore among the earliest, soon followed by China, Thailand and Malaysia – but also gave the industries of those areas a better chance to challenge Japan in other parts of the world. Japanese businessmen, aware that their labour costs, when translated into foreign currencies, were in many cases much too high, took two steps to restore their competitive position. One was to reduce the size of their labour force in Japan. The other, known as 'hollowing out', was to transfer manufacturing to countries where labour, though sufficiently skilled, was cheaper. Japanese products began to be

marketed under labels that described them as 'made in Korea', 'made in Singapore', even 'made in Britain'. This involved in many instances a transfer of technology and know-how that was bound to improve the competitiveness of potential rivals.

Despite this, Japan in the 1980s had the world's second strongest industrial economy. Production of steel was greater than that of the United States. So was that of automobiles: some six million units were exported every year. Exports as a whole produced a large and rising trade surplus, much of it used to finance investment overseas. As a result, Japan became a major international creditor for the first time in her modern history. Prosperity, it was predicted, would last well into the final decade of the century.

The prediction was wrong. At the beginning of the 1990s, property prices, which had been raised to unsustainable levels by generous lending policies on the part of financial institutions, suddenly fell. Banks were left with huge outstanding loans, many of them irrecoverable. Credit grew tighter. The government made the situation worse by raising taxes to strengthen revenue. From this point on, Japan moved rapidly into recession. Business confidence declined, unemployment began to rise, consumption fell. In the summer of 1992 the Tokyo stock exchange index stood at less than half its earlier peak.

Government efforts to restore the situation in the next six years were unsuccessful. By 1998 the financial structure was looking more and more fragile, the yen had weakened, cabinets were shaky. The Liberal Democrats suffered an electoral defeat, the prime minister resigned. To all appearances the 'economic miracle' was at an end.

Thirty years of prosperity, starting in the 1960s, brought about far-reaching changes in Japanese life. It carried forward the urbanisation, begun in the Edo period, to the point where three-quarters of Japanese already lived in towns and cities by 1973. Still more worked in them, for every city had its spreading fringe of suburbs and dormitory areas. Even some country-dwellers,

nominally farmers, commuted to urban types of employment. Officially, farmers made up 9 per cent of the population by 1980, but they contributed less than 3 per cent to the national product. Underlining the statistics, an urban and suburban belt spread westward along the Pacific coast from Tokyo, stretching more than 300 miles to Osaka, then farther west along the northern shores of the Inland Sea. One can travel all the way by rail and rarely get a glimpse of genuine countryside. Elsewhere the concentration is less dense, but this is because so much of Japan's terrain is mountainous, providing neither industrial nor farming land.

Employees of Japan's largest firms, together with office workers, form a large proportion of the residents in these urban areas. They fall into three categories. At the top is management, characterised by what is known as the 'salaryman' (*sarariman*). He is usually recruited, like his equivalents in the state bureaucracy, from male university graduates (few women have found a place in their ranks, though the number has slowly been increasing). Recruitment and starting salary depend on the reputation of the candidate's university, more than on the academic attainment of the individual; promotion is by seniority, except that the less efficient are diverted to the fringes as they near the top; loyalty to the company, measured by conscientious attendance and long hours, is held to be a primary virtue. Salaries have not as a rule been generous at any level, but other advantages exist to compensate: job security (usually known as 'life employment'), regular bonuses, company housing, health and pension schemes. Wives, whose husbands more often than not are late home from the office, are left to deal with the home and the children's education. They have little to do with the husband's 'business' life.

A little lower in the scale come the members of the company's 'permanent' workforce, though the social distinction is not sharply drawn. Having a less prestigious education than the *sarariman*, they nevertheless enjoy the same expectation of life employment, subject to job changes and retraining, plus a similar range of employee benefits. These are the workers most likely to

be unionised. Revision of the labour laws between 1945 and 1947 gave employees the right to organise and strike, as well as guaranteeing a health insurance scheme and accident compensation. By the end of 1948 there were 34,000 separate unions with nearly 7 million members, two-fifths of the industrial workforce; but strikes, coupled with the participation of union leaders in radical politics, attracted the hostility of both conservative cabinets and American military government. The 'red purge' of 1950–51 checked the trend, leaving most trade unions as 'company' unions, concerned almost wholly with wages and working conditions. This has remained true ever since, though the labour movement as a whole has had its ups and downs.

A large part of a company's workforce – as much as half in some cases – is described as 'temporary': that is, does not have a guarantee of life employment. Traditionally it is also paid less well, though differentials have narrowed in recent years. Those who belong to this category of workers can be hired and fired with relative impunity, as the fortunes of the business fluctuate, so their presence constitutes an economic safety valve, increasing job security for the rest; and since they are the ones least likely to be unionised, their disabilities are not as much a cause of turbulence as one might otherwise expect.

Medium and smaller companies, engaged perhaps in subcontracting, or in the distribution and service industries, have remained to a greater extent family owned and differently structured. They tend to have a smaller 'permanent' workforce, to employ more family labour, to offer lower pay. They, too, therefore contribute to economic flexibility, part of a general pattern that has kept formal unemployment remarkably low. It remains low by European standards, even if one takes account of the concealed unemployment to which the system in practice leads.

Since 1990, while Japan has been in recession, not all characteristics of the business world have remained the same. There has been a reduced commitment to lifetime employment at almost all levels. Sometimes salarymen change jobs voluntarily, looking for better opportunities. Sometimes they are subject to com-

pulsory early retirement. More women are being employed, often part time and usually at lower pay than men. This has gone hand in hand with an increase in divorce, perhaps in middle age or later, when the children have left home and wives can think of taking up jobs again. None of this would be particularly surprising in Europe or America. In Japan it suggests that the social habits always thought to be part of the 'economic miracle' are not immutable. As Japanese society continues to evolve, it becomes more and more like that of other capitalist countries.

One thing that has not changed is preoccupation with the 'ladder' of education. In Meiji the state education system was designed to train a skilled and biddable population, some members of which could expect by virtue of ability to make their way upward through the ranks of a powerful bureaucracy. Occupation policy set out to reform both the structure and the ethos, though it was more successful with the former than with the latter. Education became the principal means of recruiting a business élite that was almost as bureaucratic as the state's. Attempts to put greater emphasis on freedom of access, variety and individual attainment, by contrast, fell all too often by the wayside, despite a very great increase in the number of universities and colleges. As a result, education is still seen primarily as the route to success in life, not as a means of self-fulfilment. Entry to one of the best universities, whether state or private, is considered a career advantage second to none. It is most likely to be attainable by those who attend one of the better schools. Since these, like the universities, choose their students by competitive examination, the 'struggle to achieve' is pushed back even into primary education. Parents make savings from the family budget to pay for children as young as five to go to special cramming classes in the evenings and school holidays. University entrance is known as the 'examination hell'.

This underlines the importance of a feature of modern Japanese life that began with the Meiji reforms: the break with hereditary status as the determinant of a person's 'place' in society. Another significant feature, this time looking back to the Edo period, has

been a rising standard of living. Those who governed Japan between 1868 and 1945 were more concerned with the nation's strength than with the people's welfare, except in so far as the latter was an element in the former. After defeat, the economy became psychologically more important; and one element underlying this was a widespread desire to secure a better life, itself a form of revulsion against the past. Japanese not only looked for higher incomes. They also sought to spend them in new ways, ways that had more in common with the tastes of Edo townsmen (*chōnin*) than with the traditions of the samurai that had shaped so much of what could 'properly' be done in the 1930s.

The affluence that derived from industrial growth spread to all levels of the population through higher wages, bonuses and profits (Japan is not to any great extent a *rentier* society). Real wages in 1970 were comfortably more than double the prewar norm. One consequence was the ability to buy a range of more expensive foodstuffs, bringing unmistakable increases in the height and weight of the younger generation. The national rugby team, though still smaller as a rule than its opponents, is not now disastrously outweighted. Girls are no longer universally tiny – and they are better dressed, mostly in the western style. Even so, a much smaller proportion of the household budget has been needed in recent years for food and clothing than was true in the nineteenth century. Housing is expensive, especially in the cities, but it still leaves more for the costs of education and entertainment, including television sets and hi-fi, even private cars. Most of the consumer durables are much like those to be found elsewhere. They are, after all, Japanese exports.

In fact, in material things Japanese life is with few exceptions a replica of western life. So it is in much else. People watch imported movies, dubbed in Japanese. They flock to concerts by western classical orchestras and pop groups. They eat western snacks and meals (Japanese food is more expensive). In addition, Japan produces conductors, violinists and ballet dancers of note, who perform throughout the world. Japanese painters of reputation are as likely to be influenced by the French Impressionists

as they are by the classical art of the Japanese school.

So far has this development gone that it is doubtful whether one should continue to call the civilisation of Europe and America 'western' when writing of Japan. To most Japanese it is so normal a part of everyday life that they accept it as their own, something they are free to modify if they wish, just as much as Italians or Americans. In other words, there is now a Japanese version of modern culture, just as there are national variants elsewhere.

Tradition has changed in response to the shift of emphasis, but has not been completely overwhelmed. For the most part it is found in isolated pockets, instead of comprising a pervasive element running through society as a whole. Most adjustments tend to be those that will increase the appeal to a popular audience. Kabuki, for example, has become brisker, indulging even more than in the past in showmanship. *Sumō* tournaments have reduced the amount of preliminary ritual before their bouts for the benefit of the television cameras. Woodblock prints have found a market in Christmas cards. *Ikebana* seeks out rare and more colourful flowers; its most 'modern' exhibitions have been known to include bicycle wheels (shorn of their tyres) in the arrangements. Yet in some respects – in the transmission of skills, or the relationship of master and 'disciple' – the traditional arts and sports remain highly conservative. The methods of public presentation have changed much more than social attitudes.

This is not entirely true of language. For a hundred years or more, Japanese has been adjusting to the social needs thrown up by time, as well as to the demands of fashion and technology: simplifying its structure and to a limited degree its writing forms, borrowing words and phrases from a variety of other languages, inventing new expressions of its own. This has made much of classical and medieval literature, both poetry and prose, harder for the present generation to understand. The *Tale of Genji*, for example, is best known in a twentieth-century Japanese 'translation'. Against that, what is now written by novelists, scholars and commentators of every kind can reach a very much wider audience. To this end, form and style have also been greatly

modified. It is possible today to buy any number of books, fictional, technical, or educational, published as *manga*, that is, the kind of strip-cartoons that were developed for the less serious pages of the daily papers.

One disadvantage of a language that loses touch with much of the literature of the past is that it cuts off many people from a knowledge of the history and ideas of their country before the present age. Outside the schools the task of explaining them in Japan has fallen more and more to those whose first concern is entertainment in television and film. Their interests are inevitably selective. The life of the samurai is a favoured topic, as it has long been. It appears in productions that range from what used to be called 'B class movies' to the glossier serials of the major TV channels. At a more elevated level, it is the subject of films that gave Kurosawa Akira a world reputation as a director. *Rashōmon* is a tale (much revised) from *Konjaku monogatari* (Chapter 4), *The Seven Samurai* one that is set in the Sengoku wars (Chapter 7), *Ran* a version of the *King Lear* story with the principals converted into Japanese feudal lords. This is fiction, but the historical detail is meticulous. Also historical are many discussions of Japan's response to the West that can be heard on current affairs pro-grammes or read in magazines. Some years ago there was a long documentary film about the Tokyo war crimes trials that drew many customers to cinemas in the cities. Japan can hardly be said to lack a consciousness of the past, albeit an impressionistic one.

Yet the strength and influence of the old religions is difficult to assess. Visit festivals and you will see throngs of visitors, including many family groups. Go to a shrine or temple at other times and most of the few who are there are likely to be elderly (or tourists). True, Buddhism and Shinto have given birth to so-called 'new religions' since 1945, but this might be as much a sign of weakness as of vigour. Zen has acquired a role in management training, Shinto in the siting of factories and office blocks. Lip-service is paid to the value of Confucian ethics by economists and right-wing politicians. Nevertheless, the impression remains that Japan has been overwhelmingly secular in its thought ever since Toku-

gawa times. A survey in 1983 concluded that less than a third of Japanese admitted to having a personal faith.

The most straightforward explanation of the changes in postwar Japan is that they have simply been another phase of continuing modernisation, a convergence of institutions, attitudes and culture with those of other industrial states. From this point of view, there are parallels with what took place after Japan began to adopt Chinese civilisation in the sixth and seventh centuries. Prince Shōtoku then did not know the extent of what he was setting in train. *Mutatis mutandis*, nor did Commodore Perry in 1853.

GLOSSARY

Ashigaru Foot-soldiers. During the Sengoku period (q.v.), *ashigaru* emerged as the lowest-ranking members of the feudal class, having status below that of samurai proper. They served as the rank and file of a feudal army, or as clerks, guards and messengers in time of peace.

Asuka period The period extending from the formal arrival of Buddhism in Japan (supposedly AD 552) to the founding of Nara in 710. Art historians use 645 as its terminal date.

Azuchi period The period in the second half of the sixteenth century when Oda Nobunaga was hegemon in Japan, taking its name from his castle on the shores of Lake Biwa. It is commonly combined with the years of Toyotomi Hideyoshi's supremacy, named after his castle on the outskirts of Kyoto, to provide a label, Azuchi-Momoyama, for the last thirty or forty years of the century.

Bakufu The *de facto* central administration of Japan under a Shogun (q.v.). First established in simple form by Minamoto Yoritomo towards the end of the twelfth century, it became more elaborate in later periods, especially under the Tokugawa, when it was staffed by some hundreds of samurai officials. The separate phases of its history are identified either by reference to the place where its headquarters was located (Kamakura Bakufu, Muromachi Bakufu, Edo Bakufu) or, in the case of the last two, by the name of the family holding power as Shogun (Ashikaga Bakufu, Tokugawa Bakufu).

Bushi See under Samurai.

Chōnin Townsmen. The non-samurai inhabitants of feudal towns (merchants, artisans, labourers) in the late medieval and Edo periods.

Daijōkan The Council of State, as established under direct imperial rule, first in Nara and Heian, then briefly in the Meiji

period. Its senior minister was the Daijō-daijin (sometimes translated 'Chancellor').

Daimyo A feudal lord of the later medieval and Edo periods, defined as one who held land rated at 10,000 or more *koku* (see *Kokudaka*). Historians describe daimyo of the late fifteenth and sixteenth centuries as Sengoku daimyo, implying that the institution was not then fully developed. Daimyo of the Edo period were divided into *fudai daimyō* (direct vassals of the Tokugawa) and *tozama daimyō* ('outside' daimyo, usually having greater independence and larger lands, but not allowed to hold Bakufu office).

Edo period The period when the Tokugawa ruled Japan as Shogun from their capital, Edo (modern Tokyo); customarily taken to have begun with the battle of Sekigahara in 1600 (though Ieyasu did not become Shogun until 1603) and to have ended with the fall of the Tokugawa in January 1868.

E-maki Picture scrolls, covering a wide range of subjects. Originally introduced from China during Nara, they became a characteristically Japanese art form from the twelfth century onwards.

Era-name (nengō) A calendrical system, adopted from China in the seventh century, in which short periods of time are given labels (*nengō*), chosen by the imperial court for their auspicious character. Years are identified by their serial place within them: thus Taika 1 = 645, Taika 2 = 646, and so on until the *nengō* is changed. In early centuries *nengō* were changed whenever events were thought to call for it, but in modern times Japan has followed Chinese practice in making them coincide with imperial reigns. The Meiji period, Taishō period and Shōwa period (q.v.) all had single *nengō*, which have posthumously become the emperor's reign-title. The practice continues.

Fudai daimyō See under Daimyo.

Fukoku-kyōhei 'Enrich the country, strengthen the army'. Originally a Chinese tag, it was modified in Japan during the second half of the nineteenth century to be the slogan under which a commercial-industrial economy was to be established and the country's military establishment reformed on western lines.

Gokenin Housemen; vassals of a feudal lord. In the Edo period, the lowest level of those with full samurai rank (cf. Samurai).

Gōshi Country samurai. Those who in the sixteenth century (after Hideyoshi's Sword Hunt) were allowed to remain in the village and continue to cultivate land, instead of moving to their lord's castle town. They lost status as a result, ranking below those of full samurai standing.

Hatamoto Bannermen. Samurai of superior status to the majority of *gokenin* (q.v.).

Heian period The period when the imperial court still ruled Japan from the emperor's capital of Heian (later known as Kyoto), i.e. from the late eighth to the late twelfth centuries.

Kamakura period The period 1185 to 1333, when the Bakufu controlled Japan from a capital in Kamakura. Cf. Bakufu.

Kami Deities of the Shinto pantheon, usually translated 'gods and goddesses' (without distinction of sex), though not all were anthropomorphic.

Kampaku One of the principal offices used by the Fujiwara to dominate the imperial court after 880. It can be described as regent to an adult emperor. Cf. Sesshō.

Kangō The 'tally' used to identify official Japanese tribute ships in missions to China during the Muromachi period. It consisted of a slip, stamped with the Chinese imperial seal, which bore the two ideographs making up the name Japan. This would be torn in half, one retained in China, the other handed to the Japanese envoy then visiting China. A future envoy would be required to bring the matching half to establish his authenticity.

Kokudaka A form of measurement of land in terms of its annual yield, expressed in units of *koku* (c.5 bushels) of rice. The system came into use in the sixteenth century as a means of assessing land values that was simpler to estimate and more meaningful in feudal terms than money.

Meiji period The reign of the Meiji emperor, properly 1867–1912, but usually taken to start with the overthrow of the Tokugawa in January 1868. Cf. Era-name.

Momoyama period See under Azuchi period.

Muromachi period The years 1336–1573, when the Ashikaga Shogun claimed to exercise authority in Japan from their headquarters in the Muromachi district of Kyoto.

Namboku period The years 1336–92, when Japan had two rival imperial lines. The northern court, supported by the Ashikaga, was in Kyoto. The southern court, comprising Go-Daigo and his descendants, was in exile in the mountains south of the Nara plain. The latter were eventually recognised as legitimate.

Nara period The years 710–84, when the imperial court was located at Nara (Heijō).

Nengō See Era-name.

Ritsuryō **system** The set of institutions, laid down in legal codes and statutes (*ritsuryō*), by which Japan was governed in the eighth and ninth centuries.

Rōjū Elder. The title of members of the senior Tokugawa council in the Edo period, as well as those holding similar office in some daimyo territories.

Sakoku 'Closed country'. The policy of national seclusion, instituted by Tokugawa Iemitsu between 1633 and 1639, by which Japanese were banned from trading or travelling overseas (though some exceptions were made with respect to Ryukyu and southern Korea). Asian traders were still allowed to come to Japanese ports under strict regulation, but among Europeans only the Dutch were given this privilege. The restrictions ended after 1854, when Commodore Perry concluded an agreement 'opening' Japanese ports.

Samurai Members of the feudal military class, usually, though not necessarily, those who were not lords; more formally described as *bushi*. First became a significant element in Japanese society in the late Heian period (q.v.). In time a number of subdivisions took shape, varying in rank and status: see *Gokenin, Gōshi, Hatamoto*.

Sankin-kōtai 'Alternate attendance'. The system, based on Ashikaga precedents, but finalised by the third Tokugawa Shogun, Iemitsu, requiring feudal lords to reside part of the time in the

Shogun's capital. Under the Tokugawa, they were required to spend at least half their time in Edo (in yearly or six-monthly periods, depending on the location of their domains).

Sengoku period The years of civil war from *c.*1460 to 1560; the label derives from Chinese history, where it is usually translated 'Warring States'. The civil wars in Japan continued in fact until 1600, but the last part of the period is more often called Azuchi-Momoyama (q.v.).

Sesshō Regent to an under-age emperor. One of the offices used by the Fujiwara to dominate the imperial court from the late ninth century (cf. Kampaku).

Shōen A private landholding (often misleadingly translated 'manor'). Complex structures of land rights, held under different legal arrangements, which came into existence in the Heian period as a means of escape from the burdens associated with the *ritsuryō* system. Characteristic of Japanese landholding in the medieval period, they were finally broken up by the Sengoku wars.

Shogun Abbreviation of *Sei-i-tai-shōgun*, 'barbarian-subduing generalissimo'. This was originally an imperial title, bestowed on the commanders of forces that were employed against the turbulent frontier tribes of the north, but it was taken by Japan's *de facto* feudal rulers from the late twelfth century to give a supposed legitimacy to their power (cf. Bakufu).

Shōwa period The reign of the Shōwa emperor (Hirohito), 1926–89. Cf. Era-name.

Shuin-sen Red seal ships. Japanese junks (some foreign owned) that were licensed to trade to the ports of south China and Southeast Asia in the late sixteenth and early seventeenth centuries. Permits, each for a single voyage, were first issued under the vermillion seal (*shuin*) by Hideyoshi in 1590. Tokugawa Iemitsu brought the practice to an end in 1635 as part of his policy of 'closing' the country (cf. *Sakoku*).

Shūshin 'Ethics'. The course in Confucian ethics and nationalist ideology, taught in Japanese schools from the Meiji period to 1945.

Sonnō-jōi 'Honour the emperor, repel the barbarian'. The slogan under which mid-nineteenth-century samurai activists set out to rally opposition to the foreign treaties and Tokugawa rule.

Taishō period The reign of the Taishō emperor, 1912–26. Cf. Era-name.

Tozama daimyō See under Daimyo.

Ukiyo 'Floating world'. Term used to describe the life and culture of *chōnin* of the cities of the Edo period, typically the world of actors and courtesans.

Wakō Japanese pirates, in particular those (not all Japanese) who attacked the coasts of China and Korea between the thirteenth and sixteenth centuries.

Yamato The oldest Japanese name for Japan. In historic times, the name of a province extending southward from Nara.

Zaibatsu 'Financial cliques'. More specifically, the large family owned financial-commercial-industrial combines of modern Japan before 1945.

BIBLIOGRAPHY

This list includes no books in Japanese. Although the work of Japanese scholars provides the foundation for almost all modern publications on Japanese history in western languages, this one is not primarily intended for those who can read Japanese, so a few Japanese works are listed in translation, but not otherwise. Section A cites a small number of general works, from which readers can obtain more detail than is given in the text. Most contain useful bibliographies of their own. Section B adds a selection of translations and more specialist studies, chosen for the light they throw on particular periods or aspects of Japanese history. The list as a whole is not intended to be exhaustive or representative.

Section A: General works

The most considerable English-language treatment of Japanese history is *The Cambridge History of Japan* (Cambridge: Cambridge University Press, 1988–). It is eventually to consist of 6 volumes, but vol. 2 has not yet appeared. Among works by individuals, the best is that by George Sansom, *A History of Japan* (3 vols, London: Cresset, 1958, 1961, 1964). The same author's earlier book, *Japan: A short cultural history* (rev. edn, London: Cresset, 1962; first published in 1931), is in some respects out of date, but is still worth reading for its insights on many topics (especially Buddhism, perhaps). Both Sansom's books end with the Edo period. For a general survey of the modern period, see W. G. Beasley, *The Rise of Modern Japan* (London: Weidenfeld and Nicolson, 1990). Ryusaku Tsunoda (ed.), *Sources of Japanese Tradition* (New York: Columbia University Press, 1958; later issued as a paperback in 2 vols) provides a range of translations on a wide variety of subjects, both political and cultural, for the premodern and modern periods.

The following books all examine more limited aspects of Japanese history over long periods of time: Takeo Yazaki, *Social Change and the City in Japan* (Tokyo: Japan Publications, 1968); Joseph M. Kitagawa, *Religion in Japanese History* (New York: Columbia University Press, 1966); Shuichi Kato, *A History of Japanese Literature* (3 vols, London: Macmillan, 1979–83); Donald Keene (ed.), *Anthology of Japanese Literature* (London: Allen and Unwin, 1956); Robert Treat Paine and Alexander Soper, *The Art and Architecture of Japan* (Harmondsworth: Penguin, 1955); Akiyama Terukazu, *Japanese Painting* (Cleveland, Ohio: Skira, 1961); Sugimoto Masayoshi and David L. Swain, *Science and Culture in Traditional Japan, AD 600–1854* (Cambridge, Mass: MIT, 1978).

Section B: *Translations and specialist studies*

(1) ANCIENT PERIOD

The most useful of the early chronicles, translated by W. G. Aston, is *Nihongi: Chronicles of Japan from the earliest times to AD 697* (reprint, London: Allen and Unwin, 1956 [1896]). Also of interest (though not easy to find) is R. Tsunoda and C. C. Goodrich, *Japan in the Chinese Dynastic Histories* (South Pasadena, Calif.: Perkins, 1951). Of J. E. Kidder's works on prehistoric Japan, *Early Japanese Art* (London: Thames and Hudson, 1964) concentrates on the tomb culture. Edwin O. Reischauer, *Ennin's Travels in T'ang China* (New York: Ronald, 1955), gives an account of a Japanese tribute mission to China in the ninth century. On Heian art and society there are two good studies: Rose Hempel, *The Heian Civilization of Japan* (Oxford: Phaidon, 1983), and Ivan Morris, *The World of the Shining Prince: Court life in ancient Japan* (London: Oxford University Press, 1964; Harmondsworth: Penguin, 1969). Helen Craig McCullough has translated a chronicle of the period: *Ōkagami, the Great Mirror: Fujiwara Michinaga (966–1027) and his times* (Princeton, NJ: Princeton University

Press, 1980). The most famous piece of prose literature of Heian, Murasaki Shikibu's novel *The Tale of Genji*, has most recently been translated by Edward Seidensticker (Harmondsworth: Penguin, 1981).

(2) MEDIEVAL PERIOD (C. 1150–1550)

John W. Hall, *Government and Local Power in Japan 500 to 1700* (Princeton, NJ: Princeton University Press, 1966), is an important study of political institutions in the context of feudalism. More colourful in its subject-matter is Paul Varley, *Warriors of Japan as Portrayed in the War Tales* (Honolulu: Hawaii University Press, 1994). Several medieval chronicles have been translated: Delmer M. Brown and Ichiro Ishida, *The Future and the Past: A translation and study of the Gukanshō* (Berkeley, Calif.: California University Press, 1979); Paul Varley, *A Chronicle of Gods and Sovereigns: Jinnō Shōtōki of Kitabatake Chikafusa* (New York: Columbia University Press, 1980); Helen Craig McCullough, *The Taiheiki* (New York: Columbia University Press, 1959). Wang Yi-t'ung, *Official Relations between China and Japan 1368–1549* (Cambridge, Mass: Harvard University Press, 1953), though not very readable, is the best-documented account in English of Ashikaga relations with the mainland. Marion Ury, *Tales of Times Now Past* (Berkeley, Calif.: California University Press, 1979), translates sixty-two tales from *Konjaku monogatari*, providing a representative sample of medieval fiction. On art, Shimizu Yoshiaki (ed.), *Japan: The shaping of daimyo culture 1185–1868* (London: Thames and Hudson, 1989), is the annotated catalogue of a very good exhibition, while Hideo Okudaira, *Emaki: Japanese picture scrolls* (Rutland and Tokyo: Tuttle, 1962), describes a medieval art form that is of immense value to the historian. Both books are lavishly illustrated.

(3) EARLY MODERN PERIOD (C. 1550–1850)

Japanese history from the sixteenth century has an extensive literature in English as well as Japanese, which makes it more difficult to choose books for inclusion here. One theme has been that of the Tokugawa political structure, widely held to be distinctive, if not unique. The chapters on the subject by John W. Hall and Harold Bolitho in vol. 4 of the *Cambridge History* provide the best summary. More controversial has been the question of how far social and economic change in the Edo period paved the way for later modernisation. A recent survey is Chie Nakane and Shinzaburō Ōishi, *Tokugawa Japan: The social and economic antecedents of modern Japan* (Tokyo: Tokyo University Press, 1990). Gilbert Rozman has made a comparison of Chinese and Japanese cities and towns in *Urban Networks in Ch'ing China and Tokugawa Japan* (Princeton, NJ: Princeton University Press, 1973). An older but still useful work is Charles Sheldon, *The Rise of the Merchant Class in Tokugawa Japan 1600–1868* (rev. edn, New York, 1973 [1958]). Ronald Dore has examined the role of education in *Education in Tokugawa Japan* (London: Routledge, 1965). Maruyama Masao considers some of the implications of intellectual history in this context: *Studies in the Intellectual History of Tokugawa Japan*, trans. Mikiso Hane (Princeton, NJ, and Tokyo: Princeton University Press and Tokyo University Press, 1974). Eiko Ikegami has more recently analysed the effect of changing circumstance on the samurai code in *The Taming of the Samurai* (Cambridge, Mass.: Harvard University Press, 1995).

Much of Edo prose fiction is a commentary on contemporary society. See, for example, Howard Hibbett, *The Floating World in Japanese Fiction* (Oxford: Oxford University Press, 1959), which includes some translated material, and G. W. Sargent, *The Japanese Family Storehouse . . . Translated from the 'Nippon Eitai-gura' of Ihara Saikaku* (Cambridge: Cambridge University Press, 1959). Art is very well illustrated in William Watson (ed.), *The Great Japan Exhibition: Art of the Edo period 1600–1868* (London: Royal Academy of Arts, 1981). On the woodblock print, the Edo art

form best known in the West, see Sadao Kikuchi, *A Treasury of Japanese Wood Block Prints, Ukiyo-e* (New York: Crown, 1969).

Another major topic is that of Japan's relationship with the outside world before and during the years of national seclusion. George Sansom, *The Western World and Japan* (New York and London: Knopf, 1950), is a perceptive survey of the cultural aspects, in particular. Michael Cooper (ed.), *They Came to Japan: An anthology of European reports on Japan 1543–1640* (London: Thames and Hudson, 1965), offers some fascinating sidelights. George Elison, *Deus Destroyed: The image of Christianity in early modern Japan* (Cambridge, Mass.: Harvard University Press, 1973), examines Japanese anti-Christian sentiment; Ronald P. Toby, *State and Diplomacy in Early Modern Japan* (Princeton, NJ: Princeton University Press, 1984), takes a revisionist look at the nature of seclusion; and Donald Keene, *The Japanese Discovery of Europe 1720–1830* (rev. edn, Stanford, Calif.: Stanford University Press, 1969; first published 1952), is chiefly concerned with 'Dutch studies' in Japan.

(4) THE MODERN PERIOD (FROM C. 1850)

The general works cited in Section A deal quite fully with the main strands of modern political and economic history. They can usefully be supplemented by Oka Yoshitake, *Five Political Leaders of Modern Japan: Itō Hirobumi, Ōkuma Shigenobu, Hara Takashi, Inukai Tsuyoshi, Saionji Kimmochi* (Tokyo: Tokyo University Press, 1986), since such biographies are hard to come by in English. The reforms carried out after 1945 have been reconsidered in some detail in Robert E. Ward and Sakamoto Yoshikazu, *Democratizing Japan: The Allied Occupation* (Honolulu: Hawaii University Press, 1987). An earlier book by Kazuo Kawai, *Japan's American Interlude* (Chicago, Ill.: Chicago University Press, 1960), provides a moderately conservative Japanese viewpoint on the same subject. Readers who have a technical interest in economic questions would do well to seek guidance elsewhere, but W. W. Lockwood, *The Economic Development of Japan: Growth and structural change*

1868–1938 (Princeton, NJ and Oxford: Princeton University Press and Oxford University Press, 1955), is an admirable introduction, jargon-free and non-mathematical. The postwar years have been abandoned to the economists.

Japan's response to the West in the mid-nineteenth century, which has played a key part in modern history, has been widely studied. Marius Jansen, *Sakamoto Ryōma and the Meiji Restoration* (Princeton, NJ: Princeton University Press, 1961), looks in some detail at the samurai activists of the 1860s. W. G. Beasley, *Japan Encounters the Barbarian: Japanese travellers in America and Europe* (New Haven, Conn.: Yale University Press, 1995), is a study of the Japanese who went overseas as diplomats or students, in order to learn about the West (plus some of their predecessors). In *The Autobiography of Fukuzawa Yukichi* (reprint, New York: Columbia University Press, 1966 [1934]), one such traveller gives his own account of his motives and experiences. An historical novel by Shimazaki Tōson, *Yo-ake Mae*, translated by William Naff under the title *Before the Dawn* (Honolulu: Hawaii University Press, 1987), reconstructs local attitudes to the events of the Restoration years in a rural part of Japan.

More analytically, Carol Gluck, *Japan's Modern Myths* (Princeton, NJ: Princeton University Press, 1985), traces some of the later repercussions of the stimulus given in this period to Japanese nationalism, while Robert K. Hall (ed.), *Kokutai no Hongi*, trans. J. O. Gauntlett (Cambridge, Mass.: Harvard University Press, 1949), makes available a major text used for the 'ethics' course in schools in the twentieth century. Herbert Passin, *Society and Education in Japan* (reprint, Tokyo: Kodansha, 1982 [1965]), treats education more widely, starting from the Edo period and including a number of translated documents.

Foreign policy after the Restoration has inevitably come in for a great deal of attention. Ian Nish, *Japanese Foreign Policy 1869–1942* (London: Routledge, 1977), provides an excellent introduction. There are several studies of important aspects of the subject: Marius Jansen, *Japan and China: From war to peace, 1894–1972* (Chicago, Ill.: Rand McNally, 1975); W. G. Beasley, *Japanese*

Imperialism 1894–1945 (Oxford: Clarendon, 1987); Ramon Myers and Mark Peattie, *The Japanese Colonial Empire 1895–1945* (Princeton, NJ: Princeton University Press, 1984); Peter Duus, Ramon Myers and Mark Peattie, *The Japanese Informal Empire in China 1895–1937* (Princeton, NJ: Princeton University Press, 1989). On the Pacific War and its origins there are many books, some of them polemical. John Toland, *The Rising Sun: The rise and fall of the Japanese empire 1936–1945* (London: Cassell, 1971), is one of the more sober. Saburō Ienaga, *Japan's Last War* (Oxford: Blackwell, 1979), exemplifies the viewpoint of the Japanese liberal left, while Joyce Lebra (ed.), *Japan's Greater East Asia Co-Prosperity Sphere in World War II* (Kuala Lumpur: Oxford University Press, 1975) provides some very much needed documentary material.

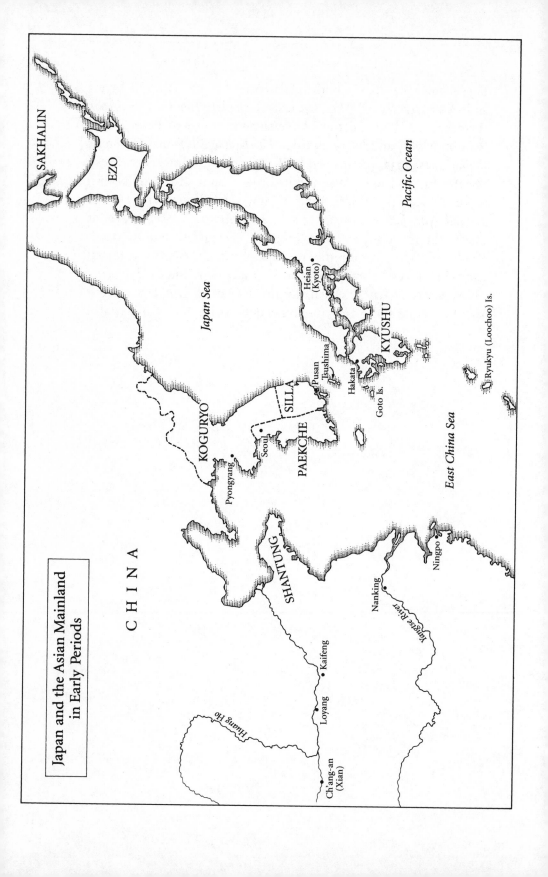

Japan and the Asian Mainland
in Early Periods

CHINA

SAKHALIN

EZO

Japan Sea

Pacific Ocean

KOGURYO

Pyongyang

Seoul

SILLA

PAEKCHE

Pusan

Tsushima

Heian
(Kyoto)

KYUSHU

Hakata

Goto Is.

Ryukyu (Loochoo) Is.

East China Sea

SHANTUNG

Ningpo

Nanking

Yangtse River

Kaifeng

Loyang

Ch'ang-an
(Xian)

Huang Ho

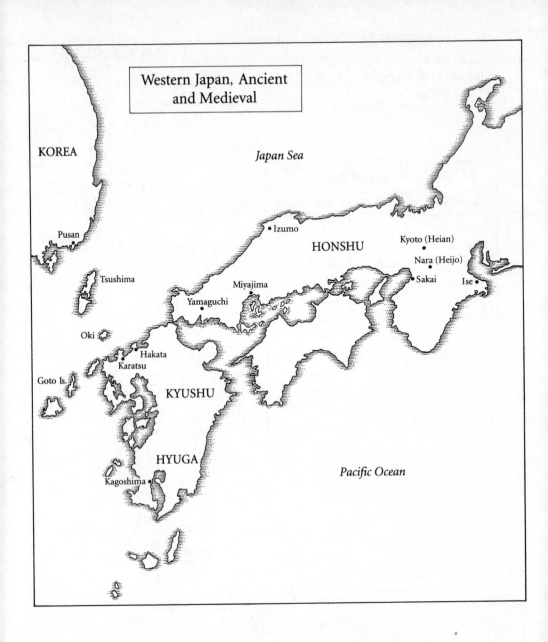

Western Japan, Ancient and Medieval

KOREA

Japan Sea

Pusan

HONSHU

• Izumo

Kyoto (Heian) •

Nara (Heijo) •

Tsushima

Miyajima

• Sakai

Ise •

Yamaguchi

Oki

Hakata

Karatsu

KYUSHU

Goto Is.

HYUGA

Pacific Ocean

Kagoshima •

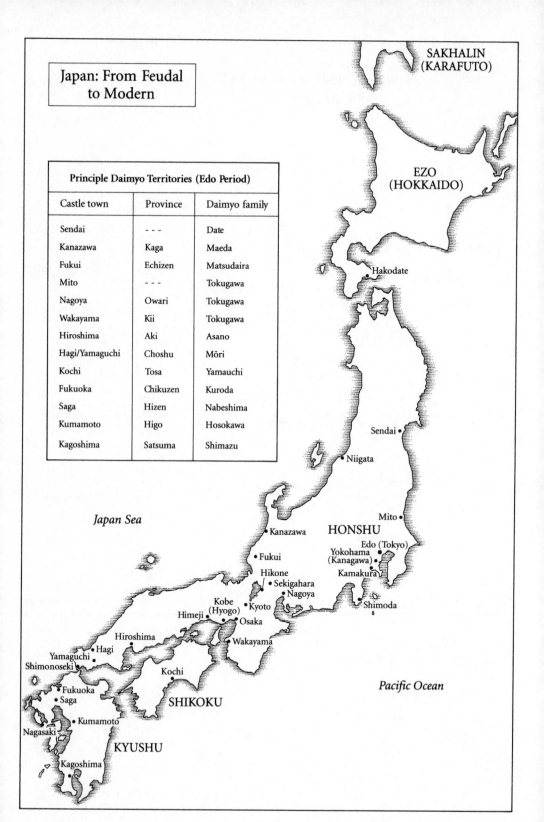

Japan: From Feudal to Modern

Principle Daimyo Territories (Edo Period)

Castle town	Province	Daimyo family
Sendai	- - -	Date
Kanazawa	Kaga	Maeda
Fukui	Echizen	Matsudaira
Mito	- - -	Tokugawa
Nagoya	Owari	Tokugawa
Wakayama	Kii	Tokugawa
Hiroshima	Aki	Asano
Hagi/Yamaguchi	Choshu	Mōri
Kochi	Tosa	Yamauchi
Fukuoka	Chikuzen	Kuroda
Saga	Hizen	Nabeshima
Kumamoto	Higo	Hosokawa
Kagoshima	Satsuma	Shimazu

SAKHALIN
(KARAFUTO)

EZO
(HOKKAIDO)

Hakodate

Sendai

Niigata

Japan Sea

Mito

HONSHU

Kanazawa

Edo (Tokyo)
Yokohama
(Kanagawa)

Fukui

Kamakura

Hikone
Sekigahara
Nagoya

Shimoda

Kobe
(Hyogo) Kyoto

Himeji   Osaka

Wakayama

Hiroshima

Hagi

Yamaguchi

Shimonoseki

Kochi

Pacific Ocean

Fukuoka
Saga

SHIKOKU

Kumamoto

Nagasaki

KYUSHU

Kagoshima

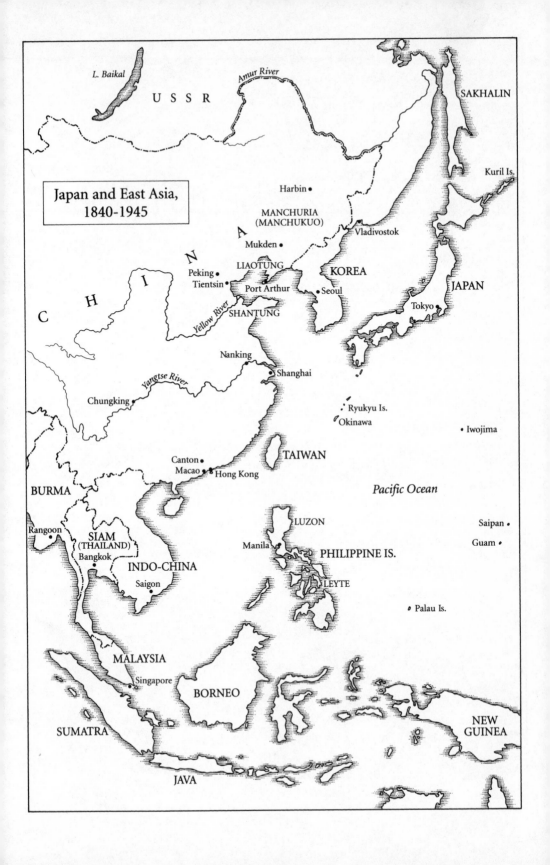

Japan and East Asia,
1840-1945

L. Baikal

U S S R

Amur River

SAKHALIN

Kuril Is.

Harbin

MANCHURIA
(MANCHUKUO)

C H I N A

Vladivostok

Mukden

LIAOTUNG

KOREA

JAPAN

Peking

Tientsin

Port Arthur

Seoul

Tokyo

SHANTUNG

Yellow River

Nanking

Shanghai

Yangtse River

Chungking

Ryukyu Is.

Okinawa

Iwojima

Canton

Macao

Hong Kong

TAIWAN

Pacific Ocean

BURMA

Rangoon

SIAM
(THAILAND)

Bangkok

INDO-CHINA

Saigon

LUZON

Manila

PHILIPPINE IS.

Saipan

Guam

LEYTE

Palau Is.

MALAYSIA

Singapore

BORNEO

NEW
GUINEA

SUMATRA

JAVA

INDEX

Abe Masahiro, 192
agriculture: early, 63, 65–6, 96; Edo
  period, 152–3, 159, 162–3, 165;
  modern, 242, 258, 261
Akechi Mitsuhide, 123–4
Akutagawa Ryūnosuke, 74
Alcock, Rutherford, 195, 197
'alternate attendance', see sankin-kōtai
Amaterasu, 3–5, 17, 29, 47, 105–6, 178
America, see United States
Amida (Amitabha), 47, 70, 75, 100,
  101, 104
Amidism, 70–1, 100–1, 172
ancestor worship, 16, 173
Andō Hiroshige, 187
Anglo-Japanese alliance, 234, 237, 239
anti-monopoly law, 153, 259
Antoku, emperor, 80, 81
Arai Hakuseki, 175, 176
architecture: ancient, 31–2, 33–4, 56;
  feudal, 110–12, 113, 169–70,
  183–4; modern, 225
army: 1868–1930, 213, 232, 234–5,
  238–9, 241; 1930–45, 243–4, 246–
  7, 248; political activities of, 218,
  236–7, 240, 242–4, 249; after 1945,
  252, 255
art: early, 56–9, 75–7; Buddhist
  influence on, 56–8, 75; medieval,
  98–9, 110–15; after 1600, 183–7,
  226, 265–6
Asakura Toshikage, 118, 121–2, 123
ashigaru, 118, 121, 155; glossary, 269
Ashikaga house, 79, 89–91, 93, 94, 97,
  105, 118; fall of, 116, 117, 122–3
Ashikaga Takauji, 89–90, 93, 94, 106,
  108, 118
Ashikaga Yoshiaki, 122–3, 130
Ashikaga Yoshimasa, 99, 112, 115
Ashikaga Yoshimitsu, 91, 94, 99, 103,
  109, 111

Ashikaga Yoshinori, 96–7
Asia, policy towards: after 1905,
  236–9, 242–6
astronomy, 52–3, 176, 203
Asuka period, 30, 31; glossary, 269
atom bombs, 231, 249
Australia, 247
Azuchi period, 124; castle, 183;
  glossary, 269

baishin, 154
Bakufu: glossary, 269; see separately
  under Kamakura period,
  Muromachi period, Edo period
balance of payments, postwar, 260, 261
Ban Dainagon e-kotoba, 77
banking, modern, 223, 224, 261
Bank of Japan, 223
Bashō, see Matsuo Bashō
Betavia, 138
be, 14
Benkei, 81
biwa, 49, 60, 107
bodhisattvas, 41, 46, 47, 48, 71, 75
Bolshevik Revolution, 238
bonsai, 99, 115
Britain, relations with: 1840–68, 190–
  1, 192–3, 197–200, 204–5, 206–7;
  1868–1930, 230, 234, 236, 238, 239;
  1930–45, 245–6, 247
bronze age, 8
Buddhism: introduction of, 13, 20–1,
  41–2, 42–6, 51; and Shinto, 18, 42–
  8; after mid-Heian, 70–1, 88, 100–
  4, 172, 267
Buddhist sects, see Hossō, Jōdo, Jōdo
  Shinshū, Kegon, Nichiren, Ritsu,
  Shingon, Tendai, Zen
bugaku, 59–60
bugyō, 126, 132
Buke Shohatto, 130–1, 132

bureaucracy: Nara and Heian, 26–9, 39; feudal, 96, 133, 156, 157–8; modern, 215, 217, 221, 253, 256, 258, 259
burial mounds (*kofun*), 6, 9–10
Burma campaign, 247, 248
bushi, see samurai
Bushidō, 156–7
business leaders, in postwar politics 255–6
Buson, *see* Yosa Buson
butsudan, 172
Byōdōin, 75

cabinet system, modern, 215, 217, 218, 253
calendars, Chinese, 23–4, 51, 52–3
Canada, 238
capital cities, early, 30–4, 79
castles, 121, 126, 128–9, 130, 132, 183
censorship, 151, 179, 211
Ch'ang-an, 30, 32, 49, 53, 69
Chang Tso-lin, 240
cha-no-yu, see tea ceremony
Chiang Kai-shek, 239–40, 244
Chikamatsu Monzaemon, 179, 181
China, relations with: early, 6, 12–13, 48–50; medieval, 87–8, 94–5, 103, 134, 135–9, 143–4; Edo period, 139–40, 151, 188, 196; after 1868, 231, 231–2, 237–8, 239–40; after 1930, 243–4, 245, 247, 248, 254, 255
China, and the West, after 1840, 188, 189–90, 193, 234
Chōjū-giga, 77
chōka, 56
chōnin: Edo period, 153, 166–7, 170; urban culture of, 171, 179–87, 265; glossary, 269
Choshu, 93, 155, 196; and the anti-Tokugawa movement, 198, 199–200, 201–3; students sent abroad, 206–7; and Meiji government, 211–12, 216
Christian Century, 134, 147–50

Christianity: arrival of, 147–8; impact on Japan, 147, 149, 150, 151; persecution of, 149, 203; and Meiji thought, 229
chronicles, early, 2–3, 5, 11–12, 16
Chu Hsi, 172–3, 174, 175
Chūai, emperor, 12
Chungking government, 244
Chūshingura, 157, 182
cities, *see* towns and cities
clothing, 32, 169, 225
coal and iron, 234–5
Cocks, Richard, 137–8
Cold War, 252, 253, 254, 255, 257
commerce, domestic: before 1850, 96, 153, 163, 168–9
Confucianism: in early periods, 29, 37, 47, 51–2; in Edo period, 158, 159, 166, 172–6; in modern Japan, 228, 267; *see also* Neo-Confucianism
constitution: Meiji, 214, 216–17, 217–18; postwar, 253
copper exports, 135, 137, 141
'co-prosperity', 238, 247–8
Co-prosperity Sphere, *see* Greater East Asia Co-prosperity Sphere
cotton trade, 142, 165, 169, 224
court ranks, 21, 23, 27–9, 153–4
culture: prehistoric, 2, 8–9, 16–18, 60; early Chinese influence on, 1, 2–3, 9–10, 13, 16, 44–6, 48–60, 62, 76; decline of same, 69–77, 98–9; medieval renewal of, 102–3, 113–15, 171, 172–6; popular (pre-modern), 2, 99, 171, 179–82, 185–7; (modern), 227, 265–6; western influence on, 2, 225–7, 229, 265–6

Daigoji, 58
Daijō-daijin, 25, 94, 124, 215
Daijōkan: Nara period, 25; Meiji period, 211–12, 215; glossary, 269
daikan, 133, 162
daimyo: rise of, 120–2; categories of, 129, 130, 154; control of, 125–6, 129–32; in Edo period, 153–5; after 1868, 211–13, 219; glossary, 270

Dannoura, battle of, 81
Daruma (Bodhidarma), 102
Dazaifu, 26
'democratisation', postwar, 252–4, 254–5
Deshima, 140–1, 150, 203
diaries, Heian, 71–2, 76
Diet (parliament): Meiji, 217, 218, 220; postwar, 253
Dōgen, 102, 172
drama, traditional, see Kabuki, Kyōgen, Nō; for modern drama, see theatre and film
Dutch, see Holland
'Dutch studies' (Rangaku), 185, 203–4, 205
dynastic cycle, Chinese, 19–20, 178
dynastic histories, Chinese, 6, 13

Echizen, 102, 118, 121–2
'economic miracle', postwar, 257–61
Edo (city), 194
Edo period, 79, 129–33, 152–70, 171–87, 188–203; Bakufu in, 79, 130–3, 153–6, 200–3; glossary, 270
education: Nara and Heian, 37, 51–2; Edo, 158–9, 168–9, 174, 176; modern, 221–2, 228–9, 253–4, 264
Education Rescript (1890), 228–9
Egami Namio, 10–11
Eiga monogatari, 74
E-ingakyō, 59
Eisai, 102, 172
electoral system, modern, 217, 218, 253, 256–7
Elgin, Lord, 194–5
e-maki, 59, 71, 76–7, 107, 112, 184, 185; glossary, 270
emperor, authority of: early periods, 4–5, 14–15, 19–20, 23, 29–30, 36–9; medieval period, 79, 82–3, 84–6, 89–91; Edo period, 131–2, 202–3; modern period, 212, 215, 217, 249, 253
emperor: divine descent of, 4–5, 19–20, 29–30, 78, 178; in modern

politics, 217, 227, 228, 252
'emperor system', 218
emperors, abdication of, 37–8
employment structure, postwar, 262–4
England, relations with: before 1840, 137, 138, 140, 150; after 1840, see under Britain
'enlightenment', 209
Ennin, 47–8
Enryakuji, 45, 47, 101, 102, 123
epidemics, 43, 63
era-names (nengō), 23–4; glossary, 270
Europe, relations with: 1500–1700, 134, 136–8, 140–1
Ezo, see Hokkaido

feudalism: origins of, 66–9, 78–9; 1180–1500, 2, 79–97; after 1500, 152–3, 153–8
feudal debt, Edo period, 159–61
firearms, introduction of, 123, 137
flower arrangement, see ikebana
foreign advisers and employees: Meiji period, 213, 216, 217, 221, 223, 225–6
Foreign Ministry, 239, 240
foreign relations, after 1850, 190–200, 203–9, 230–50
foreigners, attacks on (1860s), 197–8, 199
Forty-seven Ronin, 157, 182
France, relations with: after 1850, 191, 194, 195, 200, 202, 205; after 1894, 232, 234, 238, 239
friars, Catholic, 149
fudai daimyo, 129, 130, 132, 154; glossary, 270 (under daimyō)
Fujiwara (city), 30
Fujiwara house, and the imperial court, 20, 28, 34–9, 106
Fujiwara Michinaga, 36, 69
Fujiwara Mototsune, 35, 36
Fujiwara no Fubito, 34
Fujiwara Seika, 173–4
Fujiwara Takanobu, 75, 110

Fujiwara Yoshifusa, 35
fukoku-kyōhei, 208–9; glossary, 270
Fukuchi Genichiro, 206
Fukuzawa Yukichi, 206

gagaku, 59–60
Ganjin (Chien-chen), 44, 57
gekokujō, 116, 152
genin, 65
Genji monogatari (Tale of Genji), 72–3,
   76, 77, 107, 112, 266
genre painting, 185–7
Genshin, 70–1
Germany, relations with, 231, 232,
   234, 237, 245
gigaku, 59, 60
Ginkakuji, 112
go, 39
Goa, 136, 137
Godai Tomoatsu, 207–8, 212, 224
Go-Daigo, emperor, 89–91, 106, 108
Go-Hōjō, 125 and note
gokenin, 82, 83, 84, 85–7, 88, 93, 130;
   glossary, 271
Go-Saga, emperor, 89
Go-Sanjō, emperor, 38, 66
gōshi, 127; glossary, 271
Go-Shirakawa, emperor, 39
Go-Toba, emperor, 84, 85
government, central: Asuka and Nara,
   21–30; Heian, 34–40; medieval,
   82–3, 85, 88, 89–90, 94, 96–7; after
   1550, 125–7, 130–3; modern, 210–
   16, 244, 251, 253–4
government, provincial and local:
   before 1150, 26, 37, 40, 64, 66, 68;
   1150–1850, 83–4, 92–3, 133;
   modern, 212–13, 215, 253–4
gozan, 103
Greater East Asia Co-prosperity
   Sphere, 247–8
Gros, Baron, 194
Guadalcanal, 248
Guam, 246, 248
Gukanshō, 105–6, 107
gunki monogatari, 74, 107

Hachiman, 46, 47, 58
Hagakure, 157
haiku, 180–1
Hakata, 87–8, 120, 135, 139
Hakodate, 192
han, 120–2
Han dynasty, 10, 12
haniwa, 9
Harris, Townsend, 193–5, 197
Hasegawa Tōhaku, 184
hatamoto, 130, 133, 155; glossary, 271
Hayashi Razan, 174
Heian (city), 33–4
Heian period, 33–4, 34–40; glossary,
   271
Heiji incident, 39
Heijō, *see* Nara
Heike monogatari, 108, 109, 179, 181
hibachi, 170
Hidetada, *see* Tokugawa Hidetada
Hideyori, *see* Toyotomi Hideyori
Hideyoshi, *see* Toyotomi Hideyoshi
Hikone, 129, 154
Himeji, 129
Hi no Maru, 196
Hirado, 137, 140, 150
Hirata Atsutane, 177, 178
Hirohito (Shōwa emperor), 242, 246,
   249–50, 251
Hiroshige, *see* Andō Hiroshige
Hiroshima, 249
Hishikawa Moronobu, 186
historical writing, 2–3, 15, 21, 55, 74–
   5, 104–8, 175
Hizen, 212
Hōjō house, 80, 84–5, 88–9, 90, 105,
   114; *see also* Go-Hōjō
Hōjō Tokimasa, 80, 84
Hōjō Tokimune, 87, 114
Hōjō Yasutoki, 85
Hōjō Yoshitoki, 84
Hokkaido (Ezo), 1, 210
Holland, relations with: before 1640,
   137, 138, 140–1, 150; after 1840,
   190, 192, 193, 195, 246–7; *see also*
   'Dutch studies'

Hōnen, 100, 101, 172
Hong Kong, 190, 194, 246, 247
honke, 65
'horse-rider' theory, 9–11
Hōryūji, 21, 44, 58, 75
Hosokawa house, 93
Hossō sect, 44
Hotta Masayoshi, 193, 194
Hyogo (Kobe), 194
Hyuga, 4, 5

Ichinotani, battle of, 81
ideology, modern, 211, 227–9
Iemitsu, *see* Tokugawa Iemitsu
Ieyasu, *see* Tokugawa Ieyasu
Ihara Saikaku, 179–80, 182, 186, 226
Ii house, 154
Ii Naosuke, 192, 194, 195, 197, 198
ikebana, 99, 115, 183, 266
Ikeda (Okayama) house, 155
Ike no Taiga, 184
Iki Is., 1
ikki, 119
Ikkō sect, 119, 123; cf. Jōdo Shinshū
   sect
Imagawa domain, 122
immigration, early periods, 11, 14, 16,
   32, 51
imperial court: as government, 21–30,
   34–9; social and cultural life of, 39–
   40, 219; in Edo period, 153–4, 194,
   198, 202–3
imperial regalia, 4–5, 81, 106
Indonesia, 246, 247
industry: modern, 211, 222–5, 235–6,
   241–2, 244–5; postwar, 251, 257,
   259–60, 261
Ingyō, emperor, 15
In-no-Chō, 38
Inō Tadataka (Chūkei), 203
Inoue Kaoru, 206
Ippen, 101, 112
iron, introduction of, 8, 11
irrigation, 11, 13, 51, 64, 65, 163
Ise, 5, 17, 29
Ise monogatari, 73

Italy, relations with, 245
Itō Hirobumi, 206, 207, 212, 215, 221,
   223; and the Meiji Constitution,
   216–17, 218, 228; and foreign
   policy, 232, 236
Iwakura embassy, 206, 209, 213, 214,
   216
Iwakura Tomomi, 211, 216–17, 218
Iwasaki Yatarō, 224
Iwojima, 249
Izanagi and Izanami, 3
Izumo, 4, 17

Jesuits, 147–9
Jien, 105–6
Jimmu, emperor, 5
Jingikan, 29–30, 227–8
jingū, 16
Jingū, empress, 12, 13, 58
jingū-ji, 47
Jinnō Shōtōki, 106–7
jitō, 83–4, 85, 86–7, 88, 92–3
Jizō (Ksitigarbha), 71, 75
Jōdo (Pure Land) sect, 100–1, 111
Jōdo Shinshū (True Pure Land) sect,
   100–1, 119
Jōmon culture, 8–9

kabane, 14–15
Kabuki drama, 157, 166–7, 181–2,
   226, 266
Kaga (Kanazawa), 119, 129, 165,
   167–8
Kagoshima, 146, 147, 166;
   bombardment of, 199, 200, 201
Kaifeng, 61
Kaifūsō, 55
kakemono, 113, 114, 185
Kakuyu, 77
Kamakura Daibutsu, 111
Kamakura period, 79–89; Bakufu in,
   79, 82–6, 88–9; culture of, 102–4,
   105–6, 108, 110–11, 112; glossary,
   271
kami, 16–18, 29, 37, 44, 46–7, 48, 88;
   glossary, 271

kamikaze, 88, 248
Kammu, emperor, 33
Kamo Mabuchi, 177
Kampaku, 35–6, 39, 89, 131–2;
  glossary, 271
Kanami, 109
kangō, 95; glossary, 271
Kanō Eitoku, 183; school of, 183–4,
  185
Kanto, and the military class, 67, 80,
  82, 94, 95, 125, 128–9
Kara-e, 75
Karafuto, *see* Sakhalin
karō, 155
Katō Kiyomasa, 143
Katsura villa, 170
Katsushika Hokusai, 187
Kazan, emperor, 38
Kegon sect, 44
Keidanren, 256
kemari, 39
Kenchōji, 103, 111
Khubilai Khan, 87, 88
Kibi no Mabiki, 49–50
Kido Takayoshi (Kōin), 211, 213, 214,
  232
Kii (Wakayama), 166
Kinkakuji, 111
Ki no Tsurayuki, 71–2
Kitabatake Chikafusa, 106–7
Kitagawa Utamaro, 186
kōan, 102
Kōfukuji, 44, 101, 110
kofun, 6, 9–10
Koguryŏ, 12–13, 20, 24
Kojiki, 2–3, 11, 16, 29, 55, 177
Kokinshū, 71
kokudaka, 126–7, 129, 130; glossary,
  271
Kokugaku, 178
kokujin, 118–19, 120, 121
Kōmyō, empress, 50–1
Konishi Yukinaga, 143–4
Konjaku monogatari, 73–4, 108, 267
Korea: and early Japanese history, 1,
  2–3, 8–11, 11–13, 49, 51, 60;

relations with, ancient period,
  12–13, 20, 24, 48, 50; feudal period,
  87–8, 141–5, 151, 174; after 1868,
  214, 231–2, 234–5
Korean War, 258
Kōryūji, 21
Kotoku, emperor, 23, 43
Koya, Mt., 45, 75
kubunden, 62, 64, 66
Kuge Shohatto, 131–2
Kujō Kanezane, 83, 105
Kūkai, 45–6, 50, 58
Kumazawa Banzan, 174, 176
Kunaishō, 25
kuni, 14
Kuroda Nagamasa, 143
Kurosawa Akira, 74, 267
Kusanagi, 4, 81
Kusunoki Masashige, 91, 108
Kwantung Army, 236, 240, 243
Kyōgen, 108–10
Kyōgoku, empress, 23
Kyoto (formerly Heian), 164, 165
Kyushu: in early history, 4–5, 6–7, 8,
  24, 50, 87–8; in medieval period,
  95, 124; and foreign relations, 42–
  3, 147–8, 199, 201–3

landholding: after Taika Reform, 23,
  61–2, 62–4; medieval period, 82,
  84–7, 91–2, 118–19, 120–2; after
  1580, 125–7, 129–30; after 1868,
  213–14
language, 2–3, 13, 54–5, 178–9,
  266–7
League of Nations, 239, 243
legal system, *ritsuryō*, 25–6; Edo, 167–
  8; modern, 215–16, 254
Leyte, 248
Liaotung (Kwantung), 232, 234, 235,
  236
Liberal Democrat Party (LDP), 256–
  7, 261
lifestyles, modern, 225, 227, 229, 252,
  265–6
Li Po, 103

literature: Nara and Heian, 54–6, 71–4; medieval, 98–9, 104–10; Edo, 178–82; modern, 226–7, 266–7
London Protocol, 198
Lotus Sutra (Hokke-kyō), 45, 104
Loyang, 30

Macao, 136–7, 140
MacArthur, Gen. Douglas, 248–9, 252
Maeda house, 129
magatama, 4, 10
Manchu (Ch'ing) dynasty, 139, 236–7
Manchukuo, 243
Manchuria, 234, 235–6, 236–7, 239–40, 242; Japanese seizure of, 243, 245
mandala, 58
Mandate of Heaven (t'ien-ming), 29, 106
Mandokoro, 83, 96
manga, 267
Manila, 137, 138, 139, 246, 247, 248
Manyōshū, 55–6, 71, 177
mappō, 70
Maruyama Masao, 174
Maruyama Ōkyo, 184
Masanobu, see Okumura Masanobu
Matsudaira Ieyasu, see Tokugawa Ieyasu
Matsuo Bashō, 179, 180–1, 184
matsuri, 17–18
matsurigoto, 17–18
medicine: Chinese, 49, 51, 53–4, 176; western, 203
Meiji emperor (Mutsuhito), 202, 210
Meiji period, 210–11, 211–29, 230–7; glossary, 271
Meiji Restoration, 200–3, 210
merchants, pre-modern, 96, 160–1, 164, 170
metsuke, 133
Midway Is., 246
Mikawa, 125
military occupation, postwar, 252–4, 258
military science, Edo period, 204

military service: ancient period, 25, 63, 66–7; modern, 213
Minamoto house, 68–9, 79–80, 84, 90, 106
Minamoto Yoritomo, 80–4, 93, 99, 105, 108, 129
Minamoto Yoshiie, 68–9
Minamoto Yoshinaka, 80–1, 108
Minamoto Yoshitsune, 81–2, 108
Ming dynasty, 94–5, 98, 135, 136, 172
mining rights (China), 234, 235, 236
Minister of the Left, see Sadaijin
Minister of the Right, see Udaijin
Ministry of International Trade and Industry (MITI), 259
mirrors, ancient period, 4–5, 8, 10
missions to America and Europe (after 1859), 198, 204–6, 207–8, 221
Mito scholars, 175
Mitsubishi, 223, 224, 259
Mitsui, 223, 259
Miyajima, 69
Mommu, emperor, 27, 34
Momoyama period, 124; glossary, 269 (under Azuchi)
Monchūjo, 83, 85
Mongol invasions, 87–8, 104, 112, 185
monogatari, Heian period, 71, 72–4, 76, 77
Mononobe, 14, 28, 42
Mōri house, 119, 123, 128, 155
Mōri Motonari, 119
Mōri Terumoto, 142
Moronobu, see Hishikawa Moronobu
Mosse, Alfred, 217
Motoda Eifu, 228
Motoori Norinaga, 177–8
Mukden, 240, 243
muraji, 15
Murasaki Shikibu, 72–3
Muretsu, emperor, 15
Muromachi period, 79, 90–7; Bakufu in, 79, 90–1, 93–7; culture of, 103, 106–7, 108–10, 113–15; glossary, 272

music: before 1850, 49, 59–60; modern, 225–6, 265
Musō Soseki, 103

Nagai Kafū, 227
Nagasaki, 133, 136–7, 139, 166, 194, 249; Chinese merchants at, 139–40, 150, 184; and Christianity, 147, 148, 149; *see also* Deshima
Nagoya, 118, 129, 165
Naka-no-Ōe, 23, 24
Nakatomi clan, 14, 21, 42
Nakatomi no Kamatari, 23, 28, 34, 44
Namboku wars, 90–1; glossary, 272
Nanking, 243, 244
Nanzenji, 103
Nara city, 30–3
Nara Daibutsu, 44, 57
Nara period, 24–33; glossary, 272
Nara plain, in early history, 5, 6–7, 9–10, 11, 30
Nara university, ancient period, 51–2
nationalism, 2, 104, 196; *see also* ultranationalism
Natsume Sōseki, 227
navy: after 1868, 213, 232, 234–5, 239, 241; after 1930, 243, 244, 246, 252, 255; in politics, 218, 246, 247, 248
nembutsu, 100, 101, 104
nengō, *see* era-name
Neo-Confucianism, 103, 172–6
Netherlands, *see* Holland
New Order in East Asia, 244–5
Nichiren sect, 104
Nihongi, *see* Nihon Shoki
Nihon Shoki (*Nihongi*), 2, 11, 15, 16, 29, 43, 55
Niigata, 194
Nijō, emperor, 39
Nijō castle, 132
Nikko shrine, 132, 184
Nimitz, Adm. Chester, 247, 248
Ningpo, 94, 95
Ninigi, 4–5
Nintoku, emperor, 9, 10, 11, 14, 15
Nishihara loans, 237–8

Nobunaga, *see* Oda Nobunaga
Nō drama, 99, 108–10, 182, 226
novels: pre-modern, 72–3, 180, 182, 186; modern, 226–7

Oda Nobunaga, 117, 118, 119, 120, 122–4
Odawara, 125
Ōe Hiromoto, 83, 99
Ogyū Sorai, 174, 176, 177
oil supplies, 245, 246, 259–60
Ōjin, emperor, 5, 10, 11–12, 14
Ōkagami, 74–5
Okayama domain, 155
Okinawa, 249
Ōkubo Toshimichi, 211, 213, 214–15, 216, 223
Okumura Masanobu, 186
omi, 15
Ōmura Sumitada, 147, 148
Open Door (China), 236, 239
Opium War, 189–90, 190–1
Osaka: before 1616, 123, 128–9, 130, 132; later Edo period, 133, 139, 165, 194
Ōtomo Sōrin, 147
Ōuchi house, 93, 99, 114, 119, 135
Owari (Nagoya), 118, 129, 165

Pacific War, 231, 246–50; peace moves, 248–50
Paekche, 12–13, 20, 24
painting: before 1550, 58–9, 110, 112–14; Edo period, 182–7; modern, 226, 265–6
Parhae, 50
Parkes, Harry, 195
Peace Preservation Law, 218
peace treaty (1951–2), 254, 259
Pearl Harbor, 246, 247
peasant revolt, 119, 159, 163–4, 220
peerage, modern, 220, 252
Perry, Cdre. Matthew, 191–2, 197, 204, 268
Philippine Is., 247, 248; *see also* Manila

piracy, Japanese, 95, 135–6, 142; *see
also wakō*
Po Chü-i, 55
poetry: in Chinese, 55, 179; in
Japanese, 55–6, 71, 114, 180–1
poetry contests, 39, 112, 126
political institutions: Chinese
influence on, 20–30, 36–7, 61–2,
98–9; western influence on, 210,
213–18, 251, 252–4
political parties: after 1868, 218, 241,
242, 245; after 1945, 251, 254–6,
257
population, 26, 32–3, 154, 159, 165–6
Port Arthur, 234, 235
Portsmouth, Treaty of, 235
Portugal, early relations with, 123,
136–7, 138, 140, 148, 150
Potsdam declaration, 249
prefectures (*ken*), 212
prehistory, 7–11
Press Law, 218
Prince of Wales, HMS, 246
printing and publishing, 112–13, 179,
185, 266–7
prints, woodblock, 185–7, 226, 266
Privy Council, 215
Pu Yi, 243
Public Works, Ministry of, 223
puppet theatre, 181
'purges', postwar, 252, 255, 263
Pusan, 142, 143, 144, 145
Pyongyang, 143

railways: in Japan, 223, 224, 235; in
China, 234, 235, 236, 247
Rangaku, *see* 'Dutch studies'
Rashōmon, 30, 74, 267
recession, after 1990, 257, 259–60
regents: to emperors, 35–6, 39; to
Shogun, 84, 194
rekishi monogatari, 74–5, 107–8
religion, *see separately* Buddhism,
Christianity, Confucianism, Shinto
renga, 114, 180
Repulse, HMS, 246

retired emperors (*In*), 38–9
rice cultivation, 6, 8–9, 64, 65
'reverse course', 255
Rinzai sect, 102–3
Ritsu sect, 44
ritsuryō system, 24–30, 47, 62–4;
glossary, 272
Roches, Léon, 202
Roesler, Hermann, 217
Rōjū, 132; glossary, 272
Rokuhara Tandai, 85
Rokumeikan, 225
rōnin, 157
Russia, relations with: 1850–68, 192,
193, 195, 205, 206; 1894–1930, 231,
232, 234–5, 238; after 1930, 245,
249, 254, 255
Russo-Japanese War, 234–5, 236
Ryoanji, 112
ryōke, 65, 67
Ryō no Gige, 27
Ryukyu (Loochoo), relations with:
before 1850, 7–8, 141, 145–6

Sadaijin (Minister of the Left), 25, 28
Saga, 35
Saichō, 45, 50
Saigō Takamori, 202, 211, 214
Saikaku, *see* Ihara Saikaku
Saipan, 248
Sakai, 120
sake, 96
Sakhalin (Karafuto), 1, 235, 238
sakoku, 151; glossary, 272
samisen, 181
samurai (*bushi*): origins and character,
66–9, 79, 82, 121, 127; Edo period,
131, 153, 154, 155–60, 161, 174–5;
after 1868, 213, 214, 219–20;
glossary, 272
samurai code (Bushidō), 67, 82, 131,
156–7
Samurai-dokoro, 82, 96
Sanjō Sanetomi, 211
sankin-kōtai, 132, 155, 165; glossary,
273

Satsuma, 124, 146, 155, 166; and the anti-Tokugawa movement, 198–9, 200, 201–3; students sent abroad, 206–7; and Meiji government, 211–12, 214; *see also* Shimazu house

science and technology: Chinese, 51, 52–4, 176; western, 147, 148, 159, 203–4, 258

sculpture, 44, 56–8, 110, 111

seclusion, national, *see sakoku*

security pact, American-Japanese, 254, 255, 256

Seiwa, emperor, 35

Sekigahara, battle of, 128, 129, 198

Self Defence Force (SDF), 255

Sengoku period, 117–22; glossary, 273

Sen no Rikyū, 184

Seoul, 143, 144

seppuku, 157

Sesshō, 35–6, 131–2; glossary, 273

Sesshū, 113–14, 184

Settsu, 26

Shaka (Sakyamuni), 44

shamans, 18, 47

Shanghai, 243, 244

Shantung, 8, 234, 237

Sharaku, 186–7

Shiba house, 118

Shiba Kōkan, 203

Shibusawa Ei'ichi, 208, 224

Shidehara Kijūrō, 239, 240, 242, 246

Shigisan engi, 76, 77, 112, 185

shiki, 65, 84, 86, 91, 126

Shikken, 84

Shimabara rebellion, 150

Shimazaki Tōson, 227

Shimazu house, 93, 116, 124, 128, 129, 155

Shimoda, 192, 193, 197

Shimonoseki bombardment, 199–200, 201

Shimonoseki, Treaty of, 232, 234

Shingon sect, 45, 58, 71, 75

Shinran, 100, 101, 172

Shinshū sect, *see* Jōdo Shinshū sect, *also* Ikkō sect

Shinto: in early periods, 2, 16–18, 42–3, 46–8, 88; revival of (Edo period), 176–8; in modern period, 227–8, 252, 267

Shirakawa, emperor, 38

shipping, modern, 223, 224

shishi (samurai activists), 196, 199, 200

shōen: growth of, 61–2, 64–6; after 1185, 83–4, 85–7, 91, 126; glossary, 273

Shogun: office of, 79, 83, 84–5, 89–90, 117; in Edo period, 130, 154, 174–5, 202–3; glossary, 273; cf. Bakufu

Shōmu, emperor, 50

Shoshidai, 132

Shōsōin, 31, 50–1, 59, 114

Shōtoku, Prince, 21–2, 23, 42–3, 44, 75, 268

Shōwa period, 242, 251; glossary, 273; cf. Hirohito, emperor

Shōwa Restoration, 242–3

shrines, 17, 29, 46, 47

shugo, 83–4, 85, 92, 118

shugo-daimyō, 92–3, 96

shuin-sen, 138–9, 150; glossary, 273

shūshin, 228, 252; glossary, 274

Siberian expedition, 238–9

Silk Road, 51

silk trade: pre-modern, 50, 95, 135, 137, 139, 140, 141; after 1860, 189, 196, 223, 224

Silla, 12–13, 20, 24

silver exports, 137, 139, 140, 141

Singapore, 246, 247

slump (1929–30), effects of, 241–2

Sō (Tsushima), 141–2, 144–5

Soami, 112

social structure: Nara and Heian, 27–9, 32–3, 39–40, 52, 62–3, 64–6, 66–9; medieval period, 78–9, 82, 86–7, 91–2, 118–22, 126–7; Edo period, 152–3, 153–9, 161–70; after 1868, 211, 219–21, 222–3, 224–5, 252, 262–3

Soga clan, 14, 21, 22–3, 30, 34, 42–3

sonnō-jōi, 196–7, 208; glossary, 274
Sōtatsu, *see* Tawaraya Sōtatsu
Sōtō sect, 102
Southeast Asia, relations with: after
    1930, 231, 245–6, 246–7, 258,
    260–1
South Manchuria Railway, 235, 236
Spain, early relations with, 137, 138,
    140, 150
standards of living, 168–9, 265
students: sent to China, 21, 22, 23, 49–
    50; sent to the West, 204, 206–7,
    208
Suez Canal, 209
Sugawara Michizane, 36–7, 69, 112
suiboku, 113
Sui dynasty, 20, 21
Suiko, empress, 21
Sujin, emperor, 5
Sumiyoshi, 48
sumō wrestling, 39, 266
Sung dynasty, 61; culture of, 61, 98,
    103, 115, 172–4
Susa-no-o, 3–4, 18
Sword Hunt (Hideyoshi), 127, 161,
    164
swordsmanship, Edo period, 158, 159,
    183

Taiheiki, 108, 179
Taihō Code, 24
Taika Reform, 23–4
Taira house, 68–9, 79–81, 82, 90, 106,
    108
Taira Kiyomori, 80, 81, 108
Taira Masakado, 68
Tairō, 128, 194
Taishō society, 241; glossary, 274
Taiwan, 232, 234
Takachiho, Mt., 4
Takamatsuzuka tomb, 10
Taketori monogatari, 73
Tanegashima, 136
T'ang dynasty, 22, 23, 24, 27, 30, 61,
    62; culture of, 57, 76, 115
tanka, 56

tatami, 169
Tawaraya Sōtatsu, 184
taxation: Nara and Heian, 23, 28, 62–
    4, 66; feudal period, 84, 86–7, 96,
    162–3; modern, 213–14, 220
tea ceremony (*cha-no-yu*), 99, 103,
    114–15, 126, 135, 183, 184
television, 265, 266, 267
Temmu, emperor, 24, 26, 28, 29
Tendai sect, 45, 47, 70, 71, 101, 102,
    104
Tenji, emperor, 24, 28
tennō, 16
Tenryūji, 103
terakoya, 168, 176
Terashima Munenori, 206, 207
textile industry, modern, 223, 224, 259
theatre and film, after 1868, 226, 265,
    267
'thought control', 218, 229
t'ien-ming, 29, 106
Tōdaiji, 31, 43, 44, 46, 57, 101, 110
Tōhaku, *see* Hasegawa Tohaku
Tōjō Hideki, 238, 247
Tokaido, 129, 187
tokonoma, 113, 170
Tokugawa Hidetada, 129, 130, 131,
    145, 149, 150
Tokugawa house, 79, 117, 129–30,
    154; overthrow of, 196–203, 210
Tokugawa Iemitsu, 129, 132, 149, 150
Tokugawa Iemochi, 195
Tokugawa Iesada, 194
Tokugawa Ieyasu, 117, 122, 124, 125,
    174; rise to power and policies of,
    128–32; and foreign relations, 139,
    143, 145, 149
Tokugawa Nariaki, 192, 194, 195
Tokugawa Yoshinobu (Keiki), 194,
    202, 210
Tokushi yoron, 175
Tokyo, made capital, 212
tomo, 14
torii, 46
Tosa, 212, 224
Tosa nikki, 71–2

Tosa school (painting), 184, 185
Tōshōdaiji, 31, 44, 57
towns and cities: before 1600, 30–4,
  120, 121, 164; Edo period, 153,
  164–6; after 1868, 225, 261–2
townsmen, *see chōnin*
Toyokuni, *see* Utagawa Toyokuni
Toyotomi Hideyori, 128–9, 149
Toyotomi Hideyoshi, 117, 123–7, 128,
  129, 130, 152; and foreign relations,
  136, 138, 142–4, 146, 148–9, 231;
  death of, 144
tozama daimyō, 130, 154, 166; glossary,
  270 (under *daimyō*)
trade: with China, pre-modern, 50,
  94–5, 96, 120, 135–41; modern,
  232, 234, 236; with Korea, pre-
  modern, 50, 142, 144–5; modern,
  236; with Southeast Asia, 138–9,
  140, 146; with Europe and
  America, 136–8, 140–1, 148,
  150–1, 196, 259–61
trade disputes, postwar, 260
trade unions, 218, 263
tradition, influence in modern Japan,
  171, 225, 226, 227, 228–9, 251,
  266–7
Trans-Siberian railway, 234, 238
treaties (1854–8): negotiation of, 191–
  5; opposition to, 194, 196–201;
  revision of, 230–1
treaty port system, 190, 194, 195–6,
  200–1, 232, 239
tribute missions: to China, early, 21,
  22, 48–50, 55, 62, 69; 1400–1550,
  94–5, 103, 134; to Japan from Korea
  and Ryukyu, 50, 145, 146
tribute system, Chinese, 23, 48–50,
  141, 144, 146
Tsukiyomi, 3–4
Tsushima, 1, 141–2, 144–5
Tsushima Straits, battle of, 235
Twenty-one Demands, 237
Tycoon (Taikun), 130, 145

Uda, emperor, 36–7

Udaijin (Minister of the Right), 25,
  28
uji, 14, 17
uji-gami, 17
ukiyo, 168, 180, 186–7; glossary, 274
ultranationalism, 241–2, 252
'unequal treaties', *see* treaties (1854–8)
United Nations, 252
United States, relations with: 1853–
  73, 191–5, 199–200, 204–5, 208–9;
  1894–1930, 231, 234, 235, 236, 237,
  238, 239; after 1930, 245–6, 252–4,
  255, 256, 258
universities, modern, 221–2
University College London, 207
Usa shrine, 46, 47
Utagawa Toyokuni, 187
Utamaro, *see* Kitagawa Utamaro

Vairocana, 44, 47
vassalage, 67–8, 155, 156–7
Versailles conference, 239
village society: medieval, 119–20, 121,
  127; Edo, 156, 161–4; modern, 220,
  225
Vladivostock, 234–5, 238

Wa (Wo), 6
waka, 56
wakō, 95, 135–6, 138, 142, 143;
  glossary, 274
Wang Yang-ming, 172, 174
war crimes trials, 252, 267
warfare, pre-modern, 79, 90–1,
  117–18
warriors, *see* samurai
Wei chih, 6–7, 11

Xavier, Francis, 147

Yakushiji, 31, 57–8, 59
Yamaga Sokō, 175–6
Yamagata Aritomo, 215
Yamaguchi, 93, 99, 113–14
Yamatai, 6–7

Yamato: region, 5, 6–7; kingdom, 9–11, 11–15; glossary, 274
Yamato-e, 75, 184
Yayoi culture, 8–9
Yi dynasty, 141, 142
Yi Sun-sin, 143
yōgaku (western studies), 159, 203–4
Yokohama (Kanagawa), 192, 194, 199, 200
Yokohama Specie Bank, 223
Yōrō Code, 24–5, 43
Yosa Buson, 184, 185

Yoshida Shigeru, 255
Yoshida Shōin, 197
Yoshino, 91, 106
Yung Lo, 94
Yūryaku, emperor, 13

zaibatsu, 252–3; glossary, 274
zazen, 102
Zeami, 109
Zen Buddhism, 101–2, 267; cultural influence of, 98, 102–3, 111, 113–15, 172, 173–4, 183

1 (4/00)

4/00

For Minnie

WHO ALONE CREATED THE OPPORTUNITY

AND FOR MY LITTLE DAUGHTER

Judith

WHO SABOTAGED IT DAILY

CONTENTS

PREFACE   xvii

Book I

FROM A CUP OF HEMLOCK TO THE INQUISITION

THE EXAMINED LIFE: *Socrates*   3
   THE APOLOGY:
      Before the Verdict   5
      After the Verdict and Before the Sentence   22
      After the Sentence of Death   25

I PAUL THE PRISONER OF JESUS CHRIST: *St. Paul*   28
   "WHOM I HAVE BEGOTTEN IN MY BONDS"   31
   "I KNOW HOW TO BE ABASED . . . HOW TO ABOUND"   32

THE EIGHTH SPIRIT: *Boethius*   37
   THE CONSOLATION OF PHILOSOPHY   38

BOOKKEEPER OF WONDERLAND: *Marco Polo*   50
   OF THE NOBLE AND MAGNIFICENT CITY OF KIN-SAI   52

PRINCE AND POET: *James I of Scotland*   65
   THE COMING OF LOVE   66

PROTESTANT PIONEER: *John Huss*   70
   THE DREAM OF JOHN HUSS   71
   THE COUNCIL   71
   THE OBSTINATE HERETIC   72

THE PRIVATE VOICE: *Jeanne D'Arc*   75
   THE TRIAL OF JEANNE D'ARC   77

ALAS, POOR YORICK! *François Villon*   99
   THE DUNGEON OF MEUN-SUR-LOIRE. SUMMER OF 1461:
      The Debate Between the Heart and the Body of Villon   100

PITY, TERROR, AND THE LAST JOKE. WINTER OF 1463:

Quatrain   103
The Epitaph in the Form of a Ballade   103
Ballade of the Appeal of Villon   104
The Request of Villon   105

GOD'S AMBASSADOR: *Christopher Columbus*   107
LETTER TO THE NURSE JUANA DE LA TORRES   109

A JURIST IN JAIL: *Hugo Grotius*   119
OF THE LEGAL CONDITION OF PERSONS   120

FOR THINKING IN ASTRONOMY: *Galileo Galilei*   123
GALILEO'S RECANTATION   125

FIRST SAINT OF THE MODERN WORLD: *Giordano Bruno*   127
BRUNO TO THE INQUISITORS   128

I WILL NOT BE SILENT: *Tommaso Campanella*   136
THE CITY OF THE SUN   137

Book II

A COMPANY OF ENGLISHMEN

A WITTY SAINT IN A HAIR SHIRT: *Thomas More*   155
A PROVOKING WIFE   156
THE WOLF, THE ASS, AND THE FOX   158
TALKATIVE NUN AND TALKATIVE WIFE   162
LOVE OF FLATTERY   163
GODLY MEDITATION   166
LETTER TO HIS DAUGHTER MARGARET   168

HAMLET WITHOUT THE PRINCE: *Henry Howard, Earl of Surrey*   169
LAMENT FOR HIS LOST BOYHOOD   170
A SATIRE ON LONDON, THE MODERN BABYLON   172

JOHN DONNE—ANNE DONNE—UNDONE: *John Donne*   174
"MY SUBMISSION, MY REPENTANCE"   176
"IT HATH MUCH PROFITED ME THAT I AM DEJECTED"   177
"AS THE DEVIL IN THE ARTICLE"   178

VIRTUE IN A NAUGHTY WORLD: *George Wither*   179
   IN PRAISE OF POETRY   181
   SATIRE TO KING JAMES   186

MOST LOFTIE, INSOLENT, AND PASSIONATE: *Walter Raleigh*   188
   THE LIE   191
   PREFACE TO THE HISTORY OF THE WORLD   194
   THE CONCLUSION   198
   THE PASSIONATE MAN'S PILGRIMAGE   199
   A LETTER TO HIS WIFE   201
   EVEN SUCH IS TIME   203

THE AXE'S EDGE: *Charles I of England*   204
   CHARLES I TO THE PRINCE OF WALES   206

PRISON AS A GENTLEMAN'S ART: *Richard Lovelace*   216
   TO ALTHEA. FROM PRISON   217
   THE VINTAGE TO THE DUNGEON   218
   A MOCK-SONG   219
   TO LUCASTA. FROM PRISON   220

THE PRIGGISH LITTLE CLERK: *James Howell*   223
   "I WAS COMMITTED TO THE FLEET"   224
   "YOU WRITE TO ME OF WIVING"   225
   "AND SO I FELL A-THINKING HOW . . . TO MAKE MY LAST WILL"   227
   "A PARCEL OF INDIAN PERFUME . . . BUT WE CALL IT TOBACCO"   229
   A PERFECT DESCRIPTION OF THE PEOPLE AND COUNTRY OF SCOTLAND   231

THE CHIEF OF SINNERS: *John Bunyan*   237
   THE DEVIL AND JOHN BUNYAN:
     The Temptation of the Bells   239
     Of the Poor Women Sitting at a Door in the Sun   240
     Thou Art My Love, Thou Art My Love   242
     Sell Him, Sell Him, Sell Him   243
     The Hound of Heaven   245
     City of the Living God   246
   VANITY FAIR   246

THE MAN IN LEATHER: *George Fox*   255
   FROM THE JOURNALS OF GEORGE FOX:

The Interview with Oliver Cromwell   258

"a nasty, stinking place"   260

"why don't ye imprison the Book?"   263

THE PEOPLE'S ANCIENT AND JUST LIBERTIES ASSERTED IN THE TRIAL OF *William Penn* AND *William Mead*   271

    WILLIAM PENN TO THE ENGLISH READER   271

    THE TRIAL   273

PILLORY WITH FLOWERS: *Daniel Defoe*   289

    A HYMN TO THE PILLORY   292

Book III

CONSCIENCE OF THE NEW WORLD

FORTY THEOCRATS AND A WOMAN: *Anne Hutchinson*   307

    THE EXAMINATION OF MRS. ANNE HUTCHINSON   309

Book IV

A CYCLE OF REVOLUTIONS

QUEEN OF THE GIRONDISTS: *Madame Roland*   343

    SELF-PORTRAIT   344

    THE COMMUNE OF PARIS: MAY 31, 1793   349

    "FOR WHOM I DESIRED LIBERTY"   353

PITY AND THE GUILLOTINE: *Camille Desmoulins*   356

    "A 'C' AND A 'D', OUR TWO NAMES"   357

    "I DIE THE VICTIM OF THOSE JESTS"   358

THE BLOOD OF A POET: *André Chénier*   363

    SAINT-LAZARE (in French)   364

    SAINT-LAZARE (in English)   365

THE CONSPIRACY OF THE EQUALS: *Gracchus Babeuf*   370

    "A SACRIFICE THAT FRIENDSHIP CAN MAKE": BABEUF'S REQUEST   372

FOUNDING FATHERS' POOR RELATION: *Thomas Paine*   377
APPEAL TO THE CONVENTION   380
MEMORIAL ADDRESSED TO JAMES MONROE   382

A GIBBET AND A GENTLEMAN: *Major John André*   392
TWO LETTERS TO GEORGE WASHINGTON:
   "The person in your possession is Major John André"   394
   "not to die on a gibbet"   395

A PRISONER OF WAR: *Mordecai Sheftall*   396
CAPTURE OF MORDECAI SHEFTALL, & ETC.   397

THE FIRST OF THE BLACKS: *Toussaint L'Ouverture*   400
MEMOIR OF GENERAL TOUSSAINT L'OUVERTURE, WRITTEN BY HIMSELF   402

THE PRISONER OF EUROPE: *Napoleon*   426
ELBA: A CORRESPONDENCE   429
AS THEMISTOCLES DID   437
ST. HELENA: A DIARY   438

Book V

IRISH TESTAMENT

THE PATRIOT: *Robert Emmet*   449
SPEECH IN THE DOCK   451

A PRISONER WITH A DIARY: *John Mitchel*   458
A BLAST AGAINST MACAULAY AND BACON   459
DOPPELGANGER AND THE EGO   470

IRELAND OR ISOLDE: *Charles Stewart Parnell*   483
PARNELL TO KATHERINE O'SHEA   485

OF THE IRISH EARTH: *Michael Davitt*   489
LECTURES TO A PET BLACKBIRD, OR THE ANATOMY OF THE UNDERWORLD:
   Preface to a Blackbird   490
   First Lecture to a Blackbird, Or the Thievocracy   491
   Second Lecture to a Blackbird, Or a Lesson in Slang   495
   Third Lecture to a Blackbird, Or Birds in a Cage   498
   Epilogue to a Blackbird   505

BALFOUR'S CRIMINAL: *Wilfrid Scawen Blunt*   506

IN VINCULIS:
Sonnets Written in an Irish Prison, 1888   507

EASTER RISING 1916: *Padraic Pearse*   516
THE WAYFARER   517

THE SHIRT OF NESSUS: *Roger Casement*   518
"IF IT BE TREASON . . ."   520

THE COUNTESS AND THE PEOPLE: *Constance Markievicz*   531

LETTERS TO EVA GORE-BOOTH:
Of Bills, Wigs, and Naptha Balls   533
Of Poems, Wild Geese, and Blake   536
"the brown wind of Connaught"   540
"president of so many things"   543

Book VI

THE NINETEENTH CENTURY

THE WIT IN THE DUNGEON: *Leigh Hunt*   549
THE FABLE OF THE FISH   552
OF THE UNPHILOSOPHICAL CONDUCT OF SIR HUMPHREY DAVY   554
BONAPARTE FALLEN AND LONDON IN APRIL   560
ELBA'S ONE HUNDRED AND ONE ROUNDS OF CANNON   563

EIGHT MILLIONS OF FREE PEOPLE: *An American Oration*   568
"I RECITE THESE THINGS, MY COUNTRYMEN, THAT YOU MAY KNOW HOW
TO PRIZE LIBERTY"   568

YANKEE PERFECTIONIST: *William Lloyd Garrison*   572
TO THE EDITOR OF THE BOSTON COURIER   575
A CARD: TO MR. FRANCIS TODD, MERCHANT, OF NEWBURYPORT, MASSACHU-
SETTS   575
FREEDOM OF THE MIND   576

OF DECEMBER 2, 1859: *John Brown*   578
THE CROSS-EXAMINATION OF JOHN BROWN FOR THE ASSAULT ON HARPER'S
FERRY   581

THE LAST SPEECH   589
JOHN BROWN'S WILL   590
ONE MORE SENTENCE   591

DROLL STORY: *Honoré de Balzac*   592
"THIS IS ONE OF THE THOUSAND ACCIDENTS OF OUR PARISIAN LIFE" 594

THE CRIME AND THE PUNISHMENT: *Fyodor Dostoevsky*   601
FROM THE PETER-AND-PAUL FORTRESS   603
A LETTER FROM SIBERIA   611

LITTLE FATHER AND THE PENITENT: *Michael Bakunin*   622
CONFESSION TO THE CZAR   625
BAKUNIN AS "IMPLORING CRIMINAL"   643

THE BOHEMIAN AND THE CRUCIFIX: *Paul Verlaine*   648
LE CIEL (in French)   649
AUTRE (in French)   650
O MON DIEU, VOUS M'AVEZ BLESSÉ D'AMOUR (in English)   651

MRS. GRUNDY AND THE FAT BOY: *Oscar Wilde*   654
"I SIT BETWEEN GILLES DE RETZ AND THE MARQUIS DE SADE"   656
"I DON'T DEFEND MY CONDUCT, I EXPLAIN IT"   658
FROM DE PROFUNDIS   660

GRANDEE OF THE GAS-LIGHT ERA: *O. Henry*   669
JABBERWOCKY FOR MARGARET   671

Book VII

IN OUR TIME

MY HONOR! MY HONOR! *Alfred Dreyfus*   681
LETTERS TO LUCIE   684
FROM THE DIARY ON DEVIL'S ISLAND   689

A SPANISH DREYFUS: *Francisco Ferrer*   694
"I BEG EVERY EDITOR"   696
"I WILL TRY TO TELL YOU ABOUT MY CASE"   698
AN INTERRUPTED LETTER   704
TESTAMENT OF A RATIONALIST   705
EDUCATION: FOR SOLEDAD   706

THE GREAT PRISONERS : *Contents*

CONVICT No. 9653: *Eugene V. Debs* 707
"DEAR SIR AND BROTHER" 709
"YOUR HONOR" 713

THE POLITICAL MAN: *Vladimir Ilyich Lenin* 718
BOOKS, BOOKS, AND THE WRONG UNDERWEAR 720

RED ROSA: *Rosa Luxemburg* 726
LETTERS TO SONIA LIEBKNECHT:
Corsica 728
Double Cage 729
Life is indivisible 730
"I belong more to the titmice than to my 'comrades'" 731
"this huge lunatic asylum" 733
State of joy . . . and pity 736
Birds 738
Free Soon 740

LETTERS TO HANS:
"kindness and pride" 740
Of economics and lake nostalgia 743
Botany 745
A Wasp 747
The Prism 747
Lonely 749

THE BATTLE AND THE BOOK: *Adolf Hitler* 753
YEARS OF STUDY AND SUFFERING IN VIENNA 755

I WAS A GERMAN: *Ernst Toller* 761
LETTERS:
To Fritz von Unruh 764
To Tessa 764
To Mrs. L. 766
To Tessa 767
To Tessa 769
To the Governor of the Fortress 770
To Professor Theodor Lessing 772
To Romain Rolland 772
To Stefan Zweig 773

THEY CAUGHT A TARTAR: *Georgi Dimitrov* 775
NOTES FOR A SPEECH 776

THE GREAT PRISONERS : *Contents*

A Good Shoemaker and a Poor Fish Peddler:
Nicola Sacco and *Bartolomeo Vanzetti* 781

THE LETTERS OF NICOLA SACCO:
"the good red rose" 784
"this spontaneous affection" 785
"terrible I said yes, but beauty at the same time" 786
"you don't know, Ines" 787
"remember this, Dante" 789

THE LETTERS OF BARTOLOMEO VANZETTI:
"a meditation perhaps" 792
"little of abdom and much of heart" 794
"if tragedy is compelled to us" 796
"please let me speak of Italy" 799
"the right of love" 801
"the reasons why I tell you, young Comrade" 803

Give Us This Day Our Daily Bread: *Odell Waller* 805
FROM SUNUP UNTIL SUNDOWN 806

The Terrible Meek: *Mohandas K. Gandhi* 810
SCHOOL DAYS 811

The Pandit Socialist: *Jawaharlal Nehru* 822
NEHRU KI JAI! 823
GANDHI FASTS 830

Queen Revenge at Riom: *Léon Blum* 835
LÉON BLUM TO HIS JUDGES AT RIOM:
"You invite a man already condemned to answer the indictment
of your tribunal" 838
"The present trial is no longer the trial of France . . . It will become
fatally the trial of the Republic" 841

A Note of Thanks 853

Acknowledgments and Sources
PART I 855
PART II 858

Bibliography 861

Index of Authors and Works 873

XV

PREFACE

I

THE great prisoners assembled in this book have never before sat down together under one literary roof. My experiment with their illustrious ghosts—with the banners of the jailbirds—has a scheme of judgments but not "a moral." It will not seriously digress from a literary intention to tempt anyone to act on Henry Thoreau's principle (Thoreau spent one night in a cell) that at a time when men and women are unjustly imprisoned, the place for just men and women is also in prison. In short, this is no invitation to the reader to hurry and do penance in the nearest jail. When the chaplain of a German concentration camp of our time asked a newcomer with a clerical collar, "Brother, why are you in prison?" he replied, "Brother, why are you out of prison?" The second question is one which I cannot afford to put to any but myself.

This collection of heroisms and heresies, this nonconformist tradition, this unfolding conscience of western man, this variety of human experience— "this happy breed of men" in spite of all appearances—sustained me like an antitoxin during the worst years of the Fascist disease and the war. If the literature in this book can extend the imagination of a few readers by a narrow margin—letting the moral lesson take care of itself—I shall have justified my experiment well enough. I would like to begin, however, by offering up on the altar of irony a passage by Victor Hugo which celebrates the happiness of the best of all centuries, the twentieth: "In the twentieth century war will be dead, the scaffold will be dead, and dogma will be dead; but man will live. For all, there will be but one country—that country the whole earth; for all, there will be but one hope—that hope the whole heaven. All hail, then, to that noble twentieth century, which shall own our children, and which our children shall inherit."

Noble, warless, undogmatic twentieth century—all hail!

This anthology, a selection from the body of literature which has been written in prison (together with a few memorable trials), is—I believe—the first effort of its kind and scope. The burlesque thought may well occur:

why the writings of prisoners—and not the masterpieces of left-handed or redheaded men? I confess to having begun with some doubts of my own rather than any desire to trade in novelty or benefit from melodrama. If my slight innovation among books calls for an explanation, I have tried—in some sixty-five analytical introductions distributed throughout this anthology as the structure rose step by step—to justify with facts and judgments the value of my arbitrary formula: that every selection which follows be written or spoken by a prisoner of society.

While I have attempted to deal with each contributor according to the logic of his individual case, the ensemble has—I believe—some of the qualities of a common denominator. This is perhaps not an orthodox "anthology." I have not adhered with fidelity to any historical or critical rule of anthology-making—*anthos* (flower) and *lego* (gather)—unless what I have plucked here, in a phrase by Nathaniel Hawthorne, is a kind of black flower: "the black flower of our civilization, a prison." Private taste did not always rule the almost inevitable choices. I have gone after something narrower or wider than standards of excellence in literature. I have tried to put into a prison of my own the spirit and the essence of moments of great public crisis. If the formula for selection seemed arbitrary at the start of the experiment, it rapidly justified itself for me. It led at once to the great main highway of history and tradition, and—without flattering our western world—to the places of public tragedy.

It is not by choice that so much genius falls into my net—I should feel more comfortable with smaller fish. But the struggle for a soul, for dignity or liberty, the adventure in humanism (or its perversion), the revolution in free inquiry (or in prejudice)—all that is war, the oldest, the fiercest, and the longest war. It has wounded leviathans and great whales and a few man-eating sharks, coloring with bile and blood the oceans as well as the provincial frog ponds and the muddy swamps. The book unfolded by its own inevitability—I was not drawn to but rather embarrassed by the elite of literature and the eloquent vanguard of public speech falling into the ranks. If the great names appear here, and some of the great papers and manifestoes of the spirit, it is because what began as an experimental formula for exploring a bypath of literature flowered into an odd but effective commentary on our intellectual adventure in the west.

My catch is in and the net full. Let philosophers or historians, churchmen or inquisitors, sibyls or psychiatrists, Marxists or Freudians, judges or jail-wardens, Providence or the Comic Spirit, explain. Nothing has needed ex-

planation more than this congregation of heroes and heretics, as "terrible as an army with banners." What has been the common denominator of a decade's statecraft and commotion? Look into any newspaper, examine mountains of sentences by foreign correspondents, tabulate their vocabulary: is not their most recurrent word—for individuals as for whole nations—the word *prisoner?* Here is a body of prison literature which speaks for itself in great flashes of introspection. It can surprise no one that on a hundred scattered pages the timeless becomes as topical and recognizable as this morning's news. On these shocks of recognition I rest my case that, from Socrates to our own day, we shall have traced a recognizable tradition: the black flower of prison.

Doubtless this book could have taken any of a half-dozen forms. It might have assembled pieces exposing prison life, drawn from the writings of the very men who are being presented in quite another aspect than that of prison reformers. It might have laid more extensive emphasis on autobiography, or on historical narration, or on pure literary excellence, or exclusively on the changing climate of ideas. But I have spent quite as much time in rejecting as in choosing my literature written in prison, in order to project, with every form and content available—whether a fragment of philosophy, or a private letter, a diary or a trial—the mood and substance of the nonconformist tradition. To me at least the cumulative effect of all that was said and written in a prison is very impressive.

Perhaps nothing since John Foxe's *Book of Martyrs,* first published in English in 1563, has attempted to frame for modern minds the "Actes and Monuments of these latter and perilous Dayes." I have shunned its mood of somber martyrology. Nothing was easier than to rescue from all these great prisoners and prisons every kind of affirmation, exaltation, poetry, anger, irony, and even laughter. What else could have resulted from the collaboration of Socrates, Huss, Columbus, Galileo, Bruno, Campanella, Anne Hutchinson, More, Bunyan, Fox, Madame Roland, Paine, Garrison, Brown, Dostoevsky, Bakunin, Lenin, Rosa Luxemburg, Toller, Gandhi, and Nehru?

I have made no special effort to reward genius with commensurate space, or compensate for years of imprisonment with a proportionate allotment of pages. I have followed consciously and consistently no general rule of measurement. If *The Examination of Mrs. Anne Hutchinson* is here in its entirety, that is because it traces, as I think, the native roots of the American adventure. I have introduced so much of Irish protest literature—the whole neat cycle from Robert Emmet to Padraic Pearse—because it is brilliant and

reflects a homogeneous group in revolt. I offer so large a slice of Michael Bakunin's *Confession to the Czar* because (as it happens) this is the first opportunity to read in English—rather than in Russian, German, French, and even Catalan—a comprehensive portion of a very remarkable human document. James Howell is here in some quantity simply because I find him so entertaining; Toussaint L'Ouverture because his strange military *Memoir* to Napoleon is virtually inaccessible and omitted by his biographers; John Mitchel because I look forward gaily to astonishing people who have never enjoyed that Irishman's muscular and mocking prose; Balzac because his droll experience in jail is a generous sample of the *comédie humaine;* Dostoevsky because the prison correspondence which I reproduce is the very heartbeat of his great art; the letters of Rosa Luxemburg, Ernst Toller, Sacco and Vanzetti because they quiver in every nerve with the terror of our days. In contrast to the grey tones of Mrs. Hutchinson's trial, there is that boisterous morality play in noisy primary colors wonderfully enacted by William Penn and his stubborn jury in Old Bailey. There is a specimen from the cancer which is *Mein Kampf* because I cannot exclude Adolf Hitler from his legitimate niche in the world of prison letters. Gandhi and Nehru are here because they were once again political prisoners while this anthology was in progress.

The opening selection of this book, Socrates' *Apology,* is the record of the man who created the first stages of the intellectual and moral tradition of Europe. The closing selection is a defense of republican France spoken by Léon Blum at his trial in Riom and proves that the moral and intellectual tradition of Europe was never in greater peril. Through the last section of this anthology our own crisis tolls like a warning bell in pages occupied at opposite poles by Lenin and Hitler, by a shoemaker and a fish peddler and an obscure sharecropper, by Gandhi and Nehru and a captive statesman of France.

II

I am aware of no unifying principle which can link Bunyan and Marco Polo, or Bruno and Balzac, or Lenin and Verlaine. Yet here they are, together, between the covers of one book. I take refuge in Shakespeare—to Falstaff's question, "How now, lad! is the wind in that door, i' faith? must we all march?" Bardolph answers with simplicity and finality, "Yea, two and two, Newgate fashion." I lean on Bardolph's logic: yea, two and two, Newgate fashion.

As for first principles, I leave them to philosophers and psychiatrists. I am content with the lesser common denominators which link the rebellious theologies of Huss, Bruno, Bunyan, Fox, Garrison, Brown, Bakunin, and Lenin; the pranks of irony which connect Marco Polo, Villon, Columbus, Raleigh, and Defoe; the prejudice which singles out Dreyfus, Blum, Sacco and Vanzetti; the cycles of revolution which join Madame Roland, Babeuf, Paine, Emmet, Toussaint L'Ouverture, Napoleon, Hitler, Gandhi, and Nehru; and the persuasion of the Inner Voice which makes Socrates an ancestor of his two daughters in Time, Jeanne D'Arc and Mrs. Anne Hutchinson.

And what about John Donne, George Wither, James Howell, Honoré de Balzac, Fyodor Dostoevsky, Paul Verlaine, Oscar Wilde, and O. Henry? They are also here: shall we shrug them off with the reflection by which De Quincey considers murder as one of the fine arts? "A sad thing it was, no doubt, very sad; but *we* can't mend it. Therefore let us make the best of a bad matter; and, as it is impossible to hammer anything out of it for moral purposes, let us treat it aesthetically, and see if it will turn out to account in that way."

In an anthology which by its own logic must deal, alas, with nothing less than the universe unlimited, the opportunity and danger of slicing up Time and Tradition sentimentally are a very wide trap. To be sure, when the foundations of society are threatened, an eschatological nostalgia for Tradition takes possession of the community—of "Heartbreak House." Englishmen actually dramatized this homesickness in 1942. Was Time sentimentalized when the steps of St. Paul's Cathedral were turned into a stage from which "an anthology of poetry and music," in praise of England, was presented to London workers? The sandbags which sheltered buildings from bombs were the stall seats. The street from which traffic had been drained was the pit. Those who could not see the faces of the players heard their voices through clusters of loudspeakers pouring out episodes of English experience, in schoolbook fashion: England's beginnings, Magna Carta, the Napoleonic crisis, days of Queen Victoria. . . . Virginia Woolf, who has been accused of sentimentalizing Time, has parodied such a ritual. In her last book, before she sought death in the Ouse River, Mrs. Woolf introduced her historical pageant as the dominating element of a single summer's day in an English village. The period of *Between the Acts* is June 1939 and its pageant a travesty of Time. An audience sits through a series of parodies: "Merrie England"; Age of Queen Elizabeth; Age of Reason; the Nineteenth Century represented by a Victorian constable with a truncheon in hand and the

Century illustrated by the device of a missionary's romance; "Present Time: Ourselves" in which every kind of village mirror—silver mirror and cracked—is literally turned by the players upon the audience—"laughed at by looking-glasses." This spectacle which the guests watch but never quite understand has the effect of splintering rather than uniting the villagers. A gramophone scratches out nostalgic period tunes; cows wander over the English lawns; choruses mumble against the wind; and one of the characters expresses the mild nihilism of her recognition of the pageantry but not the irony by murmuring: ". . . scenes from English history. . . ." Sometimes the Period quickly peters out under the director's burden of sustaining the illusion, of making a right transition, and then—the cows take over the responsibility of History: "The cows annihilated the gap; bridged the distance; filled the emptiness and continued the emotion." The audience becomes tired of the whole baffling business and impatient to return to the fragmentary identities from which it started, when twelve airplanes drone over their heads. It is of course June 1939. Oblivious to symbolism in a country sky, a clergyman devoted to the piety of wiring the village church with electricity informs the audience that the pageant has raised exactly thirty-six pounds, ten shillings, and eighteen pence . . . the inconclusive end.

After such reflections on the futility of making packages of tradition, I would like to declare my anxiety to avoid making village pageants of history and to avoid treating literature "as a commodity destined for instructional, narcotic, patriotic, religious, humorous and other household uses."[1] But I still have some courage to consider, in the framework of my own panorama in this collection, how the stretches of Time flow between Socrates, Jeanne D'Arc, and Mrs. Anne Hutchinson—for example—how these three, whose differences are as complete as the cultures of Athens, the village of Domrémy, and Massachusetts Bay Colony, coincide in a little phrase. "An unexamined life is not worth living," said Socrates; and "I would rather die after that defence than live upon your terms." Asked how she knew that God would send the French a great victory, Jeanne said, "I know by a revelation to me"; and as for submitting to the Church Militant, "she thought that our Lord and the Church were all one, and therein they ought not to make difficulties for her: 'Why do you make difficulties when it is all one?'" And when a provincial New England Synod (as against a worldly Athenian court) accused Anne Hutchinson of "keeping two public

---

[1] *A Pamphlet Against Anthologies*, by Laura Riding and Robert Graves, Doubleday, Doran & Co., 1928—required reading for every anthologist.

lectures every week in her home" and of reproaching ministers for not preaching "a covenant of grace"—and hated the woman for a haughty and fierce carriage, for her nimble wit and voluble tongue—she, too, retreated to the authority of Voices, those Voices which spoke to her predecessors in trouble.. She named her authority "the voice of my beloved" and begged for freedom "to see the atheism of my heart," answering with certainty that she knew whereof she spoke "by an immediate revelation." The great Greek philosopher of free inquiry; a village girl obsessed by visions of St. Margaret and St. Catherine; a housewife in a colonial wilderness weighing a covenant of free grace against a covenant of works—each held passionately to a daemon, or a private voice, or an immediate revelation.

I have referred to "shocks of recognition," recognition not of the possibility that history may repeat itself, but of the relevance of the remotest past to the morning newspaper. Thus, with a contemporary's concern, what else can the reader of John Huss' fifteenth-century letters do than think harder of the fate of modern Czechoslovakia—and laugh, heartily I trust, when he reads what a younger Benito Mussolini said about Huss in a carefully forgotten biography: "I cherish the hope," writes Mussolini, "that it may arouse in the minds of its readers a hatred of every form of spiritual and secular tyranny, whether it be theocratic or Jacobine." Consider also the fifteenth-century voices of Jeanne D'Arc. They speak, as it happens, exclusively in French. Asked if St. Margaret speaks in the English tongue, she answers: "Why should she speak English when she is not on the English side?" There was, of course, a profundity in Jeanne's country simplicity, more than the University of Paris and professional inquisitors could suffer. We are likely to inquire how far Jeanne's logic on languages still bore on later circumstances in France which imprisoned the policies of a Marshal Henri Philippe Pétain and M. Pierre Laval.

Leigh Hunt went to jail for no extraordinary crime or even virtue, but he spent his two prison years industriously editing a liberal journal into which he poured a criticism of the Napoleonic crisis. For example, he attacked Sir Humphrey Davy, a British subject, for accepting an academic prize and a passport from Napoleon. Hunt castigated him on the grounds that men of art and science had a special responsibility before tyrants—and not alone because England was at war with Napoleon (or because Sir Humphrey was, as it happened, traveling comfortably through the enemy's continent with a new wife). Pursuing his journalistic quarry (at his editorial desk in jail), Hunt felt the pulse of the sudden new peace in Europe—it was

an April day in London. Bonaparte had fallen and the imprisoned editor of *The Examiner* speculated on the chances of the emperor's happiness at Elba. What a nostalgia this century-old speculation in an English periodical arouses in reverse, when in the midst of our own war it is projected into the future around Adolf Hitler. Nostalgia deepens with the rereading of Napoleon's journal. How startling it is—after all the debates with History on St. Helena, all those séances with Glory—to hear Napoleon murmuring wistfully in the boredom of an armchair: "What shall we read tonight? You all agree on the Bible? It is really most edifying; they wouldn't guess what we're doing, in Europe!"

The shock of recognition hits the reader of that extraordinary *Confession to the Czar* by Michael Bakunin with its familiar and historical Panslavism. The fascination of this document is in its ambiguity. Is the Panslav hope really shared between the revolutionist Bakunin and the autocratic Nicholas I? Or is it toyed with shyly only for a moment between the half-sincere penitent prisoner and the Little Father of Holy Russia? Between them, the professional conspirator and the professional tyrant, could they not—ventures Bakunin with his pen as he "confesses"—take the national dogma out of the hands of adventurers (like Bakunin himself)? Could *they* not revitalize the Panslav dream of Russians, Poles, and Czechs? All considerations of democracy are, after all, secondary: "I wanted a republic," confides Bakunin. "But of what kind? Not a parliamentary republic . . . all that narrow, cleverly interwoven, vapid political catechism of Western liberals never won my admiration, nor my sympathy, nor even my respect. . . ."

Boethius and More are here; Columbus and Raleigh; Galileo and Bruno and Campanella; Bunyan and Fox and Penn; Garrison and Brown; Verlaine and Wilde; Dreyfus and Blum; Babeuf and Lenin; Rosa Luxemburg, Toller, Desmoulins and Chenier; Gandhi and Nehru; the uncrowned Negro emperor Toussaint L'Ouverture and the Negro sharecropper Odell Waller.

They add up to a considerable commotion in the world's public affairs and to a large measure of punishment. Yet the reader of this anthology has not been summoned to a mourners' bench. There is no carbolic acid smell of prison in the botanical and zoological letters of the revolutionist Rosa Luxemburg. There is only the most miraculous idealism in Campanella's utopian dungeon dream, *The City of the Sun*. Jawaharlal Nehru and Walter Raleigh are jailbirds of rare sensibility who sit down to the quiet composition of world histories. From Bruno, Bunyan, Fox, and Toller the issue is

only courage, defiance, and in each case a passionate brand of piety. "If anyone needs persuading that liberty cannot exist differently from the way it has lived and always will live in history, a perilous and fighting life," says Benedetto Croce, "let him for a moment consider a world of liberty without obstacles, without menaces and without oppressions of any kind; immediately he will look away from this picture with horror as being something worse than death, an infinite boredom . . . what is then the anguish that men feel for liberty that has been lost, the invocations, the lost hopes, the words of love and anger which come from the hearts of men in certain moments and in certain ages of history? . . . these are not philosophical nor historical truths, nor are they errors or dreams; they are movements of moral conscience; they are history in the making." As I review a long list of prisoners, only Camille Desmoulins, Oscar Wilde, and Alfred Dreyfus shed hot self-pitying tears, and certainly no one begrudges them their private grief; but they are counterbalanced by others who adopted a policy expressed by Sénancour: "It may be that after this life we shall perish utterly, but if that is our fate, let us so live that annihilation will be unjust."

III

I have chosen some sixty-five and omitted at least as many names with a place in significant prison-written literature. Because this experiment is pioneer work, an account of exploration may be of some interest. Where and how I staked out my claim will become apparent if I leave a rough chart of the land reserves beyond my own fences. But I have by no means exhausted even the variety of jail writings by the sixty-five—over the same ground, any other anthologist, with other criteria or temperament, can easily work out a literary counterpoint of a different complexion. And beyond the area of these sixty-five there stretches a country which, like Christian's in *The Pilgrim's Progress,* is a wilderness with infinite surprises.

There is one price of admission: a conscience for determining what is really prison-written literature. The exploring anthologist must attend to the dissents and quarrels of the scholars and weigh their doubts and opinions. He must track down some prowling myths—that *Don Quixote* was written in jail by Cervantes is a myth abetted, I think, by Carlyle. He will find some prison letters enjoying a reputation but no English translation. He will find antique translations which are only the mummified bones of some alien masterpiece—and, if he wants the best of prison-written literature

represented, where can he find the talent (or for that matter the money to pay for it) to do justice to a Tasso, Quevedo, Voltaire, or Verlaine?

There is not much use in chronicling the names of men known to fame only because of their martyrdom. Alas, there are many of them, God rest their souls. And I have tried to protect the reader (and myself) from those who were mere pawns in a game of injustice—for as everybody knows, and Shaw puts so well, "martyrdom is the only way in which a man can become famous without ability." Yet only because of limitations of space and unavailability in English some really distinguished prison literature had to be omitted. (Unavailability in adequate translation, rather than a wider dispensation of injustice in England and America, accounts for the predominance in this book of English-speaking contributors over those who speak French, Italian, Spanish, German, and Russian.)

The *Henriade* and the *Oedipe* of Voltaire, fruits of hospitality in the Bastille, dry up in existing translation; so do the celebrated prison *Meditations* of Savonarola. If the poetry which Toyohiko Kagawa, the contemporary Japanese reformer and Tolstoyan Christian, wrote in jail (where he may be again) has sensibility, I fear the translator has not proved it. There is not enough of the witty Quevedo in English to trace the satires and the "visions" with which that genius amused himself in a Spanish dungeon three hundred years ago. This is how I must justify the absence of Savonarola, Quevedo, Voltaire, and Kagawa.

I regret my inability to corroborate by research a claim by Prince Kropotkin, in a sentence of his *Memoirs,* that it was in a French jail at Lyons that the great anarchist worked hard on his article for the *Encyclopaedia Britannica.* For the present at any rate, the respectability of the *Britannica* remains untainted by evidence that in its inventory of anarchism it is perpetuating a jailbird's contribution. I had fond hopes of borrowing a specimen of prison literature from the *Encyclopaedia Britannica* itself.

Mirabeau, the celebrated "prisoner of Vincennes" is not introduced with all his youthful gambling, his angry father, and his amours. The *Enquiries concerning lettres de cachet* which Mirabeau wrote in prison and the *Memoirs* which he composed in the Chateau d'If (the fort in which Dumas imprisoned the Count of Monte Cristo) are too limited, and those famous letters to his mistress Sophie (for my taste, at least) too mawkish—let the reader explore them at his own risk.

The obscenities of the Marquis de Sade ascetically written in the discomforts of the Bastille have no place, I suppose, in this book. I have discreetly

left out the notorious "scandal letter" to Queen Elizabeth and other works ascribed to Mary, Queen of Scots. Her writing in captivity is the football of partisans and scholars, and I am overwhelmed by too many dilemmas.

The urbane rondels of Charles d'Orléans are not here because I offer enough of the royal style in the poetry of James I of Scotland. Certainly there is more passionate genius in the contemporary verse of Villon. "Sleepe, Death's allye, oblivion of teares," the lovely and moving poetry of *St. Peter's Complaint* by the martyred Robert Southwell is absent because M. Mario Praz throws doubt on its prison origin.

The poetry of James Montgomery, Thomas Cooper, and William Cowper's pious translation of Madame Guyon, is left out because, in my opinion, it is all deadly dull—though the lives of that fighting Chartist, Thomas Cooper, and of the amazing lady in the Bastille, Madame Guyon de la Mothe, the friend of Fénélon and practitioner of "quietism," are, to be sure, anything but dull. Similarly the lives and other works of Lady Jane Grey, Hugh Latimer, William Prynne, Algernon Sidney, and Pierre Joseph Proudhon are vastly more interesting than what they happened to have said or written in prison. The jail products of Francis Bacon, John Wilkes, Lavoisier, Aaron Burr, and Mazzini—chiefly letters—are slender items. Nevertheless, I remain somewhat uneasy at having passed by a few rare specimens of prison creation: the letter to Archbishop Laud by the pilloried and ear-pruned William Prynne who dubbed the theater "the Divells Chappells," John Wilkes' notes from his jail to his daughter Polly who was in Paris, and Lavoisier's resigned and pathetic little letter written before the guillotine cut off his head (a head of which someone remarked that it took only a moment to sever it, but perhaps a hundred years would not suffice to reproduce its kind). Three sonnets credited to Machiavelli by Villari, at a period when the great philosopher of tyrannical statecraft himself suffered the rack and jail, are probably not his own at all—or if they are, would not add very much to his reputation among his contemporary admirers.

I should put into this inventory some additional evidences of prison letters. A playful sentence in the preface to *Don Quixote* ("you may suppose it the child of disturbance, engendered in some prison") and a lugubrious reference to Cervantes by Carlyle ("sitting in gaol, with one arm left him") are responsible for a myth. But there is no proof, I believe, that *Don Quixote* is prison literature, though possibly it was conceived and planned in jail at Seville. Cervantes was committed there for not being able to pay back to the treasury the public taxes which he had collected as an official and then

entrusted to a bankrupt merchant. Nor can I find evidence that during three months' confinement in that prison he also composed, as some believe, his tales *Rinconete and Cortadillo* and *The Jealous Estremian*. About Cervantes we know what he tells us himself: "He that you see here [Cervantes wrote in the preface to one of these tales] with an aquiline face, with chestnut hair, smooth and open forehead, with cheerful eyes, hooked nose, though it is well proportioned, his beard of silver, though twenty years ago it was gold, his moustaches large, his mouth small, his teeth scanty, for he has only six, and even they do not match, his body between two extremes, neither large nor small, his complexion healthy, rather fair than brown, somewhat round at the shoulders, and not very smart on his feet; he, I say, is the image of the author of *La Galatea* and of *Don Quixote* . . . and who is called commonly Miguel de Cervantes Saavedra. He was a soldier many years, and for five and a half years a captive, during which he learned the art of patience in adversity." What, if anything, did he create with his art of patience in adversity? After military adventures in which he gave a good account of himself, Cervantes fell into Moorish captivity which lasted from 1575 to 1580. The story of his efforts to escape assembles the ingredients of the wildest romances: wicked and treacherous Moorish guides, caves and gardens, executions and Christian frigates to the rescue. It is probable that Cervantes wrote a number of plays to drive away the tedium and despair of fellow prisoners. But it is more certain that in 1577 he sent to Mateo Vasquez, the Spanish king's secretary, a rhymed epistle which not only recounted his adventures but also proposed a stratagem for cleaning out that nest of pirates in North Africa where some 20,000 European captives languished in misery. The rhymed epistle had no effect on the resolution of Philip II or the immediate fortunes of Cervantes; but however undistinguished the prison verse of that magnificent storyteller, it tells us what befell the absent left hand of *Don Quixote's* historian in the bloody battle of Lepanto.

Nor have I been able to find a suitable place in my crowded gallery for the great mystic of Spanish literature, John of the Cross. He wrote much of his *Song of the Spirit* in the Toledo dungeon where he landed (a reformer in the footsteps of St. Theresa) in the war between the Calced and Discalced Carmelites. His passionate Hebraic metaphors were borrowed from the gaiety of the *Song of Songs* and the salty imagery of lovers was distilled for an ascetic adoration of God. The canticles of this saintly poet and rebellious friar, called St. John of the Cross, lay in the laps of the nuns of

Discalced long before they were held in the hands of secular readers in Spain or abroad.

With the English Quakers well represented in this collection by George Fox and William Penn, one need only mention the existence of numberless prison tracts, particularly those by Isaac Penington, and by that startling man of sacred blasphemy, James Nayler—a tortured and heaven-intoxicated figure entering Bristol town on horseback as the "Lord God of Sabaoth." The practical authorities locked up this dizzy incarnation in the cell of a jail. Nor can my framework offer a suitable place for the Leveller tracts of John Lilburne and others (so many of them labored and written down in the prisons of England), though they belong with the most extraordinary literature of politics.

Other curious documents of jailbirds with a pen may be noted. There is Sir John Eliot's political treatise, *The Monarchie of Man,* and his defense, *An Apology for Socrates,* which he wrote in the Tower where Charles I placed him as a man "desperate in mind and fortune." Consider also the very strange case of the English parson, farmer, lawyer, member of Parliament, and above all philologist, John Horne Tooke. He sat in more than one jail—once for a whole year for signing an advertisement soliciting subscriptions for the relief of relatives of Americans "murdered by the king's troops at Lexington and Concord"—another time, in 1794, when the English Tories were frightened by the French Revolution and Tooke was tried, but unsuccessfully, for high treason. A philologist in a cell, he put up the most remarkable of all defenses I have yet encountered in the rhetoric of jailbirds and nonconformists, in elaborating a prison-written evidence that he was the "victim of two prepositions and a conjunction!"

I have left out of these pages that supreme moral and literary curiosity, the notorious English divine and embezzler Dr. William Dodd, for the simple reason that the best he offered the world during his prison years was written by quite another and more respectable doctor—Samuel Johnson. This delectable Dodd was a fashionable preacher married to an extravagant wife. As one of the king's chaplains, he tutored the youth who was to become the Earl of Chesterfield. By Mrs. Dodd's indiscretion in offering 3000 guineas to the wife of the Lord Chancellor for a vacant benefice, the Dodds were disgraced and soon exiled themselves to the Continent. Old habit reasserted itself when the repatriated Dr. Dodd, still preaching, forged a bond and collected 4200 pounds from his former pupil, Lord Chesterfield. The sensational trial at Old Bailey plucked at the heartstrings of Londoners.

While Dr. Dodd, who had already written copiously and fashionably on Shakespeare and on Virtue, was covering paper with one of the dullest exercises in self-pity and blank verse (his *Thoughts in Prison*), Dr. Samuel Johnson was writing Dodd's speeches for the judge and jury and his petitions to nobility and royalty. Nothing-could save the divine from swinging by the neck at Tyburn in 1777—neither his sonnets, nor Dr. Johnson's speeches, not even a mass petition for mercy fortified by 23,000 signatures.

Honoré Daumier sat honorably and worked industriously in a jail. For caricaturing as "Gargantua" the political and physical corpulence of Louis Philippe, the artist spent six months in the Sainte-Pélagie. Charles Philipon, who employed Daumier on his comic weeklies, had with his own pencil drawn the *roi bourgeois* as a fathead. This was the famous caricature of a *poire* in evolution—pun and symbol of Louis Philippe-pear-fathead—which Philipon defended in court with animation. He was fined 6000 francs for his graphic pun on Louis Philippe's pear-shaped head. Philipon complied with the law by publishing the text of the verdict in his paper—on the front page and *in the shape of a typographical pear!* For his sins, Honoré Daumier sat in the Sainte-Pélagie serenely enough, busy over the now lost lithographs of a series called *L'imagination*. Here is a piece of Daumier's mild irony communicated to a fellow artist in a letter of October 8, 1832:

My dear Genron: I am obliged to write to you since I can't see you, because I'm at Sainte-Pélagie—nothing very serious. There's a great deal of noise being made right now, I simply must go see what it's all about. . . . Right back—it was nothing much, some Carlists fighting each other; those people are always fighting, not for honor but for petty reasons, for money. Well, here I am in Sainte-Pélagie, a charming place which not everybody enjoys. I rather like it—you know me— there's nothing I like better than being in the opposition. I assure you I'd get along well enough here if thinking of my family didn't muddy the charms of sweet solitude. . . . I tell you this prison will not be unpleasant to think about later, though I could do with a little more ink, as my inkhorn is nearly empty and I have to dip at every stroke, which is a nuisance. Apart from this, I've got pretty much everything I need. I work four times as hard in this boarding-house as I did at my Dad's. But I'm fed up with the crowd of citizens who beg me to sketch their portraits. I'm cross and sad and even mortified because you can't come to see your friend *la Gouape* now labelled *Gargantua*. I was born to be saddled with nicknames—people remembered my caricature better than my name, and *Gargantua* has stuck to me from the moment I settled down here. . . . *Adieu la Gouape*. . . . Don't write about politics, the letters are opened. . . .

Across the Channel in England, Benjamin Robert Haydon, the painter, who was lodged in the King's Bench only for his never-ending money

troubles, used his imprisonment for the advancement of art by petitioning parliament to appoint "a committee to inquire into the state of encouragement of historical painting." This man, so respected by young John Keats and admired by literary contemporaries for his literary paintings, achieved the rather curious distinction of having put on canvas, in one of His Majesty's jails for debtors, a picture (the "Mock Election") which George IV himself bought from the impoverished artist for five hundred pounds. Haydon's *Journal,* so full of the genius which he should not have squandered on heroic biblical canvases, does not fail to give us a few lively pages from his prison diary.

There is the amusing *affaire* Borrow. George Borrow came to Catholic Spain during the civil war of the 1830's "to be liberal in *giving* New Testaments" propagated by the British and Foreign Bible Society and "to ascertain how far the minds of the people were prepared to receive the truths of Christianity." As his readers know, Borrow had some entertaining adventures in which the distribution of Bibles played a rather minor role. After preparing *Saint Luke* in Basque and in the Gypsy language ("He will convert all Spain by means of the Gypsy language"), the authorities of Madrid made the mistake of putting him in jail. His rather thoughtful warden told him with a bow and in graceful Castilian: "You will find matters here not altogether below the attention of a philosophic mind." Borrow fully appreciated the opportunity of cultivating—philosophically—thieves' slang and other data, particularly as the British Legation was advising him to be in no hurry to get out (he wasn't) before receiving the apologies due to a British subject. As Spanish embarrassment increased before British indignation, so did this Bible-missionary's satisfaction: "They have put me in prison for their pleasure, and I intend to remain here for my own." Among the letters to the Bible Society which he incorporated into *The Bible in Spain,* which had George Borrow written with "a philosophic mind" from jail?

What about Gerard Winstanley, John Harrington, Kosciusko, Schiller, Blanqui, Max Stirner, Trotzky, Eamon de Valera (and so many others filling my notebooks with the unresolved question)—what have they written in prison?

I have not dug into every archaeological site on my way. Even when some prison writings required no resurrection by research they were sacrificed often to the need of imposing reasonable limits on this book. Thus I have omitted Maxim Gorky, Bertrand Russell, and Benito Mussolini. Unlike the author of *Mein Kampf,* Benito Mussolini as the pious writer of a biography

of John Huss is a candidate on the side of the angels. When in 1911 Italy went to war with Turkey over Libya, Mussolini was violently opposed to wars of expansion and thanked the State for shutting him up in the Forli Citadel where, housed and fed at the public expense, he finished his book on John Huss. In later years, in an atmosphere of glory, not a trace of his indiscreet passion for the anti-Teutonic Bohemian thinker was to be found in Italy. As for Maxim Gorky, he was jailed in the Peter-and-Paul fortress during the crisis of 1905 where he filled a notebook with his play, *Children of the Sun;* while Bertrand Russell was imprisoned during the war hysteria of 1918 in Brixton Prison where he composed his *Introduction to Mathematical Philosophy.* I have left out the wholesale company of prisoners in the Moscow Trials whose confessions, whether spontaneous or prefabricated, "shook the world" (remembering John Reed's title to a book) more than "ten days."

The mind at work in a jail is an ingenious thing and the spirit of a man pushed into a blind alley manufactures some adventurous cryptograms. I offer contrasting examples of this inventiveness from the prison experiences of Denis Diderot and Pastor Martin Niemöller. Diderot was imprisoned at Vincennes in 1749 for his atheist essay *Letter on the Blind* and for sneering at the mistress of a minister of state. In his prison he received visitors like Rousseau as well as a Madame de Puisieux. He accepted the favors of each but jealousy and ennui did not spare him—jealousy which made him scale the walls of his jail to find Madame de Puisieux at a neighborhood festival exactly in the circumstances which he dreaded—ennui because he was without pen and paper. The philosopher milked invention from necessity and left this recipe on the walls of Vincennes for all its future tenants:

INK IS MADE WITH SLATE, GROUND TO A VERY
FINE POWDER, AND A PEN OF A TOOTHPICK.

Martin Niemöller's cryptogram is a mere scratch on paper. Before complete silence closed on him at the Moabit Prison, this German pastor, who had climbed from a U-boat into a pulpit and descended from it into a concentration camp, was able to send only one written message to the outside world. Among the censored and innocuous trifles in one of his letters to his wife, he made these marks with his pen:

II Kor. 4:16.

It is a key to a sentence in *Corinthians* which reads: "Wherefore we faint not; but though our outward man is decaying, yet our inward man is

renewed day by day." Martin Niemöller's prison document is shorter than Diderot's recipe for making ink and, alas for the twentieth century, it lacks the gaiety.[1]

IV

A fragment from *Corinthians* smuggled out of a concentration camp by Martin Niemöller, Léon Blum's logic in the courtroom of Riom, Ernst Toller's verse plays in prison: place all these communications together and discover (in the lines of W. H. Auden) that

> Ironic points of light
> Flash out wherever the Just
> Exchange their messages

The Just were exchanging their messages, but there was no guarantee that they would be delivered at our doors. There was no guarantee that our addresses would be found in good order, that names below doorbells would be clearly written out, that there would always be someone at home who was responsible. The messages were stacked up high and were marked urgent. They came from Warsaw, Lidice, India, a jail in Massachusetts, a courtroom in France, from boatloads of refugees at the bottom of the Mediterranean. The postage was always interesting. A product of the crisis like Arthur Koestler confessed a nightmare which was the archetype of our day for nightmares. He found us bewitched, our doorbells broken, a dream-barrier stifling the sound of all messages: "There is a dream which keeps coming back to me at almost regular intervals; there is a busy road at no more than ten yards distant; I scream for help but nobody hears me, the crowd walks past laughing and chatting." Koestler preached a fraternity of short-term pessimists whose "chief aim will be to create oases in the inter-regnum desert," even as a few years before him Ignazio Silone advocated a society of friends and brothers as guardians of the "seed beneath the snow."

If freedom were a species of sensitive plant, then a monastery of pious brothers might well coddle its roots during the storm; if freedom were a formula in a destructible document, a fraternity of friendly pessimists might shelter it from arson, waiting as Koestler recommended "without sectarian blinkers for the first signs of the new horizontal movement" among the people so that "when it comes, they will assist its birth." Yet this "waiting without sectarian blinkers" was itself a kind of transcendental sublimation of reality. For the world suddenly teemed with guerrilla bands fighting on the

---

[1] *His political silence having been broken by liberation, Niemöller exposed a cloven hoof.*

outskirts of organized armies and with underground partisans on the periphery of established parties. For better or worse, the future of freedom seemed to lie in the experimental hands of these new men, men who knew grief, anger, and hope, and no devices for sublimating them. These partisans were now sacrificing themselves everywhere—whether to the present strategy alone or the future order, it was not yet clear. "Sacrifice signifies neither amputation nor repentance," said Antoine de Saint-Exupéry. "It is in essence an act. It is the gift of one's self to the being of which one forms a part." In a Europe which was one vast prison and which still required the initiative and example of individual sacrifices for its ultimate liberation, Saint-Exupéry speculated beyond the exigencies of the moment: "We had bit by bit introduced a code for the collectivity which neglected the existence of man. That code explains clearly why the individual should sacrifice himself for the community. It does not explain clearly and without ambiguity why the community should sacrifice itself for a single member, why it is equitable that a thousand die to deliver a single man from unjust imprisonment. . . ."

What is freedom? There are answers in the metaphysics, politics, economics, and semantics of freedom and a discussion was only recently presented by some forty scholars of such distinction as Benedetto Croce, Alfred North Whitehead, Paul Tillich, Etienne Gilson, Bertrand Russell, Charles Beard, Gaetano Salvemini, John Dewey, Franz Boas, J. B. S. Haldane, Henri Bergson, and Jacques Maritain.[2] The symposium was an exhibition of the subject's profound theoretical complexity and it is simpler (if only experimental) to treat of freedom in the shape of confession and direct speech from the great prisoners to ourselves—which is one aspect of this anthology. If, however, instead of asking what freedom is, we inquire whether there is an error abroad in the world which is the source of all inquisitions, Dr. Reinhold Niebuhr replies: there is such an error. He is examining the effects of the man whom someone defined as the type that "regards itself as entrusted by an inscrutable providence with the sacred guardianship of the one Truth in the midst of the world. It is of the type which stands in the world . . . but yet while in the world it stands there with the single task of subjecting the world . . . to the dominion of this one everlasting truth— truth remote from all fluctuations due to individuality and existence."[3] And

[2] *Freedom: Its Meaning,* Edited by Ruth Nanda Anshen, Harcourt, Brace & Co., 1940.
[3] *The Nature and Destiny of Man: A Christian Interpretation,* Reinhold Niebuhr, v. 1: Human Nature; v. 2: Human Destiny, Charles Scribner's Sons, 1941, Nisbet & Co. Ltd., London, 1943.

Niebuhr remarks that "mere men cannot have this truth 'remote from all fluctuations due to individuality and existence.' This error is the root of all Inquisitions." I think that there are only a few prisoners in this anthology whose own concept of the truth (rather than their judges' or inquisitors' truth) is so absolute—perhaps only Napoleon, Hitler, and in a measure, on the side of the angels: Lenin and Gandhi. Almost all the others in this book are subject to the fluctuations and humility of doubt. "However we twist or turn," says Reinhold Niebuhr, "whatever instruments or pretensions we use, it is not possible to establish the claim that we have the truth. We may have it; and yet we do not have it. And we will have it the more purely in fact if we know that we have it only in principle. Our toleration of truths opposed to those which we confess is an expression of the spirit of forgiveness in the realm of culture. Like all forgiveness, it is possible only if we are not too sure of our own virtue." In all his enormous humility, even Gandhi, our own closest approximation to a saint, is sure of his virtue, a little too proud in the conviction that "in experiments of faith there are no failures." But are there not?

In this special context of an anthology of literature written in prison, I have penciled a few speculative genealogical lines from Socrates to Mrs. Anne Hutchinson, from Boethius to Thomas More, from Raleigh to Nehru, from Dreyfus to Blum. Certainly, these are not family trees in the genealogy of freedom. I do not know what a Puritan Mrs. Hutchinson would see mirrored of herself in Socrates' mask of Silenus, or a sceptical Nehru in the rococo of a Raleigh. What has the nonconformist sensibility of Léon Blum in common with the lifelong correctness of poor Alfred Dreyfus? These individuals are after all united only by a misfortune and a tragic adventure. And if there is any excuse (for me) in a play of illusion which classifies them historically in pairs or groups, it is that these prisoners, centuries or miles apart, are nevertheless collaborators in all history at once, the history of protest and freedom. Croce who warns us against the illusion of descriptive labels and classification in history, puts the matter with great charm: "People suffering from those illusions should go to learn from lovers, who are always persuaded that the beloved, and their own love, is indeed a thing new and unique in the world—and in being thus persuaded are much nearer the truth." "In history," he says, "everything lasts only in so far as everything changes."

Can I avoid the temptation (and the risk) of drawing a conclusion from a labor which has consumed several years of research? A project which began

as an exploration—without a map and only a compass, as it were—has taken on a shape and character. The great prisoners, a host of individuals plucked from every human circumstance, stand together, I think not without inevitability: their role as prisoners is often narrower than the whole role they played in history, literature, philosophy, or religion; but note how in their separate crises they go straight to the heart of their own being, how they show the traits and the values by which they are recognizable in any other context as politicians or priests or poets.

Very little in the network of events for 1942, 1943, and 1944 seemed remote or alien to the subject matter of these pages. The living contemporary world with its millions of prisoners, its death camps and lime kilns and human gas chambers, its refugees in all the ports and cellars, its quislings and patriots and all its fierce partisan passions, has had sufficient variety to match any past terror and atrocity in historical narration. As in Koestler's nightmare which was the interpretive fable of those years, the newspapers screamed and—between the paid advertisements—the radios performed in five-minute inventories. Will it add something to our awareness of these years if those who have spoken well on the old human themes communicate the experience of their crises in the midst of our own?

I am ending these comments at the climax of the conflict: Paris, Brussels, Copenhagen, Oslo, Stockholm, Amsterdam, Vienna, Prague, Warsaw, Athens, and Rome are yet prisoners of war. In this morning's newspaper I have read the dispatch of a foreign correspondent with an eye for the debris of warfare. Gravely he reports the survival of ten painted Benedictine figures on the face of a mural in the ruined Abbey of Mount Cassino—Amor Dei, Charitas, Discretio, Patientia, Humilitias, Paupertas, Castitas, Obedentia, Conversio, and Stabilitas. This patch of mural plaster in an umbombed basement is more miraculous than the whole dead ghetto of Warsaw: its painted images and mottoes survive. . . . Exile and imprisonment, homelessness and hunger, death and humiliation have given new vitality to an old ironical phrase. When the Abbé Sieyès (who was so correct during the excesses of another crisis in history that he confided his bitterness and cowardice only to his diary) was asked, "What did you do during the Terror?" he answered drily, "I lived." If by any chance this book should reach the hands of young men and women who are still making free decisions, they may learn, I trust, why mere survival is not enough, why those who cannot survive except on their own terms are often luckier. In the coming practice of freedom, in the re-established equilibrium of liberties,

we can use an awareness of the whole range of our experiences and tradition. Judging by evidence in this book, it is plain enough that none need be overtaxed with nostalgia for any golden age of sweet reasonableness. No sentimentality or hero worship will help us decide how to use "blood, sweat and tears" as a future discipline. In this sphere of action no savior, no reformation can expiate for our sins; no hero in history, no revolution can grant us unlimited dividends of life, liberty and the pursuit of happiness. When the complaining words of Job are ended, the Voice Out of the Wilderness warns him: "Who is this that darkeneth counsel by words without knowledge? Gird up now thy loins like a man." The old legacy, the old currency of freedom is always expended. The perilous and fighting life always renews itself. When its impact on a generation of men is exhausted, the old dramas of inquisition and freedom remain tragedies which have only the power of catharsis and consolation. They will be re-enacted after us again and again, each Job always repeating his fresh performance outside the kingdom of God, and each inquisitor outside the last judgment.

ISIDORE ABRAMOWITZ

New York
May 19, 1944

This was our climate of ideas and alarms. One blessed morning we saw it as if it were changing: "When Paris fell something died in Europe, now it rises again and something comes to life." A private weather chart of the long years before liberation, my comments explain at least the private emotion behind this project—and I beg leave to let my preface stand unamended.

August 23, 1944

Book I

From a Cup of Hemlock to the Inquisition

SOCRATES

ST. PAUL

BOETHIUS

MARCO POLO

JAMES I OF SCOTLAND

JOHN HUSS

JEANNE D'ARC

FRANCOIS VILLON

CHRISTOPHER COLUMBUS

HUGO GROTIUS

GALILEO GALILEI

GIORDANO BRUNO

TOMMASO CAMPANELLA

Book I

From a Cup of Hemlock to the Inquisition

SOCRATES

AL-RAZI

BOETHIUS

MARCO POLO

ROGER THE SCHOLAR

OMAR KHAN

JEANNE D'ARC

FRANCOIS VILLON

CHRISTOPHER COLUMBUS

HUGO GROTIUS

GALILEO GALILEI

GIORDANO BRUNO

TOMÁS DE TORQUEMADA

THE EXAMINED LIFE:

Socrates

THE APOLOGY: *Before the Verdict*

After the Verdict and Before the Sentence

After the Sentence

~~~~~~

It is an outward casing he wears, similarly to the sculptured Silenus. But if you opened his inside, you cannot imagine how full he is, good cup-companions, of sobriety. I tell you, all the beauty a man may have is nothing to him; he despises it more than any of you can believe; nor does wealth attract him, nor any sort of honor that is the envied prize of the crowd. All these possessions he counts as nothing worth, and all of us as nothing, I assure you; he spends his whole life in chaffing and make game of his fellow-men. Whether any one else has caught him in a serious moment and opened him, and seen the images inside, I know not; but I saw them one day, and thought them so divine and golden, so perfectly fair and wondrous, that I simply had to do as Socrates bade me.

<div align="right">PLATO'S <em>Symposium</em></div>

S OCRATES is the first man whose intellectual and ideal world is known to us," writes René Kraus. And is it not just that in this company the voice of Socrates should be the first? Is he not still on trial? And all those accused of making new gods or listening to new voices, have they not always been on trial with Socrates, always paraphrasing his *Apology?* We belong to a generation which has returned to (if indeed it ever escaped) a crisis of which Paul Valéry said in 1919: "An extraordinary shudder has lately passed through the marrow of Europe. It perceived in all its thinking substance that it recognized itself no longer." After a quarter of a century, in the second and greater crisis, we had accumulated reasons to doubt the permanence of nearly everything with which the Socratic mind was associated. So much was quickly corrupted or destroyed: human lives, communities, states, institutions, consciousness itself. To Greece in particular (added Valéry) we were indebted for "a method of thinking which tends to relate all things to man, to the complete man; he becomes the *system of references* by which all things must be finally measured." And after the shudder which passed through the marrow of Europe after 1939? If there are those who still have a wish to unite around a reliable and reasonable patron saint, they are in desperate need of repeating with Erasmus: *Sancte Socrates, ora pro nobis.*

When the *Apology* was spoken before his judges, Socrates was seventy

<div align="center">3</div>

years old and Plato thirty. Socrates had seen the Peloponnesian War and four revolutions in Athens. It was a time of instability and change, a period of purges and refugees. Herodotus was only fifteen years older than Socrates and Thucydides an exact contemporary. In the middle period of Socrates' Life, Aeschylus wrote the *Oresteia* and Sophocles the *Antigone*, literature in which men and their sins still submitted to the retribution of the gods. Euripides wrote the *Alcestis, Medea, Hippolytus,* and *Suppliants,* in which the fate of man was already presented as conditioned by will, effort, and natural circumstance. In the *Clouds* Aristophanes drew a devastating caricature of Socrates when the philosopher was not yet fifty years old, and in the *Euthyphro, Apology, Crito,* and *Phaedo,* Plato wrote an apotheosis just a few years after Socrates' trial.

The charges were heresy against the state religion and corruption of the youth. Socrates professed the divine guidance of a *daemon.* He had beaten everyone in argument with irony and reason. He had embarrassed politicians, orators, and poets. As A. D. Lindsay says, "if Socrates were right, politics and rhetoric and poetry must go." Against the *daemon* and irony of the accused, were the five hundred and one judges defending democracy and piety and poetry? Was Socrates (who in the *Euthyphro* presses hard for a true definition of piety, in the *Crito* refuses to cheat the state of his life by escaping, and in the *Phaedo* submits in reconciliation with death) guilty? Was he preparing the ground for revolution by asking what is justice? virtue? courage? piety? the real good?

This Socrates, who had announced that his implacable *daemon* had forbidden him to engage in politics, to desert philosophy, or to take back pupils who had once left him, was already well tarred and feathered with the brush of a great conservative comic genius. In Aristophanes' *Clouds* Socrates was presented to Athenians as an impostor, treading on air, suspended in a surrealist basket—a "thinking ship." Of the five hundred and one judges, two hundred and eighty-one voted against Socrates; and how many of these voted for or against him because of the claims of philosophy or religion or poetry? Even Athens, which also accused Euripides of impiety and Alcibiades of profaning the mysteries, could not reasonably lay claim to five hundred philosophers—all of them judges. Years later, when charged with paying honors to a mortal, Aristotle, unlike Socrates, left Athens to save the Athenians from sinning a second time against philosophy. And the Emperor Julian wrote this in a letter to a philosopher: "The achievements of Alexander the Great are outdone in my opinion by Socrates the son of Sophronis-

cus. It is to him I ascribe the wisdom of Plato, the fortitude of Antisthenes, the generalship of Xenophon. . . . Who ever found salvation in the victories of Alexander? . . . Whereas it is thanks to Socrates that all who find salvation in philosophy are being saved even now."

Two sentences spoken by Socrates are worth more than any speculation about his innocence or guilt: "I would rather die after that defence than live upon your terms" and "An unexamined life is not worth living." They place Socrates at once among the martyrs of free inquiry. He was neither a preacher of discreet morality, nor a dialectician of "free thought," nor the philosophical court jester of a golden age. But as A. E. Taylor puts it, "Socrates created the intellectual and moral tradition by which Europe has ever since lived. . . . For more than two thousand years it has been the standing assumption of the civilized European man that he has a *soul*, something which is the seal of his normal waking intelligence and moral character, and that, since this *soul* is either identical with himself or at any rate the most important thing about him, his supreme business in life is to make the most of it and do the best for it." This Socratic doctrine begs our age for disciples; it promises an order in which no one need speak before judges an *Apology* for independent criticism, for intellectual freedom, for "the examined life." I repeat: is it not just that in this company the voice of Socrates should be the first?

THE APOLOGY
Before the Verdict

I DO not know, men of Athens, what you have felt in listening to my accusers, but they almost made even me forget myself, they spoke so plausibly. And yet, I may say, they have not spoken one word of truth. And of all the lies they told, I wondered most at their saying that you ought to be on your guard against being misled by me, as I was a great speaker. To feel no shame when they knew that they would be refuted immediately by my own action, when I show you that I am not a great speaker at all,—that did seem to me the height of their audacity; unless perhaps they mean by a great speaker a man who speaks the truth. If that is their meaning, I should agree that I am an orator, though not like them. For they, as I have told you, have said little

or nothing that is true; from me you will hear the whole truth. Not, I assure you, that you will get fine arguments like theirs, men of Athens, decked out in splendid phrases, no, but plain speech set forth in any words that come to hand. I believe what I have to say is true, and I ask that none of you should look for anything else. Indeed, gentlemen, it would hardly suit my age to come before you like a boy, with a made-up speech. And yet, I do ask one thing of you, and I ask it very earnestly: if you find I speak in my defence just as I have been accustomed to speak over the bankers' tables in the market-place,—as many of you have heard me, there and elsewhere; do not be surprised at it, and do not interrupt. For this is how the matter stands. This is the first time I have ever been in a lawsuit, and I am seventy years old,—so I am really an entire stranger to the language of this place. Now, just as you would have forgiven me, I am sure, had I been actually a foreigner, if I had spoken in the tongue and manner to which I had been born, so I think I have a right to ask you now to let my way of speaking pass—be it good or bad—and to give your minds to this question and this only, whether what I say is right or not. That is the virtue of the judge, as truth is the virtue of the orator.

Now in making my defence, men of Athens, it will be well for me to deal first with the first false accusations and my first accusers, and afterwards with those that followed. For I have had many accusers who have come before you now for many years, and have not said one word of truth, and I fear them more than Anytus and his supporters, though they are formidable too. But the others, gentlemen, are still more to be feared, I mean the men who took most of you in hand when you were boys, and have gone on persuading you ever since, and accusing me—quite falsely—telling you that there is a man called Socrates, a philosopher, who speculates about the things in the sky, and has searched into the secrets of the earth, and makes the worse appear the better reason. These men, Athenians, the men who have spread this tale abroad, they are the accusers that I fear: for the listeners think that those who study such matters must be atheists as well. Besides, these accusers of mine are many, and they have been at this work for many years, and that, too, when you were at an age at which you would be most ready to believe them, for you were young, some of you mere striplings, and judgment has really gone by default, since there was no one to make the defence. And what is most troublesome of all, it is impossible even to find out their names, unless there be a comedian among them. As for those who have tried to persuade you through envy and prejudice, some, it is true, convincing others

because they were convinced themselves,—these are the hardest to deal with of all. It is not possible to call up any of them here and cross-examine them: one is compelled, as it were, to fight with shadows in making one's defence, and hold an inquiry where there is nobody to reply. So I would have you understand with me that my accusers have been, as I say, of two kinds: those who have just brought this charge against me, and others of longer standing, of whom I am speaking now; and I ask you to realise that I must defend myself against the latter first of all, for they were the first whom you heard attack me, and at much greater length than these who followed them. And now, I presume, I must make my defence, men of Athens, and try in the short time I have before me to remove from your minds this calumny which has had so long to grow. I could wish for that result, and for some success in my defence, if it would be good for you and me. But I think it a difficult task, and I am not unaware of its nature. However, let the result be what God wills; I must obey the law, and make my defence.

Let us begin from the beginning and see what the accusation is that gave birth to the prejudice on which Meletus relied when he brought this charge. Now, what did they say to raise this prejudice? I must treat them as though they were prosecutors and read their affidavit: "Socrates, we say, is a trouble to the State. He is guilty of inquiring into the things beneath the earth, and the things of the firmament, he makes the worse appear the better reason, and he teaches others so." That is the sort of thing they say: you saw it yourselves in the comedy of Aristophanes,—a character called Socrates carried about in a basket, saying that he walked on air, and talking a great deal more nonsense about matters of which I do not understand one word, great or small. And I do not say this in contempt of such knowledge, if any one is clever at those things. May Meletus never bring so grave a charge against me! But in truth, gentlemen, I have nothing to do with these subjects. I call you yourselves,—most of you,—to witness: I ask you to instruct and tell each other,—those of you who have ever heard me speak, and many of you have,—tell each other, I say, if any of you have ever heard one word from me, small or great, upon such themes; and you will realise from this that the other tales people tell about me are of the same character.

There is, in fact, no truth in them at all, nor yet in what you may have heard from others, that I try to make money by my teaching. Now here again, I think it would be a great thing if one could teach men as Gorgias of Leontini can, and Prodicus of Keos, and Hippias of Elis. They can all go to every one of our cities, and take hold of the young men,—who are able, as it

is, to associate free of charge with any of their fellow-citizens they may choose,—and they can persuade them to leave this society for theirs and pay them money and be very grateful to them too. Why, there is another philosopher here from Paros; he is in town, I know: for I happened to meet a friend of mine who has spent more money on sophists than all the rest put together,—Callias the son of Hipponicus. Now I put a question to him,—he has two sons of his own,—"Callias," I said, "if your two sons were only colts or bullocks we could have hired a trainer for them to make them beautiful and good, and all that they should be; and our trainer would have been, I take it, a horseman or a farmer. But now that they are human beings, have you any trainer in your mind for them? Is there any one who understands what a man and a citizen ought to be? I am sure you have thought of it, because you have sons of your own. Is there any one," I said, "or not?" "Oh yes," said he, "certainly there is." "Who is he?" I asked, "and where does he come from and how much does he charge?" "Euenus," he answered, "from Paros; five minas a head." And I thought Euenus the happiest of men if he really has that power and can teach for such a moderate fee. Now I should have been set up and given myself great airs if I had possessed that knowledge; but I do not possess it, Athenians.

Some of you will say perhaps:—"But, Socrates, what can your calling be? What has given rise to these calumnies? Surely, if you had done nothing more than any other man, there would not have been all this talk, had you never acted differently from other people. You must tell us what it is, that we may not be left to make our own theories about you."

That seems to me a fair question, and I will try to show you myself what it can be that has given me my name and produced the calumny. Listen to me then. Some of you may think I am in jest, but I assure you I will only tell the truth. The truth is, men of Athens, that I have won my name because of a kind of wisdom, nothing more nor less. What can this wisdom be? The wisdom, perhaps, that is proper to man. It may really be that I am wise in that wisdom: the men I have just named may have a wisdom greater than man's,—or else I know not what to call it. Certainly I do not possess it myself; whoever says I do lies, and speaks to calumniate me. And pray, gentlemen, do not interrupt me: not even if you think I boast. The words that I say will not be my own; I will refer you to a speaker whom you must respect. The witness I will bring you of my wisdom,—if such it really is,—and of its nature, is the god whose dwelling is at Delphi. Now you knew Chairephon, I think. He was my friend from boyhood, and the friend of your

8

democracy; he went with you into exile, and came back with you.[1] And you know, I think, the kind of man Chairephon was—how eager in everything he undertook. Well, he made a pilgrimage to Delphi, and had the audacity to ask this question from the oracle: and now I beg you, gentlemen, do not interrupt me in what I am about to say. He actually asked if there was any man wiser than I. And the priestess answered, No. I have his brother here to give evidence of this, for Chairephon himself is dead.

Now see why I tell you this. I am going to show you how the calumny arose. When I heard the answer, I asked myself: What can the god mean? What can he be hinting? For certainly I have never thought myself wise in anything, great or small. What can he mean then, when he asserts that I am the wisest of men? He cannot lie of course: that would be impossible for him. And for a long while I was at a loss to think what he could mean. At last, after much thought, I started on some such course of search as this. I betook myself to one of the men who seemed wise, thinking that there, if anywhere, I should refute the utterance, and could say to the oracle: "This man is wiser than I, and you said I was the wisest." Now when I looked into the man—there is no need to give his name—it was one of our citizens, men of Athens, with whom I had an experience of this kind—when we talked together I thought, "This man seems wise to many men, and above all to himself, but he is not so;" and then I tried to show him that he thought he was wise, but he was not. Then he got angry with me, and so did many who heard us, but I went away and thought to myself, "Well, at any rate I am wiser than this man: probably neither of us knows anything of beauty or of good, but he thinks he knows something when he knows nothing, and I, if I know nothing, at least never suppose that I do. So it looks as though I really were a little wiser than he, just in so far as I do not imagine myself to know things about which I know nothing at all." After that I went to another man who seemed to be wiser still, and I had exactly the same experience: and then he got angry with me too, and so did many more.

Thus I went round them all, one after the other, aware of what was happening and sorry for it, and afraid that they were getting to hate me: but still I felt I must put the word of the god first and foremost, and that I must

---

[1] In 404 B.C. after the submission to Sparta, the democratic government of Athens was overthrown. A body of thirty oligarchs, appointed at first provisionally, got practically the whole power into their hands and acted with great injustice and cruelty. The leading democrats of those who escaped judicial murder went into exile, but in a year's time effected a re-entry, partly by force of arms, and established the democracy again.

go through all who seemed to have any knowledge in order to find out what the oracle meant. And by the Dog, men of Athens,—for I must tell you the truth,—this was what I experienced. As I went on with the quest the god had imposed on me, it seemed to me that those who had the highest reputation were very nearly the most deficient of all, and that others who were thought inferior came nearer being men of understanding. I must show you, you see, that my wanderings were a kind of labour of Hercules to prove to myself that the oracle was right. After I had tried the statesmen I went to the poets,—tragedians, writers of lyrics, and all,—thinking that there I should take myself in the act and find.I really was more ignorant than they. So I took up the poems of theirs on which they seemed to have spent most pains, and asked them what they meant, hoping to learn something from them too. Now I am really ashamed to tell you the truth; but tell it I must. On the whole, almost all the bystanders could have spoken better about the poems than the men who made them. So here again I soon perceived that what the poets make is not made by wisdom, but by a kind of gift and inspiration, as with the prophets and the seers: they, too, utter many glorious sayings, but they understand nothing of what they say. The poets seemed to me in much the same state; and besides, I noticed that on account of their poetry they thought themselves the wisest of men in other matters too, which they were not. So I left them also, thinking that I had just the same advantage over them as over the politicians.

Finally I turned to the men who work with their hands. I was conscious I knew nothing that could be called anything; and I was quite sure I should find that they knew a great many wonderful things. And in this I was not disappointed; they did know things that I did not, and in this they were wiser than I. But then, gentlemen, the skilled artisans in their turn seemed to me to have just the same failing as the poets. Because of his skill in his own craft every one of them thought that he was the wisest of men in the highest matters too, and this error of theirs obscured the wisdom they possessed. So that I asked myself, on behalf of the oracle, whether I would ᶦ rather be as I am, without their wisdom and without their ignorance, or like them in both. And I answered for myself and for the oracle that it was better for me to be as I am.

It was this inquiry, men of Athens, that gave rise to so much enmity against me, and that of the worst and bitterest kind: a succession of calumnies followed, and I received the surname of the Wise. For those who meet me think me wise wherever I refute others; but, sirs, the truth may be that

God alone has wisdom, and by that oracle he may have meant just this, that human wisdom is of little or no account. It seems as though he had not been speaking of Socrates the individual; but had merely used my name for an illustration, as if to say: "He, O men, is the wisest of you all, who has learnt, like Socrates, that his wisdom is worth nothing." Such has been my search and my inquiry ever since up to this day, in obedience to the god, whenever I found any one—fellow-citizen or foreigner—who might be considered wise: and if he did not seem so to me I have borne God witness, and pointed out to him that he was not wise at all. And through this incessant work I have had no leisure for any public action worth mentioning, nor yet for my private affairs, but I live in extreme poverty because of this service of mine to God.

And besides this, the young men who follow me, those who have most leisure,—sons of our wealthiest citizens,—they take a keen delight themselves in hearing people questioned, and they often copy me and try their hand at examining others on their own account; and, I imagine, they find no lack of men who think they know something but know little or nothing at all. Now those whom they examine get angry—not with themselves, but with me—and say that there is a man called Socrates, an utter scoundrel, who is ruining the young. And when any one asks them what he does or what he teaches, they have really nothing whatever to say, but so as not to seem at a loss they take up the accusations that lie ready to hand against all philosophers, and say that he speaks of the things in the heavens and beneath the earth and teaches men not to believe in the gods and to make the worse appear the better reason. The truth, I imagine, they would not care to say, namely, that they have been convicted of claiming knowledge when they have none to claim. And being, as I think they are, ambitious, energetic, and numerous, well-organized and using great powers of persuasion, they have gone on calumniating me with singular persistence and vigour till your ears are full of it all. After them Meletus attacked me and Anytus and Lycon,—Meletus on behalf of the poets, Anytus for the artisans and the statesmen, Lycon for the orators,—so that, as I said at first, I should be greatly surprised if in the short time before me I could remove the prejudice that has grown to be so great. There, men of Athens, that is the truth;—I have not hidden one thing from you, great or small; I have not kept back one word. Yet I am fairly sure that I have roused hostility by so doing, which is in itself a proof that what I say is true, and that the calumnies against me are of this nature, and the reasons those I have

given. And if you look into the matter,—now or afterwards,—you will find it to be so.

Well, that is a sufficient defence in answer to my first accusers. Now I must try to defend myself against Meletus,—the good man and the patriot, as he calls himself,—and the rest who followed. These are my second accusers, and let us take up their affidavit in its turn. It runs somewhat as follows: Meletus asserts that Socrates is guilty of corrupting the young and not believing in the gods in whom the city believes, but in some strange divinities. That is the sort of charge, and let us take it point by point. He does really say that I am guilty of corrupting the young. But I answer, men of Athens, that Meletus is guilty of an unseemly jest, bringing men to trial on a frivolous charge, pretending that he cares intensely about matters on which he has never spent a thought. That this is so I will try to prove.

Come here, Meletus, and tell me: you really think it of importance that our young men should be as good as possible? "I do indeed." Well, will you tell the court who it is that makes them better? It is plain that you must know since you have given the matter thought. You have found, so you say, the man who corrupts them in me; you have accused me and brought me to trial before these judges: go on and point out to them who it is that makes them better. See, Meletus, you are silent and have not a word to say: and now, are you not ashamed? Is not this proof enough of what I say, that you have never thought of it at all? Yet once more, my friend, I ask you, who is it makes them better? "The laws." No, my good fellow, that is not what I ask: I ask what *man* makes them better, and he, of course, must know the laws already. "Well, then, Socrates, I say these judges are the men." Really, Meletus, can these men really teach our youth and make them better? "Most certainly they can." All of them, do you mean, or only some? "All of them." Splendid! Splendid! What a wealth of benefactors! And what of the audience? Can they do so or not? "Yes, they can do so too." And what about the Councillors? "Yes, the Councillors too." Well, Meletus, what of the Assembly and those who sit there? They do not corrupt our young men, I suppose? All of them too, you would say, make them better? "Yes, all of them too." Then it really seems that all the Athenians except me can make men good, and that I alone corrupt them. Is that what you mean? "That is exactly what I mean." What a dreadful fate to be cursed with! But answer me: have you the same opinion in the case of horses? Do you think that those who make them better consist of all mankind, with the exception of one single individual who ruins them? Or, on the contrary, that there is

only one man who can do them good, or very, very few, the men, namely, who understand them? And that most people, if they use horses and have to do with them, ruin them? Is it not so, Meletus, with horses and all other animals too? Of course it is, whether you and Anytus admit it or not. It would be well, and more than well, with our youth if there was only one man to corrupt them and all the others did them good. However, Meletus, you show us clearly enough that you have never considered our young men: you have made it quite plain that you care nothing about them, that you have never given a thought to the cause for which you have brought me here.

But tell us now, Meletus, I entreat you, is it better to live in an evil city or a good? Answer us, my friend: it is not a hard question after all. Do not bad men do evil to their nearest neighbours and good men good? "Yes, of course." Well, is there any man who would rather be injured than aided by his fellows? Answer me, my good man. Indeed the law says you must. Is there any one who wishes to be harmed? "Certainly not." Well, you accuse me, we know, of corrupting the youth and making them worse: do you suppose that I do it intentionally or unintentionally? "Intentionally, I have no doubt." Really and truly, Meletus? Is a man of your years so much wiser than a man of mine that you can understand that bad men always do some evil, and good men some good to those who come nearest to them, while I have sunk to such a depth of folly that I am ignorant of it and do not know that if I make one of my fellows wicked I run the risk of getting harm from him,—and I bring about this terrible state of things intentionally, so you say? I do not believe you, Meletus, nor can any one else, I think. Either I do not corrupt them at all, or if I do, it is done unintentionally, so that in either case you are wrong. And if I do it unintentionally, it is not legal to bring me here for such involuntary errors; you ought to have taken me apart and taught me and reproved me in private; for it is evident that when I learn the truth I shall cease to do what I have done in ignorance. But you shrank from meeting me and teaching me,—you did not choose to do that: you brought me here where those should be brought who need punishment, not those who need instruction.

Well, men of Athens, it has been plain for some time that Meletus, as I say, has never spent a thought on these matters,—not one, great or small. Nevertheless, you must tell us, Meletus, how you think I corrupt the youth. No doubt, as you say in the indictment, by teaching them not to believe in the gods in whom our city believes but in some new divinities. Is not that

how you say I ruin them? "Certainly, I do say so, as strongly as I can." Then, in the name of those gods of whom we speak, explain yourself more clearly to me and to the court. I have not been able to discover whether you say I teach belief in divinities of some kind, in which case I do after all believe in gods, and am not an utter atheist, and so far I am not guilty; only they are not the gods in which the city believes, they are quite different, and that is your charge against me. Or perhaps you mean to say that I do not believe in gods of any kind, and that I teach others so. "Yes, that is what I say; you do not believe in them at all." Meletus, you astound me. What makes you say so? Then I do not even believe that the sun and the moon are gods as other men believe? "Most certainly, gentlemen of the court, most certainly; for he says the sun is stone and the moon earth." My dear Meletus, do you imagine you are attacking Anaxagoras? Or do you think so little of the jury, do you fancy them so illiterate as not to know that the books of Anaxagoras, the philosopher of Clazomenae, are full of all these theories? The young men, we are to suppose, learn them all from me, when they can buy them in the theatre for tenpence at the most and laugh at Socrates if he should pretend that they were his, especially when they are so extraordinary. Now tell me in heaven's name, is this really what you think?—that I believe in no god at all? "In none at all." I cannot believe you, Meletus, I cannot think you can believe yourself. Men of Athens, I think this man an audacious scoundrel, I consider he has framed this indictment in a spirit of sheer insolence, aggression, and arrogance. One would think he was speaking in riddles, to try "whether the wise Socrates will discover that I am jesting and contradicting myself, or whether I shall deceive him and all who hear me." For he surely contradicts himself in his own indictment, almost as if he said: "Socrates is guilty of not believing in gods but believing in them." Such words can only be in jest.

Look at the matter with me, gentlemen of the court, and see how it appears to me. And you must answer us, Meletus, and you sirs, I ask you, as I asked you at first, not to interrupt me if I put the questions in my usual way. Now is there any man, Meletus, who believes that human things exist, but not human beings? Let him answer, sirs, but do not allow him only to interrupt. Is there any one who does not believe in horses but does believe in their trappings? Or who does not believe in flute players but does believe in flutes? There cannot be, my worthy man; for if you will not answer, I must tell you myself and tell the court as well. But answer this at least: is there any one who believes in things divine and disbelieves in divinities?

"No, there is not." How kind of you to answer at last, under pressure from the court! Well, you admit that I believe in things divine, and that I teach others so. They may be new or they may be old, but at the least, according to your own admission, I do believe in things that are divine, and you have sworn to this in your deposition. And if I believe in things divine I must believe in divinities as well. Is that not so? Indeed it is; for since you will not answer I must assume that you assent. And do we not believe that divinities are gods, or the sons of gods? You admit this? "Yes, certainly." Well, now if I believe in divinities, as you grant I do, and if divinities are gods of some kind, then this is what I meant when I said you were speaking in riddles and jesting with us, saying that I do not believe in gods and yet again that I do, since I believe in divinities. Again if these divinities are the bastards of the gods, with nymphs and other women for their mothers, as people say they are,—what man is there who could believe in sons of gods and not in gods? It would be as absurd as to believe in the offspring of horses and of asses, and not believe in horses and asses too. No, Meletus, it can only be that you were testing me when you drew up that charge, or else it was because you could find nothing to accuse me of with any truth. There is no possible way by which you could persuade any man of the least intelligence to doubt that he who believes in things divine and godlike must believe in divinities and gods, while he who disbelieves the one must disbelieve the other.

However, men of Athens, I do not think much defence is needed to show that I am innocent of the charge Meletus has made; I think I have now said enough; but what I told you before, namely, that there is deep and widespread enmity against me, that, you must remember, is perfectly true. And this is what will overthrow me, if I am overthrown, not Meletus nor yet Anytus, but the prejudices and envy of the majority, forces that have overthrown many a good man ere now, and will, I imagine, overthrow many more; there is little fear that it will end with me. But maybe some of you will say to me: "And are you not ashamed of a practice that has brought you to the verge of death?" But I have a good answer to give him. "You are not right, my friend," so I would say, "if you think that a man of any worth at all, however slight, ought to reckon up the chances of life and death, and not consider one thing and one alone, and that is whether what he does is right or wrong, a good man's deed or a craven's." According to you, the sons of the gods who died at Troy would have been foolish creatures, and the son of Thetis above all, who thought so lightly of danger compared with the least disgrace, that, when he was resolved to kill Hector and when his

mother, goddess as she was, spoke to him, to this effect, if I remember right: "My son, if you avenge the slaughter of your friend Patroclus, and kill Hector, you will die yourself:—

'After the fall of Hector, death is waiting for you;' "—

those were her words. But he, when he heard, thought scorn of death and danger: he was far more afraid to live a coward's life and leave his friend unavenged. "Come death then!" he answered, "when I have punished the murderer, that I may not live on here in shame,—

'Here by my longships lying, a burden for earth to bear!' "

Do you think that that man cared for death or danger? Hear the truth, men of Athens! The post that a man has taken up because he thought it right himself or because his captain put him there, that post, I believe, he ought to hold in face of every danger, caring no whit for death or any other peril in comparison with disgrace.

So it would be a strange part for me to have played, men of Athens, if I had done as I did under the leaders you chose for me, at Potidæa and Amphipolis and Delium, standing my ground like any one else where they had posted me and facing death, and yet, when God, as I thought and believed, had set me to live the life of philosophy, making inquiry into myself and into others, I were to fear death now, or anything else whatever, and desert my post. It would be very strange; and then, in truth, one would have reason to bring me before the court, because I did not believe in the gods, since I disobeyed the oracle and was afraid of death, and thought I was wise where I was not. For to fear death, sirs, is simply to think we are wise when we are not so: it is to think we know what we know not. No one knows whether death is not the greatest of all goods that can come to man; and yet men fear it as though they knew it was the greatest of all ills. And is not this the folly that should be blamed, the folly of thinking we know what we do not know? Here, again, sirs, it may be that I am different from other men, and if I could call myself wiser than any one in any point, it would be for this, that as I have no real knowledge about the world of Death, so I never fancy that I have. But I do know that it is evil and base to do wrong and disobey the higher will, be it God's or man's. And so for the sake of evils, which I know right well are evils, I will never fear and never fly from things which are, it may be, good. Therefore, though you should acquit me now and refuse to listen to Anytus when he says that either I ought never to have

been brought here at all, or else, now that I have been, it is impossible not to sentence me to death, assuring you that if I am set at liberty, your sons will at once put into practice all that I have taught them, and all become entirely corrupt—if, in face of this, you should say to me, "Socrates, for this once we will not listen to Anytus; we will set you free, but on this condition, that you spend your time no longer in this search, and follow wisdom no more. If you are found doing it again you will be put to death." If, I repeat, you were to set me free on that condition, I would answer you: Men of Athens, I thank you and I am grateful to you, but I must obey God rather than you, and, while I have life and strength, I will never cease to follow wisdom, and urge you forward, explaining to every man of you I meet, speaking as I have always spoken, saying, "See here, my friend, you are an Athenian, a citizen of the greatest city in the world, the most famous for wisdom and for power; and are you not ashamed to care for money and money-making and fame and reputation, and not care at all, not make one effort, for truth and understanding and the welfare of your soul?" And should he protest, and assert he cares, I will not let him go at once and send him away free: no! I will question him and examine him, and put him to the proof, and if it seems to me that he has not attained to virtue, and yet asserts he has, I will reproach him for holding cheapest what is worth most, and dearer what is worth less. This I will do for old and young,—for every man I meet,—foreigner and citizen,—but most for my citizens, since you are nearer to me by blood. It is God's bidding, you must understand that; and I myself believe no greater blessing has ever come to you or to your city than this service of mine to God. I have gone about doing one thing and one thing only,—exhorting all of you, young and old, not to care for your bodies or for money above or beyond your souls and their welfare, telling you that virtue does not come from wealth, but wealth from virtue, even as all other goods, public or private, that man can need. If it is by these words that I corrupt our youth, then these words do harm; but if any one asserts that I say anything else, there is nothing in what he says. In face of this I would say, "Men of Athens, listen to Anytus or not, acquit me or acquit me not, but remember that I will do nothing else, not if I were to die a hundred deaths."

No! do not interrupt me, Athenians; keep the promise I asked you to give, —not to interrupt what I had to say, but to hear it to the end. I believe it will do you good. I am about to say something else for which you might shout me down, only I beg you not to do so. You must understand that if

you put me to death when I am the kind of man I say I am, you will not injure me so much as your own selves. Meletus or Anytus could not injure me; they have not the power. I do not believe it is permitted that a good man should be injured by a bad. He could be put to death, perhaps, or exiled, or disfranchised, and it may be Meletus thinks, and others think, that these are terrible evils, but I do not believe they are. I think it far worse to do what he is doing now,—trying to put a man to death without a cause. So it comes about, men of Athens, that I am far from making my defence for my own sake, as might be thought: I make it for yours, that you may not lose God's gift by condemning me. For if you put me to death you will not easily find another of my like; one, I might say,—even if it sounds a little absurd,—who clings to the city at God's command, as a gadfly clings to a horse; and the horse is tall and thorough-bred, but lazy from his growth, and he needs to be stirred up. And God, I think, has set me here as something of the kind,—to stir you up and urge you, and prick each one of you and never cease, sitting close to you all day long. You will not easily find another man like that; and, sirs, if you listen to me you will not take my life But probably you have been annoyed, as drowsy sleepers are when suddenly awakened, and you will turn on me and listen to Anytus, and be glad to put me to death; and then you will spend the rest of your life in sleep, unless God, in his goodness, sends you another man like me. That I am what I say I am, given by God to the city, you may realise from this: it is not the way of a mere man to leave all his own affairs uncared for and all his property neglected during so many years, and go about your business all his life, coming to each individual man, as I have come, as though I were his father or his elder brother, and bidding him think of righteousness. If I had got any profit by this, if I had taken payment for these words, there would have been some explanation for what I did; but you can see for yourselves that my accusers—audacious in everything else—have yet not had the audacity to bring witnesses to assert that I have ever taken payment from any man, or ever asked for it. The witness I could bring myself in my own poverty, would be enough, I think, to prove I speak the truth.

It may perhaps seem strange that while I have gone about in private to give this counsel, and have been so busy over it, yet I have not found it in my heart to come forward publicly before your democracy and advise the State. The reason is one you have heard me give before, at many times and in many places; and it is this: I have a divine and supernatural sign that comes to me. Meletus referred to it scoffingly in his indictment, but, in truth,

it has been with me from boyhood, a kind of voice that comes to me; and, when it comes, it always holds me back from what I may intend to do; it never urges me forward. It is this which has stopped me from taking part in public affairs; and it did well, I think, to stop me. For you may be sure, men of Athens, if I had attempted to enter public life, I should have perished long ago, without any good to you or to myself. Do not be angry with me if I tell you the truth. No man will ever be safe who stands up boldly against you, or against any other democracy, and forbids the many sins and crimes that are committed in the State; the man who is to fight for justice—if he is to keep his life at all—must work in private, not in public.

I will give you a remarkable proof of this, a proof not in words, but in what you value—deeds. Listen, and I will tell you something that happened to me, and you may realise from it that I will never consent to injustice at any man's command for fear of death, but would die on the spot rather than give way. What I have to tell you may seem an arrogant tale and a commonplace of the courts, but it is true.

You know, men of Athens, that I have never held any other office in the State, but I did serve on the Council. And it happened that my tribe, Antiochis, had the Presidency at the time you decided to try the ten generals who had not taken up the dead after the fight at sea.[2] You decided to try them in one body, contrary to law, as you all felt afterwards. On that occasion I was the only one of the Presidents who opposed you, and told you not to break the law; and I gave my vote against it; and when the orators were ready to impeach and arrest me, and you encouraged them and hooted me, I thought then that I ought to take all risks on the side of law and justice, rather than side with you, when your decisions were unjust, through fear of imprisonment or death. That while the city was still under the democracy. When the oligarchy came into power, the Thirty, in their turn, summoned me with four others to the Rotunda, and commanded us to fetch Leon of Salamis from that island, in order to put him to death: the sort of commands they often gave to many others, anxious as they were to incriminate all they could. And on that occasion I showed, not by words only, that for death, to put it bluntly, I did not care one straw,—but I did care, and to the

---

[2] This was after the sea-fight of Arginusæ, 406 B.C., one of the last Athenian successes in the Peloponnesian war. In spite of the success, twenty-five ships were lost. Their crews were not saved, and it was felt that the generals—eight in number—must have been careless in the matter. The popular indignation was extreme; the case was tried in the Assembly, and the generals were sentenced to death in a body. This was contrary to recognised law, as each should have been tried separately.

full, about doing what was wicked and unjust. I was not terrified then into doing wrong by that government in all its power: when we left the Rotunda, the other four went off to Salamis and brought Leon back, but I went home. And probably I should have been put to death for it if the government had not been overthrown soon afterwards. Many people will confirm me in what I say.

Do you believe now that I should have lived so long as this, if I had taken part in public affairs and done what I could for justice like an upright man, putting it, as I was bound to put it, first and foremost? Far from it, men of Athens. Not I, nor any other man on earth. And all through my life you will find that this has been my character,—in public, if ever I had any public work to do, and the same in private,—never yielding to any man against right and justice, though he were one of those whom my calumniators call my scholars. But I have never been any one's teacher. Only, if any man, young or old, has ever heard me at my work and wished to listen, I have never grudged him my permission; I have not talked with him if he would pay me, and refused him if he would not; I am ready for questions from rich and poor alike, and equally ready to question them should they care to answer me and hear what I have to say. And for that, if any one is the better or any one the worse, I ought not to be held responsible; I never promised instruction, I never taught, and if any man says he has ever learnt or heard one word from me in private other than all the world could hear, I tell you he does not speak the truth.

What then can it be that makes some men delight in my company? You have heard my answer, sirs. I told you the whole truth when I said their delight lay in hearing men examined who thought that they were wise but were not so; and certainly it is not unpleasant. And I, as I believe, have been commanded to do this by God, speaking in oracles and in dreams, in every way by which divine grace has ever spoken to man at all and told him what to do. That, men of Athens, is the truth, and easy to verify. For if it were really the case that I corrupt our young men and have corrupted them, then surely, now that they are older, if they have come to understand that I ever meant to do them harm when they were young, some of them ought to come forward here and now, to accuse and punish me, or if they did not care to come themselves, some who are near to them—their fathers, or their brothers, or others of their kin,—ought to remember and punish it now, if it be true that those who are dear to them have suffered any harm from me. In fact, there are many of them here at this very moment; I can see

them for myself; there is Crito, my contemporary, who belongs to the same deme as I, the father of Critobulus there; and here is Lusanias of Sphettos, the father of Æschines, who is beside him; and Antiphon of Kephisia, the father of Epigenes; and others too whose brothers have spent their time with me, Nicostratus, the son of Theozotides, brother of Theodotus. Theodotus is dead; so it cannot be his entreaty that has stopped his brother. And Paralus is here, the son of Demodocus, whose brother Theages was; and Adeimantus, the son of Ariston, whose brother Plato I see, and Aiantodorus with his brother Apollodorus too. And I could tell you of many more, one of whom at least Meletus should have called as a witness in his attack; or, if he forgot then, let him call one now, and I will stand aside, and he can speak if he has anything to say. But, gentlemen, you will find precisely the reverse; you will find them all prepared to stand by me, the man who has done the harm, the man who has injured their nearest and dearest, as Meletus and Anytus say. Those, perhaps, who are ruined themselves might have some reason for supporting me, but those who are uncorrupted,—men of advancing years, their relatives,—what other reason could they have for their support except the right and worthy reason that they know Meletus is lying and I am speaking the truth?

There, gentlemen, that is on the whole what I had to say in my defence, with something more, perhaps, to the same effect. Now there may be a man among you who will feel annoyed if he remembers his own conduct when undergoing a trial far less serious than this of mine; how he prayed and supplicated the judges with floods of tears, and brought his little children into court to rouse as much pity as possible, and others of his family and many of his friends; but I, it would appear, will not do anything of the kind, and that in the face, as it might seem, of the utmost danger. Such a man, it may be, observing this, will harden himself against me; this one fact will enrage him and he will give his vote in anger. If this is so with any of you,—I do not say it is, but if it is,—I think it would be reasonable for me to say, "I too, my good man, have kindred of my own, I too was not born, as Homer says, 'from stock or stone,' but from men, so that I have kinsfolk and sons also, three sons,—the eldest of them is already a stripling, the other two are children. And yet I do not intend to bring one of them here, or entreat you to acquit me." And why is it that I will not do anything of the kind? Not from pride, men of Athens, nor from disrespect for you: nor is it because I am at peace about death; it is for the sake of my honour and yours and the honour of the city. I do not think it fitting that I should do such

21

things, a man of my years, and with the name I bear; it may be true or false, but at any rate it is believed that Socrates is in some way different from most other men. And if those among you who bear a name for wisdom or courage or any other virtue were to act like this, it would be disgraceful. I have seen it often in others, when they came under trial, men of some repute, but who behaved in a most extraordinary way, thinking, apparently, that it would be a fearful thing for them to die; as though they would be immortal if you did not put them to death. Such men, I think, bring disgrace upon the city, and any stranger might suppose that the Athenians who bore the highest name for virtue, who had been chosen out expressly for office and reward, were no whit better than women. We must not behave so, men of Athens, those of us who are thought to be of any worth at all, and you must not allow it, should we try: you must make it plain, and quite plain, that you will be more ready to condemn the man who acts these pitiful scenes before you and makes the city absurd, than him who holds his peace.

Even putting honour aside, gentlemen, it does not seem to me right to supplicate a judge and gain acquittal so: we ought rather to instruct him and convince him. The judge does not sit here to grant justice as a favour, but to try the case; he has sworn, not that he will favour those he chooses, but that he will judge according to the law. So we should not teach you to break your oath, and you should not let yourselves be taught. Neither of us would reverence the gods if we did that. Therefore you must not expect me, men of Athens, to act towards you in a way which I do not think seemly or right or reverent—more especially when I am under trial for impiety, and have Meletus here to face. For plainly, were I to win you over by my entreaties, and have you do violence to your oath, plainly I should be teaching you not to believe in the gods, and my own speech would accuse me unmistakably of unbelief. But it is far from being so; for I believe, men of Athens, as not one of my accusers believes, and I leave it to you and to God to decide my case as may be best for me and you.

After the Verdict and Before the Sentence

THERE are many reasons, men of Athens, why I feel no distress at what has now occurred, I mean your condemnation of me. It is not unexpected; on the contrary, I am surprised at the number of votes on either side. I did not think it would be so close. I thought the majority would be great; but in fact,

so it appears, if only thirty votes had gone otherwise, I should have been acquitted. Against Meletus, as it is, I appear to have won, and not only so, but it is clear to every one that if Anytus and Lycon had not come forward to accuse me, he would have been fined a thousand drachmas, for he would not have obtained a fifth part of the votes.

The penalty he fixes for me is, I understand, death. Very good. And what am I going to fix in my turn, men of Athens? It must be, must it not, what I deserve? Well, then, what do I deserve to receive or pay because I chose not to sit quiet all my life, and turned aside from what most men care for,—money-making and household affairs, leadership in war and public speaking, and all the offices and associations and factions of the State,—thinking myself, as a matter of fact, too upright to be safe if I went into that life? So I held aloof from it all; I should have been of no use there to you or to myself, but I set about going in private to each individual man and doing him the greatest of all services—as I assert—trying to persuade every one of you not to think of what he had but rather of what he was, and how he might grow wise and good, nor consider what the city had, but what the city was, and so with everything else in the world. What, then, do I deserve for this? A reward, men of Athens, if I am really to consider my deserts, and a reward, moreover, that would suit me. And what reward would suit a poor man who has been a public benefactor, and who is bound to refrain from work because of his services in exhorting you? There could be nothing so suitable, men of Athens, as a place at the table in the Presidents' Hall; far more suitable than if any of you had won a horse-race at Olympia or a chariot race. The Olympian victor brings you fancied happiness, but I bring you real: he does not need maintenance, but I do. If I am to fix what I deserve in all fairness, then this is what I fix:—a place at the table in the Presidents' Hall.

Perhaps when I say this you will feel that I am speaking much as I spoke about entreaties for pity, that is to say, in a spirit of pride; but it is not so, Athenians. This is how it is: I am convinced that I have never done wrong to any man intentionally, but I cannot convince you; we have only had a little time to talk together. Had it been the custom with you, as with other nations, to spend not one day but many on a trial for life and death, I believe you would have been convinced; but, as matters are, it is not easy to remove a great prejudice in a little time.

Well, with this conviction of mine that I have never wronged any man, I am far from meaning to wrong myself by saying that I deserve any harm, or assigning myself anything whatever of the kind. What should I be afraid

of? Of suffering what Meletus has assigned, when I say that I do not know, after all, whether it is not good? And to escape it I am to choose what I know quite well is bad? And what punishment should I fix? Imprisonment? Why should I live in prison, slave to the Eleven[3] of the day? Or should I say a fine, with imprisonment until I pay it? But then there is just the difficulty I mentioned a moment ago: I have no money to pay a fine. Or am I to say exile? You might, I know, choose that for my punishment. My love of life would indeed be great if I were so blind as not to see that you, my own fellow-citizens, have not been able to endure my ways and words, you have found them too trying and too heavy to bear, so that you want to get rid of them now. And if that is so, will strangers put up with them? Far from it, men of Athens. And it would be a grand life for a man of my years to go into exile and wander about from one city to another. For well I know that wherever I went the young men would listen to my talk as they listen here; and if I drove them away, they would drive me out themselves and persuade their elders to side with them, and if I let them come, their fathers and kindred would banish me on their account.

Perhaps some one will say: "But, Socrates, cannot you leave us and live in peace and quietness?" Now that is just what it is hardest to make you, some of you, believe. If I were to say that this would be to disobey God, and therefore I cannot hold my peace, you would not believe me; you would say I was using my irony. And if I say again that it is in fact the greatest of all goods for a man to talk about virtue every day, and the other matters on which you have heard me speaking and making inquiry into myself and others: if I say that the life without inquiry is no life for man—you would believe that even less. Yet it is so, even as I tell you—only it is not easy to get it believed. Moreover, I am not accustomed to think myself deserving of punishment. However, if I had had any money I should have fixed a price that I could pay, for that would not have harmed me at all; but as it is, since I have no money—unless perhaps you would consent to fix only so much as I could afford to pay? Perhaps I might be able to pay one mina silver; and I will fix the fine at that. But Plato here, gentlemen, and Crito, and Critobulus, and Apollodorus, beg me to say thirty minas, and they tell me they will guarantee it. So I will fix it at this sum, and these men, on whom you can rely, will be sureties for the amount.

---

[3] The Eleven formed a board consisting of a secretary and ten members appointed by lot every year. They had charge of the prisons and superintended executions.

After the Sentence of Death

You have hastehed matters a little, men of Athens, but for that little gain you will be called the murderers of Socrates the Wise by all who want to find fault with the city. For those who wish to reproach you will insist that I am wise, though I may not be so. Had you but waited a little longer, you would have found this happen of itself: for you can see how old I am, far on in life, with death at hand. In this I am not speaking to all of you, but only to those who have sentenced me to death. And to them I will say one thing more. It may be, gentlemen, that you imagine I have been convicted for lack of arguments by which I could have convinced you, had I thought it right to say and do anything in order to escape punishment. Far from it. No; convicted I have been, for lack of—not arguments, but audacity and impudence, and readiness to say what would have been a delight for you to hear, lamenting and bewailing my position, saying and doing all kinds of things unworthy of myself, as I consider, but such as you have grown accustomed to hear from cthers. I did not think it right then to behave through fear unlike a free-born man, and I do not repent now of my defence; I would far rather die after that defence than live upon your terms. As in war, so in a court of justice, not I nor any man should scheme to escape death by any and every means. Many a time in battle it is plain the soldier could avoid death if he flung away his arms and turned to supplicate his pursuers, and there are many such devices in every hour of danger for escaping death, if we are prepared to say and do anything whatever. But, sirs, it may be that the difficulty is not to flee from death, but from guilt. Guilt is swifter than death. And so it is that I, who am slow and old, have been caught by the slower-paced, and my accusers, who are clever and quick, by the quick-footed, by wickedness. And now I am to go away, under sentence of death from you: but on them truth has passed sentence of unrighteousness and injustice. I abide by the decision, and so must they. Perhaps indeed, it had to be just so: and I think it is very well.

And now that that is over I desire to prophesy to you, you who have condemned me. For now I have come to the time when men can prophesy —when they are to die. I say to you, you who have killed me, punishment will fall on you immediately after my death, far heavier for you to bear—I call God to witness!—than your punishment of me. For you have done this thinking to escape the need of giving any account of your lives: but exactly the contrary will come to pass, and so I tell you. Those who will call you to

25

account will be more numerous,—I have kept them back till now, and you have not noticed them,—and they will be the harder to bear inasmuch as they are younger, and you will be troubled all the more. For if you think that by putting men to death you can stop every one from blaming you for living as you should not live, I tell you you are mistaken; that way of escape is neither feasible nor noble; the noblest way, and the easiest, is not to maim others, but to fit ourselves for righteousness. That is the prophecy I give to you who have condemned me, and so I leave you.

But with those who have acquitted me I should be glad to talk about this matter, until the Archons are at leisure and I go to the place where I am to die. So I will ask you, gentlemen, to stay with me for the time. There is no reason why we should not talk together while we can, and tell each other our dreams. I would like to show you, as my friends, what can be the meaning of this that has befallen me. A wonderful thing, my judges,—for I may call you judges, and not call you amiss,—a wonderful thing has happened to me. The warning that comes to me, my spiritual sign, has always in all my former life been most incessant, and has opposed me in most trifling matters, whenever I was about to act amiss; and now there has befallen me, as you see yourselves, what might really be thought, as it is thought, the greatest of all evils. And yet, when I left my home in the morning, the signal from God was not against me, nor when I came up here into the court, nor in my speech, whatever I was about to say; and yet at other times it has often stopped me in the very middle of what I was saying; but never once in this matter has it opposed me in any word or deed. What do I suppose to be the reason? I will tell you. This that has befallen me is surely good, and it cannot possibly be that we are right in our opinion, those of us who hold that death is an evil. A great proof of this has come to me: it cannot but be that the well-known signal would have stopped me, unless what I was going to meet was good.

Let us look at it in this way too, and we shall find much hope that it is so. Death must be one of two things: either it is to have no consciousness at all of anything whatever, or else, as some say, it is a kind of change and migration of the soul from this world to another. Now if there is no consciousness at all, and it is like sleep when the sleeper does not dream, I say there would be a wonderful gain in death. For I am sure if any man were to take that night in which he slept so deeply that he saw no dreams, and put beside it all the other nights and days of his whole life, and compare them, and say how many of them all were better spent or happier than that one night,—I am sure that not the ordinary man alone, but the King of

Persia himself, would find them few to count. If death is of this nature I would consider it a gain; for the whole of time would seem no longer than one single night. But if it is a journey to another land, if what some say is true and all the dead are really there, if this is so, my judges, what greater good could there be? If a man were to go to the House of Death, and leave all these self-styled judges to find the true judges there, who, so it is said, give justice in that world,—Minos and Rhadamanthus, Æacus and Triptolemus, and all the sons of the gods who have done justly in this life,— would that journey be ill to take? Or to meet Orpheus·and Musæus, Hesiod and Homer, what would you give for that, any of you? I would give a hundred deaths if it is true. And for me especially it would be a wonderful life there, if I met Palamedes, and Ajax, the son of Telamon, or any of the men of old who died by an unjust decree: to compare my experience with theirs would be full of pleasure, surely. And best of all, to go on still with the men of that world as with the men of this, inquiring and questioning and learning who is wise among them, and who may think he is, but is not. How much would one give, my judges, to question the hero who led the host at Troy, or Odysseus, or Sisyphus, or any of the countless men and women I could name? To talk with them there, and live with them, and question them, would be happiness unspeakable. Certainly there they will not put one to death for that; they are far happier in all things than we of this world, and they are immortal for evermore,—if what some say is true.

And you too, my judges, must think of death with hope, and remember this at least is true, that no evil can come to a good man in life or death, and that he is not forgotten of God; what has come to me now has not come by chance, but it is clear to me that it was better for me to die and be quit of trouble. That is why the signal never came to turn me back, and I cannot say that I am altogether angry with my accusers and those who have condemned me. Yet it was not with that intention that they condemned and accused me; they meant to do me harm, and they are to be blamed for that. This much, however, I will ask of them. When my sons come of age, sirs, will you reprove them and trouble them as I troubled you, if you think they care for money or anything else more than righteousness? And if they seem to be something when they are really nothing, reproach them as I reproached you for not seeking what they need, and for thinking they are somewhat when they are worth nothing. And if you do this, we shall have received justice at your hands, my sons and I.

But now it is time for us to go, I to death, and you to iife; and which of us goes to the better state is known to none but God.

27

I PAUL THE PRISONER OF JESUS CHRIST:

St. Paul

"WHOM I HAVE BEGOTTEN IN MY BONDS"

(The Epistle of Paul to Philemon)

"I KNOW BOTH HOW TO BE ABASED . . . HOW TO ABOUND"

(The Epistle of Paul to the Philippians)

What was Paul? He was not a saint. The dominant feature of his character is not goodness. He was haughty, pertinacious, aggressive . . . his expressions were harsh; he deemed himself absolutely in the right; he clung to his opinions; he quarrelled with different persons. He was not learned. It may even be said that he greatly injured science by his paradoxical contempt for reason, by his eulogy upon apparent folly, by his apotheosis of transcendental absurdity. Nor was he a poet either. His writings, works of the greatest originality, are without charm. Their form is harsh, and almost always devoid of grace. What was he then? . . . He was an eminent man of action; of powerful soul, progressive, enthusiastic; a conqueror, a missionary, a propagator. ERNEST RENAN, *Saint Paul*

The modern condemnation of the Apostle as an obscurantist who corrupted the simple gospel of the Nazarene with harsh and difficult dogmas, is the dregs of doctrinaire study of Paul, mostly in the tired brains of gifted amateurs. . . . Paul is essentially first and foremost a hero of religion. The theological element in him is secondary; naiveté in him is stronger than reflection; mysticism stronger than dogmatism; Christ means more to him than Christology, God more than the doctrine of God. He is far more a man of prayer, a witness, a confessor and a prophet, than a learned exegete and close-thinking scholastic.

ADOLF DEISSMANN, *Paul, a Study in Social and Religious History*

Behold I shew you a mystery; We shall not all sleep, but we shall all be changed, in a moment, in the twinkling of an eye, at the last trump: for the trumpet shall sound, and the dead shall be raised incorruptible, and we shall be changed. For this corruptible must put on incorruption, and this mortal put on immortality, then shall be brought to pass the saying that is written, Death is swallowed up in victory. O death where is thy sting? O grave where is thy victory?

First Letter from Paul, the Apostle, to the Christians in Corinth

WE TURN to Paul in a unique private moment of his stormy public life, in his prison in Rome, writing the letter to Philemon. It is dispatched on an impulse without the characteristic Pauline dialectic passion, without doctrine, without allegory, and without his mystery. The slave Onesimus has run away (perhaps not empty-handed) from his Christian

28

master Philemon. Onesimus has fled into the intricate human maze of the great port of Ephesus; then, probably arrested and put into prison, he comes to meet Paul. The little letter which he was to carry from Paul to Philemon begs for forgiveness and reconciliation. Its argument is delicate in the ordinary worldly sense, written as between two men of whom one has property and the other a show of respect for it. Yet Paul's diplomacy goes out sweetly with a touch of divine grace. Let Philemon forgive his runaway slave Onesimus, whom Paul might indeed have retained "in the bonds of the Gospel," except "that thy benefit should not be as it were of necessity, but willingly." If Onesimus robbed Philemon, if he wronged him, let Philemon put it to Paul's account; and did not Philemon, by virtue of his new Christian soul, owe his teacher Paul "even thine own self besides?" There exists a comparable pagan letter by Pliny the Younger who writes to Sabinianus: "Your freedman . . . threw himself at my feet and clung there with as much submission as he could have done at yours. . . . He sincerely repents of his fault and I am persuaded that he is thoroughly reformed." Gracefully Pliny begs: "If he should incur your displeasure hereafter, you will have so much the stronger plea in excuse for your anger, as you shew yourself more exorable to him now." And with expert urbanity he pleads as between men of cultivated sensibility: "Allow something to his youth, to his tears, and to your own natural mildness of temper . . . for a man of your benevolence of heart cannot be angry without feeling great uneasiness." Between them, Paul and Pliny, though with similar tact for property, measure a great difference, the difference between Judeo-Christian and Greek. But as Adolf Deissmann warns us in connection with Paul's letter to Philemon, "If one regards this precious leaf as a tract on the attitude of Christianity to slavery, he misses his way not only in historical criticism but also in human taste." Paul is at work, certainly, on the private salvation of the souls of a master and his slave, not on the public morality of Roman law. This little letter to Philemon is alone among the Pauline epistles a wholly private matter, but it is public speech in this: that Paul preaches freedom through love rather than law and revolution. There have been those who have seen in Paul either a liberator from a harsh old law, or from man's own will, or from reliance on mere works of merit. If Paul called to liberty, his condition was that it should not be used "for an occasion to the flesh" but for love. He lived and preached this riddle: Paul is a prisoner because he is a Christian, a Christian because he is a prisoner of Jesus Christ.

Paul's letters from his prison in Rome (presenting enormous historical and

critical difficulties to scholars) include those sent to the Philippians, the Colossians, to Philemon, and perhaps the one to the Ephesians. They are part of that great Pauline campaign of correspondence, the most revolutionary in effect ever written, whose exposition of man, sin, and death shaped the character of Christianity and made of it a world religion. They were written by a man who was stoned, whipped, starved, shipwrecked, often imprisoned, and always pricked by "a thorn in the flesh." They burn fiercely with the intuition of an apostle who saw Jesus plain only in a vision, but a vision which pursued him relentlessly: "As he journeyed, he came near Damascus: and suddenly there shone round about him a light from heaven, and he fell to the earth, and heard a voice saying unto him, 'Saul, Saul, why persecutest thou me?' And he said, 'Who art thou, Lord?' And the Lord said, 'I am Jesus whom thou persecutest: it is hard for thee to kick against the goad.' And he trembling and astonished said, 'Lord, what would thou have me do?' And the Lord said unto him, 'Arise and go into the city, and it shall be told thee what thou must do.' And the men who journeyed with him stood speechless, hearing a voice, but seeing no man. And Saul arose from the earth; and when his eyes were opened, he saw no man: but they led him by the hand, and brought him into Damascus. And he was three days without sight, and neither did he eat or drink." This is the bare narrative of Paul's conversion and this is the fountainhead of his mystery.

But Paul, a prisoner in Rome, was also a citizen of Rome. Consciously or unconsciously, this prisoner, dictating his last letters, was conquering the universality of the empire with the universality of the Kingdom of God, missing no Roman institutional lessons. He warned the Colossians against the intellectual atmosphere which might corrupt their first faith. And if the language, style, and doctrine of the letter to the Ephesians is not only Pauline but also Paul's, he expounded to them, precisely from Rome, a doctrine which made Christ "the head over all things to the Church." And he wrote to the Philippians a message almost as simple and tender as the little note to Philemon: "Whatsoever things are true, whatsoever things are honest, whatsoever things are just, whatsoever things are pure, whatsoever things are lovely, whatsoever things are of good report; if there be any virtue, and if there be any praise, think on these things." If to Socrates only "the examined life" was worth living, for Paul, in the grip of his mystery, there was not even any question as between living and dying, since, for Paul, "It is not I that live but Christ that liveth in me."

"WHOM I HAVE BEGOTTEN IN MY BONDS"[1]

UNTO *Philemon our dearly beloved, and fellowlaborer, and to our beloved Apphia, and Archippus our fellowsoldier, and to the Church in thy house: Grace to you, and peace, from God our Father and the Lord Jesus Christ.*

I thank my God, making mention of thee always in my prayers, hearing of thy love and faith, which thou hast toward the Lord Jesus, and toward all saints; that the communication of thy faith may become effectual by the acknowledging of every good thing which is in you in Christ Jesus. For we have great joy and consolation in thy love, because the bowels of the saints are refreshed by thee, brother.

Wherefore, though I might be much bold in Christ to enjoin thee that which is convenient, yet for love's sake I rather beseech thee, being such an one as Paul the aged, and now also a prisoner of Jesus Christ. I beseech thee for my son Onesimus, whom I have begotten in my bonds: which in time past was to thee unprofitable, but now profitable to thee and to me: whom I have sent again: thou therefore receive him, that is, mine own bowels: whom I would have retained with me, that in thy stead he might have ministered unto me in the bonds of the Gospel: but without thy mind would I do nothing; that thy benefit should not be as it were of necessity, but willingly. For perhaps he therefore departed for a season, that thou shouldest receive him for ever; not now as a bondservant, but above a bondservant, a brother beloved, specially to me, but how much more unto thee, both in the flesh, and in the Lord? If thou count me therefore a partner, receive him as myself. If he hath wronged thee, or oweth thee ought, put that on mine account. I Paul have written it with mine own hand, I will repay it: albeit I do not say to thee how thou owest unto me even thine own self besides. Yea, brother, let me have joy of thee in the Lord: refresh my bowels in the Lord.

Having confidence in thy obedience I wrote unto thee, knowing that thou wilt also do more than I say. But withal prepare me also a lodging: for I trust that through your prayers I shall be given unto you.

There salute the Epaphras, my fellowprisoner in Christ Jesus; Marcus, Aristarchus, Demas, Lucas, my fellowlaborers.

The grace of our Lord Jesus Christ be with your spirit. Amen.

Paul, a prisoner of Jesus Christ,
and Timothy our brother.

[*from Rome, circa 60 A.D.*]

---

[1] *The Epistle of Paul to Philemon.*

"I KNOW HOW TO BE ABASED . . . HOW TO ABOUND"[2]

To ALL *the saints in Christ Jesus which are at Philippi, with the bishops and deacons:*
Grace be unto you, and peace, from God our Father, and from the Lord Jesus Christ.

I thank my God upon every remembrance of you, always in every prayer of mine for you all making request with joy, for your fellowship in the Gospel from the first day until now; being confident of this very thing, that He which hath begun a good work in you will perform it until the day of Jesus Christ: even as it is meet for me to think this of you all, because I have you in my heart; inasmuch as both in my bonds, and in the defence and confirmation of the Gospel, ye all are partakers of my grace. For God is my record, how greatly I long after you all in the bowels of Jesus Christ. And this I pray, that your love may abound yet more and more in knowledge and in all judgment. That ye may approve things that are excellent; that ye may be sincere and without offence till the day of Christ; being filled with the fruits of righteousness, which are by Jesus Christ, unto the glory and praise of God.

But I would ye should understand, brethren, that the things which have happened unto me have fallen out rather unto the furtherance of the Gospel; so that my bonds in Christ are manifest in all the palace, and in all other places; and many of the brethren in the Lord, waxing confident by my bonds, are much more bold to speak the Word without fear.

Some indeed preach Christ even of envy and strife; and some also of good will. The one preach Christ of contention, not sincerely, supposing to add affliction to my bonds: but the other of love, knowing that I am set for the defence of the Gospel. What then? notwithstanding, every way, whether in pretence, or in truth, Christ is preached; and I therein do rejoice, yea, and will rejoice. For I know that this shall turn to my salvation through your prayer, and the supply of the Spirit of Jesus Christ, according to my earnest expectation and my hope, that in nothing I shall be ashamed, but that with all boldness, as always, so now also Christ shall be magnified in my body, whether it be by life, or by death.

For to me to live is Christ, and to die is gain. But if I live in the flesh, this is the fruit of my labour: yet what I shall choose I wot not. For I am in a

---

[2] *The Epistle of Paul the Apostle to the Philippians.*

strait betwixt two, having a desire to depart, and to be with Christ; which is far better: nevertheless to abide in the flesh is more needful for you. And having this confidence, I know that I shall abide and continue with you all for your furtherance and joy of faith; that your rejoicing may be more abundant in Jesus Christ for me by my coming to you again.

Only let your conversation be as it becometh the Gospel of Christ: that whether I come and see you, or else be absent, I may hear of your affairs, that ye stand fast in one spirit, with one mind striving together for the faith of the Gospel; and in nothing terrified by your adversaries: which is to them an evident token of perdition, but to you of salvation, and that of God. For unto you it is given in the behalf of Christ, not only to believe on Him, but also to suffer for His sake; having the same conflict which ye saw in me, and now hear to be in me.

If there be therefore any consolation in Christ, if any comfort of love, if any fellowship of the Spirit, if any bowels and mercies, fulfil ye my joy, that ye be likeminded, having the same love, being of one accord, of one mind. Let nothing be done through strife or vainglory; but in lowliness of mind let each esteem other better than themselves. Look not every man on his own things, but every man also on the things of others. Let this mind be in you, which was also in Christ Jesus. Who, being in the form of God, thought it not robbery to be equal with God: but made Himself of no reputation, and took upon Him the form of a servant, and was made in the likeness of men; and being found in fashion as a man, He humbled Himself, and became obedient unto death, even the death of the cross. Wherefore God also hath highly exalted Him, and given Him a name which is above every name, that at the name of Jesus every knee should bow, of things in heaven, and things in earth, and things under the earth; and that every tongue should confess that Jesus Christ is Lord, to the glory of God the Father.

Wherefore, my beloved, as ye have always obeyed, not as in my presence only, but now much more in my absence, work out your own salvation with fear and trembling. For it is God Who worketh in you both to will and to do of His good pleasure. Do all things without murmurings and disputings: that ye may be blameless and harmless, the sons of God, without rebuke, in the midst of a crooked and perverse nation, among whom ye shine as lights in the world, holding forth the word of life; that I may rejoice in the day of Christ, that I have not run in vain, neither laboured in vain. Yea, and if I be offered upon the sacrifice and service of your faith, I joy, and rejoice with you all. For the same cause also do ye joy, and rejoice with me.

But I trust in the Lord Jesus to send Timothy shortly unto you, that I also may be of good comfort, when I know your state. For I have no man like-minded, who will naturally care for your state. For all seek their own, not the things which are Jesus Christ's. But ye know the proof of him, that, as a son with the father, he hath served with me in the Gospel. Him therefore I hope to send presently, so soon as I shall see how it will go with me. But I trust in the Lord that I also myself shall come shortly. Yet I supposed it necessary to send to you Epaphroditus, my brother, and companion in labour, and fellowsoldier, but your Apostle, and he that ministered to my wants. For he longed after you all, and was full of heaviness, because that ye had heard that he had been sick. For indeed he was sick nigh unto death: but God had mercy on him; and not on him only, but on me also, lest I should have sorrow upon sorrow. I sent him therefore the more carefully, that, when ye see him again, ye may rejoice, and that I may be the less sorrowful. Receive him therefore in the Lord with all gladness; and hold such in reputation: because for the work of Christ he was nigh unto death, not regarding his life, to supply your lack of service toward me.

Finally, my brethren, rejoice in the Lord. To write the same things to you, to me indeed is not grievous, but for you it is safe.

Beware of dogs, beware of evil workers, beware of the concision. For we are the circumcision, which worship God in the spirit, and rejoice in Christ Jesus, and have no confidence in the flesh. Though I might also have confidence in the flesh.

If any other man thinketh that he hath whereof he might trust in the flesh, I more: circumcised the eighth day, of the stock of Israel, of the tribe of Benjamin, an Hebrew of the Hebrews; as touching the law, a Pharisee; concerning zeal, persecuting the Church; touching the righteousness which is in the law, blameless.

But what things were gain to me, those I counted loss for Christ. Yea doubtless, and I count all things but loss for the excellency of the knowledge of Christ Jesus my Lord: for Whom I have suffered the loss of all things, and do count them but dung, that I may win Christ and be found in Him, not having mine own righteousness, which is of the law, but that which is through the faith of Christ, the righteousness which is of God by faith; that I may know Him, and the power of His resurrection, and the fellowship of His sufferings, being made conformable unto His death; if by any means I might attain unto the resurrection of the dead. Not as though I had already attained, either were already perfect: but I follow after, if that I may appre-

hend that for which also I am apprehended of Christ Jesus. Brethren, I count not myself to have apprehended: but this one thing I do, forgetting those things which are behind, and reaching forth unto those things which are before, I press toward the mark for the prize of the high calling of God in Christ Jesus. Let us therefore, as many as be perfect, be thus minded: and if in any thing ye be otherwise minded, God shall reveal even this unto you. Nevertheless, whereto we have already attained, let us walk by the same rule, let us mind the same thing.

Brethren, be followers together of me, and mark them which walk so as ye have us for an ensample. For many walk, of whom I have told you often, and now tell you even weeping, that they are the enemies of the cross of Christ: whose end is destruction, whose God is their belly, and whose glory is in their shame, who mind earthly things. For our conversation is in heaven; from whence also we look for the Saviour, the Lord Jesus Christ: Who shall change our vile body, that it may be fashioned like unto His glorious body, according to the working whereby He is able even to subdue all things unto Himself.

Therefore, my brethren dearly beloved and longed for, my joy and crown, so stand fast in the Lord, my dearly beloved.

I beseech Euodias, and beseech Syntyche, that they be of the same mind in the Lord. And I intreat thee also, true yokefellow, help those women which laboured with me in the Gospel, with Clement also, and with other my fellowlabourers, whose names are in the book of life.

Rejoice in the Lord alway: and again I say, Rejoice. Let your moderation be known unto all men. The Lord is at hand. Be careful for nothing; but in every thing by prayer and supplication with thanksgiving let your requests be made known unto God. And the peace of God, which passeth all understanding, shall keep your hearts and minds through Christ Jesus.

Finally, brethren, whatsoever things are true, whatsoever things are honest, whatsoever things are just, whatsoever things are pure, whatsoever things are lovely, whatsoever things are of good report; if there be any virtue, and if there be any praise, think on these things. Those things, which ye have both learned, and received, and heard, and seen in me, do: and the God of peace shall be with you.

But I rejoiced in the Lord greatly, that now at the last your care of me hath flourished again; wherein ye were also careful, but ye lacked opportunity. Not that I speak in respect of want: for I have learned, in whatsoever state I am, therewith to be content. I know both how to be abased, and I

know how to abound: every where and in all things I am instructed both to be full and to be hungry, both to abound and to suffer need. I can do all things through Christ Who strengtheneth me. Notwithstanding ye have well done, that ye did communicate with my affliction. Now ye Philippians know also, that in the beginning of the Gospel, when I departed from Macedonia, no church communicated with me as concerning giving and receiving, but ye only. For even in Thessalonica ye sent once and again unto my necessity. Not because I desire a gift: but I desire fruit that may abound to your account. But I have all, and abound: I am full, having received of Epaphroditus the things which were sent from you, an odour of a sweet smell, a sacrifice acceptable, wellpleasing to God. But my God shall supply all our need according to His riches in glory by Christ Jesus.

Now unto God and Our Father be glory for ever and ever. Amen.

Salute every saint in Christ Jesus. The brethren which are with me greet you. All the saints salute you, chiefly they that are of Caesar's household.

The grace of our Lord Jesus Christ be with you all. Amen.

Paul and Timothy,
the servants of Jesus Christ.

[*from Rome, circa 61 A.D.*]

THE EIGHTH SPIRIT:

Boethius·

THE CONSOLATION OF PHILOSOPHY

AN EIGHTH place of honor is conferred on Boethius by one of his great lovers, Dante, when in the tenth canto of *Paradiso* the poet meets the twelve supreme theologians. Dante (himself to become an exile in need of comfort), who had read Boethius' *Consolation of Philosophy* after the loss of Beatrice, assigns to him the eighth place in Paradise among the company which includes Thomas Aquinas, Albertus Magnus, and Peter Lombard:

> The saintly soul that shows
> The world's deceitfulness, to all who hear him,
> Is with the sight of all the good that is
> Blest there. The limbs whence it was driven lie
> Down in Cieldauro, and from martyrdom
> And exile came it here.

Boethius' misfortunes were cruel but brief. Theodoric, Ostrogoth emperor and a Christian of the Arian heresy, had patronized each of Boethius' many talents, in mechanics, music, astronomy, finance, philosophy, and government. In a time when Graeco-Roman civilization was giving up its ghost, Boethius was stubbornly busy with plans for reconciling Plato with Aristotle and religion with reason. His humanist program came to a sudden stop when Theodoric, suspecting a conservative Catholic senate of opposing his Arianism and of negotiating with Byzantium against his rule in Italy, began to clean out his house of rebellion. For defending one of the senators accused of secret correspondence with Justin I, Boethius was himself thrown into a dungeon at Pavia. The charges were treason and, for good measure, also the practice of the black arts. In the brief interval of imprisonment before his execution in 524, Boethius was assailed by all the old tormenting doubts of Job. Could he, Boethius, in the evil of his dungeon, justify the moral government of the universe? Could he, the lover of Philosophy, the servant of Reason, justify the ways of God to man? His answer was the *Consolation of Philosophy,* the allegory which captured the hearts and the imagination of the Middle Ages and which found eager translators in King Alfred, Chaucer, and even Queen Elizabeth. The poem opens with the

revelation to Boethius of "a woman's form, whose countenance was full of majesty, whose eyes shone as with fire and in power of insight surpassed the eyes of men, whose colour was full of life, whose strength was yet intact though she was so full of years that none would ever think that she was subject to such age as ours." This was his mistress, Philosophy, who had consoled other victims before him, Socrates, Anaxagoras, Zeno, and Seneca. She expounds to Boethius the nature of good and evil, and, stage by stage, climbs with him to rarer regions, to the mountain-top of Divine Intelligence. The whole rising, ecstatic journey of thirty-nine songs alternating with thirty-nine prose passages, curiously never leads off the "pagan" philosophic road to some Christian shrine by the wayside; Jesus is never mentioned in the dialogue between Philosophy and Boethius. But in its last flight upwards the work ends like a grand choral with a hymn to God: "Hopes are not vainly put in God, nor prayers in vain offered: if these are right, they cannot but be answered. Turn therefore from vice: ensue virtue: raise your soul to upright hopes: send up on high your prayers from this earth. If you would be honest, great is the necessity enjoined upon your goodness, since all you do is done before the eyes of an all-seeing Judge."

THE CONSOLATION OF PHILOSOPHY

WHILE I was pondering thus in silence, and using my pen to set down so tearful a complaint, there appeared standing over my head a woman's form, whose countenance was full of majesty, whose eyes shone as with fire and in power of insight surpassed the eyes of men, whose colour was full of life, whose strength was yet intact though she was so full of years that none would ever think that she was subject to such age as ours. One could but doubt her varying stature, for at one moment she repressed it to the common measure of a man, at another she seemed to touch with her crown the very heavens: and when she had raised higher her head, it pierced even the sky and baffled the sight of those who would look upon it. Her clothing was wrought of the finest thread by subtle workmanship brought to an indivisible piece. This had she woven with her own hands, as I afterwards did learn by her own shewing. Their beauty was somewhat dimmed by the dulness of long neglect, as is seen in the smoke-grimed masks of our ancestors. On the border below was inwoven the symbol II, on that above was to be read a Θ.[1]

---

[1] II and Θ are the first letters of the Greek words denoting Practical and Theoretical, the two divisions of philosophy.

And between the two letters there could be marked degrees, by which, as by the rungs of a ladder, ascent might be made from the lower principle to the higher. Yet the hands of rough men had torn this garment and snatched such morsels as they could therefrom. In her right hand she carried books, in her left was a sceptre brandished.

When she saw that the Muses of poetry were present by my couch giving words to my lamenting, she was stirred a while; her eyes flashed fiercely, and said she, 'Who has suffered these seducing mummers to approach this sick man? Never do they support those in sorrow by any healing remedies, but rather do ever foster the sorrow by poisonous sweets. These are they who stifle the fruit-bearing harvest of reason with the barren briars of the passions: they free not the minds of men from disease, but accustom them thereto. I would think it less grievous if your allurements drew away from me some uninitiated man, as happens in the vulgar herd. In such an one my labours would be naught harmed, but this man has been nourished in the lore of Eleatics and Academics; and to him have ye reached? Away with you, Sirens, seductive unto destruction! leave him to my Muses to be cared for and to be healed.'

Their band thus rated cast a saddened glance upon the ground, confessing their shame in blushes, and passed forth dismally over the threshold. For my part, my eyes were dimmed with tears, and I could not discern who was this woman of such commanding power. I was amazed, and turning my eyes to the ground I began in silence to await what she should do. Then she approached nearer and sat down upon the end of my couch: she looked into my face heavy with grief and cast down by sorrow to the ground, and then she raised her complaint over the trouble of my mind in these words.

'Ah me! how blunted grows the mind when sunk below the o'erwhelming flood! Its own true light no longer burns within, and it would break forth to outer darkness. How often care, when fanned by earthly winds, grows to a larger and unmeasured bane. This man has been free to the open heaven: his habit has it been to wander into the paths of the sky: his to watch the light of the bright sun, his to inquire into the brightness of the chilly moon; he, like a conqueror, held fast bound in its order every star that makes its wandering circle, turning its peculiar course. Nay, more, deeply has he searched into the springs of nature, whence came the roaring blasts that ruffle the ocean's bosom calm: what is the spirit that makes the firmament resolve; wherefore does the evening star sink into the eastern wave but to rise from the radiant East; what is the cause which so tempers the season of

Spring that it decks the earth with rose-blossoms; whence comes it to pass that Autumn is prolific in the years of plenty and overflows with teeming vines: deeply to search these causes was his wont, and to bring forth secrets deep in Nature hid.

'Now he lies there; extinct his reason's light, his neck in heavy chains thrust down, his countenance with grievous weight downcast; ah! the brute earth is all he can behold.

'But now,' said she, 'is the time for the physician's art, rather than for complaining.' Then fixing her eyes wholly on me, she said, 'Are you the man who was nourished upon the milk of my learning, brought up with my food until you had won your way to the power of a manly soul? Surely I had given you such weapons as would keep you safe, and your strength unconquered; if you had not thrown them away. Do you know me? Why do you keep silence? Are you dumb from shame or from dull amazement? I would it were from shame, but I see that amazement has overwhelmed you.'

When she saw that I was not only silent, but utterly tongue-tied and dumb, she put her hand gently upon my breast, and said, 'There is no danger: he is suffering from drowsiness, that disease which attacks so many minds which have been deceived. He has forgotten himself for a moment and will quickly remember, as soon as he recognizes me. That he may do so, let me brush away from his eyes the darkening cloud of thoughts of matters perishable.' So saying, she gathered her robe into a fold and dried my swimming eyes.

Then was dark night dispelled, the shadows fled away, and my eyes received returning power as before. . . .

In such a manner were the clouds of grief scattered. Then I drew breath again and engaged my mind in taking knowledge of my physician's countenance. So when I turned my eyes towards her and fixed my gaze upon her, I recognized my nurse, Philosophy, in whose chambers I had spent my life from earliest manhood. And I asked her, 'Wherefore have you, mistress of all virtues, come down from heaven above to visit my lonely place of banishment? Is it that you, as well as I, may be harried, the victim of false charges?' 'Should I,' said she, 'desert you, my nursling? Should I not share and bear my part of the burden which has been laid upon you from spite against my name? Surely Philosophy never allowed herself to let the innocent go upon their journey unbefriended. Think you I would fear calum-

nies? that I would be terrified as though they were a new misfortune? Think you that this is the first time that wisdom has been harassed by dangers among men of shameless ways? In ancient days before the time of my child, Plato, have we not as well as nowadays fought many a mighty battle against the recklessness of folly? And though Plato did survive, did not his master, Socrates, win his victory of an unjust death, with me present at his side? When after him the followers of Epicurus, and in turn the Stoics, and then others did all try their utmost to seize his legacy, they dragged me, for all my cries and struggles, as though to share me as plunder; they tore my robe which I had woven with mine own hands, and snatched away the fragments thereof: and when they thought I had altogether yielded myself to them, they departed. And since among them were to be seen certain signs of my outward bearing, others ill-advised did think they wore my livery: thus were many of them undone by the errors of the herd of uninitiated. But if you have not heard of the exile of Anaxagoras, nor the poison drunk by Socrates, nor the torture of Zeno, which all were of foreign lands, yet you may know of Canius, Seneca, and Soranus, whose fame is neither small nor passing old. Naught else brought them to ruin but that, being built up in my ways, they appeared at variance with the desire of unscrupulous men.[2] So it is no matter for your wonder if, in this sea of life, we are tossed about by storms from all sides; for to oppose evil men is the chief aim we set before ourselves. Though the band of such men is great in numbers, yet is it to be contemned: for it is guided by no leader, but is hurried along at random only by error running riot everywhere. If this band when warring against us presses too strongly upon us, our leader, Reason, gathers her forces into her citadel, while the enemy are busied in plundering useless baggage. As they seize the most worthless things, we laugh at them from above, untroubled by the whole band of mad marauders, and we are defended by that rampart to which riotous folly may not hope to attain.

'*He who has calmly reconciled his life to fate, and set proud death beneath his feet, can look fortune in the face, unbending both to good and bad: his countenance unconquered he can shew. . . . Fear nought, and hope nought: thus shall you have a weak man's rage disarmed. But whoso fears with trembling, or desires aught from them, he stands not firmly rooted,*

---

[2] Anaxagoras went into exile from Athens about 450 B.C. Socrates was executed by the Athenian state, 399 B.C. Zeno of Elea was tortured by Nearchus, tyrant of Elea, about 440 B.C. Canius was put to death by Caligula, c. 40 A.D. Seneca was driven to commit suicide by Nero, 65 A.D. Soranus was condemned to death by Nero, 66 A.D.

but dependent: thus has he thrown away his shield; he can be rooted up, and he links for himself the very chain whereby he may be dragged.'

'Are such your experiences, and do they sink into your soul?' she asked. Do you listen only as "the dull ass to the lyre"? Why do you weep? Wherefore flow your tears? "Speak, nor keep secret in thine heart." If you expect a physician to help you, you must lay bare your wound.'

Thus did I rally my spirit till it was strong again, and answered, 'Does the savage bitterness of my fortune still need recounting? Does it not stand forth plainly enough of itself? Does not the very aspect of this place strike you? Is this the library which you had chosen for yourself as your sure resting-place in my house? Is this the room in which you would so often tarry with me expounding the philosophy of things human and divine? Was my condition like this, or my countenance, when I probed with your aid the secrets of nature, when you marked out with a wand the courses of the stars, when you shaped our habits and the rule of all our life by the pattern of the universe? Are these the rewards we reap by yielding ourselves to you? Nay, you yourself have established this saying by the mouth of Plato, that commonwealths would be blessed if they were guided by those who made wisdom their study, or if those who guided them would make wisdom their study. By the mouth of that same great man did you teach that this was the binding reason why a commonwealth should be governed by philosophers, namely that the helm of government should not be left to unscrupulous or criminal citizens lest they should bring corruption and ruin upon the good citizens. Since, then, I had learned from you in quiet and inaction of this view, I followed it further, for I desired to practise it in public government. You and God Himself, who has grafted you in the minds of philosophers, are my witnesses that never have I applied myself to any office of state except that I might work for the common welfare of all good men. Thence followed bitter quarrels with evil men which could not be appeased, and, for the sake of preserving justice, contempt of the enmity of those in power, for this is the result of a free and fearless conscience. How often have I withstood Conigastus [3] to his face, whenever he has attacked a weak man's fortune! How often have I turned by force Trigulla, the overseer of the Emperor's household, from an unjust act that he had begun or even carried out! How many times have I put my own authority in danger by protecting those wretched people who were harried with unending false charges by

---

[3] Conigastus and Trigulla were favourite officers of the Emperor, Theodoric, the Goth: they used their influence with him for the oppression of the weak.

the greed of barbarian Goths which ever went unpunished! Never, I say, has any man depraved me from justice to injustice. My heart has ached as bitterly as those of the sufferers when I have seen the fortunes of our subjects ruined both by the rapacity of persons and the taxes of the state. Again, in a time of severe famine, a grievous, intolerable sale by compulsion was decreed in Campania, and devastation threatened that province. Then ·I undertook for the sake of the common welfare a struggle against the commander of the Imperial guard; though the king was aware of it, I fought against the enforcement of the sale, and fought successfully. Paulinus was a man who had been consul: the jackals of the court had in their own hopes and desires already swallowed up his possessions, but I snatched him from their very gaping jaws. I exposed myself to the hatred of the treacherous informer Cyprian, that I might prevent Albinus, also a former consul, being overwhelmed by the penalty of a trumped-up charge. Think you that I have raised up against myself bitter and great quarrels enough? But I ought to have been safer among those whom I helped; for, from my love of justice, I laid up for myself among the courtiers no resource to which I might turn for safety. Who, further, were the informers ·upon whose evidence I was banished? One was Basilius: he was formerly expelled from the royal service, and was driven by debt to inform against me. Again, Opilio and Gaudentius had been condemned to exile by the king for many unjust acts and crimes: this decree they would not obey, and they sought sanctuary in sacred buildings, but when the king was aware of it, he declared that if they departed not from Ravenna before a certain day, they should be driven forth branded upon their foreheads. What could be more stringent than this? Yet upon that very day information against me was laid by these same men and accepted. Why so? Did my character deserve this treatment? Or did my prearranged condemnation give credit and justification to my accusers? Did Fortune feel no shame for this? If not for innocence calumniated, at any rate for the baseness of the calumniators?

'Would you learn the sum of the charges against me? It was said that "I had desired the safety of the Senate." You would learn in what way. I was charged with "having hindered an informer from producing papers by which the Senate could be accused of treason." What think you, my mistress? Shall I deny it lest it shame you? Nay, I did desire the safety of the Senate, nor shall ever cease to desire it. Shall I confess it? Then there would have been no need to hinder an informer. Shall I call it a crime to have wished for the safety of that order? By its own decrees concerning myself it has estab-

lished that this is a crime. Though want of foresight often deceives itself, it cannot alter the merits of facts, and, in obedience to the Senate's command, I cannot think it right to hide the truth or to assent to falsehood.

'However, I leave it to your judgment and that of philosophers to decide how the justice of this may be; but I have committed to writing for history the true course of events, that posterity may not be ignorant thereof. I think it unnecessary to speak of the forged letters through which I am accused of "hoping for the freedom of Rome." Their falsity would have been apparent if I had been free to question the evidence of the informers themselves, for their confessions have much force in all such business.

'But what avails it? No liberty is left to hope for. Would there were any! I would answer in the words of Canius, who was accused by Caius Caesar, Germanicus' son, of being cognizant of a plot against himself: "If I had known of it, you would not have."

'And in this matter grief has not so blunted my powers that I should complain of wicked men making impious attacks upon virtue: but at this I do wonder, that they should hope to succeed. Evil desires are, it may be, due to our natural failings, but that the conceptions of any wicked mind should prevail against innocence while God watches over us, seems to me unnatural. Wherefore not without cause has one of your own followers asked, "If God is, whence come evil things? If He is not, whence come good?"

'Again, let impious men, who thirst for the blood of the whole Senate and of all good citizens, be allowed to wish for the ruin of us too whom they recognize as champions of the Senate and all good citizens: but surely such as I have not deserved the same hatred from the members of the Senate too?

'Since you were always present to guide me in my words and my deeds, I think you remember what happened at Verona. When King Theodoric, desiring the common ruin of the Senate, was for extending to the whole order the charge of treason laid against Albinus, you remember how I laboured to defend the innocence of the order without any care for my own danger? You know that I declare this truthfully and with no boasting praise of self. For the secret value of a conscience, that approves its own action, is lessened somewhat each time that it receives the reward of fame by displaying its deeds. But you see what end has fallen upon my innocency. In the place of the rewards of honest virtue, I am suffering the punishments of an ill deed that was not mine. And did ever any direct confession of a crime find its judges so well agreed upon exercising harshness, that neither the liability of the human heart to err, nor the changeableness of the fortune of all man-

kind, could yield one dissentient voice? If it had been said that I had wished to burn down temples, to murder with sacrilegious sword their priests, that I had planned the massacre of all good citizens, even so I should have been present to plead guilty or to be convicted, before the sentence was executed. But here am I, nearly five hundred miles away, without the opportunity of defending myself, condemned to death and the confiscation of my property because of my too great zeal for the Senate. Ah! well have they deserved that none should ever be liable to be convicted on such a charge! Even those who laid information have seen the honour of this accusation, for, that they might blacken it with some criminal ingredient, they had need to lie, saying that I had violated my conscience by using unholy means to obtain offices corruptly. But you, by being planted within me, dispelled from the chamber of my soul all craving for that which perishes, and where your eyes were looking there could be no place for any such sacrilege. For you instilled into my ears, and thus into my daily thoughts, that saying of Pythagoras, "Follow after God." Nor was it seemly that I, whom you had built up to such excellence that you made me as a god, should seek the support of the basest wills of men. Yet, further, the innocent life within my home, my gathering of most honourable friends, my father-in-law Symmachus,[4] a man esteemed no less in his public life than for his private conscientiousness, these all put far from me all suspicion of this crime. But—O the shame of it! —it is from you that they think they derive the warrant for such a charge, and we seem to them to be allied to ill-doing from this very fact that we are steeped in the principles of your teaching, and trained in your manner of life. Thus it is not enough that my deep respect for you has profited me nothing, but you yourself have received wanton contumely from the hatred that had rather fallen on me. Yet besides this, is another load added to my heap of woes: the judgment of the world looks not to the deserts of the case, but to the evolution of chance, and holds that only this has been intended which good fortune may chance to foster: whence it comes that the good opinion of the world is the first to desert the unfortunate. It is wearisome to recall what were the tales by people told, or how little their many various opinions agreed. This alone I would fain say: it is the last burden laid upon us by unkind fortune, that when any charge is invented to be fastened upon unhappy men, they are believed to have deserved all they have to bear. For kindness I have received persecutions; I have been

---

[4] Symmachus was executed by Theodoric at the same time as Boethius.

driven from all my possessions, stripped of my honours, and stained for ever in my reputation. I think I see the intoxication of joy in the sin-steeped dens of criminals: I see the most abandoned of men intent upon new and evil schemes of spying: I see honest men lying crushed with the fear which smites them after the result of my perilous case: wicked men one and all encouraged to dare every crime without fear of punishment, nay, with hope of rewards for the accomplishment thereof: the innocent I see robbed not merely of their peace and safety, but even of all chance of defending themselves. So then I may cry aloud:—

'Founder of the star-studded universe, resting on Thine eternal throne whence Thou turnest the swiftly rolling sky, and bindest the stars to keep Thy law; at Thy word the moon now shines brightly with full face, ever turned to her brother's light, and so she dims the lesser lights; or now she is herself obscured, for nearer to the sun her beams shew her pale horns alone. Cool rises the evening star at night's first drawing nigh: the same is the morning star who casts off the harness that she bore before, and paling meets the rising sun. When winter's cold doth strip the trees, Thou settest a shorter span to day. And Thou, when summer comes to warm, dost change the short divisions of the night. Thy power doth order the seasons of the year, so that the western breeze of spring brings back the leaves which winter's north wind tore away; so that the dog-star's heat makes ripe the ears of corn whose seed Arcturus watched. Naught breaks that ancient law: naught leaves undone the work appointed to its place. Thus all things Thou dost rule with limits fixed: the lives of men alone dost Thou scorn to restrain, as a guardian, within bounds. For why does Fortune with her fickle hand deal out such changing lots? The hurtful penalty is due to crime, but falls upon the sinless head: depraved men rest at ease on thrones aloft, and by their unjust lot can spurn beneath their hurtful heel the necks of virtuous men. Beneath obscuring shadows lies bright virtue hid: the just man bears the unjust's infamy. They suffer not for forsworn oaths, they suffer not for crimes glozed over with their lies. But when their will is to put forth their strength, with triumph they subdue the mightiest kings whom peoples in their thousands fear. O Thou who dost weave the bonds of Nature's self, look down upon this pitiable earth! Mankind is no base part of this great work, and we are tossed on Fortune's wave. Restrain, our Guardian, the engulfing surge, and as Thou dost the unbounded heaven rule, with a like bond make true and firm these lands.'

46

While I grieved thus in long-drawn pratings, Philosophy looked on with a calm countenance, not one whit moved by my complaints. Then said she, 'When I saw you in grief and in tears I knew thereby that you were unhappy and in exile, but I knew not how distant was your exile until your speech declared it. But you have not been driven so far from your home; you have wandered thence yourself: or if you would rather hold that you have been driven, you have been driven by yourself rather than by any other. No other could have done so to you. For if you recall your true native country, you know that it is not under the rule of the many-headed people, as was Athens of old, but there is one Lord, one King, who rejoices in the greater number of his subjects, not in their banishment. To be guided by his reins, to bow to his justice, is the highest liberty. Know you not that sacred and ancient law of your own state by which it is enacted that no man, who would establish a dwelling-place for himself therein, may lawfully be put forth? For there is no fear that any man should merit exile, if he be kept safe therein by its protecting walls. But any man that may no longer wish to dwell there, does equally no longer deserve to be there. Wherefore it is your looks rather than the aspect of this place which disturb me. It is not the walls of your library, decked with ivory and glass, that I need, but rather the resting-place in your heart, wherein I have not stored books, but I have of old put that which gives value to books, a store of thoughts from books of mine. As to your services to the common weal, you have spoken truly, though but scantily, if you consider your manifold exertions. Of all wherewith you have been charged either truthfully or falsely, you have but recorded what is well known. As for the crimes and wicked lies of the informers, you have rightly thought fit to touch but shortly thereon, for they are better and more fruitfully made common in the mouth of the crowd that discusses all matters. You have loudly and strongly upbraided the unjust ingratitude of the Senate: you have grieved over the charges made against myself, and shed tears over the insult to my fair fame: your last outburst of wrath was against Fortune, when you complained that she paid no fair rewards according to deserts: finally, you have prayed with passionate Muse that the same peace and order, that are seen in the heavens, might also rule the earth. But you are overwhelmed by this variety of mutinous passions: grief, rage, and gloom tear your mind asunder, and so in this present mood stronger measures cannot yet come nigh to heal you. Let us therefore use gentler means, and since, just as matter in the body hardens into a swelling,

47

so have these disquieting influences, let these means soften by kindly handling the unhealthy spot, until it will bear a sharper remedy.

'When the sign of the crab doth scorch the field, fraught with the sun's most grievous rays, the husbandman that has freely intrusted his seed to the fruitless furrow, is cheated by the faithless harvest-goddess; and he must turn him to the oak tree's fruit.

'When the field is scarred by the bleak north winds, wouldst thou seek the wood's dark carpet to gather violets? If thou wilt enjoy the grapes, wouldst thou seek with clutching hand to prune the vines in spring? 'Tis in autumn Bacchus brings his gifts. Thus God marks out the times and fits to them peculiar works: He has set out a course of change, and lets no confusion come. If aught betake itself to headlong ways, and leaves its sure design, ill will the outcome be thereto.'

'First then,' she continued, 'will you let me find out and make trial of the state of your mind by a few small questions, that so I may understand what should be the method of your treatment?'

'Ask,' said I, 'what your judgment would have you ask, and I will answer you.'

Then said she, 'Think you that this universe is guided only at random and by mere chance? or think you there is any rule of reason constituted in it?'

'No, never would I think it could be so, nor believe that such sure motions could be made at random or by chance. I know that God, the founder of the universe, does overlook His work; nor ever may that day come which shall drive me to abandon this belief as untrue.'

'So is it,' she said, 'and even so you cried just now, and only mourned that mankind alone has no part in this divine guardianship: you were fixed in your belief that all other things are ruled by reason. Yet, how strange! how much I wonder how it is that you can be so sick though you are set in such a health-giving state of mind! But let us look deeper into it: I cannot but think there is something lacking. Since you are not in doubt that the universe is ruled by God, tell me by what method you think that government is guided?'

'I scarcely know the meaning of your question; much less can I answer it.'

'Was I wrong,' said she, 'to think that something was lacking, that there was some opening in your armour, some way by which this distracting

48

disease has crept into your soul? But tell me, do you remember what is the aim and end of all things? what the object to which all nature tends?'

'I have heard indeed, but grief has blunted my memory.'

'But do you not somehow know whence all things have their source?'

'Yes,' I said; 'that source is God.'

'Is it possible that you, who know the beginning of all things, should not know their end? But such are the ways of these distractions, such is their power, that though they can move a man's position, they cannot pluck him from himself or wrench him from his roots. But this question would I have you answer: do you remember that you are a man?'

'How can I but remember that?'

'Can you then say what is a man?'

'Need you ask? I know that he is an animal, reasoning and mortal; that I know, and that I confess myself to be.'

'Know you naught else that you are?' asked Philosophy.

'Naught,' said I.

'Now,' said she, 'I know the cause, or the chief cause, of your sickness. You have forgotten what you are. Now therefore I have found out to the full the manner of your sickness, and how to attempt the restoring of your health. You are overwhelmed by this forgetfulness of yourself: hence you have been thus sorrowing that you are exiled and robbed of all your posses-sions. You do not know the aim and end of all things; hence you think that if men are worthless and wicked, they are powerful and fortunate. You have forgotten by what methods the universe is guided; hence you think that the chances of good and bad fortune are tossed about with no ruling hand. These things may lead not to disease only, but even to death as well. But let us thank the Giver of all health, that your nature has not altogether left you. We have yet the chief spark for your health's fire, for you have a true knowledge of the hand that guides the universe: you do believe that its government is not subject to random chance, but to divine reason. There-fore have no fear. From this tiny spark the fire of life shall forthwith shine upon you. But it is not time to use severer remedies, and since we know that it is the way of all minds to clothe themselves ever in false opinions as they throw off the true, and these false ones breed a dark distraction which con-fuses the true insight, therefore will I try to lessen this darkness for a while with gentle application of easy remedies, that so the shadows of deceiving passions may be dissipated, and you may have power to perceive the bright-ness of true light.'

BOOKKEEPER OF WONDERLAND:
Marco Polo

~~~~~~

And so, being in prison in Genoa, he made a Book, concerning the great wonders of the World, i.e., concerning such of them as he had seen. And what he told in the Book was not as much as he had really seen, because of the tongues of detractors, who, being ready to impose their own lies on others, are over hasty to set down as lies what they in their perversity disbelieve, or do not understand. And because there are many great and strange things in that Book, which are reckoned past all credence, he was asked by his friends on his death-bed to correct the Book by removing everything that went beyond the facts. To which his reply was that he had not told *one-half* of what he had really seen.

JACOPO OF ACQUI, *Imago Mundi* (quoted by Sir Henry Yule)

MARCO POLO is a complete realist taking careful notes in an alien world. He is a sober, patient, tactful, and modest merchant of Venice at the court of Kublai Khan. He is a bookkeeper conscientiously entering into his accounts risks and profits, geography and sociology, bits of decoration and of splendor. The observed fact, the odd detail, and the marvelous item, are all set down in his passionless report. The finished mosaic of Marco Polo's tale is so attractive that it has the effect of making the mechanics, the artistry and the tyranny of Kublai Khan seem superior to the contemporary civilization of the West. A mere by-product of the commercial mission of the Polos was the Pope's greetings to the Asiatic emperor whose predecessors had threatened Christian Europe. This was a Europe in which Louis IX of France had bought from Baldwin II of Constantinople the crown of thorns worn by Jesus (for some time pawned in the Venice of the Polos) as well as "the baby linen of the Son of God, the lance, the sponge and the chain of His passion, the reed of Moses, and part of the skull of St. John the Baptist." The Polos who went doggedly eastward on business were citizens of Venice which vied with Genoa for the trade of the Near East and the comfortable profits accruing from the stream of holy pilgrimage to Palestine. When Marco Polo returned with the million wonders of the eastern world on his tongue—a tired traveler speaking his native Italian with an accent, and ready to begin a new life at forty—he was caught in the struggle between the Venetians and the Genoese. In 1296, the survivor of a hundred hardships found himself a prisoner of war in the underground rooms of a palace in

Genoa together with other Venetians and a few Pisans. He found distraction in entertaining his companions, and even his jailers, with episodes of his adventure. His remarkable stories won him indulgence and respect—but neither freedom nor exactly credence. When a literary fellow prisoner, one Rustichello of Pisa, an old hand at Arthurian romances, offered to relieve the storyteller of the fatigue of repeated recitals by setting down the whole adventure on parchment, Marco Polo, with the approval of the warring Genoese, sent to Venice for his old travel notes. From this collaboration in a dungeon the *Description of the World* was born in bad French, attained a Latin translation, later the vulgar Italian dialects, and rapidly all tongues that could tell a tale. This "description of the world," like one of those dreams which extracts from something unreal the appearance of a meticulous reality, gave Europeans a sudden introduction to Persia, India, China, and Tartary. Centuries later, this dream of riches and wonder had the honor of being carried in the baggage of Christopher Columbus, hopefully annotated in his own hand, and so real to the Admiral of the Indies that he could write home under its spell: "large ships of the Grand Khan come here."

Marco Polo, bookkeeper of wonderland, never lets us into the private feelings of his decades of service in an alien land, where he was governor of a city, an engineer of artillery, a minister without portfolio, as it were, and a kind of court savant to Kublai Khan. Did he, while accumulating profits and tales, ever feel the bitterness which T. E. Lawrence, for example, felt among the Arabs, that "a man who gives himself to be a possession of aliens leads a Yahoo life, having bartered his soul to a brute master?" Perhaps Marco Polo on business and in exile was too busy for the luxuries of introspection. His *Description of the World* is all the better for its primary colors. It is like one of those medieval tapestries—Flemish, French or Italian; in reds, yellows, blues, oranges, and silver-gilt thread; with flowers, birds, animals, unicorns and palaces—all of it orderly and very pleasant. Coleridge, dozing over the marvelous tale, composed his lines:

> In Xanadu did Kubla Khan
> A stately pleasure-dome decree:
> Where Alph, the sacred river, ran
> Through caverns measureless to man
> Down to a sunless sea.
> So twice five miles of fertile ground
> With walls and towers were girdled round:

And here were gardens bright with sinuous rills
Where blossomed many an incense-bearing tree;
And here were forests ancient as the hills,
Enfolding sunny spots of greenery.

OF THE NOBLE AND MAGNIFICENT CITY OF KIN-SAI

UPON leaving Va-giu you pass, in the course of three days' journey, many towns, castles, and villages, all of them well inhabited and opulent. The people are idolaters, and the subjects of the grand khan, and they use paper money and have abundance of provisions. At the end of three days you reach the noble and magnificent city of Kin-sai, a name that signifies "the celestial city," and which it merits from its preeminence to all others in the world, in point of grandeur and beauty, as well as from its abundant delights, which might lead an inhabitant to imagine himself in paradise. This city was frequently visited by Marco Polo, who carefully and diligently observed and inquired into every circumstance respecting it, all of which he entered in his notes, from whence the following particulars are briefly stated. According to common estimation, this city is an hundred miles in circuit. Its streets and canals are extensive, and there are squares, or market-places, which, being necessarily proportioned in size to the prodigious concourse of people by whom they are frequented, are exceedingly spacious. It is situated between a lake of fresh and very clear water on the one side, and a river of great magnitude on the other, the waters of which, by a number of canals, large and small, are made to run through every quarter of the city, carrying with them all the filth into the lake, and ultimately to the sea. This, whilst it contributes much to the purity of the air, furnishes a communication by water, in addition to that by land, to all parts of the town; the canals and the streets being of sufficient width to allow of boats on the one, and carriages in the other, conveniently passing, with articles necessary for the consumption of the inhabitants. It is commonly said that the number of bridges, of all sizes, amounts to twelve thousand. Those which are thrown over the principal canals and are connected with the main streets, have arches so high, and built with so much skill, that vessels with their masts can pass under them, whilst, at the same time, carts and horses are passing over their heads,—so well is the slope from the street adapted to the height of the arch. If they were not in fact so numerous, there would be no convenience of crossing from one place to another.

Beyond the city, and enclosing it on that side, there is a fosse about forty miles in length, very wide, and full of water that comes from the river before mentioned. This was excavated by the ancient kings of the province, in order that when the river should overflow its banks, the superfluous water might be diverted into this channel; and to serve at the same time as a measure of defence. The earth dug out from thence was thrown to the inner side, and has the appearance of many hillocks surrounding the place. There are within the city ten principal squares or market-places, besides innumerable shops along the streets. Each side of these squares is half a mile in length, and in front of them is the main street, forty paces in width, and running in a direct line from one extremity of the city to the other. It is crossed by many low and convenient bridges. These market-squares (two miles in their whole dimension) are at the distance of four miles from each other. In a direction parallel to that of the main street, but on the opposite side of the squares, runs a very large canal, on the nearer bank of which capacious warehouses are built of stone, for the accommodation of the merchants who arrive from India and other parts, together with their goods and effects, in order that they may be conveniently situated with respect to the market-places. In each of these, upon three days in every week, there is an assemblage of from forty to fifty thousand persons, who attend the markets and supply them with every article of provision that can be desired. There is an abundant quantity of game of all kinds, such as roebucks, stags, fallow deer, hares, and rabbits, together with partridges, pheasants, francolins, quails, common fowls, capons, and such numbers of ducks and geese as can scarcely be expressed; for so easily are they bred and reared on the lake, that, for the value of a Venetian silver groat, you may purchase a couple of geese and two couple of ducks. There, also, are the shambles, where they slaughter cattle for food, such as oxen, calves, kids, and lambs, to furnish the tables of rich persons and of the great magistrates. As to people of the lower classes, they do not scruple to eat every other kind of flesh, however unclean, without any discrimination. At all seasons there is in the markets a great variety of herbs and fruits, and especially pears of an extraordinary size, weighing ten pounds each, that are white in the inside, like paste, and have a very fragrant smell. There are peaches also, in their season, both of the yellow and the white kind, and of a delicious flavour. Grapes are not produced there, but are brought in a dried state, and very good, from other parts. This applies also to wine, which the natives do not hold in estimation, being accustomed to their own liquor prepared from rice and spices. From the sea,

which is fifteen miles distant, there is daily brought up the river, to the city, a vast quantity of fish; and in the lake also there is abundance, which gives employment at all times to persons whose sole occupation it is to catch them. The sorts are various according to the season of the year, and, in consequence of the offal carried thither from the town, they become large and rich. At the sight of such an importation of fish, you would think it impossible that it could be sold; and yet, in the course of a few hours, it is all taken off, so great is the number of inhabitants, even of those classes which can afford to indulge in such luxuries, for fish and flesh are eaten at the same meal. Each of the ten market-squares is surrounded with high dwelling-houses, in the lower part of which are shops, where every kind of manufacture is carried on, and every article of trade is sold; such, amongst others, as spices, drugs, trinkets, and pearls. In certain shops nothing is vended but the wine of the country, which they are continually brewing, and serve out fresh to their customers at a moderate price. The streets connected with the market-squares are numerous, and in some of them are many cold baths, attended by servants of both sexes, to perform the offices of ablution for the men and women who frequent them, and who from their childhood have been accustomed at all times to wash in cold water, which they reckon highly conducive to health. At these bathing places, however, they have apartments provided with warm water, for the use of strangers, who, from not being habituated to it, cannot bear the shock of the cold. All are in the daily practice of washing their persons, and especially before their meals.

In other streets are the habitations of the courtesans, who are here in such numbers as I dare not venture to report, and not only near the squares, which is the situation usually appropriated for their residence, but in every part of the city they are to be found, adorned with much finery, highly perfumed, occupying well-furnished houses, and attended by many female domestics. These women are accomplished, and are perfect in the arts of blandishment and dalliance, which they accompany with expressions adapted to every description of person, insomuch that strangers who have once tasted of their charms, remain in a state of fascination, and become so enchanted by their meretricious arts, that they can never divest themselves of the impression. Thus intoxicated with sensual pleasures, when they return to their homes they report that they have been in Kin-sai, or the celestial city, and pant for the time when they may be enabled to revisit paradise. In other streets are the dwellings of the physicians and the astrologers, who also give

instructions in reading and writing, as well as in many other arts. They have apartments also amongst those which surround the market-squares. On opposite sides of each of these squares there are two large edifices, where officers appointed by the grand khan are stationed, to take immediate cognisance of any differences that may happen to arise between the foreign merchants, or amongst the inhabitants of the place. It is their duty likewise to see that the guards upon the several bridges in their respective vicinities (of whom mention shall be made hereafter) are duly placed, and in cases of neglect, to punish the delinquents at their discretion.

On each side of the principal street, already mentioned as extending from one end of the city to the other, there are houses and mansions of great size, with their gardens, and near to these, the dwellings of the artisans, who work in shops, at their several trades; and at all hours you see such multitudes of people passing and repassing, on their various avocations, that the providing food in sufficiency for their maintenance might be deemed an impossibility; but other ideas will be formed when it is observed that, on every market-day, the squares are crowded with tradespeople, who cover the whole space with the articles brought by carts and boats, for all of which they find a sale. By instancing the single article of pepper, some notion may be formed of the whole quantity of provisions, meat, wine, groceries, and the like, required for the consumption of the inhabitants of Kin-sai; and of this, Marco Polo learned from an officer employed in the grand khan's customs, the daily amount was forty-three loads, each load being two hundred and forty-three pounds.

The inhabitants of the city are idolaters, and they use paper money as currency. The men as well as the women have fair complexions, and are handsome. The greater part of them are always clothed in silk, in consequence of the vast quantity of that material produced in the territory of Kin-sai, exclusively of what the merchants import from other provinces. Amongst the handicraft trades exercised in the place, there are twelve considered to be superior to the rest, as being more generally useful; for each of which there are a thousand workshops, and each shop furnishes employment for ten, fifteen, or twenty workmen, and in a few instances as many as forty, under their respective masters. The opulent principals in these manufactories do not labour with their own hands, but, on the contrary, assume airs of gentility and affect parade. Their wives equally abstain from work. They have much beauty, as has been remarked, and are brought up with delicate and languid habits. The costliness of their dresses, in silks and

jewellery, can scarcely be imagined. Although the laws of their ancient kings ordained that each citizen should exercise the profession of his father, yet they were allowed, when they acquired wealth, to discontinue the manual labour, provided they kept up the establishment, and employed persons to work at their paternal trades. Their houses are well built and richly adorned with carved work. So much do they delight in ornaments of this kind, in paintings, and fancy buildings, that the sums they lavish on such objects are enormous. The natural disposition of the native inhabitants of Kin-sai is pacific, and by the example of their former kings, who were themselves unwarlike, they have been accustomed to habits of tranquillity. The management of arms is unknown to them, nor do they keep any in their houses. Contentious broils are never heard among them. They conduct their mercantile and manufacturing concerns with perfect candour and probity. They are friendly towards each other, and persons who inhabit the same street, both men and women, from the mere circumstance of neighbourhood, appear like one family. In their domestic manners they are free from jealousy or suspicion of their wives, to whom great respect is shown, and any man would be accounted infamous who should presume to use indecent expressions to a married woman. To strangers also, who visit their city in the way of commerce, they give proofs of cordiality, inviting them freely to their houses, showing them hospitable attention, and furnishing them with the best advice and assistance in their mercantile transactions. On the other hand, they dislike the sight of soldiery, not excepting the guards of the grand khan, as they preserve the recollection that by them they were deprived of the government of their native kings and rulers.

On the borders of the lake are many handsome and spacious edifices belonging to men of rank and great magistrates. There are likewise many idol temples, with their monasteries, occupied by a number of monks, who perform the service of the idols. Near the central part are two islands, upon each of which stands a superb building, with an incredible number of apartments and separate pavilions. When the inhabitants of the city have occasion to celebrate a wedding, or to give a sumptuous entertainment, they resort to one of these islands, where they find ready for their purpose every article that can be required, such as vessels, napkins, table-linen, and the like, which are provided and kept there at the common expense of the citizens, by whom also the buildings were erected. It may happen that at one time there are a hundred parties assembled there, at wedding or other feasts, all of whom, notwithstanding, are accommodated with separate rooms or

pavilions, so judiciously arranged that they do not interfere with or incom-
mode each other. In addition to this, there are upon the lake a great number
of pleasure vessels or barges, calculated for holding ten, fifteen, to twenty
persons, being from fifteen to twenty paces in length, with a wide and flat
flooring, and not liable to heel to either side in passing through the water.
Such persons as take delight in the amusement, and mean to enjoy it, either
in the company of their women or that of their male companions, engage
one of these barges, which are always kept in the nicest order, with proper
seats and tables, together with every other kind of furniture necessary for
giving an entertainment. The cabins have a flat roof or upper deck, where
the boatmen take their place, and by means of long poles, which they thrust
to the bottom of the lake (not more than one or two fathoms in depth),
they shove the barges along, until they reach the intended spot. These
cabins are painted within-side of various colours and with a variety of
figures; all parts of the vessel are likewise adorned with painting. There are
windows on each side, which may either be kept shut, or opened, to give an
opportunity to the company, as they sit at table, of looking out in every
direction and feasting their eyes on the variety and beauty of the scenes as
they pass them. And truly the gratification afforded in this manner, upon
the water, exceeds any that can be derived from the amusements on the
land; for as the lake extends the whole length of the city, on one side, you
have a view, as you stand in the boat, at a certain distance from the shore,
of all its grandeur and beauty, its palaces, temples, convents, and gardens,
with trees of the largest size growing down to the water's edge, whilst at
the same time you enjoy the sight of other boats of the same description, continually passing you, filled in like manner with parties in pursuit of amusement. In fact, the inhabitants of this place, as soon as the labours of the day
have ceased, or their mercantile transactions are closed, think of nothing else
than of passing the remaining hours in parties of pleasure, with their wives
or their mistresses, either in these barges, or about the city in carriages, of
which it will here be proper to give some account, as constituting one of the
amusements of these people.

It must be observed, in the first place, that the streets of Kin-sai are all
paved with stones and bricks, and so likewise are all the principal roads extending from thence through the province of Manji, by means of which
passengers can travel to every part without soiling their feet; but as the
couriers of his majesty, who go on horseback with great speed, cannot make
use of the pavement, a part of the road, on one side, is on their account left

unpaved. The main street of the city, of which we have before spoken, as leading from one extremity to the other, is paved with stone and brick to the width of ten paces on each side, the intermediate part being filled up with small gravel, and provided with arched drains for carrying off the rain-water that falls, into the neighbouring canals, so that it remains always dry. On this gravel it is that the carriages are continually passing and repassing. They are of a long shape, covered at top, have curtains and cushions of silk, and are capable of holding six persons. Both men and women who feel disposed to take their pleasure, are in the daily practice of hiring them for that purpose, and accordingly at every hour you may see vast numbers of them driven along the middle part of the street. Some of them proceed to visit certain gardens, where the company are introduced, by those who have the management of the place, to shady recesses contrived by the gardeners for that purpose; and here the men indulge themselves all day in the society of their women, returning home, when it becomes late, in the manner they came.

It is the custom of the people of Kin-sai, upon the birth of a child, for the parents to make a note, immediately, of the day, hour, and minute at which the delivery took place. They then inquire of an astrologer under what sign or aspect of the heavens the child was born; and his answer is likewise committed carefully to writing. When therefore he is grown up, and is about to engage in any mercantile adventure, voyage, or treaty of marriage, this document is carried to the astrologer, who, having examined it, and weighed all the circumstances, pronounces certain oracular words, in which these people, who sometimes find them justified by the event, place great confidence. Of these astrologers, or rather magicians, great numbers are to be met with in every market-place, and no marriage is ever celebrated until an opinion has been pronounced upon it by one of that profession.

It is also their custom, upon the death of any great and rich personage, to observe the following ceremonies. The relations, male and female, clothe themselves in coarse dresses, and accompany the body to the place appointed for burning it. The procession is likewise attended by performers on various musical instruments, which are sounded as it moves along, and prayers to their idols are chanted in a loud voice. When arrived at the spot, they throw into the flame many pieces of cotton-paper, upon which are painted representations of male and female servants, horses, camels, silk wrought with gold, as well as of gold and silver money. This is done, in consequence of their belief that the deceased will possess in the other world all these con-

veniences, the former in their natural state of flesh and bones, together with the money and the silks. As soon as the pile has been consumed, they sound all the instruments of music at the same time, producing a loud and long-continued noise; and they imagine that by these ceremonies their idols are induced to receive the soul of the man whose corpse has been reduced to ashes, in order to its being regenerated in the other world, and entering again into life.

In every street of this city there are stone buildings or towers, to which, in case of a fire breaking out in any quarter (an accident by no means un-usual, as the houses are mostly constructed of wood), the inhabitants may remove their effects for security. By a regulation which his majesty has estab-lished, there is a guard of ten watchmen stationed, under cover, upon all the principal bridges, of whom five do duty by day and five by night. Each of these guard-rooms is provided with a sonorous wooden instrument as well as one of metal, together with a *clepsydra* (*horiuolo*), by means of which latter the hours of the day and night are ascertained. As soon as the first hour of the night is expired, one of the watchmen gives a single stroke upon the wooden instrument, and also upon the metal *gong* (*bacino*), which an-nounces to the people of the neighbouring streets that it is the first hour. At the expiration of the second, two strokes are given; and so on progressively, increasing the number of strokes as the hours advance. The guard is not allowed to sleep, and must be always on the alert. In the morning, as soon as the sun begins to appear, a single stroke is again struck, as in the evening, and so onwards from hour to hour. Some of these watchmen patrol the streets, to observe whether any person has a light or fire burning after the hour appointed for extinguishing them. Upon making the discovery, they affix a mark to the door, and in the morning the owner of the house is taken before the magistrates, by whom, if he cannot assign a legitimate excuse for his offence, he is condemned to punishment. Should they find any person abroad at an unseasonable hour, they arrest and confine him, and in the morning he is carried before the same tribunal. If, in the course of the day, they notice any person who from lameness or other infirmity is unable to work, they place him in one of the hospitals, of which there are several in every part of the city, founded by the ancient kings, and liberally endowed. When cured, he is obliged to work at some trade. Immediately upon the appearance of fire breaking out in a house, they give the alarm by beating on the wooden machine, when the watchmen from all the bridges within a certain distance assemble to extinguish it, as well as to save the effects of

the merchants and others, by removing them to the stone towers that have been mentioned. The goods are also sometimes put into boats, and conveyed to the islands in the lake. Even on such occasions the inhabitants dare not stir out of their houses, when the fire happens in the night-time, and only those can be present whose goods are actually removing, together with the guard collected to assist, which seldom amounts to a smaller number than from one to two thousand men. In cases also of tumult or insurrection amongst the citizens, the services of this police guard are necessary; but, independently of them, his majesty always keeps on foot a large body of troops, both infantry and cavalry, in the city and its vicinity, the command of which he gives to his ablest officers, and those in whom he can place the greatest confidence, on account of the extreme importance of this province, and especially its noble capital, which surpasses in grandeur and wealth every other city in the world. For the purposes of nightly watch, there are mounds of earth thrown up, at the distance of above a mile from each other, on the top of which a wooden frame is constructed, with a sounding board, which being struck with a mallet by the guard stationed there, the noise is heard to a great distance. If precautions of this nature were not taken upon occasions of fire, there would be danger of half the city being consumed; and their use is obvious also in the event of popular commotion, as, upon the signal being given, the guards at the several bridges arm themselves, and repair to the spot where their presence is required.

When the grand khan reduced to his obedience the province of Manji, which until that time had been one kingdom, he thought proper to divide it into nine parts, over each of which he appointed a king or viceroy, who should act as supreme governor of that division, and administer justice to the people. These make a yearly report to commissioners acting for his majesty, of the amount of the revenue, as well as of every other matter pertaining to their jurisdiction. Upon the third year they are changed, as are all other public officers. One of these nine viceroys resides and holds his court in the city of Kin-sai, and has authority over more than a hundred and forty cities and towns, all large and rich. Nor is this number to be wondered at, considering that in the whole of the province of Manji there are no fewer than twelve hundred, containing a large population of industrious and wealthy inhabitants. In each of these, according to its size and other circumstances, his majesty keeps a garrison, consisting, in some places, of a thousand, in others of ten or twenty thousand men, accordingly as he judges the city to be, in its own population, more or less powerful. It is not to be

understood that all these troops are Tartars. On the contrary, they are chiefly natives of the province of Cathay. The Tartars are universally horsemen, and cavalry cannot be quartered about those cities which stand in the low, marshy parts of the province, but only in firm, dry situations, where such troops can be properly exercised. To the former, he sends Cathaians, and such men of the province of Manji as appear to have a military turn; for it is his practice to make an annual selection amongst all his subjects of such as are best qualified to bear arms; and these he enrolls to serve in his numerous garrisons, that may be considered as so many armies. But the soldiers drawn from the province of Manji he does not employ in the duty of their native cities; on the contrary, he marches them to others at the distance of perhaps twenty days' journey, where they are continued for four or five years, at the expiration of which they are allowed to return to their homes, and others are sent to replace them. This regulation applies equally to the Cathaians. The greater part of the revenues of the cities, paid into the treasury of the grand khan, is appropriated to the maintenance of these garrisons. When it happens that a city is in a state of rebellion (and it is not an uncommon occurrence for these people, actuated by some sudden exasperation, or when intoxicated, to murder their governors), a part of the garrison of a neighbouring city is immediately despatched with orders to destroy the place where such guilty excesses have been committed; whereas it would be a tedious operation to send an army from another province, that might be two months on its march. For such purposes, the city of Kin-sai constantly supports a garrison of thirty thousand soldiers; and the smallest number stationed at any place is one thousand.

It now remains to speak of a very fine palace that was formerly the residence of king Facfur, whose ancestors enclosed with high walls an extent of ground ten miles in compass, and divided it into three parts. That in the centre was entered by a lofty portal, on each side of which was a magnificent colonnade, on a flat terrace, the roofs of which were supported by rows of pillars, highly ornamented with the most beautiful azure and gold. The colonnade opposite to the entrance, at the further side of the court, was still grander than the others, its roof being richly adorned, the pillars gilt, and the walls on the inner side ornamented with exquisite paintings, representing the histories of former kings. Here, annually, upon certain days consecrated to the service of their idols, king Facfur was accustomed to hold his court, and to entertain at a feast his principal nobles, the chief magistrates, and the opulent citizens of Kin-sai. Under these colonnades

might be seen, at one time, ten thousand persons suitably accommodated at table. This festival lasted ten or twelve days, and the magnificence displayed on the occasion, in silks, gold, and precious stones, exceeded all imagination; for every guest, with a spirit of emulation, endeavoured to exhibit as much finery as his circumstances would possibly allow. Behind the colonnade last mentioned, or that which fronted the grand portal, there was a wall, with a passage, that divided this exterior court of the palace from an interior court, which formed a kind of large cloister, with its rows of pillars sustaining a portico that surrounded it, and led to various apartments for the use of the king and queen. These pillars were ornamented in a similar manner, as were also the walls. From this cloister you entered a covered passage or corridor, six paces in width, and of such a length as to reach to the margin of the lake. On each side of this there were corresponding entrances to ten courts, in the form of long cloisters, surrounded by their porticoes, and each cloister or court had fifty apartments, with their respective gardens, the residence of a thousand young women, whom the king retained in his service. Accompanied sometimes by his queen, and on other occasions by a party of these females, it was his custom to take amusement on the lake, in barges covered with silk, and to visit the idol temples on its borders. The other two divisions of this seraglio were laid out in groves, pieces of water, beautiful gardens stored with fruit-trees, and also enclosures for all sorts of animals that are the objects of sport, such as antelopes, deer, stags, hares, and rabbits. Here likewise the king amused himself, in company with his damsels, some in carriages and some on horseback. No male person was allowed to be of these parties, but on the other hand, the females were practised in the art of coursing with dogs, and pursuing the animals that have been mentioned. When fatigued with these exercises, they retired into the groves on the banks of the lake, and there quitting their dresses, rushed into the water in a state of nudity, sportively swimming about, some in one direction and some in another, whilst the king remained a spectator of the exhibition. After this they returned to the palace. Sometimes he ordered his repast to be provided in one of these groves, where the foliage of lofty trees afforded a thick shade, and was there waited upon by the same damsels. Thus was his time consumed amidst the enervating charms of his women, and in profound ignorance of whatever related to martial concerns, the consequence of which was, that his depraved habits and his pusillanimity enabled the grand khan to deprive him of his splendid possessions,

and to expel him with ignominy from his throne as has been already stated. All these particulars were communicated to me, when I was in that city, by a rich merchant of Kin-sai, then very old, who had been a confidential servant of king Facfur, and was acquainted with every circumstance of his life. Having known the palace in its original state, he was desirous of conducting me to view it. Being at present the residence of the grand khan's viceroy, the colonnades are preserved in the style in which they had formerly subsisted, but the chambers of the females had been suffered to go to ruin, and the foundations only were visible. The wall likewise that enclosed the park and gardens was fallen to decay, and neither animals nor trees were any longer to be found there.

At the distance of twenty-five miles from this city, in a direction to the northward of east, lies the sea, near to which is a town named Gan-pu, where there is an extremely fine port, frequented by all the ships that bring merchandise from India. The river that flows past the city of Kin-sai forms this port, at the place where it falls into the sea. Boats are continually employed in the conveyance of goods up and down the river, and those intended for exportation are there put on board of ships bound to various parts of India and of Cathay.

Marco Polo, happening to be in the city of Kin-sai at the time of making the annual report to his majesty's commissioners of the amount of revenue and the number of inhabitants, had an opportunity of observing that the latter were registered at one hundred and sixty *tomans* of fire-places, that is to say, of families dwelling under the same roof; and as a *toman* is ten thousand, it follows that the whole city must have contained one million six hundred thousand families, amongst which multitude of people there was only one church of Nestorian Christians. Every father of a family, or housekeeper, is required to affix a writing to the door of his house, specifying the name of each individual of his family, whether male or female, as well as the number of his horses. When any person dies, or leaves the dwelling, the name is struck out, and upon the occasion of a birth, it is added to the list. By these means the great officers of the province and governors of the cities are at all times acquainted with the exact number of the inhabitants. The same regulation is observed throughout the province of Cathay as well as of Manji. In like manner, all the keepers of inns and public hotels inscribe in a book the names of those who take up their occasional abode with them, particularising the day and the hour of their arrival and departure; a

copy of which is transmitted daily to those magistrates who have been spoken of as stationed in the market-squares. It is a custom in the province of Manji, with the indigent class of the people, who are unable to support their families, to sell their children to the rich, in order that they may be fed and brought up in a better manner than their own poverty would admit.

PRINCE AND POET:

James I of Scotland

THE COMING OF LOVE

~~~~~~

IN SCOTCH anthologies, James I still rules a few pages of poetry, in Chaucerian stanzas and with an emotion borrowed from Boethius. A lad of twelve on his way from Scotland to France, he was captured at sea by English sailors and presented to Henry IV. For the next eighteen years he was a tame bird in a golden cage, alternately a captive in the Tower and in several comfortable royal quarters. Nominally king of Scotland, his place was usurped by his uncle and later his cousin. But in his gilded captivity he exercised in manly sports, music, philosophy and poetry. By 1423 the Scotch came around to negotiating for his release and signed a treaty whereby 60,000 marks were to be paid out "for his maintenance in Engand" and young James was to wed an English lady. He married Jane Beaufort, brought his bride to Scotland, broke a Stewart conjugal tradition by remaining faithful to her all his life, subdued the nobles, pacified Scotland, and was murdered for his pains.

The *Kingis Quair* is a love poem of 197 stanzas, an allegory in the courtly manner which was the natural expression of a susceptible Chaucerian reader. Having sat down with old Boethius, meditated on the reverses of fortune, invoked the muses and begun a poem, the captive prince walks to the window of his garden and there beholds the lady Jane Beaufort. This allegory of love, through the license of sleep, is carried away to the palace of Venus, hostess of lovers. It travels on to Minerva, Good Hope, and Fortune. The royal poet receives counsel of virtue as an insurance against failure in love, and finally a turtle dove brings him a branch with a message of encouragement, and his lady grants her consent.

Over this musical allegory, sometimes freshly felt through the established mode, the scholars have had their abstruse quarrel. Was it written in the eighteenth year of his captivity, when James saw Jane Beaufort plain ("beauty eneuch to make a world to dote") in a garden of Windsor Castle in May, or after he returned to Scotland? And was it really written by James himself? The odds are still in favor of James and the period of captivity, the dissenters numerically few. Only one sceptical reflection will be permitted here: that "if Chaucer's Palamon had never seen Emelye from the tower in

Athens, perhaps James would not have seen Lady Jane Beaufort from his prison window." But surely everybody knows that nature imitates art.

THE COMING OF LOVE

Bewailing in my chamber thus alone,
Despaired of all joy and remedy,
For-tirit of my thought and woe-begone,
Unto the window gan I walk in hy
To see the world, and folk that went forby
As for the time; though I of mirthis food
Might have no more, to look it did me gude.

Now was there made fast by the towris wall
A garden fair, and in the corneris set
Ane herbere green, with wandis long and small
Railit about, and so with treis set
Was all the place, and hawthorn hedges knet,
That life was none walking there forby
That might within scarce ony wight aspye.

So thick the boughis and the leavis green
Beshadit all the alleys that there were,
And myddis every herbere might be seen
The sharpë, grenë, swetë junipere,
Growing so fair with branches here and there,
That, as it semed to a life without,
The boughis spread the herbere all about.

And on the smalë, grenë, twistis sat
The lytel swetë nightingale and sang,
So loud and clere the hymnis consecrat

Stanzas 30-45, *Kingis Quair*

for-tirit, tired out   *herbere*, ground with turf
in hy, in haste   *aspye*, observe
forby, past   *twistis*, twigs

Of luvis use, now soft, now loud among,
That all the garden and the wallis rong
Right of their song, and in the copill next
Of their sweet harmony, and lo! the text:

'Worship ye that luvaris bene this May,
For of your bliss the kalendis are begonne,
And sing with us, Away, winter, away!
Come summer come, the swete season and sun!
Awake for shame that have your heavenis won,
And amorously lift up your hedis all,
Thank Luve that list you to his mercy call.'

When they this song had sung a lytil thrawe,
They stent awhile, and therewith unafraid,
As I beheld and cast myne eyne alaw,
From bough to bough they hoppit and they played,
And freshly in their birdis kind arraid
Their fetheris new, and fret them in the sun,
And thankit Luve, that had their makis won.

This was the planë ditee of their note,
And therewithal unto my self I thought,
'What life is this, that makis birdis dote?
What may this be, how cometh it of ought,
What needeth it to be so dear ybought?
It is nothing, trow I, bot feignit cheer,
And that men list to counterfeiten cheer.'

Eft wold I think, 'O Lord, what may this be,
That Luve is of so noble might and kind,
Luving his folk, and such prosperitee
Is it of him, as we in bookis find?
May he our hertis setten and unbind?
Hath he upon our hertis such maistry,
Or is all this bot feignit fastasye?

---

copill, couplet   *thrawe,* time
list, is pleased   *stent,* stopped

'For gif he be of so great excellence,
That he of every wight hath cure and charge,
What have I guilt to him or doon offence,
That I am thrall, and birdis gone at large,
Sen him to serve he might set my courage?
And gif he be noght so, then may I seyne,
What makis folk to jangle of him in vain?

'Can I noght ellis find; bot gif that he
Be lord, and as a god may live and reign,
To bind and loose, and maken thrallis free
Then wold I pray his blissful grace benign
To able me unto his service digne,
And evermore for to be one of tho
Him truly for to serve in weill and woe.'

And therewith kest I down myne eye again
Where as I saw, walking under the tower,
Full secretly, new comin her to playne,
The fairest and the freshest yongë flour
That ever I saw methought before that hour.
For which sudden abate, anon asterte
The blude of all my body to my hert.

And though I stood abaisit tho a lyte,
No wonder was, for why, my wittis all
Were so ourcome with plesance and delight
Only through letting of myne eyen fall,
That suddenly my hert became her thrall
For ever, of free will, for of menace
There was no token in her swetë face.

And in my head I drew ryght hastily,
And eft-sonës I lent it forth again,
And saw her walk that verray womanly

---

gif, if   *abate,* drew away
seyne, say   *asterte,* returned
jangle, talk   *lyte,* little
playne, clear   *eft-sonës,* very soon

68

With no wight mo bot only women twain.
Then gan I study in myself and seyne:
'A! sweet, are ye a warldly creature,
Or heavenly thing in likeness of nature?

'Or are ye God Cupidis owin princesse,
And cummyn are to loose me out of band?
Or are ye verray Nature the goddess
That have depaynted with your heavenly hand
This garden full of flowris as they stand?
What sall I think, alas! what reverence
Sall I minister to your excellence?

'Gif ye a goddess be, and that ye like
To do me pain, I may it not asterte:
Gif ye be worldly wight that doth me sike,
Why list God make you so, my dearest hert,
To do a sely prisoner thus smert,
That luvis you all, and wot of noght bot woe?
And therefore, mercy sweet, sen it is so.'

When I a lytel thraw had made my moan,
Bewailing myne infortune and my chance,
Unknawin how or what was best to doon,
So fer I fallen was in luvis dance,
That suddenly my wit, my contenance,
My hert, my will, my nature and my mynd
Was changit clene right in anothir kynd.

---

sike, sigh
sely, simple, weak

PROTESTANT PIONEER:

John Huss

THE DREAM OF JOHN HUSS   THE COUNCIL   THE OBSTINATE HERETIC

~~~~~~

If this man is a heretic, it is difficult to see where under the sun you will find a true Christian.

MARTIN LUTHER, *Letters of Huss*

IN THE autumn of 1414 John Huss set out in all good faith from Bohemia to honor the invitation of the Council of Constance. He was guarded by his friends and disciples and rode in a cart on a pile of his dissident books. Behind him lay a turbulent life, ahead of him the stake. He had welded into one national movement a protest against the Church and the Germans. His forge was the University of Prague, the anvil his crowded Bethlehem Chapel, and one of his hammers the doctrine of an Englishman, Wycliffe. By 1410 the Church had excommunicated him and interdicted the rebellious people of Prague; and two years later, when he pressed the war against indulgences, he was forced to retire to seclusion where he wrote *De Ecclesia*. As Wycliffe had taught that an evil priest was devoid of spiritual power, and that superfluous ecclesiastical wealth had better be divided among the poor, so Huss echoed that the elect owe fidelity only to Christ and need not follow an erring Pope. The Hussite doctrine, a two-edged sword, grew into a national *and* ecclesiastical war. Phrases like "putting off the pomp and lordship of this world" were the euphemism of revolt, a patriotic vocabulary in the doctrine of Wycliffe and Huss which was both new and nationalist—English and Czech. Huss had himself nourished the common speech of the Bohemian people, revised a translation of the Bible, and even gave those audiences which flocked to the sermons in the Bethlehem Chapel a number of Bohemian versions of the old Latin hymns. And like Czech statesmen in other crises five hundred years later, Huss searched for political ties with the Slavic peoples and regarded a Polish victory over the Knights of the Teutonic Order as a piece of Czech good luck. But the Council of Constance, to which Huss was riding on his cart with a baggage of books, was a trap, rather than (as he hoped) a platform. His last writing was a series of moving letters to his friends from the cell of his prison before he went to the stake on July 6, 1415. It is with malice and pleasure that one can quote today a forgotten line from a discreetly

forgotten book by Benito Mussolini, who, when languishing in the Forli Citadel as an objector to the conquest of Tripoli in 1911, wrote in his florid biography of John Huss: "I cherish the hope that it may arouse in the minds of its readers a hatred of every form of spiritual and secular tyranny, whether it be theocratic or Jacobine."

THE DREAM OF JOHN HUSS

EXPOUND my dream last night. I dreamed that they wanted to destroy all the pictures of Christ in the Bethlehem,[1] and they succeeded. Next morning I saw many painters at work on finer and more numerous pictures, upon which I gazed with gladness. And the painters, together with a vast crowd, were crying out: "Let the bishops come now and hurt us." Whereupon the crowd rejoiced, and I with them. And when I awoke I found that I was laughing.

THE COUNCIL

I, MASTER JOHN HUSS, in hope, servant of Christ, and ardently desiring that believers in Christ may not, when I shall have ceased to live, find in my death an opportunity for scandal, and look on me as an obstinate heretic, do take to witness Jesus Christ, for the sake of whose word I have wished to die; and I leave in writing the remembrance of these things for the friends of truth.

I had often declared, both in private, in public, and before the Council, that I would consent to an inquiry, and would submit myself to instruction, abjuration, and punishment, if it was demonstrated to me that I had written, taught, or disseminated, any thing contrary to the truth. But fifty doctors, who stated that they were deputed by the Council, having been frequently corrected by me, and even in public, for having falsely extracted articles from my works, refused me any private explanation, and declared that they would not confer with me, saying *You ought to submit yourself to the decision of the Council*. And the Council mocked when, in the public audi-

---

[1] On the walls of his Bethlehem Chapel at Prague, Huss had caused to be painted up at various times some arguments and theses, once even a long treatise. The dream was described in a letter to Peter Maldoniewitz and was interpreted by John de Chlum, another friend, as "more than an allegory . . . a prophecy."

ence, I quoted the words of Christ and the holy doctors; at one time they reproached me with misunderstanding them, and, at another, the doctors insulted me. . . .

An English doctor, who had already said to me in private, that Wycliffe had wished to annihilate all science, and had filled his books and his logic with errors, began to discourse on the multiplication of the body of Christ in the consecrated host, and, as his arguments were weak, he was told to be silent; then he cried out: "This man deceives the Council; take care that the Council be not led into error as it was by Berenger." When he was silent, another discussed noisily concerning the created and common essence. All began to clamour against him. I then demanded that he might be heard, and said to him, "You argue well; I will answer you most willingly." He also broke down, and he added in a sullen voice: *"This man is a heretic."* The Seignior Wenceslaus Duba, John de Chlum, and Peter the notary, valiant champions and friends of the truth, know what clamours, what unworthy raillery and blasphemies were poured upon me in this assembly. Stunned by so much noise, I said, "I thought there was to be found in this Council more decency, more piety, and more discipline." All then began to listen, for the Emperor had commanded silence to be observed.

The cardinal who presided said to me—"You spoke more humbly in your prison." I answered—"It is true; for then no one clamoured against me, and now they are all vociferous." He added—"Will you submit to an investigation?" "I consent to it," replied I, "within the limits which I have fixed." "Take this for the result of the inquiry," resumed the cardinal, "that the doctors have declared the articles extracted from your books to be errors, which you ought to efface, in abjuring those already testified against you by witnesses." The Emperor afterwards said—"This will soon be committed to writing for you, and you will answer it." "Let that be done at the next audience," said the cardinal; and the sitting closed. God knows how many trials I have suffered since!

THE OBSTINATE HERETIC

A MULTITUDE of people have come to exhort me, and amongst them many doctors, but few brethren, as the Apostle has said. They were prodigal in their counsels and phrases; they told me, that I could and I ought to abjure my scruples in submitting my will to the Holy Church, which the Council

represents; but not one of them can avoid the difficulty, when I place him in my situation, and ask him, if, being certain of having never preached, or defended, or entertained heresy, he could, in safe conscience, formally confess that he abjured an error which he never supported. Some of them stated, that it was not necessary to abjure, but merely to renounce the heresy held or not held; others maintain, that to abjure signifies to deny what is attested rightly or erroneously. I would willingly swear, I replied to them, that I have never preached, held, or defended, the errors which are imputed to me; and that I will never preach, hold, or defend them. And when I spoke thus, they immediately retired.

Others insist that, supposing a man really innocent were found in the Church, and this man, through humility, confess himself guilty, he would be well deserving: thereupon some one cited, amongst the ancient fathers, a certain saint, in whose bed had been covertly put a prohibited book. Inculpated and examined on this subject, the saint denied the fault, but his enemies answered, "Thou hast concealed the book, and put it in thy bed;" and this book having been found there, the saint confessed himself culpable. Some supported this opinion by the example of a certain holy woman, who lived in a monastery in the disguise of a man. She was accused of being the father of a child. She confessed it, and kept the child: her innocence was afterwards discovered with her sex. Many other means were also proposed to me.

An Englishman addressed me thus, "Were I in your place, I would abjure; for in England, all the masters, and all men held in consideration, who were suspected of adhering to the opinions of Wycliffe, have been severally cited before the archbishop, and have abjured."

Lastly, yesterday they were all agreed in engaging me to place myself at the mercy of the Council.

Paletz came at my entreaty, for I desired to confess to him. I asked the commissioners, and those who exhorted me, to give me for confessor either him or another. And I said, "Paletz is my principal adversary; I wish to confess to him; or, at least, give me in his stead a man qualified to hear me: I conjure you to do so in the name of the Lord." This last desire was accorded: I confessed to a monk, who piously and most patiently listened to me; he gave me absolution, and counselled me, but did not enjoin me, to follow the advice of others.

Paletz came: he wept with me when I besought him to pardon me for having uttered before him some offensive words, and especially for having

called him a forger of writings. And as I reminded him that, in a public audience, when he heard me deny the articles cited by the witnesses, he rose up and cried: "This man does not believe in God,"—he denied it, but truly he said it, and perhaps you heard him do so. I reminded him, in what manner he said to me in prison, in presence of the Commissioners, "Since the birth of Christ, no heretic has written more dangerously than Wycliffe and thou." He also insisted, that all those who have read my sermons are infected with the error concerning the sacrament of the altar. He has now denied it, adding, "I did not say all, but a great number." And yet it is certain that he said it. And when I took him up by saying, "Oh! Master Paletz, how much you wrong me in accusing my auditory of heresy!" he did not reply anything, and he exhorted me, like the others, always repeating, that through me and mine much harm had been done. He told me, also, that he possessed a letter addressed to the Bohemians, in which was written, that, at the Chateau, I sang some verses on my captivity. In the name of Heaven, take great care of my letters: do not let them be carried to any clerical person, and let our Seigniors only trust some laymen. Inform me whether they accompany the Emperor. Jesus Christ, by his grace, preserves me unmoveable in my first resolution.

JOHN HUSS, *in hope, servant of God.*

THE PRIVATE VOICE:

Jeanne D'Arc

THE TRIAL OF JEANNE D'ARC

A vision of the statue before Rheims Cathedral appears.

JOAN. Is that funny little thing me too?

CHARLES. That is Rheims Cathedral where you had me crowned. It must be you.

JOAN. Who has broken my sword? My sword was never broken. It is the sword of France.

DUNOIS. Never mind. Swords can be mended. Your soul is unbroken; and you are the soul of France.

BERNARD SHAW, *Saint Joan*

SOCRATES in the old, Anne Hutchinson in the new world, and other nonconformist souls, heard private voices to which authority raised its solemn objections. But only in the case of Jeanne D'Arc was the *national language* of the private voice a matter of serious concern to authority. The voices spoke to her in French—in her adolescence at Domrémy, on her journey to the Dauphin, during the siege of Orleans and the crowning of Charles VII, through her capture by the Burgundians, her purchase by the English, her trial and death. In 1429 (as in 1942) listening to such a *French* voice in France was both heroic and heretical. France was torn by the English invaders and the civil war of two native factions. In the forests and swamps, bands of partisans—noblemen, peasants, and shoemakers—practiced sabotage. After Jeanne turned the tide at Orleans, Paris was still in English hands. The English who needed usable proof that their defeats and frustrations were the results not of God's will but of witchcraft; the University of Paris which suffered from Jeanne's war of national defence; and the Church Militant which through political pressure was presented with a case of heresy, combined to destroy the mutual enemy of all three. In the end, Jeanne D'Arc's two great judges, the English and the Church, reversed themselves and canonized her almost simultaneously in the 1920's—one as heroine, the other as saint.

In the English secular canonization—in the dramatic workshop of Bernard Shaw—Jeanne D'Arc is translated into plain Joan, with no villain in that modern mystery play, not even the Inquisitor. Under the spell of Shaw's comic spirit the institutions do the talking and rationalizing—the Church and Inquisition against "protestantism" (her voices), the Feudal System

75

against "nationalism" (her concept of France), the heresies for which she was burned. Since "she claimed to be the ambassador and plenipotentiary of God" and "she lectured, talked down, and overruled statesmen and prelates . . . there were only two opinions about her: one that she was miraculous, the other that she was unbearable." Hence the whole truth about her is that she was both miraculous and unbearable, in short the Shavian definition of a saint. This Joan is neither the rationalized figure of Anatole France, nor the "unimpeachable American schoolteacher in armor" of Mark Twain. The Church, says Shaw, "could not tolerate her pretensions without either waiving its authority or giving her a place beside the Trinity during her lifetime and in her teens," so it did what it could under the circumstances, had her burned and then quarantined her "protestantism" by granting her the privileges of a saint.

In the actual trial the ecclesiastical court pointed out "how serious and dangerous it is curiously to examine the things which are beyond one's understanding, and to believe in new things . . . and even to invent new and unusual things, for demons have a way of introducing themselves into suchlike curiosities." The soul of Jeanne D'Arc was truly in a perilous adventure of curiosity and belief. She held fast to the assurance of her personal salvation, certain of being received into Paradise, though as the learned faculty of the University of Paris demonstrated, with considerable wisdom, "on this earthly journey no pilgrim knows." Asked if she were in God's grace, she answered, "If I am not, God put me there, and if I am, God keep me there"—an answer which evaded a point in theology with excessive common sense. Asked if Saint Michael appeared to her naked, she replied, "Do you think that God has not wherewithal to clothe him?"—an answer which transferred the burden of modesty to God. Asked if Saint Margaret spoke to her in English, she asked with simplicity, "Why should she speak English when she is not of the English party?" She gave her judges no loophole for escape from the necessary conclusion that by limiting her testimony, and the area of their inquiry, to bounds set by herself—bounds which left her voices and visions matters of direct reference to God—she was by their law a heretic. And when the theologians of the City of Paris (who were in the hands of the English invaders) accused her of "the spilling of human blood," and charged her with professing that her saints and angels, being anti-English, spoke French, when all Christendom knew that the law of love had no national boundary, they, the theologians and inquisitors, introduced a

logic into the trial of Rouen in 1431 which would be of some service to the judges of Riom in 1942.

THE TRIAL OF JEANNE D'ARC

IN THE NAME OF THE LORD, AMEN

HERE BEGIN THE PROCEEDINGS IN MATTER OF FAITH AGAINST A DEAD
WOMAN, JEANNE, COMMONLY KNOWN AS THE MAID

IT HAS pleased divine Providence that a woman of the name of Jeanne, commonly called *The Maid,* should be taken and apprehended by famous warriors within the boundaries and limits of our diocese and jurisdiction. The reputation of this woman had already gone forth into many parts: how, wholly forgetful of womanly honesty, and having thrown off the bonds of shame, careless of all modesty of womankind, she wore with an astonishing and monstrous brazenness, immodest garments belonging to the male sex; how, moreover, her presumptuousness had grown until she was not afraid to perform, to speak, and to disseminate many things contrary to the Catholic faith and hurtful to the articles of the orthodox belief. And by so doing, as well in our diocese as in several other districts of this kingdom, she was said to be guilty of no inconsiderable offenses. These things having come to the knowledge of our mother the University of Paris, and of brother Martin Billorin, vicar-general of the lord Inquisitor of Heretical Error, they immediately summoned the illustrious prince, the Duke of Burgundy and the noble lord Jean de Luxembourg, who at this time held the said woman in their power and authority, in the name of the vicar-general above mentioned, and under penalty of law, to surrender and dispatch to us, as ordinary judge, the woman so defamed and suspected of heresy. . . .

Wednesday, February 21st. The First Public Session
First Inquiry After the Oath

. . . When she had thus taken the oath the said Jeanne was questioned by us about her name and surname. To which she replied that in her own country she was called Jeannette, and after she came to France, she was called Jeanne. Of her surname she said she knew nothing. Consequently she was questioned about the district from which she came. She replied she was born in the village of Domrémy, which is one with the village of Greux; and in Greux is the principal church.

Asked about the name of her father and mother, she replied that her father's name was Jacques d'Arc, and her mother's name Isabelle.

Asked where she was baptized, she replied it was in the church of Domrémy.

Asked who were her godfathers and godmothers, she said one of her godmothers was named Agnes, another Jeanne, another Sibylle; of her godfathers, one was named Jean Lingué, another Jean Barrey: she had several other godmothers, she had heard her mother say.

Asked what priest had baptized her, she replied that it was Master Jean Minet, as far as she knew.

Asked if he was still living, she said she believed he was.

Asked how old she was, she replied she thought nineteen. She said moreover that her mother taught her the *Paternoster, Ave Maria,* and *Credo;* and that no one but her mother had taught her her *Credo.*

Asked by us to say her *Paternoster,* she replied that if we would hear her in confession then she would gladly say it for us. And as we repeatedly demanded that she should repeat it, she replied that she would not say her *Paternoster* unless we would hear her in confession. Then we told her that we would gladly send one or two notable men, speaking the French tongue, to hear her say her *Paternoster,* etc.; to which the said Jeanne replied that she would not say it to them, except in confession.

Whereupon we, the aforementioned bishop, forbade Jeanne to leave the prison assigned to her in the castle of Rouen without our authorization under penalty of conviction of the crime of heresy. She answered that she did not accept this prohibition, adding that if she escaped, none could accuse her of breaking or violating her oath, since she had given her oath to none. Then she complained that she was imprisoned with chains and bonds of iron. We told her that she had tried elsewhere and on several occasions to escape from prison, and therefore, that she might be more safely and securely guarded, an order had been given to bind her with chains of iron. To which she replied: "It is true that I wished and still wish to escape, as is lawful for any captive or prisoner." . . .

Thursday, February 22nd. Second Session

. . . The said Jeanne was then brought before us there, and we admonished and required her, under penalty of law, to take the oath that she had taken the day before; and to swear to speak the truth, absolutely and simply, on

everything which she was asked in the respect of the matter of which she was accused and defamed. To which she replied that she had taken an oath yesterday, and that should suffice.

Then we required her to swear; for none, not even a prince, could refuse to take oath when required in matter of faith. She answered again: "I swore yesterday; that should be quite enough. You overburden me." At last she swore to speak the truth on that which concerned the faith.

Whereupon the distinguished professor of sacred theology, master Jean Beaupère, at our order and command questioned the said Jeanne as follows:

And first he exhorted her to answer truly, as she had sworn, what he should ask her. To which she replied: "You may well ask me such things, that to some I shall answer truly, and to others I shall not." And she added, "If you were well informed about me, you would wish me to be out of your hands. I have done nothing except by revelation."

Asked how old she was when she left her father's house, she said she could not vouch for her age.

Asked if in her youth she had learned any craft, she said yes, to sew and spin: and in sewing and spinning she feared no woman in Rouen. And moreover she confessed that for dread of the Burgundians she left her father's house and went to the town of Neufchâteau, in Lorraine, to the house of a certain woman called *La Rousse,* where she stayed about a fortnight. She added too, that as long as she was at home with her father, she saw to the ordinary domestic tasks; and that she did not go to the fields to look after the sheep and other animals.

Asked if she confessed her sins once a year, she said yes, to her own curé; and when he was prevented, she confessed to another priest, with his permission. Sometimes, too, twice or thrice perhaps, she confessed to mendicant friars: but that was in the town of Neufchâteau. And she received the sacrament of the Eucharist at Easter.

Asked if, at other feasts than Easter, she received the said sacrament of the Eucharist, she told the interrogator to continue to the next question. Afterwards she declared that at the age of thirteen she had a voice from God to help her and guide her. And the first time she was much afraid. And this voice came towards noon, in summer, in her father's garden: and the said Jeanne had [not] fasted on the preceding day. She heard the voice on her right, in the direction of the church; and she seldom heard it without a light. This light came from the same side as the voice, and generally there was a great light. When she came to France she often heard the voice.

Asked how she could see the light of which she spoke, since it was at the side, she made no reply, and went on to other things. She said that if she was in a wood she easily heard the voices come to her. It seemed to her a worthy voice, and she believed it was sent from God; when she heard the voice a third time she knew that it was the voice of an angel. She said also that this voice always protected her well and that she understood it well.

Asked what instruction this voice gave her for the salvation of her soul: she said it taught her to be good and to go to church often; and it told her that she must come to France. And, Jeanne added, Beaupère would not learn from her, this time, in what form that voice appeared to her. She further said that this voice told her once or twice a week that she should leave and come to France, and that her father knew nothing of her leaving. She said that the voice told her to come, and she could no longer stay where she was; and the voice told her again that she should raise the siege of the city of Orleans. She said moreover that the voice told her that she, Jeanne, should go to Robert de Baudricourt, in the town of Vaucouleurs of which he was captain, and he would provide an escort for her. And the said Jeanne answered that she was a poor maid, knowing nothing of riding or fighting. She said she went to an uncle of hers, and told him she wanted to stay with him for some time; and she stayed there about eight days. And she told her uncle she must go to the said town of Vaucouleurs, and so her uncle took her.

Then she said that when she reached Vaucouleurs she easily recognized Robert de Baudricourt, although she had never seen him before; and she knew him through her voice, for the voice had told her it was he. And the said Jeanne told Robert she must come to France. The said Robert twice refused to hear her and repulsed her; the third time he listened to her and gave her an escort. And the voice had told her that it would be so.

Then she declared that the duke of Lorraine ordered that she should be taken to him; and she went to him and told him she wished to go to France. And the duke questioned her about the recovery of his health; but she said she knew nothing about that; and she spoke to him little concerning her journey. She told the duke nevertheless to send his son and some men to escort her to France, and she would pray to God for his health. She visited him with a safe conduct and returned to the town of Vaucouleurs.

She declared that, on her departure from Vaucouleurs, she wore the habit of a man, and carried a sword which Robert de Baudricourt had given her, but no other arms; and accompanied by a knight, a squire, and four serv-

ants, she reached the town of Saint Urbain, where she slept in an abbey. She said that on her journey she passed through Auxerre, and she heard Mass in the principal church there; and from that time she frequently heard her voices, including the one already mentioned.

Required to say by what advice she took to man's dress, she several times refused to answer. Finally she answered that she charged no one with that; and several times she answered variously.

She said that Robert de Baudricourt had sworn those who accompanied her to conduct her well and safely. "Go," said Robert to Jeanne, as she departed, "Go, and come what may."

Jeanne said furthermore that she knows very well that God loves the duke of Orleans; and so she had more revelations concerning him than any man alive, except him whom she calls her king. She said also that it was altogether necessary to change her women's clothes for men's. She believed that her counsel said well.

She said that she sent to the English at Orleans letters telling them to depart, as shown in the copy of the letters which had been read to her in this town of Rouen, except two or three words in the copy: for example, where in this copy it read *Surrender to the Maid* it should read *Surrender to the King*. There are also these words, *body for body* and *chieftain of war*, which were not in the original letters.

After this the said Jeanne told that she went without hindrance to him whom she calls her king. And when she had arrived at Ste. Catherine de Fierbois, then she sent first to Chinon, where he whom she calls her king was. She reached Chinon towards noon and lodged at an inn; and after dinner she went to him whom she calls king, who was at the castle. She said that when she entered her king's room she recognized him among many others by the counsel of her voice, which revealed him to her. She told him she wanted to make war on the English.

Asked whether, when the voice showed her her king, there was no light, she answered: "Pass on to the next question." Asked if she saw no angel above the king, she answered: "Spare me that. Continue." She said also that before the king put her to work he had several apparitions and beautiful revelations.

Asked what revelations and apparitions the king had, she answered: "I will not tell you. It is not now the time to tell you; but send to the king and he will tell you."

Then Jeanne said that her voice had promised her that as soon as she

should come to the king he would receive her. She said also that those of her party knew well that the voice was sent to Jeanne from God, and they saw and knew this voice. She said further that her king and several others heard and saw the voices which came to the said Jeanne; and there were present Charles de Bourbon, and two or three others.

Then Jeanne said that there is not a day when she does not hear this voice; and she has much need of it. She said she never asked of it any final reward but the salvation of her soul. The voice told her to remain at Saint-Denis in France, and the said Jeanne wished to remain; but against her will the lords took her away. However, if she had not been wounded, she would not have left; she was wounded in the trenches before Paris, after she left Saint-Denis; but recovered in five days. Further she confessed that she caused an assault to be made before Paris.

And when she was asked if that day were a feast day, she answered she thought it certainly was.

Asked if she thought it was a good thing to do, she answered: "Pass on." When this was over, as it appeared to us sufficient for one day, we postponed the affair until the following Saturday, at eight o'clock in the morning.

February 24th. Third Session

. . . Then, at our order, she was questioned by the distinguished doctor Jean Beaupère above mentioned, who first asked her when she had last taken food and drink. She answered that since yesterday noon she had not taken either.

Asked when she had heard the voice come to her, she answered: "I heard it yesterday and today."

Asked at what hour yesterday she had heard this voice, she answered that she had heard it three times: once in the morning, once at vespers, and once when the *Ave Maria* was rung in the evening. And often she heard it more frequently than she said.

Asked what she was doing yesterday morning when the voice came to her, she said she was sleeping and the voice awakened her.

Asked if the voice woke her by touching her on the arm, she answered that it was without touching her.

Asked if the voice was actually in the room, she said she did not know, but it was in the castle.

Asked if she did not thank it and kneel down, she answered that she

thanked it, but she was sitting on the bed, and she put her hands together; and this was after she asked counsel of it. Whereupon the voice told her to answer boldly.

Asked what the voice had said when she was awakened, she answered that she asked the voice to counsel her in her replies, telling the voice to beseech therein the counsel of Our Lord. And the voice told her to answer boldly and God would comfort her.

Asked if it had not spoken certain words to her before she questioned it, she replied that the voice spoke certain words, but she did not understand them all. However, when she awakened from her sleep, the voice told her to answer boldly.

Then she said to us, the aforementioned bishop: "You say that you are my judge; take good heed of what you do, because, in truth, I am sent by God, and you put yourself in great peril," in French *'en grant dangier.'*

Asked if she knows she is in God's grace, she answered: "If I am not, may God put me there; and if I am, may God so keep me. I should be the saddest creature in the world if I knew I were not in His grace." She added, if she were in a state of sin, she did not think that the voice would come to her; and she wished every one could hear the voice as well as she did. She thought she was about thirteen when the voice came to her for the first time.

Asked whether in her youth she had played in the fields with the other children, she answered that she certainly went sometimes, but she did not know at what age.

Asked if the people of Domrémy sided with the Burgundians or the other party, she answered that she only knew one Burgundian; and she would have been quite willing for him to have his head cut off, that is if it had pleased God.

Asked if at Maxey the people were Burgundians or enemies of the Burgundians, she answered they were Burgundians.

Asked if the voice told her in her youth to hate the Burgundians, she answered that since she had known that the voices were for the king of France, she did not like the Burgundians. She said the Burgundians will have war unless they do as they ought; she knows it from her voice.

Asked if it was revealed to her in her early years that the English should come to France, she answered that the English were already in France when the voices began to come to her.

Asked if she was ever with the children who fought for her party, she

answered no, as far as she remembered; but she sometimes saw certain children from Domrémy, who had fought against those from Maxey, returning wounded and bleeding.

Asked whether in her youth she had any great intention of defeating the Burgundians, she answered that she had a great desire and will for her king to have his kingdom.

Asked if she had wanted to be a man when it was necessary for her to come to France, she said she had answered elsewhere.

Asked if she took the animals to the fields, she said that she had answered elsewhere; and that since she had grown up, and had reached understanding, she did not generally look after the beasts, but helped to take them to the meadows and to a castle called the Island, for fear of the soldiers; but she does not recall whether or not she tended them in her youth.

Then she was questioned about a certain tree growing near her village. To which she answered that, fairly near Domrémy, there was a certain tree called the Ladies' Tree, and others called it the Fairies' Tree; and near by is a fountain. And she has heard that people sick of the fever drink of this fountain and seek its water to restore their health; that, she has seen herself; but she does not know whether they are cured or not. She said she has heard that the sick, when they can rise, go to the tree and walk about it. It is a big tree, a beech, from which they get the fair May, in French *le beau may;* and it belongs, it is said, to Pierre de Bourlemont, knight. She said sometimes she would go playing with the other young girls, making garlands for Our Lady of Domrémy there; and often she had heard the old folk say (not those of her family) that the fairies frequented it. And she heard a certain Jeanne, the wife of mayor Aubery of Domrémy, her godmother, say that she had seen the fairies; but she herself doesn't know whether it is true or not. As far as she knew, she said, she never saw the fairies at the tree. Asked if she saw them elsewhere, she does not know at all. She had seen the young girls putting garlands on the branches of the tree, and she herself sometimes hung them there with the other girls; sometimes they took them away, and sometimes they left them there.

She said that since she learned that she must come to France, she had taken as little part as possible in games or dancing; and did not know whether she had danced near the tree since she had grown to understanding. Although on occasions she may well have danced there with the children, she more often sang than danced. There is also a wood, called the oak-wood, in French *le Bois-chesnu,* which can be seen from her father's door; not

more than half a league away. She does not know, nor has she ever heard, that the fairies repair there; but she has heard from her brother that in the country around it is said she received her message at the tree; but she says she did not, and she told him quite the contrary. Further, she says, when she came to the king, several people asked her if there were not in her part of the country a wood called the oak-wood; for there was a prophecy which said that out of this wood would come a maid who should work miracles; but Jeanne said that she put no faith in that.

Asked if she wanted a woman's dress, she answered: "Give me one. I will take it and go: otherwise I will not have it, and am content with this, since it pleases God that I wear it."

Tuesday, February 27th. Fourth Session

... Asked whether the voice which spoke to her was that of an angel, or of a saint, male or female, or straight from God, she answered that the voice was the voice of St. Catherine and of St. Margaret. And their heads were crowned in a rich and precious fashion with beautiful crowns. "And to tell this," she said, "I have God's permission. If you doubt it, send to Poitiers where I was examined before."

Asked how she knew they were these two saints, and how she knew one from the other, she answered she knew well who they were, and easily distinguished one from the other.

Asked how she knew one from the other, she answered she knew them by the greeting they gave her. She said further that a good seven years have passed since they undertook to guide her. She said also she knows the saints because they tell her their names.

Asked if the said saints are dressed in the same cloth, she answered: "I will tell you no more now; I have not leave to reveal it. If you do not believe me, send to Poitiers!" She said also that there were some revelations made directly to the king of France, and not to those who question her.

Asked if the saints are the same age, she answered that she had not leave to say.

Asked if the saints spoke at the same time, or one after another, she answered: "I have not leave to tell you; nevertheless I have always had counsel from both."

Asked which one appeared first, she answered: "I did not recognize them immediately; I knew well enough once, but I have forgotten; if I had leave

I would gladly tell you. It is written down in the register at Poitiers." She added that she had received comfort from St. Michael.

Asked which of the apparitions came to her first, she answered that St. Michael came first.

Asked whether it was a long time ago that she first heard the voice of St. Michael, she answered: "I do not speak of St. Michael's voice, but of his great comfort."

Asked which was the first voice which came to her when she was about thirteen, she answered that it was St. Michael whom she saw before her eyes; and he was not alone, but accompanied by many angels from heaven. She said also that she came into France only by the instruction of God.

Asked if she saw St. Michael and these angels corporeally and in reality, she answered: "I saw them with my bodily eyes as well as I see you; and when they left me, I wept; and I fain would have had them take me with them too." . . .

March 1st. Fifth Session

. . . She said that before seven years are past the English will lose a greater stake than they did at Orleans, for they will lose everything in France. She adds that the said English will suffer greater loss than ever they did in France; and it will be a great victory which God will send the French.

Asked how she knew this, she answered: "I know by a revelation made to me, and within seven years it will happen: and I am much vexed that it should be so long postponed." She said also that she knew it by revelation as well as she knew we were at that moment before her.

Asked when it will happen, she said she knew neither the day nor the hour.

Asked in what year it will happen, she answered: "You will not learn that: nevertheless I heartily wish it might be before St. John's Day."

Asked whether she said it would happen before Martinmas in winter, she answered that she had said that before Martinmas in winter many things would be seen; and it might be that the English would be overthrown.

Asked what she told John Grey, her guard, about Martinmas, she answered: "I have told you."

Asked through whom she knew that this would come to pass, she answered that she knew through St. Catherine and St. Margaret. Asked if St. Gabriel was with St. Michael when he came to her, she answered she did not remember.

Asked if since the last Tuesday she had not spoken with St. Catherine and St. Margaret, she answered yes, but she does not know at what time.

Asked on what day, she answered, yesterday and today; "there is no day but I hear them."

Asked if she always saw them in the same dress, she answered she always sees them in the same form; and their heads are richly crowned. Of their other clothing she does not speak: of their robes she knows nothing.

Asked how she knew whether her apparition was man or woman, she answered she knew for certain, she recognized them by their voices, and they revealed themselves to her; nor did she know anything but by revelation and God's command.

Asked what part of them she saw, she answered the face.

Asked if the saints which appeared to her had hair, she answered: "It is well to know that they have."

Asked if there were anything between their crowns and their hair, she answered no.

Asked if their hair were long and hung down, she answered: "I do not know." She added that she did not know whether they appeared to have arms or other members. She said they spoke very well and beautifully; and she understood them very well.

Asked how they spoke if they had no other members, she answered: "I leave that to God." She said the voice was gentle, soft and low, and spoke in French.

Asked if St. Margaret spoke in the English tongue, she answered: "Why should she speak English when she is not on the English side?" . . .

. . . Asked what she had done with her mandrake, she answered that she has no mandrake, and never did have; but has heard that near her village there was one, though she has never seen it. She said also that she had heard it called a dangerous and evil thing to keep; nor does she know its use.

Asked where the mandrake grows, of which she has heard speak, she said in the earth, near the tree, but she does not know the spot. She said that over the mandrake, she has heard, a hazel grows.

Asked what she has heard about the mandrake, she answered that she has heard it attracts money, but she does not believe it. And the voices never told her anything about this.

Asked in what form St. Michael appeared, she answered that she did not see his crown, and she knows nothing of his apparel.

Asked if he was naked, she answered: "Do you think God has not where-withal to clothe him?" . . .

In Prison. Monday, March 12th. The Vicar of the Lord Inquisitor is summoned according to the tenor of his new commission

. . . Asked whether she spoke to Our Lord when she promised Him to keep her virginity, she answered that it ought to be quite enough to promise it to those who were sent from Him, namely St. Catherine and St. Margaret.

Asked what persuaded her to summon a man from the town of Toul for breach of promise, she answered: "I did not have him summoned; it was he who summoned me; and I swore before the judge to tell the truth." And moreover, she said, she had made no promise to this man. She added that the first time she heard her voice she vowed to keep her virginity as long as it should please God; and she was then thirteen years old, or thereabouts. She said her voices assured her that she would win her case at Toul.

Asked if she had not spoken to her priest or any other churchman of the visions which she claimed to have she answered no, save to Robert de Baudricourt and to her king. She added that her voices did not compel her to conceal them, but she was afraid of revealing them, afraid that the Burgundians might hinder her journey; and in particular she feared that her father would stop her.

Asked if she believed it was right to leave her father and mother without permission, when she should honor her father and mother, she answered that in all other things she was obedient to them, except in this journey; but afterwards she wrote to them, and they forgave her.

Asked whether she thought she had committed a sin when she left her father and mother, she answered that since God commanded, it was right to do so. She added that since God commanded, if she had had a hundred parents, or had been the king's daughter, she would have gone nevertheless.

Asked whether she asked her voices if she should tell her father and mother of her going, she answered that as for her father and mother, the voices were well pleased that she should tell them, but for the difficulty they would have raised if she had done so; and as for herself, she would not have told them for anything. She said the voices left it to her to tell her father and mother, or be silent. . . .

Wednesday, March 14th

... She says that she asked three things of her voices: one was her deliver-ance; the second was that God should aid the French and keep the towns which were under their control; and the third was the salvation of her soul. She asks that if she is taken to Paris she may have a copy of the questions and of her replies, so that she may give them to the people at Paris and say to them "Thus was I questioned at Rouen, and here are my replies," and may not be worried again over so many questions.

And then since she had said that we the aforenamed bishop were exposing ourselves to great peril, in French *en grant dangier,* by bringing her to trial, she was asked what that meant, and to what peril or danger we exposed ourselves, we and the others. She answered that she had said to us the afore-said bishop, "You say that you are my judge; I do not know if you are; but take good heed not to judge me ill, because you would put yourself in great peril. And I warn you so that if God punish you for it I shall have done my duty in telling you."

Asked what the danger or peril was, she answered that St. Catherine told her she would have aid, and she does not know whether this will be her deliverance from prison, or if, whilst she is being tried, some tumult might come through which she can be delivered. And she thinks it will be one or the other. And beyond this the voices told her she will be delivered by a great victory; and then they said: "Take everything peacefully: have no care for thy martyrdom; in the end thou shalt come to the Kingdom of Paradise." And this her voices told her simply and absolutely, that is, without faltering. And her martyrdom she called the pain and adversity which she suffers in prison; and she knows not whether she shall yet suffer greater adversity, but therein she commits herself to God.

Asked whether, since her voices had told her that in the end she should go to Paradise, she has felt assured of her salvation, and of not being damned in hell, she answered that she firmly believed what the voices told her, namely that she will be saved, as firmly as if she were already there.

Asked whether after this revelation she believed that she could not commit mortal sin, she answered: "I do not know; but in everything I commit my-self to God." And when she was told that this was an answer of great weight, she answered that she held it for a great treasure. ...

Saturday, March 17, in prison

. . . Asked if she would submit [her deeds and words] to the decision of the Church, she answered: "I commit myself to Our Lord, Who sent me, to Our Lady, and to all the Blessed Saints of Paradise." And she thought that Our Lord and the Church were all one, and therein they ought not to make difficulties for her. "Why do you make difficulties when it is all one?"

Then she was told that there is a Church Triumphant, where God is with the saints and the souls who are already saved; and also the Church Militant, that is Our Holy Father the Pope, vicar of God on earth, the Cardinals, the prelates of the Church, and the clergy and all the good Christians and Catholics: and this Church in good assembly cannot err and is governed by the Holy Spirit. Therefore she was asked if she would submit to the Church Militant, namely the Church on earth which is so called. She answered that she came to the King of France in God's name, and in the names of the Blessed Virgin and of all the Blessed Saints of Paradise, and of the Church Victorious above, and at their command; to that Church she submitted all her good deeds and all she had done or should do. And concerning her submission to the Church Militant she would answer nothing more. . . .

. . . Asked how she knew that St. Catherine and St. Margaret hated the English, she answered: "They love those whom God loves, and hate whom He hates."

Asked if God hated the English, she answered that of God's love or His hatred for the English, or of what He would do to their souls, she knew nothing, but she was certain that, excepting those who died there, they would be driven out of France, and God would send victory to the French and against the English.

Asked if God was for the English when they were prospering in France, she answered that she knew not whether God hated the French, but she believed it was His will to suffer them to be beaten for their sins, if they were in a state of sin. . . .

Wednesday, May 23rd. Jeanne's faults are expounded to her by master Pierre Maurice. The trial is concluded

I

Firstly, Jeanne, you have said that from the age of thirteen years or thereabouts you have had revelations and apparitions of angels, of St. Catherine

and St. Margaret, whom you have frequently seen with your bodily eyes; and that they have often spoken with you and told you many things set forth at length in your trial.

On this point the clerks of the University of Paris and others have considered the manner and end of these revelations, the matter of the things revealed, and the quality of your person: and having considered everything relevant they declare that it is all false, seductive, pernicious, that such revelations and apparitions are superstitious and proceed from evil and diabolical spirits.

II

You have said that your king received a sign by which he knew that you were sent from God, that it was St. Michael, in the company of a host of angels, some with crowns, others with wings, and St. Catherine and St. Margaret were among them, coming to you in the town and castle of Chinon. They all mounted the stair of the castle in your company up to the chamber of your king, before whom the angel who bore the crown bowed. At another time you said this crown, which you call a sign, was given to the archbishop of Reims, who presented it to your king, before many princes and lords whom you have named.

Regarding this article, the clergy say it is not probable, but rather a presumptuous, misleading and pernicious lie, an undertaking contrary and derogatory to the dignity of angels.

III

You have said that you recognized the angels and saints by the good counsel, comfort and doctrine they gave you; by the fact that they told you their names and the saints greeted you; moreover, that you believe it was St. Michael who appeared to you; that their words and deeds are good; all of which you believe as firmly as you hold the faith of Jesus Christ.

Regarding this article, the clergy say that the signs were not sufficient for the recognition of the angels and saints, that you believed lightly and affirmed rashly, that, moreover, in the comparison you make you deviate from the faith.

IV

You have said you are certain of future and contingent events, that you have known where things were hidden, that you recognized men you had never seen, through the voices of St. Catherine and St. Margaret.

Regarding this article, the clergy find superstition, divination, presumptuous assertions and vain boasting.

V

You have said that you wore and still wear man's dress at God's command and to His good pleasure, for you had instruction from God to wear this dress, and so you have put on a short tunic, jerkin, and hose with many points. You even wear your hair cut short above the ears, without keeping about you anything to denote your sex, save what nature has given you. And often you have in this apparel received the Sacrament of the Eucharist. And although you have many times been admonished to put it off, you would not, saying that you would rather die than put off this dress, unless it were God's command; and that if you were still in this dress and with those of your own party, it would be for the great welfare of France. You say also that nothing could persuade you to take an oath not to wear this dress and bear these arms; and for all this you plead divine command.

Regarding such matters, the clergy declare that you blaspheme against God, despising Him and His sacraments, that you transgress divine law, Holy Scripture and the canons of the Church, that you think evil and err from the faith, that you are full of vain boasting, that you are given to idolatry and worship yourself and your clothes, according to the customs of the heathen.

VI

You have often said that in your letters you have put these names JHESUS MARIA, and the sign of the cross, to warn those to whom you wrote not to do what was indicated in the letter. In other letters you boasted that you would kill all those who did not obey you, and that by your blows would the favor of the Lord be seen. Also you have often said that all your deeds were by revelation and according to divine command.

In regard to such affirmations, the clergy declare you to be a traitor, per-

fidious, cruel, desiring human bloodshed, seditious, an instigator of tyranny, a blasphemer of God's commandments and revelations.

VII

You have said that according to revelations vouchsafed you at the age of seventeen, you left your parents' house against their will, driving them almost mad. You went to Robert de Baudricourt, who, at your request, gave you a man's dress and a sword, also men-at-arms to take you to your king. And when you came to the king, you told him that his enemies should be driven away, you promised to bring him into a great kingdom, to make him victorious over his foes, and that for this God had sent you. These things you say you accomplished in obedience to God and according to revelation.

Regarding such things, the clergy declare that you have been irreverent to your father and mother, thereby disobeying God's commandment, that you have given occasion for scandal, that you have blasphemed; that you have erred from the faith; and that you have made a rash and presumptuous promise.

VIII

You have said that of your own will you hurled yourself from the tower of Beaurevoir, preferring to die rather than be delivered into the hands of the English and live after the destruction of Compiègne. And although St. Catherine and St. Margaret forbade you to leap, you could not restrain yourself. And in spite of the great sin you have committed in offending these saints, you knew by your voices that after your confession your sin was forgiven.

This act the clergy declare you committed because of cowardice verging on despair and possibly suicide. In this matter you also uttered a rash and presumptuous statement in asserting that your sin is forgiven, and you err from the faith touching the doctrine of free will.

IX

You have said that St. Catherine and St. Margaret promised to lead you to Paradise provided that you preserved the virginity which you vowed and promised them, and that you are as well assured of it as if you had already

entered into the glory of the Blessed. You believe you have not committed mortal sin, and it seems to you that if you were in mortal sin the saints would not visit you daily as they do.

Such an assertion the clergy declare to be a pernicious lie, presumptuous and rash, that it contains a contradiction of what you had previously said, and that finally your beliefs err from the true Christian faith.

X

You have declared that you know well that God loves certain living persons better than you, and that you learned this by revelation from St. Catherine and St. Margaret; also that those saints speak French, not English, as they are not on the side of the English. And since you knew that your voices were for your king, you began to dislike the Burgundians.

Such matters the clergy pronounce to be a rash and presumptuous assertion, a superstitious divination, a blasphemy uttered against St. Catherine and St. Margaret, and a transgression of the commandment to love our neighbors.

XI

You declared that to those whom you call St. Michael, St. Catherine and St. Margaret, you did reverence, bending the knee, taking off your cap, kissing the ground on which they trod, vowing to them your virginity: that you believed in the instruction of these saints, whom you invoked, kissed and embraced, as soon as they appeared to you, without seeking counsel from your priest or from any other ecclesiastic. And, notwithstanding, you believe these voices came from God as firmly as you believe in the Christian religion and the Passion of Our Lord Jesus Christ. Moreover, you said that if any evil spirit should appear to you in the form of St. Michael you would know such a spirit and distinguish him from the saint. And again you said, that of your own accord, you have sworn not to reveal the sign you gave to your king. And finally you added: "Save at God's command."

Now touching these matters, the clergy affirm that if you had the revelations and saw the apparitions of which you boast in such a manner as you say, then you are an idolatress, an invoker of demons, an apostate from the faith, a maker of rash statements, a swearer of an unlawful oath.

XII

And you have said that if the Church wished you to disobey the orders you say God gave you, nothing would induce you to do so; that you know that all the deeds of which you have been accused in your trial were wrought according to the command of God and that it was impossible for you to do otherwise. Touching these deeds, you refuse to submit to the judgment of the Church on earth or of any living man, and will submit therein to God alone. And, moreover, you declared that this reply itself was not made of your own accord but by God's command; in spite of the article of faith, *Unam Sanctam Ecclesiam Catholicam,* having been many times declared before you, and notwithstanding that it behooves all Christians to submit their deeds and sayings to the Church Militant especially all that concerns revelations and similar matters.

Wherefore the clergy declare you to be schismatic, an unbeliever in the unity and authority of the Church, apostate and obstinately erring from the faith.

Now when these assertions with the qualifications of the University of Paris had thus been related and explained to Jeanne she was finally admonished in French by the same doctor to think very carefully over her acts and sayings, especially in the light of the last article. He spoke to her thus:

"Jeanne, dearest friend, it is now time, near the end of your trial to think well over all that has been said. Although you have four times already, by the lord bishop of Beauvais, by the lord vicar of the Inquisitor, by other doctors sent to you on their behalf, been most diligently admonished for the honor and reverence of God, for the faith and law of Jesus Christ, for the tranquillity of their consciences, and the alleviation of the scandal you have caused, to the salvation of your body and soul; although you have been shown the perils to which you expose your body and soul if you do not reform yourself and your sayings and correct them by submitting your acts and your words to the Church, and by accepting her judgment, nevertheless up till now you have not wished to listen.

"Now although many of your judges would have been satisfied with the evidence collected against you, in their anxiety for the salvation of your body and soul they have submitted your sayings for examination to the University of Paris, the light of all knowledge and the extirpator of errors. When the lord judges received the deliberations of the University they de-

cided that you should to this end be once more admonished, warned of your errors, scandals and other crimes, and that we should beg, exhort and advise you by the bowels of Our Lord Jesus Christ who suffered cruel death for the redemption of mankind, to correct your words and submit them to the judgment of the Church, as every loyal Christian is bound and obliged to do. Do not permit yourself to be separated from Our Lord Jesus Christ who created you to be a partaker in His glory; do not choose the way of eternal damnation with the enemies of God who daily endeavor to disturb men, counterfeiting often the likeness of Christ, His angels and His saints, who they profess and affirm themselves to be, as is shown more fully in the lives of the Fathers and in the Scriptures. Therefore if such apparitions have appeared to you, do not believe them: more than that, put away the belief or imagination you had in such things, and believe rather in the words and opinions of the University of Paris and other doctors who, being well acquainted with the law of God and the Holy Scriptures, have concluded that no faith should be given to such apparitions or in any extraordinary apparition or forbidden novelty which is not supported by Holy Scripture or sign or miracle, none of which you have.

"You have believed these apparitions lightly, instead of turning to God in devout prayer to grant you certainty; and you have not consulted prelates or learned ecclesiastics to enlighten yourself: although, considering your condition and the simplicity of your knowledge, you ought to have done so. Take this example: suppose your king had appointed you to defend a fortress, forbidding you to let any one enter. Would you not refuse to admit whoever claimed to come in his name but brought no letters or authentic sign? Likewise Our Lord Jesus Christ, when He ascended into Heaven, committed the government of His Church to the apostle St. Peter and his successors, forbidding them to receive in the future those who claimed to come in His name but brought no other token than their own words. So you should not have put faith in those which you say came to you, nor ought we to believe in you, since God commands the contrary.

"First, Jeanne, you should consider this: if when you were in your king's domain, a soldier or other person born in his realm or fealty had arisen and said, 'I will not obey the king or submit to any of his officers,' would you not have said this man should be condemned? What shall you say of yourself, who, brought up in the faith of Christ by the sacrament of baptism, have become the daughter of the Church and the spouse of Christ, if you do

not obey Christ's officers, that is to say, the prelates of the Church? What judgment shall you deliver upon yourself? Cease, I pray you, from uttering these things if you love your Creator, your precious spouse and your salvation; obey the Church and submit to its judgment; know that if you do not, if you persevere in this error, your soul will be condemned to eternal punishment and perpetual torture, and I do not doubt that your body will come to perdition.

"Let not human pride and empty shame, which perhaps constrain you, hold you back because you fear that if you do as I advise you will lose the great honors which you have known. For the honor of God and the salvation of your body and soul must come first: you will lose all if you do not as I say, for you will separate yourself from the Church and from the faith you swore in the holy sacrament of baptism, you cut the authority of Our Lord from the Church which is nevertheless led, ruled and governed by His spirit and authority. For He said to the prelates of the Church: 'He that heareth you heareth Me, he that despiseth you despiseth Me.' Therefore if you will not submit to the Church you separate yourself in fact, and if you will not submit to her you refuse to submit to God, and you err in respect of this article: *Unam Sanctam Ecclesiam.* What the Church is, and her authority, has been sufficiently explained to you already in former admonitions.

"Therefore, in view of all these things, on behalf of your judges the lord bishop of Beauvais and the lord vicar of the Inquisitor, I admonish, beg and exhort you by the pity you have for the passion of your Creator, by the love you bear for the salvation of your body and soul, correct and amend these errors, return to the way of truth, by obedience to the Church and submission in all things to her judgment and decision. By so doing you will save your soul and redeem, as I hope, your body from death; but if you do not, if you persist, know that your soul will be overwhelmed in damnation and I fear the destruction of your body. From these ills may Our Lord preserve you!"

After Jeanne had been admonished in this manner and had heard these exhortations she replied thereto in this way: "As for my words and deeds, which I declared in the trial, I refer to them and will maintain them."

Asked if she thinks she is not bound to submit her words and deeds to the Church Militant or any one other than God, she answered: "I will maintain that manner of speech which I always said and held in the trial."

She said that if she were condemned and she saw the fire and the faggots

alight and the executioner ready to kindle the fire, and she herself were in it, she would say nothing else and would maintain until death what she said in the trial.

Then we her judges asked the Promoter and Jeanne whether they had anything further to say. They answered that they had not. Then we proceeded to conclude the proceedings according to the formula of a certain schedule which we the said bishop held in our hands, and of which the tenor follows:

We, competent judges in this trial, as we esteem and declare ourselves in so far as it is necessary, according to your refusal to say anything further, WE DECLARE THE TRIAL ENDED; and, this conclusion pronounced, we assign tomorrow as the day on which you shall hear us give justice and pronounce sentence, which shall afterwards be carried out and proceeded with according to law and reason. . . .

ALAS, POOR YORICK!

François Villon

THE DEBATE BETWEEN THE HEART AND BODY   QUATRAIN

THE EPITAPH IN THE FORM OF A BALLADE

BALLADE OF THE APPEAL OF VILLON   THE REQUEST OF VILLON

Where be your gibes now? your gambols? your songs? your flashes of
merriment; that were wont to set the table on a roar? Not one now,
to mock your own grinning? quite chop-fallen?
               Hamlet

THOUGH he inspires sentimental pity—in the phrase of Hilaire Belloc:
"if you desire one word to use as an antithesis of the word sentimental,
use the word Villon."

We know Villon from criminal records and from Victorian translations,
an impossible synthesis. He was born in the year when Joan was burned
at the stake; in the *Ballade of Dead Ladies* he lamented her as *"Jehanne la
bonne Lorraine."* He was a bad lot in a bitter age, an age settling the long
accounts of The Hundred Years' War. Living by his wits in France of the
fifteenth century, of the invader Goddams (the English), in the underworld
of the Coquillards, in the shadow of the gibbet, in the brothels of Paris, in
the taverns and the hostile countryside, he was an outlawed partisan fighter
at war with society.

Only a major poet could have supported the intolerable burden, at once
personal and patriotic, of such a theme as *"Je ris en pleurs";* but the tears
were hot and the jokes good, both salted. He committed homicide in the
streets, robbed the sacristy of a college, annoyed bishops and harlots, borrowed from dukes and bandits, wandered in exile, and rotted in prisons.
The Ballade of the Hanged shows that he was as intimate with the terror
of death as with the humiliations of poverty. Out of this terror and disorder
he tortured all the macabre jests of the *Great Testament* and the *Ballades,*
and put into the mouth of his mother, kneeling before "a painted heaven
where harps and lutes adore," the very agony of medieval piety.

Stevenson called Villon "a merry-andrew, who has found a certain despicable eminence over human respect and human affection by perching
himself astride upon the gallows," and "the first wicked sans-culotte." In
Christian experience the gallows of the thief is a neighbor of the cross. As

99

for the "wicked sans-culotte," there is Villon's defense in *Straight Tip to All Cross Coves* (in the dress supplied by W. E. Henley):

> Suppose you try a different tack,
> And on the square you flash your flag?
> At penny-a-lining make your wack,
> Or with the mummers mug and gag?
> For nix, for nix the dibbs you bag!
> At any graft, no matter what,
> Your merry goblins soon stravag:
> Booze and the blowens cop the lot.

> *The Moral*

> It's up the spout and Charley Wag
> With wipes and tickers and what not.
> Until the squeezer nips your scrag,
> Booze and the blowens cop the lot.

TWO SESSIONS WITH VILLON

The Dungeon of Meun-sur-Loire. Summer of 1461

Monseigneur Thibault d'Aussigny, Bishop of Orleans, having charged François Villon, clerk and Master of Arts, with sacrilege (possibly the theft of a votive lamp in the church at Baccon-sur-Loire) and forced evidence by "lashings of water," had him committed to the lower dungeon of the Meun prison. Villon composed the *Epistle in Form of a Ballade to His Friends.* That summer, thirty years after the death of Joan of Arc, her beloved Dauphin, Charles VII, died, and Louis XI, crowned at Rheims, was making his way toward Orleans, freeing prisoners at each royal station. Before Louis reached Meun on October 20, and liberated Villon for his masterpiece, *The Great Testament,* the heart and body of the unhappy prisoner engaged in a metaphysical debate:

THE DEBATE BETWEEN THE HEART AND BODY OF VILLON

'What do I hear?' ' 'Tis I, thy weary heart,
Which holds on now by but a single thread.
Strength is no more, I cannot clearly think

ALAS, POOR YORICK! : *François Villon*

As I see thee, O body, skulking there,
Like a poor cur which shivers in the wind.'
'Desiring what?' 'What foolish wills hold sweet.'
'Why dost thou feel so sad?' 'I share thy grief.'
'Leave me in peace.' 'And why?' 'I will repent.'
'When pray?' 'When wisdom comes to me.'
'I say no more.' 'I'll gladly miss thy words.'

'What thinkest thou? A shining light thou art!
Thirty years old—age of worn-out mule.
Art thou a child?' 'Nay, nay!' 'Is it then lust
That holds thee captive in remorseless grip?
Dost thou know nothing?' 'Oh, yes, well I know
Life's disappointments and her many griefs.'
'And is that all?' 'Why, what more can I say?
But if it's not enough, I'll speak some more.'
'But thou art lost!' 'Yet will I try to rise.'
'I say no more.' 'I'll gladly miss thy words.'

'Thy sorrows smite me when they strike at thee,
If thou wert feeble-witted or a dolt
That might excuse thy folly, lessen guilt,
But if thou canst distinguish good from ill
Either thy head is harder than a flint
Or shame delights you more than honour's praise.
What dost thou answer to that argument?'
'I shall be free from grief when I am dead!'
'Cold comfort, that! What eloquence divine!
I say no more.' 'I'll gladly miss thy words.'

'Whence, then, thy wretchedness?' 'It's my ill luck,
For I was born 'neath Saturn's evil frown;
On me he placed these burdens, I believe.'
'Oh fool, the master makes the slave obey,
For Solomon has written in his scroll,

"The wise man" (so he says) "has ample power
O'er threatening planets and whate'er they bring." '
'That will I ne'er believe, they fashioned me.'
'What do you say?' 'Indeed, 'tis my belief.'
'I say no more.' 'I'll gladly miss thy words.'

Envoy

'You wish to live?' 'God grant I have the strength!'
'You must—' 'Must what?' 'You must at once repent
And read—' 'Read what?' 'All sorts of learned books,
And shun loose company.' 'That will I do.'
'And don't forget!' 'I'll bear it well in mind.'
'Expect too much and disappointment comes.
I say no more.' 'I'll gladly miss thy words.'

Pity, Terror, and the Last Joke. Winter of 1463

One night in the autumn of 1462, Villon, hungry for his supper, invited himself to the house of one Robin Dogis and sat at his table with Hutin du Moustier, a hard-boiled police officer, and Roger Pichard, who was shortly to end on the gibbet. Returning to Villon's room to finish the festivities, the drunken quartet stopped at the lighted street-window of a most respectable citizen of Paris. In a spirit of social criticism, Pichard moved closer, to spit his contempt at the dull and honest scribblers inside the law-office. The result was a violent brawl in the dark from which Villon slipped away at the start. The authorities seized Dogis in his home, du Moustier in the arms of the disturbed clerks, Pichard in the sanctuary of a church, and Villon in bed. All were imprisoned in the Châtelet, Villon the least guilty but with the blackest *dossier* on his black past. They decided to seize an opportunity to finish him off, gave him the water treatment, and sentenced him to hanging and strangling. Villon's first preparation for a death which seemed impending with such certainty was the bitter jest, *The Quatrain*. Purged of obscenity and joking, he composed *The Ballade of the Hanged*. Then pity and terror gave way to a frantic hope of saving his neck. Miraculously, the Court of Parliament annulled his death sentence on January 3, 1463, banishing him from Paris for ten years, and Villon burst into a self-congratulatory song, *The Ballade to Etienne Garnier*. Garnier was the man who kept the prisoners' register. Villon's humor rising with his luck, he sent to the Parliament a grateful and extravagant *Request of Villon* for three days' grace to prepare for that journey into oblivion from which we have no more *Ballades* or bitter jokes.

QUATRAIN

Que Feit Villon Quand Il Fut Jugé a Mourir

Je suis Françoys, dont il me poise,
Né de Paris emprès Pontoise,
Et d'une corde d'une toise
Sçaura mon col que mon cul poise.

[I am François, luckless jay,
Born at Paris, Ponthoise way,
My neck, looped up beneath the tree,
Will learn how heavy buttocks be.]

THE EPITAPH IN THE FORM OF A BALLADE

Which Villon made for himself and his companions while waiting to be hanged with them.
(Commonly known as *The Ballade of the Hanged*.)

You who still live, though night has dimmed our day,
    Do not make hard your hearts to us who die:
For if with grieving hearts you hear this lay
    The sooner will God's anger pass you by;
    Five or six comrades dangling in the sky,
How flaps the flesh we fed so tenderly,
Bestripped and rotten for all men to see!
    This our sad fate doth loud for pity call,
So let none mock (our bones will pardoned be!)
    But ever pray that God will pardon all.

Brothers we claim you, by our side then stay,
    Do not despise us, though we hang so high
By justice slain; for some foolish stray,
    All cannot tread the paths which straight do lie.
Pray for us, brothers, to the Christ on high.
Dear Virgin-born, all may come near to Thee;
Keep us secure from Hell's dread agony,
    That from Thy grace we may not hopeless fall.
Trouble us not, for dead, yes, dead are we!
    But ever pray that God will pardon all.

ALAS, POOR YORICK! : *François Villon*

Dried by the sun are we, black from its ray;
Washed clean and spotless, for the rains come nigh.
Close hang the ravens and the vultures grey,
To feast upon and hollow out each eye,
Even for beard and eyebrow they will sigh.
No rest for us who, spinning ceaselessly,
Obey the wind and pay the law's last fee,
More pecked of birds than fruit on garden wall.
Therefore, in mercy, look not scornfully,
But ever pray that God will pardon all.

Envoy

Prince Jesus, Lord, heed now our misery,
Preserve us all from Hell's dread seigneury,
We do not crave so harsh a ruler's call.
Friends, I implore you, banish cruelty,
But ever pray that God will pardon all.

BALLADE OF THE APPEAL OF VILLON

Written when he learned that the Parlement of Paris had commuted his sentence of death
to one of banishment for ten years.

What about my last appeal,
  Garnier, was I foolish, eh?
Every beast protects its weal,
  Struggles hard when snared, I lay,
  To escape and get away.
Round my neck a rope they'd snap,
  Gallows fruit must soon decay!
No time that to shut my trap!

Had I owned a royal seal,
  Been a Bourbon, a Capet,
I would not their torture feel,
  But you know their gentle way!
  When with wicked malice, they,

Falsehood's guile in ermine wrap,
　　Trick me foully, then I'll say,
　　'No time that to close my trap!'

Don't you think that sense I'd steal
　　(When my skies appeared so grey)?
Louder than a mouse to squeal,
　　And they heard me, too, hurray!
　　Men think quickly when at bay,
When the notary did rap,
　　'You'll be hanged, my lad, next day.'
No time that to close my trap!

Envoy

Prince, if I had not called, 'Nay,'
Stark I'd stand (a sore mishap!),
　　Like a scarecrow 'mid the hay.
No time that to close my trap!

THE REQUEST OF VILLON

Presented to the Court of Parlement in the form of a ballade.

All my five senses, ears and mouth and eyes,
　　My nose and you, O sense of touch so dear;
Each weary limb on which disgrace still lies,
　　In your own fashion bring your praises near.
　　Dear sovereign Court by whose grace we are here,
Who kept our feet from fell Misfortune's maze;
The tongue cannot enough thy fame emblaze
　　Nor offer thanks as each one humbly should:
Wherefore to thee our voices glad we raise,
　　Sister of Angels, Mother of the Good.

O wound yourself, O heart, when Memory plies
　　Her lash; do not more grim and hard appear

105

Than that grey mighty rock 'neath Eastern skies,
  Whence water gushed at word from Jewish seer.
  Shed tears, O heart, and draw to mercy near,
A humble heart which sighs with glad amaze.
The Court, with Holy Empire leagued, now praise,
  Which comforts strangers who defenceless stood;
Pilgrim who treads dear Heaven's holiest ways,
  Sister of Angels, Mother of the Good.

Each of my teeth, forgetting strength or size,
  Leap forward now and call with lusty cheer,
Louder than organ calls or trumpet cries,
  Even forget to masticate or fear!
  Remember that I was in durance drear.
My liver, lungs, and heart that lifeblood pays;
My body, too, vile as where filth decays,
  Viler than pig 'mid slime in distant wood,
Ere worse befall you, bring your praiseful lays,
  Sister of Angels, Mother of the Good.

Envoy

O Prince, now grant your servant three short days
That he may seek again his folks' kind gaze,
  Without them he lacks money, yea, and food
O Court triumphal, your decree he prays,
  Sister of Angels, Mother of the Good.

The poems by Villon are translated by Lewis Wharton.

GOD'S AMBASSADOR:
Christopher Columbus
LETTER TO THE NURSE JUANA DE LA TORRES

If in these days, some reckless airman resolved to fly to Mars and actually set out: and if, on his way, he discovered a hitherto unknown planet and returned with the story of this new star—bringing news of unfamiliar beings, animals, and plants unknown before, that thrived in that strange air; of dimensions and proportions that made everything to which our eyes had been accustomed hitherto, seem dwarfish: this would about represent the revolution in the human imagination evoked by the discoveries of Columbus. For such, indeed, was its main effect: a revolution in the imagination.

JACOB WASSERMANN, *Christopher Columbus*

For it is as the achievement of a flower, pure, white, waxlike and fragrant, that Columbus' infatuated course must be depicted, especially when compared with the acrid and poisonous apple which was later by him to be proved. No more had Columbus landed, the flower once ravished, than it seemed as if heaven itself had turned upon this man for disturbing its repose.

WILLIAM CARLOS WILLIAMS, *In the American Grain*

THE first bold, blind voyage of Columbus near the turn of the fifteenth century opened up more than the islands and continents of America; it made a revolution in the imagination of Europeans. "The time had come," says de Madariaga gracefully, "when mankind, which had lived for centuries with its hands joined upwards in a yearning, vertical gesture, the shape of its cathedral windows, had to lower its arms, disjoin its hands and make them active in horizontal, tumultuous and creative activities." An immense restlessness was awakened out of the old lethargy and a great energy was released into the making of the brave new world, a world which was to be neither Europe nor America, "but that world which the discovery of the American Continent was to bring forth in the minds of men." Once the miracle of the discovery was accomplished, Columbus, its all too human and frail catalytic agent, was finished. By 1500, only *eight* years after the date of the discovery, Columbus was a dejected prisoner in irons. It was the beginning of the end. He had three voyages behind him, and he had lately sent back to Spain news of rebellion in Española, of finding marvelous pearls, and of the fresh discovery of a big river which, considering the violence that had been committed against the unknown and against the boundaries of possibility, might in fact be one of the four rivers of Paradise.

With more reason, it was a river leading to Hell. All this news reached the court of Spain; evidence was also accumulating in the hands of Ferdinand and Isabella which showed too plainly that their Admiral of the Ocean Sea had no talents for ruling the lands which he had with such passionate faith wrested from timeless obscurity. In Española he was bogged down in a swamp of administrative problems—of slavery, salaries, tough characters, and ultimately rebellion. He could not extricate himself from the mismanagement of men and of government in Española, as easily as only a few years before he had skirted the danger zone of heresy, when they had cited against his enterprise the dogmas of the Church and the opinions of the saints: that it was rash to look in the antipodes for a race of men with their heels in the air, belonging to a nation not descended from old Adam. Rebellion and wretched statecraft were the heresies by which Columbus was destroyed. He had outlived his mission, usefulness, and ability. That the curtain was already coming down on the Admiral of the Ocean Sea, and a moral shadow settling even on his discovery, was evident at the Spanish court: "There go the Admiral's sons," people said, "the mosquitoes of the man who found lands of vanity and deceit, which are the tomb and misery of Castilians." And very soon the royal commissioner, Francisco de Bobadilla, brought back Columbus himself in fetters, though only his cook, and no one else in rebellious Española, would put those irons on the Admiral's feet.

The letter which gives us Columbus' impassioned version of the events in Española was addressed by the humiliated prisoner in chains—in whom humility was now all his pride—to Juana de la Torres who had been the nurse of Ferdinand and Isabella's son, Prince John. She was the sister of that Antonio de Torres who was prominent in several of the voyages to the Indies. To her, therefore, a lady so strategically located between the heart of the queen and a partner in his enterprise, he could open his mind, offer a vindication of his errors, and a confession of his whole soul. It is a strange and revealing letter; Columbus himself valued it. God was his witness that he had succeeded in baring in the Indies "a new heaven and a new earth." How could anyone confuse that new heaven and earth with the administrative mess in Española? They had burdened his weary shoulders with the government of a dissolute people. What had his service, one that "every day is more famous," profited him but shame and anguish? How in the name of justice could Bobadilla, even by royal decree, replace him, Columbus, who was "governor by privilege?" Who had brought him to this pass but a vaga-

bond people, merchants who could buy a woman as one buys a farm, men "who did not deserve baptism in the eyes of God?" Had he, then, appropriated gold, when the truth was that he had carefully laid aside for their majesties "grains as large as a goose's egg, and a hen's egg, and a pullet's egg?" At home they regarded him, the Admiral of the Ocean Sea, as some petty governor set to rule over a petty island, when by the will of God he had given Spain "another world." No, he ought to be judged as a knight of the sword, and judged by men of action, not by a Bobadilla. His pain, his irons, were dear to him. Let God punish ingratitude and wrongs.

Ferdinand and Isabella were duly remorseful and touched by this sorrowing rhetoric, but Columbus succeeded only in postponing the inevitable and inglorious last curtain. In the words of de Madariaga: "It had to be. For had not Don Quixote de la Mancha come home a prisoner in a wooden cage? How could Don Cristobal de Cipango come home but in the jail in which reality encloses all those knights who do not respect it?"

LETTER TO THE NURSE JUANA DE LA TORRES

MOST VIRTUOUS LADY: If it be something new for me to complain of the world, its custom of maltreating me is of very old standing. A thousand battles have I fought with it, and I have withstood all until now when neither arms nor wit avail me. With cruelty, it has cast me down to the depth. Hope in Him Who created all men sustains me; His succour has been always very near. On one occasion, and that not long ago, when I was deeply distressed, He raised me with His divine arm, saying: 'O man of little faith, arise, it is I, be not afraid!'

I came with such earnest love to serve these princes, and I have served with a service that has never been heard or seen. Of the new heaven and of the new earth, which Our Lord made, as St. John writes in the Apocalypse, after He had spoken of it by the mouth of Isaiah, He made me the messenger and He showed me where to go. In all there was incredulity, and to the queen my lady He gave the spirit of understanding and great courage, and He made her the heiress of all, as His dear and very loved daughter. I went to take possession of all this in her royal name. All wished to cover the ignorance in which they were sunk, hiding their little knowledge by speaking of difficulties and expense. Her Highness on the contrary approved and supported the enterprise as far as she was able. Seven years were spent

in discussion and nine in performance. Remarkable and memorable events took place in that time. Of all this, there had been no conception.

I came to be, and I am, such that there is none so vile as not to dare to insult me. Throughout the world, it will be counted virtue in any that he is not able to consent to this reviling. If I had violently seized the Indies or the land made holy because in it there is to-day the fame of the altar of St. Peter, and had given them to the Moors, they could not have shown greater enmity towards me in Spain. Who would believe such a thing of a land where there has always been so great nobility?

I would very gladly rid myself of the whole business if it were honourable towards my Queen for me to do so. The support of Our Lord and Her Highness has caused me to persevere in it, and in order somewhat to mitigate the grief that death has brought upon her, I entered upon a new voyage to a new heaven and a new earth, which up to then had lain hidden, and if this, like the other voyages of the Indies, be not regarded there, it is no wonder, for through my exertions it has come to knowledge. The Holy Spirit inspired St. Peter and the other Twelve with him, and they all wrestled here below, and many were their labours and great their weariness; in the end, they were victorious in all. I believed that this voyage to Paria would be some appeasement on account of the pearls and the finding of gold in Española. I ordered the people to gather and to fish for the pearls, and with them an agreement was made concerning my return for them, and as I understood it, they should amount to the measure of a *fanega*. If I have not written this to Their Highnesses, it was because I wished first to have the matter of the gold settled.

This issued for me as many other things have issued. I should not have lost them or my honour, if I had sought my own advantage and if I had allowed Española to be ruined, or if my privileges and the agreements made with me had been respected. And I say also as much concerning the gold, which I had by then collected and which with so great loss of life and with so many labours, I have brought in perfectly.

When I went on the voyage to Paria, I found almost half the people in Española in revolt, and they have made war on me to this day, as if I had been a Moor, and at the same time there has been a serious conflict with the Indians. It was then that Ojeda came and he endeavoured to put the seal on this state of affairs, saying that Their Highnesses had sent him with promises of gifts and franchises and wages. He gathered a great following, for in all Española there are few who are not vagabonds, and there is no one with

a wife and children. This Ojeda troubled me greatly and it was necessary that he should be sent away; and he went, declaring that he would speedily return with more ships and men, and that he had left the royal person of the queen at the point of death.

At this time there arrived Vicente Yañez; he caused tumult and suspicions, but no damage. The Indians spoke of many other caravels at the cannibal islands and in Paria, and afterwards there was a report of six other caravels which a brother of the alcalde commanded, but this was due to malice. And this was already at a time when there was now very little hope that Their Highnesses would ever send ships to the Indies, and when we did not expect them, and when they said generally that Her Highness was dead.

At this time one Adrian attempted to revolt again as before, but Our Lord would not permit his evil purpose to be carried into effect. I had resolved in my own mind not to touch a hair of anyone's head, and owing to his ingratitude, I was not able to save him, as I had intended to do. I would not have done less to my own brother, if he had desired to kill me and to deprive me of the lordship which my king and queen had given into my keeping. This Adrian, as is now demonstrated, had sent Don Fernando to Xaragua to assemble some of his followers, and there was there a dispute with the alcalde, whence arose a deadly quarrel, but the purpose was not attained. The alcalde arrested him and some of his band, and the fact was that he punished them without my having ordered it. They were prisoners, awaiting a caravel in which they were to go; the news of Ojeda, whom I have mentioned, caused hope to be lost that it would come any more.

For six months I had been ready to leave to come to Their Highnesses with the good news of the gold and to escape from having to govern a dissolute people, who have no fear of God or of their king and queen, and who are full of folly and malice. I should have been able to pay the people with six hundred thousand maravedis, and for this purpose, I had four *contos* from the tithes and something over, besides the third from the gold.

Before my departure I many times prayed Their Highnesses that they would send there at my cost someone who might have charge of the administration of justice, and after I had found the alcalde in revolt, I asked this again, or for some men or at least for some servant, bearing their letters, since my reputation is such that although I were to build churches and hospitals, they would always be called lairs for robbers. They have now at last made provision, and it has been very different from that which the

business demanded; let that be, since it is their pleasure. I was there for two years without being able to secure any provision in my favour or in favour of those who were there, and he brings a purseful; whether all will be employed for their service, God knows. Already there are franchises for twenty years, which is the age of a man, and gold is collected, so that a man has the value of five marks in four hours, of which I will speak more at length hereafter.

It would be a charity if it were to please Their Highnesses to put to shame a mob of those who know my weariness, for their evil speaking has done me the greater injury, so that my great service has not profited me, and my preservation of their property and dominion. So I should regain my honour and I should be renowned throughout the world, for the matter is of the kind that every day is more famous and in higher esteem.

At this time the comendador Bobadilla came to Santo Domingo. I was in the Vega and the adelantado was in Xaragua where this Adrian had made his attempt, but already all was settled and the land prosperous and in all peace. On the day after his arrival, he created himself governor and appointed officials and performed executive acts, and he proclaimed franchises for the collection of gold and remitted tithes, and granted a general indulgence for everything else for twenty years, which as I say is the age of a man. And he declared that he was come to pay everyone, although they have not served duly up to this day. And he published abroad that he was to send me back in fetters and my brothers, as he has done, and that I was never to go there more, nor any other of my family, saying a thousand unjust and insulting things of me.

All this was on the day after he arrived, as I have said, I being absent at a distance and knowing nothing of it or of his coming. Some letters of Their Highnesses, signed in blank, of which he brought a quantity, he filled up and sent to the alcalde and to his company with compliments and flattery. To me he never sent a letter or a messenger, nor has he done so down to this day.

Consider what a man who held my position was to think! Honour and favour to one who proved to be robbing Their Highnesses of their lordship and who had done so much evil and damage! And disgrace for one who had supported it through so great perils! When I learned this, I believed that this would be as the affair of Ojeda, or of one of the others. I refrained myself when I knew of a certainty from the friars that Their Highnesses had sent him. I wrote that his coming was welcome, and that I was prepared to

go to the court, and that I had put up for sale all that I possessed, and that in the matter of the franchises, there should be no haste, for I would immediately give him this and the government absolutely, and so I wrote to the religious. Neither he nor they gave me an answer, but he adopted a hostile attitude, and he compelled as many as went there to swear to him as governor; they told me, for twenty years.

As soon as I knew of these franchises, I thought to repair so great an error and that he would be content. Without necessity and reason, he had given so great a thing and to a vagabond people, that which would have been an excessive grant to a man who had brought out a wife and children. I proclaimed by word of mouth and by letters that he was not empowered to make use of his provisions, since mine were of greater authority, and I showed the grants brought by Juan Aguado. All this that I did was in order to gain time, that Their Highnesses might be informed of the state of the country and that they might have occasion to order that in the matter which might be for their service.

It is not advantageous to them that such franchises should be proclaimed in the Indies. It is a favour to the inhabitants who have acquired residence, for to them are given the best lands and at a low estimate they will be worth two hundred thousand maravedis at the end of the four years, when the time of residence is completed, without a single sod being turned in them. I would not so speak if the settlers were married men, but there are not six among them all whose aim is not to amass as much as they can and to return home speedily. It would be well that people should come from Castile, and only such as are well known, and that the country should be peopled with honest men.

I had agreed with these settlers that they should pay a third of the gold and the tithes, and this at their request, and they received it as a great favour from Their Highnesses. I blamed them when I heard that they were departing from it, and they expected that he would make another such as I had done, but the contrary was the case. He irritated them against me, saying that I wished to deprive them of that which Their Highnesses had given to them, and he laboured that they should hurl accusations at me, and he achieved this and that they should write to Their Highnesses that they should not send me again as governor, and so I pray for myself and for all who belong to me, while there is not another people, and he ordered an inquiry to be made into my misdeeds, which were such as were never known in hell.

Our Lord is there, Who saved Daniel and the Three Children with so much wisdom and power, and with such a manifestation, as was pleasing to Him, for His honour. I should have known how to remedy all this and the rest that is said and that has passed since I have been in the Indies, if I had admitted a wish to procure my own good for myself, and it had been honourable for me to do so. But the maintenance of justice and the extension of the lordship of Their Highnesses up to now has brought me to the depth.

Now at the time when so much gold is found, there is a dispute whether there is more to be gained by going about robbing or by going to the mines. For one woman moreover a hundred castellanos are given, as if for a farm, and this is very common, and there are now many merchants who go seeking for girls; nine or ten are now for sale; for women of all ages, there is a good price to be had.

I declare that the violence of the evil speaking of disaffected persons has done me more injury than my service has profited me; it is an evil example for the present and for the future. I make oath that a number of men have gone to the Indies who did not deserve baptism in the eyes of God and man, and now they are returning thither, and he connives at it.

I declare that in saying that the comendador could not grant franchises, I did that which he wished, although I told him that it was to gain time until Their Highnesses should have an account of the land and come to see and to command that which would be to their service.

He has made all hostile to me, and it appears, from that which he has done and from his methods, that he came already very inflamed against me, and it is said that he has spent much to come on this business; I know of this no more than I have heard. I never heard that a *pesquisidor* [1] should gather rebels and bring them as witnesses against one who was governing them, and others without faith and unworthy of it. If Their Highnesses would command a general inquiry to be made there, I declare to you that they would find it a great marvel that the island has not been swallowed up.

I believe that you will remember that when the storm drove me without sails into Lisbon, I was falsely accused as having gone there to the king in order to give the Indies to him. Afterwards Their Highnesses knew the contrary and that it was all malice. Although I have little knowledge, I do not know who regards me as so dull that I do not know that even if the Indies were mine, I should not be able to maintain myself without the aid of a

---

[1] A special judge, appointed to hold an inquiry into acts of administration.

prince. If this be so, where could I have better support and security against being driven out from them entirely than in the king and queen, our sovereigns, who from nothing have set me in such honour and who are the most exalted princes in the world by sea and land? And they know how I have served them and they preserve my privileges and rewards for me, and if any infringe them, Their Highnesses increase them to my advantage, as was seen in the case of Juan Aguado, and they command much honour to be done me, and as I have said, Their Highnesses have received services from me and have taken my sons to be their servants,[2] which could in nowise have happened with another prince, for where there is no love, all else is lacking.

I have now spoken so against a malicious calumny severely and against my wish, for it is a matter which I would not recall even in my dreams. The comendador Bobadilla has with malice wished openly to exhibit his methods and actions in this matter, but with the utmost ease I will make it appear that his small understanding and his great cowardice, united with his inordinate greed, have caused him to fail in this. I have already said how I wrote to him and to the friars, and immediately, as I said to him, I set out utterly alone, because all the people were with the adelantado, and also in order to disarm his suspicion. When he knew this, he threw Don Diego, as a prisoner, loaded with fetters, into a caravel, and to me when I arrived he did the same, and to the adelantado when he came. I have not spoken more to him, nor, up to this day, has he allowed anyone to speak with me, and I make oath that I could not think why I was a prisoner.

His first care was to take the gold, which he had without measuring or weighing it, and, I being absent, he said that he wished to pay the people from it, and, as I have heard, he took the first part for himself, and that he would appoint new persons to superintend the exchange. Of this gold I had put aside certain specimens, grains as large as a goose's egg, and a hen's egg, and a pullet's egg, and of many shapes, which some persons had collected in a little while and with which Their Highnesses would have been pleased, and in order that they might realize the nature of the business from a number of great stones, full of gold. This was the first that he maliciously took for himself, that Their Highnesses might not consider this business as anything until he had feathered his own nest, which he hastened to do. The gold, which was to be melted, diminished in the fire; a chain which weighed

---

[2] Diego and Ferdinand Columbus had become pages in the court after the first voyage of Columbus.

up to twenty marks has never been seen. I have been more aggrieved in the matter of the gold than even in that of the pearls, because I have not brought it to Your Highnesses.

The comendador showed energy always in everything that he thought would injure me. I have already said that with six hundred thousand maravedis I should have paid everyone without defrauding anyone, and I had more than four *contos* from the tithes and from police dues, without touching the gold. He made some gifts which are laughable, although I believe that he rewarded himself first; there Their Highnesses will know the truth when they command him to render an account, especially if I may be present at it. He says continually that a great sum is due, and it is that amount which I have stated and even less.

I have been very much aggrieved in that there has been sent to inquire into my conduct a man who knew that, if the report which he sent back were very damaging, he would remain in charge of the government. Would that it had pleased Our Lord that Their Highnesses had sent him or another two years ago, for I know that then I should have been free from scandalous abuse and infamy, and I should not have been deprived of my honour or have lost it. God is just, and He will cause it to be known by whom and how it was done.

At home they judge me as a governor sent to Sicily or to a city or two under settled government, and where the laws can be fully maintained, without fear of all being lost; and at this I am greatly aggrieved. I ought to be judged as a captain who went from Spain to the Indies to conquer a people, warlike and numerous, and with customs and beliefs very different from ours, a people, living in highlands and mountains, having no settled dwellings, and apart from us; and where, by the will of God, I have brought under the dominion of the king and queen, our sovereigns, another world, whereby Spain, which was called poor, is now most rich. I ought to be judged as a captain, who, for so long a time, down to this day, has borne arms, never laying them down for an hour, and by knights of the sword and by men of action, and not by men of letters, unless they had been as the Greeks or Romans, or as others of the present day of whom there are so many and so noble in Spain, for in any other way I am greatly aggrieved, because in the Indies there is neither a town nor any settled dwelling.

To the gold and pearls the gate is already opened, and they may surely expect a quantity of all, precious stones and spices and a thousand other things. And would that never more ill might come to me, so that I might

undertake the great voyage, and so make the negotiation for Arabia Felix as far as Mecca, as I wrote to Their Highnesses by Antonio de Torres, in my answer concerning the division of the sea and land with the Portuguese, and afterwards I would go to Colucuti, as I have said and laid down in writing in the monastery of la Mejorada.

The news of the gold which I said that I would give is that, on the day of the Nativity, being greatly afflicted owing to my struggles with evil Christians and with the Indians, and being on the verge of leaving all and escaping with my life, if possible, Our Lord miraculously consoled me and said: 'Take courage, be not dismayed nor fear; I will provide for all; the seven years, the term of the gold, are not passed, and in this and in the rest I will give thee redress.' On that day I learned that there were eighty leagues of land and in every part of them mines; it now appears that they are all one. Some have collected a hundred and twenty castellanos in a day, others ninety, and it has risen to two hundred and fifty. To collect from fifty to seventy, and many others from fifteen to fifty, is held to be a good day's work, and many continue to collect it; the average is from six to twelve, and any who falls below this is not content. The opinion of all is that, were all Castile to go there, however inexpert a man might be, he would not get less than a castellano or two a day, and so it is up to the present time. It is true that he who has an Indian collects this amount, but the matter depends on the Christian.

Observe the discretion of Bobadilla! He gave all for nothing and four *contos* of tithes without reason and without being asked, and without first giving notice to Their Highnesses! And this is not the only damage that has been done. I know that my errors have not been committed with intention to do ill, and I believe that Their Highnesses will credit me when I say so. And I know and see that they are merciful to one who maliciously does them disservice. I believe and regard as very certain that they will treat me much better and with more kindness, for I have fallen into error innocently and under compulsion, as they will hereafter know fully, and that I am their humble servant, and they will regard my services and will every day know better that they have been greatly to their advantage. They will weigh all in the balance, as Holy Scripture tells us the good will be weighed with the evil on the day of judgment. If still they command that another judge me, which I do not expect, and that there be an inquiry concerning the Indies, I pray them humbly that they send there two persons, conscientious and honourable, at my expense, and they will easily find that now gold is won

at the rate of five marks in four hours. Be this as it may, it is very necessary that they should make provision in the matter.

The comendador, on arriving at Santo Domingo, took up his residence in my house. All that he found there, he appropriated for himself; well and good, perhaps he had need of it; a pirate never treated a merchant so. Concerning my papers I complain most, that they have been taken from me by him, and that I have never been able to recover one, and those which would have been most useful to me in my defence, he has most carefully concealed. Observe the just and honest pesquisidor. Whatever he may have done, they tell me that he has ceased to regard justice and is acting as a despot. Our Lord God lives, with His power and wisdom, as in the past, and above all things, He punishes ingratitude and wrongs.

A JURIST IN JAIL:

Hugo Grotius

OF THE LEGAL CONDITION OF PERSONS

IN THE memorable career of the great father of international law there is an imprisonment of twenty months during which Hugo Grotius applied himself to writing a legal classic. Generations of judges, never sentenced to prison, have carefully studied it. In 1618, Protestant Netherlands was torn between ardent Arminians (who believed in free will) and ardent Gomarians or Calvinists (who believed in predestination). Religious and political issues became mixed in the struggle for sovereignty between the smaller provinces and Holland. Grotius was on the unpopular, the Arminian side, and found himself condemned to a life sentence in the Castle of Loevstein. The Arminian heresy of free will was checked, the advocates of centralized government won the day, and Grotius had the leisure to write both verse and jurisprudence in jail. In verse he wrote some works in Christian apologetics, defending dogmas common to the various confessions (an advanced and progressive attitude), and a treatise to be used, it seems, by sailors to drive away boredom on the high seas and help repel the arguments of "heathen, Jews and Mohammedans." But the chief prison work was one of the two books on which his fame rests, the *Introduction to the Jurisprudence of Holland,* which, as a legal scholar points out, may be read for its theory of natural law more fully worked out in the celebrated *De juri belli ac pacis,* or for a picture of seventeenth-century Netherlands, or, considering the vanity of lawyers, because "an apt citation from Grotius may give weight or ornament to an argument." From these busy tasks and his castle-jail Grotius was released by the ingenuity of a clever wife, who, sharing his captivity, persuaded the great jurist to hide himself in a trunk filled with borrowed books and a month's dirty linen. When the castle's soldiers, probably Calvinists, complained that the trunk was so heavy "there must be an Arminian in it," Madame Grotius joked with considerable presence of mind about the "heaviness" of Arminian books, and saved the founder of the modern science of the law of nations for his future labors in exile.

OF THE LEGAL CONDITION OF PERSONS

1. In order to understand the rights of persons to things, since law exists between persons, to whom the right belongs, and between things, over which the right extends, we must treat first of the legal condition of persons, secondly of the legal condition of things.

2. The legal condition of persons is distinguished as arising either from what is essential or from what is accidental.

3. The essential distinction between persons is that some are yet unborn, others are born.

4. Unborn persons are held to be persons, to their advantage not to their disadvantage.

5. Such persons only are held to be born as have a body fit to contain a reasonable soul. Monstrous births are not held to be human: the practice in these Provinces is to smother such immediately.

6. Persons actually born are male or female: what are called hermaphrodites are referred to one or other sex according to the prevailing character.

7. Accidental distinctions are such as exist between persons in law, consisting either in a mutual relation between men or in a quality.

8. This mutual relation takes, indeed, its shape from the civil laws, but has its origin in natural law. For natural law teaches us that children, having derived their existence, under God, from their parents, owe to them all honour, gratitude and submission. Moreover the female sex is generally colder and more moody than the male sex, and less fitted for affairs which require understanding: therefore the male sex is given by nature a sort of authority over women. For it belongs to the wisest to rule; but nothing but confusion would result, if all men were to rule over all women: besides which, the upbringing of children could not be properly cared for, unless every one knew his own children; which could not be the case, if a woman were at the same time to have relations with more than one man. From all this comes the necessity of marriage; and since undivided love is stronger, and the principle of community seems to demand that if a woman is bound to one man, a man, in turn, should be bound to one woman, hence the original institution of marriage was between one man and one woman. Further, in order that the upbringing of children, which demands the care of both parents, should not be neglected, and to increase the mutual confidence of the spouses, the first institution was that marriage should be indissoluble, and by this original institution the Germans abide. From this

authority of husband over wife and of parent over child has arisen family government, which in time extended its range, since persons who could not very well take care of themselves voluntarily placed themselves under the government of wise or powerful heads of families. But since children, being incapable during childhood of governing themselves, were also not wise enough to choose for themselves a governor, parents desired their friends to care for the children, when they were dead. Then, as the human race increased, and men came to live in great societies for mutual advantage, it was found that such large numbers of men could not conveniently come together for the discussion of matters of common interest and that the direction of such common interests could be more fittingly effected by chosen representatives. But since peoples had not everywhere the same disposition or aims, it came about that in some places the community entrusted matters of less importance to a representative, retaining most matters in its own hands, from which came democracy; in other places commercial communities, not caring to be troubled with government, have left it to men preeminent in understanding and wealth; hence aristocracy (or oligarchy): finally, in many places for the avoidance of dissension and other difficulties, power has been made over to one man; and this is the origin of monarchy or kingship. And since the law of nature could not have determined everything, these rulers, as observed above, have made further laws for the common good: these rulers, then, finding that parents sometimes left young children without having appointed any guardians to them and that persons of full age by reason of various defects might be unfitted to manage themselves or their affairs, provided for these contingencies. Now, since the law of nature had given parents power over their children, and husbands power over their wives, but could not define how far this power should extend in every case that might arise; and since men come, some sooner, some later, to the use of understanding and ability to rule themselves, and the age of capacity could not be precisely fixed in each individual, and yet a general limit of age must be fixed which would apply if not in all, at all events in the majority of, cases; consequently all these matters, left undefined by the law of nature, have been defined by the civil law, and variously in various countries. Further, since experience teaches that crime, increasing in enormity from day to day, cannot be restrained save by severe punishments, there has been introduced in various countries in addition to the punishment of death, and punishments consisting in ignominy, physical pain and pecuniary loss, also the punishment of slavery, that is loss of freedom, whereby

one man, deemed to have renounced the reason of man and become like to a beast, is subjected not merely to the authority of others, but actually becomes an object of property. This punishment was particularly employed against those who by force, that is by unjust war, after the manner of beasts had injured others in person and in goods. In other countries, however, slavery has not been introduced, or, having been introduced, has been disused, as being too severe. From all of which we may understand how it is that, though all men are equal by birth (saving the duty of children to their parents), nevertheless, not without reason, one man has been subjected to the direction and authority of another. To come now to the civil law of Holland, this distinguishes persons in their mutual relation as persons of full capacity and persons of limited capacity.

FOR THINKING IN ASTRONOMY:

Galileo Galilei

GALILEO'S RECANTATION

And lest some should persuade ye, lords and commons, that these arguments of learned men's discouragement at this your order are mere flourishes, and not real, I could recount what I have seen and heard in other countries, where this kind of inquisition tyrannizes, when I have sat among their learned men (for that honour I had) and been counted happy to be born in such a place of philosophic freedom as they supposed England was, while they themselves did nothing but bemoan the servile condition into which learning amongst them was brought: that this was it which had damped the glory of Italian wits; that nothing had been there written now these many years but flattery and fustian. There it was that I found and visited the famous Galileo grown old, a prisoner to the Inquisition for thinking in astronomy otherwise than the Franciscan and Dominican licensers thought. And though I knew that England then was groaning loudest under the prelatical yoke, nevertheless I took it as a pledge of future happiness that other nations were so persuaded of her liberty.

> JOHN MILTON, *Areopagitica: A Speech for the Liberty of Unlicensed Printing, to the Parliament of England*

A POSTHUMOUS story about Galileo presents him on his knees before the inquisitors, abjuring his conviction that the earth moves around the sun, and then rising with an involuntary phrase on his lips: *e pur si muove*—but it does move! This vicarious barb of wit is just, but apocryphal. What Galileo had seen through his telescope refuted Ptolemy and supported Copernicus, both of whom in fact "contradicted" Scripture. Through the telescope, which showed no heavenly bodies moved by angels, Galileo saw the mountains and the inequality of the moon's surface and the sunlight reflected from the earth. The Milky Way was translated from mythology into an intelligible arrangement of stars, while the revolution of Jupiter's satellites, Saturn's ring, the phases of Venus, and the spots of the sun became arguments for the Copernican theory and the new astronomy. As a mere hypothesis the Copernican idea might have been tolerated in manuscript, but an attack on the Aristotelian axiom of the incorruptibility of the heavens was an attack on Heaven itself. "Write freely," Galileo was advised, "but keep outside the sacristy"; and in 1616 he was forbidden to "hold, teach or defend" the theory that the shining sun is immovable in the center of the universe and that the earth, favored by the grace of God, has a diurnal motion of rotation. Nothing he saw through the telescope which scrutinized

123

the heavens of the Bible ever deflected Galileo from his lifelong position as a sincere Catholic, and in his Copernican cosmology his religious faith remained as immovable as the sun. But the memory of the condemnation and warning of 1616 was weakened by many friendly audiences with the Pope, praise of his piety, the grant of an ecclesiastical pension, the optimism of his friends, and above all by hope for leniency. In 1632 he rashly published the *Dialogue on Two Principal Systems of the World,* the Ptolemaic and Copernican, a three-cornered discussion by Salviate (Galileo), Sagredo (an open-minded listener), and an Aristotelian disciple, Simplicio (the dull brain of the party). It may have appeared to some that it was the Pope himself who was the Simplicio of the symposium, but none could deny that Galileo had broken his word pledged to silence on Copernicus. The boldness of the hopeful old man had to be punished, for as de Sanctis characterizes the *Dialogue:*

> The "effectual theory" of Machiavelli, the "natural light" of Bruno, the "experimental method" of Telesio, the "sweet liberty for truth" of Campanella, are all summarized in the splendid words of Galileo: "Oh, vile cowardice of servile intellects, enslaved with their own conceit!" But the good Simplicio, the Aristotelian pedant, like Bruno's Polinnio is perplexed: "But in case we recede from Aristotle," he says, "whom then shall we have for our guide in philosophy?" And Galileo answers him quietly: "Only the blind require a guide . . . The man that hath eyes in his head and in his mind, those shall he use as his guide."

The official reaction was inexorable; nothing could alter the command of the Inquisition, neither Galileo's seventy years, nor his infirmities, nor the dangers of traveling to Rome through a raging plague. Galileo's arrival on a litter in 1633 and his defence were not exactly heroic. In successive examinations he claimed ignorance of the admonition of 1616, then admitted some taint of disobedience; then asserted he had not really held the Copernican theory since the ecclesiastical reproof; and protested that in sixteen years he had forgotten the injunction not to hold or teach the heretical opinion. He said: "My error has been, and I confess it, one of vainglorious ambition and of pure ignorance and inadvertence." And he said: "I am here in your hands, do with me what you please." In the Church of Santa Maria sopra Minerva, on his knees, he read the words of the recantation. Ptolemy won over Copernicus, Aristotle was vindicated, and the universe was safe. The old man went into the seclusion of a strict exile "vehemently suspected of heresy" and instructed to recite once a week for three years the seven penitential psalms. John Milton on his Italian trip visited Galileo in 1638,

by now a blind astronomer who had scraped the moon's secrets with his telescope—a telescope which, as Marjorie Nicolson speculates, disclosed to Milton "the new conception of the heavens and of space which is reflected in *Paradise Lost.*" The records of Galileo's trial went into the files of the Inquisition, in later years traveled to Paris with the loot of Napoleon, re-turned to Rome from the private library of Louis Philippe, and came to the light of day only after the most delicate hesitation of the authorities. In 1820 a Catholic professor at Rome, having published a little book which took the Copernican theory for granted, was asked by the Censor, as a condition for receiving the imprimatur, to treat it as a mere hypothesis. It was the nineteenth century—the professor refused. But the authorities also hesitated to affirm a stationary earth—it was the nineteenth century. Thus it was that his books, the motion of the earth, and the stability of the sun were officially restored to Galileo.

GALILEO'S RECANTATION

I, GALILEO GALILEI, son of the late Vincenzio Galilei of Florence, aged 70 years, tried personally by this court, and kneeling before You, the most Eminent and Reverend Lord Cardinals, Inquisitors-General throughout the Christian Republic against heretical depravity, having before my eyes the Most Holy Gospels, and laying on them my own hands; I swear that I have always believed, I believe now, and with God's help I will in future believe all which the Holy Catholic and Apostolic Church doth hold, preach, and teach. But since I, after having been admonished by this Holy Office entirely to abandon the false opinion that the Sun was the centre of the universe and immoveable, and that the Earth was not the centre of the same and that it moved, and that I was neither to hold, defend, nor teach in any manner whatever, either orally or in writing, the said false doctrine; and after hav-ing received a notification that the said doctrine is contrary to Holy Writ, I did write and cause to be printed a book in which I treat of the said al-ready condemned doctrine, and bring forward arguments of much efficacy in its favour, without arriving at any solution: I have been judged vehe-mently suspected of heresy, that is, of having held and believed that the Sun is the centre of the universe and immoveable, and that the Earth is not the centre of the same, and that it does move.

Nevertheless, wishing to remove from the minds of your Eminences and

all faithful Christians this vehement suspicion reasonably conceived against me, I abjure with a sincere heart and unfeigned faith, I curse and detest the said errors and heresies, and generally all and every error and sect contrary to the Holy Catholic Church. And I swear that for the future I will neither say nor assert in speaking or writing such things as may bring upon me similar suspicion; and if I know any heretic, or one suspected of heresy, I will denounce him to this Holy Office, or to the Inquisitor and Ordinary of the place in which I may be. I also swear and promise to adopt and observe entirely all the penances which have been or may be by this Holy Office imposed on me. And if I contravene any of these said promises, protests. or oaths, (which God forbid!) I submit myself to all the pains and penalties which by the Sacred Canons and other Decrees general and particular are against such offenders imposed and promulgated. So help me God and the Holy Gospels, which I touch with my own hands. I, Galileo Galilei, aforesaid have abjured, sworn, and promised, and hold myself bound as above; and in token of the truth, with my own hand have subscribed the present schedule of my abjuration, and have recited it word by word. In Rome, at the Convent della Minerva, this 22d day of June, 1633.

I, GALILEO GALILEI, *have abjured as*
above, with my own hand.

FIRST SAINT OF THE MODERN WORLD:
Giordano Bruno

BRUNO TO THE INQUISITORS

So in looking for men of cŏnsciousness in that Italy of Arcadia—for men, that is, who had life in them, for men who had faith and conviction and love of humanity and of right, and zeal for truth and for knowledge—we must turn to those "new men" of Bacon, those first saints of the modern world, the men who carried in their breasts a new Italy and a new literature.

FRANCESCO DE SANCTIS, *History of Italian Literature*

BRUNO lived and died for this heresy: "I hold that there is an infinite universe." He began his career as a refugee from the priesthood; he was under a cloud for impious views on transubstantiation and the immaculate conception. He ended up with a deepening religious experience, in which he found God—a God, who able to produce one small familiar world, was also capable of producing an infinite number of other worlds besides. For the inquisitors who at last caught and tried him, Bruno's religion therefore embraced an infinity too much. In all the years between his first and last crisis, he was a vagabond of the renaissance, agitating every congregation of scholars, in Geneva, Lyons, Toulouse, Montpellier, Paris, London, and Frankfört, sowing philosophy and science, making a restless world more restless, charting the subversive islands of the learned and disputatious with the passion of a Columbus and an Apostle. The earth was his mother, he was fond of saying, and the sun his father. Pursued by homelessness and poverty, he dubbed himself an "Academician of no Academy at all, known as the Disgusted One," and took refuge in his mission for the gospel of Infinity and an intellectual love of God. The manners of an Apostle are not pleasant, as the pedants of Oxford University found out when Bruno invited himself to lecture on Copernicus, with a self-advertisement in which he presented himself as a:

Doctor of a more scientific theology, professor of a purer and less harmful learning, known in the chief universities of Europe, a philosopher approved and honourably received, a stranger with none but the uncivilized and the ignoble, a wakener of sleeping winds, tamer of presumptuous and obstinate ignorance, who in all respects professes a general love of man, and cares not for the Italian more than for the Briton, male more than female, the mitre more than the crown, the toga more than the coat of mail, the cowled more than the uncowled; but loves

127

him who in intercourse is the more peaceable, polite, friendly and useful—
(Brunus) whom only propagators of folly and hypocrites detest, whom the honourable and studious love, whom noble minds applaud.

This amazing self-congratulatory visiting card of a philosopher is the
renaissance passport of a militant and unhappy man among "doctors of
grammar," Bruno's defense mechanism among the respectable. From' this
violent self-assertion Bruno distilled the allegories and speculations of a
God-intoxicated angel: everything has soul, all things are alive, the universe
is of infinite dimensions and worlds without end, set in infinite space. Nothing in it exists in Aristotelian bondage: nothing is fixed or nailed down, all
is fluid and in motion, all is moved from within, divinity very close inside,
but none outside, a triumph over matter and asceticism and the supernatural. The difference between "the ass that carries the sacraments and the
holy things themselves" is everything. "Leave the shadows and embrace the
substance; change not thy present for the future. You are like the dog in
the fable that let the meat fall into the river while he desired the shadow
of that which he held in his mouth. It was never yet the counsel of a wise
or shrewd person to lose one good in order to get another. Why do you go
far off for a Paradise when you have found Paradise in yourselves?"

The inquisitors of the Church who tried him in 1592 and kept him imprisoned until his execution in 1600, carefully extracted from his writings
eight heresies, none as impious in its implications for the pre-Columbian
and pre-Copernican world as the heresy defined by the historian of Italian
culture, Francesco de Sanctis: "In Bruno," he says, "not only do 'the heavens
declare the glory of God,' but the heavens are themselves divine by their own
virtue, by their own intrinsic divineness. It is the rehabilitation of matter
or of Nature. No longer is Nature the enemy of the spirit, and execrated.
Nature is divine . . . 'the generation of God.'"

BRUNO TO THE INQUISITORS

MY NAME is Giordano, of the family of Bruni, of the city of Nola, twelve
miles from Naples. I was born and brought up in that city, and my profession was and is letters and the sciences. My father's name was Giovanni,
and my mother Fraulissa Savolina, and my father was a soldier by profession; he is dead, and my mother also. I am about forty-four years of age; I
was born, as far as I have heard, in May in the year '48; and I remained in

Naples acquiring learning, logic, and dialectics until I was fourteen; and I used to attend the public lectures of one who was called the Sarnese; and I went privately to learn logic from an Augustinian father called Fra Theophilo da Vairano, who afterwards taught metaphysics in Rome; and at about fourteen or fifteen years of age I took the habit of St. Dominic in the monastery or convent of St. Dominic at Naples, and was invested by a Father, who was then Prior of the convent, named Maestro Ambrosio Pasqua; and, the year of probation ended, I was admitted by himself to the profession, which I solemnly made in the same convent; and I do not think that any one else made profession at the same time, except a lay brother; and afterwards I was promoted to holy orders, and in due time to the priesthood; and I sang my first mass in Campagna, a town of the same kingdom, far from Naples, staying at the time in a convent of the same Order, dedicated to St. Bartholomew. And I continued in this habit of St. Dominic, celebrating mass and the divine offices, and under obedience to the superiors of the same religion, and to the Priors of the monasteries, and convents in which I was, until the year '76, which was the year following the year of the Jubilee, when, being in Rome, in the convent of the Minerva, under obedience to Maestro Sisto de Luca, Procurator of the Order, where I had gone to present myself because I had been proceeded against twice at Naples, first, for having given away certain figures and images of saints, retaining a crucifix only, whence it was imputed to me that I despised the images of the saints; and also for having said to a novice who was reading the *History of the Seven Joys* in verse, that he should rid himself of that, and rather read some other book, as the *Life of the Holy Fathers.* The which suit was renewed at the time that I went to Rome; with other articles which I do not know. For which reason I left a religious life, and, putting off the habit, went to Noli, in the Genoese territory, where, by teaching grammar to boys, I supported myself for four or five months.

I remained at Noli, as I have said, about four months, teaching grammar to boys and reading astronomy with certain gentlemen; and then I left, and went first to Savona, where I remained about a fortnight, and from Savona to Turin, where, not finding entertainment to my satisfaction, I came by the Po to Venice, where I remained for a month and a half in the Frezzaria, lodging in the house of a man in the Arsenal, and I do not know his name; and whilst I was here I caused a certain small book, entitled *Of the Signs of the Times,* to be printed, and had this work printed to get a little money together to be able to support myself, the which work I first showed to the

Reverend Father Maestro Renigio of Florence; and leaving this, I went to Padua, where, finding some fathers of the Dominican Order, acquaintances of mine, they persuaded me to wear the habit again, although I had not wished to return to a religious life; but it appeared to them more convenient to wear the habit than not; and with this intention I went to Bergamo, and had a gown made for myself of common white cloth, and over it I put the scapulary which I had kept when I left Rome, and in this habit I took the road for Lyons; and when I was at Chambéry, going to lodge at the convent of the Order, and seeing myself very coldly treated, and discoursing upon this with an Italian Father who was there, he said, 'Be warned, for you will find no sort of kindness in these parts, and the farther you go the less you will find;' therefore I turned towards Geneva, and on arriving there went to lodge at the inn; and shortly after the Marchese de Vico, a Neapolitan, who was staying in that city, asked me who I was, and if I desired to remain and to profess the religion of that city; to whom, after I had given account of myself, and of the cause for which I had left the religious life, I added that I did not intend to follow the creed of this city, because I did not know what religion it was; and that therefore I rather desired to remain there, and to live at liberty and to be in a place of safety, than for any other reason, and being recommended in any case to put off that habit which I wore, I took those clothes and caused a pair of breeches to be made for myself, with other things, and the said Marquis, with other Italians, gave me a sword, a hat, a cloak, and other things necessary to clothe me, procuring these that I might be enabled to support myself and to correct for the printers, in which employment I remained about two months, going sometimes, however, to the preaching and sermons of such Italians and Frenchmen as taught and preached in that city. Many times, amongst others, I heard the readings and sermons of Nicolo Balbani of Lucca, who read the Epistles of St. Paul and preached the Gospels; but being told that I could not remain there longer if I was not disposed to embrace the religion of the citizens, without doing which I had no more help to expect from them, I resolved to go away, and I went to Lyons, where I remained a month; and not finding means of gaining sufficient to live by and for my needs, I went from there to Toulouse, where there is a famous school, and having made acquaintance with men of learning, I was invited to lecture to different scholars on the use of the globes and astronomy, which I did, and I delivered philosophical lectures for perhaps six months; and meanwhile the place of ordinary lecturer on philosophy in that city, which is given by general vote,

being vacant, I sought to take my degree, which I did as master of arts, and thus presented myself to the said general vote, and was admitted and approved, and afterwards I delivered lectures in that city for two years continually on the text of Aristotle, *De Anima,* with other lectures on philosophy; and then, because of the civil wars, I departed and went to Paris, where I proposed to give an extraordinary lecture to make a name for myself, and to show such powers as I had, and I gave thirty lectures on the thirty divine attributes from St. Thomas, from the first part; and then being desired to take an ordinary lectureship, I refused, and would not accept it, because the public lecturers of this city usually go to mass and to the other divine offices, and I have always avoided this, knowing that I was excommunicated because I left the religious life and put off the habit; for although in Toulouse I held that ordinary lectureship, I was not obliged to go to mass, as I should have been in the said city of Paris if I had accepted the said ordinary lectureship; and I acquired such fame by giving that extraordinary lecture, that King Henry III had me called one day to ask me whether the memory which I had and which I taught was natural or came by magic arts; to whom I gave satisfaction, and he perceived, both by what I told him and by what I caused him to accomplish himself, that it was not by art magic, but by science; and after this I had a book printed *De Memoria,* under the title of *Umbris Idearum,* which I dedicated to his Majesty, and on this occasion he made me lecturer-extraordinary and a pensioner; and I continued to lecture in that city, as I have said, about five years, and because of the tumults afterwards, I took leave, and, with letters from the same King, I went to England to stay with his Majesty's ambassador, who was called the Sr. Della Malviciera, by name Michel de Castelnovo, in whose dwelling I did nothing, but passed for his gentleman. I remained two years and a half in England, not attending at this time also where mass was said in the house, nor going to mass out of doors, nor to sermons, for the aforesaid reason; and the ambassador returning to France to the court, I accompanied him to Paris, where I remained for another year, keeping company with those lords whom I knew, however at my own expense for the greatest part of the time; and leaving Paris because of the tumults, I went away to Germany. I went first to Mez *alias* Magonsa (Mayence), which is an archiepiscopal city, and the first electorate of the empire, where I remained for twelve days; and not finding suitable entertainment there, or at Vispure (Würzburg), a place not far off, I went to Wittenberg in Saxony, where I found two factions, one of philosophers

who were Calvinists, and the other of theologians who were Lutherans; and a doctor among the latter who was called Alberigo Gentile a Marchegiano, whom I had known in England, a professor of law, received me with kindness and presented me as lecturer on the *Organon* of Aristotle, and I gave other lectures on philosophy for two years, in which time the old Duke was succeeded by his son, who being a Calvinist and his father a Lutheran, began to favour the party opposed to those who favoured me, so that I went away, and went to Prague, and remained there six months, and whilst I was there I had a book on *Geometry* printed, which I presented to the Emperor, from whom I received a gift of three hundred thalers, and with this money I left Prague and remained for a year at the Julia Academy in Brunswick, where the death of the Duke [margin, "Who was a heretic,"] occurring at this time, at his obsequies, together with many others of the university, I made an oration, for which his son and successor gave me eighty crowns of that place; and I departed and went to Frankfort to have two books printed, one *De Minimo,* and the other *De Numero, Monade, et Figura,* &c.; and in Frankfort I remained for about six months, lodging in the convent of the Carmelites, the place assigned to me by the printer, who was obliged to give me lodging; and from Frankfort, as I have said in my other examination, invited by Ser Zuane Mocenigo, I came seven or eight months ago to Venice, where that which I have recounted in my other examination then took place, and I went again to Frankfort, leaving this to have my other works printed, and one in particular on the *Seven Liberal Arts,* . . . hoping to obtain leave to resume the clerical habit without entering the religious life; and at this chapter held here during the past few days, where there were many Neapolitan fathers of the Order, I have spoken of this matter, in particular with Father Fra Domenico de Nocera, Father Fra Serafino, bachelor of arts, of Nocera, and with Fra Giovanni, of I know not what place, but he is from the kingdom of Naples, and with another, who also himself quitted the religious life, but a short while ago he resumed the habit; he is of Atripalda, but I do not know his name—in religion he is called Fra Felice; and besides these fathers I have spoken with Zuane Mocenigo, who also promised to help me in all things which were right. I have said that I wished to present myself at the feet of his Holiness with some of my approved works, having some others which I do not approve, meaning thereby to say, that there are certain works of mine composed by me and printed which I do not approve, because in them I have spoken and discoursed too philosophically, dishonestly, and not altogether as a good

Christian; and in especial I know that in some of these works I have taught and held certain things philosophically which ought to be attributed to the power, wisdom, and goodness of God, according to the Christian faith, founding my doctrine upon sense and reason, and not upon faith; and this is for the generality, and for particulars I refer to my writings, for I do not now recall any precise article or particular doctrine which I may have taught, but I will reply according as I shall be questioned and as I shall remember.

Being at Frankfort last year, I had two letters from the Signor Giovanni Mocenigo, a Venetian gentleman, in which he invited me to come to Venice, desiring, according to what he wrote to me, that I should teach him the art of memory and invention, promising to treat me well, and that I should be content with him; and so I came about seven or eight months ago; and I have taught him various terms relating to these two sciences, at first living elsewhere, and then with him in his own house; and it appearing to me that I had done and taught him enough, and as much as I ought, of those things which he desired of me, and meditating a return to Frankfort to print some works of mine, last Thursday, in order that I might depart, I took leave of him; and on this, suspecting that rather than go to Frankfort, as I said, I wished to leave his house in order to teach other persons the same sciences which I had taught to him and others, he entreated me with much earnestness to remain; and I continually insisting that I would go, he first began to complain that I had not taught him as much as I had promised, and then to threaten me, by telling me that if I would not remain willingly, he would find a way to compel me to stay.

He insisted upon it that I should remain, and I insisted that I must go; and he first began to complain that I had not taught him as much as I was under engagement to do, and he then threatened and said, if I would not remain willingly, he would force me to stay; and on the night of the day following, which was Friday, seeing that I persisted in my resolution, and that I had arranged my affairs and had taken measures to dispatch what was mine to Frankfort, he came when I was in bed, under pretence of wishing to speak with me, and he was followed by his servant called Bartolo, with, if I mistake not, five or six others, who were, I believe, the gondoliers of persons living in that neighbourhood, and they forced me to rise from my bed and brought me to a garret, and locked me into it, Ser Giovanni himself saying that if I would remain and teach him the terms of the memory of

words and the terms of geometry which he had required from me at the beginning, he would set me at liberty, otherwise a worse thing would befall me. [Bruno then gives the account of his capture, concluding with his arrival in the prisons of the Holy Office] . . . where I believe myself to have been brought by means of the said Ser Giovanni, who being angry, for the reason I have already given, has brought an accusation against me.

[Being asked if he had a memorandum of all the books which he had printed, and if he remembered their subjects and doctrine, Bruno responded:] I have made a list of all those books which I have given to be printed, and also of those which I have composed and which are not yet printed, and which I was revising to give them to the press as soon as I should have opportunity, either at Frankfort or elsewhere, the which note and list is this. . . . The subject of all these books, speaking generally, is philosophical matter, differing according to the titles of the said books; as may be seen in them all, I have always defined things philosophically, and according to natural principles and the light of Nature, not having regard chiefly to that which ought to be held according to the faith; and I believe that nothing can be found in them by which I can be condemned for professing rather to desire to attack religion than to exalt philosophy, although I may have uttered many impious things founded on my natural light.

[Asked whether, publicly or privately, in the lectures given by him in different places, according to what he had said above in his other examinations, he had ever taught, held, or disputed any article contrary or repugnant to the Catholic faith, and according to the terms of the holy Roman Church, he replied:] I have taught nothing directly against the Christian Catholic religion, although I have done so indirectly, as was determined in Paris, where, however, I was permitted to hold certain disputations under the title of 'A Hundred and Twenty Articles against the Peripatetics and other Ordinary Philosophers,' printed by permission of the Superiors; and I was allowed to treat them according to natural principles, not prejudicing the truth according to the light of faith, in which fashion the books of Aristotle and Plato may be read and taught; for they in the same way are indirectly contrary to the faith—indeed, much more contrary than the articles philosophically propounded and defended by me, all of which may be known by what is printed in these last Latin books at Frankfort, called *De Minimo, De Monade, De Immenso et Innumerabilis,* and in part of *De*

Compositione Imaginum; and in these books particularly may be seen my intention and what I have held.

I hold that there is an infinite universe, which is the effect of the Infinite Divine Power, because I esteem it to be a thing unworthy of the Divine Goodness and Power that, being able to produce another world, and an infinite number of others besides this world, it should produce one finite world. With regard to the personality of the Holy Spirit, I stand within the boundaries of philosophy; and though I do not remember to have given in writing or in speech any sign that I do not hold these doctrines, I do not understand the Divine Spirit to be a Third Person, except in the manner of Pythagoras and of Solomon, as the soul of the universe or contributive (*assistente*) to the universe. From this Spirit, which is One, all being flows; there is one truth and one goodness penetrating and governing all things. In Nature are the thoughts of God. They are made manifest in figures and vestiges to the eye of sense; they are reproduced in our thoughts, where alone we can arrive at consciousness of true being. We are surrounded by eternity and by the uniting of love. There is but one centre, from which all species issue, as rays from a sun, and to which all species return. There is but one celestial expanse, where the stars choir forth unbroken harmony. In the circle, which comprehends in itself the beginning and the end, we have the figure of true being; and circular motion is the only enduring form of motion. From this Spirit, which is called the Life of the Universe, proceed the life and soul of everything which has soul and life,—the which life, however, I understand to be immortal, as well in bodies as in their souls, all being immortal, there being no other death than division and congregation; which doctrine seems to be expressed in Ecclesiastes, where it is said nothing is new under the sun.

"I WILL NOT BE SILENT":
Tommaso Campanella

THE CITY OF THE SUN

"Ass that you are," said friends and enemies alike to Campanella, "you do not know how to live; you do not speak in the name of God." And for emblem he took a bell with *"Non tacebo"*—"I will not be silent"—engraved on it.

FRANCESCO DE SANCTIS, *History of Italian Literature*

THE work of Campanella began with the death of the anti-Aristotelian philosopher Bernadino Telesio, whom, under Dominican discipline, he was not permitted to meet in life, and upon whose bier he tenderly left a prayer, a poem, and his gratitude. "Telesio delighted me," Campanella said, "both on account of the liberty of his philosophy, and because he depended on the nature of things, not on the sayings of men." He paid the price for this enthusiasm for the experimental method of natural philosophy by losing his youthful manuscripts to the Inquisition and, for a while, his liberty. So far was he unregenerate, that he entered into nothing less than a political conspiracy which, with the aid of the Turks, might free Naples from Spanish tyranny. Combining the offenses of a revolutionist in politics with those of a heretic in philosophy, Campanella was committed to prison where he stayed fully twenty-seven years, virtually a lifetime. The thought, the passion, even the idealism that poured out of that captivity, is one of the miracles of the mind. "My veins and arteries were broken," he wrote in one of the poems of *Le Cantiche* which were accumulating in his dungeon for fourteen years, "and my bones were cracked on the wooden horse . . . full six pounds of my blood was drunk by the earth . . . I was buried in a hole without light or air, but with only stench and damp, and perpetual night and cold." And again from his prison: "Six and six years I have spent in pain, with my every sense afflicted, and my limbs tortured seven times, and compelled to listen to the blasphemies and lies of fools; and the sun denied to my eyes, my nerves stretched, my bones disjointed, my flesh torn; with nastiness where I lie, with iron chains hung on me, with blood flowing, and with cruel fear, and with little to eat and filthy at that." Curiously, he remained strictly orthodox, a lifelong apologist for the Pope's temporal power, nevertheless a dangerous man with a megalomania about his destiny, one who had plotted a revolution with the hope, it

136

was said, of setting up a communist commonwealth among the mountains of his native Calabria, and a philosophic constitution for a Naples free from Spain. The miracle was that out of the early torture and prison darkness came his utopia *City of the Sun* (in 1602), and that after all the years of confinement, when news filtered into his jail that Galileo was on trial, he composed (in 1616) his *Defence of Galileo,* a courageous and passionate pamphlet for the Copernican astronomy and for free scientific investigation.

Fundamentally Campanella stood between two worlds. On the one hand, he eulogized Telesio who "with the unerring arrow from thy quiver thou dost kill the tyrant of intellects (Aristotle) in the midst of his sophists, and givest [*libertà dolce alla verità*] sweet liberty to truth"; on the other hand, he clung to tradition and to an astrological magic. That theocratic utopia *City of the Sun* is the miscegenation of medievalism and the brave new world of senses and experiment—"sweet liberty to truth" ingeniously smothered by duty and pious statism. His world of eugenical Solarians is full of light and no heat, a Monastery rather than a City, a kind of astrological chart in which children, love, art, opinion and passion revolve obediently around a Father Confessor who is at once supreme Reason and sacred Eunuch. It is not a utopia for Italians, least of all Calabrians. But this cold communism of wealth and wives does glow with a peculiar fervor for order, labor, physical cleanliness and human equality. "All work they call discipline," we are told about his Solarians, "and thus they say that it is honourable to go on foot, to do any act of nature, to see with the eye, and to speak with the tongue; and when there is need, they distinguish philosophically between tears and spittle." What a manly, what a wise, what a humane inscription for the façade of a new supreme court whose judges, at once philosophers and physicians, will "distinguish philosophically between tears and spittle"!

THE CITY OF THE SUN

A Poetical Dialogue Between a Grandmaster of the Knights Hospitallers and a Genoese Sea Captain, His Guest

G.M. Prithee, now, tell me what happened to you during that voyage?

Capt. I have already told you how I wandered over the whole earth. In the course of my journeying I came to Taprobane, and was compelled to go ashore at a place, where through fear of the inhabitants I remained in a

wood. When I stepped out of this I found myself on a large plain immediately under the equator.

G.M. And what befell you here?

Capt. I came upon a large crowd of men and armed women, many of whom did not understand our language, and they conducted me forthwith to the City of the Sun.

(He then describes how the city is built on a high hill, divided into seven rings named after the planets, and the beauty of the palaces, galleries, and temple.)

G.M. I pray you, worthy hero, explain to me their whole system of government; for I am anxious to hear it.

Capt. The great ruler among them is a priest whom they call by the name HOH, though we should call him Metaphysic. He is the head over all, in temporal and spiritual matters, and all business and lawsuits are settled by him, as the supreme authority. Three princes of equal power—viz., Pon, Sin and Mor—assist him, and these in our tongue we should call POWER, WISDOM and LOVE. To POWER belongs the care of all matters relating to war and peace. He attends to the military arts, and, next to Hoh, he is ruler in every affair of a warlike nature. He governs the military magistrates and the soldiers, and has the management of the munitions, the fortifications, the storming of places, the implements of war, the armories, the smiths and workmen connected with matters of this sort.

But WISDOM is the ruler of the liberal arts, of mechanics, of all sciences with their magistrates and doctors, and of the discipline of the schools. As many doctors as there are, are under his control. There is one doctor who is called Astrologus; a second, Cosmographus; a third, Arithmeticus; a fourth, Geometra; a fifth, Historiographus; a sixth, Poeta; a seventh, Logicus; an eighth, Rhetor; a ninth, Grammaticus; a tenth, Medicus; an eleventh, Physiologus; a twelfth, Politicus; a thirteenth, Moralis. They have but one book, which they call Wisdom, and in it all the sciences are written with conciseness and marvellous fluency of expression. This they read to the people after the custom of the Pythagoreans. It is Wisdom who causes the exterior and interior, the higher and lower walls of the city to be adorned with the finest pictures, and to have all the sciences painted upon them in an admirable manner. On the walls of the temple and on the dome, which is let down when the priest gives an address, lest the sounds of his voice, being scattered, should fly away from his audience, there are pictures of

stars in their different magnitudes, with the powers and motions of each, expressed separately in three little verses.

(He describes the mathematical, geographical, biological, artistic, and historical murals on the walls of the temple.)

There are magistrates, who announce the meaning of the pictures, and boys are accustomed to learn all the sciences, without toil and as if for pleasure; but in the way of history only until they are ten years old.

LOVE is foremost in attending to the charge of the race. He sees that men and women are so joined together, that they bring forth the best offspring. Indeed, they laugh at us who exhibit a studious care for our breed of horses and dogs, but neglect the breeding of human beings. Thus the education of the children is under his rule. So also is the medicine that is sold, the sowing and collecting of fruits of the earth and of trees, agriculture, pasturage, the preparations for the months, the cooking arrangements, and whatever has any reference to food, clothing, and the intercourse of the sexes. Love himself is ruler, but there are many male and female magistrates dedicated to these arts.

Metaphysic then with these three rulers manages all the above-named matters, and even by himself alone nothing is done; all business is discharged by the four together, but in whatever Metaphysic inclines to the rest are sure to agree.

G.M. Tell me, please, of the magistrates, their services and duties, of the education and mode of living, whether the government is a monarchy, a republic, or an aristocracy.

Capt. This race of men came there from India, flying from the sword of the Magi, a race of plunderers and tyrants who laid waste their country, and they determined to lead a philosophic life in fellowship with one another. Although the community of wives is not instituted among the other inhabitants of their province, among them it is in use after this manner. All things are common with them, and their dispensation is by the authority of the magistrates. Arts and honours and pleasures are common, and are held in such a manner that no one can appropriate anything to himself.

They say that all private property is acquired and improved for the reason that each one of us by himself has his own home and wife and children. From this self-love springs. For when we raise a son to riches and dignities, and leave an heir to much wealth, we become either ready to grasp at the property of the state, if in any case fear should be removed from

the power which belongs to riches and rank; or avaricious, crafty, and hypocritical, if any one is of slender purse, little strength, and mean ancestry. But when we have taken away self-love, there remains only love for the state.

G.M. Under such circumstances no one will be willing to labour, while he expects others to work, on the fruit of whose labours he can live, as Aristotle argues against Plato.

Capt. I do not know how to deal with that argument, but I declare to you that they burn with so great a love for their fatherland, as I could scarcely have believed possible; and indeed with much more than the histories tell us belonged to the Romans, who fell willingly for their country, inasmuch as they have to a greater extent surrendered their private property. I think truly that the friars and monks and clergy of our country, if they were not weakened by love for their kindred and friends, or by the ambition to rise to higher dignities, would be less fond of property, and more imbued with a spirit of charity towards all, as it was in the time of the Apostles, and is now in a great many cases.

G.M. St. Augustine may say that, but I say that among this race of men, friendship is worth nothing; since they have not the chance of conferring mutual benefits on one another.

Capt. Nay, indeed. For it is worth the trouble to see that no one can receive gifts from another. Whatever is necessary they have, they receive it from the community, and the magistrate takes care that no one receives more than he deserves. Yet nothing necessary is denied to any one. Friendship is recognized among them in war, in infirmity, in the art contests, by which means they aid one another mutually by teaching. Sometimes they improve themselves mutually with praises, with conversation, with actions and out of the things they need. All those of the same age call one another brothers. They call all over twenty-two years of age, fathers; those who are less than twenty-two are named sons. Moreover, the magistrates govern well, so that no one in the fraternity can do injury to another.

G.M. And how?

Capt. As many names of virtues as there are amongst us, so many magistrates there are among them. There is a magistrate who is named Magnanimity, another Fortitude, a third Chastity, a fourth Liberality, a fifth Criminal and Civil Justice, a sixth Comfort, a seventh Truth, an eighth Kindness, a tenth Gratitude, an eleventh Cheerfulness, a twelfth Exercise, a thirteenth Sobriety, etc. They are elected to duties of that kind, each one

to that duty for excellence in which he is known from boyhood to be most suitable. Wherefore among them neither robbery nor clever murders, nor lewdness, incest, adultery, or other crimes of which we accuse one another, can be found. They accuse themselves of ingratitude and malignity when any one denies a lawful satisfaction to another, of indolence, of sadness, of anger, of scurrility, of slander, and of lying, which curseful thing they thoroughly hate. Accused persons undergoing punishment are deprived of the common table, and other honours, until the judge thinks that they agree with their correction.

G.M. Tell me the manner in which the magistrates are chosen.

Capt. You would not rightly understand this, unless you first learned their manner of living. That you may know then, men and women wear the same kind of garment, suited for war. The women wear the toga below the knee, but the men above. And both sexes are instructed in all the arts together. When this has been done as a start, and before their third year, the boys learn the language and the alphabet on the walls by walking round them. They have four leaders, and four elders, the first to direct them, the second to teach them, and these are men approved beyond all others. After some time they exercise themselves with gymnastics, running, quoits, and other games, by means of which all their muscles are strengthened alike. Their feet are always bare, and so are their heads as far as the seventh ring. Afterwards they lead them to the offices of the trades, such as shoemaking, cooking, metal working, carpentry, painting, etc. In order to find out the bent of the genius of each one, after their seventh year, when they have already gone through the mathematics on the walls, they take them to the readings of all the sciences; there are four lectures at each reading, and in the course of four hours the four in their order explain everything.

For some take physical exercise or busy themselves with public services or functions, others apply themselves to reading. Leaving these studies all are devoted to the more abstruse subjects, to mathematics, to medicine, and to other sciences. There is continual debate and studied argument amongst them, and after a time they become magistrates of those sciences or mechanical arts in which they are the most proficient; for every one follows the opinion of his leader and judge, and goes out to the plains to the works of the field, and for the purpose of becoming acquainted with the pasturage of the dumb animals. And they consider him the more noble and renowned who has dedicated himself to the study of the most arts and knows how to practise them wisely. Wherefore they laugh at us in that we consider our

workmen ignoble, and hold those to be noble who have mastered no pursuit; but live in ease, and are so many slaves given over to their own pleasure and lasciviousness; and thus as it were from a school of vices so many idle and wicked fellows go forth for the ruin of the state.

The rest of the officials, however, are chosen by the four chiefs, Hoh, Pon, Sin and Mor, and by the teachers of that art over which they are fit to preside. And these teachers know well who is most suited for rule. Certain men are proposed by the magistrates in council, they themselves not seeking to become candidates, and he opposes who knows anything against those brought forward for election, or if not, speaks in favour of them. But no one attains to the dignity of Hoh except him who knows the histories of the nations, and their customs and sacrifices and laws, and their form of government, whether a republic or a monarchy. He must also know the names of the lawgivers and the inventors in science, and the laws and the history of the earth and the heavenly bodies. They think it also necessary that he should understand all the mechanical arts, the physical sciences, astrology and mathematics. (Nearly every two days they teach our mechanical art. They are not allowed to overwork themselves, but frequent practice and the paintings render learning easy to them. Not too much care is given to the cultivation of languages, as they have a goodly number of interpreters who are grammarians in the state.) But beyond everything else it is necessary that Hoh should understand metaphysics and theology; that he should know thoroughly the derivations, foundations and demonstrations of all the arts and sciences; the likeness and difference of things; necessity, fate, and the harmonies of the universe; power, wisdom, and the love of things and of God; the stages of life and its symbols; everything relating to the heavens, the earth and the sea; and the ideas of God, as much as mortal man can know Him. He must also be well read in the Prophets and astrology. And thus they know long beforehand who will be Hoh. He is not chosen to so great a dignity unless he has attained his thirty-fifth year. And this office is perpetual, because it is not known who may be too wise for it or who too skilled in ruling.

G.M. Who indeed can be so wise? If even any one has a knowledge of the sciences it seems that he must be unskilled in ruling.

Capt. The very question I asked them and they replied thus: "We, indeed, are more certain that such a very learned man has the knowledge of governing, than you who place ignorant persons in authority, and consider them suitable merely because they have sprung from rulers or have been

chosen by a powerful faction. But our Hoh, a man really the most capable to rule, is for all that never cruel nor wicked, nor a tyrant, inasmuch as he possesses so much wisdom. This, moreover, is not unknown to you, that the same argument cannot apply among you, when you consider that man the most learned who knows most of grammar, or logic, or of Aristotle or any other author. For such knowledge as this of yours much servile labour and memory work is required, so that a man is rendered unskilful; since he has contemplated nothing but the words of books and has given his mind with useless result to the consideration of the dead signs of things. Hence he knows not in what way God rules the universe, nor the ways and customs of Nature and the nations. Wherefore he is not equal to our Hoh. For that one cannot know so many arts and sciences thoroughly, who is not esteemed for skilled ingenuity, very apt at all things, and therefore at ruling especially. This also is plain to us that he who knows only one science, does not really know either that or the others, and he who is suited for only one science and has gathered his knowledge from books, is unlearned and unskilled. But this is not the case with intellects prompt and expert in every branch of knowledge and suitable for the consideration of natural objects, as it is necessary that our Hoh should be. Besides in our state the sciences are taught with a facility (as you have seen) by which more scholars are turned out by us in one year than by you in ten, or even fifteen. Make trial, I pray you, of these boys." In this matter I was struck with astonishment at their trustful discourse and at the trial of their boys, who did not understand my language well. Indeed it is necessary that three of them should be skilled in our tongue, three in Arabic, three in Polish, and three in each of the other languages, and no recreation is allowed them unless they become more learned. For that they go out to the plain for the sake of running about and hurling arrows and lances, and of firing harquebuses, and for the sake of hunting the wild animals and getting a knowledge of plants and stones, and agriculture and pasturage; sometimes the band of boys does one thing, sometimes another.

They do not consider it necessary that the three rulers assisting Hoh should know other than the arts having reference to their rule, and so they have only a historical knowledge of the arts which are common to all. But their own they know well, to which certainly one is dedicated more than another. Thus Power is the most learned in the equestrian art, in marshalling the army, in marking out of camps, in the manufacture of every kind of weapon and of warlike machines, in planning stratagems, and in

every affair of a military nature. And for these reasons, they consider it necessary that these chiefs should have been philosophers, historians, politicians, and physicists. Concerning the other two triumvirs, understand remarks similar to those I have made about Power.

G.M. I really wish that you would recount all their public duties, and would distinguish between them, and also that you would tell clearly how they are all taught in common.

Capt. They have dwellings in common and dormitories, and couches and other necessaries. But at the end of every six months they are separated by the masters. Some shall sleep in this ring, some in another; some in the first apartment, and some in the second; and these apartments are marked by means of the alphabet on the lintel. There are occupations, mechanical and theoretical, common to both men and women, with this difference, that the occupations which require more hard work, and walking a long distance, are practised by men, such as ploughing, sowing, gathering the fruits, working at the threshing floor, and perchance at the vintage. But it is customary to choose women for milking the cows, and for making cheese. In like manner, they go to the gardens on the outskirts of the city both for collecting the plants and for cultivating them. In fact, all sedentary and stationary pursuits are practised by the women, such as weaving, spinning, sewing, cutting the hair, shaving, dispensing medicines, and making all kinds of garments. They are, however, excluded from working in wood and the manufacture of arms. If a woman is fit to paint, she is not prevented from doing so; nevertheless, music is given over to the women alone, because they please the more, and of a truth to boys also. But the women have not the practice of the drum and the horn.

And they prepare their feasts and arrange the tables in the following manner. It is the peculiar work of the boys and girls under twenty to wait at the tables. In every ring there are the suitable kitchens, barns, and stores of utensils for eating and drinking, and over every department an old man and an old woman preside. These two have at once the command of those who serve, and the power of chastising, or causing to be chastised, those who are negligent or disobedient; and they also examine and mark each one, both male and female, who excels in his or her duties.

All the young people wait upon the older ones who have passed the age of forty, and in the evening when they go to sleep the master and mistress command that those should be sent to work in the morning, upon whom in succession the duty falls, one or two to separate apartments. The young peo-

ple, however, wait upon one another, and that alas! with some unwilling-
ness. They have first and second tables, and on both sides there are seats. On
one side sit the women, on the other the men; and as in the refectories of the
monks, there is no noise. While they are eating a young man reads a book
from a platform, intoning distinctly and sonorously, and often the magistrates question them upon the more important parts of the reading. And
truly it is pleasant to observe in what manner these young people, so beautiful and clothed in garments so suitable, attend to them, and to see at the
same time so many friends, brothers, sons, fathers and mothers all in their
turn living together with so much honesty, propriety and love. So each
one is given a napkin, a plate, fish, and a dish of food. It is the duty of the
medical officers to tell the cooks what repasts shall be prepared on each day,
and what food for the old, what for the young, and what for the sick. The
magistrates receive the full-grown and fatter portion, and they from their
share always distribute something to the boys at the table who have shown
themselves more studious in the morning at the lectures and debates concerning wisdom and arms. And this is held to be one of the most distinguished honours. For six days they ordain to sing with music at table.
Only a few, however, sing; or there is one voice accompanying the lute and
one for each other instrument. And when all alike in service join their
hands, nothing is found to be wanting. The old men placed at the head of
the cooking business and of the refectories of the servants praise the cleanliness of the streets, the houses, the vessels, the garments, the workshops and
the warehouses.

They wear white undergarments to which adheres a covering, which is at
once coat and legging, without wrinkles. The borders of the fastenings are
furnished with globular buttons, extended round and caught up here and
there by chains. The coverings of the legs descend to the shoes and are continued even to the heels. Then they cover the feet with large socks, or as if
it were half-buskins fastened by buckles, over which they wear a half-boot,
and besides, as I have already said, they are clothed with a toga. And so
aptly fitting are the garments, that when the toga is destroyed, the different
parts of the whole body are straightway discerned, no part being concealed.
They change their clothes for different ones four times in the year, that is
when the sun enters respectively the constellations Aries, Cancer, Libra and
Capricorn, and according to the circumstances and necessity as decided by
the officer of health. The keepers of clothes for the different rings are wont
to distribute them, and it is marvellous that they have at the same time as

many garments as there is need for, some heavy and some slight, according to the weather. They all use white clothing, and this is washed in each month with lye or soap, as are also the workshops of the lower trades, the kitchens, the pantries, the barns, the storehouses, the armories, the refectories and the baths. Moreover, the clothes are washed at the pillars of the peristyles, and the water is brought down by means of canals which are continued as sewers. In every street of the different rings there are suitable fountains, which send forth their water by means of canals, the water being drawn up from nearly the bottom of the mountain by the sole movement of a cleverly contrived handle. There is water in fountains and in cisterns, whither the rain water collected from the roofs of the houses is brought through pipes full of sand. They wash their bodies often, according as the doctor and master command. All the mechanical arts are practised under the peristyles, but the speculative are carried on above in the walking galleries and ramparts where are the more splendid paintings, but the more sacred ones are taught in the temple. In the halls and wings of the rings there are solar timepieces and bells, and hands by which the hours and seasons are marked off.

G.M. Tell me about their children.

Capt. When their women have brought forth children, they suckle and rear them in temples set apart for all. They give milk for two years or more as the physician orders. After that time the weaned child is given into the charge of the mistresses, if it is a female, and to the masters, if it is a male. And then with other young children they are pleasantly instructed in the alphabet, and in the knowledge of the pictures, and in running, walking and wrestling; also in the historical drawings, and in languages; and they are adorned with a suitable garment of different colours. After their sixth year they are taught natural science, and then the mechanical sciences. The men who are weak in intellect are sent to farms, and when they have become more proficient some of them are received into the state. And those of the same age and born under the same constellation are especially like one another in strength and appearance, and hence arises much lasting concord in the state, these men honouring one another with mutual love and help. Names are given to them by Metaphysicus, and that not by chance but designedly, and according to each one's peculiarity, as was the custom among the ancient Romans. Wherefore one is called Beautiful (*Pulcher*), another the Big-nosed (*Naso*), another the Fat-legged (*Cranipes*), another Crooked (*Torvus*), another Lean (*Macer*), and so on. But when they have

become very skilled in their professions and done any great deed in war or in time of peace, a cognomen from art is given to them, such as Beautiful, the great painter (*Pulcher, Pictor Magnus*), the golden one (*Aureus*), the excellent one (*Excellens*), or the strong (*Strenuus*); or from their deeds, such as Naso the Brave (*Nason Fortis*), or the cunning, or the great, or very great conqueror; or from the enemy any one has overcome, Africanus, Asiaticus, Etruscus; or if any one has overcome Manfred or Tortelius, he is called Macer Manfred or Tortelius, and so on. All these cognomens are added by the higher magistrates, and very often with a crown suitable to the deed or art, and with the flourish of music. For gold and silver is reckoned of little value among them except as material for their vessels and ornaments, which are common to all.

G.M. Tell me, I pray you, is there no jealousy among them or disappointment to that one who has not been elected to a magistracy, or to any other dignity to which he aspires?

Capt. Certainly not. For no one wants either necessaries or luxuries. Moreover, the race is managed for the good of the commonwealth and not of private individuals, and the magistrates must be obeyed. They deny what we hold—viz., that it is natural to man to recognize his offspring and to educate them, and to use his wife and house and children as his own. For they say that children are bred for the preservation of the species and not for individual pleasure, as St. Thomas also asserts. Therefore the breeding of children has reference to the commonwealth and not to individuals, except in so far as they are constituents of the commonwealth. And since individuals for the most part bring forth children wrongly and educate them wrongly, they consider that they remove destruction from the state, and therefore, for this reason, with most sacred fear, they commit the education of the children, who as it were are the element of the republic, to the care of magistrates; for the safety of the community is not that of a few. And thus they distribute male and female breeders of the best natures according to philosophical rules. Plato thinks that this distribution ought to be made by lot, lest some men seeing that they are kept away from the beautiful women, should rise up with anger and hatred against the magistrates; and he thinks further that those who do not deserve cohabitation with the more beautiful women, should be deceived whilst the lots are being led out of the city by the magistrates, so that at all times the women who are suitable should fall to their lot, not those whom they desire. This shrewdness, however, is not necessary among the inhabitants of the City of the Sun. For with

147

them deformity is unknown. When the women are exercised they get a clear complexion, and become strong of limb, tall and agile, and with them beauty consists in tallness and strength. Therefore, if any woman dyes her face, so that it may become beautiful, or uses high-heeled boots so that she may appear tall, or garments with trains to cover her wooden shoes, she is condemned to capital punishment. But if the women should even desire them, they have no facility for doing these things. For who indeed would give them this facility? Further, they assert that among us abuses of this kind arise from the leisure and sloth of women. By these means they lose their colour and have pale complexions, and become feeble and small. For this reason they are without proper complexions, use high sandals, and become beautiful not from strength, but from slothful tenderness. And thus they ruin their own tempers and natures, and consequently those of their offspring. Furthermore, if at any time a man is taken captive with ardent love for a certain woman, the two are allowed to converse and joke together, and to give one another garlands of flowers or leaves, and to make verses. But if the race is endangered, by no means is further union between them permitted. Moreover, the love born of eager desire is not known among them; only that born of friendship.

Domestic affairs and partnership are of little account, because, excepting the sign of honour, each one receives what he is in need of. To the heroes and heroines of the republic, it is customary to give the pleasing gifts of honour, beautiful wreaths, sweet food or splendid clothes, while they are feasting. In the daytime all use white garments within the city, but at night or outside the city they use red garments either of wool or silk. They hate black as they do dung, and therefore they dislike the Japanese, who are fond of black. Pride they consider the most execrable vice, and one who acts proudly is chastised with the most ruthless correction. Wherefore no one thinks it lowering to wait at table or to work in the kitchen or fields. All work they call discipline, and thus they say that it is honourable to go on foot, to do any act of nature, to see with the eye, and to speak with the tongue; and when there is need, they distinguish philosophically between tears and spittle.

Every man who, when he is told off to work, does his duty, is considered very honourable. It is not the custom to keep slaves. For they are enough, and more than enough, for themselves. But with us, alas! it is not so. In Naples there exist seventy thousand souls, and out of these scarcely ten or fifteen thousand do any work, and they are always lean from overwork and

are getting weaker every day. The rest become a prey to idleness, avarice, ill-health, lasciviousness, usury and other vices, and contaminate and corrupt very many families by holding them in servitude for their own use, by keeping them in poverty and slavishness, and by imparting to them their own vices. Therefore public slavery ruins them; useful works, in the field, in military service and in arts, except those which are debasing, are not cultivated, the few who do practise them doing so with much aversion. But in the City of the Sun, while duty and work is distributed among all, it only falls to each one to work for about four hours every day. The remaining hours are spent in learning joyously, in debating, in reading, in reciting, in writing, in walking, in exercising the mind and body, and with play. They allow no game which is played while sitting, neither the single die nor dice, nor chess, nor others like these. But they play with the ball, with the sack, with the hoop, with wrestling, with hurling at the stake. They say, moreover, that grinding poverty renders men worthless, cunning, sulky, thievish, insidious, vagabonds, liars, false witnesses, etc.; and that wealth makes them insolent, proud, ignorant, traitors, assumers of what they know not, deceivers, boasters, wanting in affection, slanderers, etc. But with them all the rich and poor together make up the community. They are rich because they want nothing, poor because they possess nothing; and consequently they are not slaves to circumstances, but circumstances serve them. And on this point they strongly recommend the religion of the Christians, and especially the life of the Apostles.

G.M. This seems excellent and sacred, but the community of women is a thing too difficult to attain. The holy Roman Clement says that wives ought to be common in accordance with the apostolic institution, and praises Plato and Socrates, who thus teach, but the Glossary interprets this community with regard to obedience. And Tertullian agrees with the Glossary, that the first Christians had everything in common except wives.

Capt. These things I know little of. But this I saw among the inhabitants of the City of the Sun that they did not make this exception. And they defend themselves by the opinion of Socrates, of Cato, of Plato, and of St. Clement, but, as you say, they misunderstand the opinions of these thinkers. And the inhabitants of the solar city ascribe this to their want of education, since they are by no means learned in philosophy. Nevertheless, they send abroad to discover the customs of nations, and the best of these they always adopt. Practice makes the women suitable for war and other duties. Thus they agree with Plato, in whom I have read these same things. The reason-

ing of our Cajetan does not convince me, and least of all that of Aristotle. This thing, however, existing among them is excellent and worthy of imita-tion—viz., that no physical defect renders a man incapable of being service-able except the decrepitude of old age, since even the deformed are useful for consultation. The lame serve as guards, watching with the eyes which they possess. The blind card wool with their hands, separating the down from the hairs, with which latter they stuff the couches and sofas; those who are without the use of eyes and hands give the use of their ears or their voice for the convenience of the state, and if one has only one sense, he uses it in the farms. And these cripples are well treated, and some become spies, telling the officers of the state what they have heard.

> *(He describes how the Solarians, advocates of liberty, train for warfare, in which they are always the victors; their military strategy; their limited commerce; the treatment of strangers and applicants for citizenship; the manner in which all citizens participate in agriculture and the "waggons fitted with sails"; the breeding of animals; their science of navigation and mechanical rafts; their dietary, hygienic and legal system.)*

G.M. Now you ought to tell me about their priests, their sacrifices, their religion, and their belief.

Capt. The chief priest is Hoh, and it is the duty of all the superior magis-trates to pardon sins. Therefore the whole state by secret confession, which we also use, tell their sins to the magistrates, who at once purge their souls and teach those that are inimical to the people. Then the sacred magistrates themselves confess their own sinfulness to the three supreme chiefs, and to-gether they confess the faults of one another, though no special one is named, and they confess especially the heavier faults and those harmful to the state. At length the triumvirs confess their sinfulness to the Hoh himself, who forthwith recognizes the kinds of sin that are harmful to the state, and succours with timely remedies. Then he offers sacrifices and prayers to God. And before this he confesses the sins of the whole people, in the presence of God, and publicly in the temple, above the altar, as often as it had been necessary that the fault should be corrected. Nevertheless, no transgressor is spoken of by his name. In this manner he absolves the people by advising them that they should beware of sins of the aforesaid kind. Afterwards he offers sacrifice to God, that He should pardon the state and absolve it of its sins, and to teach and defend it. Once in every year the chief priests of each

separate subordinate state confess their sins in the presence of Hoh. Thus he is not ignorant of the wrongdoings of the provinces, and forthwith he removes them with all human and heavenly remedies.

(He continues to describe religious rites and astronomical science which conditions the arts of breeding, agriculture and general public policy; how the learned priests disbelieve in Aristotle and feel bound to no Father but God.)

They are in doubt whether there are other worlds beyond ours, and account it madness to say there is nothing. Nonentity is incompatible with the infinite entity of God. They lay down two principles of metaphysics, entity which is the highest God, and nothingness which is the defect of entity. Evil and sin come of the propensity to nothingness; the sin having its cause not efficient, but in deficiency. Deficiency is, they say, of power, wisdom or will. Sin they place in the last of these three, because he who knows and has the power to do good is bound also to have the will, for will arises out of them. They worship God in Trinity, saying God is the supreme Power, whence proceeds the highest Wisdom, which is the same with God, and from these comes Love, which is both Power and Wisdom; but they do not distinguish between persons by name, as in our Christian law, which has not been revealed to them. This religion, when its abuses have been removed, will be the future mistress of the world, as great theologians teach and hope. Therefore Spain found the New World (though its first discoverer, Columbus, greatest of heroes, was a Genoese), that all nations should be gathered under one law. We know not what we do, but God knows, whose instruments we are. They sought new regions for lust of gold and riches, but God works to a higher end. The sun strives to burn up the earth, not to produce plants and men, but God guides the battle to great issues. His the praise, to Him the glory!

G.M. Oh, if you knew what our astrologers say of the coming age, and of our age, that has in it more history within a hundred years than all the world had in four thousand years before! Of the wonderful inventions of printing and guns, and the use of the magnet, and how it all comes of Mercury, Mars, the Moon, and the Scorpion!

Capt. Ah, well! God gives all in His good time! They astrologize too much.

Book II
A Company of Englishmen

THOMAS MORE

HENRY HOWARD, EARL OF SURREY

JOHN DONNE

GEORGE WITHER

WALTER RALEIGH

CHARLES THE FIRST

RICHARD LOVELACE

JAMES HOWELL

JOHN BUNYAN

GEORGE FOX

WILLIAM PENN

DANIEL DEFOE

A WITTY SAINT IN A HAIR SHIRT:

Sir Thomas More

A PROVOKING WIFE   THE WOLF, THE ASS, AND THE FOX

TALKATIVE NUN AND TALKATIVE WIFE   LOVE OF FLATTERY

GODLY MEDITATION   LETTER TO HIS DAUGHTER, MARGARET

~~~~~~

When Sir Thomas More had continued a good while in the Tower, my lady his wife obtained license to see him. Who at her first coming, like a simple ignorant woman, and somewhat worldly too, with this manner of salutation bluntly saluted him: "What the good year, Master More," quoth she: "I marvel that you, that have been always hitherto taken for so wise a man, will now so play the fool to lie here in this close filthy prison, and be content thus to be shut up among mice and rats, when you might be abroad at your liberty and with the favour and goodwill both of the King and his Council, if you would but do as all the Bishops and the best learned of this realm have done. And seeing you have at Chelsey a right fair house, your library, your gallery, your garden, your orchard and all other necessaries so handsome about you, where you might in the company of me your wife, your children and household, be merry, I muse what a'God's name you mean here still thus fondly to tarry."

ROPER'S *Life of More*

WHEN Henry the Eighth's prisoner, Sir Thomas More, took off his habitual shirt of hair, which he wore secretly under his robes of dignity because he was a modest man, he could not shed his wit because that article was closer to his piety than the hair shirt. "Wait," he said on the block, "till I put aside my beard, for *that* never committed treason." Between the apologists for King Henry and the English Reformation and the apologists for Thomas More and his conscience, the beard of the great master has been often and vigorously pulled, but not yet plucked. English historians (and More's second wife) regretted that he did not take Henry's oath of supremacy and so endorse a reformation which More's own learning and that of Erasmus, Colet, and Fisher was bringing on anyway. What was at the bottom of his behavior? Had the author of *Utopia* hardened with age into a reactionary and renegade, and had he lost his sense of proportion and of humor, when he turned down the invitation to the wedding of Henry the Eighth and Anne Boleyn? For Professor R. W. Chambers (More's interpreter and knight-errant in England), not the Catholic dogma that the primacy of the Pope was instituted by God was the fundamental issue, but More's martyred principle "to look first to God, and after God unto the King."

155

Accordingly, More, like his beloved friend Erasmus who dedicated to him the *Praise of Folly*, was a European; a man "defending the right of the individual soul, against the command of the civil power, to hold any dogma at all"; a patriot of the renaissance if not of Henry's England; a scholar in search of a Christendom united without violence; a Catholic collectivist in the service of reason and Christian learning, as against the Baconian "Protestant man of science." So Thomas More died for the right of individual conscience—"the most civil of martyrs," says Professor Chambers. This issue of conscience is debated in *The Dialogue of Comfort* which Thomas More wrote in the Tower, a work sheltering the autobiography of the imprisoned author in the disguise of a holy and humorous old Hungarian nobleman (Antony) who instructs his nephew (Vincent) in the proper conduct of a Catholic under the Turkish (that is Henry's) threat of conquest and persecution. Into those recipes of comfort against tribulation, mixed with all the ingredients which make up an ascetic faith, Thomas More slyly drops a number of rich sugarplums of wit in the form of parables. They reveal what gay human laughter Thomas More hid under his shirt of hair, as the *Utopia* reveals the contrary, what stern discipline he hid under the guise of a radical social experiment. Karl Kautsky, the socialist, admired Thomas More, and Professor Chambers refers to a very curious letter, sent, he says, by the Karl Marx-Engels Institute of the U.S.S.R. seeking information about the great communist Sir Thomas More from the Sisters of Beaufort Street Convent whose devotions consist in praying for the soul of the martyr. In the parables of *A Provoking Wife; The Wolf, the Ass, and the Fox; Talkative Nun and Talkative Wife*, and *Love of Flattery*, there is not much information about the "communist," but a great deal about a witty saint in a hair shirt. His son-in-law, William Roper, added his portrait to Holbein's canvas in praising More as:

A manne of singular virtue and of a clear unspotted conscience, (as witnesseth Erasmus) more pure and white then the whitest snow, and of such an angelicall witt, as England, he sayth, never had the like before, and never shall againe.

A PROVOKING WIFE

Antony. There was here in Buda, in King Ladislaus' days, a good, poor, honest man's wife: this woman was so fiendish that the devil, perceiving her

nature, put her in the mind that she should anger her husband so sore, that she might give him occasion to kill her, and then he should be hanged for her.

Vincent. This was a strange temptation indeed. What the devil should she be the better then?

Antony. Nothing but that it eased her shrewd stomach before, to think that her husband should be hanged after. And peradventure if you look about the world and consider it well, you shall find more such stomachs than a few. Have you never heard no furious body plainly say, that to see some such man have a mischief, he would with good will be content to lie as long in hell as God liveth in heaven?

Vincent. Forsooth, and some such have I heard of.

Antony. This mind of his was not much less mad than hers, but rather haply the more mad of the twain: for the woman peradventure did not cast so far peril therein. But to tell you now to what good pass her charitable purpose came: as her husband (the man was a carpenter) stood hewing with his chip-axe upon a piece of timber, she began after her old guise so to revile him, that the man waxed wrath at last, and bade her get in or he would lay the helm of his axe about her back, and said also, that it were little sin even with that axe-head to chop off that unhappy head of hers that carried such an ungracious tongue therein. At that word the devil took his time, and whetted her tongue against her teeth, and when it was well sharped, she sware to him in very fierce anger: "By the mass, I would thou wouldst: here lieth my head, lo! (and therewith down she laid her head upon the same timber log) if thou smite it not off, I beshrew thy heart." With that, likewise, as the devil stood at her elbow, so stood (as I heard say) his good angel at his, and gave him ghostly courage, and bade him be bold and do it. And so the good man up with his chip-axe, and at a chop chopped off her head indeed. There were standing other folk by, which had a good sport to hear her chide, but little they looked for this chance, till it was done ere they could let it. They said they heard her tongue babble in her head, and call evil names twice after the head was from the body. At the leastwise afterward unto the king thus they reported all, except only one, and that was a woman, and she said that she heard it not.

Vincent. Forsooth, this was a wonderful work. What became, Uncle, of the man?

Antony. The king gave him his pardon.

Vincent. Verily he might in conscience do no less.

Antony. But then was it farther almost at another point, that there should have been a statute made, that in such case there should never after pardon be granted, but, the truth being able to be proved, no husband should need any pardon, but should have leave by the law to follow the sample of the carpenter, and do the same.

Vincent. How happed it, Uncle, that the good law was left unmade?

Antony. How happed it? As it happeth, Cousin, that many more be left unmade as well as it, and within a little as good as it too, both here and in other countries; and, sometimes some worse made in their stead. But (as they say) the let of that law was the queen's grace, God forgive her soul! it was the greatest thing, I ween, good lady, that she had to answer for when she died, for surely, save for that one thing, she was a full blessed woman.

THE WOLF, THE ASS, AND THE FOX

Antony. My mother had, when I was a little boy, a good old woman that took heed to her children; they called her Mother Maud: I trow, you have heard of her.

Vincent. Yea, yea, very much.

Antony. She was wont, when she sat by the fire with us, to tell us that were children many childish tales. I remember me that among other of her fond tales, she told us once, that the ass and the wolf came on a time to confession to the fox. The poor ass came to shrift in the shrovetide, a day or two before Ash Wednesday; but the wolf would not come to confession until he saw first Palm Sunday past, and then foded yet forth farther until Good Friday. The fox asked the ass before he began *Benedicite,* wherefore he came to confession so soon before Lent began. The poor beast answered him again: for fear of deadly sin if he should lose his part of any of those prayers that the priest in the cleansing days prayeth for them that are confessed already. Then in his shrift he had a marvellous grudge in his inward conscience, that he had one day given his master a cause of anger, in that, that with his rude roaring before his master arose, he had awaked him out of his sleep, and bereaved him out of his rest. The fox for that fault, like a good discreet confessor, charged him to do so no more, but lie still and sleep like a good son himself, till his master were up and ready to go to work, and so should he be sure, that he should not wake him no more.

To tell you all the poor ass's confession, it were a long work, for every-

thing that he did was deadly sin with him, the poor soul was so scrupulous. But his wise wily confessor accounted them for trifles, as they were, and sware afterward unto the badger, that he was so weary to sit so long and hear him, that saving for the manners' sake, he had liever have sitten all the while at breakfast with a good fat goose. But when it came to the penance giving, the fox found that the most weighty sin in all his shrift was gluttony, and therefore he discreetly gave him in penance, that he should never for greediness of his own meat do any other beast any harm or hindrance, and then eat his meat, and study for no more.

Now, as good Mother Maud told us, when the wolf came to confession to Father Reynard (for that was, she said, the fox's name) upon Good Friday, his confessor shook his great pair of beads upon him almost as big as bowls, and asked him wherefore he came so late. "Forsooth, Father Reynard," quoth he, "I must needs tell you the truth: I come (you wot well) therefor, I durst come no sooner, for fear lest you would for any gluttony have given me in penance to fast some part of this Lent." "Nay, nay," quoth Father Fox, "I am not so unreasonable: for I fast none of it myself. For I may say to thee, son, between us twain here in confession, it is no commandment of God this fasting, but an invention of man. The priests make folk fast and put them to pain about the moonshine in the water, and do but make folk fools: but they shall make me no such fool, I warrant thee, son. For I eat flesh all this Lent, myself I. Howbeit, indeed, because I will not be occasion of slander, I therefore eat it secretly in my chamber, out of sight of all such foolish brethren as for their weak scrupulous·conscience would wax offended withal, and so would I counsel you to do." "Forsooth, Father Fox," quoth the wolf, "and so I thank God I do, so near as I can. For when I go to my meat, I take none other company with me, but such sure brethren as are of mine own nature, whose consciences are not weak, I warrant you, but their stomachs as strong as mine." "Well, then, no matter," quoth Father Fox.

But when he heard after by his confession, that he was so great a ravener, that he devoured and spent sometime so much victual at one meal, as the price thereof would well find some poor man with his wife and children almost all the week; then he prudently reproved that point in him, and preached him a process of his own temperance, which never used, as he said, to pass upon himself the value of sixpence at a meal, no nor yet so much neither. "For when I bring home a goose," quoth he, "not out of the poulterer's shop, where folk find them out of their feathers ready plucked, and see which is the fattest and yet for sixpence buy and choose the best,

but out of the housewife's house at the first hand, which may somewhat better cheap afford them, you wot well, than the poulterer may, nor yet cannot be suffered to see them plucked, and stand and choose them by day, but am fain by night to take at adventure, and when I come home, am fain to do the labour to pluck her myself: yet for all this, though it be but lean, and I ween not well worth a groat, serveth it me somewhat for all that, both dinner and supper too. And therefore, as for that you live of raven, therein can I find no fault: you have used it so long, that I think you can do none other. And therefore were it folly to forbid it you, and (to say the truth) against good conscience too. For live you must, I wot well, and other craft can you none; and therefore, as reason is, must you live by that. But yet, you wot well, too much is too much, and measure is a merry mean, which I perceive by your shrift you have never used to keep. And therefore, surely, this shall be your penance: that you shall all this year now pass upon yourself the price of sixpence at a meal, as near as your conscience can guess the price."

Their shrift have I showed you, as Mother Maud showed it us. But now serveth for our matter the conscience of them both, in the true performing of their penance. The poor ass after his shrift, when he waxed a hungered, saw a sow lie with her pigs well lapped in new straw, and near he drew and thought to have eaten of the straw. But anon his scrupulous conscience began therein to grudge him. For while his penance was, that for greediness of his meat he should do none other body harm; he thought he might not eat one straw thereof, lest for lack of that straw some of those pigs might hap to die for cold. So held he still his hunger, till one brought him meat. But when he should fall thereto, then fell he yet in a far further scruple; for then it came in his mind that he should yet break his penance, if he should eat any of that either, since he was commanded by his ghostly father, that he should not for his own meat hinder any other beast. For he thought, that if he eat not that meat, some other beast might hap to have it, and so should he by the eating of it peradventure hinder another. And thus stood he still fasting, till when he told the cause, his ghostly father came and informed him better, and then he cast off that scruple, and fell mannerly to his meat, and was a right honest ass many a fair day after.

Now this wolf had cast out in confession all his old raven, and then hunger pricked him forward, that he should begin all afresh. But yet the prick of conscience withdrew and held him back, because he would not for breaking of his penance take any prey for his mealtide that should pass the price of sixpence. It happed him then as he walked prowling for his gear

about, he came where a man had in few days before cast off two old, lean, and lame horses, so sick, that no flesh was there left on them; and the one, when the wolf came by, could scant stand upon his legs, and the other already dead, and his skin ripped off and carried away. And as he looked upon them suddenly, he was first about to feed upon them, and whet his teeth on their bones. But as he looked aside, he spied a fair cow in a close walking with her young calf by her side. And as soon as he saw them, his conscience began to grudge him against both those two horses. And then he sighed, and said unto himself: "Alas! wicked wretch that I am, I had almost broken my penance ere I was ware. For yonder dead horse, because I never saw no dead horse sold in the market, and I should even die therefore, I cannot devise what price I should set upon him; but in my conscience I set him far above sixpence, and therefore I dare not meddle with him. Now, then, is yonder quick horse, of likelihood worth a great deal of money: for horses be dear in this country, specially such soft amblers; for I see by his face he trotteth not, nor can scant shift a foot. And therefore I may not meddle with him, for he very far passeth my sixpence. But kine this country here hath enough, but money have they very little; and therefore, considering the plenty of the kine, and the scarcity of the money, as for yonder cow seemeth unto me in my conscience worth not past a groat, an she be worth so much. Now, then, as for her calf, is not so much as she by half. And therefore, while the cow is in my conscience worth but fourpence, my conscience cannot serve me for sin of my soul to appraise her calf above twopence, and so pass they not sixpence between them both. And therefore them twain may I well eat at this one meal, and break not my penance at all." And so therefore he did, without any scruple of conscience.

If such beasts could speak now, as Mother Maud said they could then, some of them would, I ween, tell a tale almost as wise as this, wherein, save for the minishing of old Mother Maud's tale, else would a shorter process have served. But yet, as peevish as the parable is, in this it serveth for our purpose, that the fear of a conscience somewhat scrupulous, though it be painful and troublous to him that hath it, like as this poor ass had here, is less harm yet, than a conscience over large, or such as for his own fantasy the man list to frame himself, now drawing it narrow, now stretching it in breadth, after the manner of a cheverel point, to serve on every side for his own commodity, as did here the wily wolf. But such folk are out of tribulation, and comfort need they none, and therefore are they out of our matter. But those that are in the night's fear of their own scrupulous conscience, let

them be well ware, as I said, that the devil, for weariness of the one, draw them not into the other; and while he would flee from Scylla, draw him into Charybdis. He must do as doth a ship that should come into an haven, in the mouth whereof lie secret rocks under the water on both sides. If he be by mishap entered in among them that are on the one side, and cannot tell how to get out: he must get a substantial cunning pilot, that so can conduct him from the rocks that are on that side, that yet he bring him not into those that are on the other side, but can guide him in the midway.

TALKATIVE NUN AND TALKATIVE WIFE

Antony. Between you and me, it fared as it did once between a nun and her brother. Very virtuous was this lady, and of a very virtuous place, a close religion, and therein had been long, in all which time she had never seen her brother, which was in like wise very virtuous, and had been far off at an university, and had there taken the degree of doctor in divinity. When he was come home he went to see his sister, as he that highly rejoiced in her virtue. So came she to the grate that they call, I trow, the locutory, and after their holy watch-word spoken on both the sides, after the manner used in that place, the one took the other by the tip of the finger (for hand would there be none wrungen through the grate), and forthwith began my lady to give her brother a sermon of the wretchedness of this world, and the frailty of the flesh, and the subtle slights of the wicked fiend, and gave him surely good counsel, saving somewhat too long, how he should be well ware in his living, and master well his body for saving of his soul; and yet, ere her own tale came all at an end, she began to find a little fault with him, and said: "In good faith, Brother, I do somewhat marvel that you, that have been at learning so long, and are doctor, and so learned in the law of God, do not now at our meeting, while we meet so seldom, to me that am your sister and a simple, unlearned soul, give of your charity some fruitful exhortation. For I doubt not but you can say some good thing yourself." "By my troth, good Sister," quoth her brother, "I cannot for you. For your tongue hath never ceased, but said enough for us both." And so, Cousin, I remember, that when I was once fallen in, I left you little space to say aught between. But now, will I, therefore, take another way with you; for I shall of our talking drive you to the one-half.

Vincent. Now, forsooth, Uncle, this was a merry tale. But now if you

make me talk the one-half, then shall you be contented far otherwise than there was of late a kinswoman of your own, but which will I not tell you; guess her an you can. Her husband had much pleasure in the manner and behaviour of another honest man, and kept him therefore much company; by the reason whereof he was at his mealtime the more oft from home. So happed it on a time that his wife and he together dined or supped with that neighbour of theirs, and then she made a merry quarrel to him for making her husband so good cheer out a-door, that she could not have him at home. "Forsooth, mistress," quoth he (as he was a dry merry man), "in my company nothing keepeth him but one; serve you him with the same, and he will never be from you." "What gay thing may that be?" quoth our cousin then. "Forsooth, mistress," quoth he, "your husband loveth well to talk, and when he sitteth with me, I let him have all the words." "All the words!" quoth she. "Marry that I am content; he shall have all the words with a good will, as he hath ever had. But I speak them all myself, and give them all to him; and for aught that I care for them, so he shall have them still. But otherwise to say, that he shall have them all, you shall keep them still, rather than he get the half."

LOVE OF FLATTERY [1]

Vincent. When I was first in Almaine, Uncle, it happed me to be somewhat favoured with a great man of the church, and a great state, one of the greatest in all that country there. And indeed whosoever might spend as much as he might in one thing and other, were a right great estate in any country of Christendom. But glorious was he very far above all measure, and that was great pity, for it did harm and made him abuse many great gifts that God had given him. Never was he satiate of hearing his own praise. So happed it one day, that he had in a great audience made an oration in a certain manner, wherein he liked himself so well, that at his dinner he sat on thorns, till he might hear how they that sat with him at his board would commend it. And when he had sitten musing a while, devising (as I thought after) on some pretty proper way to bring it in withal, at last, for lack of a better (lest he should have letted the matter too long) he brought it even bluntly forth, and asked us all that sat at his board's end (for at his own

---

[1] This story is generally supposed to apply to Cardinal Wolsey.

mess in the midst there sat but himself alone), how well we liked his oration that he had made that day. But in faith, Uncle, when that problem was once proposed, till it was full answered, no man I ween ate one morsel of meat more: every man was fallen in so deep a study, for the finding of some exquisite praise. For he that should have brought out but a vulgar and common commendation would have thought himself shamed for ever.

Then said we our sentences by row as we sat, from the lowest unto the highest in good order, as it had been a great matter of the common weal in a right solemn council. When it came to my part (I will not say it for no boast, Uncle), methought, by our lady! for my part I quit myself pretty well. And I liked myself the better, because methought my words (being but a stranger) went yet with some grace in the Almaine tongue, wherein, letting my Latin alone, me listed to show my cunning. And I hoped to be liked the better, because I saw that he that sat next me, and should say his sentence after me, was an unlearned priest: for he could speak no Latin at all. But when he came forth for his part with my lord's commendation, the wily fox had been so well accustomed in court with the craft of flattery that he went beyond me too far. And then might I see by him, what excellency a right mean wit may come to in one craft, that in all his whole life studieth and busieth his wit about no more but that one. But I made after a solemn vow to myself, that if ever he and I were matched together at that board again, when we should fall to our flattery I would flatter in Latin, that he should not contend with me no more. For though I could be content to be outrun of a horse, yet would I no more abide it to be outrun of an ass. But, Uncle, here began now the game: he that sat highest, and was to speak the last, was a great beneficed man, and not a doctor only, but also somewhat learned indeed in the laws of the Church. A world it was to see how he marked every man's word that spake before him, and it seemed that every word, the more proper that it was the worse he liked it, for the cumbrance that he had to study out a better to pass it. The man even sweat with the labour, so that he was fain in the while now and then to wipe his face. Howbeit in conclusion, when it came to his course, we that had spoken before him, had so taken all up among us before, that we had not left him one wise word to speak after.

Antony. Alas! good man, among so many of you, some good fellow should have lent him one.

Vincent. It needed not, as hap was, Uncle, for he found out such a shift, that in his flattering he passed us all the many.

164

Antony. Why, what said he, Cousin?

Vincent. By our Lady! Uncle, not one word. . . . For when he saw that he could find no word of praise that would pass all that had been spoken before already, the wily fox would speak never a word, but as he were ravished unto heavenward with the wonder of the wisdom and eloquence that my lord's grace had uttered in that oration, he fetched a long sigh with an oh! from the bottom of his breast, and held up both his hands, and lifted up his head, and cast up his eyes into the welkin and wept.

Antony. Surely, Cousin, as Terence saith, such folks make men of fools even stark mad, and much cause have their lords to be right angry with them.

Vincent. God hath indeed, and is, I ween: but as for their lords, Uncle, if they would after wax angry with them therefor, they should in my mind do them very great wrong, when it is one of the things that they specially keep them for. For those that are of such vainglorious mind (be they lords or be they meaner men) can be much better content to have their contents commended, then amended; and require their servants and their friend never so specially to tell them the very truth, yet shall he better please them if he speak them fair, than if he tell them truth. And in good faith, Uncle, the self-same prelate that I told you my tale of, I dare be bold to swear it (I know it so surely), had on a time made of his own drawing a certain treaty, that should serve for a league between that country and a great prince. In which treaty, himself thought that he had devised his articles so wisely, and indited them so well, that all the world would allow them. Whereupon longing sore to be praised, he called unto him a friend of his, a man well learned, and of good worship, and very well expert in those matters, as he that had been divers times ambassador for that country, and had made many such treaties himself. When he took him the treaty, and that he had read it, he asked him how he liked it, and said: "But I pray you heartily tell me the very truth." And that he spake so heartily, that the other had weened he would fain have heard the truth, and in trust thereof he told him a fault therein. At the hearing whereof, he swore in great anger: "By the mass! thou art a very fool." The other afterward told me, that he would never tell him truth again.

Antony. Without question, Cousin, I cannot greatly blame him: and thus themself make every man mock them, flatter them, and deceive them: those, I say, that are of such vainglorious mind. For if they be content to hear the truth, let them then make much of those that tell them the truth, and with-

draw their ear from them that falsely flatter them, and they shall be more truly served than with twenty requests, praying men to tell them true. King Ladislaus, our Lord assoil his soul, used much this manner among his servants. When any of them praised any deed of his, or any condition in him, if he perceived that they said but the truth, he would let it pass by uncontrolled. But when he saw that they set a gloss upon it for his praise of their own making beside, then would he shortly say unto them: "I pray thee, good fellow, when thou sayest grace at my board, never bring in *Gloria Patri* without a *sicut erat;* that is to wit, even as it was, and none otherwise: and lift me not up with no lies, for I love it not." If men would use this way with them, that this noble king used, it would minish much of their false flattery.

I can well allow, that men should commend (keeping them within the bounds of truth) such things as they see praiseworthy in other men, to give them the greater courage to the increase thereof. For men keep still in that point one condition of children, that praise must prick them forth; but better it were to do well, and look for none. Howbeit, they that cannot find in their heart to commend another man's good deed, show themself either envious, or else of nature very cold and dull. But out of question, he that putteth his pleasure in the praise of the people hath but a fond phantasy. For if his finger do but ache of an hot blain, a great many men's mouths blowing out his praise will scantly do him among them all half so much ease as to have one little boy to blow upon his finger.

GODLY MEDITATION

GIVE me thy grace, good Lord,
To set the world at nought. •
To set my mind fast upon thee
And not to hang upon the blast of men's mouths.
To be content to be solitary.
Not to long for worldly company.
Little and little utterly to cast off the world
And rid my mind of all the business thereof.
Not to long to hear of any worldly things.
But that the hearing of worldly fantasies may be
　　to me displeasant.
Gladly to be thinking of God,

Piteously to call for his help.

To lean unto the comfort of God.

Busily to labour to love him.

To know mine own vilitie and wretchedness.

To humble and meeken myself under the mighty
hand of God.

To bewail my sins passed,

For the purging of them, patiently to suffer
adversity.

Gladly to bear my purgatory here.

To be joyful of tribulations.

To walk the narrow way that leadeth to life.

To bear the cross with Christ.

To have the last thing in remembrance.

To have ever afore mine eye, my death, that
is ever at hand.

To make death no stranger to me.

To foresee and consider the everlasting fire of
hell.

To pray for pardon before the judge come.

To have continually in mind, the passion that
Christ suffered for me.

For his benefits uncessantly to give him thanks.

To buy the time again, that I before have lost.

To abstain from vain confabulations.

To eschew light foolish mirth and gladness.

Recreations not necessary to cut off.

Of worldly substance, friends, liberty, life and all
to set the loss at right nought, for the winning
of Christ.

To think my most enemies my best friends.

For the brethren of Joseph could never have done
him so much good with their love and favour,
as they did with their malice and hatred.

These minds are more to be desired of every
man, than all the treasure of all the princes and
kings Christian and heathen, were it gathered
and laid together all upon one heap.

LETTER TO HIS DAUGHTER, MARGARET

OUR LORD bless you, good daughter, and your good husband, and your little boy, and all yours, and all my children, and all my God-children, and all our friends. Recommend me when ye may, to my good daughter Cecily, whom I beseech our Lord to comfort. And I send her my blessing, and to all her children, and pray her to pray for me. I send her an handkercher: and God comfort my good son her husband. My good daughter Daunce hath the picture in parchment, that you delivered me from my lady Coniers, her name is on the back-side. Show her that I heartily pray her that you may send it in my name to her again, for a token from me to pray for me. I like special well Dorothy Colley, I pray you be good unto her. I would wit whether this be she that you wrote me of. If not yet I pray you be good to the other as you may in her affliction, and to my good daughter Joan Alleyn too. Give her I pray you some kind answer, for she sued hither to me this day to pray you be good to her. I cumber you good Margaret much, but I would be sorry, if it should be any longer than tomorrow. For it is Saint Thomas even, and the octave of Saint Peter: and therefore tomorrow long I to go to God: it were a day very meet and convenient to me. I never liked your manner toward me better, than when you kissed me last: for I love when daughterly love and dear charity, hath no leisure to look to worldly courtesy. Farewell my dear child, and pray for me, and I shall for you and all your friends, that we may merrily meet in heaven. I thank you for your great cost. I send now my good daughter Clement her algorism stone, and I send her and my godson and all hers, God's blessing and mine. I pray you at time convenient recommend me to my good son John More. I liked well his natural fashion. Our Lord bless him and his good wife my loving daughter, to whom I pray him to be good as he hath great cause: and that if the land of mine come to his hand, he break not my will concerning his sister Daunce. And our Lord bless Thomas and Austin and all they that have—[2]

---

[2] The letter breaks off abruptly. Dorothy Colley and Joan Alleyn were Margaret's maid and friends. Thomas and Austin were grandsons, children of John More. Clement's "algorism stone" was for arithmetic, apparently a slate. The letter was written to Margaret the day before his last and sent along with his shirt of hair since More was "not willing to have it seen."

HAMLET WITHOUT THE PRINCE:
Henry Howard, Earl of Surrey

LAMENT FOR HIS LOST BOYHOOD

A SATIRE ON LONDON, THE MODERN BABYLON

~~~~~~

AN ADHERENT of the English Reformation remarked about Surrey: "It ys the most folish prowde boye that ys in Englande." The son of the powerful Duke of Norfolk, he was heir to the conservatism of nobility and religion on which the dictatorship of Henry VIII was encroaching. But the future belonged to the new capitalism, to the families which made their fortunes by breeding sheep rather than aristocrats, by manufacturing cloth, and from the church lands which Henry had confiscated. The future belonged to men of commercial energy, not to the scions of the old privileges and of Catholic tradition. Surrey had only thirty years to live, dangerously, proudly, and brilliantly. He pioneered in all the arts of a gentleman: contempt for upstarts, refinement of manners, boldness of dress, the Italian sonnet, and the new blank verse. After Sir Thomas Wyatt's death, Surrey was a real prince—but only in English poetry, a mild by-product of his total ambition. The dictatorship of Henry VIII undermined the humanism of the milder reformers and the literary renaissance of the poets. It chopped off the talented heads of Thomas More and John Fisher, and put into prison Thomas Wyatt and Hugh Latimer. It was not at all a healthy climate for "the most folish prowde boye that ys in Englande." The first occasion for Surrey's disgrace came in 1537 with his return from a campaign against the Pilgrimage of Grace, a rebellion to obtain restitution of property to the church. In the royal park at Hampton Court he struck a courtier who accused him of secret sympathy with the Catholic insurgents. He was imprisoned in Windsor Castle, where he wrote the *Lament for His Lost Boyhood*. In 1542 he was committed to the Tower for a brawl which he ingenuously attributed to "the fury of reckless youth." In 1543 young Surrey-Hamlet turned into a Villon with an unprecedented adventure: he was charged with having eaten flesh in Lent and having spent a riotous London night with companions (including young Wyatt, son of the poet), who broke windows with stone-bows. The victims of this aristocratic slumming party were the humble apprentices of Cheapside. The smashed windowpanes be-

169

longed, significantly, to Protestant burghers who had made their new fortunes after the suppression of the monasteries. Surrey was sent to the Fleet where he composed his defence and apology for vandalism, *Satire on London, The Modern Babylon.* Is this poem a pious and flaming Catholic indictment of London sinners, or does it show the twenty-six-year-old Surrey with his tongue in his cheek? He was to have just one more battle with the new order. As Henry VIII was dying, surrounded by whispers concerning the succession of a Regent during the minority of Prince Edward, Surrey and his father, the Duke of Norfolk, were indicted for treason. All that young Surrey had accumulated now stood against him—his Italian polish, his adherence to the old tradition, the charge that he had brazenly assumed the royal coat of arms, as well as the curious testimony of his sister that he had advised her to become the king's mistress to promote her brother's ambition. But his real crime lay in a condition beyond his control—the potential danger to Henry VIII's succession in a family as proud and conservative and powerful as the Duke of Norfolk's. He was executed. So died Surrey, who with the older poet Wyatt had "newly crept out of the schooles of Dante, Arioste, and Petrarch, and greatly polished our rude and homely manner of vulgar poesie."

LAMENT FOR HIS LOST BOYHOOD

So CRUEL prison how could betide, alas,
As proud Windsor, where I in lust and joy,
With a Kinges son, my childish years did pass,
In greater feast than Priam's sons of Troy.
Where each sweet place returns a taste full sour.
The large green courts, where we were wont to hove,
With eyes cast up into the maiden's tower,
And easy sighs, such as folk draw in love.
The stately seats, the ladies bright of hue,
The dances short, long tales of great delight;
With words and looks, that tigers could but rue:
Where each of us did plead the other's right.
The palme-play, where, despoiled for the game,
With dazed eyes oft we by gleams of love
Have missed the ball, and got sight of our dame,

To bait her eyes, which kept the leads above.
The gravelled ground, with sleeves tied on the helm,
On foaming horse, with swords and friendly hearts;
With chere, as though one should another whelm,
Where we have fought, and chased oft with darts.
With silver drops the mead yet spread for ruth,
In active games of nimbleness and strength,
Where we did strain, trained with swarms of youth,
Our tender limbs, that yet shot up in length.
The secret groves, which oft we made resound
Of pleasant plaint, and of our ladies' praise;
Recording oft what grace each one had found,
What hope of speed, what dread of long delays.
The wild forest, the clothed holts with green;
With reins availed, and swift y-breathed horse,
With cry of hounds, and merry blasts between,
Where we did chase the fearful hart of force.
The void walls eke, that harboured us each night:
Wherewith, alas! reviveth in my breast
The sweet accord, such sleeps as yet delight;
The pleasant dreams, the quiet bed of rest;
The secret thoughts, imparted with such trust,
The wanton talk, the divers change of play;
The friendship sworn, each promise kept so just,
Wherewith we past the winter night away.
And with this thought the blood forsakes the face;
The tears berain my cheeks of deadly hue:
The which, as soon as sobbing sighs, alas!
Up-supped have, thus I my plaint renew:
'O place of bliss! renewer of my woes!
Give me account, where is my noble fere?
Whom in thy walls thou dost each night enclose;
To other lief; but unto me most dear.'
Echo, alas! that doth my sorrow rue,
Returns thereto a hollow sound of plaint.
Thus I alone, where all my freedom grew,
In prison pine, with bondage and restraint:

And with remembrance of the greater grief,
To banish the less, I find mv chief relief.

A SATIRE ON LONDON, THE MODERN BABYLON

LONDON! hast thou accused me
Of breach of laws? the root of strife!
Within whose breast did boil to see,
So fervent hot, thy dissolute life;
That even the hate of sins that grow
Within thy wicked walls so rife,
For to break forth did convert so,
That terror could it not repress.
The which, by words, since preachers know
What hope is left for to redress,
By unknown means it liked me
My hidden burthen to express.
Whereby it might appear to thee
That secret sin hath secret spite;
From justice' rod no fault is free,
But that all such as work unright
In most quiet, are next ill rest.
In secret silence of the night
This made me, with a rechless breast,
To wake thy sluggards with my bow:
A figure of the Lord's behest,
Whose scourge for sin the Scriptures shew.
That as the fearful thunder's clap
By sudden flame at hand we know;
Of pebble stones the soundless rap,
The dreadful plague might make thee see
Of God's wrath that doth thee enwrap.
That pride might know, from conscience free,
How lofty works may her defend;
And envy find, as he hath sought,
How other seek him to offend:
And wrath taste of each cruel thought,

The just shape higher in the end:
And idle sloth, that never wrought,
To heaven his spirit lift may begin:
And greedy lucre live in dread,
To see what hate ill got goods win.
The letchers, ye that lusts do feed,
Perceive what secrecy is in sin:
And gluttons' hearts for sorrow bleed,
Awaked, when their fault they find:
In loathsome vice each drunken wight,
To stir to God this was my mind.
Thy windows had done me no spight;
But proud people that dread no fall,
Clothed with falsehood, and unright
Bred in the closures of thy wall,
Wrested to wrath my fervent zeal
Thou hast; to strife, my secret call.
Indured hearts no warning feel.
O! shameless whore! is dread then gone?
Be such thy foes, as meant thy weal?
O! member of false Babylon!
The shop of craft! the den of ire!
Thy dreadful doom draws fast upon.
Thy martyrs' blood by sword and fire,
In heaven and earth for justice call.
The Lord shall hear their just desire!
The flame of wrath shall on thee fall!
With famine and pest lamentably
Stricken shall be thy lechers all.
Thy proud towers, and turrets high
Enemies to God, beat stone from stone:
Thine idols burnt that wrought iniquity:
When, none thy ruin shall bemoan;
But render unto the righteous Lord,
That so hath judged Babylon,
Immortal praise with one accord.

"JOHN DONNE—ANNE DONNE—UNDONE":
John Donne

> For Godsake hold your tongue, and let me love,
>   Or chide my palsie, or my gout,
>   My five gray haires, or ruin'd fortune flout,
>   With wealth your state, your minde with Arts improve,
>   Take you a course, get you a place,
>   Observe his honour or his grace,
>   Or the Kings reall, or his stamped face
>   Contemplate, what you will, approve,
>   So you will let me love.
>
> JOHN DONNE, *The Canonization*

THE Lord Keeper of the Great Seal of England, Sir Thomas Egerton, attracted by the learning, languages, and wit of young John Donne made him his chief secretary in 1597. Amidst the domestic urbanity and intelligence of York House, Master Donne was treated with courtesy and had a place at the table and in the bright table talk. He was a vivacious and complicated young man, capable of adroit but respectful sallies with the ladies—a poet who had lost his innocence.

Both his secretarial task and distinguished employer were rapidly maturing his worldly experience when John Donne became attracted to Anne More, a daughter of Sir George More. She lived at York House because she had been temporarily adopted by Sir George's sister, Lady Egerton. Anne was sixteen years old when her aunt's death left her exposed both to the cares of managing York House and the clandestine admiration and able strategy of the brilliant young secretary. Two events hastened a climax: the impending remarriage of the Lord Keeper, and Anne's recall from his home by her own family. In a number of sonnets Donne communicated the daily dilemma of his heart to his good friends Christopher and Samuel Brooke. Three weeks before the Christmas of 1601, John Donne and Anne More were secretly married—Christopher generously giving away the bride by proxy, and his brother Samuel, who had just taken orders almost as if for this purpose, performing the rites.

By marrying off a minor without her father's consent, John, Christopher,

174

and Samuel ran the gauntlet of both the Common and the Canon Law. The romantic impulse appeased, it became necessary to discover a mediator between the bridegroom and his father-in-law, one who could reconcile the irreconcilable—the fury and vanity of Sir George More, Knight. John Donne found a mediator in Henry Percy, a friend of Essex and later of Raleigh, an intellectual person with no prejudices in matrimonial conventions, a gentleman with a taste for the exotic scene, especially if it were the face of a scandalized father. Percy brought to Sir George from the very worried bridegroom a piece of written casuistry about the marriage with Anne which did not at all appease him: "So long since as her being at York House this had foundation," Donne said of the affair, "and so much then of promise and contract built upon it as, without violence to conscience, might not be shaken. . . . I humbly beseech you, so to deal in it as the persuasions of Nature, Reason, Wisdom, and Christianity shall inform you." Sir George was promptly informed by Nature—he was terribly angry. He did not stop to consult either Reason, Wisdom, or Christianity. Vengefully he sought to prevail over his brother-in-law, Sir Thomas Egerton, to deprive the poet of his bread-and-butter post. He found swifter satisfaction in having John Donne and the two Brookes put into jail.

Mrs. Donne, who was held prisoner by her father, received a note from her husband in which one unhappy line rhymed: "John Donne—Anne Donne—Undone." Meanwhile Sir George and Sir Thomas received Donne's despairing and remorseful cries of appeal from Fleet Prison, with the result that the bridegroom was transferred into a domestic semi-captivity at his chambers in the Strand. From here Donne sent his father-in-law still another (and rather curious) communication. As Donne humbled, Sir George subsided. There were conciliatory ladies who, appreciating Donne better than did Sir George, hastened to congratulate the angry parent on having acquired so brilliant a husband for his Anne. In due course, Sir George was so far reconciled that he actually joined Donne in vain pleading with Sir Thomas Egerton for the secretarial position which was lost only when the scandal became irrevocably public. In the end, the court of the Archbishop of Canterbury confirmed the marriage of John Donne to Anne More. In so doing, the ecclesiastical court showed that it was not aware of the kind of poetry Donne had been writing, or perhaps it would have hesitated in pronouncing that clandestine marriage sacred. A contemporary critic observes with some irony that "Donne was married to Anne More in 1601, 'three weeks before Christmas', and *The Progresse of the Soule*, in

which he releases some of his bitterest statements against women, is dated by himself, '16. Augusti 1601' "!

"MY SUBMISSION, MY REPENTANCE"

To the right wor. Sir Geo. More, kt.

Sir,—The inward accusations in my conscience, that I have offended you beyond any ability of redeeming it by me, and the feeling of my Lord's heavy displeasure following it, forceth me to write, though I know my fault make my letters very ungracious to you.

Almighty God, whom I call to witness that all my grief is that I have in this manner offended you and Him, direct you to believe that which out of an humble and afflicted heart I now write to you. And since we have no means to move God, when He will not hear our prayers, to hear them, but by praying, I humbly beseech you to allow by His gracious example my penitence so good entertainment, as it may have a belief and a pity.

Of nothing in this one fault that I hear said to me can I disculp myself, but of the contemptuous and despiteful purpose towards you, which I hear is surmised against me. But for my dutiful regard to my late Lady, for my religion, and for my life, I refer myself to them that may have observed them. I humbly beseech you to take off these weights, and to put my fault into the balance alone, as it was done without the addition of these ill reports, and though then it will be too heavy for me, yet then it will less grieve you to pardon it.

How little and how short the comfort and pleasure of destroying is, I know your wisdom and religion informs you. And though perchance you intend not utter destruction, yet the way through which I fall towards it is so headlong, that, being thus pushed, I shall soon be at bottom, for it pleaseth God, from whom I acknowledge the punishment to be just, to accompany my other ills with so much sickness as I have no refuge but that of mercy, which I beg of Him, my Lord, and you, which I hope you will not repent to have afforded me, since all my endeavours and the whole course of my life shall be bent to make myself worthy of your favour and her love, whose peace of conscience and quiet I know must be much wounded and violenced if your displeasure sever us.

I can present nothing to your thoughts which you knew not before, but my submission, my repentance, and my hearty desire to do anything satis-

176

factory to your just displeasure. Of which I beseech you to make a charitable use and construction. From the Fleet, 11th Feb. 1601[2].—Yours in all faithful duty and obedience,

J. DONNE.

"IT HATH MUCH PROFITED ME THAT I AM DEJECTED"

To EXCUSE my offence, or so much to resist the just punishment for it, as to move your Lordship to withdraw it, I thought till now were to aggravate my fault. But since it hath pleased God to join with you in punishing thereof with increasing my sickness, and that He gives me now audience by prayer, it emboldeneth me also to address my humble request to your Lordship, that you would admit into your favourable consideration how far my intentions were from doing dishonour to your Lordship's house, and how unable I am to escape utter and present destruction, if your Lordship judge only the effect and deed.

My services never had so much worth in them as to deserve the favours wherewith they were paid; but they had always so much honesty as that only this hath stained them. Your justice hath been merciful in making me know my offence, and it hath much profited me that I am dejected. Since then I am so entirely yours, that even your disfavours have wrought good upon me. I humbly beseech you that all my good may proceed from your Lordship, and that since Sir George More, whom I leave no humble way unsought to regain, refers all to your Lordship, you would be pleased to lessen that correction which your just wisdom hath destined for me, and so to pity my sickness and other misery as shall best agree with your honourable disposition.

Almighty God accompany all your Lordship's purposes, and bless you and yours with many good days. Fleet, 12 Febr. 1601[2].—Your Lordship's most dejected and poor servant.

JOHN DONNE.

To the Right Honourable my very good
L. and Master Sr. THOMAS EGERTON,
Knight, L. Keeper of the Great Seal
of England.

"AS THE DEVIL IN THE ARTICLE"

SIR,—From you, to whom next to God I shall owe my health, by enjoying by your mediation this mild change of imprisonment, I desire to derive all my good fortune and content in this world; and therefore, with my most unfeigned thanks, present to you my humble petition that you would be pleased to hope that, as that fault which was laid to me of having deceived some gentlewoman before, and that of loving a corrupt religion, are vanished and smoked away (as I assure myself, out of their weakness they are), and that as the devil in the article of our death takes the advantage of our weakness and fear, to aggravate our sins to our conscience, so some uncharitable malice hath presented my debts double at least.

How many of the imputations laid upon me would fall off, if I might shake and purge myself in your presence! But if that were done, of this offence committed to you I cannot acquit myself, of which yet I hope that God (to whom for that I heartily direct many prayers) will inform you to make that use, that as of evil manners good laws grow, so out of disobedience and boldness you will take occasion to show mercy and tenderness. And when it shall please God to soften your heart so much towards us as to pardon us, I beseech you also to undertake that charitable office of being my mediator to my Lord, whom as upon your just complaint you found full of justice, I doubt not but you shall also find full of mercy, for so is the Almighty pattern of Justice and Mercy equally full of both.

My conscience, and such affection as in my conscience becomes an honest man, emboldeneth me to make one request more, which is, that by some kind and comfortable message you would be pleased to give some ease of the afflictions which I know your daughter in her mind suffers, and that (if it be not against your other purposes) I may with your leave write to her, for without your leave I will never attempt anything concerning her. God so have mercy upon me, as I am unchangeably resolved to bend all my courses to make me fit for her, which if God and my Lord and you be pleased to strengthen, I hope neither my debts, which I can easily order, nor anything else shall interrupt. Almighty God keep you in His favour, and restore me to His and yours.

From my chamber, whither by your favour I am come, 13th Feb. 1601[2].

J. DONNE.

To the Right Worshipful
Sir GEORGE MORE, *Knight.*

VIRTUE IN A NAUGHTY WORLD:

George Wither

IN PRAISE OF POETRY

SATIRE TO KING JAMES

GEORGE WITHER, a man obsessed by virtue in a naughty world, was locked up in the Marshalsea when he was seven-and-twenty, and inside Newgate at three-and-seventy. He left behind him, for the anthologists, some of the most delightful and spontaneous of English poems, and also some of the dullest in the language. The source of his lifelong difficulties was not so much his conversion from royalism to puritanism, as an uncompromising talent for getting into trouble, whether under James I, Charles I, the Commonwealth, or the Restoration. *Abuses Stript and Whipt* (its dedication reads: "To Him-selfe George Wither wisheth all happiness") was an exercise in satire against the vices of the time. Although it *stript* and *whipt* only abstractions like Revenge, Ambition, and Lust, some hint in the satire seems to have gotten under a thin skin. This adventure furnished Wither with his first introduction to the Marshalsea in 1614. There he consoled himself with writing *The Shepherd's Hunting,* which caused Charles Lamb (who rescued his reputation from bankruptcy) to say: "The prison-notes of Wither are finer than the wood-notes of most of his poetical brethren." Wither's later difficulties were with the Stationers' Company, with his booksellers, and with Ben Jonson's "drunken conclave." In the Civil War he was captured by royalists at the head of a parliamentary troop which he had raised by selling his estate, and he owed his life to the intervention of Sir John Denham who pleaded mockingly that so long as Wither lived in the flesh, he, Denham, could not be accounted the worst living poet in England. Somehow Wither survived this devastating generosity. But he got into trouble for admitting—during the Cromwell regime—the possibility of a restoration, and—when the restoration was accomplished—for being too frank in expressing his fears in reverse. We find him in Newgate from 1660 to 1663, busy writing that portion of his work which no one reads. To use a pun known to himself, the freshness of his verse had "withered" since *The Shepherd's Hunting* of his first confinement in the Marshalsea. He was now an old man chiding the City of London from a cell in Newgate:

179

And, possibly, another Generation
Will heed, that I am somewhat to the Nation,
Deserving better, then than to lie I should
Within a Jail, at seventy-three years old,
For acting and designing nothing worse
Then, how to save them from a greater curse.

He had written fashionable satires and passionate puritan diatribes and many pious hymns, eclogues, epigrams, sonnets, a history of the plague, rhymed petitions to parliament, warnings and proclamations—so wordy an output that it has never been collected in one edition. From a dusty grave in Pope's *The Dunciad,* Lamb rescued "wretched Withers" without covering his faults with charity: "Wither seems to have contemplated to a degree of idolatry his own possible virtue. He is forever anticipating persecution and martyrdom; fingering, as it were, the flames, to try how he can bear them. Perhaps his premature defiance sometimes made him obnoxious to censures, which he could otherwise have slipped by." But George Wither, who made virtue too garrulous to frighten the vices of his age, and never once rivaled his great contemporary Milton in the politics of liberty, left behind him such pleasant lines as:

Shall I wasting with despair
Die because a woman's fair?

and his rich *Christmas Carol,* and the enthusiasm of his youth (the youth of English poetry) recorded in a Marshalsea cell:

It is known what thou canst do,
For it is not long ago
When that Cuddy, thou, and I,
Each the other's skill to try,
At Saint Dunstan's charmèd well,
(As some present there can tell)
Sang upon a sudden theme,
Sitting by the crimson stream;
Where if thou didst well or no
Yet remains the song to shew.

IN PRAISE OF POETRY

[In the five eclogues of *The Shepherd's Hunting*, Philarete (George Wither),
Willy (William Browne), Cuddy (Christopher Brooke), and Alexis (William Ferrar) discuss a poet's imprisonment. The following selection is
from the fourth eclogue whose climax is the celebrated eulogy of poetry.]

Philarete. Willy! what may those men be,
   Are so ill to malice thee?

Willy. Some are worthy-well esteem'd;
   Some without worth are so deem'd;
   Others of so base a spirit,
   They have no esteem or merit.

Philarete. What's the wrong?

Willy.   A slight offence,
   Wherewithal I can dispense;
   But hereafter, for their sake,
   To myself I'll music make.

Philarete. What, because some clown offends,
   Wilt thou punish all thy friends?

Willy. Do not, Phil, misunderstand me:
   Those that love me may command me;
   But thou know'st I am but young,
   And the pastoral I sung
   Is by some suppos'd to be,
   By a strain, too high for me:
   So they kindly let me gain
   Not my labour for my pain.
   Trust me, I do wonder why
   They should me my own deny.
   Though I'm young, I scorn to flit
   On the wings of borrowed wit.

From *The Shepherd's Hunting: Being certain Eclogues written during the time of the
Author's Imprisonment in the Marshalsea*. By George Wither, Gentleman. (Dedicated)
To those Honoured, Noble and right Virtuous Friends, my Visitants in Marshalsea: And
to all other my unknown Favourers, who either privately or publicly wished me well in
my imprisonment. London. 1622.

I'll make my own feathers bear me.
Yet I'll keep my skill in store,
Till I've seen some winters more.

Philarete. But in earnest mean'st thou so?
Then thou art not wise, I trow:
Better shall advise thee, Pan,
For thou dost not rightly then:
That's the ready way to blot
All the credit thou hast got.
Rather in thy age's prime
Get another start of Time;
And make those that so fond be,
Spite of their own dullness, see
That the sacred Muses can
Make a child in years a man.[1]
It is known what thou canst do;
For it is not long ago,
When that Cuddy, thou, and I,
Each the other's skill to try,
At Saint Dunstan's charmèd well,[2]
As some present there can tell,
Sang upon a sudden theme,
Sitting by the crimson stream;
Where, if thou didst well or no,
Yet remains the song to shew.
Much experience more I've had,
Of thy skill, thou happy lad!
And would make the world to know it,
But that time will further shew it.
Envy makes their tongues now run

---

[1] "A good motto for the Life of Chatterton," remarks Charles Lamb.

[2] "*Saint Dunstan's charmèd well.* The Devil Tavern, Fleet-Street, where Child's Place now stands, and where, within the memory of the Editor, about eighteen years ago, a sign hung of the Devil and Saint Dunstan. Ben Jonson made this a famous place of resort for poets, by drawing up a set of *Leges Conviviales* which were engraven in marble over the chimney-piece in the room called APOLLO. One of Drayton's poems is called *The Sacrifice to Apollo;* it is addressed to the Priests or wits of Apollo, and is a kind of poetical paraphrase upon the *Leges Conviviales.* This tavern to the very last kept up a room of that name." Annotation by Charles Lamb.

More than doubt of what is done;
For that needs must be thy own,
Or to be some other's known;
But how then will't suit unto
What thou shalt hereafter do?
Or I wonder, where is he
Would with that song part to thee.
Nay, were there so mad a swain,
Could such glory sell for gain,
Phoebus would not have combin'd
That gift with so base a mind.
Never did the Nine impart
The sweet secrets of their art
Unto any that did scorn,
We should see their favours worn.
Therefore unto those that say,
Where they pleas'd to sing a lay,
They could do't and will not tho',
This I speak, for this I know
None e'er drank the Thespian spring,
And knew how, but he did sing.
For, that once infus'd in man,
Makes him shew't, do what he can;
Nay, those that do only sip,
Or but even their fingers dip
In that sacred fount, poor elves!
Of that brood will shew themselves.
Yea, in hope to get them fame,
They will speak, though to their shame.
Let those, then, at thee repine,
That by their wits measure thine:
Needs those songs must be thine own,
And that one day will be known.
That poor imputation too,
I myself do undergo;
But it will appear ere long,
That 'twas Envy sought our wrong;
Who, at twice ten, have sung more

Than some will do at four score.
Cheer thee, honest Willy! then,
And begin thy song again.

Willy.　Fain I would, but I do fear,
When again my lines they hear,
If they yield they are my rhymes,
They will feign some other crimes;
And 'tis not safe vent'ring by,
When we see Detraction lie;
For, do what I can, I doubt
She will pick some quarrel out;
And I oft have heard defended
Little said is soon amended.

Philarete. See'st thou not, in clearest days,
Oft thick fogs cloud Heaven's rays?
And that vapours which do breathe
From the Earth's gross womb beneath,
Seem unto us with black steams
To pollute the Sun's bright beams
And yet vanish into air,
Leaving it, unblemish'd fair?
So, my Willy! shall it be
With Detraction's breath on thee:
It shall never rise so high,
As to stain thy poesy.
As that sun doth oft exhale
Vapours from each rotten vale,
Poesy so sometime drains
Gross conceits from muddy brains;
Mists of envy, fogs of spite,
'Twixt men's judgments and her light;
But so much her power may do,
That she can dissolve them too.
If thy verse do bravely tower,
As she makes wing, she gets power;
Yet the higher she doth soar,
She's affronted still the more,

Till she to the high'st hath past;
Then she rests with Fame at last.
Let nought therefore thee affright;
But make forward in thy flight.
For if I could match thy rhyme,
To the very stars I'd climb;
Then begin again, and fly
Till I reach'd eternity.
But, alas, my Muse is slow:
For thy place she flags too low;
Yea, the more's her hapless fate,
Her short wings were clipt of late;
And poor I, her fortune ruing,
Am myself put up a mewing.
But if I my cage can rid,
I'll fly where I never did;
And though for her sake I'm crost,
Though my best hopes I have lost,
And knew she would make my trouble
Ten times more than ten times double;
I should love and keep her too,
'Spite of all the world could do . . .

She doth tell me where to borrow
Comfort in the midst of sorrow,
Makes the desolatest place
To her presence be a grace,
And the blackest discontents
To be pleasing ornaments.
In my former days of bliss,
Her divine skill taught me this,
That from everything I saw,
I could some invention draw;
And raise pleasure to her height
Through the meanest object's sight;
By the murmur of a spring,
Or the least bough's rustling;
By a daisie, whose leaves spread,

Shut when Titan goes to bed;
Or a shady bush or tree;
She could more infuse in me,
Than all nature's beauties can
In some other wiser man.
By her help I also now
Make this churlish place allow
Some things, that may sweeten gladness
In the very gall of sadness:
The dull loneness, the black shade
That these hanging vaults have made;
The strange music of the waves,
Beating on these hollow caves;
This black den, which rocks emboss,
Over-grown with eldest moss;
The rude portals that give light,
More to terror than delight;
This my chamber of neglect,
Wall'd about with disrespect;
From all these, and this dull air,
A fit object for despair,
She hath taught me, by her might,
To draw comfort and delight.
Therefore, thou best earthly bliss:
I will cherish thee for this.

SATIRE TO KING JAMES

WHAT once the Poet said, I may avow,
'Tis a hard thing not to write Satires now;
Since what we speak (abuse so reigns in all),
Spite of our hearts, will be satirical.

Know, I am he that enter'd once the list,
'Gainst all the world to play the Satyrist;

Fragment from a Satire, written to the King's most Excellent Majesty, By George Wither, When he was Prisoner in the Marshalsea, for his first Book. London. 1622.

'Twas I that made my measures, rough and rude,
Dance, arm'd with whips, amidst the multitude;
And unappalled with my damned scrowls,
Teaz'd angry Monsters in their lurking-holes.
I've play'd with wasps and hornets without fears,
Till mad they grew, and swarm'd about my ears;
I've done it, and methinks 'tis such brave sport,
I may be stung, but ne'er be sorry for't;
For all my grief is that I was so sparing,
And had no more in't worth the name of daring.
He that will tax these times must be more bitter:
Tart lines of vinegar and gall are fitter.

"MOST LOFTIE, INSOLENT, AND PASSIONATE":
Sir Walter Raleigh

THE LIE   PREFACE TO THE HISTORY OF THE WORLD

THE CONCLUSION   THE PASSIONATE MAN'S PILGRIMAGE

A LETTER TO HIS WIFE   EVEN SUCH IS TIME

RALEIGH seems dominated by no critical or rebellious idea and belongs to no revisionist movement. He carries no clear passport to his long martyrdom in the Tower. He baffles analysis. He is an Elizabethan paradox even to Elizabethans. It was easier to shower him with epithets than to justify him even to an Elizabethan age—"ambitious Raleigh," "exuberant Raleigh," "flamboyant Raleigh"—a sport in adjectives begun with Puttenham's familiar sentence: "I find Sir Walter Rawleygh's vayne the most loftie, insolent and passionate. . . ." But the very ingredients in Raleigh are explosive: action and intellect, pride and inquiry, greed and humanism. To explain his downfall, we must recall that he lived in an age of uncertain fortunes and sudden treachery, that he was ruled by pride and politics. However, neither pride nor politics, but force of imagination, made of him a kind of heretic, an explorer of himself as of continents. Raleigh was above all a sceptic. A paragon of courtiers, he was capable of writing:

> Say to the court it glowes
> And shines like rotten wood.

Father of the imperialist dream, he could say nevertheless:

> Give me my Scallop shell of quiet
> My staffe of Faith to walk upon.

A modern student of Raleigh, Miss Agnes M. C. Latham, remarks how difficult it is "to believe in him," how even to his own age he seemed "so monstrously proud, so dangerously subtle, and in the end so horribly wronged." Queen Elizabeth believed in Raleigh as long as he remained chained to her by titles, wine monopolies, properties, and homage. The queen willingly granted him no leave of absence from her favors. She could put him in the Tower for a love affair and turn his honeymoon into a jail sentence. It was not the flattery of Raleigh's long poem, *Ocean's Love to Cynthia,* that brought him out of prison, but the embarrassment of

"Cynthia" after a piratical prize had docked in England, whose treasures no one could protect from the general looting as imperiously and efficiently as the prisoner in the Tower. Of course "Ocean" wisely and prudently gave "Cynthia" the lion's share of the loot. But after 1592, through the exploration of Guiana, the expedition against Cadiz, and all his other enterprises, Raleigh, still fallen from favor, had become in the words of Miss Latham "less of a courtier, more of a man." In Parliament he spoke up for free trade, for the repeal of monopolies, and for religious toleration; he tried to stem the persecution of extreme Puritans ("the law is hard that taketh life or sendeth into banishment").

"Cynthia" died and Raleigh never impressed James I, who followed her, with anything but a capacity for mischief. In 1603 Raleigh was implicated in the charges of treasonable conspiracy with Roman Catholic Spain; had Raleigh been charged with exactly the opposite, an unlawful greed for Spanish possessions and a too eager inquiry into established religion, the trial and investigation, in which his friends turned against him, would have been less wide of the mark. But, however paradoxical the charges, James was determined to get rid of Raleigh and make peace with Spain. Condemned to death, reprieved, dispossessed, Raleigh made the Tower his home for thirteen long years, the lowest tide of his fortunes and perhaps the highest tide of his brooding spirit. He settled down to working at chemical and medical experiments, tracts in morals and philosophy, and an extraordinary history of mankind from Adam and Eve. Of this scientist in the Tower who concocted an elixir to cure him of a mortal fever, Prince Henry, Raleigh's friend and pupil, said "only my father could keep such a bird in the cage"; and of the history with which Raleigh hoped to impress and soften the learned James, that sovereign coldly remarked that it was much "too saucy in censuring the acts of kings." This history of all the world, the length of thirty modern novels, an unfinished exploration more remarkable than Raleigh's physical voyages of discovery to the Americas, was launched on a sea of naïveté, proclaiming as its aim to ascertain nothing less than "how Kings and Kingdoms have flourished and fallen; and for what virtue and piety God made prosperous, and for what vice and deformity he made wretched." The history contains such gems of the inquiring and critical mind as this: "Sure I am, that the discoverie of a truth formerly unknowne, doth rather convince man of ignorance, than nature of errour." *The History of the World* ends, as it begins, with great music. It anticipates John Mil-

ton's yet unborn style. It sets down the most fitting judgment of Raleigh himself: "O eloquent, just, and mighty Death! whom none could advise, thou hast persuaded; what none hath dared, thou hast done; and whom all the world hath flattered, thou only hast cast out of the world and despised; thou has drawn together all the far-stretched greatness, all the pride, cruelty, and ambition of man, and covered it all over with these two narrow words, *Hic jacet!*"

Raleigh was a prisoner on parole when James released him for the impossible expedition of 1616, the crafty terms of which allowed him to rob Guiana of its gold but admonished him to keep the peace with Spain at all costs. This expedition for a mythical gold mine was at once a death warrant for Raleigh and a shrewd opportunity to placate Spain with the execution of the Don Quixote who was sailing straight into inevitable failure. Irony was exploited to its limit when Raleigh was sacrificed to Spain not for the sins of the gold mine expedition, but on the charges of 1603 that he had conspired treason *with* Spain!

The flattering courtier of Elizabeth and the submissive victim of James was not a militant protestant either in doctrines of religion or politics. Miss Latham finds that "everything he did seems to have been tainted by a curious impermanence"—his exploration, colonization, poetry and position —"it is as though all his power was vested in himself, in his compelling individuality; he could not depute it." He could no more rid himself of the habit of thought and scepticism, than of the fever of action and the malady of ambition. He was the friend of Marlowe, Ben Jonson, Spenser, Chapman. His full repertory of friendships included alchemists, astrologers, mathematicians, historians, sea captains, explorers, cosmographers, wits, and poets. He founded a literary society which Shakespeare dubbed "The School of Night" and a Jesuit critic called "Sir Walter Rawley's School of Atheisme." It ranged among problems of theology, astronomy, geography, and chemistry, and achieved notoriety through the downfall of Raleigh and the death of Marlowe. To contemporaries who did not appreciate high-flown intellectual research, this ballad, broadcast through England, carried conviction:

> Raleigh doth time bestride,
> He sits 'twixt wind and tide,
> Yet uphill he cannot ride,
> For all his bloody pride. . . .

> He seeks taxes in the tin,
> He polls the poor to the skin,
> Yet he vows 'tis no sin,
> Lord for the pity!

T. S. Eliot remarks of Elizabethan England that "it was a period of dissolution and chaos; and in such a period any emotional attitude which seems to give a man something firm, even if it be only the attitude of 'I am myself alone,' is eagerly taken up . . . the Senecan attitude of Pride, the Montaigne attitude of Scepticism, and the Machiavellian attitude of Cynicism, arrived at a kind of fusion in the Elizabethan individualism." To the question of what it was that Raleigh believed, and why such a gifted man—one who anticipated both the metaphysical style of John Donne and the commercial style of imperialism—could not save his neck from the chopping block, there are probably more answers than are contained in King James' foreign policy. Perhaps "most loftie, insolent and passionate" Raleigh rose as high as he ever did in this one brave sentence of his history: "But for my selfe, I shall never be perswaded that GOD hath shut up all light of Learning within the lanthorne of *Aristotles* braines." In those dull days in the Tower he explored territory farther than Guiana and fortresses stronger than Cadiz.

THE LIE

> Goe soule the bodies guest
> Upon a thanklesse arrant,
> Feare not to touch the best,
> The truth shall be thy warrant:
> Goe since I needs must die,
> And give the world the lie.

"The poem professes to have been written at the point of death. Hence it has been dated 1618, the year when Ralegh died, or 1603, the year he was condemned. Neither date is correct because there is a copy in MS. . . . written about 1596. . . . In 1592 Ralegh was in disgrace over the affair of Elizabeth Throckmorton. He was in the Tower, never in the slightest danger of his life, but doubtless very wretched, regretting that he ever put trust in princes. This seems the likeliest date if his claim to the poem is accepted." *The Poems of Sir Walter Ralegh,* edited by Agnes M. C. Latham, p. 156.

Say to the Court it glowes
    And shines like rotten wood.
Say to the Church it showes
    What's good, and doth no good.
If Church and Court reply
    Then give them both the lie.

Tell potentates they live
    Acting by others' action,
Not loved unlesse they give,
    Not strong but by a faction.
If potentates reply,
    Give potentates the lie.

Tell men of high condition,
    That manage the estate,
Their purpose is ambition,
    Their practise onely hate:
And if they once reply,
    Then give them all the lie.

Tell them that brave is most,
    They beg for more by spending,
Who in their greatest cost
    Like nothing but commending.
And if they make reply,
    Then give them all the lie.

Tell zeale it wants devotion,
    Tell love it is but lust,
Tell time it meets but motion,
    Tell flesh it is but dust.
And wish them not reply
    For thou must give the lie.

Tell age it daily wasteth,
    Tell honour how it alters.

Tell beauty how she blasteth,
　Tell favour how it falters.
And as they shall reply
　Give every one the lie.

Tell wit how much it wrangles
　In tickle points of nyceness,
Tell wisedome she entangles
　Her selfe in over wiseness,
And when they doe reply
　Straight give them both the lie.

Tell phisicke of her boldnes,
　Tell skill it is pretention:
Tell charity of coldnes,
　Tell law it is contention,
And as they doe reply
　So give them still the lie.

Tell fortune of her blindnesse,
　Tell nature of decay,
Tell friendship of unkindnesse,
　Tell justice of delay.
And if they will reply
　Then give them all the lie.

Tell arts they have no soundnesse,
　But vary by esteeming,
Tell schooles they want profoundnes
　And stand so much on seeming.
If arts and schooles reply,
　Give arts and schooles the lie.

Tell faith it's fled the citie,
　Tell how the country erreth,
Tell manhood shakes off pittie
　Tell vertue least preferred.
And if they doe reply,
　Spare not to give the lie.

So when thou hast as I
Commanded thee, done blabbing,
Because to give the lie
Deserves no lesse than stabbing,
Stab at thee he that will
No stab thy soule can kill.

PREFACE TO THE HISTORY OF THE WORLD

How unfit and how unworthie a choice I have made of my selfe, to undertake a work of this mixture, mine owne reason, though exceedingly weak, hath sufficiently resolved me. For, had it been begotten then with my first dawne of day, when the light of common knowledge began to open it selfe to my younger years, and before my wound received either from fortune or time; I might yet well have doubted that the darkness of Age and Death would have covered over both it and me long before the performance. For, beginning with the Creation, I have proceeded with the *History of the World;* and lastly purposed (some few sallies excepted) to confine my discourse within this our renowned island of Great Britain. I confesse that it had better sorted with my disability, the better part of whose times are run out in other travailes, to have set together, as I could, the unjointed and scattered frame of our English affairs, than of the universal; in whom, had there been no other defect (who am all defect) than the time of the day, it were enough; the day of a tempestuous life drawn on to the very evening ere I began. But those inmost and soule-piercing wounds, which are ever aking while uncured, with the desire to satisfy those friends which I have tried by the fire of adversity; the former enforcing, the latter persuading; have caused me to make my thoughts legible, and my selfe the subject of every opinion, wise or weake.

To the world I present them, to which I am nothing indebted, neither have others that were (Fortune changing) sped much better in any age. For Prosperity and Adversity have evermore tied and untied vulgar affections. And as we see it in experience, that dogs do alwaies bark at those they know not, and that it is in their nature to accompany one another in those clamours; so it is with the inconsiderate multitude, who wanting that virtue which we call Honesty in all men, and Charity in Christian men, condemn without hearing, and wound without offence given. . . . This vanity of vul-

gar opinion it was that gave St. Augustine Argument to affirm, That he feared the praise of good men and detested that of evil; and herein no man hath given a better rule than this of Seneca, "Let us satisfie our own consciences, and not trouble ourselves with fame; be it never so ill, it is to be despised, so we deserve well!"

For my selfe, if I have in anything served my Country, and prized it before my private, the generall acceptation can yield me no other profit at this time than doth a faire sunshine day to a Seaman after shipwreck; and the contrary no other harme than an outrageous tempest after the port attained. I know that I lost the love of many for my fidelity towardes Her, whom I must still honor in the dust though further than the defence of Her excellent person. I never persecuted any man. Of those that did it, and by what device they did it, He that is the Supreme Judge of all the world hath taken the account. . . .

To me it belongs in the first part of this preface, following the common and approved custome of those who have left the memories of time past to after ages, to give as neare as I can the same right to History which they have done. Yet seeing that therein I should but borrow other men's wordes, I will not trouble the reader with the repetition. True it is that among many other benefits for which it hath been honoured, in this one it triumpheth over all humane knowledge, that it hath given us life in our understanding, since the world it selfe had life and beginning even too: yea, it hath triumphed over time, which besides it nothing but eternity hath triumphed over, for it hath carried our knowledge over the vast and devouring space of so many thousands of yeares, and given so fair and piercing eyes to our minde, that we plainely behold living now as we had lived then, that great World, "Magni Dei sapiens opus," the wise work (saith Hermes) of a great God, as it was then, when but new to it selfe. By it, I say, it is that we live in the very time when it was created; we behold how it is governed; how it was covered with waters, and againe repeopled. How Kings and Kingdoms have flourished and fallen; and for what virtue and piety God made prosperous, and for what vice and deformity he made wretched, both the one and the other. And it is not the least debt which we owe unto History, that it hath made us acquainted with our dead Ancestors, and out of the depth and darkenesse of the earth delivered us their memory and fame. In a word we may gather out of History a policy no less wise than eternall, by the comparison and application of other men's forepassed miseries, with our owne like errors and ill-deservings.

But it is neither of Examples, the most lively instructions, nor the words of the wisest men, nor the terror of future torments, that hath yet so wrought in our blind and stupefied mindes, as to make us remember that the infinite eye and wisdome of God doth pierce through all our pretences; as to make us remember that the justice of God doth require none other accuser than our owne consciences, which neither the false beauty of our apparent actions, nor all the formality which (to pacifie the mindes of men) we put on, can in any or the least kind cover from his knowledge. And so much did that Heathen wisdome confesse, no way as yet qualified by the knowledge of a true God. "If any" (saith Euripides) "having in his life committed wickednesse, think he can hide it from the everlasting gods, he thinks not well."

To repeat God's judgments in particular upon those of all degrees which have played with his mercies would require a volume apart, for the Sea of examples hath no bottom. The marks, set on private men, are with their bodies cast into the earth, and their fortunes written onely in the memories of those that lived with them, so as they who succeed, and have not seen the fall of others, do not fear their owne faults. God's judgments upon the great and greatest have been left to posterity, first by those happy lands which the Holy Ghost hath guided; and secondly by their virtue, who have gathered the acts and ends of men, mighty and remarkable in the world. . . .

Seeing the first bookes of the following story have undertaken the discourse of the first Kings and Kingdomes, and that it is impossible for the short life of a Preface to travaile after and over-take farr-off Antiquity, and to judge of it; I will for the present examine what profit hath been gathered by our owne Kings and their Neighbour Princes, who having beheld both in divine and humane letters the successe of infidelity, injustice, and cruelty, have (notwithstanding) planted after the same pattern. . . .

Now for Henry VIII.: If all the pictures and patterns of a mercilesse prince were lost in the world, they might all again be painted to the life out of the story of this king. For how many servants did he advance in haste (but for what virtue no man could suspect) and with the change of his fancy ruined again, no man knowing for what offence? To how many others of more desert gave he abundant flowers, from whence to gather honey, and in the end of harvest burnt them in the hive? How many wives did he cut off and caste off as his fancy and affection changed? How many Princes of the blood (whereof some of them for age could hardly crawl towards the block), with a world of others of all degrees (of whome our common chronicles have kept the account), did he execute? Yea, on his very

death-bed, when he was at the point to have given his account to God for the abundance of blood already spilt, he imprisoned the Duke of Norfolk the father, and executed the Earl of Surrey the sonne; the one whose deservings he knew not how to value, having never omitted anything that concerned his own honour and the King's service, the other never having committed anything worthie of his least displeasure; the one exceeding valiant and advised, the other no lesse valiant than learned, and of excellent hope.

But besides the sorrows which he heaped upon the fatherlesse and widowes at home, and besides the vain enterprises abroad, wherein it is thought that he consumed more treasure than all our victorious kings did in their severall conquests; what causeless and cruel warres did he make upon his owne nephew King James the fift? What Lawes and Wills did he devise, to establish this Kingdome in his owne issues, using his sharpest weapons to cut off and cut down those branches which sprang from the same roote that him selfe did. And in the end (notwithstanding these his so many irreligious provisions) it pleased God to take away all his owne, without increase, though for themselves in their severall kindes, all Princes of eminent virtue. For these Wordes of Samuel to Agag, King of the Amalekites, have been verified upon many others: "As thy sword hath made other women childlesse; so shall thy mother be childlesse among other women. . . ."

Oh, by what plots, by what forswearings, betrayings, oppressions, imprisonments, tortures, poysonings, and under what reasons of state and politic subtlety have these forenamed Kings, both strangers and of our owne Nation, pulled the vengeance of God upon themselves, upon theirs and upon their prudent ministers! and in the end have brought those things to pass for their enemies, and seen an effect so directly contrarie to all their owne counsells ánd cruelties, as the one could never have hoped for themselves, and the other never have succeeded if no such opposition had ever been made. God hath said it and performed it ever, "I will destroy the wisdome of the wise."

But what of all this? and to what end do we lay before the eyes of the living the fall and fortunes of the dead, seeing the world is the same that it hath bin, and the children of the present time will still obey their parents? It is in the present time that all the wits of the world are exercised. To hold the times we have, we hold all things lawful, and either we hope to hold them forever, or at least we hope that there is nothing after them to be hoped for. . . .

I know that it will be said by many, that I might have beene more pleas-

ing to the Reader if I had written the story of mine own times, having been permitted to draw water as near the Well-head as another. To this I answered that whosoever in writing a Modern History shall follow truth too near the heeles, it may haply strike out his teeth. There is no Mistresse or Guide that hath lead her followers and servants into greater miseries. He that goes after her too far off, loseth her sight, and loseth him selfe; and he that walks after her at middle distance, I know not whether I should call that kind of course temper or baseness. It is true that I never travailed after men's opinions, when I might have made the best use of them: and I have now too few days remaining to imitate those that either out of extreme ambition, or extreme cowardice, or both, do yet (when death hath them on his shoulders) flatter the world betweene the bed and the grave. . . .

But these discourses are idle. I know that as the charitable will judge charitably, so against those, *qui gloriantur in malitia,* my present adversity hath disarmed me. I am on the ground already, and therefore have not far to fall, and for rising again, as in the naturall privation there is no recession to habit, so it is seldom seen in the privation politic.

I do therefore forbear to style my Readers Gentle, Courteous, and Friendly, thereby to beg their good opinions, or to promise a second and third volume (which I also intend) if the first receive grace and good acceptance. For that which is already done may be thought enough, and too much, and it is certaine, let us claw the Reader with never so many courteous phrases, yet shall we ever more be thought fooles that write foolishly. For conclusion, all the hope I have lies in this, that I have already found more ungentle and uncourteous Readers of my love towards them, and well deserving of them, than ever I shall do againe. For had it been otherwise, I should hardly have had this leisure to have made my selfe a foole in print.

THE CONCLUSION

For the rest, if we seeke a reason of the succession and continuance of this boundlesse ambition in mortall men, we may add to that which has been already said that the Kings and Princes of the World have alwayes laid before them the actions but not the ends of those great Ones which preceded them. They are always transported with the glorie of the one, but they never mind the miserie of the other, till they find the experience in themselves. They neglect the advice of God while they enjoy life, or hope it; but they

follow the counsell of Death upon his first approach. It is he that puts into man all the wisdom of the world, without speaking a word; which God with all the works of his Law promises or threats doth not infuse. Death that hateth and destroyeth man is beleeved. God which hath made him and loves him is always deferred. "I have considered," saith Solomon, "all the workes that are under the Sunne, and behold all is vanity and vexation of spirit": but who believes it, till Death tells it us? It was death which, opening the conscience of Charles the fift, made him enjoin his sonne Philip to restore Navarre; and King Francis the first of France, to command that justice should be done upon the Murderers of the Protestants in Merindol and Cabrieres which till then he neglected. It is therefore Death alone that can make man suddenly to know himselfe. He tells the proud and insolent that they are but Abjects, and humbles them at the instant, makes them cry, complain, and repent, yea, even to hate their forepassed happinesse. He takes the account of the rich, and proves him a beggar, a naked beggar which hath interest in nothing but in the gravell that fills his mouth. He holds a Glass before the eyes of the most beautiful, and makes them see therein their own deformitie and rottenness; and they acknowledge it.

O eloquent, just, and mightie Death! whom none could advise, thou hast perswaded; what none hath dared, thou hast done; and whom all the world hath flattered, thou only hast cast out of the world and despised. Thou hast drawne together all the farre-stretched greatnesse, all the pride, crueltie, and ambition of man, and covered it all over with these two narrow words, "Hic jacet."

THE PASSIONATE MAN'S PILGRIMAGE

> Give me my Scallop shell of quiet,
> My staffe of Faith to walke upon,
> My scrip of Joy, immortal diet,
> My bottle of salvation:
> My Gowne of Glory, hopes true gage,
> And thus Ile take my pilgrimage.
>
> Blood must be my bodies balmer,
> No other balme will there be given

Whilst my soule like a white Palmer
Travels to the land of heaven,
Over the silver mountaines,
Where sprung the Nectar fountaines:
And there Ile kisse
The Bowle of blisse,
And drink my eternall fill
On every milken hill.
My soule will be a drie before,
But after it, wi'l nere thirst more.

And by the happie blissful way
More peacefull Pilgrims I shall see,
That have shooke off their gownes of clay,
And goe appareld fresh like mee.
Ile bring them first
To slake their thirst,
And then to tast those Nectar suckets
At the cleare wells
Where sweetness dwells,
Drawne up by Saints in Christall buckets.

And when our bottles and all we,
Are fild with immortalitie:
Then the holy paths weele travell
Strewde with Rubies thicke as gravell,
Seelings of Diamonds, Saphire floores,
High walles of Corall and Pearle Bowres.

From thence to heavens Bribeles hall
Where no corrupted voyces brall,
No Conscience molten into gold,
No forg'd accusers bought and sold,
Nor cause deferd, nor vaine spent Journey,
For there Christ is the Kings Atturney:
Who pleades for all without degrees,
And he hath Angells, but no fees.

When the grand twelve million Jury,
Of our sinnes with sinfull fury,
Gainst our soules blacke verdicts give,
Christ pleades his death, and then we live,
Be thou my speaker taintles pleader,
Unblotted Lawyer, true proceeder,
Thou movest salvation even for almes:
Not with a bribed Lawyers palmes.

And this is my eternall plea,
To him that made Heaven, Earth and Sea,
Seeing my flesh must die so soone,
And want a head to dine next noone,
Just at the stroke when my vaines start and spred
Set on my soule an everlasting head.
Then am I readie like a palmer fit,
To tread those blest paths which before I writ.

A LETTER TO HIS WIFE

You shall nowe receive (my dear Wife) my last Wordes in these my last lines. My love I send you that you may keep it when I am Dead, and my Counsell, that you may remember it when I am no more. I would not by my will present you with sorrows, dear Bess, let them go into the Grave with me and be buried in the dust: And seeing it is not the Will of God that ever I shall see you more in this Life, bear it patiently and with a heart like thy selfe.

First I send you all the thanks which my heart can conceive, or my Wordes can express, for your manie travels and care taken for me; which though they have not taken effect as you wished, yet my Debt to you is not the less; but pay it I never shall in this World.

Secondly, I beseeche you for the love you bear me Living, do not hide your selfe many Days after my Death, but by your Travels seek to help your miserable Fortunes and the Right of your poor Child. Thy Mournings cannot avayl me, I am but Dust.

Thirdly, you shall understand that my Land was conveyed (bona fide) to my Child; the writings were drawn at Midsummer was Twelve months; my

honest Cousin Brett can testifie so much and Dalberie too can remember somewhat therein: And I trust my Blood will quench their Malice that have thus cruelly murthered me; and that they will not seek also to kill thee and thine with extream Poverty. To what Friend to direct thee I knowe not, for all mine have left me in the true Time of Tryall; And I plainely perceive that my Death was determined from the first Day; most sorry I am, God knows, that being thus surprized with Death, I can leave you in no better Estate. God is my Witnesse I meant you all my office of wines, or all that I could have purchased by selling it; half my Stuff and all my Jewels, but some one for the Boy; but God hath prevented all my resolutions, even that Great God that ruleth all in all; But if you can live free from Want, care for no more; the rest is but vanity, love God and begin betimes to repose your selfe on him; and therein shall you find true and lasting riches, and endless Comfort; For the rest, when you have travelled and wearied your Thoughts over all sorts of worldly Cogitation, you shall but sit down by sorrow in the end. Teach your Son also to love and fear God, whilst he is yet young, that the feare of God may grow up with him: and then God will be a Husband to you, and a Father to him; a Husband and Father that cannot be taken from you.

Bayly oweth me 200*l*. and Adrian Gilbert 600*l*. In Jersey also I have much money owing me; besides the arrearages of the Wines will pay my debts; and howsoever you do, for my Soul's sake pay all poor Men. When I am gone no doubt you shall be sought to by many; for the world thinks that I was very rich. But take heed of the pretences of men and of theire affections; for they last not but in honest and worthie men; and no greater Misery can befall you in this Life than to become a Prey and afterwards to be despised. I speake not this, God knows, to disswade you from Marriage; for it will be best for you, both in respect of this World and of God. As for me I am no more yours, nor you mine; Death has cut us asunder; and God hath divyded me from the World, and you from me.

Remember your poore Child, for his Father's sake; who chose you and loved you in the happiest time. Get those Letters, if it be possible, which I writt to the Lords, wherein I sued for my Life. God is my witness, it was for you and yours that I desired Lyfe; but it is true that I disdain my selfe for begging it, for know it, dear Wife, that you Son is the son of a true man, and one who in his own respect despiseth Death, and all his misshapen and ugly Formes. I cannot write much: God he knoweth how hardly I steal this Time, while others sleep; and it is also high time that I should separate

my Thoughts from the world. Beg my dead Bodye which living was denied thee; and either lay it at Shirburne (if the Land continue) or in Exeter church by my Father and Mother; I can· say no more, Time and Death call me away.

The Everlasting, Powerful, Infinite and Omnipotent God; that Almighty God who is Goodness it selfe; the true Life and true Light, keep thee and thine, have Mercy on me and teach me to forgive my Persecutors and Accusers, and send us to meet in his glorious Kingdom. My dear Wife, farewell, bless my poor Boy, pray for me and let my good God hold you both in His Arms.

Written with the dying hand of sometime your Husband, but now alas overthrowne.

Yours that was but now not my owne,

WALTER RALEIGH.

EVEN SUCH IS TIME

Even such· is Time, which takes in trust
Our Youth, our Joys, and all we have,
And payes us but with earth and dust,
Who in the· darke and silent grave,
When we have wandred all our wayes,
Shuts up the story of our dayes:
And from which Earth and Grave and Dust
The Lord shall raise me up I trust.

"Manuscripts and printed books are alike unanimous in assigning to Ralegh this famous verse, supposed to have been written the night before he died. But though both traditions, that it is Ralegh's and that he wrote it in 1618, are of the strongest, fresh evidence has recently come to light pointing to a different date and a different occasion. . . . If it is true that Ralegh wrote the lines in his Bible in 1618, the first three words and the concluding couplet are all that had not been written before in a lighter mood. But the knowledge that he was recasting old work makes the date if anything more probable, for the poem becomes less of a psychological curiosity, and it is characteristic of his sombre temper that even his love songs could at will supply an epitaph." *The Poems of Sir Walter Ralegh,* edited by Agnes M. C. Latham, p. 165 ff.

THE AXE'S EDGE:

CHARLES I TO THE PRINCE OF WALES

~~~~~~

He nothing common did or mean
Upon that memorable scene;
But with his keener eye
The axe's edge did try:
Nor called the gods with vulgar spite
To vindicate his helpless right,
But bowed his comely head
Down as upon a bed.
ANDREW MARVELL, *A Horatian Ode
upon Cromwell*

THE equestrian statue of Charles I which stands in Charing Cross had in its time been sold by the Commonwealth to a brazier who worked a miracle. This legendary brazier sold its metal flesh for small mementos to the pious, yet the statue was still intact at the Restoration of Charles II. We are not called upon to explain this brazier's magical or commercial secret; nor to decide whether the court which condemned Charles had the legal authority to do so; nor to decide for what principle or piety Charles died with such memorable dignity. In any case, Charles stands overwhelmed in the shadow of Cromwell, a reserved and rather intellectual monarch who in his years of captivity among the Scots and the English read Launcelot Andrews' sermons, Hooker's *Ecclesiastical Polity,* Spenser's *Faerie Queen* and the plays of Shakespeare. He is a "royal actor" on a "tragic scaffold" even to the puritan Andrew Marvell who wrote the best remembered lines about him. Charles left a royal document of touching simplicity and grace for the edification of the Prince of Wales who was to be restored as Charles II. At his trial Charles Stuart, "Tyrant, Traitor, Murderer, and publick Enemy to the good People of this Nation," spoke well and, at the end, pathetically:

King: Will you hear me a word, Sir?
President: Sir, you are not to be heard after Sentence.
King: No, Sir?
President: No, Sir, by your favor. Guard, withdraw your Prisoner.
King: I may speak after Sentence, by your favor, Sir, I may speak after

Sentence, ever. By your favor, hold: the Sentence, Sir—I say Sir, I do—I am not suffer'd to speak, expect what Justice other People will have.

There is a moment in any revolution when the cry "expect what Justice other People will have" has an ominous sound. But, except for the Jacobites who still lay wreaths in Charing Cross, time has tamed the grievance of Charles Stuart and reduced it to that mild nostalgia in the lines from Shakespeare's *Richard II:*

> For God's sake, let us sit upon the ground
> And tell sad stories of the death of kings.

A word portrait of Charles by a contemporary [1] may be quoted for our present purpose: "He was no great scholar, his learning consisted more in what he had seen than what he had studied; his judgment was good and better than that of most of his Ministers. The misfortune was that he seldom depended upon it, unless in matters of his own religion, wherein he was always very stiff. His arguing was beyond measure civil and patient. He would seldom or never contradict any man angrily, but would always say, 'By your favour, I think otherwise'; or, 'I am not of your opinion.' He would discourage any bold address to him, and did not love strangers; and, whilst he was upon the throne, he would permit none to enter abruptly with him into business. He was wiser than most of his Council, yet so unhappy as seldom to follow his own judgment. He would always, whilst in his Court, be addressed to by proper Ministers, and still kept up the dignity of his Court, limiting all persons to places suitable for their employment, and quality; and would there only hear them, unless he called for them in particular. Besides the ladies and women who attended the King, he permitted no Minister to have his wife at Court. He spake but slowly, and would stammer a little when he began to speak eagerly. He seldom or never made his own dispatches till his latter days, but would still mend or alter them; and to that purpose he found it better to be a cobbler than a shoemaker. As to his religion, he was very positive in it, and would bear no arguments against it."

---

[1] *Memoirs and Reflections upon the Reigns and Governments of King Charles the First and King Charles the Second,* by Sir Richard Bulstrode, a soldier, diplomat, author, and lesser Pepys, who lived 101 years from 1610 to 1711. For the quotation I am indebted to J. G. Muddiman's *Trial of King Charles the First,* London & Edinburgh, William Hodge & Co. Ltd.

CHARLES I TO THE PRINCE OF WALES

SON: If these papers, with some others, wherein I have set down the private reflections of my conscience, and my most impartial thoughts, touching the chief passages which have been most remarkable, or disputed in my late troubles, come to your hands, to whom they are chiefly designed, they may be so far useful to you, as to state your judgement aright in what hath passed; whereof a pious use is the best can be made; and they may also give you some directions how to remedy the present distempers, and prevent (if God will) the like for time to come.

It is some kind of deceiving and lessening the injury of my long restraint, when I find my leisure and solitude have produced something worthy of myself, and useful to you; that neither you, nor any other, may hereafter measure my cause by the success, nor my judgement of things by my misfortunes, which I count the greater by far, because they have so far lighted upon you and some others whom I have most cause to love as well as myself, and of whose unmerited sufferings I have a greater sense than of my own.

But this advantage of wisdom you have done above most princes; that you have begun, and now spent some years of discretion in the experience of troubles, and exercise of patience, wherein piety and all virtues, both moral and political, are commonly better planted to a thriving, as trees set in winter, than in warmth and serenity of times, or amidst those delights which usually attend princes' courts in times of peace and plenty, which are prone either to root up all plants of true virtue and honour, or to be contented only with some leaves and withering formalities of them without any real fruits, such as tend to the public good, for which princes should always remember they are born, and by Providence designed.

The evidence of which different education the Holy Writ affords us in the contemplation of David and Rehoboam, the one prepared by many afflictions for a flourishing kingdom, the other softened by the unparalleled prosperity of Solomon's court; and so corrupted to the great diminution, both for peace, honour, and kingdom, by those flatteries, which are as inseparable from prosperous princes as flies are from fruit in summer, whom adversity, like cold weather, drives away.

I had rather you should be Charles *le bon,* than *le grand,* good, than great; I hope God hath designed you to be both; having so early put you into that exercise of His grace and gifts bestowed upon you, which may best weed out all vicious inclinations, and dispose you to those princely en-

dowments and employments, which will most gain the love, and intend the welfare of those over whom God shall place you.

With God, I would have you begin and end, who is King of Kings, the sovereign disposer of the kingdoms of the world, who pulleth down one and setteth up another.

The best government and highest sovereignty you can attain to is to be subject to Him, that the sceptre of His word and spirit may rule in your heart.

The true glory of princes consists in advancing God's glory, in the maintenance of true religion and the Church's good; also in the dispensation of civil power, with justice and honour to the public peace.

Piety will make you prosperous, at least it will keep you from becoming miserable; nor is he much a loser that loseth all, yet saveth his own soul at last.

To which centre of true happiness, God (I trust) hath and will graciously direct all these black lines of affliction which He hath been pleased to draw on me, and by which He hath (I hope) drawn me nearer to Himself. You have already tasted of that cup whereof I have liberally drunk; which I look upon as God's physic, having that in healthfulness which it wants in pleasure.

Above all, I would have you, as I hope you are already, well grounded and settled in your religion, the best profession of which I have ever esteemed that of the Church of England, in which you have been educated; yet I would have your own judgement and reason now sealed to that sacred bond which education hath written, that it may be judiciously your own religion, and not other men's custom or tradition which you profess.

In this I charge you to persevere, as coming nearest to God's word for doctrine, and to the primitive examples for government, with some little amendment which I have otherwhere expressed, and often offered, though in vain. Your fixation in matters of religion will not be more necessary for your soul's than your kingdom's peace, when God shall bring you to them.

For I have observed, that the devil of rebellion doth commonly turn himself into an angel of reformation; and the old serpent can pretend new lights, when some men's consciences accuse them for sedition and faction, they stop its mouth with the name and noise of religion; when piety pleads for peace and patience, they cry out zeal.

So that, unless in this point you be well settled, you shall never want temptations to destroy you and yours, under pretension of reforming matters

of religion; for that seems even to the worst of men, as the best and most auspicious beginning of their worst designs.

Where, besides the novelty which is taken enough with the vulgar, every one hath an affectation, by seeming forward to an outward reformation of religion, to be thought zealous; hoping to cover those irreligious deformities whereto they are conscious, by a severity of censuring other men's opinions and actions.

Take heed of abetting any factions, or applying to any public discriminations in matters of religion, contrary to what is in your judgement and the churches well settled; your partial adhering as head to any one side gains you not so great advantage in some men's hearts (who are prone to be of their King's religion) as it loseth you in others; who think themselves and their profession first despised, then persecuted by you; take such a course as may either with calmness and charity quite remove the seeming differences and offences by impartiality, or so order affairs in point of power that you shall not need to fear or flatter any faction.

For, if ever you stand in need of them, or must stand to their courtesy, you are undone. The serpent will devour the dove; you may never expect less of loyalty, justice, or humanity than from those who engage in religious rebellions; their interest is always made God's, under the colours of piety, ambitious policies march, not only with greatest security, but applause as to the populacy; you may hear from them Jacob's voice, but you shall feel they have Esau's hands.

Nothing seemed less considerable than the Presbyterian faction in England for many years, so compliant they were to public order; nor, indeed, was their party great either in Church or State as to men's judgements; but as soon as discontents drove men into sidings, as ill humours fall to the disaffected part, which causes inflammations, so did all at first who affected any novelties adhere to that side, as the most remarkable and specious note of difference (then) in point of religion.

All the lesser factions at first were officious servants to Presbytery, their great master, till time and military success, discovering to each their peculiar advantages invited them to part stakes; and leaving the joint stock of uniform religion, they pretended each to drive for their party the trade of profits and preferments to the breaking and undoing not only of the Church and State, but even of Presbytery itself, which seemed and hoped at first to have engrossed all.

Let nothing seem little or despicable to you in matters which concern religion and the Church's peace, so as to neglect a speedy reforming and effectually suppressing errors and schisms; what seem at first but as a hand-breadth, by seditious spirits, as by strong winds, are soon made a cover and darken the whole heaven.

When you have done justice to God, your own soul and His Church in the profession and preservation of truth and unity in religion, the next main hinge on which your prosperity will depend and move, is that of civil justice, wherein the settled laws of these kingdoms, to which you are rightly heir, are the most excellent rules you can govern by, which by an admirable temperament give very much to subjects industry, liberty, and happiness; and yet reserve enough to the majesty and prerogative of any king who owns his people as subjects, not as slaves, whose subjection as it preserves their property, peace, and safety, so it will never diminish your rights, nor their ingenious liberties; which consist in the enjoyment of the fruits of their industry and the benefit of those laws to which themselves have consented.

Never charge your head with such a crown as shall, by its heaviness, oppress the whole body, the weakness of whose parts cannot return anything of strength, honour, or safety to the head, but a necessary debilitation and ruin.

Your prerogative is best showed and exercised in remitting rather than exacting the rigour of the laws; there being nothing worse than legal tyranny.

In these two points of preservation of established religion and laws, I may (without vanity) turn the reproach of my sufferings, as to the world's censure, into the honour of a kind of martyrdom, as to the testimony of my own conscience; the troubles of my kingdoms, having nothing else to object against me but this, that I prefer religion and laws established before those alterations they propounded.

And so indeed I do, and ever shall, till I am convinced by better arguments than what hitherto have been chiefly used towards me—tumults, armies, and prisons.

I cannot yet learn that lesson, nor I hope ever will you, that it is safe for a King to gratify any faction with the perturbation of the laws, in which is wrapt up the public interest and the good of the community.

How God will deal with me, as to the removal of these pressures and indignities, which His justice, by the very unjust hands of some of my

subjects, hath been pleased to lay upon me I cannot tell; nor am I much solicitous what wrong I suffer from men, while I retain in my soul what I believe is right before God.

I have offered all for reformation and safety that in reason, honour, and conscience I can, reserving only what I cannot consent unto without an irreparable injury to my own soul, the Church, and my people, and you also as the next and undoubted heir of my kingdoms.

To which, if the Divine Providence, to whom no difficulties are insuperable, shall in His due time, after my decease, bring you as I hope He will, my counsel and charge to you is, that you seriously consider the former real or objected miscarriages which might occasion my troubles, that you may avoid them.

Never repose so much upon any man's single counsel, fidelity, and discretion, in managing affairs of the first magnitude (that is, matters of religion and justice), as to create in yourself or others a diffidence of your own judgement, which is likely to be always more constant and impartial to the interests of your crown and kingdom than any man's.

Next beware of exasperating any factions by the crossness and asperity of some men's passions, humours, or private opinions employed by you, grounded only upon the differences in lesser matters, which are but the skirts and suburbs of religion.

Wherein a charitable connivance and Christian toleration often dissipates their strength, whom rougher opposition fortifies, and puts the despised and oppressed party into such combinations as may most enable them to get a full revenge on those that count their persecutors, who are commonly assisted by that vulgar commiseration which attends all that are said to suffer under the notion of religion.

Provided the differences amount not to an insolent opposition of laws and government, or religion established as to the essentials of them; such motions and mimings are intolerable.

Always keep up solid piety, and those fundamental truths which mend both hearts and lives of men with impartial favour and justice.

Take heed that outward circumstances and formalities of religion devour not at all, or the best encouragements of learning, industry, and piety; but with an equal eye and impartial hand distribute favours and rewards to all men, as you find them for their real goodness both in abilities and fidelity worthy and capable of them.

This will be sure to gain you the hearts of the best and the most, too;

who, though they be not good themselves, yet are glad to see the severer ways of virtue at any time sweetened by temporal rewards.

I have, you see, conflicted with different and opposite factions (for so I must needs call and count all those that act not in any conformity to the laws established in Church and State): no sooner have·they by force subdued what they counted their common enemy (that is all those that adhered to the laws and to me), and are secured from that fear, but they are divided to so high a rivalry as sets them more at defiance against each other than against their antagonist.

Time will dissipate all factions, when once the rough hours of private men's covetous and ambitious designs shall discover themselves; which were at first wrapt up and hidden under the soft and smooth pretensions of religion, reformation, and liberty: as the wolf is not cruel, so he will be more justly hated, when he shall appear no better than a wolf under sheep's clothing.

But as for the seduced train of the vulgar, who, in their simplicity, follow those disguises, my charge and counsel to you is, that as you need no palliations for any designs (as other men), so you study really to exceed (in true and constant demonstrations of goodness, piety, and virtue towards the people) even all those men, that make the greatest noise and ostentation of religion; so you shall neither fear any detection (as they do, who have but the face and mask of goodness), nor shall you frustrate the just expectations of your people, who cannot in reason promise themselves so much good from any subject's novelties as from the virtuous constancy of their King.

When these mountains of congealed factions shall, by the sunshine of God's mercy and the splendour of your virtues, be thawed and dissipated, and the abused vulgar shall have learned that none are greater oppressors of their estates, liberties, and consciences than those men, that entitle themselves the patrons and vindicators of them, only to usurp power over them; let, then, no passion betray you to any study of revenge upon those whose own sin and folly will sufficiently punish them in due time. But as soon as the forked arrow of factious emulations is drawn out, use all princely arts and clemency to heal the wounds that the smart of the cure may not equal the anguish of the hurt.

I have offered acts of indemnity and oblivion, to so great a latitude, as may include all, that can but suspect themselves to be any way obnoxious to the laws, and which might serve to exclude all future jealousies and insecurities.

I would have you always propense to the same way, whenever it shall be

desired and accepted, let it be granted, not only as an act of state policy and necessity, but of Christian charity and choice.

It is all I have now left me, a power to forgive those that have deprived me of all; and I thank God I have a heart to do it, and joy as much in this grace, which God hath given me, as in all my former enjoyments; for this is a greater argument of God's love to me than any prosperity can be. Be confident (as I am) that the most of all sides, who have done amiss, have done so, not out of malice, but misinformation, or misapprehension of things.

None will be more loyal and faithful to me and you, than those subjects who, sensible of their errors and our injuries, will feel, in their own souls, most vehement motives to repentance, and earnest desire to make some reparations for their former defects.

As your quality sets you beyond any duel with any subject, so the nobleness of your mind must raise you above the meditating any revenge, or executing your anger upon the many.

The more conscious you shall be to your own merits upon your people, the more prone you will be to expect all love and loyalty from them, and to inflict no punishment upon them for former miscarriages; and you will have more inward complacency in pardoning one, than in punishing a thousand.

This I write to you, not despairing of God's mercy, and my subjects' affections towards you, both which I hope you will study to deserve; yet we cannot merit of God but by His own mercy.

If God shall see fit to restore me, and you after me, to those enjoyments which the laws have assigned to us, and no subjects, without an high degree of guilt and sin can divest us of; then may I have better opportunity when I shall be so happy to see you in peace, to let you more fully understand the things that belong to God's glory, your own honour, and the kingdom's peace.

But if you never see my face again, and God will have me buried in such a barbarous imprisonment and obscurity (which the perfecting some men's designs requires) wherein few hearts that love me are permitted to exchange a word or a look with me, I do require and entreat you as your father and your King, that you never suffer your heart to receive the least check against or disaffection from the true religion established in the Church of England.

I tell you I have tried it, and, after much search and many disputes, hath

concluded it to be the best in the world, not only in the community, as Christian, but also in the special notion, as reformed, keeping the middle way between the pomp of superstitious tyranny, and the meanness of fantastic anarchy.

Not but that (the draught being excellent as to the main, both for doctrine and government, in the Church of England) some lines, as in very good figures, may haply need some sweetening, or polishing, which might here have easily been done by a safe and gentle hand, if some men's precipitancy had not violently demanded such rude alterations, as would have quite destroyed all the beauty and proportions of the world.

The scandal of the late troubles which some may object and urge to you against the Protestant religion established in England, is easily answered to them, or your own thoughts in this, that scarce any one who hath been a beginner, or an active persecutor of this late war against the Church, the laws, and me, either was or is a true lover, embracer, or practiser of the Protestant religion established in England, which neither gives such rules, nor ever before set such examples.

'Tis true, some heretofore had the boldness to present threatening petitions to their princes and Parliaments, which others of the same faction (but of worse spirits) have now put in execution; but let not counterfeit and disorderly zeal abate your value and esteem of true piety; both of them are to be known by their fruits; the sweetness of the vine and the fig-tree is not to be despised, though the brambles and thorns should pretend to bear figs and grapes, thereby to rule over the trees.

Nor would I have you to entertain any aversion or dislike of Parliaments, which, in their right constitution with freedom and honour, will never hinder or diminish your greatness, but will rather be an interchanging of love, loyalty, and confidence, between a prince and his people.

Nor would the events of this black Parliament have been other than such (however much biased by factions in the elections) if it had been preserved from the insolencies of popular dictates, and tumultuary impressions; the sad effects of which will no doubt make all Parliaments after this more cautious to preserve that freedom and honour which belongs to such assemblies (when once they have fully shaken off this yoke of vulgar encroachment), since the public interest consists in the mutual and common good both of prince and people.

Nothing can be more happy for all than, in fair, grave, and honourable

ways, to contribute their counsels in common, enacting all things by public consent, without tyranny or tumults. We must not starve ourselves, because some have surfeited of wholesome food.

And if neither I nor you be ever restored to our right, but God, in His severest justice, will punish my subjects with continuance in their sin, and suffer them to be deluded with the prosperity of their wickedness, I hope God will give me and you that grace which will teach and enable us to want, as well as to wear a crown, which is not worth taking up, or enjoying upon sordid, dishonourable, and irreligious terms.

Keep you to true principles of piety, virtue, and honour; you shall never want a kingdom.

A principal point of your honour will consist in your deferring all respect, love, and protection to your mother, my wife, who hath many ways deserved well of me, and chiefly in this, that having been a means to bless me with so many hopeful children (all which, with their mother, I recommend to your love and care), she hath been content with incomparable magnanimity and patience to suffer both for and with me and you.

My prayer to God Almighty is (whatever becomes of me, who am, I thank God, wrapt up and fortified in my own innocency, and His grace) that He would be pleased to make you an anchor, or harbour rather, to these tossed and weather-beaten kingdoms; a repairer, by your wisdom, justice, piety, valour, of what the folly and wickedness of some men have so far ruined, as to leave nothing entire in Church or State, to the Crown, the nobility, the clergy, and the Commons, either as to laws, liberties, estates, order, honour, conscience, or lives.

When they have destroyed me (for I know not how far God may permit the malice and cruelty of my enemies to proceed, and such apprehensions some men's words and actions have already given me) as I doubt not my blood will cry aloud for vengeance to Heaven; so I beseech God not to pour out His wrath upon the generality of the people who have either deserted me, or engaged me, through the artifice and hypocrisy of their leaders, whose inward horror will be their first tormentor, nor will they escape exemplary judgements.

For those that loved me, I pray God they may have no miss of me when I am gone; so much I wish and hope that all good subjects may be satisfied with the blessings of your presence and virtues.

For those that repent of any defects in their duty toward me, as I freely forgive them in the word of a Christian King, so I believe you will find them

214

truly zealous to repay, with interest, that loyalty and love to you which was due to me.

In sum, what good I intended do you perform, when God shall give you power: much good I have offered, more I proposed to Church and State, if times had been capable of it.

The deception will soon vanish, and the vizards will fall off apace; this mark of religion on the face of rebellion (for so it now plainly appears since my restraint and cruel usage, that they fought not for me, as was pretended) will not long serve to hide some men's deformities.

Happy times, I hope, attend you, wherein your subjects, by their miseries, will have learned that religion to their God, and loyalty to their King, cannot be parted without both their sin and infelicity.

I pray God bless you and establish your kingdoms in righteousness, your soul in true religion, and your honour in the love of God and your people.

And if God will have disloyalty perfected by my destruction, let my memory ever, with my name, live in you; as of your father, that loves you, and once a King of three flourishing kingdoms; whom God thought fit to honour, not only with the sceptre and government of them, but also with the suffering many indignities and an untimely death for them; while I studied to preserve the rights of the Church, the power of the laws, the honour of my crown, the privilege of Parliaments, the liberties of my people and my own conscience, which I thank God, is dearer to me than a thousand kingdoms.

I know God can—I hope He will—restore me to my rights. I cannot despair, either of His mercy, or my people's love and pity.

At worst, I trust I shall but go before you to a better kingdom, which God hath prepared for me, and me for it, through my Saviour Jesus Christ, to whose mercy I commend you, and all mine.

Farewell, till we meet, if not on earth, yet in Heaven.

PRISON AS A GENTLEMAN'S ART:

Richard Lovelace

TO ALTHEA FROM PRISON   THE VINTAGE TO THE DUNGEON

A MOCK-SONG   TO LUCASTA FROM PRISON

LOVELACE, "the handsomest man of his times," an Adonis of royalism, wrote his best political poems under titles addressed to ladies. Whether in love or in uniform, in verse or in jail, he remembered he was a Gentleman. He maintained this decorum in politics and rhyme throughout the Civil War and until he died two years before the Restoration. He polished up that cavalier paradox that stonewalls do not a prison make nor iron bars a cage. When the rupture between Charles I and Parliament took place and Lovelace petitioned Commons for the royalists in Kent in 1642, he took up his first residence within stonewalls in the Gatehouse, writing *To Althea from Prison* and *The Vintage to the Dungeon*. Notwithstanding Althea and the vintage, after seven weeks of imprisonment Lovelace wrote to Commons that "your petitioner beeinge confined here in the Spring-tide of Action" while there was rebellion in Ireland, he would much prefer even "a conditionall freedome." [1] Having obtained the conditional release on a huge bond, he could only cool his heels in London under the watchful eye of Parliament, spending his fortune in furnishing royalist forces, always a man who, as long as he had any money or property that could be turned into money, was generous to "ingenious men in want, whether scholars, musicians, soldiers." By 1646 he found himself able to join the forces of Charles I and stayed with them until the royalist reverses drove him out of England with the well-bred stoic lines to Lucasta:

---

[1] ". . . your petitioner beeinge confined here in the Spring-tide of Action, when open Rebellion treads on the late peacefull bosome of his Maiesties Kingdome of Ireland." On the late peaceful bosom of His Majesty's Kingdom of Ireland, in 1635, the lord-deputy Strafford had begun a general system of extortion, and Irish money went into the making of an army for the oppression of the Scotch and English too. The recall of Strafford's iron grip made insurgence safer in Ireland and a civil war was on the point of breaking out. The years of slaughter and revenge, 1641 and 1642, were bloody, but nothing compared to Cromwell's coming campaign of 1649–1650. This, then, was the "Spring-tide of Action" for which Lovelace was begging "a conditionall freedome" from the Gatehouse where he was writing so charmingly of Althea and "Liberty."

> Tell me not, Sweet, I am unkinde,
> That from the Nunnerie
> Of thy chaste breast, and quiet minde,
> To Warre and Armes I flie.

He returned in the crisis of 1648 and was committed to Peterhouse Prison. The king's cause now shattered, Lovelace lost his charm and almost his decorum in the rhymed grief of *A Mock-Song* and *To Lucasta from Prison*. He polished up a new conceit, begging for liberty not from his prison but from his Lucasta; and everything being lost, Parliament, Religion, Property, what was left "but th' only spring/ Of all our loves and joyes, the KING"? In 1649 Lovelace came out of Peterhouse Prison, the Lucasta poems in his hand, to face a new and strange England, Cromwell's Commonwealth. In a prefatory poem to this collection edited in jail, Andrew Marvell comforted Lovelace against the "word-peckers," "paper-rats," and "book-scorpions," with this consoling, if ribald, reminder of a cavalier age:

> But when the beauteous ladies came to know,
> That their deare Lovelace was endanger'd so:
> Lovelace, that thaw'd the most congealed brest,
> He who lov'd best, and them defended best,
> Whose hand so rudely grasps the steely band,
> Whose hands so gently melts the ladies hand,
> They all in mutiny, though yet undrest,
> Sally'd, and would in his defence contest.

TO ALTHEA
FROM PRISON
Song
Set by Dr John Wilson

> WHEN Love with unconfined wings
>   Hovers within my Gates;
> And my divine *Althea* brings
>   To whisper at the Grates:
> When I lye tangled in her haire,
>   And fetter'd to her eye;
> The Birds that wanton in the Aire,
>   Know no such Liberty.

When flowing Cups run swiftly round
　　With no allaying *Thames,*
Our carelesse heads with Roses bound,
　　Our hearts with Loyall Flames;
When thirsty griefe in Wine we steepe,
　　When Healths and draughts go free,
Fishes that tipple in the Deepe,
　　Know no such Liberty.

When, like committed Linnets, I
　　With shriller throat shall sing
The sweetnes, Mercy, Majesty,
　　And glories of my KING;
When I shall voyce aloud, how Good
　　He is, how Great should be;
Inlarged Winds that curle the Flood,
　　Know no such Liberty.

Stone Walls doe not a Prison make,
　　Nor Iron bars a Cage;
Mindes innocent and quiet take
　　That for an Hermitage;
If I have freedome in my Love,
　　And in my soule am free;
Angels alone that sore above,
　　Injoy such Liberty.

THE VINTAGE TO THE DUNGEON

A Song

Set by Mr William Lawes

SING out, pent soules, sing cheerfully!
Care Shackles you in Liberty:
Mirth frees you in Captivity:
　　Would you double fetters adde?
　　Else why so sadde?

Chorus

Besides your pinion'd armes youl finde
Griefe too can manakell the minde.

Live then Pris'ners uncontrol'd;
Drinke oth' strong, the Rich, the Old,
Till Wine too hath your Wits in hold
    Then if still your jollitie
    And throats are free;

Chorus

Tryumph in your Bonds and Paines,
And daunce to th' Musick of your Chaines.

A MOCK-SONG

Now *Whitehall's* in the grave,
    And our *Head* is our slave,
The bright pearl in his close shell of Oyster;
    Now the *Miter* is lost,
    The proud *Praelates,* too, crost,
And all *Rome's* confin'd to a Cloyster:
    He, that *Tarquin* was styl'd,
    Our white Land's exil'd,
        Yea, undefil'd;
Not a Court *Ape's* left to confute us;
    Then let your Voyces rise high,
    As your Colours did flye,
        And flour'shing cry:
Long live the brave Oliver-Brutus.

Now the *Sun* is unarm'd,
    And the *Moon* by us charm'd,
All the *Stars* dissolv'd to a Jelly;
    Now the *Thighs* of the Crown
    And the *Arms* are lopp'd down,

And the *Body* is all but a Belly,
 Let the *Commons* go on.
The Town is our own,
 We'l rule alone:
For the *Knights* have yielded their Spent-gorge;
 And an order is tane
 With HONY SOIT profane,
 Shout forth amain:
For our Dragon hath vanquish'd the St. *George.*

TO LUCASTA
FROM PRISON

An Epode

Long in thy Shackels, liberty
I ask not from these walls, but thee;
Left for a while, another bride,
To fancy all the world beside.

Yet e're I doe begin to love,
See! How I all my objects prove;
Then my free Soule to that confine,
'Twere possible I might call mine.

First I would be in love with *Peace,*
And her rich swelling breasts increase;
But how alas! how may that be,
Despising Earth, she will love me?

Faine would I be in love with *War,*
As my deare Just avenging star;
But War is lov'd so ev'ry where,
Ev'n He disdaines a Lodging here.

Thee and thy wounds I would bemoane,
Faire thorough-shot *Religion;*
But he lives only that kills thee,
And who so bindes thy hands, is free.

I would love a *Parliament*
As a maine Prop from Heav'n sent;
But ah! Who's he, that would be wedded
To th' fairest body that's beheaded,

Next would I court my *Liberty,*
And then my Birth-right, *Property;*
But can that be, when it is knowne,
There's nothing you can call your owne?

A *Reformation* I would have,
As for our griefes a Sov'raigne salve;
That is, a cleansing of each wheele
Of State, that yet some rust doth feele.

But not a reformation so,
As to reforme were to ore'throw,
Like Watches by unskilfull men
Disjoynted, and set ill againe.

The *Publick Faith* I would adore,
But she is banke-rupt of her store:
Nor how to trust her can I see,
For she that couzens all, must me.

Since then none of these can be
Fit objects for my Love and me;
What then remaines, but th' only spring
Of all our loves and joyes, the KING.

He who, being the whole Ball
Of Day on Earth, lends it to all;
When seeking to ecclipse his right,
Blinded, we stand in our owne light

And now an universall mist
Of Error is spread or'e each breast
With such a fury edg'd, as is
Not found in th' inwards of th' Abysse

Oh from thy glorious Starry Waine
Dispense on me one sacred Beame,
To light me where I soone may see
How to serve you, and you trust me!

THE PRIGGISH LITTLE CLERK:

James Howell

"I WAS COMMITTED TO THE FLEET" "YOU WRITE TO ME OF
WIVING" "AND SO I FELL A-THINKING HOW . . . TO MAKE MY
LAST WILL" "A PARCEL OF INDIAN PERFUME . . . BUT WE CALL
IT TOBACCO" A PERFECT DESCRIPTION OF THE PEOPLE AND
COUNTRY OF SCOTLAND

Montaigne and "Howel's Letters" are my bedside books. If I wake at night, I have
one or other of them to prattle me to sleep again. They talk about themselves for
ever, and don't weary me. I like to hear them tell their old stories over and óver
again. I read them in the dozy hours, and only half remember them. I am informed
that both of them tell coarse stories. I don't heed them. It was the custom of their
time. . . . I love, I say, and scarce ever tire of hearing, the artless prattle of those
two dear old friends, the Perigourdin gentleman and the priggish little Clerk of King
Charles's Council.
WILLIAM MAKEPEACE THACKERAY, "On Two Children in Black,"
in *Roundabout Papers*

IN AN apology for his celibacy, Howell informs us that he "came tumbling into the world a pure cadet, a true cosmopolite, not born to land,
lease, house or office." He lived a long life through the reigns of James I and
Charles I and Cromwell and the Restoration. He traveled through Europe
in multiple roles, as a commercial agent, a diplomat, and a connoisseur of
men, cities, and anecdotes. He laid up a rich foundation of experiences for
the eight years of prison writing in the Fleet (between 1643 and 1651) to
which Parliament committed him, either because of his loyalty to and spying for King Charles, or because of his debts, or for all of these. He demonstrated a flowery devotion to the first and second King Charles, but retained
the generous capacity for sandwiching between his two sovereigns homage
for Oliver Cromwell too. In politics a lover of "one man power," in
pamphleteering a bottomless inkwell, in poetry a bore, in domesticity a
bachelor, in travel a guidebook, in friendship an artist, in spelling a reformist, in journalism one of the earliest Englishmen to live by the pen, in autobiography a gold mine, this "priggish little Clerk" is a literary brother to
John Evelyn and Samuel Pepys and literary father to Steele and Addison.
He is all that A. C. Harwood has said of him so aptly: "an amateur scholar,
an amateur poet, an amateur philosopher, an amateur politician, and an

223

amateur antiquarian, and very gravely does he cry, 'Gee up,' to all his four horses."

The *Epistolae Ho-Elianae* or *The Familiar Letters* were arranged in the Fleet Prison as correspondence which Howell professed to have written to his friends—letters on language, religion, wines, tobacco, the Copernican theory, Presbyterianism, marriage, and nearly everything else. Scholarship has found some of the dates of these "letters" quite impossible, their historical authority faulty, and much of the alleged correspondence probably fictitious. But the art itself, exercised "to relieve his necessities" in the Fleet Prison, is wholly delightful and hence justified. In these delicious letters, we meet with Raleigh returning bankrupt from Guiana; we travel through "Venice the rich, Padua the learned, Bologna the fat, Rome the holy, Naples the gentle, Genoa the proud, Florence the fair, and Milan the great"; we stumble over mention of "Doctor Harvey, who is my physician"; we are treated to a sermon against swearing, and to what my Lord Keeper Bacon thought of the tall French Ambassador on February 2, 1621: "'Sir,' said Bacon, 'tall men are like high houses of four to five storys, wherein commonly the uppermost room is worst furnished.'"

"I WAS COMMITTED TO THE FLEET"

To the Earl of B., from the Fleet

My Lord,

I was lately come to London upon some occasions of mine own, and I had been divers times in Westminster Hall, where I conversed with many Parliament men of my acquaintance, but one morning betimes there rushed into my chamber five armed men with swords, pistols and bills, and told me they had a warrant from the Parliament for me. I desired to see their warrant, they denied it; I desired to see the date of it, they denied it; I desired to see my name in the warrant, they denied all; at last one of them pulled a greasy paper out of his pocket, and showed me only three or four names subscribed, and no more. So they rushed presently into my closet, and seized on all my papers and letters and anything that was manuscript, and many printed books they took also, and hurled all into a great hair trunk, which they carried away with them. I had taken a little physic that morning, and with very much ado they suffered me to stay in my chamber with two

guards upon me till evening, at which time they brought me before the committee for examination, where I confess I found good respect, and being brought up to the close committee, I was ordered to be forthcoming till some papers of mine were perused, and Mr Corbet was appointed to do it. Some days after I came to Mr Corbet, and he told me that he had perused them, and could find nothing that might give offence. Hereupon I desired him to make a report to the House accordingly, which (as I was told) he did very fairly; yet such was my hard hap that I was committed to the Fleet, where I am now under close restraint. And, as far as I see, I must lie at dead anchor in this Fleet a long time, unless some gentle gale blow thence to make me launch out. God's will be done, and amend the times, and make up these ruptures which threaten so much calamity. So I am your lordship's most faithful (though now afflicted) servitor,

Fleet, November 20, 1643.

J. H.

"YOU WRITE TO ME OF WIVING"

To Tho. Young, Esq.

I received yours of the fifth of March, and it was as welcome to me as the flowers in May, which are now coming on apace. You seem to marvel I do not marry all this while, considering I am past the meridian of my age, and that to your knowledge there have been overtures made me of parties above my degree. Truly in this point I will deal with you as one should do with his confessor. Had I been disposed to have married for wealth without affection or for affection without wealth, I had been in bonds before now; but I did never cast my eyes upon any yet that I thought I was born for, where both these concurred. It is the custom of some (and it is a common custom) to choose wives by the weight, that is, by their wealth. Others fall in love with light wives, I do not mean venerean lightness, but in reference to portion. The late Earl of Salisbury gives a caveat for this, "that beauty without a dowry (without that *unguentum indicum*) is as a gilded shell without a kernel"; therefore he warns his son to be sure to have something with his wife, and his reason is, "because nothing can be bought in the market without money." Indeed it is very fitting that *he* or *she* should have wherewith to support both, according to their quality, at least to keep the wolf from the door, otherwise it were a mere madness to marry; but he who hath enough

of his own to maintain a wife, and marrieth only for money, discovereth a poor sordid disposition. There is nothing that my nature disdains more than to be a slave to silver or gold, for though they both carry the King's face, yet they shall never reign over me, and I would I were free from all other infirmities as I am from this. I am none of those mammonists who adore white and red earth, and make their prince's picture their idol that way: such may be said to be under a perpetual eclipse, for the earth stands always betwixt them and the fair face of heaven. Yet my genius prompts me that I was born under a planet not to die in a lazaretto. At my nativity my ascendant was that hot constellation of Cancer about the midst of the dog days, as my ephemerides tells me; Mars was then predominant. Of all the elements fire sways most in me. I have many aspirings, and airy odd thoughts swell often in me, according to the quality of the ground whereon I was born, which was the belly of a huge hill situated southeast, so that the house I came from (besides my father's and mother's coat) must needs be illustrious, being more obvious to the sunbeams than ordinary. I have upon occasion of a sudden distemper, sometimes a madman, sometimes a fool, sometimes a melancholy odd fellow to deal withal: I mean myself, for I have the humours within me that belong to all three; therefore who would cast herself away upon such a one? Besides, I came tumbling out into the world a pure cadet, a true cosmopolite, not born to land, lease, house or office. It is true I have purchased since a small spot of ground upon Parnassus which I hold in fee of the Muses, and I have endeavoured to manure it as well as I could, though I confess it hath yielded me little fruit hitherto. And what woman would be so mad as to take that only for her jointure?

But to come to the point of wiving, I would have you know that I have, though never married, divers children already, some French, some Latin, one Italian, and many English; and though they be but poor brats of the brain, yet are they legitimate, and Apollo himself vouchsafed to co-operate in their production. I have exposed them to the wide world to try their fortunes; and some out of compliment would make me believe they are long-lived.

But to come at last to your kind of wiving, I acknowledge that marriage is an honourable condition, nor dare I think otherwise without profaneness, for it is the epithet the holy text gives it. Therefore it was a wild speech of the philosopher to say that "if our conversation could be without women angels would come down and dwell amongst us." And a wilder speech it was of the cynic, when, passing by a tree where a maid had made herself away, wished "that all trees might bear such fruit." But to pass from these

moth-eaten philosophers to a modern physician of our own, it was a most unmanly thing in him, while he displays his own religion to wish that there were a way to propagate the world otherwise than by conjunction with women (and Paracelsus undertakes to show him the way), whereby he seems to repine (though I understand he was wived a little after) at the honourable degree of marriage, which I hold to be the prime link of human society, the chiefest happiness of mortals, and wherein heaven hath a special hand.

But I wonder why you write to me of wiving, when you know I have much ado to man or maintain myself, as I told you before; yet notwithstanding that the better part of my days are already threaded upon the string of time, I will not despair but I may have a wife at last that may perhaps enable me to build hospitals. For although nine long lustres of years have now passed over my head, and some winters more (for all my life, considering the few sunshines I have had, may be called nothing but winters), yet, I thank God for it, I find no symptom of decay, either in body, senses or intellectuals. But writing thus extravagantly, methinks I hear you say that this letter shows I begin to dote and grow idle, therefore I will display myself no further unto you at this time.

To tell you the naked truth, my dear Tom, the highest pitch of my aim is, that by some condition or other, I may be enabled at last (though I be put to sow the time that others use to reap) to quit scores with the world, but never to cancel that precious obligation wherein I am indissolubly bound to live and die your true constant friend,

From the Fleet, 28 of April 1645.   J. H.

"AND SO I FELL A-THINKING HOW . . . TO MAKE MY LAST WILL"

To Sir Edward Sa., Knight

SIR EDWARD,

I had a shrewd disease hung lately upon me, proceeding, as the physicians told me, from this long reclused life and close restraint, which had much wasted my spirits and brought me low. When the crisis was past I began to grow doubtful that I had but a short time to breathe in this elementary world, my fever still increasing, and finding my soul weary of this muddy

mansion, and methought more weary of this prison of flesh than this flesh was of this prison of the Fleet. Therefore, after some gentle slumbers, and unusual dreams about the dawnings of the day, I had a lucid interval, and so I fell a-thinking how to put my little house in order and to make my last will. Hereupon my thoughts ran upon Grunnius Sophista's last testament, who having nothing else to dispose of but his body, he bequeathed all the parts thereof in legacies, as his skin to the tanners, his bones to the dice-makers, his guts to the musicians, his fingers to the scriveners, his tongue to his fellow-sophisters (which were the lawyers of those times), and so forth. As he thus dissected his body, so I thought to divide my mind into legacies, having, as you know, little of the outward pelf and gifts of fortune to dis-pose of, for never any was less beholden to that blind baggage. In the high-est degree of theoretical contemplation I made an entire sacrifice of my soul to her Maker who by infusing created her, and by creating infused her to actuate this small bulk of flesh with an unshaken confidence of the redemp-tion of both in my Saviour, and consequently of the salvation of the one and the resurrection of the other. My thoughts then reflected upon divers of my noble friends, and I fell to proportion unto them what legacies I held most proper. I thought to bequeath unto my Lord of Cherberry and Sir K. Digby that little philosophy and knowledge I have in the mathematics; my histori-cal observations and critical researches I made into antiquity, I thought to bequeath unto Dr Usher, Lord Primate of Ireland; "My Observations Abroad," and "Inspection into Foreign States" I thought to leave to my Lord G. D.; my poetry, such as it is, to Mistress A. K., who, I know, is a great minion of the Muses. "School Languages" I thought to bequeath unto my dear mother the University of Oxford; my "Spanish" to Sir Lewis Dives and Master Endymion Porter, for though they are great masters of that language, yet it may stead them something when they read "La Picara Justina." My "Italian" to the worthy company of Turkey and Levantine merchants, from divers of whom I have received many noble favours. My "French" to my most honoured lady, the Lady Cor, and it may help her something to under-stand Rabelais. The little smattering I have in the Dutch, British, and my English I did not esteem worth the bequeathing. My love I had bequeathed to be diffused among all my dear friends, especially those that have stuck unto me in this my long affliction. My best natural affections betwixt the Lord B. of Br., my brother Howell, and my three dear sisters, to be trans-ferred by them to my cousins their children. This little sackful of bones I thought to bequeath to Westminster Abbey, to be interred in the cloister within the south side of the garden, close to the wall, where I would have

desired Sir H. F. (my dear friend) to have inlaid a small piece of black marble and caused .this motto to have been insculped upon it, *Hucusque peregrinus, heic domi,* or this, which I would have left to his choice, *Hucusque erraticus, heic fixus,* and instead of strewing my grave with flowers I would have desired him to have grafted thereon some little tree of what sort he pleased that might have taken root downward to my dust, because I have been always naturally affected to woods and groves and those kind of vegetables, insomuch that if there were any such thing as a Pythagorean metempsychosis I think my soul would transmigrate into some tree when she bids this body farewell.

By these extravagancies and odd chimeras of my brain, you may well perceive that I was not well, but distempered, especially in my intellectuals. According to the Spanish proverb, *"Siempre desvarios con la calentura."* Fevers have always their fits of dotage. Among those to whom I had bequeathed my dearest love, you were one to whom I had intended a large proportion, and that love which I would have left you then in legacy, I send you now in this letter, for it hath pleased God to reprieve me for a longer time to creep upon this earth, and to see better days I hope, when this black dismal cloud is dispelled; but come foul or fair weather, I shall be as formerly your most constant, faithful servitor,

Fleet, 26 March 1643.   J. H.

"A PARCEL OF INDIAN PERFUME . . . BUT WE CALL IT TOBACCO"

To Henry Hopkins, Esq.

To usher in again old Janus, I send you a parcel of Indian perfume, which the Spaniard calls the holy herb, in regard of the various virtues it hath, but we call it tobacco. I will not say it grew under the King of Spain's window, but I am told it was gathered near his gold mines of Potosi (where they report that in some places there is more of that ore than earth), therefore it must needs be precious stuff. If moderately and seasonably taken (as I find you always do), it is good for many things; it helps digestion taken awhile after meat, it makes one void rheume, break wind, and keeps the body open. A leaf or two being steeped overnight in a little white wine is a vomit that never fails in its operation. It is a good companion to one that converseth with dead men, for if one hath been poring long upon a book, or

is toiled with the pen and stupefied with study, it quickeneth him, and dispels those clouds that usually overset the brain. The smoke of it is one of the wholesomest scents that is against all contagious airs, for it o'ermasters all other smells, as King James, they say, found true when, being once ahunting, a shower of rain drove him into a pigsty for shelter, where he caused a pipeful to be taken on purpose. It cannot endure a spider or a flea, with such-like vermin, and if your hawk be troubled with any such, being blown into his feathers it frees him. It is good to fortify and preserve the sight, the smoke being let in round about the balls of the eyes once a week, and frees them from all rheums, driving them back by way of repercussion. Being taken backward, it is excellent good against the cholic, and taken into the stomach, it will heat and cleanse it; for I could instance in a great lord (my Lord of Sunderland, President of York), who told me that he taking it downward into his stomach, it made him cast up an impostume, bag and all, which had been a long time engendering out of a bruise he had received at football, and so preserved his life for many years. Now to descend from the substance of the smoke to the ashes, it is well known that the medicinal virtues thereof are very many but they are so common that I will spare the inserting of them here. But if one would try a petty conclusion how much smoke there is in a pound of tobacco, the ashes will tell him, for let a pound be exactly weighed, and the ashes kept charily and weighed afterward, what wants of a pound weight in the ashes cannot be denied to have been smoke, which evaporated into air. I have been told that Sir Walter Raleigh won a wager of Queen Elizabeth upon this nicety.

The Spaniards and Irish take it most in powder or smutchin, and it mightily refreshes the brain, and I believe there is as much taken this way in Ireland as there is in pipes in England. One shall commonly see the serving maid upon the washing block, and the swain upon the ploughshare, when they, overtired with labour, take out their boxes of smutchin and draw it into their nostrils with a quill, and it will beget new spirits in them, with a fresh vigour to fall to their work again. In Barbary and other parts of Africa it is wonderful what a small pill of tobacco will do, for those who use to ride post through the sandy deserts, where they meet not with anything that is potable or edible sometimes three days together, they use to carry small balls or pills of tobacco, which being put under the tongue, it affords them a perpetual moisture, and takes off the edge of the appetite for some days.

If you desire to read with pleasure all the virtues of this modern herb, you must read Doctor Thorus' *Poetologia,* an accurate piece couched in a strenuous heroic verse full of matter, and continuing its strength from first

to last, insomuch that for the bigness it may be compared to any piece of antiquity, and in my opinion is beyond Βατραχομυομαχία, or γαλεωμυομαχία.

So I conclude these rambling notions, presuming you will accept this small argument of my great respects unto you. If you want paper to light your pipe, this letter may serve the turn, and if it be true what the poets frequently sing, that affection is fire, you shall need no other than the clear flames of the donor's love to make ignition, which is comprehended in this distich:

> *Ignis amor si fit, tobaccum accendere nostrum,*
> *Nulla petenda tibi fax nisi dantis amor.*

> If love be fire, to light this Indian weed,
> The donor's love of fire may stand in stead.

So I wish you, as to myself, a most happy New Year; may the beginning be good, the middle better, and the end best of all. Your most faithful and truly affectionate servant,

Fleet, 1 January 1646.

                                                                    J. H.

A PERFECT DESCRIPTION OF THE PEOPLE AND COUNTRY OF SCOTLAND
By James Howel, Gent. London,
Printed for F-S. 1649 [1]

FIRST; for the Country, I must confess, it is good for those that possess it, and too bad for others, to be at the charge to conquer it. The Ayr might be

---

[1] This anti-Scotch tract by James Howell, dated 1649 (he was then in his sixth year in Fleet Prison) "descends into invective so bitter and so coarse that its date alone can excuse it." Almost a hundred years later John Wilkes reprinted it in his August 28, 1762, issue of the *North Briton,* at the time of the agitation against Lord Bute, a Scotch Tory, with the following sly preface: "Sir, I enclose a very great curiosity, which I desire you to reprint verbatim. It will shew the present age how unjust the last was in their sentiments of the people and country of Scotland, and that the prejudices against the inhabitants of the northern part of this island were not conceived by the English yesterday." In extenuation of Howell's ill-natured pamphlet against the Scotch, let us say here that he wrote another against the Dutch, that he wrote nonsense about Jews, that he was himself a Welshman, that he was unmarried (see his letter on wiving), and that this generally good-natured, pious, and correct man had during his eight-year imprisonment confessed: "By these extravagancies and odd chimeras of my brain, you may well perceive that I was not well, but distempered, especially in my intellectuals."

wholesome, but for the stinking people that inhabit it. The ground might be fruitful, had they wit to manure it.

Their Beasts be generally small, Women onely excepted; of which sort, there are none greater in the whole world. There is great store of Fowl too, as foulhouses, foul sheets, foul-linen, foul-dishes and pots, foul-trenchers, and napkins; with which sort, we have been forced to say, as the children did with their fowl in the wilderness. They have good store of fish too, and good for those that can eat it raw; but if it come once into their hands, it is worse then if it were three days old. For their Butter and Cheese, I will not meddle withal at this time, nor no man else at any time, that loves his life.

They have great store of Deer, but they are so far from the place where I have been, that I had rather beleeve, then go to disprove it: I confess, all the Deer I meet withal, was dear Lodgings, dear Horse-meat, and dear Tobacco, and *English* Beer.

As for Fruit, for their Gransire *Adam's* sake, they never planted any; and for other Trees, had *Christ* been betrayed in this Countrey, (as doubtless he should, had he come as a stranger) *Judas* had sooner found the Grace of Repentance, then a Tree to hang himself on.

They have many Hills, wherein they say is much treasure, but they shew none of it; Nature hath onely discovered to them some Mines of Coals, to shew to what end he created them.

I see little Grass, but in their Pottage: The Thistle is not given them of nought, for it is the fairest flower in their Garden. The word Hay is Heathen-Greek unto them; neither man nor beast knows what it means.

Corn is reasonable plenty at this time, for since they heard of the King's coming, it hath been as unlawful for the common people to eat Wheat, as it was in the old time for any, but the Priests, to eat Shew bread. They prayed much for his coming, and long fasted for his welfare; but in the more plainer sense, that he might fare the better, all his followers were welcome, but his guard; for those they say, are like *Pharaoh's* lean Kine, and threaten dearth wheresoever they come: They could perswade the Footmen, that Oaten cakes would make them long winded; and the children of the Chappel they have brought to eat of them, for the maintenance of their voyces.

They say our Cooks are too sawcy, and for Grooms and Coach-men, they wish them to give to their Horses, no worse than they eat themselves; they commend the brave mindes of the Pentioners, and the Gentlemen of the Bed-Chamber, which choose rather to go to Taverns, then to be always eat-

ing of the King's Provision; they likewise do commend the Yeomen of the Buttery and Sellar, for their readiness, and silence, in that they will hear twenty knocks, before they will answer one. They perswade the Trumpetters, that fasting is good for men of that quality; for emptiness, they say, causes wind, and wind causes a Trumpet to sound well.

The bringing of Heraulds, they say, was a needless charge, they all know their pedegrees wel enough; and the Harbengers might have been spared, sithence they brought so many Beds with them; and of two evils, since the least should be chosen, They wish the beds might remain with them, and poor Harbengers keep their places, and do their office, as they return: His Hangings, they desire might likewise be left as Reliques, to put them in minde of His Majesty; and they promise to dispense with the Wooden Images, but for those Graven Images in his new beautified Chappel, they threaten to pull down soon after his departure, and to make of them a burnt-offering, to appease the indignation they imagined conceived against them in the Brest of the Almighty, for suffering such Idolatry to enter into their Kingdom; The Organ, I think, will find mercy, because (as they say) there is some affinity between them and the Bag-pipes.

The Shipper that brought the singing-men, with their Papistical Vestments, complains that he hath been much troubled with a strange singing in his head, ever since they came aboard his Ship. For remedy whereof, the Parson of the Parish hath perswaded him to sell that prophane Vessel, and to distribute the money among the faithful Brethren.

For his Majesties entertainment, I must needs ingenuously confess, he was received into the Parish of *Edenburg* (for a City, I cannot call it) with great shouts of joy, but no shews of charge for Pageants; they hold them idolatrous things, and not fit to be used in so reformed a place; from the Castle they gave him some peeces of Ordnance, which surely he gave them, since he was King of *England;* and at the entrance of the Town, they presented him with a Golden Bason, which was carried before him on mens shoulders to his palace, I think, from whence it came. His Majesty was conveyed by the Younkers of the Town, which were some hundred Halberds, (dearly shall they rue it, in regard of the charge) to the Cross, and so to the high Church, where the onely Bell they had, stood on tip-toe to behold his sweet face, where I must intreat you to spare him, for an hour I lost him.

In the mean time to report the Speeches of the people, concerning his never-exampled entertainment, were to make this discourse too tedious unto

233

you, as the Sermon was to those that were constrained to endure it. After the Preachment, he was conducted by the same Halberds, unto His Palace, of which I forbear to speak, because it was a place sanctified by His divine Majesty, onely I wish it had been better Walled, for my friends sake that waited on him.

Now I will begin briefly to speak of the people, according to their degrees and qualities; for the Lords Spiritual, they may well be termed so indeed; for they are neither Fish nor Flesh, but what it shall please their earthly God, the King, to make them. Obedience is better than Sacrifice, and therefore they make a mock at Martyrdom, saying, That Christ was to die for them, and not they for him. They will rather subscribe, then surrender, and rather suspence with small things, then trouble themselves with great disputation; they will rather acknowledge the King to be their head, then want wherewith to pamper their bodies.

They have taken great pains and trouble to compass their Bishopricks, and they will not leave them for a trifle; for the Deacons, whose defects will not lift them up to dignities, all their study is to disgrace them that have gotten the least degree above them; and because they cannot Bishop, they proclaim they never heard of any. The Scriptures, say they, speak of Deacons and Elders, but not a word of Bishops. Their Discourses are full of detraction; their Sermons nothing but railing; and their conclusions, nothing but Heresies and Treasons. For their Religion they have, I confess they have it above reach, and God willing I will never reach for it.

They Christen without the Cross, Marry without the Ring, receive the Sacrament without reverence, die without repentance, and bury without Divine Service; they keep no Holy-days, nor acknowledge any Saint, but Saint *Andrew,* who they said, got that honor by presenting Christ with an Oaten Cake, after his fourty days fast. They say likewise, that he that translated the Bible, was the son of a Maulster, because it speaks of a miracle done by Barley Loaves, whereas they swear they were Oaten Cakes, and that no other bread of that quantity, could have sufficed so many thousands.

They use no prayer at all, for they say it is needless, God knows their mindes without prattling; and what he doth, he loves to do it freely. Their Sabbaths exercise, is a preaching in the Forenoon, and a persecuting in the Afternoon; they go to Church in the Forenoon to hear the Law, and to the Crags and Mountains in the Afternoon to louze themselves.

They hold their Noses, if you talk of Bear-baiting, and stop their Ears, if you speak of a Play: Fornication they hold but a pastime, wherein mans

ability is approved, and a womans fertility discovered: At Adultery.they shake their heads, Theft they rail at, Murther they wink at, and Blasphemy they laugh at; they think it impossible to loose the way to Heaven, if they can but leave *Rome* behind them.

To be opposite to the Pope, is to be presently with God: to conclude, I am perswaded, That if God and his Angels, at the last day, should come down in their whitest Garments, they would run away, and cry, The children of the Chappel are come again to torment us, let us flie from the abomination of these Boys, and hide ourselves in the Mountains.

For the Lords Temporal and Spiritual, temporizing Gentlemen, if I were apt to speak of any, I could not speak much of them, onely I must let you know, they are not Scotishmen, for assoon as they fall from the brest of the beast their mother, their careful sire posts them away for *France,* where as they pass the Sea sucks from them, that which they have suckt from their rude dams; there they gather, new flesh, new blood, new manners, and there they learn to put on their cloaths, and then return into their Countries, to wear them out; there they learn to stand, to speak, and to discourse, and congee, to court women, and to complement with men.

They spared of no cost to honor the King, nor for no complemental courtesie to welcome their Country-men; their followers, are their fellows, their wives their slaves, their horses their masters, and their swords their judges; by reason whereof, they have but few laborers, and those not very rich: their Parliaments hold but three days, their Statutes three lines, and their Suits are determined in a manner in three words, or very few more, etc.

The wonders of their Kingdom are these; the Lord Chancellor, he is beleeved; the Master of the Rolls, well spoken of; and the whole Councel, who are the Judges for all Causes, are free from suspition of corruption. The Country, although it be mountainous, affords no Monsters, but Women, of which the greatest sort, (as Countesses, and Ladies) are kept like Lyons in Iron grates; the Merchants wives are also prisoners, but not in so strong a hold; they have Wooden Cages, like our Boar Franks, through which, sometimes peeping to catch the Air, we are almost choaked with the Sight of them; the greatest madness amongst the men is Jealousie; in that they fear what no man that hath but two of his sences will take from them.

The Ladies are of opinion, that Susanna could not be chast, because she bathed so often. Pride is a thing bred in their bones, and their flesh naturally abhors cleanliness; their breath commonly stinks of Pottage, their linen of Piss, their hands of Pigs turds, their body of sweat, and their splay-feet, never

offend in Socks. To be chained in marriage with one of them, were to be tied to a dead carkass, and cast into a stinking ditch; Formosity and a dainty face, are things they dream not of.

The Oyntments they most frequently use amongst them, are Brimstone and Butter for the Scab, and oyl of Bays, and tavesacre. I protest, I had rather be the meanest servant of the two to my Pupils Chamber-maid, then to be the Master Minion to the fairest Countess I have yet discovered. The sin of curiosity of oyntments, is but newly crept into the Kingdom, and I do think will not long continue.

To draw you down by degrees from the Citizens Wives, to the Country Gentlewomen, and convey you to common Dames in Sea-coal Lane, that converse with Rags and Marrow-bones, are things of Mineral race; every whore in *Houndsditch* is an *Helena;* and the greasie Bauds in *Turnbal*-street, are Greekish Dames, in comparison of these. And therefore to conclude, The men of old did no more wonder, that the great *Messia* should be born in so poor a Town, as *Bethlem* in *Judea* then I do wonder, that so brave a Prince as King *James,* should be born in so stinking a Town as *Edenburg,* in Lousy *Scotland.*

THE CHIEF OF SINNERS:

John Bunyan

THE DEVIL AND JOHN BUNYAN:

The Temptation of the Bells
Of the Poor Women Sitting at a Door in the Sun
Thou Art My Love, Thou Art My Love
Sell Him, Sell Him, Sell Him
The Hound of Heaven
City of the Living God

VANITY FAIR

~~~~~~

As I walked through the wilderness of this world, I lighted on a certain place where was a Den, and I laid me down in that place to sleep: and, as I slept, I dreamed a dream. I dreamed, and behold I saw a man clothed with rags, standing in a certain place, with his face from his own house, a book in his hand, and a great burden upon his back. I looked, and saw him open the book and read therein; and, as he read, he wept, and trembled; and not being able longer to contain, he brake out with a lamentable cry, saying, "What shall I do?"

JOHN BUNYAN, *The Pilgrim's Progress*

RECENT studies have explored behind the religious appearances of seventeenth-century radicals: Levellers, Diggers, Quakers, Baptists, Ranters and others. Bunyan takes his place in that congregation, a typical tinker among all the eloquent tinkers, cobblers, and tailors of the people who preached the millennium to exorcise high prices, tithes, landlords, and the whips over nonconformist heads during the Restoration. The Devil whom Bunyan threw out of his tormented bowels in *Grace Abounding to the Chief of Sinners,* and the Celestial City which was the reward of his Pilgrim's Progress, were (in the re-evaluation of the scholars) religious triumphs amidst social and economic discontent. *Grace Abounding* is the autobiography of a conversion, while *Pilgrim's Progress* is Bunyan's confession in allegorical dress. These books are the two poles of Bunyan's twelve years of imprisonment. They project a seventeenth-century nonconformist pilgrimage. Here is John Bunyan in the role of Christian escaping the *City of Destruction,* tumbling into the *Slough of Despond,* opening *Doubting Castle,* skirting *Worldly-wise, Save-all, By-ends, Money-love,* persevering towards the millennial land of harps, crowns, palms, and song. William York

Tindall calls this rich fantasy of escape "that lower-class dream of relief and triumph which occupied the fancies of the theocratic Baptists," and of those tinkers, tailors and cobblers, among whom Bunyan was the chief of sinners, "subjected by society for their trade, illiteracy, poverty, and presumption, and their class-conscious campaign of preaching against the rich and the powerful in behalf of the oppressed." Bunyan's lifetime extends from the reign of Charles I to the flight of James II, traversing all the convulsions of the age of Cromwell. His enormous bulk of prison writing coincides with the Great Plague and the Fire of London. "As I walked through the wilderness of this world, I lighted on a certain place where was a Den"—those haunting words, almost an echo of Dante, with which *Pilgrim's Progress* begins. That Den is literally Bunyan's jail, from which he escapes in a dream, a pilgrim with a great burden on his back and "a lamentable cry, saying, 'What shall I do?'"—the Protestant cry for salvation by grace. *Grace Abounding* is a unique testament of personal spiritual conflict, and *Pilgrim's Progress* a proletarian novel in which the poor, having lost the earth to the respectable, the rich, and to Satan, win the class struggle on a more advantageous battleground: heaven. Before his judges, in 1660, the specific indictment against Bunyan was that he had "devilishly and perniciously abstained from coming to church to hear Divine service, and is a common upholder of several unlawful meetings and conventicles, to the great disturbance and distraction of the good subjects of this kingdom." He rejected the parish church and the *Common Prayer Book*. Asked "What do you count prayer?" he said, "When a man prayeth, he doth, through a sense of those things which he wants." Asked to state the things he wanted, he said "to meet together, and to pray, and exhort one another." Bunyan recounts that one of the polished judges called this affirmation "pedlar's French." He reports the following dialogue between the judges and his wife who came to petition at the next assizes:

Justice Chester. My lord, said Justice Chester, he is a pestilent fellow, there is not such a fellow in the country again.

Justice Twisdon. What, will your husband leave preaching? If he will do so, then send for him.

Woman. My lord, said she, he dares not leave preaching, as long as he can speak.

Twis. See here, what should we talk any more about such a fellow? Must he do what he lists? He is a breaker of the peace.

Wom. She told him again, that he desired to live peaceably, and to follow his calling, that his family might be maintained; and, moreover, said, My lord, I have

four small children that cannot help themselves, of which one is blind, and have nothing to live upon, but the charity of good people.

Justice Hale. Hast thou four children? said Judge Hale; thou art but a young woman to have four children.

Wom. My lord, said she, I am but mother-in-law to them, having not been married to him yet full two years. Indeed, I was with child when my husband was first apprehended; but being young, and unaccustomed to such things, said she, I being smayed at the news, fell into labour, and so continued for eight days, and then was delivered, but my child died.

Hale. Whereat, he looking very soberly on the matter, said, Alas, poor woman!

Twis. But Judge Twisdon told her, that she made poverty her cloak; and said, moreover, that he understood I was maintained better by running up and down a-preaching, than by following my calling.

Hale. What is his calling? said Judge Hale.

Answer. Then some of the company that stood by said, A tinker, my lord.

Wom. Yes, said she, and because he is a tinker, and a poor man, therefore he is despised, and cannot have justice.

Hale. Then Judge Hale answered, very mildly, saying, I tell thee, woman, seeing it is so, that they have taken what thy husband spake for a conviction; thou must either apply thyself to the king, or sue out his pardon, or get a writ of error.

Chest. But when Justice Chester heard him give her this counsel; and especially, as she supposed, because he spoke of a writ of error, he chafed, and seemed to be very much offended; saying, My lord, he will preach and do what he lists.

Wom. He preacheth nothing but the Word of God, said she.

Twis. He preach the Word of God! said Twisdon; and withal she thought he would have struck her; he runneth up and down, and doth harm.

Wom. No, my lord, said she, it is not so; God hath owned him, and done much good by him.

Twis. God! said he; his doctrine is the doctrine of the devil.[1]

THE DEVIL AND JOHN BUNYAN [2]

The Temptation of the Bells

Now, you must know, that before this I had taken much delight in ringing, but my conscience beginning to be tender, I thought such practice was but vain, and therefore forced myself to leave it, yet my mind hankered; wherefore I should go to the steeple house, and look on it, though I durst not ring.

---

[1] From *A Relation of Bunyan's Imprisonment.*
[2] From *Grace Abounding to the Chief of Sinners.*

But I thought this did not become religion neither, yet I forced myself, and would look on still; but quickly after, I began to think, How, if one of the bells should fall? Then I chose to stand under a main beam, that lay over-thwart the steeple, from side to side, thinking there I might stand sure, but then I should think again, should the bell fall with a swing, it might first hit the wall, and then rebounding upon me, might kill me for all this beam. This made me stand in the steeple door; and now, thought I, I am safe enough; for, if a bell should then fall, I can slip out behind these thick walls, and so be preserved notwithstanding.

So, after this, I would yet go to see them ring, but would not go farther than the steeple door; but then it came into my head, How, if the steeple itself should fall? And this thought, it may fall for aught I know, when I stood and looked on, did continually so shake my mind, that I durst not stand at the steeple door any longer, but was forced to flee, for fear the steeple should fall upon my head.

Of the Poor Women Sitting at a Door in the Sun

BUT upon a day, the good providence of God did cast me to Bedford, to work on my calling; and in one of the streets of that town, I came where there were three or four poor women sitting at a door in the sun, and talking about the things of God; and being now willing to hear them discourse, I drew near to hear what they said, for I was now a brisk talker also myself in the matters of religion, but now I may say, I heard, but I understood not; for they were far above, out of my reach; for their talk was about a new birth, the work of God on their hearts, also how they were convinced of their miserable state by nature; they talked how God had visited their souls with his love in the Lord Jesus, and with what words and promises they had been refreshed, comforted, and supported against the temptations of the devil. Moreover, they reasoned of the suggestions and temptations of Satan in particular; and told to each other by which they had been afflicted, and how they were borne up under his assaults. They also discoursed of their own wretchedness of heart, of their unbelief; and did contemn, slight, and abhor their own righteousness, as filthy and insufficient to do them any good.

And methought they spake as if joy did make them speak; they spake with such pleasantness of Scripture language, and with such appearance of grace in all they said, that they were to me as if they had found a new

world, as if they were people that dwelt alone, and were not to be reckoned among their neighbours.

At this I felt my own heart began to shake, as mistrusting my condition to be naught; for I saw that in all my thoughts about religion and salvation, the new birth did never enter into my mind, neither knew I the comfort of the Word and promise, nor the deceitfulness and treachery of my own wicked heart. As for secret thoughts, I took no notice of them; neither did I understand what Satan's temptations were, nor how they were to be withstood and resisted, etc.

Thus, therefore, when I had heard and considered what they said, I left them, and went about my employment again, but their talk and discourse went with me; also my heart would tarry with them, for I was greatly affected with their words, both because by them I was convinced that I wanted the true tokens of a truly godly man, and also because by them I was convinced of the happy and blessed condition of him that was such a one.

Therefore I should often make it my business to be going again and again into the company of these poor people, for I could not stay away; and the more I went amongst them, the more I did question my condition; and as I still do remember, presently I found two things within me, at which I did sometimes marvel, especially considering what a blind, ignorant, sordid, and ungodly wretch but just before I was; the one was a very great softness and tenderness of heart, which caused me to fall under the conviction of what by Scripture they asserted; and the other was a great bending in my mind to a continual meditating on it, and on all other good things which at any time I heard or read of.

By these things my mind was now so turned, that it lay like a horse leech at the vein, still crying out, Give, give; yea, it was so fixed on eternity, and on the things about the kingdom of heaven, that is, so far as I knew, though as yet, God knows, I knew but little; that neither pleasures, nor profits, nor persuasions, nor threats, could loosen it, or make it let go his hold; and though I may speak it with shame, yet it is in very deed a certain truth, it would then have been as difficult for me to have taken my mind from heaven to earth, as I have found it often since to get it again from earth to heaven. . . .

About this time, the state and happiness of these poor people at Bedford was thus, in a dream or vision, represented to me. I saw, as if they were set on the sunny side of some high mountain, there refreshing themselves with

the pleasant beams of the sun, while I was shivering and shrinking in the cold, afflicted with frost, snow, and dark clouds. Methoughts, also, betwixt me and them, I saw a wall that did compass about this mountain; now, through this wall my soul did greatly desire to pass; concluding, that if I could, I would go even into the very midst of them, and there also comfort myself with the heat of their sun.

About this wall I thought myself, to go again and again, still prying as I went, to see if I could find some way or passage, by which I might enter therein; but none could I find for some time. At the last, I saw, as it were, a narrow gap, like a little doorway in the wall, through which I attempted to pass; but the passage being very strait and narrow, I made many efforts to get in, but all in vain, even until I was well-nigh quite beat out, by striving to get in; at last, with great striving, methought I at first did get in my head, and after that, by a sidling striving, my shoulders, and my whole body; then was I exceeding glad; and went and sat down in the midst of them, and so was comforted with the light and heat of their sun.

Thou Art My Love, Thou Art My Love

In this condition I went a great while; but when comforting time was come, I heard one preach a sermon upon those words in the Song, "Behold, thou *art* fair, my love; behold, thou *art* fair." But at that time he made these two words, "My love," his chief and subject matter; from which, after he had a little opened the text, he observed these several conclusions: 1. That the church, and so every saved soul, is Christ's love, when loveless. 2. Christ's love without a cause. 3. Christ's love when hated of the world. 4. Christ's love when under temptation, and under desertion. 5. Christ's love from first to last.

But I got nothing by what he said at present, only when he came to the application of the fourth particular, this was the word he said: If it be so, that the saved soul is Christ's love when under temptation and desertion; then, poor tempted soul, when thou art assaulted and afflicted with temptation, and the hidings of God's face, yet think on these two words, "My love," still.

So as I was a-going home, these words came again into my thoughts; and I well remember, as they came in, I said thus in my heart, What shall I get by thinking on these two words? This thought had no sooner passed

through my heart, but the words began thus to kindle in my spirit, "Thou art my love, thou art my love," twenty times together; and still as they ran thus in my mind, they waxed stronger and warmer, and began to make me look up; but being as yet between hope and fear, I still replied in my heart, But is it true, but is it true? At which, that sentence fell in upon me, He "wist not that it was true which was done by the angel."

Then I began to give place to the word, which, with power, did over and over make this joyful sound within my soul, Thou art my love, thou art my love; and nothing shall separate thee from my love; and with that, Rom. viii. 39 came into my mind. Now was my heart filled full of comfort and hope, and now I could believe that my sins should be forgiven me; yea, I was now so taken with the love and mercy of God, that I remember I could not tell how to contain till I got home; I thought I could have spoken of his love, and of his mercy to me, even to the very crows that sat upon the ploughed lands before me, had they been capable to have understood me; wherefore I said in my soul, with much gladness, Well, I would I had a pen and ink here, I would write this down before I go any farther, for surely I will not forget this forty years hence; but alas! within less than forty days, I began to question all again; which made me begin to question all still.

Sell Him, Sell Him, Sell Him

AND now I found, as I thought, that I loved Christ dearly; oh! methought my soul cleaved unto him, my affections cleaved unto him. I felt love to him as hot as fire; and now, as Job said, I thought I should die in my nest; but I did quickly find that my great love was but little, and that I, who had, as I thought, such burning love to Jesus Christ, could let him go again for a very trifle; God can tell how to abase us, and can hide pride from man. Quickly after this my love was tried to purpose.

For after the Lord had, in this manner, thus graciously delivered me from this great and sore temptation, and had set me down so sweetly in the faith of his holy gospel, and had given me such strong consolation and blessed evidence from heaven touching my interest in his love through Christ; the tempter came upon me again, and that with a more grievous and dreadful temptation than before.

And that was, To sell and part with this most blessed Christ, to exchange him for the things of this life, for anything. The temptation lay upon me for

the space of a year, and did follow me so continually that I was not rid of it one day in a month, no, not sometimes one hour in many days together, unless when I was asleep.

And though, in my judgment, I was persuaded that those who were once effectually in Christ, as I hoped, through his grace, I had seen myself, could never lose him for ever—for "the land shall not be sold for ever, for the land *is* mine," saith God—yet it was a continual vexation to me to think that I should have so much as one such thought within me against a Christ, a Jesus, that had done for me as he had done; and yet then I had almost none others, but such blasphemous ones.

But it was neither my dislike of the thought, nor yet any desire and endeavour to resist it that in the least did shake or abate the continuation, or force and strength thereof; for it did always, in almost whatever I thought, intermix itself therewith in such sort that I could neither eat my food, stoop for a pin, chop a stick, or cast mine eye to look on this or that, but still the temptation would come, Sell Christ for this, or sell Christ for that; sell him, sell him.

Sometimes it would run in my thoughts, not so little as a hundred times together, Sell him, sell him, sell him; against which I may say, for whole hours together, I have been forced to stand as continually leaning and forcing my spirit against it, lest haply, before I were aware, some wicked thought might arise in my heart that might consent thereto; and sometimes also the tempter would make me believe I had consented to it, then should I be as tortured upon a rack for whole days together.

This temptation did put me to such scares, lest I should at sometimes, I say, consent thereto, and be overcome therewith, that by the very force of my mind, in labouring to gainsay and resist this wickedness, my very body also would be put into action or motion by way of pushing or thrusting with my hands or elbows, still answering as fast as the destroyer said, Sell him; I will not, I will not, I will not, I will not; no, not for thousands, thousands, thousands of worlds. Thus reckoning lest I should in the midst of these assaults; set too low a value of him, even until I scarce well knew where I was, or how to be composed again.

At these seasons he would not let me eat my food at quiet; but, forsooth, when I was set at the table at my meat, I must go hence to pray; I must leave my food now, and just now, so counterfeit holy also would this devil be. When I was thus tempted, I should say in myself, Now I am at my meat, let me make an end. No, said he, you must do it now, or you will displease

God, and despise Christ. Wherefore I was much afflicted with these things; and because of the sinfulness of my nature, imagining that these things were impulses from God, I should deny to do it, as if I denied God; and then should I be as guilty, because I did not obey a temptation of the devil, as if I had broken the law of God indeed.

But to be brief, one morning, as I did lie in my bed, I was, as at other times, most fiercely assaulted with this temptation, to sell and part with Christ; the wicked suggestion still running in my mind, Sell him, sell him, sell him, sell him, sell him, as fast as a man could speak; against which also, in my mind, as at other times, I answered, No, no, not for thousands, thousands, thousands, at least twenty times together. But at last, after much striving, even until I was almost out of breath, I felt this thought pass through my heart, Let him go, if he will! and I thought also, that I felt my heart freely consent thereto. Oh, the diligence of Satan! Oh, the desperateness of man's heart!

The Hound of Heaven

Now I should find my mind to flee from God, as from the face of a dreadful judge; yet this was my torment, I could not escape his hand: "It is a fearful thing to fall into the hands of the living God." But blessed be his grace, that scripture, in these flying sins, would call as running after me, "I have blotted out, as a thick cloud, thy transgressions; and, as a cloud, thy sins: return unto me, for I have redeemed thee." This, I say, would come in upon my mind, when I was fleeing from the face of God; for I did flee from his face, that is, my mind and spirit fled before him; by reason of his highness, I could not endure; then would the text cry, "Return unto me"; it would cry aloud with a very great voice, "Return unto me, for I have redeemed thee." Indeed, this would make me make a little stop, and, as it were, look over my shoulder behind me, to see if I could discern that the God of grace did follow me with a pardon in his hand, but I could no sooner do that, but all would be clouded and darkened again by that sentence, "For you know how that afterward, when he would have inherited the blessing, he found no place of repentance, though he sought it carefully with tears." Wherefore I could not return, but fled, though at sometimes it cried, "Return, return," as if it did holloa after me. But I feared to close in therewith, lest it should not come from God; for that other, as I said, was still sounding in my conscience, "For you know how that afterward, when he would have inherited the blessing, he was rejected."

City of the Living God

AFTER I had been in this condition some three or four days, as I was sitting by the fire, I suddenly felt this word to sound in my heart, I must go to Jesus; at this my former darkness and atheism fled away, and the blessed things of heaven were set within my view. While I was on this sudden thus overtaken with surprise, Wife, said I, is there ever such a scripture, I must go to Jesus? She said she could not tell, therefore I sat musing still to see if I could remember such a place; I had not sat above two or three minutes but that came bolting in upon me, "And to an innumerable company of angels," and withal, Hebrews the twelfth, about the mount Sion, was set before mine eyes.

Then with joy I told my wife, O now I know, I know! But that night was a good night to me, I never had but few better; I longed for the company of some of God's people that I might have imparted unto them what God had showed me. Christ was a precious Christ to my soul that night; I could scarce lie in my bed for joy, and peace, and triumph, through Christ; this great glory did not continue upon me until morning, yet that twelfth of the author to the Hebrews was a blessed scripture to me for many days together after this.

The words are these, "Ye are come unto mount Sion, and unto the city of the living God, the heavenly Jerusalem, and to an innumerable company of angels, to the general assembly and church of the firstborn, which are written in heaven, and to God the Judge of all, and to the spirits of just men made perfect, and to Jesus the mediator of the new covenant, and to the blood of sprinkling, that speaketh better things than *that of* Abel." Through this blessed sentence the Lord led me over and over, first to this word, and then to that, and showed me wonderful glory in every one of them. These words also have oft since this time been great refreshment to my spirit. Blessed be God for having mercy on me.

VANITY FAIR [3]

THEN I saw in my dream, that when they were got out of the wilderness, they presently saw a town before them, and the name of that town is *Vanity;*

---

[3] From *Pilgrim's Progress.*

and at the town there is a fair kept, called *Vanity Fair:* it is kept all the year long; it beareth the name of *Vanity Fair,* because the town where it is kept is lighter than vanity; and also because all that is there sold, or that cometh thither, is vanity. As is the saying of the wise, *all that cometh is vanity.*

This fair is no new-erected business, but a thing of ancient standing; I will shew you the original of it.

Almost five thousand years agone, there were pilgrims walking to the *Celestial City,* as these two honest persons are: and *Beelzebub, Apollyon,* and *Legion* with their companions, perceiving by the path that the pilgrims made, that their way to the city lay through this town of *Vanity,* they contrived here to set up a fair; a fair wherein should be sold all sorts of vanity, and that it should last all the year long: therefore at this fair are all such merchandise sold, as houses, lands, trades, places, honours, preferments, titles, countries, kingdoms, lusts, pleasures, and delights of all sorts, as whores, bawds, wives, husbands, children, masters, servants, lives, blood, bodies, souls, silver, gold, pearls, precious stones, and what not.

And, moreover, at this fair there is at all times to be seen juggling cheats, games, plays, fools, apes, knaves, and rogues, and that of every kind.

Here are to be seen, too, and that for nothing, thefts, murders, adulteries, false swearers, and that of a blood-red colour.

And as in other fairs of less moment, there are the several rows and streets, under their proper names, where such and such wares are vended; so here likewise you have the proper places, rows, streets, (viz., countries and kingdoms,) where the wares of this fair are soonest to be found. Here is the *Britain Row,* the *French Row,* the *Italian Row,* the *Spanish Row,* the *German Row,* where several sorts of vanities are to be sold. But, as in other fairs, some one commodity is as the chief of all the fair, so the ware of *Rome* and her merchandise is greatly promoted in this fair; only our *English* nation, with some others, have taken a dislike thereat.

Now, as I said, the way to the *Celestial City* lies just through this town where this lusty fair is kept; and he that will go to the city, and yet not go through this town, must needs *go out of the world.* The Prince of princes himself, when here, went through this town to his own country, and that upon a fair day too; yea, and as I think, it was *Beelzebub,* the chief lord of this fair, that invited him to buy of his vanities; yea, would have made him lord of the fair, would he but have done him reverence as he went through the town. Yea, because he was such a person of honour, *Beelzebub* had him

from street to street, and shewed him all the kingdoms of the world in a little time, that he might, if possible, allure the Blessed One to cheapen and buy some of his vanities; but he had no mind to the merchandise, and therefore left the town, without laying out so much as one farthing upon these vanities. This fair, therefore, is an ancient thing, of long standing, and a very great fair. Now these pilgrims, as I said, must needs go through this fair. Well, so they did: but, behold, even as they entered into the fair, all the people in the fair were moved, and the town itself as it were in a hubbub about them; and that for several reasons: for—

First, The pilgrims were clothed with such kind of raiment as was diverse from the raiment of any that traded in that fair. The people, therefore, of the fair, made a great gazing upon them: some said they were fools, some they were bedlams, and some they are outlandish men.

Secondly, And as they wondered at their apparel, so they did likewise at their speech; for few could understand what they said; they naturally spoke the language of Canaan, but they that kept the fair were the men of this world; so that, from one end of the fair to the other, they seemed barbarians each to the other.

Thirdly, But that which did not a little amuse the merchandisers was, that these pilgrims set very light by all their wares; they cared not so much as to look upon them; and if they called upon them to buy, they would put their fingers in their ears, and cry, *Turn away mine eyes from beholding vanity,* and look upwards, signifying that their trade and traffic was in heaven.

One chanced mockingly, beholding the carriage of the men, to say unto them, What will ye buy? But they, looking gravely upon him, answered, *We buy the truth.* At that there was an occasion taken to despise the men the more; some mocking, some taunting, some speaking reproachfully, and some calling upon others to smite them. At last things came to a hubbub and great stir in the fair, insomuch that all order was confounded. Now was word presently brought to the great one of the fair, who quickly came down, and deputed some of his most trusty friends to take these men into examination, about whom the fair was almost overturned. So the men were brought to examination; and they that sat upon them, asked them whence they came, whither they went, and what they did there, in such an unusual garb? The men told them that they were pilgrims and strangers in the world, and that they were going to their own country, which was the heavenly *Jerusalem,* and that they had given no occasion to the men of the

town, nor yet to the merchandisers, thus to abuse them, and to let them in their journey, except it was for that, when one asked them what they would buy, they said they would buy the truth. But they that were appointed to examine them did not believe them to be any other than bedlams and mad, or else such as came to put all things into a confusion in the fair. Therefore they took them and beat them, and besmeared them with dirt, and then put them into the cage, that they might be made a spectacle to all the men of the fair.

Behold *Vanity Fair!* the pilgrims there
Are chain'd and stand beside:
Even so it was our Lord pass'd here,
And on Mount Calvary died.

There, therefore, they lay for some time, and were made the objects of any man's sport, or malice, or revenge, the great one of the fair laughing still at all that befell them. But the men being patient, and not rendering railing for railing, but contrariwise, blessing, and giving good words for bad, and kindness for injuries done, some men in the fair that were more observing, and less prejudiced than the rest, began to check and blame the baser sort for their continual abuses done by them to the men; they, therefore, in angry manner, let fly at them again, counting them as bad as the men in the cage, and telling them that they seemed confederates, and should be made partakers of their misfortunes. The other replied that, for aught they could see, the men were quiet, and sober, and intended nobody any harm; and that there were many that traded in their fair that were more worthy to be put into the cage, yea, and pillory too, than were the men they had abused. Thus, after divers words had passed on both sides, the men behaving themselves all the while very wisely and soberly before them, they fell to some blows among themselves, and did harm one to another. Then were these two poor men brought before their examiners again, and there charged as being guilty of the late hubbub that had been in the fair. So they beat them pitifully, and hanged irons upon them, and led them in chains up and down the fair, for an example and a terror to others, lest any should speak in their behalf, or join themselves unto them. But *Christian* and *Faithful* behaved themselves yet more wisely, and received the ignominy and shame that was cast upon them, with so much meekness and patience, that it won to their side, though but few in comparison of the rest, several of the men in the fair. This put the other party yet into greater rage, insomuch that they

concluded the death of these two men. Wherefore they threatened, that the cage nor irons should serve their turn, but that they should die, for the abuse they had done, and for deluding the men of the fair.

Then were they remanded to the cage again, until further order should be taken with them. So they put them in, and made their feet fast in the stocks.

Here, therefore, they called again to mind what they had heard from their faithful friend *Evangelist,* and were the more confirmed in their way and sufferings by what he told them would happen to them. They also now comforted each other, that whose lot it was to suffer, even he should have the best of it; therefore each man secretly wished that he might have that preferment: but committing themselves to the all-wise disposal of Him that ruleth all things, with much content, they abode in the condition in which they were, until they should be otherwise disposed of.

Then a convenient time being appointed, they brought them forth to their trial, in order to their condemnation. When the time was come, they were brought before their enemies and arraigned. The judge's name was Lord *Hategood.* Their indictment was one and the same in substance, though somewhat varying in form, the contents whereof were this:—

'That they were enemies to and disturbers of their trade; that they had made commotions and divisions in the town, and had won a party to their own most dangerous opinions, in contempt of the law of their prince.'

> Now, *Faithful,* play the man, speak for thy God:
> Fear not the wickeds' malice; nor their rod!
> Speak boldly, man, the truth is on thy side:
> Die for it, and to life in triumph ride.

Then *Faithful* began to answer, that he had only set himself against that which hath set itself against Him that is higher than the highest. And, said he, as for disturbance, I make none, being myself a man of peace; the parties that were won to us, were won by beholding our truth and innocence, and they are only turned from the worse to the better. And as to the king you talk of, since he is *Beelzebub,* the enemy of our Lord, I defy him and all his angels.

Then proclamation was made, that they that had aught to say for their lord the king against the prisoner at the bar, should forthwith appear and give in their evidence. So there came in three witnesses, to wit, *Envy, Superstition,* and *Pickthank.* They were then asked if they knew the prisoner at

the bar; and what they had to say for their lord the king against him.

Then stood forth *Envy*, and said to this effect: My Lord, I have known this man a long time, and will attest upon my oath before this honourable bench that he is—

Judge. Hold! Give him his oath. (So they sware him.) Then he said—

Envy. My Lord, this man, notwithstanding his plausible name, is one of the vilest men in our country. He neither regardeth prince nor people, law nor custom; but doth all that he can to possess all men with certain of his disloyal notions, which he in the general calls principles of faith and holiness. And, in particular, I heard him once myself affirm that Christianity and the customs of our town of *Vanity* were diametrically opposite, and could not be reconciled. By which saying, my Lord, he doth at once not only condemn all our laudable doings, but us in the doing of them.

Judge. Then did the Judge say to him, Hast thou any more to say?

Envy. My Lord, I could say much more, only I would not be tedious to the court. Yet, if need be, when the other gentlemen have given in their evidence, rather than anything shall be wanting that will despatch him, I will enlarge my testimony against him. So he was bid to stand by.

Then they called *Superstition,* and bid him look upon the prisoner. They also asked, what he could say for their lord the king against him. Then they sware him; so he began.

Super. My Lord, I have no great acquaintance with this man, nor do I desire to have further knowledge of him; however, this I know, that he is a very pestilent fellow, from some discourse that, the other day, I had with him in this town; for then, talking with him, I heard him say, that our religion was naught, and such by which a man could by no means please God. Which sayings of his, my Lord, your Lordship very well knows, what necessarily thence will follow, to wit, that we do still worship in vain, are yet in our sins, and finally shall be damned; and this is that which I have to say.

Then was *Pickthank* sworn, and bid say what he knew, in behalf of their lord the king, against the prisoner at the bar.

Pick. My Lord, and you gentlemen all, This fellow I have known of a long time, and have heard him speak things that ought not to be spoke; for he hath railed on our noble prince *Beelzebub,* and hath spoken contemptibly of his honourable friends, whose names are the Lord *Old Man,* the Lord *Carnal Delight,* the Lord *Luxurious,* the Lord *Desire of Vain Glory,* my old Lord *Lechery,* Sir *Having Greedy,* with all the rest of our nobility; and he hath said, moreover, That if all men were of his mind, if possible, there is

not one of these noblemen should have any longer a being in this town. Besides, he hath not been afraid to rail on you, my Lord, who are now appointed to be his judge, calling you an ungodly villain, with many other such like vilifying terms, with which he hath bespattered most of the gentry of our town.

When this *Pickthank* had told his tale, the Judge directed his speech to the prisoner at the bar, saying, Thou runagate, heretic, and traitor, hast thou heard what these honest gentlemen have witnessed against thee?

Faith. May I speak a few words in my own defence?

Judge. Sirrah! sirrah! thou deservest to live no longer, but to be slain immediately upon the place; yet, that all men may see our gentleness towards thee, let us hear what thou, vile runagate, hast to say.

Faith. 1. I say, then, in answer to what Mr. *Envy* hath spoken, I never said aught but this, That what rule, or laws, or customs, or people, were flat against the Word of God, are diametrically opposite to Christianity. If I have said amiss in this, convince me of my error, and I am ready here before you to make my recantation.

2. As to the second, to wit, Mr. *Superstition,* and his charge against me, I said only this, That in the worship of God there is required a Divine faith; but there can be no Divine faith without a Divine revelation of the will of God. Therefore, whatever is thrust into the worship of God that is not agreeable to Divine revelation, cannot be done but by a human faith, which faith will not be profitable to eternal life.

3. As to what Mr. *Pickthank* hath said, I say (avoiding terms, as that I am said to rail, and the like) that the prince of this town, with all the rabblement, his attendants, by this gentleman named, are more fit for a being in hell, than in this town and country: and so, the Lord have mercy upon me!

Then the Judge called to the jury, (who all this while stood by, to hear and observe:) Gentlemen of the jury, you see this man about whom so great an uproar hath been made in this town. You have also heard what these worthy gentlemen have witnessed against him. Also you have heard his reply and confession. It lieth now in your breasts to hang him or save his life; but yet I think meet to instruct you into our law.

There was an Act made in the days of Pharaoh the Great, servant to our prince, that lest those of a contrary religion should multiply and grow too strong for him, their males should be thrown into the river. There was also an Act made in the days of Nebuchadnezzar the Great, another of his servants, that whosoever would not fall down and worship his golden image,

should be thrown into a fiery furnace. There was also an Act made in the days of Darius, that whoso, for some time, called upon any god but him, should be cast into the lions' den. Now the substance of these laws this rebel has broken, not only in thought, (which is not to be borne,) but also in word and deed, which must therefore needs be intolerable.

For that of Pharaoh, his law was made upon a supposition, to prevent mischief, no crime being yet apparent; but here is a crime apparent. For the second and third, you see he disputeth against our religion; and for the treason he hath confessed, he deserveth to die the death.

Then went the jury out, whose names were, Mr. *Blind-man,* Mr. *No-good,* Mr. *Malice,* Mr. *Love-lust,* Mr. *Live-loose,* Mr. *Heady,* Mr. *High-mind,* Mr. *Enmity,* Mr. *Liar,* Mr. *Cruelty,* Mr. *Hate-light,* and Mr. *Implacable;* who every one gave in his private verdict against him among themselves, and afterwards unanimously concluded to bring him in guilty before the Judge. And first, among themselves, Mr. *Blind-man,* the foreman, said, I see clearly that this man is a heretic. Then said Mr. *No-good,* Away with such a fellow from the earth. Ay, said Mr. *Malice,* for I hate the very looks of him. Then said Mr. *Love-lust,* I could never endure him. Nor I, said Mr. *Live-loose,* for he would always be condemning my way. Hang him, hang him, said Mr. *Heady.* A sorry scrub, said Mr. *High-mind.* My heart riseth against him, said Mr. *Enmity.* He is a rogue, said Mr. *Liar.* Hanging is too good for him, said Mr. *Cruelty.* Let us despatch him out of the way, said Mr. *Hate-light.* Then said Mr. *Implacable,* Might I have all the world given me, I could not be reconciled to him; therefore, let us forthwith bring him in guilty of death. And so they did; therefore he was presently condemned to be had from the place where he was, to the place from whence he came, and there to be put to the most cruel death that could be invented.

They, therefore, brought him out, to do with him according to their law; and, first, they scourged him, then they buffeted him, then they lanced his flesh with knives; after that, they stoned him with stones, then pricked him with their swords; and, last of all, they burned him to ashes at the stake. Thus came *Faithful* to his end.

Now I saw that there stood behind the multitude a chariot and a couple of horses, waiting for *Faithful,* who (so soon as his adversaries had despatched him) was taken up into it, and straightway was carried up through the clouds, with sound of trumpet, the nearest way to the *Celestial Gate.*

Brave *Faithful,* bravely done in word and deed;
Judge, witnesses, and jury have, instead
Of overcoming thee, but shewn their rage: *
When they are dead, thou'lt live from age to age.

But as for *Christian,* he had some respite, and was remanded back to prison. So he there remained for a space; but He that overrules all things, having the power of their rage in his own hand, so wrought it about, that *Christian* for that time escaped them, and went his way; and as he went, he sang, saying—

Well, *Faithful,* thou hast faithfully profest
Unto thy Lord; with whom thy shalt be blest,
When faithless ones, with all their vain delights,
Are crying out under their hellish plights:
Sing, *Faithful,* sing, and let thy name survive;
For, though they killed thee, thou art yet alive.

THE MAN IN LEATHER:

George Fox

FROM THE JOURNALS OF GEORGE FOX:

The Interview with Oliver Cromwell

A Nasty, Stinking Place

Why Don't Ye Imprison the Book?

~~~~~~

Never such a plant was bred in England.

Thus when God doth work, who shall let it? and this I knew experimentally.

GEORGE FOX

GEORGE FOX makes his way through the English countryside of the seventeenth century in plain leather breeches. As he puts it: "The Lord's everlasting power was over the world, and reached to the hearts of people, and made both priests and professors tremble. It shook the earthly and airy spirit in which they held their profession of religion and worship, so that it was a dreadful thing when it was told them, *'The man in leather breeches is come.'*" The man in leather: the unpaid priest; the repudiation of the oath ("Swear not at all, but keep to Yea and Nay"); the new rebellious and unceremonious grammar of *Thee* and *Thou* ("without any respect to rich or poor, great or small"); the denial of hat-honor ("an honor invented by men in the fall and the alienation from God")—these were the aggressive weapons of Quakerism, and "Oh! the rage and scorn, the heat and fury that arose! Oh! the blows, punchings, beatings, and imprisonments that we underwent for not putting off our hats to men!" But there was in Fox's preaching to the people a novelty that stirred deeper than issues of oaths and grammar. It was a doctrine free from the self-torture of sin, and divorced from the devil, a devil otherwise very busy in the seventeenth century. "When I was in prison," Fox tells, "divers professors came to discourse with me, and I had a sense before they spoke that they came to plead for sin and imperfection. . . . They could not endure to hear of purity, and of victory over the devil . . . they pleaded for unholiness." From this doctrine of the covered head and the inward light flowed all the Quaker symbols of dress and decorum. To the Calvinist it was a serious heresy and Quakers were hanged in Boston. But the equalitarianism that made no distinction of

255

sex or position, that covered its head and undressed its grammar, that abandoned liturgy and worshiped in silence, that was hostile to sin and friendly to perfection, appealed to the poor ("the dregs of the common people") and to the lower middle class—to the dissolving periphery of all the ranters, shakers, and seekers. The Friends were jailed by the thousands and they prospered. When they were deprived of their preachers, they could embarrass the ingenuity of learned lawyers by assembling in the innocence—and legality!—of an absolute silence.

With the simplicity of genius Fox says: "I came to know God experimentally, and was as one who hath a key and doth open." Knowing God experimentally, he did not, like John Bunyan who knew God rather fearfully, carry a heavy burden on his back. Fox was no refugee from the City of Destruction—or from any city. The pattern of his life is one of action, movement, aggression. The fruit of his imprisonments, his *Short Journal* and *Great Journal*, are intense pictures of seventeenth-century England in motion—and commotion. He breaks into the churches dubbed "steeple-houses," heckles the "professors" with great gusto, marches into the crowds of the market places, tramps the streets of all the towns, climbs a haystack for a pulpit, drinks from a pool in the ditch and sleeps in the bushes, preaches in the alehouse and the fair and the courtroom and the jails, reaches out energetically to the commoners of England and the chambers of Oliver Cromwell and the wilderness of the untamed Indians of America from the West Indies to Long Island. He writes, says Josiah Royce, "as the soldier records his campaigns." Between 1649 and 1675 Fox went to jail eight times. In 1649, the year when Charles I was beheaded, Fox interrupted a preacher in a "steeple-house" and was committed to the first of a series of "nasty stinking" prisons in which he spent a total of six years. In 1650 he served six months for "blasphemy" and another six months for refusing to bear arms, because he "lived in the virtue of that life and power that took away the occasion of all wars." Set at liberty, this man of extraordinary energy and aggression had one of the memorable experiences of his life while entering the town of Lichfield. In his own words: "I lifted up my head and espied three steeple-house spires, and they struck at my life." He had an uncontrollable impulse to take off his shoes and hand them to some shepherds in the field:

Then I walked on about a mile till I came into the town, and as soon as I was got within the town the word of the Lord came to me again, to cry, "Woe unto the bloody city of Lichfield!" So I went up and down the streets, crying with a

loud voice, "Woe to the bloody city of Lichfield!" It being market-day, I went into the market-place, and to and fro in several parts of it, and made stands, crying as before, "Woe to the bloody city of Lichfield!" And no one laid hands on me; but as I went thus crying through the streets, there seemed to me to be a channel of blood running down the streets, and the market-place appeared like a pool of blood.

Following two strenuous years of Quaker activity, he returned to another jail whose prisoners "were exceeding lousy," where he was beaten for approaching the window, and where he won a curious singing contest ("in the Lord's power") against a fiddler fetched by the jailer to compete with his song: "But my voice drowned them and confounded them; that made them give over fiddling and go their ways." He was arrested, as so often, on suspicion of plotting against the state, though he had protested that "our books are against sedition and seditious men and seditious books and seditious teachers and seditious ways," and had cleared his skirts both of the politics of the Protectorate and the exiled monarchy. In 1660, when Charles II arrived in England and Fox was again pursued, fifteen foolish constables watched the prisoner by the fire on the hearth lest the notorious and magical Quaker fly up the chimney. After 1664, in the darkest days of persecution, he served again nearly three years; and the last imprisonment, for attending a meeting and refusing the oath of allegiance, came in 1673. Over a quarter of the turbulent seventeenth century (so instructive to our twentieth), George Fox came to know "experimentally" both God and the filthiest jails in England. William James who scrutinizes Fox in *The Varieties of Religious Experience* pays his religion this tribute: "In a day of shams, it was a religion of veracity rooted in spiritual inwardness, and a return to something more like the gospel of truth than men had ever known in England." George Fox, the shoe apprentice, the man in leather, carefully impartial between monarchy and the Puritan revolution, was in revolt against authority and compulsion, whatever its source. This manly apostle, covered by a hat and obsessed by an intimacy with God, filled the English market-places and his remarkable journals with the rude and salty speech of the people: *"the evil-minded man walked huffing up and down the room"*; *"he was civil but dark in Egypt"*; *"they all kicked and yelled, and roared, and raged, and ran against the life and spirit"*; *"professors began to jangle"*; *"very rude, and wild, and airy they were"*; and *"they fell, like an old rotten house."*

FROM THE JOURNALS OF GEORGE FOX [1]

The Interview with Oliver Cromwell

And after I was brought before him, he was pretty moderate, and said he wished me no more hurt than his own soul, which I said if he did, he went against his own soul; and so bid him hear the voice of God and harden not his heart, for that kept him from hardness of heart, and he saw it was true.

THE SHORT JOURNAL

Now I was carried up a prisoner by Captain Drury from Leicester; and when we came to Harborough, he asked me if I would go home and stay a fortnight. I should have my liberty, he said, if I would not go to nor keep meetings. I told him I could not promise any such thing. Several times on the road did he ask, and try me after the same manner, and still I gave him the same answers. So he brought me to London, and lodged me at the Mermaid over against the Mews at Charing-Cross. As we travelled, I was moved of the Lord to warn people at the inns and places where I came of the day of the Lord that was coming upon them.

After Captain Drury had lodged me at the Mermaid, he left me there, and went to give the Protector an account of me. When he came to me again, he told me the Protector required that I should promise not to take up a carnal sword or weapon against him or the Government. And I should write it in what words I saw good, and set my hand to it. I said little in

---

[1] The *Short Journal*, a preliminary draft of the *Great Journal* and the earliest personal narrative of his life, was dictated by George Fox to Thomas Lower, his stepson-in-law and fellow-prisoner, during the imprisonment in Lancaster Jail in 1663-4. The *Short Journal* is less full and attentive to chronology than the *Great Journal*, closing with the year 1664 when Fox had been about one year in jail. Rufus M. Jones says that the *Great Journal* was begun and largely composed in Worcester Jail (1674) and completed up to the year 1675 at Swarthmore Hall: "It is probable that the recital of Fox's life for fifty-one years engaged his attention during his imprisonment, and that, at home at Swathmoor, he was able to gather together the incidents of his life, recorded in notebooks and various writings, and dictate the results to his son-in-law, Thomas Lower, in the form which has come down to us and which was printed *in extenso* by the Cambridge University Press in 1911 To complete a Journal of the life of George Fox during the next sixteen years, his editors, Thomas Ellwood and others, shortly after his death gathered information from various sources and formed a continuous narrative, which they cast into autobiographical form." The Cambridge edition of 1911 refers to the tradition that the *Great Journal* was originally dictated in Worcester Jail, but concludes that it could not have been completed before Fox's release and that the narrative portions were probably written at Swarthmore Hall. To our present selections from the *Great Journal* we have attached corresponding key sentences from the *Short Journal*, thus combining the skeleton material definitely composed in jail with the fuller version planned during the later imprisonment and edited at Swarthmore Hall.

reply to Captain Drury. But the next morning I was moved of the Lord to write a paper "To the Protector by the Name of Oliver Cromwell," wherein I did in the presence of the Lord God declare that I did deny the wearing or drawing of a carnal sword, or any other outward weapon, against him or any man: and that I was sent of God to stand a witness against all violence, and against the works of darkness; and to turn people from darkness to light; and to bring them from the occasion of war and fighting to the peaceable gospel, and from being evil-doers which the magistrates' swords should be a terror to. When I had written what the Lord had given me to write, I set my name to it, and gave it to Captain Drury to hand to Oliver Cromwell, which he did.

Then after some time Captain Drury brought me before the Protector himself at Whitehall. It was in a morning, before he was dressed, and one Harvey, who had come a little among Friends, but was disobedient, waited upon him. When I came in, I was moved to say, "Peace be in this house"; and I bid him to keep in the fear of God, that he might receive wisdom from Him, that by it he might be directed, and order all things under his hand to God's glory. I spake much to him of Truth, and much discourse I had with him about religion; wherein he carried himself very moderately. But he said we quarreled with priests, whom he called ministers. I told him I did not quarrel with them, but they quarreled with me and my friends. . . . As I spake, he several times said it was very good and it was the truth. . . . Many words I had with him, but people coming in, I drew a little back; and as I was turning, he caught me by the hand, and with tears in his eyes, said, "Come again to my house, for if thou and I were but an hour of a day together, we should be nearer one to the other"; adding that he wished me no more ill than he did his own soul; and I bid him hearken to God's voice, that he might stand in His counsel and obey it; and if he did so, that would keep him from hardness of heart; but if he did not hear God's voice, his heart would be hardened. He said it was true. Then I went out; and when Captain Drury came out after me, he told me his Lord Protector said I was at liberty, and might go whither I would. "And my Lord says," he says, "you are not a fool, and said he never saw such a paper in his life" as I had sent him. Then I was brought into a great hall, where the Protector's gentlemen were to dine; and I asked them what they brought me thither for. They said it was by the Protector's order that I might dine with them. I bid them let the Protector know I would not eat a bit of his bread, nor drink a sup of his drink. When he heard this he said, "Now I see there is a people risen

and come up that I cannot win either with gifts, honours, offices, or places; but all other sects and people I can." It was told him again that we had forsaken our own, and were not likely to look for such things from him.

THE GREAT JOURNAL *(after the arrest in Leicestershire in 1654)*

"A Nasty, Stinking Place"

It was called Doomsdale, because many received their end there and died in it and we were kept a great while prisoners in that Town and castle, I think a great part or the most part of a year.

THE SHORT JOURNAL

Now the Assize being over, and we settled in prison upon such a commitment, that we were not likely to be soon released, we brake off from giving the jailer seven shillings a-week each for our horses, and seven for ourselves; and sent our horses out into the country. Upon which he grew very wicked and devilish; and put us down into Doomsdale, a nasty, stinking place, where they used to put witches and murderers, after they were condemned to die. The place was so noisome, that it was said few that went in ever came out again alive. There was no house of office in it; and the excrements of the prisoners that from time to time had been put there, had not been carried out (as we were told) for many years. So that it was all like mire, and in some places to the top of the shoes in water and piss; and he would not let us cleanse it, nor suffer us to have beds or straw to lie on. At night some friendly people of the town brought us a candle and a little straw, and we burnt a little of our straw to take away the stink. The thieves lay over our heads, and the head jailer in a room by them, over us also. Now it seems the smoke went up into the jailer's room, which put him into such a rage that he took the pots of excrements of the thieves, and poured them through a hole upon our heads in Doomsdale; whereby we were so bespattered that we could not touch ourselves or one another. And the stink increased upon us, so that what with that, and what with smoke, we had nearly been choked and smothered. We had the stink under our feet before, but now we had it on our heads and backs also; and he, having quenched our straw with the filth he poured down, had made a great smother in the place. Moreover he railed at us most hideously, calling us "hatchet-faced dogs," and such strange names as we had never heard in our lives. In this

manner were we fain to stand all night, for we could not sit down, the place was so full of filthy excrements. A great while he kept us after this manner before he would let us cleanse it, or suffer us to have any victuals brought in but what we had through the grate. Once a lass brought us a little meat, and he arrested her for breaking his house, and sued her in the town Court for breaking the prison. Much trouble he put the young woman to, whereby others were so discouraged that we had much to do to get water or drink or victuals. Near this time we sent for a young woman, Anne Downer, from London (that could write, and take things well in short-hand), to get and dress our meat for us, which she was very willing to do, it being also upon her spirit to come to us in the love of God; and she was very serviceable to us.

The head-jailer, we were informed, had been a thief, and was branded in the hand and in the shoulder; his wife, too, had been branded in the hand for some wickedness. The under-jailer had been branded in the hand and shoulder; and his wife in the hand also. Colonel Bennet, who was a Baptist teacher, having purchased the jail and lands belonging to the Castle, had placed this head-jailer therein. The prisoners, and some wild people, talked of spirits that haunted Doomsdale, and how many died in it; thinking perhaps to terrify us therewith. But I told them that if all the spirits and devils in hell were there, I was over them in the power of God, and feared no such thing.

By this time the General Quarter Sessions drew nigh; and the jailer still carrying himself basely and wickedly towards us, we drew up our sufferings and sent it to the Sessions at Bodmin; upon reading of which the justices gave order that Doomsdale door should be opened and that we should have liberty to cleanse it, and to buy our meat in the town. We also sent a copy of our sufferings to the Protector, setting forth how we were taken and committed by Major Ceely, and abused by Captain Keate as aforesaid, and the rest in order, whereupon the Protector sent down an order to Captain Fox, governor of Pendennis Castle, to examine the matter about the soldiers abusing us, and striking me. . . .

One of the Protector's chaplains, told him they could not do George Fox a greater service for the spreading of his principles in Cornwall than to imprison him there. And indeed my imprisonment there was of the Lord, and for His service in those parts: for after the Assizes were over, and it was known we were likely to continue prisoners, several Friends from most parts of the nation came into the country to visit us. . . . One time there

came a soldier to us; and whilst one of our friends was admonishing of him and exhorting him to sobriety, &c., I saw him begin to draw his sword. Whereupon I stepped to him and told him what a shame it was to offer to draw his sword upon a naked man; and a prisoner; and how unfit and unworthy he was to carry such a weapon; and that if he should have offered such a thing to some men, they would have taken his sword from him, and have broken it to pieces. So he was ashamed, and went his way; and the Lord's power preserved us.

Another time, about the eleventh hour at night, the jailer being half drunk, came and told me he had got a man now to dispute with me (this was when we had leave to go a little into the town). As soon as he spake these words, I felt there was mischief intended to my body. All that night and the next day I lay down on a grass-plat to slumber, and I felt something still about my body; and I started up and struck at it in the power of the Lord, and yet still it was about my body. Then I arose and walked into the Castle Green, and the under-keeper came to me and told me there was a maid would speak with me in the prison. I felt a snare in his words too, therefore I went not into the prison, but to the grate, and looking in, I saw a man that was lately brought to prison for being a conjurer, and he had a knife in his hand. I spake to him, and he threatened to cut my chops (as he said); but being within the jail, he could not come at me. This was the jailer's great disputant. I went soon after into the jailer's house, and found him at breakfast; and he had then got his conjurer out with him. I told the jailer his plot was discovered. Then he got up from the table, and struck his napkin away in a rage; and I left them and went away to my chamber; for at this time we were out of Doomsdale. At the time the jailer had said the dispute should be, I went down and walked in the court (the place appointed) till about the eleventh hour, but nobody came. Then I went up to my chamber again, and after a while I heard one call for me. I stepped to the stairs' head, and there I saw the jailer's wife upon the stairs, and the fortune-teller at the bottom of the stairs, holding his hand behind his back and in a great rage. I asked him, "Man, what hast thou in thy hand behind thy back? Pluck thy hand before thee," said I; "let us see thy hand and what thou hast in it." Then in a rage he plucked forth his hand with a naked knife in it. I shewed the jailer's wife the wicked design of her husband and herself against me; for this was the man they had brought to dispute of the things of God. . . .

Now in Cornwall, Devonshire, Dorsetshire and Somersetshire, Truth be-

gan mightily to spread, and many were turned to Christ Jesus and His free teaching; for many Friends that came to visit us were drawn forth to declare the truth in those counties; which made the priests and professors rage, and they stirred up the magistrates to ensnare Friends. They placed watches in the streets and highways, on pretence of taking up all suspicious persons; under which colour they stopped and picked up the Friends that travelled in and through those counties to visit us in prison. . . .

At the Assize divers justices came to us and were pretty civil, and reasoned of the things of God soberly, having a pity towards us. Captain Fox, governor of Pendennis Castle, came and looked me in the face, and said not a word; but went to his company, and told them he never saw a simpler man in his life. I called after him, and said, "Stay, man, we will see who is the simpler man." But he went his way; a light chaffy man.

THE GREAT JOURNAL *(imprisonment of 1656)*

"Why Don't Ye Imprison the Book?"

They asked me if I would take the Oath of Allegiance. I told them I never took the Oath in my life. I could not swear this was my coat; if a man took it, I could not swear that he was the man . . . I told them our Allegiance did not lie in Oaths but in truth and faithfulness. For they had experience enough of men's swearing one way and then another and breaking their Oaths, but our yea was our yea, and our nay was nay. And so they cried, take him away Gaoler. And so I bid them take Notice it was in obedience to Christ's Commands that I suffered. And so I was sent to prison where now I am with eight more.

THE SHORT JOURNAL

NEXT day toward the eleventh hour, I was called again to hear the sentence; and Margaret Fell being called first to the Bar, had counsel to plead, who found many errors in her indictment; whereupon, after the judge had acknowledged them, she was set by. Then the judge asked what they could say to my indictment. I was not willing to let any man plead for me, but to speak to it myself, and indeed, though Margaret had some that pleaded for her, yet she spake as much herself as she would. But before I came to the Bar, I was moved in my spirit to pray that God would confound their wickedness and envy, set His truth over all, and exalt His Seed. The thundering Voice said, "I have glorified thee and will glorify thee again." And I was so filled full of glory that my head and ears were full of glory, and then when the trumpets and judges came up again, they all appeared as

dead men under me. And the Lord heard and answered, and did confound them in their proceedings against me; and though they had most envy against me, yet the most gross errors were found in my indictment.

Now, I having put by others from pleading for me, the judge asked me what I had to say why he should not pass sentence upon me. I told him I was no lawyer, but I had much to say, if he would have patience to hear. At that he laughed, and others laughed also, and said, "Come, what have you to say? he can say nothing." "Yes," said I, "I have much to say, have but the patience to hear me." Then I asked him whether the oath was to be tendered to the King's subjects, or to the subjects of foreign princes. He said, "To the subjects of this realm." Then said I, "Look at the indictment, and ye may see that ye have left out the word *subject:* so not having named me in the indictment as a subject, ye cannot premunire me for not taking the oath." Then they looked over the statute and the indictment, and saw that it was as I said; and the judge confessed it was an error.

I told him I had something else to stop his judgment; and I desired him to look what day the indictment said the oath was tendered to me at the Sessions there. They looked, and said it was the eleventh day of January. "What day of the week were the Sessions held on?" said I. "On a Tuesday," said they. Then said I, "Look at your almanacs, and see whether there were any Sessions held at Lancaster on the eleventh day of January." So they looked, and found that the eleventh was the day called Monday, and that the Sessions were on the day called Tuesday, which was the twelfth day of that month. "Look ye now," said I, "ye have indicted me for refusing the oath in the Quarter Sessions held at Lancaster on the eleventh day of January last, and the justices have sworn that they tendered me the oath in open Sessions here that day, and the jury upon their oaths have found me guilty thereupon; and yet ye see there were no Sessions held in Lancaster that day." Then the judge, to cover the matter, asked whether the Sessions did not begin on the eleventh. But some in the Court answered, "No; the Sessions held but one day, and that was the twelfth." Then the judge said this was a great mistake, and an error. Some of the justices were in a great rage at this, and were ready to have gone off the Bench; they stamped and said, "Who hath done this? somebody hath done it on purpose"; and a great heat was amongst them. Then said I, "Are not the justices here, that have sworn to this indictment, forsworn men in the face of the country? But this is not all," said I, "I have more yet to offer why sentence should not be given against me."

264

Then I asked in what year of the King the last Assize here was holden, which was in the month called March last. The judge said, "It was in the sixteenth year of the King." "But," said I, "the indictment says it was in the fifteenth year." They looked and found it so. This also was acknowledged to be another error. Then they were all in a fret again, and could not tell what to say; for the judge had sworn the officers of the Court that the oath was tendered to me at the Assize mentioned in the indictment. "Now," said I, "is not the Court here forsworn also, who have sworn that the oath was tendered to me at the Assize holden here in the fifteenth year of the King, when it was in his sixteenth year, and so they have sworn a year false?" The judge bid them look whether Margaret Fell's indictment was so or not. They looked, and found it was not so.

I told the judge I had more yet to offer to stop sentence; and asked him whether all the oath ought to be put into the indictment or no. "Yes," said he, "it ought to be all put in." "Then," said I, "compare the indictment with the oath, and there thou mayst see these words, viz., *or by any authority derived, or pretended to be derived from him, or his see,* left out of the indictment, which is a principal part of the oath, and in another place the words *heirs and successors* are left out." The judge acknowledged these also to be great errors. "But," said I, "I have not yet done; I have something further to allege." "Nay," said the judge, "I have enough, you need say no more." "If," said I, "thou hast enough, I desire nothing but law and justice at thy hands, for I don't look for mercy." "You must have justice," said he, "and you shall have law." Then I asked, "Am I at liberty and free from all that hath ever been done against me in this matter?" "Yes," said the judge, "you are free from all that hath been done against you. But then," starting up in a rage, he said, "I can put the oath to any man here, and I will tender you the oath again." I told him he had examples enough yesterday of swearing and false-swearing, both in the justices and the jury; for I saw before mine eyes that both justices and jury had forsworn themselves. The judge asked me if I would take the oath. I bid him do me justice for my false imprisonment all this while; for what had I been imprisoned so long for? and I told him I ought to be set at liberty. "You are at liberty," said he, "but I will put the oath to you again." Then I turned me about and said, "All people, take notice, this is a snare, for I ought to be set free from the jailer and from this Court." But the judge cried, "Give him the book"; and the sheriff and the justices cried, "Give him the book." Then the power of darkness rose up in them like a mountain; and a clerk lifted up a book to me. I

stood still and said, "If it be a Bible, give it me into my hand." "Yes, yes," said the judge and justices, "give it him into his hand." So I took it and looked in it, and said, "I see it is a Bible; I am glad of it."

Now he had caused the jury to be called, and they stood by; for after they had brought in their former verdict, he would not dismiss them, though they desired it; but told them he could not dismiss them yet, for he should have business for them, and therefore they must attend and be ready when they were called. When he said so, I felt his intent that if I was freed he would come on again. So I looked him in the face, and the witness of God started up in him, and made him blush when he looked at me again, for he saw that I saw him. Nevertheless, hardening himself, he caused the oath to be read to me, the jury standing by; and when it was read, he asked me whether I would take the oath or not. Then said I, "Ye have given me a book here to kiss and to swear on, and this book which ye have given me to kiss, says, 'Kiss the Son'; and the Son says in this book, 'Swear not at all'; and so says also the apostle James. Now, I say as the book says, and yet ye imprison me; how chance ye do not imprison the book for saying so? How comes it that the book is at liberty amongst you, which bids me not swear, and yet ye imprison me for doing as the book bids me? Why don't ye imprison the book?" Now as I was speaking this to them, and held up the Bible open in my hand, to shew them the place in the book where Christ forbids swearing, they plucked the book out of my hand again; and the judge said, "Nay, but we will imprison George Fox." Yet this got abroad over all the country as a by-word that they gave me a book to swear on that commanded me not to swear at all; and that the Bible was at liberty, and I in prison for doing as the Bible said.

Now when the judge still urged me to swear, I told him I never took oath, covenant, or engagement in my life, but my yea or nay was more binding to me than an oath was to many others; for had they not had experience how little men regarded an oath; and how they had sworn one way and then another; and how the justices and Court had forsworn themselves now. I told him I was a man of a tender conscience, and if they had any sense of a tender conscience, they would consider that it was in obedience to Christ's command that I could not swear. "But," said I, "if any of you can convince me, that after Christ and the Apostle had commanded not to swear, they did alter that command and commanded Christians to swear, then ye shall see I will swear." There being many priests by, I said, "If ye cannot do it, let your priests stand up and do it." But not one of the priests made any an-

swer. "Oh!" said the judge, "all the world cannot convince you." "No," said I; "how is it like the world should convince me? for 'the whole world lies in wickedness'; but bring out your spiritual men, as ye call them, to convince me." Then both the sheriff and the judge said, "The angel swore in the Revelations." I replied, "When God bringeth in His first-begotten Son into the world, He saith, 'Let all the angels of God worship Him'; and He saith, 'Swear not at all.'" "Nay," said the judge, "I will not dispute." Then I spake to the jury, telling them it was for Christ's sake that I could not swear, and therefore I warned them not to act contrary to that of God in their consciences, for before His judgment-seat they must all be brought. And I told them, "As for plots, and persecution for religion and Popery, I do deny them in my heart; for I am a Christian, and shall shew forth Christianity amongst you this day. It is for Christ's sake I stand, for it is *Lotish shabiun becoll daber.*" [2] And they all gazed and there was a great calm. More words I had both with the judge and jury before the jailer took me away.

In the afternoon I was brought up again, and put among the thieves a pretty while, where I stood with my hat on till the jailer took it off. Then the jury having found this new indictment against me for not taking the oath, I was called to the Bar; and the judge asked me what I would say for myself. I bid them read the indictment, for I would not answer to that which I did not hear. The clerk read it, and as he read the judge said, "Take heed it be not false again"; but he read it in such a manner that I could hardly understand what he read. When he had done, the judge asked me what I said to the indictment. I told him that at once hearing so large a writing read, and at such a distance that I could not distinctly hear all the parts of it, I could not well tell what to say to it; but if he could let me have a copy, and give me time to consider it, I would answer it. This put them to a little stand; but after a while the judge asked me what time I would have. I said, "Till the next Assize." "But," said he, "what plea will you now make? are you guilty or not guilty?" I said, "I am not guilty at all of denying swearing obstinately and wilfully; and as for those things mentioned in the oath, as Jesuitical plots and foreign powers, I utterly deny them in my heart; and if I could take any oath, I should take that; but I never took any oath in my life." The judge said I said well; "but," said he, "the King is sworn, the Parliament is sworn, I am sworn, the justices are sworn, and the law is preserved by oaths." I told him they had had sufficient experience of men's

---

[2] The Hebrew means "Ye shall not swear by anything."

swearing, and he had seen how the justices and jury had sworn wrongly the other day; and if he had read in the *Book of Martyrs* how many of the martyrs had refused to swear, both within the time of the ten persecutions and in Bishop Bonner's days, he might see that to deny swearing in obedience to Christ's command was no new thing. He said he wisht the laws were otherwise. I said, "Our Yea is yea, and our Nay is nay; and if we transgress our yea and our nay, let us suffer as they do, or should do, that swear falsely." This I told him we had offered to the King, and the King said it was reasonable. After some further discourse, they committed me to prison again, there to lie till the next Assize; and Colonel Kirkby gave order to the jailer to keep me close, and suffer no flesh alive to come at me, for I was not fit, he said, to be discoursed with by men.

Then I was put into a tower, where the smoke of the other rooms came up so thick, that it stood as dew upon the walls, and sometimes it was so thick that I could hardly see the candle when it burned; and I being locked under three locks, the under-jailer, when the smoke was great, would hardly be persuaded to come up to unlock one of the upper doors, for fear of the smoke, so that I was almost smothered. Besides, it rained in upon my bed; and many times, when I went to stop out the rain in the cold winter season, my shift would be as wet as muck with the rain that came in upon me. And the place being high and open to the wind, sometimes as fast as I stopt it, the wind, being high and fierce, would blow it out again. In this manner did I lie all that long cold winter, till the next Assize; in which time I was so starved with cold and rain, that my body was greatly swelled, and my limbs much numbed.

The Assize began on the 16th day of the month called March, 1664–5. The same judges, Twisden and Turner, coming down again, Judge Twisden sate this time on the Crown Bench, and before him I was had. Now I had informed myself of the errors in this indictment also. For though at the Assize before, Judge Turner had said to the officers in Court, "Pray see that all the oath be in the indictment, and that the word *subject* be in, and that the day of the month and the year of the King be put in right; for it is a shame that so many errors should be seen and found in the face of the country"; yet there were many errors, and those great ones, in this indictment as well as in the former. Surely the hand of the Lord was in it to confound their mischievous work against me and to blind them therein; insomuch, that although after the indictment was drawn at the former Assize the judge examined it himself and tried it with the clerks, yet the word *subject* was

left out of this indictment also, the day of the month was put in wrong, and several material words of the oath were left out; yet they went on confidently against me, thinking all was safe and well.

When I was set to the Bar, and the jury called over to be sworn, the clerk asked me first whether I had any objection to make against any of the jury. I told him I knew none of them. Then, having sworn the jury, they swore three of the officers of the Court to prove that the oath was tendered to me at the last Assizes, according to the indictment. "Come, come," said the judge, "it was not done in a corner." Then he asked me what I had said to it, or whether I had taken the oath at the last Assize. I told him what I had said, viz., that the book they gave me to swear on says, "Swear not at all"; and I repeated more of what I had formerly said to them, as it now came to my remembrance. Whereupon the judge said, "I will not dispute with you, but in point of law." "Then," said I, "I have something to speak to the jury concerning the indictment." He told me I must not speak to the jury, but if I had anything to say, I must speak to him. Then I asked him whether the oath was to be tendered to the King's subjects only, or to the subjects of foreign princes. He replied, "To the subjects of this realm; for I will speak nothing to you," said he, "but in point of law." "Then," said I, "look in the indictment, and thou mayest see that the word *subject* is left out of this indictment also. And therefore seeing the oath is not to be tendered to any but the subjects of this realm, and ye have not put me in as a subject, the Court is to take no notice of this indictment." I had no sooner spoken than the judge cried, "Take him away, jailer, take him away." So I was presently hurried away. The jailer and people looked when I should be called for again; but I was never brought to the Court any more, though I had many other great errors to assign in the indictment.

After I was gone, the judge asked the jury if they were agreed. They said, "Yes," and found for the King against me, as I was told. But I was never called to hear sentence given, nor was any given against me that I could hear of. For I heard that when they had looked more narrowly into the indictment, they saw it was not good: and the judge having sworn the officers of the Court that the oath was tendered me at the Assize before, such a day, according as was set in the indictment, and that being the wrong day, I should have proved the officers of the Court forsworn men again, if the judge would have suffered me to plead to the indictment; which was thought to be the reason why he hurried me away so soon. It seems, when I was hurried away so, they recorded me as a premunired person, though I

was never brought to hear the sentence or knew of it; which was very illegal. For they ought not only to have had me present to hear the sentence given, but also to have asked me first what I could say why sentence should not be given against me. But they knew I had so much to say, that they could not give sentence if they heard it.

THE GREAT JOURNAL *(Lancaster imprisonment, 1664)*

THE PEOPLE'S ANCIENT AND JUST LIBERTIES ASSERTED IN THE TRIAL OF

William Penn
William Mead

AT THE SESSIONS HELD AT THE OLD BAILEY, IN LONDON,

THE 1ST, 3D, 4TH, AND 5TH OF SEPTEMBER, 1670, AGAINST

THE MOST ARBITRARY PROCEDURE OF THAT COURT

WILLIAM PENN TO THE ENGLISH READER

IF EVER it were time to speak, or write, it is now; so many strange occurrences requiring both.

How much thou art concerned in this ensuing trial, (where not only the prisoners, but the fundamental Laws of England, have been most arbitrarily arraigned) read, and thou mayest plainly judge.

Liberty of conscience is counted a pretence for rebellion; and religious assemblies, routs and riots; and the defenders of both are by them reputed factious and disaffected.

Magna charta is magna far— with the recorder of London; and to demand right, an affront to the court.

Will and power are their great charter; but to call for England's, is a crime, incurring the penalty of the bale-dock and nasty hole; nay, the menace of a gag, and iron shackles too.

The jury (though proper judges of law and fact) they would have overruled in both: as if their verdict signified no more, than to echo back the illegal charge of the bench. And because their courage and honesty did more than hold pace with the threat and abuse of those who sat as judges (after two days and two nights restraint for a verdict) in the end they were fined and imprisoned for giving it.

Oh! what monstrous and illegal proceedings are these! Who reasonably can call his coat his own, when property is made subservient to the will and interest of his judges? Or, who can truly esteem himself a free man, when all pleas for liberty are esteemed sedition, and the laws that give and maintain them, so many insignificant pieces of formality.

And what do they less than plainly tell us so, who at will and pleasure

break open our locks, rob our houses, raze our foundations, imprison our persons, and finally deny us justice to our relief? As if they then acted most like Christian men, when they were most barbarous, in ruining such as are really so; and that no sacrifice could be so acceptable to God, as the destruction of those that most fear him.

In short, that the conscientious should only be obnoxious, and the just demand of our religious liberty the reason why we should be denied our civil freedom (as if to be a Christian and an Englishman were inconsistent); and that so much solicitude and deep contrivance should be employed only to ensnare and ruin so many ten thousand conscientious families (so eminently industrious, serviceable, and exemplary; whilst murders can so easily obtain pardon, rapes be remitted, public uncleanness pass unpunished, and all manner of levity, prodigality, excess, profaneness, and atheism, universally connived at, if not in some respect manifestly encouraged) cannot but be detestibly abhorrent to every serious and honest mind.

Yet that this lamentable state is true, and the present project in hand, let London's recorder, and Canterbury's chaplain, be heard.

The first, in his public panegyrick upon the Spanish Inquisition, 'highly admiring the prudence of the Romish church in the erection of it, as an excellent way to prevent schism.' Which unhappy expression at once passeth sentence, both against our fundamental laws, and Protestant reformation.

The second, in his printed mercenary discourse against toleration, asserting for a main principle, 'That it would be less injurious to the government to dispense with profane and loose persons, than to allow a toleration to religious dissenters.'—It were to overdo the business to say any more, where there is so much said already.

And therefore to conclude, we cannot chuse but admonish all, as well persecutors to relinquish their heady, partial, and inhuman persecutions (as what will certainly issue in disgrace here, and inevitable condign punishment hereafter); as those who yet dare express their moderation (however out of fashion, or made the brand of fanaticism) not to be huffed, or menaced out of that excellent temper, to make their parts and persons subject to the base humours and sinister designs of the biggest mortal upon earth; but reverence and obey the eternal just God, before whose great tribunal all must render their accounts, and where he will recompense to every person according to his works.

THE TRIAL

As there can be no observation, where there is no action; so it is impossible there shall be a judicious intelligence without due observation.

And since there can be nothing more reasonable than a right information, especially of public acts; and well knowing how industrious some will be to misrepresent this trial, to the disadvantage of the cause and prisoners; it was thought requisite, in defence of both, and for the satisfaction of the people, to make it more public. Nor can there be any business wherein the people of England are more concerned, than in that which relates to their civil and religious liberties, questioned in the persons before named at the Old Bailey, the first, third, fourth and fifth of September 1670.

There being present on the bench, as justices,

SAM. STARLING, *mayor.*	JOHN ROBINSON, *alderm.*
JOHN HOWELL, *recorder.*	JOSEPH SHELDEN, *alderm.*
THO. BLUDWORTH, *alderm.*	RICHARD BROWN,
WILLIAM PEAK, *alderm.*	JOHN SMITH, *sheriffs.*
RICHARD FORD, *alderm.*	JAMES EDWARDS,

The citizens of London that were summoned for jurors, appearing, were impanelled; viz.

Cle. Call over the jury.

Cry. Oyes, Thomas Veer, Ed. Bushel, John Hammond, Charles Milson, Gregory Walklet, John Brightman, Will. Plumstead, Henry Henly, James Damask, Henry Michel, Will. Lever, John Baily.

The form of the Oath.

'You shall well and truly try, and true deliverance make betwixt our sovereign lord the king, and the prisoners at the bar, according to your evidence. So help you God.'

The Indictment.

'That William Penn, gent. and William Mead, late of London, linen-draper, with divers other persons to the jurors unknown, to the number of three hundred, the 15th day of August, in the 22d year of the king, about eleven of the clock in the forenoon of the same day, with force and arms, &c.

273

in the parish of St. Bennet Gracechurch, in Bridge-ward, London, in the street called Gracechurch-street, unlawfully and tumultuously did assemble and congregate themselves together, to the disturbance of the peace of the said lord the king: and the aforesaid William Penn and William Mead, together with other persons to the jurors aforesaid unknown, then and there so assembled and congregated together; the aforesaid William Penn, by agreement between him and William Mead before made, and by abetment of the aforesaid William Mead, then and there, in the open street, did take upon himself to preach and speak, and then and there did preach and speak, unto the aforesaid William Mead, and other persons there in the street aforesaid, being assembled and congregated together; by reason whereof a great concourse and tumult of people in the street aforesaid, then and there, a long time did remain and continue, in contempt of the said lord the king, and of his law; to the great disturbance of his peace, to the great terror and disturbance of many of his liege people and subjects, to the ill example of all others in the like case offenders, and against the peace of the said lord the king, his crown and dignity.'

What say you William Penn, and William Mead? Are you guilty, as you stand indicted, in manner and form as aforesaid, or not guilty?

Penn. It is impossible that we should be able to remember the indictment *verbatim,* and therefore we desire a copy of it, as is customary on the like occasions.

Rec. You must first plead to the indictment, before you can have a copy of it.

Penn. I am unacquainted with the formality of the law, and therefore before I shall answer directly, I request two things of the court. First, That no advantage may be taken against me, nor I deprived of any benefit, which I might otherwise have received. Secondly, That you will promise me a fair hearing, and liberty of making my defence.

Court. No advantage shall be taken against you: you shall have liberty; you shall be heard.

Penn. Then I plead not guilty, in manner and form.

Cle. What sayest thou, William Mead? Art thou guilty in manner and form, as thou standest indicted, or not guilty?

Mead. I shall desire the same liberty as is promised to William Penn.

Court. You shall have it.

Mead. Then I plead not guilty, in manner and form.

The Court adjourned until the afternoon.

Cry. Oyes, &c.

Cle. Bring William Penn and William Mead to the bar.

Observ.[1] The said prisoners were brought, but were set aside, and other business prosecuted. Where we cannot chuse but observe, that it was the constant and unkind practice of the court to the prisoners, to make them wait upon the trials of felons and murderers, thereby designing, in all probability, both to affront and tire them. After five hours attendance, the court broke up, and adjourned to the third instant.

The third of September 1670, the Court sat.

Cry. Oyes, &c.

Mayor. Sirrah, Who bid you put off their hats? Put on their hats again.

Obser. Whereupon one of the officers putting the prisoners hats upon their heads (pursuant to the order of the court) brought them to the bar.

Record. Do you know where you are?

Penn. Yes.

Rec. Do you know it is the king's court?

Penn. I know it to be a court, and I suppose it to be the king's court.

Rec. Do you know there is respect due to the court?

Penn. Yes.

Rec. Why do you not pay it then?

Penn. I do so.

Rec. Why do you not put off your hat then?

Penn. Because I do not believe that to be any respect.

Rec. Well, the court sets forty marks a-piece upon your heads, as a fine, for your contempt of the court.

Penn. I desire it may be observed, that we came into the court with our hats off (that is, taken off) and if they have been put on since, it was by order from the bench; and therefore not we, but the bench, should be fined.

Mead. I have a question to ask the recorder: Am I fined also?

Rec. Yes.

Mead. I desire the jury, and all people, to take notice of this injustice of the recorder, who spake not to me to pull off my hat, and yet hath he put

---

[1] The Observer is, of course, William Penn himself.

a fine upon my head. O! fear the Lord, and dread his power, and yield to the guidance of his Holy Spirit; for he is not far from every one of you.

The Jury sworn again.

Obser. J. Robinson, lieutenant of the Tower, disingenuously objected against Edward Bushel, as if he had not kissed the book, and therefore would have him sworn again; though indeed it was on purpose to have made use of his tenderness of conscience, in avoiding reiterated oaths, to have put him by his being a juryman, apprehending him to be a person not fit to answer their arbitrary ends.

The clerk read the indictment as aforesaid.

Cle. Call James Cook into the court, give him his oath.

Cle. James Cook, lay your hand upon the book; 'The evidence you shall give to the court, betwixt our sovereign the king, and the prisoners at the bar, shall be the truth, and the whole truth, and nothing but the truth. So help you God,' &c.

Cook. I was sent for from the Exchange, to go and disperse a meeting in Gracious-street, where I saw Mr. Penn speaking to the people, but I could not hear what he said, because of the noise. I endeavoured to make way to take him, but I could not get to him for the croud of people. Upon which Captain Mead came to me, about the kennel of the street, and desired me to let him go on; for when he had done, he would bring Mr. Penn to me.

Court. What number do you think might be there?

Cook. About three or four hundred people.

Court. Call Richard Read, give him his oath.

Read being sworn, was asked, What do you know concerning the prisoners at the bar?

Read. My lord, I went to Gracious-street, where I found a great croud of people, and I heard Mr. Penn preach to them; and I saw Captain Mead speaking to Lieutenant Cook, but what he said I could not tell.

Mead. What did William Penn say?

Read. There was such a great noise, that I could not tell what he said.

Mead. Jury, observe this evidence; he saith, he heard him preach; and yet saith, he doth not know what he said.

Jury, take notice, he swears now a clean contrary thing to what he swore before the mayor, when we were committed: for now he swears that he saw me in Gracious-street, and yet swore before the mayor, when I was com-

mitted, that he did not see me there. I appeal to the mayor himself if this be not true? (But no answer was given.)

Court. What number do you think might be there?

Read. About four or five hundred.

Penn. I desire to know of him what day it was?

Read. The 14th day of August.

Penn. Did he speak to me, or let me know he was there? For I am very sure I never saw him.

Cle. Crier, call —— —— into the court.

Court. Give him his oath.

—— My lord, I saw a great number of people, and Mr. Penn I suppose was speaking. I saw him make a motion with his hands, and heard some noise, but could not understand what he said. But for Captain Mead, I did not see him there.

Rec. What say you, Mr. Mead? Were you there?

Mead. It is a maxim in your own law, *nemo tenetur accusare seipsum;* which if it be not true Latin, I am sure that it is true English, 'that no man is bound to accuse himself.' And why dost thou offer to ensnare me with such a question? Doth not this shew thy malice? Is this like unto a judge, that ought to be counsel for the prisoner at the bar?

Rec. Sir, hold your tongue; I did not go about to ensnare you.

Penn. I desire we may come more close to the point, and that silence be commanded in the court.

Cry. Oyes! All manner of persons keep silence, upon pain of imprisonment.—Silence in the court.

Penn. We confess ourselves to be so far from recanting, or declining to vindicate the assembling of ourselves, to preach, pray, or worship the eternal, holy, just God, that we declare to all the world, that we do believe it to be our indispensable duty to meet incessantly upon so good an account; nor shall all the powers upon earth be able to divert us from reverencing and adoring our God, who made us.

Brown. You are not here for worshipping God, but for breaking the law. You do yourselves a great deal of wrong in going on in that discourse.

Penn. I affirm I have broken no law, nor am I guilty of the indictment that is laid to my charge. And to the end the bench, the jury, and myself, with those that hear us, may have a more direct understanding of this procedure, I desire you would let me know by what law it is you prosecute me, and upon what law you ground my indictment.

Rec. Upon the common law.

Penn. Where is that common law?

Rec. You must not think that I am able to run up so many years, and over so many adjudged cases, which we call common law, to answer your curiosity.

Penn. This answer I am sure is very short of my question; for if it be common, it should not be so hard to produce.

Rec. Sir, will you plead to your indictment?

Penn. Shall I plead to an indictment that hath no foundation in law? If it contain that law you say I have broken, why should you decline to produce that law, since it will be impossible for the jury to determine, or agree to bring in the verdict, who have not the law produced, by which they should measure the truth of this indictment, and the guilt, or contrary, of my fact.

Rec. You are saucy, fellow. Speak to the indictment.

Penn. I say it is my place to speak to matter of law. I am arraigned a prisoner; my liberty, which is next to life itself, is now concerned. You are many mouths and ears against me; and if I must not be allowed to make the best of my case, it is hard. I say again, unless you shew me, and the people, the law you ground your indictment upon, I shall take it for granted your proceedings are merely arbitrary.

Obser. At this time several upon the bench urged hard upon the prisoner to bear him down.

Rec. The question is, Whether you are guilty of this indictment?

Penn. The question is not whether I am guilty of this indictment, but whether this indictment be legal. It is too general and imperfect an answer, to say it is the common law, unless we both knew where, and what it is. For where there is no law, there is no transgression; and that law which is not in being, is so far from being common, that it is no law at all.

Rec. You are an impertinent fellow. Will you teach the court what law is? It is *lex non scripta;* that which many have studied thirty or forty years to know; and would you have me tell you in a moment?

Penn. Certainly, if the common law be so hard to be understood, it is far from being very common. But if the Lord Coke, in his 'Institutes,' be of any consideration, he tells us, 'That common law is common right; and that common right is the great charter privileges, confirmed 9 Hen. 3. 29. 25 Edw. 1. 1. 2 Edw. 3. 8.' Coke Inst. 2, p. 56.

Rec. Sir, you are a troublesome fellow, and it is not for the honour of the court to suffer you to go on.

Penn. I have asked but one question, and you have not answered me; though the rights and privileges of every Englishman be concerned in it.

Rec. If I should suffer you to ask questions till to-morrow morning, you would be never the wiser.

Penn. That is according as the answers are.

Rec. Sir, we must not stand to hear you talk all night.

Penn. I design no affront to the court, but to be heard in my just plea. And I must plainly tell you, that if you will deny me the Oyer of that law, which you suggest I have broken, you do at once deny me an acknowledged right, and evidence to the whole world your resolution to sacrifice the privileges of Englishmen to your sinister and arbitrary designs.

Rec. Take him away. My lord, if you take not some course with this pestilent fellow, to stop his mouth, we shall not be able to do any thing to-night.

Mayor. Take him away, take him away; turn him into the bale-dock.

Penn. These are but so many vain exclamations. Is this justice, or true judgment? Must I therefore be taken away because I plead for the fundamental laws of England? However, this I leave upon your consciences, who are of the jury, (and my sole judges) that if these ancient fundamental laws, which relate to LIBERTY and PROPERTY, (and are not limited to particular persuasions in matters of religion) must not be indispensably maintained and observed, 'who can say he hath a right to the coat upon his back?' Certainly our liberties are openly to be invaded; our wives to be ravished; our children slaved; our families ruined; and our estates led away in triumph, by every sturdy beggar, and malicious informer, as their trophies, but our (pretended) forfeits for conscience sake. The Lord of heaven and earth will be judge between us in this matter.

Rec. Be silent there.

Penn. I am not to be silent in a case wherein I am so much concerned; and not only myself, but many ten thousand families besides.

Obser. They having rudely haled him into the bale-dock, William Mead they left in court, who spake as followeth.

Mead. You men of the jury, here I do now stand to answer to an indictment against me, which is a bundle of stuff, full of lies and falsehood; for therein I am accused that I met *vi & armis, illicitè & tumultuosè.* Time was, when I had freedom to use a carnal weapon, and then I thought I

279

feared no man; but now I fear the living God, and dare not make use thereof, nor hurt any man; nor do I know I demeaned myself as a tumultuous person. I say, I am a peaceable man; therefore it is a very proper question what William Penn demanded in this case, 'An Oyer of the law on which our indictment is grounded.'

Rec. I have made answer to that already.

Mead. [Turning his face to the jury, said] You men of the jury, who are my judges, if the recorder will not tell you what makes a riot, a rout, or an unlawful assembly, Coke, he that once they called the Lord Coke, tells us what makes a riot, a rout, and an unlawful assembly.—'A riot is when three, or more, are met together to beat a man, or to enter forcibly into another man's land, to cut down his grass, his wood, or break down his pales.'

Obser. Here the recorder interrupted him, and said, 'I thank you, sir, that you will tell me what the law is.' (Scornfully pulling off his hat.)

Mead. Thou mayest put on thy hat; I have never a fee for thee now.

Brown. He talks at random; one while an Independent, another while some other religion, and now a Quaker, and next a Papist.

Mead. Turpe est doctori cum culpa redarguit ipsum.

Mayor. You deserve to have your tongue cut out.

Rec. If you discourse in this manner, I shall take occasion against you.

Mead. Thou didst promise me I should have fair liberty to be heard. Why may I not have the privilege of an Englishman? I am an Englishman; and you might be ashamed of this dealing.

Rec. I look upon you to be an enemy to the laws of England, which ought to be observed and kept; nor are you worthy of such privileges as others have.

Mead. The Lord is judge between me and thee in this matter.

Obser. Upon which they took him away into the bale-dock, and the recorder proceeded to give the jury their charge, as followeth.

Rec. You have heard what the indictment is; it is for preaching to the people, and drawing a tumultuous company after them; and Mr. Penn was speaking. If they should not be disturbed, you see they will go on. There are three or four witnesses that have proved this, that he did preach there, that Mr. Mead did allow of it. After this, you have heard by substantial witnesses what is said against them. Now we are upon the matter of fact, which you are to keep to and observe, as what hath been fully sworn, at your peril.

Obser. The prisoners were put out of the court, into the bale-dock, and the

charge given to the jury in their absence. At which W. P. with a very raised voice, (it being a considerable distance from the bench) spake.

Penn. I appeal to the jury, who are my judges, and this great assembly, whether the proceedings of the court are not most arbitrary, and void of all law, in offering to give the jury their charge in the absence of the prisoners. I say, it is directly opposite to, and destructive of, the undoubted right of every English prisoner, as Coke, in the 2 Inst. 29. on the chapter of Magna Charta, speaks.

Obser. The recorder being thus unexpectedly lashed for his extrajudicial procedure, said, with an enraged smile,

Rec. Why ye are present, you do hear: do you not?

Penn. No thanks to the court, that commanded me into the bale-dock. And you of the jury take notice, that I have not been heard, neither can you legally depart the court, before I have been fully heard; having at least ten or twelve material points to offer, in order to invalidate their indictment.

Rec. Pull that fellow down; pull him down.

Mead. Are these according to the rights and privileges of Englishmen, that we should not be heard, but turned into the bale-dock, for making our defence, and the jury to have their charge given them in our absence? I say, these are barbarous and unjust proceedings.

Rec. Take them away into the hole. To hear them talk all night, as they would, that I think doth not become the honour of the court; and I think you (i. e. the jury) yourselves would be tired out, and not have patience to hear them.

Obser. The jury were commanded up to agree upon their verdict, the prisoners remaining in the stinking hole. After an hour and a half's time, eight came down agreed, but four remained above; the court sent an officer for them, and they accordingly came down. The bench used many unworthy threats to the four that dissented; and the recorder, addressing himself to Bushel, said, Sir, you are the cause of this disturbance, and manifestly shew yourself an abettor of faction; I shall set a mark upon you, Sir.

J. Robinson. Mr. Bushel, I have known you near these fourteen years; you have thrust yourself upon this jury, because you think there is some service for you. I tell you, you deserve to be indicted more than any man that hath been brought to the bar this day.

Bushel. No, Sir John; there were threescore before me; and I would willingly have got off, but could not.

Bludw. I said, when I saw Mr. Bushel, what I see is come to pass: for I knew he would never yield. Mr. Bushel, we know what you are.

Mayor. Sirrah, you are an impudent fellow; I will put a mark upon you.

Obser. They used much menacing language, and behaved themselves very imperiously to the jury, as persons not more void of justice, than sober education. After this barbarous usage, they sent them to consider of bringing in their verdict; and after some considerable time they returned to the court. Silence was called for, and the jury called by their names.

Cle. Are you agreed upon your verdict?

Jury. Yes.

Cle. Who shall speak for you?

Jury. Our foreman.

Cle. Look upon the prisoners at the bar: how say you? Is William Penn guilty of the matter whereof he stands indicted in manner and form, or not guilty?

Foreman. Guilty of speaking in Gracious-street.

Court. Is that all?

Foreman. That is all I have in commission.

Rec. You had as good say nothing.

Mayor. Was it not an unlawful assembly? You mean he was speaking to a tumult of people there?

Foreman. My lord, this was all I had in commission.

Obser. Here some of the jury seemed to buckle to the questions of the court; upon which Bushel, Hammond, and some others, opposed themselves, and said, 'They allowed of no such word, as an unlawful assembly, in their verdict.' At which the recorder, mayor, Robinson, and Bludworth, took great occasion to vilify them with most opprobrious language; and this verdict not serving their turns, the recorder expressed himself thus:

Rec. The law of England will not allow you to depart, till you have given in your verdict.

Jury. We have given in our verdict, and we can give in no other.

Rec. Gentlemen, you have not given in your verdict, and you had as good say nothing. Therefore go and consider it once more, that we may make an end of this troublesome business.

Jury. We desire we may have pen, ink, and paper.

Obser. The court adjourns for half an hour; which being expired, the court returns, and the jury not long after.

The prisoners were brought to the bar, and the jurors names called over.

Cle. Are you agreed of your verdict?

Jury. Yes.

Cle. Who shall speak for you?

Jury. Our foreman.

Cle. What say you? Look upon the prisoners: Is William Penn guilty in manner and form, as he stands indicted, or not guilty?

Foreman. Here is our verdict (holding forth a piece of paper to the clerk of the peace, which follows):

We the jurors, hereafter named, do find William Penn to be guilty of speaking or preaching to an assembly, met together in Gracious-street, the 14th of August last 1670; and that William Mead is not guilty of the said indictment.

Foreman, Thomas Veer,	Charles Milson,
Edward Bushel,	Gregory Walklet,
John Hammond,	John Baily,
Henry Henly,,	William Lever,
Henry Michel,	James Damask,
John Brightman,	William Plumstead.

Obser. This both mayor and recorder resented at so high a rate, that they exceeded the bounds of all reason and civility.

Mayor. What! will you be led by such a silly fellow as Bushel! an impudent canting fellow? I warrant you, you shall come no more upon juries in haste: you are a foreman indeed! (addressing himself to the foreman) I thought you had understood your place better.

Rec. Gentlemen, you shall not be dismissed, till we have a verdict that the court will accept; and you shall be locked up, without meat, drink, fire and tobacco. You shall not think thus to abuse the court; we will have a verdict, by the help of God, or you shall starve for it.

Penn. My jury, who are my judges, ought not to be thus menaced. Their verdict should be free, and not compelled. The bench ought to wait upon them, but not forestall them. I do desire that justice may be done me, and that the arbitrary resolves of the bench may not be made the measure of my jury's verdict.

Rec. Stop that prating fellow's mouth, or put him out of the court.

Mayor. You have heard that he preached; that he gathered a company of

tumultuous people; and that they do not only disobey the martial power, but the civil also.

Penn. It is a great mistake; we did not make the tumult, but they that interrupted us. The jury cannot be so ignorant, as to think that we met there with a design to disturb the civil peace; since, 1st, we were by force of arms kept out of our lawful house, and met as near it in the street as the soldiers would give us leave: and, 2dly, because it was no new thing, nor with the circumstances expressed in the indictment, but what was usual and customary with us. It is very well known, that we are a peaceable people, and cannot offer violence to any man.

Obser. The court being ready to break up, and willing to huddle the prisoners to their jail, and the jury to their chamber, Penn spake as follows:

Penn. The agreement of twelve men is a verdict in law; and such a one being given by the jury, 'I require the clerk of the peace to record it, as he will answer it at his peril.' And if the jury bring in another verdict contrary to this, I affirm they are perjured men in law. [And looking upon the jury, said] 'You are Englishmen; mind your privilege, give not away your right.'

Bushel. Nor will we ever do it.

Obser. One of the jurymen pleaded indisposition of body, and therefore desired to be dismissed.

Mayor. You are as strong as any of them. Starve then, and hold your principles.

Rec. Gentlemen, you must be content with your hard fate; let your patience overcome it; for the court is resolved to have a verdict, and that before you can be dismissed.

Jury. We are agreed, we are agreed, we are agreed.

Obser. The court swore several persons to keep the jury all night, without meat, drink, fire, or any other accommodation. They had not so much as a chamber-pot, though desired.

Cry. Oyes, &c.

Obser. The court adjourned till seven of the clock next morning (being the fourth instant, vulgarly called Sunday); at which time the prisoners were brought to the bar, the court sat, and the jury called in, to bring in their verdict.

Cry. Oyes, &c.—Silence in the court, upon pain of imprisonment.

The jury's names called over.

Cle. Are you agreed upon your verdict?

Jury. Yes.

284

Cle. Who shall speak for your

Jury. Our foreman.

Cle. What say you? Look upon the prisoners at the bar: Is William Penn guilty of the matter whereof he stands indicted, in manner and form as aforesaid, or not guilty?

Foreman. William Penn is guilty of speaking in Gracious-street.

Mayor. To an unlawful assembly?

Bushel. No, my lord, we give no other verdict than what we gave last night: we have no other verdict to give.

Mayor. You are a factious fellow; I'll take a course with you.

Bludw. I knew Mr. Bushel would not yield.

Bushel. Sir Thomas, I have done according to my conscience.

Mayor. That conscience of yours would cut my throat.

Bushel. No, my lord, it never shall.

Mayor. But I will cut yours as soon as I can.

Rec. He has inspired the jury; he has the spirit of divination; methinks I feel him. I will have a positive verdict, or you shall starve for it.

Penn. I desire to ask the recorder one question: Do you allow of the verdict given of William Mead?

Rec. It cannot be a verdict, because you are indicted for a conspiracy; and one being found not guilty, and not the other, it could not be a verdict.

Penn. If not guilty be not a verdict, then you make of the jury, and magna charta, but a mere nose of wax.

Mead. How! Is not guilty no verdict?

Rec. No, it is no verdict.

Penn. I affirm, that the consent of a jury is a verdict in law. And if William Mead be not guilty, it consequently follows, that I am clear; since you have indicted us of a conspiracy, and I could not possibly conspire alone.

Obser. There were many passages that could not be taken, which passed between the jury and the court. The jury went up again, having received a fresh charge from the bench, if possible to extort an unjust verdict.

Cry. Oyes, &c.—Silence in the court.

Court. Call over the jury.—[Which was done.]

Cle. What say you? Is William Penn guilty of the matter whereof he stands indicted in manner and form aforesaid, or not guilty?

Foreman. Guilty of speaking in Gracious-street.

Rec. What is this to the purpose? I say I will have a verdict. [And speak-

285

ing to E. Bushel said] You are a factious fellow; I will set a mark upon you. And whilst I have any thing to do in the city, I will have an eye upon you.

Mayor. Have you no more wit, than to be led by such a pitiful fellow? I will cut his nose.

Penn. It is intolerable that my jury should be thus menaced! Is this according to the fundamental law? Are not they my proper judges by the great charter of England? What hope is there of ever having justice done, when juries are threatened, and their verdicts rejected? I am concerned to speak, and grieved to see such arbitrary proceedings. Did not the lieutenant of the Tower render one of them worse than a felon? And do you not plainly seem to condemn such for factious fellows, who answer not your ends? Unhappy are those juries, who are threatened to be fined, and starved and ruined, if they give not in their verdicts contrary to their consciences.

Rec. My lord, you must take a course with that same fellow.

Mayor. Stop his mouth. Jailer, bring fetters, and stake him to the ground.

Penn. Do your pleasure; I matter not your fetters.

Rec. Till now I never understood the reason of the policy and prudence of the Spaniards in suffering the Inquisition among them. And certainly it will never be well with us, till something like the Spanish inquisition be in England.

Obser. The jury being required to go together, to find another verdict, and stedfastly refusing it (saying, they could give no other verdict than what was already given) the recorder in great passion was running off the bench, with these words in his mouth, 'I protest I will sit here no longer to hear these things.' At which the mayor calling, 'Stay, stay,' he returned and directed himself unto the jury, and spake as followeth:

Rec. Gentlemen, we shall not be at this pass always with you. You will find the next sessions of parliament there will be a law made, that those that will not conform, shall not have the protection of the law. Mr. Lee, draw up another verdict, that they may bring it in special.

Lee. I cannot tell how to do it.

Jury. We ought not to be returned; having all agreed, and set our hands to the verdict.

Rec. Your verdict is nothing; you play upon the court. I say, you shall go together, and bring in another verdict, or you shall starve; and I will have you carted about the city, as in Edward the Third's time.

Foreman. We have given in our verdict, and all agreed to it. And if we give in another, it will be a force upon us to save our lives.

Mayor. Take them up.

Officer. My lord, they will not go up.

Obser. The mayor spoke to the sheriff, and he came off his seat, and said:

Sher. Come, gentlemen, you must go up; you see I am commanded to make you go.

Obser. Upon which the jury went up; and several were sworn to keep them without any accommodation, as aforesaid, till they brought in their verdict.

Cry. Oyes, &c. The court adjourns till to-morrow morning, at seven of the clock.

Obser. The prisoners were remanded to Newgate, where they remained till next morning, and then were brought into the court; which being sat, they proceeded as followeth:

Cry. Oyes, &c.—Silence in the court, upon pain of imprisonment.

Clerk. Set William Penn and William Mead to the bar. Gentlemen of the jury, answer to your names; Thomas Vere, Edward Bushel, John Hammond, Henry Henly, Henry Michel, John Brightman, Charles Milson, Gregory Walklet, John Baily, William Lever, James Damask, William Plumstead; are you all agreed of your verdict?

Jury. Yes.

Clerk. Who shall speak for you?

Jury. Our foreman.

Clerk. Look upon the prisoners: What say you? Is William Penn guilty of the matter whereof he stands indicted, in manner and form, &c. or not guilty?

Foreman. You have there read in writing already our verdict, and our hands subscribed.

Obser. The clerk had the paper, but was stopped by the recorder from reading of it; and he commanded to ask for a positive verdict.

Foreman. If you will not accept of it, I desire to have it back again.

Court. That paper was no verdict; and there shall be no advantage taken against you by it.

Clerk. How say you? Is William Penn guilty, &c. or not guilty?

Foreman. Not guilty.

Clerk. How say you? Is William Mead guilty, &c. or not guilty?

Foreman. Not guilty.

Clerk. Then hearken to your verdict. You say that William Penn is not guilty in manner and form, as he stands indicted: you say that William Mead is not guilty in manner and form, as he stands indicted; and so you say all.

Jury. Yes, we do so.

Obser. The bench being unsatisfied with the verdict, commanded that every person should distinctly answer to their names, and give in their verdict; which they unanimously did, in saying, Not guilty, to the great satisfaction of the assembly.

Rec. I am sorry, gentlemen, you have followed your own judgments and opinions, rather than the good and wholesome advice which was given you. God keep my life out of your hands: but for this the court fines you forty marks a man, and imprisonment till paid. [At which Penn stepped up towards the bench, and said]

Penn. I demand my liberty, being freed by the jury.

Mayor. No! you are in for your fines.

Penn. Fines! for what?

Mayor. For contempt of the court.

Penn. I ask, if it be according to the fundamental laws of England, that any Englishman should be fined, or amerced, but by the judgment of his peers or jury? Since it expressly contradicts the fourteenth and twenty-ninth chapter of the great charter of England, which says, 'No freeman ought to be amerced, but by the oath of good and lawful men of the vicinage.'

Rec. Take him away, take him away, take him out of the court.

Penn. I can never urge the fundamental laws of England, but you cry, Take him away, take him away. But it is no wonder, since the Spanish inquisition hath so great a place in the recorder's heart. God Almighty, who is just, will judge you for all these things.

Obser. They haled the prisoners to the bale-dock, and from thence sent them to Newgate, for non-payment of the fines; and so were their jury.

[William Penn's father, who was ill and had only a few days to live, paid the fines and the two prisoners were released. But the rebellious jurymen kept clamoring for their liberty every six hours until they obtained it on a writ of *habeas corpus*. Led by juryman Bushel, they promptly sued the mayor and the recorder, Starling and Howell, for illegal imprisonment. In the Court of Common Pleas busy lawyers planned and argued for a whole year and at last twelve wise judges unanimously made a decision, important in English law, establishing the sacred right of juries to bring in a verdict according to conscience. Edward Bushel (whose name is commemorated on a tablet beside those of Penn, Mead, and juror Thomas Vere) wrested from that court the valuable opinion that judges "may try to open the eyes of jurors, but not to lead them by the nose."]

PILLORY WITH FLOWERS:

Daniel Defoe

A HYMN TO THE PILLORY

~~~~~~

> Tell them, the men that placed him here,
> Are scandals to the Times,
> Are at a loss to find his guilt,
> And can't commit his crimes.
> DANIEL DEFOE, *A Hymn to the Pillory*

FOR launching one of the great literary hoaxes, and for the ambiguities of irony in his pamphlet *The Shortest Way with the Dissenters* Daniel Defoe paid the first of his two visits to jail. The circumstances arose at the beginning of Queen Anne's reign when a bill to disqualify dissenters from civil employment was being debated in Parliament. The High Church party, then in power, was determined at last to abolish Occasional Conformity. This was a rather curious practice in double standards which permitted a Lord Mayor in all his official paraphernalia to attend services in the established church, and immediately after in his nonconformist chapel. It allowed any dissenter with a flexible conscience (and a job) to take the Anglican communion perfunctorily, but purge his soul afterwards in his nonconformist meetinghouse. Though a kind, if cynical, compromise, the practice of Occasional Conformity was nevertheless attacked both by extremist churchmen (so-called high flyers) and by the more scrupulous dissenters who scorned "Christians of an amphibious nature." Defoe, a dissenter and son of a dissenter, had already written in disapproval of the paradox of Occasional Conformity. Now he proposed to set a rather extraordinary trap for the intolerant, with bait which they would relish but not suspect. Perhaps the Whigs, and the rising politician Robert Harley, were in the background of the great hoax when Defoe published *The Shortest Way with the Dissenters*. Writing it anonymously, in the disguise of a high flyer, his tongue in his cheek, and his ingenious pen dripping with irony, Defoe called for the utter extermination of the dissenters. He carried the arguments of the most intolerant churchman to the furthest limits of their logic, crudity, and absurdity:

This is the time to pull up this heretical weed of sedition, that has so long disturbed the peace of our Church, and poisoned the good corn. But, says another hot and cold objector, this is renewing fire and faggot . . . this will be cruelty in

289

its nature, and barbarous to all the world. I answer, it is cruelty to kill a snake or a toad in cold blood, but the poison of their nature makes it a charity to our neighbours to destroy those creatures, not for any personal injury received, but for prevention; not for the evil they have done, but the evil they may do. Serpents, toads, vipers, &c. . . . shall any land be given to such wild creatures? Some beasts are for sport, and the huntsmen give them advantages of ground; but some are knocked on the head by all possible ways of violence and surprise. I do not prescribe fire and faggot, but, as Scipio said of Carthage, *"Delenda est Carthago,"* they are to be rooted out of the nation. . . . If one law were made, and punctually executed, that whoever was found at a conventicle should be banished the nation, and the preacher be hanged, we should soon see an end of the tale. They would all come to church; and our age would make us all one again.

The irony would have had happier results if Defoe's assumed ferocity had been less subtle. He should have given it the burlesque title of a "Modest proposal for preventing the dissenters from being a burden to their country by having them fattened and boiled for the relief of paupers." As it happened, *The Shortest Way* had so familiar a ring among the extremists of the High Church party, that instead of seeing in it their shame and the *reductio ad absurdum* of their position, they, *mirabile dictu,* at once appropriated it as their authentic voice. Meanwhile the unhappy dissenters, falling into the trap set for their enemies, trembled with fear at its bloodthirsty contents. When Defoe realized that his satire had boomeranged, he issued *An Explanation* and revealed the dissenter's signature behind his hoax on the high flyers. Then the churchmen raged; the Whigs held their sides with laughter; and, worst of all, the dissenters, unyielding in their suspicion, and still trembling, could only say of Defoe that "he must have a very transforming maw or a very good slight of hand, that will spew up claret or blood, Knives or Daggers, and at the same time to make us believe 'tis all the same wine and sugar-plums that he swallow'd before." Between the grindstones of public rage, Defoe was suddenly very much alone, very much frightened, and in hiding from an order for his arrest by the secretary of state. This official suspected that the hoax was a conspiracy by the Whigs and by Harley to discredit the party in power with laughter. From his refuge in the house of a French weaver, Defoe made frantic efforts to reach the authorities, the Queen, Harley, the dissenters, anybody who might help him save his wife, his seven children, his tile business, and particularly his neck from the pillory which he very much dreaded. On January 10, 1703, the *London Gazette* carried the following public notice and physical description of the fugitive:

PILLORY WITH FLOWERS : *Daniel Defoe*

Whereas Daniel De Foe, alias De Foe, is charged with writing a scandalous and seditious pamphlet, entitled, *The Shortest Way with the Dissenters*. He is a middle-sized, spare man, about fifty years old, of a brown complexion, and dark brown coloured hair, but wears a wig; a hooked nose, a sharp chin, grey eyes, and a large mole near his mouth; was born in London, and for many years was a hose-factor in Freeman's Yard in Cornhill; and now is the owner of the brick and pantile works near Tilbury Fort in Essex; whoever shall discover the said Daniel De Foe to one of Her Majesties principal Secretaries of State, or any of her Majesties justices of the peace, so he may be apprehended, shall have a reward of £50, which Her Majesty has ordered immediately to be paid upon such discovery.

Five months later his hiding place was betrayed by an informer who collected his £50 and Defoe went to Newgate whose pickpockets and prostitutes he would portray in his books with memorable fidelity. He was tried and condemned to pay a fine, to be pilloried three times, to be imprisoned indefinitely, and to find sureties for his good behavior during seven years of probation. William Penn, the Quaker, who interceded for him at court, did not, however, get very far with an undecided Queen. Nonconformist clergymen, who visited Newgate to pray with a horse thief who was due for the gallows, snubbed poor Defoe who begged them for equal ministrations. He quaked with a vision of the pillory, its humiliations and physical terrors: "Gaols, pillories, and such like, with which I have been so much threatened," he confessed, "have convinced me I want passive courage, and I shall never for the future think myself injured if I am called a coward." This bold "coward" who had dared so much and so far, now dared desperately once more. He threatened to make certain interesting revelations—and at once stirred the Whigs into a belated pledge that, if he submitted to the pillory discreetly, they would organize his protection and guarantee him a gay and heroic martyrdom. Equal to the bargain, Defoe revealed no important secrets, dipped his pen into vinegar and dashed off *A Hymn to the Pillory* which was to be hawked in the streets of London in the hour of his disgrace. For three days he was pilloried successively in Cornhill, Cheapside, and Temple Bar. Grateful for the trick played on the high flyers, and for a jolly lampoon on the pillory, the London crowd (which could just as easily burn down dissenters' meetinghouses as lionize the celebrated trickster of the day) canonized Defoe by pelting him with flowers instead of the customary rotten eggs, and by draining beer mugs instead of emptying chamber pots. The pillory, the flowers, the beer, and the triumph pledged by the

PILLORY WITH FLOWERS : *Daniel Defoe*

Whigs and by Harley (for whom he was shortly to edit *The Review*[1]), marked a birthday party for a great decision on the part of Defoe, "The Age's Humble Servant." "Neither he nor the mob," observes Professor Trent, "knew that the experience marked a turning point in the career of one of the most variously, though not nobly, gifted men England has ever produced." It was the birthday of Harley's man Friday.

A HYMN TO THE PILLORY

HAIL hieroglyphic State Machine,
Contrived to punish Fancy in:
Men, that are men, in thee can feel no pain;
And all thy insignificants disdain.
Contempt, that false new word for Shame,
Is without a crime an empty name!
A Shadow to amuse mankind;
But never frights the wise or well-fixed mind:
Virtue despises human scorn
And scandals Innocence adorn.

Exalted on thy Stool of State,
What prospect do I see of sovereign Fate;
How the inscrutables of Providence,
Differ from our contracted sense,
Here, by the errors of the Town,
The fools look out and knaves look on!
Persons or Crimes find here the same respect;

---

[1] The first numbers of *The Review*, a very remarkable journal, and *The Storm*, a literary curiosity of the first order, have until recently been assigned to Defoe's writing period in Newgate (where he wrote *A Hymn to the Pillory*, began his political poem *Jure Divino*, dashed off a few controversial tracts, and edited his previous works) Professor Trent says: "It was held until recently that Defoe remained at Newgate until August 1704, although more careful examination of *The Review* would have led to a different conclusion. Research in other newspapers and the publication of his correspondence with Harley have now made it clear that he was released, through Harley's good offices, about 1 November 1703. This disposes of the story that *The Review* was founded while its editor was in prison, and it also absolves us from the necessity of supposing that, when, in his volume on the great storm, Defoe described devastations of which he had been an eyewitness, he was drawing on his imagination." (Professor W. P. Trent in *The Cambridge History of English Literature*, volume 9.)

292

And Vice does Virtue oft correct,
The undistinguished fury of the street,
With mob and malice, mankind greet:
No bias can the rabble draw;
But Dirt throws dirt, without respect to Merit or to Law

Sometimes, the air of Scandal to maintain,
Villains look from thy lofty Loops in vain:
But who can judge of Crimes, by Punishment,
Where Parties rule, and L[aw]'s subservient?
Justice, with change of Interest learns to bow;
And what was Merit once, is Murder now:
Actions receive their tincture from the Times,
And as they change, are Virtues made, or Crimes.
Thou art the State-Trap of the law,
But neither canst keep knaves, nor honest men in awe:
These are too hardened in offence,
And those upheld by innocence.

How have thy opening Vacancies received
In every Age, the criminals of State?
And how has Mankind been deceived,
When they distinguish crimes by fate?
Tell us, Great Engine, how to understand
Or reconcile the Justice of the land;
How Bastwick, Prynne, Hunt, Hollingsby, and Pye,
Men of unspotted honesty;
Men that had Learning, Wit, and Sense,
And more than most men have had since,
Could equal title to thee claim,
With Oates and Fuller, men of later fame:
Even the learned Selden saw
A prospect of thee, through the law:
He had thy lofty Pinnacles in view,
But so much honour never was thy due:
Had the great Selden triumphed on thy stage,
Selden, the honour of his Age,
No man would ever shun thee more

Or grudge to stand where SELDEN stood before.
Thou art no Shame to Truth and Honesty,⎫
Nor is the character of such defaced by thee, ⎬
  Who suffer by oppressive injury.   ⎭
  Shame, like the exhalations of the sun,
  Falls back where first the motion was begun.
And he who, for no crime shall on thy Brows appear,
Bears less reproach than they who placed him there.

But if Contempt is on thy Face entailed,
  Disgrace itself shall be ashamed;
Scandal shall blush, that it has not prevailed
  To blast the man it has defamed.
Let all that merit equal punishment,
Stand there with him, and we are all content.

There would the famed S[ACHEVERE]LL stand,
With trumpet of sedition in his hand,
Sounding the first *Crusado* in the land.
  He, from a Church of England pulpit first
    All his Dissenting brethren curst;
    Doomed them to SATAN for a prey;
    And first found out *The Shortest Way;*
With him, the wise Vice-Chancellor of the Press,
Who, though our Printers licenses defy,
    Willing to show his forwardness,
    Blessed it with his authority;
He gave the Church's sanction to the Work,
As Popes bless colours for troops which fight the Turk.
  Doctors in Scandal, these are grown,
For red-hot Zeal and furious Learning known:
Professors in Reproach and highly fit,
For Juno's Academy, Billingsgate.
  Thou, like a *True-born English* tool, ⎫
  Hast from their Composition stole,   ⎬
And now art like to smart, for being a fool:⎭
And as of English men, 'twas always meant,
They're better to improve, than to invent;

294

Upon their model, thou hast made
A Monster makes the World afraid.

With them, let all the Statesmen stand,
Who guide us with unsteady hand:
Who armies, fleets, and men betray
And ruin all, *The Shortest Way.*
Let all those soldiers stand in sight,
Who're willing to be paid, and not to fight.
Agents and Colonels, who false musters bring,
To cheat their country first, and then, their King:
Bring all your coward Captains of the fleet;
Lord! what a crowd will there be, when they meet?

They who let POINTI 'scape to Brest,
Who all the gods of Carthagena blest.
Those who betrayed our Turkey Fleet,
Or injured TALMASH sold at Camaret.
Who missed the squadron from Toulon,
And always came too late, or else too soon;
All these are heroes whose great actions claim
Immortal honours to their dying fame;
And ought not to have been denied
On thy great Counterscarp, to have their valour tried.

Why have not these, upon thy swelling Stage,
Tasted the keener justice of the Age;
If 'tis because their crimes are too remote,
Whom leaden-footed Justice has forgot;
Let's view the modern scenes of fame,
If Men and Management are not the same;
When fleets go out with money and with men,
Just time enough to venture home again.
Navies prepared to guard the insulted coast;
And convoys settled, when our ships are los:.
Some heroes lately come from sea,
If they were paid their due, should stand with thee;
Papers too should their deeds relate

295

To prove the justice of their fate.
Their deeds of war, at Port St. Mary's done;
And set the Trophies by them, which they won:
Let Or[mon]d's *Declaration* there appear,
He'd certainly be pleased to see them there.
Let some good limner represent
The ravished nuns, the plundered town,
The English honour now misspent;
The shameful coming back, and little done!

The Vigo men should next appear
To triumph on thy Theatre;
They who, on board the great Galoons had been,
Who robbed the Spaniards first, and then the Queen:
Set up the praises, to their valour due;
How Eighty Sail had beaten Twenty-two.
Two troopers so, and one dragoon
Conquered a Spanish boy at Pampelune.
Yet let them Or[mon]d's conduct own,
Who beat them first on shore, or little had been done:
What unknown spoils from thence are come,
How much was brought away; how little, home.
If all the thieves should on thy Scaffold stand
Who robbed their masters in Command;
The multitude would soon outdo
The City crowds of Lord Mayor's Show.

Upon thy Penitential Stools,
Some people should be placed, for fools:
As some, for instance, who, while they look on,
See others plunder all, and they get none.
Next the Lieutenant General,
To get the Devil, lost the De'il and all:
And he, some little badge should bear
Who ought, in justice, to have hanged them there:
This had his honour more maintained
Than all the spoils at Vigo gained.

Then clap thy wooden Wings for joy,
And greet the Men of Great Employ!
The authors of the Nation's discontent,
And scandal of a Christian Government.
Jobbers, and Brokers of the City Stocks,
With forty thousand tallies at their backs;
Who make our Banks and Companies obey,
Or sink them all *The Shortest Way.*
The intrinsic value of our Stocks
Is stated in their calculating books,
The imaginary prizes rise and fall
As they command who toss the ball;
Let them upon thy lofty Turrets stand,
With bear-skins on the back, Debentures in the hand!
And write in capitals upon the post,
That here they should remain
Till this enigma they explain:
How Stocks should fall, when Sales surmount the cost;
And rise again when ships are lost.

Great Monster of the Law, exalt thy head;
Appear no more in masquerade,
In homely phrase, express thy discontent,
And move it in the approaching Parliament:
Tell them, how Paper went, instead of Coin;
With interest Eight per cent., and discount Nine.
Of Irish transport debts unpaid,
Bills false endorsed, and long accounts unmade.
And tell them all the Nation hopes to see, ⎫
They'll send the guilty down to thee; ⎬
Rather than those who write their history. ⎭

Then bring those Justices upon thy bench,
Who vilely break the Laws they should defend;
And upon Equity intrench
By punishing the crimes they will not mend.
Set every vicious Magistrate
Upon thy sumptuous Chariot of the State;
There, let them all in triumph ride,

Their purple and their scarlet laid aside.
Let no such Bridewell Justices protect,
 As first debauch the Whores which they correct:
  Such who with oaths and drunk'ness sit,
 And punish far less crimes than they commit:
  These, certainly, deserve to stand,
With Trophies of Authority in either hand.

Upon thy Pulpit, set the drunken Priest,
Who turns the Gospel to a daily jest;
Let the Fraternity degrade him there,
  Lest they like him appear:
There let him his *memento mori* preach,
And by example, not by doctrine, teach.

   *   *   *   *   *

If a poor Author has embraced thy Wood,
Only because he was not understood;
They punish Mankind but by halves,
  Till they stand there,
Who false to their own principles appear;
  And cannot understand themselves.
Those Nimshites, who with furious zeal drive on,
And build up Rome to pull down Babylon;
The real Authors of *The Shortest Way,*
Who for destruction, not conversion pray:
  There let those Sons of Strife remain,
  Till this Church Riddle they explain;
How at Dissenters they can raise a storm,
  But would not have them all conform;
For there, their certain ruin would come in,
And Moderation, which they hate, begin.
Some Churchmen next should grace thy Pews,
Who talk of Loyalty they never use:
Passive Obedience well becomes thy Stage,
For both have been the Banter of the Age.
  Get them but once within thy reach,
Thou'lt make them practise what they used to teach.

Next bring some Lawyers to thy Bar,
By innuendo, they might all stand there;
There let them expiate that guilt,
And pay for all that blood their tongues have spilt;
  These are the Mountebanks of State,
Why, by the slight of tongue, can crimes create,
And dress up trifles in the robes of Fate.
  The Mastiffs of a Government,
To worry and run down the innocent;
  The Engines of infernal Wit,
  Covered with cunning and deceit:
Satan's sublimest attribute they use,
  For first they tempt, and then accuse;
No vows or promises can bind their hands,
  Submissive Law obedient stands:
When Power concurs, and lawless Force stands by,
He's lunatic that looks for Honesty.

  There sat a man of mighty fame,
Whose actions speak him plainer than his name;
In vain he struggled, he harangued in vain,
To bring in Whipping sentences again:
And to debauch a milder Government,
With *abdicated* kinds of punishment.
  No wonder he should Law despise,
  Who Jesus Christ Himself denies;
  His actions only now direct,
  What we when he is made a Judge expect:
Set L[ove]ll next to his Disgrace
With Whitney's horses staring in his face;
There let his Cup of Penance be kept full,
Till he's less noisy, insolent, and dull.

When all these heroes have passed o'er thy Stage,
And thou hast been the Satire of the Age;
Wait then a while, for all those Sons of Fame,
Whom present Power has made too great to name:
Fenced from thy Hands, they keep our Verse in awe,

Too great for Satire, and too great for Law.
As they their Commands lay down,
They all shall pay their homage to thy Cloudy Throne:
And till within thy reach they be,
Exalt them in effigy.

The martyrs of the by-past reign,
For whom new Oaths have been prepared in vain;
SHE[RLOC]K's disciple, first by him trepanned,
He for a k[nave], and they for f[ool]s should stand.
Though some affirm he ought to be excused,
Since to this day, he had refused;
And this was all the frailty of his life,
He damn'd his conscience, to oblige his wife.
But spare that Priest, whose tottering conscience knew
That if he took but one, he'd perjure two;
Bluntly resolved he would not break them both,
And swore, by G[o]d he'd never take the Oath;
Hang him, he can't be fit for thee,
For his unusual honesty.

Thou Speaking Trumpet of men's fame,
Enter in every Court thy claim;
Demand them all, for they are all thy own,
Who swear to three Kings, but are true to none.
Turn-coats of all sides are thy due,
And he who once is false is never true:
To-day can swear, to-morrow can abjure;
For Treachery's a crime no man can cure.
Such, without scruple, for the Time to come,
May swear to all the Kings in Christendom;
But he's a mad man will rely
Upon their lost fidelity.

They that, in vast employments rob the State,
Let them in thy Embraces, meet their fate;
Let not the millions, they by fraud obtain
Protect them from the scandal, or the pain:

They who from mean beginnings grow
To vast estates, but God knows how;
Who carry untold sums away
From little Places, with but little pay:
Who costly palaces erect,
The thieves that built them to protect:
The gardens, grottoes, fountains, walks, and groves
Where Vice triumphs in pride, and lawless loves;
Where mighty luxury and drunk'ness reigned,
Profusely spend what they profanely gained:
Tell them, their *Mene Tekel's* on the wall,
Tell them, the nation's money paid for all.

Advance thy double Front, and show,
And let us both the Crimes and Persons know:
Place them aloft upon thy Throne,
Who slight the nation's business for their own;
Neglect their posts, in spite of double pay,
And run us all in debt *The Shortest Way*.

* * * * *

What need of Satire to reform the Town?
Or Laws to keep our vices down?
Let them to Thee due homage pay,
This will reform us all *The Shortest Way*.
Let them to thee, bring all the knaves and fools,
Virtue will guide the rest by rules;
They'll need no treacherous friends, no breach of faith,
No hired evidence with their infecting breath;
No servants masters to betray,
Or Knights of the Post, who swear for pay;
No injured Author'll on thy steps appear,
Not such as *wou'd* be rogues, but such as *are*.

The first Intent of Laws
Was to correct the Effect, and check the Cause;
And all the Ends of Punishment,
Were only future mischiefs to prevent.

But Justice is inverted when
Those Engines of the Law,
Instead of pinching vicious men,
Keep honest ones in awe;
Thy business is, as all men know,
To punish villains, not to make men so.

Whenever then, thou art prepared
To prompt that vice, thou should'st reward,
And by the terrors of thy grisly Face
Make men turn rogues to shun disgrace;
The End of thy Creation is destroyed;
Justice expires of course, and Law's made void.

What are thy terrors? that, for fear of thee,
Mankind should dare to sink their honesty?
He's bold to impudence that dare turn knave,
The scandal of thy company to save:
He that will crimes he never knew confess,
Does, more than if he know those crimes, transgress:
And he that fears thee, more than to be base;
May want a heart, but does not want a face.

Thou, like the Devil dost appear,
Blacker than really thou art, by far:
A wild chimeric notion of Reproach;
Too little for a crime, for none too much.
Let none th' indignity resent;
For Crime is all the shame of Punishment.

Thou Bugbear of the Law stand up and speak,
Thy long misconstrued silence break,
Tell us, who 'tis, upon thy Ridge stands there,
So full of fault, and yet so void of fear;
And from the Paper in his hat,
Let all mankind be told for what:

Tell them it was because he was too bold,
And told those truths which should not have been told.
  Extol the Justice of the land,
Who punish what they will not understand.
  Tell them he stands exalted there
  For speaking what we would not hear;
  And yet he might have been secure,
Had he said less, or would he have said more.
  Tell them that this is his reward,
  And worse is yet for him prepared,
Because his foolish virtue was so nice,
As not to sell his friends, according to his friends' advice.

  And thus he's an example made,
To make men of their honesty afraid;
  That for the Time to come, they may
More willingly, their friends betray:
Tell them, the men that placed him here,
Are sc[anda]ls to the Times,
  Are at a loss to find his guilt,
  And can't commit his crimes.

FINIS

Book III
Conscience of the New World

THE TRIAL OF MRS. ANNE HUTCHINSON

Time: November 7 and 8, 1637
Place: The General Court at Newtown,
Massachusetts Bay Colony

FORTY THEOCRATS AND A WOMAN:

Anne Hutchinson

THE EXAMINATION OF MRS. ANNE HUTCHINSON

The court also sent for Mrs. Hutchinson, and charged her with divers matters, as her keeping two public lectures every week in her home, whereto sixty or eighty persons did usually resort, and for reproaching most of the ministers (viz., all except Mr. Cotton) for not preaching a covenant of free grace, and that they had not the seal of the spirit, nor were able ministers of the New Testament; which were clearly proved against her, though she sought to shift it off. And, after many speeches to and fro, at last she was so full as she could not contain, but vented her revelations. . . .

WINTHROP'S *Journal*

Unless one keeps in mind the social forces that found it convenient to array themselves in Puritan garb, the clear meaning of it all will be lost in the fogs of Biblical disputation, and some of the ablest men the English race has ever bred will be reduced to crabbed theologians involved in tenuous subtleties and disputing endlessly over absurd dogmas.

V. L. PARRINGTON, *The Colonial Mind*

THE trial of the conscience of Anne Hutchinson—of her beloved "voice" and revelations—was a crisis in the rise of New England. The symbolic protagonists at her trial were doctrines: "the covenant of works" and "the covenant of grace," salvation by ministry and authority against salvation through the free inner light. The human protagonists were the big and little men of the church-state of Massachusetts Bay Colony and the group around Mrs. Hutchinson (her brother Wheelwright, already indicted, Sir Harry Vane, and others) constituting almost an incipient party of another creed. Anne Hutchinson had neither the originality nor the depth of mind of Roger Williams, but she had intelligence, wit, pride, stubbornness, and opinions. To her forty judges sitting in the General Court at Newtown in November 1637 she appeared as "a woman of haughty and fierce carriage, of a nimble wit and active spirit, and a very voluble tongue, more bold than a man." That she was a spirited woman in a masculine theocracy, and that she referred her revelations to "the voice of my beloved," were almost equal sources of heresy. Before the examining New England synod, which had sat for twenty-four days to draw up a list of eighty-two heresies, "some blasphemous, others erroneous, and all unsafe," with "nine unwholesome expres-

307

sions," Anne Hutchinson appeared as her own defense counsel. Behind the subtleties of theology, and beyond all the display of wit and prejudice and jealousy, her plea was for freedom of conscience, and the right to go straight from her heart, without benefit of clergy, to the source of her revelation: to distinguish between the visible public and invisible private experience; to "see the atheism of my heart"; and "to distinguish between the voice of my beloved and the voice of Moses." Asked, "How do you know that that was the spirit?" she replied: "By an immediate revelation." "How! an immediate revelation," they exclaimed, and she said, "By the voice of his own spirit to my soul. . . . Having seen him which is invisible I fear not what man can do unto me. . . . Now if you condemn me for speaking what in my conscience I know to be truth I must commit myself unto the Lord."

To Governor John Winthrop, who was steward both of godly and temporal business on the Bay, this state of affairs was "the most desperate enthusiasm in the world," though as V. L. Parrington fondly exonerates him, "Godliness has its own special temptations and it would be ungenerous to bear ill-will against so generous a man." To the ministers who witnessed against Anne Hutchinson, whose spiritual quality as ministers she had measured to their discredit against John Cotton's, the odd and rebellious revelations of her heart were more bearable than her too free tongue. She had followed the doctrine and footsteps of John Cotton into New England and he had responded with sympathy to his pupil's doctrine of the inner light, but on her day of trial he stood there, in embarrassment and chaos and indecision, a kind man lacking courage to stand by her, because he could not stand alone. The curious aspect of this trial was not the defection of godly men. It was rather that after she checkmated the charge that she supported the Antinomian teachings of Wheelwright, and checkmated the charge that the meetings in her home were something unlawful and impious, she was swept away in a *voluntary* confession of her "revelations." She was angry, she was desperate to justify herself, she was ill, she was with child. Was she betrayed by the fatigue of her pregnancy, or pride of spirit, or an uncontrollable desire to lay herself bare, or by the ambition to proselytize even her judges? She at once provided these judges with the heresy which they could not, perhaps would not, themselves outline: she martyred herself by a little speech to the court, rather than by the weight of the evidence and the credibility of the excited witnesses. She handed that court in Newtown, on a silver platter, the unguarded confession of her heresy. A few months later, with the abnormal delivery of her dead child, she was to provide the Rever-

308

end John Cotton, at one of his public lectures, with the sad and indecent details of her "monstrous birth." This miscarriage of her womb, and later the slaughter of the Hutchinsons by the Indians comforted the uneasy consciences of those who had cast her out as "a Hethen and a Publican" and "as a Leper."

We have no assurance that had Anne Hutchinson won her trial and established her doctrine of direct communion and inner experience, religious toleration and its political counterpart would have been born sooner from the schisms of the Puritan fortress on Massachusetts Bay. But within the hard Puritan dogma, in its Calvinistic shell, lay the old seed of Lutheran justification by faith that had to break out, in the New World, into a revolutionary spiritual freedom. It was an idealism that burned with both light and heat in English individuals like Roger Williams, Anne Hutchinson, Thomas Hooker, Harry Vane, Oliver Cromwell, and John Milton. The trials of Roger Williams and Anne Hutchinson; the doctrinal duels between "a covenant of works" and "a covenant of grace"; the tempestuous little synods of Protestant inquisition in New England; the great irony of fostering fellowship by excommunication into the Indian wilderness; the Calvinistic thunder and lightning over the stout and bloody heads of Antinomians and Quakers, were, after all, only prophetic of an incipient New England democracy.

THE EXAMINATION OF MRS. ANNE HUTCHINSON

GOVERNOR JOHN WINTHROP
DEPUTY GOVERNOR THOMAS DUDLEY
REV. JOHN COTTON, *teacher of Boston Church*
MR. JOHN ENDICOTT *of Salem, assistant to the Court*
MRS. ANNE HUTCHINSON, *accused*

Ministers and Witnesses

MR. HUGH PETERS *of Salem*
MR. JOHN WILSON *of Boston*
MR. THOMAS WELD *of Roxbury*
MR. GEORGE PHILLIPS *of Watertown*

MR. ZECHARIAH SIMMES *of Charlestown*
MR. THOMAS SHEPHARD *of Cambridge*
MR. JOHN ELIOT *of Roxbury*
MR. RICHARD MATHER *of Dorchester*

Assistants, Elders, Magistrates, Deputies, and Etc.

MR. INCREASE NOWELL, *assistant*
MR. ISRAEL STOUGHTON, *assistant*
MR. ROGER HARLAKENDEN, *assistant*
MR. JOHN COGGESHALL, *deputy*
MR. WILLIAM COLBORN, *deputy and ruling elder of Boston Church*
MR. THOMAS LEVERET, *ruling elder of Boston Church*

CAPT. WILLIAM JENNISON, *deputy of Ipswich*
MR. WILLIAM CODDINGTON, *treasurer of Massachusetts Bay*
MR. BRADSTREET, *assistant*
MR. BROWN, *deputy and ruling elder of Watertown*
MR. BISHOP, *deputy*

MR. COLLICUT, *deputy and merchant of Boston*

Villagers and partisans of the "Covenant of Grace" and the "Covenant of Works"

TIME: *November 7 and 8, 1637*
PLACE: *The General Court at Newtown in the Province of Massachusetts-Bay*

The Examination of Mrs. Anne Hutchinson at the court at Newtown [1]

Mr. Winthrop, governor. Mrs. Hutchinson, you are called here as one of those that have troubled the peace of the commonwealth and the churches here; you are known to be a woman that hath had a great share in the promoting and divulging of those opinions that are causes of this trouble, and to be nearly joined not only in affinity and affection with some of those the court had taken notice of and passed censure upon, but you have spoken divers things as we have been informed very prejudicial to the honour of the churches and ministers thereof, and you have maintained a meeting and an assembly in your house that hath been condemned by the general assembly as a thing not tolerable nor comely in the sight of God nor fitting for your sex, and notwithstanding that was cried down you have continued the same, therefore we have thought good to send for you to understand how things are, that if you be in an erroneous way we may reduce you that so you may become a profitable member here among us, otherwise if you be obstinate in your course that then the court may take such course that you may trouble

---

[1] Reprinted by permission of the President and Fellows of Harvard College from Thomas Hutchinson's *The History of the Colony and Province of Massachusetts-Bay*, edited by Lawrence Shaw Mayo, Harvard University Press, Cambridge, Massachusetts, 1936. (Punctuation and discrepancies in spelling of names have been preserved.)

us no further, therefore I would intreat you to express whether you do not assent and hold in practice to those opinions and factions that have been handled in court already, that is to say, whether you do not justify Mr. Wheelwright's sermon and the petition.

Mrs. Hutchinson. I am called here to answer before you but I hear no things laid to my charge.

Gov. I have told you some already and more I can tell you. (Mrs. H.) Name one Sir.

Gov. Have I not named some already?

Mrs. H. What have I said or done?

Gov. Why for your doings, this you did harbour and countenance those that are parties in this faction that you have heard of. (Mrs. H.) That's matter of conscience, Sir.

Gov. Your conscience you must keep or it must be kept for you.

Mrs. H. Must not I then entertain the saints because I must keep my conscience.

Gov. Say that one brother should commit felony or treason and come to his brother's house, if he knows him guilty and conceals him he ·is guilty of the same. It is his conscience to entertain him, but if his conscience comes into act in giving countenance and entertainment to him that hath broken the law he is guilty too. So if you do countenance those that are transgressors of the law you are in the same fact.

Mrs. H. What law do they transgress?

Gov. The law of God and of the state.

Mrs. H. In what particular?

Gov. Why in this among the rest, whereas the Lord doth say honour thy father and thy mother.

Mrs. H. Ey Sir in the Lord. (Gov.) This honour you have broke in giving countenance to them.

Mrs. H. In entertaining those did I entertain them against any act (for there is the thing) or what God hath appointed?

Gov. You knew that Mr. Wheelwright did preach this sermon and those that countenance him in this do break a law.

Mrs. H. What law have I broken?

Gov. Why the fifth commandment.

Mrs. H. I deny that for he saith in the Lord.

Gov. You have joined with them in the faction.

Mrs. H. In what faction have I joined with them?

Gov. In presenting the petition.

Mrs. H. Suppose I had set my hand to the petition what then? (Gov.) You saw that case tried before.

Mrs. H. But I had not my hand to the petition.

Gov. You have councelled them. (Mrs. H.) Wherein?

Gov. Why in entertaining them.

Mrs. H. What breach of law is that Sir?

Gov. Why dishonouring of parents.

Mrs. H. But put the case Sir that I do fear the Lord and my parents, may not I entertain them that fear the Lord because my parents will not give me leave?

Gov. If they be the fathers of the commonwealth, and they of another religion, if you entertain them then you dishonour your parents and are justly punishable.

Mrs. H. If I entertain them, as they have dishonoured their parents I do.

Gov. No but you by countenancing them above others put honor upon them.

Mrs. H. I may put honor upon them as the children of God and as they do honor the Lord.

Gov. We do not mean to discourse with those of your sex but only this; you do adhere unto them and do endeavor to set forward this faction and so you do dishonour us.

Mrs. H. I do acknowledge no such thing neither do I think that I ever put any dishonour upon you.

Gov. Why do you keep such a meeting at your house as you do every week upon a set day?

Mrs. H. It is lawful for me so to do, as it is all your practices and can you find a warrant for yourself and condemn me for the same thing? The ground of my taking it up was, when I first came to this land because I did not go to such meetings as those were, it was presently reported that I did not allow of such meetings but held them unlawful and therefore in that regard they said I was proud and did despise all ordinances, upon that a friend came unto me and told me of it and I to prevent such aspersions took it up, but it was in practice before I came therefore I was not the first.

Gov. For this, that you appeal to our practice you need no confutation. If your meeting had answered to the former it had not been offensive, but I will say that there was no meeting of women alone, but your meeting is of another sort for there are sometimes men among you.

312

Mrs. H. There was never any man with us.

Gov. Well, admit there was no man at your meeting and that you was sorry for it, there is no warrant for your doings, and by what warrant do you continue such a course?

Mrs. H. I conceive there lyes a clear rule in Titus, that the elder women should instruct the younger and then I must have a time wherein I must do it.

Gov. All this I grant you, I grant you a time for it, but what is this to the purpose that you Mrs. Hutchinson must call a company together from their callings to come to be taught of you?

Mrs. H. Will it please you to answer me this and to give me a rule for them I will willingly submit to any truth. If any come to my house to be instructed in the ways of God what rule have I to put them away?

Gov. But suppose that a hundred men come unto you to be instructed will you forbear to instruct them?

Mrs. H. As far as I conceive I cross a rule in it.

Gov. Very well and do you not so here?

Mrs. H. No Sir for my ground is they are men.

Gov. Men and women all is one for that, but suppose that a man should come and say Mrs. Hutchinson I hear that you are a woman that God hath given his grace unto and you have knowledge in the word of God I pray instruct me a little, ought you not to instruct this man?

Mrs. H. I think I may. —— Do you think it not lawful for me to teach women and why do you call me to teach the court?

Gov. We do not call you to teach the court but to lay open yourself.

Mrs. H. I desire you that you would then set me down a rule by which I may put them away that come unto me and so have peace in so doing.

Gov. You must shew your rule to receive them.

Mrs. H. I have done it.

Gov. I deny it because I have brought more arguments than you have.

Mrs. H. I say, to me it is a rule.

Mr. Endicot. You say there are some rules unto you. I think there is a contradiction in your own words. What rule for your practice do you bring, only a custom in Boston.

Mrs. H. No Sir that was no rule to me but if you look upon the rule in Titus it is a rule to me. If you convince me that it is no rule I shall yield.

Gov. You know that there is no rule that crosses another, but this rule crosses that in the Corinthians. But you must take it in this sense that elder

women must instruct the younger about their business and to love their husbands and not to make them to clash.

Mrs. H. I do not conceive but that it is meant for some publick times.

Gov. Well, have you no more to say but this?

Mrs. H. I have said sufficient for my practice.

Gov. Your course is not to be suffered for, besides that we find such a course as this to be greatly prejudicial to the state, besides the occasion that it is to seduce many honest persons that are called to those meetings and your opinions being known to be different from the word of God may seduce many simple souls that resort unto you, besides that the occasion which hath come of late hath come from none but such as have frequented your meetings, so that now they are flown off from magistrates and ministers and this since they have come to you, and besides that it will not well stand with the common wealth that families should be neglected for so many neighbours and dames and so much time spent, we see no rule of God for this, we see not that any should have authority to set up any other exercises besides what authority hath already set up and so what hurt comes of this you will be guilty of and we for suffering you.

Mrs. H. Sir I do not believe that to be so.

Gov. Well, we see how it is we must therefore put it away from you or restrain you from maintaining this course.

Mrs. H. If you have a rule for it from God's word you may.

Gov. We are your judges, and not you ours and we must compel you to it.

Mrs. H. If it please you by authority to put it down I will freely let you for I am subject to your authority.

Mr. Bradstreet. I would ask this question of Mrs. Hutchinson, whether you do think this is lawful? for then this will follow that all other women that do not are in a sin.

Mrs. H. I conceive this is a free will offering.

Bradst. If it be a free will offering you ought to forbear it because it gives offence.

Mrs. H. Sir, in regard of myself I could, but for others I do not yet see light but shall further consider of it.

Bradst. I am not against all women's meetings but do think them to be lawful.

Mr. Dudley, dep. gov. Here hath been much spoken concerning Mrs. Hutchinson's meetings and among other answers she saith that men come

not there, I would ask you this one question then, whether never any man was at your meeting?

Gov. There are two meetings kept at their house.

Dep. Gov. How; is there two meetings?

Mrs. H. Ey Sir, I shall not equivocate, there is a meeting of men and women and there is a meeting only for women.

Dep. gov. Are they both constant?

Mrs. H. No, but upon occasions they are deferred.

Mr. Endicot. Who teaches in the men's meetings none but men, do not women sometimes?

Mrs. H. Never as I heard, not one.

Dep. gov. I would go a little higher with Mrs. Hutchinson. About three years ago we were all in peace. Mrs. Hutchinson from that time she came hath made a disturbance, and some that came over with her in the ship did inform me what she was as soon as she was landed. I being then in place dealt with the pastor and teacher of Boston and desired them to enquire of her, and then I was satisfied that she held nothing different from us, but within half a year after, she had vented divers of her strange opinions and had made parties in the country, and at length it comes that Mr. Cotton and Mr. Vane were of her judgment, but Mr. Cotton hath cleared himself that he was not of that mind, but now it appears by this woman's meeting that Mrs. Hutchinson hath so forestalled the minds of many by their resort to her meeting that now she hath a potent party in the country. Now if all these things have endangered us as from that foundation and if she in particular hath disparaged all our ministers in the land that they have preached a covenant of works, and only Mr. Cotton a covenant of grace, why this is not to be suffered, and therefore being driven to the foundation and it being found that Mrs. Hutchinson is she that hath depraved all the ministers and hath been the cause of what is fallen out, why we must take away the foundation and the building will fall.

Mrs. H. I pray Sir prove it that I said they preached nothing but a covenant of works.

Dep. Gov. Nothing but a covenant of works, why a Jesuit may preach truth sometimes.

Mrs. H. Did I ever say they preached a covenant of works then?

Dep. Gov. If they do not preach a covenant of grace clearly, then they preach a covenant of works.

315

Mrs. H. No sir, one may preach a covenant of grace more clearly than another, so I said.

D. Gov. We are not upon that now but upon position.

Mrs. H. Prove this then Sir that you say I said.

D. Gov. When they do preach a covenant of works do they preach truth?

Mrs. H. Yes Sir, but when they preach a covenant of works for salvation, that is not truth.

D. Gov. I do but ask you this, when the ministers do preach a covenant of works do they preach a way of salvation?

Mrs. H. I did not come hither to answer to questions of that sort.

D. Gov. Because you will deny the thing.

Mrs. H. Ey, but that is to be proved first.

D. Gov. I will make it plain that you did say that the ministers did preach a covenant of works.

Mrs. H. I deny that.

D. Gov. And that you said they were not able ministers of the new testament, but Mr. Cotton only.

Mrs. H. If ever I spake that I proved it by God's word.

Court. Very well, very well.

Mrs. H. If one shall come unto me in private, and desire me seriously to tell them what I thought of such an one. I must either speak false or true in my answer.

D. Gov. Likewise I will prove this that you said the gospel in the letter and words holds forth nothing but a covenant of works and that all that do not hold as you do are in a covenant of works.

Mrs. H. I deny this for if I should so say I should speak against my own judgment.

Mr. Endicot. I desire to speak seeing Mrs. Hutchinson seems to lay something against them that are to witness against her.

Gover. Only I would add this. It is well discerned to the court that Mrs. Hutchinson can tell when to speak and when to hold her tongue. Upon the answering of a question which we desire her to tell her thoughts of she desires to be pardoned.

Mrs. H. It is one thing for me to come before a public magistracy and there to speak what they would have me to speak and another when a man comes to me in a way of friendship privately there is difference in that.

Gov. What if the matter be all one.

Mr. Hugh Peters. That which concerns us to speak unto as yet we are

316

sparing in unless the court command us to speak, then we shall answer to Mrs. Hutchinson notwithstanding our brethren are very unwilling to answer.

Govern. This speech was not spoken in a corner but in a public assembly, and though things were spoken in private yet now coming to us, we are to deal with them as public.

Mr. Peters. We shall give you a fair account of what was said and desire that we may not be thought to come as informers against the gentlewoman, but as it may be serviceable for the country and our posterity to give you a brief account. This gentlewoman went under suspicion not only from her landing, that she was a woman not only difficult in her opinions, but also of an intemperate spirit. What was done at her landing I do not well remember, but as soon as Mr. Vane and ourselves came this controversy began yet it did reflect upon Mrs. Hutchinson and some of our brethren had dealt with her, and it so fell out that some of our ministry doth suffer as if it were not according to the gospel and as if we taught a covenant of works instead of a covenant of grace. Upon these and the like we did address ourselves to the teacher of that church, and the court then assembled being sensible of these things, and this gentlewoman being as we understood a chief agent, our desire to the teacher was to tell us wherein the difference lay between him and us, for the spring did then arise as we did conceive from this gentlewoman, and so we told him. He said that he thought it not according to God to commend this to the magistrates but to take some other course, and so going on in the discourse we thought it good to send for this gentlewoman, and she willingly came, and at the very first we gave her notice that such reports there were that she did conceive our ministry to be different from the ministry of the gospel, and that we taught a covenant of works, &c. and this was her table talk and therefore we desired her to clear herself and deal plainly. She was very tender at the first. Some of our brethren did desire to put this upon proof, and then her words upon that were. The fear of man is a snare why should I be afraid. These were her words. I did then take upon me to ask her this question. What difference do you conceive to be between your teacher and us? She did not request us that we should preserve her from danger or that we should be silent. Briefly, she told me there was a wide and a broad difference between our brother Mr. Cotton and our selves. I desired to know the difference. She answered that he preaches the covenant of grace and you the covenant of works and that you are not able ministers of the new testament and know no more than the apostles did before the resurrection of Christ. I did then put it to her,

What do you conceive of such a brother? She answered he had not the seal of the spirit. And other things we asked her but generally the frame of her course was this, that she did conceive that we were not able ministers of the gospel. And that day being past our brother Cotton was sorry that she should lay us under a covenant of works, and could have wished she had not done so. The elders being there present we did charge them with her, and the teacher of the place said they would speak further with her, and after some time she answered that we were gone as far as the apostles were before Christ's ascension. And since that we have gone with tears some of us to her.

Mrs. H. If our pastor would shew his writings you should see what I said, and that many things are not so as is reported.

Mr. Wilson. Sister Hutchinson, for the writings you speak of I have them not, and this I must say I did not write down all that was said and did pass betwixt one and another, yet I say what is written I will avouch.

Dep. Gov. I desire that the other elders will say what Mr. Peters hath said.

Mr. Weld. Being desired by the honored court, that which our brother Peters had spoken was the truth and things were spoken as he hath related and the occasion of calling this sister and the passages that were there among us. And myself asking why she did cast such aspersions upon the ministers of the country though we were poor sinful men and for ourselves we cared not but for the precious doctrine we held forth we could not but grieve to hear that so blasphemed. She at that time was sparing in her speech. I need not repeat the things they have been truly related. She said the fear of man is a snare and therefore I will speak freely and she spake her judgment and mind freely as was before related, that Mr. Cotton did preach a covenant of grace and we a covenant of works. And this I remember she said we could not preach a covenant of grace because we were not sealed, and we were not able ministers of the new testament no more than were the disciples before the resurrection of Christ.

Mr. Phillips. For my own part I have had little to do in these things only at that time I was there and yet not being privy to the ground of that which our brother Peters had mentioned but they procuring me to go along with them telling me that they were to deal with her; at first she was unwilling to answer but at length she said there was a great deal of difference between Mr. Cotton and we. Upon this Mr. Cotton did say that he could have wished that she had not put that in. Being asked of particulars she did instance in Mr. Shepherd that he did not preach a covenant of grace clearly and she instanced our brother Weld. Then I asked her of myself (being she spake

318

rashly·of them all) because she never heard me at all. She likewise said that we were not able ministers of the new testament and her reason was because we were not sealed.

Mr. Simmes. For my own part being called to speak in this case to discharge the relation wherein I stand to the commonwealth and that which I stand in unto God, I shall speak briefly. For my acquaintance with this person I had none in our native country, only I had occasion to be in her company once or twice before I came, where I did perceive that she did slight the ministers of the word of God. But I came along with her in the ship, and it so fell out that we were in the great cabin together and therein did agree with the labours of Mr. Lothrop and myself, only there was a secret opposition to things delivered. The main thing that was then in hand was about the evidencing of a good estate, and among the rest about that place in John concerning the love of the brethren. That which I took notice of was the corruptness and narrowness of her opinions, which I doubt not but I may call them so, but she said, when she came to Boston there would be something more seen than I said, for such speeches were cast about and abused as that of our saviour, I have many things to say but you cannot bear them now. And being come and she desiring to be admitted a member, I was desired to be there, and then Mr. Cotton did give me full satisfaction in the things then in question. And for things which have been here spoken, as far as I can remember they are the truth, and when I asked her what she thought of me, she said alas you know my mind long ago, yet I do not think myself disparaged by her testimony and I would not trouble the court, only this one thing I shall put in, that Mr. Dudley and Mr. Haines were not wanting in the cause after I had given notice of her.

Mr. Wilson. I desire you would give me leave to speak this word because of what has been said concerning her entrance into the church. There was some difficulty made, but in her answers she gave full satisfaction to our teacher and myself, and for point of evidencing justification by sanctification she did not deny, but only justification must be first. Our teacher told her then that if she was of that mind she would take away the scruple; for we thought that matter, for point of order we did not greatly stand upon, because we hoped she would hold with us in that truth as well as the other.

Mr. Shephard. I am loth to speak in this assembly concerning this gentlewoman in question, but I can do no less than speak what my conscience speaks unto me. For personal reproaches I take it a man's wisdom to conceal.

Concerning the reproaches of the ministry of our's there hath been many in the country, and this hath been my thoughts of that. Let men speak what they will not only against persons but against ministry, let that pass, but let us strive to speak to the consciences of men, knowing that if we had the truth with us we shall not need to approve our words by our practice and our ministry to the hearts of the people, and they should speak for us and therefore I have satisfied myself and the brethren with that. Now for that which concerns this gentlewoman at this time I do not well remember every particular, only this I do remember that the end of our meeting was to satisfy ourselves in some points. Among the rest Mrs. Hutchinson was desired to speak her thoughts concerning the ministers of the Bay. Now I remember that she said that we were not able ministers of the new testament. I followed her with particulars, she instanced myself as being at the lecture and hearing me preach when as I gave some means whereby a christian might come to the assurance of God's love. She instanced that I was not sealed. I said why did she say so. She said because you put love for an evidence. Now I am sure she was in an error in this speech for if assurance be an holy estate than I am sure there are not graces wanting to evidence it.

Mr. Eliot. I am loth to spend time therefore I shall consent to what hath been said. Our brethren did intreat us to write and a few things I did write the substance of which hath been here spoken and I have it in writing, therefore I do avouch it.

Mr. Shephard. I desire to speak this word, it may be but a slip of her tongue, and I hope she will be sorry for it, and then we shall be glad of it.

Dep. Gov. I called these witnesses and you deny them. You see they have proved this and you deny this, but it is clear. You said they preached a covenant of works and that they were not able ministers of the new testament; now there are two other things that you did affirm which were that the scriptures in the letter of them held forth nothing but a covenant of works and likewise that those that were under a covenant of works cannot be saved

Mrs. H. Prove that I said so. (Gov.) Did you say so?

Mrs. H. No Sir it is your conclusion.

D. Gov. What do I do charging of you if you deny what is so fully proved.

Gov. Here are six undeniable ministers who say it is true and yet you deny that you did say that they did preach a covenant of works and that they were not able ministers of the gospel, and it appears plainly that you have

spoken it, and whereas you say that it was drawn from you in a way of friendship, you did profess then that it was out of conscience that you spake and said The fear of man is a snare, wherefore shall[2] I be afraid, I will speak plainly and freely.

Mrs. H. That I absolutely deny, for the first question, was thus answered by me to them. They thought that I did conceive there was a difference between them and Mr. Cotton. At the first I was somewhat reserved, then said Mr. Peters I pray answer the question directly as fully and as plainly as you desire we should tell you our minds. Mrs. Hutchinson we come for plain dealing and telling you our hearts. Then I said I would deal as plainly as I could, and whereas they say I said they were under a covenant of works and in the state of the apostles why these two speeches cross one another. I might say they might preach a covenant of works as did the apostles, but to preach a covenant of works and to be under a covenant of works is another business.

Dep. Gov. There have been six witnesses to prove this and yet you deny it.

Mrs. H. I deny that these were the first words that were spoken.

Gov. You make the case worse, for you clearly shew that the ground of your opening your mind was not to satisfy them but to satisfy your own conscience.

Mr. Peters. We do not desire to be so narrow to the court and the gentlewoman about times and seasons, whether first or after, but said it was.

Dep. Gov. For that other thing I mentioned for the letter of the scripture that it held forth nothing but a covenant of works, and for the latter that we are in a state of damnation, being under a covenant of works, or to that effect, these two things you also deny. Now the case stands thus. About three quarters of a year ago I heard of it, and speaking of it there came one to me who is not here, but will affirm if it need be, as he did to me that he did hear you say in so many words. He set it down under his hand and I can bring it forth when the court pleases. His name is subscribed to both these things, and upon my peril be it if I bring you not in the paper and bring the minister (meaning Mr. Ward) to be deposed.

Gov. What say you to this, though nothing be directly proved yet you hear it may be.

Mrs. H. I acknowledge using the words of the apostle to the Corinthians unto him, that they that were ministers of the letter and not the spirit did

---

[2] The first edition gives "should" instead of "shall."

preach a covenant of works. Upon his saying there was no such scripture, then I fetched the bible and shewed him this place 2 Cor. iii. 6. He said that was the letter of the law. No said I it is the letter of the gospel.

Gov. You have spoken this more than once then.

Mrs. H. Then upon further discourse about proving a good estate and holding it out by the manifestation of the spirit he did acknowledge that to be the nearest way, but yet said he, will you not acknowledge that which we hold forth to be a way too wherein we may have hope; no truly if that be a way it is a way to hell.

Gov. Mrs. Hutchinson, the court you see hath laboured to bring you to acknowledge the error of your way that so you might be reduced, the time now grows late, we shall therefore give you a little more time to consider of it and therefore desire that you attend the court again in the morning.

The next morning.

Gov. We proceeded the last night as far as we could in hearing of this cause of Mrs. Hutchinson. There were divers things laid to her charge, her ordinary meetings about religious exercises, her speeches in derogation of the ministers among us, and the weakening of the hands and hearts of the people towards them. Here was sufficient proof made of that which she was accused of in that point concerning the ministers and their ministry, as that they did preach a covenant of works when others did preach a covenant of grace, and that they were not able ministers of the new testament, and that they had not the seal of the spirit, and this was spoken not as was pretended out of private conference, but out of conscience and warrant from scripture alledged the fear of man is a snare and seeing God had given her a calling to it she would freely speak. Some other speeches she used, as that the letter of the scripture held forth a covenant of works, and this is offered to be proved by probable grounds. If there be any thing else that the court hath to say they may speak.

Mrs. H. The ministers come in their own cause. Now the Lord hath said that an oath is the end of all controversy; though there be a sufficient number of witnesses yet they are not according to the word, therefore I desire they may speak upon oath.

Gov. Well, it is in the liberty of the court whether they will have an oath or no and it is not in this case as in case of a jury. If they be satisfied they have sufficient matter to proceed.

322

Mrs. H. I have since I went home perused some notes out of what Mr. Wilson did then write and I find things not to be as hath been alledged.

Gov. Where are the writings?

Mrs. H. I have them not, it may be Mr. Wilson hath.

Gov. What are the instructions that you can give, Mr. Wilson?

Mr. Wilson. I do say that Mr. Vane desired me to write the discourse out and whether it be in his own hands or in some body's else I know not. For my own copy it is somewhat imperfect, but I could make it perfect with a little pains.

Gov. For that which you alledge as an exception against the elders it is vain and untrue, for they are no prosecutors in this cause but are called to witness in the cause.

Mrs. H. But they are witnesses of their own cause.

Gov. It is not their cause but the cause of the whole country and they were unwilling that it should come forth, but that it was the glory and honour of God.

Mrs. H. But it being the Lord's ordinance that an oath should be the end of all strife, therefore they are to deliver what they do upon oath.

Mr. Bradstreet. Mrs. Hutchinson, these are but circumstances and adjuncts to the cause, admit they should mistake you in your speeches you would make them to sin if you urge them to swear.

Mrs. H. That is not the thing. If they accuse me I desire it may be upon oath.

Gov. If the court be not satisfied they may have an oath.

Mr. Nowel. I should think it convenient that the country also should be satisfied because that I do hear it affirmed, that things which were spoken in private are carried abroad to the publick and thereupon they do under-value the ministers of congregations.

Mr. Brown. I desire to speak. If I mistake not an oath is of a high nature, and it is not to be taken but in a controversy, and for my part I am afraid of an oath and fear that we shall take God's name in vain, for we may take the witness of these men without an oath.

Mr. Endicot. I think the ministers are so well known unto us, that we need not take an oath of them, but indeed an oath is the end of all strife.

Mrs. H. There are some that will take their oaths to the contrary.

Mr. Endicot. Then it shall go under the name of a controversy, therefore we desire to see the notes and those also that will swear.

Gov. Let those that are not satisfied in the court speak.

[*Many say. —— We are not satisfied.*]

Gov. I would speak this to Mrs. Hutchinson. If the ministers shall take an oath will you sit down satisfied?

Mrs. H. I can't be notwithstanding oaths satisfied against my own conscience.

Mr. Stoughton. I am fully satisfied with this that the ministers do speak the truth but now in regard of censure. I dare not hold up my hand to that, because it is a course of justice, and I cannot satisfy myself to proceed so far in a way of justice, and therefore I should desire an oath in this as in all other things. I do but speak to prevent offence if I should not hold up my hand at the censure unless there be an oath given.

Mr. Peters. We are ready to swear if we see a way of God in it.

[*Here was a parley between the deputy governor and Mr. Stoughton about the oath.*]

Mr. Endicot. If they will not be satisfied with a testimony an oath will be in vain.

Mr. Stoughton. I am persuaded that Mrs. Hutchinson and many other godly-minded people will be satisfied without an oath.

Mrs. H. An oath Sir is an end of all strife and it is God's ordinance.

Mr. Endicot. A sign it is what respect she hath to their words, and further, pray see your argument, you will have the words that were written and yet Mr. Wilson saith he writ not all, and now you will not believe all those godly ministers without an oath.

Mrs. H. Mr. Wilson did affirm that which he gave in to the governor that then was to be true. (some reply) But not all the truth.

Mr. Wilson. I did say so far as I did take them they were true.

Mr. Harlakenden. I would have the spectators take notice that the court doth not suspect the evidence that is given in, though we see that whatever evidence is brought in will not satisfy, for they are resolved upon the thing and therefore I think you will not be unwilling to give your oaths.

Gov. I see no necessity of an oath in this thing seeing it is true and the substance of the matter confirmed by divers, yet that all may be satisfied, if the elders will take an oath they shall have it given them.

Dep. Gov. Let us join the things together that Mrs. Hutchinson may see what they have their oaths for.

Mrs. H. I will prove by what Mr. Wilson hath written that they never heard me say such a thing.

Mr. Sims. We desire to have the paper and have it read.

Mr. Harlakenden. I am persuaded that is the truth that the elders do say and therefore I do not see it necessary how to call them to oath.

Gov. We cannot charge any thing of untruth upon them.

Mr. Harlakenden. Besides, Mrs. Hutchinson doth say that they are not able ministers of the new testament.

Mrs. H. They need not swear to that.

Dep. Gov. Will you confess it then.

Mrs. H. I will not deny it or say it.

Dep. Gov. You must do one.

Mrs. H. After that they have taken an oath, I will make good what I say.

Gov. Let us state the case and then we may know what to do. That which is laid to Mrs. Hutchinson's charge is this, that she hath traduced the magistrates and ministers of this jurisdiction, that she hath said the ministers preached a covenant of works and Mr. Cotton a covenant of grace, and that they were not able ministers of the gospel, and she excuses it that she made it a private conference and with a promise of secrecy, &c. now this is charged upon her, and they therefore sent for her seeing she made it her table talk, and then she said the fear of man was a snare and therefore she would not be affeared of them.

Mrs. H. This that your self hath spoken, I desire that they may take their oaths upon.

Gov. That that we should put the reverend elders unto is this that they would deliver upon oath that which they can remember themselves.

Mr. Shepard. I know no reason of the oath but the importunity of this gentlewoman.

Mr. Endicot. You lifted up your eyes as if you took God to witness that you came to entrap none and yet you will have them swear.

Mr. Harlakenden. Put any passage unto them and see what they say.

Mrs. H. They say I said the fear of man is a snare, why should I be afraid. When I came unto them, they urging many things unto me and I being backward to answer at first, at length this scripture came into my mind 29th Prov. 15. The fear of man bringeth a snare, but whoso putteth his trust in the Lord shall be safe.

Mr. Harlakenden. This is not an essential thing.

Gov. I remember his testimony was this.

Mrs. H. Ey, that was the thing that I do deny for they were my words and they were not spoken at the first as they do alledge.

Mr. Peters. We cannot tell what was first or last, we suppose that an oath

325

is an end of all strife and we are tender of it, yet this is the main thing against her that she charged us to be unable ministers of the gospel and to preach a covenant of works.

Gover. You do understand the thing, that the court is clear for we are all satisfied that it is truth but because we would take away all scruples, we desire that you would satisfy the spectators by your oath.

Mr. Bishop. I desire to know before they be put to oath whether their testimony be of validity.

Dep. Gov. What do you mean to trouble the court with such questions. Mark what a flourish Mrs. Hutchinson puts upon the business that she had witnesses to disprove what was said and here is no man to bear witness.

Mrs. H. If you will not call them in that is nothing to me.

Mr. Eliot. We desire to know of her and her witnesses what they deny and then we shall speak upon oath. I know nothing we have spoken of but we may swear to.

Mr. Sims. Ey, and more than we have spoken to.

Mr. Stoughton. I would gladly that an oath should be given that so the person to be condemned should be satisfied in her conscience and I would say the same for my own conscience if I should join in the censure ——

[*Two or three lines in the MS are defaced and not legible.*]

Mr. Coggeshall. I desire to speak a word—It is desired that the elders would confer with Mr. Cotton before they swear.

Govern. Shall we not believe so many godly elders in a cause wherein we know the mind of the party without their testimony?

Mr. Endicot to Mr. Coggeshall. I will tell you what I say. I think that this carriage of your's tends to further casting dirt upon the face of the judges.

Mr. Harlakenden. Her carriage doth the same for she doth not object any essential thing, but she goes upon circumstances and yet would have them sworn.

Mrs. H. This I would say unto them. Forasmuch as it was affirmed by the deputy that he would bring proof of these things, and the elders they bring proof in their own cause, therefore I desire that particular witnesses be for these things that they do speak.

Gov. The elders do know what an oath is and as it is an ordinance of God so it should be used.

Mrs. H. That is the thing I desire and because the deputy spake of witnesses I have them here present.

Mr. Colborn. We desire that our teacher may be called to hear what is said. —— [*Upon this Mr. Cotton came and sat down by Mrs. Hutchinson.*]

Mr. Endicot. This would cast some blame upon the ministers—Well, but whatsoever he will or can say we will believe the ministers.

Mr. Eliot, Mr. Shepard. We desire to see light why we should take an oath.

Mr. Stoughton. Why it is an end of all strife and I think you ought to swear and put an end to the matter.

Mr. Peters. Our oath is not to satisfy Mrs. Hutchinson but the court.

Mr. Endicot. The assembly will be satisfied by it.

Dep. Gov. If the country will not be satisfied you must swear.

Mr. Shepard. I conceive the country doth not require it.

Dep. Gov. Let her witnesses be called.

Gov. Who be they?

Mrs. H. Mr. Leveret and our teacher and Mr. Coggeshall.

Gov. Mr. Coggeshall was not present.

Mr. Coggeshall. Yes but I was, only I desired to be silent till I should be called.

Gov. Will you Mr. Coggeshall say that she did not say so?

Mr. Coggeshall. Yes I dare say that she did not say all that which they lay against her.

Mr. Peters. How dare you look into the court to say such a word?

Mr. Coggeshall. Mr. Peters takes upon him to forbid me. I shall be silent.

Mr. Stoughton. Ey, but she intended this that they say.

Gov. Well, Mr. Leveret, what were the words? I pray speak.

Mr. Leveret. To my best remembrance when the elders did send for her, Mr. Peters did with much vehemency and intreaty urge her to tell what difference there was between Mr. Cotton and them, and upon his urging of her she said. The fear of man is a snare, but they that trust upon the Lord shall be safe. And being asked wherein the difference was, she answered that they did not preach a covenant of grace so clearly as Mr. Cotton did, and she gave this reason of it because that as the apostles were for a time without the spirit so until they had received the witness of the spirit they could not preach a covenant of grace so clearly.

Gov. Don't you remember that she said they were not able ministers of the new testament?

Mrs. H. Mr. Weld and I had an hour's discourse at the window and then I spake that, if I spake it.

Mr. Weld. Will you affirm that in the court? Did not I say unto you, Mrs.

Hutchinson, before the elders. When I produced the thing, you then called for proof. Was not my answer to you, leave it there, and if I cannot prove it you shall be blameless?

Mrs. H. This I remember I spake, but do not you remember that I came afterwards to the window when you was writing and there spake unto you.

Mr. Weld. No truly. (Mrs. H.) But I do very well.

Gov. Mr. Cotton, the court desires that you declare what you do remember of the conference which was at that time and is now in question.

Mr. Cotton. I did not think I should be called to bear witness in this cause and therefore did not labour to call to remembrance what was done; but the greatest passage that took impression upon me was to this purpose. The elders spake that they had heard that she had spoken some condemning words of their ministry, and among other things they did first pray her to answer wherein she thought their ministry did differ from mine, how the comparison sprang I am ignorant, but sorry I was that any comparison should be between me and my brethren and uncomfortable it was, she told them to this purpose that they did not hold forth a covenant of grace as I did, but wherein did we differ? why she said that they did not hold forth the seal of the spirit as he doth. Where is the difference there? say they, why saith she speaking to one or other of them, I know not to whom. You preach of the seal of the spirit upon a work and he upon free grace without a work or without respect to a work, he preaches the seal of the spirit upon free grace and you upon a work. I told her I was very sorry that she put comparisons between my ministry and their's, for she had said more than I could myself, and rather I had that she had put us in fellowship with them and not have made that discrepancy. She said, she found the difference. Upon that there grew some speeches upon the thing and I do remember I instanced to them the story of Thomas Bilney in the book of martyrs how freely the spirit witnessed unto him without any respect unto a work as himself professes. Now upon this other speeches did grow. If you put me in mind of any thing I shall speak it, but this was the sum of the difference, nor did it seem to be so ill taken as it is and our brethren did say also that they would not so easily believe reports as they had done and withall mentioned that they would speak no more of it, some of them did; and afterwards some of them did say they were less satisfied than before. And I must say that I did not find her saying they were under a covenant of works, nor that she said they did preach a covenant of works.

328

Gov. You say you do not remember, but can you say she did not speak so —— [*Here two lines again defaced.*]

Mr. Cotton. I do remember that she looked at them as the apostles before the ascension.

Mr. Peters. I humbly desire to remember our reverend teacher. May it please you to remember how this came in. Whether do you not remember that she said we were not sealed with the spirit of grace, therefore could not preach a covenant of grace, and she said further you may do it in your judgment but not in experience, but she spake plump that we were not sealed.

Mr. Cotton. You do put me in remembrance that it was asked her why cannot we preach a covenant of grace? Why, saith she, because you can preach no more than you know, or to that purpose, she spake. Now that she said you could not preach a covenant of grace I do not remember such a thing. I remember well that she said you were not sealed with the seal of the spirit.

Mr. Peters. There was a double seal found out that day which never was.

Mr. Cotton. I know very well that she took the seal of the spirit in that sense for the full assurance of God's favour by the holy ghost, and now that place in the Ephesians doth hold out that seal.

Mr. Peters. So that was the ground of our discourse concerning the great seal and the little seal.

Mr. Cotton. To that purpose I remember somebody speaking of the difference of the witness of the spirit and the seal of the spirit, some to put a distinction called it the broad seal and the little seal. Our brother Wheelwright answered if you will have it so be it so.

Mrs. H. Mr. Ward said that.

[*Some three or four of the ministers. Mr. Wheelwright said it.*]

Mr. Cotton. No, it was not brother Wheelwright's speech but one of your own expressions, and as I remember it was Mr. Ward.

Mr. Peters. - - - - - -

Mr. Cotton. Under favour I do not remember that.

Mr. Peters. Therefore her answer clears it in your judgment but not in your experience.

Mrs. H. My name is precious and you do affirm a thing which I utterly deny.

D. Gov. You should have brought the book with you.

Mr. Nowell. The witnesses do not answer that which you require.

Gov. I do not see that we need their testimony any further. Mr. Cotton hath expressed what he remembered, and what took impression upon him, and so I think the other elders also did remember that which took impression upon them.

Mr. Weld. I then said to Mrs. Hutchinson when it was come to this issue, why did you let us go thus long and never tell us of it?

Gov. I should wonder why the elders should move the elders of our congregation to have dealt with her if they saw not some cause.

Mr. Cotton. Brother Weld and brother Shepard, I did not then clear myself unto you that I understood her speech in expressing herself to you that you did hold forth some matter in your preaching that was not pertinent to the seal of the spirit —— [*Two lines defaced.*]

Dep. Gov. They affirm that Mrs. Hutchinson did say they were not able ministers of the new testament.

Mr. Cotton. I do not remember it.

Mrs. H. If you please to give me leave I shall give you the ground of what I know to be true. Being much troubled to see the falseness of the constitution of the church of England, I had like to have turned separatist; whereupon I kept a day of solemn humiliation and pondering of the thing; this scripture was brought unto me—he that denies Jesus Christ to be come in the flesh is antichrist—This I considered of and in considering found that the papists did not deny him to be come in the flesh, nor we did not deny him—who then was antichrist? Was the Turk antichrist only? The Lord knows that I could not open scripture; he must by his prophetical office open it unto me. So after that being unsatisfied in the thing, the Lord was pleased to bring this scripture out of the Hebrews. He that denies the testament denies the testator, and in this did open unto me and give me to see that those which did not teach the new covenant had the spirit of antichrist, and upon this he did discover the ministry unto me and ever since, I bless the Lord, he hath let me see which was the clear ministry and which the wrong. Since that time I confess I have been more choice and he hath left me to distinguish between the voice of my beloved and the voice of Moses, the voice of John Baptist and the voice of antichrist, for all those voices are spoken of in scripture. Now if you do condemn me for speaking what in my conscience I know to be truth I must commit myself unto the Lord.

Mr. Nowel. How do you know that that was the spirit?

Mrs. H. How did Abraham know that it was God that bid him offer his son, being a breach of the sixth commandment?

330

Dep. Gov. By an immediate voice.

Mrs. H. So to me by an immediate revelation.

Dep. Gov. How! an immediate revelation.

Mrs. H. By the voice of his own spirit to my soul. I will give you another scripture, Jer. 46. 27, 28—out of which the Lord shewed me what he would do for me and the rest of his servants.—But after he was pleased to reveal himself to me I did presently like Abraham run to Hagar. And after that he did let me see the atheism of my own heart, for which I begged of the Lord that it might not remain in my heart, and being thus, he did shew me this (a twelvemonth after) which I told you of before. Ever since that time I have been confident of what he hath revealed unto me.

[*Obliterated*] another place out of Daniel chap. 7 and he and for us all, wherein he shewed me the sitting of the judgment and the standing of all high and low before the Lord and how thrones and kingdoms were cast down before him. When our teacher came to New-England it was a great trouble unto me, my brother Wheelwright being put by also. I was then much troubled concerning the ministry under which I lived, and then that place in the 30th of Isaiah was brought to my mind. Though the Lord give thee bread of adversity and water of affliction yet shall not thy teachers be removed into corners any more, but thine eyes shall see thy teachers. The Lord giving me this promise and they being gone there was none then left that I was able to hear, and I could not be at rest but I must come hither. Yet that place of Isaiah did much follow me, though the Lord give thee the bread of adversity and water of affliction. This place lying I say upon me then this place in Daniel was brought unto me and did shew me that though I should meet with affliction yet I am the same God that delivered Daniel out of the lion's den, I will also deliver thee.—Therefore I desire you to look to it, for you see this scripture fulfilled this day and therefore I desire you that as you tender the Lord and the church and commonwealth to consider and look what you do. You have power over my body but the Lord Jesus hath power over my body and soul, and assure yourselves thus much, you do as much as in you lies to put the Lord Jesus Christ from you, and if you go on in this course you begin you will bring a curse upon you and your posterity, and the mouth of the Lord hath spoken it.

Dep. Gov. What is the scripture she brings?

Mr. Stoughton. Behold I turn away from you.

Mrs. H. But now having seen him which is invisible I fear not what man can do unto me.

331

Gov. Daniel was delivered by miracle do you think to be deliver'd so too?

Mrs. H. I do here speak it before the court. I look that the Lord should deliver me by his providence.

Mr. Harlakenden. I may read scripture and the most glorious hypocrite may read them and yet go down to hell.

Mrs. H. It may be so.

Mr. Bartholomew. I would remember one word to Mrs. Hutchinson among many others. She knowing that I did know her opinions, being she was at my house at London, she was afraid I conceive or loth to impart herself unto me, but when she came within sight of Boston and looking upon the meanness of the place, I conceive, she uttered these words, if she had not a sure word that England should be destroyed her heart would shake. Now it seemed to me at that time very strange that she should say so.

Mrs. H. I do not remember that I looked upon the meanness of the place nor did it discourage me, because I knew the bounds of my habitation were determined, &c.

Mr. Bartholomew. I speak as a member of the court. I fear that her revelations will deceive.

Gov. Have you heard of any of her revelations?

Mr. Barthol. For my own part I am sorry to see her now here and I have nothing against her but what I said was to discover what manner of spirit Mrs. Hutchinson is of; only I remember as we were once going through Paul's church yard she then was very inquisitive after revelations and said that she had never had any great thing done about her but it was revealed to her beforehand. (Mrs. H.) I say the same thing again.

Mr. Bartholomew. And also that she said that she was come to New-England but for Mr. Cotton's sake. As for Mr. Hooker (as I remember) she said she liked not his spirit, only she spake of a sermon of his in the low countries wherein he said thus—it was revealed to me yesterday that England should be destroyed. She took notice of that passage and it was very acceptable with her.

Mr. Cotton. One thing let me intreat you to remember, Mr. Bartholomew, that you never spake anything to me.

Mr. Barth. No Sir, I never spake of it to you and therefore I desire to clear Mr. Cotton.

Gov. There needs no more of that.

Mr. Barth. Only I remember her eldest daughter said in the ship that she

332

had a revelation that a young man in the ship should be saved, but he must walk in the ways of her mother.

Mr. Sims. I could say something to that purpose, for she said—then what would you say if we should be at New-England within these three weeks, and I reproved her vehemently for it.

Mr. Elliot. That speech of Mr. Hooker's which they alledge is against his mind and judgment.[3]

Mr. Sims. I would intreat Mrs. Hutchinson to remember, that the humble he will teach—I have spoken before of it and therefore I will leave the place with her and do desire her to consider of many expressions that she hath spoken to her husband, but I will not enlarge myself.

Mr. Endicot. I would have a word or two with leave of that which hath thus far been revealed to the court. I have heard of many revelations of Mrs. Hutchinson's, but they were reports, but Mrs. Hutchinson I see doth maintain some by this discourse, and I think it is a special providence of God to hear what she hath said. Now there is a revelation you see which she doth expect as a miracle. She saith she now suffers and let us do what we will she shall be delivered by a miracle. I hope the court takes notice of the vanity of it and heat of her spirit. Now because her reverend teacher is here I should desire that he would please to speak freely whether he doth condescend to such speeches or revelations as have been here spoken of, and he will give a great deal of content.

Mr. Cotton. May it please you Sir. There are two sorts of revelations, there are [defaced] or against the word besides scripture both which [defaced] tastical and tending to danger more ways than one —— there is another sort which the apostle prays the believing Ephesians may be made partakers of, and those are such as are breathed by the spirit of God and are never dispensed but in a word of God and according to a word of God, and though the word revelation be rare in common speech and we make it uncouth in our ordinary expressions, yet notwithstanding, being understood in the scripture sense I think they are not only lawful but such as christians may receive and God bear witness to it in his word, and usually he doth express it in the ministry of the word and doth accompany it by his spirit, or else it is in the reading of the word in some chapter or verse and whenever it comes it comes flying upon the wings of the spirit.

---

[3] Mr. Elliot was mistaken. The passage from his sermon is in print and Mr. Hooker avowed it afterwards at Hartford. Magn. B. iii, P. 62.

Mr. Endicot. You give me satisfaction in the thing and therefore I desire you to give your judgment of Mrs. Hutchinson; what she hath said you hear and all the circumstances thereof.

Mr. Cotton. I would demand whether by a miracle she doth mean a work above nature or by some wonderful providence for that is called a miracle often in the psalms.

Mrs. H. I desire to speak to our teacher. You know Sir what he doth declare though he doth not know himself [*something wanting.*] now either of these ways or at this present time it shall be done, yet I would not have the court so to understand me that he will deliver me now even at this present time.

Dep. Gov. I desire Mr. Cotton to tell us whether you do approve of Mrs. Hutchinson's revelations as she hath laid them down.

Mr. Cotton. I know not whether I do understand her, but this I say, if she doth expect a deliverance in a way of providence—then I cannot deny it.

Dep. Gov. No Sir we did not speak of that.

Mr. Cotton. If it be by way of miracle then I would suspect it.

Dep. Gov. Do you believe that her revelations are true?

Mr. Cotton. That she may have some special providence of God to help her is a thing that I cannot bear witness against.

Dep. Gov. Good Sir I do ask whether this revelation be of God or no?

Mr. Cotton. I should desire to know whether the sentence of the court will bring her to any calamity, and then I would know of her whether she expects to be delivered from that calamity by a miracle or a providence of God.

Mrs. H. By a providence of God I say I expect to be delivered from some calamity that shall come to me.

Gover. The case is altered and will not stand with us now, but I see a marvellous providence of God to bring things to this pass that they are. We have been hearkening about the trial of this thing and now the mercy of God by a providence hath answered our desires and made her to lay open her self and the ground of all these disturbances to be by revelations, for we receive no such made out of the ministry of the word

and so one scripture after another, but all this while there is no use of the ministry of the word nor of any clear call of God by his word, but the ground work of her revelations is the immediate revelation of the spirit and not by the ministry of the word, and that is the means by which she hath

334

very much abused the country that they shall look for revelations and are not bound to the ministry of the word, but God will teach them by immediate revelations and this hath been the ground of all these tumults and troubles, and I would that those were all cut off from us that trouble us, for this is the thing that hath been the root of all the mischief.

Court. We all consent with you.

Gov. Ey it is the most desperate enthusiasm in the world, for nothing but a word comes to her mind and then an application is made which is nothing to the purpose, and this is her revelations when it is impossible but that the word and spirit should speak the same thing.

Mr. Endicot. I speak in reference to Mr. Cotton. I am tender of you Sir and there lies much upon you in this particular, for the answer of Mr. Cotton doth not free him from that way which his last answer did bring upon him, therefore I beseech you that you'd be pleased to speak a word to that which Mrs. Hutchinson hath spoken of her revelations as you have heard the manner of it. Whether do you witness for her or against her.

Mr. Cotton. This is that I said Sir, and my answer is plain that if she doth look for deliverance from the hand of God by his providence, and the revelation be in a word or according to a word, that I cannot deny.

Mr. Endicot. You give me satisfaction.

Dep. Gov. No, no, he gives me none at all.

Mr. Cotton. But if it be in a way of miracle or a revelation without the word that I do not assent to, but look at it as a delusion, and I think so doth she too as I understand her.

Dep. Gov. Sir, you weary me and do not satisfy me.

Mr. Cotton. I pray Sir give me leave to express my self. In that sense that she speaks I dare not bear witness against it:

Mr. Nowell. I think it is a devilish delusion.

Gover. Of all the revelations that ever I read of I never read the like ground laid as is for this. The Enthusiasts and Anabaptists had never the like.

Mr. Cotton. You know Sir, that their revelations broach new matters of faith and doctrine.

Gover. So do these and what may they breed more if they be let alone. I do acknowledge that there are such revelations as do concur with the word but there hath not been any of this nature.

Dep. Gov. I never saw such revelations as these among the Anabaptists, therefore am sorry that Mr. Cotton should stand to justify her.

Mr. Peters. I can say the same and this runs to enthusiasm, and I think that is very disputable which our brother Cotton hath spoken [*wanting*] an immediate promise that he will deliver them [*wanting*] in a day of trouble.

Gover. It overthrows all.

Dep. Gov. These disturbances that have come among the Germans have been all grounded upon revelations, and so they that have vented them have stirred up their hearers to take up arms against their prince and to cut the throats of one another, and these have been the fruits of them, and whether the devil may inspire the same into their hearts here I know not, for I am fully persuaded that Mrs. Hutchinson is deluded by the devil, because the spirit of God speaks truth in all his servants.

Gov. I am persuaded that the revelation she brings forth is delusion.

[*All the court but some two or three ministers cry out we all believe it— we all believe it.*]

Mr. Endicot. I suppose all the world may see where the foundation of all these troubles among us lies.

Mr. Eliot. I say there is an expectation of things promised, but to have a particular revelation of things that shall fall out, there is no such thing in the scripture.

Gov. We will not limit the word of God.

Mr. Collicut. It is a great burden to us that we differ from Mr. Cotton and that he should justify these revelations. I would intreat him to answer concerning that about the destruction of England.

Gov. Mr. Cotton is not called to answer to any thing but we are to deal with the party here standing before us.

Mr. Bartholomew. My wife hath said that Mr. Wheelwright was not acquainted with this way until that she imparted it unto him.

Mr. Brown. Inasmuch as I am called to speak, I would therefore speak the mind of our brethren. Though we had sufficient ground for the censure before, yet now she having vented herself and I find such flat contradiction to the scripture in what she saith, as to that in the first to the Hebrews—God at sundry times spake to our fathers—For my part I understand that scripture and other scriptures of the Lord Jesus Christ, and the apostle writing to Timothy saith that the scripture is able to make one perfect—therefore I say the mind of the brethren—I think she deserves no less a censure than hath been already past but rather something more. for this is the foundation of all

336

mischief and of all those bastardly things which have been overthrowing by that great meeting. They have all come out from this cursed fountain.

Gov. Seeing the court hath thus declared itself and hearing what hath been laid to the charge of Mrs. Hutchinson and especially what she by the providence of God hath declared freely without being asked, if therefore it be the mind of the court, looking at her as the principal cause of all our trouble, that they would now consider what is to be done to her. ——

Mr. Coddington. I do think that you are going to censure therefore I desire to speak a word.

Gov. I pray you speak.

Mr. Coddington. There is one thing objected against the meetings. What if she designed to edify her own family in her own meetings may none else be present?

Gov. If you have nothing else to say but that, it is pity Mr. Coddington that you should interrupt us in proceeding to censure.

Mr. Coddington. I would say more Sir, another thing you lay to her Charge is her speech to the elders. Now I do not see any clear witness against her, and you know it is a rule of the court that no man may be a judge and an accuser too. I do not speak to disparage our elders and their callings, but I do not see any thing that they accuse her of witnessed against her, and therefore I do not see how she should be censured for that. And for the other thing which hath fallen from her occasionally by the spirit of God, you know the spirit of God witnesses with our spirits, and there is no truth in scripture but God bears witness to it by his spirit, therefore I would entreat you to consider whether those things you have alledged against her deserve such censure as you are about to pass, be it to banishment or imprisonment. And again here is nothing proved about the elders, only that she said they did not teach a covenant of grace so clearly as Mr. Cotton did, and that they were in the state of the apostles before the ascension. Why I hope this may not be offensive nor any wrong to them.

Gov. Pass by all that hath been said formerly and her own speeches have been ground enough for us to proceed upon.

Mr. Coddington. I beseech you do not speak so to force things along, for I do not for my own part see any equity in the court in all your proceedings. Here is no law of God that she hath broken nor any law of the country that she hath broke, and therefore deserves no censure, and if she say that the elders preach as the apostles did, why they preached a covenant of grace and

337

what wrong is that to them, for it is without question that the apostles did preach a covenant of grace, though not with that power, till they received the manifestation of the spirit, therefore I pray consider what you do, for here is no law of God or man broken.

Mr. Harlakenden. Things thus spoken will stick. I would therefore that the assembly take notice that here is none that condemns the meeting of christian women; but in such a way and for such an end that it is to be detested. And then tho' the matter of the elders be taken away yet there is enow besides to condemn her, but I shall speak no further.

Dep. Gov. We shall be all sick with fasting.

Mr. Colburn. I dissent from censure of banishment.

Mr. Stoughton. The censure which the court is about to pass in my conscience is as much as she deserves, but because she desires witness and there is none in way of witness therefore I shall desire that no offence be taken if I do not formally condemn her because she hath not been formally convicted as others are by witnesses upon oath.

Mr. Coddington. That is a scruple to me also, because Solomon saith, every man is partial in his own cause, and here is none that accuses her but the elders, and she spake nothing to them but in private, and I do not know what rule they had to make the thing publick, secret things ought to be spoken in secret and publick things in publick, therefore I think they have broken the rules of God's word.

Gov. What was spoken in the presence of many is not to be made secret.

Mr. Coddington. But that was spoken but to a few and in private.

Gov. In regard Mr. Stoughton is not satisfied to the end all scruples may be removed we shall desire the elders to take their oaths.

[*Here now was a great whispering among the ministers, some drew back others were animated on.*]

Mr. Eliot. If the court calls us out to swear we will swear.

Gov. Any two of you will serve.

Mr. Stoughton. There are two things that I would look to discharge my conscience of, 1st to hear what they testify upon oath and 2dly to ———

Gov. It is required of you Mr. Weld and Mr. Eliot.

Mr. Weld, Mr. Eliot. We shall be willing.

Gov. We'll give them their oaths. You shall swear to the truth and nothing but the truth as far as you know. So help you God. What you do remember of her speak, pray speak.

[*Mr. Peters held up his hand also.*]

338

Mr. Eliot. I do remember and I have it written, that which she spake first was, the fear of man is a snare, why should she be afraid but would speak freely. The question being asked whether there was a difference between Mr. Cotton and us, she said there was a broad difference. I would not stick upon words—the thing she said—and that Mr. Cotton did preach a covenant of grace and we of works and she gave this reason—to put a work in point of evidence is a revealing upon a work. We did labour then to convince her that our doctrine was the same with Mr. Cotton's: She said no, for we were not sealed. This is all I shall say.

Gov. What say you Mr. Weld?

Mr. Weld. I will speak to the things themselves—these two things ı am fully clear in—she did make a difference in three things, the first I was not so clear in, but that she said this I am fully sure of, that we were not able ministers of the new testament and that we were not clear in our experience because we were not sealed.

Mr. Eliot. I do further remember this also, that she said we were not able ministers of the gospel because we were but like the apostles before the ascension.

Mr. Coddington. This was I hope no disparagement to you.

Gov. Well, we see in the court that she doth continually say and unsay things.

Mr. Peters. I was much grieved that she should say that our ministry was legal. Upon which we had a meeting as you know and this was the same she told us that there was a broad difference between Mr. Cotton and us. Now if Mr. Cotton do hold forth things more clearly than we, it was our grief we did not hold it so clearly as he did, and upon those grounds that you have heard.

Mr. Coddington. What wrong was that to say that you were not able ministers of the new testament or that you were like the apostles—methinks the comparison is very good.

Gov. Well, you remember that she said but now that she should be delivered from this calamity.

Mr. Cotton. I remember she said she should be delivered by God's providence, whether now or at another time she knew not.

Mr. Peters. I profess I thought Mr. Cotton would never have took her part.

Mr. Stoughton. I say now this testimony doth convince me in the thing, and I am fully satisfied the words were pernicious, and the frame of her spirit doth hold forth the same.

339

Gov. The court hath already declared themselves satisfied concerning the things you hear, and concerning the troublesomness of her spirit and the danger of her course amongst us, which is not to be suffered. Therefore if it be the mind of the court that Mrs. Hutchinson for these things that appear before us is unfit for our society, and if it be the mind of the court that she shall be banished out of our liberties and imprisoned till she be sent away, let them hold up their hands.

[*All but three.*]

Those that are contrary minded hold up yours,

[*Mr. Coddington and Mr. Colborn, only.*]

Mr. Jennison. I cannot hold up my hand one way or the other, and I shall give my reason if the court require it.

Gov. Mrs. Hutchinson, the sentence of the court you hear is that you are banished from out of our jurisdiction as being a woman not fit for our society, and are to be imprisoned till the court shall send you away.

Mrs. H. I desire to know wherefore I am banished?

Gov. Say no more, the court knows wherefore and is satisfied.

Book IV

A Cycle of Revolutions

MADAME ROLAND

CAMILLE DESMOULINS

ANDRÉ CHÉNIER

GRACCHUS BABEUF

THOMAS PAINE

MAJOR JOHN ANDRÉ

MORDECAI SHEFTALL

TOUSSAINT L'OUVERTURE

NAPOLEON

QUEEN OF THE GIRONDISTS:
Madame Roland

THE salon of Madame Roland, whose refreshments were a pitcher of water and a sugar bowl, patriotism and virtue, was designed, like her famous *Mémoirs*, to "aid an understanding of the human heart and teach great lessons to sensitive people." In the role of a priestess of sensibility, this charming queen of the Girondists ruled her elderly husband, the minister, ruled the secret but virtuous passion of her heart for a younger man, and presided over a coterie of republican politicians. Plutarch provided the heroic models, the books of Rousseau the emotions, and Madame Roland the tact and genius required to transform revolutionary politicians into purists and philosophers. The result was that Madame Roland did not ballast either her salon or herself against the coming storms of the Revolution. Danton and Robespierre acquired the habit of staying away. The salon of the Rolands became a Noah's Ark perched very high on classical books and rocks of idealism, a school of character taught by a handsome woman who believed that "it is the art of people of character to lend it to those who lack it." But the ingredients of character dispensable in Madame Roland's salon were not adequate to supply the needs of the whole French Revolution, not even sufficient to save herself from destruction. "The best patriots," she observed in 1791 during the struggle between the conservatives and the radicals, "seem to me more concerned with their own petty glory . . . they are all mediocre men . . . it is not wit they lack, but soul." A year later she lectured the man who did not visit her salon, Robespierre: "Your prejudices grieved me, and in order to have none myself, I hoped that I would come to know your reasons." Following the "second revolution" in the summer of 1792 she wrote: "My friend Danton directs everything; Robespierre is his puppet, Marat holds his torch and dagger; this savage tribune rules. . . . You know my enthusiasm for the Revolution, well, it has now turned to shame!" By December she was writing, "I know not what the morrow will bring . . . I have sent my daughter off to the country and put my small affairs in order as if for a great journey . . . the villain Danton . . . the barker Marat. . . ." She was jailed in June and guillotined in November,

offering the Revolution that parting shot of a high-minded salon, the epigram of liberalism: "O Liberty! what crimes are committed in thy name!" During the five months among the austere rituals of her prison life, she had put down on paper *An Appeal to Impartial Posterity,* paying her last respects to Rousseau by remembering the life and zest of his *Confessions* as she was unfolding and finishing her own. She rejected an opportunity of escaping from the Revolution's ugly knife, an escape that would have shown a lack of dignity before the models which she adored in Plutarch ("Plutarch had prepared me to become a republican"), and before that posterity which, as she hoped, would be persuaded by her beautiful stoicism that virtue justifies itself completely before villains and assassins. No excursion into stormy politics as queen of the Girondists, not even the harsh exigencies of the Revolution, could alter the fact, which she died to prove, that Madame Roland was a philosopher.

SELF-PORTRAIT

This, perhaps, is as proper a place as any to introduce my portrait. At fourteen years, as now, my stature was about five feet, for I had completed my growth; my leg and foot were well formed; the hips full and bold; the chest large, and the bust well rounded; my shoulders of an elegant *tournure;* my carriage firm and graceful, my step light and quick. Such was the first *coup d'oeil.* As to my face, there was nothing in it specially striking of itself, save perhaps the fresh color, the tenderness and expression. To go into details, "Where," it may be asked, "is the beauty?" Not a feature is regular, but all please. The mouth is rather large—one sees a thousand that are prettier; but where is there a smile more sweet and engaging? The eye is scarcely large enough, and its iris is of a grayish hue; but, though somewhat prominently set, it is frank, lively, and tender, crowned by delicately pencilled brown eyebrows (the color of my hair), and its expression varies with the changing emotions of the soul whose activity it reflects; grave and haughty, at times it imposes; but it charms oftener, and is always animated. The nose gave me some uneasiness; I thought it too full at the end, but, regarded with the rest, and especially in profile, it did not detract from the general effect of the face. The ample forehead, at that age exposed and unhidden by the hair, with arched eyebrows, and veins in the form of the Greek γ, that dilated at the slightest emotion, dignified an *ensemble* remote enough from the insig-

nificance of so many faces. As for the chin, which was slightly retiring, it has the precise characteristics attributed by physiognomists to the voluptuary. Indeed, when I combine all the peculiarities of my character, I doubt if ever an individual was more formed for pleasure, or has tasted it so little. The complexion was clear rather than fair; its lively colors were frequently heightened by a sudden effervescence of the blood, occasioned by nerves the most sensitive; the skin soft and smooth; the arms finely rounded; the hand elegant without being small, because the fingers, long and slender, announce dexterity and preserve grace; teeth white and well ranged; and, lastly, the plenitude and plumpness of perfect health: such are the gifts with which nature had endowed me. I have lost many of them, particularly such as depend upon bloom and fulness of figure; but those which remain are sufficient to conceal, without any assistance of art, five or six years of my age, and the persons who see me must be informed of what it is, to believe me more than two or three and thirty. It is only since my beauty has faded that I have known what was its extent; while in its bloom I was unconscious of its worth, and perhaps this ignorance augmented its value. I do not regret its loss, because I have never abused it; but if my duty could accord with my taste to leave less ineffective what remains of it, I certainly should not be mortified. My portrait has frequently been drawn, painted, and engraved, but none of these imitations gives an idea of my person; it is difficult to seize, because I have more soul than figure, more expression than features. This an inferior artist cannot express; it is probable even that he would not perceive it. My face kindles in proportion to the interest with which I am inspired, in the same manner as my mind is developed in proportion to the mind with which I have to act. I find myself so dull with some people, that, perceiving the abundance of my resources with persons of talent, I have imagined, in my simplicity, that to them alone I was indebted for it. I generally please, because I dislike to offend; but it is not granted to all to find me handsome, or to discover what I am worth. I can imagine an old coxcomb, enamored of himself, and vain of displaying his slender stock of science, fifty years in acquiring, who might see me for ten years together without discovering that I could do more than cast up a bill, or cut out a shirt. Camille Desmoulins was right when he expressed his amazement, that "at my age, and with so little beauty," I had still what he calls adorers. I have never spoken to him, but it is probable that with a personage of his stamp I should be cold and silent, if I were not absolutely repulsive. But he missed the truth in supposing me to hold a court. I hate gallants as much as I

despise slaves, and I know perfectly how to baffle your complimenters. I have need, above all things, of esteem and benevolence; admire me afterwards if you will, but I cannot live without being respected and cherished: this seldom fails from those who see me often, and who possess, at the same time, a sound understanding and a heart.

That desire to please, which animates a youthful breast and excites so delicious an emotion at the flattering looks of which we perceive ourselves the object, was oddly combined with my timid reserve and the austerity of my principles; and, displayed in my dress, it lent my person a charm that was strictly peculiar. Nothing could be more decent than my dress, nothing more modest than my deportment. I wished them to announce propriety and grace; and from the commendations that were bestowed upon me, I flattered myself that I succeeded. Meanwhile, that renunciation of the world, that contempt of its pomps and vanities, so strongly recommended by Christian morality, ill accorded with the suggestions of nature. Their contradictions at first tormented me, but my reasonings necessarily extended to rules of conduct, as to articles of faith. I applied myself with equal attention to the investigation of what I was to do, and the examination of what I ought to believe. The study of philosophy, considered as the science of manners and the basis of happiness, became indeed my only study, and I referred to it all my readings and observation.

In metaphysics and moral systems I experienced the same feeling as in reading poems, when I fancied myself transformed into the personage of the drama that had most analogy to myself, or that I most esteemed. I accordingly adopted the propositions the novelty or brilliance of which had most impressed me, and these I held until others more novel or more profound superseded them. Thus, in the controversial class, I enrolled myself with the Port-Royal school; their logic and austerity accorded with my character, while I felt an instinctive aversion for the sophistical and pliant doctrine of the Jesuits. While I was examining the sects of the ancient philosophers, I gave the palm to the Stoics. I endeavored, like them, to maintain that pain was no evil. This folly, indeed, could not last, but I nevertheless persisted in determining not to permit myself to be conquered by suffering; and the small experiments I had occasion to make persuaded me that I could endure the greatest torments without uttering a cry. The night of my marriage overturned the confidence I had till then preserved: it must, however, be allowed, that surprise in certain cases is to be counted for something, and that a novice in this philosophy may be expected to hold himself more firm against an ill

that is foreseen, than against one that takes him by surprise, and where the exact contrary was looked for.

During two months that I studied Descartes and Malebranche, I had considered my kitten, when she mewed, merely as a piece of mechanism performing its movements; but in thus habitually separating sensation from its manifestations, I became a mere anatomist, and found no longer anything attractive or interesting in the world. I thought it infinitely more delightful to furnish everything with a soul; and indeed, rather than dispense with it, I should have adopted the system of Spinoza. Helvetius did me considerable injury by annihilating all my most ravishing illusions; everywhere he posited a mean and revolting self-interest. Yet what sagacity! what luminous development! I persuaded myself that Helvetius delineated mankind as they had been disfigured and depraved by an erroneous and vicious form of society, and I judged it useful to be acquainted with his system, as a security against the knaveries of the world; but I was upon my guard against adopting his principles respecting man in the abstract, and applying them to the appreciation of my own actions. I would not so undervalue and degrade myself: I felt myself capable of a generosity, of which he did not admit the possibility. With what delight did I oppose to his system the great exploits of history, and the virtues of the heroes it has celebrated! I never read the recital of a glorious deed but I said to myself: "It is thus I would have acted." I became a passionate lover of republics, in which I found the most virtues to admire and the most men to esteem. I became convinced that this form of government was the only one capable of producing such virtues and such characters. I felt myself not unequal to the former; I repulsed with disdain the idea of uniting myself to a man inferior to the latter; and I demanded, with a sigh, why I was not born amidst these republics.

About this time we made an excursion to Versailles, my mother, my uncle, Mademoiselle d'Hannache, and myself. This journey had no other object than to show me the court and the place it inhabited, and to amuse me with its pageantry. We lodged in the palace. Madame le Grand, nurse to the Dauphin, well known to my uncle Bimont, through her son, of whom I shall have occasion to speak, being absent, lent us her apartments. They were in the attic story, in the same corridor with those of the Archbishop of Paris, and so close to them that it was necessary for that prelate to speak in a low tone of voice to avoid being overheard by us; the same precaution was requisite on our part. Two chambers indifferently furnished, over one of which it was contrived to lodge a valet, and the avenue to which was ren-

dered insupportable by its obscurity and its odors, were the habitation which a duke and peer of France did not disdain to occupy, that he might have the honor of cringing every morning before their majesties; and this servile prelate, meanwhile, was no other than the austere Beaumont. For one entire week we were constant spectators of the life of the inmates of the château, sometimes separated, and sometimes united, their masses, promenades, card parties, and the whole round of presentations.

Our acquaintance with Madame le Grand facilitated our admission; while Mademoiselle d'Hannache, penetrated with confidence everywhere, ready to batter down with her name whoever should oppose any resistance, and fancying they must read in her grotesque countenance the ten generations of her genealogy. She recollected two or three *gardes du roi,* whose pedigrees she recounted with minuteness, proving herself precisely the relation of him whose name was the most ancient, and who seemed to possess most consideration at court. The spruce figure of a little clergyman like Bimont, and the imbecile hauteur of the ugly d'Hannache, were not wholly out of place at Versailles; but the unrouged face of my respectable mother, and the sober decency of my apparel, announced that we were *bourgeois;* and if my youth or my eyes drew forth a word or two, they were modulated with a tone of condescension that gave me no less offence than the compliments of Madame de Boismorel. Philosophy, imagination, sentiment, and calculation were all equally exercised in me upon this occasion. I was not insensible to the effects of sumptuousness and magnificence, but I felt indignant that they should be employed to exalt certain individuals already too powerful from circumstances and totally insignificant in themselves. I preferred seeing the statues in the gardens to the personages of the court; and my mother inquiring if I was pleased with my visit, "Yes," replied I, "if only it be soon over; a few days longer, and I shall so perfectly detest these people that I shall not know what to do with my hatred."

"What harm do they do you?"

"They give me the feeling of injustice, and oblige me every moment to contemplate absurdity." I sighed to think of Athens, where I could have equally enjoyed the fine arts without being wounded with the spectacle of despotism; in imagination I walked in Greece, I assisted at the Olympic games, and I grieved to find myself a Frenchwoman. Impressed with everything which the great age of the republics had presented to me, I overlooked the troubles that disturbed them; I forgot the death of Socrates, the exile of Aristides, the condemnation of Phocion. I did not know that Heaven had

348

destined me to be a witness of crimes similar to those of which they were the victims, and to participate in the glory of a persecution of the same kind, after having professed their principles.

THE COMMUNE OF PARIS: MAY 31, 1793

IT WAS half after five in the evening, when six men armed came to our house. One of them read to Roland an order of the *revolutionary committee,* by the authority of which they came to apprehend him. 'I know no law,' said Roland, which constitutes the authority you cite to me, and I shall obey no orders proceeding from it. If you employ violence, I can only oppose to you the resistance of a man of my years; but I shall protest against it to the last moment.'—'I have no order to employ violence,' replied the person, 'and I will leave my colleagues here, whilst I go and report your answer to the council of the commune.'

Immediately it occurred to me, that it would be well to announce this circumstance to the convention with some noise, in order to prevent the arrest of Roland, or to obtain his prompt release, if this should be carried into execution. To communicate the thought to my husband, write a letter to the president, and set out, was the business of a few minutes. My servant was absent; I left a friend, who was in the house, with Roland; and stepped alone into a hackney-coach, which I ordered to proceed as fast as possible to the Carrouzel. The court of the Tuileries was filled with armed men. I crossed, and flew through the midst of them like a bird. I was dressed in a morning gown, and had put on a black shawl, and a veil. On my arrival at the doors of the outer halls, which were all shut, I found sentinels, who allowed no one to enter, or sent me by turns from one door to another. In vain I insisted on admission: at length I bethought myself of employing such language, as might have been uttered by some devotee of Robespierre: 'but, citizens, in this day of salvation for our country, in the midst of those traitors we have to fear, you know not of what importance some notes I have to transmit to the president may be. Let me at least see one of the messengers, that I may entrust them to him.'

The door opened, and I entered into the petitioners hall. I inquired for a messenger of the house. 'Wait till one comes out:' said one of the inner sentinels. A quarter of an hour passed away: I perceived Rôze, the person who brought me the decree of the convention, which invited me to repair to

the bar, on occasion of the ridiculous accusation of Viard, whom I overwhelmed with confusion: now I solicited permission to appear there, and
announced Roland to be in danger, with which the public weal was connected. But circumstances were no longer the same, though my rights were
equal: before invited, now a suppliant, could I expect the same success?
Rôze took charge of my letter; understood the subject of my impatience; and
repaired to lay it on the table, and urge its being read. An hour elapsed. I
walked hastily backwards and forwards: every time the door opened my eyes
were cast towards the hall, but it was immediately shut by the guard: a fearful noise was heard at intervals: Rôze again appeared.—'Well!'—'Nothing
has been done yet. A tumult I cannot describe prevails in the assembly.
Some petitioners, now at the bar, demand the *two-and-twenty* to be apprehended: I have just assisted Rabaud to slip out without being seen: they
are not willing he should make the report of the commission of *twelve:* he
has been threatened: several others are escaping: there is no knowing what
will be the event.'—'Who is the president now?'—'Héraut-Séchelles.'—'Ah!
my letter will not be read. Send some deputy to me, with whom I can speak
a few words.'—'Whom?'—'Indeed I have been little acquainted, or have little esteem for any, but them, who are proscribed. Tell Vergniaux I am inquiring for him.'

Rôze went in quest of him. After a considerable time he appeared. We
talked together for ten minutes. He went back into the hall, returned, and
said to me: 'In the present state of the assembly, I dare not flatter you, you
have little to hope. If you get admission to the bar, you may obtain a little
more favour as a woman; but the convention can do no more good.'—'It
can do every thing:' exclaimed I: 'for the majority of Paris seeks only to
know what it has to do. If I were admitted, I would venture to say, what you
could not without exposing yourself to an accusation. I fear nothing; and if I
cannot save Roland, I will utter with energy truths, which will not be useless to the republic. Inform your worthy colleagues: a burst of courage may
have a great effect, and at least will set a great example.'—In fact, I was in
that temper of mind, which imparts eloquence: warm with indignation,
superiour to all fear, my bosom glowing for my country, the ruin of which
I foresaw, every thing dear to me in the world exposed to the utmost danger,
feeling strongly, expressing my sentiments with fluency, too proud not to
utter them with dignity, I had subjects in which I was highly interested to
discuss, possessed some means of defending them, and was in a singular sit-

uation for doing it with advantage.—'But, at any rate, your letter cannot be read this hour or two: a plan of a decree, forming six articles, is going to be discussed: petitioners, deputed by the sections, wait at the bar: think what an attempt!'—'I will go home, then, to hear what has passed; and will immediately return: so tell our friends.'—'Most of them are absent: they show themselves courageous, when they are here; but they are deficient in assiduity.'—'That is unfortunately too true.'

I quitted Vergniaux: I flew to Louvet's: I wrote a note to inform him of what was going on, and what I foresaw. I flung myself into a hackney-coach, and ordered it home. The poor horses answered not the speed of my wishes. Soon we were met by some battalions, whose march stopped us: I jumped out of the coach, paid the coachman, rushed through the ranks, and made off. This was near the Louvre. I ran to our house, which was opposite St. Côme, in Harp-street. The porter whispered me, that Roland was gone into the landlord's, at the bottom of the court. Thither I repaired, in a profuse perspiration. A glass of wine was brought me, and I was told, that the bearer of the *mandate* of arrest having returned, without being able to procure a hearing at the council, Roland had persisted in protesting against his orders; and that these good people had demanded his protest in writing, and had then withdrawn: after which Roland went through the landlord's apartment, and got out of the house the back way. I did the same to find him, to inform him of what I had done, and to acquaint him with the steps I meant to pursue. At the first house to which I repaired, I found him not: in the second I did. From the solitariness of the streets, which were illuminated, I presumed it was late; yet this did not prevent my design of returning to the convention. There I would have appeared ignorant of Roland's escape, and spoken as I had before intended. I was about to set off on foot, without being conscious, that it was past ten o'clock, and that I was out that day for the first time since my illness, which demanded rest and the bath. A hackney-coach was brought me. On approaching the Carrouzel, I saw nothing more of the armed force: two pieces of cannon, and a few men, were still at the gate of the national palace: I went up to it, and found the sitting was dissolved!

What, on the day of an insurrection, when the sound of the alarm-bell scarcely ceases to strike the ear, when forty thousand men in arms surrounded the convention only two hours before, and petitioners threatened its members from the bar, the assembly is not permanent!—Surely then it is completely subjugated! it has done every thing, that it was ordered! The

351

revolutionary power is so mighty, that the convention dares not oppose it, and it has no need of the convention!

'Citizens,' said I to some sans-culottes collected round a cannon, 'has every thing gone well?'—'O wonderfully! they embraced, and sung the hymn of the Marseilles, there, under the tree of liberty.'—'What, then, is the right side appeased?'—'Faith, it was obliged to listen to reason.'—'And what of the committee of twelve?'—'It is kicked into the ditch.'—'And the *twenty-two?*'—'The municipality will cause them to be taken up.'—'Good: but can it?'—'Is it not the sovereign? It was necessary it should, to set those b—— of traitors right, and support the commonwealth.'—'But will the departments be well pleased to see their representatives * * * *'—'What are you talking of? the Parisians do nothing but in concert with the departments: they have said so to the convention.'—'That is not too clear, for, to know their will, the primary assemblies should have met.'—'Were they wanting on the 10th of August? Did not the departments approve what Paris did then? They do the same now: it is Paris that saves them.'—'That ruins them rather, perhaps.'

I had crossed the court, and arrived at my hackney-coach, as I finished this dialogue with an old sans-culotte, no doubt well paid to tutor the dupes. A pretty dog pressed close at my heels:—'Is the poor creature yours?' said the coachman to me, with a tone of sensibility very rare amongst his fellows, which struck me extremely.—'No: I know nothing of him:' answered I gravely, as if I were speaking of a man, and already thinking of something else: 'you will set me down at the galleries of the Louvre.' There I intended to call on a friend, with whom I would consult on the means of getting Roland out of Paris. We had not gone a dozen yards before the coach stopped. 'What is the matter?' said I to the coachman.—'Ah, he has left me; like a fool; and I wanted to keep him for my little boy. He would have been highly pleased with him. Wheugh! Wheugh! Wheugh!'—I recollected the dog: it was gratifying to me to have for a coachman, at such an hour, a man of a good heart, of feeling, and a father. 'Endeavour to catch him:' said I: 'you shall put him into the coach, and I will take care of him for you.'—The good man, quite delighted, caught the dog, opened the door, and gave him to me for a companion. The poor animal appeared sensible that he had found protection and an asylum: I was greatly caressed by him, and I thought of that tale of Sandi, in which is described an old man, weary of his fellow creatures, and disgusted with their passions, who retired to a wood, in which he constructed himself a dwelling, of which he sweetened the solitude

by means of some animals, who repaid his cares with testimonies of affection, and with a species of gratitude, to which he confined himself, for want of meeting with its like amongst mankind.

Pasquier had just gone to bed. He rose: I proposed to him my plan. We agreed, that he should come to me the next day after seven o'clock, and I would inform him where to find his friend. I returned to my coach: it was stopped by the sentry, at the post of the Woman of Samaria. 'Have a little patience:' whispered the good coachman to me, turning back on his seat: 'it is the custom at this time of night.'—The serjeant came, and opened the door. 'Who is here?'—'A woman.'—'Whence do you come?'—'From the convention.'—'It is very true:' added the coachman, as if he feared, I should not be credited.—'Whither are you going?'—'Home.'—'Have you no bundles?'—'I have nothing. See.'—'But the assembly has broken up.'—'Yes: at which I am very sorry, for I had a petition to make.'—'A woman! at this hour! it is very strange: it is very imprudent.'—'No doubt it is not a very common occurrence: I must have had strong reasons for it.'—'But, madam, alone?'—'How, sir, alone! Do you not see I have innocence and truth with me? what more is necessary?'—'I must submit to your reasons.'—'And you do well:' replied I, in a gentler tone: 'for they are good.'

The horses were so fatigued, that the coachman was obliged to pull them by the bridle, to get them up the hill, in the street in which I resided. I got home: I dismissed him: and I had ascended eight or ten steps, when a man, close at my heels, who had slipped in at the gate unperceived by the porter, begged me to conduct him to citizen Roland.—'To his apartment, with all my heart, if you have any thing of service to him to impart: but to him is impossible.'—'This evening he will certainly be apprehended.'—'They must be very dexterous, who accomplish it.'—'You give me great pleasure; for it is an honest citizen who accosts you.'—'I am glad of it:' said I, and went on, without well knowing what to think of the adventure.

"FOR WHOM I DESIRED LIBERTY"

[Draft of a defense intended to be read to the Tribunal, written at the Conciergerie the night after her examination.]

... I KNOW that in revolutions, law, as well as justice, is often forgotten; and the proof of it is, that I am here. I owe my trial to nothing but the prejudices and violent animosities which arise in times of great agitation, and which

are generally directed against those who have been placed in conspicuous situations, or are known to possess any energy or spirit. It would have been very easy for my courage to put me out of the reach of the sentence which I foresaw; but I thought that it rather became me to undergo it; I thought that I owed this example to my country; I thought that if I were to be condemned, it was right to leave tyranny all the odium of sacrificing a woman whose crime was that of possessing some small talents which she never misapplied, a zealous desire for the good of mankind, and courage enough to acknowledge her unfortunate friends, and to do homage to virtue at the risk of her life. Those minds that have any claim to greatness are capable of divesting themselves of selfish considerations; they feel that they belong to the whole human race; and their views are directed towards posterity alone. I am the wife of a virtuous man exposed to perfection; I was the friend of men who have been proscribed and immolated by delusion, and the hatred of jealous mediocrity. It is necessary that I should perish in my turn, because it is a rule with tyranny to sacrifice those whom it has grievously oppressed, and to annihilate the very witnesses of its misdeeds. I have this double claim to death from your hands, and I expect it. When innocence walks to the scaffold, at the command of error and perversity, every step she takes is an advance towards glory. May I be the last victim sacrificed to the furious spirit of party! I shall quit with joy this unfortunate earth, which swallows up the friends of virtue, and drinks the blood of the just.

Truth! friendship! my country! sacred objects, sentiments dear to my heart, accept my last sacrifice. My life was devoted to you, and you will render my death easy and glorious.

Just heaven! enlighten this unfortunate people for whom I desired liberty. . . . Liberty!—It is for the noble minds, who despise death, and who know how upon occasion to give it to themselves. It is not for those weak beings who enter into a composition with guilt, and cover their selfishness and cowardice with the name of prudence. It is not for those corrupted men who rise from the bed of debauchery, or from the mire of indigence to feast their eyes upon the blood that streams from the scaffold. It is for the wise people who delight in humanity, practise justice, despise their flatterers, and respect the truth. As long as you are not such a people, O my fellow-citizens! you will talk in vain of liberty; instead of liberty you will have nothing but licentiousness, of which you will all fall victims in your turns: you will ask for bread; dead bodies will be given you, and at last you will bow down your necks to the yoke.

I have neither concealed my sentiments nor my opinions. I know that a Roman lady was sent to the scaffold for having lamented the loss of her son; I know that in times of delusion and party rage, he who dares avow himself the friend of the condemned or of the proscribed exposes himself to share their fate. But I despise death; I never feared any thing but guilt, and I will not purchase life at the expense of a base subterfuge. Woe to the times! woe to the people among whom the doing homage to disregarded truth can be attended with danger, and happy he who in such circumstances is bold enough to brave it!

It is now your part to see whether it answer your purpose to condemn me without proof, upon mere matter of opinion, and without the support of any law whatever.

PITY AND THE GUILLOTINE:

Camille Desmoulins

"A 'C' AND A 'D,' OUR TWO NAMES"

"I DIE THE VICTIM OF THOSE JESTS"

~~~~~~

No, this Liberty descended from Heaven is not a nymph of the Opera, not a red cap, a dirty shirt, or rags and tatters. Liberty is happiness, reason, equality; she is justice, she is embodied in the Declaration of Rights, in your sublime Constitution! Do you wish me to recognize her, to fall at her feet, to shed my blood in her service? Open the doors of the prisons to those 200,000 citizens whom you call "suspects"; because in the Declaration of Rights there is no house of suspicion, there are only houses of detention; there are no suspected persons, only those convicted of crimes fixed by law. And do not believe that this measure would be harmful to the Republic. It would be the most Revolutionary measure that you could possibly take. . . .

CAMILLE DESMOULINS, *Vieux Cordelier*, No. 4

THE pen of Camille Desmoulins was mightier than the Girondists; it destroyed them with a tract. Having lived by a pen which was his sword, Desmoulins died by the guillotine. From the same cart which carried Danton to the execution, on a street lined by citizens who used to riot for a copy of his writings, Desmoulins cried: "You are deceived, citizens. Citizens, your preservers are being sacrificed. It was I, who in '89, called you to arms. I raised the first cry of liberty. My crime, my only crime has been pity." Desmoulins' historical claim was true: he was the hero of 1789 who had pointed to the Bastille from the top of a table in the Palais Royal. He thereafter considered himself a legitimate father of the Revolution. And it was true: Desmoulins was the best pamphleteer of the Revolution; with his clever brains and deadly inky barbs Danton destroyed Brissot, and in turn Robespierre destroyed Danton. Desmoulins survived the bloody party struggle between the "Gironde" and the "Mountain," but did not escape the dangers created by his own journalism. "He thought he was setting off fireworks," says Sainte-Beuve, "and little guessed what a fire he had started, a fire in which he was to perish, child that he was, while joyously lighting his fuses." It is said that Desmoulins was overcome in the courtroom by the verdict against the Girondists: "O my God, I am the one who is killing them, my [pamphlet] *Brissot Unmasked!*" This was the beginning of a counter-revolution, a counter-revolution of pity which was inspired by Danton and embodied by Desmoulins in the issues of his periodical *Vieux Corde-*

lier. Under the thin pretext of translating his favorite Tacitus, he attacked the Terrorists and the Ultras who had filled the jails to the bursting point. Behind the innocence of classical allusions, Desmoulins gave the counter-revolution a mask of pity, and called for a Committee of Clemency to give France relief from the terrorist "Law of Suspects." His pity made first-rate satire against the clichés of the Terror. He repeated *Suspect! Suspect! Suspect!* ad nauseam: Were you rich? he wrote. Ah, but there was danger that the people would be corrupted by your gifts: *Suspect!* Were you poor? Nobody is so enterprising as he who has nothing: *Suspect!* Were you melancholy? shabby? Doubtless you were bothered by the prosperous state of public affairs: *Suspect!* Virtuous and austere? Good, a new Brutus, whose pallor is a criticism of the state: *Suspect!.* A philosopher, an orator, or a poet? Might he not steal fame from those who governed? *Suspect!* But if you were struck by the absurdity of all this chaos and panic, then you might come to believe that the real counter-revolution was working by means of the fake and terrorist patriots. This brief for the innocent sold 50,000 copies at once; citizens fought for it at the bookstore and auctioned it off to each other at a *louis* a copy. It was read in the prisons by unhappy wretches who caught a glimpse of hope in the pity of the Dantonists; it was also read by those who considered themselves insulted and the Revolution betrayed. "All the counter-revolutionaries clapped their hands," says Louis Blanc whose hero is Robespierre, "all boasted to spread the news abroad that Camille Desmoulins had traced the history of his own epoch; against his will, the generous but rash writer had, in giving hope to the innocent, served the calculations of hatred." On March 31, 1794, Desmoulins was arrested along with Danton and all their friends in the "faction of indulgence," that counter-revolution of pity. Passing from history with less dignity than Danton, Desmoulins left a heartbreaking farewell to his wife Lucile (but she did not receive his letter before her own execution)—and a piece of minor blasphemy. When asked his age by the Revolutionary Tribunal, Desmoulins replied: "I am thirty-three, the age of the Sans-culotte Jesus, a critical age for every patriot." But he was older; he was really thirty-four.

"A 'C' AND A 'D,' OUR TWO NAMES"

Ma chère Lucile, ma vesta, mon ange,

Destiny leads my eyes from my prison over that garden where I passed eight years in following you. A glimpse of the Luxembourg brings back to

me a crowd of memories of my love. I am alone, but never deserted by thoughts, imagination, almost by the sense of the bodily presence of you, your mother, my little Horace.

I have written this first letter only to beg for some necessary things. But I am going to pass all my time in prison writing to you; because I have no need to take up my pen for my defence. My justification is complete in my eight Republican volumes. They are a good pillow, upon which my conscience rests, awaiting the tribunal and posterity.

Oh, my good Lolotte, speak of other things! I throw myself on my knees, I try to embrace you, where is my poor Loulou . . . ?

Send me a water glass, the one on which there is a "C" and a "D," our two names. Send me a pair of sheets, and a book in duodecimo which I bought a few days ago at Charpentier's, and in which there are blank pages made expressly for notes. This book treats of the immortality of the soul. I have need to persuade myself that there is a God, more just than men, and that I shall not fail to see you again. Do not be too much affected by my ideas, dearest. I do not yet despair of men and of my liberation; yes, my well-beloved, we shall be able to meet yet once more in the garden of the Luxembourg. But send me that book. Good-by, Lucile! Good-by, Horace! I cannot embrace you, but through my tears it seems to me that I am holding you against my breast.

YOUR CAMILLE.

"I DIE THE VICTIM OF THOSE JESTS"

5 heures du matin
1ᵉʳ avril (1794)

KIND sleep has eased my misfortune and I do not feel my captivity, heaven has had pity on me. Only a little while ago I saw you all in a dream, I embraced you and Horace. . . . But our little one had lost an eye through some infection which had settled there and in my distress I woke up. I found myself in my cell, day was dawning. I saw you no longer and could not hear you and I arose so that I might speak to you at least in writing. But when I opened my windows, the thought of my loneliness, the terrible bars, the bolts which separate us, pushed the strength out of my soul. I burst into tears, I sobbed, crying Lucile, Lucile!

Last night I had the same experience and my heart was moved when I saw

your mother in the gardens below. An impulse threw me on my knees against the bars, my hands were clasped as though imploring her pity, she, who must have mourned on your breast. I saw her grief yesterday by her handkerchief and by her veil, which she lowered because she could not bear the sight. When you both come again, sit closer together so that I can see you better. It seems to me there is no danger. My spy-glass is not very good.

I beg you, send me the picture. Let your painter pity me, who suffer only for having had too much pity for others. Let him give you two sittings a day. In the horror of my jail, the day when I receive your portrait will be a holiday, a day of rejoicing. And until then send me a lock of hair to wear near my heart. Dear Lucile, I have returned to the springtime of my love for you when the mere fact that anyone came from you was enough to make him important to me. Today when the citizen who carried my letter to you returned: "Well, you have seen her?" I asked, as I used to say to the Abbé Laudréville, and I caught myself looking at him as though some sign of you clung to his clothes, on his person. He has a charitable soul, since he gave you my letter without erasures. I shall see him when he comes, twice a day, in the morning and the evening. This message of my sorrows becomes as dear to me as would formerly have been a messenger for my pleasures.

I have discovered a crack in my cell. I put my ear to it and heard a sigh. I whispered a few words and heard the voice of a sick man suffering. He asked my name. I told him. "My God!" he cried falling back on his bed, and I recognized distinctly the voice of Fabre d'Eglantine: "Yes, I am Fabre. You here! Has, then, the counter-revolution arrived?"

We did not dare to talk for fear that hatred would grudge us this poor consolation of speaking together, and that if anyone should overhear us we should be separated and more strictly confined; because he has a room with a fireplace, and mine would be sufficiently comfortable if a cell could ever be called so.

Dearest, you cannot imagine what it is to be in solitary confinement, without knowing the reason, without having been interrogated, without a single newspaper. It is to be both living and dead—alive in a coffin. They say innocence is calm and courageous. Oh my dear Lucile, my innocence is often feeble, a father's, a son's, a husband's.

If it was Pitt or Cobourg who treated me so severely; but my comrades!—Robespierre, who signed the order for my imprisonment—the Republic, after all I have done for her! This is my reward for so many virtues and sacrifices for her sake!

When I entered here I saw Hérault-Séchelles, Simon, Ferroux, Chaumette, Antonelle; they are less unhappy; not one of them is in solitary confinement. It is I who have called down on myself for the past five years so many hatreds and perils for the sake of the Republic, I, who have preserved my poverty in the midst of the Revolution, I, who in the whole world have to ask pardon only from you, my dear Lolotte, and to whom you have granted it, because you know that my heart, for all its faults, is not unworthy of you; it is I who am thrown into a cell, alone, as though I were a conspirator—by men who call themselves my friends, who call themselves Republicans. Socrates drank hemlock, but at least he saw in his prison his friends and his wife. How much harder it is to be separated from you! The worst criminal would be too severely punished if he were torn from a Lucile by anything except death, a separation which would be bitter only for a moment; but a guilty man would not have been your husband and you have loved me only because I have existed for nothing but the happiness of my countrymen.

They are calling me. . . .

At this moment the Commissaries of the Republic came to interrogate me —only one question: whether I had conspired against the Republic. . . . What mockery—how can they so insult the purest Republican feeling? I realize my fate, farewell! You see in me a victim of the barbarism and ingratitude of man. My last moments will not dishonor you. My fears were well-founded after all, my premonitions true. I married a wife made saintly by her virtue, I was a good husband, a good son, I would have been a good father. I take with me the esteem and the pity of all true Republicans, of all virtuous and free men. I die at thirty-four, but it is a miracle that for five years I should have passed so many precipices of the Revolution without falling, and that I am still alive. I rest my head calmly on the pillow of my all too numerous writings. They all breathe the same love of humanity, the same wish to make my countrymen free and happy. The ax cannot touch *them*. I see that power intoxicates all men and that they all say with Dionysius of Syracuse: "Tyranny is a fine epitaph." Console yourself, unhappy widow. The epitaph of your poor Camille is more glorious: it is that of Cato and Brutus, the murderers of tyrants.

Dear Lucile, I was born to make verses and to defend the miserable. Where I am now fighting for my life, I defended four years ago for whole nights a mother of ten children who could find no pleader. Facing the jurors who are now murdering me, I once appeared, when my father had already lost a great lawsuit, suddenly like a miracle before the seats of the

360

judges. Weeping was no crime then. I knew how to move them with emotion and I won a case which my father had lost. Well, that is the kind of conspirator I am, I never was any other! I was born to make you happy, to build a Tahiti in the hearts of those whom we both love. I dreamed the dreams of the Abbé Saint-Pierre. I dreamed of a Republic which all the world would have adored. I could not believe that men are so fierce and so unjust. How could I imagine that a few written sallies against comrades would wipe out the memory of all my services? I cannot hide from myself that I die the victim of those jests and of my friendship for Danton. I thank my murderers that they let me die with him and Philippeaux; and since my colleagues have been so cowardly as to abandon us and to lend an ear to calumnies which I do not know, but which I am told are of the gravest nature, I can say that we die the victims of our courage in denouncing two traitors and of our love for truth. The freedom of the press and opinion has no longer any defenders. We will die as the last Republicans, though we had to die on our own swords like Cato, if there were no guillotine.

Forgive me, my dear love, my true life—lost when we were separated, for occupying myself with memories. I ought rather to make you forget. My Lucile, my good Loulou, I beg you, do not cry out, it would rend my heart even in the grave. Live for Horace, speak to him of me, you will tell him what he cannot yet understand, that I would have loved him much. In spite of my martyrdom, I believe that there is a God. My blood will wash out my sins, my human weakness, and for what is good in me, for my virtues, my love of Liberty, God will reward me. I shall see you again some day, Lucile! Is death so great a misfortune when it delivers me from the sight of so much suffering?

Good-by, my life, my soul, my heaven on earth! I leave you in the care of good friends, all the compassionate and virtuous men who remain. Good-by Lucile, my very dear Lucile! Good-by Horace! . . . Good-by father! The shores of my life are slipping. I see you still, Lucile, my beloved. My bound hands embrace you and my eyes see you as I die.

This is the letter which never reached Lucile. Racing with time, Camille Desmoulins wrote part of the next issue of the *Vieux Cordelier*, the seventh, and composed, against his official accuser, *Notes upon the Report of Saint-Just:*

"If I could print in my turn . . . If they would leave me only two days in which to compose No. 7, how I would confound M. le Chevalier Saint-Just! . . . But Saint-Just writes at his leisure, in his bath, in his dressing-room; he meditates on my assassination for fifteen days; and I, I have nowhere even to place my writing-case; I have only a few hours left in which to defend my life . . ."

PITY AND THE GUILLOTINE : *Camille Desmoulins*

It was Saint-Just who delivered the charges before the Revolutionary Tribunal. With two names like Danton and Desmoulins on the benches of the accused, Saint-Just had to warn: "The Republic is the people and not the renown of a few men." Lucile could not reach Robespierre whose name was signed both to her certificate of marriage and Camille's death warrant—the signatures just three years apart. Lucile to Robespierre:

"Camille saw the growth of your pride . . . But he recoiled from the idea of accusing his old college friend, the companion of his labors. That hand which has often pressed yours, forsook the pen before its time, because it could no longer hold it to trace your praises. And you have sent him to death! You have then understood his silence!"

What an imprudent letter! Accused of plotting against the National Convention (when all her passion was concentrated in the Luxembourg and on Camille's prison window), Lucile was destroyed two days after her husband's execution by the same knife which finished him. She reached the platform of the guillotine the companion of Hébert's widow, who was less brave. What a strange and belated friendship between the widows of Hébert and Desmoulins, whose husbands had sought each other's annihilation. How often had Hébert sneered at Desmoulins for having married "a rich wife." And Desmoulins had written to Hébert:

"I will only say one word about my wife. I have always believed in the immortality of the soul. After the many sacrifices of personal interests which I have made to liberty and for the happiness of the people, I have said, at the height of the persecution: 'There must be some recompense for virtue elsewhere.' But my marriage is so happy, my domestic bliss so great, that I feared to have received my recompense already upon earth, and I almost lost my confidence in immortality. But your persecutions, your rage against me, your cowardly calumnies have restored all my hope."

No profound theology, to be sure, but still an original dilemma with regard to immortality and matrimony—almost as if, without hesitation, it were really better to be happily married than immortal.

THE BLOOD OF A POET:

André Chénier

SAINT-LAZARE

~~~~~~

THE fate of André Chénier, whose head rolled off the guillotine at thirty-one, is the kind which inspires the trimmings of an opera: "ladies, gentlemen, servants, pages, peasants, republican soldiers, masqueraders, judges, jurymen, prisoners, etc." He deserves better than this tinsel before the golden horseshoe. The child of a Greek mother whose salon in Paris drew Lavoisier and David, he dreamed of classic idylls and elegies. The critics, whom he was to remind of Keats and Shelley, could not decide whether he was the last of the Greeks or the first of the romantics. Chénier had at least two unlimited enthusiasms: to condense Diderot's encyclopedia in the manner of Lucretius, and to reform the Jacobin terror by writing articles for the papers. He composed an ode to Charlotte Corday. In the name of constitutional authority, when the air of the revolution was most combustible, he attacked "a few hundred idlers massing in a garden or at a public spectacle, a party or two of bandits, pillaging shops—these (with what effrontery) are called the people. The most insolent despots of history never received from their most sycophantic courtiers a viler or more tiresome flattery than that with which, every day the writers and orators of these Jacobin societies (the scourge of France) intoxicate two or three thousand usurpers of the sovereignty of the Nation." In the prison of Saint-Lazare he wrote at white heat, on sheets which left his cell under dirty linen, the best poetry of his short life. Characteristically his indignation was divided between the fate of a seductive duchess portrayed in *La Jeune Captive* and the unpleasant ways of history which were chided in *Saint-Lazare*. Robespierre, who could not forgive Chénier's insults in the *Journal de Paris*, himself had only a few days left before joining the poet's angry ghost.

SAINT-LAZARE

Comme un dernier rayon, comme un dernier zéphire
  Animent la fin d'un beau jour,
Au pied de l'échafaud j'essaye encor ma lyre;
  Peut-être est-ce bientôt mon tour;
Peut-être avant que l'heure en cercle promenée
  Ait posé sur l'émail brillant,
Dans les soixante pas où sa route est bornée,
  Son pied sonore et vigilant,
Le sommeil du tombeau pressera ma paupière!
  Avant que de ses deux moitiés
Ce vers que je commence ait atteint la dernière,
  Peut-être en ces murs effrayés
Le messager de mort, noir recruteur des ombres,
  Escorté d'infâmes soldats,
Ébranlant de mon nom ces longs corridors sombres,
  Où, seul, dans la foule à grands pas
J'erre, aiguisant ces dards persécuteurs du crime,
  Du juste trop faibles soutiens,
Sur mes lèvres soudain va suspendre la rime;
  Et, chargeant mes bras de liens,
Me traîner, amassant en foule à mon passage
  Mes tristes compagnons reclus,
Qui me connaissaient tous avant l'affreux message,
  Mai qui ne me connaissent plus.
Eh bien! j'ai trop vécu. Quelle franchise auguste,
  De mâle constance et d'honneur
Quels exemples sacrés, doux à l'âme du juste,
  Pour lui quelle ombre de bonheur,
Quelle Thémis terrible aux têtes criminelles,
  Quels pleurs d'une noble pitié,
Des antiques bienfaits quels souvenirs fidèles,
  Quels beaux échanges d'amitié,
Font digne de regrets l'habitacle des hommes?
  La Peur blême et louche est leur dieu.
Le désespoir! . . . la feinte! . . . Ah! lâches que nous sommes,
  Tous, oui, tous. Adieu, terre, adieu.

SAINT-LAZARE

As a last ray of light, last waft of zephyr's wings,
  Brighten a lovely day's decline,
Even on the scaffold's step I'll seek to tune my strings;
  Perchance the next turn will be mine.
Perchance before Time's self, who marches round and round,
  On the smooth dial's face has set,
Within the sixty steps whereby his course is bound,
  His foot that strikes the hour when met,
The slumbers of the tomb will weigh my eyelids down.
  Ere from my lips imperfect falls
My song, nor end is heard the unfinished work to crown,
  Perchance within these startled walls
The messenger of death, the Shades' grim monitor,
  Escorted by his foul patrol,
Will waken with my name this long, dark corridor
  Where mid the crowd I wander sole,
And polish bright my darts to meet the face of crime,
  Frail arms the just man to assist.
Suddenly on my lips he may arrest a rhyme,
  With fetters bind me, wrist to wrist,
And drag me through the crowds who throng to watch me go,
  Sad comrades in captivity,
All of whom knew me well ere came the fatal blow,
  But who no more my face will see.
Ah, well! I've lived too long. What pride in truth heart-whole,
  Of manly faith and constancy
What blest examples dear to every good man's soul,
  What gleam of fortune come near by,
What Judge to punish crime rising in majesty,
  What tears a noble grief lets fall,
Of antique benefits what loyal memory,
  What sweet exchange at true love's call,
Make worthy of regret men's habitat on earth?
  Pale fear's their god, of aspect fell.
Despair! . . . Deceit! . . . Ah, me! cowards are we from birth,
  All, all. Farewell, this earth, farewell.

Vienne, vienne, la mort! Que la mort me délivre!
Ainsi donc, mon coeur abattu
Cède au poids de ses maux? Non, non, puissé-je vivre!
Ma vie importe à la vertu
Car l'honnête homme enfin, victime de l'outrage,
Dans les cachots, près de cercueil,
Relève plus altiers son front et son langage
Brillant d'un généreux orgueil.
S'il est écrit aux cieux que jamais une épée
N'étincellera dans mes mains,
Dans l'encre et l'amertume une autre arme trempée
Peut encor servir les humains.
Justice, vérité, si ma bouche sincère,
Si mes pensers les plus secrets
Ne froncèrent jamais votre sourcil sévère,
Et si les infâmes progrès,
Si la risée atroce ou (plus atroce injure!)
L'encens de hideux scélérats
Ont pénétré vos couers d'une longue blessure,
Sauvez-moi; conservez un bras
Qui lance votre foudre, un ami qui vous venge.
Mourir sans vider mon carquois!
Sans percer, sans fouler, sans petrir dans leur fange,
Ces bourreaux barbouilleurs de lois!
Ces vers cadavéreux de la France asservie,
Égorgée. . . . O mon cher trésor!
O ma plume! fiel! bile! horreur, dieux de ma vie!
Par vous seuls je respire encor,
Comme la poix brûlante agitée en ses veines
Ressuscite un flambeau mourant.
Je souffre, mais je vis. Par vous, loin de mes peines,
D'espérance un vaste torrent
Me transporte. Sans vous, comme un poison livide,
L'invincible dent du chagrin,
Mes amis opprimés, du menteur homicide
Les succès, le sceptre d'airain,
Des bons proscrits par lui la mort ou la ruine,
L'opprobre de subir sa loi,

Come death, come welcome death, and my deliverance give.
Does then my heart, worsted in strife,
Sink neath its load of ill? No, no, would I might live!
Virtue sets store upon my life.
An honourable man, victim of hate and fear,
In prison cell, by the grave's side,
Holds higher still his head, and speaks in tones more clear,
Glowing with all a generous pride.
If by God's will no sword shall from its scabbard leap,
To glitter when I deal a blow,
This other arm, the pen in ink and gall I steep,
May help to serve man here below.
Justice and truth, if words fallen from my lips sincere,
Thoughts I have nursed in secrecy
Have never brought a frown upon your brows severe,
And if the march of infamy,
Atrocious laughter, or (worse insult to endure)
Praise from a monstrous crime-stained band
Have driven in your hearts wounds that are hard to cure,
Save me! Sustain a stout right hand
To hurl your bolts, a friend to render blood for blood.
To die, with arrows yet unspent!
Unpierced, untrampled on, unmortared in their mud
Those who our laws have fouled and rent,
Cadaverous worms who feed on France stretched in her gore,
Their victim! . . . O thou treasure rare,
My pen! Malice and wrath, horror, gods I adore!
Through you alone I breathe heaven's air,
Even as the burning pitch, hid in the torch's veins,
When shaken wakes a dying gleam.
I suffer, but I live. Far, far from all my pains,
Through you, hope in a rushing stream
Transports me. Without you, like poison purple-dyed
Chagrin's sharp tooth naught can withstand,
The oppression of my friends, the lying homicide,
Brass sceptre of success in hand,
Good men whom he condemns to loss of all, even life,
By shameful law of lawless men,

Tout eût tari ma vie, ou contre ma poitrine
  Dirigé mon poignard. Mais quoi?
Nul ne resterait donc pour attendrir l'histoire
  Sur tant de justes massacrés;
Pour consoler leur fils, leurs veuves, leur mémoire;
  Pour que des brigands abhorrés
Frémissent aux portraits, noirs de leur ressemblance,
  Pour descendre jusqu'aux enfers
Chercher le triple fouet, le fouet de la vengeance,
  Déjà levé sur ces pervers;
Pour cracher sur leur noms, pour chanter leur supplice!
  Allons, étouffe tes clameurs;
Souffre, ô couer gros de haine, affamé de justice,
  Toi, Vertu, pleurs si je meurs.

All had dried up my life, or driven their steely knife
   Deep in my very heart. What then?
None would remain to win the heart of history
   For all these just men done to death,
Console their widows, sons, their memory;
   To check the abhorred brigands' breath
Before dark portraits drawn to show them as they stand;
   To plunge down even into hell,
To seek the triple whip, whip for the Avenger's hand,
   Now raised to serve these perverts well;
To spit upon their names, gloat o'er their suffering!
   Come, stifle now thy bitter cry;
Suffer, heart big with hate, for justice famishing.
   Thou, Virtue, weep, if I should die.

THE CONSPIRACY OF THE EQUALS:
Gracchus Babeuf

"A SACRIFICE THAT FRIENDSHIP CAN MAKE": BABEUF'S REQUEST

~~~~~~

THE Conspiracy of the Equals was a revolution within a revolution, the swan song of the Terror and the Thermidor. As the young star of Bonaparte was rising, Babeuf prophesied: "We are the last Frenchmen, we are the last energetic Republicans, the reign of royalist terror begins. . . ." By the paradox which converts the last into the first, the Conspiracy of the Equals, of the *Égaux,* the *Babouvistes,* was the first modern political agitation for a socialist program whose heirs were 1848 and 1871. Before the fall of Robespierre, Babeuf played only a minor role. Afterwards, none too innocently entangled in politics, he mingled adroitly his journalistic attacks on both the Terror and the Thermidoreans, gathering around him the defeated and disgruntled old partisans: the "tail of Robespierre." In the name of the liquidated Constitution of 1793 he launched in his *Le Tribun du Peuple* an idea which was more alien to the dying French Revolution than the unborn Industrial Revolution—his doctrine of economic equality. He worked in poverty: "I sacrificed my post and devoted myself to the defence of the rights of the people alone. My wife and my son, aged nine years, both of whom are as republican and zealous as their husband and father, undertake to second me with all their might. They are making the same sacrifices. They are engaged day and night at Guffroy's, my printer's, in folding, distributing, and sending out the paper. Our home is deserted. Two other young children, one of them only three years of age, have been left shut up at home all day for a month past. . . . There is no food to cook at home; ever since the paper has gone on, we have lived on bread, grapes, and nuts."[1] For his violent attacks, rather than his communist doctrine, he found himself in jail, a school of insurrection filled with old Jacobins, a place where Babeuf could compare notes and digest his theory of equality. From his prison this ancestor of communism smuggled out its first crude political manifesto: "Babeuf, the Tribune of the People, to his Fellow-Citizens." In the world outside the crisis was mounting: financial panic, a shortage of bread and meat, five hundred thousand Parisians in need of relief, and Thermidorean

---

[1] Quoted by Albert Mathiez, *After Robespierre,* Knopf, 1931.

370

leaders who were acquiring fat estates and moneyed mistresses. (Babeuf's *Tribun*: "Why conceal the fact any longer that Tallien, Fréron, and Bentabole decide the destiny of men while reclining indolently on eider down and roses, at the side of princesses? Those who have become their better halves were under arrest about the time of the 9th Thermidor; these men went and said to them: 'Do you want to escape the guillotine? Then accept the offer of my hand.' The high and mighty ladies replied: 'It is better to marry than to be beheaded,' and here they are making our laws!" [2]) Liberated by an amnesty, Babeuf plunged into an underground conspiracy. The Society of the Pantheon, which was put out of business by a young officer named Bonaparte, went under cover into a subterranean vault lit by torches and awakened by angry echoes. The Directory planted its spies among the old Jacobins and the new communists, much less afraid of their curious gospel of equality than they were delighted with an opportunity to use the conspiracy as a threat against potential defection to the royalists. The Directory was not very much disturbed by a fantastic idea which proclaimed that "in the social order conceived by the committee, the country shall seize upon the new-born individual, never to leave him till his death; it shall watch over his first moments, shall assure the milk and the care of her who gave him birth, shall guard him from all that might injure his health and enervate his body, shall shield him from a false tenderness, and shall take him, by the hand of his mother, to the national home, where he shall acquire virtue and the illumination necessary to be a true citizen." The *Babouvistes* anticipated all the classical instruments of agitation: underground cells, manifestoes, street meetings, posters, songs (*"mourant de faim, mourant de froid"*), propaganda in the army, economic doctrine, the call to the *ouvrier* and the working class faubourgs. The *Tribun* collapsed with its forty-third number and the *Manifesto of the Equals* was put down on paper a century too soon:

People of France! During fifteen centuries you have lived as slaves. . . . It is scarcely six years that you have begun to breathe, in the expectation of independence, happiness, equality! . . . From time immemorial it has been repeated, with hypocrisy, that *men are equal;* and from time immemorial the most degrading and the most monstrous inequality ceaselessly weighs on the human race. . . . Today when it is demanded with a stronger voice, they reply to us: "Be silent, wretches! Equality of fact is nothing but a chimera; be contented with conditional equality; you are all equal before the law. *Canaille,* what do you want more?"

---

[2] Quoted by Albert Mathiez, *op. cit.*

What do we want more? . . . We demand real equality or death. . . . The French Revolution is but a precursor of another and a greater and more solemn revolution which will be the last! . . . We aim at something more sublime and more equitable —the common good, or the community of goods. . . . We demand, we would have, the communal enjoyment of the fruits of the earth, fruits which are for everyone! We declare that we can no longer suffer, with the enormous majority of men, labor and sweat in the service and for the good pleasure of a small minority! Enough and too long have less than a million individuals disposed of that which belongs to more than twenty millions of their kind! Let this great scandal, that our grandchildren will hardly believe existed, cease! Let the revolting distinction of rich and poor disappear, once and for all, the distinction of great and small, of masters and valets, of governors and governed. Let there be no other difference between human beings than those of age and sex. Since all have the same needs and the same faculties, let there be one education for all, one food for all. . . . Never has a vaster design been conceived or been put into execution. From time to time some men of genius have spoken of it in a low and trembling voice. Not one of them has had the courage to tell the whole truth. . . . The moment has arrived for founding the Republic of Equals. . . .

Babeuf was mistaken, it was not the moment for the Republic of Equals. The fences around private property had been safe even under Robespierre and Marat; they were firmer under the Directory which became alarmed only at the clever organizing talent of the *Babouvistes* and so put Babeuf to death.

"A SACRIFICE THAT FRIENDSHIP CAN MAKE": BABEUF'S REQUEST

Greetings, dear Felix: [3]

Don't alarm yourself on seeing these lines traced by my hand. I know that all that bears the imprint of relations with me gives the right to disquietude. I am the man whom all shun; whom all regard as dangerous. However, my conscience tells me that I am pure; and my true friends, that is, certain just

---

[3] Felix Lepelletier (a brother of the assassinated hero of the Revolution), a well-to-do member of the secret committee of insurrection of the Conspiracy of the Equals. The committee included Babeuf, Debon, Darthé, Sylvain Maréchal, and others, as well as Filippo Michele Buonarroti (a descendant of Michelangelo and an exile from Italy) who lived long enough to become the connecting link between the *Babouvistes* and the socialists of the July Monarchy whose memoirs appeared in London, in 1836, as *Buonarroti's History of Babeuf's Conspiracy for Equality, with the Author's Reflections on the Causes and Character of the French Revolution and his Estimate of the Leading Men and Events of that Epoch, Also his Views of Democratic Government, Community of Property and Political and Social Equality.*

men, know also that I have nothing for which to reproach myself. If even they shun me, it is not from any real aversion which I inspire in them, but it is the effect of the factitious terror inspired upon them by malice, lest by chance they should be reputed criminals, and treated as such. In this position the consideration which I owe to good men prescribes to me the interdiction of all intercourse with them, in order to avoid giving them the smallest alarm. But urgent considerations, such as present themselves naturally to the thoughts of a man on the brink of the tomb, have decided me to make one more advance towards one of my fellow citizens whom I especially esteem. I do this the more willingly inasmuch as I am sure to run no other risk than that, perhaps, of somewhat disquieting him. It is a sacrifice that friendship can make. I shall lighten it in reassuring you, as quickly as possible, my good Felix, that there is nothing to fear. I was certain, in getting this epistle conveyed to you, the last that I shall address to you, that it would overcome without peril all the obstacles that might come between you and me.

Behold us, then, without doubt, more at ease with one another—you to read me, I to conclude what I have to tell you! I have built my text, in speaking to you, on friendship. I have called you friend! I have believed, and I believe, that I may do so. It is by this title that I address you in confidence —respecting do you know what?—my testament, and last recommendation.

I make the following assumptions subordinate to its execution—that proscription will not always pursue you; that the tyrants, sated with my blood and that of some of my unhappy companions, will be contented, and their own policy will not counsel them, perhaps, to do what they at first appeared to propose doing, namely, to make a hecatomb of all republicans. On the other hand, it might still happen, after my martyrdom, that fortune will tire of striking our country, and then that her true children may breathe in peace. If it is otherwise, I lose all hope as to what shall survive me. Then all will perish in the vast cataclysm that crime against virtue and justice will engender. The work of the good, their memory, their families, will fall into eternal night, and be involved in one universal destruction. Then, again, all is said: I need take no more care for those who are still dear to me, whom my thought has followed up to the repose of nothingness, the last inevitable end of all that exists.

It is on the first supposition that I am acting, my friend. I believe I have remained worthy of the esteem of men who are as just as you are. I have not seen you in the ranks of those evil Machiavellian politicians who multiply

my sufferings a hundredfold, and are looking forward to my death. The traitors! In causing those for whom they appeared to have interested themselves most to appear in a cowardly and shameful light, they have pictured me—whose every public act has testified to the rectitude, to the purity of my intentions; to me, whose sighs and tenderness ever for unfortunate humanity are painted in unequivocal traits!—me, who have worked with such courage and devotion for the enfranchisement of my brothers!—me, who in this sublime enterprise have had at the moment of misfortune, following on the great success which attests that I have at least brought some intelligence to the work before me!—they have pictured me, I say, either as a miserable dreamer in oblivion, or as a secret instrument of the perfidy of the enemies of the people. They have not blushed to agree with the tyrants as to the culpability of the most generous efforts to break down slavery and to cause the horrible misery of the country to cease. They have not blushed, finally, to seek to cast upon me alone this capital offence, in ornamenting it with all the accessories by which they thought to be able effectively to give it the colour of crime; and, nevertheless, I myself had the delicacy to compromise no one by name, only involving in the charge brought against me the coalition of all the democrats of the entire Republic, because I thought it at first useful to strike at despotism with terror, and because I thought it would be an insult to any democrat not to present him as a participant in an enterprise so obligatory for him as that of the re-establishment of equality! What have they gained, these false brothers, these apostates from our holy doctrine? What have they gained by this evil system which they appear to regard as the *non plus ultra* of cleverness? They have gained nothing beyond dishonour to themselves, to discredit revolutionaries with the people, who necessarily always disperse when they see themselves abandoned by their leaders. They have also succeeded in encouraging the enemy by the spectacle of such weakness. They have succeeded, finally, in precipitating the more rapidly their own protégés into the abyss. You have not taken part in these turpitudes, my friend. You have already begun to render to us the tribute of homage, which a just posterity will pay in full. * * * * *

I have no need to assure you that, in my complete devotion to the people, I have not thought of my personal affairs, neither have I ever forecast as to what might happen in the case of the failure that has now befallen me. I leave children and a wife, and I leave them without a cent, without the means of livelihood. No! for a man like Felix, it will certainly not be too onerous a legacy to impose upon him, to charge him to aid these unhappy creatures in

not dying of want. * * * * * You will permit me to give a little more in detail what I wish to be done for the unfortunates that I am abandoning. My two sons: the elder, as far as I can judge from the little that has been done for his education, will not have a great aptitude for the sciences. This would seem also to argue that he will not have the ambition to play any important rôle in the political arena. Hence he may pass his life quietly, and thus avoid the painful lot and misfortunes of his father. This boy has at least an excellent judgment and an independent spirit, the result of all the ideas in which he has been nourished. I have sounded him as to what he would like to be. Workman, he replied, but workman of the most independent class possible, and he cited that of the printer. He was not so far wrong, perhaps, and I desire nothing more than that he should follow his tastes. I can say nothing as regards his younger brother, who is too young as yet to decide anything as to his capacities; but if I have ground to hope that you will do as much for him as for the elder, I am content. Gracchus Babeuf has never been ambitious for himself or for his children. He has only been anxious to procure some good for the people. He would be too fortunate if he knew that his children were by way of becoming some day good and peaceable artisans, among the classes of which society has always need, and which consequently can never be wanting to her.

As regards my wife, in the face of the fact that she only has the domestic virtues and the simple qualities belonging to the mother of a family, all that will be necessary to preserve her from a pitiable want will be very little. It will suffice to advance her some small sum to place her in a position to undertake one of those minor occupations such as furnish all that is necessary to keep a small family.

And now, my good friend, I will ask of you one more favour. The nature of my trial and its slow progress tell me that I have still a certain number of days to live before that day when I shall go to sleep myself on the bed of honour, to expiate the acts which render me supremely culpable in the eyes of the enemies of humanity. I can wish, for my consolation, that my wife and my children might accompany me, so to say, to the foot of the altar where I shall be immolated; that will do me much more good than a confessor. Place them, I pray of you, in a position to make the journey, so that I shall not be deprived of this last satisfaction.

My body will return to earth. There will remain no more of me than a sufficient quantity of projects, notes, and sketches of democratic and revolutionary writings, all tending to the last aim, to the complete philanthropic

system for which I die. My wife will be able to collect them all; and one day, when the persecution shall have slackened, when perchance good men shall breathe again, with freedom enough to be able to cast a few flowers on our tomb, when people will have come to think again on the means of procuring to the human race the happiness we have proposed for it, you may look into those fragments, and present to all the disciples of Equality, to those of our friends who preserve our principles in their hearts—you may present to them, I say, for the benefit of my memory, a selection of these divers fragments, containing all that the corrupt of today call my dreams. I have finished. I embrace you and bid you adieu.[4]   G. BABEUF.

---

[4] Babeuf and Darthé were executed, seven other leaders were exiled, including Buonarroti. But Felix Lepelletier escaped imprisonment by the Directory and fulfilled his obligation to Babeuf's orphans. Babeuf's English biographer, E. B. Bax (a friend of William Morris at whose suggestion the English life was written) records that Lepelletier adopted Emile, who eventually joined the Spanish patriots in their struggle for independence. In Spain, Emile met Georges Grisel, the spy planted by the Directory in the Conspiracy of Equals. He promptly challenged him to a duel and avenged his father by killing him. The later history of Emile, who was to follow the dignified and independent vocation of printer, was a series of failures, as a bookseller in Lyons and Jacobin newspaper publisher in Paris. He seems to have joined the imperial cause of Napoleon I and emigrated to America when the empire fell. Babeuf's other son, Caius, was killed in battle during the first invasion of French territory in 1814, and Camille committed suicide from the Vendôme column in 1815 at the sight of the Cossacks entering Paris. The political, like the physical, offspring of Babeuf, those of 1848 and 1871, were also unfortunate. Of the *Babouvistes* Marx and Engels were to point to the "necessary failure of those early attempts at direct action" and blame them on "the embryonic state of the proletariat and . . . the absence of the material conditions for its emancipation." In 1938 a left-wing periodical, *Science and Society,* was to discover a "spiritual tie between the Bolsheviks and the *Babouvistes.*"

FOUNDING FATHERS' POOR RELATION:

Thomas Paine

APPEAL TO THE CONVENTION

MEMORIAL TO JAMES MONROE

On the 14th July, 1793, the anniversary of the French Revolution was celebrated, with every demonstration of joy and congratulation, at Philadelphia. The following toasts were drunk upon the occasion: 1. The Day 2. The French Republick 3. Victory to the French Armies over the Foes to Liberty 4. Liberty or Death 5. The Fair of France and America may each weave a Cap of Liberty for a Husband 6. The United States, may they prove an Asylum to all oppressed Patriots 7. The Rights of Man 8. Liberty and Equality 9. The Memory of those who have fallen in Defence of Liberty 10. May the People in the different Nations of the World soon follow the glorious examples of France and America, in asserting their lawful sovereignty, in Opposition to the Usurpation of Kings 11. Universal Liberty to all Mankind 12. The 4th of July, 1776 13. May Truth prevail over Prejudice 14. A Revolution, upon just Principles, throughout the World 15. Honour to those who have the Impulse and Spirit to exert it in the Cause of Liberty 16. Destruction to Mr. Burke's "Corinthian Pillar of Polished Society" 17. May those Kings and Supporters of Kings who have persecuted Men for the Defence of Liberty soon meet their just Reward 18. A Revolution and Freedom to the Nations of South America 19. An Abolition of every Kind of Slavery 20. May the Kings of Europe exchange their Crowns for the Cap of Liberty. . . .

From TOM PAINE'S JESTS [1]

THE old conspiracy against Tom Paine has not yet been dissipated and his friends have not altogether torn him from the embrace of village atheists. His American citizenship, by which he was rescued from a Jacobin jail, is not yet in very good standing. He was guilty of having too keen a nose for the crisis of revolution, too sharp a tongue with the idiom of common sense, and a brain too busy for the rights of man. Naturally the tory has burned him in effigy—and the orthodox democrat has tried hard to live him down. John Adams called him "the filthy Tom Paine," which Theodore Roosevelt echoed with "the filthy little atheist." Time is rubbing out the libelous portrait of a Bohemian pamphleteer with a bottle of whiskey and is revealing one of the most original of republican imaginations. After the now

---

[1] *Tom Paine's Jests:* Being An Entirely New And Select Collection Of Patriotick Bon Mots, Repartees, Anecdotes, Epigrams, Observations, & Etc. On Political Subjects. By Thomas Paine And Other Supporters Of The Rights Of Man. London. 1793.

respectable eighteenth-century axioms of Tom Paine on government and deism are discounted, there remains some singular speculation on property, labor and social planning which is still fresh and alive in the competition of ideas. "Personal property is the effect of society"—anticipates Henry George. "The accumulation of personal property is, in many instances, the effect of paying too little for the labor that produced it; and the consequence for which is that the working hand perishes in old age, and the employer abounds in affluence"—conveys Paine's notion of the class struggle. "It is not charity but a right, not bounty but justice, that I am pleading for"—pleads, in a measure, for the principle of social security.

In 1787, with the American Revolution behind him, with *Common Sense* and the *Crisis* papers the literary property of Americans, Tom Paine returned to Europe. He carried his reputation to Europe, as well as his model for an iron bridge, and rediscovered in London and Paris the excitement of great events. To counterbalance Burke's *Reflections on·the Revolution in France* he wrote *The Rights of Man*. The reformers, the radicals and the workingmen's societies read him hungrily in cheap editions, while Thomas Holcroft wrote in great excitement to William Godwin: "Hey, for the new Jerusalem! The Millennium! And peace and eternal beatitude be unto the soul of Thomas Paine." But the royalties of that revolutionary pamphlet were paid out to Tom Paine neither in peace nor beatitude. There were readers on both sides of the Atlantic who were embarrassed, antagonized, and deeply enraged by the pamphleteer, the internationalist, the agitator. Through the timely warning of William Blake, Paine escaped arrest by fleeing to France, though it turned out to be a jump from the frying pan into the fire, from the English terror against civil liberties into the coming French terror against life itself. The French National Assembly granted Paine honorary citizenship along with Washington, Hamilton, Madison, Priestley, Bentham and other republicans. Feted, applauded, kissed on both cheeks, the fugitive found a haven among the middle-of-the-road Girondists of the French Revolution. He collaborated with Condorcet, Danton and others in planning the abortive Constitution of 1793, but he disgusted the Jacobins by pleading for the life of Louis XVI. His light went out with the fall of the Girondists and he sat down to his most vilified writing, the dull scientific deism of *The Age of Reason*. For its sins he was to be refused a Quaker burial or any consecrated ground and he rested a while in an infidel's corner of his farm in New Rochelle. But his bones, which William Cobbett (in a penitent mood) later hauled off to England for some scheme of sanctifica-

tion, were lost to the graveyard and won by a furniture dealer—after Lord
Byron had written the jingle:

> For digging up your Bones, Tom Paine,
> Will Cobbett has done well;
> You'll visit him on earth again,
> He'll visit you in hell.

Tom Paine had his rehearsal of hell in a Jacobin prison, the Luxembourg,
where he was committed under a hysterical law against foreigners. From
this jail he wrote to the French Convention but the Committee of Public
Safety suppressed the appeal. Three of its members had received the impression from Gouverneur Morris, the American minister, that Paine's imprisonment was not being contested, while in Robespierre's handwriting a
rather curious sentence found its way into an order that Paine should "be
decreed of accusation for the interests of America as well as of France." In
the "interests of America" Gouverneur Morris was deep in a plot to rescue
the poor French king. That American gentleman had a nostalgia for royalty.
The Senate which nearly rejected Morris' appointment by Washington knew
nothing of the sophisticated peccadilloes of its cultivated but cynical ambassador, of his simultaneous flirtations with the Jacobins and the monarchists.
Morris despised Citizen Paine as a Bohemian nonconformist and crackpot,
disliked him for being a kind of unofficial and rival ambassador to the revolution, and so wrote home with calculated carelessness to Secretary Jefferson: "Lest I forget it, I must mention that Thomas Paine is in prison, where
he amuses himself with publishing a pamphlet against Jesus Christ . . . I
believe he thinks that I ought to claim him as an American citizen." Morris
did not press the matter of citizenship too hard. When war broke out between England and France, Morris, whose sympathies were with England,
and those in America who were weighing treaty obligations to France
against advantages of reconciliation with England, found the case of Tom
Paine's jailing something of a nuisance. The recall of Citizen Genet from
Washington and of Gouverneur Morris from Paris brought the new American minister, James Monroe, to Paine's rescue. In the Luxembourg where he
was pondering the second part of *The Age of Reason,* Paine saw hundreds
led out daily to the guillotine, among them Desmoulins and Danton. After
ten months of imprisonment he had the once crowded jail and its ghosts
almost to himself. Monroe not only helped to release him but sheltered and
nursed him. Paine had the satisfaction of being eulogized once again by the

French (André Chénier read the eulogy) and particularly of declining a pension. The adventure developed in Paine a bitterness against George Washington, whom he reminded in a letter that, when the revolution was established in America, he, Thomas Paine, had journeyed to propagate it abroad, while Washington rested at home on his laurels; he, Paine, became a prisoner, Washington a President. In the words of John Dos Passos, the trouble with Tom Paine was "that he never formed the knack that successful men have of encrusting themselves in official niches. He didn't have the respectable coloration of the country gentleman that protected many of the great libertarians of the time. His function was to observe events with the gazette in his hand from his seat in the coffeehouse or tavern and say his say and let his private life go to hell, and it did."

APPEAL TO THE CONVENTION

Citizens, Representatives: If I should not express myself with the energy I used formerly to do, you will attribute it to the very dangerous illness I have suffered in the prison of the Luxembourg. For several days I was insensible of my own existence; and though I am much recovered, it is with exceeding great difficulty that I find power to write you this letter.

But before I proceed further, I request the Convention to observe: that this is the first line that has come from me, either to the Convention or to any of the committees since my imprisonment—which is approaching to eight months. Ah, my friends, eight months' loss of liberty seems almost a lifetime to a man who has been, as I have been, the unceasing defender of liberty for twenty years.

I have now to inform the Convention of the reason of my not having written before. It is a year ago that I had strong reason to believe that Robespierre was my inveterate enemy, as he was the enemy of every man of virtue and humanity. The address that was sent to the Convention some time about last August from Arras, the native town of Robespierre, I have always been informed was the work of that hypocrite and the partisans he had in the place.

The intention of that address was to prepare the way for destroying me, by making the people declare (though without assigning any reason) that I had lost their confidence; the address, however, failed of success, as it was immediately opposed by a counter-address from St. Omer, which declared the direct contrary. But the strange power that Robespierre, by the most consummate hypocrisy and the most hardened cruelties, had obtained, ren-

380

dered any attempt on my part to obtain justice not only useless but dangerous; for it is the nature of tyranny always to strike a deeper blow when any attempt has been made to repel a former one. This being my situation, I submitted with patience to the hardness of my fate and waited the event of brighter days. I hope they are now arrived to the nation and to me.

Citizens, when I left the United States in the year 1787 I promised to all my friends that I would return to them the next year; but the hope of seeing a revolution happily established in France, that might serve as a model to the rest of Europe, and the earnest and disinterested desire of rendering every service in my power to promote it, induced me to defer my return to that country, and to the society of my friends, for more than seven years.

This long sacrifice of private tranquillity, especially after having gone through the fatigues and dangers of the American Revolution which continued almost eight years, deserved a better fate than the long imprisonment I have silently suffered. But it is not the nation but a faction that has done me this injustice. Parties and factions, various and numerous as they have been, I have always avoided. My heart was devoted to all France, and the object to which I applied myself was the Constitution. The plan which I proposed to the Committee, of which I was a member, is now in the hands of Barrère, and it will speak for itself.

It is perhaps proper that I inform you of the cause assigned in the order for my imprisonment. It is that I am "a foreigner"; whereas, the *foreigner* thus imprisoned was invited into France by a decree of the late National Assembly, and that in the hour of her greatest danger, when invaded by Austrians and Prussians. He was, moreover, a citizen of the United States of America, an ally of France, and not a subject of any country in Europe, and consequently not within the intentions of any decree concerning foreigners. But any excuse can be made to serve the purpose of malignity when in power.

I will not intrude on your time by offering any apology for the broken and imperfect manner in which I have expressed myself. I request you to accept it with the sincerity with which it comes from my heart; and I conclude with wishing fraternity and prosperity to France, and union and happiness to her representatives.

Citizens, I have now stated to you my situation, and I can have no doubt but your justice will restore me to the liberty of which I have been deprived.

THOMAS PAINE.

Luxembourg, Thermidor 19, 2nd Year of the French Republic, one and indivisible.

MEMORIAL ADDRESSED TO JAMES MONROE, MINISTER FROM THE UNITED STATES TO THE FRENCH REPUBLIC

I ADDRESS this memorial to you, in consequence of a letter I received from a friend, 18°Fructidor (September fourth), in which he says, "Mr. Monroe has told me, that he has no orders [meaning from the American Government] respecting you; but I am sure he will leave nothing undone to liberate you; but, from what I can learn, from all the late Americans, you are not considered either by the Government, or by the individuals, as an American citizen. You have been made a French citizen, which you have accepted, and you have further made yourself a servant of the French Republic; and, therefore, it would be out of character for an American Minister to interfere in their internal concerns. You must therefore either be liberated out of compliment to America, or stand your trial, which you have a right to demand."

This information was so unexpected by me, that I am at a loss how to answer it. I know not on what principle it originates; whether from an idea that I had voluntarily abandoned my citizenship of America for that of France, or from any article of the American Constitution applied to me. The first is untrue with respect to any intention on my part; and the second is without foundation, as I shall show in the course of this memorial.

The idea of conferring honor of citizenship upon foreigners, who had distinguished themselves in propagating the principles of liberty and humanity, in opposition to despotism, war and bloodshed, was first proposed by me to Lafayette, at the commencement of the French Revolution, when his heart appeared to be warmed with those principles. My motive in making this proposal, was to render the people of different nations more fraternal than they had been, or then were. I observed that almost every branch of science had possessed itself of the exercise of this right, so far as it regarded its own institution.

Most of the academies and societies in Europe, and also those of America, conferred the rank of honorary member, upon foreigners eminent in knowledge, and made them, in fact, citizens of their literary or scientific republic, without affecting or anyways diminishing their rights of citizenship in their own country or in other societies: and why the science of government should not have the same advantage, or why the people of one nation should not,

382

by their representatives, exercise the right of conferring the honor of citizenship upon individuals eminent in another nation, without affecting *their* rights of citizenship, is a problem yet to be solved.

I now proceed to remark on that part of the letter, in which the writer says, that *from what he can learn from all the late Americans, I am not considered in America, either by the Government or by the individuals, as an American citizen.*

In the first place I wish to ask, what is here meant by the Government of America? The members who compose the Government are only individuals, when in conversation, and who, most probably, hold very different opinions upon the subject. Have Congress as a body made any declaration respecting me, that they now no longer consider me as a citizen? If they have not, anything they otherwise say is no more than the opinion of individuals, and consequently is not legal authority, nor anyways sufficient authority to deprive any man of his citizenship. Besides, whether a man has forfeited his rights of citizenship, is a question not determinable by Congress, but by a court of judicature and a jury; and must depend upon evidence, and the application of some law or article of the Constitution to the case. No such proceeding has yet been had, and consequently I remain a citizen until it be had, be that decision what it may; for there can be no such thing as a suspension of rights in the interim.

I am very well aware, and always was, of the article of the Constitution which says, as nearly as I can recollect the words, that "any citizen of the United States, who shall accept any title, place, or office, from any foreign king, prince, or state, shall forfeit and lose his right of citizenship of the United States."

Had the article said, that *any citizen of the United States, who shall be a member of any foreign convention, for the purpose of forming a free constitution, shall forfeit and lose the right of citizenship of the United States,* the article had been directly applicable to me; but the idea of such an article never could have entered the mind of the American Convention, and the present article is altogether foreign to the case with respect to me. It supposes a government in active existence, and not a government dissolved; and it supposes a citizen of America accepting titles and offices under that government, and not a citizen of America who gives his assistance in a convention chosen by the people, for the purpose of forming a government *de nouveau* founded on their authority.

The late Constitution and Government of France was dissolved the tenth

of August, 1792. The National Legislative Assembly then in being, supposed itself without sufficient authority to continue its sittings, and it proposed to the departments to elect not another legislative assembly, but a convention for the express purpose of forming a new constitution. When the Assembly were discoursing on this matter, some of the members said, that they wished to gain all the assistance possible upon the subject of free constitutions; and expressed a wish to elect and invite foreigners of any nation to the Convention, who had distinguished themselves in defending, explaining and propagating the principles of liberty.

It was on this occasion that my name was mentioned in the Assembly. (I was then in England.) After this, a deputation from a body of the French people, in order to remove any objection that might be made against my assisting at the proposed convention, requested the Assembly, as their representatives, to give me the title of French citizen; after which, I was elected a member of the Convention, in four different departments, as is already known.

The case, therefore, is, that I accepted nothing from any king, prince or state, nor from any government: for France was without any government, except what arose from common consent, and the necessity of the case. Neither did I *make myself a servant of the French Republic,* as the letter alluded to expresses; for at that time France was not a republic, not even in name. She was altogether a people in a state of revolution.

It was not until the Convention met that France was declared a republic, and monarchy abolished; soon after which a committee was elected, of which I was a member,[2] to form a constitution, which was presented to the Convention [and read by Condorcet, who was also a member] the fifteenth and sixteenth of February following, but was not to be taken into consideration till after the expiration of two months, and if approved of by the Convention, was then to be referred to the people for their acceptance, with such additions or amendments as the Convention should make.

In thus employing myself upon the formation of a constitution, I certainly did nothing inconsistent with the American Constitution. I took no oath of allegiance to France, or any other oath whatever. I considered the citizenship they had presented me with as an honorary mark of respect paid to me not only as a friend to liberty, but as an American citizen. My acceptance of that, or of the deputyship, not conferred on me by any king, prince or state,

---

[2] Sieyès, Paine, Brissot, Danton, Condorcet, Petion, Barrère, Vergniaud, Gensonne.

but by a people in a state of revolution and contending for liberty, required no transfer of my allegiance or of my citizenship from America to France. There I was a real citizen, paying taxes; here, I was a voluntary friend, employing myself on a temporary service. Every American in Paris knew that it was my constant intention to return to America, as soon as a constitution should be established, and that I anxiously waited for that event.

I know not what opinions have been circulated in America. It may have been supposed there that I had voluntarily and intentionally abandoned America, and that my citizenship had ceased by my own choice. I can easily [believe] there are those in that country who would take such a proceeding on my part somewhat in disgust. The idea of forsaking old friendships for new acquaintances is not agreeable. I am a little warranted in making this supposition by a letter I received some time ago from the wife of one of the Georgia delegates in which she says: "Your friends on this side the water cannot be reconciled to the idea of your abandoning America."

I have never abandoned her in thought, word or deed; and I feel it incumbent upon me to give the assurance to the friends I have in that country and with whom I have always intended and am determined, if the possibility exists, to close the scene of my life. It is there that I have made myself a home. It is there that I have given the services of my best days. America never saw me flinch from her cause in the most gloomy and perilous of her situations; and I know there are those in that country who will not flinch from me. If I have enemies (and every man has some) I leave them to the enjoyment of their ingratitude.[3]

It is somewhat extraordinary that the idea of my not being a citizen of America should have arisen only at the time that I am imprisoned in France because, or on the pretense that, I am a foreigner. The case involves a strange contradiction of ideas. None of the Americans who came to France while I

---

[3] I subjoin in a note, for the sake of wasting the solitude of a prison, the answer that I gave to the part of the letter above mentioned. It is not inapplicable to the subject of this Memorial; but it contains somewhat of a melancholy idea, a little predictive, that I hope is not becoming true so soon.

"You touch me on a very tender point when you say that my friends on your side the water cannot be reconciled to the idea of my abandoning America. They are right. I had rather see my horse Button eating the grass of Borden-Town or Morrisania than see all the pomp and show of Europe.

"A thousand years hence (for I must indulge a few thoughts) perhaps in less, America may be what Europe now is. The innocence of her character, that won the hearts of all nations in her favor, may sound like a romance and her inimitable virtues as if it had never been. The ruin of that liberty which thousands bled for or struggled to obtain may just furnish materials for a village tale or extort a sigh from rustic sensibility, while the

was in liberty had conceived any such idea or circulated any such opinion; and why it should arise now is a matter yet to be explained. However discordant the late American Minister G. M. [Gouverneur Morris] and the late French Committee of Public Safety were, it suited the purpose of both that I should be continued in arrestation. The former wished to prevent my return to America, that I should not expose his misconduct; and the latter, lest I should publish to the world the history of its wickedness. While that Minister and the Committee continued I had no expectation of liberty. I speak here of the Committee of which Robespierre was member.

I ever must deny, that the article of the American Constitution already mentioned, can be applied either verbally, intentionally, or constructively, to me. It undoubtedly was the intention of the Convention that framed it, to preserve the purity of the American Republic from being debased by foreign and foppish customs; but it never could be its intention to act against the principles of liberty, by forbidding its citizens to assist in promoting those principles in foreign countries; neither could it be its intention to act against the principles of gratitude.

France had aided America in the establishment of her revolution, when invaded and oppressed by England and her auxiliaries. France in her turn was invaded and oppressed by a combination of foreign despots. In this situation, I conceived it an act of gratitude in me, as a citizen of America, to render her in return the best services I could perform.

I came to France (for I was in England when I received the invitation) not to enjoy ease, emoluments and foppish honors, as the article supposes; but to encounter difficulties and dangers in defense of liberty; and I must question whether those who now malignantly seek (for some I believe do) to turn this to my injury, would have had courage to have done the same thing. I am sure Gouverneur Morris would not. He told me the second day after my arrival (in Paris), that the Austrians and Prussians, who were then

---

fashionable of that day, enveloped in dissipation, shall deride the principle and deny the fact.

"When we contemplate the fall of Empires and the extinction of the nations of the Ancient World, we see but little to excite our regret than the mouldering ruins of pompous palaces, magnificent museums, lofty pyramids and walls and towers of the most costly workmanship; but when the Empire of America shall fall, the subject for contemplative sorrow will be infinitely greater than crumbling brass and marble can inspire. It will not then be said, here stood a temple of vast antiquity; here rose a babel of invisible height; or there a palace of sumptuous extravagance; but here, Ah, painful thought! the noblest work of human wisdom, the grandest scene of human glory, the fair cause of Freedom rose and fell. Read this, and then ask if I forget America." [THOMAS PAINE]

at Verdun, would be in Paris in a fortnight. "I have no idea," said he, "that seventy thousand disciplined troops can be stopped in their march by any power in France."

Besides the reasons I have already given for accepting the invitations to the Convention, I had another that has reference particularly to America, and which I mentioned to Mr. Pinckney the night before I left London to come to Paris: "That it was to the interest of America that the system of European governments should be changed and placed on the same principle with her own." Mr. Pinckney agreed fully in the same opinion. I have done my part toward it.

It is certain that governments upon similar systems agree better together than those that are founded on principles discordant with each other; and the same rule holds good with respect to the people living under them. In the latter case they offend each other by pity, or by reproach; and the discordancy carries itself to matters of commerce. I am not an ambitious man, but perhaps I have been an ambitious American. I have wished to see America the *Mother Church* of government, and I have done my utmost to exalt her character and her condition.

I have now stated sufficient matter to show that the article in question is not applicable to me; and that any such application to my injury, as well in circumstances as in right, is contrary both to the letter and intention of that article, and is illegal and unconstitutional. Neither do I believe that any jury in America, when they are informed of the whole of the case, would give a verdict to deprive me of my rights upon that article. The citizens of America, I believe, are not very fond of permitting forced and indirect explanations to be put upon matters of this kind.

I know not what were the merits of the case with respect to the person who was prosecuted for acting as prize master to a French privateer, but I know that the jury gave a verdict against the prosecution. The rights I have acquired are dear to me. They have been acquired by honorable means, and by dangerous service in the worst of times, and I cannot passively permit them to be wrested from me. I conceive it my duty to defend them, as the case involves a constitutional and public question, which is, how far the power of the Federal Government extends, in depriving any citizen of his rights of citizenship, or of suspending them.

That the explanation of national treaties belongs to Congress is strictly constitutional; but not the explanation of the Constitution itself, any more than the explanation of law in the case of individual citizens. These are

altogether judiciary questions. It is, however, worth observing, that Congress, in explaining the article of the treaty with respect to French prizes and French privateers, confined itself strictly to the letter of the article. Let them explain the article of the Constitution with respect to me in the same manner, and the decision, did it appertain to them, could not deprive me of my rights of citizenship, or suspend them, for I have accepted nothing from any king, prince, state or government.

You will please observe that·I speak as if the Federal Government had made some declaration upon the subject of my citizenship; whereas the fact is otherwise; and your saying that you have in order respecting me is a proof of it. Those therefore who propagate the report of my not being considered as a citizen of America by Government, do it to the prolongation of my imprisonment, and without authority; for Congress, *as a government,* has neither decided upon it, nor yet taken the matter into consideration; and I request you to caution such persons against spreading such reports. But be these matters as they may, I cannot have a doubt that you will find and feel the case very different, since you have heard what I have to say, and known what my situation is [better] than you did before your arrival.

But it was not the Americans only, but the Convention also, that knew what my intentions were upon that subject. In my last discourse delivered at the Tribune of the Convention, January 19, 1793, on the motion for suspending the execution of Louis XVI, I said (the Deputy Bancal read the translation in French):

"It unfortunately happens that the person who is the subject of the present discussion, is considered by the Americans as having been the friend of their revolution. His execution will be an affliction to them, and it is in your power not to wound the feelings of your ally. Could I speak the French language I would descend to your bar, and in their name become your petitioner to respite the execution of the sentence.

"As the Convention was elected for the express purpose of forming a Constitution, its continuance cannot be longer than four or five months more at furthest; and, if after my *return to America,* I should employ myself in writing the history of the French Revolution, I had rather record a thousand errors on the side of mercy than be obliged to tell one act of severe justice.

"Ah citizens! give not the tyrant of England the triumph of seeing the man perish on a scaffold who had aided my much-loved America."

Does this look as if I had abandoned America? But if she abandons me in the situation I am in, to gratify the enemies of humanity, let that disgrace

be to herself. But I know the people of America better than to believe it, though I undertake not to answer for every individual.

When this discourse was pronounced, Marat launched himself into the middle of the hall and said that "I voted against the punishment of death because I was a Quaker." I replied that "I voted against it both morally and politically."

I certainly went a great way, considering the rage of the times, in endeavoring to prevent that execution. I had many reasons for so doing. I judged, and events have shown that I judged rightly, that if they once began shedding blood, there was no knowing where it would end; and as to what the world might call *honor*, the execution would appear like a nation killing a mouse; and in a political view, would serve to transfer the hereditary claim to some more formidable enemy. The man could do no more mischief; and that which he had done was not only from the vice of his education, but was as much the fault of the nation in restoring him after he had absconded June 21, 1791, as it was his.

I made the proposal for imprisonment until the end of the war and perpetual banishment after the war, instead of the punishment of death. Upwards of three hundred members voted for that proposal. The sentence for absolute death (for some members had voted the punishment of death conditionally) was carried by a majority of twenty-five out of more than seven hundred.

I return from this digression to the proper subject of my memorial.

Painful as the want of liberty may be, it is a consolation to me to believe that my imprisonment proves to the world that I had no share in the murderous system that then reigned. That I was an enemy to it, both morally and politically, is known to all who had any knowledge of me; and could I have written French as well as I can English, I would publicly have exposed its wickedness and shown the ruin with which it was pregnant. They who have esteemed me on former occasions, whether in America or in Europe, will, I know, feel no cause to abate that esteem, when they reflect that *imprisonment with preservation of character is preferable to liberty with disgrace.*

I here close my memorial and proceed to offer you a proposal that appears to me suited to all the circumstances of the case; which is that you reclaim me conditionally, until the opinion of Congress can be obtained on the subject of my citizenship of America; and that I remain in liberty under your protection during that time.

I found this proposal upon the following grounds:

First, you say you have no orders respecting me; consequently, you have no orders *not* to reclaim me; and in this case you are left discretionary judge whether to reclaim or not. My proposal therefore unites a consideration of your situation with my own.

Secondly, I am put in arrestation because I am a foreigner. It is therefore necessary to determine to what country I belong. The right of determining this question cannot appertain exclusively to the Committee of Public Safety or General Surety; because I appeal to the Minister of the United States, and show that my citizenship of that country is good and valid, referring at the same time, through the agency of the Minister, my claim of right to the opinion of Congress. It being a matter between two governments.

Thirdly. France does not claim me for a citizen; neither do I set up any claim of citizenship in France. The question is simply whether I am or am not a citizen of America. I am imprisoned here on the decree for imprisoning foreigners because, say they, I was born in England.

I say in answer that, though born in England, I am not a subject of the English Government any more than any other American who was born, as they all were, under the same government, or than the citizens of France are subjects of the French monarchy under which they were born. I have twice taken the oath of abjuration to the British King and Government and of allegiance to America—once as a citizen of the State of Pennsylvania in 1776, and again before Congress, administered to me by the President, Mr. Hancock, when I was appointed Secretary in the office of Foreign Affairs in 1777.

The letter before quoted in the first page of this memorial, says, "It would be out of character for an American Minister to interfere in the internal affairs of France." This goes on the idea that I am a citizen of France, and a member of the Convention, which is not the fact. The Convention have declared me to be a foreigner; and consequently the citizenship and the election are null and void. It also has the appearance of a decision, that the article of the Constitution, respecting grants made to American citizens by foreign kings, princes or states, is applicable to me; which is the very point in question, and against the application of which I contend.

I state evidence to the Minister, to show that I am not within the letter or meaning of that article; that it cannot operate against me; and I apply to him for the protection that I conceive I have a right to ask and to receive. The internal affairs of France are out of the question with respect to my application or his interference. I ask it not as a citizen of France, for I am not one:

I ask it not as a member of the Convention, for I am not one; both these, as before said, have been rendered null and void; I ask it not as a man against whom there is any accusation, for there is none; I ask it not as an exile from America, whose liberties I have honorably and generously contributed to establish; I ask it as a citizen of America, deprived of his liberty in France, under the plea of being a foreigner; and I ask it because I conceive I am entitled to it upon every principle of constitutional justice and national honor.

But though I thus positively assert my claim because I believe I have a right to do so, it is perhaps most eligible, in the present situation of things, to put that claim upon the footing I have already mentioned; that is, that the Minister reclaims me conditionally until the opinion of Congress can be obtained on the subject of my citizenship of America, and that I remain in liberty under the protection of the Minister during that interval.

(Signed)   THOMAS PAINE.

N.B. I should have added that as Gouverneur Morris could not inform Congress of the cause of my arrestation, as he knew it not himself, it is to be supposed that Congress was not enough acquainted with the case to give any directions respecting me when you came away.

T. P.

A GIBBET AND A GENTLEMAN:
Major John André
TWO LETTERS TO GEORGE WASHINGTON:
"The person in your possession is Major John André"
"not to die on a gibbet"

~~~~~~

IF BENEDICT ARNOLD is, as Carl Van Doren calls him, "the Iago of traitors," then Major John André is the Mercutio of spies. While Benedict Arnold saved his neck in the conspiracy to betray the American Revolution, André gambled with his life and left a legend. The balladmakers and the playwrights have been generous to André. He has been compensated by fame with monuments on *both* sides of the Revolution. Except for a brief and unpleasant rendezvous with a gibbet, Major John André was a gentleman who enjoyed a great many of the fortunes of war and not a few of the accomplishments of fashion. A very young man, he became the trusted aide of Sir Henry Clinton and the brain of British headquarters in America which co-ordinated all the secret information regarded as necessary to sever the head of the Revolution from its body. When André was not busy as a soldier or conspirator, the Loyalists of New York and "the little society of Third and Fourth Streets" in Philadelphia knew him for a delightful master of ceremonies. On the occasion when General Howe gave way to General Clinton amidst the British frivolities of the *Meschianza* (a festival of dances, music, and fireworks) Major André proved himself as valiant on the ballroom floor as in the field. He could write a prologue to a play, design a Turkish costume, sketch the *Meschianza* ladies, and compose some of those satirical ballads for the gazettes of the day, in one of which, *The Cow-Chase,* André ridiculed General Anthony Wayne and his "dung-born tribes."

> All wondrous proud in arms they came!
> What hero could refuse
> To tread the rugged path to fame,
> Who had a pair of shoes?

The web spun by Benedict Arnold around the American Revolution was fatal to John André but gave the young Englishman opportunities for fame lacking in a drawing room. Captured in Tarrytown as a spy in the Arnold-Clinton negotiations, and hung on a gibbet by an enemy who agreed with

Alexander Hamilton that "never did a man suffer death with more justice, or deserve it less," he won a corner in Westminster Abbey to which *The Cow-Chase* alone would certainly not have entitled him. Before his execution in 1780 he wrote two gallant letters to General George Washington. An officer and a gentleman, he begged another officer and gentleman, though a rebel, not to judge appearances by their face value; he was not a common spy. But André's vindication was posthumous. In England his friend, Miss Anna Seward, wrote a *Monody on Major André* dedicated to Sir Henry Clinton and praised by Dr. Johnson. In America it is now too difficult to remember anything about the young man but his virtues. Thirteen days after André's execution, Benedict Arnold, who could have waited a little longer, sent to Sir Henry Clinton a bill for treason which mentioned £10,000. But, then, at a sale of autograph letters in 1926, a single André item sold for $1250—and the inscription on his *American* monument one hundred years later was a minor miracle of sublimation:

Here died, October 2, 1780
Major JOHN ANDRÉ, of the British army
who, entering the American lines
on a secret mission to Benedict Arnold
for the surrender of West Point
was taken a prisoner, tried and condemned as a Spy.
His death,
though according to the stern code of war,
moved even his enemies to pity:
and both armies mourned the fate
of one so young and so brave.
In 1821 his remains were removed to
Westminster Abbey.
A hundred years after the execution
this stone was placed above the spot where he lay,
by a citizen of the United States against which he fought,
not to perpetuate the record of strife,
but in token of those better feelings
which have since united two nations,
one in race, in language and in religion,
in the hope that the friendly understanding
will never be broken.

A GIBBET AND A GENTLEMAN : *John André*

TWO LETTERS TO GEORGE WASHINGTON

"The person in your possession is Major John André"

Salem, September 24th, 1780.

SIR, What I have as yet said concerning myself was in the justifiable attempt to be extricated. I am too little accustomed to duplicity to have succeeded. I beg your Excellency will be persuaded that no alteration in the temper of my mind, or apprehension for my safety, induces me to take the step of addressing you, but that it is to rescue myself from an imputation of having assumed a mean character for treacherous purposes or self-interest; a conduct incompatible with the principles that actuate me, as well as with my condition in life. It is to vindicate my fame that I speak, and not to solicit security. The person in your possession is Major John André, adjutant general to the British army.

The influence of one commander in the army of his adversary is an advantage taken in war. A correspondence for this purpose I held, as confidential (in the present instance) with his Excellency Sir Henry Clinton. To favor it, I agreed to meet, upon ground not within the posts of either army, a person who was to give me intelligence. I came up in the *Vulture* man-of-war for this effect, and was fetched by a boat from the ship to the beach. Being here, I was told that the approach of day would prevent my return, and that I must be concealed until the next night. I was in my regimentals, and had fairly risked my person.

Against my stipulations, my intention, and without my knowledge beforehand, I was conducted within one of your posts. Your Excellency may conceive my sensation on this occasion, and must imagine how much more must I have been affected by a refusal to re-conduct me back the next night as I had been brought. Thus become a prisoner, I had to concert my escape. I quitted my uniform, and was passed another way in the night, without the American posts, to neutral ground, and informed I was beyond all armed parties, and left to press for New York. I was taken to Tarrytown by some volunteers. Thus, as I have had the honor to relate, was I betrayed (being adjutant general of the British army) into the vile condition of an enemy in disguise within your posts.

Having avowed myself a British officer, I have nothing to reveal but what relates to myself, which is true on the honor of an officer and a gentleman. The request I have to make to your Excellency, and I am conscious I address

myself well, is, that in any rigor policy may dictate, a decency of conduct may work that, though unfortunate, I am branded with nothing dishonorable, as no motive could be mine but in service of my king, and as I was involuntarily an impostor. Another request is, that I may be permitted to write an open letter to Sir Henry Clinton, and another to a friend for clothes and linen.

I take the liberty to mention the condition of some gentlemen at Charleston, who, being either on parole or under protection, were engaged in a conspiracy against us. Though their situation is not similar, they are objects who may be set in exchange for me, or are persons whom the treatment I receive might affect. It is no less, Sir, in a confidence of the generosity of your mind, than on account of your superior station, that I have chosen to importune you with this letter.

I have the honour to be, with great respect, Sir,

Your Excellency's most obedient and most humble servant,

JOHN ANDRÉ, *Adjutant General.*

"not to die on a gibbet" [1]

October 1.

SIR, Buoyed above the terror of death by the consciousness of a life devoted to honourable pursuits, and stained with no action that can give me remorse, I trust that the request I make to your Excellency at this serious period, and which is to soften my last moments, will not be rejected. Sympathy towards a soldier will surely induce your Excellency, and a military tribunal, to adopt the mode of my death to the feelings of a man of honour. Let me hope, Sir, if aught in my character impresses you with esteem towards me, if aught in my misfortunes marks me as the victim of policy and not of resentment, I shall experience the operation of these feelings in your breast by being informed I am not to die on a gibbet.

I have the honour, etc., etc.

JOHN ANDRÉ.

---

[1] This letter was afterwards paraphrased by N. P. Willis in verses whose third stanza reads:

Thine is the power to give,
Thine to deny;
Joy for the hour I live,
Calmness to die.

By all the brave should cherish,
By my dying breath,
I ask that I may perish
By a soldier's death.

A PRISONER OF WAR:

Mordecai Sheftall

IN THE charter which the English king granted to the Trustees of Georgia, liberty of conscience was guaranteed to all save "Papists," though the Trustees also harbored prejudices against rum and lawyers. In the second vessel which arrived in James Oglethorpe's colony there were forty hopeful settlers who were neither "Papists" nor lawyers nor rum lovers. The Trustees, who probably never expected that Jews would seek to come within the boundaries of their publicized toleration, were unfriendly to them. Some were poor German Jews to whom the Trustees, commissioned "to assist the needy and respectable families from England," especially objected. Others were Portuguese Jews, many of them refugees from the Inquisition, bearing names like Nuñez, Bornal, de Olivera, Lopez de Crasto, Molena, Moranda, Cohen del Monte, Minis, de Lyon, Sheftall. But James Oglethorpe sheltered them all, and thus Mordecai Sheftall was born to a Jewish settler, among the first white freeborn children native to Georgia. Sheftall left the mark of his energy and respectability on the social life of Savannah. He championed the American cause—the name of Sheftall, as "Chairman of Rebel Parochial Committee," appearing beside a Cohen and a Minis in a list of persons disqualified by the British from holding any office of trust in the province, because of a "most audacious, wicked, and unprovoked rebellion." Sheftall was appointed commissary general to the troops of Georgia and he figured as a staff officer in the Continental line of the Georgia brigade, and in the defense of Savannah when it was attacked in 1778. The fortunes of war reduced him to the miseries of a prison ship. Risking his neck, he resisted unsportsmanlike inducements from the enemy to make him deflect his loyalties, and the British spoke of him as "a very great rebel." With three patriots who shared his prison he observed the ceremonies and anniversaries of a Savannah society, Sheftall being chosen its president-in-exile. He survived all his trials and returned to his niche in the memories and history of old Georgia. From his captivity he brought home in his pocket, for the Sheftall family album as it were, an artless diary of a little corner of the great Revolution.

CAPTURE OF MORDECAI SHEFTALL, DEPUTY COMMIS-
SARY GENERAL OF ISSUES TO THE CONTINENTAL
TROOPS FOR THE STATE OF GEORGIA, VIZ., 1778,
DECEMBER 29TH:

THIS day the British troops, consisting of about 3500 men, including two
battalions of Hessians, under the command of Lieutenant-Colonel Archi-
bald Campbell, of the 71st regiment of Highlanders, landed early in the
morning at Brewton Hill, two miles below the town of Savannah, where
they met with very little opposition before they gained the height. At about
three o'clock in the afternoon they entered, and took possession of the town
of Savannah, when I endeavored, with my son Sheftall, to make our escape
across Musgrove Creek, having first premised that an intrenchment had been
thrown up there in order to cover a retreat, and upon seeing Colonel Samuel
Elbert and Major James Habersham trying to make their escape that way.
But on our arrival at the creek, after having sustained a very heavy fire of
musketry from the light infantry under the command of Sir James Baird,
during the time we were crossing the Common, without any injury to either
of us, we found it high water; and my son, not knowing how to swim, and
we, with about one hundred and eighty-six officers and privates, being
caught, as it were, in a pen, and the Highlanders keeping up a constant fire
on us, it was thought advisable to surrender ourselves prisoners. We accordingly did, and which was no sooner done than the Highlanders plundered
every one amongst us, except Major Low, myself and son, who, being foremost, had an opportunity to surrender ourselves to the British officer, namely,
Lieutenant Peter Campbell. He disarmed us as we came into the yard
formerly occupied by Mr. Moses Nunes. During this business Sir James
Baird was missing; but, on his coming into the yard, he mounted himself
on the stepladder which was erected at the end of the house, and sounded
his brass bugle horn, which the Highlanders no sooner heard than they all
got about him, and he addressed himself to them in Highland language
when they all dispersed, and finished plundering such of the officers and
men as had been fortunate enough to escape their first search. This over we
were marched in file, guarded by the Highlanders and York Volunteers,
who had come up before we marched, when we were paraded before Mrs.
Goffe's door, on the Bay, where we saw the greatest part of the army drawn
up. From there, after some time we were all marched through the town to

the courthouse, which was very much crowded, the greatest part of the officers they had taken being here collected, and indiscriminately put together. I had been here about two hours, when an officer, who I afterwards learned to be Major Crystie, called for me by name, and ordered me to follow him, which I did, with my blanket and shirt under my arm, my clothing and my son's which were in my saddlebags having been taken from my horse, so that my wardrobe consisted of what I had on my back.

On our way to the white guardhouse we met with Colonel Campbell, who inquired of the major how he had got there. On his naming me to him, he desired that I might be well guarded, as I was a very great rebel. The Major obeyed his orders, for, on lodging me in the guardhouse, he ordered the sentry to guard me with a drawn bayonet, and not to suffer me to go without the reach of it; which orders were strictly complied with, until a Mr. Gild Busler, their Commissary-General, called for me, and ordered me to go with him to my stores, that he might get some provisions for our people, who, he said, were starving, not having eaten anything for three days, which I contradicted, as I had victualled them that morning for the day. On our way to the office where I used to issue the provisions, he ordered me to give him information of what stores I had in town, and what I had sent out of town, and where. This I declined doing, which made him angry. He asked me if I knew that Charlestown was taken. I told him no. He then called us poor, deluded wretches, and said "Good God! how you are deluded by your leaders!" When I inquired of him who had taken it and when he said General Grant, with ten thousand men, and that it had been taken eight or ten days ago, I smiled, and told him it was not so, as I had a letter in my pocket that was written in Charlestown but three days ago by my brother. He replied we had been misinformed. I then retorted that I found they could be misinformed by their leaders as well as we could be deluded by ours. This made him so angry, that when he returned me to the guardhouse, he ordered me to be confined amongst the drunken soldiers and Negroes, where I suffered a great deal of abuse, and was threatened to be run through the body, or as they termed it, "skivered" by one of the York Volunteers; which threat he attempted to put into execution three times during the night, but was prevented by one Sergeant Campbell.

In this situation I remained two days without a morsel to eat, when a Hessian officer named Zaltman, finding that I could talk his language, removed me to his room, and sympathized with me on my situation. He permitted me to send to Mrs. Minis who sent me some victuals. He also per-

mitted me to go and see my son, and to let him come and stay with me. He introduced me to Captain Kappel, also a Hessian, who treated me very politely. In this situation I remained until Saturday morning, the 2nd of January, 1779, when the Commander, Colonel Innis, sent his orderly for me and my son to bring us to his quarters, which was James Habersham's house, where on the top of the steps I met with Captain Stanhope, of the *Raven* sloop of war, who treated me with the most illiberal abuse; and, after charging me with having refused the supplying of the King's ships with provisions, and of having shut the church door, together with many ill-natured things, ordered me on board the prison ship, together with my son. I made a point of giving Mr. Stanhope suitable answers to his impertinent treatment, and then turned from him, and inquired for Colonel Innis. I got his leave to go to Mrs. Minis for a shirt she had taken to wash for me as it was the only one I had left, except the one on my back, and that was given me by Captain Kappel, as the British soldiers had plundered both mine and my son's clothes. This favor he granted me under guard; after which I was conducted on board one of the flat boats, and put on board the prison ship *Nancy,* commanded by Captain Samuel Tait, when the first thing that presented itself to my view was one of our poor continental soldiers lying on the ship's main deck in the agonies of death, and who expired in a few hours. After being presented to the Captain with mine and the rest of the prisoners' names, I gave him in charge what paper money I had, and my watch. My son also gave him his money, to take care of. He appeared to be a little more civil after this confidence placed in him, and permitted us to sleep in a stateroom—that is, the Rev. Moses Allen, myself and son. In the evening we were served with what was called our allowance, which consisted of two pints and a half, and a half gill of rice, and about seven ounces of boiled beef per man. We were permitted to choose our mess mates and I accordingly made choice of Capt. Thomas Fineley, Rev. Mr. Allen, Mr. Moses Valentonge, Mr. Daniel Flaherty, myself and son, Sheftall Sheftall.

THE FIRST OF THE BLACKS:
Toussaint L'Ouverture

MEMOIR OF GENERAL TOUSSAINT L'OUVERTURE,

WRITTEN BY HIMSELF

~~~~~~

> Toussaint, the most unhappy man of men!
> Whether the whistling Rustic tend his plough
> Within thy hearing, or thy head be now
> Pillowed in some deep dungeon's earless den;—
> O miserable Chieftain! where and when
> Wilt thou find patience? Yet die not; do thou
> Wear rather in thy bonds a cheerful brow:
> Though fallen thyself, never to rise again,
> Live, and take comfort. Thou hast left behind
> Powers that will work for thee; air, earth, and skies;
> There's not a breathing of the common wind
> That will forget thee; thou hast great allies;
> Thy friends are exaltations, agonies,
> And love, and man's unconquerable mind.
>
> WILLIAM WORDSWORTH, *To Toussaint L'Ouverture*

THE French Revolution's cry of *Liberty* found an echo in the revolt of the slaves of San Domingo. As Bonaparte was rising from the wreckage and ashes of Thermidor, Toussaint L'Ouverture—historically just as remarkable a phenomenon as the First Consul himself—was already well planted to challenge slavery and white supremacy in the colony. Ending in personal failure, the great Negro leader (who had been a slave till he was forty-five) succeeded for a time in thwarting the powers of France, Spain, and England. Defeated only by a piece of treachery, he left behind him the means of a swift and ruthless liberation under his successor Dessalines. Although it is not true that in the fantastic contest between Toussaint L'Ouverture and Napoleon Bonaparte, the Negro protagonist addressed a message *"To the First of the Whites from the First of the Blacks,"* that legendary salutation has a historical logic. Moreover, the flavor of irony plays over the issue between them: it was, after all, *the First of the Blacks,* though he perished in Bonaparte's dungeon, who won, if only posthumously, in the revolt against *the First of the Whites.* When the Bastille was being assaulted by the people of Paris, San Domingo was the great slave market of the world. The sweat of half a million slaves was the oil for its exotic colonial civiliza-

400

tion. The revolt of the San Domingo Negroes in 1791 took place at the cross-roads of a number of forces—conflicts of color, caste, property; the struggle for power among royalist whites, republican whites, Jacobins and· anti-Jacobins, free mulattoes and enslaved blacks, and beyond this sordid incestuous ant-hill the rival imperialisms of the greatest powers on earth: Spain, England, France. The result was a series of unspeakable brutalities, and finally insurrection. The Declaration of Rights had proclaimed that all men are born free and equal; visitors from France to San Domingo freely distributed the fraternal embrace of the Revolution; the "people of color" were decreed citizenship and votes; but the victorious bourgeoisie of the Revolution remained too long in confusion about the disposition of colonial property, that is to say the slaves and sons of slaves. Out of this chaos rose the leadership of Toussaint L'Ouverture. In twelve years every cycle of power was defeated, mulatto and white, monarchist and republican, Spanish, British, and French. The leadership came from a self-taught slave who had taken to heart the words of the Abbé Reynal when he wrote: "The Negroes lack but a chief. Where is the great man? He will appear; we have no doubt of it. He will show himself; he will unfurl the sacred standard of liberty." Toussaint L'Ouverture did more; he won and tamed a state, ruling it as much with primitive decorum as with his fierce dictatorial discipline. Having abolished slavery, he commanded that a constitution be written for free black men and had the unfortunate audacity to send a sample copy to General Bonaparte. The First Consul's answer to the black constitution was a punitive expedition under his brother-in-law General Leclerc, who never really defeated Toussaint L'Ouverture but succeeded in sending him to Napoleon's dungeon in the Fort de Joux only by treachery after an armistice. The dungeon quickly killed him and there is reason to suspect that he was deliberately starved to death. The autobiographical document which belongs to Toussaint L'Ouverture's captivity seems as much an *apologia* to Bonaparte for L'Ouverture's resistance to General Leclerc's expedition to restore slavery in San Domingo, as the desire of the old soldier to record his campaigns on paper. It was not long before his old comrade-in-arms, General Dessalines, avenged his death on white Frenchmen with the greatest brutality. The free Negro state of Haiti was born—only eight months after Toussaint L'Ouverture was dead. Among Napoleon's archives there exists in the hand of the unfortunate messenger who carried the black constitution to Paris (and whom Napoleon banished to a little island named Elba), a portrait of the Negro leader when his genius was in full flower:

THE FIRST OF THE BLACKS : *Toussaint L'Ouverture*

At the head of so many resources is a man the most active and tireless of whom one can possibly have any idea; it is the strictest truth to say that he is everywhere and, above all, in that spot where a sound judgment and danger make it essential for him to be; his great sobriety, the faculty accorded to him alone of never taking a rest, the advantage he enjoys of being able to start at once with the work in his office after wearisome journeys, of replying to a hundred letters a day and tiring out his secretaries; more than that, the art of tantalizing and confusing everybody even to deceit: all this makes of him a man so superior to all around him that respect and submission reach the limits of fanaticism in a vast number of heads. He has imposed on his brothers in San Domingo a power without bounds. He is the absolute master of the island and nothing can counteract his wishes, whatever they may be, although some distinguished men, but very few blacks among them, know what are his plans and view them with great fear.

MEMOIR OF GENERAL TOUSSAINT L'OUVERTURE, WRITTEN BY HIMSELF [1]

It is my duty to render to the French Government an exact account of my conduct. I shall relate the facts with all the simplicity and frankness of an old soldier, adding to them the reflections that naturally suggest themselves. In short, I shall tell the truth, although it be against myself.

The colony of Santo Domingo, of which I was commander, enjoyed the greatest tranquillity; agriculture and commerce flourished there. The island had attained a degree of splendor which it had never seen before. And all this—I have to say it—was my work.

Nevertheless, as we were upon a war footing, the Commission had published a decree ordering me to take all necessary measures to prevent the enemies of the Republic from penetrating into the island. Accordingly, I ordered all the commanders of the sea-ports not to permit any ships of war

---

[1] From *Toussaint L'Ouverture: A Biography and Autobiography,* by John R. Beard, James Redpath, publisher, Boston, 1863: "The existence of these Memoirs was first mentioned by the venerable Abbé Grégoire, bishop of Blois, in his curious and entertaining work entitled *The Literature of the Negroes.* In 1845, the journal *La Presse* published fragments of them; and at that time some persons seemed to doubt their authenticity. But, quite recently, through the friendly medium of M. Fleutelot, member of the University of France, I was enabled to obtain from Gen. Desfourneaux a copy of these Memoirs which he had in his possession. Still later, after much research, I succeeded in discovering the original Manuscript in the General Archives of France . . . all written in the hand of the First of the Blacks." The French original may be found in *Histoire de Toussaint Louverture* by H. P. Sannon, Imprimerie Aug. Heraux, Port-Au-Prince, Haiti, 1933: "*On est ici en présence d'un mémoire justificatif.*" M. Sannon refers to carton A. F. IV, 1213 of the National Archives in Paris.

to enter into the roadstead, except they were known and had obtained permission from me. If it should be a squadron, no matter from what nation, it was absolutely prohibited from entering the port, or even the roadstead, unless I should myself know where it came from, and the port from which it sailed.

This order was in force, when, on the 26th of January, 1802, a squadron appeared before the Cape. At that time I had left this town to visit the Spanish part, Santo Domingo, for the purpose of inspecting the agriculture. On setting out from Maguâna, I had dispatched one of my aides-de-camp to Gen. Dessalines, Commander-in-chief of the departments of the West and South, who was then at St. Marc, to order him to join me at Gonaïves, or at St. Michel, to accompany me on my journey.

At the time of the squadron's appearance, I was at Santo Domingo, from which place I set out, three days after, to go to Hinche. Passing by Banique, arriving at Papayes, I met my aide-de-camp Couppé and an officer sent by Gen. Christophe, who brought me a letter from the general, by which he informed me of the arrival of the French squadron before the Cape, and assured me that the General-in-chief commanding this squadron had not done him the honor to write to him, but had only sent an officer to order him to prepare accommodations for his forces; that Gen. Christophe having demanded of this officer whether he was the bearer of letters to him or of dispatches for the General-in-chief, Toussaint L'Ouverture, requesting him to send them to him, that they might reach him at once, this officer replied to him, that he was not charged with any, and that it was not, in fact, a question concerning Gen. Toussaint. "Surrender the town," he continued; "you will be well recompensed; the French Government sends you presents." To which Gen. Christophe replied, "Since you have no letters for the General-in-chief nor for me, you may return and tell your general that he does not know his duty; that it is not thus that people present themselves in a country belonging to France."

Gen. Leclerc having received this answer, summoned Gen. Christophe to deliver the place to him, and, in case of refusal, warned him that on the morning of the next day he should land fifteen thousand men. In response to this, Gen. Christophe begged him to wait for Gen. Toussaint L'Ouverture, to whom he had already sent the intelligence, and would do so the second time, with the greatest celerity. In fact, I received a second letter, and hastened to reach the Cape, in spite of the overflowing of the Hinche, hoping to have the pleasure of embracing my brothers-in-arms from Europe, and

403

to receive at the same time the orders of the French Government; and in order to march with greater speed, I left all my escorts. Between St. Michel and St. Raphaël, I met Gen. Dessalines and said to him, "I have sent for you to accompany me on my tour to Port-de-Paix, and to Môle; but that is useless now. I have just received two letters from Gen. Christophe, announcing the arrival of the French squadron before the Cape."

I communicated to him these letters, whereupon he told me that he had seen from St. Marc six large vessels making sail for the coast of Port Républicain; but he was ignorant of what nation they were. I ordered him then to repair promptly to this port, since it was possible that Gen. Christophe having refused the entrance of the Cape to the general commanding the squadron, the latter might have proceeded to Port Républicain in the hope of finding me there; should this prove true, I ordered him, in advance, to request the general to wait for me, and to assure him that I would go first to the Cape in the hope of meeting him there, and in case I should not find him there, I would repair at once to Port Républicain to confer with him. I set out for the Cape, passing by Vases, the shortest road. On arriving upon the heights of the Grand Boucan, in the place called the Porte-Saint-Jacques, I perceived a fire in the town on the Cape. I urged my horse at full speed to reach this town, to find there the general commanding the squadron, and to ascertain who had caused the conflagration. But, on approaching, I found the roads filled with the inhabitants who had fled from this unfortunate town, and I was unable to penetrate farther because all the passages were cannonaded by the artillery of the vessels which were in the roadstead. I then resolved to go up to the Fort of Bel-Air, but I found this fort evacuated likewise, and all the pieces of cannon spiked.

I was, consequently, obliged to retrace my steps. After passing the hospital, I met Gen. Christophe, and asked him who had ordered the town to be fired. He replied that it was he. I reprimanded him severely for having employed such rigorous measures. "Why," said I to him, "did you not rather make some military arrangements to defend the town until my arrival?" He answered, "What do you wish, general? My duty, necessity, the circumstances, the reiterated threats of the general commanding the squadron, forced me to it. I showed the general the orders of which I was the bearer, but without avail." He added, "that the proclamations spread secretly in the town to seduce the people, and instigate an uprising, were not sanctioned by military usage; that if the commander of the squadron had truly pacific intentions, he would have waited for me; that he would not have employed

the means which he used to gain the commander of the Fort of Boque, who is a drunkard; that he would not in consequence have seized this fort; that he would not have put to death half of the garrison of Fort Liberty; that he would not have made a descent upon Acul, and that, in a word, he would not have committed at first all the hostilities of which he was guilty."

Gen. Christophe joined me, and we continued the route together. On arriving at Haut-du-Cap, we passed through the habitations of Breda as far as the barrier of Boulard, passing by the gardens. There I ordered him to rally his troops, and go into camp on the Bonnet until further orders, and to keep me informed of all the movements he made. I told him that I was going to Héricourt; that there, perhaps, I should receive news from the commander of the squadron; that he would doubtless deliver to me the orders of the Government; that I might even meet him there; that I should then ascertain the reasons which had induced him to come in this manner; and, that, in case he was the bearer of orders from the government, I should request him to communicate them to me, and should in consequence make arrangements with him.

Gen. Christophe left me then to repair to the post which I had assigned to him; but he met a body of troops who fired upon him, forced him to dismount from his horse, plunge into the river, and cross it by swimming.

After separating from Gen. Christophe, I had at my side Adjutant-General Fontaine, two other officers, and my aide-de-camp, Couppé, who went in advance; he warned me of the troops on the road. I ordered him to go forward. He told me that this force was commanded by a general. I then demanded a conference with him. But Couppé had not time to execute my orders; they fired upon us at twenty-five steps from the barrier. My horse was pierced with a ball; another ball carried away the hat of one of my officers. This unexpected circumstance forced me to abandon the open road, to cross the savanna and the forests to reach Héricourt, where I remained three days to wait for news of the commander of the squadron, again without avail.

But, the next day, I received a letter from Gen. Rochambeau, announcing "that the column which he commanded had seized upon Fort Liberty, taken and put to the sword a part of the garrison, which had resisted; that he had not believed the garrison would steep its bayonets in the blood of Frenchmen; on the contrary, he had expected to find it disposed in his favor." I replied to this letter, and, manifesting my indignation to the general, asked to know, "Why he had ordered the massacre of those brave soldiers who had

only followed the orders given them; who had, besides, contributed so much to the happiness of the colony and to the triumph of the Republic. Was this the recompense that the French Government had promised them?"

I concluded by saying to Gen. Rochambeau, that "I would fight to the last to avenge the death of these brave soldiers, for my own liberty, and to re-establish tranquillity and order in the colony."

This was, in fact, the resolution I had taken after having reflected deliberately upon the report Gen. Christophe had brought me, upon the danger I had just run, upon the letter of Gen. Rochambeau, and finally upon the conduct of the commander of the squadron.

Having formed my resolution, I went to Gonaïves. There I communicated my intentions to Gen. Maurepas, and ordered him to make the most vigorous resistance to all vessels which should appear before Port-de-Paix, where he commanded; and, in case he should not be strong enough,—having only half of a brigade,—to imitate the example of Gen. Christophe and afterward withdraw to the Mountain, taking with him ammunition òf all kinds; there to defend himself to the death.

I then went to St. Marc to visit the fortifications. I found that the news of the shameful events which had just taken place had reached this town, and the inhabitants had already fled. I gave orders for all the resistance to be made that the fortifications and munitions would allow of.

As I was on the point of setting out from this town to go to Port-au-Prince and the southern part to give my orders, Captains Jean-Philippe Dupin and Isaac brought me dispatches from Paul L'Ouverture, who commanded at Santo Domingo. Both informed me that a descent had just been made upon Oyarsaval, and that the French and Spaniards who inhabited this place had risen and cut off the roads from Santo Domingo. I acquainted myself with these dispatches. In running over the letter of Gen. Paul and the copy of Gen. Kerverseau's to the commander of the place of Santo Domingo, which was enclosed in it, I saw that this general had made the overture to the commander of the place, and not to Gen. Paul, as he should have done, to make preparations for the landing of his force. I saw also the refusal given by Gen. Paul to this invitation, until he should receive orders from me. I replied to Gen. Paul that I approved his conduct, and ordered him to make all possible effort to defend himself in case of attack; and even to make prisoners of Gen. Kerverseau and his force, if he could. I returned my reply by the captains just mentioned. But foreseeing, on account of the interception of the roads, that they might be arrested and their dispatches

demanded, I gave them in charge a second letter, in which I ordered Gen. Paul to use all possible means of conciliation with Gen. Kerverseau. I charged the captains, in case they should be arrested, to conceal the first letter and show only the second.

My reply not arriving as soon as he expected, Gen. Paul sent another black officer with the same dispatches in duplicate. I gave only a receipt to this officer, and sent him back. Of these three messengers two were black and the other white. They were arrested, as I had anticipated; the two blacks were assassinated in violation of all justice and right, contrary to the customs of war; their dispatches were sent to Gen. Kerverseau, who concealed the first letter, and showed to Gen. Paul only the second, in which I had ordered him to enter into negotiations with Gen. Kerverseau. It was in consequence of this letter that Santo Domingo was surrendered.

Having sent off these dispatches, I resumed my route toward the South. I had hardly set forward when I was overtaken by an orderly, coming up at full speed, who brought me a package from Gen. Vernet and a letter from my wife, both announcing to me the arrival from Paris of my two children and their preceptor, of which I was not before aware. I learned also that they were bearers of orders for me from the First Consul. I retraced my steps and flew to Ennery, where I found my two children and the excellent tutor whom the First Consul had had the goodness to give them. I embraced them with the greatest satisfaction and ardor. I then inquired if they were bearers of letters from the First Consul for me. The tutor replied in the affirmative, and handed me a letter which I opened and read about half through; then I folded it, saying that I would reserve the reading of it for a more quiet moment. I begged him then to impart to me the intentions of the Government, and to tell me the name of the commander of the squadron, which I had not yet been able to ascertain. He answered, that his name was Leclerc; that the intention of the Government toward me was very favorable, which was confirmed by my children, and of which I afterwards assured myself by finishing the letter of the First Consul. I observed to them, nevertheless, that if the intentions of the Government were pacific and good regarding me and those who had contributed to the happiness which the colony enjoyed, Gen. Leclerc surely had not followed nor executed the orders he had received, since he had landed on the island like an enemy, and done evil merely for the pleasure of doing it, without addressing himself to the commander or making known to him his powers. I then asked Citizen Coisnon, my children's tutor, if Gen. Leclerc had not given him a dispatch for

me or charged him with something to tell me. He replied in the negative, advising me, however, to go to the Cape to confer with the general; my children added their solicitations to persuade me to do so. I represented to them, "that, after the conduct of this general, I could have no confidence in him; that he had landed like an enemy; that, in spite of that, I had believed it my duty to go to meet him in order to prevent the progress of the evil; that he had fired upon me, and I had run the greatest dangers; that, in short, if his intentions were as pure as those of the Government which sent him, he should have taken the trouble to write to me to inform me of his mission; that, before arriving in the roadstead, he should have sent me an advice-boat with you, sir, and my children,—that being the ordinary practice,—to announce their arrival, and to impart to me his powers; that, since he had observed none of these formalities, the evil was done, and therefore I should refuse decidedly to go in search of him; that, nevertheless, to prove my attachment and submission to the French Government, I would consent to write a letter to Gen. Leclerc. I shall send to him," I continued, "by Mr. Granville, a worthy man, accompanied by my two children and their tutor, whom I shall charge to say to Gen. Leclerc, that it is absolutely dependent upon himself whether this colony is entirely lost, or preserved to France; that I will enter into all possible arrangements with him; that I am ready to submit to the orders of the French Government; but that Gen. Leclerc shall show me orders of which he is bearer, and shall, above all, cease from every species of hostility."

In fact, I wrote the letter, and the deputation set out. In the hope that after the desire I had just manifested to render my submission, order would again be restored, I remained at Gonaïves till the next day. There I learned that two vessels had attacked St. Marc; I proceeded there and learned that they had been repulsed. I returned then to Gonaïves to wait for Gen. Leclerc's reply. Finally, two days after, my two children arrived with the response so much desired, by which the general commanded me to report in person to him, at the Cape, and announced that he had furthermore ordered his generals to advance upon all points; that his orders being given, he could not revoke them. He promised, however, that Gen. Boudet should be stopped at Artibonite; I concluded then, that he did not know the country perfectly, or had been deceived; for, in order to reach Artibonite, it was necessary to have a free passage by St. Marc, which was impossible now, since the two vessels which had attacked this place had been repulsed. He added, further, that they should not attack Môle, only blockade it, since this

place had already surrendered. I replied then plainly to the general, "that I should not report to him at the Cape; that his conduct did not inspire me with sufficient confidence; that I was ready to deliver the command to him in conformity with the orders of the First Consul, but that I would not be his lieutenant-general." I besought him again to let me know his intentions, assuring him that I would contribute everything in my power to the re-establishment of order and tranquillity. I added, in conclusion, that if he persisted in his invasion, he would force me to defend myself, although I had but few troops. I sent him this letter with the utmost dispatch, by an orderly, who brought me back word, "that he had no reply to make and had taken the field."

The inhabitants of Gonaïves then asked my permission to send a deputation to Gen. Leclerc, which I accorded to them, but he retained the deputation.

The next day I learned that he had taken, without striking a blow and without firing a gun, Dondon, St. Raphaël, St. Michel and Marmelade, and that he was prepared to march against Ennery and Gonaïves.

These new hostilities gave rise to new reflections. I thought that the conduct of Gen. Leclerc was entirely contrary to the intentions of the Government, since the First Consul, in his letter, promised peace, while the general made war. I saw that, instead of seeking to arrest this evil, he only increased it. "Does he not fear," I said to myself, "in pursuing such conduct, to be blamed by his Government? Can he hope to be approved by the First Consul, that great man whose equity and impartiality are so well known, while I shall be disapproved?" I resolved then to defend myself, in case of attack; and in spite of my few troops, I made my dispositions accordingly.

* * * * *

[The Memoir continues with an account of the subsequent strategy. Toussaint L'Ouverture ordered Gonaïves to be burned and marched against General Rochambeau's column of 4000 men. He left General Dessalines to face General Leclerc and himself planned a diversion into the northern parts to retake what had been seized: "by this manoeuvre, I should force the general to retrace his steps and make arrangements with me to preserve this beautiful colony to the Government." At Ennery he found a proclamation of General Leclerc pronouncing him an outlaw, but confident that he had done no wrong, that the disorder was occasioned by General Leclerc himself, and believing himself to be the legitimate commander of the island, he counteracted the insulting proclamation by a declaration that it was precisely Bonaparte's brother-in-law who was the outlaw on the island. He then recaptured a number of towns and nearly the person of

General Leclerc, whom, he says, he would have sent back to the First Consul in Paris, "rendering to him an exact account of his conduct, and praying him to send me another person worthy of his confidence, to whom I could deliver up the command." Towns were burned down, prisoners killed under attack, inhabitants uprooted from their native grounds.]

All these disasters happened just at the time that Gen. Leclerc came. Why did he not inform me of his powers before landing? Why did he land without my order and in defiance of the order of the Commission? Did he not commit the first hostilities? Did he not seek to gain over the generals and other officers under my command by every possible means? Did he not try to instigate the laborers to rise, by persuading them that I treated them like slaves, and that he had come to break their chains? Ought he to have employed such means in a country where peace and tranquillity reigned?—in a country which was in the power of the Republic?

If I did oblige my fellow-countrymen to work, it was to teach them the value of true liberty without license; it was to prevent corruption of morals; it was for the general happiness of the island, for the interest of the Republic. And I had effectually succeeded in my undertaking, since there could not be found in all the colony a single man unemployed, and the number of beggars had diminished to such a degree that, apart from a few in the towns, not a single one was to be found in the country.

If Gen. Leclerc's intentions had been good, would he have received Golart into his army, and given to him the command of the 9th demi-brigade,—a corps that he had raised at the time that he was chief of battalion? Would he have employed this dangerous rebel, who caused proprietors to be assassinated in their own dwelling-places; who invaded the town of Môle-Saint-Nicolas; who fired upon Gen. Clerveaux, who commanded there; upon Gen. Maurepas and his brigade commander; who made war upon the laborers of Jean-Rabel, from the *Moustiques* and the heights of Port-de-Paix; who carried his audacity so far as to oppose me when I marched against him to force him to submit to his chief, and to retake the territory and the town which he had invaded! The day that he dared to fire upon me, a ball cut the plume from my hat; Bondère, a physician, who accompanied me, was killed at my side, my aides-de-camp were unhorsed. In short, this brigand, after being steeped in every crime, concealed himself in a forest; he only came out of it upon the arrival of the French squadron. Ought Gen. Leclerc to have raised likewise to the rank of brigade commander another rebel, called L'Amour Desrances, who had caused all the inhabitants of the Plain of

Cul-de-Sac to be assassinated; who urged the laborers to revolt; who pillaged all this part of the island; against whom, only two months before the arrival of the squadron, I had been obliged to march, and whom I forced to hide in the forests? Why were rebels and others amicably received, while my subordinates and myself, who remained steadfastly faithful to the French Government, and who had maintained order and tranquillity, were warred upon? Why was it made a crime to have executed the orders of the Government? Why was all the evil which had been done and the disorders which had existed imputed to me? All these facts are known by every inhabitant of St. Domingo. Why, on arriving, did they not go to the root of the evil? Had the troops which gave themselves up to Gen. Leclerc received the order from me? Did they consult me? No. Well! those who committed the wrong did not consult me. It is not right to attribute to me more wrong than I deserve.

I shared these reflections with some prisoners which I had. They replied that it was my influence upon the people which was feared, and that these violent means were employed to destroy it. This caused me new reflections. Considering all the misfortunes which the colony had already suffered, the dwellings destroyed, assassinations committed, the violence exercised even upon women, I forgot all the wrongs which had been done me, to think only of the happiness of the island and the interest of the Government. I determined to obey the order of the First Consul, since Gen. Leclerc had just withdrawn from the Cape with all his forces, after the affair of Crête-à-Pierrot.

Let it be observed that up to this time I had not been able to find an instant in which to reply to the First Consul. I seized with eagerness this momentary quiet to do so. I assured the First Consul of my submission and entire devotion to his orders, but represented to him "that if he did not send another older general to take command, the resistance which I must continue to oppose to Gen. Leclerc would tend to increase the prevalent disorder."

I remembered then that Gen. Dessalines had reported to me that two officers of the squadron—one an aide-de-camp of Gen. Boudet, the other a naval officer, accompanied by two dragoons, sent to stir up a rebellion among the troops—had been made prisoners at the time of the evacuation of Port-au-Prince. I ordered them to be brought before me, and, after conversing with them, sent them back to Gen. Boudet, sending by them a letter with the one which I had written to the First Consul. Just as I was sending off these two officers, I learned that Gen. Hardy had passed Coupe-à-l'Inde

with his army, that he had attacked my possessions, devastated them, and taken away all my animals, among them a horse named Bel-Argent, which I valued very highly. Without losing time, I marched against him with the force I had. I overtook him near Dondon. A fierce engagement took place, which lasted from eleven in the morning till six in the evening.

Before setting out, I had ordered Gen. Dessalines to join the troops which had evacuated Crête-à-Pierrot, and go into camp at Camp-Marchand, informing him that after the battle I should proceed to Marmelade.

Upon my arrival in that place, I received the reply of Gen. Boudet, which he sent me by my nephew Chancy, whom he had previously made prisoner. That General assured me that my letter would easily reach the First Consul, that, to effect this, he had already sent it to•Gen. Leclerc, who had promised him to forward it. Upon the report of my nephew, and after reading the letter of Gen. Boudet, I thought I recognized in him a character of honesty and frankness worthy of a French officer qualified to command. Therefore I addressed myself to him with confidence, begging him to persuade Gen. Leclerc to enter upon terms of conciliation with me. I assured him that ambition had never been my guide, but only honor; that I was ready to give up the command in obedience to the orders of the First Consul, and to make all necessary sacrifices to arrest the progress of the evil. I sent him this letter by my nephew Chancy, whom he kept with him. Two days after, I received a letter sent in haste by an orderly, announcing to me that he had made known my intentions to Gen. Leclerc, and assuring me that the latter was ready to make terms with me, and that I could depend upon the good intentions of the Government with regard to me.

The same day, Gen. Christophe communicated to me a letter which he had just received from a citizen named Vilton, living at the Petite-Anse, and another from Gen. Hardy, both asking him for an interview. I gave permission to Gen. Christophe to hold these interviews, recommending him to be very circumspect.

Gen. Christophe did not meet this appointment with Gen. Hardy, for he received a letter from Gen. Leclerc, proposing to him another rendezvous. He sent me a copy of this letter and of his reply, and asked my permission to report himself at the place indicated; which I granted, and he went.

Gen. Christophe, on his return, brought me a letter from Gen. Leclerc, saying that he should feel highly satisfied if he could induce me to concert with him, and submit to the orders of the Republic. I replied immediately that I had always been submissive to the French Government, as I had in-

variably borne arms for it; that if from the beginning I had been treated as I should have been, not a single shot would have been fired; that peace would not have been even disturbed in the island, and that the intention of the Government would have been fulfilled. In short, I showed to Gen. Leclerc, as well as to Gen. Christophe, all my indignation at the course which the latter had pursued, without orders from me.

The next day, I sent to Gen. Leclerc my Adjutant-General Fontaine, bearer of a second letter, in which I asked for an interview at Héricourt, which he refused. Fontaine assured me, however, that he had been well received. I was not discouraged. I sent the third time my aide-de-camp, Couppé and my secretary Nathand, assuring him that I was ready to give up the command to him, comformably to the intentions of the First Consul. He replied, that an hour of conversation would be worth more than ten letters, giving me his word of honor that he would act with all the frankness and loyalty that could be expected of a French general. At the same time a proclamation from him was brought me, bidding all citizens to regard as null and void that article of the proclamation of Feb. 16, 1802, which made me an outlaw. "Do not fear," he said in this proclamation, "you and your generals, and the people who are with you, that I shall search out the past conduct of any one; I will draw the veil of oblivion over the events which have taken place at Santo Domingo; I imitate, in so doing, the example which the First Consul gave to France on the 11th of November. In future, I wish to see in the island only good citizens. You ask repose; after having borne the burden of government so long, repose is due you; but I hope that in your retirement you will use your wisdom, in your moments of leisure, for the prosperity of Santo Domingo."

After this proclamation and the word of honor of the general, I proceeded to the Cape. I submitted myself to Gen. Leclerc in accordance with the wish of the First Consul; I afterward talked with him with all the frankness and cordiality of a soldier who loves and esteems his comrade. He promised me forgetfulness of the past and the protection of the French Government. He agreed with me that we had both been wrong. "You can, General," he said to me, "retire to your home in perfect security. But tell me if Gen. Dessalines will obey my orders, and if I can rely upon him?" I replied that he could; that Gen. Dessalines might have faults, like every man, but that he understood military subordination. I suggested to him, however, that for the public good and to reëstablish the laborers in their occupations, as they were at the time of his arrival in the island, it was necessary that Gen. Dessalines

should be recalled to his command at Saint Marc, and Gen. Charles Belair to L'Arcahaye, which he promised me should be done. At eleven in the evening, I took leave of him and withdrew to Héricourt, where I passed the night with Gen. Fressinet, and set out the next morning for Marmelade.

The third day after, I received a letter from Gen. Leclerc, bidding me discharge my foot-guards and horse-guards. He addressed to me also an order for Gen. Dessalines; I acquainted myself with it and sent it to Gen. Dessalines, telling him to comply with it. And that I might the better fulfil the promises that I had made Gen. Leclerc, I requested Gen. Dessalines to meet me half-way between his house and mine. I urged him to submit, as I had done; I told him that the public interest required me to make great sacrifices, and that I was willing to make them; but as for him, he might keep his command. I said as much to Gen. Charles, also to all the officers with them; finally, I persuaded them, in spite of all the reluctance and regret they evinced, to leave me and go away. They even shed tears. After this interview, all returned to their own homes. Adjutant-General Perrin, whom Gen. Leclerc had sent to Dessalines with his orders, found him very ready to comply with them, since I had previously engaged him to do so in our interview. As we have seen, a promise was made to place Gen. Charles at L'Arcahaye; however, it was not done.

It was unnecessary for me to order the inhabitants of Dondon, St. Michel, St. Raphaël and Marmelade to return to their homes, since they had done so as soon as I had taken possession of these communities; I only advised them to resume their usual occupations. I ordered also the inhabitants of Plaisance and the neighboring places, to return home and begin their labor, too. They expressed fears that they might be disturbed. Therefore I wrote to Gen. Leclerc, reminding him of his promise, and begging him to attend to their execution. He replied, that his orders were already given upon that subject. Meanwhile, the commander of this place had divided his forces and sent detachments into all the districts, which had alarmed the laborers and compelled them to flee to the mountains. I proceeded to Ennery and acquainted Gen. Leclerc with these things, as I had promised him. In this town I found a great many laborers from Gonaïves, whom I persuaded to return home. Before I left Marmelade, I ordered the commander of that place to restore the artillery and ammunition to the commander of Plaisance, in conformity to the desire of Gen. Leclerc. I also ordered the commander at Ennery to return the only piece of artillery there, and also the ammunition, to the commander of Gonaïves.

I then employed myself in rebuilding my houses which had been burned. In a house in the mountains, which had escaped the flames, I had to prepare a comfortable lodging for my wife, who was still in the woods where she had been obliged to take refuge.

While engaged in these occupations, I learned that 500 troops had arrived, to be stationed at Ennery, a little town, which, until then, could not have had more than 50 armed men as a police force; and that a very large detachment had also been sent to St. Michel. I hastened to the town. I saw that all my houses had been pillaged and even the coffers of my laborers carried off. At the very moment when I was entering my complaint to the commander, I pointed out to him the soldiers loaded with fruit of all kinds, even unripe fruit; I also showed him the laborers who, seeing these robberies, were fleeing to other houses in the mountains. I gave an account to Gen. Leclerc of what was going on, and observed to him that the measures which were being taken, far from inspiring confidence, only increased distrust; that the number of troops which he had sent was very considerable, and could only be an injury to agriculture and the inhabitants. I then returned to my house in the mountains.

The next day I received, in this house, a visit from the commander at Ennery, and I saw very clearly that this soldier, instead of making me a visit of politeness, had come to my house merely to reconnoitre my dwelling and the avenues about it, that he might seize me the more easily when he received the order to do so. While talking with him, I was informed that several soldiers had gone with horses and other beasts of burden to one of my residences near the town, where a god-daughter of mine was residing, and had taken away the coffee and other provisions found there. I made complaint to him; he promised me to put a stop to these robberies and to punish severely those who had been guilty of them. Fearing that my house in the mountains inspired only distrust, I determined to remove to that very house which had just been pillaged, and almost totally destroyed, but two hundred paces from the town. I left my wife in the house which I had prepared for her. I was now occupied in laying out new plantations to replace those which had been destroyed, and in preparing necessary materials for reconstructing my buildings. But every day I experienced new robberies and new vexations. The soldiers came to my house in such large numbers that I dared not have them arrested. In vain I bore my complaints to the commander. I received no satisfaction. Finally, I determined, though Gen. Leclerc had not done me the honor to answer my two former letters upon this subject, to

write him a third, which I sent to him at the Cape by my son Placide, for greater security. This, like the others, elicited no reply. But the chief of the staff told me that he would make his report. Some time after, the commander, having come to see me again, one afternoon, found me at the head of my laborers, employed in directing the work of reconstruction. He himself saw my son Isaac drive away several soldiers who had just come to the gate to cut down the bananas and figs. I repeated to him the most earnest complaints. He still promised to stop these disorders. During three weeks that I stayed in this place, I witnessed daily new ravages; every day I received visits from people who came as spies, but they were all witnesses that I was engaged solely in domestic labors. Gen. Brunet himself came, and found me occupied in the same manner. Notwithstanding my conduct, I received a letter from Gen. Leclerc, which, in place of giving me satisfaction in regard to the complaints which I had made to him, accused me of keeping armed men within the borders of Ennery, and ordered me to send them away. Persuaded of my innocence, and that evil-disposed people had deceived him, I replied that I had too much honor to break promises which I had made, and that when I gave up the command to him, it was not without reflection; that, moreover, I had no intention of trying to take it back. I assured him, besides, that I had no knowledge of armed men in the environs of Ennery, and that for three weeks I had been constantly at work on my own place. I sent my son Isaac to give him an account of all the vexations I suffered, and to warn him that if he did not put an end to them, I should be obliged to leave the place where I was living, and go to my ranche in the Spanish part.

One day, before I received any answer from Gen. Leclerc, I was informed that one of his aides-de-camp, passing by Ennery, had told the commander that he was the bearer of an order for my arrest, addressed to Gen. Brunet. Gen. Leclerc having given his word of honor and promised the protection of the French Government, I refused to believe the report; I even said to some one who advised me to leave my residence, that I had promised to stay there quietly, working to repair the havoc that had been made; that I had not given up the command and sent away my troops to act so foolishly now; that I did not wish to leave home, and if they came to arrest me, they would find me there; that, besides, I would not give credence to the calumny.

The next day I received a second letter from Gen. Leclerc, by my son whom I sent to him, which read thus:—

THE FIRST OF THE BLACKS : *Toussaint L'Ouverture*

"Army of St. Domingo,
"Headquarters at Cap Français, June 5, 1802.

"The Gen.-in-Chief to Gen. Toussaint.—

"Since you persist, Citizen-General, in thinking that the great number of troops stationed at Plaisance (the Secretary probably wrote Plaisance by mistake, meaning Ennery) frightens the laborers of that district, I have commissioned Gen. Brunet to act in concert with you, and to place a part of these troops in the rear of Gonaïves and one detachment at Plaisance. Let the laborers understand, that, having taken this measure, I shall punish those who leave their dwellings to go to the mountains. Let me know, as soon as this order has been executed, the results which it produces, because, if the means of persuasion which you employ do not succeed, I shall use military measures. I salute you."

The same day I received a letter from Gen. Brunet, of which the following is an extract:—

"Army of Saint Domingo,
"Headquarters at Georges, June 7, 1802.

"Brunet, Gen. of Division, to the Gen. of Division, Toussaint L'Ouverture:

"Now is the time, Citizen-General, to make known unquestionably to the General-in-chief that those who wish to deceive him in regard to your fidelity are base calumniators, and that your sentiments tend to restore order and tranquillity in your neighborhood. You must assist me in securing free communication to the Cape, which has been interrupted since yesterday, three persons having been murdered by fifty brigands between Ennery and Coupe-à-Pintade. Send in pursuit of these murderers men worthy of confidence, whom you are to pay well; I will keep account of your expenses.

"We have arrangements to make together, my dear General, which it is impossible to do by letter, but which an hour's conference would complete. If I were not worn out by labor and petty cares, I should have been the bearer of my own letter to-day; but not being able to leave at this time, will you not come to me? If you have recovered from your indisposition, let it be to-morrow; when a good work is to be done, there should be no delay. You will not find in my country-house all the comforts which I could desire before receiving you, but you will find the sincerity of an honest man who desires only the prosperity of the colony and your own happiness. If Madame

Toussaint, whom I greatly desire to know, wishes to take the journey, it will give me pleasure. If she needs horses, I will send her mine. I repeat, General, you will never find a sincerer friend than myself.

"With confidence in the Captain-General, with friendship for all who are under him, and hoping that you may enjoy peace,

"I cordially salute you.

(Signed) "BRUNET.

"P. S. Your servant who has gone to Port-au-Prince passed here this morning; he left with his passport made out in due form."

That very servant, instead of receiving his passport, was arrested, and is now in prison with me.

After reading these two letters, although not very well, I yielded to the solicitations of my sons and others, and set out the same night to see Gen. Brunet, accompanied by two officers only. At eight in the evening I arrived at the General's house. When he met me, I told him that I had received his letter, and also that of the General-in-chief, requesting me to act with him, and that I had come for that purpose; that I had not brought my wife, as he requested, because she never left home, being much occupied with domestic duties, but if sometime, when he was travelling, he would do her the honor of visiting her, she would receive him with pleasure. I said to him that, being ill, my stay must be short, asking him, therefore, to finish our business as soon as possible, that I might return.

I handed him the letter of Gen. Leclerc. After reading it, he told me that he had not yet received any order to act in concert with me upon the subject of the letter; he then excused himself for a moment, and went out, after calling an officer to keep me company. He had hardly left the room when an aide-de-camp of Gen. Leclerc entered, accompanied by a large number of soldiers, who surrounded me, seized me, bound me as a criminal, and conducted me on board the frigate Créole.

I claimed the protection which Gen. Brunet, on his word of honor, had promised me, but without avail. I saw him no more. He had probably concealed himself to escape my well-merited reproaches. I afterward learned that he treated my family with great cruelty; that, immediately after my arrest, he sent a detachment of troops to the house where I had been living with a part of my family, mostly women, children, and laborers, and ordered them to set it on fire, compelling the unhappy victims to fly half-naked to the

woods; that everything had been pillaged and sacked; that the aide-de-camp of Gen. Brunet had even taken from my house fifty-five ounces of gold belonging to me, and thirty-three ounces belonging to one of my nieces, together with all the linen of the family.

Having committed these outrages upon my dwelling, the commander at Ennery went, at the head of one hundred men, to the house occupied by my wife and nieces, and arrested them, without giving them time to collect any of their effects. They were conducted like criminals to Gonaïves and put on board the frigate Guerrière.

When I was arrested, I had no extra clothing with me. I wrote to my wife, asking her to send me such things as I should need most to the Cape, hoping I should be taken there. This note I sent by an aide-de-camp of Gen. Leclerc, begging that it might be allowed to pass; it did not reach its destination, and I received nothing.

As soon as I was taken on board the Créole, we set sail, and, four leagues from the Cape, found the Héros, to which they transferred me. The next day, my wife and my children, who had been arrested with her, arrived there also. We immediately set sail for France. After a voyage of thirty-two days, during which I endured not only great fatigue, but also every species of hardship, while my wife and children received treatment from which their sex and rank should have preserved them, instead of allowing us to land, they retained us on board sixty-seven days.

After such treatment, could I not justly ask where were the promises of Gen. Leclerc? where was the protection of the French Government? If they no longer needed my services and wished to replace me, should they not have treated me as white French generals are always treated? They are warned when they are to be relieved of their command; a messenger is sent to notify them to resign the command to such and such persons; and in case they refuse to obey, measures are taken to compel them; they can then justly be treated as rebels and sent to France.

I have, in fact, known some generals guilty of criminally neglecting their duties, but who, in consideration of their character, have escaped punishment until they could be brought before superior authority.

Should not Gen. Leclerc have informed me that various charges had been brought against me? Should he not have said to me, "I gave you my word of honor and promised you the protection of the Government; to-day, as you have been found guilty, I am going to send you to that government to give an account of your conduct"? Or, "Government orders you to submit; I

convey that order to you"? I have not been so treated; on the other hand, means have been employed against me which are only used against the greatest criminals. Doubtless, I owe this treatment to my color; but my color, —my color,—has it hindered me from serving my country with zeal and fidelity? Does the color of my skin impair my honor and my bravery?

But even supposing that I was a criminal, and that Government had ordered my arrest, was it necessary to employ a hundred riflemen to arrest my wife and children in their own home, without regard to their sex, age, and rank; without humanity and without charity? Was it necessary to burn my houses, and to pillage and sack my possessions? No. My wife, my children, my family had no responsibility in the matter; they were not accountable to the Government; it was not lawful to arrest them.

Gen. Leclerc's authority was undisputed; did he fear me as a rival? I can but compare him to the Roman Senate, pursuing Hannibal to the very depths of his retreat.

Upon the arrival of the squadron in the colony, they took advantage of my absence to seize a part of my correspondence, which was at Port-Républicain; another portion, which was in one of my houses, has also been seized since my arrest. Why have they not sent me with this correspondence to give an account of my movements? They have taken forcible possession of my papers in order to charge me with crimes which I have never committed; but I have nothing to fear; this correspondence is sufficient to justify me. They have sent me to France destitute of everything; they have seized my property and my papers, and have spread atrocious calumnies concerning me. Is it not like cutting off a man's legs and telling him to walk? Is it not like cutting out a man's tongue and telling him to talk? Is it not burying a man alive?

In regard to the Constitution, the subject of one charge against me: Having driven from the colony the enemies of the Republic, calmed the factions and united all parties; perceiving, after I had taken possession of St. Domingo, that the Government made no laws for the colony, and feeling the necessity of police regulations for the security and tranquillity of the people, I called an assembly of wise and learned men, composed of deputies from all the communities, to conduct this business. When this assembly met, I represented to its members that they had an arduous and responsible task before them; that they were to make laws adapted to the country, advantageous to the Government, and beneficial to all,—laws suited to the localities, to the character and customs of the inhabitants. The Constitution must be sub-

mitted for the sanction of the Government, which alone had the right to adopt or reject it. Therefore, as soon as the Constitution was decided upon and its laws fixed, I sent the whole, by a member of the assembly, to the Government, to obtain its sanction. The errors or faults which this Constitution may contain cannot therefore be imputed to me. At the time of Leclerc's arrival, I had heard nothing from the Government upon this subject. Why to-day do they seek to make a crime of that which is no crime? Why put truth for falsehood, and falsehood for truth? Why put darkness for light and light for darkness?

In a conversation which I had at the Cape with Gen. Leclerc, he told me that while at Samana he had sent a spy to Santo Domingo to learn if I was there, who brought back word that I was. Why did he not go there to find me and give me the orders of the First Consul, before commencing hostilities? He knew my readiness to obey orders. Instead of this, he took advantage of my absence at St. Domingo to proceed to the Cape and send troops to all parts of the colony. This conduct proves that he had no intention of communicating anything to me.

If Gen. Leclerc went to the colony to do evil, it should not be charged upon me. It is true that only one of us can be blamed; but however little one may wish to do me justice, it is clear that he is the author of all the evils which the island has suffered, since, without warning me, he entered the colony, which he found in a state of prosperity, fell upon the inhabitants, who were at their work, contributing to the welfare of the community, and shed their blood upon their native soil. That is the true source of the evil.

If two children were quarrelling together, should not their father or mother stop them, find out which was the aggressor, and punish him, or punish them, if they were both wrong? Gen. Leclerc had no right to arrest me; Government alone could arrest us both, hear us, and judge us. Yet Gen. Leclerc enjoys liberty, and I am in a dungeon.

Having given an account of my conduct since the arrival of the fleet at St. Domingo, I will enter into some details of previous events.

Since I entered the service of the Republic, I have not claimed a penny of my salary; Gen. Laveaux, Government agents, all responsible persons connected with the public treasury, can do me this justice, that no one has been more prudent, more disinterested than I. I have only now and then received the extra pay allowed me; very often I have not asked even this. Whenever I have taken money from the treasury, it has been for some public use; the governor (*l'ordonnateur*) has used it as the service required. I remember that

once only, when far from home, I borrowed six thousand francs from Citizen Smith, who was governor of the Department of the South.

I will sum up, in a few words, my conduct and the results of my administration. At the time of the evacuation of the English, there was not a penny in the public treasury; money had to be borrowed to pay the troops and the officers of the Republic. When Gen. Leclerc arrived, he found three millions, five hundred thousand francs in the public funds. When I returned to Cayes, after the departure of Gen. Rigaud, the treasury was empty; Gen. Leclerc found three millions there; he found proportionate sums in all the private depositories on the island. Thus it is seen that I did not serve my country from interested motives; but, on the contrary, I served it with honor, fidelity, and integrity, sustained by the hope of receiving, at some future day, flattering acknowledgments from the Government; all who know me will do me this justice.

I have been a slave; I am willing to own it; but I have never received reproaches from my masters.

I have neglected nothing at Santo Domingo for the welfare of the island; I have robbed myself of rest to contribute to it; I have sacrificed everything for it. I have made it my duty and pleasure to develop the resources of this beautiful colony. Zeal, activity, courage—I have employed them all.

The island was invaded by the enemies of the Republic; I had then but a thousand men, armed with pikes. I sent them back to labor in the field, and organized several regiments, by the authority of Gen. Laveaux.

The Spanish portion had joined the English to make war upon the French. Gen. Desfourneaux was sent to attack Saint Michel with well-disciplined troops of the line; he could not take it. General Laveaux ordered me to the attack; I carried it. It is to be remarked that, at the time of the attack by Gen. Desfourneaux, the place was not fortified, and that when I took it, it was fortified by bastions in every corner. I also took Saint-Raphaël and Hinche, and rendered an account to Gen. Laveaux. The English were intrenched at Pont-de-l'Ester; I drove them from the place. They were in possession of Petite Rivière. My ammunition consisted of one case of cartridges which had fallen into the water on my way to the attack; this did not discourage me. I carried the place by assault before day, with my dragoons, and made all the garrison prisoners. I sent them to Gen. Laveaux. I had but one piece of cannon; I took nine at Petite Rivière. Among the posts gained at Petite Rivière, was a fortification defended by seven pieces of cannon, which I attacked, and carried by assault. I also conquered the Spaniards

intrenched in the camps of Miraut and Dubourg at Verrettes. I gained a famous victory over the English in a battle which lasted from six in the morning until nearly night. This battle was so fierce that the roads were filled with the dead, and rivers of blood were seen on every side. I took all the baggage and ammunition of the enemy, and a large number of prisoners. I sent the whole to Gen. Laveaux, giving him an account of the engagement. All the posts of the English upon the heights of Saint Marc were taken by me; the walled fortifications in the mountains of Fond-Baptiste and Délices, the camp of Drouët in the Matheux mountains, which the English regarded as impregnable, the citadels of Mirebalais, called the Gibraltar of the island, occupied by eleven hundred men, the celebrated camp of l'Acul-du-Saut, the stone fortifications of Trou-d'Eau, three stories high, those of the camp of Décayette and of Beau-Bien—in short, all the fortifications of the English in this quarter were unable to withstand me, as were those of Neybe, of Saint Jean de la Maguâna, of Las Mathas, of Banique and other places occupied by the Spaniards; all were brought by me under the power of the Republic. I was also exposed to the greatest dangers; several times I narrowly escaped being made prisoner; I shed my blood for my country; I received a ball in the right hip which remains there still; I received a violent blow on the head from a cannon-ball, which knocked out the greater part of my teeth, and loosened the rest. In short, I received upon different occasions seventeen wounds, whose honorable scars still remain. Gen. Laveaux witnessed many of my engagements; he is too honorable not to do me justice: ask him if I ever hesitated to endanger my life, when the good of my country and the triumph of the Republic required it.

If I were to record the various services which I have rendered the Government, I should need many volumes, and even then should not finish them; and, as a reward for all these services, I have been arbitrarily arrested at St. Domingo, bound, and put on board ship like a criminal, without regard for my rank, without the least consideration. Is this the recompense due my labors? Should my conduct lead me to expect such treatment?

I was once rich. At the time of the revolution, I was worth six hundred and forty-eight thousand francs. I spent it in the service of my country. I purchased but one small estate upon which to establish my wife and family. To-day, notwithstanding my disinterestedness, they seek to cover me with opprobrium and infamy; I am made the most unhappy of men; my liberty is taken from me; I am separated from all that I hold dearest in the world,— from a venerable father, a hundred and five years old, who needs my as-

sistance, from a dearly-loved wife, who, I fear, separated from me, cannot endure the afflictions which overwhelm her, and from a cherished family, who made the happiness of my life.

On my arrival in France I wrote to the First Consul and to the Minister of Marine, giving them an account of my situation, and asking their assistance for my family and myself. Undoubtedly, they felt the justice of my request, and gave orders that what I asked should be furnished me. But, instead of this, I have received the old half-worn dress of a soldier, and shoes in the same condition. Did I need this humiliation added to my misfortune?

When I left the ship, I was put into a carriage. I hoped then that I was to be taken before a tribunal to give an account of my conduct, and to be judged. Far from it; without a moment's rest I was taken to a fort on the frontiers of the Republic, and confined in a frightful dungeon.

It is from the depths of this dreary prison that I appeal to the justice and magnanimity of the First Consul. He is too noble and too good a general to turn away from an old soldier, covered with wounds in the service of his country, without giving him the opportunity to justify himself, and to have judgment pronounced upon him.

I ask, then, to be brought before a tribunal or council of war, before which, also, Gen. Leclerc may appear, and that we may both be judged after we have both been heard; equity, reason, law, all assure me that this justice cannot be refused me.

In passing through France, I have seen in the newspapers an article concerning myself. I am accused in this article of being a rebel and a traitor, and, to justify the accusation, a letter is said to have been intercepted in which I encouraged the laborers of St. Domingo to revolt. I never wrote such a letter, and I defy any one to produce it, to tell me to whom it was addressed, and to bring forward the person. As to the rest of the calumny, it falls of itself; if I had intended to make war, would I have laid down my arms and submitted? No reasonable man, much less a soldier, can believe such an absurdity.

If the Government had sent a wiser man, there would have been no trouble; not a single shot would have been fired.

Why did fear occasion so much injustice on the part of Gen. Leclerc? Why did he violate his word of honor? Upon the arrival of the frigate Guerrière, which brought my wife, why did I see on board a number of people who had been arrested with her? Many of these persons had not fired a shot. They were innocent men, fathers of families, who had been torn

from the arms of their wives and children. All these persons had shed their blood to preserve the colony to France; they were officers of my staff, my secretaries, who had done nothing but by my orders; all, therefore, were arrested without cause.

Upon landing at Brest, my wife and children were sent to different destinations, of both of which I am ignorant. Government should do me more justice: my wife and children have done nothing and have nothing to answer for; they should be sent home to watch over our interests. Gen. Leclerc has occasioned all this evil; but I am at the bottom of a dungeon, unable to justify myself. Government is too just to keep my hands tied, and allow Gen. Leclerc to abuse me thus, without listening to me.

Everybody has told me that this Government was just; should I not, then, share its justice and its benefits?

Gen. Leclerc has said in the letter to the minister, which I have seen in the newspaper, that I was waiting for his troops to grow sick, in order to make war and take back the command. This is an atrocious and abominable lie: it is a cowardly act on his part. Although I may not have much knowledge or much education, I have enough good sense to hinder me from contending against the will of my Government; I never thought of it. The French Government is too strong, too powerful, for Gen. Leclerc to think me opposed to it, who am its servant. It is true, that when Gen. Leclerc marched against me, I said several times that I should make no attack, that I should only defend myself, until July or August; that then I would commence in my turn. But, afterward, I reflected upon the misfortunes of the colony and upon the letter of the First Consul; I then submitted.

I repeat it again: I demand that Gen. Leclerc and myself be judged before a tribunal; that Government should order all my correspondence to be brought; by this means my innocence, and all that I have done for the Republic will be seen, although I know that several letters have been intercepted.

First Consul, father of all soldiers, upright judge, defender of innocence, pronounce my destiny. My wounds are deep; apply to them the healing remedy which will prevent them from opening anew; you are the physician; I rely entirely upon your justice and wisdom!

THE PRISONER OF EUROPE:
Napoleon

ELBA: A CORRESPONDENCE   AS THEMISTOCLES DID

ST. HELENA: A DIARY

~~~~~~

"What shall we do in that desolate place?" asked the Emperor. "Sire," I replied, "we shall live on the past. Do we not enjoy the lives of Caesar and Alexander? We shall have better than that: you will re-read yourself, Sire." Of course," answered Napoleon. "We shall write our memoirs. Yes, we shall have to work. Work, moreover, is a scythe of Time. After all, one must fulfil one's destiny—that is my great principle. Let mine be accomplished."

LAS CASES, *Mémorial de Saint-Hélène*

His genius was far-reaching and agile; his intelligence, vast in extent but common and vulgar in character, embraced humanity, but did not rise above it. He thought what every grenadier in the army thought; but he thought it with unprecedented force. He loved the game of chance, and it pleased him to tempt fortune by urging pigmies in their hundreds and thousands against each other. It was the game of a child as big as the world.

ANATOLE FRANCE, *The Revolt of the Angels*

IN A political cartoon by Cruikshank, Napoleon is shown chained in a cage pulled by a husky cossack, with the caption: "The Elbaronian Emperor going to take possession of his new territory." Another caricature deposits him on a rockbound coast surrounded by wild-eyed natives, one of whom, a thick-lipped and full-breasted savage (to whom Napoleon is ruefully murmuring, "Ah woe is me, seeing what I see"), says with simple hospitality, "Come, cheer up, my little Nicky, I'll be your Empress." Still another cartoon, projecting "The Robinson Crusoe of the island of Elba," shelters him from the sun under an umbrella, and from indignity in a dead lion's skin. In English music halls a vulgar song with a dreadful pun celebrated:

Little Nap Horner
Up in a corner
Dreading his doleful doom;
He who gave t'other day
Whole kingdoms away
Now is glad to find Elba room.

In a riot of caricatures Napoleon figured as a waxwork manikin, a whipped top, a caged ape, a Robinson Crusoe, a shuttlecock, and a jay plucked of its

plumes. None of these political barbs really hit the bull's-eye. The bare facts of the Elban interlude were more devastating than the distortions of caricaturists. Napoleon landed on the little island to the accompaniment of cheers, guitars, and innocent excitement. From the first moment to the last, he invested at Elba the energy of a dispossessed emperor in the duties of a provincial mayor. He established at least five residences, connected them laboriously by roads, chose a proper flag for the little empire, surveyed the island's mines, salvaged a lilliputian navy, imported an army of seven hundred veterans and drilled them with superfluous vitality. He reorganized the customs, raised the duty on corn, renewed the salt and fishing monopoly, strengthened fortifications, repaired barracks, planted vines, introduced the silkworm, drained the swamps, and paved the streets. When in addition to Generals Bertrand, Dalesme, Drouot, and the others, his court was increased by Madame, his mother (who brought her own furniture), and his favorite sister Princess Pauline, Napoleon carefully avoided the burlesque of a Sancho Panza by not yielding as much as an inch the starchy formalities of the Tuileries. He ruled by writing endless orders-of-the-day on note paper, even if the person addressed might be close at hand or in the very next chamber. In an excess of energy, he played with the idea of colonizing a petty neighboring island and making it into a model settlement, but that miniature imperialistic scheme ended as a penitentiary for bored and insubordinate grenadiers. He talked of making Elba a center of art and science, but the bugaboo of his days, the sad need for stringent economy, drove him instead to reducing the number of body servants and putting down a villagers' revolt against the payment of taxes in arrears. Balls, banquets, and theatricals were needed to drive away the ennui of the guards in the dullness of Elba—"a fine place for a fox to live in," they grumbled. He converted a church into a theater, an irreverent venture which was paid for by selling lifetime privileges in the stalls to the gullible and flattered islanders. With his mother and sister he played at dominoes, chess, and cards, not unconcerned about his little winnings. When his mother exclaimed, "Napoleon, you are cheating," he would say, "Madame, you are rich, you can afford to lose, but I am poor and must win." He arrested the disease of penury and boredom by returning to France for the Hundred Days and for Waterloo, the English caricaturing him on the broad shoulders of a flying devil, crying: "Here I come, my lads, I'll set you to work again."

But the six years on St. Helena were a sad business; Napoleon and his entourage worked skillfully day and night to make of it the crucifixion of a

Prometheus. "The universe watches us," he declared. "We remain the martyrs of an immortal cause. Millions of men weep for us; our country sighs; and glory is in mourning." St. Helena was all talk, talk, and grievance, and a masterpiece of living theater. Generals, majors, lieutenants, physicians, wives, and valets; each conscious of a noble immolation for the Emperor, kept an ear cocked on Immortality—and a thick secret diary to make sure of it. St. Helena was a school for Boswells, and a factory for that Napoleonic mythology which has made French politics and literature from 1815 down to the days of Vichy.[1] Las Cases, Montholon, Gourgaud, Bertrand, O'Leary, each in his own fashion, in Bainville's words, "reconciled devotion with advertisement," while Napoleon was "like an author revising his writings when he has achieved the full powers of his style." Las Cases, Montholon, and Gourgaud spoke only to the Emperor—and Napoleon spoke directly to History: "I closed up the gulf of anarchy and restored order. I cleansed the Revolution, exalted peoples, and strengthened kings. I stimulated all worthy ambitions, rewarded all achievements, and extended the bounds of glory. All this is indeed something!" But what if History should rake up the charges of despotism, dictatorship, and war? "My despotism? But it will be demonstrated that dictatorship was absolutely necessary. Will I be charged with having restricted liberty? But it will be proved that license, anarchy, and the greatest disorders were still prevalent. Will I be accused of having been too fond of war? But it will be shown that I was always the one attacked. Will I be charged with having aspired to universal monarchy? But it will be seen that this was only the work of fortuitous circumstances, our enemies themselves having led me to it step by step." To guide History into such sweet reasonableness, he dictated seven volumes of his *Memoirs* to Montholon and Gourgaud, and each day reduced the Revolution and the glory of his campaigns to brilliant small talk. With an eye for the effect on Europe, the supreme occupation of the prisoner and exiles on St. Helena was grievance—against the climate, the rocks, the provisions,

---

[1] *The New York Times,* September 25, 1942: "The French National Committee, executive organization of the Fighting French Forces, has assumed responsibility for the upkeep of the house and the grounds where Napoleon lived and died in exile. The upkeep hitherto has been met by the French Government, but the caretaker, George Collin, has notified General Charles de Gaulle that he cannot remain faithful to the memory of Napoleon and loyal to the Vichy Government at the same time. . . . M. Collin has written to General de Gaulle as follows: 'I cannot support the humiliation of being in direct contact with a government of traitors that tramples on the honor of France and the will of its people.' Recently a Fighting French ship put in at St. Helena. Its captain and crew planted a willow tree near Napoleon's tomb and raised the Tricolor with the Cross of Lorraine, the Fighting French emblem."

428

the limitations on Napoleon's movements and correspondence and visitors, and the character of Sir Hudson Lowe, the governor who violated common sense with an excess of caution. But then Gourgaud had readily admitted that if the Governor of St. Helena were an angel, they would still complain of him. And St. Helena did not foster the growth of angels. As the diaries fattened and the notebooks filled, the atmosphere of competition for Napoleon's attention, as well as the natural trials of captivity, began to disintegrate the loyalties of the disciples and to corrupt even their nostalgia for glory. They spied on each other, they suspected, they hated, they quarreled, they looked forward to the day of liberation and the publication of their diaries, souvenirs, and memoirs. The disciples who survived these civil wars on St. Helena began to measure the remaining span of bondage to the sick Emperor. He liberated them by dying. When in 1840 the body of Napoleon was exhumed from its island grave for a tomb in the Paris of Louis Philippe, it was Bertrand, Gourgaud, Las Cases, and Marchand who assisted in the public rites which, in the words of Octave Aubry, "stuffed the monarchy of July into the lion's skin." Las Cases was old and blind, Gourgaud was gray, Bertrand was tired of living, only Marchand was fifty. They wept over their past, their sacrifices, their crown of thorns, their canonization and their glory. And Paris shouted *"Vive l'Empereur"* over the superman of whom Victor Hugo said that "God was bored with him."

ELBA: A CORRESPONDENCE

Fréjus, April 27, 1814. To General Count Dalesme, Commandant of the Island of Elba:

Circumstances having led me to renounce the French throne, sacrificing my rights to the welfare and interests of my country, I have reserved for myself the sovereignty and proprietorship of the island of Elba, with the fortresses of Porto Ferrajo and Porto Longone; and the powers have agreed to this arrangement. I am therefore sending General Drouot, so that you may make over the island to him without delay, with its stores of food and ammunition, and all the properties belonging to my Imperial Domain. Announce this new order of things to the inhabitants, and tell them that I have chosen the island for my residence because I know the kindness of their character and the excellence of their climate. They will always be an object of liveliest interest to me.

Porto Ferrajo, May 7, 1814. To General Drouot:

You must find out from the sub-prefect in what the civil government of the country consists. Have the flag of the island run up in all the parishes on Sunday, and make a kind of holiday of that day. . . . The hoisting of the flag should be announced to Naples, Rome, Tuscany, and Genoa. . . .

Porto Ferrajo, May 7, 1814. Order to General Drouot:

Request the Commissar of the Navy, the Captain of the Port, and the Commander of the French Navy to report tomorrow. We shall have them point out boats, feluccas, etc., belonging to the island, and draw up an account taking possession; dating from tomorrow, I shall assume responsibility for them. . . . If no difficulties are raised, we shall keep one of the schooners, but I shall not insist on it.

Elba, May 28, 1814. Note for General Drouot:

The fleet must be organized on the lines I laid down. No dining allowances will be given. The brig "Inconstant" will have the same crew as the schooner. M. Taillade will be in command of this vessel, but without any increase of pay. The 18 marines of My Guard who are here will be counted on the strength of the Navy. As we no longer have the "Light Woman," M. Rich will be put in command of one of the feluccas belonging to the mine. The command of the other will be given to M. Carnavali, the chief coxswain. He will therefore be included on the strength, filling one of the posts already created. Representations must be made as to the forwarding of the mine vessels here as soon as possible. Their crews can continue to serve them. I need these two vessels at once. They will be named the "Fly" and the "Bee."

Porto Ferrajo, June 10, 1814. To General Bertrand:

It is my intention to appoint the mayor of Porto Longone commandant of my palace at Porto Longone. He must perform the functions of commandant, *concierge,* keeper of the robes, and overseer of the gardens. He will receive a salary of 600 francs. . . .

Elba, June 14, 1814. To Grand Marshal Bertrand:

The naval Budget should include a heading for "Upkeep of vessels." The provisional grant under this head will be 600 francs, assigned as follows:—

For a copper compass for My cutter   50 francs
For cushions, tapestry, curtains, etc.   450 francs
For greasing the "Caroline," paint-
    ing the cutters, and other neces-
    sary expenses................... 100 francs

Give orders that My cutter has all the necessary work done on it before the end of the week.

Note: Porto Ferrajo, June 17, 1814

As the theater is to be demolished some day, it is not my intention to do anything which will greatly increase the expenses.

[*A few days later:*]

I return the plan of the house. There is not room on the first floor for more than three apartments; a large apartment of eight rooms, one of six rooms for the Empress, and another of three rooms. . . .

Porto Ferrajo, July 17, 1814. Note for the Grand Marshal:

Write to my brother Lucien that I have received his letter of June 11; that I am pleased with the sentiments which he expresses; that he must not be astonished if he does not receive a reply from me, because I write to no one. I have not written even to Madame [*his mother*].

Note: July 28:

I keep up three schooners with sixteen sailors each, and a brig which has sixty. This naval force is necessary to watch the coasts and to drive off the Algerian corsairs. . . . [*same day:*] As I am not sufficiently well lodged to give *fêtes,* I shall await the arrival of the Empress and the Princess Pauline, whom I expect in the first days of September, to have fireworks. I wish the parish to pay the expenses of a ball to be given in the public square, where a ballroom in wood can be constructed, and the officers of the Imperial Guard be invited. In the neighborhood of the ballroom an orchestra must be established for the soldiers to dance to, and the parish must take care to have some barrels of wine for them to drink. I also wish the parish to arrange the wedding of two young people whom it must endow. The Grand Marshal and the authorities must be present at this marriage, which must take place after high mass.

Porto Ferrajo, August 9, 1814. To General Bertrand:

Colonel Laczinski, who is going to leave today for Leghorn, will go from there to Aix, and will take with him a letter from me to the Empress. Write to Meneval to inform him that I expect the Empress at the end of the month, that I wish her to send me my son, and that it is singular that I have no news of her, which comes from letters being intercepted; that this ridiculous order is probably due to some subaltern, and cannot come from her father; at all events, that no one has any authority over the Empress and my son.

La Madone, August 23, 1814. To General Bertrand:

I arrived here at nine o'clock; it is now five, and I am going out shooting. One does not feel the heat here. Two shutters are wanting for my bedroom; try and send them tomorrow. Also send me two lanterns to put at the door of my tent. There are three iron beds here. I have ordered one to be brought from Marciana for Madame. There are fifteen mattresses, with blankets and sheets, which is all that is required. Madame can come to Marciana, if she likes, and lodge in the house of the mayor. She might start on Thursday, at five in the morning. . . . Send on a *valet de chambre,* a footman and a lady's maid, a cook and Cipriani, to get her house and her breakfast ready. In the mayor's house Madame will have a room for herself and one for her ladies, one for her maids and one for her men servants. If the Sieur Colonna accompanies Madame he will be lodged in the town. In this house there is sufficient furniture. I have had a chest of drawers placed in her apartments. There is enough linen for both of us. Major Roul will be attached to me as orderly officer. His pay will be 200 francs a month. He will accompany Madame, as well as the chamberlain Ventini. I think there are things enough for Madame's kitchen and mine. There are also candles and lights enough. The kitchen can be established in the house. Send three curtains for Madame's room. The rods are here. Send us also fire-irons, tongs, shovels, &c. People who say it is necessary to have fires in the evening are right.

P.S. The *valet de chambre* has some stuff for making curtains, which he is going to take to Madame's house.

La Madone, August 26, 1814. To General Bertrand:

I think that I asked you to write to the Princess Pauline not to bring her piano master with her, but only a good singer and a good songstress, seeing that we have here a good violin player and a good pianist. . . . [*same day:*]

One of my mules was recently drowned, which is a loss; this was due to the absence of a small pump in the stable; have one of those in store repaired.

La Madone, September 2, 1814. To General Bertrand:
Write to the Princess Pauline that I have received all the letters from Naples; tell her that I feel much hurt that my letters should have been forwarded open, as if I were a prisoner; that I find this conduct ridiculous and insulting. . . .

September 6, 1814. Order to General Bertrand:
We are in need of ordinary chairs for all our establishments; you must decide upon a model for the chairs to cost five francs each, and a model for the arm-chairs and sofas at a price in proportion, and buy them at Pisa, to the amount of 1000 francs. Choose the most suitable models from those they make at Pisa.

September 6, 1814. Note:
I see with pain that men are always at work on the Vantini House [*rented by Madame, Napoleon's mother*], which is all the more disagreeable seeing that it does not belong to me. It is proper that the note of the expenditure which has been ordered by Madame should be presented to her, so that she shall pay; that is the only way of making her abstain from ordering anything more, nothing being less urgent than all this raising of walls and placing of iron railings.

Longone, September 9, 1814. To General Drouot:
Give orders that when the sailors of My Guard go on board My cutters, they are always to take with them their sabres, muskets, and two clips of cartridges in their cartridge-cases. Racks must be fitted in the cutters to hold these weapons.

Porto Longone, September 9, 1814. To General Bertrand:
I thank you for the pamphlets which I have just received; make a collection of those which are *for* and those which are *against;* one of these days I will run over them all. I have received a very tender letter from the King of Naples; he pretends having written to me several times, but I doubt it; it appears that affairs between France and Italy turn his head and make him tender. Send me a list of persons whom the Princess Pauline is bringing with her. . . .

433

Elba, October 15, 1814. To Grand Marshal Bertrand:

I have received your report on Supplementary Expenditure for the month of September.

Gardens. Reprimand the gardener for employing three men all the month on a garden the size of my hand, and 11 grenadiers for loading up a few cartfuls of earth. I disapprove of the proposed expenditure on turf during October: I would rather have grass seed. The gardener must bargain with the grenadiers to load earth at so much a cubic metre, and use just enough carts to keep them constantly employed. I don't think this ought to cost more than 80 francs. Similarly the O.C. Engineers must bargain with the grenadiers for the excavation of the gardens. I estimate the cost at 400 francs. I therefore allow 480 francs for the Supplementary Estimates for the gardens during October.

Stables. I can't allow more than 600 francs a month. It's impossible to do things on the same scale in this country as in Paris. Chauvin and the deputy-chamberlain must agree, and arrange matters accordingly. They can have the shoeing done on account, and it certainly won't cost more than 200 francs a month. They can treat the other expenses in the same way, provided they keep within the limit of 600 francs. I can't give more than 150 francs for the side-saddle.

Stores. This account is in a great muddle. The ordinary expenditure should suffice for a watchman (whom I don't see put down), 2 or 3 women in permanent employment, and a valet who can also do upholstering. I should like this last, if possible, to be the man who came with Madame. Conti, who supplied the furniture, ought not to be employed any more in the Stores. Have a separate account made for all the items under the head of "carriage of Princess Pauline's things." I refuse to pay the 280 francs demanded by the Stores department for petty cash. I can only allow 40 francs. Have an estimate made out for the ordinary expenditure of the Stores during October, as well as one for Supplementary Expenditure. As Saint-Martin and the Princess's apartment are being furnished, the Supplementary Estimates for October are likely to be higher than in other months: my provisional esti-. mate is 800 francs. Make out a list of the proper charges for carriage from the fleet at Longone to the citadel at Merciana and to La Madone, and from the fleet to the palace of Porto Ferrajo. The Stores department will conform to this tariff; but it must be strictly forbidden to employ the carrier for any transport work that can be done by our own vehicles.

November 16, 1814. Order to General Drouot:

[*When his taxgatherers were assaulted by the people of Capoliveri, led by their priest, Napoleon sent Major Colombani with two hundred men to escort the police back to the rebellious village, and ordered:*] Each man will have three packets of cartridges. Major Colombani will arrest the priest who has been the leader of the riot, and two others. He will remain with his column at Capoliveri until the contributions are paid. He will find lodgings with the fifty inhabitants who are most in arrears. The sieur Bigischi, secretary-general of the Intendant, will go there with a letter from the Intendant to establish the fact of the bad behavior, arrest three chiefs of the revolt, and compel immediate payment of the contributions; otherwise it may be the worse for Capoliveri. He must make the town understand that. He must manage so as to arrive only an hour before the troops, and if the local notabilities are able to induce the inhabitants to be reasonable the police alone will enter the town.

Porto Ferrajo, January 3, 1815. Note for the Balls to Be Given During the Carnival:

Sunday, the 8th, there will be a ball in the grand saloon. It is necessary that the invitations should be made out tomorrow and the list submitted to His Majesty. The invitations should extend all over the island, without however comprising more than 200 persons. They must be issued for 9 o'clock. There will be refreshments without ices, considering the difficulties in procuring them. There will be a supper served at midnight. All this must not cost more than 40 pounds. Sunday, the 15th, the Academy can open its theater and give a fancy ball. The 22nd following I can give another ball. The 29th, the theater can give a second fancy ball. During the holidays there can be two fancy balls given, one in the theater and one at the palace. . . .

Porto Ferrajo, January 31, 1815. To General Bertrand:

[*General Bertrand having submitted for appropriation a bill for eight blinds for the drawing room of the Princess Pauline, Napoleon decided:*] Not having ordered this expense, which has not been carried to the budget, the Princess must pay it. It will be the same with all expenses of this kind, made before they have been approved. [*The princess having furnished the linen, the whole expense was about 2 pounds 10 shillings.*]

Note: February 3, 1815:

I see that the Cardinal proposes an expenditure of 5600 francs for the opera

of Porto Ferrajo. Inquire if the band of the guard could not form an orchestra, and Gaudiano be leader; that would reduce the expenses to 2600 francs a month. The note gives a list of four men only, who cannot form a company. There must be women; the Cardinal announced several. . . .

Order (ten days before leaving Elba):
The brig is to be sent to drydock for overhauling: the copper gone over, the water leaks and gaps stopped, the keel recalked—in short, everything necessary to make it seaworthy. It is to be painted like an English brig. . . . Rearm the brig; provision it with sea-biscuits, rice, vegetables, cheese; the liquor supply is to be half wine and half *eau-de-vie;* provide enough water for one hundred and twenty men for three months. There is to be enough salt meat for fifteen days; and plenty of wood. Make absolutely certain that nothing is overlooked or forgotten.

Porto Ferrajo, February 26, 1815. To General Lapi:
I am leaving the island of Elba. I have been extremely satisfied with the conduct of the inhabitants. I confide to them the safety of this country, to which I attach a great importance. I cannot give them a greater mark of confidence than in leaving my mother and my sister in their care, after the departure of the troops. The members of the Junta, and all the inhabitants of the island, may count upon my affection and upon my special protection.

NAPOLEON.

[*Napoleon left Elba on February 26, landed in France on March 1, and reached Paris on the 20th.*]

Paris, March 23, 1815. To General Count Bertrand, Grand Marshal of the Palace:
Send Bernotti post-haste to the Isle of Elba. Entrust him with news for the island. He must sail from Toulon. Write to Lapi telling him to run up the tricolour. Recover from Elba any of my things that are worth sending. I am anxious to have my Corsican horse, if it is not ill, and can be sent back. The canary travelling-carriage, the big carriage, and two of the state coaches, are worth the trouble of returning, as well as my underwear. I am presenting my library to the town, along with my house: the house will do for a casino, but the library must be left in it.

436

AS THEMISTOCLES DID

Isle d'Aix, July 14, 1815. To the Prince Regent of England:
Your Royal Highness: victimized by the factions which divide my country, and by the hostility of the European powers, I have ended my political career; and I come, as Themistocles did, to claim a seat by the hearth of the British people. I put myself under the protection of British law—a protection which I claim from Your Royal Highness, as the strongest, the stubbornest, and the most generous of my foes.

NAPOLEON.

Aboard the Bellerophon, July 31, 1815. To Admiral Keith, Commander-in-Chief of the Channel Fleet:
. . . Upon accepting the hospitality of the *Bellerophon*, I placed myself under the protection of the laws of your country . . . I wish to live at liberty in the interior of England, under the protection and watchfulness of her laws; and I am willing to make any commitments and promises to this effect judged necessary. . . . Since I abdicated, it has been my intention to make my home either in the United States or in England. I trust, Milord, that you and the under-secretary of your government, will make an accurate report of these facts. I am placing my trust in the honor of the Prince Regent, and the laws of your country.

At Sea, on Board the Bellerophon, August 4, 1815:
I here protest solemnly before Heaven and before men against the violation of my most sacred rights, in disposing of my person and of my liberty by force. I came of my own free will on board the *Bellerophon*. I am not a prisoner; I am the guest of England. I came here myself at the instigation of the captain, who said that he had received orders from his Government to convey me to England with my suite, if that were agreeable to me. I presented myself in good faith, in order to place myself under the protection of her laws. As soon as I had placed foot on board the *Bellerophon* I was on the hearth of the British people. If the Government, in giving directions to the captain of the *Bellerophon* to receive me with my suite, wished merely to set me a trap, an ambush, it has forfeited its honor and sullied its flag. Should such an act be consummated it will be all in vain for the English to speak in future of their honesty, of their laws, and of their liberty. British good faith will be compromised by the hospitality of the *Bellerophon*.

437

I appeal to history. It will say that an enemy who for twenty years waged war against the English people came of his own accord, in his misfortune, to seek an asylum under their laws; and what greater proof could he give of his esteem and his confidence? But how did England reply to this magnanimity? She feigned to stretch out a hospitable hand to the enemy, and when he trusted himself to her good faith she immolated him!

NAPOLEON.

ST. HELENA: A DIARY [2]

October 24th, 1815. What infamous treatment they have held in store for us! This is the agony of death! To injustice, to violence, they add insult and slow torture! If I was so dangerous, why didn't they get rid of me? A few bullets in my heart or in my head would have settled it; there would have been some courage at least in such a crime! If it were not for you and for your wives I would refuse everything here save a soldier's rations. How can the Sovereigns of Europe permit the sacred nature of sovereignty to be attainted in me? Can't they see that they are killing themselves at St. Helena? I have entered their capitals as a conqueror; had I been moved by such motives, what would have become of them? They all called me their brother, and I had become so by the will of the people, the sanction of victory, the character of religion, the alliances of policy and of family.

November 16th. You don't know men; they are difficult to judge precisely. Do they know, do they realize themselves fully? Had I continued prosperous, most of those who abandoned me would probably never have suspected their own treachery. In any case, I was more deserted than betrayed; there was more weakness about me than treason; they were the regiment of St. Peter,—repentance and tears may stand at the gates! Apart from that, who has there been in history with more partisans, more friends? Who has been more popular, more beloved? Who ever left behind more ardent regrets? Look at France: might not one say that from this rock of mine I still reign over her?

25th. When I returned from Moscow, from Leipzig, it was reported in Paris that my hair had turned white; but you see it is not so, and I expect to stand worse things than those!

---

[2] This material is derived entirely from Napoleon's own words, written and spoken; but there are abbreviations, and transpositions of words and dates.

29th. My Code alone, because of its simplicity, has done more good in France than the sum total of all the laws that preceded it. My schools are preparing unknown generations. And so during my reign crime diminished rapidly, whilst on the contrary among our neighbours in England it increased with frightful rapidity. And that is enough, I think, to give a clear judgment on the two governments.

People take England on trust, and repeat that Shakespeare is the greatest of all authors. I have read him: there is nothing that compares with Racine or Corneille: his plays are unreadable, pitiful.

30th, in the garden:

It is certainly far from poor Toby here (a Negro gardener) to a King Richard! And yet the crime is no less atrocious; for, after all, this man had a family, happiness, an individual existence. And it is a horrible crime to have sent him here to finish his days under the load of slavery. But I read your looks; you think there is a similar case at St. Helena! There is not the least comparsion between the two; if the misdeed strikes higher, the victim can fall back on far greater resources. Our situation may even have good points! The Universe watches us! We stand as martyrs of an immortal cause! Millions of men weep with us, our country sighs, and glory has put on mourning! We struggle here against the tyranny of the gods, and the hopes of humanity are with us! Misfortune itself knows heroism, and glory! Only adversity was wanting to complete my career! Had I died on the throne, in the clouds of my almightiness, I would have remained a problem for many; as it is, thanks to my misfortunes, I can be judged naked.

December 6th. Well, we shall have sentries under our windows for dinner at Longwood; they would like to compel me to have a foreign officer at my table, in my room; I must not ride out on horseback without one; in a word we must not take one step, under penalty of an insult!

January 1, 1816. In this accursed island one cannot see the sun or the moon for the greater part of the year; always rain or fog. One can't ride a mile without being soaked; even the English, accustomed as they are to dampness, complain of it.

15th. We have no superfluity here, except of time.

22d. On my return from the army of Italy, Bernardin de St. Pierre came to call on me, and almost at once turned the conversation on the subject of his poverty. During my boyhood I had dreamed of nothing but Paul and Virginia, and, flattered by a confession that I assumed to be confidential

and due to. my great reputation, I speedily returned his call, and discreetly left a little roll of twenty-five louis on the mantelpiece.

* * * * *

17th. If I hadn't been fool enough to get myself beaten at Waterloo, the business was done; even now I can't see how it happened—but there, don't let's talk about it any more!

March 3d. I frightened them pretty well with my invasion of England, didn't I? What was the public talk about it at the time? Well, you may have joked about it in Paris, but Pitt wasn't laughing in London. Never was the English oligarchy in greater peril!

I had made a landing possible; I had the finest army that ever existed, that of Austerlitz; what more can be said? In four days I could have reached London; I would not have entered as a conqueror but as a liberator; I would have acted the part of William III again, but with greater generosity. The discipline of my army would have been perfect; and it would have behaved in London as it might in Paris. From there I would have operated from south to north, under the colours of the Republic, the European regeneration which later I was on the point of effecting from north to south, under monarchical forms. The obstacles before which I failed did not proceed from men but from the elements: in the south it was the sea destroyed me; and in the north it was the fire of Moscow and the ice of winter; so there it is, water, air, fire, all nature and nothing but nature; these were the opponents of a universal regeneration commanded by Nature herself! The problems of Nature are insoluble!

7th. Count Lascases Chambellan of the S. M. Longwood; into his polac: very press.

Count Lascases, Since sixt wek, y learn the english and y do not any progress. Sixt week do fourty and two day. If might have learn fivty word for day, i could know it two thousands and two hundred. It is in the diction-ary more of fourty thousand; even he could most twenty; but much of tems. For know it or hundred and twenty week which do more two years. After this you shall agree that the study one tongue is a great labour who it must do into the young aged. Longwood, this morning the seven march thursday one thousand eight hundred sixteen after nativity the Lors Jesus Christ.

11th. The Emperor of Russia is intelligent, pleasing, well-educated, can fascinate easily; but one has to be on one's guard, he is a real Greek of the later Empire.

Greece awaits a liberator. What a splendid wreath of glory is there! He can inscribe his name for eternity with those of Homer, of Plato, of Epaminondas! I myself was perhaps not far from doing it! When at the time of my campaign of Italy I touched the shores of the Adriatic, I wrote to the Directoire that I could look out over the Empire of Alexander.

The French are all critical, turbulent: they are real weathervanes at the mercy of the winds; but this fault is free from any factor of self-interest, and that is their best excuse.

31st. With St. John of Acre captured, I could have reached Constantinople and India; I would have changed the face of the world!

April 1st. I can count thirty-one conspiracies on official record, without speaking of those that remain unknown; others invent such things, I have carefully concealed all I was able to. The risk to my life was a great one, especially between Marengo and the attempt of Georges and the affair of the Duke d'Enghien.

11th. Talleyrand's face is so impassive that it is impossible to interpret it; Lannes and Murat used to say of him jokingly that if, while he was speaking with you, some one kicked him from behind, his face would show nothing.

Fouché required intrigues just as he did food. He intrigued at all times, in all places, in all manners, with all people. He was always in everybody's boots.

(O'Meara: Which is the best of the French generals?)

It is difficult to say, but it seems to me that it is Suchet; formerly it was Masséna, but he may be considered a dead man. Suchet, Clausel, and Gérard are the best French generals, in my opinion. I made my generals out of mud.

18th. In my misfortunes, I sought an asylum, and instead I have found contempt, ill-treatment, and insult. Shortly after I came on board (Admiral Cockburn's) ship, as I did not wish to sit for two or three hours guzzling down wine to make myself drunk, I got up from table, and walked out upon deck. While I was going out, he said, in a contemptuous manner:—I believe the *general* has never read Lord Chesterfield; meaning, that I was deficient in politeness, and did not know how to conduct myself at table.

19th. I have no reason to complain of the English soldiers or sailors; on the contrary, they treat me with great respect, and even appear to feel for me. Moore was a brave soldier, an excellent officer, and a man of talent.

20th. England and France have held in their hands the fate of the world, especially that of European civilization. How we have injured one another!

21st. They want to know what I wish? I ask for my freedom, or for the

executioner! Tell your Prince Regent what I say. I no longer ask for news of my son since they have had the barbarism to leave my first request unanswered.

It is hard, all the same, to find myself without money; I might make arrangements to have an annual credit on Eugène of 7000 or 8000 napoleons. He could not very well refuse; he has had perhaps more than 40 millions from me, and it would be casting a slur on his personal character to doubt him.

26th. Well, after all said and done, circumstances might have led me to accept Islam, and as that excellent Queen of France used to say: How you do go on! But I should have wanted something worth my while,—at least up to the Euphrates. A change of religion, which is unpardonable for personal motives, may perhaps be accepted when immense political results depend on it. Henry IV rightly said: Paris is worth a mass. To think that the Empire of the East, perhaps the dominion of all Asia, was the matter of a turban and a pair of baggy trousers; for really that was all it came to.

Constantinople alone is an Empire; whoever possesses it can rule the world.

28th. Had I not won at Austerlitz, I would have had the whole of Prussia on my back. Had I not triumphed at Jena, Austria and Spain would have risen behind me. Had I not succeeded at Wagram, a far less decisive victory, I had to fear that Russia would abandon me, that Prussia would revolt, and the English were already in front of Antwerp. I made a great mistake after Wagram in not striking Austria down even lower. She remained too powerful for our security; she eventually destroyed us. Austria had come into my family; and yet this marriage was fatal to me. I stepped on to an abyss covered with flowers.

29th. My dear friend, you and I, in this place, are already in the next world; we are conversing in the Elysian Fields.

May 1st. They may change, and chop, and suppress, but after all they will find it pretty difficult to make me disappear altogether. A French historian cannot very easily avoid dealing with the Empire; and, if he has a heart, he will have to give me back something of my own. I sealed the gulf of anarchy, and I unravelled chaos. I purified the revolution, raised the people, and strengthened monarchy. I stimulated every ambition, rewarded every merit, and pushed back the bounds of glory! All that amounts to something!

10th. It is most remarkable how the revolution suddenly produced so many great generals, Pichegru, Kléber, Masséna, Marceau, Desaix, Hoche; and nearly all of them rankers; but there the effort of Nature seemed to stop, she has produced nothing since.

16th. Well, my dear fellow, things got pretty hot; I was angry! They have sent me something worse than a gaoler; Sir Hudson Lowe is an executioner! Well, I received him to-day with my face of thunder, head down, and ears back! We stared like two rams on the point of butting at one another; and my emotions must have been quite violent, for I felt my left calf twitching. That is a great symptom with me, and hadn't occurred for a long time.

You say, sir, that your instructions are more terrible than those of the Admiral. Are they to kill me by the sword, or by poison? I am prepared for anything from your Minister; here I am, slaughter your victim! I don't know how you can manage the poison; but as for the sword you have already found the way. I warn you that if, as you have threatened, you intrude on my privacy, the brave 53d will not pass in except over my body. On learning of your arrival I flattered myself that I should find in you an army officer who, having been on the Continent and having witnessed its great struggles, would have behaved with propriety towards me; I made a profound mistake. Your nation, your government, you yourself, will be covered with opprobrium because of me; and your children too; that will be the verdict of posterity. What subtlety of barbarism could go further, sir, than that which led you a few days ago to invite me to your table under the qualification of General Bonaparte, to make me the amusement and the laughing-stock of your guests? Would you have cut your courtesy to the rank you were pleased to assign me? I am not General Bonaparte for you, sir; you have no more right than any other person on earth to take from me the qualifications that are mine!

They will kill me here, my dear fellow, that is quite certain!

19th. When sleeping together it is not easy to lose touch; but otherwise people are quickly strangers. And so it was that so long as that habit lasted, none of my thoughts, none of my actions, escaped Josephine; she seized, guessed, kept track of everything, which was sometimes quite awkward for me and for business. A passing quarrel put an end to it at the time of the camp of Boulogne.

Josephine was always thinking of the future, and was alarmed at her

barrenness. She realized fully that no marriage is complete and real without children; and she had married when no longer able to have any. As prosperity came, her anxiety increased; she had recourse to the medical art; she frequently pretended that success had resulted. Josephine had the excessive extravagance and disorderliness of the Creoles. Her accounts never could be balanced; she was always in debt; and we always quarrelled vigorously when the moment came for settling those debts. Even at Elba Josephine's accounts were showered on me from every part of Italy.

Another characteristic trait of Josephine was her constant attitude of negation. At any moment, at any question made to her, her first instinct was to deny, her first word was *no;* and the *no* was not exactly a lie, it was a precaution, a mere defensive; and it is just that which differentiates us from you, ladies, a fundamental distinction of sex and of education: you are made for love, and you are taught to say *no*. We, on the contrary, glory in saying *yes,* even when we should not. And there is the key of our difference in conduct. We are not and cannot be of the same sort in life.

If I were starting at night in a chaise for a distant journey, to my great astonishment there would Josephine be, waiting in it ready dressed, although it had not been arranged that she should go.—But you can't possibly come! I am going too far; it would fatigue you too much!—Not in the least, answered Josephine.—And I must start at once.—Well, I'm quite ready.—But you need a whole paraphernalia.—Not at all, she said; I have everything.—And generally I had to give in.

After all said and done, Josephine gave her husband happiness, and was always his tenderest friend, always and in all events showing submission, devotion, absolute self-sacrifice. And I have always thought of her with tender affection and keen gratitude.

Madame (Mère) was too parsimonious; it was ridiculous. I even offered her a large monthly allowance if only she would disburse it. She was quite ready to take it, but on condition she could keep it. In reality it was all merely an excess of prudence on her part; she was always afraid of finding herself penniless some day. She had known necessity, and could never free her mind from the memory of that terrible time. It is only fair to say, however, that she gave a great deal of money to her children in secret; she is such a good mother!

And yet this same woman from whom it is so difficult to extract a five franc piece would have given her all to help my return from Elba; and after Waterloo she would have given me all she possessed to help re-

444

establish my affairs; she offered it me; she would have sentenced herself to black bread without a murmur.

20th. I am sad, bored, ill; sit in that armchair, keep me company.

21st. What shall we read to-night? You all agree on the Bible? It is really most edifying; they wouldn't guess what we're doing, in Europe!

Book V
Irish Testament

ROBERT EMMET

JOHN MITCHEL

CHARLES STEWART PARNELL

MICHAEL DAVITT

WILFRID SCAWEN BLUNT

PADRAIC PEARSE

ROGER CASEMENT

CONSTANCE MARKIEVICZ

THE PATRIOT:

Robert Emmet

SPEECH IN THE DOCK

"Are you straight?"
"I am."
"How straight?"
"As straight as a rush."
"Go on, then."
"In truth, in trust, in unity and liberty."
"What have you got in your hand?"
"A green bough."
"Where did it first grow?"
"In America."
"Where did it bud?"
"In France."
"Where are you going to plant it?"
"In the Crown of Great Britain."
From the catechism of the *Society of United Irishmen*

ROBERT EMMET gave a tragic pattern to Irish luck and patriotism. The failure of his insurrection of 1803, recapitulated by Young Ireland in 1848, came to a full circle in the Easter Rising of 1916, with the English in Dublin Castle still the master. A century of ill luck between them, young Robert Emmet was the progenitor of young Padraic Pearse. But Emmet also had his Irish models: Lord Edward Fitzgerald who died in the rebellion of 1798, and Theobald Wolfe Tone who sailed into Bantry Bay in the uniform of the French revolutionary republic only to cut his throat when the invasion game was up. Emmet resurrected Tone's Society of United Irishmen, ravaged by Dublin Castle, and prepared for the work of finishing the rebellious job begun in '98. His student years in Ireland, which preceded his precocious revolutionary leadership at twenty-four, had been crowded with floggings, burnings, tortures, shootings, hangings, and rapes. Great revolutions had taken place in America and France. The very air was Jacobin; young Irishmen were making mysterious pilgrimages to Paris; and one day France would be sailing upon Ireland:

The French are in the Bay.
They'll be here without delay.

A grave young man who had gambled away his chance for a respectable pro-

449

fession in Dublin with a piece of rebellious oratory, Emmet had said to his college debating society: "When a people advancing rapidly in knowledge and power perceive at last how far their government is lagging behind them, what then, I ask, is to be done in such a case? What but to pull the government up to the people?" The interlude between his speech to a debating society and the last *Speech in the Dock*, Ireland's national treasure, was short. Emmet went to Paris, saw Talleyrand and Bonaparte, and came home to Dublin to an amateurish enterprise of manufacturing pikes, rockets, and hand grenades. If eight thousand Irish could seize Dublin Castle, if the Irish countryside could be brought to a boiling point, if in the war between England and France the French could launch another invasion, then the liberation attempted by Lord Edward Fitzgerald and Wolfe Tone would be redeemed. If not—"if a precipice is opening under my feet from which my duty will not suffer me to turn back—I am grateful for that sanguine disposition which leads me to the brink and throws me down while my eyes are still raised to the vision of happiness that my fancy formed in the air." The insurrection of 1803 failed to do more than leave a gesture and a national pattern for young Irishmen of sensibility. Emmet's rockets exploded prematurely, at the crucial moment his hand grenades were faulty, the matches for the fuses were carelessly mixed, the ladders for scaling Dublin Castle never arrived, and the revolution petered out into a riot. Even romance intruded on high Irish politics (as later in the case of Parnell and Kitty O'Shea) when the love letters of Sarah Curran to Robert Emmet fell into English hands. Emmet's death on the gallows fed the ballad literature of broken hearts with a national theme. Thomas Moore wrote:

> She is far from the land where her young hero sleeps,
> And lovers are round her sighing;
> But coldly she turns from their gaze and weeps,
> For her heart in his grave is lying.

But with the exception of the speech delivered before the presiding judge, Lord Norbury, Emmet's insurrection of 1803 was politically a failure. In 1914 Padraic Pearse, who was to re-enact the role of Emmet's martyrdom in only two years, was telling an Irish audience in New York that "no failure, judged as the world judges these things, was ever more complete, more pathetic than Emmet's. And yet he has left a prouder memory than the memory of Brian victorious at Clontarf or of Owen Roe victorious at Benburb. . . . Face to face with England in the dock at Green Street he uttered the most memorable words ever uttered by an Irish man."

SPEECH IN THE DOCK [1]

My lords: Why the sentence of the law should not be passed upon me I have nothing to say. Why the sentence which in the public mind is usually attached to that of the law ought to be reversed, I have much to say. I stand here a conspirator—as one engaged in a conspiracy for the overthrow of the British Government in Ireland; for the fact of which I am to suffer by the law, for the motives of which I am to answer before God. I am ready to do both. Were it only the fact of treason, were it that naked fact alone with which I stood charged, were I to suffer no other punishment than the death of the body—I would not obtrude upon your attention, but having received the sentence I would bow my neck in silence to the stroke. But, my lords, I well know that when a man enters into conspiracy, he has not only to combat against the difficulties of fortune, but to contend with the still more insurmountable obstacle of prejudice; and that if in the end fortune abandons him and delivers him bound into the hands of the law, his character is previously loaded with calumny and misrepresentation—for what purpose I know not, except that the prisoner thus weighed down both in mind and body, may be delivered over a more unresisting victim to condemnation.

It is well; but the victim being once obtained and firmly in your power, let him now unmanacle his reputation.

Not, my lords, that I have much to demand from you. It is a claim on your memory, rather than on your candor, that I am making.

I do not ask you to believe implicitly what I say, I do not hope that you will let my vindication ride at anchor in your breasts. I only ask you to let it float upon the surface of your recollection, till it comes to some more friendly port to receive it, and give it shelter against the heavy storms with which it is buffeted.

I am charged with being an emissary of France, for the purpose of inciting insurrection in the country and then delivering it over to a foreign enemy. It is false. I did not wish to join this country with France. I did join—I did

---

[1] "The last speech of Robert Emmet," says R. W. Postgate in *Dear Robert Emmet,* "one of the most remarkable pieces of English oratory of its kind that survives, has suffered greatly in the passage of time. Enemies have cut out what they did not desire to have preserved, friends have 'improved' it by additions of their own. Dr. Madden, the United Irishmen historian, found in his day no fewer than eleven different versions; to-day fuller investigation raises that number to a score. It can only be said, therefore, for the account that follows, that it is probably as nearly exact a text as can be found and that it is the product of considerable research and investigation."

not create—the rebellion; not for France, but for liberty. It is true, there were communications between the United Irishmen and France; it is true that, in consequence of them, the war was no surprise upon us. There is a new agent at Paris, at this moment, negotiating with the French government to obtain from them an aid sufficient to accomplish the separation of Ireland from England, and before any expedition sails, it is intended to have a treaty signed, as a guarantee, similar to that which Franklin obtained for America. Whether they will do that now, England, you may judge. But the only question with the members of the Provisional Government was whether France should come to this country as an enemy. Whether she should have any pretext for so doing. Whether the people should look to France as their only deliverer, or through the medium and control of the Provisional Government attain their object. It is not now that I discover, or that the rest of the Provisional Government of Ireland feel, what it is that binds states together. They well know, my lords, that such a disposition exists only in proportion to its mutuality of interest; and wherever that mutuality does not exist, no written articles can secure the inferior state, nor supply the means of protecting its independence.

In this view it never was the intention of the Provisional Government of Ireland to form a permanent alliance with France; well knowing that, if there is between states a permanent mutual interest, more or less, though treaties may be made, yet for the most part it is not the treaty which binds them together, but a sense of common interest, and where the interest does not exist, treaties are soon represented as unjust—they are qualified and interpreted at pleasure, and violated under any pretext. Under these views, it never was the intention to form a permanent treaty with France, and in the treaty which they did make, they had the same guarantee which America had, that an independent government should be established in the country, before the French should come. God forbid that I should see my country under the hands of a foreign power. On the contrary, it is evident from the introducing paragraph of the address of the Provisional Government of Ireland, that every hazard attending on independent effort was deemed preferable to the more fatal risk of introducing a French army into the country. For what?—When it has liberty to maintain and independence to keep, may no consideration induce it to submit.

If the French come as a foreign enemy, oh, my countrymen, meet them on the shore with a torch in one hand and a sword in the other. Receive them with all the destruction of war—immolate them in their boats before our

native soil shall be polluted by a foreign foe. If they succeed in landing, fight them on the strand, burn every blade of grass before them, as they advance; raze every house. And if you are driven to the center of your country, collect your provisions, your property, your wives and your daughters, join a circle around them—fight while two men are left, and when but one remains let that man set fire to the pile, and release himself and the families of his fallen countrymen from the tyranny of France.[2]

Deliver my country into the hands of France? Look at the proclamation—where is it stated? Is it in that part where the people of Ireland are called upon to show the world that they are competent to take their place among nations? That they have a right to claim acknowledgment as an independent country, by the satisfactory proof of their capability of maintaining their independence?—by wresting it from England with their own hands? Is it in that part where it is stated that the system has been organized within the last eight months, *without the hope of foreign assistance,* and which the renewal of hostilities has not accelerated? Is it in that part which desires England not to create a deadly national antipathy between the two countries?

Look then to another part of the proclamation—look at the military regulations: is there a word introduced from the French nomenclature? Are not all the terms English? all the appellations of the intended constituted authorities English? Why then say the system was from France? Yes—there was one argument urged, one quotation from the proclamation relied upon to prove that we must have meant to resort to France:—

"You are to show to us that you have something in reserve wherewith to crush hereafter not only a greater exertion on the part of the people, but a greater exertion rendered still greater by *foreign assistance.*"

From which an inference is drawn that foreign assistance is the support of the present system. Because you are called upon to show that your strength is such that you can put down the present attempt without bringing out all your force—to show that you have something in *reserve* wherewith to crush

---

2 Winston Churchill in the House of Commons, June 4, 1940, after Dunkirk: "We shall not flag or fail. We shall go on to the end. We shall fight in France, we shall fight on the seas and oceans, we shall fight with growing confidence and growing strength in the air, we shall defend our Island, whatever the cost may be. We shall fight on the beaches, we shall fight on the landing grounds, we shall fight in the fields and in the streets, we shall fight in the hills; we shall never surrender, and even if, which I do not for a moment believe, this Island or a large part of it were subjugated and starving, then our Empire beyond the seas, armed and guarded by the British Fleet, would carry on the struggle, until, in God's good time, the New World, with all its power and might, steps forth to the rescue and the liberation of the old."

hereafter; therefore, the conclusion drawn is, because a *future* exertion *may be* rendered greater by foreign assistance, that foreign assistance *is* the foundation of the present exertion.

But it is said, we *must* have had in view to deliver up the country to France, and this is not attempted to be proved upon any ground but that of assertion. It is not proved from our declarations or actions; because every circumstance attending the attempt which took place shows that our object was to anticipate France. How could we speak of freedom to our countrymen, how assume such an exalted motive and meditate the introduction of a power which has been the enemy of freedom wherever she appears? See how she has behaved to Switzerland, to Holland, and to Italy. Could we expect better conduct towards us? No! Let not then any man calumniate my memory by believing that I could have hoped for freedom from the government of France, or that I would have betrayed the sacred cause of the liberty of this country by committing it to the power of her most determined foe.

With regard to this, I have one observation to make. It has been stated that I came from abroad. If I had been in Switzerland, I would have fought against the French for I am certain the Swiss are hostile to the French. In the dignity of freedom I would have expired on the frontiers of that country, and they should have entered it only by passing over my lifeless corpse. But if I thought the people were favorable to the French—I have seen so much what the consequences of the failure of revolutions are: the oppression of the higher upon the lower orders of the people—I say, if I saw them disposed to admit the French, I would not join them, but I would put myself between the French and the people, not as a victim but to protect them from subjugation and endeavor to gain their confidence by sharing in their danger.

So would I have done with the people of Ireland, and so would I do if I were called upon tomorrow. Our object was to effect a separation from England. . . .

(Here Lord Norbury interrupted.)

My lord, I did say that I had nothing to offer why the sentence of the law should not pass upon me. But if that is all I am asked, that is not all I am to suffer. I have always understood it to be the duty of a judge when a prisoner has been convicted to pronounce the sentence of the law. I have also understood that judges sometimes think it their duty to hear with patience

and speak with humanity—to exhort the victim of the laws and to offer with tender benignity their opinion of the motives by which he was actuated in the crime of which he was adjudged guilty. That judges have thought this their duty so to have done I have no doubt. But where is the boasted freedom of your institutions—where is the vaunted impartiality, clemency, and mildness of your courts of justice, if an unfortunate prisoner, whom your policy and not justice is about to deliver into the hands of the execution, is not suffered to explain his motives sincerely and truly, and to vindicate the principles by which he was moved?

What I claim is this—to free my character from a foul imputation. Though you, my lord, sit there as a judge; and I stand here as a culprit, yet you are but a man, and I am a man also. And when you or any other judge speak against the motives of a dying man, I do conceive it to be the right of the dying man—that it is his duty—to vindicate his character and his views from aspersion. If I say anything contrary to the law, your lordship may stop me, and I will submit immediately upon being corrected. But it is hardly possible, when I am justifying my motives, to avoid mentioning some which must be disagreeable to those I address; all I can say is that they should have been passed over in silence. If my motives are not to be justified, nothing should be said but the pronouncing of the sentence. If I am not permitted to vindicate my motives let no man calumniate my actions. If I am permitted to go on—

(Here Lord Norbury interrupted.)

Then I have nothing more to say if I am not permitted to vindicate myself. Vindication rests upon the abstract principle and the views with which that principle was applied. I did wish to state both. I did wish to state the views which I had, without presuming to make application to anybody.

(Here Lord Norbury interrupted.)

O my country, was it personal ambition that influenced me? Had it been the soul of my action, could I not by my education and fortune, by the rank and consideration of my family, have placed myself among the proudest of your oppressors? When my spirit shall have joined those bands of martyred heroes who have shed their blood on the scaffold and in the field in the defense of their country, this is my hope: that my memory and name may serve to animate those who survive me.

THE PATRIOT : *Robert Emmet*

(Here Lord Norbury interrupted.)

I do not fear approaching the omnipotent Judge to answer for the conduct of my past life, and am I to stand appalled before a mere remnant of mortality? But, my lord, were it possible to collect all the blood that you have shed into a common reservoir—for great indeed it must be—your lordship might swim therein. What I have spoken was not intended for your lordships, whose situation I rather commiserate than envy. My expressions were for my countrymen. If there be a true Irishman present, let my last words cheer him in the hour of affliction!

(Here Lord Norbury interrupted.)

My lords, shall a dying man be denied the legal privilege of exculpating himself in the eyes of the community from a reproach therein on him during his trial, by charging him with ambition, and attempting to cast away for a paltry consideration the liberties of his country? Why then insult me, or rather, why insult justice, in demanding of me why sentence of death should not be pronounced against me? I know, my lords, that the form prescribes that you should put the question. The form also confers a right of answering. This, no doubt, may be dispensed with, and so might the whole ceremony of the trial, since sentence was already pronounced at the Castle before your jury was impaneled. Your lordships are but the priests of the oracle, and I submit; but I insist on the whole of the forms.

My lord, you are impatient for the sacrifice. The blood which you seek is not congealed by the artificial terrors which usually surround your victim; it circulates warmly and unruffled through its channels, and in a little time it will go to heaven. Be patient. I have but a few more words to say—my ministry is now ended. I am going to my cold and silent grave. I have burnt out my lamp of life. I have parted with everything that was dear to me in this life for my country's cause; I have abandoned another idol that I adored in my heart. My race is run, the grave opens to receive me and I sink into its bosom. I am ready to die. I have not been allowed to vindicate my character. I have but one request to ask at my departure from this world—it is the charity of its silence. Let there be no inscription on my tomb. Let no man write my epitaph. No man can write my epitaph, for as no man who knows my motives and character dares now to vindicate them, let not prej-

456

udice or ignorance asperse them. Let them rest in obscurity and peace until other times and other men can do justice to them. When my country takes her place among the nations of the earth, *then* shall my character be vindicated, *then* may my epitaph be written.

I have done.

A PRISONER WITH A DIARY:

John Mitchel

A BLAST AGAINST MACAULAY AND BACON

DOPPELGANGER AND THE EGO

JOHN MITCHEL'S rare *Jail Journal,* which has been flattered by partisans as "the testament of Young Ireland" and "the bible of Irish nationalism," of which Arthur Griffith said that "in the political literature of Ireland it has no peer outside Swift," is one of those badly neglected books which can do with fewer epithets and more readers. The *Jail Journal* is a product of 1848, year of revolutionary hopes. Young Ireland had crossed swords with Old Ireland and aging Daniel O'Connell. Heroes had sprung from Europe: Mazzini, Garibaldi, Kossuth, Kosciusko, and all the contagious spirits of France. The leaders of Young Ireland were excited by this continental climate beyond the Irish Sea. Their militant paper, the *Nation,* was publishing verse rendering romantic homage to Kathleen ni Houlihan and Dark Rosaleen, at the same time advising hopeful Irishmen to "look at Portugal, look at Holland, look at Sweden and Prussia." The leaders of Young Ireland—Thomas Davis, Smith O'Brien, Thomas Meagher, Gavan Duffy, John Mitchel, John Dillon, and Fintan Lalor—were stirring up their own courage and the blood of their followers with ballads and feuilletons. In a campaign of "holy hatred of English rule," Davis (who died in 1845) was saying: "Oh no! Oh no! ask us not to copy English vice, and darkness, and misery and impiety; give us the worst wigwam in Ireland and a dry potato rather than Anglicize us." But even the dry potato vanished with the Great Famine of the late 'forties and with it went the little stock of patience of Young Ireland. In the midst of the greatest Irish misery old O'Connell died on a pilgrimage to Rome, and the year 1848 at last arrived with its hot breath of revolution. In Ireland the storm broke in Tipperary, a brief and abortive rebellion. Mitchel, Meagher, and O'Brien were jailed, weighted with chains, and packed off to the ends of the earth, to Van Dieman's Land which is now Tasmania. Mitchel's *Jail Journal,* written in dismal creaking cells in the bowels of the ships which were transporting him toward Bermuda, the African coast, and finally Van Dieman's Land, is alive with manly anger, intellectual ribaldry, and a rough pictorial beauty. "On this day," runs the opening sentence,

458

"about four o'clock in the afternoon, I, John Mitchel, was kidnapped, and carried off from Dublin, in chains, as a convicted 'Felon'." Thereafter the literary prisoner poured into his record diatribes and essays, landscapes and imaginary dialogues, memories and prejudices. There is no portrait of a political rebel quite like that of the *Jail Journal*. Mitchel paid no lip service to the democratic sentiments of 1848. He thought "Socialists are something worse than wild beasts" and, eventually escaping from his exile to the United States, gave the lives of two sons to the cause of slavery and the Confederacy. He would concede no moral links between Irish independence and the abolition of slavery. Henry Ward Beecher was "an eloquent, powerful, and rowdy preacher," he said, and slavery was unpalatable only to humanitarians and universalists. There are a few pieces in the *Jail Journal* in which Mitchel whips up his prejudices into a fine prose whose eloquence comes from something more than an inexhaustible stock of Irish "holy hatred." One of these remarkable pieces is Mitchel's acrimonious attack on Macaulay's best of all centuries and on Macaulay's philistine and progressive Bacon. "Through all our nineteenth-century British literature," jibes the Young Irelander in a felon's chains, "there runs a tone of polite, though distant recognition of Almighty God, as one of the Great Powers; and though not resident, is actually maintained at His Court. Yet British civilization gives Him assurances of friendly relations; and 'our venerable Church,' and our 'beautiful liturgy,' are relied upon as a sort of diplomatic Concordat, or Pragmatic Sanction, whereby we, occupied as we are, in grave commercial and political pursuits, carrying on our business, selling our cotton, and civilizing our heathen—bind ourselves, *to let Him alone, if He lets us alone*—if He will keep looking apart, contemplating the illustrious mare-milkers, and blameless Ethiopians, and never-minding us, we will keep up a most respectable Church for Him, and make our lower orders venerate it, and pay for it handsomely, and we will suffer no national infidelity, like the horrid French."

A BLAST AGAINST MACAULAY AND BACON

June 14th, 1848. On Board H.M.S. Scourge.—Gulf-weed, Portuguese men-of-war, flying-fish.

15th.—Flying-fish, Portuguese men-of-war, Gulf-weed.

16th.—Gulf-weed, flying-fish, Portuguese men-of-war.

459

17th.—Reading—for want of something better—"Macaulay's Essays." He is a born Edinburgh Reviewer, this Macaulay; and, indeed, a type-reviewer— an authentic specimen-page of nineteenth century "literature." He has the right, omniscient tone, and air, and the true knack of administering reverential flattery to British civilization, British prowess, honour, enlightenment, and all that, especially to the great nineteenth century and its astounding civilization, that is, to his readers. It is altogether a new thing in the history of mankind, this triumphant glorification of a current century upon being the century it is. No former age, before Christ or after, ever took any pride in itself and sneered at the wisdom of its ancestors; and the new phenomenon indicates, I believe, not higher wisdom, but deeper stupidity. The nineteenth century is come, but not gone; and what now, if it should be, hereafter, memorable among centuries for something quite other than its wondrous enlightenment? Mr. Macaulay, however, is well satisfied with it for his part, and in his essay on Milton penny-a-lines thus: "Every girl who has read Mrs. Marcet's little dialogues on political economy, could teach Montague or Walpole many lessons on finance. Any intelligent man may now, by resolutely applying himself for a few years to mathematics, learn more than the great Newton knew after half a century of study and meditation"; and so on. If Pythagoras, now, could only have been introduced to Mrs. Marcet, or even to one of her premium girls, how humbly would he have sat at her feet! Could Aristotle or Hipparchus but have seen Mr. Pinnock before they died, how would they have sung *nunc dimittas!* This nineteenth-century man, and indeed the century generally, can see no difference between being told a thing—conning it in a catechism, or "little dialogue"—and knowing it; between getting by heart a list of results, what you call facts, and mastering science.

Still more edifying, even than Edinburgh wisdom, is the current Edinburgh ethics. Herein, also, the world has a new development; and as I am now about to retire a little while from the great business of this stirring age, to hide me, as it were, in a hole of the rock, while the loud-sounding century, with its steam-engines, printing-presses, and omniscient popular literature, flares and rushes roaring and gibbering by, I have a mind to set down a few of Macaulay's sentences, as a kind of land-marks, just to remind me where the world and I parted. For I do, indeed, account this Reviewer a real type and recognised spokesman of his age; and by the same token he is now, by virtue of his very reviewing, too, a Cabinet Minister.

In his essay on Lord Bacon, he freely admits the treacherous, thoroughly

false, and unprincipled character of the statesmen of that age; thinks, however, we must not be too hard on them; says, "it is impossible to deny that they committed many acts which would justly bring down, on a statesman of *our time,* censures of the most serious kind" [as that a man is a liar, an extortioner, a hypocrite, a suborner]; "but when we consider the *state of morality in their age,* and the unscrupulous character of the adversaries against whom they had to contend," etc.

And the state of morality, it seems, varies, not with the age only, but with the climate also, in a wonderful manner. For the essayist, writing of Lord Clive and his villainies in India, pleads in behalf of Clive, that "he knew he had to deal with men destitute of *what in Europe is called* honour; with men who would give any promise, without hesitation, and break any promise without shame; with men who would unscrupulously employ corruption, perjury, forgery, to compass their. ends." And *they* knew that they had to deal with men destitute of *what in Asia is called honesty*—men who would unscrupulously employ corruption, perjury, forgery, etc.—so, what were the poor men to do, on *either* side?—the state of morality was so low! When one is tempted to commit any wickedness, he ought, apparently, to ascertain this point—what is the state of morality? How range the quotations? Is this an age (or a climate) adapted for open robbery? Or does the air agree better with swindling and cheating? Or must one cant and pray, and pretend anxiety to convert the heathen—to compass one's ends? But to come back to Lord Clive, the great founder of British power in India; when the essayist comes to that point at which he cannot get over fairly telling us how Clive swindled Omichund by a forged paper, he says: "But Clive was not a man to do anything by halves [too much British energy for that]. We almost blush to write it. He forged Admiral Watson's name." *Almost blush* —but not just quite. Oh! Babington Macaulay. This approximation to blushing, on the part of the blue-and-yellow Reviewer, is a graceful, touching tribute to the lofty morality of our blessed century.

For morality, *now*—Lord bless you—ranges very high; and Religion, also: through all our nineteenth-century British literature there runs a tone of polite, though distant recognition of Almighty God, as one of the Great Powers; and though not resident, is actually maintained at His court. Yet British civilization gives Him assurances of friendly relations; and "our venerable Church," and our "beautiful liturgy," are relied upon as a sort of diplomatic Concordat, or Pragmatic Sanction, whereby we, occupied as we are, in grave commercial and political pursuits, carrying on our business,

461

selling our cotton, and civilizing our heathen—bind ourselves, *to let Him alone, if He lets us alone*—if He will keep looking apart, contemplating the illustrious mare-milkers, and blameless Ethiopians, and never-minding us, we will keep up a most respectable Church for Him, and make our lower orders venerate it, and pay for it handsomely, and we will suffer no national infidelity, like the horrid French.

For the venerable Church of England, and for our beautiful liturgy, the essayist has a becoming respect; and in his essay on Hallam's Constitutional History, I find a sentence or two on this point worth transcribing. He is writing about the villains who reformed religion in England, and the other miscreants who accomplished the Glorious Revolution, and he says: "It was, in one sense, fortunate, as we have already said, for the Church of England, that the Reformation in this country was effected by men who cared little about religion. And in the same manner it was fortunate for our civil Government that the Revolution was effected by men who cared little about their political principles. *At such a crisis* splendid talents and strong passions [by strong passions he means any kind of belief or principle] might have done more harm than good." But then he immediately adds—for we must keep up an elevated tone of morality now—"But narrowness of intellect, and flexibility of principle, *though they may be serviceable,* can never be respectable." Why not? If scoundrels and blockheads can rear good, serviceable, visible churches for the saving of men, and glorious constitutions for the governing of men, what hinders them from being respectable? What else *is* respectable? Or, indeed, what is the use of the splendid talents and the strong passions at all?——

I am wasting my time, and exasperating the natural benignity of my temper, with this oceanic review of the Edinburgh Reviewer. But my time at least is not precious just now; and I will plunge into the man's essay on Lord Bacon, which cannot fail to be the most characteristic piece of British literature in the volumes.

This must be done to-morrow; for there are two sails reported in sight on the weather-bow, which is an event of high interest at sea; besides, the sun is drawing near his evening bath—a grand imperial ceremony, at which I always *assist*.

The ships in sight are—one American and one Carthaginian.

18th.—Last night, after two bells (one o'clock), I was awakened by a great trampling, pushing, hauling, and thumping on deck. Something unusual was certainly going forward. Got up; went through the cabin, and to the

foot of the companion-ladder; found the skylights of the cabin removed, and smooth deck laid in their place—the captain out on deck—the companion-ladder blocked up at the top. *The deck was cleared for action.* I heard loud words of command. Spirit of the Constitution! Has war been declared since we came to sea? Is Baudin—is Trehouart upon us? May the Powers grant it! Oh, Trehouart, Admiral of Heaven!—lay yourself alongside here. You can easily wing our accursed paddle, or send two or three fifty-pounders into us amidships, to derange the economy of our engine-room. I ran through the lieutenant's room, telling a boy who was there to run up before me and report me to my sergeant. At the foot of one of the funnels I found a ladder that brought me on deck. Ah! there was no enemy (no friend) in sight; it was only British discipline that had started British prowess from his sleep, to practise in the dead of the night. We were alone on the wide, silent sea, and were going to bombard the moon. Four times we shelled her with our huge mortar; not, if truth must be told, with actual bombshells, but with quarter-charges of powder; four times we thundered at her with our long-gun; four times with our cannonades; and then, British energy having blotted the white moonshine awhile with his gunpowder smoke, tumbled into his hammock again. No living soul, but those on board, heard that cannonade—for fishes are notoriously deaf. On the convex of the great globe we are all alone here: and even here amongst the guns the whole effect is mean, for there is no echo, and each report is a mere *belch,* far indeed from the rever-berating thunderous roll of heavy guns alongshore. It is a pitiful pyro-techny; and the black thunder-bearing *Scourge* seems, in this silent immen-sity, but a small black spiteful spitfire doing its paltry worst to trouble the still empire of great ambrosial night. But the smoke soon melts away, drift-ing off to leeward, and the solemn Moon (unharmed apparently) looks down as mildly on ship and ocean as before the battery was opened upon her. Forgive the impudent spitfire. O soft Moon! Sink her not to the depths with a discharge of thy terrible aerolite grape—for thou, too, as I do remem-ber, art potent in artillery. "What is to become of us, mortals," saith Jean Paul, "dwelling on this bare convexity, and the Moon going round bombard-ing us with stones, like a Turk!" Let there be peace between us and thee, O Τοξοφόρα! Oh, fairest huntress Ἰοχέαιρα! Call to mind those nights on Latmos, and be gracious to mortal man. We have war-engines enough, argument enough, and diabolic rage enough, to tear, blow up, crush, and batter one another—ay, enough to glut thee in thy character of Hecate, with-out thy ordnance of meteor-stones. Needs not that thou exact human sacri-

fices, beautiful Bendis! Gentle Astarte, queen of Heaven! There be ill-favoured demons enough unto whom we may immolate our brothers—Mammon and Moloch, and the truly enlightened God of civilization, fair-spoken Belial. Do thou, O Moon! wheel thy bright orbit, weave thy mystic nodes, and fill thy horns in peace!

Fine rant this.

After breakfast, when the sun burned too fiercely on deck, went below, threw off coat and waistcoat for coolness, and began to read Macaulay on Bacon—"the great English teacher," as the reviewer calls him. And to do the reviewer justice, he understands Bacon, knows what Bacon did, and what he did not; and therefore sets small store by that illustrious Chimera's new "method" of investigating truth. He is not ignorant; but knows that Lord Bacon's discovery of the inductive "method," or *Novum Organum,* is the most genuine piece of mare's-nesting recorded in the history of letters. And, to do Bacon himself justice, for all the impudence of his title (*Instauratio Scientiarum*) and the pretentiousness of his outrageous phraseology, he hardly pretended to be the original discoverer of wisdom, to the extent that many Baconians, learned stupid asses, have pretended for him. Apart from the "induction" and the "method," and the utterly inexcusable terminology (far worse even than the coinage of Jeremy Bentham), Bacon's true distinction as a "philosopher" was *this*—I accept the essayist's description—"The philosophy which he taught was essentially new. Its object was *the good of mankind,* in the sense in which the *mass of mankind* always ·have understood, and always will understand, the word *good.* The aim of the Platonic philosopher was to raise us far above vulgar wants; the aim of the Baconian philosophy was to supply our vulgar wants. The former aim was noble; but the latter was attainable." What the mass of mankind understand by the word good is, of course, pudding and praise and profit, comfort, power, luxury, supply of vulgar wants—all, in short, which Bacon included under the word *commoda;* and to minister to mankind in these things is, according to the great English teacher, the highest aim—the only aim and end—of true philosophy or wisdom. O Plato! O Jesu!

"The former aim was noble, but the latter was attainable." On the contrary, I affirm that the former aim was both noble and, to many men, attainable; the latter not only ignoble, but to all men unattainable, and to the noblest men most.

The essayist makes himself very merry with the absurdities of what they called philosophy in times of ante-Baconian darkness. "It disdained to be

useful, and was content to be stationary. It dealt largely in theories of moral perfection, which were so sublime that they never could be more than theories; it attempts to solve insoluble enigmas; in exhortations to the attainment of unattainable frames of mind. It could not condescend to the humble office of ministering to the *comfort* of human beings."

Now the truth is, that Plato and Pythagoras did not undervalue comfort, and wealth, and human *commoda* at all; but they thought the task of attending to such matters was the business of ingenious tradespeople, and not of wise men and philosophers. If James Watt had appeared at Athens or Crotona with his steam-engine, he would certainly have got the credit of a clever person and praiseworthy mechanic—all he deserved; but they never would have thought of calling him philosopher for *that.* They did actually imagine—those ancient wise men—that it is true wisdom to raise our thoughts and aspirations above what the mass of mankind calls good—to regard truth, fortitude, honesty, purity, as the great objects of human effort, and *not* the supply of vulgar wants.

What a very poor fool Jesus Christ would have been, judged by the "new philosophy,"—for His aim and Plato's were one. He disdained to be useful in the matter of our little comforts—yes, indeed, "He could not condescend to the humble office of ministering to the comfort of human beings." On the contrary, "whatsoever things are pure, whatsoever things are holy, if there be any virtue——"

Why, good Messiah! this is the mere Academy over again. Have you considered that these are unattainable frames of mind? You offer us living bread, and water which he that drinketh shall not thirst again;—very beautiful, but too romantic. Can you help us to butter the mere farinaceous bread we have got, to butter it first on one side and then on the other?—to improve the elemental taste and somewhat too paradisiac weakness of this water? These are our vulgar wants; these are what the mass of mankind agrees to call *good.* Whatsoever things are snug, whatsoever things are influential— if there be any comfort, if there be any money, think on these things. Henceforth we acknowledge no light of the world which does not light our way to good things like these.

Almost this sounds profanely; but the profanity belongs to the essayist. His comparison of Plato's philosophy with modern inventive genius is exactly as reasonable as if he had compared the Christian religion with the same. Ancient philosophy was indeed natural religion—was an earnest

465

striving after spiritual truth and good; it dealt with the supersensuous and nobler part of man; and its "aim" was to purify his nature, and give him hope of an immortal destiny amongst the enthroned gods on sainted seats.

Just so, says the essayist; that was what they called wisdom—*this* is what I, Lord Bacon and I, call wisdom. "The *end* which the great Lord Bacon proposed to himself was *the multiplying of human enjoyments and the mitigating of human sufferings.*" Anything beyond this we simply ignore; let all the inquirings, all the aspirings of mankind stop here. Leave off dreaming of your unattainable frames of mind, and be content with the truth as it is in Bacon.

I can imagine an enlightened inductive Baconian standing by with scornful nose as he listens to the Sermon on the Mount, and then taking the Preacher sternly to task—"What mean you by all this—'Bless them that curse you'—'Love your enemies'—'Be ye perfect as your Father in Heaven is perfect!' What mortal man ever attained these frames of mind? Why not turn your considerable talents, friend, to something useful, something within reach? Can you make anything?—improve anything?—You are, if I mistake not, a carpenter by trade, and have been working somewhere in Galilee; now, have you invented any little improvement in your own respectable trade? Have you improved the saw, the lathe, the plane? Can you render the loom a more perfect machine, or make a better job of the potter's wheel? Have you in any shape economised materials, economised human labour, added to human enjoyment? Have you done, or can you show the way to do, any of all these things? *No!* Then away with him! Crucify him!"

Ah! but the enlightened Briton would say, "Now you talk of religion; that is our strong point in this admirable age and country. Is not there our venerable Church?—our beautiful liturgy? There is a *department* for all that, with the excellent Archbishop of Canterbury at the head of it. If information is wanted about the other world, or salvation, or anything in that line, you can apply at the head-office, or some of the subordinate stations.

True, there is a department, and offices, and salaries, more than enough; yet the very fact is, that modern British civilisation (which may be called the child of this great British teacher) is not only not Christian, but is not so much as Pagan. It takes not the smallest account of anything higher or greater than earth bestows. The hopeless confusion of ideas that made Bacon and Macaulay institute a comparison between ancient philosophy and modern ingenuity, is grown characteristic of the national mind and heart, and foreshadows *national death.* The mass of mankind agree to call money,

466

power, and pleasure, *good;* and behold! the Spirit of the Age has looked on it, and pronounced it very good. The highest phase of human intellect and virtue is to be what this base spirit calls a philanthropist—that is, one who, by new inventions and comfortable contrivances, mitigates human suffering, heightens human pleasure. The grandest effort of godlike genius is to augment human power—power over the elements, power over uncivilised men —and all for our own comfort. Nay, by tremendous enginery of steam and electricity, and gunpowder—by capital and the "law of progress," and the superhuman power of co-operation, this foul Spirit of the Age does veritably count upon scaling the heavens. The failure of Otus and Ephialtes, of Typhæus and Enceladus, of the builders of Shinar, never daunts him a whit— for why?—*they* knew little of co-operation; electricity and steam and the principle of the arch were utterly hidden from them; civil engineering was in its infancy; how should they not fail?

The very capital generated and circulated, and utilised on so grand a scale by civilised men now-a-days, seems to modern Britons a power mighty enough to wield worlds; and its *numen* is worshipped by them accordingly, with filthy rites. The God of mere nature will, they assure themselves, think twice before He disturbs and quarrels with such a power as this; for indeed it is faithfully believed in the City, by the moneyed circles there, that God the Father has money invested in the three-per-cents, which makes Him careful not to disturb the peace of the world, or suffer the blessed march of "civilisation" to be stopped.

Semble then, first, that the peace of the world is maintained so long as it is only the unmoneyed circle that are robbed, starved, and slain; and, second, that nothing civilises either gods or men like holding stock.

But I am strong in the belief that the portentous confusion both of language and thought, which has brought us to all this, and which is no accidental misunderstanding, but a radical confounding of the English national intellect and language, a chronic addlement of the general brain, getting steadily worse now for two hundred years, is indeed more alarming than the gibbering of Babel, and is symptomatic of a more disastrous ending. By terrible signs and wonders it shall be made known that comfort is not the chief end of man. I do affirm, I—that Capital is not the ruler of the world—that the Almighty has no pecuniary interest in the stability of the funds or the European balance of power—finally, that no engineering, civil or military, can raise man above the heavens or shake the throne of God.

On that day some nations that do now bestride the narrow world will learn lessons of true philosophy, but not new philosophy, in sackcloth and ashes. And other nations, low enough in the dust now, will arise from their sackcloth and begin a new national life—to repeat, it may be, the same crimes and suffer the same penalties. For the progress of the species is circular; or possibly in trochoidal curves, with some sort of cycloid for deferent; or more properly it oscillates, describing an arc of a circle, pendulum-wise; and even measures time (by æons) in that manner; or let us say, in one word, the world wags.

Another crimson evening is upon us. The sun, in a conflagration of clouds, flames on the very rim of Ocean. He, too, the unwearied sun, is chasing his own shadow round and round the world. "The sun also ariseth, and the sun goeth down, and hasteth to his place whence he rose. All the rivers run into the sea, yet the sea is not full; unto the place from whence the rivers came, thither they return again. The waters wear the stones: Thou washest away the things which grow out of the dust of the earth; and thou destroyest the hope of man. Thou prevailest for ever against him, and he passeth." Good night.

19*th.*—One other observation upon the "great English teacher," and then I bid him farewell. Try to measure the value of him and his teaching, even in respect of human comfort, power, and luxury, the great *end* of it all. First, he never discovered, or even thoroughly learned, or, properly speaking, knew, anything himself. He had a smattering, like Lord Brougham, of the science of his age; of the one chancellor it might be said, as it has been of the other, "if he had known a little law he would then have known a little of everything." But I crave his lordship's pardon—his, now I remember, was a nobler mission—not to toil himself, amidst laboratory fumes, forges, and furnaces, but to direct others how to toil: to survey and lay out great leading paths of investigation, to take a vast comprehensive view of the whole field of science, and allot the labourers their tasks. This man, then, living in an age of extraordinary intellectual and experimental activity— shortly after Galileo had demonstrated the true solar and planetary motions and Kepler had fixed their laws—after the telescope and the mariner's compass and the printing-press had been invented (and all *without* the *Organum*) —this smattering chancellor, who never himself discovered anything, except

468

his law, is supposed to have shown quite a new way, given quite a fresh impulse and a worthy aim to "philosophy." I want the evidence; but there is none. Therefore I dogmatically affirm that no chemist, no geologist, no mechanist, physician, astronomer, engineer, or other "philosopher," ever since Bacon's day, in any investigation or series of experiments, thought once of the *instantiæ,* or the *vindemiæ,* or any of the other uncouth verbiage which makes up that preposterous book. I affirm, further, that of those men who have really carried forward science and the arts, not one in forty ever read that book—that of those who read it not one in forty understood it—and that of those who understood it, not one at all made use of it.

Hereupon the essayist, you may be sure, would tell me that although indeed they did not read, understand, or value the teachings of that book, or know the things treated of therein by Bacon's names, yet they did pursue their inquiries, and conduct their experiments with due regard to the very instantiæ of the "Organum," and gather in their vintages by the very process our great teacher taught—yes, they did so, just as Tubal Cain and Dædalus, Archimedes, Aristotle, Columbus, and Kepler did before them, and not otherwise.

What Lord Bacon really *did,* then, the whole result and upshot of his teaching—if anything at all—was this—to cause mechanical ingenuity and experimental or empiric investigations into the laws of bodies (with a sole view to use and comfort) to be substituted for *Philosophy* and dignified with that venerable name. And the popular essayist, not being an ill-informed man, nor behind, nor before his age, acknowledges that this is what Bacon did and pronounces that he did well.

Now I am tired of Macaulay and his Essays, and see with surprise that I have filled up some fourteen pages with a tirade against him. He is, after all, a very clever and dexterous artificer in words; one of the deftest of the nineteenth century. His Lay of Horatius and his ballad of Naseby might be imposed at first upon anybody, for poems, for true Song. I took them for such myself not long ago: but the thing is impossible.

> "And what's impossible can't be,
> And never, never, comes to pass."

DOPPELGANGER AND THE EGO

[On November 7, 1848, Mitchel noted in his *Jail Journal* that someone had thrown a London newspaper into his cell which gave him news for months of digestion. The leaders of the Young Ireland Movement—Smith O'Brien, Meagher, and others—had been sentenced to death, the paper reported. The French Republic of 1848 was still standing, with the "Red Republicans" and the "Communists" having attempted another Revolution, which, Mitchel thought, might have been the death of the Republic: "Socialists are something worse than wild beasts." Alas, the gentle Lamartine had disappeared from the political scene. The Carthaginian newspapers—the Carthaginians were the English, of course—were deeply distressed over the life of the French Republic, predicting a return of the monarchy; and "the aristocracy and credit-funding plutocracy of Carthage are frightened at this near neighborhood of liberty. . . . And am I, O my God! through all these crowded years of life, to sit panting here behind an iron grating, or to die an old hound's death and rot among Bermudian blattae! Infandum!"]

Last night, as my double-goer and I—for I go double—sat in my cell smoking our pipe together, the awful shade took occasion to expostulate with me in the following terms:—"I do observe," quoth he, "a singular change in you of late days; a shadow of gloom, and almost a tinge of atrocity, staining the serene empyrean of your soul; and, what is yet sadder, I behold in you what seems to be a sort of conscious obliquity of judgment and elaborate perversity of feeling, which is—that is, it appears to me—that is, if I read you aright—which is blacker than mere natural malignity."

The Ego (puffing thick clouds).—Explain; your language is unusual.

Doppelganger.—Well, then, first: What is the meaning of all this fiery zeal of yours for the French Republic? I know well that you feel no antipathy to either a monarchical or an aristocratic government, as such; that, in fact, within your secret heart, you care very little about Republicanism in the abstract.

The Ego.—Not a rush. What then?

Doppelganger.—Then I am forced to conclude that your anxiety for the success of the French Republic springs from something else than zeal for the welfare of the human race.

The Ego.—A fig for the human race; to be sure it does.

Doppelganger.—Yes; it is born of no love for mankind, or even French mankind, but of pure hatred to England, and a diseased longing for blood and carnage. You think a republic cannot long stand in France without a European war, which would smash the credit-system, cut up commerce, and in all probability take India and Canada from the British Empire—to say nothing of Ireland.

470

The Ego.—To say nothing of Ireland? But what if I were thinking of Ireland all the time?

Doppelganger.—And for the *chance* of getting Ireland severed from Britain in the dreadful *mêlée*, do you desire to see all Europe and America plunged in desperate war? For the chance of enkindling such a war, do you delight to see a great and generous people like the French, committing themselves and their children to a wild political experiment, which, as you know, is as like to breed misery as happiness to them and theirs?

The Ego—(*laying down pipe, and raising aloft an umbrageous pillar of smoke*).—Now, listen to me, Herr Doppelganger. First, I care little, indeed, about Republicanism in the abstract; but the French Republic I watch in its growth with keen and loving interest. For Republicanism, or Monarchism, *in the abstract,* is nothing—a government is a thing that governs concrete living men under absolute extant circumstances; and I regard aristocratic and monarchic institutions, how good soever in their day and place—how defensible soever "in the abstract," as being for the Western nations of Europe worn out—that is to say, worn out for the present; and until we shall have advanced to them again, *via* barbarism, in the cyclical progress of the species. For England, for Ireland especially, I believe those institutions are far more than worn out—were worn out fifty years ago, and have only been kept seemingly alive by the commercial world, and for purposes of traffic— to stave off the inevitable bankruptcy, smash, and alteration of the style and firm; but in so sustaining a fictitious credit, and pushing trade to such desperate lengths under it, those money-making people are likened unto the man who built his house upon the sand—the longer he has been able to shore it up (building additional storeys on it all the while) the greater will be the fall of it. Secondly, I hold that in all marches and counter-marches of the human race, France of right leads the van. Your Anglo-Saxon race worships only money, prays to no other god than money, would buy and sell the Holy Ghost for money, and believes that the world was created, is sustained, and governed, and will be saved by the only one true, immutable Almighty Pound Sterling. France recognises a higher national life, aspires for ever to a grander national destiny than mere trading. France mints the circulating medium of thoughts and noble passions, and sets up poor nations in business with capital of that stamp. Paris is the great moral metropolis of mankind. Thirdly, Mein Herr, the French have no right to stipulate for their own "happiness," while they discharge this high public duty. Neither for man nor nation is happiness the end of living—least of all for those who

utter new truths and lead in new paths. Let a nation act with all the energy of its national life—do with its might what its hand findeth to do—the truth it has got to utter speak it in thunder. Therein let it find its "happiness," or nowhere.

Doppelganger.—You speak as if France were fighting the republican fight for all the world, and in advance of all the world. Apparently you forget America, and where France herself went to school to learn republicanism. At any rate, the United States were a republic before ever France was one.

The Ego.—And San Marino before the United States; but I was speaking of the great ancient *nations* of feudal Europe, and the struggle and travail that is appointed them before they can slough off the coil of their decrepit or dead aristocracies and heraldries, which have come to be humbugs—a struggle which the United States never knew, nor had need to make; for those British colonies in America, once the yoke of King George was broken, found themselves republics by the necessity of the case; they had no material there whereout to form any other sort of government. The difficulty *there* would have been to *get up* a dynasty—to find the original parents out of whom to breed an hereditary aristocracy. In short, external circumstances and agencies, and mere necessity, made America Republican. But *France*— France, with all her *circumstances,* habits, traditions, tending the other way; ancient France, Mother of Chivalry, heritage of Charlemagne's peers, environed by a whole world of monarchism, landlordism, and haughtiest gentility—tearing off the clinging curse, trampling it under foot, and fronting the naked swords of all raging Europe, while she stood forth in the simple might of manhood, uncrowned, unfrocked, untabarded, showing what, after all, men can do; then, after her own hero, in whom she trusted, lifted up his heel against her, when she was hacked and hewn almost to pieces by the knives of allied butchers, hag-ridden by the horrid ghost of a dynasty, and cheated by a "citizen king,"—cherishing still, deep in her glowing heart, the great idea, through long years, through agonies and sore travail, until the days are accomplished for the god-like birth—*this,* I apprehend, is another kind of phenomenon than the Declaration of Independence. And we ought to be thankful to the good God (you and I) that we live in the days when we may reasonably hope to see this noble work consummated, though it be in flames and blood.

Doppelganger.—You say nothing in answer to my charge, that all this enthusiasm of yours is mere hatred of England.

The Ego.—No; I scorn to answer that. But what mean you by England?—

the English people, or the English Government? Do you mean those many millions of honest people who live in England, minding their own business, desiring no better than to enjoy, in peace and security, the fruits of their own industry, and grievously devoured by taxes? Or do you mean the unholy alliance of land appropriators, and fund-men, and cotton-men, who devour them? Do you mean the British nation? or do you mean what Cobbett called the *Thing?*

Doppelganger.—By England I mean, of course, all her people, and all her institutions: tradesmen and nobles, Church and State, weavers, stockholders, pitmen, farmers, factories, funds, ships, Carlton clubs, Chartist conventions, Dissenting chapels, and Epsom races. I mean that.

The Ego.—You do? Then let me tell you it is a very unmeaning kind of lumping you make; I hold that now, and for fifty years back, the best friend to the British nation is simply he who approves himself the bitterest enemy to their government, and to all their institutions, in Church and State. And thus I claim to be, not an enemy, but a friend, of England; for the British people are what *I* call England.

Doppelganger.—Excluding, of course, those cruel capitalists, mill-owners, landlords; everybody, in short, who has anything?

The Ego.—Excluding nobody! But you are aware that in every possible condition of human society, no matter how intolerable to the great majority, no matter how grievously it may cry aloud for change, there are always many fat persons right well content with things as they are—to wit, those who thrive upon things as they are. Why, in Ireland, even, are many grave and well-dressed persons (I have seen them myself in Belfast, and even in Dublin, among the fed classes)—who say, Ireland is doing reasonably well, and likely to do well. Now, in speaking of Ireland and the Irish people, I do not exclude those persons: only set at naught their opinion, and set aside their particular interests in consideration of the vital general interest. Therefore, when I say that I would cut down and overthrow, root and branch, the whole government and social arrangements of England, I am entitled also to call myself a friend to the English people, to *all* the English people— yes, to the very money-men in Lombard Street, to the very dukes, the very bishops—I would make them all turn to some honest occupation.

Doppelganger.—Do you imagine capitalists eat their money, and so make away with it out of *rerum natura?* Or that land-proprietors devour and digest the entire produce of their estates? Or, in short, that the wealthy, be they ever so malignant, *can* use their riches otherwise than by employing the

poor, and paying them for their labour? Or do you propose to enable all the poor to live without labour or wages?

The Ego.—I am not to learn from you first principles of political economy, taken out of Dr. Whately's little primer. Perhaps you will next be urging that mill-owners are not, by nature, anthropophagous, and that landlords are not, by anatomical structure, hyænas, but men. Let us suppose all those matters you have mentioned, just proved, admitted, put out of the way: they are nothing to the purpose. But the case is this—those you call capitalists are, as a body, *swindlers*—that is to say, the "commercial world" is trading on what it knows to be fictitious capital,—keeping up a bankrupt firm by desperate shifts, partly out of mere terror at the thought of the coming crash, and partly because—what often happens in bankruptcy—those who are active in the business are making their private gains in the meantime out of the already dilapidated estate—and all this is but preparing for a heavier fall and wider-spreading ruin—the more undoubting confidence in the stability of the concern is felt by fools and pretended by knaves, so much the greater number of innocent and ignorant people will have their homes desolated at last. Again, I say that fifty years ago the Crown and Realm of Britain was a bankrupt firm, and that the hollow credit system on which it has kept itself afloat is a gigantic piece of national swindling—which must end not in ruin merely, but in utter national disgrace also.

Doppelganger.—Ah! The nation is swindling itself then! I perceive you think England must be ruined by the national debt—that huge sum of money due by herself to herself.

The Ego.—Yes—due by England to herself; that is to say, due by the millions of tax-payers to the thousands who have interest enough to get themselves made tax-eaters—that is to say, due by the workers to the idlers—due by the poor to the rich—yet, incredible to tell, incurred and created at first by the idlers and the rich, to sustain a state of things which keeps them idle and rich. In short, over and above the eternal inequalities of condition in human society, which for ever doom the many to labour that the few may eat and sleep, over and above this, British policy has thrown an additional burden of eight hundred millions or so upon the working many—placed an item of that amount on the *wrong* side of the account—to make the workers, I suppose, work the better—to make them look sharp, and mind economy—lest they should wax fat and kick, possibly kick down the whole *Thing*.

Doppelganger.—But, after all, the main question as to this national debt

is, whether the objects for which it was incurred were *to the nation* worth the money, or rather worth the inconvenience of owing the money and burdening the industry of the country with the interest of it. England was certainly saved from invasion—her vast commerce and manufactures——

The Ego.—Yes, England was saved from invasion; her institutions in Church and State, from ruin; her game-preserving aristocracy from abolition and the lamp-iron; her commerce and manufactures were kept going on a fictitious basis—and India, Canada, Ireland, were debarred of their freedom. These are the things for which the eight hundred millions were squandered —and instead of incurring a never-to-be-paid debt to avert all those sad events, I tell you that, to the English people, it had been worth many a million to effect them—every one—to the Irish people worth the best blood in their veins.

Doppelganger.—But why do you keep saying fictitious basis, fictitious capital? What is there fictitious in all this commerce? Does it not hold myriads of men employed? Does it not pay them in hard money every Saturday? Does it not keep their families in comfortable houses, and clothe and feed them as only the families of British artisans can pretend to be clothed and fed? Does it not enable them to save money and realise an independence for their old age?

The Ego.—How do they invest their savings? In buying land?

Doppelganger.—No; you know well that small properties of land are not a common commodity in the market. The soil of the British islands is not just yet cut up into little fee-farms: your revolution has to come yet.

The Ego.—How then do these hard-working men secure the money they have realised, as you tell me, for an independence in their old age?

Doppelganger.—Why, in the public funds—or, in the savings-banks, which invest it for them in the same funds. And I believe, when they wish to draw out their deposits, those banks generally pay them without demur.

The Ego.—They do—the insolvent State has not yet shut its doors. Yet I do affirm that these poor honest people are laying up their savings in a fund beyond the moon—they take debentures on the limbo of fools. Why, the *last* holders of these securities will all inevitably be robbed; that grand national swindle, which is called the "national credit" (and to keep up the "stability" of which all newspapers and organs of opinion are subsidised to express *confidence,* and to vaunt daily the infinite resources of the empire)— that national credit swindle will cheat them irremediably at last. There is

475

no money, or other wealth, in those same funds: there is absolutely nothing to meet these poor people's claims—nothing but *confidence*—and they are exchanging their hard earnings for draughts of east wind.

Doppelganger.—But how well, how wonderfully it works! Consider how many people live comfortably on the yearly produce of these same debentures, and bequeath them to their children, or exchange them for farms and merchandise—and never know that the notes are but drafts of Notus and Company upon Eurus and Sons. Consider the amount of gainful business actually done upon this great national credit—the vast interests that depend upon it. Why may it not go on and expand itself infinitely, or, at least, indefinitely?

The Ego.—Because, *Because* it is the inevitable fate of mere sublunary soap-bubbles to burst, when they are blown to a certain predestined bigness—because a lie, be it never so current, accepted, endorsed, and renewed many times, is quite sure (thank God!) to get protested at last. Is it not so written in the great book of *noster* Thomas?—Written also in the yet greater books of nature and history, with an iron pen?—"Great is Bankruptcy."

Doppelganger.—Suppose all this is true—I, at least, cannot think, without pain, of the inevitable destruction of all this teeming life and healthy, glowing action. It is a bright and stirring scene.

The Ego.—But look well at the background of this fine scene; and lo! the reeky shanks and yellow chapless skulls of Skibbereen!—and the ghosts of starved Hindoos in dusky millions.

Doppelganger.—Surely these sore evils are not incurable—by wise administration, by enlightened legislation: the ghosts and skeletons are not an essential part of the picture; not necessary to the main action of the piece.

The Ego.—Absolutely necessary—nay, becoming more and more necessary every hour. To uphold the stability of the grand central fraud, British policy must drain the blood and suck the marrow of all the nations it can fasten its desperate claws upon: and by the very nature of a bankrupt concern sustaining itself on false credit, its exertions must grow more desperate, its exactions more ruthless day by day, until the mighty smash come. The great British *Thing* cannot now do without any one of the usual sources of plunder. The British Empire (that is, the imaginary *Fund*s) could not now stand a week without India—could not breathe an hour without Ireland: the *Thing* has strained itself to such a pass that (being a sublunary soap-bubble, and not a crystalline celestial sphere), the smallest *jag* will let the wind out of it, and then it must ignominiously collapse. Or you may call this

abomination a pyramid balancing itself upon its apex—one happy kick on *any* side will turn it upside down. For ever blessed be the toe of that boot which shall administer the glorious kick!

Doppelganger.—And must every new order of things in the revolutions of eternity be brought about only through a fierce paroxysm of war? Let your mind dwell for a minute on the real horrors of war.

The Ego.—Let your mind dwell a moment on the horrors of peaceful and constitutional famine; it will need no effort of imagination, for you have *seen* the thing—and tell me which is better, to pine and whiten helplessly into cold clay, passing slowly, painfully through the stages of hungry brute-ferocity—passionless, drivelling, slavering idiocy, and dim awful unconsciousness, the shadow-haunted confines of life and death, or to pour out your full soul in all its pride and might with a hot torrent of red raging blood—triumphant defiance in your eye, and an appeal to heaven's justice on your lips—*animam exhalare opimam?* Which? Nay, whether is it better that a thousand men perish in a nation by tame beggarly famine, or that fifty thousand fall in a just war? Which is the more hideous evil—three seasons of famine-slaughter in the midst of heaven's abundance, at the point of foreign bayonets, with all its train of debasing diseases and more debasing vices, or a thirty years' war to scourge the stranger from your soil, though it leave that soil a smoking wilderness? If you have any doubt which is more horrible, look on Ireland this day. "They that be slain with the sword," saith Jeremiah the prophet, "are better than they that be slain with hunger; for these pine away, stricken through for want of the fruits of the field."

Doppelganger.—I cannot see the absolute necessity of either. Those good people may not be mere idiots, after all, who look forward to the total cessation of war.

The Ego.—

> Ου γαρ πω τουτ' εστι φιλον μακαρεσσι Θεοισν
> Φυλοπιδος ληξαι πριν κεν λυκος οιν υμεναιοι.

See Aristophanes. Let me also refer you to the Homeric verse—

Doppelganger.—Let me have none of your college quotations.

The Ego.—Then give me none of your confounded cant about cessation of war. Nature has laws. Because the Irish have been taught peaceful agitation in their slavery, *therefore* they have been swept by a plague of hunger worse than many years of bloody fighting. Because they would not fight, they have been made to rot off the face of the earth, that so they might learn

477

at last how deadly a sin is patience and perseverance under a stranger's yoke.

Doppelganger.—I hear you say so; but I want some reasons. Nature has laws; but you are not their infallible interpreter. Can you argue? Can you render a reason?

The Ego.—I never do. It is all assertion. I declaim vehemently; I dogmatise vigorously, but argue never. You have my thought. I don't want you to agree with me; you can take it or leave it.

Doppelganger.—Satisfactory; but I find the Irish people draw quite a different moral lesson from late events. They are becoming, apparently, more moral and constitutional than ever; and O'Connell's son points to "Young Ireland," hunted, chained, condemned, transported, and says: "Behold the fate of those who would have made us depart from the legal and peaceful doctrines of the Liberator!" And they hearken to him.

The Ego.—And do you read Ireland's mind in the canting of O'Connell's son? or in the sullen silence of a gagged and disarmed people? Tell me not of O'Connell's son. His father begat him in moral force, and in patience and perseverance did his mother conceive him. I swear to you there are blood and brain in Ireland yet, as the world one day shall know. God! let me live to see it. On that great day of the Lord, when the kindred and tongues and nations of the old earth shall give their banners to the wind, let this poor carcase have but breath and strength enough to stand under Ireland's immortal Green!

Doppelganger.—Do you allude to the battle of Armageddon? I know you have been reading the Old Testament of late.

The Ego.—Yes. "Who is this that cometh from Edom: with dyed garments from Bozrah? This that is glorious in his apparel, travelling in the greatness of his strength? Wherefore are thou red in thine apparel, and thy garments like him that treadeth in the wine vat? I have trodden the winepress alone, and of the people there was none with me: for I will tread them in mine anger and trample them in my fury, and their blood shall be sprinkled upon my garments, and I will stain all my raiment. For the day of vengeance is in my heart." Also an aspiration of King David haunts my memory when I think on Ireland and her wrongs: *"That thy foot may be dipped in the blood of thine enemies, and that the tongue of thy dogs may be red through the same."*

Doppelganger.—Anathema! What a grisly frame of mind!

The Ego.—Ah! the atmosphere of the world needs to be cleared by a wholesome tornado. The nimble air has grown obese and heavy; charged

with azote and laden with the deleterious miasmata of all the cants that are canted. Tell me, do you believe, or rather understand, that these neighbouring West Indian islands would soon be uninhabitable to any living creature save caymans and unclean beasts, but for an occasional hurricane?

Doppelganger.—Very true; and I observe the analogy. But I do not understand that men in the West Indies get up hurricanes, or pray to heaven for hurricanes. Remember that God, in the hollow of whose hand is the cave of all the winds, sends forth His storms when He sees fit.

The Ego.—And His wars also. The difference lies only in the secondary agencies whereby the Almighty works: when tornadoes are wanted to purify the material atmosphere, He musters and embattles the tropic air-currents from Cancer to Capricornus, be they moist, dry, dense, or rare, under their several cloud-banners; and at the blowing of the thunder-trumpet they rush blindly together, crashing calamitously through cane plantations, blowing the sails off sugar-mills, and desolating colonial banks—but when the moral tornado has to blow upon the earth—when wars and revolutions (the truest moral force) are needed to purify and vivify a comatose world, then Providence uses another kind of power—to wit, *Man.* For not more surely, not more absolutely are the winds enclosed in the hollow of the Almighty hand, than are the gusts and tempests of mortal passion, or even what we deem our coolest and best regulated resolves: and when strong indignation against oppression, when pity, and pride, and sacred wrath have grown transcendental in divine rage against falsehood and wrong, and arm for desperate battle against some hoary iniquity, then *charge* in the name of the Lord of Hosts!

Doppelganger.—But a mistake may occur. In your high-blazing transcendent fury you may chance to be fighting the devil's fight.

The Ego.—Be that at the peril of every man who goeth up to the battle.

Doppelganger.—Enough, enough! I seem to smell the steam of carnage. I envy you not your bloody dreams. Though all this were as you argue—

The Ego.—I do not argue.

Doppelganger.—Well, as you harangue; yet one is not obliged to delight in the storm of human wrath and vengeance, any more than in the wasting tornado. Though it must be that this offence come, woe unto him by whom it cometh! Oh! pity and woe, if the same be his chosen mission, wherein his soul delights. In such gloating over thoughts of dying groans and hoof-trampled corpses, and garments rolled in blood, there is something ghastly, something morbid, monomaniacal—to you surely something unnatural, for

479

you have always lived peaceably. And though we were very Manichæans, and believed that the principle of destruction, disorder, and darkness were for ever to maintain unextinguishable and infinite battle with the spirit of Order and of Good, yet I cannot think he chooses the better part who enlists under the banner of Ahriman—who loves to destroy, and builds—creates— nothing.

The Ego.—Hearken once more, O Double-goer! Consider how this habitable earth, with all its rock-built mountains and flowery plains, is for ever growing and perishing in eternal birth and death—consider how the winds, and lightnings, and storms of rain and hail, and flooded rivers, and lashing seas are for ever cutting, mining, gnawing away, confringing, colliding and comminuting the hills and the shores, yea, and the sites of high-domed cities —until every mountain shall be brought low, and every capital city shall lie deep "at the bottom of the monstrous world," where Helice and Buris, Sodom and Gomorrah lie now—this, I suppose, you call destruction—but consider further how the nether fires are daily and nightly forging, in the great central furnaces, new granite mountains, even out of that old worn rubbish; and new plains are spreading themselves forth in the deep sea, bearing harvests now only of tangled *algæ,* but destined to wave with yellow corn; and currents of brine are hollowing out foul sunless troughs, choked with obscene slime, but one day to be fair river-valleys blushing with purple clusters. Now in all this wondrous procedure can you dare to pronounce that the winds, and the lightnings, which tear down, degrade, destroy, execute a more ignoble office than the volcanoes and subterranean deeps that upheave, renew, recreate? Are the nether fires holier than the upper fires? The waters that are above the firmament, do they hold of Ahriman, and the waters that are below the firmament, of Ormuzd? Do you take up a reproach against the lightnings for that they only shatter and shiver, but never construct! Or have you a quarrel with the winds because they fight against the churches, and build them not! In all nature, spiritual and physical, do you not see that some powers and agents have it for their function to abolish and demolish and derange—other some to construct and set in order? But is not the destruction, then, as natural, as needful, as the construction?—Rather tell me, I pray you, which is construction—which destruction? This destruction *is* creation: Death is Birth and

"The quick spring like weeds out of the dead."

Go to—the revolutionary Leveller is your only architect. Therefore take

courage, all you that Jacobins be, and stand upon your rights, and do your appointed work with all your strength, let the canting fed classes rave and shriek as they will—where you see a respectable, fair-spoken Lie sitting in high places, feeding itself fat on human sacrifices—down with it, strip it naked, and pitch it to the demons: wherever you see a greedy tyranny (constitutional or other) grinding the faces of the poor, join battle with it on the spot—conspire, confederate, and combine against it, resting never till the huge mischief come down, though the whole "structure of society" come down along with it. Never you mind funds and stocks; if the price of the things called *consols* depend on lies and fraud, down with them too. Take no heed of "social disorganisation"; you cannot bring back chaos—never fear; no disorganisation in the world can be so complete but there will be a germ of new order in it: sansculottism, when she hath conceived, will bring forth venerable institutions. Never spare; work joyfully according to your nature and function; and when your work is effectually done, and it is time for the counter operations to begin, why, then, you can fall a-constructing, if you have a gift that way; if not, let others do *their* work, and take your rest, having discharged your duty. Courage, Jacobins! for ye, too, are ministers of heaven.

Doppelganger.—In one word, you wish me to believe that your desire to plunge your country into deluges of slaughter arises out of philosophical considerations altogether.

The Ego.—Entirely: I prescribe copious blood-letting upon strictly therapeutical principles.

Doppelganger.—And revenge upon England, for your own private wrong, has nothing to do with it.

The Ego.—Revenge! Private wrong! Tell me! are not my aims and desires now exactly what they were two years ago, before I had any private wrong at all? Do you perceive any difference even in point of intensity? In truth, as to the very conspirators who made me a "felon," and locked me up here, I can feel no personal hostility against them: for, personally, I know them not —never saw Lord John Russell or Lord Clarendon; would not willingly hurt them if I could. I do believe myself incapable of desiring private vengeance; at least I have never yet suffered any private wrong atrocious enough to stir up that sleeping passion. The vengeance I seek is the righting of my country's wrong, which includes my own. Ireland, indeed, needs vengeance; but this is public vengeance—public justice. Herein England is truly a great public criminal. England! all England, operating through her Government:

481

through all her organised and effectual public opinion, press, platform, pulpit, parliament, has done, is doing, and means to do, grievous wrong to Ireland. She must be punished; that punishment will, as I believe, come upon her by and through Ireland; and so will Ireland be *avenged*. "Nations are chastised for their crimes in this world; they have no future state." And never object that so the innocent children would be scourged for what the guilty fathers did; it is so for ever. A profligate father may go on sinning prosperously all his days, with high hand and heart, and die in triumphant iniquity; but his children are born to disease, poverty, misery of mind, body and estate. The fathers have eaten sour grapes, and the children's teeth are set on edge. Mysterious are the works and ways of God. Punishment of England, then, for the crimes of England—this righteous public vengeance I seek, and shall seek. Let but justice be done; let Ireland's wrong be righted, and the wrong done to me and mine is more than avenged; for the whole is greater than its part. Now, Mein Herr, you have my theory of vengeance; and for such vengeance I do vehemently thirst and burn.

Doppelganger (*musing*).—He has a great deal of reason; I do begin to be of his opinion.

The Ego.—Yes; we generally come to be of one mind in the long run. But it grows late, and we have talked long enough. Let us drink our rum-ration; and I will propose to you a national toast—(*rising up and speaking solemnly*)—"ARTERIAL DRAINAGE."

Doppelganger—(*with enthusiasm*).—"Arterial Drainage!"

The Ego.—Good night.

Doppelganger.—Hark! I hear the first mate coming with his keys. Good night.

(*Doppelganger flies out of the port-hole, between the bars. The Ego tumbles into bed.*)

IRELAND OR ISOLDE:

Charles Stewart Parnell

PARNELL TO KATHERINE O'SHEA

Come, all ye gallant Irishmen, and listen to my song,
Whilst I a story do relate of England's cruel wrong.
Before this wrong all other wrongs of Ireland do grow pale,
For they've clapped the pride of Erin's Isle into could Kilmainham Jail.

It was the tyrant Gladstone, and he said unto himself,
"I nivir will be aisy till Parnell is on the shelf.
So make the warrant out in haste and take it by the mail,
And we'll clap the pride of Erin's Isle into could Kilmainham Jail."

From *The Ballad of Could Kilmainham Jail*

THE jailing of Parnell gave Irishmen two troublesome documents: Parnell's love letters to Kitty O'Shea, and the Kilmainham Treaty. Those sentimental letters nailed a modern Tristan on the cross of scandal, and the national issue of domestic morality in the love affair nearly resulted in a civil war. As for the Kilmainham Treaty, it temporarily dampened a revolution. When in 1881 the Irish leaders of the Land League were put into Kilmainham Jail as obstructionists, Parnell had more than Ireland to worry him. His mistress, Mrs. O'Shea, was expecting his child. The "Chief," the "uncrowned king of Ireland," could allay her anxiety—and his own—only by writing to her the heretical assurance that Ireland was less important than love. Those rather commonplace letters to another man's wife by a great leader of almost epic pride are, to M. M. O'Hara, "amongst the hardest pills Parnell's biographer has to swallow. . . . One tolerates the infantile simplicities of Swift's correspondence to Stella, for they are in keeping with the freshness of his charmer, Stella, but prattling endearments," he says, "are sickening in a callous and guilty amour." How guilty Parnell's "amour" was, how compromising to leadership in Catholic Ireland, how distasteful to the Protestant morality of home rulers and Gladstone in England—all this was the passionate subject of a civil war which rent Ireland and broke the pride and life of the "Chief" at the age of forty-five. "No man is great in Ireland," Parnell grieved, "until he is 'dead and unable to do more for his country." But in the seven months at Kilmainham Jail (this was ten years before the notorious divorce case and the tragic deposition of the "Chief"

483

from leadership in Committee Room No. 15) Parnell's attention was equally divided between the *No Rent Manifesto*—and Katie's confinement. As Shane Leslie remarks, "the destiny which gave him the leadership of the Irish apparently made her its secret condition." But prison was not too uncomfortable, with Parnell playing chess and handball and William O'Brien still writing editorials for *United Ireland*,[1] with game which was poached by Irish tenants and with woolen things which were embroidered by Irish ladies all pouring solace into Kilmainham Jail. As it happened, Parnell objected to anything woven in green by Irish ladies. Parnell, who violated all orthodoxy in Irish leadership by being a landlord, handsome, proud, and a Protestant, would say: "How can you expect a country to have luck that has green for its color?" The Land League issued its *No Rent Manifesto* from jail. It declared a strike against landlords over a body of signatures whose addresses were unanimously original: Charles Stewart Parnell, President, *Kilmainham Jail;* A. J. Kettle, Honorary Secretary, *Kilmainham Jail;* Michael Davitt, Honorary Secretary, *Portland Prison;* Thomas Brennan, Honorary Secretary, *Kilmainham Jail;* Thomas Sexton, Head Organizer, *Kilmainham Jail;* Patrick Egan, Treasurer, *Paris.* Parnell had been arrested in October 1881; by February 1882 Mrs. O'Shea was delivered of a girl. The infant's illness brought to a head the deep anxiety between the lovers. This domestic crisis, and the political exertions of both Captain and Mrs. O'Shea, ended in the release of Parnell for renewed negotiations with Gladstone. As the famous Kilmainham Treaty was being negotiated in one room of the O'Shea household, the love-child was dying in another. More charitable than O'Hara and other Irishmen, St. John Ervine quotes these lines from Thomas Hardy in extenuation of Parnell and Kitty O'Shea:

> Judge them not harshly in a love
> Whose hold on them was strong;
> Sorrow therein they tasted of,
> And deeply, and too long.

---

[1] Of all the Irish political prisoners, William O'Brien (1852–1928) wielded perhaps the most prolific pen in jail. Shut up with Parnell and others in Kilmainham, O'Brien not only contrived to supply *United Ireland* with leaders and editorials, but it was he who drafted that historical document of Irish nationalism, the *No Rent Manifesto,* a jail composition smuggled out into the world outside on the back of a pink telegram. Under the Balfour regime and the Coercion Act of 1887, O'Brien was given sufficient leisure in other prisons to compose love letters to Sophie Raffalovich, the Frenchwoman who admired him at long distance from Paris and eventually married him, and also to write *When We Were Boys* on prison foolscap, a talented nationalist novel very popular in 1890 and which Mademoiselle R⸍ffalovich was most eager to translate into French.

PARNELL TO KATHERINE O'SHEA

October 21, 1881.

MY OWN DARLING WIFIE,—I wrote you a short note this afternoon, which I succeeded in getting off safely. Now after we have been all locked up safely for the night, and when everything is quiet and I am alone, I am going to send my own Queenie some news. But first I must tell you that I sleep exceedingly well, and am allowed to read the newspapers in bed in the morning, and breakfast there also, if I wish.

I want, however, to give you a little history from the commencement of my stay here.

When I heard that the detectives were asking for me a terror—one which has often been present with me in anticipation—fell upon me, for I remembered that my darling had told me that she feared it would kill her; and I kept the men out of my room while I was writing you a few hasty words of comfort and of hope, for I knew the shock would be very terrible to my sweet love.

I feared that I could not post it, but they stopped the cab just before reaching the prison and allowed me to drop the letter into a pillar-box. My only torture during those first few days was the unhappiness of my queen. I wired Mrs. S. to know how you were, but the wire was sent back with a note that it could not be delivered as she had gone to R. Finally your first letter came, and then I knew for the first time that you were safe. You must not mind my being in the infirmary. I am only there because it is more comfortable than being in a cell, and you have longer hours of association, from 8 a.m. to 8 p.m., instead of being locked up at 6 and obliged to eat by yourself. The infirmary is a collection of rooms, and each has a room to himself—Dillon is in a cell, but he is allowed as a special privilege to come over and associate with us during the daytime. I am obliged to invent little maladies for myself from day to day in order to give Dr. Kenny an excuse for keeping me in the infirmary, but I have never felt better in my life. Have quite forgotten that I am in prison, and should very much miss the rattle of the keys and the slam of the doors. The latest discovery is heart affection.

The only thing I don't like is that the Government insist upon sending a lot of police into the gaol every night, two of whom sleep against my door and two more under my window. Just at present we are all in great disgrace on account of the manifesto, and the poor warders have been most

of them dismissed and fresh ones brought in. A very strict watch is kept, and I have been obliged to exert my ingenuity to get letters out to you and to get yours in return. If Wifie is very good and becomes strong and happy again I may let her come over and see me after a time, but for five days more I am not to be allowed to see any visitor, but I will write you again about your coming. They have let us off very easily. I fully expected that we should have been scattered in different gaols through the country as a punishment, but they evidently think no other place safe enough for me. Indeed, this place is not safe, and I can get out whenever I like, but it is probably the best policy to wait to be released. And now good-night, my own dear little Wifie. Promise your husband that you will sleep well and look as beautiful when we meet again as the last time I pressed your sweet lips.

YOUR OWN HUSBAND.

November 5, 1881.

My DARLING WIFIE,—When I received your dear letter to-day I had just time to send you a few hasty lines in acknowledgment; now when everything is quiet and with your own sweet face before me I can give my thoughts up entirely to my Queen, and talk to you almost as well as if you were in my arms. It seems to me a long, long time since our hasty good-bye, although the first three weeks of my present life—which term will have been completed to-morrow morning—has seemed only a moment. I often feel very sad when I think of poor, unhappy Katie waiting for her husband who does not come any longer as he used to come, but who will come again to her and will not again leave her.

I am trying to make arrangements that my own Queenie may come to me this time. I shall ask my ruler here if I may see my cousin, "Mrs. Bligh, who is coming from England to see me," in his office, and with only himself present. After all, darling, the only way in which I could have escaped being here would have been by going to America, and then I could not have seen you at all, and I know I should not have been so happy or so comfortable in America as here, and, besides, I should have been beset by so many dangers there.

I admire supremely my life of ease, laziness, absence of care and responsibility here. My only trouble is about your health and happiness, and this has been my only trouble from the first. Queenie, then, will see that she also must try not to be so unhappy, especially as her husband's love is becoming stronger and more intense every hour and every day.

486

You will be anxious to know what my short illness was about. It was of a very unromantic kind—not the heart, but the stomach. I had not much appetite for some days, and was tempted by a turkey to eat too much, thence very severe indigestion and considerable pain for about an hour. However, "our doctor," by means of mustard and chlorodyne, got me all right again, and my appetite is now as good as ever. In fact, I have gotten over very quickly the "mal du prison" which comes on everybody sooner or later more or less severely.

One of the men in this quarter who has been here for nearly nine months, poor fellow, looks after me as if he was my—brother, I was going to say, but I will substitute Mary.[2] He makes me a soda and lemon in the morning, and then gives me my breakfast. At dinner he takes care that I get all the nicest bits and concocts the most perfect black coffee in a "Kaffee Kanne" out of berries, which he roasts and grinds fresh each day. Finally, in the evening, just before we are separated for the night, he brews me a steaming tumbler of hot whisky. He has marked all my clothes for me also, and sees that the washerwoman does not rob me. Don't you begin to feel quite jealous?

I am going to ask Katie to put her proper initials upon the inner envelope of her next letter—thus, K.P. Your writing on the outside envelope on the one which came to-day will do splendidly.

I do not think there is the least possibility of my being moved; this is the strongest place they have, and they are daily trying to increase its strength according to their own notions, which are not very brilliant. My room is very warm and perfectly dry. They wanted me to go to another, which did not face the sun, but I refused, so they did not persist.

With a thousand kisses to my own Wifie, and hoping soon to lay my head in its old place.

Good-night, my darling.

December 14, 1881.

My darling Queenie,—Your second letter reached me all right, and I can read them perfectly. But, my darling, you frighten me dreadfully when you tell me that I am "surely killing" you and our child.

I am quite well again now, my own, and was out to-day for a short time,

---

[2] Mrs. O'Shea's parlormaid.

and will take much better care of myself for the future. It was not the food, but a chill after over-heating myself at ball. But I do not intend to go back on prison fare, even nominally, again, as the announcement that we were on it has served the purpose of stimulating the subscription.

Rather than that my beautiful Wifie should run any risk I will resign my seat, leave politics, and go away somewhere with my own Queenie, as soon as she wishes; will she come? Let me know, darling, in your next about this, whether it is safe for you that I should be kept here any longer.

Your own Husband.

There can be no doubt we shall be released at opening of Parliament, but I think not sooner.

Dr. K. was allowed to be with me at night while I was ill, and we are not to be changed from our rooms.

OF THE IRISH EARTH:

Michael Davitt

LECTURES TO A PET BLACKBIRD, OR THE ANATOMY OF THE UNDERWORLD:

Preface to a Blackbird

First Lecture to a Blackbird, or The Thievocracy

Second Lecture to a Blackbird, or A Lesson in Slang

Third Lecture to a Blackbird, or Birds in a Cage

Epilogue to a Blackbird

~~~~~~

Parnell, an aristocrat; Davitt, a peasant. Parnell, bearing visibly a noble lineage; Davitt, with the marks of hard toil and cruel fate upon him. Parnell, in his young energy, unimpaired by trouble or privation; Davitt, young, too, but wrecked by the horrors of the jail. Parnell, touched with the culture of one of the ancient universities; Davitt, his own teacher at stolen moments. Parnell, with an old and historic right to political prominence in Ireland; Davitt, whose origin was lost in the confused history of the common people.

M. M. O'HARA, *Chief and Tribune: Parnell and Davitt*

THE great potato famine and a landlord's eviction gave Michael Davitt a Fenian elementary education. He improved these first lessons by losing an arm as a child laborer in an English factory, later by conspiracy and gun-running, and by spending the years of his young manhood in oakum picking, stone breaking, cart loading, and observing the rules of silence at Dartmoor Jail for six years. Fenian romanticism hardened into practical doctrine. Nevertheless he came out of his schooling a man of warm and quick sensibility, father of that Land League which told the Irish peasantry: "Hold a firm grip on your homesteads." On the day he returned to Mayo bonfires blazed on the hillside. He met Parnell and found in him "an Englishman of the strongest type, moulded for an Irish purpose." He made himself the ambassador of Irish nationalism before Fenian audiences in America and working-class circles in England. He tried to steer Irish independence between Fenian revolution and Parnell's parliamentarianism. In 1881 he began a term of fifteen months in Portland Jail, months during which the Land League which he had founded was suppressed, the *No Rent Manifesto* issued over his prison address, Parnell's Kilmainham Treaty negotiated with Gladstone, and Davitt's own campaign for land nationalization repudiated. Davitt went far from Ireland to round off his education. He learned from

Henry George and the socialists. He traveled to Pretoria during the Boer War to pay his respects to the victims of imperialism. He saw the terrible effects of the Kishineff pogrom on the Jews of Russia and became aware of the claims and the regenerative spirit of a contemporary nationalist force, the Zionist movement. He applied his broad education in Dartmoor Jail to agitation for prison reform, having brought out of his cell one of the rarest manuscripts of its kind, one which mingled an imaginative inquiry into the strange lives of thieves, swindlers, card sharpers, and confidence tricksters, with a projection of the Irish land question and the ideas of socialism. F. Hugh O'Donnell, a historian with a constitutional viewpoint in Irish politics, pays off a partisan score against Michael Davitt. Faced with this one-handed man who was neither provincial nor dull, an Irish peasant leader who had dared to remark of the proud and handsome and aristocratic Parnell that "he had neither wit nor humor, eloquence or the passion of conviction, Irish accent, appearance or mannerism," O'Donnell sketches the following not too ungracious portrait:

Thither came tall, gaunt and worn Michael Davitt, with the Socialist's dream in his eyes and unappeasable wrath against the existence of feudalism. A true brother of Tom Paine and Rousseau, and very far from O'Neils and O'Donnells, ancient and modern. An infant in Ireland but an English-trained workman copiously ill-read and uneducated by the Mechanics Institute, inspired by the hot wine of Fenianism, a finer instrument of cosmopolitan discontent has never been draped in a tattered copy of the uniform of Robert Emmet. Parnell might have been a Nationalist. Davitt was a humanitarian Jacobin. Generally speaking a truth-loving man. As fit to counsel statesmanlike patriotism as a blind fiddler to manoeuvre the Channel Fleet.[1]

LECTURES TO A PET BLACKBIRD, OR THE ANATOMY OF THE UNDERWORLD

Preface to a Blackbird

I WAS remitted to Portland Prison on the third of February, 1881. Shortly afterwards, through the kindness of the governor, a young blackbird came into my possession. For some months I relieved the tedium of my solitude by efforts to win the confidence of my companion, with the happiest results. He would stand upon my breast as I lay in bed in the morning and awaken

---

[1] Quoted by Shane Leslie in his *Studies in Sublime Failure* from *A History of the Irish Parliamentary Party* by F. Hugh O'Donnell.

me from sleep. He would perch upon the edge of my plate and share my porridge. His familiarity was such that on showing him a small piece of slate pencil, and then placing it in my waistcoat pocket, he would immediately abstract it. He would perch upon the edge of my slate as it was adjusted between my knees, and watching the course of the pencil as I wrote, would make the most amusing efforts to peck the marks from off the slate. He would "fetch and carry" as faithfully as any well-trained dog. Towards evening he would resort to his perch, the post of the iron bedstead, and there remain, silent and still, till the dawning of another day, when his chirrup would again be heard, like the voice of Nature, before the herald of civilization, the clang of the prison bell at five o'clock.

One evening as "Joe" sat upon the perch, it occurred to me to constitute him chairman and audience of a course of lectures: and with him constantly before me as the representative of my fellow creatures, I jotted down what I have substantially reproduced in the following pages.

First Lecture to a Blackbird, or The Thievocracy

To this class belongs both the higher and middle ranks of the aristocracy of crime—professional burglars, "honorable" thieves, professional swindlers, members of the "long firm," and dealers in "snide" (base coin). Ninety per cent. of this class will have more or less acquaintance with minor imprisonment before entering penal servitude, while many "professors" will reckon from two to four experiences of convict life. This class looks with contempt upon all "low" thieves, and repudiates the mean or "cadger" order of crime as discreditable to the profession of thieving. They form the most singular and interesting study of all the criminal classes. It is to them that the phrase "honor among thieves" refers. They never "round" upon each other, while they hold all "coppers" (prison informers) in detestation. They are an intelligent class of men, as a rule, though very deficient in common sense and common prudence in the regulation of their ordinary conduct when out of prison. Regard for honesty, religion, or morality they have none whatever, except what portion of the latter virtue may be comprised within the practice not to rob or betray an associate, or operate upon the working or poorer classes when prosecuting their "honorable" calling in society. Had their earlier years been identified with other than criminal associations, they would belong to the skilled artisan class of Englishmen. All the mechanical work required in a convict prison is performed by their labor.

To be considered a member of this order, and be credited with having done a "big job" in one's time, is the ambition of the less accomplished thieves, and is what they invariably report themselves to be among "flats," *i.e.,* the ignorant section of convicts who are outside the "profession." London, of course, supplies the greater portion of this class to the convict prisons, and these metropolitan adepts in crime have a very inferior opinion of all the provincial or foreign artists belonging to the same calling. Numbers of them have travelled abroad, and have tried their hands and tools in Belgium, France, and America. They all agree in the opinion that the latter is the most difficult and dangerous country in which to do a "burst" (burglary). The Yankees are admitted to be very cute in guarding their wealth, and make very little scruple in giving the contents of a revolver to any one who ventures for those of a desk or safe. I have conversed with several cracksmen who have been in Egypt, Russia, Turkey, and other foreign lands. Many of them while in prison study French, German, mechanics, and chemistry; and I have found a few clever linguists among their number. In reply to questions as to why they did not turn their energies and talents to honest and industrial pursuits, their answer, as a general rule, was that there is an amount of excitement and pleasure in the life of a cracksman unknown in that of an ordinary wage-paid toiler. Efforts to reform this class rarely if ever prove successful. Their good conduct in prison is partly the outcome of a resolve not to bring additional punishment upon themselves, or to prolong their imprisonment by insubordination, and partly the result of experience produced by former terms of imprisonment. They are generally sold or betrayed to the detectives by the abandoned creatures with whom they spend the "swag" after a successful enterprise. They declare this to be the way in which they are "lagged" (arrested), when not taken in the performance of a "job," and not through the cleverness of the detectives. They consequently hold the fair sex in far less estimation, as human beings, than either Turk or Heathen Chinee.

When a young thief belonging to the next class wishes to pass himself off on a "flat" as a professional, he will ask his auditor if he knows Nobby from the Dials, Jack Somebody from the New Cut, or Bill Somethingelse from Golden Lane; adding superlative slang encomiums to the particular forte of each, and recounting with an I-took-part-myself-in-it air such recent burglaries or clever "lifts" as may have excited unusual interest in the public press.

I well recollect the excitement which the advent of one of these sham

heroes to the exercise yard of Millbank caused among the pick-pocket fraternity, after he had announced himself as having got seven "stretch" (years) for clearing out a jeweller's shop in Manchester. He had "planted the swag" (hid the plunder) before being caught, where it would be safe until he was "chucked up" (released), when he would dispose of it in Belgium or Holland, buy a race horse, and live the life of a swell in future. Lord Wolseley, recounting his exploits amid a company of volunteers or new recruits, would not excite half the envy which this young thief, who was known as "Flash Johnson," created in the convict circle into which his sentence introduced him. He preceded me to Dartmoor, where I found his fame even more loudly trumpeted than ever, especially by Manchester "hooks" (pickpockets), who boast of being the rivals of the "Cocks," or Londoners, in the art of obtaining other people's property without paying for it. Unfortunately for fame that does not rest upon actual deeds, and for reputation not genuinely acquired, one of Flash Johnson's "pals" arrived in Dartmoor one day, in company with a fresh batch of prisoners from Millbank, and soon brought down the renown of the hitherto worshipped hero to the very dust, by relating that there was not one word of truth in Johnson's yarn; as he had been "lagged" for having "sneaked" a costermonger's barrow and contents! Johnson never lifted his diminished head again during his stay in Dartmoor; and doubtless his ambition upon regaining liberty will be to perform some "great act" which will entitle him to the envy and admiration of his companions in crime.

Not the least efficacious of the remedies proposed for the diminishing of the criminal classes would be the entire separation of the young pick-pocket of first conviction from the criminals I am treating of in this sketch of Class II while in prison.

I found many of this class to be men of very good address, possessing a fair knowledge of political and passing events, and bearing little or no trace of their following in any of their belongings, except in their use of slang expressions. They would pass in hotels or in railway trains as men of business among people who would have no experience of criminal character. They may be divided into experts or scientific, and less skilled thieves. The former make hotels, jewellers' shops, offices, and mansions where valuable plate is known to be, their field of operation; not despising lower booty should a good chance present itself of obtaining it. They will often spend weeks, and sometimes months, in maturing their plans for a big "burst," and work in partnerships of two or more, as the nature of the "job" may

require. To obtain the requisite knowledge of the interior of a place which is "spotted" for operations, the game of "sweethearting the slavey" is gone through by the best-looking member of the gang. If a certain number of interviews with a servant can thus be obtained, it becomes an easy matter to learn the habits of the household, the character for vigilance of the nearest "bobby," and the other necessary particulars for the successful carrying out of the "burst."

Burglars seldom receive more than twenty per cent of the value of their booty from the buyers to whom they dispose of it, if it happens to be in any other form than coin. A 10*l.* Bank of England note will bring but 2*l.* from a buyer, while 100*l.* worth of plate would be only worth 15*l.* or 20*l.* to the thief who would risk years of liberty in obtaining it; and so on of all other valuables. If the stories told by these criminals can be credited, many men of apparent stainless character in the commercial world owe most of their wealth to direct dealing with professional thieves.

The less skilled section of this class work in a peculiar manner, generally having a woman as an accomplice. The "lady" is often the direct agent in obtaining the "swag." She is not a prostitute, but cohabits with her partner as long as they are mutually agreeable, and profitable, to each other. The possession of one of these lady artists who may be renowned for cleverness, is an object of much desire and professional wooing among her male admirers. Two essential points in her equipment must be good looks and ladylike address and carriage, as these are the weapons with which she operates. She must, above all things, be well dressed.

Thus "rigged," she makes her descent upon a fashionable jeweller or dealer in other costly articles of female luxury, often driving to the establishment in a respectable hired carriage. Her plan is to obtain the inspection of as many valuable articles as possible before making a purchase, exhibiting a make-believed well-filled purse, etc., while engaged in examining the goods, then buying a few trifles, and pilfering whatever can be secured without the knowledge of the dealer or shopman. All the arts known to the class of mortals termed "coquettes" may be called into requisition for exercise in an enterprise of this description; while "palming" diamonds, exchanging paste for genuine jewelry, etc., form additional parts of the lady's accomplishments. The "gentleman" is usually on guard outside, ready to secure the "swag" when "Miss Courtney, of Belgravia," or "Miss Florence Beaumont, of Kensington," shall have completed her purchases and be driven away.

When the male professor tries his hand in his particular line, the lady

becomes the aide-de-camp. A Miss Brown, Jones, or Robinson, from London, Manchester, or Glasgow, puts up at some first-class country hotel, watering-place, or other such resort of fashionable people, where numerous guests are known to be staying. A Mr. Wilberforce, or some other respectable sounding name, will arrive a day before or after, at the same hotel, from some city or place in the country, and stay a week or two. No intercourse will take place between the accomplices while in the hotel, at least to the observation of the other guests. The gentleman, after becoming acquainted with the house, and discovering where the parties are located who are believed to have most cash or valuables, will go to work in day or night, as best suits his plans, and with skeleton keys help himself to whatever plunder may fall in his way. This is usually given to Miss Brown for security, who will be one of the first to report the loss of her purse, or gold watch, after the thief has absconded. As a rule, the proprietors prefer making good the damage rather than allow their hotels to figure in the papers as having harbored such characters, and thereby sustain discredit to its reputation as a safe and respectable house. Miss Brown, Jones, or Robinson leaves, of course, in a few days afterwards, loudly complaining, and resolving never to stay in another hotel without giving her jewels or valuables to the proprietor on her arrival.

The lady thief also lends assistance when a burglary is to be attempted in a street or open thoroughfare, where the "copper" patrols. To do this requires that she shall play the part of an unfortunate, to the extent of parading in the neighborhood, while she is acting as a sentinel on the policeman, during the time that her chums are making an entrance into, or clearing out, the place selected for the "burst." Should the policeman make his appearance at a critical point of the operation, the woman will feign drunkenness, "go for" the policeman's whisker, and allow herself to be taken into custody, screaming, struggling, and employing other feminine stratagems while in the act of being "run in." She may get seven, fourteen, or twenty-one days in the Bridewell for creating a disturbance in the public streets; but her confederates will, in all probability, have succeeded in their little game, through her self-sacrificing action having removed the enemy from the immediate neighborhood of the enterprise.

Second Lecture to a Blackbird, or A Lesson in Slang

. . . Not only on the walls of that-never-to-be-forgotten black hole, but on the cell-walls and doors in all my subsequent wanderings in penal life—in Millbank, Dartmoor, Portsmouth, and Portland—have I spent hours in de-

495

ciphering the records of "famous" deeds and particular "professions," dates of sentences and the penalties awarded to the strange beings who had preceded me along that slow, weary, and heartsore journey of punishment.

Fuller accounts of the professions and proficiency of the occupants would be sure to be always found upon the cell slate, written by them for the envious admiration of the prisoner who was next to be located there. These histories, invariably written in slang, have afforded me much amusement at times, and have been a means, among others, of aiding me in the mastery of the criminal vocabulary, which I have so frequently used in these sketches.

Young thieves would, of course, "blow their own horn" in narrating their sentences and exploits, by taking credit for imaginary deeds of fame, not "honestly" acquired; but old hands could be easily traced in the terse expressions which would record—

"A burst in the City. Copped while boning the swag. 7 stretch, 1869. Roll on 1876. Cheer up, pals."

Another—

"Hook. 7 ys. Roll on time."

Another—

"Bob White from the Dials. 5 stretch for slugging a copper."

"Little Dickey from the New Cut. 10 and a ticket. Put away by a moll" (sold by an unfortunate).

And such like information, on through the whole category of crime.

The great majority of convicts hide their real under assumed names, many of them having a fresh "monicker" (name) each conviction, to be dropped, for obvious reasons, upon release. The giving of names, therefore, in these sketches, reveals nothing that would injure the persons who were the bearers while undergoing their "laggings."

A letter, of which the following is an exact copy was left, by a prisoner in one of the cells which I occupied after receiving sentence in Newgate. It afforded much amusement to the officers of that prison, who kept it in that particular cell, and who called my attention to it upon my removal thereto, in order, I believe, to distract my mind from the sentence that had been passed upon me a couple of days previously.

"Shor ditch—1870.

"DEERE JIM
"i was in quod, doin 14 days when i heerd you was lagged i blakked Polly S——'s peepers who called me names she was fuddled and hit me fust, when i kolered her nut and giv her a fine slugging and her mug was all over blud the

496

spiteful thing bit me she did, an funked fight, when we were both taken by the Kopper, and the beek only giv me 14 days, and her got 21 for hitten me fust and been fuddled, cheer up Jim i am sorry wot you are lagged, and i wont pal with nobody wile your in quod. good by Jim from your tru luv   SALLY."

Whether this is the fair one whom the song of the period described—

> "Her fighting weight was thirteen stone,
> And her maiden name was Sarah,"

I know not; but her love-letter to poor Jim was the means of eliciting from me the first laugh in which I felt inclined to indulge in that early stage of penal servitude.

A pickpocket told me the history of his arrest one day in the following language:—

"I was jogging down a blooming slum in the Chapel when I butted a reeler who was sporting a red slang. I broke off his jerry and boned the clock, which was a red one, but I was spotted by a copper who claimed me. I was lugged before the beak, who gave me six doss in the Steel. The week after I was chucked up I did a snatch near St. Paul's, was collared, lagged, and got this bit of seven stretch."

In English this would read as follows:—

"As I was walking down a narrow alley in Whitechapel I ran up against a drunken man who had a gold watch-guard. I stole his watch, which was gold, but was seen by a policeman, who caught me and took me before the magistrate who gave me six months in the Bastille [Middlesex House of Detention, so named by thieves]. When I was released I attempted to steal a watch near St. Paul's, but was taken again, convicted, and sentenced to seven years' penal servitude."

The use of slang in prisons is prevalent only among the lower order of thieves, but is, of course, employed by all habitual criminals when in company, or on the theft path outside. Some of the pickpocket fraternity are so addicted to it that their true character might be inferred from its almost constant presence in their conversation.

Thieves' Latin, an improvement upon slang, is more a special criminal method of speech than the ordinary slang, and is of general use among the professional burglar and "hook" orders of thief when in pursuit of game. Its chief peculiarity consists in reversing the position of the syllables of a word containing more than one syllable, and making two syllables of all words having only one in ordinary pronunciation by adding a vowel or liquid

consonant to the first or second part of such word. By the application of this simple rule to slang words the "lingo" becomes too complicated for any but the initiated to understand. For instance, if two thieves were prowling for game, and one were to see a policeman, he would shout to his comrade—

"Islema! Ogda the opperca!" which in slang is—"Misle! Dog the copper!" otherwise—"Vanish! See the policeman!"

If a pair of confederates were in company with some "flat," or easily deceived person whom they were about to fleece, the lingo would be used as a means by which they would intercommunicate their impressions of the victim in his hearing, and give directions what was best to do in order to obtain his money—

"A uffma, ill olloswa a alewha. Itchpa the idesna, or mpo the ukedo in the obfa," would be some of the phrases needed for such an emergency.

In ordinary slang the foregoing would stand as follows—"He is a muff, and will swallow a whale. Pitch the snide, or put your duke in his fob"; and translated into English would read—"He is such a confounded ass that he will stand almost anything. Try the counterfeit coin, or pick his pocket."

As some words will not admit very well of the necessary transposition of syllables needed to disguise the talk from listening victims or enemies, the first syllables of such words, if immediately following each other, will change places, so that the first syllable, letter, or letters of the second word will become that or those of the first word, and *vice versa*. For instance, if Jack had made the discovery that a person whom himself and Bill were following had only a silver watch, the disgusting fact would be told to Jack as follows:—

"I jay, Sack, the okleblo's wack's clite," which in slang would be—"I say, Jack, the bloke's clock is only a white one"; and in English—"The fellow's watch is only silver."

The letters "J" and "s" of the words "Jack" and "say" are exchanged; the ordinary lingo rule is followed in reference to the word "bloke" and the "cl" of the word "clock," and "w" of "white" are exchanged as in the case of the letters "J" and "s."

Third Lecture to a Blackbird, or Birds in a Cage

I am not about to include in this lecture the mighty muse of a Tasso, or the amorous elegances of a Lovelace or a Waller, or other distinguished patrons of Pegasus who may have strung their lyres and sent forth tuneful song

while held in durance vile. My votaries of that steed of song are, as yet, entirely unknown to poetic fame, and I very much fear that such of their performances as a treacherous memory will permit me to rescue from the tablets of cell-doors, skilly-cans, bottoms of dinner-tins, and the less oblivious pages of whitewashed walls, will scarcely rank them among the inspired community of immortal songsters.

Chateaubriand has remarked that man or bird is never so prone to sing as when caged. Whether this be really so or not I cannot venture to say, but certain I am that the criminal "muse" would never be heard,·if—

> "Stone walls did *not* a prison make
> Nor iron bars a cage"

for jail-bird "poets." The "poetry" of prison walls, cell-doors, slates, can-bottoms, tin knives, and margins of books must, in the first place, be necessarily of a fragmentary nature, and be wanting in that descriptive power which would require for its exposition more stanzas than one, or more lines than from four to twelve—the ordinary range of most poetic flights of convict genius. In almost every other respect it must also suffer in· the important point of execution, owing chiefly to the fact that all such performances, no matter how truly inspired or instinctive with condensed thought or beauty, are held to be by prison critics—that is, warders—"defacing" the walls, doors, etc., and are made a vulgar question of bread and water to the hungry author when translated on a slip of paper in the form of a report for the final opinion of that stern reviewer, the governor. There is no prohibition, however, in regard to the use of a slate, but unfortunately my reading has been almost exclusively confined to the contents of the former more circumscribed mediums of written convict song. I noticed that Clerkenwell House of Detention failed to evoke a single poetic sentiment, or to stir a particle of the divine. fire in its inmates, while *in transitu* to liberty or other stage of imprisonment. Newgate gave birth to but a very selfish sentimentality or the severely sarcastic, notwithstanding its historic record. Millbank seemed to inspire a livelier strain, with wider sympathies, while the sarcasm which it also evoked was a means by which disappointed gourmands revenged themselves upon the culinary *chef* of that famous establishment. Dartmoor and Portsmouth gave each their peculiar idiosyncrasies to the widening stream of breathing thought and burning word. This poetic development in proportion to the degrees of captivity represented by the foregoing stages of waiting trial, conviction, probationary existence and the full crea-

tive influence of heavier tasks and fuller rations, with correspondingly growing experiences of Chateaubriand's cage, seems to bear out that famous writer's theory in a very conclusive manner.

The first book which I was given to read in Newgate had been in the hands of two poets of an opposite school of feeling when inditing their respective contributions to the spare margins of that volume. The first, who was evidently of the sentimental class, poor fellow, had written—"Good-bye, Lucy dear," throughout the book, upwards of as many times as the love-smitten hero of *As You Like It* had carved the name of Rosalind on the trees of Arden Forest, ere he ventured to clothe his feelings in more musical language, but finally dashed off—

> "Good-bye, Lucy dear,
> I'm parted from you for seven long year.
> "ALF. JONES."

This modest performance, to which the lamenting poet courageously affixed his name, contained a story of love and misfortune, and should, on that account alone, have appealed to the charitable criticism of all who might read the same. But right underneath this effort of the love-sick Jones, a sour and sceptical Jeffrey had added the following verses:—

> "If Lucy dear is like most gals,
> She'll give few sighs or moans,
> But soon will find among your pals
> Another Alfred Jones."

Like all unmerciful critics, this heartless wretch, who was evidently himself a sufferer from some fair one's slight, or perhaps evidence, refused to attach his name to his contribution, but fortunately for Lucy's *inamorato* the stigma which was thus cast upon her constancy and that of her whole sex would fall under his notice only in case of his losing Lucy again after liberation and passing through Newgate in the course of a second lagging.

The next original effusion which met my eye in Newgate, also in the sentimental strain, though of a bolder sweep than that of the poet Jones, was as follows:—

> "The judge he seven years gave me, transported to Van Diemen's Land,
> Far away from my friends and relations, and the girl with the dark velvet band."

Now, inasmuch as these lines were written in the city of London in 1869, and that neither thieves nor poets are now transported from England to any

more distant region of the world than Dartmoor, the first line of this verse amounts to a most unwarranted stretch of poetic license, being introduced only to find a rhyme for the sable ornament of the writer's lady love. *A propos* of the description which we find given of this lady, was she the only girl in existence with a dark velvet band? and did she wear it round her neck, or arm, or—but, impossible!—was it akin to the sacred ornament which gave rise to the legend, *"Honi soit qui mal y pense"?* Well for the writer that he neglected to affix his name to such a production, as the poetic censor who cut up Jones and his Lucy would have emptied all his wrath upon the anonymous writer's style and taste.

My next selection will be from the muse of Millbank, who, in consequence of change of scenery and the more advanced march of the poets on the song-inspiring journey of penal servitude, is of a more epicurean turn than her sentimental sister at Newgate. Margins of books are no longer available, however, for the preservation of amorous verse or sorrowing ditty, for reasons already hinted at, and the substitutes must become as various as the objects celebrated. On the bottom of a dinner-can, and written with a nail, I discovered the following:—

> *"Millbank* for thick shins and graft at the pump;
> *Broadmoor* for all laggs as go off their chump;
> *Brixton* for good toke and cocoa with fat;
> *Dartmoor* for bad grub but plenty of chat;
> *Portsmouth* a blooming bad place for hard work;
> *Chatham* on Sunday gives four ounce of pork;
> *Portland* is worst of the lot for to joke in—
> For fetching a lagging there's no place like *Woking.*
> "CRUTCHY QUINN, 10 and ticket."

In one respect this short, but very descriptive poem appeared to have something of a pretense to more crime than would give a prison experience sufficient to cover so much ground as eight convict establishments; but as I had the distinguished privilege of not only meeting the poet "Crutchy," but of occupying a cell next to his in Dartmoor a twelvemonth after reading the above, I discovered that he had really passed some portion of time in seven of the prisons whose praise or shortcomings he had so graphically described while doing his "separates" in Millbank for the third time.

His Celtic patronymic reminds me that I have so far left you in complete ignorance as to what is the nationality of prison poets, or in what proportion, rather, they are distributable between England, Scotland, Wales, and

Ireland. I am a firm believer in the wisdom of the German proverb, that "Neither one's country nor mankind is served by national vanity," and I have, therefore, throughout the whole of these lectures, claimed so very little of professional or poetic genius for my own country, that I am in no fear of being charged with any undue partiality. I am, however, in obedience to the behest of truth, compelled to give two-thirds of the prison poets to the land of Moore.

Crutchy Quinn, despite his surname, I found to be a Saxon, though his own story, told to me as follows, would lead to consistency with his name:—

"I am the brother of the celebrated Corporal Quinn, who took a company of Russians prisoners by his own bravery in the Crimea. I am an inventor, and to my love for the study of invention is due this, my misfortune. I once made a model of a patent diving-bell which would surpass anything of the sort ever invented before. I showed it to a gentleman in London, who had something of the same sort in his nut also. Seeing that my plan was the best, he resolved to put me away, and he did it in this manner: I was walking down Cheapside one day, when this rascal meets me, and asks my opinion of a gold chronometer which he had just purchased for twenty quid. No sooner did I take the watch in my hand than he shouted for a copper, and gave me into custody for attempting to steal it from him! Did you ever hear of such villainy before in broad daylight?" Upon repeating this story, a few days after having heard it, to a London pickpocket who "knew everybody," he gave me the following as the true history of Crutchy:—"That is all one of Crutchy's blooming yarns. He has been here twice before, and had a new monicker each time. He is not Irish, but a born Cockney, and when he has done this bit he will have spent twenty-five years of his life in quod." Crutchy sustained his reputation as a poet during the time he and I were fellow-prisoners in Dartmoor.

But returning to Millbank. There can be no doubt as to the country that gave birth to the author of the following sad couplet, which I found very appropriately inscribed upon one of the tin knives in that prison:—

"I had for my dinner, ochone! ochone!
One ounce of mutton and three ounce of bone!"

It was while studying the backs of doors and the bottoms of dinner-cans in this establishment, that I first met a convict poet in the flesh. He did me the honor of requesting me to become the critic of a piece of blank verse,

which, he declared, had elicited from the schoolmaster an opinion that Shakespeare had nothing equal to it in any of his works. I, of course, suddenly became deeply interested in the individual who could beat Shakespeare hollow, and asked how I could have the pleasure of reading his lines. "Oh, exchange slates," he replied. "Nothing easier. We can do it in the morning when the gates are unlocked for chapel." This conversation occurred while returning from prayers; so on the following morning I became possessed of his slate, and found about fifty lines of a medley, which commenced with

"When most alone we are least alone,"

containing nothing but a string of unconnected lines stolen from Milton, Shakespeare, and Young's *Night Thoughts*. This was discouraging, and would scarcely have earned for Shakespeare's rival a place among my convict poets if I had not met him again under anything but poetic circumstances. Nine years after this incident I was walking along Stephen's Green, in Dublin, one evening, when who should I see coming in an opposite direction, in company with two more individuals, but the well-remembered face of the man who claimed to have beaten the Swan of Avon in Millbank. As I had learned, while his associate in this penitentiary, of his more congenial accomplishments, I ventured to predict to the friend with whom I was chatting when this *rencontre* occurred, that some clever burglary or cheat would take place in Dublin ere many days had gone by. Two days afterwards the whole city was thrown into a state of excitement in consequence of numbers of forged 10*l*. National Bank notes having been successfully tendered to various shopkeepers and dealers ere their counterfeit character was discovered. One of the "snide pitchers" was caught, but he was not the leader of the gang—my quondam poetic neighbor of Millbank, doubtless, who had made good his escape; but if he had been caught and subjected to the poetic inspiration of Spike Island, he would, to a certainty, soon aspire to take the laurels from the brow of the author of the Melodies.

As Dartmoor was, poetically speaking, in possession of Crutchy Quinn during the whole of my sojourn in that place, truly famous for "bad grub," if not for "plenty of chat," and as I have already given a sample of his poetry, I must pass on to Portsmouth prison, which, from some cause or other, never satisfactorily explained, had the reputation of numbering more poets among its criminal population than all the other convict prisons combined. I was

told by one of these geniuses that the schoolmaster encouraged poetry among prisoners, and that once a fortnight, on book-changing days, each votary of the Portsmouth muse would leave his composition on his slate where the prison Holofernes could read it, and mark his approval or other opinion for the perusal of the author. This appeared to me as simply exquisite; and I looked forward to a long and constant enjoyment of this community of imprisoned songsters, when, unfortunately for the remainder of this lecture on prison poets, I was sent back to Dartmoor with only a few weeks' experience of my new acquaintances. Short as my stay in Portsmouth was, however, it was not altogether barren of poetic results. Upon reaching the place where my gang was employed, one morning in the July of 1872, the officer in charge bade me go to the end stack of bricks, and the prisoner who was there at work would teach me how to "skintle," *i.e.,* stack wet bricks to dry. The personage to whose teaching I was thus consigned was a little man of fifty or more years of age. Having eyed me very closely on my approach, he saluted me with the startling question, "Are you a *pôte?*"

Somewhat taken aback at the thought that there might be some connection between the composition of poetry and the manufacture of bricks hitherto undreamt of by me, I answered, "No!" "I am," was the proud and prompt reply. "Indeed!" I ventured to observe, "and have you published any works?" "No; but I have made a lot of poetry," he answered in a tone that might have applied to so many barrow-loads of bricks. "Upon what subjects have you chiefly composed?" was my next inquiry. "The pugging machine—" "But what is that, please?" I interrupted. "That is what makes the bricks," was the reply. "Holy Joe." "Who is he, pray?" "Oh! that is our chaplain." "Well?" "I have made some poetry on Pentonville, too," he continued, and immediately putting himself in an attitude of poetic frenzy, he recited—

> " 'Twas one fine morning I left Wakefield Jail,
> Meself and comrades we did cry our fill;
> Far from our friends we were now transported
> Till the same evening we reached Pentonville—"

"If you don't stop that jaw, Horgan, and allow that man to go on with his work, I'll give you a run!" broke in the anything-but-musical voice of the warder upon the poet and startled auditor; and as the threatened "run," if carried out, would entail more disagreeable consequences than the combined critical condemnation of all the literary reviews, there was no more "poetry" recited that day.

Epilogue to a Blackbird

Now, Mr. Chairman, our task is done, and your right to liberty can no longer be resisted by me. I shall feel our separation keenly; for our companionship has been to me a source of singular happiness. You have robbed solitary confinement of its inhuman features, while the little care and attention which your simple wants required at my hands, have kept in play those better attributes of poor humanity that manifest themselves in the solicitude which one being exhibits for the welfare of another, but for the exercise of which there is neither scope nor opportunity in penal servitude. But with tomorrow's advent I will surely open your cage, and you shall be as free as the air upon which your wings are longing to unfold themselves.

BALFOUR'S CRIMINAL:

Wilfrid Scawen Blunt

IN VINCULIS

~~~~~~

He was the chief public nuisance of his time. In turn he puzzled and exasperated the Foreign Office, the Irish Office and the India Office. To Pro-Consuls and Secretaries of State he was a pest. To his fellow-Squires he was a disgrace: a country gentleman born, who spent his life and substance defending subject races.

SHANE LESLIE, *Men Were Different*

THE restlessness of an Elizabethan did not spoil Wilfrid Scawen Blunt's career as a Victorian English gentleman. It only contributed to his life the romantic perspective suitable to a man who had married Byron's granddaughter, bred Arabian horses, and written sonnets. It made him an anti-Imperial Conservative—a Tory at home, but a rebel abroad. Grateful for the entertainment in Arab culture and the dignity in Irish suffering, he became a champion of their nationalisms. Lord Rosebery wrote to Queen Victoria about Blunt: "This invaluable subject of Your Majesty spends his time in masquerading like an oriental in a circus under a tabernacle outside Cairo and intriguing against the British occupation of Egypt." To the national struggles of Egypt and Ireland he added those of India and the Boers and became a full-fledged knight of premature causes. Arabia, whose dress and sanctities he had enjoyed the excitement of trying on, he called "a sacred land, the cradle of Eastern liberty and true religion." As an English politician he ran for office both in Conservative and Liberal parties, giving his allegiance only to Irish Home Rule, explaining that "at home I am a Catholic and a Tory as regards the land question and education, and in Ireland I am a Nationalist." It was for his Irish adventure that he went to jail. Defeated in the elections, he launched into unofficial political action. He founded the British Home Rule Association, made converts among Cambridge undergraduates, and wrote a sonnet on Ireland which was rejected by the editor of the *Nineteenth Century,* who remarked he never accepted poetry "except from Tennyson and Mat Arnold, and had refused Swinburne last week." From his itinerary in Ireland outlined for him by Michael Davitt, Blunt wrote letters to the *Pall Mall Gazette* which showed how much the evictions of Irish peasants had moved his warm sensibilities. His biographer, Miss Edith Finch, recounts how Blunt, the landlord, took the wise precaution of

reducing rents on his own estate in England "and left himself free to pluck the mote from the eyes of Irish landlords." At the height of the agrarian agitation worked out by William O'Brien, John Dillon, and Tim Harrington, Blunt found himself before an audience of excited Irish farmers in a "suppressed" .district, Woodford County, Galway. He had come single-handed to break the back of Irish coercion by embarrassing the government with the spectacle of a free-born Englishman who was going to exercise *his* rights of speech and assembly. Government, however, was not overcome with shame and plucked him from his platform in a country meadow before he could say "Men of Galway." The Irish lit bonfires and formed torchlight processions to show how they appreciated his martyrdom; and in England, Asquith, the Liberal Party, the whole cause of Home Rule, were scandalized and vocal. Blunt had never been so famous as a political agitator as when he became "Balfour's Criminal." He surrendered himself happily to a jail cell in Galway, and later in Kilmainham, not without the sound medical advice of Gladstone's own physician and the devout blessings of Cardinal Manning. He spent his term picking oakum, reading the Old Testament and filling its fly-leaves with the sonnets which he called *In Vinculis*. A photograph of Blunt in his prison garb, prefacing the edition of the sonnets, shows how little his manly beauty, so much like Parnell's, suffered from the indignity; and the announcement of the prison's governor that he would christen his newborn son Wilfrid Blunt, after the gentleman prisoner, proves the point made by Shane Leslie that "he was one of the few Englishmen who have been heroes in Ireland."

IN VINCULIS

Sonnets Written in an Irish Prison, 1888

To the priests and peasantry of Ireland who for three hundred years have preserved the tradition of a righteous war for faith and freedom.

I

FROM Caiaphas to Pilate I was sent,
    Who judged with unwashed hands a crime to me.
    Next came the sentence, and the soldiery
Claimed me their prey. Without, the people rent

With weeping voices the loud firmament.
And through the night from town to town passed we
Mid shouts and drums and stones hurled heavily
By angry crowds on love and murder bent.

And last the gaol.—What stillness in these doors!
The silent turnkeys their last bolts have shot,
And their steps die in the long corridors.
I am alone. My tears run fast and hot.
Dear Lord, for Thy grief's sake I kiss these floors
Kneeling; then turn to sleep, dreams trouble not.

II

Naked I came into the world of pleasure,
And naked come I to this house of pain.
Here at the gate I lay down my life's treasure,
My pride, my garments and my name with men.
The world and I henceforth shall be as twain,
No sound of me shall pierce for good or ill
These walls of grief. Nor shall I hear the vain
Laughter and tears of those who love me still.

Within, what new life waits me! Little ease,
Cold lying, hunger, nights of wakefulness,
Harsh orders given, no voice to soothe or please,
Poor thieves for friends, for books rules meaningless;
This is the grave—nay, Hell. Yet, Lord of Might,
Still in Thy light my spirit shall see light.

III

Honoured I lived e'erwhile with honoured men
In opulent state. My table nightly spread
Found guests of worth, peer, priest and citizen,
And poet crowned, and beauty garlanded.

Nor these alone, for hunger too I fed,
And many a lean tramp and sad Magdalen
Passed from my doors less hard for sake of bread.
Whom grudged I ever purse or hand or pen?

To-night, unwelcomed at these gates of woe
I stand with churls, and there is none to greet
My weariness with smile or courtly show
Nor, though I hunger long, to bring me meat.
God! what a little accident of gold
Fences our weakness from the wolves of old!

IV

How shall I build my temple to the Lord,
Unworthy I, who am thus foul of heart?
How shall I worship who no traitor word
Know but of love to play a suppliant's part?
How shall I pray, whose soul is as a mart,
For thoughts unclean, whose tongue is as a sword
Even for those it loves to wound and smart?
Behold how little I can help Thee, Lord.

The Temple I would build should be all white,
Each stone the record of a blameless day;
The souls that entered there should walk in light,
Clothed in high chastity and wisely gay.
Lord, here is darkness. Yet this heart unwise,
Bruised in Thy service, take in sacrifice.

V

A prison is a convent without God.
Poverty, Chastity, Obedience
Its precepts are. In this austere abode
None gather wealth of pleasure or of pence.

Woman's light wit, the heart's concupiscence
Are banished here. At the least warder's nod
Thy neck shall bend in mute subservience.
Nor yet for virtue—rather for the rod.

Here a base turnkey novice-master is,
    Teaching humility. The matin bell
        Calls thee to toil, but little comforteth.
None heed thy prayers or give the kiss of peace.
    Nathless, my soul, be valiant. Even in Hell
        Wisdom shall preach to thee of life and death.

VI

There are two voices with me in the night,
    Easing my grief. The God of Israel saith,
        "I am the Lord thy God which vanquisheth.
See that thou walk unswerving in my sight,
    So shall thy enemies thy footstool be.
I will avenge." Then wake I suddenly,
And, as a man new armoured for the fight,
    I shout aloud against my enemy.

Anon, another speaks, a voice of care
    With sorrow laden and akin to grief,
        "My son," it saith, "What is my will with thee?
The burden of my sorrows thou shalt share.
    With thieves thou too shalt be accounted thief,
        And in my kingdom thou shalt sup with me."

VII

Long have I searched the Earth for liberty
    In desert places and lands far abroad
Where neither Kings nor constables should be,
    Nor any law of Man, alas, or God.

Freedom, Equality and Brotherhood,
These were my quarries which eternally
Fled from my footsteps fast as I pursued,
Sad phantoms of desire by land and sea.

See, it is ended. Sick and overborne
By foes and fools, and my long chase, I lie.
Here, in these walls, with all life's souls forlorn
Herded I wait,—and in my ears the cry,
"Alas, poor brothers, equal in Man's scorn
And free in God's good liberty to die."

VIII

'Tis time, my soul, thou shouldst be purged of pride.
What men are these with thee, whose ill deeds done
Make thee thus shrink from them and be denied?
They are but as thou art, each mother's son
A convict in transgression. Here is one,
Sayest thou, who struck his fellow and he died.
And yet he weeps hot tears. Do thy tears run?
This other thieved, yet clasps Christ crucified.

Where is thy greater virtue? Thinkest thou sin
Is but crime's record on the judgment seat?
Or must thou wait for death to be bowed down?
Oh for a righteous reading which should join
Thy deeds together in an accusing sheet,
And leave thee if thou couldst, to face men's frown!

IX

Behold the Court of Penance. Four gaunt walls
Shutting out all things but the upper heaven.
Stone flags for floor, where daily from their stalls
The human cattle in a circle driven

.Tread down their pathway to a mire uneven,
Pale-faced, sad-eyed, and mute as funerals.
Woe to the wretch whose weakness unforgiven
Falters a moment in the track or falls!

Yet is there consolation. Overhead
    The pigeons build and the loud jackdaws talk,
And once in the wind's eye, like a ship moored,
A sea-gull flew and I was comforted.
Even here the heavens declare thy glory, **Lord**,
    And the free firmament thy handiwork.

X

My prison has its pleasures. Every day
    At breakfast-time, spare meal of milk and **bread**,
Sparrows come trooping in familiar way
    With head aside beseeching to be fed.
    A spider too for me has spun her thread
Across the prison rules, and a brave mouse
    Watches in sympathy the warders' tread,
These two my fellow-prisoners in the house.

But about dusk in the rooms opposite
    I see lamps lighted, and upon the blind
A shadow passes all the evening through.
    It is the gaoler's daughter fair and kind
And full of pity (so I image it)
Till the stars rise, and night begins anew.

XI

God knows, 'twas not with a fore-reasoned plan
    I left the easeful dwellings of my peace,
And sought this combat with ungodly Man,
    And ceaseless still through years that do not cease

Have warred with Powers and Principalities.
My natural soul, e'er yet these strifes began,
    Was as a sister diligent to please
And loving all, and most the human clan.

God knows it. And he knows how the world's tear
    Touched me. And He is witness of my wrath,
How it was kindled against murderers
    Who slew for gold, and how upon their path
I met them. Since which day the World in arms
Strikes at my life with angers and alarms.

XII

There are wrongs done in the fair face of heaven
    Which cry aloud for vengeance, and shall cry;
Loves beautiful in strength whose wit has striven
    Vainly with loss and man's inconstancy;
    Dead children's faces watched by souls that die;
Pure streams defiled; fair forests idly riven;
    A nation suppliant in its agony
Calling on justice, and no help is given.

All these are pitiful. Yet, after tears,
    Come rest and sleep and calm forgetfulness,
And God's good providence consoles the years.
    Only the coward heart which did not guess,
The dreamer of brave deeds that might have been,
Shall cureless ache with wounds for ever green.

XIII

To do some little good before I die;
    To wake some echoes to a loftier theme;
To spend my life's last store of industry
    On thoughts less vain than Youth's discordant dream;

To endow the world's grief with some counter-scheme
Of logical hope which through all time should lighten
  The burden of men's sorrow and redeem
Their faces' paleness from the tears that whiten;

To take my place in the world's brotherhood
  As one prepared to suffer all its fate;
To do and be undone for sake of good,
  And conquer rage by giving love for hate;
That were a noble dream, and so to cease,
Scorned by the proud but with the poor at peace.

XIV

I thought to do a deed of chivalry,
  An act of worth, which haply in her sight
Who was my mistress should recorded be
  And of the nations. And, when thus the fight
Faltered and men once bold with faces white
Turned this and that way in excuse to flee,
  I only stood, and by the foeman's might
Was overborne and mangled cruelly.

Then crawled I to her feet, in whose dear cause
  I made this venture, and "Behold," I said,
"How I am wounded for thee in these wars."
  But she, "Poor cripple, wouldst thou I should wed
A limbless trunk?" and laughing turned from me.
Yet was she fair, and her name "Liberty."

XV

Farewell, dark gaol. You hold some better hearts
  Than in this savage world I thought to find.
I do not love you nor the fraudulent arts
  By which men tutor men to ways unkind.

514

Your law is not my law, and yet my mind
Remains your debtor. It has learned to see
    How dark a thing the earth would be and blind
But for the light of human charity.

I am your debtor thus and for the pang
    Which touched and chastened, and the nights of thought
Which were my years of learning. See I hang
    Your image here, a glory all unsought,
About my neck. Thus saints in symbol hold
Their tools of death and darings manifold.

XVI

No, I will smile no more. If but for pride
    And the high record of these days of pain,
I will not be as these, the uncrucified
    Who idly live and find life's pleasures vain.
    The garment of my life is rent in twain,
Parted by love and pity. Some have died
    Of a less hurt than 'twas my luck to gain,
And live with God, nor dare I be denied.

No, I will smile no more. Love's touch of pleasure
    Shall be as tears to me, fair words as gall,
The sun as blackness, friends as a false measure,
    And Spring's blithe pageant on this earthly ball,
If it should brag, shall earn from me no praise
But silence only to my end of days.

EASTER RISING 1916:

Padraic Pearse

~~~~~~

> I write it out in verse—
> MacDonagh and MacBride
> And Connolly and Pearse,
> Now and in time to be,
> Wherever green is worn,
> Are changed, changed utterly:
> A terrible beauty is born.
>
> WILLIAM BUTLER YEATS, *Easter 1916*

THREE poets fell before the firing squad after the Easter Rising of 1916:
Thomas MacDonagh, Joseph Mary Plunkett, and Padraic Pearse who
had been made president of the provisional government of the Irish Republic. Aloof, ascetic, unmarried, saintly, scholarly, dedicated to Gaelic and a
new Irish school, Padraic Pearse lived with the ghosts of Wolfe Tone and
Robert Emmet. He wrote:

> I am Ireland
> I am older than the Old Woman of Beare.
>
> Great my glory:
> I that bore Cuchullain the valiant.
>
> Great my shame:
> My own children that sold their mother.
>
> I am Ireland:
> I am lonelier than the Old Woman of Beare.

In his school for brave new Irishmen at St. Enda's, the caption of the mural
of Cuchullain taking arms at the risk of an early death read: "I care not if
my life has only the span of a night and a day if my deeds be spoken of
by men of Ireland." Cuchullain's wish inscribed on St. Enda's walls turned
out to be prophetic of the bloody Easter Week, whose aftermath was more
effective than the rising itself. Sinn Feiners, parliamentarians, and Gaelic
Leaguers united in the body of the Irish Volunteers. The poets died in the
name of Cuchullain, and the labor leader, James Connolly, for "men of no
property." Failure and terror and wholesale execution of the leaders fol-

lowed, but Ireland was to be transformed nevertheless. Pearse wrote *The Wayfarer* in Kilmainham Jail and Yeats was to say of him shortly and neatly:

> This man had kept a school
> And rode our winged horse.

THE WAYFARER

THE beauty of the world hath made me sad,
This beauty that will pass;
Sometimes my heart hath shaken with great joy
To see a leaping squirrel in a tree,
Or a red lady-bird upon a stalk,
Or little rabbits in a field at evening,
Lit by a slanting sun,
Or some green hill where shadows drifted by
Some quiet hill where mountainy man hath sown
And soon would reap; near to the gate of Heaven;
Or children with bare feet upon the sands
Of some ebbed sea, or playing on the streets
Of little towns in Connacht,
Things young and happy.
And then my heart hath told me:
These will pass,
Will pass and change, will die and be no more,
Things bright and green, things young and happy;
And I have gone upon my way
Sorrowful.

THE SHIRT OF NESSUS:

Sir Roger Casement

"IF IT BE TREASON. . . ."

Sedition, the natural garment for an Irishman to wear, has been for a hundred years a bloodless sedition. It is this fiery shirt of Nessus that has driven our strong men mad. How to shed our blood with honor, how to give our lives for Ireland—that has been, that is the problem of Irish nationality. The day the first German comrade lands in Ireland, the day the first German warship is seen proudly breasting the waves of the Irish Sea with the flag of Ireland at her fore, that day many Irishmen must die, but they shall die in the sure peace of God that Ireland may live. (Written in November-December 1913.)

SIR ROGER CASEMENT, *The Crime Against Ireland and How the War May Right It*

UNDER the heading of *Some Neglected Morals of the Irish Rising,* G. B. Shaw has warned the English public that "no wise man now uses the word Traitor at all." The *Encyclopaedia Britannica* refers to the career of Roger Casement as that of a "British consular agent and rebel." It is a very strange and lonely career, indeed, in which scientific humanism, nationalist passion, and all the furies of melodrama intermingle—and the ends and means of life become tragically entangled. Like Hercules, the Irish hero puts on the shirt dipped in the blood of Nessus—"sedition, the natural garment for an Irishman to wear," says Roger Casement—and he wanders around in agony until he is released from pain.[1] Casement should be remembered as the British consular investigator who plunged into the African Congo and the South American Putumayo, to come back with a story about rubber that embarrassed shareholders with an exposure of the way in which their dividends were obtained. He uncovered unspeakable bestialities against Negroes and Indians, nests of sadism in which lives and rubber trees were tapped with equal ferocity. In 1913 he retired to Ireland, fatigued in the middle of his life by his explorations of the peonage, rape, murder, and amputated hands of the wretched rubber makers. Anticipating war between England and Germany, seeing in the Home Rule Bill a bribe to keep Ireland ap-

---

[1] I was reading the galley-proof for this Irish section when President Eamon de Valera brought his official condolences to the German Embassy in Dublin upon the reported death of Adolf Hitler. Only the fossil and folk-lore of protocol, the protocol of a neutrality? Or the "fiery shirt of Nessus that has driven our strong men mad?"

peased, Casement plunged into Irish political journalism. The outbreak of the war and John Redmond's recruiting of soldiers in Ireland roused him to say that "Ireland has no blood to give to any land, to any cause but that of Ireland," and he conceived the ill-fated idea of going to Germany and raising an Irish Brigade among the prisoners of war. From this point to the end, melodrama and fatalism ruled his life. The mere details of his misadventures in Germany read like a crude "international thriller," but the passion recorded in Casement's diary is not mechanical. To the German Foreign Office in the midst of an implacable war, he was a strange bird, an eccentric idealist whose nationalism had a certain nuisance value against England and some pro-German propaganda value in America. Casement wanted to believe that "at least I shall have given more to Ireland by one bold deed of open treason than Redmond and Co. after years of talk and spouting treason have gained from England; England does not mind the 'treason' of the orthodox Irish 'patriot' . . . she recognizes only action, and respects only deeds." But his human raw material for action and deeds, the candidates for the Irish Brigade among the war prisoners in Germany, startled Casement with their ghastly appearance and, in fact, their jeering. A declaration by the Germans on Irish liberation depended on the success of enrolling a number of these badly clad and shivering men—men without a spark of pro-German feeling and a great deal of suspicion for the "b—— Fenian" who came to seduce their allegiance. He put them down in his diary as "the scum of Ireland," of whom fifty-three were somehow rigged out in Irish uniforms, tailored by the Germans with emerald green facings, golden harps and shamrocks—a disorderly, ostracized and unhappy lot of human beings with absolutely nothing to do with themselves in captivity. Tortured by failure, Casement added to his diary: "I do not think the German government has any soul for great enterprise—it lacks the divine spark of imagination that has ennobled British piracy." In the end he obtained his "Treaty" in writing, but, beyond a few thousand worn-out guns, he did not receive the full military aid which Casement believed was being counted upon in Ireland for the Easter Rising of 1916. "If I fail—if Germany be defeated—still the blow struck today for Ireland must change the course of British policy towards that country. Things will never be again quite the same. The 'Irish Question' will have been lifted from the mire and mud and petty, false strife of British domestic politics into an international atmosphere. That, at least, I shall have achieved." He wrote this in his diary on his arrival in Berlin in 1914. Now the logic of his certain failure could dictate only one further step.

THE SHIRT OF NESSUS : *Roger Casement*

To stop the Easter Rising, for which he had failed to obtain arms, he landed on the Kerry coast from a German submarine, though the consequences for himself meant death. From the jail where he was waiting for the gallows, he wrote a letter to his sister describing to her what he felt when he landed in Ireland. The shirt of Nessus was loosening at last:

When I landed in Ireland that morning (about 3 a.m.) swamped and swimming ashore on an unknown strand, I was happy for the first time for over a year. Although I knew that this fate waited on me, I was for one brief spell happy and smiling once more. I cannot tell you what I felt. The sandhills were full of skylarks, rising in the dawn, the first I had heard for years—the first sound I heard through the surf was their song as I waded in through the breakers, and they kept rising all the time up to the old rath at Currshone, where I stayed and sent the others on, and all round were primroses and wild violets and the singing of the skylarks in the air, and I was back in Ireland again. As the day grew brighter I was quite happy, for I felt all the time that it was God's will that I was there.[2]

"IF IT BE TREASON. . . ."

My Lord Chief Justice, as I wish to reach a much wider audience than I see before me here, I intended to read all that I propose to say. What I shall read now is something I wrote more than twenty days ago. I may say, my lord, at once that I protest against the jurisdiction of this Court in my case on this charge, and the argument that I am now going to read is addressed not to this Court, but to my own countrymen.

There is an objection, possibly not good in law, but surely good on moral grounds, against the application to me here of this old English statute, 565 years old, that seeks to deprive an Irishman to-day of life and honour, not for "adhering to the King's enemies," but for adhering to his own people.

When this statute was passed, in 1351, what was the state of men's minds on the question of a far higher allegiance—that of a man to God and His kingdom? The law of that day did not permit a man to forsake his church or deny his God save with his life. The "heretic" then had the same doom as the "traitor."

To-day a man may forswear God and His heavenly kingdom without fear or penalty, all earlier statutes having gone the way of Nero's Edicts against the Christians, but that Constitutional phantom, "The King," can still dig

---

[2] Henry W. Nevinson, *Last Changes, Last Chances.*

up from the dungeons and torture chambers of the Dark Ages a law that takes a man's life and limb for an exercise of conscience.

If true religion rests on love, it is equally true that loyalty rests on love. The law I am charged under has no parentage in love and claims the allegiance of to-day on the ignorance and blindness of the past.

I am being tried, in truth, not by my peers of the live present, but by the peers of the dead past; not by the civilisation of the twentieth century, but by the brutality of the fourteenth; not even by a statute framed in the language of an enemy land—so antiquated is the law that must be sought to-day to slay an Irishman, whose offence is that he puts Ireland first.

Loyalty is a sentiment, not a law. It rests on love, not on restraint. The Government of Ireland by England rests on restraint and not on law; and since it demands no love it can evoke no loyalty.

But this statute is more absurd even than it is antiquated; and if it is potent to hang one Irishman, it is still more potent to gibbet all Englishmen.

Edward III. was King not only of the realm of England, but also of the realm of France, and he was not King of Ireland. Yet his dead hand to-day may pull the noose around the Irishman's neck whose Sovereign he was not, but it can strain no strand around the Frenchman's throat whose Sovereign he was. For centuries the successors of Edward III. claimed to be Kings of France, and quartered the arms of France on their royal shield down to the Union with Ireland on 1st January, 1801. Throughout these hundreds of years these "Kings of France" were constantly at war with their realm of France and their French subjects, who should have gone from birth to death with an obvious fear of treason before their eyes. But did they? Did the "Kings of France" resident here at Windsor or in the Tower of London, hang, draw, and quarter as a traitor every Frenchman for 400 years who fell into their hands with arms in his hand? On the contrary, they received embassies of these traitors, presents from these traitors, even knighthood itself at the hands of these traitors, feasted with them, tilted with them, fought with them—but did not assassinate them by law. Judicial assassination to-day is reserved only for one race of the King's subjects, for Irishmen; for those who cannot forget their allegiance to the realm of Ireland.

The Kings of England as such had no rights in Ireland up to the time of Henry VIII., save such as rested on compact and mutual obligation entered between them and certain princes, chiefs, and lords of Ireland. This form of legal right, such as it was, gave no King of England lawful power to impeach an Irishman for high treason under this statute of King Edward III. of Eng-

land until an Irish Act, known as Poyning's Law, the 10th of Henry VII., was passed in 1494 at Drogheda, by the Parliament of the Pale in Ireland, and enacted as law in that part of Ireland. But if by Poyning's Law an Irishman of the Pale could be indicted for high treason under this Act, he could be indicted only in one way and before one tribunal—by the laws of the realm of Ireland and in Ireland. The very law of Poyning's, which, I believe, applies this statute of Edward III. to Ireland, enacted also for the Irishman's defence, "All those laws by which England claims her liberty." And what is the fundamental charter of an Englishman's liberty? That he shall be tried by his peers. With all respect I assert this Court is to me, an Irishman, not a jury of my peers to try me in this vital issue, for it is patent to every man of conscience that I have a right, an indefeasible right, if tried at all, under this statute of high treason, to be tried in Ireland, before an Irish Court and by an Irish jury. This Court, this jury, the public opinion of this country, England, cannot but be prejudiced in varying degree against me, most of all in time of war. I did not land in England; I landed in Ireland. It was to Ireland I came; to Ireland I wanted to come; and the last place I desired to land in was England. But for the Attorney-General of England there is only "England"—there is no Ireland, there is only the law of England—no right of Ireland; the liberty of Ireland and of Irishmen is to be judged by the power of England. Yet for me, the Irish outlaw, there is a land of Ireland, a right of Ireland, and a charter for all Irishmen to appeal to, in the last resort, a charter that even the very statutes of England itself cannot deprive us of— nay, more, a charter that Englishmen themselves assert as the fundamental bond of law that connects the two kingdoms. This charge of high treason involves a moral responsibility, as the very terms of the indictment against myself recite, inasmuch as I committed the acts I am charged with, to the "evil example of others in the like case." What was this "evil example" I set to others in "the like case," and who were these others? The "evil example" charged is that I asserted the rights of my own country, and the "others" I appealed to to aid my endeavour were my own countrymen. The example was given not to Englishmen, but to Irishmen, and the "like case" can never arise in England, but only in Ireland. To Englishmen I set no evil example, for I made no appeal to them. I asked no Englishman to help me. I asked Irishmen to fight for their rights. The "evil example" was only to other Irishmen who might come after me, and in "like case" seek to do as I did. How, then, since neither my example nor my appeal was addressed to Englishmen, can I be rightfully tried by them?

If I did wrong in making that appeal to Irishmen to join with me in an effort to fight for Ireland, it is by Irishmen, and by them alone, I can be rightfully judged. From this Court and its jurisdiction I appeal to those I am alleged to have wronged, and to those I am alleged to have injured by my "evil example," and claim that they alone are competent to decide my guilt or my innocence. If they find me guilty, the statute may affix the penalty, but the statute does not override or annul my right to seek judgment at their hands.

This is so fundamental a right, so natural a right, so obvious a right, that it is clear the Crown were aware of it when they brought me by force and by stealth from Ireland to this country. It was not I who landed in England, but the Crown who dragged me here, away from my own country to which I had turned with a price upon my head, away from my own countrymen whose loyalty is not in doubt, and safe from the judgment of my peers whose judgment I do not shrink from. I admit no other judgment but theirs. I accept no verdict save at their hands. I assert from this dock that I am being tried here, not because it is just, but because it is unjust. Place me before a jury of my own countrymen, be it Protestant or Catholic, Unionist or Nationalist, Sinn Feineach or Orangemen, and I shall accept the verdict and bow to the statute and all its penalties. But I shall accept no meaner finding against me than that of those whose loyalty I endanger by my example and to whom alone I made appeal. If they adjudge me guilty, then guilty I am. It is not I who am afraid of their verdict; it is the Crown. If this be not so, why fear the test? I fear it not. I demand it as my right.

That, my lord, is the condemnation of English rule, of English-made law, of English Government in Ireland, that it dare not rest on the will of the Irish people, but it exists in defiance of their will—that it is a rule derived not from right, but from conquest. Conquest, my lord, gives no title, and if it exists over the body, it fails over the mind. It can exert no empire over men's reason and judgment and affections; and it is from this law of conquest without title to the reason, judgment, and affection of my own countrymen that I appeal.

My lord, I beg to say a few more words. As I say, that was my opinion arrived at many days ago while I was a prisoner. I have no hesitation in re-affirming it here, and I hope that the gentlemen of the press who did not hear me yesterday may have heard me distinctly to-day. I wish my words to go much beyond this Court.

I would add that the generous expressions of sympathy extended me from

many quarters, particularly from America, have touched me very much. In that country, as in my own, I am sure my motives are understood and not misjudged—for the achievement of their liberties has been an abiding inspiration to Irishmen and to all men elsewhere rightly struggling to be free in like cause.

My Lord Chief Justice, if I may continue, I am not called upon, I conceive, to say anything in answer to the inquiry your lordship has addressed to me why sentence should not be passed upon me. Since I do not admit any verdict in this Court, I cannot, my lord, admit the fitness of the sentence that of necessity must follow it from this Court. I hope I shall be acquitted of presumption if I say that the Court I see before me now is not this High Court of Justice of England, but a far greater, a far higher, a far older assemblage of justices—that of the people of Ireland. Since in the acts which have led to this trial it was the people of Ireland I sought to serve—and them alone—I leave my judgment and my sentence in their hands.

Let me pass from myself and my own fate to a far more pressing, as it is a far more urgent theme—not the fate of the individual Irishman who may have tried and failed, but the claims and the fate of the country that has not failed. Ireland has outlived the failure of all her hopes—and yet she still hopes. Ireland has seen her sons—aye, and her daughters too—suffer from generation to generation always for the same cause, meeting always the same fate, and always at the hands of the same power; and always a fresh generation has passed on to withstand the same oppression. For if English authority be omnipotent—a power, as Mr. Gladstone phrased it, that reaches to the very ends of the earth—Irish hope exceeds the dimensions of that power, excels its authority, and renews with each generation the claims of the last. The cause that begets this indomitable persistency, the faculty of preserving through centuries of misery the remembrance of lost liberty, this surely is the noblest cause men ever strove for, ever lived for, ever died for. If this be the case I stand here to-day indicted for, and convicted of sustaining, then I stand in a goodly company and a right noble succession.

My counsel has referred to the Ulster Volunteer movement, and I will not touch at length upon that ground save only to say this, that neither I nor any of the leaders of the Irish Volunteers who were founded in Dublin in November, 1913, had quarrel with the Ulster Volunteers as such, who were born a year earlier. Our movement was not directed against them, but against the men who misused and misdirected the courage, the sincerity, and the local patriotism of the men of the north of Ireland. On the contrary, we wel-

comed the coming of the Ulster Volunteers, even while we deprecated the aims and intentions of those Englishmen who sought to pervert to an English party use—to the mean purposes of their own bid for place and power in England—the armed activities of simple Irishmen. We aimed at winning the Ulster Volunteers to the cause of a united Ireland. We aimed at uniting all Irishmen in a natural and national bond of cohesion based on mutual self-respect. Our hope was a natural one, and if left to ourselves, not hard to accomplish. If external influences of disintegration would but leave us alone, we were sure that Nature itself must bring us together. It was not we, the Irish Volunteers, who broke the law, but a British party. The Government had permitted the Ulster Volunteers to be armed by Englishmen, to threaten not merely an English party in its hold on office, but to threaten that party through the lives and blood of Irishmen. The battle was to be fought in Ireland in order that the political "outs" of to-day should be the "ins" of to-morrow in Great Britain. A law designed for the benefit of Ireland was to be met, not on the floor of Parliament, where the fight had indeed been won, but on the field of battle much nearer home, where the armies would be composed of Irishmen slaying each other for some English party again; and the British Navy would be the chartered "transports" that were to bring to our shores a numerous assemblage of military and ex-military experts in the congenial and profitable business of holding down subject populations abroad. Our choice lay in submitting to foreign lawlessness or resisting it, and we did not hesitate to choose. But while the law breakers had armed their would-be agents openly, and had been permitted to arm them openly, we were met within a few days of the founding of our movement, that aimed at united Ireland from within, by Government action from without direct against our obtaining any arms at all. The manifesto of the Irish Volunteers, promulgated at a public meeting in Dublin on 25th November, 1913, stated with sincerity the aims of the organisation as I have outlined them. If the aims contained in that manifesto were a threat to the unity of the British Empire, then so much the worse for the Empire. An Empire that can only be held together by one section of its governing population perpetually holding down and sowing dissension among a smaller but none the less governing section, must have some canker at its heart, some ruin at its root. The Government that permitted the arming of those whose leaders declared that Irish national unity was a thing that should be opposed by force of arms, within nine days of the issue of our manifesto of goodwill to Irishmen of every creed and class, took steps to nullify our efforts by pro-

hibiting the import of all arms into Ireland as if it had been a hostile and blockaded coast. And this proclamation of the 4th December, 1913, known as the Arms Proclamation, was itself based on an illegal interpretation of the law, as the Chief Secretary has now publicly confessed. The proclamation was met by the loyalists of Great Britain with an act of still more lawless defiance—an act of widespread gun-running into Ulster that was denounced by the Lord Chancellor of England as "grossly illegal and utterly unconstitutional." How did the Irish Volunteers meet the incitements of civil war that were uttered by the party of law and order in England when they saw the prospect of deriving political profit to themselves from bloodshed among Irishmen?

I can answer for my own acts and speeches. While one English party was responsible for preaching a doctrine of hatred designed to bring about civil war in Ireland, the other, and that the party in power, took no active steps to restrain a propaganda that found its advocates in the Army, Navy, and Privy Council—in the Houses of Parliament and in the State Church—a propaganda the methods of whose expression were so "grossly illegal and utterly unconstitutional" that even the Lord Chancellor of England could find only words and no repressive action to apply to them. Since lawlessness sat in high places in England and laughed at the law as at the custodians of the law, what wonder was it that Irishmen should refuse to accept the verbal protestations of an English Lord Chancellor as a sufficient safeguard for their lives and their liberties? I know not how all my colleagues on the Volunteer Committee in Dublin reviewed the growing menace, but those with whom I was in closest co-operation redoubled, in face of these threats from without, our efforts to unite all Irishmen from within. Our appeals were made to Protestant and Unionist as much almost as to Catholic and Nationalist Irishmen. We hoped that by the exhibition of affection and goodwill on our part towards our political opponents in Ireland we should yet succeed in winning them from the side of an English party whose sole interest in our country lay in its oppression in the past, and in the present in its degradation to the mean and narrow needs of their political animosities. It is true that they based their actions, so they averred, on "fears for the Empire," and on a very diffuse loyalty that took in all the peoples of the Empire, save only the Irish. That blessed word "Empire" that bears so paradoxical a resemblance to charity! For if charity begins at home, "Empire" begins in other men's homes, and both may cover a multitude of sins. I for one was determined that Ireland was much more to me than "Empire," and that if charity begins

at home, so must loyalty. Since arms were so necessary to make our organisation a reality, and to give to the minds of Irishmen menaced with the most outrageous threats a sense of security, it was our bounden duty to get arms before all else. I decided with this end in view to go to America, with surely a better right to appeal to Irishmen there for help in an hour of great national trial than those envoys of "Empire" could assert for their week-end descents upon Ireland, or their appeals to Germany. If, as the right honourable gentleman, the present Attorney-General, asserted in a speech at Manchester, Nationalists would neither fight for Home Rule nor pay for it, it was our duty to show him that we knew how to do both. Within a few weeks of my arrival in the States the fund that had been opened to secure arms for the Volunteers of Ireland amounted to many thousands of pounds. In every case the money subscribed, whether it came from the purse of the wealthy man or the still readier pocket of the poor man, was Irish gold.

Then came the war. As Mr. Birrell said in his evidence recently laid before the Commission of Inquiry into the causes of the late rebellion in Ireland, "the war upset all our calculations." It upset mine no less than Mr. Birrell's, and put an end to my mission of peaceful effort in America. War between Great Britain and Germany meant, as I believed, ruin for all the hopes we had founded on the enrolment of the Irish Volunteers. A constitutional movement in Ireland is never very far from a breach of the constitution, as the Loyalists of Ulster had been so eager to show us. The cause is not far to seek. A constitution to be maintained intact must be the achievement and the pride of the people themselves; must rest on their own free will and on their own determination to sustain it, instead of being something resident in another land whose chief representative is an armed force—armed not to protect the population, but to hold it down. We had seen the working of the Irish constitution in the refusal of the army of occupation at the Curragh to obey the orders of the Crown. And now that we were told the first duty of an Irishman was to enter that army, in return for a promissory note, payable after death—a scrap of paper that might or might not be redeemed, I felt over there in America that my first duty was to keep Irishmen at home in the only army that could safeguard our national existence. If small nationalities were to be the pawns in this game of embattled giants, I saw no reason why Ireland should shed her blood in any cause but her own, and if that be treason beyond the seas I am not ashamed to avow it or to answer for it here with my life. And when we had the doctrine of Unionist loyalty at last— "Mausers and Kaisers and any King you like," and I have heard that at

Hamburg, not far from Limburg on the Lahn—I felt I needed no other warrant than that these words conveyed—to go forth and do likewise. The difference between us was that the Unionist champions chose a path they felt would lead to the woolsack; while I went a road I knew must lead to the dock. And the event proves we were both right. The difference between us was that my "treason" was based on a ruthless sincerity that forced me to attempt in time and season to carry out in action what I said in word—whereas their treason lay in verbal incitements that they knew need never be made good in their bodies. And so, I am prouder to stand here to-day in the traitor's dock to answer this impeachment than to fill the place of my right honourable accusers.

We have been told, we have been asked to hope, that after this war Ireland will get Home Rule, as a reward for the life blood shed in a cause which whoever else its success may benefit can surely not benefit Ireland. And what will Home Rule be in return for what its vague promise has taken and still hopes to take away from Ireland? It is not necessary to climb the painful stairs of Irish history—that treadmill of a nation whose labours are as vain for her own uplifting as the convict's exertions are for his redemption—to review the long list of British promises made only to be broken—of Irish hopes raised only to be dashed to the ground. Home Rule when it comes, if come it does, will find an Ireland drained of all that is vital to its very existence—unless it be that unquenchable hope we build on the graves of the dead. We are told that if Irishmen go by the thousand to die, not for Ireland, but for Flanders, for Belgium, for a patch of sand on the deserts of Mesopotamia, or a rocky trench on the heights of Gallipoli, they are winning self-government for Ireland. But if they dare to lay down their lives on their native soil, if they dare to dream even that freedom can be won only at home by men resolved to fight for it there, then they are traitors to their country, and their dream and their deaths alike are phases of a dishonourable phantasy. But history is not so recorded in other lands. In Ireland alone in this twentieth century is loyalty held to be a crime. If loyalty be something less than love and more than law, then we have had enough of such loyalty for Ireland or Irishmen. If we are to be indicted as criminals, to be shot as murderers, to be imprisoned as convicts because our offence is that we love Ireland more than we value our lives, then I know not what virtue resides in any offer of self-government held out to brave men on such terms. Self-government is our right, a thing born in us at birth; a thing no more to be doled out to us or withheld from us by another people than the right to life

itself—than the right to feel the sun or smell the flowers, or to love our kind. It is only from the convict these things are withheld for crime committed and proven—and Ireland that has wronged no man, that has injured no land, that has sought no dominion over others—Ireland is treated to-day among the nations of the world as if she was a convicted criminal. If it be treason to fight against such an unnatural fate as this, then I am proud to be a rebel, and shall cling to my "rebellion" with the last drop of my blood. If there be no right of rebellion against a state of things that no savage tribe would endure without resistance, then I am sure that it is better for men to fight and die without right than to live in such a state of right as this. Where all your rights become only an accumulated wrong; where men must beg with bated breath for leave to subsist in their own land, to think their own thoughts, to sing their own songs, to garner the fruits of their own labours—and even while they beg, to see things inexorably withdrawn from them—then surely it is braver, a saner and a truer thing, to be a rebel in act and deed against such circumstances as these than tamely to accept it as the natural lot of men.

My lord, I have done. Gentlemen of the jury, I wish to thank you for your verdict. I hope you will not take amiss what I said, or think that I made any imputation upon your truthfulness or your integrity when I spoke and said that this was not a trial by my peers. I maintain that I have a natural right to be tried in that natural jurisdiction, Ireland, my own country, and I would put it to you, how would you feel in the converse case, or rather how would all men here feel in the converse case, if an Englishman had landed here in England and the Crown or the Government, for its own purposes, had conveyed him secretly from England to Ireland under a false name, committed him to prison under a false name, and brought him before a tribunal in Ireland under a statute which they knew involved a trial before an Irish jury? How would you feel yourselves as Englishmen if that man was to be submitted to trial by jury in a land inflamed against him and believing him to be a criminal, when his only crime was that he had cared for England more than for Ireland?

The USHER—Oyez. My lords, the King's Justices do strictly charge and command all manner of persons to keep silence whilst sentence of death is passing upon the prisoner at the bar, upon pain of imprisonment.

The LORD CHIEF JUSTICE—Sir Roger David Casement, you have been found guilty of treason, the gravest crime known to the law, and upon evidence which in our opinion is conclusive of guilt. Your crime was that of as-

sisting the King's enemies, that is the Empire of Germany, during the terrible war in which we are engaged. The duty now devolves upon me of passing sentence upon you, and it is that you be taken hence to a lawful prison, and thence to a place of execution, and that you be there hanged by the neck until you be dead. And the Sheriffs of the Counties of London and Middlesex are, and each of them is, hereby charged with the execution of this judgment, and may the Lord have mercy on your soul.

Mr. JUSTICE AVORY—Amen!

THE COUNTESS AND THE PEOPLE:
Constance Markievicz

LETTERS TO EVA GORE-BOOTH: *Of Bills, Wigs, and Naphtha Balls*
Of Poems, Wild Geese, and Blake
"The brown wind of Connaught"
"President of so many things...."

She was neither poor nor helpless; she was not of the people; neither of their class nor their religion nor their political faith; their traditions were not her traditions; she was not part of their history but of the tail-end of the history of their exploitation. . . . All she knew was that she wanted to do something for James Malone of the Coombe and to do it she did the only thing she could think of. . . .
    SEÁN O'FAOLÁIN, *Constance Markievicz, or The Average Revolutionary*

IN 1888 she was presented at Court as Constance Gore-Booth and in 1927 she died in the public ward of a Dublin hospital as Countess Markievicz, ending her rebellious pilgrimage through Irish politics and poverty. It was an original journey of progressive conversion which, through Sinn Fein, the Irish Republican Brotherhood, the Rising of 1916, and the socialism of James Connolly, displayed gaiety and piety, if not intellectual analysis and great distinction. Constance Gore-Booth became Countess Markievicz by marrying a Polish aristocrat without politics, a sparkling boulevardier of her Bohemian art-student days in Paris. With perfect ease, he adopted Ireland, if not the English language, and spent his time in the company of wits, poets, and good drinkers, enriching the already rich saga of Dublin with anecdotes, friendships, a few paintings and a handful of plays, and much good-humored virility. The Countess, in a parallel groove, with diminishing domestic ties, continued her career as a rebel: "I saw the hollowness of all that Castle business and I wanted to do something for the people." She became a Sinn Feiner; she joined the Daughters of Ireland; she founded the scout organization of Fianna boys whom she taught to shoot; she floundered in the experiment of a co-operative; she tortured herself with the intricacies of Gaelic and Irish politics; and in an effort to live down the suspicion of being a dilettante in revolution and a slummer in virtuous emotions, she finally loosened most of her ties with respectability and security. All her jail sentences add up to some three years. During the labor strikes and crisis of 1913 she came under the

influence of Jim Larkin and especially James Connolly, turning her Dublin home, Surrey House, into a refuge for overworked strike leaders and a head-quarters for noisy Fianna boys carrying bundles of pamphlets. She organized a food kitchen for the wives and children of the wretched strikers and in-vited the cynical remarks of comfortable Dubliners about the "afternoon teas" of the Countess Markievicz. The socialism of James Connolly, however she understood it, became her religion, and his Citizen Army her passion. She preached socialism to the end of her days, certain that she had found in it the ultimate salvation of Irish nationalism and a station for her own rest-less Irish pilgrimage among the poor. Her faith always wore a gay dress; her uniform in the Citizen Army was a thing of shining buttons and bold insignia, and she was a crack shot with her pistol. The Easter Rising found her second in command, holding an isolated position in Dublin's Stephen's Green, battling as well as any man, and surrendering after Padraic Pearse himself had surrendered, and after Connolly had been wounded. In Kil-mainham Jail she heard the shots that finished off the leaders of the Rising, Pearse, MacDonagh, Plunkett, the husband of Maud Gonne, her superior officers in Stephen's Green, the captains of her Fianna boys, and the Irish-man who more than any other gave her a blueprint for faith, James Con-nolly. In a long succession of imprisonments at different stages of the Irish rebellion, in Mountjoy, Aylesbury, Holloway, and Cork, she scrubbed, laun-dered, cooked, painted, and with an undiminished zest wrote letters to her talented sister, the poet Eva Gore-Booth. When in 1919 Eamon de Valera made her a Secretary of Labor; when she went to one more prison for a sedi-tious speech and still another during the Black and Tan terror; when she wandered around Dublin in odd disguises, a homeless woman and a labor arbitrator settling disputes hurriedly between interludes with the police, the Countess Markievicz was drawing on the habits and techniques of a lifetime. All her jails and all her final homelessness gave her less pain and trouble than the ideal she had accepted from the hands of Connolly and which she kept preaching to the end and to a mere handful:—"the Worker's Republic for which Connolly died." During the strike of 1926, at sixty, Madame, the Countess, carried bags of coal on her old back up the stairs of the tenement homes in which she often cooked the meals and wiped the noses of the chil-dren. She received a great funeral from the Irish State, having taken care be-forehand to die in a public ward, in the slums where the poor could weep a requiem over her unfulfilled religion, Connolly's socialism. Seán O'Faoláin

calls it her "Gaelic synthesis that was utterly impracticable" and he adds this tender lament over the Countess Markievicz:

It was not her fault but the fault of the people, if she, out of the Big House, one of the outcasts, Anglo-Irish in every line of her body and every tone of her voice, having taken the religion of the people, having taken their cause, having taken their manners, having tried to take their language, (and when they failed her she had not uttered a word of complaint), found that when she turned to other tasks she turned to them almost alone. . . . It was an amazing ragout— Marx, and the Brehon Laws, the encyclical of Leo XIII, the Seanchas Mór, Das Kapital and the Democratic Programme of Dail Eireann. Nobody but a simple Anglo-Irishwoman could have done it, nobody but a woman who had not, in short, learned, for all her twenty years in Irish politics, that the native Irishman does not always mean what he says.

LETTERS TO EVA GORE-BOOTH

Of Bills, Wigs, and Naphtha Balls

MOUNTJOY PRISON,
DUBLIN,
May 16, 1916.

DEAREST OLD DARLING,—It was such a heaven-sent joy, seeing you. It was a new life, a resurrection, though I knew all the time that you'd try and see me, even though I'd been fighting and you hate it all so and think killing so wrong. It was so dear of Esther to come all that long way too. Susan too, for I expect lots of people will think it very awful of her. Anyhow, you are three dears and you brought sunshine to me, and I long to hug you all!

Now to business. H—— and H—— are agents for Surrey House. They wrote to me *re* giving up tenancy, and very decently secured the house, which had been left open. The house is very untidy, as I had no time to put it straight after the police raid.

My valuables are all with a friend (silver and jewelry). I am rather unhappy about the pictures. I don't want anything thrown away. Egan —— might store those pictures hanging on the walls, and my illuminated address from the Transport Union. He has some pictures of ours already.

Don't store furniture with M——: he was a brute to his men in the strike. You'll want to insist on their bringing proper boxes for the books, as they

533

are awfully careless. The china too wants care. Then there are the acting things. You'll probably want to buy a tin trunk or two, and get them packed with naphtha balls. There are wigs in the bottom of the kitchen press and in the cupboard half-way up the stairs. They want to be put by with care. The linen too, such as it is, wants to have the starch washed out before it is put by. If you could only catch Bessie ——, she knows the house so well and is such a good worker. There are a lot of crewel wools in the big press on the stairs: they want to be put with naphtha balls too. If someone could house the wigs and them I'd be thankful.

On the right of the fireplace in drawing-room is a sort of a desk. The same key fits it and the big brown press upstairs. One of my friends has the key. If you have not got it, pull out top drawer and push down and push lock back where it pokes through. Small centre drawer is locked: there is nothing in it.

Could Susan get my clothes and look after them for me? There is a little brown case with drawing things that Susan might keep for me. I told you that C—— and Co. are trying to let St. Mary's. I think my name should be suppressed and it should be let in yours.

Of course my household bills are not paid. C—— of Richmond Street is my grocer; F——, Rathmines, my baker; K——, butcher, and H——, oil-man, are both Rathmines. I owe two coal bills: one to C——, Tara St., and the other to a man I forget in Charlemont St., on the right-hand side as you face the bridge, but close to the chemist at the corner where the trams cross. I owe also a trifle to G—— of O'Connell St. for a skirt, and to the Art Decorating Co., Belfast. But there is no hurry about any of these. Don't pay anything unless you know the bill is really mine, as people have played queer tricks, gettings things on credit in my name before now.

You poor old darling. It's such a bore for you. I feel rather as if I were superintending my own funeral from the grave!

There is a very old book of music in the drawing-room. It might be valuable. If you have time, bring it to a Mr. Braid at P——, and ask his advice about selling it. I promised to let him have a look at it, as he says it is unique. I had no time to leave it with him.

I left a green canvas suit-case and a small red dressing-case with the caretaker of Liberty Hall. I've had them there some time. I dare say Peter's arrested, but he wasn't mixed up in anything, so he may be out. I left my bike knocking round the Hall too.

I miss poor 'Poppet' very much and wonder if he has forgotten me. Poor

Mrs. Connolly—I wonder where she is, and if you got him from her. I do feel so sorry for her. She was so devoted to her husband. Also she has four children at home and only the two older girls working. With regard to Bessie ——: what I had in mind for her was to start her in a small way in some work after the War. She is a beautiful laundress. Of course she would want another girl with her to do accounts, etc., but you could let her know that she is not forgotten, and the ten shillings a week is only to keep her safe and happy until something can be arranged. It's much better for people to earn their own living if they can.

Poor Bridie —— ought to get a month's wages, at least. She was arrested with me. Bessie would know where she lives: somewhere in Henrietta St. If you can't find Bessie, advertise for her in the evening paper. I hope you found Mrs. Mallin. I wish I knew, for it worries me so to think of her.

I nearly forgot the little Hall in Camden St. Mr. C— of Richmond St. is the landlord. If things quiet down, I'd like to go on paying the rent for them as hitherto. A little boy called Smith, living in Piles building, could find out. The landlord, of course, might know. He was quite nice.

I feel as if I were giving you such a lot of worries and bothers, and I feel, too, that I haven't remembered half. Anyhow, it's very economical living here! and I half feel glad that I am not treated as a political prisoner, as I would then be tempted to eat, smoke and dress at my own expense! In the meantime, all my debts will be paid, I live free, and after a time I suppose I will be allowed to write again and see a visitor. I don't know the rules. But do try to get in touch with Mrs. C—, Mrs. M—, and Bessie —— for me. I would be sorry for any of them to be hungry, and I would be sorry too if they thought I had forgotten them, for they were friends.

By the way, the garden seat and tools might be of use to Susan. There are a few decent plants, too, which she could take if she likes, and a couple of decent rose-trees.

Now, darling, don't worry about me, for I'm not too bad at all, and it's only a mean spirit that grudges paying the price.

Everybody is quite kind, and though this is not exactly a bed of roses, still many rebels have had much worse to bear. The life is colorless, the beds are hard, the food peculiar, but you might say that of many a free person's life, and when I think of what the Fenians suffered, and of what the Poles suffered in the 'sixties, I realize that I am extremely lucky. So don't worry your sweet old head. I don't know if you are still here, so I am sending this to Susan to forward.

I hope that I shall live to see you again some day and I shall live in hopes. With very much love to you three darlings. I can see your faces when I shut my eyes.

Of Poems, Wild Geese, and Blake

AYLESBURY PRISON,
February 27, 1917.

DEAREST OLD DARLING,—The sun is shining, the sky is so blue and the horrid red walls make it look bluer still, and I seem to see it shining through your golden halo and touching up your blues and greys, and then I think 'perhaps she is in a murky English fog' and I grudge it being able to touch you and envelop you in its embrace. And then I think: 'perhaps the same fog will blow over here, and will have us both in the same grip'—and so I wander on, quite drivelling.

I loved your last poem and letter. If you can think of it, do bring Mrs. Meynell's poem next visit. I am burning with curiosity: I think I told you, but can't be sure.

Please tell 'C——' not to publish any *unpublished* poems of mine without asking *me* (through you). Anything once published they can do what they like with, but there are one or two I don't want published yet awhile.

I was so glad to hear of K—— the old darling. I'm sure he's a rebel in his heart. He's one of the people I should really love to see. He and I were so very sympathetic always. Tell him I was so glad to get a message from him and give him my love. He always feels like part of the family.

The greedy starlings are making such a row on the window-ledge, fighting most rudely over the remains of my dinner.

This morning a wedge-shaped flight of wild geese flew over us as we were exercising, making their weird cackling cry, and they brought me home at once. Do you remember the wonderful monster, supposed to be a cow, that Joss concocted, to stalk them from behind or within, and how they fled shrieking for miles at the sight, and how unapproachable they were for weeks owing to the fright they got? The Trojan horse was nothing to that beast.

I have just been reading your letter again and can't help wishing that I were Percy's cow or pig!

536

Who is the D . . . at Barrington? I can't read the name, and where is Street?

Give Father Albert my love and tell him I often think of him.

Lord MacDonnell was an old friend, also his wife and nice daughter. He always impressed me as a very straight man, although he was a politician! I liked him very much.

Give Emmy my love and tell her I would have sent her a gilt-edged invitation card, but the censor won't allow me! I'd love to see her, don't let her *not* come if she *says* she is coming. Once she gets a pass she must come!

I was glad to hear of Mrs. M——, and so interested to hear that the boy is learning to draw. Perhaps I shall be able to help him, some day. Who knows?

What a lot of letters I am letting you in for, you poor old darling. It would probably upset Mrs. M—— very much, seeing me. It would bring it all back to her. They were such a devoted pair. The last things he said to me were about her.

If you are writing to any of the Hall crowd, tell them I got their cards. The Co-op. girls sent a joint one, and the N—— sent me one each. Tell them to remember me to Mrs. N—— and ask for news of her husband.

Now I'm going to write out a poem, about another jail-bird—a thrush. It's true!

He sang the song of the waking Spring,
The song of the budding tree,
Of the chrysalis cradling the butterfly's wing
And the waking to life of each earth-bound thing
That the sun comes out to free.

He sang of himself and of five blue eggs
Black-spotted and warm and alive,
Of baby-birds hopping on uncouth legs,
Of worms lying cool by the sheltered hedge.
Oh! how he would live and thrive!

He sang of the sunrise, all azure and gold,
He laughed at the prison wall.
The joy of his song made him happy and bold,

He forgot that life could be cruel and cold,
That each shadowy nook could a foe enfold.
His wings could defy them all.

In the air was the rapture of dawn and Spring
But the glittering sun was cold.
The wind from the west, with its sweet salt sting,
Was quenched from the north with his haste to bring
Clouds discoloured and lowering
Which down on the day he rolled.

White on the world the snow-flakes fall
And cold and death have their sway.
They beat on his wings in a smothering pall,
And close at the foot of the prison wall
Which loomed above him so endless and tall
Frozen to death he lay.

Away into space the storm-clouds float
And the earth is again awake.
Cold from his heart the snow-flakes float,
The reviving sun kissed his soft-dappled throat,
But it never will throb to another note
Nor thrill with a sparkling shake.

He will never build the nest of his song
Nor sing to his brooding mate.
Was he right to rejoice or was he all wrong?
Do hope and faith but to fools belong?
Is courage all a mistake?

No effort is lost though all may go wrong
And death come to shadow and change.
He gave his best, and simple and strong
Broke the darkness which lasted the winter long
With Spring-time's triumphant melodious song,
A melody wild and strange,
And the air had thrilled to his morning song,

The ripples of life and glee
That floated, all rainbow-tinted, along,
Striking a note that rang true and strong
On the strings of Eternity.

It's very long, isn't it? and they say that 'good things are done up in small parcels.'

I love your birthday poem so much. You've missed your vocation. You should be a Poet Laureate. I will make you mine!

I am sure no one had so much poetry written about them *spontaneously* before, while they were alive. Ordinary kings and queens have to pay for it, so they get rubbish.

Pegasus, being thoroughbred, will not stand a spur—even a golden one.

I wanted so to talk about Blake and about horoscopes the other day, but of course forgot about both! I wish I'd known Blake. I would love to argue about light and shade with him. He was all wrong—strange for such a great man. He took the superficial view that shadow is to soften and conceal. It never seemed to dawn on him that bad draughtsmen may use shadows for this: but a Master, such as Rembrandt, has as true an outline as Flaxman, and each shadow is a definite thing with a shape, as much so as an arm or a leg. But I must not write lectures on Art or Blake! I have no room and you no time to read.

Take care of yourself, you blessed old dear. I am very well, and luckily for me escaped my usual bad cold, which generally gets hold of me in January. The frosty weather always agrees with me.

Last night I dreamt I was walking on the cliff beyond John's Port, with a ripe cornfield with poppies on my right, when a great khaki-coloured snake rushed out of the corn and slithered down the cliff!

You didn't tell me if you found any meanings in the colours of the winds.

Molly B—— is a great girl. I wish I could write her some songs. She sings with such go and has such a nice voice. Give her my love and tell her I long to hear her sing again and I often think of the times we had together.

Give Susan my love. It's awfully good of her to help Bessie. By the way, if Bessie marries, I promised her £10 to set up. If she married, it might help things, so ask Susan to let her know I have not forgotten. I don't even know if she wants to marry!—and remember, in setting her up, I don't mind a few pounds more or less, *but her mother must not live with her*. She's a devil.

Please ask Joss to give Maeve £1 to buy an Easter egg.

You are so encouraging about my poetry, and a little bird tells me all the time that it's twaddle, and I laugh at myself and go on and inflict it on you. Now I am arriving at the 'wall' and so must pull up.

I hope you like being a 'respectable friend.'[1]

"The brown wind of Connaught"

AYLESBURY PRISON,
May 14, 1917.

DEAREST OLD DARLING,—When I came up to my cell after seeing you I found this old blue sheet, the bird's own colours! so I begin at once.

I loved your drawings. They are quite wonderful. You have a wonderful gift for line and a great imagination. All you need is the knack of wagging a pen and that is practice. You want to go on and *on* and *on*. Your figures have such grace and life. Do bring more next time.

Did I ever thank Reginald for his Easter card with its tri-colour messages? I *loved* it, and those cards of good pictures are such a help to look at.

I want you to send the following messages to Father Albert: he was such a wonderful friend.

[11 *lines deleted by the Censor.*]

I neglected this epistle to the 'Birds' Nest' all Sunday, for I suddenly got a craze to work out Clare's book-plate and it came out much nicer. I've started Esther's too, and I've got some more ideas for it and it is coming out better than I expected. I am going to do your birthday card all over again. I was really rather seedy and that is really why I went off into that wild smudging that you saw. I cannot wag a pen monotonously unless I am very fit, and I am feeling fine to-day.

I have some of Gertrude's primroses, some roses and carnations in my cell and I talk nonsense to them and they are great company.

Suddenly I heard you shouting to me this morning. I wondered so what

---

1 "The authorities supply the prisoner with the one sheet of paper permitted, on the back of which are the grim regulations. The prisoner, we are informed, is allowed to write so that she may keep in touch with her 'respectable' friends, and, being respectable, they must never be exposed to 'slang or improper expressions,' or the letter will be suppressed." —Esther Roper, *Prison Letters of Countess Markievicz.*

you were trying to tell me, for I couldn't hear. One's imagination plays one such odd tricks.[2]

Last night I dreamt too, such a strange beautiful dream. I was in an artist's house. He was a sculptor—German or Norwegian I think—and everything was very, very old, simple and massive. The windows were long, low slits with tiny panes, like some palaces in the time of the Huns and Goths, and the only picture there was of a girl, all in blue, with a mushroom hat of iridescent blue feathers, yellow-gold hair and a pale face. While I was looking at it, the figure suddenly looked down at a paper lying in its lap, and I realised that it was you! There were such lovely lilies growing in carved stone jars in that house and through the windows the sun shone on trees and a river.

I am still reading Blake diligently and I like the two you quoted immensely and I too was struck by the prophecy. Do you know 'the Song of Liberty?' It ends with:—

'Empire is no more and now the lion and the wolf shall cease.' I wonder if that is a prophecy too? I don't understand anything else in it from beginning to end! Tiriel, Har and Heva etc. also puzzle me much. I suppose they are really only fancy names for quite commonplace articles.

I have just been given F. Albert's gifts, so please say 'Thank you a thousand times' and tell him I love the beads in my own rebel colours!

No one who has not been in jail can realise what a joy it is to get a coloured picture post-card!

The *Life of S. Francis* too looks awfully interesting.

I am already looking forward to your next visit in the flesh. They are like flashes of sunlight.

Your letter still smells delicious. I have it here under my nose.

I wonder so who is acting 'tail' and who 'dog' in Dublin now.

The younger generation of rebels will have a great chance now of building up and doing things for the country. I have great faith in the young.

---

[2] Countess Markievicz' literary executor brings to my attention "a letter from Countess Markievicz to my sister. It refers to the habit the Countess and her sister Eva Gore-Booth had of getting into touch with each other at 6 P.M.—the Countess being in Aylesbury Prison and Eva at 14, Frognal Gardens, Hampstead, a distance of 30 miles as the crow flies. My sister and I were living in the same house and knew that this was a genuine instance of habitual telepathy. Eva and Con used to compare notes about it. Constance (the Countess) once told me that when she was back at home again in Ireland she was on the point of having a bad motor smash when she saw Eva and heard her say 'It's perfectly all right, Con.' Eva was at the time in London."

These last few days the trees have simply flung out their green leaves. They did it at night, so that I should not learn their secret!

The one thing I am learning here is to watch everything closely, whether it is trees or blackbeetles, birds or women.

The sparrows are delightful—like men at their best.

Someone once said 'the more I know men, the more I love my dog,' and I think I rather agree. Dogs don't lie: I don't suppose birds do!

What's G—— doing over here? and what's happening to Muncaster?

It's tragic, the way things break up and change. He spent his whole time for such years building up that place, and now I suppose the next man will either alter everything or let the whole place drop to pieces. I should like to have seen it again. It must be rather awful for G——.

Dusk is coming on and the B.B. will have finished pecking at her evening meal by now and is probably preening her feathers and wondering what I am doing.

Again, another day! and I don't know why I have delayed so long over this. Laziness and dullness, I suppose, but really, if you come to think of it, I have nothing to talk about, only vague nonsense.

The Chapel was a treat this morning, with the smell of the lilies. How I love the smell of them! I think they are your flower.

(Saturday) I have just seen the Governor. Miss Emily N—— wants to visit me. Of course I'd love to see her, but I don't want her visit to interfere with you. (I wish people would go to *you* about visiting me and let *you* arrange. I'm so afraid of someone getting your pass—by accident.) It's so impossible for me to arrange and I only want what and who is convenient to you.

Naturally I am delighted to see any friends.

There is only a week now till I see you. You probably won't get this till afterwards.

I have written one more verse to the B.B. It ends in the middle of a sentence. Here it is. Next verse not done enough to send.

Then my soul strikes the magical key-note
And the circle of wonder is born
When all beautiful thoughts that are free float
In a vortex out to the dawn,

While the air grows heavy around me
As the Presence encloses my soul
And I know that my Blue Bird has found me,
That together we rule and control.

(I *am* sorry for the Censor!)
By day I dream all sorts of vague ideas and theories about sounds, all sounds being musical notes. Echo will only call back to you when you pitch your voice on certain notes. Certain notes are re-echoed by dogs, who howl if you play to them on the violin or piano or sing them. There is a certain pitch that carries best in every different Hall. I think that there is a lot of natural magic in sounds.

That's an awfully nice photo of you drawing. I wish Esther were in the room too.

The 'brown wind of Connaught' is blowing. He will kiss you for me and ruffle your curls at sundown. He passes here on his way from Ireland.

There is a small sycamore tree here in the garden. It's not very 'paintable.'

I am having an egg for breakfast!

Alice Milligan's card was prophetic, only it's not a 'duck!'

They say there was another air raid. I hope you were not alarmed or deafened.

"President of so many things...."

AYLESBURY PRISON,
June 9, 1917.

BELOVED OLD DARLING,—How short your visit always seems and how much must always remain unsaid, unless the powers that be provide me with a brand-new and absolutely clean and unwritten tablet for my poor old memory!

I meant to have asked you where the meeting was that you could not go to, and where Dr. L. spoke.

I also wanted to tell you to ask Susan for a motto to illustrate for the book-plate she probably has, but I'd love to do her a motto.

Now don't work and worry yourself to death about me, you old blessing. I am wonderfully content and I know that all is going well with Kathleen

and that there is nothing I can do in my own country that others can't do as well.

The hours slip by, like rosary beads of dragons' teeth, with a big glowing opal bead to mark the rhythm—your visit.

Don't I drivel?

It is really very curious that you should write a poem on and give a lecture on S. Francis. For I have been thinking of him a great deal and thinking out pictures of him. I could find out very little about him here, then F. A. sent me his life—'out of the blue' as they say—and then your letter came.

I have copied your poem and decorated it already. It's very beautiful, the poem.

Did I ever tell you that 'Squidge' sent me a card? I want you to give my love and thanks to her.

I am so interested in little Doyle's horoscope. You must make it out for Janey, his mother, for me to give her if ever I get out! Perhaps you may drift across them, but I am sure she would be most interested in it and would love to have it signed by you and dated, to put by until he grows up. You have hit one nail on the head in it in a wonderful way.

What you poetically term my 'ascetic way of living' certainly has great compensations. I think that something I might call the 'subconscious self' develops only at the expense of your body—of course with the consent and desire of your will. To develop it, it is necessary to cut yourself off from a great deal of human intercourse, to work hard and eat little, and as your subconscious self emerges, it comes more and more in tune with the subconscious soul of the world, in which lie all the beauties and subtleties you speak of.

I think, too, that any friendships worth having have their roots on this plane: and, too, that this is the secret of the monastic orders and of the hermits and philosophers from the beginning of the world, especially of the Eastern mystics.

It used to puzzle me so when I read of girls—like Maud's sisters—becoming Carmelite nuns, and I could never see either the sense or the use of it. Since I have been here I understand it absolutely, and I know that for people with a vocation the compensation far outweighs the things you give up.

You ask me if the flowers last. They are wonderful. One lily—I threw it away on Monday—lasted one month and two days. I think it knew that I loved it. I am always going to keep a flower or leaf in water from one visit to another.

544

THE COUNTESS AND THE PEOPLE : *Constance Markievicz*

I am glad that I am President of so many things! I should always advise societies to choose their presidents from among jail-birds, as presidents are always such a bore and so in the way on committees! I always rather liked taking the chair, for the fun of bursting through all the red tape: and when remonstrated with, I could always corner them by saying, 'ridiculous *English* conventions! Surely an *Irish* Committee is not going to be bound by them?' Now they'll be able, on all the committees in Ireland, to waste all their precious time tying up their minds and other people's in red tape. Notices of motion about rubbish taking the place of the divine inspiration of the moment, and then all that twaddle about amendments and addenda and procedure of every kind! I wonder whether you would get dignified and shocked? It is such years since we served on committees together: not since we went out to force a Suffrage Bill through Parliament. I have no ambition to have a vote for an English Parliament, and don't suppose I would use it. I don't think that Parliaments are much use anyhow. All authority in a country always seems to get into the hands of a clique and permanent officials.

I think I am beginning to believe in anarchy. Laws work out as injustice, legalised by red tape.

You have such a lot of real good news and interesting gossip in your letter. You always manage to tell me about the things I most want to hear about.

The Fianna news was very cheering, and isn't the Doctor splendid?— when one considers that her paying patients must almost all be in the enemy's camp! I call it awfully plucky and fine of her to come out in public the way she does. It's wonderful too the amount she does for the poor. I feel so proud of having introduced her to the real Ireland. One has such wonderful luck sometimes. If another doctor hadn't suddenly lost her mother. I should never have met ours.

I think my handwriting is getting awful. I think the sort of work I do is bad for writing.

Do you ever hear of Mrs. Connolly and her daughter Ina, great friends of mine? Ask for news of them, next time you write to the doctor or any of them. Ina was a splendid girl. Ask too if the 'Feis' has come off yet.

Do you remember the verse labelled 'Introduction' at the head of Blake's *Gates of Paradise?* Judges ought to take it to heart.

I am already beginning to get excited over your next visit and to wonder whom you are going to bring.

545

I wonder if any of my visitors will ever get into jail themselves? Take my advice, and *don't you,* for you are not strong enough. Some people it would be very good for. I am sure that six months of it would do P—— a lot of good!

I saw a lovely moon the other night, and in my mind's eye began to play billiards with it. I rolled my mind into a great ball and cannoned off the moon into the B.B.'s window. If you think of it, the moon is the apex of so many triangles.

I would have loved to hear your lecture on the 'Peace of St. Francis.' You can tell me something about it, if you've room, in your next letter.

It's so funny to me to realise that I never wrote letters until I got into jail! and it's really quite an amusing game! You're so awfully good. I sometimes find it on my conscience that I give you so much to do. I must be an awful nuisance. Don't wear yourself out, that's all.

Did you ever visit the catacombs in Rome? The old paintings must be so interesting. I have just been reading about them. I have always longed to go to Rome. That and the Pyramids and perhaps the Parthenon, which you would almost have to pass; I always feel I know these places quite well.

This morning, when the flutter of wings came, at nine o'clock, I was peeling swedes. They, you may not know, are a kind of turnip largely eaten by sheep! We have been eating so many lately that I feel I shall soon begin to 'baa-baa.' But they are very good indeed. You should try them, though perhaps as a veg.[3] you already know them.

Now, darling, the limit is reached and there is no space for love which would require a very big one and remembrances to all friends. I hope Esther will be coming again soon. I long to show her the book. I know she would understand.

---

[3] Vegetarian.

Book VI
The Nineteenth Century

LEIGH HUNT

AN AMERICAN ORATION

WILLIAM LLOYD GARRISON

JOHN BROWN

HONORÉ DE BALZAC

FYODOR DOSTOEVSKY

MICHAEL BAKUNIN

PAUL VERLAINE

OSCAR WILDE

O. HENRY

THE WIT IN THE DUNGEON:
Leigh Hunt

What though, for showing truth to flatter'd state,
　Kind Hunt was shut in prison, yet has he,
　In his immortal spirit, been as free
As the sky-searching lark, and as elate.
Minion of grandeur! think you he did wait?
　Think you he naught but prison walls did see,
　Till, so unwilling, thou unturn'dst the key?
Ah, no! far happier, nobler was his fate!
In Spenser's halls he stray'd, and bowers fair,
　Culling enchanted flowers; and he flew
With daring Milton through the fields of air:
　To regions of his own his genius true
Took happy flights. Who shall his fame impair
When thou art dead, and all thy wretched crew?
　　　　　JOHN KEATS, *Written on the Day That*
　　　　　Mr. Leigh Hunt Left Prison

THE Irish of London used to celebrate St. Patrick's Day with much toasting of the Prince of Wales as a Liberal and friend of Catholics. When the mind of the old king gave way (the king who lost the American colonies), the new Prince Regent, who retained the Tory ministers of his father and a great many bad habits, now brought more hisses than applause. The year of Irish hisses, 1812, saw Napoleon's invasion of Russia and Leigh Hunt's libelous article, *The Prince on St. Patrick's Day,* which he published in *The Examiner.* Napoleon duly retreated from Russia but not Leigh Hunt from his libel in the weekly paper which he and his earnest brother John had set up in 1808. It was named after *The Examiner* of Swift, but unlike its Tory namesake, aimed chiefly "to assist in producing Reform in Parliament, liberality in opinion in general (especially freedom from superstition), and a fusion of literary taste into all subjects whatsoever. It began with being of no party; but Reform soon gave it one."

The Examiner began its career when Bonaparte had the Continent under his boots. Hunt's was an English voice directing censure both against reac-

THE WIT IN THE DUNGEON : *Leigh Hunt*

tion at home and "Boney" across the Channel. But his boldest wit spawned against the Prince Regent. He described him as "a corpulent man of fifty," "a violator of his word," "a libertine over head and ears in disgrace, a despiser of domestic ties, the companion of gamblers and demireps, a man who has just closed half a century without one single claim on the gratitude of his country, or the respect of posterity." This opinion promptly brought editor Leigh Hunt two years of martyrdom, but no leisure from journalism, in Horsemonger Lane Jail.

"If we would have the great to be what they ought," he rashly declared, "we must find some means or other to speak of them as they are." Having found means adequate enough to earn him two years in jail, Hunt was the kind of man to recall with satisfaction, in later years, that "I believe it did good, and I should have suffered far worse in the self-abasement." He added wistfully about his naughty Prince Regent, "Could I but meet him in some odd corner of the Elysian fields, where chance had room for both of us, I should first apologize to him for having been the instrument in the hand of events for attacking a fellow-creature, and then expect to hear him avow as hearty a request for having injured myself, and unjustly treated his wife." For Leigh Hunt placed the Prince Regent's sin against a free press on a level with his sin against a wife.

The period of Hunt's imprisonment, 1813–1815, saw the appearance of Jane Austen's *Pride and Prejudice* and *Mansfield Park;* Byron's *Giaour, Bride of Abydos,* and *Corsair;* Moore's *Twopenny Post Bag;* Shelley's *Queen Mab;* Southey's *Life of Nelson;* Scott's *Waverley;* and Wordsworth's *Excursion.* Hunt was editing *The Examiner* in jail as Napoleon abdicated his hold on Europe, as Edmund Kean first appeared in London, and as Shelley and Mary Godwin were leaving England for a kinder climate. Hazlitt and Lamb were faithful contributors to *The Examiner* and a half-dozen immortals paid their respects to its editor in Horsemonger Lane Jail.

Leigh Hunt's jailer, a snob who delighted in gentlemen, rescued him from the steerage quarters of the prison, and the magistrates restored his domestic felicity by permitting Mrs. Hunt and the children to join him in captivity. Though often seriously ill, he wrote his nostalgic *Hampstead Sonnets,* his *Descent of Liberty* so curiously forecasting Hardy's *The Dynasts,* his weekly leaders in *The Examiner* on Bonaparte, on Shakespeare, on military torture, on education for the poorer classes, and again on the sins of the Prince Regent.

Hunt himself papered his prison walls with a trellis of roses; colored the

ceiling with clouds and sky; camouflaged the bars with Venetian blinds; introduced books and busts and flowers and a piano. He enjoyed a grass plot and a garden and an apple tree. He was triumphant when his distinguished visitors gaped at all this—when Lamb declared there was no other such room except in a fairy tale; when Bentham came to play battledore; when Houdon arrived loaded with a work of art; when Hazlitt bustled in on editorial business; and when Byron and Moore descended for dinner. In Horsemonger Lane Jail, Mrs. Hunt gave birth to little Florimel (dutifully named after Spenser), with Leigh himself as midwife and the prison garden visible through the open door of the labor chamber. Hunt would work under an awning and shut his eyes fancying himself afar and free. He would dress up as if for a long walk, putting on his gloves, taking a book under his arm, requesting Mrs. Hunt with a laugh not to wait for dinner if he were late. Hunt observes: "We scatter an urbanity about the prison." There was indeed urbanity inside the jail, but plenty of anger on the outside, where Shelley ("I am boiling with indignation") offered to pay Hunt's fine for libel ("Oh! that I might wallow for one night in the Bank of England!"); and Keats wept ("Kind Hunt was shut in prison"); and Byron, preparing for his visit and a dinner of fish and vegetables, wrote to Moore:

> Tomorrow be with me, as soon as you can, Sir,
> All ready and dress'd, for proceeding to spunge on
> (According to compact) the wit in the dungeon—
> Pray Phoebus at length our political malice
> May not get us lodgings within the same palace . . .
> But tomorrow, at four, we will both play the Scurra,
> And you'll be Catullus, the Regent Mammura.

Byron was a gentleman about whom uneasy Mrs. Hunt had "heard something," though Leigh admonished his good wife Marianne on a lack of tolerance: "You must make allowances for the early vagaries of Lord Byron." Hunt was really grateful:

> And so adieu, dear Byron, dear to me
> For many a cause, disinterestedly . . .
> Next for that frank surprise, when Moore and you
> Came to my cage, like warblers kind and true,
> And told me, with your arts of cordial lying
> How well I looked, when you both thought me dying.

THE FABLE OF THE FISH[1]

IN THE land of the Genii, where every living creature was gifted with speech, and even some inanimate things, such as a pair of mustachios or of stirrups, could say very pretty things in public, there was a territory governed by a sultan of the name of Jee-Awj, who had under him a counsellor that was also a cadi, called El-En-Burrah. The reader perhaps never heard of cadis in the land of the Genii, but that is not my fault; that people were a desperate sort of fellows, and had as much need of a magistrate as any set of Musselmen from Cairo to Bagdad. Sultan Jee-Awj was what in the dialect of the Ginninstan was called a *Raic*, which in our language perhaps we should interpret by the phrase *Jolly Fellow:*—he could sit up, for instance, night after night, drinking the forbidden liquor and eating bang. He was also fond of dress, delighting in sumptuous vests and drawers covered with gold; his mustachios were each of them six inches long; but for all that, he did not know how to govern, and great odium was attached to persons about him of infamous lives and example. As to El-En-Burrah, he was the strangest genius in the world for a cadi; he would take off his turban, and boast that he had eaten ten times as many dishes of pilau as it would hold; he would flounce about on the seat of justice in a rage, in order to shew his impartiality; putting a husband to the torture he called a venial error and a misfortune; and he had this remarkable maxim above all others, that it was better to poison than to say any thing against poisoning. Now the Prince unfortunately met him on this ground, for he had a way of amusing himself with scattering a certain strong poison called Badex-Ampel in a river near his palace, the fishes of which were daily infected by it. The effect at last became so violent, that two of them, who had a knack of speaking their minds, could no longer forbear, but rising on the surface of the water, delivered themselves after this manner:—"We wish to be obedient to our Lord and Sultan the illustrious Jee-Awj, and we are heartily sorry for disturbing his pleasure; but if he goes on in this manner, this whole territory may be infected, and he himself die by the contagion; as the cadis therefore cannot interfere in this matter, we think it necessary to advise him ourselves, and do accordingly protest, as

---

[1] From *Sentence Against The Examiner* in *The Examiner*, No. 268, February 14, 1815, the third of a series of articles by Leigh Hunt in protest at being deprived of the society of his wife and children, at being cut off from friends, at the clanking of felons' chains in his ears, and at windows too high to see out of his prison.

strongly as fishes can, against his continuance of this fatal amusement." Jee-Awj was astonished at this remonstrance, and looked at those about him, who looked at El-En-Burrah, who seized the daring fish with an angling-rod of magic parchment which he had in his hand. Their offence was soon settled by the maxim above-mentioned, and being pronounced to have highly misdemeaned themselves, it was agreed that they should be sent among the other animals who had lately misdemeaned themselves, in whatever manner. Accordingly they were separately dismissed to a dog-kennel, where they had for their company all sorts of brute animals, some for biting people, some for breaking into sheep-folds, some for betraying their masters' houses. Their dog-kennels were very good dog-kennels, very clean, and light, and airy, and fit for dogs; but unluckily they were not at all suitable to fish, for the latter, as we all know, require an element of their own. Of one of the fish I have not heard all the particulars, and can only say that he was not a very stout fish, and went off to his prison with a contemptuous silence. The other was pretty much of as strong a spirit, but he was of a delicate and sorry kind of a body, and he lay gasping at the bottom of his kennel for want of water. "Will you change your opinions?" said his accusers. "That is impossible," said the fish, "but I should like exceedingly to change my lodging:—I have been used to living in good, free water, surrounded by the most friendly and respectable fins in the river, and if I cannot have my freedom, which I do not ask, let me at least have an element to breathe in:—put me in a tub, if you choose it, but then let it be filled with water, for I have the feelings and wants of a fish and not of a beast, and am condemned, not to death, but imprisonment." "But the law," said they, "has found you guilty of a misdemeanour, and all animals guilty of misdemeanour are condemned to a similar place." "So much the worse," replied he, "for the good sense of the lawyers; but I am not to suffer because they saw no difference between a mackerel and a mastiff." At these words a great clamor arose among the more considerate of the by-standers; but here the story abruptly breaks off, and we are not told of the result.

ON THE UNPHILOSOPHICAL CONDUCT OF SIR
HUMPHREY DAVY[2]

IN BRINGING into our columns the name of this celebrated chemist, we are not going to deviate into any private or family matters,—matters with which we have nothing to do, except where they are forced upon us by their connexion with the interests of the State. We notice the subject, partly on account of a paragraph in the *Times* of Tuesday last, which has occasioned much comment and difference of opinion, and chiefly because it involves a question as to the political conduct of men of letters and science, which notwithstanding its importance we do not remember to have seen noticed before. The paragraph, to which we allude, was as follows:—

" 'Sir Humphrey Davy and his Lady arrived at Portsmouth on Saturday, and were expected to embark on board the Collingwood cartel, for Morlaix, on their route to Paris. It is stated, that he will visit the greatest part of Europe before his return to this country, permission having been obtained from the French Government to pass through France and her dependencies.' The above is copied from an evening paper. We cannot help thinking, that while so large a portion of the Continent (Spain included) is, either through our bravery, or that of our Allies, open to the researches of science, Sir Humphrey might have spared himself the trouble of accepting any favor from the enemy of his country, by visiting France first. We should not be sorry, if Bonaparte sent him to keep company with the first victims of Corsican treachery at Verdun. Neither, we believe, would his Imperial Majesty be at all nice about it, if he thought the Professor worth keeping. But Bonaparte studies the *cui bono:* and is well aware that the *strenua inertia* of these *dirty-finger* gentry can be of no other use than that of making women and children troublesome, by the affectation and babble of knowledge."

In this vehement effusion, of gross impudence according to some, of just indignation according to others, there is something to which every one of good sense and good taste must object. Many persons may think with the

---

[2] From *Sir Humphrey Davy and His Visit to Paris* in *The Examiner*, No. 304, October 24, 1813. Sir Humphrey Davy achieved European fame as a scientist when in 1807 he expounded his discoveries before the Royal Society. Napoleon, then first consul, founded a prize of 3000 francs for the best experiments made on the galvanic fluid. Twelve months after the publication of Sir Humphrey Davy's lecture, the Institute of France awarded him the Napoleon Prize. It should be added that at the close of 1807 the scientist fell ill from his exertions in disinfecting Newgate prison and that in 1812 he married. Thereupon "other views of ambition than those presented by achievements in science had opened on his mind." While his country was at war with France, Sir Humphrey Davy traveled on the Continent by permission of Napoleon. From his cell in jail Leigh Hunt voiced his disapproval. (I have used Hunt's and *The Examiner's* spelling of Sir Humphrey's name.)

writer, that the institution of fashionable lectures on an abstruse and laborious science can be of little avail but to produce the babble he mentions, but
to say nothing of the old, ungallant affectation of classing "women and children" together, the whole conclusion of his paragraph looks like something
worse than the affectation and babble of knowledge, and rather resembles
the sturdy vulgarity of ignorance. The dignity of chemistry, as a science that
looks into the profoundest operations of nature, and its utility, as applicable
to the purposes of society, have long been so evident to the perceptions of
every intelligent man not blinded with spleen, that any vindication of it
from charges to the contrary would only be a piece of derogatory officious-
ness:—the wonder is that charges of such a kind should appear in times like
the present, from the pen of any writer who has the air of understanding his
grammar. The *strenua inertia* of the chemists, the laborious idleness, or
much ados about nothing, as the Editor of the *Times* is pleased to call them,
may do little perhaps towards bringing in my Lord Wellesley or blowing up
the Americans, whatever chemical experiments the latter may wish to make
upon us; but not to call to mind the Infernal Machines (respectable things,
if used at Paris or Dresden), the Editor may find in himself a little more
respect for the science, even by his own standard of the agreeable and useful,
if he recollects what it is that sends off the Tower guns, and by whose assistance his ink is so good and his opinions so legible.

With respect to Bonaparte's concern in the business, we wish that he studied the *cui bono* as much as the Editor says he does; but setting apart the
moral part of his wisdom, we are afraid that, of the two, he is rather the
shrewder man in a chemical point of view, and thinks the Professors of the
art well worth his keeping, as long as they can help to give éclat to his
patronage, and assistance to his military resources. So far from making ignorant conclusions with respect to the value of chemistry, it is well known, not
only that he ennobles its Professors, but that he puts them to use in his own
profession, and sets upon improving and economizing in the art of military
subsistence. Perhaps while the Editor's eyes are opening on the subject, he
may begin to suspect that even a little imitation of the "Corsican's" policy on
this head would do us no injury. The paragraph preceding his abuse of the
science, contained a melancholy account of the "trash" which formed part of
our army's subsistence in the Pyrenees; and indeed our inferiority to the
French in this particular is not less perhaps, in its degree, than theirs is to
ourselves in point of the cause for which they are fighting.

As to the select and finishing epithet of *"dirty-finger* gentry," of which he

has thought proudly enough to mark it in italics, we will not refer him to his own fingers, or to those of the gentlemen about him, when they have been brandishing their quills for an hour or two against French Courts and foreign rascality:—they hold their pens, no doubt, a little more cautiously than we do, and take care to which quarter they shed their ink. But will he abuse the fine arts, because they dirty one's fingers? Will he object to the oil-colors of the painter or the *dirt* of the sculptor? Will he say before a picture of Raphael's—"Ah, but he must have soiled his hands!"—or before the Venus de Medici—"Oh, but she was modelled in clay!" A chemist blackens his fingers, and with what sort of substances does he blacken them? With such as dirty the fingers of every soldier that handles a cartridge, with such as have blackened the hands and faces of the conquerors of St. Sebastian, with such as have brought down the eulogies of the *Times,* and deservedly, on those dirty-fingered gentry, the patriots of Spain.

But it is humiliating to one's common sense to think of answering these absurdities; and we are sorry that the proceedings of Sir Humphrey Davy are not so easily vindicated as his pursuits. Much however as we dissent from the *Times* in what it has said of the latter, we cannot help agreeing with it respecting Sir Humphrey's journey to Paris and the permission he must have sought for that purpose. We do not say that we should wish to see him detained there, or sent to keep company "with the first victims of Corsican treachery at Verdun," for we have no wish to add to such victims, or to make Bonaparte worse than he is already:—But we do think, that at a time like the present, when there are so many national, personal, and moral feelings, interested to a more than ordinary degree in the wars and politics of Europe, no Englishman, especially one of intellectual consequence, ought to accept a favor from such a man as Bonaparte, and willfully, as it were, become neuter to them all.

In giving this opinion, let us not be misunderstood. We are aware that at first sight, it may look like adding new barbarism to warfare; but reflection, we are persuaded, will shew the reverse, at least to those understandings, who, without indulging in dreams of earthly perfectibility, believe that something may be done, and every thing ought to be tried, for reducing the food and appetite of ambition.

It has been said, whenever the arts and sciences have been mentioned as influenced by a state of war—"Oh, nobody wages war with philosophers and men of letters; it would be barbarous not to respect their pursuits in the midst of hostilities; we should return to a state of barbarism if we made them

a party concerned; the republic of letters is a world of its own, and it is for the interests of mankind that it should be left at peace when all the rest of us are contending." Now these sayings are very specious, and are unquestionably dictated by benevolent motives; but while the exemption of artists and men of letters from a supposed concern in hostilities throws an air of refinement over the hostile parties, and tends, as the phrase is, to diminish the horrors of war, what if it should assist in leaving the rest of the world at the mercy of the said parties, and tend to perpetuate the horrors that remain?

That it has such a tendency, is quite clear to us. Of the two great principles that influence the whole present government of the world, the passive principle is opinion, and the active one force; in other words, mental strength is upon the whole subjected to physical; and *so far,* we not only agree with Hume that the science of government has a great deal to learn and has had little experience hitherto, in spite of all the systems of which history talks so finely, but it appears to us that society is in an absolute state of barbarism; just as if instead of resorting to courts of justice and dispassionate arbitrations, we were to settle our legal disputes with the fist, and let might create right. We all laugh now-a-days at the judgments of chivalry, by which the sword was the arbitrator of right and wrong, and any robust gentleman on horseback was sure to carry his cause before him; yet this is what we do, to this day, in the greatest and gravest disputes that can take place between man and man, and while we ridicule such a mode of settling justice between two persons, applaud it between twenty thousand. Now Force, conscious of these absurdities by which he maintains his power of playing havoc with us, and aware that Opinion, who only suffers him to do as he pleases, might choose to become the more active of the two and put an end to them, is alternately occupied in threatening and cajoling the latter: if he seems inclined to object to some of his vagaries, he shews him deaths and imprisonments, but if he will hold his tongue, he shews him a fair countenance, and if he will consent to applaud him, compliments and honors are at his service. In plain terms, those who would do what they please with mankind and make the happiness of the whole human race a secondary business to their own pleasure or aggrandizement, find it to their interest to cajole the more intelligent part of the species, well aware that if they succeed in stopping the mouths and flattering the vanities of such persons, they shall have no trouble with the remainder. The affectation therefore of exempting speculative men from their share in politics, and of shewing them the civilities of peace in the

midst of war, is not humanity in these brutal pretenders, for at that very moment they are blowing thousands of ordinary heads to pieces:—it is a policy, which they know will return to them with tenfold interest:—it is, in fact, saying to such men, "Leave us to do as we like with these fellow-creatures of yours, say not a word about us, or say a good word, if you can—and you, in return, shall walk where you please, and be honored by us in the sight of the world." It is thus that Napoleon makes Barons and Counts of the artists and men of letters about him; it is thus that he scatters his honors, wherever he can, among the literati of Europe, and that he opens the friendly arms of his territory to Sir Humphrey Davy.

And this is not the whole of the evil. The disturbers of the world are not merely left by these means to act as they please; they are not merely suffered to continue disturbers; they are flattered and encouraged to be so; and indeed if it were not for the homage of the intelligent would hardly think it worth while to possess the power of troubling us. Power without homage would be to them a load without value. If the wiser part of mankind were to draw off their praises, and leave such persons on their own proper level among inferior people, the latter would soon find themselves aground in their ambition; but as long as this mutual smirking and complimenting goes forward between the violence of the warlike and the vanity of the wise, so long it will be a useless and senseless labor to make partial complaints of this man's conquests and that man's ambition, and to object to the vicious person while we flatter the vice.

On the other hand, the consenters to these pleasant arrangements are spoiled in their turn. Their flattery and encouragement put the man upon valuing himself more and more on what he calls his greatness, and his flattery in return makes them conclude that nobody is truly wiser than he. It is notorious what lamentable progress the French Emperor has made in the hearts of some of our artists and men of letters, and no doubt of others in various parts of Europe, by this kind of mutual good dealing. It is in vain that he breaks all his fine promises about freedom, and turns despot and subjugator:—for does he not encourage the arts? It is in vain that he commits the meanest and grossest outrage in Spain:—for has he not made David a Baron? It is in vain that he drags up thousands of human beings to perish in the snows of the North, far from the agonized hearts of their wives and children:—for did he not, in his way, go and visit Wieland? These are the redeeming actions, which are not only to save him from shame, but to cover him with glory, in the eyes of the better part of the world; and who,

after this, shall affect to despise the mobs that follow after a drum or that shout at the inspiring oratory of a serjeant?

Seeing then that men of art and science, and all others who are separated from the rest of the world by their intellect, hold a station in society, from which they assist in dispensing opinion both upwards and downwards, and in regulating our tastes and discernments, it is clear that such men ought to consider their responsibility, their consciences, and their real dignity, and not tamper with the minds and happiness of their fellow-creatures for the sake of indulging a paltry vanity. It is on this ground, a wider one, we suspect, than that of the *Times,* that we object to favors from Bonaparte, and to the journey of Sir Humphrey Davy. We can discern very well for what he goes to Paris:—he may talk about so many chemical intentions as he pleases, but he goes to see and to be seen, to be hawked about among coteries and Lyceums, and to have it said, as he moves along through smiles of admiration and shrugs of obeisance, "Ah, there is the *grand philosophe, Davie!"*—"See here the interesting *Chevalier Humphrey!"* But all this time he must have no opinion about men and monarchs; he must leave the Englishman behind him; and so far from venturing to say any thing against Bonaparte, which would be indecorous, will probably be expected to say something for him, which would be but genteel. Now the consenting to act in this slavish manner, to seek for unnecessary homage in an enemy's court, and to add another instance to the list of those who have paid welcome compliments to ambition, is in our minds not only very un-English conduct, but very unphilosophical, and such as goes hard to establish that charge of foppery which is made against Sir Humphrey's character in general. But we have no wish to dwell upon this part of the subject. We content ourselves with having shewn the error and injuriousness of these compromises with worldly greatness; and do not mean to say that every man of sense is to take a violent part in politics, and to endanger his comforts like those who have embarked in the public cause. We only say that it becomes his good sense to have an opinion of his own, to set a proper value on his example, and to see the danger and unworthiness of countenancing errors of any sort, that tend to keep his fellow-creatures ignorant and unhappy.

BONAPARTE FALLEN AND LONDON IN APRIL [3]

PEOPLE are not yet recovered from the first surprise, or rather wonderment, occasioned them by the late events. The imperial Dictator of a Continent suddenly displaced from his throne, another revolution effected in France, and in favor of real freedom, a king restored to his crown, whose succession had been given up for years as a thing of hopeless remembrance, other monarchs, and even despotic ones, looking in the meantime with faces of popular feeling, people in their turn looking at *them* with surprise and regard—peace, in short, after an interval of twenty years, suddenly throwing open the intercourse between nations, and a new reasonableness of expectation given to the hopes of all lovers of improvement and happiness—all these things, coming too at a time when the whole of Christendom is keeping holiday, and when spring has returned with double luxury after a winter of unexampled severity, naturally carry people beyond their usual limits of enjoyment, and throw the common-places of life and business into the background.

Thus the world out of doors is represented to us as exhibiting a kind of perpetual fair; and luckily we can easily form a picture of it in our minds; for Attorney-Generals cannot commit one's fancy to custody, and as our imagination never sinned against the happiness of the community by flattering the * * * but a truce of these times with reflections that can do Princes no honor and give their people no pleasure We mingle with the busy pleasure of the streets; we see the joyous faces on all sides; we are carried along hither and thither through lane, square, and country road; here the little boys, looking another way, tumble against us and are off again; there the tradesman and his wife, in order to be in time, toil along under the burden of infants and bundles; here comes a country-grandmother with a huge nosegay for the little ones; there the gallant-apprentices push by, with their sweethearts under their arm, the latter in their best bonnets and their triangular pinned kerchiefs, the former looking up every now and then at the April clouds, conscious of the new hat and the glossy second-cloth; there his more tasty friend, sauntering by himself, hopes to be mistaken for a lounger; there the cavaliers of the day dance along upon horseback, the better ones exhibiting their skill and their easy persons, the others veiling the horror of being thrown by a look of serious indifference, or coming to a

---

[3] From *The Joy of the Public—Bonaparte* in *The Examiner*, No. 330, April 24, 1814.

walk as if they were past the pride of exhibiting; coaches, in the meantime, come sweeping along by the path or the curb-stone, some filled with gaping little children, others with older and placid looks, and others with beautiful faces that flash upon you as they bound by; similar appearances are at the windows and balconies; every body's object seems to please and to be pleased; the very dogs seem to think that they know as much of the business as most people; and life appears to be nothing but one scene of walking, riding, and smiling, thronged windows, dresses, handkerchiefs, green leaves, white ribbons, and flowers.

This has been the enjoyment out of doors:—but there is another species of it when people get in, and not inferior perhaps for being the quieter. How delightful to wake in the morning, and to think that there is *Peace,* to know that the work of death is not going on all over Europe, and that despotism is not only not extending itself, but has had a blow at its very roots! Then how pleasant to see in the newspapers the long-absent advertisements of mails from France, and visits to Paris! How welcome to receive the congratulations and hear the anticipated enjoyments of every body that comes in! How refreshing to the speculative politician to consider, that to a certain extent, the abuses of Government and of Government influence must now be giving way; and that Europe at large, from the various and complete experience it has had of the worst political errors, must be sincerely and calmly prepared to look after improvement! Every in-door enjoyment is bound to be double what it was, the wine to drink better, the concert to flow better; and though we are far from deprecating his just punishment and affording the moral, we should not esteem those persons the more, who could think with unmingled bitterness even of Bonaparte.

To this name one's thoughts necessarily come round. Where is he—what is he doing—how is he feeling—are questions that continue to start from everybody; and in his present situation, such a curiosity is not only natural, but laudable, and conducive to the very best purposes. We have already spoken of his future residence in Elba, and the probable turn of his thoughts there. After various reports which were contradicted one after the other, it now seems agreed that he has actually set out for that place; and if the life which he led at Fontainebleau be truly described, perhaps he is not sorry, comparatively speaking, at having taken his departure.

Think of a man, who has been used to dictate to every body, suddenly shut up with a few troops in a nook of his former dominions, and reading his doom every day in the papers which he lately had at his command. A

General or two, and a few domestics of the inferior kind, seem to have been all that remained with him. Two or three Marshals looked in at first, but it was only to advise him to be quiet, and to let him see that they were about to leave him. Here he remains, day after day, near enough to Paris to feel his pride elbowed, as it were, by the new bustle of things, yet far enough from it to be left to his new solitude and his still newer want of occupation.

The anecdotes, which are related of him under these circumstances, are natural enough upon the whole to be probable: but it is needless to repeat that, whether true or not, it is impossible to rely upon them. It is a well-imagined picture at any rate which represents him, in the first instance, at coming upon the parade at Fontainebleau, "horribly pale and thoughtful," and remaining there only a few minutes, his Generals during his stay talking among themselves loudly enough to be heard by him, and speculating, with an alarming want of attention, upon the events that had taken place. During the communication which Ney afterwards made to him of the final overthrow of his dynasty, he is described as conducting himself with cheerfulness; but upon Lefebvre's bluntly though not unfeelingly telling him that he was undone, and that he was undone because he would never listen to the advice of his servants, he is said to have been overcome and to have burst into a flood of tears. If this is true, what a multitude of new emotions must have gushed out with that flood! This may have been the first time since he set out on his ambitious projects, that he had felt the manifest voice of truth upon his ear; he was dashed back, at the moment he could least support it, with a sudden consciousness of himself and his infatuations; and it was a new sense perhaps of the friendliness which he had formerly doubted and disregarded, that came to the relief of his passionate nature, and threw him into tears.

With some persons, this will be a new proof of his want of courage; but here we must again differ from them:—with us it is rather an unexpected proof of his having something of the kindliness of human nature about him; and we only wish that he could have been acquainted with tears long since; they might have saved him many a reproach for dimming the eyes of others. If indeed it turned out that he made a practice of weeping, we should give up his manhood at once, at least in times like the present; for even then he might puzzle some of our declamatory persons by quoting classical authority for heroes being lachrymose, and talk of Aeneas, Achilles, and others, who made a point of crying and groaning whenever they found them-

selves uncomfortable. But we cannot say that we ever had a vast admiration for these personages any more than for great soldiers in general.

The most terrible anecdote however still remains, and this, we suppose, is to be convincing against him. Our readers will recollect that Bonaparte had for a long time had a favorite Mameluke, who was always about him. This personage, it seems, being of a very lofty mind, as is the custom with valets, and of a very delicate sense of honor, as is the characteristic of Mamelukes, entered his master's chamber the other day, after carefully sharpening a sword, and addressed him in the following terms:

Mameluke. Sir, after what has happened, of course you will not choose to live. I have brought you my sword. Will you use it yourself, or shall I pass it through your body? I am ready to obey your commands.

Napoleon. It does not appear to me that either of these alternatives is necessary.

Mameluke (with astonishment). Neither! What, can you endure life after such a reverse? Then pray dispatch me with the same weapon, or dismiss me from your service, for I will not live under such disgrace.

So saying, the Mameluke, without waiting either to be dispatched or dismissed, "haughtily leaves the room."

ELBA'S ONE HUNDRED AND ONE ROUNDS OF CANNON [4]

HAVING hitherto paid a good deal of attention to the proceedings of Bonaparte since his fall, thinking, as we do, that he is an object of much more rational curiosity, now that he is in a condition to turn his adversity to good purpose, than when he was abusing the vulgar admiration of the world, and only perplexing and slaughtering his species, we shall close our part, as *literary* Commissioners, by just seeing him safely in his island of exile, and then take our leave of him in common with the others.

He arrived on the isle of Elba, his new and dwindled span of dominion, on the 4th instant. The English frigate, that carried him, appeared the preceding evening off Porto Ferrajo, and his arrival having been officially communicated to the commanding officer, preparations were made during the night to receive him. The next morning, a white flag, sprinkled with bees,

---

[4] From *Bonaparte and His Arrival at Elba* in *The Examiner*, No. 335, May 29, 1814.

and charged in the middle with the united arms of himself and the island, was hoisted on the castle with the usual ceremonies; and some time after, he landed with his suite under a discharge of one hundred and one rounds of cannon. He appears to have been gaily drest, having under a blue great coat a suit richly embroidered with silver, and a round hat with a white cockade in it; but there was a sad falling off in the pomp of reception to which he has been accustomed, the bands of triumphant music, that used to burst out at his appearance, having sunk, if the account is not joking, into three fiddlers and a couple of fifes. He took up his abode for the present at the Mayoralty-house, and after reposing a little and receiving the visits of the authorities, with whom he is said to have been very lively and inquisitive, visited the different forts. The next day, still accompanied by the Allied Commissioners, he continued his survey of the island, and visited the celebrated iron mines, of which he asked the revenue. On being told the sum, he said "These livres then will be mine." "But, Sire," it was replied, "you know that by a decree, you appropriated them to the Legion of Honor." *Bonaparte:* "Where was my head when I gave this decree? But I have issued a number of foolish decrees in my lifetime!"

The French papers further inform us that there have since arrived in the port of Leghorn some small vessels from Elba, bearing the new flag, and that the populace from the shore insulted the crews for having afforded an asylum to Bonaparte. This may or may not be true; but if true, we are afraid that the Elbese will rather gather a pride from the importance attached to their master, and begin to value themselves above their neighbors, than take a counter-lesson from their reproaches. The white ground of Bonaparte's new colors, the emblem of *peace* and *innocence,* alludes perhaps to the new leaf he intends to turn over, in the tranquillity and harmlessness of his future pursuits; and the white cockade is most likely referable to this ground, and not to the Bourbons; though, if he mounted a similar decoration on his journey through France, in consequence of the popular cry, he chose the whole color perhaps as a trick by which he might afterwards explain away his compliance. The bees, which he retains, are probably intended to announce to us that he will retain his old habits of industry; for such is the heraldic import of bees, which signify also, we believe, that the person bearing them is able to be sweet to his friends and stinging to his enemies—a judicious mixture of the *glukupieron,* on which Bonaparte can hardly value himself—his sting has been much more notorious than his honey.

Immediately on his arrival, some very characteristic proclamations were

issued, which would seem as if he meant to act over his former part, at least as a sovereign, upon a sort of miniature scale. The first is signed by the French General commanding at Porto Ferrajo, and tells the inhabitants by Napoleon's direction, that their new Monarch having sacrificed his "rights" to the interests of France, had reserved to himself, with the assent of all the Allied Powers, the sovereignty and property of the Isle of Elba, and that he had selected the place in consideration of the mildness of their manners and the temperance of the climate. The General then says that the Emperor had promised to make them "the constant objects of his most lively interests," and adds, in a lofty manner, and as if he were addressing a great kingdom: "Elbese! These words require no comment; they *fix your destiny.*" This is evidently Napoleon's language; and looks like an actor, who from stage-habits cannot lower his tone to ordinary occasions.

The second Proclamation is from the Office of Signor Balbiani, Vice-Prefect, who tells the inhabitants that their wishes are accomplished, that the felicity of the island is secured, that Providence has conferred on it a signal favor, and that the first words which their august Sovereign had condescended to address to them through the medium of the public functionaries were never to be forgotten: "*I will be to you a good father, be you to me good children.*" What words from a man fresh from the exercise of civil and military despotism and from slaughters which he kept up to the last! But he scarcely seems aware of his own cant.

The last, longest, and most servile, is from the Reverend Father Giuseppe Filippo Arrighi, who, if we are to judge from his titles, is a most important person, being no less than Honorary Canon of the Cathedral of Pisa, ditto of the Metropolitan Church of Florence, and under the Bishop of Ajaccio, Vicar-General of the Isle of Elba and Principality of Piombino. Bonaparte, we should think, after being used to the pithy signatures of Archbishops and Cardinals, must feel a sickening sensation at this display of nonentities. The immediate object of the Reverend Vicar-General is to order a solemn thanksgiving in all the churches "for the precious gift which Heaven, in the abundance of its mercy, had conferred upon the inhabitants," but he takes ample occasion to be prefatory. Bonaparte is Napoleon the Great, the "Father rather than Sovereign," the "Annointed of the Lord," the "new Prince of immortal fame" who is to elevate "the island of Elba into the rank of nations." The memorable words, "I will be a good father, be you to me good children," are to form "the delight of their thoughts," and to be "impressed on their souls with transports of consolation"—above all (and here

his Reverence lets us into the secret of Elbian prosperity) "opulence is to inundate the country" and "multitudes will flock from foreign parts to behold a hero." The smallness of the things and places that are at present associated with Bonaparte leaves the absurdity of this old adulation to shift for itself; but it is melancholy to reflect that great nations have first set the example, and that very few of those persons who affect to enjoy the mock-heroic of his situation have really a right to laugh at it.

The Vicar-General, however, is right in supposing that Bonaparte's residence in the island may be useful to it, though it is curious enough that amidst all his panegyrics he can see no other advantage worth mentioning than the arrival of strangers from other parts "to behold a hero." If Bonaparte has not lost all relish or distinction of delicate praise, he must recoil at the coarse hint thus thrown out, of his being converted into a show. There is no knowing, it is true, what character he may put on next in order to obtain admiration; he may effect, for aught we know, the acme of candor and simplicity, and be easy of access to every traveller that shall choose to visit him in his library or garden; but we should not expect as much. He will not be able to conceal from himself that the curiosity he excites in his downfall is a very different one from that which he commanded during his imposing elevation; and unless he be exceedingly altered, and shall discover in his retreat the secret of true greatness, his patience will hardly stand the continual performance of an artificial philosophy. Even then indeed, by growing more disgusted with what he has been, he will grow nicer in his love of applause and tenderer to misapprehension; and must satisfy himself that his visitors come to see him in his new and more respectable character, before he can feel comfortable under their looks. However, whether he consents to see travellers or not, it is likely that he will attract them to the place of his residence, and that Elba will acquire from it an additional importance which must be sensibly felt in the dealings and connexions of so humble a territory.

The greater advantages which may accrue to the island from its new master will materially depend upon the sort of mastership he shall assume. If he contents himself with a sullen receipt of the revenues, letting everything else continue in its old state, and regarding the whole place with dislike as nothing but a compulsory habitation, Elba, with its mild inhabitants, may be only so much the worse for the introduction of a retinue of soldiers and fine servants, who, in endeavoring to make up for the loss of campaigning and of a French metropolis, may only lord it over the men and set about corrupting the females. But if, as if it would seem, he can get over the ridiculous

look of the contrast between his former and present sovereignty, if he should actually busy himself as a Prince in the welfare of his subjects, he may become a real blessing to the spot and make amends, in some measure, for the miseries he has inflicted on larger territories. He may soon become acquainted with the wants and means of all the inhabitants, he may greatly enlarge their trade and manufactures, circulate money amongst them, give them a good court to look up to, introduce to them the best enjoyments of the Continent, and render all that he bestows truly profitable by the greatest gift of all, the blessing of education. Luckily he will have no means of exercising his old trade of war; and despotism will be a needless trouble because he may here convince himself, if he has not done so before, that he can enjoy as much power as he can put to any actual purpose without it. In short, he cannot do any such harm as he has been doing to France, and he may perform upon a small scale all the good that he ought to have done. He may become what his great countryman, Paoli, hoped to have been to the Corsicans, a real father and improver. What has the man done that Providence should give him such a noble opportunity? Yet let not one's frail thoughts ask themselves this invidious question. If he was not good enough to deserve reward, he has done evil enough to want opportunities of making recompense, and here is, at least, one of them of no ordinary description.

There are one or two questions however still remaining which may interfere a little not only with the rising glories of the Elbese but with the present aspect of much greater nations. Will all this be lasting? Will Bonaparte, now that he is lodged in this island, be able to keep himself there, or be kept there by others? The Allied Powers have landed him and he has taken possession; but what guarantee has he for the possession of the place should a new war break out and one of the belligerents choose to attack it? Again, what is the pure and unbreakable talisman by which the European Sovereigns are to hold him aloof, if, with the renewal of their dynasties they are to be renewing their old tricks and taking pains once more to disgust the good sense of the community, if one Prince, rising from under oppression, is to begin plundering his neighbors, if another, restored from exile, is to set his face against the abolition of slavery and expatriation, and a third, triumphantly set free from imprisonment, is to turn upon his deliverers and with a worse than idiot mockery laugh their liberties to scorn? We trust that if some of these, unfortunately, are proved to be so doing, the intentions of others are grossly belied and that Bonaparte is not again to find his best strength in the sovereign weakness of his opponents.

EIGHT MILLIONS OF FREE PEOPLE:

An American Oration

An Oration delivered by permission on board the *Nassau*
prison-ship at Chatham, England, on the Fourth July
1814 by an American seaman prisoner of war. Printed at
Boston 1815.

"I RECITE THESE THINGS, MY COUNTRYMEN, THAT YOU MAY
KNOW HOW TO PRIZE LIBERTY"

My fellow-prisoners, and beloved countrymen,

WE ARE assembled to commemorate that ever memorable Fourth of July, 1776, when our forefathers, inspired with the love of liberty, dared to divest themselves of the shackles of tyranny and oppression: yes, my friends, on that important day these stripes were hoisted on the standard of liberty, as a signal of unity, and of their determination to fight under them, until America was numbered among the nations of the globe, as one of them, a free and independent nation. Yes, my countrymen, she was determined to spare neither blood nor treasure, until she had accomplished the grand object of her intentions; an object, my friends, which she was prompted by Heaven to undertake, and inspired by all that honour, justice, and patriotism could infuse; her armies were then in the field, with a WASHINGTON at their head, whose upright conduct and valorous deeds you have often heard related, and the memory of whom should be held sacred in the breast of every true-born American.—Let his heart beat high at the name of WASHINGTON! Sacred as the archives of heaven! for he was a man of truth, honour, and integrity, and a soldier fostered by the gods to be the saviour of his country.

The struggle was long, and arduous; but our rallying word was, "Liberty or Death!" Torrents of blood were spilt; towns and villages were burnt, and nothing but havoc, devastation and destruction was seen from one end of the continent to the other; and this was not all; but, to complete the horrid scene, an infernal horde of savage murderers was prompted by our enemy to butcher our helpless wives and children! Then did our fathers' patriotic

568

hearts swell in their bosoms, and they were ten-fold more resolved to break the yoke of the tyrant.

I recite these things, my countrymen, that you may know how to prize your liberty, that precious gem for which your fathers fought, wading in rivers of blood, until it pleased the Almighty to crown their arms with success; and, glorious to relate, America was acknowledged free and independent by all the powers of Europe. Happy period! then did our warriors exult in what they had so nobly achieved; then commerce revived, and the *thirteen stripes* were hoisted upon the tall masts of our ships, and displayed from pole to pole; emigrants flocked from many parts to taste our freedom, and other blessings heaven had bestowed upon us; our population increased to an incredible degree; our commerce flourished, and our country has been the seat of peace, plenty and happiness for many years. At length the fatal blast reached our land! America was obliged to unsheath the sword in justification of her violated rights. Our ships were captured and condemned upon frivolous pretensions; our seamen were dragged from their lawful employment; they were torn from the bosom of their beloved country; sons from their fathers; husbands from their wives and children, to serve with reluctance for many years, under the severity of a martial law. The truth of this many of you can attest to, perhaps with inward pining and a bleeding heart!

My countrymen! I did not mount this rostrum to inveigh against the British; only the demagogues, the war-faction I exclaim against. We all know, and that full well, that there are many honest, patriotic men in this country, who would raise their voices to succour us, and their *arms* too, could they do it with impunity. The sympathetic hearts of the good, feel for the oppressed in all climes. And now, my countrymen, it is more than probable that the land of your nativity will be involved in war, and deluged in blood for some time to come; yes, my friends, that happy country, which is the guardian of every thing you possess, that you esteem, near and dear, has again to struggle for her liberty. The British war-faction are rushing upon us with their fleets and armies, thinking, perhaps, to crush us in a moment. Strange infatuation! They have forgotten Bunker's Hill! They have forgotten Saratoga, and Yorktown, when the immortal WASHINGTON with his victorious army chased them through the Jerseys, under the muzzles of their ship's cannon for protection! They have forgotten that the sons of America have as good blood in their veins, and possess as sound limbs and nerves as they; strange infatuation! I repeat it, if they presume to think that eight millions of free people will be very easily divested of their liberty; my

word for it, they will not give up at the sight of their men-of-war or their redcoats; no, my friends, they will meet the lads who will play them the tune of yankee doodle, as well as they did at Lexington, or Bunker Hill. Besides, my countrymen, there is a plant in that country, (very little of which grows any where else,) the infusion of which stimulates the true sons of America to deeds of valour. There is something so fostering in the very sound of its name, that it holds superiority wherever it grows; it is a sacred plant, my friends, its name is LIBERTY, and may God grant that that plant may continue to grow in the United States of America, and never be rooted out so long as it shall please Him to continue the celestial orb to roll in yon azure expanse.

Ah! Britons! Britons! had your counsellors been just, and had they listened with attention, and followed the advice of the immortal William Pitt, Britain and America might have been one until the present hour; and they, united, in time might have given laws to the inhabitants of this terrestrial ball.

Many of you, my friends, have voluntarily embraced this loathsome prison, rather than betray your country; for by the laws of your country, to aid or give any assistance to an enemy, is treason, is punishable with death. I therefore hope that your country will reward you abundantly for your toil. And one and all let us embrace the icy arms of death, rather than cherish the least symptoms of an inclination to betray our country. Some have done it, who have pretended to be Americans, so far as to shield themselves under the name. Whether they were *real* Americans or not, it is hard for me to say; but if they were, they have put their hand to the plough, and not only looked back, but have *gone* back. I have not the least doubt but they will meet their reward; that is, they will be spurned at by those very people that laid the bait for them. Such characters will for ever be condemned, and held in detestation by both parties. Therefore all you who feel the tide of true American blood flow through your hearts, I hope never will attempt to flee from the allegiance of your country. It is cowardice, it is felony; and for all those who have done it, we may pray that the departed spirits of their fathers, who so nobly fought, bled, and fell in the conflict to gain them their liberty, will haunt them in their midnight slumbers, and that they may feel the horrors of conscience and the dread of a gallows! also, that they may have no rest, but like the dove that Noah sent out of the ark, be restless until they return to the allegiance of their country. And now, my countrymen, let us join in unison to correct our own morals; let us be sober, let us be vigilant over ourselves while in this situation. And although it is not in

our power to assist our countrymen in the present conflict, yet if we are good the power of Heaven will fight for us; for the good must merit God's peculiar care. The powers of Heaven fought for us; they assisted us to gain our liberty, it is evident from the very circumstance, that in our struggle with Great Britain for our liberty, we had no navy, or none of any consequence, yet Great Britain lost more line of battle ships in that war than she did with France, although France is a great naval power. And we should be thankful to God for all the blessings he hath bestowed upon us from time to time, and in particular for the blessings of that unity which we are recently informed prevails among our countrymen in America; united they stand, nor will the powers of hell be able to overthrow them. And now let us appeal to the God of Sabaoth, that is, the God of armies—let us appeal to Him who holds the balance, and weighs the events of battles and of realms, and by his decision we must abide. And may He grant us health, peace and unity in this our disagreeable situation; and let us all join in concord to praise the Ruler and Governor of the universe. Amen. Amen.[1]

---

[1] *Under the spell of this anonymous orator, we may recall that* The Star-Spangled Banner *was written in 1814 when Francis Scott Key was virtually a prisoner of war. Under a flag of truce he was negotiating the release of a fellow-townsman by the British Fleet just when it was busy planning the attack on Fort McHenry and Baltimore. As every schoolboy knows, Key endured his celebrated agony of suspense—a patriot's purgatory—until he saw "proof through the night that our flag was still there." According to Chief Justice Taney's account of the birth of the national ballad, in the 1857 edition of* Poems of the late Francis S. Key, Esq.: *"When I had read it and expressed my admiration, I asked him how he found time, in the scenes he had been passing through, to compose such a song? He said he commenced it on the deck of their vessel, in the fervor of the moment, when he saw the enemy hastily retreating to their ships, and looked at the flag he had watched for so anxiously as the morning opened; that he had written some lines, or brief notes that would aid him in calling them to mind, upon the back of a letter which he happened to have in his pocket; and for some of the lines, as he proceeded, he was obliged to rely altogether on his memory; and that he finished it in the boat on his way to the shore, and wrote it out as it now stands, at the hotel, on the night he reached Baltimore, and immediately after he arrived. He said that on the next morning, he took it to Judge Nicholson [his brother-in-law], to ask him what he thought of it, that he was so much pleased with it, that he immediately sent it to a printer, and directed copies to be struck off in hand-bill form; and that he, Mr. Key, believed it to have been favorably received by the Baltimore public."*

YANKEE PERFECTIONIST:
William Lloyd Garrison

TO THE EDITOR OF THE "BOSTON COURIER"

TO MR. FRANCIS TODD, MERCHANT

FREEDOM OF THE MIND

~~~~~~

I am in earnest—I will not equivocate—I will not excuse—I will not retreat a single inch—AND I WILL BE HEARD.

William Lloyd Garrison

> There's Garrison, his features very
> Benign for an incendiary.
>
> *James Russell Lowell*

WHEN a passionate Yankee of five-and-twenty, William Lloyd Garrison, was made the editor of a nomadic newspaper with a name as long as a caravan, *The Genius of Universal Emancipation,* a true genius for trouble came to the city of Baltimore, port of slave shipping. Reporting a commonplace phenomenon on the docks of 1829, the young editor brought attention to a respectable citizen, Mr. Francis Todd of Newburyport, Massachusetts, whose good ship, the *Francis,* was loading for New Orleans seventy-five slaves chained in a narrow place between the decks. Garrison's language and typography were bold: "The men who have the wickedness to participate therein for the purpose of heaping up wealth, should be ☞ SENTENCED TO SOLITARY CONFINEMENT FOR LIFE ☜ *they are the enemies of their own species—highway robbers and murderers;* and their final doom will be, unless they speedily repent, *to occupy the lowest depths of perdition."* Not unnaturally, the feelings of Mr. Francis Todd of Newburyport were hurt, and he caused editor Garrison to be put into the Baltimore jail with the apologetic remark that he, Francis Todd, "should have preferred another kind of freight, but as freights were dull, times hard, and money scarce, he was satisfied with the bargain." Garrison was not satisfied. On the threshold of a hydra-headed career that was to bring down on him a tar-and-feather mob in Boston and "protective arrest" in 1835; that was to include a battle with the churches and his old friends; a universal reformism which embraced tobacco, capital punishment, prohibition, woman suffrage, Indian rights, prostitution, disunion from the South, *and* Abolition;

572

as well as that dramatic moment when Garrison was to burn publicly copies of the Fugitive State Law and the Constitution of the United States in the same pot, he was schooling himself fast in his present apprenticeship for his life-long mission to act "as an antidote to American complacency." (He was to remark, "Sir, slavery will not be overthrown without excitement, a most tremendous excitement.") From his cell in the Baltimore jail he waged a seven-weeks' war of abolition. He wrote a pamphlet on his trial, "cards" to his judge, his prosecuting attorney, and his accuser, youthful sonnets on the satisfaction of being in jail, and of course letters to the press. The excitement of the young man of twenty-five, whose Yankee will was being tempered into the sharpest abolitionist sword, was aroused by the impudent slave-traders who were invading even the sanctuary of his jail in Baltimore. When a rich, northern, abolitionist businessman, Arthur Tappan (for whose respectable body a southern state would have given a reward of $20,000 and whose ears to another southern state were worth $3000) finally rescued young Garrison from jail by paying $100, the young editor founded a paper of his own, the famous *Liberator,* and treated his readers to the following account of his apprenticeship in Baltimore:

During my late incarceration in Baltimore prison, four men came to obtain a runaway slave. He was brought out of his cell to confront his master, but pretended not to know him—did not know that he had ever seen him before—could not recollect his name. Of course the master was exceedingly irritated. "Don't you remember," said he, "when I gave you, not long since, thirty-nine lashes under the apple-tree? Another time, when I gave you a sound flogging in the barn? Another time, when you were scourged for giving me the lie, by saying that the horse was in a good condition?"

"Yes," replied the slave, whose memory was thus quickened, "I do recollect. You have beaten me cruelly without a cause; you have not given me enough to eat and drink; and I don't want to go back again. I wish you to sell me to another master—I had rather even go to Georgia than to return home."

"I'll let you know, you villain," said the master, "that *my* wishes, and not *yours,* are to be consulted. I'll learn you how to run away again."

The other men advised him to take the black home, and cut him up in inch pieces for his impudence, obstinacy, and desertion—swearing tremendously all the while. The slave was ordered back to his cell.

I had stood speechless during this singular dialogue, my blood boiling in my veins, and my limbs trembling with emotion. I now walked up to the gang, and, addressing the master as calmly as possible, said—

"Sir, what right have you to that poor creature?"

He looked up in my face very innocently, and replied—

"My father left him to me."

"Suppose," said I, "your father had broken into a bank and stolen ten thousand dollars, and safely bequeathed the sum as a legacy: could you conscientiously keep the money? For myself, I had rather rob any bank to an indefinite amount than kidnap a fellow-being, or hold him in bondage: the crime would be less injurious to society, and less sinful in the sight of God."

The man and his crew were confounded. What! to hear such sentiments in Maryland,—and in jail, too! Looking them full in the face, and getting no reply, I walked a few steps to the door. After a brief consultation, the master came up to me and said—

"Perhaps you would like to buy the slave, and give him his liberty?"

"Sir, I am a poor man; and were I ever so opulent, it would be necessary, on your part, to make out a clear title to the services of the slave before I could conscientiously make a bargain."

After a pause, he said—

"Well, sir, I can prove from the Bible that slavery is right."

"Ah!" replied I, "that is a precious book—the rule of conduct. I have always supposed that its spirit was directly opposed to everything in the shape of fraud and oppression. However, sir, I should be glad to hear your text."

He somewhat hesitatingly muttered out—"Ham—Noah's curse, you know."

"O, sir, you build on a very slender foundation. Granting, even—what remains to be proved—that the Africans are the descendants of Ham, Noah's curse was a *prediction* of future servitude, and not an *injunction* to oppress. Pray, sir, is it a careful desire to fulfil the Scriptures, or to make money, that induces you to hold your fellow-men in bondage?"

"Why, sir," exclaimed the slavite, with unmingled astonishment, "do you really think that the slaves are beings like ourselves?—that is, I mean do you believe that they possess the same faculties and capacities as the whites?"

"Certainly, sir," I responded. "I do not know that there is any moral or intellectual quality in the curl of the hair or the color of the skin. I cannot conceive why a black man may not as reasonably object to my color, as I to his. Sir, it is not a black face that I detest, but a black heart—and I find it very often under a white skin."

"Well, sir," said my querist, "how would you like to see a black man President of the United States?"

"As to that, sir, I am a true republican, and bow to the will of the majority. If the people prefer a black President, I shall cheerfully submit; and if he be qualified for the station, may peradventure give him my vote."

"How should you like to have a black man marry your daughter?"

"I am not married—I have no daughter. Sir, I am not familiar with *your* practices; but allow me to say, that slaveholders generally should be the last persons to affect fastidiousness on that point; for they seem to be enamoured with *amalgamation*."

Thus ended the dialogue.

TO THE EDITOR OF THE *BOSTON COURIER*[1]

Baltimore,
May 12, 1830.

Dear Sir: I salute you from the walls of my prison! So weak is poor human nature, that commonly, the larger the building it occupies, the more it is puffed up with inordinate pride. I assure you, that, notwithstanding the massive dimensions of this superstructure—its imperishable strength, its redundant passages, its multicapsular apartments—I am as humble as any occupant of a ten-foot building in our great Babel;—which frame of mind, my friends must acknowledge, is very commendable. It is true, I am not the owner of this huge pile, nor the grave lord-keeper of it; but then, I pay no rent—am bound to make no repairs—and enjoy the luxury of independence divested of its cares. . . .

Now, don't look amazed because I am in confinement. I have neither broken any man's head nor picked any man's pocket, neither committed highway robbery nor fired any part of the city. Yet, true it is, I am in prison, as snug as a robin in his cage; but I sing as often, and quite as well, as I did before my wings were clipped. To change the figure: here I strut, the lion of the day; and, of course, attract a great number of visitors, as the exhibition is gratuitous—so that between the conversation of my friends, the labors of my brain, and the ever-changing curiosities of this huge menagerie, time flies astonishingly swift. Moreover, this is a capital place to sketch the lights and shadows of human nature. Every day, in the gallery of my imagination, I hang up a fresh picture. I shall have a rare collection at the expiration of my visit.

[ENCLOSURE FOR THE "COURIER"]

A CARD: TO MR. FRANCIS TODD, MERCHANT, OF NEWBURYPORT, MASSACHUSETTS

Sir: As a New England man, and a fellow townsman, I am ashamed of your conduct. How could you suffer your noble ship to be freighted with the wretched victims of slavery? Is not this horrible traffic offensive to God, and

---

[1]Joseph Tinker Buckingham.

revolting to humanity? You have a wife—Do you love her? You have children—If one merchant should kidnap, another sell, and a third transport them to a foreign market, how would you bear this bereavement? What language would be strong enough to denounce the abettor? You would rend the heavens with your lamentations! There is no sacrifice so painful to parents as the loss of their offspring. So cries the voice of nature!

Take another case. Suppose you and your family were seized on execution, and sold at public auction: a New Orleans planter buys your children—a Georgian, your wife—a South Carolinian, yourself: would one of your townsmen (believing the job to be a profitable one) be blameless for transporting you all thither, though familiar with all these afflicting circumstances?

Sir, I owe you no ill-will. My soul weeps over your error. I denounced your conduct in strong language—but did not you deserve it? Consult your Bible and your heart. I am in prison for denouncing slavery in a free country! You, who have assisted in oppressing your fellow-creatures, are permitted to go at large, and to enjoy the fruits of your crime! *Cui prodest scelus, is fecit.*

You shall hear from me again. In the meantime, with mingled emotions, &c., &c.

WILLIAM LLOYD GARRISON

Baltimore Jail, May 13, 1830.

FREEDOM OF THE MIND [2]

HIGH walls and huge the BODY may confine,
    And iron grates obstruct the prisoner's gaze,
    And massive bolts may baffle his design,
    And vigilant keepers watch his devious ways:
Yet scorns th'immortal MIND this base control!
    No chains can bind it, and no cell enclose:

---

[2] Verse written by young Garrison on the wall of his cell in the Baltimore Jail. He decorated those walls with another, *Sonnet To Sleep*, and explained to the editor for whom he copied it from the original place: "I send you a Sonnet which I pencilled on the wall of my room the morning after my incarceration. It is a little bulletin showing in what manner I rested during the preceding night." He wrote a third sonnet, *The Guiltless Prisoner*, presumably on paper, which somewhat exaggerated the young man's situation:

Though beat—imprisoned—put to open shame—
Time shall embalm and magnify thy name.

Swifter than light, it flies from pole to pole,
  And, in a flash, from earth to heaven it goes!
It leaps from mount to mount—from vale to vale
  It wanders, plucking honeyed fruits and flowers;
It visits home, to hear the fireside tale,
  Or in sweet converse pass the joyous hours:
'Tis up before the sun, roaming afar,
  And, in its watches, wearies every star!

OF DECEMBER 2, 1859:

John Brown

THE CROSS-EXAMINATION OF JOHN BROWN

THE LAST SPEECH   JOHN BROWN'S WILL

ONE MORE SENTENCE

~~~~~~

Well, no, I don't suppose he could get four-and-sixpence a day for being hung, take the year round; but then he stands a chance to save a considerable part of his soul, —and *such* a soul!—when *you* do not. No doubt you can get more in your market for a quart of milk than for a quart of blood, but that is not the market that heroes carry their blood to.

THOREAU, *A Plea for Captain John Brown*

LIKE a stroke of lightning which brought a whole landscape into instantaneous relief, the hanging of John Brown on December 2, 1859 was a moment of sharp revelation. On that day his impetuous vision of an insurrection by fugitive slaves was spent; his bloody sins in the Kansas massacre were shriven by the martyrdom on the gallows. He died with dignity, and the satisfaction that God had approved him and his assault on Harper's Ferry without any reservations. Then he became the bone of contention between those who were sure that he was mad because there were legal affidavits to prove it, and those who were sure he was prophetic because the Civil War proved it. Of course, the Civil War was not an insurrection of slaves and the effect of John Brown was best defined by himself when he said, "I am worth now infinitely more to die than to live"—in the words of Stephen Vincent Benét:—

> And lived his month so, busily.
> A month of trifles building up a legend
> And letters in a pinched, firm handwriting
> Courageous, scriptural, misspelt and terse,
> Sowing a fable everywhere they fell
> While the town filled with troops.

The hanging stirred the nation. It stirred pro-slavery Democrats against "Black Republicans." It caught both the militant and mild abolitionists with their defenses down. It soon echoed in Concord, Boston, New Bedford,

Manchester, New York, and Philadelphia. The bells tolled, the churches and the townhalls filled, the editors wrote editorials and the diarists set down their private emotions.

Thoreau, who in 1846 had gone to jail rather than pay the poll tax, was one of the first to seize a platform. John Brown had been one of the favorite three to impress him with manliness—Brown, the Indian guide in Maine, and Walt Whitman. In his private journal Thoreau wrote:

Though we wear no crape, the thought of that man's position and probable fate is spoiling many a man's day here at the North for other thinking. If any one who has seen him here can pursue successfully any other train of thought, I do not know what he is made of. If there is any such who gets his normal allowance of sleep, I will warrant him to fatten easily under any circumstances which do not touch his body or purse. I put a piece of paper and a pencil under my pillow, and when I could not sleep, I wrote in the dark.

What Thoreau wrote "in the dark" was put together hurriedly and bitterly into *A Plea for Captain John Brown* and read to the villagers of Concord, the townspeople of Worcester, and Theodore Parker's audience in Boston. Thoreau, who considered himself too transcendental to be a joiner, now said: "For once we are lifted out of the dust of politics into the region of truth and manhood." In another private journal, Bronson Alcott measured these events very earnestly from day to day—on May 8, Brown had the platform in the Town Hall of Concord, Massachusetts, and "our best people listen to his words: Emerson, Thoreau, Judge Hoar, my wife"—on October 23: "this deed of his, so surprising, so mixed, so confounding to most persons, will go down as an impulse to freedom and humanity"—on October 30 when Thoreau read his indignation publicly—on November 2, after the verdict of death: "Sanborn takes tea with us and tells us many things about Brown, all to the credit of the man and the hero"—on November 4: "Assort my Baldwin apples and get them ready for customers. Thoreau calls and reports about the reading of his lecture on Brown at Boston and Worcester"—and finally on December 2, 1859, after the memorial meeting in Concord:

Ellen Emerson sends me a fair copy of hers of the Martyr Service. 2 P.M. Meet at Town Hall. Our townspeople present mostly, and many from the adjoining towns. Simon Brown, Chairman. Readings by Thoreau, Emerson, Bowers, Keyes, and Alcott, and Sanborn's dirge is sung by the company, standing. The bells are not rung. I think not more than one or two of Brown's friends wished them to be. I did not. It was more fitting to signify our sorrow in the subdued tones, and silent, than by any clamor of steeples and the awakening of angry feelings. Any conflict is needless as unamiable between neighbors, churchmen, and

statesmen. The services are affecting and impressive; distinguished by modesty, simplicity, and earnestness; worthy alike of the occasion and of the man.

Thomas Wentworth Higginson, plotting an escape for Brown who however stubbornly refused it, wrote to his "Dearest Mother" on October 27: "I don't feel sure that his acquittal or rescue would do half as much good as his being executed." On November 5 Higginson spoke of the "money, shoes, gloves, handkerchiefs, kisses and counsel" which Mrs. Brown was receiving from friends, and on November 22 Higginson wrote to his mother about "a man in Winchendon offering to adopt one of the daughters and teach her telegraphy," and added, "The whole thing is having a tremendous influence on public sentiment." Longfellow recorded in his diary: "This will be a great day in our history; the date of a new Revolution,—quite as much needed as the old one." Emerson spoke of John, Brown as "that new saint." Whittier wrote a poem which was to appear in the *Independent* of December 22:

Perish with him the folly that seeks through evil good!
Long live the generous purpose unstained with human blood!
Not the raid of midnight terror, but the thought which underlies;
Not the borderer's pride of daring, but the Christian's sacrifice.

William Lloyd Garrison announced that: "In firing his gun, he has merely told us what time of the day it is. It is high noon, thank God!" Horace Greeley said: "I think the end of slavery is ten years nearer than it seemed a few weeks ago." At the funeral Wendell Phillips declared that Brown "has loosened the roots of the slave system; it only breathes,—it does not live—hereafter," though in Troy, Kansas, Abraham Lincoln was remarking on December 2, 1859, that:

Old John Brown has been executed for treason against a State. We cannot object, even though he agreed with us in thinking slavery wrong. That cannot excuse violence, bloodshed and treason. It could avail him nothing that he might think himself right.

From across the seas Victor Hugo had fired a gun of rhetoric with the words: "The conscience of mankind is an open eye; let the court at Charlestown understand—Hunter and Parker, the slave-holding jurymen, the whole population of Virginia—that they are watched." And in the United States one American wrote to another American [1] on December 3, 1859: "Poor

---

[1] George Hoadley to Salmon P. Chase, quoted by Oswald Garrison Villard in his biography of John Brown.

old John Brown, God sanctify his death to our good, and give us a little of his courage, piety and self-sacrificing spirit, with more brains!"

THE CROSS-EXAMINATION OF JOHN BROWN FOR THE ASSAULT ON HARPER'S FERRY

[In the afternoon of October 19, 1859, a lucky reporter of the *New York Herald* attended the cross-examination of prisoner John Brown who lay wounded, alongside one of his companions, in the armory at Harper's Ferry. "There have been few more dramatic scenes in American history," says Oswald Garrison Villard, "few upon which the shadows of coming events were more ominously cast. The two wounded prisoners, their hair clotted and tangled, their faces, hands and clothing powder-stained and blood-smeared, lay upon what the reporter of the *New York Herald*, who preserved for posterity this interview, called their 'miserable shakedowns, covered with old bedding.' Near them stood Robert E. Lee, J. E. B. Stuart, Senator J. M. Mason, Governor Wise, Congressman Vallandigham of Ohio, Colonel Lewis Washington, Andrew Hunter, Congressman Charles James Faulkner of Virginia, nearly all destined soon to play important roles, the first four in the Confederacy that was to come into being." The verbatim report of the proceedings appeared in the *New York Herald* of Friday, October 21, 1859, under these headlines:

THE HARPER'S FERRY OUTBREAK

Verbatim Report Of The Questioning Of Old Brown
By Senator Mason, Congressman Vallandigham, Etc.
He Refuses To Disclose The Names Of His Abettors, Etc.
He Declares That He Received His Wounds After Surrendering, Etc.]

Senator Mason. Can you tell us who furnished money for your expedition?

John Brown. I furnished most of it myself; I cannot implicate others. It is by my own folly that I have been taken. I could easily have saved myself from it, had I exercised my own better judgment rather than yielded to my feelings.

Mason. You mean if you had escaped immediately?

Brown. No. I had the means to make myself secure without any escape; but I allowed myself to be surrounded by a force by being too tardy. I should have gone away; but I had thirty odd prisoners, whose wives and daughters were in tears for their safety, and I felt for them. Besides, I wanted to allay the fears of those who believed we came here to burn and kill. For this reason I allowed the train to cross the bridge, and gave them full liberty to pass on. I did it only to spare the feelings of those passengers and their families, and to allay the apprehensions that you had got here in your

vicinity a band of men who had no regard for life and property, nor any feelings of humanity.

Mason. But you killed some people passing along the streets quietly.

Brown. Well, sir, if there was anything of that kind done, it was without my knowledge. Your own citizens who were my prisoners will tell you that every possible means was taken to prevent it. I did not allow my men to fire when there was danger of killing those we regarded as innocent persons, if I could help it. They will tell you that we allowed ourselves to be fired at repeatedly, and did not return it.

A Bystander. That is not so. You killed an unarmed man at the corner of the house over there at the water-tank, and another besides.

Brown. See here, my friend; it is useless to dispute or contradict the report of your own neighbors who were my prisoners.

Mason. If you would tell us who sent you here,—who provided the means, —that would be information of some value.

Brown. I will answer freely and faithfully about what concerns myself,— I will answer anything I can with honor,—but not about others.

Mr. Vallandigham (who had just entered). Mr. Brown, who sent you here?

Brown. No man sent me here; it was my own prompting and that of my Maker, or that of the Devil,—whichever you please to ascribe it to. I acknowledge no master in human form.

Vallandigham. Did you get up the expedition yourself?

Brown. I did.

Vallandigham. Did you get up this document that is called a Constitution?

Brown. I did. They are a constitution and ordinances of my own contriving and getting up.

Vallandigham. How long have you been engaged in this business?

Brown. From the breaking out of the difficulties in Kansas. Four of my sons had gone there to settle, and they induced me to go. I did not go there to settle, but because of the difficulties.

Mason. How many are there engaged with you in this movement?

Brown. Any questions that I can honorably answer I will,—not otherwise. So far as I am myself concerned, I have told everything truthfully. I value my word, sir.

Mason. What was your object in coming?

Brown. We came to free the slaves, and only that.

A Volunteer. How many men, in all, had you?

Brown. I came to Virginia with eighteen men only, besides myself.

Volunteer. What in the world did you suppose you could do here in Virginia with that amount of men?

Brown. Young man, I do not wish to discuss that question here.

Volunteer. You could not do anything.

Brown. Well, perhaps your ideas and mine on military subjects would differ materially.

Mason. How do you justify your acts?

Brown: I think, my friend, you are guilty of a great wrong against God and humanity,—I say it without wishing to be offensive,—and it would be perfectly right for any one to interfere with you so far as to free those you wilfully and wickedly hold in bondage. I do not say this insultingly.

Mason. I understand that.

Brown. I think I did right, and that others will do right who interfere with you at any time and at all times. I hold that the Golden Rule, "Do unto others as ye would that others should do unto you," applies to all who would help others to gain their liberty.

Lieutenant Stuart. But don't you believe in the Bible?

Brown. Certainly I do.

. . . . . .

Mason. Did you consider this a military organization in this Constitution? I have not yet read it.

Brown. I did, in some sense. I wish you would give that paper close attention.

Mason. You consider yourself the commander-in-chief of these "provisional" military forces?

Brown. I was chosen, agreeably to the ordinance of a certain document, commander-in-chief of that force.

Mason. What wages did you offer?

Brown. None.

Stuart. "The wages of sin is death."

Brown. I would not have made such a remark to you if you had been a prisoner, and wounded, in my hands.

A Bystander. Did you not promise a Negro in Gettysburg twenty dollars a month?

Brown. I did not.

Mason. Does this talking annoy you?

Brown. Not in the least.

Vallandigham. Have you lived long in Ohio?

Brown. I went there in 1805. I lived in Summit County, which was then Portage County. My native place is Connecticut; my father lived there till 1805.

Vallandigham. Have you been in Portage County lately?

Brown. I was there in June last.

Vallandigham. When in Cleveland, did you attend the Fugitive Slave Law Convention there?

Brown. No. I was there about the time of the sitting of the court to try the Oberlin rescuers. I spoke there publicly on that subject; on the Fugitive Slave Law and my own rescue. Of course, so far as I had any influence at all, I was supposed to justify the Oberlin people for rescuing the slave, because I have myself forcibly taken slaves from bondage. I was concerned in taking eleven slaves from Missouri to Canada last winter. I think I spoke in Cleveland before the Convention. I do not know that I had conversation with any of the Oberlin rescuers. I was sick part of the time I was in Ohio with the ague, in Ashtabula County.

Vallandigham. Did you see anything of Joshua R. Giddings there?

Brown. I did meet him.

Vallandigham. Did you converse with him?

Brown. I did. I would not tell you, of course, anything that would implicate Mr. Giddings; but I certainly met with him and had conversations with him.

Vallandigham. About that rescue case?

Brown. Yes; I heard him express his opinions upon it very freely and frankly.

Vallandigham. Justifying it?

Brown. Yes, sir; I do not compromise him, certainly, in saying that.

Vallandigham. Will you answer this: Did you talk with Giddings about your expedition here?

Brown. No, I won't answer that; because a denial of it I would not make, and to make any affirmation of it I should be a great dunce.

Vallandigham. Have you had any correspondence with parties at the North on the subject of this movement?

Brown. I have had correspondence.

A Bystander. Do you consider this a religious movement?

Brown. It is, in my opinion, the greatest service man can render to God.

Bystander. Do you consider yourself an instrument in the hands of Providence?

Brown. I do.

Bystander. Upon what principle do you justify your acts?

Brown. Upon the Golden Rule. I pity the poor in bondage that have none to help them: that is why I am here; not to gratify any personal animosity, revenge, or vindictive spirit. It is my sympathy with the oppressed and the wronged, that are as good as you and as precious in the sight of God.

Bystander. Certainly. But why take the slaves against their will?

Brown. I never did.

Bystander. You did in one instance, at least.

[Stephens, the other wounded prisoner, here said, "You are right. In one case I know the Negro wanted to go back."]

Bystander. Where did you come from?

Stephens. I lived in Ashtabula County, Ohio.

Vallandigham. How recently did you leave Ashtabula County?

Stephens. Some months ago. I never resided there any length of time; have been through there.

Vallandigham. How far did you live from Jefferson?

Brown. Be cautious, Stephens, about any answers that would commit any friend. I would not answer that.

[Stephens turned partially over with a groan of pain, and was silent.]

Vallandigham. Who are your advisers in this movement?

Brown. I cannot answer that. I have numerous sympathizers throughout the entire North. ..

Vallandigham. In northern Ohio?

Brown. No more there than anywhere else; in all the free States.

Vallandigham. But you are not personally acquainted in southern Ohio?

Brown. Not very much.

A Bystander. Did you ever live in Washington City?

Brown. I did not. I want you to understand, gentlemen, and [to the reporter of the "Herald"] you may report that,—I want you to understand that I respect the rights of the poorest and weakest of colored people, oppressed by the slave system, just as much as I do those of the most wealthy and powerful. That is the idea that has moved me, and that alone. We expected no reward except the satisfaction of endeavoring to do for those in distress and greatly oppressed as we would be done by. The cry of dis-

tress of the oppressed is my reason, and the only thing that prompted me to come here.

Bystander. Why did you do it secretly?

Brown. Because I thought that necessary to success; no other reason.

Bystander. Have you read Gerrit Smith's last letter?

Brown. What letter do you mean?

Bystander. The "New York Herald" of yesterday, in speaking of this affair, mentions a letter in this way:—

"Apropos of this exciting news, we recollect a very significant passage in one of Gerrit Smith's letters, published a month or two ago, in which he speaks of the folly of attempting to strike the shackles off the slaves by the force of moral suasion or legal agitation, and predicts that the next movement made in the direction of Negro emancipation would be an insurrection in the South."

Brown. I have not seen the "New York Herald" for some days past; but I presume, from your remark about the gist of the letter, that I should concur with it. I agree with Mr. Smith that moral suasion is hopeless. I don't think the people of the slave States will ever consider the subject of slavery in its true light till some other argument is resorted to than moral suasion.

Vallandigham. Did you expect a general rising of the slaves in case of your success?

Brown. No, sir; nor did I wish it. I expected to gather them up from time to time, and set them free.

Vallandigham. Did you expect to hold possession here till then?

Brown. Well, probably I had quite a different idea. I do not know that I ought to reveal my plans. I am here a prisoner and wounded, because I foolishly allowed myself to be so. You overrate your strength in supposing I could have been taken if I had not allowed it. I was too tardy after commencing the open attack—in delaying my movements through Monday night, and up to the time I was attacked by the Government troops. It was all occasioned by my desire to spare the feelings of my prisoners and their families and the community at large. I had no knowledge of the shooting of the Negro Heywood.

Vallandigham. What time did you commence your organization in Canada?

Brown. That occurred about two years ago; in 1858.

Vallandigham. Who was the secretary?

Brown. That I would not tell if I recollected; but I do not recollect. I

think the officers were elected in May, 1858. I may answer incorrectly, but not intentionally. My head is a little confused by wounds, and my memory obscure on dates, etc.

Dr. Biggs. Were you in the party at Dr. Kennedy's house?

Brown. I was the head of that party. I occupied the house to mature my plans. I have not been in Baltimore to purchase caps.

Dr. Biggs. What was the number of men at Kennedy's?

Brown. I decline to answer that.

Dr. Biggs. Who lanced that woman's neck on the hill?

Brown. I did. I have sometimes practised in surgery when I thought it a matter of humanity and necessity, and there was no one else to do it; but I have not studied surgery.

Dr. Biggs. It was done very well and scientifically. They have been very clever to the neighbors, I have been told, and we had no reason to suspect them, except that we could not understand their movements. They were represented as eight or nine persons; on Friday there were thirteen.

Brown. There were more than that.

Q. Where did you get arms? *A.* I bought them.

Q. In what State? *A.* That I will not state.

Q. How many guns? *A.* Two hundred Sharpe's rifles and two hundred revolvers,—what is called the Massachusetts Arms Company's revolvers, a little under navy size.

Q. Why did you not take that swivel you left in the house? *A.* I had no occasion for it. It was given to me a year or two ago.

Q. In Kansas? *A.* No. I had nothing given to me in Kansas.

Q. By whom, and in what State? *A.* I decline to answer. It is not properly a swivel; it is a very large rifle with a pivot. The ball is larger than a musket ball; it is intended for a slug.

Reporter. I do not wish to annoy you; but if you have anything further you would like to say, I will report it.

Brown. I have nothing to say, only that I claim to be here in carrying out a measure I believe perfectly justifiable, and not to act the part of an incendiary or ruffian, but to aid those suffering great wrong. I wish to say, furthermore, that you had better—all you people at the South—prepare yourselves for a settlement of this question, that must come up for settlement sooner than you are prepared for it. The sooner you are prepared the better. You may dispose of me very easily,—I am nearly disposed of now; but this question is still to be settled,—this Negro question I mean; the end

of that is not yet. These wounds were inflicted upon me—both sabre cuts on my head and bayonet stabs in different parts of my body—some minutes after I had ceased fighting and had consented to surrender, for the benefit of others, not for my own. I believe the Major would not have been alive; I could have killed him just as easy as a mosquito when he came in, but I supposed he only came in to receive our surrender. There had been loud and long calls of "surrender" from us,—as loud as men could yell; but in the confusion and excitement I suppose we were not heard. I do not think the Major, or any one, meant to butcher us after we had surrendered.

An Officer. Why did you not surrender before the attack?

Brown. I did not think it was my duty or interest to do so. We assured the prisoners that we did not wish to harm them, and they should be set at liberty. I exercised my best judgment, not believing the people would wantonly sacrifice their own fellow-citizens, when we offered to let them go on condition of being allowed to change our position about a quarter of a mile. The prisoners agreed by a vote among themselves to pass across the bridge with us. We wanted them only as a sort of guarantee of our own safety,—that we should not be fired into. We took them, in the first place, as hostages and to keep them from doing any harm. We did kill some men in defending ourselves, but I saw no one fire except directly in self-defence. Our orders were strict not to harm any one not in arms against us.

Q. Brown, suppose you had every nigger in the United States, what would you do with them? *A.* Set them free.

Q. Your intention was to carry them off and free them? *A.* Not at all.

A Bystander. To set them free would sacrifice the life of every man in this community.

Brown. I do not think so.

Bystander. I know it. I think you are fanatical.

Brown. And I think you are fanatical. "Whom the gods would destroy they first make mad," and you are mad.

Q. Was it your only object to free the Negroes? *A.* Absolutely our only object.

Q. But you demanded and took Colonel Washington's silver and watch? *A.* Yes; we intended freely to appropriate the property of slaveholders to carry out our object. It was for that, and only that, and with no design to enrich ourselves with any plunder whatever.

Bystander. Did you know Sherrod in Kansas? I understand you killed him.

Brown. I killed no man except in fair fight. I fought at Black Jack Point and at Osawatomie; and if I killed anybody, it was at one of these places.

THE LAST SPEECH [2]

I HAVE, may it please the Court, a few words to say.

In the first place, I deny everything but what I have all along admitted,— the design on my part to free the slaves. I intended certainly to have made a clean thing of that matter, as I did last winter, when I went into Missouri and there took slaves without the snapping of a gun on either side, moved them through the country, and finally left them in Canada. I designed to have done the same thing again, on a larger scale. That was all I intended. I never did intend murder, or treason, or the destruction of property, or to excite or incite slaves to rebellion, or to make insurrection.

I have another objection: and that is, it is unjust that I should suffer such a penalty. Had I interfered in the manner which I admit, and which I admit has been fairly proved (for I admire the truthfulness and candor of the greater portion of the witnesses who have testified in this case),—had I so interfered in behalf of the rich, the powerful, the intelligent, the sc called great, or in behalf of any of their friends,—either father, mother, brother, sister, wife, or children, or any of that class,—and suffered and sacrificed what I have in this interference, it would have been all right; and every man in this court would have deemed it an act worthy of reward rather than punishment.

This court acknowledges, as I suppose, the validity of the law of God. I see a book kissed here which I suppose to be the Bible, or at least the New Testament. That teaches me that all things whatsoever I would that men should do to me, I should do even so to them. It teaches me, further, to 're-member them that are in bonds, as bound with them.' I endeavored to act up to that instruction. I say, I am yet too young to understand that God is any respecter of persons. I believe that to have interfered as I have done— as I have always freely admitted I have done—in behalf of His despised poor, was not wrong, but right. Now, if it is deemed necessary that I should forfeit my life for the furtherance of the ends of justice, and mingle my blood further with the blood of my children and with the blood of millions

---

[2] Delivered in the court at Charlestown, Virginia, on November 2, 1859, and published on the following day in the *New York Herald*.

in this slave country whose rights are disregarded by wicked, cruel, and unjust enactments,—I submit; so let it be done!

Let me say one word further.

I feel entirely satisfied with the treatment I have received on my trial. Considering all the circumstances, it has been more generous than I expected. But I feel no consciousness of guilt. I have stated from the first what was my intention, and what was not. I never had any design against the life of any person, nor any disposition to commit treason, or excite slaves to rebel, or make any general insurrection. I never encouraged any man to do so, but always discouraged any idea of that kind.

Let me say, also, a word in regard to the statements made by some of those connected with me. I hear it has been stated by some of them that I have induced them to join me. But the contrary is true. I do not say this to injure them, but as regretting their weakness. There is not one of them but joined me of his own accord, and the greater part of them at their own expense. A number of them I never saw, and never had a word of conversation with, till the day they came to me; and that was for the purpose I have stated.

Now I have done.

JOHN BROWN'S WILL

CHARLESTOWN, JEFFERSON COUNTY, VA., Dec. 1, 1859.

I GIVE to my son John Brown, Jr., my surveyor's compass and other surveyor's articles, if found; also, my old granite monument, now at North Elba, N. Y., to receive upon its two sides a further inscription, as I will hereafter direct; said stone monument, however, to remain at North Elba so long as any of my children and my wife may remain there as residents.

I give to my son Jason Brown my silver watch, with my name engraved on inner case.

I give to my son Owen Brown my double-spring opera-glass, and my rifle-gun (if found), presented to me at Worcester, Mass. It is globe-sighted and new. I give, also, to the same son $50 in cash, to be paid him from the proceeds of my father's estate, in consideration of his terrible suffering in Kansas and his crippled condition from his childhood.

I give to my son Salmon Brown $50 in cash, to be paid him from my father's estate, as an offset to the first two cases above named.

I give to my daughter Ruth Thompson my large old Bible, containing the family record.

I give to each of my sons, and to each of my other daughters, my son-in-law, Henry Thompson, and to each of my daughters-in-law, as good a copy of the Bible as can be purchased at some bookstore in New York or Boston, at a cost of $5 each in cash, to be paid out of the proceeds of my father's estate.

I give to each of my grandchildren that may be living when my father's estate is settled, as good a copy of the Bible as can be purchased (as above) at a cost of $3 each.

All the Bibles to be purchased at one and the same time for cash, on the best terms.

I desire to have $50 each paid out of the final proceeds of my father's estate to the following named persons, to wit: To Allan Hammond, Esq., of Rockville, Tolland County, Conn., or to George Kellogg, Esq., former agent of the New England Company at that place, for the use and benefit of that company. Also, $50 to Silas Havens, formerly of Lewisburg, Summit County, Ohio, if he can be found. Also, $50 to a man of Stark County, Ohio, at Canton, who sued my father in his lifetime, through Judge Humphrey and Mr. Upson of Akron, to be paid by J. R. Brown to the man in person, if he can be found; his name I cannot remember. My father made a compromise with the man by taking our house and lot at Munroville. I desire that any remaining balance that may become my due from my father's estate may be paid in equal amounts to my wife and to each of my children, and to the widows of Watson and Oliver Brown, by my brother.

JOHN BROWN.

JOHN AVIS, *Witness.*

ONE MORE SENTENCE [3]

I John Brown am now quite certain that the crimes of this *guilty land:* will never be purged away; but with Blood. I had *as I now think:* vainly flattered myself that without *very much* bloodshed; it might be done.

---

[3] Handed to one of his guards in the jail on the morning of his execution, December 2, 1859.

DROLL STORY:

Honoré de Balzac

"THIS IS ONE OF THE THOUSAND ACCIDENTS OF OUR PARISIAN LIFE"

"THIS is one of the thousand accidents of our Parisian life," Balzac was writing to Madame Evelina Hanska in the Ukraine. He was referring to his sudden lock-up in the "Hotel des Haricots"—a "hotel" derisively named after its standard dish of beans for impecunious jailbirds. Under Louis Philippe, whose bourgeois monarchy Balzac detested, all citizens were compelled to do guard duty for one or two nights a month. Those too poor to afford the vacation, and those too proud to "paddle in the mud" (as Werdet, Balzac's publisher, described the maneuvers), preferred the lock-up and the beans. Nothing could induce Balzac to put on the uniform of Louis Philippe. He had always managed to escape from the knapsack and the mud by timely bribes. Suddenly the busy novelist was granted, by an incorruptible agent of the National Guard, a week's pause in an unpleasant cell to consider his debts, his lawsuits, his schemes, his passions, to finish *Lily of the Valley,* and to send Madame Hanska in the boredom of her distant Russian château the latest news of Balzac's personal *comédie humaine.*

Enter Eugène Sue into this "Hotel des Haricots"—another fugitive in the spring of 1836 from Louis Philippe's monthly mud-paddling. The death of his father had given Sue a fortune, and his early romantic novels had increased it. This was some ten years before the humble man in the street was devouring the Fourierism of *The Mysteries of Paris.* Under lock and key in the company of Sue, Balzac had a leisurely opportunity to pity this rich and self-satisfied man, and to report to Madame Hanska the very worst about him: that "he no longer thinks of literature" and "he does not wish to marry." Nevertheless, he profited by the occasion to obtain from Eugène Sue another one of those passionately sought autographs of famous men for which Balzac was Madame Hanska's faithful agent.[1]

---

[1] Eugène Sue's autograph consisted of three little drawings: a horse, a horseman, and a marine. For the benefit of Madame Hanska, Balzac wrote under the first: *"Songler allant au bois";* under the second: *"Houp! là!"*; and under the third: *"Ceci est une marine."* Songler was the name of a horse which Balzac then owned. Over the whole prison souvenir Balzac wrote: *"Fait en prison à l'hôtel Bazancourt, où nous etions punis pour (n') avoir pas monté la garde, par les epiciers de Paris."* Punished, says Balzac, by the grocers of Paris.

The Parisian letter, which first the police and then Eugène Sue had interrupted, was addressed to a lady of quality whom Balzac loved for seventeen years, and called Madame de Balzac for only five months. Madame Hanska, the *"L'Étrangère"* of the celebrated Balzac correspondence, was the wife of a rich, old, and ailing man at the other end of Europe. In a château near Kiev, she lived less patiently with boredom than Chekov's Three Sisters, a boredom dissipated by infrequent travels and by those extraordinary letters that passed between her and the novelist who adored her. Balzac, who wanted not only to be famous but also to be loved ("believe me, youth and beauty are something"), first met Madame Hanska in 1833 at an auspicious moment. Balzac, says J. H. Floyd, had "grown weary of poor Duchesse d'Abrantes, about to cease his intimacy with Madame de Berny, having been rejected by Mademoiselle de Trumilly, and having suffered bitterly at the hands of the Duchesse de Castries." Thus Honoré de Balzac became Madame Hanska's "moujik," her dear "Honorenski." A little stout man of thirty-three who could devour one hundred oysters at a sitting, with the passion of a Napoleon for the great "human comedy" which he was constructing ("in that young Coliseum now constructing there is no sun"), he at once wrote to a dear and understanding, but never jealous friend, Madame Carraud, about his Polish aristocrat, Madame Hanska:

I must go climbing to Aix. I must run after someone who is perhaps only laughing at me—one of those aristocratic women you doubtless dislike; one of those exquisite beauties in whom one supposes, immediately, beautiful souls—a true duchess, disdainful, loving, subtle, coquettish. I have never seen the like of her. The woman of one's dreams!

The Balzac dream: *la femme de trente ans!*

The *Lily of the Valley* which Balzac was finishing in jail creates a Madame de Mortsauf who spends many years of renunciation explaining to a young man (who resembles Balzac) a virtue torn between passion and duty. When Madame Hanska's husband, suffering from "blue devils" like the husband in the *Lily of the Valley* which celebrates purity, at last died in 1841, Balzac wrote to her that he had not "in [his] most cruel moments stained [his] soul with evil wishes." He visited her in 1842, after an absence of eight long years, but she did not become his wife until 1850, *seventeen years* after their first meeting on a gay promenade in Neufchâtel. The luxurious house in Paris to which this Jacob brought his Rachel—a mansion which the newlyweds could not enter without the help of a locksmith because

Balzac's caretaker had quite suddenly gone mad from the excitement of preparation—and the illness which quickly killed the bridegroom are not as noteworthy and curious as the triumph felt by Honoré de Balzac before he died. For five months, this creator of passionate characters, this great lord of the imagination, was happy because he could claim as Madame de Balzac a lady who was, it seems, the grandniece of Queen Marie Leczinska, queen consort of Louis XV!

"THIS IS ONE OF THE THOUSAND ACCIDENTS OF OUR PARISIAN LIFE"

PARIS, April 23, 1836.

Cara. I receive to-day your number 8 with twenty days' interval. How many things have happened in twenty days! Yes, I have delayed writing, but intentionally. I wanted to send you only good news, and my affairs have been getting worse and worse. I have none but dreadful combats to relate to you, struggles, sufferings, useless measures taken, nights without sleep. To listen to my life a demon would weep.

Reading the last paragraphs of your letter I said to myself, "Well, I will write to her, even if to sadden her." Sorrow has a strong life, too strong perhaps.

My lawsuit is not yet tried. I must wait six days more for a verdict, unless the trial is still further postponed. The matter of the "Contes Drolatiques" is not decided. The shares of the "Chronique" are difficult to dispose of. So, my embarrassments redouble. For two months, since I have had so much business, I have done little work; here are two months lost; that is to say, the goose with the golden eggs is ill. Not only am I discouraged, but the imagination needs rest. A journey of two months would restore me. But a journey of two months means ten thousand francs, and I cannot have that sum when, on the contrary, I am behindhand with just that money. My liberation retreats; my dear independence comes not.

"Le Livre Mystique" is little liked here; the sale of the second edition does not go off. But in foreign countries it is very different; there the feeling is passionate. I have just received a very graceful letter from a Princess Angelina Radziwill, who envies you your dedication, and says it is all of

594

life for a woman to have inspired that book. I was very pleased for you. *Mon Dieu!* if you could have seen how in my quivering there was nothing personal. How happy I was to feel myself full of pride for you! What a moment of complete pleasure, and all unmixed! I shall thank the princess for you and not for myself—as we give treasures to a doctor who saves a beloved person. Besides, this is the first testimony to my success which has reached me from abroad.

Cara, write me quickly if you have any very trustworthy person in Saint Petersburg, because I have the means, or shall have, to send you those manuscripts through the French embassy. They can instantly reach Saint Petersburg; but from there to you, you must find the intermediary.

My letter was interrupted by the arrival of a commissary of police and two agents, who arrested me, and took me to the prison of the National Guard, where I am at this moment, and where I continue my letter peacefully. I am here for five days. I shall celebrate the birthday of the King of the French. But I lose the fine fireworks I intended to go and see!

My publisher [Werdet] has come, and given me an explanation of the non-arrival of the "Livre Mystique" to your hands. It is forbidden by the censor. So now I don't know what we shall do. Is it not singular that the person to whom it is dedicated should be the only one who has not read it? You must find out what is proper to do about it. I await your orders.

Here are all my ideas put to flight. This prison is horrid; all the prisoners are together. It is cold, and we have no fire. The prisoners are of the lowest class, they are playing cards and shouting. Impossible to have a moment's tranquillity. They are mostly poor workmen, who cannot give two days of their time to guard duty without losing the subsistence of their families; and here and there are a few artists and writers, for whom this prison is even better than the guard-house. They say the beds are dreadful.

I have just got a table, a sofa, and a chair, and I am in a corner of a great, bare hall. Here I shall finish the "Lys dans la Vallée." All my affairs are suspended; and this happens on a day when my paper appears, and almost on the eve of the 30th, when I have three thousand francs to pay.

This is one of the thousand accidents of our Parisian life; and every day the like happens in all business. A man on whom you count to do you a service is in the country, and your plan fails. A sum that should have been paid to you is not paid. You must make ten tramps to find some one (and often at the last moment) for the success of some important matter. You can never imagine how much agony accompanies these hours, these days, lost.

Many a time I have lain down wearied,—incapable of undertaking to write a single word, of thinking my most dear ideas!

I cannot too often repeat it—it is a battle equal to those of war; the same fatigues under other forms. No real benevolence, no succour. All is protestation without efficacy. I have vanquished for six years, even seven; well, discouragement lays hold upon me when only one quarter of my debt remains to be paid, the last quarter. I don't know what to do. My life stops short before those last four thousand ducats.

Monday, 25th.

I have again interrupted my letter for forty-eight hours. Just as I was writing the word *ducats* Eugène Sue arrived. He is imprisoned for forty-eight hours. We have spent them together, and I would not continue this letter before him. He talked to me of his occupations, of his fortune. He is rich, and sheltered from everything. He no longer thinks of literature; he lives for himself alone; he has developed a complete selfishness; he does nothing for others, all for himself; he wants, at the end of his day, to be able to say that all that he has done, and all that has been done was for him. Woman is merely an instrument; he does not wish to marry. He is incapable of feeling any sentiment. I listened to all this tranquilly, thinking of my interrupted letter. It pained me for him. Oh! these forty-eight hours were all I needed to prove to me that men without ambition love no one. He went away, without thanking me for having sacrificed for him the concession I had obtained of being alone in the dormitory; for his admission came near compromising the little comforts a few friends had extracted for me from the inflexible staff of grocers, anxious to club all classes together in this fetid galley. I am going to bed.

Saturday, 30.

Great news! The bill for the lateral canal in the Lower Loire, which will go from Nantes to Orléans, has passed the Chamber of Deputies, and will be presented, May 3, to the Chamber of Peers, where the Marquis de la Place, the friend of all pupils of the École Polytechnique, has promised my brother-in-law to have it passed. So, there are my sister and her husband attaining, after ten years' struggle, to their ends. You know I told you at Geneva about that fine enterprise. Now, the only point is to find the twenty-

six millions. But that is nothing after what has been done. The stock will be rated so high that money will not be lacking.

At this moment I have a hope on my own account. That is to buy the grant of the grantee, M. de Villevêque, and try to make something on it by selling to a banker. My brother-in-law has just left my prison to try and arrange this affair. If I have this luck, I might in two months make a couple of hundred thousand francs, which would heal all my wounds. It is especially in political warfare that money is the nerve.

Sue drew caricatures with pen and ink on a bit of paper to which he put his name; so I send it to you as autograph. It will remind you of my seven days in prison.

Here, I am dying of consuming activity, while, from what you say, you are living in stagnation, without aliment, without your emotions of travel, which makes you desire either travel or complete solitude. What you tell me of Anna delights me; I had some fears for that frail health, but the fears came from my affection, for I know that these organizations, apparently weak, are sometimes of astonishing power.

I have just written to Hammer; he asked me for a second copy of "Le Livre Mystique." I shall send him two; and as our dear Hammer is as patient as a goat that is strangling herself, and thinks that books can go as fast as the post, I shall request him to send you one by the first opportunity. That's a first attempt, I'll try ten more, and out of ten there may be a lucky chance.

I have the set of pearls for you. But how can I send them?

When I leave the prison I shall go and see Madame Kisseleff. That will be number two of my chances.

Apropos, if you find a safe opportunity remember my tea, for there is none good in Paris. I tasted yours (Russian, I mean) a few days ago, and I am shameless enough to remind you of this. "Norma" has had little success here.

The gracefulness you have put into your last letter received here, to console me for the grief of knowing that the "Lys" was published in its first proof [in Russia] I cannot accept as author. The French language admits nothing that comforts the heart of M. Honoré de Balzac. You will say so with me when you hold the book and read it. However it be, the Apollo and the Diana are more beautiful than blocks of marble. The young man, the Oaristes, is more graceful than a skeleton, and we prefer the peach to the peach-stone, though that may contain a million of peaches.

I have much distress, even enormous distress in the direction of Madame

de Berny; not from her directly, but from her family. It is not of a nature to be written. Some evening at Wierzchownia, when the wounds are scars, I will tell it to you in murmurs that the spiders cannot hear, for my voice shall go from my lips to your heart. They are dreadful things, that scoop into life to the bone, deflowering all, and making one doubt of all, except of you for whom I reserve these sighs.

Oh! what repressions there are in my heart! Since I left Vienna all my sufferings, of all kinds, of all natures, have redoubled. Sighs sent through space, sufferings endured in secret, sufferings unperceived! My God! I who have never done ill, how many times have I said to myself, "One year of Diodati, and the lake!" How often have I thought, "Why not be dead on such a day, at such an hour?" Who is in the secret of so many inward storms, of so much passion lost in secret? Why are the fine years going, pursuing hope, which escapes, leaving nought behind but an indefatigable ardour of re-hoping? During this burning year, when at every moment all seems ending, and no end comes, desires lay hold upon me to flee this crater which makes me fear a withered end—to flee it to the ends of the earth.

I am the Wandering Jew of Thought, always afoot, always marching, without rest, without enjoyments of the heart, with nothing but that which leaves a memory both rich and poor, with nothing that I can wrest from the future. I beg from the future, I stretch my hands to it. It casts me—not an obole, but—a smile that says, "To-morrow."

PARIS, May 1, 1836.

This is the day on which last year I said to myself, "I am going there!" Last evening, I left my window for sadness overcame me. Sleep drove away the grief.

I have worked much to-day. I shall close this letter this evening; I will see if I have forgotten to tell you any facts of the last twenty days, when I have been like a shuttlecock between two battledores. I am going to set to work at the difficult passages in the "Lys." I must finish the chapter entitled, "First Loves." I think that I have undertaken literary effects that are extremely difficult to render. What work! What ideas are buried in this book! It is the poetic pendant of the "Médecin de campagne." I like all you write to me of the little events of your existence at Kiev: the name of Vandernesse, the little lady, etc. But I would like your letters still better if you would write me ten lines a day; no, not ten lines, but a word, a sentence. You have all your time, and I have only hours stolen from sleep to offer you. You are the

luxury of the heart, the only luxury that does not ruin, but brings with it nature's own simplicity, riches, poverty,—in short, all!

Alas! not being at home to-day I cannot enclose to you any autograph, and I have some interesting ones: Talma, Mademoiselle Mars, all sorts of people; I shall have one of Napoleon, one of Murat, etc. You will see that when a matter concerns the documentary treasures of Wierzchownia we have great constancy in our ideas.

To-day I have worked much; I shall spend the night on the completion of the "Lys"; for I have still thirty *feuilles* of my writing to do, which is one quarter of the book. After that I must finish the "Héritiers Boirouge" for Madame Béchet, who is married and become Madame Jacquillart; and next, give "La Torpille" in June to the "Chronique," without which we go to the bad. You see it is impossible that I should budge from here before September; there is nothing to be said; those things must be done. After that I shall have no money, I shall only have fulfilled my engagements. So I don't know which way to turn; what with notes falling due, no receipts, and no friend to advance me funds, what will become of me? Either some lucky chance or perish. Hitherto luck has served me.

Just now I am particularly overwhelmed because I counted on the conclusion of the affair of the "Cent Contes Drolatiques" which gave me thirty thousand francs and would have quieted everything. But the longer it goes, the less it ends. I am more than disheartened, I am crazy about it.

There, then, are my affairs. Much work to finish, no money to receive, much money to pay. Am I to be stopped in the midst of my career? What can I attempt?

My brother-in-law came back this morning. M. Lainé de Villevêque asks to reflect upon this sale. He asks three days; and that is the least a man should take to decide so important a matter. I have offered him twenty thousand ducats for his position as grantee, but in ready money. I hope that Rossini will get Aguado to lend it to me, and that I can then resell the position to Rothschild for the double or treble, out of which those scamps will still make five or six millions. There's a pretty smile; the first that fortune has bestowed upon me.

You see that in my next letter I shall have very interesting things to tell you: the canal affair; my lawsuit and the "Lys," and finally "Les Drolatiques," which will be either a complete failure or a piece of business done; in such matters I must have a "yes" or a "no."

Adieu, *cara;* do not make yourself unhappy about all this. I have broad

shoulders, the courage of a lion, strength of character, and if, at times, melancholy lays hold upon me, I look at the future, I believe in something good—though the years do pass with cruel rapidity; and what years! Ah, the beautiful years! Shall I ever again see the Lake of Geneva, or Neufchâtel?

Well, adieu; till ten days hence. You will know all that should be said for me and of me to those about you.

THE CRIME AND THE PUNISHMENT:

Fyodor Dostoevsky

FROM THE PETER-AND-PAUL FORTRESS

A LETTER FROM SIBERIA

This man had once been led out with others to the scaffold and a sentence of death was read over him. He was to be shot for a political offence. Twenty moments later a reprieve was read to them, and they were condemned to another punishment instead. Yet the interval between those two sentences, twenty minutes or at least a quarter of an hour, he passed in the fullest conviction that he would die in a few minutes. . . . He remembered it all with extraordinary distinctness and used to say that he never would forget those minutes.

DOSTOEVSKY, *The Idiot*

IF, TO explain the Dostoevsky doctrine of suffering, the authorship of *Crime and Punishment, The Idiot,* and *The Possessed,* we had no knowledge of the adventure which sent the great Russian master into eight years of prison and exile, we should somehow have to invent it. The roots of Dostoevsky's art and religion were nourished in prison. He entered it with a half-baked social enthusiasm; he came forth with a complete and conservative philosophy of the destiny of Russia and the Russian people. Almost at the start of the great catastrophe of his life he reported to his brother Michael: "I have gone through much; I mean, I have gone through much in myself; and now there are the things I am going to see and go through. There will be much to be written." As a member of the Petrashevsky Circle and the Dourov Circle of intellectuals of the mid-nineteenth century, was Dostoevsky a radical? In 1848 the February Revolution in Paris made every young Russian who read the newspapers a radical, that is to say a speculator in theories. The friends of Petrashevsky talked, lounged, recited, smoked, exchanged forbidden books, criticized the censor, deplored serfdom, discussed Fourier, poverty, Christianity, society, defined socialism, drank tea, and believed in mankind. The already famous twenty-seven-year-old author of *Poor Folk* would read aloud the notorious letter of the critic Belinsky to the novelist Gogol in which the Russian bureaucrats and autocrats were denounced as robbers and the Orthodox Church as a prop of the knout. A few bold souls proposed the ultimate in the annals of crime against the Throne: a secret printing press. The whole Petrashevsky conspiracy of indignation,

with a membership of some thirty young men, was nipped in the bud when the police spies had filled their copybooks. With his strangely abnormal health, his mysterious headaches, elations and depressions, haemorrhoids and hypochondria, Dostoevsky spent months in the Peter-and-Paul fortress, writing plans for a novel and a play, the short story *A Little Hero,* waiting for that fantastic climax which the vanity and charity of Nicholas I begot. The imaginative and playful Emperor commuted the death sentence of the Petrashevsky criminals to imprisonment and exile with careful orders, however, for a mock execution which would teach them a lesson at once in obedience and gratitude. The youthful theorists, talkers, tea-drinkers, Fourierists, smokers, abolitionists, poetasters, and lovers of mankind were led to the firing squad. The death sentence was read to them with solemnity and emphasis. The priest held up the cross. The first batch of three was tied to posts. In the last second of organized sadism the scheduled reprieve duly arrived with an imperial flourish. Death was mechanically commuted to imprisonment and the fine artistry of Nicholas I had made a little masterpiece of *grand guignol* with a dash of Christian charity. One prisoner promptly went mad without gratitude, others spoke on their knees the thankful words which the Emperor expected; Dostoevsky was later to put his emotion into the mouth of Myshkin in *The Idiot.* The mild radical in Dostoevsky died and the disciple of law and order was born. In the Siberian prison where he stayed for four years in ten-pound chains, he discovered the virtues of the Russian people among thieves and murderers, and, far from rebelling against his fate, Dostoevsky felt he was expiating original sin, and learning for the first time, among criminals and saints, the moral laws which govern men, their hearts, and their true politics. He was to say later: "Petrashevsky's disciples sowed many seeds. . . . Our exile was just; the *people* would have condemned us." After four years of prison he submitted to four years of Siberian exile in a soldier's uniform, contrite, Slavophil, a complete patriot. Whatever it was, evil or accidental, that had brought him there, the "people" changed him, the New Testament fed him; he was a true Russian. He informed his brother Michael that he now had many new needs and hopes. "To my soul, all is clear. I see my whole future, and all that I shall accomplish, plainly before me. I am content with my life. I fear only men and tyranny"—but not the insulted and the injured, the crucified and the underground souls. From Siberia he confessed to a lady who was pious: "I want to say to you about myself, that I am a child of this age, a child of unfaith and scepticism, and probably (indeed I know it) shall remain so to the end of

my life." But already he stated the problem that was to torment his art twenty-five years later: "If anyone could prove to me that Christ is outside the truth, and if the truth really did exclude Christ, I should prefer to stay with Christ and not with the truth."

FROM THE PETER-AND-PAUL FORTRESS

July 18, 1849

Dear Brother,

. . . At last you are free,[1] and I can vividly imagine how happy you were when you saw your family again. How impatiently they must have awaited you! I seem to see that your life is beginning to shape itself differently. With what are you now occupied, and, above all, what are your means of support? Have you work, and of what sort? Summer is indeed a burden in the town. You tell me only that you have taken a new house; and probably it is much smaller. It is a pity you couldn't spend the whole summer in the country. I thank you for the things you sent; they have relieved and diverted me. You write, my dear fellow, that I must not lose heart. Indeed, I am not losing heart at all; to be sure, life here is very monotonous and dreary, but what else could it be? And after all it isn't invariably so tedious. The time goes by most irregularly, so to speak—now too quickly, now too slowly. Sometimes I have the feeling that I've grown accustomed to this sort of life, and that nothing matters very much. Of course, I try to keep all alluring thoughts out of my head, but can't always succeed; my early days, with their fresh impressions, storm in on my soul, and I live all the past over again. That is in the natural order of things. The days are now for the most part bright, and I am somewhat more cheerful. The rainy days, though, are unbearable, and on them the casemate looks terribly grim. I have occupation, however. I do not let the time go by for naught; I have made out the plots of three tales and two novels; and I am writing a novel now, but avoid over-working. Such labor, when I do it with great enjoyment (I have never worked so much *con amore* as now), has always agitated me and affected my nerves. While I was working in freedom I was always obliged to diversify my labors with amusements; but here the excitement consequent on work has to evaporate unaided. My health is good, except for the haemorrhoids, and the shattered

---

[1] Michael Dostoevsky, also a member of the Petrashevsky Circle, was arrested but quickly released.

state of my nerves, which keeps up a constant *crescendo*. Now and then I get attacks of breathlessness, my appetite is as unsatisfactory as ever, I sleep badly, and have morbid dreams. I sleep about five hours in the daytime, and wake four times at least every night. This is the only thing that really bothers me. The worst of all are the twilight hours. By nine o'clock it is quite dark here. I often cannot get to sleep until about one or two in the morning, and the five hours during which I have to lie in darkness are hard to bear. They are injuring my health more than anything else. When our case will be finished I can't say at all, for I have lost all sense of time, and merely use a calendar upon which I stroke out, quite passively, each day as it passes: "That's over!" I haven't read much since I've been here: two descriptions of travel in the Holy Land, and the works of Demetrius von Rostov. The latter interested me very much; but that kind of reading is only a drop in the ocean; any other sorts of books would, I imagine, quite extraordinarily delight me, and they might be very useful, for thus I could diversify my own thoughts with those of others, or at all events capture a different mood.

There you have all the details of my present existence—I have nothing else to tell you. I am glad that you found your family in the best of health. Have you written of your liberation to Moscow? It is a pity that nothing is done there. How I should like to spend at least one day with you! It is now three months since we came to this fortress: what may not still be in store for us! Possibly I shall not, the whole summer through, see so much as one green leaf. Do you remember how in May they would take us to walk in the little garden? The green was just beginning then, and I couldn't help thinking of Reval, where I was with you about that season, and of the garden belonging to the Engineering College. I imagined that you *must* be making the same comparison, so sad was I. And I should like to see a lot of other people besides. Whom do you see most of now? I suppose everybody's in the country. But our brother Andrey must surely be in town? Have you seen Nikolya? Greet them all from me. Kiss all your children for me. Greet your wife, and tell her that I am greatly touched by her thinking of me. Don't be too anxious on my account. I have but one wish—to be in good health; the tedium is a passing matter, and cheerfulness depends in the last resort upon myself. Human beings have an incredible amount of endurance and will to live; I should never have expected to find so much in myself; now I know it from experience. Farewell! I hope that these few lines will give you much pleasure. Greet everyone you see whom I have known—forget no one. I have not forgotten anybody. What can the children be thinking of me, and how do

they explain to themselves my disappearance! Farewell. If you can at all manage it, send me the *O.Z.*[2] Then I should at any rate have something to read. Write me a few lines—it would extraordinarily cheer me.

Till next time!

August 27, 1849

I rejoice that I may answer you, dear brother, and thank you for sending the books. I rejoice also that you are well, and that the imprisonment had no evil effects upon your constitution. I am most particularly grateful to you for the *O.Z.* But you write far too little, and my letters are much more comprehensive than yours. This only by the way—you'll do better next time.

I have nothing definite to tell you about myself. As yet I know nothing whatever about our case. My *personal* life is as monotonous as ever; but they have given me permission to walk in the garden, where there are almost seventeen trees! This is a great happiness for me. Moreover, I am given a candle in the evenings—that's my second piece of luck. The third will be mine if you answer as soon as possible, and send me the next number of the *O.Z.* I am in the same position as a country subscriber, and await each number as a great event, like some landed proprietor dying of boredom in the provinces. Will you send me some historical works? That would be splendid. The best of all would be the Bible (both Testaments). I need one. Should it prove possible, send it in a French translation. But if you could add as well a Slav edition, it would be the height of bliss.

Of my health I can tell you nothing good. For a month I have been living almost exclusively on castor oil. My haemorrhoids have been unusually tormenting; moreover I detect a pain in the breast that I have never had before. My nervous irritability has notably increased, especially in the evening hours; at night I have long, hideous dreams, and latterly I have often felt as if the ground were rocking under me, so that my room seems like the cabin of a steamer. From all this I conclude that my nerves are increasingly shattered. Whenever formerly I had such nervous disturbances, I made use of them for writing; in such a state I could write much more and much better than usual; but now I refrain from work that I may not utterly destroy myself. I took a rest of three weeks, during which time I wrote not at all; now I have begun again. But anyhow, all this is nothing: I can stick it out to the end. Perhaps I shall get quite right again.

---

[2] *Otetchestvennia Zapiski*, or *Annals of the Fatherland.*

THE CRIME AND THE PUNISHMENT : *Fyodor Dostoevsky*

You most tremendously astonish me when you write that you believe they know nothing of our adventure in Moscow. I have thought it over, and come to the conclusion that that's quite impossible. They simply *must* know, and I attribute their silence to another reason. And that was, after all, to be expected. Oh, it's quite clear. . . .

September 14, 1849

I have received, dear brother, your letter, the books (Shakespeare, the Bible, and the *O.Z.*) and the money (ten roubles): thank you for all. I am glad that you are well. I go on as before. Always the same digestive troubles and the haemorrhoids. I don't know if all this will ever leave me. The autumn months, which I find so trying, are drawing near, and with them returns my hypochondria. The sky is already grey; my health and good heart are dependent on those little tatters of blue that I can see from my casemate. But at any rate I'm alive, and comparatively well. This fact I maintain: therefore I beg you to think of my state as not wholly grievous. My health *is* at present good. I had expected worse, and now I see that I have so much vitality in me that it simply won't allow itself to be exhausted.

Thank you again for the books. They divert me at all events. For almost five months I have been living exclusively on my own provisions—that is to say, on my own head alone and solely. That machine is still in working order. But it is unspeakably hard to think *only,* everlastingly to think, without any of those external impressions which renew and nourish the soul. I live as though under the bell of an air-pump, from which the air is being drawn. My whole existence has concentrated itself in my head, and from head has drifted into my thoughts, and the labor of those thoughts grows more arduous every day. Books are certainly a mere drop in the ocean, still they do always help me; while my own work, I think, consumes my remains of strength. Nevertheless it gives me much happiness.

I have read the books you sent. I am particularly thankful for the Shakespeare. That was a good idea of yours. The English novel in the *O.Z.* is very good. On the other hand, Turgenev's comedy is unpardonably bad. Why has he always such ill-luck? Is he fated to ruin every work of his which runs to more than one printed sheet? I simply could not recognize him in this comedy. Not a trace of originality; everything in the old, worn-out groove. He has said it all before, and much better. The last scene is puerile in its feebleness. Here and there one thinks to see signs of talent, but only for want of something better. How splendid is the article on the Banks—and how uni-

versally true! I thank all who remember me; greet your Emilie Fyodorovna from me, our brother Andrey too, and kiss the children, who, I greatly hope, are better. Truly I don't know, brother, when and how we shall meet again! Farewell, and please don't forget me. Write to me, even if it can't be for a fortnight. Till next time!

Pray do not be anxious about me. If you can get hold of any books, send them.

> THE PETER-AND-PAUL FORTRESS
> *December 22, 1849.*

Michail Michailovich Dostoevsky
Nevsky Prospect, opposite Gryazny Street
in the house of Neslind.

Brother, my precious friend! all is settled! I am sentenced to four years' labor in the fortress (I believe, of Orenburg) and after that to serve as a private. To-day, the 22nd of December, we were taken to the Semionov Drill Ground. There the sentence of death was read to all of us, we were told to kiss the Cross, our swords were broken over our heads, and our last toilet was made (white shirts). Then three were tied to the pillar for execution. I was the sixth. Three at a time were called out; consequently, I was in the second batch and no more than a minute was left me to live. I remembered you, brother, and all yours; during the last minute you, you alone, were in my mind, only then I realised how I love you, dear brother mine! I also managed to embrace Plescheyev and Durov who stood close to me and to say good-bye to them. Finally the retreat was sounded, and those tied to the pillar were led back, and it was announced to us that His Imperial Majesty granted us our lives. Then followed the present sentences. Palm alone has been pardoned, and returns with his old rank to the army.

I was just told, dear brother, that to-day or to-morrow we are to be sent off. I asked to see you. But I was told that this was impossible; I may only write you this letter: make haste and give me a reply as soon as you can. I am afraid that you may somehow have got to know of our death-sentence. From the windows of the prison-van, when we were taken to the Semionov Drill Ground, I saw a multitude of people; perhaps the news reached you, and you suffered for me. Now you will be easier on my account. Brother! I have not become downhearted or low-spirited. Life is everywhere life, life in ourselves, not in what is outside us. There will be people near me, and to be a *man* among people and remain a man for ever, not to be downhearted

nor to fall in whatever misfortunes may befall me—this is life; this is the task of life. I have realised this. This idea has entered into my flesh and into my blood. Yes, it's true! The head which was creating, living with the highest life of art, which had realised and grown used to the highest needs of the spirit, that head has already been cut off from my shoulders. There remain the memory and the images created but not yet incarnated by me. They will lacerate me, it is true! But there remains in me my heart and the same flesh and blood which can also love, and suffer, and desire, and remember, and this, after all, is life. *On voit le soleil!* Now, good-bye, brother! Don't grieve for me!

Now about material things: my books (I have the Bible still) and several sheets of my manuscript, the rough plan of the play and the novel (and the finished story *A Little Hero*) have been taken away from me, and in all probabilitý will be got by you. I also leave my overcoat and old clothes, if you send to fetch them. Now, brother, I may perhaps have to march a long distance. Money is needed. My dear brother, when you receive this letter, and if there is any possibility of getting some money, send it me at once. Money I need now more than air (for one particular purpose). Send me also a few lines. Then if the money from Moscow comes,—remember me and do not desert me. Well, that is all! I have debts, but what can I do?

Kiss your wife and children. Remind them of me continually; see that they do not forget me. Perhaps, we shall yet meet some time! Brother, take care of yourself and of your family, live quietly and carefully. Think of the future of your children. . . . Live positively. There has never yet been working in me such a healthy abundance of spiritual life as now. But will my body endure? I do not know. I am going away sick, I suffer from scrofula. But never mind! Brother, I have already gone through so much in life that now hardly anything can frighten me. Let come what may! At the first opportunity I shall let you know about myself. Give the Maikovs my farewell and last greetings. Tell them that I thank them all for their constant interest in my fate. Say a few words for me, as warm as possible, as your heart will prompt you, to Eugenia Petrovna. I wish her much happiness, and shall ever remember her with grateful respect. Press the hands of Nikolay Apollonovich and Apollon Maikov, and also of all the others. Find Yanovsky. Press his hand, thank him. Finally, press the hands of all who have not forgotten me. And those who have forgotten me—remember me to them also. Kiss our brother Kolya. Write a letter to our brother Andrey and let him know about

me. Write also to Uncle and Aunt. This I ask you in my own name, and greet them for me. Write to our sisters: I wish them happiness.

And maybe, we shall meet again some time, brother! Take care of yourself, go on living, for the love of God, until we meet. Perhaps some time we shall embrace each other and recall our youth, our golden time that was, our youth and our hopes, which at this very instant I am tearing out from my heart with my blood, to bury them.

Can it indeed be that I shall never take a pen into my hands? I think that after the four years there may be a possibility. I shall send you everything that I may write, if I write anything, my God! How many imaginations, lived through by me, created by me anew, will perish, will be extinguished in my brain or will be spilt as poison in my blood! Yes, if I am not allowed to write, I shall perish. Better fifteen years of prison with a pen in my hands!

Write to me more often, write more details, more, more facts. In every letter write about all kinds of family details, of trifles, don't forget. This will give me hope and life. If you knew how your letters revived me here in the fortress. These last two months and a half, when it was forbidden to write or receive a letter, have been very hard on me. I was ill. The fact that you did not send me money now and then worried me on your account; it meant you yourself were in great need! Kiss the children once again; their lovely little faces do not leave my mind. Ah, that they may be happy! Be happy yourself too, brother, be happy!

But do not grieve, for the love of God, do not grieve for me! Do believe that I am not downhearted, do remember that hope has not deserted me. In four years there will be a mitigation of my fate. I shall be a private soldier, —no longer a prisoner, and remember that some time I shall embrace you. I was to-day in the grip of death for three-quarters of an hour; I have lived it through with that idea; I was at the last instant and now I live again!

If any one has bad memories of me, if I have quarrelled with any one, if I have created in any one an unpleasant impression—tell them they should forget it, if you manage to meet them. There is no gall or spite in my soul; I should dearly love to embrace any one of my former friends at this moment. It is a comfort, I experienced it to-day when saying good-bye to my dear ones before death. I thought at that moment that the news of the execution would kill you. But now be easy, I am still alive and shall live in the future with the thought that some time I shall embrace you. Only this is now in my mind.

What are you doing? What have you been thinking to-day? Do you know about us? How cold it was to-day!

Ah, if only my letter reaches you soon. Otherwise I shall be for four months without news of you. I saw the envelopes in which you sent money during the last two months; the address was written in your hand, and I was glad that you were well.

When I look back at the past and think how much time has been wasted in vain, how much time was lost in delusions, in errors, in idleness, in ignorance of how to live, how I did not value time, how often I sinned against my heart and spirit,—my heart bleeds. Life is a gift, life is happiness, each minute might have been an age of happiness. *Si jeunesse savait!* Now, changing my life, I am being reborn into a new form. Brother! I swear to you that I shall not lose hope, and shall preserve my spirit and heart in purity. I shall be reborn to a better thing. That is my whole hope, my whole comfort!

The life in prison has already sufficiently killed in me the demands of the flesh which were not wholly pure; I took little heed of myself before. Now privations are nothing to me, and, therefore, do not fear that any material hardship will kill me. This cannot be! Ah! To have health!

Good-bye, good-bye, my brother! When shall I write you again? You will receive from me as detailed an account as possible of my journey. If I can only preserve my health, then everything will be right!

Well, good-bye, good-bye, brother! I embrace you closely, I kiss you closely. Remember me without pain in your heart. Do not grieve, I pray you, do not grieve for me! In the next letter I shall tell you how I go on. Remember then what I have told you: plan out your life, do not waste it, arrange your destiny, think of your children. Oh, to see you, to see you! Good-bye! Now I tear myself away from everything that was dear; it is painful to leave it! It is painful to break oneself in two, to cut the heart in two. Good-bye! Good-bye! But I shall see you, I am convinced—I hope; do not change, love me, do not let your memory grow cold, and the thought of your love will be the best part of my life. Good-bye, good-bye, once more! Good-bye to all! —Your brother   FYODOR DOSTOEVSKY.

Dec. 22, 1849.

At my arrest several books were taken away from me. Only two of them were prohibited books. Won't you get the rest for yourself? But there is this request: one of the books was *The Work of Valerian Maikov:* his critical

essays—Eugenia Petrovna's copy. It was her treasure, and she lent it me. At my arrest I asked the police officer to return that book to her, and gave him the address. I do not know if he returned it to her. Make enquiries! I do not want to take this memory away from her. Good-bye, good-bye, once more!—Your   F. DOSTOEVSKY.

On the margins:
   I do not know if I shall have to march or go on horses. I believe I shall go on horses. Perhaps!

Once again press Emily Fiodorovna's hand, kiss the little ones. Remember me to Krayevsky: perhaps . . .

Write me more particularly about your arrest, confinement, and liberation.

A LETTER FROM SIBERIA [3]

OMSK, *February 22, 1854.*

AT LAST I can talk with you somewhat more explicitly, and, I believe, in a more reasonable manner. But before I write another line I *must* ask you: Tell me, for God's sake, why you have never written me a single syllable till now? Could I have expected this from you? Believe me, in my lonely and isolated state, I sometimes fell into utter despair, for I believed that you were no longer alive; through whole nights I would brood upon what was to become of your children, and I cursed my fate because I could not help them. But whenever I heard for certain that you were still alive, I would get furious (this happened, however, only in times of illness, from which I have suffered a very great deal), and begin to reproach you bitterly. Then

---

[3] To his brother Michael. The inclusion of this extraordinary letter, written not in the prison fortress but in semi-captivity, requires some justification. It was dispatched four years after the letter to his brother sent on the terrible day appointed for the mock execution. From 1850 to 1854 Dostoevsky served his sentence of hard labor in chains in the prison fortress at Omsk. On the completion of the first half of the sentence, the chains were struck off, on February 15, 1854. In a week Dostoevsky was to inaugurate the second half of his sentence: four years of Siberian exile in uniform. He was enlisted as a private in the Seventh Siberian Regiment of the Line. The first of his letters in exile, this contains in a nutshell not only the matter in the yet unwritten *House of the Dead* but the entire spiritual and literary development of Dostoevsky—through *Crime and Punishment* of 1865, *The Idiot* of 1868, *The Possessed* of 1870, and *The Brothers Karamazov* of 1879.

those states of mind would pass, and I would excuse you, I would exert myself to find a justification for you, and grow tranquil as soon as I discovered any—nor did I ever for a moment utterly lose faith in you: I know that you love me, and keep me in kindly remembrance. I wrote you a letter through our official staff; you simply must have got it; I expected an answer from you, and received none. Were you then forbidden to write to me? But I know that letters are allowed, for every one of the political prisoners here gets several in the year. Even Dourov had some; and we often asked the officials how it stood about correspondence, and they declared that people had the right to send us letters. I think I have guessed the real reason for your silence. You were too lazy to go to the police-office, or if you did go once, you took the first "No" for an answer—given you, probably, by some functionary or other who knew nothing rightly about the matter. Well, you have caused me a great deal of selfish anxiety, for I thought: If he won't take any trouble about a letter, he certainly won't either about more important things! Write and answer me as quickly as possible; write, without awaiting an opportunity, *officially,* and be as explicit and detailed as you possibly can. I am like a slice cut from a loaf nowadays; I long to grow back again, but can't. *Les absents ont toujours tort.* Is that saying to come true of us two? But be easy in your mind: I trust you.

It is a week now since I left the prison. I am sending this letter in the strictest secrecy; say not a syllable about it to anyone. I shall send you an official one too, through the staff of the Siberian Army Corps. Answer the official one instantly, but this—on the first suitable occasion. You must, though, write very circumstantially in the official letter of what you have been doing during these four years. For my part I should like to be sending you volumes. But as my time scarcely suffices for even this sheet, I shall tell you only the most important thing.

What *is* the most important? What was the most important to me in the recent past? When I reflect, I see that even to tell that, this sheet is far too small. How can I impart to you what is now in my mind—the things I thought, the things I did, the convictions I acquired, the conclusions I came to? I cannot even attempt the task. It is absolutely impracticable. I don't like to leave a piece of work half done; to say only a part is to say nothing. At any rate, you now have my detailed report in your hands: read it, and get from it what you will. It is my duty to tell you all, and so I will begin with my recollections. Do you remember how we parted from one another, my dear beloved fellow? You had scarcely left me when we three, Dourov,

Yastrchembsky, and I, were led out to have the irons put on. Precisely at midnight on that Christmas Eve (1849), did chains touch me for the first time. They weigh about ten pounds, and make walking extraordinarily difficult. Then we were put into open sledges, each alone with a gendarme, and so, in four sledges—the orderly opening the procession—we left Petersburg. I was heavy-hearted, and the many different impressions filled me with confused and uncertain sensations. My heart beat with a peculiar flutter, and that numbed its pain. Still, the fresh air was reviving in its effect, and, since it is usual before all new experiences to be aware of a curious vivacity and eagerness, so *I* was at the bottom quite tranquil. I looked attentively at all the festively-lit houses of Petersburg, and said good-bye to each. They drove us past your abode, and at Krayevsky's the windows were brilliantly lit. You had told me that he was giving a Christmas party and tree, and that your children were going to it, with Emilie Fyodorovna; I did feel dreadfully sad as we passed that house. I took leave, as it were, of the little ones. I felt so lonely for them, and even years afterwards I often thought of them with tears in my eyes. We were driven beyond Yaroslavl; after three or four stations we stopped, in the first grey of morning, at Schlüsselburg, and went into an inn. There we drank tea with as much avidity as if we had not touched anything for a week. After the eight months' captivity, sixty versts in a sledge gave us appetites of which, even to-day, I think with pleasure.

I was in a good temper, Dourov chattered incessantly, and Yastrchembsky expressed unwonted apprehensions for the future. We all laid ourselves out to become better acquainted with our orderly. He was a good old man, very friendly inclined towards us; a man who has seen a lot of life; he had travelled all over Europe with despatches. On the way he showed us many kindnesses. His name was Kusma Prokofyevitch Prokofyev. Among other things he let us have a covered sledge, which was very welcome, for the frost was fearful.

The second day was a holiday; the drivers, who were changed at the various stations, wore cloaks of grey German cloth with bright red belts: in the village-streets there was not a soul to be seen. It was a splendid winter-day. They drove us through the remote parts of the Petersburg, Novgorod, and Yaroslavl Governments. There were quite insignificant little towns, at great distances from one another. But as we were passing through on a holiday, there was always plenty to eat and drink. We drove—drove terribly. We were warmly dressed, it is true, but we had to sit for ten hours at a time in the sledges, halting at only five or six stations: it was almost unendurable. I

froze to the marrow, and could scarcely thaw myself in the warm rooms at the stations. Strange to say, the journey completely restored me to health. Near Perm, we had a frost of forty degrees during some of the nights. I don't recommend that to you. It was highly disagreeable. Mournful was the moment when we crossed the Ural. The horses and sledges sank deep in the snow. A snow-storm was raging. We got out of the sledges—it was night—and waited, standing, till they were extricated. All about us whirled the snow-storm. We were standing on the confines of Europe and Asia; before us lay Siberia and the mysterious future—behind us, our whole past; it was very melancholy. Tears came to my eyes. On the way, the peasants would stream out of all the villages to see us; and although we were fettered, prices were tripled to us at all the stations. Kusma Prokofyevitch took half our expenses on himself, though we tried hard to prevent him; in this way each of us, during the whole journey, spent only fifteen roubles.

On January 12 (1850) we came to Tobolsk. After we had been paraded before the authorities, and searched, in which proceeding all our money was' taken from us, myself, Dourov, and Yastrchembsky were taken into one cell; the others, Spyechnyov, etc., who had arrived before us, were in another section, and during the whole time we hardly once saw each other. I should like to tell you more of our six days' stay in Tobolsk, and of the impressions it made upon me. But I haven't room here. I will only tell you that the great compassion and sympathy which was shown us there, made up to us, like a big piece of happiness, for all that had gone before. The prisoners of former days (and still more their wives) cared for us as if they had been our kith and kin. Those noble souls, tested by five-and-twenty years of suffering and self-sacrifice! We saw them but seldom, for we were very strictly guarded; still, they sent us clothes and provisions, they comforted and encouraged us. I had brought far too few clothes, and had bitterly repented it, but *they* sent me clothes. Finally we left Tobolsk, and reached Omsk in three days.

While I was in Tobolsk, I gathered information about my future superiors. They told me that the Commandant was a very decent fellow, but that the Major, Krivzov, was an uncommon brute, a petty tyrant, a drunkard, a trickster—in short, the greatest horror that can be imagined. From the very beginning, he called both Dourov and me blockheads, and vowed to chastise us bodily at the first transgression. He had already held his position for two years, and done the most hideous and unsanctioned things; two years later, he was court-martialled for them. So God protected me from him. He used

to come to us mad drunk (I never once saw him sober), and would seek out some inoffensive prisoner and flog him on the pretext that he—the prisoner—was drunk. Often he came at night and punished at random—say, because such and such an one was sleeping on his left side instead of his right, or because he talked or moaned in his sleep—in fact, anything that occurred to his drunken mind. I should have had to break out in the long run against such a man as that, and it was he who wrote the monthly reports of us to Petersburg.

I had made acquaintance with convicts in Tobolsk; at Omsk I settled myself down to live four years in common with them. They are rough, angry, embittered men. Their hatred for the nobility is boundless; they regard all of us who belong to it with hostility and enmity. They would have devoured us if they only could. Judge then for yourself in what danger we stood, having to cohabit with these people for some years, eat with them, sleep by them, and with no possibility of complaining of the affronts which were constantly put upon us.

"You nobles have iron beaks, you have torn us to pieces. When you were masters, you injured the people, and now, when it's evil days with you, you want to be our brothers."

This theme was developed during four years. A hundred and fifty foes never wearied of persecuting us—it was their joy, their diversion, their pastime; our sole shield was our indifference and our moral superiority, which they were forced to recognize and respect; they were also impressed by our never yielding to their will. They were for ever conscious that we stood above them. They had not the least idea of what our offence had been. We kept our own counsel about that, and so we could never come to understand one another; we had to let the whole of the vindictiveness, the whole of the hatred, that they cherish against the nobility, flow over us. We had a very bad time there. A military prison is much worse than the ordinary ones. I spent the whole four years behind dungeon walls, and only left the prison when I was taken on "hard labour." The labour was hard, though not always; sometimes in bad weather, in rain, or in winter during the unendurable frosts, my strength would forsake me. Once I had to spend four hours at a piece of extra work, and in such frost that the quicksilver froze; it was perhaps forty degrees below zero. One of my feet was frost-bitten. We all lived together in one barrack-room. Imagine an old, crazy wooden building, that should long ago have been broken up as useless. In the summer it is unbearably hot, in the winter unbearably cold. All the boards are

rotten. On the ground filth lies an inch thick; every instant one is in danger of slipping and coming down. The small windows are so frozen over that even by day one can hardly read. The ice on the panes is three inches thick. The ceilings drip, there are draughts everywhere. We are packed like herrings in a barrel. The stove is heated with six logs of wood, but the room is so cold that the ice never once thaws; the atmosphere is unbearable—and so through all the winter long. In the same room, the prisoners wash their linen, and thus make the place so wet that one scarcely dares to move. From twilight till morning we are forbidden to leave the barrack-room; the doors are barricaded; in the ante-room a great wooden trough for the calls of nature is placed; this makes one almost unable to breathe. All the prisoners stink like pigs; they say that they can't help it, for they must live, and are but men. We slept upon bare boards; each man was allowed one pillow only. We covered ourselves with short sheepskins, and our feet were outside the covering all the time. It was thus that we froze night after night. Fleas, lice, and other vermin by the bushel. In the winter we got thin sheepskins to wear, which didn't keep us warm at all, and boots with short legs; thus equipped, we had to go out in the frost.

To eat we got bread and cabbage-soup: the soup should, by the regulations, have contained a quarter-pound of meat per head; but they put in sausage-meat, and so I never came across a piece of genuine flesh. On feast-days we got porridge, but with scarcely any butter. On fast-days—cabbage and nothing else. My stomach went utterly to pieces, and I suffered tortures from indigestion.

From all this you can see for yourself that one couldn't live there at all without money; if I had had none, I should most assuredly have perished; no one could endure such a life. But every convict does some sort of work and sells it, thus earning, every single one of them, a few pence. I often drank tea and bought myself a piece of meat; it was my salvation. It was quite impossible to do without smoking, for otherwise the stench would have choked one. All these things were done behind the backs of the officials.

I was often in hospital. My nerves were so shattered that I had some epileptic fits—however, that was not very often. I have rheumatism in my legs now, too. But except for that, I feel right well. Add to all these discomforts, the fact that it was almost impossible to get one's self a book, and that when I did get one, I had to read it on the sly; that all around me was incessant malignity, turbulence, and quarrelling; then perpetual espionage, and the impossibility of ever being alone for even an instant—and so with-

out variation for four long years: you'll believe me when I tell you that I was not happy. And imagine, in addition, the ever-present dread of drawing down some punishment on myself, the irons, and the utter oppression of spirits—and you have the picture of my life.

I won't even try to tell you what transformations were undergone by my soul, my faith, my mind, and my heart in those four years. It would be a long story. Still, the eternal concentration, the escape into myself from bitter reality, did bear its fruit. I now have many new needs and hopes of which I never thought in other days. But all this will be pure enigma for you, and so I'll pass to other things. I will say only one word: Do not forget me, and do help me. I need books and money. Send them me, for Christ's sake.

Omsk is a hateful hole. There is hardly a tree here. In summer—heat and winds that bring sandstorms; in winter—snow-storms. I have scarcely seen anything of the country round. The place is dirty, almost exclusively inhabited by military, and dissolute to the last degree. I mean the common people. If I hadn't discovered some human beings here, I should have gone utterly to the dogs. Constantine Ivanovitch Ivanov is like a brother to me. He has done everything that he in any way could for me. I owe him money. If he ever goes to Petersburg, show him some recognition. I owe him twenty-five roubles. But how can I repay his kindness, his constant willingness to carry out all my requests, his attention and care for me, just like a brother's? And he is not the only one whom I have to thank in that way. Brother, there are very many noble natures in the world.

I have already said that your silence often tortured me. I thank you for the money you sent. In your next letter (even if it's "official," for I don't know yet whether it is possible for me to correspond with you)—in your next, write as fully as you can of all your affairs, of Emilie Fyodorovna, the children, all relations and acquaintances; also of those in Moscow—who is alive and who is dead; and of your business: tell me with what capital you started it,[4] whether it is lucrative, whether you are in funds, and finally, whether you will help me financially, and how much you will send me a year. But send no money with the official letter—particularly if I don't find a covering address. For the present, give Michael Petrovitch as the consignor of all packets (you understand, don't you?). For the time I have some money, but I have no books. If you can, send me the magazines for this year, or at any rate the *O. Z.* But what I urgently need are the following; I need

---

[4] Michael Dostoevsky had at this time a tobacco and cigarette factory.

(very necessary) ancient historians (in French translations); modern historians: Guizot, Thierry, Thiers, Ranke, and so forth; national studies, and the Fathers of the Church. Choose the cheapest and most compact editions. Send them by return. They have ordered me to Semipalatinsk, which lies on the edge of the Kirghiz steppes; I'll let you have the address. Here is one for the present, anyhow; ",Semipalatinsk, Siberian Regiment of the Line, Seventh Battalion, Private F. Dostoevsky." That's the official style. To this one send your letters. But I'll give you another for the books. For the present, write as Michael Petrovitch. Remember, above all things, I need a German dictionary.

I don't know what awaits me at Semipalatinsk. I don't mind the service much. But what I *do* care about is—exert yourself for me, spend yourself for me with somebody or other. Could they not transfer me in a year or two to the Caucasus? Then I should at least be in European Russia! This is my dearest desire, grant it me, for Christ's sake! Brother, do not forget me! I write and scold you and dispose of your very property! But my faith in you is not yet extinguished. You are my brother, and you used to love me. I need money. I must have something to live on, brother. These years shall not have been in vain. I want money and books. What you spend on me will not be lost. If you give me help, you won't be robbing your children. If I live, I'll repay you with interest—oh, a thousandfold. In six years, perhaps even sooner, I shall surely get permission to print my books. It may indeed be quite otherwise, but I don't write recklessly now. You shall hear of me again.

We shall see one another some day, brother. I believe in that as in the multiplication-table. To my soul, all is clear. I see my whole future, and all that I shall accomplish, plainly before me. I am content with my life. I fear only men and tyranny. How easily might I come across a superior officer who did not like me (there are such folk!), who would torment me incessantly and destroy me with the rigours of service—for I am very frail and of course in no state to bear the full burden of a soldier's life. People try to console me: "They're quite simple sort of fellows there." But I dread simple men more than complex ones. For that matter, men everywhere are just— men. Even among the robber-murderers in the prison, I came to know some men in those four years. Believe me, there were among them deep, strong, beautiful natures, and it often gave me great joy to find gold under a rough exterior. And not in a single case, or even two, but in several cases. Some

inspired respect; others were downright fine. I taught the Russian language and reading to a young Circassian—he had been transported to Siberia for robbery with murder. How grateful he was to me! Another convict wept when I said good-bye to him. Certainly I had often given him money, but it was so little, and his gratitude so boundless. My character, though, was deteriorating; in my relations with others I was ill-tempered and impatient. They accounted for it by my mental condition, and bore all without grumbling. Apropos: what a number of national types and characters I became familiar with in the prison! I lived *into* their lives, and so I believe I know them really well. Many tramps' and thieves' careers were laid bare to me, and, above all, the whole wretched existence of the common people. Decidedly I have not spent my time there in vain. I have learnt to know the Russian people as only a few know them. I am a little vain of it. I hope that such vanity is pardonable.

Brother! Be sure to tell me of all the most important events in your life. Send the official letter to Semipalatinsk, and the unofficial—whither you soon shall know. Tell me of all our acquaintances in Petersburg, of literature (as many details as possible), and finally of our folks in Moscow. How is our brother Kolya? What (and this is much more important) is sister Sacha doing? Is Uncle still alive? What is brother Andrey about? I am writing to our aunt through sister Vera. For God's sake, keep this letter a dead secret, and burn it; it might compromise various people. Don't forget, dear friend, to send me books. Above all things histories and national studies, the *O. Z.*, the Fathers of the Church, and church-histories. Don't send all the books at once, though as soon after one another as possible. I am dispensing your money for you as if it were my own; but only because your present situation is unknown to me. Write fully about your affairs, so that I may have some idea of them. But mark this, brother: books are my life, my food, my future! For God's sake, don't abandon me. I pray you! Try to get permission to send me the books quite openly. But be cautious. If it can be done openly, send them openly. But if it can't, then send them through brother Constantine Ivanovitch, to his address. I shall get them. Constantine Ivanovitch, by-the-bye, is going this very year to Petersburg; he'll tell you everything. What a family he has! And what a wife! She is a young girl, the daughter of the Decembrist Annenkov. Such a heart, such a disposition— and to think of what they've all been through! I shall set myself, when I go to Semipalatinsk in a week, to find a new covering address. I am not quite

strong yet, so must remain here a while. (Send me the Koran, and Kant's "Critique of Pure Reason"), and if you have the chance of sending anything *not* officially, then be sure to send Hegel—but particularly Hegel's "History of Philosophy." Upon that depends my whole future. For God's sake, exert yourself for me to get me transferred to the Caucasus; try to find out from well-informed people whether I shall be permitted to print my works, and in what way I should seek this sanction. I intend to try for permission in two or three years. I beg you to sustain me so long. Without money I shall be destroyed by military life. So please!

Perhaps in the beginning the other relatives would support me too? In that case they could hand the money to you, and you would send it to me. In my letters to Aunt and to Vera, though, I never ask for money. They can guess themselves that I want it, if they think about me at all.

Filippov, before he left for Sebastopol, gave me twenty-five roubles. He left them with the Commandant, Nabokov, and I knew nothing about it beforehand. He thought that I should have no money. A kind soul! All our lot are doing not so badly in banishment. Toll has done his time, and now lives quite tranquilly in Tomsk. Yastrchembsky is in Tara; his time is drawing to an end. Spyechnyov is in the Irkutsk Government; he has won general liking and respect there. That man's is a curious destiny! Wherever, and in whatever circumstances, he may appear, even the most inaccessible people show him honour and respect. Petrashevsky is now and then not in his right mind; Monbelli and Loov are well; poor Grigoryev has gone clean out of his senses and is in hospital. And how goes it with you? Do you still see a great deal of Mme. Plestcheiev? What is her son doing? From prisoners who passed through here, I heard that he is alive and in the fortress at Orsk, and that Golovinsky has long been in the Caucasus. How goes your literature, and your interest in literature? Are you writing anything? What is Krayevsky about, and what are your relations with him? I don't care for Ostrovsky; I have read nothing by Pissemsky; Drushinin I loathe. I was enchanted with Eugénie Tur. I like Krestovsky too.

I should like to have written much more; but so much time has gone by that even this letter was somewhat difficult to write. But it really cannot be that our relation is altered in any respect. Kiss your children. Can they remember Uncle Fedya at all? Greet all acquaintances—but keep this letter a dead secret. Farewell, farewell, dear fellow! You shall hear from me again, and perhaps even see me. Yes—we shall most certainly see one another again! Farewell. Read attentively all that I write to you. Write to me as

often as possible (even if officially). I embrace you and all yours more times
than I can count.

Thy

DOSTOEVSKY.

P.S.—Have you received my children's story,[5] that I wrote in the fortress?
If it is in your hands, don't do anything with it, and show it to no one. Who
is Tschernov, that wrote a "Double" in 1850?
Till next time!

Thy

DOSTOEVSKY.

---

[5] He means "The Little Hero." The story did not appear till 1857 (in the *O. Z.*, under
the pseudonym "M—y.").

LITTLE FATHER AND THE PENITENT:
Michael Bakunin

CONFESSION TO THE CZAR

BAKUNIN AS "IMPLORING CRIMINAL"

His career was barren of concrete result. "He spent his whole life," said his friend Vyrubov, "playing the part of Sisyphus, continually preparing political and social revolutions, which no less continually collapsed on his shoulders." Yet it is scarcely relevant to speak of his failure to achieve, when the whole idea of achievement was alien to his character and purpose. Reichel once asked him what he would do if he succeeded in realizing all his plans and creating everything he had dreamed of. "Then," he replied, "I should at once begin to pull down again everything I had made." Bakunin is one of the completest embodiments in history of the spirit of liberty—the liberty which excludes neither license nor caprice, which tolerates no human institution, which remains an unrealised and unrealisable ideal, but which is almost universally felt to be an indispensable part of the highest manifestations and aspirations of humanity.

E. H. CARR, *Michael Bakunin*

WHETHER it is the seed of dictatorship or a flower of romanticism, a comedy of errors or a work of art in conspiracy, the life of Michael Bakunin is without doubt a life of great proportions. This Russian bull invaded western Europe in 1840; by 1876 when he was spent and dead and harmless, a great many china shops had been rattled and antiques broken. It was Bakunin's aim to set on fire an alleged libertarian instinct and to convince a small army of conspirators that the passion for destruction is also a creative passion—when it is Bakuninist. Though his career was essentially an almost singlehanded conspiracy against the governments of the world— emperors and kings and all the chiefs of police, though vanity made of him a dictator, he was faithful to a dogma of millennian liberty: "My dear," he wrote to a friend, not without sincerity, "I shall die and the worms will eat me, but I want our idea to triumph. I want the masses of humanity to be really emancipated from all authorities and from all heroes present and to come." But in 1840 he did not begin with an anarchist ideal, he began with Russian orthodoxy and some German metaphysics. Excess of energy drove him from the small comforts of a nobleman's provincial estate into the bohemianism of the cosmopolitan west, and into years of wandering, idling, borrowing, theorizing, agitating, imprisonment, insurrection, rivalry, in-

trigue, and disillusionment. He crossed the paths of nearly all the vital figures of the century, Herzen and Ogarev, Turgenev and Wagner, Ruge and Herwegh, Marx and Engels, Proudhon and Louis Blanc and Nechaev, Bettina von Arnim and George Sand, Emperor Nicholas and Emperor Francis Joseph, Guizot and Louis Philippe, Garibaldi and Mazzini. When he was not himself the progenitor of nationalist revolution, he was at least the midwife—for Czechs, Serbs, Croats, Poles, Germans, Swiss, French, and Italians. Before the father of implacable revolutionary anarchism bid farewell to nationalism, he spent a passionate apprenticeship in the service of the idea of a grand Pan-Slavic revolt and federation. From the Austrian and Russian wreckage there would one day rise a sweet Pan-Slavic harmony liberating the latent mystical virtues of Russians, Poles, and Czechs. He was obsessed with this idea when the French uprising of 1848 burst on his horizon with the first opportunity for direct revolutionary action. The barricades of furniture, the red flags, and the long processions intoxicated him. He surpassed himself. "He preached destruction so long as there was anything left to destroy," remarks his English biographer, E. H. Carr, "he preached rebellion—even when there was nothing left to rebel against . . . 'What a man!' exclaimed Caussidière. 'On the first day of the revolution, he is a perfect treasure; on the second, he ought to be shot.'" From the fast receding fever of Paris Bakunin, a veteran of barricades, returned to his old agitation among the Poles and the Czechs. He participated in the insurrections of Prague and Dresden and then disappeared for a whole decade into Saxon, Austrian, and Russian imprisonment. In the Peter and Paul fortress he wrote his *Confession to the Czar,* and won, by degrees of self-abasement, exile to Siberia and a chance to escape by way of America to the western world again. Returned to Europe, he eventually renounced the Pan-Slav illusion, nationalism, the mysticism of Mazzini, the respectability of Herzen, the dictatorship of God, and all "patriotic-bourgeois rhetoric." He built a new illusion, a new God, and a new rhetoric, a *Revolutionary Catechism* for an International Brotherhood. Seduced for a time by the youth and amorality of Sergei Nechayev, the new Bakuninist preached that "all soft and enervating feelings of relationship, friendship, love, gratitude, even honor, must be stifled in him by a cold passion for the revolutionary cause." The communists and Karl Marx, against whom Bakunin lost the struggle for power in the ranks of the First International, were wrong with their quest for political power. A revolutionary elite, a revolutionary party (an echo of Babeuf's Conspiracy of the Equals which was the swan song of the

French Revolution), a hundred disciplined secret leaders, were capable of planning the strategy of world revolution and "the development and organization of the non-political, social, and anti-political power of the working masses." The revolution must be social rather than political, anti-authoritarian, against centralized government, spontaneous, passionate, not from above but from below, a heroic impulse towards destruction rather than a calculated philosophical theory. Yet paradoxically Bakuninism hid under its impulsive rhetoric a party and a dictator. In the ironic characterization by Max Nomad, Bakuninism "had to resort to the immemorial device of Hassan, the fig vendor, who shouted: 'Hassan's figs are biggest of all figs; Hassan's figs are ten times as big as they are!' Hassan-Bakunin simply shouted: 'Bakunin's revolution is better than that of the other revolutionists; Bakunin's government is no government.'"

Bakunin wrote his *Confession to the Czar* in that long and unhappy prison interlude which lay between his Pan-Slavic period and the last formative years of revolutionary anarchism. Nicholas I had dispatched Count Orlov to the Peter and Paul fortress to ask the prisoner Bakunin to write out his life, not as to a stern judge but as to his confessor, one of the most unusual collaborations in revolutionary politics, even in Russia. They were undoubtedly both flattered:—the Little Father with his world-celebrated penitent, and the Pan-Slavist Bakunin with his royal confessor. Here was intellectual melodrama of the very first rank. The play called for grand histrionics, self-abasement, flattery, flagellation—and between the lines of humility, a sly projection of beliefs which a misunderstood penitent and a wise confessor might discover in each other to their mutual surprise and, who knows, satisfaction. After all, where but in the Czar himself, in the Little Father of Holy Russia, could one find a more perfect recipient of the Pan-Slavic dream and dogma? Indeed, Bakunin had never made a fetish of democratic scruples or institutions, and life in the Peter and Paul fortress made any considerations of pride or dignity very impracticable indeed. It would be just sufficient to cheat the Little Father of any hopes that Bakunin would turn informer, and then butter his disappointment with homage. In the summer of 1851 Bakunin sat down to his task and poured out his life on paper in some 30,000 words. "There was in my character a radical defect," he reflected aloud, "love for the fantastic, for out-of-the-way, unheard-of adventures, for undertakings which open up an infinite horizon and whose end no man can foresee." Would the Little Father be disarmed by the romantic apology for his life? "In Western Europe, wherever you turn, you

see everywhere decay." Why should the Russian emperor object to this? "I did not succeed in becoming either a German or a Frenchman. On the contrary, the longer I lived abroad, the more deeply did I feel that I was a Russian and should never cease to be a Russian." True, he had plotted revolutions: "I wanted a republic. But of what kind? Not a parliamentary republic . . . all that narrow, cleverly interwoven, vapid political catechism of Western liberals never won my admiration, nor my sympathy, nor even my respect; and at that time I began to despise them still more, seeing the fruits of parliamentary forms in France, in Germany, and even at the Slav Congress." His revolution in Bohemia? It would have liberated and united all the Slavs and harmed only the despised Germans, the Hapsburg monarchy . . . "all clubs, all newspapers, all the manifestation of a gabby anarchy would likewise have been suppressed. Everything was to be subjected to a dictatorial power." His sins?—contempt for the Germans, a Pan-Slav dream, a revolution and an anti-parliamentary dictatorship. Though Bakunin never explicitly said it in so many words, the Little Father might himself have dreamt of leadership in a Pan-Slav federation which would regenerate Europe. . . . On Bakunin's prison manuscript, which the Russian Revolution retrieved from the dust seventy years later, the Czar had put down thoughtfully in the margins such remarks as "true"; "a striking truth"; "an incontestable truth"; "every sinner can be saved by repentance, if it is sincere"; a note for the heir to the throne: "it is worth your while to read this—it is very curious"; but he remarked of Bakunin, "He is a good fellow and clever: he ought to be kept behind prison bars."

CONFESSION TO THE CZAR

Your Imperial Majesty, All-Merciful Czar!

When I was being transported from Austria to Russia, knowing the severity of Russian laws, knowing Your relentless hatred of anything resembling disobedience, to say nothing of open rebellion against the will of Your Imperial Majesty—knowing also the full weight of my crimes, which I had no hope, or even intention of concealing or minimizing before judgment— I said to myself that the only thing left for me to do was to endure until the end; and I prayed God for the strength to drink with dignity and without ignoble frailty the bitter cup which I had myself prepared. . . .

I cannot tell You, Sire, how astounded and how deeply touched I have been by the courteous, humane and indulgent treatment which met me as soon as I reached the Russian frontier! I had expected a different reception. All that I saw and heard, all that I experienced during the entire journey from the Kingdom of Poland to the Fortress of Peter and Paul was so contrary to my fearful expectations, was in such conflict with everything that I myself, believing rumors, had thought and said and written about the cruelty of the Russian Government, that, doubting for the first time the truth of my previous conceptions, I asked myself in amazement: Have I been guilty of calumny? My two months' stay in the Fortress of Peter and Paul has finally convinced me how utterly unfounded many of my old prejudices were.

Please do not think, Sire, that, encouraged by such humane treatment, I should be nursing some false or idle hope. I understand full well that the severity of laws does not exclude the love of mankind, and that the reverse is also true: love of mankind does not interfere with the strict execution of the law. I know the greatness of my crimes and, having lost the right to hope, I hope no more,—and to tell the truth, Sire, I have aged so much and grown so heavy of soul during the last years that there is hardly anything I wish for.

Count Orlov has declared to me, in the name of Your Imperial Majesty, that You, Sire, desire me to write to You a full Confession of all my misdeeds. Sire! I have not deserved such benevolence, and I blush to remember all that I have dared to say and write concerning the implacable severity of Your Imperial Majesty.

How shall I write? What shall I say to the dreadful Russian Czar, the terrible and zealous Guardian of the law? My confession to You, as my Sovereign, would have been couched in the following few words: "Sire! I am guilty on every count before Your Imperial Majesty and before the laws of my country. You know my crimes, and that which You know is sufficient to condemn me, according to the law, to the severest form of punishment which exists in Russia. I have been in open revolt against You, Sire, and against Your Government; I have dared to oppose You as an enemy, I have written, spoken, set people's minds against You, wherever and however I could. What more is needed? Order to have me tried and punished, Sire; both Your trial and Your punishment will be legal and just."—What else could I have written to my Sovereign?

But Count Orlov said a thing to me, in the name of Your Imperial

Majesty, which has shaken my soul and has moved me to the bottom of my heart: "Write," he said to me, "Write to the Czar as if you were speaking to your Father Confessor."

Yes, Sire, I shall tell You my sins as I would to a father confessor, from whom a man expects pardon not for this world, but for the next; I pray God that He inspire me with simple, sincere and heart-felt words, without cunning or flattery, worthy, in short, of finding their way to the heart of Your Imperial Majesty.

I beg of You two things only, Sire! First, do not doubt the truth of my words; I swear to You that not a lie, nor the thousandth part of a lie, shall flow from my pen. Secondly, I implore You, Sire, do not demand that I confess other men's sins to You. In a confessional no man discloses the sins of others, but only his own. Out of the terrible shipwreck I have suffered, I have salvaged one good thing only: my honor, and the knowledge that, in order to save myself or to lighten my lot, I have nowhere, neither in Saxony nor in Austria, been an informer. On the contrary the knowledge of having betrayed a confidence, or even of having repeated a word carelessly spoken in my presence, would be more painful to me than torture itself. And in Your own eyes, Sire, I prefer to be a criminal deserving the cruelest punishment, rather than a scoundrel.

I shall now begin my Confession.

[*Bakunin describes his boyhood and youth in Russia, his trip abroad, and his early revolutionary activities.*]

Until 1846 my sins had not been intentional but rather light-minded and, I might say, youthful; though a man in years, I long remained an inexperienced youth. From that time on, however, I began to sin consciously, deliberately, and with a more or less definite purpose in mind. Sire! I shall make no attempt to excuse my inexcusable crimes, nor speak to You of a belated repentance: repentance in my position is just as useless as the repentance of a sinner after death; I shall simply tell You the facts, without concealing or softening a single one.

[*Bakunin was in contact with Polish democrats, who wished to free their country from Russian domination. His own aim was a revolution in Russia and the subsequent formation of a Pan-Slavic Federation. Co-operation with the Poles didn't jell; they mistrusted him, some thought him a secret agent of the Russian Government. Exiled from Paris for a revolutionary speech he*]

went to Brussels, where he met more Poles, some German and Belgian communists, English Chartists and French democrats. He remained in Belgium until the Revolution of 1848.]

At last the February Revolution broke out. As soon as I learned that they were fighting in Paris I set out for France, having borrowed a passport from an acquaintance just in case. But no passport was necessary: the first words which we heard at the frontier were: *"La République est proclamée à Paris"* ("The Republic has been proclaimed in Paris.") I had goose-flesh all over when I heard this news; I reached Valenciennes on foot, because the railroad had been wrecked; everywhere there were crowds, shouts of delight, red banners in all the streets, squares, and on all public buildings. From there I had to make a detour, the railroad having been wrecked in many places, and arrived in Paris February 26, on the third day after the proclamation of the Republic. I was happy while traveling—what shall I say to You, Sire, of the impression Paris made on me! This enormous city, the center of European enlightenment, had suddenly transformed itself into the wilds of Caucasus: on every street, almost at every spot, one saw barricades, piled up like mountains and reaching to the roofs, and on them, in the midst of stones and broken furniture, like the Caucasians in their mountain passes, the workers in their picturesque blouses, blackened with gun-powder and armed from head to foot; fat shopkeepers, *épiciers,* glanced fearfully out of their windows, their faces made stupid by terror; on the streets, on the boulevards, not a carriage to be seen; all the dandies, young and old, had vanished, all the hateful society lions with their canes and lorgnettes, and in their place were my noble *ouvriers* (workers) in triumphant, jubilant throngs, waving red banners, singing patriotic songs, intoxicated with their victory! And in the midst of this limitless freedom, this wild rapture, everybody was so gentle, compassionate, humane, honest, modest, polite, courteous, witty, that only in France—and even in France, only in Paris—could such a thing be possible! Later I lived with workers for over a week in the *caserne de Tournons* (Tournons barracks), a few steps away from the Luxembourg Palace; these barracks had formerly been used by the Municipal Guard, but at that time, together with many others, they were transformed into a fortress of red republicanism, housing Caussidière's guard. I was living there at the invitation of a democrat I knew, who was in command of a detachment of 500 workers. I thus had an opportunity to observe and study these last from morning till night. Sire! I assure You, in no class of society, at no time or

place, have I ever found so much noble self-sacrifice, so much truly touching honesty, so much natural tact, and so much courteous gaiety, combined with so much heroism, as in these simple uneducated people, who always have been and always will be a thousand times better than all their leaders! . . .

Sire! I am unable to give you a clear report of the month I spent in Paris, because it was a month of spiritual intoxication. Not I alone, but all around were drunk: some with mad fear, others with mad delight and madder hopes. I used to get up at four or five in the morning, and go to bed at two; I was on my feet all day, took part in absolutely all meetings, gatherings, clubs, processions, promenades, demonstrations; in a word, I was absorbing the heady revolutionary atmosphere through all my senses, through all my pores. It was a feast without beginning or end; I saw everybody there and yet I saw nobody, because all were lost in one innumerable moving throng; I spoke with everyone and remembered neither what I said to them nor what they said to me, because at every step there were new objects, new adventures, new reports. Of great assistance in keeping up and increasing the general fervor was the news which kept coming from the rest of Europe. One heard constantly: *"On se bat à Berlin; le roi a pris la fuite, après avoir prononcé un discours!—On s'est battu à Vienne, Metternich s'est enfui, la République y est proclamée!—Toute l'Allemagne se soulève. Les Italiens ont triomphé à Milan et à Venise; les Autrichiens ont subi une honteuse défaite! —La République y est proclamée; toute l'Europe devient République . . . vive la République!"* ("They are fighting in Berlin; the King is in flight, after having made a speech! There has been fighting in Vienna, Metternich has fled, the Republic has been proclaimed there! The whole of Germany is rising. The Italians have triumphed in Milan and in Venice; the Austrians have suffered a shameful defeat! The Republic has been proclaimed there; all Europe is becoming a republic. . . . Long live the Republic!")

[*Bakunin denies several accusations which had been made against him: of having been an agent of Ledru-Rollin, and of having plotted against the life of Nicholas I.*]

But it is time to return to my own story. After two or three weeks of such drunkenness, I sobered up somewhat and began to ask myself: what should I do now? Not in Paris, not in France is my vocation, my place is on the Russian frontier; the Polish émigrés are rushing there now, to prepare for war against Russia; I too must be there in order to work at the same

time on the Russians and on the Poles, in order to prevent this war from becoming a war of Europe against Russia, *"pour refouler ce peuple barbare dans les déserts de l'Asie,"* ("To drive this barbaric people back into the deserts of Asia") as they sometimes said; I must do my best to make this not a war of Germanized Poles against the Russian people, but a Slavic war, a war of free united Slavs against the Russian Emperor. . . .

Having taken some money from Flocon, I went to Caussidière for a passport; however, I got from him not one passport, but two, in case of need; one in my own name, and the other in a false one, since I wished as much as possible to conceal my presence in Germany and in the Duchy of Posen. Then, having dined at Herwegh's and having received from him letters and messages to Baden democrats, I got into a stagecoach and set off for Strasbourg. Had anyone in the stagecoach questioned me concerning the purpose of my journey, and had I wished to reply, we might have had the following conversation:

"Why are you traveling?"

"To raise a rebellion."

"Against whom?"

"Against the Emperor Nicholas."

"By what means?"

"I don't quite know myself."

"Where are you bound now?"

"For the Duchy of Posen."

"Why there, precisely?"

"Because I've heard from the Poles that there is more life there now, more movement, and that it is easier to work on the Kingdom of Poland from there than from Galicia."

"What funds have you?"

"Two thousand francs."

"And hopes of funds?"

"Nothing definite, but perhaps I shall find some."

"Have you friends and connections in the Duchy of Posen?"

"With the exception of a few young men, whom I used to meet rather frequently at the Berlin University, I don't know a soul there."

"Have you any letters of recommendation?"

"Not one."

"How do you expect, without funds and all alone, to combat the Russian Czar?"

LITTLE FATHER AND THE PENITENT : *Michael Bakunin*

"The Revolution is on my side, and in Posen I hope not to be alone any longer."

"All the Germans are now clamoring against Russia, praising the Poles, and preparing, together with them, to fight the Russian Empire. You are a Russian, can you join forces with them?"

"God forbid! As soon as the Germans dare to set foot on Slavic soil I shall become their implacable enemy; but I am going to Posen precisely in order to oppose the unnatural union of Poles and Germans against Russia."

"But surely the Poles alone are no match for the power of Russia?"

"Alone, no, but in union with other Slavs they would be, especially should I succeed in arousing the Russians in the Kingdom of Poland. . . ."

"On what do you base your hopes, have you any connections with the Russians?"

"None; I place my hope in propaganda and in the mighty spirit of revolution, which now rules the world!"

Aside from the greatness of my crime, it must seem laughable to You, Sire, that I, nameless, powerless, alone, set out to combat You, the Great Czar of a great empire! I see my madness clearly now, and would myself laugh at it, were I in a mood for laughter. . . . But at that time I saw nothing, reflected about nothing, but pushed on like one possessed into obvious disaster. If anything can to some extent excuse not the criminality, but the absurdity of my escapade, it is the fact that I was leaving drunken Paris, that I was drunk myself, and all were drunk around me!

[*But Bakunin failed to make satisfactory progress with the Poles: they distrusted him, and he disliked them. After some weeks of idleness he decided to attend the Pan-Slavic Congress which was to be held in Prague.*]

Although my expectations were not fully realized, neither was I altogether deceived. The Slavs are children politically, but I discovered an incredible freshness in them, and incomparably more natural intelligence and energy than the Germans possess. It was touching to behold their first meeting, their childlike but profound delight; one might have said that members of the same family, scattered over the whole world by a terrible fate, were here for the first time coming together again after a long and bitter separation. They wept, they laughed, they embraced each other, and their tears, their joy, their friendly greetings contained no empty phrases, no lies, no pompous bombast; all was simple, sincere, and holy. In Paris I had been captivated by the democratic exaltation, the heroism of the popular masses; here, on the other hand,

I was enthralled by the sincerity and warmth of this plain but profound Slavic emotion. I myself felt the heart of a Slav awakening within me, so that at first I almost quite forgot the democratic sympathies which were my tie with Western Europe. The Poles looked down on the other Slavs from the heights of their political importance, and held themselves rather aloof, smiling a little. As for me, I mingled with them, and lived among them, and shared their joys with my whole heart; and for this I was beloved by them and enjoyed almost general confidence.

The feeling which dominates the Slavs is their hatred for the Germans. The forceful, though discourteous, expression "God-damned German," which is spoken in almost exactly the same way in all Slav languages, produces an incredible effect on every Slav: I have tried out its power several times, and have seen it work on the Poles themselves. . . . Hatred of the Germans was the inexhaustible subject of all conversations. It served as a greeting between strangers: when two Slavs met, the first words they exchanged were always directed against the Germans, as if they wished to reassure each other that they were both good genuine Slavs. Hatred of the Germans is the primary foundation for a Slav union and for mutual understanding among the Slavs; it is so strong, so deeply engraved in the heart of every Slav that I still feel persuaded, Sire, that sooner or later, in one way or another, and no matter what form European political relations may take, the Slavs will free themselves from German oppression and a time will come when there will no longer be any Prussian, or Austrian, or Turkish Slavs.

The importance of the Pan-Slavic Congress, in my opinion, lay in the fact that this was the first meeting, the first acquaintance, the first attempt of the Slavs to get together and to understand one another. As for the Congress itself, like all modern congresses and gatherings, it was quite empty of all meaning.

[*The political aims and desires of the Czechs, Poles, and Southern Slavs diverged too widely to permit the Congress to achieve any concrete results. Bakunin tried, vainly, to convince them that the thing for them to do was to free themselves from German domination and form a Pan-Slavic union, which Russia, after a revolution, would join. He quotes from one of the speeches he made at the Congress:*]

"But no less mistaken are those who look to the Russian Czar for help in the restoration of Slavic independence. The Russian Czar has formed a new close alliance with the Austrian dynasty, not for you but against you, not in

order to help you but in order to force you, as well as all other rebellious Austrian subjects, to return to the old subjection, to the old unquestioning obedience. The Emperor Nicholas likes neither popular freedom nor constitutions: you have seen a living example of that in Poland. . . . There is no room for you now in the bosom of the Russian Empire: you want life, and there dead silence reigns; you demand independence, mobility, and there you will find mechanical obedience; you wish renovation, elevation, education, liberation, and there nothing is to be seen but death, darkness, and slave labor. By entering the Russia of Emperor Nicholas, you would have entered the tomb of all popular life and all freedom. It is true that without Russia no Slav union, no Slav power is complete; but it would be madness to expect salvation and aid to the Slavs from present-day Russia. What is left for you then? Unite at first without Russia, not excluding her, but awaiting her, hoping for her prompt liberation; and she will be moved by your example, and you will become the liberators of the Russian people, which in its turn will then become your power and your shield."

[Bakunin explains how, without organization or funds, he expected to bring about a revolution in Russia.]

I am not a charlatan by nature, Sire; on the contrary, nothing repels me so much as charlatanism, nor have I ever lost the love of simple, unadulterated truth; but the unfortunate, unnatural position—for which, of course, I myself was to blame—forced me at times to be a charlatan against my will. Without connections, without funds, alone with my plans in the midst of a crowd of strangers, I had only one fellow-champion, my faith, and I kept saying to myself that faith moves mountains, destroys obstacles, conquers the invincible and does the impossible; that faith alone is half the success, half the victory, for, coupled with a strong will, it creates the circumstances, creates the men, gathers, joins and unites the masses into a single power and a single soul; I kept saying to myself that, believing as I did in the Russian Revolution, and having made others, Europeans, especially Slavs, and latterly Russians, believe in it, I would make the revolution in Russia possible and indispensable. In short, I wanted to believe, and wanted others to believe.

[Penitent or not, Bakunin proceeds to tell the Czar a few home truths about his Empire and its administration.]

As one looks around the world, one finds everywhere a great deal of evil,

oppression and corruption, and in Russia, perhaps, even more than in other states. This is not because people in Russia are worse than in Western Europe; on the contrary, I believe that the Russians are better, kinder, more spacious of soul, than the Westerners. But in the West there are remedies against evil: information, public opinion, and finally, freedom, which ennobles and elevates all men. These remedies do not exist in Russia. Western Europe at times seems worse to us because there every evil appears on the surface, few things remaining hidden. In Russia, on the contrary, every illness is driven inwards, and eats away the inner composition of the public organism. In Russia the chief motive power is fear, and fear kills all life, all intelligence, every noble emotion. It is difficult and painful for a man who loves truth to live in Russia, for a man who loves his neighbor, who respects equally in all human beings the dignity and independence of the immortal soul—a man, in short, who suffers not only from the oppression of which he is himself the victim, but also from the oppression which hits his neighbor! Russian public life is a chain of oppression: the man high up oppresses the one under him; the latter endures it, not daring to complain, but in his turn oppresses the man below, who also endures and also avenges himself on his subordinates. Worst off are the common people, the poor Russian *moujiks,* who, being at the very bottom of the social ladder, cannot themselves oppress anybody, but must suffer oppression from all, just as the old Russian proverb has it: "Only the lazy don't beat *us!*"

People steal and take bribes and do wicked things for money all over the world—in France, and in England, and in honest Germany; but in Russia, I believe, more than in any other state. In the West the corrupt seldom remain hidden, for a thousand eyes are upon each man, and each man may call public attention to theft or injustice, in which case no ministry is powerful enough to protect the wrongdoer. In Russia, on the other hand, it may happen that everybody knows the thief, the oppressor, the man who accepts pay for wrongdoing; everybody knows, yet everybody remains silent, being afraid; and the authorities too are silent, knowing that they are not blameless themselves, and everybody is concerned only with keeping the Minister, and the Czar, from finding out. And the Czar is far away, Sire, just as God is high up! (*Russian proverb*). In Russia it is difficult and almost impossible for an official not to be a thief. First of all, everybody around him steals; habit soon becomes second nature, and what at first aroused indignation and repulsion soon becomes natural, unavoidable, indispensable. Second, a sub-

ordinate must himself in one form or another frequently offer gratuities to his superior. Finally, if a man should get the notion of remaining honest, both his comrades and his superiors would hate him; at first they might call him a character, a standoffish, unsociable person; then, if he refused to mend his ways, stamp him as a liberal or dangerous free-thinker; they wouldn't rest until they had crushed and ruined him altogether. . . .

Fear alone is not effective against this all-devouring illness. It may stun and deter for a time, but only for a short time. A man gets used to everything, even to fear: Vesuvius is surrounded with villages, and that very spot where Herculaneum and Pompeii are buried is inhabited today. . . . It is even so with the Russian officials, Sire! They know how terrible is your wrath and how severe your punishments when the news of some theft or injustice reaches you; they tremble at the mere thought of your anger, yet still continue to steal, to oppress and to do wrong! They do so partly because it is difficult to give up an old and ingrained habit, partly because each one of them is tied up, connected with and obligated to others who have stolen and are still stealing with him, and most of all because each one consoles himself with the thought that he is so careful and has such excellent protection from above, that his misdeeds will never reach your ears.

Fear alone is ineffective. Against this evil other remedies are needed: the nobility of feeling, the independence of thought, the proud fearlessness which goes with a clear conscience, the respect for human dignity in oneself and in others, and finally, public contempt of dishonest and cruel men, a public shame, a public conscience! But these qualities flourish only where there is room and freedom for the soul, and not where slavery and fear are in the saddle. These qualities are feared in Russia not because they are disliked, but lest they bring free-thinking with them. . . .

I used to be especially amazed and troubled by the unfortunate situation of the so-called common people, the kindly and generally oppressed Russian *moujiks*. I felt more liking for them than for any other class, immeasurably more than for the weak and wanton Russian nobility. It was on them that I based all my hopes of resurrection, all my faith in the great future of Russia; it was in them that I saw spontaneity, greatness of soul, a clear intelligence untouched by foreign corruption—in short, the strength of Russia; and I used to think, what might this people not become if it were given freedom and property, if it were taught to read and write! And I kept asking myself why the present government—an absolute government, armed

with tremendous force, not.bound, in law or reality, by any rival right, by any foreign power—did not use its omnipotence for the liberation, the elevation, the education of the Russian people?

[*Bakunin, the Czar's prisoner, realizes that a good subject of the Czar has no right to ask such a question. He realizes further that statecraft and state policies are matters too complicated to be grasped by the ordinary mind "without having been prepared by special training, special atmosphere, close acquaintance and constant practice." After repenting his aberrations for a while, he continues to relate them.*]

In a word, Sire, I convinced myself that Russia, in order to save her honor and her future, had to have a revolution, overthrow your power, destroy the monarchist form of government, and, having thus freed herself from internal slavery, had to place herself at the head of the Slav movement, taking up arms against the Austrian Emperor, the Prussian King, the Sultan of Turkey, and, if need be, against Germany and the Magyars as well—in short, against the whole world—for the final liberation of all Slavs from foreign subjection. Half of Prussian Silesia, a large part of Western and Eastern Prussia, in short, all lands where Slav languages and Polish are spoken, would have to break away from Germany. My fancies went even further: I thought, I hoped, that the Magyar nation, forced by circumstances, by its isolated position in the midst of Slavic tribes, and also by its nature, which is Eastern rather than Western, that all Moldavians and Wallachians and, finally, even Greece, would join the Slavic Union, thus a single free Eastern state would arise, an Eastern Empire reborn, distinct from the West though not hostile to it, with Constantinople as its capital.

This is how far my revolutionary expectations went! Yet these were not the plans of personal ambition, Sire, I swear—and hope that you will soon be convinced of that. But first I must answer the question: what form of government did I desire to see in Russia? It is very difficult for me to reply to this, since my ideas on this subject were vague and indefinite. Having spent eight years abroad I knew that I did not know Russia, and said to myself that it was not for me, particularly when I was outside Russia, to determine the laws and forms of her new existence. I saw that in Western Europe, where social conditions are defined clearly enough, where there is far more general understanding of public affairs than in Russia—I saw that even there no one was able to foresee not only the constant forms the future might take but even the changes which tomorrow would bring. I said to

myself: no one knows Russia now, neither the Europeans nor the Russians themselves, because Russia is silent; she is silent not because she has nothing to say, but merely because she is bound and gagged. Let her arise and speak, and then we shall know what she thinks and what she wishes; she herself will show us what laws and institutions she requires.

[Bakunin feels that the parliamentary form of government would not do for Russia, both because of his dislike for "the narrow, cunningly-fashioned political catechism of western liberals" and because nineteenth-century "democracy" would exclude the great peasant masses from direct participation.]

I think that Russia, more than any other country, would need a strong dictatorship, which would devote itself exclusively to the elevation and education of the popular masses; a dictatorship free in policy and spirit, but without a parliament; printing books of a free nature, but without freedom of the press; surrounded by sympathizers, enlightened by their advice, strengthened by their voluntary collaboration, but not limited by anybody or anything. I told myself that the whole difference between such a dictatorship and the Czarist government would lie in the fact that the former, because of the spirit in which it was founded, would have to strive to make its existence unnecessary as soon as possible, having as its purpose only the freedom, independence, and gradual maturity of the people; whereas the Czarist government must on the contrary work to keep its existence from ever becoming superfluous, and must therefore maintain its subjects in a state of constant childhood.

What would come after the dictatorship I did not know; nor did I believe that anyone could have foretold that.

[Bakunin denies that he ever thought of himself as the dictator.]

I will not say that I am devoid of ambition, but it has never dominated me; on the contrary, I had to force myself, I had to overcome my natural reluctance, whenever I was preparing to speak in public, or even to write for publication. Neither did I have any of these tremendous vices *à la Danton* or *à la Mirabeau,* that violent, insatiable corruption which is ready to set the whole world topsy-turvy for its own satisfaction. And what I had of egoism consisted entirely in the need for movement, the need for action. There has always been a radical defect in my character: the love of the fantastic, of unheard-of, extraordinary adventures, of undertakings which open up a

limitless horizon and whose end none can foresee. I felt stifled and nauseated in ordinary, tranquil surroundings. People generally seek tranquillity and regard it as the highest good; but I was driven to despair by it; my soul was in a state of constant excitement, requiring action, movement and life.

[*The unsuccessful Pan-Slavic Congress in Prague was cut short by a revolution in which Bakunin, though he did not believe in its success and had advised against it, naturally took part. When the revolution failed he fled to Germany. Pursued by the rumor that he was a secret agent of the Russian government, he kept away from the German democrats, but established connections with Czechs and Poles. Still penniless, still without any organization backing him, he conceived an audacious plan of a thorough-going revolution in Bohemia, which would destroy all old records and divide the land among the peasants. A preliminary step would be the organization of several secret societies. While Bakunin, with two Polish associates, Geltman and Kryszanovsky, was waiting in Dresden for a summons from his confederates in Prague, a revolution broke out in Dresden itself. Tempted to flee, he felt that such a course would be dishonorable since, as the head of the Prague conspiracy, he had put others in danger, and had to share it with them. He remained while the revolution was going on. So he took part in it. . . .*]

On the day of the election of the Provisional Government my activity was limited to giving advice. This was, I believe, May 4th. The Saxon troops were conducting a parley; I advised Tschirner (*democrat member of the Provisional Government*) not to let himself be deceived, since it was clear that the Government was merely trying to gain time, expecting Prussian aid. I advised Tschirner to cut short the meaningless negotiations, to waste no time, and to take advantage of the weakness of the troops by seizing all of Dresden. I even offered to collect all my Polish acquaintances, of whom there were many in Dresden at that time, and together with them to lead the populace, who were demanding weapons, to the Arsenal. A whole day was lost in parleying. On the next day Tschirner remembered my advice and my offer, but the circumstances had already changed: the bourgeois had gone home with their rifles, the populace had cooled, not many of the *Freischarren* had arrived as yet, but the first Prussian battalions had already, I believe, made their appearance. However, swayed by his request, and still more by his promises, I found Geltman and Kryszanovsky, and, not without difficulty, persuaded them to take part in the Dresden revolution with me, explaining to them what favorable consequences its successful course

might have for the revolution in Bohemia, which we were expecting. They agreed, and brought with them to the City Hall, where the Provisional Government was installed, another Pole, an officer whom I did not know. We then concluded a sort of contract with Tschirner: he declared to us, first of all, that if the revolution was successful he would not be satisfied merely with a recognition of the Frankfurt Parliament and the Frankfurt Constitution, but would proclaim a democratic republic; second, he undertook to be our aid and faithful ally in all our Slavic enterprises; he promised us money, weapons, in a word, anything we might need for the Bohemian revolution. He only asked us to say nothing of all this.to Todt and Haeubner (*the two remaining members of the Provisional Government, more reactionary than himself*) whom he called traitors and reactionaries.

Thus we—Geltman, Kryszanovsky, the above-mentioned Polish officer, and myself—took up residence in the room of the Provisional Government, behind a screen. Our position was a most peculiar one: we represented a sort of general staff of the Provisional Government, which executed all our demands without a murmur; but Lieutenant Heinse, who was the chief of the national guard, acted and commanded the revolutionary forces independently, without taking orders from us or even from the Provisional Government. He looked upon us with open hostility, almost with hatred, and not only did not carry out a single one of our directions, which came to him in the form of orders from the Provisional Government, but did precisely the opposite, so that all our efforts were in vain. During a whole day we asked for nothing more than 500 or even 300 men, whom we wanted to lead to the Arsenal ourselves, and were unable to collect fifty, not because they were unavailable, but because Heinse would admit no one to us, and instead, as soon as fresh forces arrived, would scatter them over the whole of Dresden. I was certain then, and am still convinced that Heinse was acting as a traitor, and fail to understand how he could have been convicted as a state criminal. He assisted in the victory of the army far more than did the army itself which, as I have mentioned, behaved with great timidity.

On the next day, I think it was May 6th, my Poles and Tschirner all disappeared. This happened as follows.

Haeubner. . . . I cannot think of that man without profound sorrow! I had not met him before, but learned to know him during these few days; in such circumstances people get to know each other quickly. I have seldom seen a man purer, nobler, or more honest. Neither through his character, tendencies, nor conceptions was he meant for revolutionary activity; he was of

a mild and peaceful nature, he had just married and was passionately in love with his wife. He felt a far stronger inclination to write sentimental verses to her than to take part in the Provisional Government in which he, as well as Todt, was trapped like a rat. That he was a member of the government was the fault of his constitution-loving friends who, taking advantage of his willingness to sacrifice himself and wishing to paralyze Tschirner's democratic plans, got him elected. He himself saw in this revolution a lawful, holy war for German unity, of which he was an ardent and somewhat dreamy worshipper; he felt that he did not have the right to refuse a dangerous post, and so accepted it. Having once accepted, he wanted to play his part honestly to the very end, and indeed made the supreme sacrifice for what he held to be true and right. I shall say no word of Todt; he was demoralized from the very start by the contradiction between his position today and that of yesterday, and made several attempts to flee. But I must say a little about Tschirner. Tschirner was the generally recognized chief of the democratic party in Saxony; he was the instigator, tutelary genius and leader of the revolution, and he fled at the first threat of danger, he fled, moreover, frightened by a false rumor; in short, he showed himself before friends and enemies alike to be a coward and scoundrel. Later he reappeared; but I felt ashamed even to talk to him, and from that time on I dealt more with Haeubner, whom I had grown to like and respect with all my heart. The Poles also disappeared; they probably felt that they had to save themselves for the sake of the Polish fatherland. Since that time I did not see another Pole. This was my last farewell to the Polish nation. But I have interrupted my tale.

Well, Haeubner and I went to the barricades, partly in order to give fresh courage to the fighters, partly in order to find out at least something of how matters stood, a point on which no one among the troops of the Provisional Government had any information. When we returned we were told that Tschirner and the Poles, frightened by a false alarm, had felt it necessary to retire and had left word advising us to do the same. Haeubner decided to remain, and so did I; later Tschirner returned, and still later Todt; but the latter remained only a short while and vanished once more.

I remained not because I hoped for success. Things had been so thoroughly ruined by Messrs. Tschirner and Heinse that only a miracle could save the democrats. It was impossible to restore order. Everything was in such a state of confusion that no one knew what to do, where to go, nor whom to ask. I expected defeat, and remained partly because I could not find it in me to

abandon poor Haeubner, who sat there like a lamb picked for slaughter; but still more because, as a Russian, more than all the others subject to vile suspicions and calumniated more than once, I felt myself obliged, as Haeubner did, to see it through until the end.

I am unable, Sire, to give you a detailed report of the three or four days which I spent in Dresden after the flight of the Poles. I bustled about a great deal, gave advice, gave orders, was practically the whole Provisional Government all by myself, in short, I did all I could to save the ruined and, apparently, dying revolution; I did not sleep, or eat, or drink, I didn't even smoke, I was completely exhausted, and could not leave the room of the Government even for a minute, fearing that Tschirner would run away again and leave my Haeubner alone. Several times I called together the barricade chiefs, trying to restore order and to gather strength for the attack; but Heinse kept nipping all my measures in the bud, so that all my tense and feverish activity was in vain. Several of the communist barricade leaders took it into their heads to burn Dresden, and did in fact fire several houses. I never gave any orders to that effect; however, I should have agreed to it, had I thought that the fires could save the Saxon revolution. I have never been able to understand that greater pity should be taken on houses and inanimate objects, than on people. . . .

I did not order the burning, but neither did I permit the city to be surrendered to the army under the pretext of putting out the fires. When it became obvious that we could no longer hold Dresden, I suggested to the Provisional Government that we blow ourselves up together with the City Hall; I had enough gunpowder for that. But they said no; Tschirner fled once more, and I have not seen him since. Haeubner and I, having sent everywhere orders for a general retreat, waited for a certain length of time until our orders were carried out, and then retired together with the forces, taking with us all our gunpowder, all the ammunition, and our wounded. I still fail to understand how we succeeded, or rather, why we were permitted to stage not a flight, but a regular, orderly retreat, when it would have been so easy to crush us to powder in the open field. I might have thought that humanitarian impulses deterred the army leaders, were I capable, after all that I have seen and heard, before and after my imprisonment, of believing that they had any. I explain this occurrence as follows: everything is relative in this world, and German troops, even as German governments, were created to combat the German democrats.

However, although we retired in decent order, our men were quite de-

moralised. Having reached Freiburg and wishing to continue the war on the Bohemian frontier—I was still hoping for a Bohemian uprising—we tried to encourage them and to reorganize them, but this was impossible. They were all tired, exhausted, without any faith in success; and we ourselves were holding on anyhow, with a last effort, a last painful tension. In Chemnitz, instead of the help we had expected, we met with betrayal; reactionary citizens seized us in our beds at night and took us to Altenburg, in order to give us over into the hands of the Prussian army. The Saxon committee of inquiry expressed surprise later that I had allowed myself to be taken, and had made no attempt to free myself. It might, in fact, have been possible to escape from the citizens; but I was worn out and exhausted spiritually even more than physically, and was altogether indifferent to what might happen to me. I merely destroyed my pocket notebook along the way, and hoped that, like Robert Blum in Vienna, I would be shot in a few days. I was afraid of only one thing: being surrendered into the hands of the Russian Government. My hope did not come true; another fate awaited me. Thus has ended my empty, useless and criminal existence, and I can only thank God that He stopped me in time along the broad highway that leads to all crimes.

My confession is finished, Sire! It has unburdened my soul. I have tried to put down all my sins, and to omit nothing essential; if I have forgotten anything, it was not on purpose. Whatever there may be in the testimonies, accusations and denunciations made against me that contradicts what I have said here will be definitely false, and either a mistake or a calumny.

Now I once again address my Sovereign and, falling at the feet of Your Imperial Majesty, implore you:

Sire! I am a great criminal who does not deserve clemency! I know this, and were I condemned to death, I should accept it as a worthy punishment, I should almost welcome it: for death would release me from a burdensome and unbearable existence. But Count Orlov said to me in the name of Your Imperial Majesty that capital punishment does not exist in Russia. Therefore I implore you, Sire, if this is possible under the law and if the plea of a criminal can touch the heart of Your Imperial Majesty, Sire, do not make me rot in perpetual imprisonment! Do not chastise me with a German punishment for my German sins! Let the hardest of hard labor be my lot, and I shall accept it gratefully, as a mercy; the harder the work, the easier it will be for me to forget myself in it! In solitary confinement, on the other hand, one remembers everything, and remembers it uselessly; both thought and

memory become indescribable torture and live for a long time, live against one's will, and, dying never, die each day of sorrow and inaction. Nowhere was I so well taken care of, neither in the Fortress of Koenigstein nor in Austria, as here in the Fortress of Peter and Paul, and God grant every free man that he have a superior as kind and humanitarian as the one whom, to my great good fortune, I have found here! Yet in spite of all this, were I given the choice, it seems to me that I would prefer not only death, but even corporal punishment to life imprisonment in the fortress.

One more request, Sire! Grant me the permission for the last time to see and bid farewell to my family, if not to all of them, then at least to my old father, my mother, and my favorite sister, of whom I don't even know whether she is still alive.

Grant me these two great mercies, All-merciful Czar, and I shall bless Providence which has freed me from the hands of the Germans in order to place me in the fatherly hands of Your Imperial Majesty.

Having lost the right to call myself a faithful subject of Your Imperial Majesty, I sign, in all sincerity,

Penitent Sinner,
MICHAEL BAKUNIN.

[The *Confession*, long buried in the Russian archives, was edited by Viateslav Polonsky and published by Gosizdat, Moscow, U.S.S.R., in 1921. The translation was made especially for this anthology—and done for the first time into English at such length—by VALENTINE SNOW.]

BAKUNIN AS "IMPLORING CRIMINAL"

[*Several years later, in a letter written to Herzen from Siberia, Bakunin refers to his Confession, saying that in it he betrayed no one, that it was "written with great firmness and audacity, and for that very reason" pleased the Czar. He remarks further: "I desired one thing only: not to become reconciled, not to resign myself, not to change, not to abase myself by seeking consolation in an illusion; to keep ablaze until the very end the holy flame of rebellion." Of the letter to Czar Alexander II, which may have been fresher in his mind, having been written on February 14, 1857, there is no mention. It accomplished what the Confession had failed to do: his sentence was changed to exile in Siberia. And when, a few years later, he escaped, the flame of rebellion blazed again. The letter to Alexander II follows.*]

LITTLE FATHER AND THE PENITENT : *Michael Bakunin*

Your Imperial Majesty, All-Merciful Czar!

The many favors shown to me by Your unforgettable and generous Father and by Your Majesty, You are pleased today to augment by a new favor, undeserved by me, but accepted with deepest gratitude: the permission to write to You. But what can a criminal write to his Sovereign, if not a plea for clemency? Thus, Sire, I am permitted to appeal to Your mercy, I am permitted to hope. Before justice any hope on my part would be madness; but before Your mercy, Sire, how can hope be madness? My weak, tormented heart is ready to believe that the present favor is half of forgiveness; and I must summon all my courage in order not to be carried away by this seductive but premature and possibly vain hope.

However, no matter what the future may bring me, I now implore for permission to open my heart to Your Majesty, to speak to You, Sire, as sincerely as I once did to Your Late Father, when His Majesty deigned to hear a full confession of my life and my actions. I carried out the will of the Late Sovereign, transmitted to me by Count Orlov, to confess to Him as a sinner does to his Father Confessor, in all honesty, and although my confession, written, as I remember, while I was still dazed by my recent past, could not, by its spirit, win the approval of the Czar, I have never, never had reason to regret my sincerity; on the contrary, I can ascribe to it alone, next to the Czar's own generosity, the merciful alleviation of my imprisonment. And now too, Sire, I cannot and will not base my hope of the possibility of pardon on anything but complete and open frankness on my part.

When I was brought from Austria to Russia in 1851, having forgotten the mildness of my country's laws, I expected death, knowing that I had fully deserved it. This expectation did not depress me too much; I even wished to take prompt leave of an existence whose future could hold forth no promise. The thought that I would pay for my mistakes with my life reconciled me to my past; and, awaiting death, I almost felt that I was in the right.

Through the generosity of the Late Czar it was deemed well to prolong my life and to lighten my fate in my imprisonment. This was a great mercy, and yet the clemency of the Czar turned into the worst of punishments for me. Having said good-bye to life, I had to return to it again, in order to discover how much greater moral suffering is than any physical pain. Had my imprisonment been made inflexibly severe, had I been forced to undergo great deprivations, I might, perhaps, have borne it more easily; but imprisonment alleviated in the extreme left full freedom to my thoughts and

turned them into torture. The family ties which I had considered forever broken, and which were resumed through the magnanimous permission to see my family, renewed in me the love of life itself: my embittered heart softened gradually under the warm breath of their love; the cold indifference which I at first had taken for tranquillity was gradually replaced by a warm interest in the fate of the family from whom I had long been separated; and in my soul there awakened—together with regret for lost happiness and peaceful home life—profound, inexpressibly painful sorrow for the possibility, destroyed forever through my own mad fault, of some day becoming, like my five brothers, the support of my home, the useful and active servant of my country. The testament of my dying father, whom I never ceased to love and respect with all my heart, even while I was acting in a manner totally opposed to his instructions, his last blessing, brought to me by my mother under condition of a sincere repentance on my part, found in me a heart which had been moved and prepared long before.

Sire! Solitary confinement is the most terrible of punishments. Without hope it would be worse than death: it is a death in life, a conscious, slow and daily realized deterioration of all the bodily, moral and mental powers; one feels oneself growing more wooden, feeble, stupid, every day, and a hundred times a day one calls for death as salvation. But this cruel solitude has at least one great and certain advantage: it places a man face to face with truth and with himself. In the tumult of the world, in the turmoil of events, it is easy to fall prey to the alluring phantom of ambition; but in the forced inactivity of imprisonment, in the sepulchral silence of constant solitude, it is impossible to deceive oneself for long. If a man has but a spark of truth in him, he will surely see his whole past life in its proper light and meaning; and if this life was empty, useless and harmful, as mine has been, he will become his own executioner. No matter how painful the merciless discussion with oneself, regarding oneself, may be, no matter how torturous the thoughts which it engenders, having once begun, it is impossible to stop it. I know this through eight years' experience.

Sire! What name shall I give to my past existence? Wasted in fruitless and chimerical striving, it ended in crime. And yet, I was neither self-seeking nor evil; I loved ardently the good and the true; but false premises, false reasoning and sinful ambition led me into criminal errors; and having once entered upon the wrong path, I felt it my duty and a point of honor to follow it to the end. It brought me to an abyss, from which only the all-powerful and saving hand of Your Majesty can rescue me.

Do I deserve such clemency? To this I can say only one thing: during my eight years of imprisonment, and especially lately, I have suffered torments which I had never previously supposed possible. It was not the loss and privation of worldly delights which tormented me, but the realization that I myself had condemned myself to insignificance, that I had accomplished nothing in my life save crime, that I had been unable even to assist my family, to say nothing of my great country, against which I had dared to raise a traitorous and helpless hand. Thus the Czar's very mercy, the very love and tender care of my relatives, which I had in no way deserved, became a new torture for me: I envied my brothers who could by action prove their love for our mother, who could serve You, Sire, and Russia. But when, at the Czar's call all Russia arose against her united enemies, when, together with the others, my five brothers too took up their arms and, leaving our old mother and their small children, risked their lives to defend their fatherland, then I cursed my errors, delusions and crimes, which were condemning me to a shameful, though involuntary, inaction at a time when I could and should have served my Czar and my country; then my situation became unbearable, despair possessed me, and I had but one plea: death or freedom.

Sire! What more shall I say? If I could begin my life all over again, I should chart a different course, but, alas! the past cannot be brought back. If I could make up for my past by action, I should implore You for a chance to do so: my spirit would not quail before the salutatory hardships of purifying service; I should be glad to wash off my crimes with sweat and blood. But my physical strength is far from corresponding to the strength and freshness of my emotions and desires; illness has made me good for nothing. Although I am not yet old in years, being forty-four, the last years of imprisonment have exhausted all my reserves of vitality, have crushed what remained to me of youth and health. I must consider myself an old man, and feel that I have not much of life left. I do not regret a life which must pass without activity or profit; only one desire is still alive within me: to breathe free air into my lungs for the last time, to glance at the clear sky, the verdant fields; to see my father's house, to kneel at his grave and, devoting the rest of my days to my mother who is in constant sorrow for me, to prepare in a worthy manner for death.

I am not ashamed, Sire, to confess to You my weakness; I admit frankly that the thought of dying alone in prison frightens me, frightens me far more than death itself, and from the bottom of my heart and soul I pray Your Majesty to spare me, if possible, this last and heaviest punishment.

No matter what sentence may await me, I resign myself to it submissively in advance, as wholly just, and I hope that I may be permitted now for the last time to express to You, Sire, my profound gratitude to Your unforgettable Father and to Your Majesty for all the favors shown me.

Imploring criminal,

MICHAEL BAKUNIN.

February 14, 1857.

[Translated from the Russian by VALENTINE SNOW.]

THE BOHEMIAN AND THE CRUCIFIX:
Paul Verlaine

LE CIEL   AUTRE   O MON DIEU

WITHOUT hypocrisy Verlaine made a career ot the sacred and profane, and continuously one element was the inspiration of the other. A bohemian of the boulevards, he wrote great Catholic poetry; a primitive worshiper of his Savior, he made subtle music for "adolescent Satans" indulging in "the seven sins of the five senses." The rhythms which cannot be translated from French into English are what Harold Nicolson calls "hermaphroditic" (the label applies to Verlaine morally as well): "The effect obtained is one of fluid simplicity and of plaintive impotence, and that, after all, was the effect which he himself desired." [1] The familiar Verlaine legend, of the poet in middle age, the Verlaine of the cafés and the hospitals, with the bald head and the bearded monkey-face, came after the memorable poems had already been written, many of them in a Belgian jail. The Verlaine legend came after the sordid crisis with his wife Mathilde and his infatuation with Arthur Rimbaud. It was in his later years that Verlaine obligingly consented to be the "Falstaff of the Boulevard St. Michel," "sodden, untidy, argumentative, shameless, cowardly, orgiac, naïf, decadent and religious." But the first experiment in decadence and religion belongs to the period of Verlaine's elopement with Arthur Rimbaud. It led to a quarrel, a shooting, and a jail in Mons. It brought Verlaine a legal separation from his wife, a cell with a copper crucifix and a conventional lithograph of the Sacred Heart—and finally the conversion. For Rimbaud, *"ange et démon,"* the interlude with Verlaine was followed by that expression of utter contempt for literature, morality, and his companion: *A Season in Hell*—and then by final and complete silence. But Verlaine remained in the monastic rigor of his Belgian jail at Mons for two years, alternating between enthusiasms for bawdy and religious poetry. In a penitent mood of self-pity for his youth he wrote:

> —Qu'as-tu fait, ô toi que voilà
> Pleurant sans cesse,
> Dit, qu'as-tu fait, toi que voilà
> De ta jeunesse?

---

[1] *Le Ciel* and *Autre,* which simply evaporate in translation, are offered in French.

and, that mood spent, turned an amused glance at his fellow jailbirds—"Samsons without Delilahs"—for whose company he had a nostalgic taste: *"Allons, frères, bons vieux voleurs,/Doux vagabonds"*—"Come, brothers, good old thieves, pickpockets in the pink of condition, good old friends. Let's smoke philosophically, let's make the rounds peacefully: no harm in doing nothing." The conversion came in a great flood of tears before a crude lithograph of the Sacred Heart, and it resulted in the poetry of *Sagesse,* including the ten sonnets which form a dialogue between Verlaine and his Savior:

> Mon Dieu m'a dit: Mon fils, il faut m'aimer. Tu vois
> Mon flanc percé, mon coeur qui rayonne et qui saigne. . . .

When Verlaine left the jail in Mons in January 1875, an official wrote into his prison record this practical judgment without benefit of rhyme:

> *Character,* weak;
> *Reform,* probable;
> *Trade Learned,* none.

And of Verlaine's invitation to Rimbaud—"Let us love one another in Jesus"—the *ange et démon,* who understood him, remarked: "Verlaine arrived the other day, with a rosary in his claws. . . . Three hours afterwards, he had denied his God and reopened the ninety-eight wounds of Our Savior."

LE CIEL [2]

> LE CIEL est, par-dessus le toit,
> Si bleu, si calme!
> Un arbre, par-dessus le toit,
> Berce sa palme.
>
> La cloche, dans le ciel qu'on voit,
> Doucement tinte.
> Un oiseau sur l'arbre qu'on voit
> Chante sa plainte.

---

[2] "Par-dessus le mur de devant ma fenêtre (j'avais une fenêtre, une vraie! munie, par exemple, de longs et rapprochés barreaux), au fond de la si triste cour où s'ébattait, si j'ose ainsi parler, mon mortel ennui, je voyais, c'était en août, se balancer la crime aux feuilles voluptuesement frémissantes de quelque haut peuplier d'un square ou d'un boulevard voisin. En même temps m'arrivaient des rumeurs lointaines, adoucies, de fêtes (Bruxelles est la ville la plus bonhommement rieuse et rigoleuse que je sache). Et je fis, à ce propos, ces vers qui se trouvent dans *Sagesse*. . . ." Verlaine, *Mes Prisons.*

Mon Dieu, mon Dieu, la vie est là,
    Simple et tranquille,
Cette paisable rumeur-là
    Vient de la ville!

—Qu'as-tu fait, ô toi que voilà
    Pleurant sans cesse,
Dit, qu'as-tu fait, toi que voilà
    De ta jeunesse?

AUTRE [3]

La cour se fleurit de souci
    Comme le front
    De tous ceux-ci
    Qui vont en rond
En flageolant sur leur fémur
    Débilité
    Le long du mur
    Fou de clarté.

Tournez, Samsons sans Dalila,
    Sans Philistin,
    Tournez bien la
    Meule au destin;
Vaincu risible de la loi,
    Mouds tour à tour
    Ton coeur, ta foi
    Et ton amour!

Ils vont! et leurs pauvres souliers
    Font un bruit sec,
    Humiliés,
    La pipe au bec.

---

[3] "Un fois par jour, le matin, les prévenus, par sections, descendaient dans une cour pavée, 'ornée' au milieu d'un petit 'jardin' tout en la fleur jaune nommée souci, munis de leur seau . . . mieux et pis qu'hygiénique, qu'il devaient vider à un endroit designé et rincer avant de commencer leur promenade à la queue-leu-leu sous l'oeil d'un gardien tout au plus humain. J'ai fait là-dessus des strophes . . ." Verlaine, *Mes Prisons*.

Pas un mot ou bien le cachot,
Pas un soupir.
Il fait si chaud
Qu'on croit mourir.

J'en suis de ce cirque effaré,
Soumis d'ailleurs
Et préparé
A tous malheurs:
Et pourquoi si j'ai contristé
Ton voeu têtu,
Société,
Me choierais-tu?

Allons, frères, bons vieux voleurs,
Doux vagabonds,
Filous en fleurs,
Mes chers, mes bons,
Fumons philosophiquement,
Promenons-nous
Paisiblement:
Rien faire est doux.

O MON DIEU, VOUS M'AVEZ BLESSÉ D'AMOUR
(*From Sagesse* [4])

O MY God, thou hast wounded me with love,
Behold the wound, that is still vibrating,
O my God, thou hast wounded me with love.

O my God, thy fear hath fallen upon me,
Behold the burn is there, and it throbs aloud,
O my God, thy fear hath fallen upon me.

---

[4] *Sagesse* represents "what was best in Verlaine during his months of imprisonment, but it does not represent all that he then composed. Practically the whole of *Parallèlement,* with its series of bawdy poems, was written at Mons, and so also was a great portion of what was later to figure in *Jadis et naguère*. It was at one time Verlaine's intention to publish the whole collection in one volume to be entitled *Cellulairement,* and to interlard among the religious poems of *Sagesse* the pieces which now figure in his more pagan publications." Harold Nicolson, *Paul Verlaine*, Houghton Mifflin.

O my God, I have known that all is vile
And that thy glory has stationed itself in me,
O my God, I have known that all is vile.

Drown my soul in floods, floods of thy wine,
Mingle my life with the body of thy bread,
Drown my soul in floods, floods of thy wine.

Take my blood, that I have not poured out,
Take my flesh, unworthy of suffering,
Take my blood, that I have not poured out.

Take my brow, that has only learned to blush,
To be the footstool of thine adorable feet,
Take my brow, that has only learned to blush.

Take my hands, because they have laboured not
For coals of fire and for rare frankincense,
Take my hands, because they have laboured not.

Take my heart, that has beaten for vain things,
To throb under the thorns of Calvary,
Take my heart, that has beaten for vain things.

Take my feet, frivolous travellers,
That they may run to the crying of thy grace,
Take my feet, frivolous travellers.

Take my voice, a harsh and a lying noise,
For the reproaches of thy Penitence,
Take my voice, a harsh and a lying noise.

Take mine eyes, luminaries of deceit,
That they may be extinguished in the tears of **prayer,**
Take mine eyes, luminaries of deceit.

Alas, thou, God of pardon and promises,
What is the pit of mine ingratitude,
Alas, thou, God of pardon and promises.

God of terror and God of holiness,
Alas, my sinfulness is a black abyss,
God of terror and God of holiness.

Thou, God of peace, of joy and delight,
All my tears, all my ignorances,
Thou, God of peace, of joy and delight.

Thou, O God, knowest all this, all this,
How poor I am, poorer than any man,
Thou, O God, knowest all this, all this.

And what I have, my God, I give to thee.

[*Translated by* ARTHUR SYMONS.]

MRS. GRUNDY AND THE FAT BOY:
Oscar Wilde

"I SIT BETWEEN GILLES DE RETZ AND THE MARQUIS DE SADE"

"I DON'T DEFEND MY CONDUCT, I EXPLAIN IT"

FROM DE PROFUNDIS

~~~~~~

On November 13th, 1895, I was brought down here from London. From two o'clock till half-past two on that day I had to stand on the centre platform of Clapham Junction in convict dress, and handcuffed, for the world to look at. I had been taken out of the hospital ward without a moment's notice being given to me. Of all possible objects I was the most grotesque. When people saw me they laughed. Each train as it came up swelled the audience. Nothing could exceed their amusement. That was, of course, before they knew who I was. As soon as they had been informed they laughed still more. For half an hour I stood there in the grey November rain surrounded by a jeering mob.

For a year after that was done to me I wept every day at the same hour and for the same space of time. . . .   OSCAR WILDE, *De Profundis*

PUNCH represented Oscar Wilde as a Fat Boy saying to Mrs. Grundy: "I want to make your flesh creep!" After a series of skirmishes, Mrs. Grundy won the last battle in the criminal courts and scored a victory against the Fat Boy. But even as she triumphed with a sermon and a prison sentence she had unwittingly hung one more icon in the gallery of her martyrs. Oscar Wilde was tried for homosexuality and wit, an act of vengeance on the part of Mrs. Grundy in an area where revenge is a quack medicine. For no sooner had the official conscience been appeased than the public flesh ceased to creep and began to tingle. By a law of compensation which has benefited Byron, Shelley, Wilde, and others, the victims of Mrs. Grundy never fail to collect their reparations with interest from posterity. The other side of the case between Oscar Wilde and Mrs. Grundy was put very sensibly by G. B. Shaw when he remarked that, "The world has been in some ways so unjust to him that one must be careful not to be unjust to the world." It is true that Wilde worked more industriously at courting his destruction than at making what he called art. Neither *Dorian Gray*, nor *Intentions*, nor all the sparkling plays, nor *The Soul of Man Under Socialism*, not even *De Profundis* and *The Ballad of Reading Gaol*, are sufficient justification of

654

Oscar Wilde's amoral personal comedy. And the aesthetic snobbism of *Punch's* Fat Boy just about matches the moral snobbism of *Punch's* Mrs. Grundy. If pity is in order at the fall of such genius as Oscar Wilde's (Wilde: "No man of my position can fall into the mire of life without getting a great deal of pity from his inferiors"), the pity lies in the stupidity which does not recognize the really dangerous enemies of society. "Wilde was a conventional man," says Shaw, "his unconventionality was the pedantry of convention."

The trial at the Old Bailey in 1895 came as a climax to a series of sensations. The sentimentality of *Dorian Gray* had been shocking. The carnations tinted green in the buttonholes of young men applauding *Lady Windermere's Fan* at the St. James Theater had been shocking. The bright paradoxes of the essays in *Intentions* and the nakedness of *Salamé* had been shocking. And the contest between the angry father of young Lord Alfred Douglas, the Marquis of Queensberry, and Oscar Wilde, was the most violent public shock of them all. The general facts of that trial are already notorious. The Marquis of Queensberry wrote down the "hideous word" on his calling card so plainly that Wilde knew at once that "the tower of ivory is assailed by the foul thing." He might have escaped the legal consequences of his friendships with grooms and bellboys but not when he was caught as a target between two quite extraordinary passions. "The hatred of your father," Wilde wrote accusingly long afterwards to Lord Alfred Douglas, "was of such stature that it entirely outstripped, overgrew and overshadowed your love for me. . . . The idea of your being the object of a terrible quarrel between your father and a man of my position seemed to delight you." It certainly delighted Mrs. Grundy when Queensberry, quite able to justify the "hideous word," turned his defense into a further prosecution. Some of the most provoking lines that Oscar Wilde ever addressed to Mrs. Grundy he delivered in the witness box of his trial. Asked by the prosecutor whether one of his stories was immoral, he replied with candor that it was worse—it was badly written. Asked whether he ever adored any young man, he answered truthfully that he had never given adoration to anybody but himself. Pressed to justify the phraseology of one of his intimate letters, he replied that it was a beautiful letter and that anyway a great deal depended on the way it was read. Asked if he had often written letters in the same style, he said that he did not repeat himself in style. But when the violent cross-examination turned from art and correspondence to young valets and grooms, the comic spirit of Oscar Wilde wilted. He lost the trial and his "wonderful life." His new life in prison for two miserable years, the reversal of his bril-

liant and sensual past, might have been calculated with sadistic nicety by someone more imaginative than Mrs. Grundy. The enforced silence, the impoverished food, the plank bed, and the picking of oakum with sore fingers were only the ordinary prison routine. He tried to rescue himself by exercise in humility and only invented a new manner of pride. He poured it all out in the never fully published *De Profundis*. "To me reformation in morals are as meaningless and vulgar as Reformations in theology," he wrote into his prison ledger, "but while to propose to be a better man is a piece of unscientific cant, to have become a deeper man is a privilege of those who have suffered." He sought depth in new phrases, such as that the supreme vice is shallowness, and whatever is realized is right: "I can claim on my side that if I realize what I have suffered, society should realize what it has inflicted on me; and that there should be no bitterness on either side." At this point in his wretchedness, he rose miles higher than Mrs. Grundy.

To a warden in Reading Gaol who had shown him some little kindness he wrote a note of thanks on a torn bit of paper. Written as it was by one of the wittiest and proudest persons in English letters, it measures the depths of piteousness to which he was reduced by Mrs. Grundy:

My dear friend: What have I to write about except that if you had been an officer in Reading Prison a year ago my life would have been much happier. Every one tells me I am looking much happier. That is because I have a good friend who gives me the *Chronicle* and *promises* me ginger biscuits!

o. w.

"I SIT BETWEEN GILLES DE RETZ AND THE MARQUIS DE SADE"

H. M. PRISON, READING
after September 1896

. . . For myself, my dear Robbie, I have little to say that can please you. The refusal to commute my sentence has been like a blow from a leaden sword. I am dazed with a dull sense of pain. I had fed on hope, and now anguish, grown hungry, feeds her fill on me as though she had been starved of her proper appetite. There are, however, kinder elements in this evil prison air than before: sympathies have been shown to me, and I no longer feel entirely isolated from humane influences, which was before a source of terror and trouble to me. And I read Dante, and make excerpts and notes

for the pleasure of using a pen and ink. And it seems as if I were better in many ways, and I am going to take up the study of German. Indeed, prison seems to be the proper place for such a study. There is a thorn, however—as bitter as that of St. Paul, though different—that I must pluck out of my flesh in this letter. It is caused by a message you wrote on a piece of paper for me to see. I feel that if I kept it secret it might grow in my mind (as poisonous things grow in the dark) and take its place with other terrible thoughts that gnaw me. . . . Thought to those that sit alone and silent and in bonds, being no 'winged living thing,' as Plato feigned it, but a thing dead, breeding what is horrible like a slime that shows monsters to the moon.

I mean, of course, what you said about the sympathies of others being estranged from me, or in danger of being so, by the deep bitterness of my feelings: and I believe that my letter was lent and shown to others. . . . Now, I don't like my letters shown about as curiosities: it is most distasteful to me. I write to you freely as to one of the dearest friends I have, or have ever had: and, with a few exceptions, the sympathy of others touches me, as far as its loss goes, very little. No man of my position can fall into the mire of life without getting a great deal of pity from his inferiors; and I know that when plays last too long, spectators tire. My tragedy has lasted far too long; its climax is over; its end is mean; and I am quite conscious of the fact that when the end does come I shall return an unwelcome visitant to a world that does not want me; a *revenant,* as the French say, and one whose face is grey with long imprisonment and crooked with pain. Horrible as are the dead when they rise from their tombs, the living who come out from tombs are more horrible still. Of all this I am only too conscious. When one has been for eighteen terrible months in a prison cell, one sees things and people as they really are. The sight turns one to stone. Do not think that I would blame any one for my vices. My friends had as little to do with them as I had with theirs. Nature was in this matter a stepmother to all of us. I blame them for not appreciating the man they ruined. As long as my table was red with wine and roses, what did they care? My genius, my life as an artist, my work, and the quiet I needed for it, were nothing to them. I admit I lost my head. I was bewildered, incapable of judgment. I made the one fatal step. And now I sit here on a bench in a prison cell. In all tragedies there is a grotesque element. You know the grotesque element in mine. Do not think I do not blame myself. I curse myself night and day for my folly in allowing something to dominate my life. If there was an echo in these

walls, it would cry 'Fool' for ever. I am utterly ashamed of my friendships.
. . . For by their friendships men can be judged. It is a test of every man.
And I feel poignant abasement of shame for my friendships . . . of which
you may read a full account in my trial.

It is to me a daily source of mental humiliation. Of some of them I never
think. They trouble me not. It is of no importance. . . . Indeed my entire
tragedy seems to be grotesque and nothing else. For as a result of my having
suffered myself to be thrust into a trap . . . in the lowest mire of Malebolge,
I sit between Gilles de Retz and the Marquis de Sade. In certain places no
one, except those actually insane, is allowed to laugh: and indeed, even in
their case, it is against the regulations for conduct: otherwise I think I would
laugh at that. . . . For the rest, do not let any one suppose that I am credit-
ing others with unworthy motives. They really had no motives in life at all.
Motives are intellectual things. They had passions merely, and such passions
are false gods that will have victims at all costs and in the present case have
had one wreathed with bay. Now I have plucked the thorn out—that little
scrawled line of yours rankled terribly. I now think merely of your getting
quite well again, and writing at last the wonderful story of . . . And send
from me all that in my thoughts and feelings is good, and whatever of remembrance and reverence she will accept, to the lady of Wimbledon, whose
soul is a sanctuary for those who are wounded and a house of refuge for
those in pain. Do not show this letter to others—nor discuss what I have
written in your answer. Tell me about that world of shadows I loved so
much. And about the life and the soul tell me also. I am curious of the
things that stung me; and in my pain there is pity.

Yours,
OSCAR

"I DON'T DEFEND MY CONDUCT, I EXPLAIN IT"

April 1st, 1897.

My Dear Robbie,—I send you a MS. separate from this, which I hope will
arrive safely. As soon as you have read it, I want you to have it carefully
copied for me. There are many causes why I wish this to be done. One will
suffice. I want you to be my literary executor in case of my death, and to
have complete control of my plays, books, and papers. As soon as I find I

have a legal right to make a will, I will do so. My wife does not understand my art, nor could be expected to have any interest in it, and Cyril is only a child. So I turn naturally to you, as indeed I do for everything, and would like you to have all my works. The deficit that their sale will produce may be lodged to the credit of Cyril and Vivian. Well, if you are my literary executor, you must be in possession of the only document that gives any explanation of my extraordinary behaviour. . . . When you have read the letter, you will see the psychological explanation of a course of conduct that from the outside seems a combination of absolute idiocy with vulgar bravado. Some day the truth will have to be known—not necessarily in my lifetime . . . but I am not prepared to sit in the grotesque pillory they put me into, for all time; for the simple reason that I inherited from my father and mother a name of high distinction in literature and art, and I cannot for eternity allow that name to be degraded. I don't defend my conduct. I explain it. Also there are in my letter certain passages which deal with my mental development in prison, and the inevitable evolution of my character and intellectual attitude towards life that has taken place: and I want you and others who still stand by me and have affection for me to know exactly in what mood and manner I hope to face the world. Of course from one point of view I know that on the day of my release I shall be merely passing from one prison into another, and there are times when the whole world seems to me no larger than my cell and as full of terror for me. Still I believe that at the beginning God made a world for each separate man, and in that world which is within us we should seek to live. At any rate you will read those parts of my letter with less pain than the others. Of course I need not remind you how fluid a thing thought is with me—with us all—and of what an evanescent substance are our emotions made. Still I do see a sort of possible goal towards which, through art, I may progress. It is not unlikely that you may help me.

As regards the mode of copying: of course it is too long for any amanuensis to attempt: and your own handwriting, dear Robbie, in your last letter seems specially designed to remind me that the task is not to be yours. I think that the only thing to do is to be thoroughly modern and to have it typewritten. Of course the MS. should not pass out of your control, but could you not get Mrs. Marshall to send down one of her typewriting girls— women are the most reliable as they have no memory for the important— to Hornton Street or Phillimore Gardens, to do it under your supervision? I assure you that the typewriting machine, when played with expression, is not

more annoying than the piano when played by a sister or near relation. Indeed many among those most devoted to domesticity prefer it. I wish the copy to be done not on tissue paper but on good paper such as is used for plays, and a wide rubricated margin should be left for corrections. . . . If the copy is done at Hornton Street the lady typewriter might be fed through a lattice in the door, like the Cardinals when they elect a Pope; till she comes out on the balcony and can say to the world: 'Habet Mundus Epistolam'; for indeed it is an Encyclical letter, and as the Bulls of the Holy Father are named from their opening words, it may be spoken of as the *'Epistola: in Carcere et Vinculis.'* . . . In point of fact, Robbie, prison life makes one see people and things as they really are. That is why it turns one to stone. It is the people outside who are deceived by the illusions of a life in constant motion. They revolve with life and contribute to its unreality. We who are immobile both see and know. Whether or not the letter does good to narrow natures and hectic brains, to me it has done good. I have 'cleansed my bosom of such perilous stuff'; to borrow a phrase from the poet whom you and I once thought of rescuing from the Philistines. I need not remind you that mere expression is to an artist the supreme and only mode of life. It is by utterance that we live. Of the many, many things for which I have to thank the Governor there is none for which I am more grateful than for his permission to write fully and at as great a length as I desire. For nearly two years I had within a growing burden of bitterness, of much of which I have now got rid. On the other side of the prison wall there are some poor black soot-besmirched trees that are just breaking out into buds of an almost shrill green. I know quite well what they are going through. They are finding expression.

Ever yours,

OSCAR

FROM DE PROFUNDIS

WHERE there is sorrow there is holy ground. Some day people will realize what that means. They will know nothing of life till they do. —— and natures like his can realize it. When I was brought down from my prison to the Court of Bankruptcy, between two policemen, —— waited in the long dreary corridor that, before the whole crowd, whom an action so sweet and simple hushed into silence, he might gravely raise his hat to me, as, hand-

cuffed and with bowed head, I passed him by. Men have gone to heaven for smaller things than that. It was in this spirit, and with this mode of love, that the saints knelt down to wash the feet of the poor, or stooped to kiss the leper on the cheek. I have never said one single word to him about what he did. I do not know to the present moment whether he is aware that I was even conscious of his action. It is not a thing for which one can render formal thanks in formal words. I store it in the treasure-house of my heart. I keep it there as a secret debt that I am glad to think I can never possibly repay. It is embalmed and kept sweet by the myrrh and cassia of many tears. When wisdom has been profitless to me, philosophy barren, and the proverbs and phrases of those who have sought to give me consolation as dust and ashes in my mouth, the memory of that little, lovely, silent act of love has unsealed for me all the wells of pity: made the desert blossom like a rose, and brought me out of the bitterness of lonely exile into harmony with the wounded, broken, and great heart of the world. When people are able to understand, not merely how beautiful ———'s action was, but why it meant so much to me, and always will mean so much, then, perhaps, they will realize how and in what spirit they should approach me. . . .

The poor are wise, more charitable, more kind, more sensitive than we are. In their eyes prison is a tragedy in a man's life, a misfortune, a casualty, something that calls for sympathy in others. They speak of one who is in prison as of one who is 'in trouble' simply. It is the phrase they always use, and the expression has the perfect wisdom of love in it. With people of our own rank it is different. With us, prison makes a man a pariah. I, and such as I am, have hardly any right to air and sun. Our presence taints the pleasures of others. We are unwelcome when we reappear. To revisit the glimpses of the moon is not for us. Our very children are taken away. Those lovely links with humanity are broken. We are doomed to be solitary, while our sons still live. We are denied the one thing that might heal us and keep us, that might bring balm to the bruised heart, and peace to the soul in pain. . . .

I must say to myself that I ruined myself, and that nobody great or small can be ruined except by his own hand. I am quite ready to say so. I am trying to say so, though they may not think it at the present moment. This pitiless indictment I bring without pity against myself. Terrible as was what the world did to me, what I did to myself was far more terrible still.

I was a man who stood in symbolic relations to the art and culture of my age. I had realized this for myself at the very dawn of my manhood, and had forced my age to realize it afterwards. Few men hold such a position in

their own lifetime, and have it so acknowledged. It is usually discerned, if discerned at all, by the historian, or the critic, long after both the man and his age have passed away. With me it was different. I felt it myself, and made others feel it. Byron was a symbolic figure, but his relations were to the passion of his age and its weariness of passion. Mine were to something more noble, more permanent, of more vital issue, of larger scope.

The gods had given me almost everything. But I let myself be lured into long spells of senseless and sensual ease. I amused myself with being a *flâneur*, a dandy, a man of fashion. I surrounded myself with the smaller natures and the meaner minds. I became the spendthrift of my own genius, and to waste an eternal youth gave me a curious joy. Tired of being on the heights, I deliberately went to the depths in the search for new sensation. What the paradox was to me in the sphere of thought, perversity became to me in the sphere of passion. Desire, at the end, was a malady, or a madness, or both. I grew careless of the lives of others. I took pleasure where it pleased me, and passed on. I forgot that every little action of the common day makes or unmakes character, and that therefore what one has done in the secret chamber one has some day to cry aloud on the housetop. I ceased to be lord over myself. I was no longer the captain of my soul, and did not know it. I allowed pleasure to dominate me. I ended in horrible disgrace. There is only one thing for me now, absolute humility.

I have lain in prison for nearly two years. Out of my nature has come wild despair; an abandonment to grief that was piteous even to look at; terrible and impotent rage; bitterness and scorn; anguish that wept aloud; misery that could find no voice; sorrow that was dumb. I have passed through every possible mood of suffering. Better than Wordsworth himself I know what Wordsworth meant when he said—

> 'Suffering is permanent, obscure, and dark
> And has the nature of infinity.'

But while there were times when I rejoiced in the idea that my sufferings were to be endless, I could not bear them to be without meaning. Now I find hidden somewhere away in my nature something that tells me that nothing in the whole world is meaningless, and suffering least of all. That something hidden away in my nature, like a treasure in a field, is Humility.

It is the last thing left in me, and the best: the ultimate discovery at which I have arrived, the starting-point for a fresh development. It has come to me right out of myself, so I know that it has come at the proper time. It

662

could not have come before, nor later. Had any one told me of it, I would have rejected it. Had it been brought to me, I would have refused it. As I found it, I want to keep it. I must do so. It is the one thing that has in it the elements of life, of a new life, a *Vita Nova* for me. Of all things it is the strangest. One cannot acquire it, except by surrendering everything that one has. It is only when one has lost all things, that one knows that one possesses it.

Now I have realized that it is in me, I see quite clearly what I ought to do; in fact, must do. And when I use such a phrase as that, I need not say that I am not alluding to any external sanction or command. I admit none. I am far more of an individualist than I ever was. Nothing seems to me of the smallest value except what one gets out of oneself. My nature is seeking a fresh mode of self-realization. That is all I am concerned with. And the first thing that I have got to do is to free myself from any possible bitterness of feeling against the world.

I am completely penniless, and absolutely homeless. Yet there are worse things in the world than that. I am quite candid when I say that rather than go out from this prison with bitterness in my heart against the world, I would gladly and readily beg my bread from door to door. If I got nothing from the house of the rich I would get something at the house of the poor. Those who have much are often greedy; and those who have little often share. I would not a bit mind sleeping in the cool grass in summer, and when winter came on sheltering myself by the warm close-thatched rick, or under the penthouse of a great barn, provided I had love in my heart. The external things of life seem to me now of no importance at all. You can see to what intensity of individualism I have arrived—or am arriving rather, for the journey is long, and 'where I walk there are thorns.'

Of course I know that to ask alms on the highway is not to be my lot, and that if ever I lie in the cool grass at night-time it will be to write sonnets to the moon. When I go out of prison, R—— will be waiting for me on the other side of the big iron-studded gate, and he is the symbol, not merely of his own affection, but of the affection of many others besides. I believe I am to have enough to live on for about eighteen months at any rate, so that if I may not write beautiful books, I may at least read beautiful books; and what joy can be greater? After that, I hope to be able to recreate my creative faculties.

But were things different: had I not a friend left in the world; were there not a single house open to me in pity; had I to accept the wallet and ragged

cloak of sheer penury: as long as I am free from all resentment, hardness and scorn, I would be able to face the life with much more calm and confidence than I would were my body in purple and fine linen, and the soul within me sick with hate.

And I really shall have no difficulty. When you really want love you will find it waiting for you.

I need not say that my task does not end there. It would be comparatively easy if it did. There is much more before me. I have hills far steeper to climb, valleys much darker to pass through. And I have to get it all out of myself. Neither religion, morality, nor reason can help me at all.

Morality does not help me. I am a born antinomian. I am one of those who are made for exceptions, not for laws. But while I see that there is nothing wrong in what one does, I see that there is something wrong in what one becomes. It is well to have learned that.

Religion does not help me. The faith that others give to what is unseen, I give to what one can touch, and look at. My gods dwell in temples made with hands; and within the circle of actual experience is my creed made perfect and complete: too complete, it may be, for like many or all of those who have placed their heaven in this earth, I have found in it not merely the beauty of heaven, but the horror of hell also. When I think about religion at all, I feel as if I would like to found an order for those who *cannot* believe: the Confraternity of the Faithless, one might call it, where on an altar, on which no taper burned, a priest, in whose heart peace had no dwelling, might celebrate with unblessed bread and a chalice empty of wine. Every thing to be true must become a religion. And agnosticism should have its ritual no less than faith. It has sown its martyrs, it should reap its saints, and praise God daily for having hidden Himself from man. But whether it be faith or agnosticism, it must be nothing external to me. Its symbols must be of my own creating. Only that is spiritual which makes its own form. If I may not find its secret within myself, I shall never find it: if I have not got it already, it will never come to me.

Reason does not help me. It tells me that the laws under which I am convicted are wrong and unjust laws, and the system under which I have suffered a wrong and unjust system. But, somehow, I have got to make both of these things just and right to me. And exactly as in Art one is only concerned with what a particular thing is at a particular moment to oneself, so it is also in the ethical evolution of one's character. I have got to make everything that has happened to me good for me. The plank bed, the loathsome food,

the hard ropes shredded into oakum till one's finger-tips grow dull with pain, the menial offices with which each day begins and finishes, the harsh orders that routine seems to necessitate, the dreadful dress that makes sorrow grotesque to look at, the silence, the solitude, the shame—each and all of these things I have to transform into a spiritual experience. There is not a single degradation of the body which I must not try and make into a spirit-ualizing of the soul.

I want to get to the point when I shall be able to say quite simply, and without affectation, that the two great turning-points in my life were when my father sent me to Oxford, and when society sent me to prison. I will not say that prison is the best thing that could have happened to me: for that phrase would savour of too great bitterness towards myself. I would sooner say, or hear it said of me, that I was so typical a child of my age, that in my perversity, and for that perversity's sake, I turned the good things of my life to evil, and the evil things of my life to good.

What is said, however, by myself or by others, matters little. The im-portant thing, the thing that lies before me, the thing that I have to do, if the brief remainder of my days is not to be maimed, marred, and incom-plete, is to absorb into my nature all that has been done to me, to make it part of me, to accept it without complaint, fear, or reluctance. The supreme vice is shallowness. Whatever is realized is right.

* * * * *

I don't regret for a single moment having lived for pleasure. I did it to the full, as one should do everything that one does. There was no pleasure I did not experience. I threw the pearl of my soul into a cup of wine. I went down the primrose path to the sound of flutes. I lived on honeycomb. But to have continued the same life would have been wrong because it would have been limiting. I had to pass on. The other half of the garden had its secrets for me also. Of course all this is foreshadowed and prefigured in my books. Some of it is in *The Happy Prince,* some of it in *The Young King,* notably in the passage where the bishop says to the kneeling boy, 'Is not He who made misery wiser than thou art?' a phrase which when I wrote it seemed to me little more than a phrase; a great deal of it is hidden away in the note of doom that like a purple thread runs through the texture of *Dorian Gray;* in *The Critic as Artist* it is set forth in many colours; in *The Soul of Man* [*Under Socialism*] it is written down, and in letters too easy to read; it is one of the refrains whose recurring *motifs* make *Salomé* so like a piece of music

and bind it together as a ballad; in the prose poem of the man who from the bronze of the image of the 'Pleasure that liveth for a moment' has to make the image of the 'Sorrow that abideth for ever' it is incarnate. It could not have been otherwise. At every single moment of one's life one is what one is going to be no less than what one has been. Art is a symbol, because man is a symbol.

It is, if I can fully attain to it, the ultimate realization of the artistic life. For the artistic life is simply self-development. Humility in the artist is his frank acceptance of all experiences, just as love in the artist is simply the sense of beauty that reveals in the world its body and its soul. In *Marius the Epicurean* Pater seeks to reconcile the artistic life with the life of religion, in the deep, sweet, and austere sense of the word. But Marius is little more than a spectator: an ideal spectator indeed, and one to whom it is given 'to contemplate the spectacle of life with appropriate emotions,' which Wordsworth defines as the poet's true aim; yet a spectator merely, and perhaps a little too much occupied with the comeliness of the benches of the sanctuary to notice that it is the sanctuary of sorrow that he is gazing at.

I see a far more intimate and immediate connection between the true life of Christ and the true life of the artist; and I take a keen pleasure in the reflection that long before sorrow had made my days her own and bound me to her wheel I had written in *The Soul of Man* that he who would lead a Christ-like life must be entirely and absolutely himself, and had taken as my types not merely the shepherd on the hillside and the prisoner in his cell, but also the painter to whom the world is a pageant and the poet for whom the world is a song. I remember saying to André Gide, as we sat together in some Paris *café*, that while metaphysics had but little interest for me, and morality absolutely none, there was nothing that either Plato or Christ had said that could not be transferred immediately into the sphere of Art and there find its complete fulfilment.

* * * * *

I am to be released, if all goes well with me, towards the end of May, and hope to go at once to some little seaside village abroad with R—— and M——.

The sea, as Euripides says in one of his plays about Iphigenia, washes away the stains and wounds of the world.

I hope to be at least a month with my friends, and to gain peace and balance, and a less troubled heart, and a sweeter mood. I have a strange longing

666

for the great simple primeval things, such as the sea, to me no less of a mother than the Earth. It seems to me that we all look at Nature too much, and live with her too little. I discern great sanity in the Greek attitude. They never chattered about sunsets, or discussed whether the shadows on the grass were really mauve or not. But they saw that the sea was for the swimmer, and the sand for the feet of the runner. They loved the trees for the shadow that they cast, and the forest for its silence at noon. The vineyard-dresser wreathed his hair with ivy that he might keep off the rays of the sun as he stooped over the young shoots, and for the artist and the athlete, the two types that Greece gave us, they plaited with garlands the leaves of the bitter laurel and of the wild parsley, which else had been of no service to men.

We call ours a utilitarian age, and we do not know the uses of any single thing. We have forgotten that water can cleanse, and fire purify, and that the Earth is mother to us all. As a consequence our art is of the moon and plays with shadows, while Greek art is of the sun and deals directly with things. I feel sure that in elemental forces there is purification, and I want to go back to them and live in their presence.

Of course to one so modern as I am, *'Enfant de mon siècle,'* merely to look at the world will be always lovely. I tremble with pleasure when I think that on the very day of my leaving prison both the laburnum and the lilac will be blooming in the gardens, and that I shall see the wind stir into restless beauty the swaying gold of the one, and make the other toss the pale purple of its plumes so that all the air shall be Arabia for me. Linnaeus fell on his knees and wept for joy when he saw for the first time the long heath of some English upland made yellow with the tawny aromatic blossoms of the common furze; and I know that for me, to whom flowers are part of desire, there are tears waiting in the petals of some rose. It has always been so with me from my boyhood. There is not a single color hidden away in the chalice of a flower, or the curve of a shell, to which, by some subtle sympathy with the very soul of things, my nature does not answer. Like Gautier, I have always been one of those *'pour qui le monde visible existe.'*

Still, I am conscious now that behind all this beauty, satisfying though it may be, there is some spirit hidden of which the painted forms and shapes are but modes of manifestation, and it is with this spirit that I desire to become in harmony. I have grown tired of the articulate utterances of men and things. The Mystical in Art, the Mystical in Life, the Mystical in Nature this is what I am looking for. It is absolutely necessary for me to find it somewhere.

All trials are trials for one's life, just as all sentences are sentences of death; and three times have I been tried. The first time I left the box to be arrested, the second time to be led back to the house of detention, the third time to pass into a prison for two years. Society, as we have constituted it, will have no place for me, has none to offer; but Nature, whose sweet rains fall on unjust and just alike, will have clefts in the rocks where I may hide, and secret valleys in whose silence I may weep undisturbed. She will hang the night with stars so that I may walk abroad in the darkness without stumbling, and send the wind over my footprints so that none may track me to my hurt: she will cleanse me in great waters, and with bitter herbs make me whole.

GRANDEE OF THE GAS-LIGHT ERA:
O. Henry
JABBERWOCKY FOR MARGARET

THE pseudonym of William Sydney Porter was born in a Spartan short-story course of thirty-nine months' duration in an Ohio penitentiary. "I am like Lord Jim," O. Henry later remarked, "because we both made one fateful mistake at the supreme crisis of our lives, a mistake from which we could not recover." The son of a doctor who wasted his career on a perpetual-motion water wheel, young Porter read *The Arabian Nights* and *The Anatomy of Melancholy*. He gyrated in the "whirligig of fortune" as clerk, bookkeeper, draftsman, bank teller, columnist in the image of Eugene Field and George Ade, and storyteller in the manner of Bret Harte. Charged with the embezzlement of about $1000 as bank teller in Austin, Texas, his first sensible impulse—he was a husband and father—was to answer the probably exaggerated accusation. His second impulse was to flee to New Orleans, and from extradition to Honduras. The jack-of-all-trades of Austin; the refugee stevedore who unloaded bananas in New Orleans; the laughing man in spotless white ducks who buffooned in Latin America; and the prison druggist who soaked up the argot and life stories of penitentiary inmates—each of these successive O. Henry roles fed O. Henry fables.

For the fugitive bank teller (who wrote it down later in *Cabbages and Kings*), "tales of the Spanish Main" were still real. He noted how "the tintype man, the enlarged photograph brigand, the kodaking tourist, and the scouts of the gentle brigade of fakirs have found it out, and carry on the work. The hucksters of Germany, France, and Sicily now bag its small change across the counters." Exiled in Trujillo, Porter tried a little huckstering himself in the company of Al Jennings, a bank and train robber of the old West. If we can believe Al Jennings' fantastic record of their comic opera meeting on a dock in Trujillo (*Jennings:* Are you the American consul? *O. Henry:* No, but what caused you to leave in a hurry? *Jennings:* Perhaps the same reason as yours!), the American exiles at once planned coconut and indigo plantations—and a campaign for the presidency. That summer, full of the nostalgia of July the Fourth, Jennings, Porter, the American consul—and on Porter's suggestion the English consul, too ("a devil of a fine joke")—sang the *Star-Spangled Banner* before the Governor's mansion. As full of

drink as of patriotism, Jennings and Porter became involved in "a revolution" through a series of confused antics in the public square, and unwittingly "saved the republic." The republic duly thanked them, but to conciliate the rebels, asked "the disturbers of the revolution" to clear out of the country.

News of the desperate illness of his wife, Athol, brought Porter back to Austin. The authorities set the fugitive free on bond. After Athol's death, his case at last came up for a trial in which his flight was interpreted as a confession of guilt. He seemed utterly indifferent to the outcome and was convicted by a jury which probably considered all banking folks thieves.

As the prison's druggist, Porter came to meet with nearly every type of prisoner, but he decidedly preferred the society of western outlaws. He met the original of Jimmy Valentine who never lived to be reformed. The inmates were worked nearly to death and revived by the old water-cure. They caught consumption as easily as colds. To Mrs. Roach, the mother-in-law who took his eight-year-old daughter Margaret into her care, Porter wrote: "From 200 to 300 men are marched in each day . . . in single file past the doctor and he prescribes for each 'on the fly.' The procession passes the drug counter and the medicines are handed out to each one as they march without stopping the line." In this setting he wrote some twelve stories and lived intimately with very remarkable characters. Sunk in the mire of political patronage, the prison was managed by a few brainy convicts. The old Al Jennings was there, and robber Billy Raidler, the terror of Indian Territory. "Every man in prison is writing a story," exaggerated Jennings. When Bill Porter read *A Christmas Chaparral Gift* to the oddest literary society ever assembled in America, Billy Raidler remarked: "Damn you, Porter, I never did it in my life before; by God, I didn't know what a tear looked like." Jennings has left a record of their Sunday Recluse Club, an astonishing project in stolen banquets and virile conversation, of which Bill Porter was allegedly the king. When in 1901 Porter, like Jimmy Valentine, received his suit of clothes, the warden's solemn handshake, and a pittance for train fare, he could add seventy dollars earned by stories written in jail.

Porter began by imitating Bret Harte, but with the prison signature "O. Henry" he became distinctive. In the O. Henry design for living, any conventional soul might make a sharp turn around the corner and meet with the marvelous and unexpected. As Carl Van Doren remarks, "anybody can be the hero of an O. Henry episode, provided the right event happens to him." The fables whose characters O. Henry dressed in the costumes of "cowboys"

and "tramps" and "crooks" and "shop girls" sparkle with argot and malapropisms. In contrast to his contemporaries, Stephen Crane, Frank Norris, and Jack London, O. Henry wrote (to use his own vernacular pun) like an "Esau who swapped his copyright for a partridge."

But the letters to Margaret were not meant to earn money or to please the hard-hearted editors of New York. They were written for a little girl, eight years old, who was a woman of thirty before her father told her the facts of his jail sentence. Porter fell into the role of a Lewis Carroll writing letters to Alice. He tried to shield with Jabberwocky the facts which a child could not be told. He had always been embarrassed by solemnity. To the question, "What do you think about the hereafter?" he had once replied:

> I had a little dog and his name was Rover,
> And when he died, he died all over.

JABBERWOCKY FOR MARGARET

Hello, Margaret:

Don't you remember me? I'm a Brownie, and my name is Aldibirontiphostiphornikophokos. If you see a star shoot and say my name seventeen times before it goes out, you will find a diamond ring in the track of the first blue cow's foot you see go down the road in a snowstorm while the red roses are blooming on the tomato vines. Try it some time. I know all about Anna and Arthur Dudley, but they don't see me. I was riding by on a squirrel the other day and saw you and Arthur Dudley give some fruit to some trainmen. Anna wouldn't come out. Well good-bye, I've got to take a ride on a grasshopper. I'll just sign my first letter— "A."

July 8, 1898.

My Dear Margaret:

You don't know how glad I was to get your nice little letter to-day. I am so sorry I couldn't come to tell you good-bye when I left Austin. You know I would have done so if I could have.

Well, I think it's a shame some men folks have to go away from home to work and stay away so long—don't you? But I tell you what's a fact. When I come home next time I'm going to stay there. You bet your boots I'm getting tired of staying away so long.

I'm so glad you and Munny are going to Nashville. I know you'll have a fine ride on the cars and a good time when you get to Uncle Bud's. Now you must have just the finest time you can with Anna and the boys and tumble around in the woods and go fishing and have lots of fun. Now, Margaret, don't you worry any about me, for I'm well and fat as a pig and I'll have to be away from home a while yet and while I'm away you can just run up to Nashville and see the folks there.

And not long after you come back home I'll be ready to come and I won't ever have to leave again.

So you be just as happy as you can, and it won't be long till we'll be reading Uncle Remus again of nights.

I'll see if I can find another one of Uncle Remus's books when I come back. You didn't tell me in your letter about your going to Nashville. When you get there you must write me a long letter and tell me what you saw on the cars and how you like Uncle Bud's stock farm.

When you get there I'll write you a letter every week, for you will be much nearer to the town I am in than Austin is.

I do hope you will have a nice visit and a good time. Look out pretty soon for another letter from me.

I think about you every day and wonder what you are doing. Well, I will see you again before very long.

Your loving

PAPA.

August 16, 1898.

My Dear Margaret:

I got your letter yesterday, and was mighty glad to hear from you. I think you must have forgotten where you were when you wrote it, for you wrote "Austin, Texas" at the top of it. Did you forget you had gone to Tennessee?

The reason why I have not written you a letter in so long is that I didn't know the name of the postoffice where you and Munny were going until I got her letter and yours yesterday. Now that I know how to write I will write you a letter every Sunday and you will know just when you are going to get one every week. Are you having a nice time at Aunt Lilly's?

Munny tells me you are fat and sassy and I am glad to hear it. You always said you wanted to be on a farm. You must write and tell me next time what kind of times you have and what you do to have fun.

I'd have liked to see the two fish you caught. Guess they were most as long

672

as your little finger, weren't they? You must make Munny keep you up there till the hot weather is over before you go back to Austin. I want you to have as good times as you can, and get well and strong and big but don't get as big as Munny because I'm afraid you'd lick me when I come home.

Did you find Dudley and Arthur much bigger than they were when they were in Austin? I guess Anna is almost grown now—or thinks she is—which amounts to about the same thing.

February 14, 1900.

Dear Margaret:

It has been quite a long time since I heard from you. I got a letter from you in the last century, and a letter once every hundred years is not very often. I have been waiting from day to day, putting off writing to you, as I have been expecting to have something to send you, but it hasn't come yet, and I thought I would write anyhow.

I am pretty certain I will have it in three or four days, and then I will write to you again and send it to you.

I hope your watch runs all right. When you write again be sure and look at it and tell me what time it is, so I won't have to get up and look at the clock.

With much love,

PAPA.

May 17, 1900.

Dear Margaret:

It has been so long since I heard from you that I'm getting real anxious to know what is the matter. Whenever you don't answer my letters I am afraid you are sick, so please write right away when you get this. Tell me something about Pittsburg and what you have seen of it. Have they any nice parks where you can go or is it all made of houses and bricks? I send you twenty nickels to spend for anything you want.

Now, if you will write me a nice letter real soon I will promise to answer it the same day and put another dollar in it. I am very well and so anxious to be with you again, which I hope won't be very long now.

With much love, as ever

PAPA.

October 1, 1900.

Dear Margaret:

I got your very nice, long letter a good many days ago. It didn't come straight to me, but went to a wrong address first. I was very glad indeed to hear from you, and very, very sorry to learn of your getting your finger so badly hurt. I don't think you were to blame at all, as you couldn't know just how that villainous old "hoss" was going to bite. I do hope that it will heal up nicely and leave your finger strong. I am learning to play the mandolin, and we must get you a guitar, and we will learn a lot of duets together when I come home, which will certainly not be later than next summer, and maybe earlier.

I suppose you have started to school again some time ago. I hope you like to go, and don't have to study too hard. When one grows up, a thing they never regret is that they went to school long enough to learn all they could. It makes everything easier for them, and if they like books and study they can always content and amuse themselves that way even if other people are cross and tiresome, and the world doesn't go to suit them.

You mustn't think that I've forgotten somebody's birthday. I couldn't find just the thing I wanted to send, but I know where it can be had, and it will reach you in a few days. So, when it comes you'll know it is for a birthday remembrance.

I think you write the prettiest hand of any little girl (or big one, either) I ever knew. The letters you make are as even and regular as printed ones. The next time you write, tell me how far you have to go to school and whether you go alone or not.

I am busy all the time writing for the papers and magazines all over the country, so I don't have a chance to come home, but I'm going to try to come this winter. If I don't I will by summer sure, and then you'll have somebody to boss and make trot around with you.

Write me a letter whenever you have some time to spare, for I am always glad and anxious to hear from you. Be careful when you are on the streets not to feed shucks to strange dogs, or pat snakes on the head or shake hands with cats you haven't been introduced to, or stroke the noses of electric car horses.

Hoping you are well and your finger is getting all right, I am, with much love, as ever,

PAPA.

Dear Margaret:

Here are two or three more pictures, but they are not very good. Munny says you are learning very fast at school. I'm sure you're going to be a very smart girl, and I guess I'd better study a lot more myself or you will know more than I will. I was reading to-day about a cat a lady had that was about the smartest cat I ever heard of. One day the cat was asleep and woke up. He couldn't see his mistress, so he ran to a bandbox where she kept the hat she wore when she went out, and knocked the top off to see if it was there. When he found it was there he seemed to be contented and lay down and went to sleep again. Wasn't that pretty bright for a cat? Do you think Nig would do anything that smart?

You must plant some seeds and have them growing so you can water them as soon as it gets warm enough. Well, I'll write you another letter in a day or two. So good-bye till then.

Your loving

PAPA.

My Dear Margaret:

I ought to have answered your last letter sooner, but I haven't had a chance. It's getting mighty cool now. It won't be long before persimmons are ripe in Tennessee. I don't think you ever ate any persimmons, did you? I think persimmon pudden (not pudding) is better than cantaloupe or watermelon either. If you stay until they get ripe you must get somebody to make you one.

If it snows while you are there you must try some fried snowballs, too. They are mighty good with Jack Frost gravy.

You must see how big and fat you can get before you go back to Austin.

When I come home I want to find you big and strong enough to pull me all about town on a sled when we have a snow storm. Won't that be nice? I just thought I'd write this little letter in a hurry so the postman would get it and when I'm in a hurry I never can think of anything to write about. You and Munny must have a good time, and keep a good lookout and don't let tramps or yellowjackets catch you. I'll try to write something better next time. Write soon.

Your loving

PAPA.

November 12.

My Dear Margaret:

Did you ever have a pain right in the middle of your back between your shoulders? Well, I did just then when I wrote your name, and I had to stop a while and grunt and twist around in my chair before I could write any more. Guess I must have caught cold. I haven't had a letter from you in a long time. You must stir Munny up every week or two and make her send me your letter. I guess you'd rather *ride* the pony than *write* about him, wouldn't you? But you know I'm always so glad to get a letter from you even if it's only a teentsy weentsy one, so I'll know you are well and what you are doing.

You don't want to go to work and forget your old Pop just because you don't see much of him just now, for he'll come in mighty handy some day to read Uncle Remus to you again and make kites that a cyclone wouldn't raise off the ground. So write soon.

With love as ever,

PAPA.

My Dear Margaret:

I ought to have answered your letter some time ago, but you know how lazy I am. I'm very glad to hear you are having a good time, and I wish I was with you to help you have fun. I read in the paper that it is colder in Austin than it has been in many years, and they've had lots of snow there too. Do you remember the big snow we had there once? I guess everybody can get snow this winter to fry. Why don't you send me some fried snow in a letter? Do you like Tennessee as well as you did Texas? Tell me next time you write. Well, old Christmas is about to come round again. I wish I could come and light up the candles on the Christmas tree like we used to. I wouldn't be surprised if you haven't gotten bigger than I am by now, and when I come back and don't want to read Uncle Remus of nights, you can get a stick and make me do it. I saw some new Uncle Remus books a few days ago and when I come back I'll bring a new one, and you'll say "thanky-doo, thankydoo." I'm getting mighty anxious to see you again, and for us to have some more fun like we used to. I guess it won't be much longer now till I do, and I want to hear you tell all about what times you've had. I'll bet you haven't learned to button your own dress in the back yet, have you?

I hope you'll have a jolly Christmas and lots of fun—Geeminy! don't I

wish I could eat Christmas dinner with you! Well, I hope it won't be long till we all get home again. Write soon and don't forget your loving,

PAPA.

My Dear Margaret:

Here it is summertime, and the bees are blooming and ·the flowers are singing and the birds making honey, and we haven't been fishing yet. Well, there's only one more month till July, and then we'll go, and no mistake. I thought you would write and tell me about the high water around Pittsburg some time ago, and whether it came up to where you live, or not. And I haven't heard a thing about Easter, and about the rabbits' eggs—but I suppose you have learned by this time that eggs grow on egg plants and are not laid by rabbits.

I would like very much to hear from you oftener; it has been more than a month since you wrote. Write soon and tell me how you are, and when school will be out, for we want plenty of holidays in July so we can have a good time. I am going to send you something nice the last of this week. What do you guess it will be?

Lovingly,

PAPA.

Book VII

In Our Time

ALFRED DREYFUS

FRANCISCO FERRER

EUGENE V. DEBS

LENIN

ROSA LUXEMBURG

ADOLF HITLER

ERNST TOLLER

GEORGI DIMITROV

NICOLA SACCO

BARTOLOMEO VANZETTI

ODELL WALLER

GANDHI

JAWAHARLAL NEHRU

LÉON BLUM

MY HONOR! MY HONOR!

Alfred Dreyfus

LETTERS TO LUCIE

FROM THE DIARY ON DEVIL'S ISLAND

~~~~~~

As to the men I accuse, I do not know them, I have never seen them, I feel neither resentment nor hatred against them. For me they are only entities, emblems of social malfeasance. The action I take here is simply a revolutionary step designed to hasten the explosions of truth and justice.

I have one passion only, for light, in the name of humanity which has borne so much and has a right to happiness. My burning protest is only the cry of my soul. Let them dare then to carry me to the court of appeals, and let there be an inquest in the full light of the day.

I am waiting.

EMILE ZOLA, *J'Accuse!*[1]

THE affaire Dreyfus, whose giant web entangled an obscure little man with a stubborn sense of honor, was a civil war between forces which never published an armistice. Today nearly all the primary actors are dead, but as in the Oberammergau Passion Play the pious cast always has heirs. The old period names of the anti-Dreyfusards have taken on such new labels as Laval, Doriot, Déat. One unfortunate little Dreyfus multiplied into many, and the anti-democratic, anti-Semitic heirs of the affaire survived the free republic itself.

Between the arrest of Captain Alfred Dreyfus in 1894 on the charge of selling French Army secrets, and his rehabilitation in 1906, the case accumulated layer upon layer of mystery, melodrama, crime and passion. There is enough in that story to satisfy nearly every taste for the human comedy; Balzac would have found employment for thirty more astonishing books. On the backdrop of the affaire we find the lurid colors of the Panama Canal scandal and the accompanying anti-Semitism of Edouard Drumont. On the capacious stage are some rare masterpieces of evil genius: the cynical adventurer Esterhazy for whose *bordereau* Dreyfus was convicted; Henry the quiet and sinister forger at work with his bottle of invisible ink in the very Intelligence Bureau of the General Staff; Du Paty De Clam with a brain inflamed by the shilling shockers of crime (Zola: "haunted by romantic in-

---

[1] From the translation by Matthew Josephson.

681

trigues, devouring serial novels, titillating himself with stolen papers, anonymous letters, strange trysts, mysterious women who come by night to sell crushing testimony, secrets of state"). There is honest Picquart who stumbled into his discovery of the real traitor Esterhazy, and who swallowed the bitter medicine of official persecution with a sort of fatalism. There is the Army Staff, inbred and haughty, with its sacred fetish of infallibility. There are the deputies, cabinet officers, and magistrates of the republic on the puppet strings of fear and politics; the mob turned into "cannibals"; the socialists hesitating between the claims of abstract justice and those of class and the electorate; the frightened and assimilated Jews of position offering to the world pathetic and irrelevant proof that Dreyfus was really a man of honor. There are the embattled camps of the intellectuals: on one side of the barricade of words, Maurras, Drumont, Barrès, Lemaitre, the old Copée; on the other side, many captains leading a small and scattered army, such as Zola, Jaurès, Clemenceau, Bernard Lazare and Joseph Reinach and Lucien Herr, Anatole France, George Sorel, Romain Rolland, Charles Peguy, Octave Mirbeau, Rostand and Sardou, Prévost, Proust, Lecomte, Charpentier, Duclaux, Claude Monet—the sensitive bourgeois world and its savants; the anti-Semitic clerical clique with its generals and a battery of newspapers; the socialists trailing Jaurès; and a chorus of foreigners heard all the way from America to "barbarous" Russia.

The thick chronology of events is melodramatic in the extreme: the passionate scenes; the miscellaneous actors in the streets and the salons and Parliament; the antiphonal choruses; the whole scale of moods of rage and indignation, duels of honor, lawsuits, speeches, articles, pamphlets, revelations, photostats, confessions, exposures, suicides, flights, and riots. Dreyfus condemned by a secret dossier; inquisitive Picquart banished for discovering the treason of Esterhazy; Zola's bombshell *J'Accuse!* and Jaurès' explosion in the Chamber of Deputies; Zola tried for libel and condemned; Esterhazy, skinning the inheritance of a provincial nephew, blackmailing even the president of the republic, and strutting before his mistress and the press; Esterhazy tried before a sham court-martial and acquitted; Zola in flight; Clemenceau in a duel with Drumont, and Picquart in a duel with the forger Henry; Picquart arrested; Henry confessing his forgeries and committing suicide; Esterhazy betrayed and abandoned, fleeing from France, shouting his confession from a hole in exile; Dreyfus recalled from the dead but once more condemned; the wave of indignation against France from every vocal quarter; the split among the Dreyfusards between those who wanted a par-

don and those who wanted the certificate of justice; the pardon (Zola: "All it has done is to lump together in a single stinking pardon men of honor and hoodlums"); the amnesty of all the peripheral lawsuits that stifled the courts; the death of Zola, accidentally asphyxiated by carbon monoxide; the gestures of rehabilitation for Dreyfus and the translation of Zola's ashes to the Pantheon, with Dreyfus shot by a diehard; the diehard acquitted; and in 1931 the fists, the stinkbombs, and the catcalls at the première of the play *L'Affaire Dreyfus* by René Kestner; and in 1935 the death of Dreyfus and that epitaph of the *Action Française*: "The famous champions of justice and truth of forty years ago have left no disciples."

The echoes of the affaire are still eloquent. Picquart addressing a general on his discovery:

What is it to *you,* if that Jew stays on Devil's Island?
But, General, he is innocent.
It is a case we can't reopen. General Mercier and General Saussier are involved in it.
But since he's innocent!
If you say nothing, no one will be the wiser.
What you have just said is an abomination, General! I don't know what I shall do, but in any event I will not carry this secret to my grave.

Esterhazy writing to his mistress about his friends and protectors on the General Staff of the Army:

Ah! these filthy fellows with their cowardly and anonymous gossip, who go from woman to woman retailing their savory bits from brothels—and always finding listeners. What a sad figure they would make in the red sun of battle, with Paris taken by assault and delivered over to the pillage of a hundred thousand drunken soldiers. That's a fête to dream of, and may it come to pass!

This anecdote from the sofas of polite society:

A physician, speaking to some friends of mine about Dreyfus, chanced to remark, "I'd like to torture him." "And I wish," rejoined one of the ladies, "that he were innocent. Then he'd suffer more!"

And Anatole France, at Zola's funeral, unwilling to be censored by Madame Zola in the interests of discretion:

Let us envy him: he brought honor to his country and the world by the extent of his labors and by a noble act. Let us envy him: his genius and his heart made for him the greatest of all destinies. In him lived for a moment the conscience of humanity.

A Viennese journalist with deep and sad eyes, Theodore Herzl, filled

with "a curious excitement" by the affaire, balancing the charges against the emancipated Jewish officer, Dreyfus, with "the almost pathological hunger for honor" of his class, digesting the lesson for his own future in political Zionism, writing:

> The Dreyfus case embodies more than a judicial error; it embodies the desire of the vast majority of the French to condemn a Jew, and to condemn all Jews in this one Jew. Death to the Jews! howled the mob, as the decorations were being ripped from the captain's coat. . . . Where? In France. In republican, modern, civilized France, a hundred years after the Declaration of the Rights of Man. The French people, or at any rate the greater part of the French people, does not want to extend the rights of man to Jews. The edict of the great Revolution has been revoked.

And at the ceremonies of July 20, 1906, at half-past one in the afternoon, when Dreyfus is made a chevalier of the Legion of Honor, in a quadrangle of the Ecole Militaire, with the bands, the cavalry, the ritual and the drums, the spectators shouted optimistically:

"*Vive Dreyfus! . . . Vive Picquart! . . . Vive la République!*"

LETTERS TO LUCIE

CHERCHE-MIDI PRISON
Thursday morning, December 6, 1894

I AM waiting impatiently for a letter from you. You are my hope and my consolation. But for you my life would no longer be worth living. I shudder when I think that they could accuse me of a crime so horrible, so monstrous. My whole being revolts against it. To have labored all my life with but a single object, revenge against the infamous despoiler of our cherished Alsace, and to be accused of treason—no, my beloved, that my poor mind cannot understand. Do you remember my telling you that, when I was in Mulhouse some ten years ago in September, I heard passing under my window a German band celebrating the anniversary of Sedan? I experienced such anguish that I swore to devote all my strength and ability to the service of my country against the enemy who thus outraged the feelings of Alsatians.

No, no, I won't go on, for I shall become mad, and I must keep my reason. My life has henceforth but one aim: to find the wretch who betrayed his country, to find the traitor for whom there is no punishment too severe. . . . Never has a man gone through the torture I endure. No physical suffering

684

can be compared to the spiritual anguish I feel when my thoughts go back to that accusation. Were it not for my honor—honor I must defend—I swear to you I had rather be dead—death at least would be oblivion. . . .

ALFRED

CHERCHE-MIDI PRISON
Tuesday, December 18, 1894

Ma bonne chérie:

At last I am approaching the end of my sufferings, the end of my torture. Tomorrow I shall appear before my judges, my head high, my soul at peace.

The trials that I have undergone, terrible as they have been, have purified my heart. I shall come back to you a nobler man. My only wish is to devote what remains of my life to you, to my children, to our dear families.

I told you that I have been through frightful attacks of hysteria. The thought of an accusation of such enormity has brought upon me attacks of raging madness.

I am ready to stand before my fellow soldiers as a soldier who has nothing for which to reproach himself. My innocence they will see in my face, read in my eyes; they will be convinced of it, as all those who know me have been convinced.

I have devoted all my strength and ability to the service of my country, and I have nothing to fear.

You may sleep peacefully, my dear, you need have no anxiety. Think only of our joy at being soon in one another's arms again, forgetful of these sad and melancholy days. . . .

ALFRED

[*The letter which follows was written by Dreyfus after his conviction by the Court-Martial, December 22.*]

CHERCHE-MIDI PRISON
December 23, 1894

My dearest:

I suffer much, but pity you more than myself. I know how much you love me. Your heart must bleed. For my part, my beloved, my thoughts have always been of you, by night and by day.

To be innocent, to have lived a stainless life, and yet to be convicted of the most heinous crime a soldier can commit—what could be more terrible

685

than this! At times it seems to me that I am the sport of some horrible nightmare.

It is for you alone that I have borne up until today. It is for you alone, my beloved, that I have endured this long torture. Will my strength endure until the end? I do not know. Only you can give me courage. It is your love alone that can give me strength. . . .

I have signed my request for a review of the case.

I dare not speak to you of the children. The memory of them is breaking my heart. . . .

My sorrow is so great, my heart so bitter that, but for the memory of you and the fear of adding to your grief, I should already have taken my life. . . .

What you must do before all else, no matter what becomes of me, is to move heaven and earth to discover the truth, to vindicate my name which has been dragged in the mire—even if it be necessary to spend every cent of our fortune. We must wipe out that unmerited stain, whatever the cost.

I have no courage to write you more now. . . .

Mille et mille baisers.

ALFRED

[*Before the public military degradation of Dreyfus.*]

CHERCHE-MIDI PRISON
Thursday noon, January 3

Ma chérie:

I am told that my supreme humiliation is to take place day after tomorrow. I expected this news and was prepared for it. Nonetheless it was a terrible blow. I will bear up—I promised you I would. I will find the strength that I need in your love, in the affection of all of you, in the memory of our dear children, in the high hope that some day the truth will be known. But I must feel the warmth of your affection. I must feel that you are fighting with me, that you are searching always and unceasingly for the truth. . . .

ALFRED

SANTÉ PRISON
Saturday, January 5, 1895

My dearest:

I have not the heart to tell you what I have gone through today. That would only add to your own suffering, already so bitter.

686

MY HONOR! MY HONOR! : *Alfred Dreyfus*

When I promised you to live, when I promised you to bear up until my name has been vindicated, I made the greatest sacrifice possible for a man of feeling and integrity, whose honor has been shorn from him. Pray God that my physical strength will not desert me! My spiritual strength is unimpaired, my conscience is clear and sustains me, but I am reaching the end of my endurance and my physical powers are ebbing. . . .

Leave no stone unturned, my dearest, to find the real culprit; don't slacken your efforts for a single instant. This is my only hope in the midst of this horrible tragedy of which I am the victim. . . .

ALFRED

SALVATION ISLANDS

Tuesday, March 12, 1895

Ma chère Lucie:

On Thursday, February 21, some hours after you left, I was taken to Rochefort and there embarked.

I shan't tell you of my voyage! I was transported as the vile wretch whom I represent would merit; that was only just. One can accord no pity to a traitor; he is the lowest of all scoundrels. So long as I represent this wretch, I can only approve these measures. My situation here is to be understood in the same light.

But your heart will tell you all that I have suffered, and that I suffer now. It is horrible. It is only my spirit which keeps me alive and which gives me hope that I shall soon see the triumphant day of vindication. It is that alone which gives me the strength to live. Without honor, a man is unworthy to live.

You who are truth itself, you swore to me on the day of my departure that you were sure of succeeding soon. I only kept alive during this terrible voyage, and I only live now, because of this promise of yours—and this you must remember.

I landed just a few minutes ago, and I secured permission to send you a cable. I am hastily writing these few words, which will go on the fifteenth by the English mail. It is a comfort to speak to you in this way—you whom I love so deeply. There are two mails a month for France—one by an English boat on the fifteenth, and one by a French boat on the third. There are likewise two mails a month coming to the Islands, one French and one English. Find out what the dates are and write me by both.

What I must say to you yet again is that, if you would have me live, bring

about my vindication. Mere personal convictions, no matter what their character, help me not at all; they do not change my situation. What is essential is a judgment of rehabilitation.

When I agreed to live on after this tragic affair, I made for you the greatest sacrifice possible for a man of courage. I did it because of the conviction you have given me that truth inevitably comes to light. It is for you then, my dear, to do everything humanly possible in order to discover the truth.

Wife and mother, this is a task to move the hearts of wives and mothers, and induce them to yield the key to this terrible mystery. I must have my honor, if you wish me to live. That we must have for our dear children, too. Your sentiments are affecting your logic and that is never good. A judgment exists. Nothing will be altered in our tragic situation, until that judgment is reviewed. . . .

ALFRED

When you have good news for me, send a cablegram. Each day I await it like the coming of the Messiah.

SALVATION ISLANDS
February 5, 1897

Chère et bonne Lucie:

It is always with the same deep and poignant emotion that I receive your dear letters. Your December letters have just been given to me.

Why should I speak to you of my sufferings? You must know what they are—stored up unendingly, without a truce which might restore my strength and fortify my courage and my mind, so shaken and exhausted: I told you that my confidence extended equally to all my supporters, and that I had the certain conviction that my appeal had been heard. I know you all, and am convinced that you will not fail in your duty.

One thing more I wish to add. There must not be brought into this terrible affair any acrimony or bitterness toward individuals. I repeat what I said at the beginning: the *patrie* rises above all the passions of men. Subjected to the worst torment and to the most frightful insults, when the beast in man is roused to ferocity and his reason made to stagger beneath the rush of burning blood—under these provocations, I have thought of death, I have wished for it, often I have summoned it with all my strength. But my lips were ever tightly sealed, for I wished to die, not only an innocent man, but a good and loyal Frenchman who had never for an instant forgotten his duty to his country. . . .

688

MY HONOR! MY HONOR! : *Alfred Dreyfus*

My dear Lucie:

Since the few lines I wrote you on May 6, I have been awaiting each day the news of the end of our horrible martyrdom, for I had hoped that the Court would finally strike a balance between its duty to render justice and its respect for human rights.

For the sake of the good name of our dear France in the eyes of the world, I deeply regret the renewal in our century of the grievous spectacle presented before 1789, when innocent men were sacrificed to legal procedure and the delays of justice—procedure and delays against which rose the protests of all the writers of the eighteenth century—and with them the protests of certain magistrates, like the *Avocat Général* Sirven, the upright Malesherbes, and before them, the most illustrious of all, Montesquieu, who wished that henceforth justice should be tempered with humanity. . . .

ALFRED

Cablegram

CAYENNE, JUNE 6, 1899

MME. DREYFUS. SALVATION ISLANDS. JUNE 5. HEART AND SOUL WITH YOU. CHILDREN. ALL. I LEAVE FRIDAY. AWAIT WITH GREAT JOY HAPPY MOMENT OF EMBRACING YOU. KISSES TO ALL. ALFRED.

[*Dreyfus left his island on June 9, 1899, and caught sight of the shores of France on June 30.*]

FROM THE DIARY ON DEVIL'S ISLAND

My Diary
(*To Be Handed To My Wife*)

Sunday, April 14, 1895

TODAY I begin the diary of my sad and tragic life. Indeed, only today have I paper at my disposal. Each sheet is numbered and signed so that I cannot use it without its being known. I must account for every bit of it. But what

could I do with it? Of what use could it be to me? To whom would I give it? What secret have I to confide to paper? Questions and enigmas!

Until now I have worshipped reason, I have believed there was logic in things and events, I have believed in human justice! Anything irrational and extravagant found difficult entrance into my brain. Oh, what a breaking down of all my beliefs and of all sound reason!

What fearful months I have passed, what sad months still await me!

During these five days, when, in the disarray of mind and senses which was the consequence of the iniquitous sentence passed on me, I had resolved to kill myself, my dear wife, with her undaunted devotion and courage, made me realize that it is because I am innocent that I have not the right to abandon her or wilfully to desert my post. I know she was right, and that this was my duty; but yet I was afraid,—yes, afraid of the atrocious mental sufferings the future had in store for me. Physically I felt myself strong enough; a pure conscience gave me superhuman strength. But the mental and physical tortures have been worse than I feared, and today I am broken in body and spirit.

However, I yielded to my wife. I lived! But what a life! I underwent first the worst punishment which can be inflicted on a soldier,—a punishment worse than any death—then, step by step, I traversed the horrible path which brought me thither, by the Santé Prison and the depot of the Ile de Ré, suffering without flinching the insults and cries, but leaving a fragment of my heart at every turn of the road.

My conscience bore me up; my reason said to me each day: "The truth at last will shine forth triumphant; in a century like ours the light cannot long remain concealed." But alas! each day brought with it a new deception. The light not only did not shine forth, but everything was done to dim it.

I am still in the closest confinement. All my correspondence is read and checked off at the Ministry, and often not forwarded. They even forbade my writing to my wife about the investigations which I wished to counsel her to have made. It is impossible for me to defend myself.

I thought that, once in my exile, I might find, if not rest—this I cannot have till my honor is restored—at least some tranquillity of mind and life, which might help me to wait for the day of rehabilitation. What a new and bitter disappointment!

After a voyage of fifteen days shut up in a cage, I first remained for four days in the roadstead of the Isles du Salut without going on deck, in the midst of tropical heat. My brain and my whole being melted away in despair.

MY HONOR! MY HONOR! : *Alfred Dreyfus*

When I was landed, I was shut up in a room of the prison, with closed blinds, prohibited from speaking to any one, alone with my thoughts, with the *régime* of a convict. My correspondence had first to be sent to Cayenne. I do not yet know if it came to hand.

Since I landed a month ago, I have remained in my pen without once leaving it, in spite of all the bodily fatigue of my painful journey. Several times I all but went crazy; I had congestion of the brain, and I conceived such a horror of life that the temptation came to me to have no care of myself and so put an end to my martyrdom. This would have been deliverance and the end of my troubles, for I should not have perjured myself, as my death would have been natural.

The remembrance of my wife and of my duty toward my children has given me strength to pull myself together. I am not willing to nullify her efforts and abandon her in her mission of seeking out the truth and the guilty man. For this reason, in spite of my fierce distaste of seeing a new face, which would be sure to be inimical, I asked for the doctor.

At last, after thirty days of this close confinement, they came to fetch me to the Ile du Diable, where I shall enjoy a semblance of liberty. By day I shall be able to walk about in a space less than half an acre, followed step by step by the guards; at nightfall (between six and half-past o'clock) I shall be shut up in my hut, thirteen feet square, closed by a door made of iron bars, through which relays of guards will look at me all the night long. . . .

*   *   *   *   *

September 27, 1895

Such torment finally passes the bounds of human strength. It renews each day the poignancy of the agony. It crushes the innocent man alive into the tomb.

Ah, I leave the consciences of those men who have condemned me on the sole evidence of a suspected handwriting, without any tangible proofs, without witnesses, without a motive to make so infamous an act conceivable, to be their judges.

If only after my condemnation they had resolutely and actively followed out as they had promised me in the name of the Minister of War, the investigations to unmask the guilty man!

And then there is a way through diplomatic channels.

A government has all the machinery necessary to investigate such a mystery; it is morally compelled to do it.

691

MY HONOR! MY HONOR! : *Alfred Dreyfus*

Ah, human nature with its passion and hatreds, with its moral hideousness!

Ah, men, to whom, compared with their selfish interests all else matters little!

Justice is a good thing—when there is plenty of time and nobody is inconvenienced!

Sometimes I am so despairing, so worn out, that I have a longing to lie down and passively let my life ebb away, I cannot by my own act hasten the end. I have not, I shall never have, that right.

The misery of my situation is becoming too unbearable.

It must end! My wife must make her voice heard—the voice of the innocent crying out for justice.

If I had only my own life to struggle for, I should strive no longer; but it is for our honor that I live and must struggle inch by inch to the end.

Bodily pains are nothing; heartache is the terrible thing.

*   *   *   *   *

October 1, 1895

I no longer know how to write down my feelings; the hours seem centuries to me.

October 5, 1895

I have received letters from home. Always nothing! From all these letters rises such an agonized cry of suffering that my whole being is shaken to the depths.

I have just written the following letter to the President of the Republic:

Accused, and then condemned, on the evidence of handwriting, for the most infamous crime which a soldier can commit, I have declared, and I declare once again, that I did not write the letter which was charged against me, and that I have never forfeited my honor.

For a year I have been struggling alone in the consciousness of my innocence, against the most terrible fatality which can pursue a man. I do not speak of physical sufferings; they are nothing; the sorrows of the heart are everything. To suffer thus is frightful in itself, but to feel that those who are dear to me are suffering with me is the crowning agony. My whole family writhes under punishment inflicted for an abominable crime which I never committed.

I do not come to beg for grace, or favors, or alleviating assurances; what I ask is that light, revealing and penetrating light, may be thrown upon this cabal of which my family and I are the unhappy victims.

MY HONOR! MY HONOR! : *Alfred Dreyfus*

That I live on, Monsieur le Président, is because the sacred duty which I have to fulfil toward my own upholds me; otherwise I should long since have succumbed under a burden too heavy for human shoulders.

In the name of my honor, torn from me by an appalling error, in the name of my wife, in the name of my children—oh, Monsieur le Président, at this last thought alone my father's heart, the heart of a loyal Frenchman and an honorable man, is pierced with grief—I ask justice from you; and this justice that I beg of you with all my soul, with all the strength of my heart, with hands clasped in prayer, is that you search out the secret of this tragic history, and thus put an end to the martyrdom of a soldier and of a family to whom their honor is all.

I am writing also to Lucie, bidding her to act on her side with energy and resolution, for this cruelty will in the end destroy us all.

They tell me that I think more of the suffering of others than of my own. Ah, yes, assuredly, for if I were alone in the world, if I allowed myself to think only of myself, long since my tongue would have been silenced forever. It is the thought of Lucie and my children that gives me strength.

Ah, my darling children, to die is a small matter, could I but know before I die that your name had been cleared of this stain!

*   *   *   *   *

Thursday, September 10, 1896

I am so utterly weary, so broken down in body and soul, that today I stop my diary, not being able to foresee how long my strength will hold out, or what day my brain will succumb under the weight of so great a burden.

I finish it by addressing to the President of the Republic this supreme appeal, in case strength and sanity fail before the end of this horrible tragedy:

Monsieur le Président de la République: I take the liberty of asking you that this diary, written day by day, be handed to my wife.

There will be found in it, perhaps, Monsieur le Président, cries of anger, of fear, at the most awful condemnation that ever befell a human being—a human being who never forfeited his honor. I no longer feel the courage to reread it, to retrace the bitter journey.

Today I have no recriminations to make against anyone; each one has thought himself acting on the fulness of right and conscience.

I simply declare once more that I am innocent of this abominable crime, and I ask ever and again for this one thing, always the same thing—that the search for the culprit who is the real author of this base crime be diligently prosecuted.

And when he is discovered, I beseech that the compassion which so great a misfortune as mine inspires may be given to my dear wife and my darling children.

A SPANISH DREYFUS:

Francisco Ferrer

"I BEG EVERY EDITOR"   "I WILL TRY TO TELL YOU ABOUT MY CASE"

AN INTERRUPTED LETTER

TESTAMENT OF A RATIONALIST   EDUCATION: FOR SOLEDAD

Everybody knows full well that Ferrer's sole crime consists in this: he founded schools.

ANATOLE FRANCE

THE numerous martyrs to education, whether through bigotry or experiment, are after all our children. Their patron saint might well be that remarkable Francisco Ferrer who, when executed by a Spanish firing squad in 1909, could think of nothing better to do to save his soul than to cry: "Long live the Modern School!" With one stroke of "freethinking," this complete rationalist probably went straight to heaven, to some corner reserved for unregenerate Catalonians. Ferrer's story begins with the abortive revolution of 1879 which drove him into exile. For many years he supported himself by teaching Spanish, until he met his most earnest pupil, Mlle. Meunier, a wealthy Frenchwoman of firm Catholic persuasion. He convinced her that her countryman, Alfred Dreyfus, was an innocent man, and that the *Escuela Moderna*, the New School, would shake the foundations of injustice in the world much sooner than the revolution. During his exile a gentler creed had mushroomed in the dark and he had come to distrust the violence of egoistic revolutionaries. He would devote himself to the moral and intellectual training of children in science, peace, and brotherhood. The money of Mlle. Meunier enabled him to establish in Catholic Spain a system of schools where the rational method of the natural sciences was substituted for the old traditional teaching. A kind of Tolstoyan anarchist, Ferrer gathered teachers who told the children of workers in Barcelona, and elsewhere in Spain, that militarism was a crime, that capitalism was bad for the workers, and that centralization of government was an evil. Aiming at the co-education of the social classes, he hoped that both the poor child and the rich child, reading the same allegorical and scientific textbook, would be infected by the same passionate resentment against poverty and superstition. Without firing a shot, the revolution would take place in the hearts of the chil-

694

dren of the human race and, as in Aesop's fable, crown the patient tortoise, education, with the laurels of the hare, revolution. Ferrer's "Modern, Scientific, and Rational School," the *Escuela Moderna* whose fame spread in Europe and America, was soon launching tiny philosophers who were writing down in their copybooks the most unusual sentiments. Here are two examples:

The police arrest unhappy people who have stolen a loaf of bread for their family; they take them to prison, and thus make the misery greater.

The pious say that we must not believe in science or practice its teachings. They say there is an all-powerful God; in that case, if he can do everything, why does he suffer the rich to exploit the poor?

These were the agnostic questions stimulated in the minds of the children of the *Escuela Moderna* of Catholic and royalist Spain when, in 1906, the anarchist Morral, a friend of Ferrer and a librarian of his school, foolishly and with a bad aim, threw a bomb at the bridal carriage of the king and queen. Anyone of Ferrer's brighter children could have proven by a little composition in his copybook why the librarian's act of terrorism was illogical, but the school was promptly closed and Ferrer was jailed for a year. A better opportunity to involve Ferrer in criminal complicity came in 1909, with the Revolution of July in Barcelona, when Spain was waging war in Morocco. In a trial which copied the classic treatment given to Dreyfus, a military council found him guilty of being "head of the insurrection" and condemned him to death. "They were profoundly convinced," remarks William Archer, "that he was morally responsible for the revolt, that he was through his opinions and teachings the moral 'author and chief' of the 'revolution'; but the law had unfortunately omitted to make such 'moral' authorship a capital crime." There were riots in Paris and protest meetings in London, Rome, Berlin, Brussels, Lisbon, Marseilles, Toulon, Lyons, Genoa, Venice, and Naples; in the United States, Cuba, South America, Australia, India, and Japan. Spanish goods could not be unloaded at European ports. The "author and chief" of the *Escuela Moderna* was eulogized around the world by the indignant public voices of the day before yesterday: Sudermann, Maeterlinck, Anatole France, Ernst Haeckel, Maxim Gorky, Havelock Ellis, Edward Carpenter, Jack London, Upton Sinclair, Emma Goldman, and Hutchins Hapgood. In the phrase of Leonard D. Abbott, he is remembered by his friends in a little school in New Jersey, an offspring of the *Escuela Moderna,* as "the morning star of an aborted Spanish revolution."

A SPANISH DREYFUS : *Francisco Ferrer*

"I BEG EVERY EDITOR"

[To the Spanish Republican paper, *El Pais.*]

CELULAR PRISON, BARCELONA,
October 7, 1909.

To the Managing Editor of El Pais.

Dear Sir:—Though my *incommunicado* was withdrawn six days ago, it was not until yesterday that I was allowed to read the papers—a thing I had demanded from the very first. On reading the monstrous falsehoods printed about me, I hasten to address this rectification to you and ask you to do me the great honor of publishing it in your worthy columns.

I shall begin by declaring it is untrue that I took any part whatsoever, either as leader or otherwise, in the events of the last week in July (there is no charge against me in the documents of my case).

Nevertheless, the Judge has not lost any time trying to find proofs of my culpability. In the first place, he questioned the 3,000 prisoners taken, it seems, from throughout Catalonia, to find out if they knew me or had received any money or orders from me. None could reply in the affirmative.

Very soon after, a detailed investigation was made at Mongat and Premia, where, it is said, I had overthrown everything. The authorities there were questioned, also a number of persons who might be in a position to help justice. They were asked what part I had taken in the events. In the inquiries there is a great deal of talk of an armed band, of shooting, dynamite, an explosion, of a carriage that went back and forth between Mongat and Premia, and of some cyclists who constantly kept carrying Ferrer's orders to the insurgents. Everybody says this, but nobody can swear to the Judge that he saw the armed band, the carriage, the cyclists, or heard the shooting and explosions. *All merely repeat that they heard these things spoken of.*

Not finding any proof against me, the court ordered a search of my home at Mongat, though two had already been made—one on August 11 by about twenty police and the *guardia civil,* which lasted twelve hours; another on August 27 by six police, which lasted three days and two nights. According to disclosures made by the police, the minister sent more than 400 telegrams ordering the latter search, and there will be much to say about it. The last time the court had the search made by two engineering officers and some engineering soldiers, who sounded the walls of the main house and outhouses,

696

and destroyed whatever it seemed necessary to them to destroy. They made plans of the house and explored the water pipes. As on the previous occasions, however, they could find no proof of what they were hunting for.

When the Judge did not know where to discover the proof he wanted, he had the happy idea of calling upon Ugarte, since Ugarte had gone to Barcelona to make an investigation by order of the Government. The attorney of the Supreme Court replied, like the people of Premia, that *he had heard* that I was the director of the entire movement, and that he was only echoing a rumor general in Barcelona. This was the last step the Judge took.

What do you think of that?

Is it serious and worthy of Spain?

What will be said of us in view of such facts?

I should add that I strongly protest against the conduct of the police, which during my trial at Madrid three years ago behaved in an inadmissible fashion, lowering itself to *falsify* documents in the hope of ruining me. Now it is doing even worse things, which will come to light at the trial.

I also protest against the seizure of my clothes. They have taken everything, from my underdrawers to my hat, and have made me wear wretched things, in which I must appear before the Judge of the private examination and the prison officers. The last time I saw the Judge I asked him in vain for a suit of my own to wear at the trial. He replied that all my effects had been confiscated. I could not even get a few pocket handkerchiefs.

I must also protest against my detention during the month of the *incommunicado* in one of those dungeons called *"riguroso castigo,"* in which the sanitary conditions are so dreadful that if I had not always enjoyed splendid health and did not possess a will which lets me rise above these human ills, I should have died before the *incommunicado* ended.

I beg every editor, not only Republican and Liberal editors, but also all who rise above political passion and possess a feeling of justice, to reproduce this protest, in order, in a degree, to dispel the vile atmosphere by which I have been encompassed, and so facilitate my lawyer's task with the tribunal that is to try me.

F. FERRER.

A SPANISH DREYFUS : *Francisco Ferrer*

"I WILL TRY TO TELL YOU ABOUT MY CASE"

[To a friend living in Paris, Charles Malato.]

CELULAR PRISON, BARCELONA,
October 1, 1909.

Dear Charles.—The *incommunicado* in force for a month has just been withdrawn, but I have not been allowed to read a thing yet, not a letter or a paper. Instead of putting me in the department for political offenders, they have put me in a cell for criminals, in which I have been locked up all day without being able to get news of myself to any one at all. It is night now, and it is by the kindness of an employee that I can write to you.

I will try to tell you about my case. From my letter of August 10-12 you are aware that I had not the slightest knowledge of the project for a general strike on July 26 to signify the protest against the Moroccan campaign. And I do not know how the rumor could have gotten about that I was the promoter of the strike. Who set the rumor afloat? Was it the Lerrouxist Republicans, because the movement, according to *L'Humanité,* had its roots in the Workmen's Federation? The Lerrouxists are eager to make it appear that I am their enemy, since, according to them, I protected the Workmen's Federation, which was fighting them.

Was it the clericals, who saw in the strike a fine occasion for calling me over the coals again? I think both sides were interested in hurting me. However that may be, I did not take any care in the matter, as I knew I had had no share in the movement and thought I should be let alone. But a member of my family came home one day thoroughly frightened. She had been at Alella and had heard a girl say I had been at Premia engaged in burning a convent at the head of a band of incendiaries. The girl did not give this information second-hand. Not at all. She said it was with her own eyes she had seen me setting fire to the convent. Who is that girl? Is she the servant at a school conducted by monks in Alella (my native village, very near Mongat), or is she the servant of one of the numerous clergy at Alella? This gave me food for thought. You will remember that no convent at Premia was burned, and that at the time I was not in Premia.

For this reason I prepared to leave my home the next day to go to friends for several days and let the excitement blow over. Several days later I wanted to appear before a Judge who had summoned me, but the friends with whom

698

I was dissuaded me. They told me to wait awhile, since the Judge gave me twenty days' time. But on August 29 I read in the paper that Ugarte, the Attorney-General, who had been at Barcelona to conduct an investigation and had returned to Madrid, had said on leaving the palace after he had read his report that I was the organizer of the revolutionary movement at Barcelona and the coast villages. I could no longer contain myself, and, contrary to my friends' advice, I decided to go to the authorities to protest against the rumors and assertions, no matter how high the source from which they sprang. I left my friends' home the night of August 31 to take the inland railroad. I am not known on that line, and I thought I should be able to reach Barcelona without hindrance and give myself up freely. But I did not reckon with the *somaten* [1] of my village. I had to walk twelve kilometers to the railroad station, and on my way there the *somaten* arrested me, and despite my entreaties to take me to the Judge who had summoned me, he took me to the Governor of Barcelona. Those peasants, all of whom knew me, were disgustingly savage, especially one of my own age, Bernadas Miralta, with whom I had played as a child. He tied my wrists tight with a rope, and several times he threatened to shoot my brains out, because, he said, I was the wickedest man on earth. So he had heard everywhere, he said, and that is what he had read in the papers.

They stood guard over me for six hours in the town hall. Once I asked for a drink. I had been talking the whole time. They brought me a *botijo* of fresh water, but Bernadas would not untie my hands to let me help myself. He offered to pour the water down my mouth himself. I refused, and he had the water taken away. I did not get a drink. I tell you this just to give you an idea of the state of mind of the clericals with regard to me.

In my interview with the Governor of Barcelona, when I declared my innocence, he replied that the reading of the books of the Modern School might very well have been one of the prime causes of the rebellion. Therefore I was responsible. At the *Jefatura* of the police I was made to pass through the Bertillon system. Then they deprived me of all my clothes, underwear and all, from my hat to my shoes, and, to the astonishment even of the employees, since it was the first time they had seen such a thing, they gave me newly bought clothes. The entire outfit cost fifteen francs. Some of it was too small. I couldn't get the waistcoat to button, while the trousers were fifteen centimeters too long. The cap could have done for an Apache

---

[1] The *somaten* is an armed guard, an institution of the villagers to protect their property against thieves.

Indian. In this disguise I was sent to the Judge and to prison! Two police-men accompanied me in the closed wagon in which I was taken to prison. The wagon jolted so much and so often that the policemen wondered what was the matter. Finally they opened a little window to ask the coachmen why they were going so fast, and where they were going. The coachmen an-swered that they had been ordered to make a wide detour in order not to meet the workmen who were leaving the factories just then (it was noon). They had also been ordered to drive the horses at a swift trot without stop-ping for anything.

Now, as to my first examination by the Judge, the Commandant Vicente Llivina y Fernandez. It took place the evening of the day I was arrested, September 1st. He asked me how I had spent the 24th, 25th and 26th of July. I replied that on the 24th and 25th I had not left Mongat, and I told him in detail about my stay in Barcelona on the 26th (just as I wrote about it to you in my letter of August 10-12).[2] I spoke of my surprise when I learned that a general strike had been declared. Then he asked me to say if I thought the strike and revolt had been managed and led by anybody, and, if so, by whom. I explained what I had read in *L'Humanité* (the first fortnightly issue in August). I advise you to read it if you haven't as yet. I advised the Judge to read it. The account seems to me to have been written by one of three or four persons who initiated the movement, he so thoroughly explains everything that happened. The Judge then asked me about many more things. I had the impression that he was animated by the spirit by which

---

[2] Following is the version of Ferrer's account of the way he spent the 26th of July as it appears in the prosecutor's report:

"He declares that after he was acquitted in the case relating to Morral's attempt, he was kept under constant and close surveillance by the police; which did not trouble him. That he did not leave Mongat either on July 24th or 25th, or four or five days before, but that he did leave it on July 26th, at 8 o'clock, to go to Barcelona, where he had various matters to attend to. That among other things he wanted to find out how much a new work would cost him. That then he went to his office in Barcelona, where he found the engraver awaiting him. That next he left his office and went to all the other places on foot. That he entered the Café Suisse intending to lunch there, but did not, because the waiter gave him an unpleasant reception. That he ordered a box with a dress in it for his wife to be sent to the station before ten minutes past six, because he thought he would leave by the 6.10 train. That he could not leave, the road having been cut off, and that he decided to return to Mongat on foot; which he did, after having dined. That he reached Mongat at five o'clock in the morning, and did not leave it until July 29 in the morning, when he went to live with some friends, in the hope that the people's feelings would have calmed down. For he had heard that a girl of Alella had said that he had put himself at the head of revolutionaries, who had burned a convent at Premia. He added that he did not wish to mention the name of the family that had harbored him, and that he had been arrested by the *somaten* of Alella on the road from Masnou."

every Judge should be, by the desire to get at the truth and nothing but the truth. So I said to myself I should not remain in prison long. But the 2d and the 3d and the 4th and the 5th passed, and the Judge did not visit me again. That perplexed me. The 6th came, and I was called to an interview. There was a different Judge, also a commandant, a very correct man, Valerio Raso, in whom I soon detected a Becerra del Toro of infamous memory. Polite, very gentlemanly, apparently a good man, but too much taken with his office, too inquisitorial in his treatment of the accused. Such qualities make those men forget that they are judges who must seek the truth on all sides, not on one side alone.

Valerio Raso began by having two army physicians examine my body for any traces of a recent bruise, or wound, or scar. He recalled to the physicians their oath to tell the truth, and they went at the examination of me from head to foot with such particularity that if by ill chance I had hurt myself in some way at home, if I had had the least scratch, nothing would have availed me. I should have been shot to death without delay. Since they could find nothing suspicious on my body, they took to searching my head, as if they intended to count my hairs. The same with my hands. They examined each nail, one by one. They were looking to see if my hair or nails had been scorched. That would have been proof that I had been present at the conflagration of the convents. Suppose I had burned myself while smoking or while lighting a fire at home. At the end of the visit the Judge sent me back to my cell.

The new Judge questioned me on the 9th. He asked me if I had been at the People's Palace in Barcelona on the 26th (the People's Palace is the Lerrouxist centre), and at Masnou and Premia on the 26th, and why I had gone there. I told him the truth. He did not seem to attach much importance to this, but paid a good deal of attention to a brief biography of myself which I had sent to Furnemont in 1907 upon his request. Furnemont wanted it for publication in the Almanac of the International Federation of Free Thought issued that year. Since I had previously told the Judge that I took no part in the activity of any political or revolutionary party, but devoted myself solely to a rationalist education, he thought he had caught me in a contradiction, because in my biography I had made revolutionary statements. I showed him his error. I had spoken of my revolutionary ideas in 1885, and had added that now I had faith in nothing but education, etc. Then he laid stress on a letter I wrote to Lerroux in 1889, asking him to become the leader of the Republican movement in Spain. I told him that then I had not yet been entirely cured of active interest in political questions. The next significant thing, in

his opinion, was a letter from Estevanez in 1906, answering Morral about a book he had asked for and a receipt for making a certain mortar. I told him all that had been discussed and passed upon at my trial in 1906–1907. The last thing he trumped up was something awful, a revolutionary leaflet that the police had found in my home, a leaflet I had never seen. It looked old. The Judge told me the leaflet had been found in the presence of my brother, my sister-in-law, and Soledad. I told him that if what he said was so, I did not know how the leaflet had gotten into my house, but I could assure him I had never seen it. The writer of the leaflet spoke of burning the convents, wiping the churches out of existence, and destroying the banks and everything else. You see, my friend, that this leaflet was the very thing. If I could have been proved to have been the author of it and to have distributed it myself, as the Judge maintained he knew I had, that would have been all they wanted. I realized they wished at all costs to make me responsible for everything, though I had done absolutely nothing.

After the Judge left I had plenty of time to think about that cursed leaflet, for ten days passed before the Judge returned. When I saw him on the 19th, at my second examination, I protested against the presence of that leaflet in my case. I said it was a mistake on the part of the police or the Judge to say that the leaflet had been found in my family's presence. I knew it had not, since the search made at Mongat on August 11 in my family's presence, in the presence of a lieutenant of the *guardia civil,* and of two persons in authority in the locality, though twelve hours were spent reading all my papers, had brought out only three things which were seized: a letter from Charles Albert to my brother, a letter from Anselmo Lorenzo speaking of a loan of 900 pesetas I had made to the Workmen's Federation when it rented its quarters, and a key several years old belonging to Lerroux. That is to say, they found nothing. The Judge promised me to file my protest, but I have heard nothing about it since.

The questioning that day, the 19th, turned on the draft of a revolutionary appeal I made in 1892 during the Free Thought Congress at Madrid. The Judge would see in it a great coincidence between what I wrote then and what happened in July, 1909, seventeen years later. It was in vain that I called his attention to the fact that there was no coincidence at all, that the draft had never been printed, and I had not thought of it since. He stuck to his notion, saying he had spent nights until three o'clock in the morning studying the draft word for word and searching for its true meaning. What was I to do? He went away leaving me in great anguish of spirit. I promised

myself that at the next examination I should protest with all my might against that desire to find proofs in my past to account for present events. I also made up my mind to protest against the accusations made against me by Lerrouxist Republicans in Masnou and Premia, about which I will tell you immediately. I could not carry out my purpose. To-day the Judge came only to announce that he had finished his report of my case, and that one of these days I should be tried by the military tribunal. He asked me to choose a defender from among the list of officers, none of whom I knew. I protested in vain. I told him I had much to say against the actions of the police, who had offered money to a person that knew me to make her state something against me, and I had much to say about the motives that had impelled the Lerrouxists to declare against me. The Judge allowed me nothing, saying that the military law is not like the civil law. Then all's over! I am going to be tried. Tried (?) some fine day, by men, I greatly fear, whose minds are not sufficiently unprejudiced calmly to judge of the deeds with which I am charged.

Here, according to the Judge, is the serious thing against me:

On Wednesday, the 28th of July, I went to Masnou, a village two kilometers distant from Mas Germinal, to get shaved, as I was in the habit of doing twice a week. As soon as I reached the barber's the shop filled up with people to see me, as the rumor was current that I was directing the movement at Barcelona—a circumstance of which I was not aware. I quickly made those people understand that I had nothing to do with it at all,—but, on the contrary, was wanting to get news from Barcelona, to learn if the shops were open, as I wanted to go see my book shop as soon as the strike was over. Just then a towboat passed with some people belonging in Masnou who were coming from Barcelona and who were to land at Premia, a village two kilometers beyond Masnou, they not being allowed to land at Masnou. Then I asked a certain Puig Llarch,—who had just stated that he had succeeded in calming a crowd that had wanted to go to excess in its demonstration, on which account he had been congratulated by the Mayor of Masnou,—if he cared to go to Premia with me to learn something about the state of things in Barcelona from some of the people just arriving from there. This Llarch is the president of the Republican Committee of Masnou. He accepted, and we went to Premia; but the people had not yet landed, and we returned, he to Masnou and I to Mongat. Naturally, during the five or ten minutes that we remained in Premia, we were surrounded by a good many persons who asked us for news, and we them, as one does in such circum-

stances anywhere. Very well! They want to make a big thing out of this visit, because this Puig of Masnou declared to the authorities that I had proposed to him to further the Barcelona movement and to burn the convent and the church at Masnou—which is not at all true. Afterwards, the Republican Mayor of Premia, one Casas, who appears to have been among the people that came around us, comes and declares that I had proposed to him to proclaim the republic at Premia and to burn the convent and the church—which is also false. The Judge confronted me with these two scoundrels, who persisted in what they had said despite my protests, in which I reminded them that we had simply exchanged the usual words of the day: "What is going on? What do you know about, here or there? What are the people saying?"

I shall continue with my account to-morrow if I can. I am too tired to keep on now. All I shall add is, that the month of the *incommunicado* was very hard. In an infected place, without air or light and convicts' fare to eat, one must be very strong indeed to have pulled through.

Regards to all, all, all.

F. FERRER.

AN INTERRUPTED LETTER

[To his companion, Soledad Villafranca.]

FORTRESS OF MONTJUICH
Barcelona 12/10/1909

. . . MY IMPRESSIONS of this new abode are excellent. The Governor-General has been very amiable, and has installed me in the best cell in the fortress. The officers and the soldiers themselves are polite and full of attentions for me. That is why I am much better off here than at the Celular.

I have a clean and fresh room with so much sun and air that, if only you were here, I should want nothing more.

But you may say, do you never think of the death which the Prosecutor demanded for you, and which your enemies desire? Not at all, my wife, not at all. Who could think of death in so much, and so brilliant, sunshine? Blessed be the sun that is the light of my chamber, and you too, Sol, who light up my soul and my conscience, for the love of the truth and the desire of good with which it is filled. No, I have no time to think of death; I will

704

think only of life, of the life which we shall live anew when I have obtained justice; for one day justice will be done me. I will think only of Mongat, of the books of the *Escuela,* of the new scope that will be given to the cause of rational education, and of the immense happiness that will fill our life. . . .

Do not suffer, my life, or let your companions in exile suffer, in thinking me ill or unhappy.

Never was a prisoner defended as I was. For my Defender pleaded not only my cause, but also that of our dear *Escuela Moderna* and our educational work, with such ardor and passion that I assure you, my Sol, that I could die contented, sure that my work, which is my life, will not die. And so long as my work lives, what does my death matter?

Tell me, did you read the defense published in *Las Noticias* which I sent you? Did it make you weep? Did they weep, the others, in reading it? For my part, yesterday, when I saw my Defender, I told him how great had been my emotion in read. . . .

Here, my beloved, the arrival of the Commandant, Valerio Raso, interrupts me. He comes to tell me that I am to be placed *en Capilla,* and. . . .

In my letter of yesterday I already bade you farewell. *Te amo y amo á cuantos me amaran.*

F. FERRER.

TESTAMENT OF A RATIONALIST

[The following is part of Ferrer's will which gave elaborate instructions on the disposition of his money and the furtherance of his educational plans.]

. . . I PROTEST with all possible energy against the unexpected position in which I have been placed, declaring my conviction that my innocence will be publicly acknowledged in a very short time. I desire that on no occasion, whether near or remote, nor for any reason whatsoever, shall demonstrations of a political or religious character be made before my remains, as I consider the time devoted to the dead would be better employed in improving the condition of the living, most of whom stand in great need of this.

As for my remains, I regret that there is no crematory in this town, as there is in Milan, Paris, and so many other cities, as I should have asked that they should be incinerated there, while expressing the hope that at no distant date cemeteries will disappear for the benefit of health, and be replaced by

crematories or some other system that may even better admit of the rapid destruction of corpses.

I also wish my friends to speak little or not at all about me, because idols are created when men are praised, and this is very bad for the future of the human race. Acts alone, no matter by whom committed, ought to be studied, praised, or blamed. Let them be praised in order that they may be imitated when they seem to contribute to the common weal; let them be censured when they are regarded as injurious to the general well-being, so that they may not be repeated. . . .

EDUCATION: FOR SOLEDAD

[Towards the end, he set himself to write his last thoughts on the *Escuela Moderna*. It was interrupted by his execution.]

THE man was right who, being asked at what age the education of a child should begin, replied, "From the moment of the birth of his grandfather." He did not even exaggerate; for we carry with us from our birth so many atavistic faults and prejudices, that, if we want to trace them to their origin, we should have to go much further back than two generations.

This consideration ought not, however, to influence education any further than in impressing on us the importance of a very great patience, seeing how gradual is every modification in the moral state whether of masses or of individuals. . . . Let us not forget, as we make a beginning in modern education, that its results can only be relative in the first generation, but that, as it is continued from generation to generation, a day will come when parents and teachers find the soil well tilled from the outset, as the children will have begun to be educated from the birth of their grandparents.

[He goes on to insist on the fundamental importance of two things: physical hygiene and the relations of children with their comrades.]

The physical hygiene which we recommend is that which is urged on us by the greatest hygienists and sanctioned by experience. It ought to begin with daily baths. Unfortunately. . . .

[He is interrupted.]

I cannot continue, they are taking my life.

F. F.

CONVICT NO. 9653:

Eugene V. Debs

"DEAR SIR AND BROTHER"

"YOUR HONOR"

∿∿

Debs was the tenderest of strong men. . . . He was tall and long of finger like a New Hampshire farmer, and yet just as vivid, intense and exuberant with amiability as the French. A French Yankee is what he was.

MAX EASTMAN, *Heroes I Have Known*

THE legacy of Gene Debs of Terre Haute, Indiana, is the memory of his love affair with the American people. He is perhaps the only American radical who survives the violence of strikes, the partisanship of schisms, and the rhetoric of the platform with a title of "lover." "He was a tall shamblefooted man," says John Dos Passos, "had a sort of gusty rhetoric that set on fire the railroad workers in their pineboarded halls/made them want the world he wanted/a world brothers might own/where everybody would split even." That was in the violent eighteen-nineties of the Pullman Strike, still the frontier days of American trade unionism, when strikes were broken by government injunction and baptized in blood. Debs had resigned from the Brotherhood of Locomotive Firemen and built up an industrial organization of railroad workers, the American Railway Union. That union had a song for Debs:

> The Union train is coming fast
> chuca, choo, chuca, choo!
> She's humming down the line, at last,
> chuca, choo, chuca, choo!
> Then blow the whistle, clear the track—
> You'd better stand a little back.
>
> * * * * *
>
> Our engineer is E. V. Debs,
> On him there are no spider webs;
> And no one, now, the fact denies,
> That on our union are no flies.[1]

Despite the fight of Governor John P. Altgeld of Illinois, the federal courts and the troops smashed the union and the song. Not even the oratory of

---

[1] *Eugene V. Debs: A Man Unafraid*, McAlister Coleman.

CONVICT NO. 9653 : *Eugene V. Debs*

Clarence Darrow could save Debs from going to Woodstock Jail for six months. In his jail Debs was wooed by partisans of every shade of radical opinion. He became a socialist without dogma. Each schism on the left would claim him without the conviction that it enjoyed a monopoly. He left Woodstock Jail on the shoulders of union workers who sang, "We'll hang Judge Woods to a sour apple tree," and settled down to the second half of his career, the evangelization of the socialist idea. When in 1920, a tired man of sixty-five, he was the Socialist Party's candidate for president for the fifth time, Debs was in the Atlanta Penitentiary—United States convict No. 9653 —because on a Sunday afternoon, in a park at Canton, Ohio, during the socialist convention of 1918, he had made plain his stand against the war. Socialist headquarters had been raided, pacifists had been arrested, meetings had been forbidden, and even his native Terre Haute had grown cool to Debs. He was indicted for trying to obstruct a world war with pacifist irony. Even the great champion of civil liberties, Justice Oliver Wendell Holmes, a veteran with fond memories of the Civil War, found in Debs' Sunday afternoon speech in the park an incitement against recruiting an army. In the presidential election of 1920, nearly a million Americans cast their votes for convict No. 9653. The presidential winner, Harding, commuted Debs' sentence a year later but did not restore his citizenship. As in 1895, he returned from jail to Terre Haute, Indiana, in the midst of the excitement of his followers. In 1895, he was forty; in 1921, he was sixty-six and a very sick man. John Dos Passos has etched this memorable American print of Debs' homecoming from the Atlanta Penitentiary:

> And they brought him back to die in Terre Haute
> to sit on his porch in a rocker with a cigar in his mouth,
> beside him American Beauty roses his wife fixed in a bowl;
> and the people of Terre Haute and the people of Indiana and the people of the Middle West were fond of him and afraid of him and thought of him as an old kindly uncle who loved them, and wanted to be with him and to have him give them candy,
> but they were afraid of him as if he had contracted a social disease, syphilis or leprosy, and thought it was too bad.[2]

---

[2] *The 42nd Parallel.*

CONVICT NO. 9653 : *Eugene V. Debs*

"DEAR SIR AND BROTHER"

WOODSTOCK, ILL.,
August 29, 1895.

Mr. Ed. H. Evinger,
Labor Day Committee, Terre Haute, Ind.

Dear Sir and Brother:—I am in receipt of your esteemed favor of the 19th inst., in which you say: 'We have been unable to get a representative labor speaker for our Labor Day celebration and the committee ordered me to ask you to write us a letter to be read on the occasion.'

In responding to your request I am disposed to recite a page of what all Christendom proclaims 'sacred history.'

There existed some twenty-five hundred years ago a king clothed with absolute power, known as Darius, who ruled over the Medes and the Persians. He was not a usurper like William A. Woods, the United States Circuit Judge. Darius was royal spawn. His right to rule was what kings then, as now, claimed to be a 'divine right.' All the people in Darius' empire were slaves. The will of the king was absolute. What the king said was law, just as we now find in the United States of America that what a United States judge says is law. Darius, the Persian despot, could imprison at will; the same is true of Woods, the despot. There is absolutely no difference. Do I hear an exception? Allow me to support my indictment by authority that passes current throughout the Republic. Only a few days ago the venerable Judge Trumbull, one of the most eminent jurists and statesmen America has ever produced, wrote these burning words: 'The doctrine announced by the Supreme Court in the Debs case, carried to its logical conclusion, places every citizen at the mercy of any prejudiced or malicious federal judge, who may think proper to imprison him.' This states the case of the officers of the American Railway Union in a nutshell. They violated no law, they committed no crime, they have not been charged, nor indicted, nor tried, and yet they were arbitrarily sentenced and thrust in jail and what has happened to them will happen to others who dare protest against such inhumanity as the monster Pullman practiced upon his employees and their families.

More than twenty-five hundred years have passed to join the unnumbered centuries since Darius lived and reigned, and now in the United States we have about four score Darius despots, each of whom may at his will, whim

709

or pleasure, imprison an American citizen—and this grim truth is up for debate on Labor Day.

It will be remembered that during the reign of Darius there was a gentleman by the name of Daniel whom the king delighted to honor. The only fault that could be found with Daniel was that he would not worship the Persian gods, but would, three times a day, go to his window, looking toward Jerusalem, and pray. This was his crime. It was enough. The Persians had a religion of their own. They had their gods of gold, brass, stone, clay, wood, anything from a mouse to a mountain, and they would not tolerate any other god. They had, in modern parlance, an 'established church,' and as Daniel, like Christ, would not conform to the Persian religion, 'the presidents of the kingdom, the governors and the princes, the counselors and the captains,' or as in these later days the corporations, the trusts, the syndicates and combines, concluded to get rid of Daniel and they persuaded Darius to issue an injunction that no man should 'ask a petition of any God or man for thirty days save of thee, O King'—and the king, à la Woods, issued the decree. But Daniel, who was made of resisting stuff, disregarded the injunction and still prayed as before to his God. Daniel was a hero. In the desert of despotism he stands forever:

> As some tall cliff that lifts its awful form,
> Swells from the vale and midway leaves the storm:
> Though round its breast the rolling clouds are spread,
> Eternal sunshine settles on its head.

But the bigots triumph for a time. The king's decree must stand, and Daniel, as a penalty for prayer, must be cast into the lions' den and the bigots, the plutocratic pirates and parasites of that period, thought that would be the end of Daniel. They chuckled as in fancy they heard the lions break his bones and lap his blood. They slept well and dreamed of victory. Not so with the king. He knew he had been guilty of an act of monstrous cruelty and in this the old Persian despot was superior to Woods. The king could not sleep and was so pained over his act that he forbade all festivities in his palace. In this he showed that he was not totally depraved. The king had a lurking idea that somehow Daniel would get out of the lions' den unharmed and that he would overcome the intrigues of those who had conspired to destroy him. Early in the morning he went to the mouth of the den. Daniel was safe. His God, unlike the Supreme Court, having found Daniel innocent of all wrongdoing, locked the jaws of the lions and Daniel stood before the king wearing the redemption of truth, more royal than a princely

diadem. Then the king who had been deceived by the enemies of Daniel, the sycophants and the vermin of power, gave his wrath free rein and had them cast into the lions' den where they were devoured by the ferocious beasts.

History repeats itself. I am not a Daniel, but I am in jail, by the decree of the autocrat. I appealed from one despot to a whole bench for justice, and the appeal was unheeded. I and my associates were innocent. There was no stain of crime upon our record but neither innocence nor constitution was of any avail. To placate the corporations, the money power, the implacable enemies of labor, we were sent to prison and here alone, contemplating the foul wrong inflicted upon me and my associate officials of the American Railway Union, with my head and heart and hand nerved for the task, I write this letter to be read on Labor Day to friends and neighbors in the city of my birth.

It is not a wail of despondency nor of despair. The cause for which I have been deprived of my liberty was just and I am thrice armed against all my enemies. To bear punishment for one's honest convictions is a glorious privilege and requires no high order of courage.

No judicial tyrant comes to my prison to inquire as to my health or my hopes, but one sovereign does come by night and by day, with words of cheer. It is the sovereign people—the uncrowned but sceptered ruler of the realm. No day of my imprisonment has passed that the bars and bolts and doors of the Woodstock Jail have not been bombarded by messages breathing devotion to the cause of liberty and justice, and as I read and ponder these messages and as I grasp the hands of friends and catch the gleam of wrath in their defiant eyes and listen to their words of heroic courage, I find it no task to see the wrath of the sovereign people aroused and all opposition to the triumphant march of labor consigned to oblivion, and as an earnest of this from every quarter come announcements that the American Railway Union is growing in membership and strength, destined at an early day to be, as it deserves to be, an organization, which by precept, example, and principle will ultimately unify railroad labor in the United States and make it invincible. There is a mighty mustering of all the forces of labor throughout the country. Labor is uniting in one solid phalanx to secure justice for labor. When this time comes, and coming it is, peacefully, I hope, no judicial despot will dare to imprison an American citizen to please corporations. When this time comes, and coming it is as certain as rivers flow to the sea, Bullion and Boodle will not rule in Congress, in legislatures and in courts, and legislators and judges and other public officers will not be controlled, as

many of them are, by the money power. There is to come a day, aye, a labor day, when from the center to the circumference of our mighty Republic, from the blooming groves of orange to waving fields of grain, from pine-lands of Maine to the Pacific Coast, the people shall be free, and it will come by the unified voice and vote of the farmer, the mechanic, and the laborer in every department of the country's industries.

I notice in your letter that you say: 'We have been unable to get a representative labor speaker for our Labor Day celebration,' and here let me say that on Labor Day all men who wear the badge of labor are 'representative speakers'—not 'orators,' perhaps, as the term is accepted to mean, and yet orators in fact, from whose lips fall 'thoughts that breathe and words that burn'; coming warm from the heart, they reach the heart and fan zeal in a great cause into a flame that sweeps along like a prairie fire. It has been the good fortune of labor to produce from its ranks men who, though unlearned in the arts of oratory, were yet orators of the highest order, if effect instead of fluency is considered. It is the occasion that makes the orator as it is the battle that makes the veteran. Mark Antony said: 'I am no orator like Brutus,' but when he showed Cæsar's mantle to the populists of Rome and pointed out where the conspirators' daggers had stabbed Caesar, the oratory of Brutus paled before his burning words. And every man, however humble he may esteem himself, may on Labor Day hold up the Constitution of the United States and point to where the judicial dagger stabbed liberty to death, and make the people cry out for the reënthronement of the Constitution— and Terre Haute has a hundred such orators.

I write in the hurry and press of business. Before me are a hundred letters demanding replies. I pass them by to respond to an appeal from my home, and in fancy, as I write, I am with you. I am at home again. My father bending beneath the weight of many years salutes me. My mother, whose lullaby songs nestle and coo in the inner temple of my memory, caresses me—her kiss baptizes me with joy and as if by enchantment:

> Years and sin and folly flee,
> And leave me at my mother's knee.

In this mood I write with the hope that the celebration at Terre Haute will inspire renewed devotion to the interests of labor, and with a heart full of good wishes, I subscribe myself,

Yours fraternally,

E. V. DEBS.

Dict. E. V. D.

712

"YOUR HONOR"

[Spoken to the court before sentence was passed.]

YOUR HONOR, years ago I recognized my kinship with all living beings, and I made up my mind that I was not one bit better than the meanest of earth. I said then, I say now, that while there is a lower class, I am in it; while there is a criminal element, I am of it; while there is a soul in prison, I am not free.

If the law under which I have been convicted is a good law, then there is no reason why sentence should not be pronounced upon me. I listened to all that was said in this court in support and justification of this law, but my mind remains unchanged. I look upon it as a despotic enactment in flagrant conflict with democratic principles and with the spirit of free institutions.

I have no fault to find with this court or with the trial. Everything in connection with this case has been conducted upon a dignified plane, and in a respectful and decent spirit—with just one exception. Your Honor, my sainted mother inspired me with a reverence for womanhood that amounts to worship. I can think with disrespect of no woman; and I can think with respect of no man who can. I resent the manner in which the names of two noble women [3] were bandied with in this court. The levity and the wantonness in this instance were absolutely inexcusable. When I think of what was said in this connection, I feel that when I pass a woman, even though it be a sister of the street, I should take off my hat and apologize to her for being a man.

Your Honor, I have stated in this court that I am opposed to the form of our present government; that I am opposed to the social system in which we live; that I believed in the change of both—but by perfectly peaceable and orderly means.

Let me call your attention to the fact this morning that in this system five per cent of our people own and control two-thirds of our wealth; sixty-five per cent of the people, embracing the working class who produce all wealth, have but five per cent to show for it.

Standing here this morning, I recall my boyhood. At fourteen, I went to work in the railroad shops; at sixteen, I was firing a freight engine on a railroad. I remember all the hardships, all the privations, of that early day, and

---

[3] Rose Pastor Stokes and Kate Richard O'Hare.

from that time until now, my heart has been with the working class. I could have been in Congress long ago. I have preferred to go to prison. The choice has been deliberately made. I could not have done otherwise. I have no regret.

In the struggle—the unceasing struggle—between the toilers and producers and their exploiters, I have tried, as best I might, to serve those among whom I was born, with whom I expect to share my lot until the end of my days.

I am thinking this morning of the men in the mills and factories; I am thinking of the women who, for a paltry wage, are compelled to work out their lives; of the little children who, in this system, are robbed of their childhood, and in their early tender years, are seized in the remorseless grasp of mammon, and forced into the industrial dungeons, there to feed the machines while they themselves are being starved body and soul. I can see them dwarfed, diseased, stunted, their little lives broken, and their hopes blasted, because in this high noon of our twentieth century civilization money is still so much more important than human life. Gold is god and rules in the affairs of men. The little girls, and there are a million of them in this country—this the most favored land beneath the bending skies, a land in which we have vast areas of rich and fertile soil, material resources in inexhaustible abundance, the most marvelous productive machinery on earth, millions of eager workers ready to apply their labor to that machinery to produce an abundance for every man, woman and child—and if there are still many millions of our people who are the victims of poverty, whose life is a ceaseless struggle all the way from youth to age, until at last death comes to their rescue and stills the aching heart, and lulls the victim to dreamless sleep, it is not the fault of the Almighty, it can't be charged to nature; it is due entirely to an outgrown social system that ought to be abolished not only in the interest of the working class, but in a higher interest of all humanity.

When I think of these little children—the girls that are in the textile mills of all description in the east, in the cotton factories of the south—when I think of them at work in a vitiated atmosphere, when I think of them at work when they ought to be at play or at school, when I think that when they do grow up, if they live long enough to approach the marriage state, they are unfit for it. Their nerves are worn out, their tissue is exhausted, their vitality is spent. They have been fed to industry. Their lives have been coined into gold. Their offspring are born tired. That is why there are so many failures in our modern life.

CONVICT NO. 9653 : *Eugene V. Debs*

Your Honor, the five per cent of the people that I have made reference to constitute that element that absolutely rules our country. They privately own all our public necessities. They wear no crowns; they wield no sceptres; they sit upon no thrones; and yet they are our economic masters and our political rulers. They control this government and all of its institutions. They control the courts.

And your Honor, if you will permit me, I wish to make just one correction. It was stated here that I had charged that all federal judges are crooks. The charge is absolutely untrue. I did say that all federal judges are appointed through the influence and power of the capitalistic class and not the working class. If that statement is not true, I am more than willing to retract it.

If the five per cent of our people who own and control all of the sources of wealth, all of the nation's industries, all of the means of our common life, it is they who declare war; it is they who make peace; it is they who control our destiny. And so long as this is true, we can make no just claim to being a democratic government—a self-governing people.

I believe, your Honor, in common with all Socialists, that this nation ought to own and control its industries. I believe, as all Socialists do, that all things that are jointly needed and used ought to be jointly owned—that industry, the basis of life, instead of being the private property of the few and operated for their enrichment, ought to be the common property of all, democratically administered in the interest of all.

John D. Rockefeller has today an income of sixty million dollars a year, five million dollars a month, two hundred thousand dollars a day. He does not produce a penny of it. I make no attack upon Mr. Rockefeller personally. I do not in the least dislike him. If he were in need and it were in my power to serve him, I should serve him as gladly as I would any other human being. I have no quarrel with Mr. Rockefeller personally, nor with any other capitalist. I am simply opposing a social order in which it is possible for one man who does absolutely nothing that is useful to amass a fortune of hundreds of millions of dollars, while millions of men and women who work all of the days of their lives secure barely enough for an existence.

This order of things cannot always endure. I have registered my protest against it. I recognize the feebleness of my effort, but, fortunately, I am not alone. There are multiplied thousands of others who, like myself, have come to realize that before we may truly enjoy the blessings of civilized life, we must reorganize society upon a mutual and cooperative basis; and to this

715

end we have organized a great economic and political movement that spread over the face of all the earth.

There are today upwards of sixty million Socialists, loyal, devoted, adherents to this cause, regardless of nationality, race, creed, color or sex. They are all making common cause. They are all spreading the propaganda of the new social order. They are waiting, watching and working through all the weary hours of the day and night. They are still in the minority. They have learned how to be patient and abide their time. They feel—they know, indeed—that the time is coming, in spite of all opposition, all persecution, when this emancipating gospel will spread among all the peoples, and when this minority will become the triumphant majority and, sweeping into power, inaugurate the greatest change in history.

In that day we will have the universal commonwealth—not the destruction of the nation, but, on the contrary, the harmonious cooperation of every nation with every other nation on earth. In that day war will curse this earth no more.

I have been accused, your Honor, of being an enemy of the soldier. I hope I am laying no flattering unction to my soul when I say that I don't believe the soldier has a more sympathetic friend than I am. If I had my way there would be no soldier. But I realize the sacrifices they are making, your Honor. I can think of them. I can feel for them. I can sympathize with them. That is one of the reasons why I have been doing what little has been in my power to bring about a condition of affairs in this country worthy of the sacrifices they have made and that they are now making in its behalf.

Your Honor, in a local paper yesterday there was some editorial exultation about my prospective imprisonment. I do not resent it in the least. I can understand it perfectly. In the same paper there appears an editorial this morning that has in it a hint of the wrong to which I have been trying to call attention. (Reading) "A senator of the United States receives a salary of $7,500—$45,000 for the six years for which he is elected. One of the candidates for senator from a state adjoining Ohio is reported to have spent through his committee $150,000 to secure the nomination. For advertising he spent $35,000; for printing $30,000; for traveling expenses, $10,000 and the rest in ways known to political managers.

"The theory is that public office is as open to a poor man as to a rich man. One may easily imagine, however, how slight a chance one of ordinary resources would have in a contest against this man who was willing to spend more than three times his six years' salary merely to secure a nomination.

716

Were these conditions to hold in every state, the senate would soon become again what it was once held to be—a rich men's club.

"Campaign expenditures have been the subject of much restrictive legislation in recent years, but it has not always reached the mark. The authors of primary reform have accomplished some of the things they set out to do, but they have not yet taken the bank roll out of politics."

They never will take it out of politics, they never can take it out of politics, in this system.

Your Honor, I wish to make acknowledgment of my thanks to the counsel for the defense. They have not only defended me with exceptional legal ability, but with a personal attachment and devotion of which I am deeply sensible, and which I can never forget.

Your Honor, I ask no mercy. I plead for no immunity. I realize that finally the right must prevail. I never more clearly comprehended than now the great struggle between the powers of greed on the one hand and upon the other the rising hosts of freedom.

I can see the dawn of a better humanity. The people are awakening. In due course of time they will come to their own.

When the mariner, sailing over tropic seas, looks for relief from his weary watch, he turns his eyes towards the southern cross, burning luridly above the tempest-vexed ocean. As the midnight approaches, the southern cross begins to bend, and the whirling worlds change their places, and with starry finger-points the Almighty marks the passage of time upon the dial of the universe, and though no bell may beat the glad tidings, the lookout knows that the midnight is passing—that relief and rest are close at hand.

Let the people take heart and hope everywhere, for the cross is bending, the midnight is passing, and joy cometh with the morning. . . .

THE POLITICAL MAN:

Vladimir Ilyich Lenin

BOOKS, BOOKS, AND THE WRONG UNDERWEAR

Lenin was a *zoon politikon* through and through. No one's life was more entirely political, more completely identified with one political task. His biography and the history of the Russian Revolution are inseparable, and he is more reducible to his work than any other man in history.

D. S. MIRSKY, *Lenin*

THE prisoner who was deported into Siberian exile called himself Ulia-nov and he returned from that school of revolution matured as Lenin. In fourteen months of imprisonment and three years of exile not an iota of his energy was wasted and nothing was deflected from his ultimate objective, the revolution. On the eve of his arrest in December 1895, a new underground newspaper, *The Workers' Cause,* was to bring the restless St. Petersburg proletariat to political consciousness. They were to be agitated by the militancy of a "League of Struggle for the Emancipation of the Working Class." Before his copy for the newspaper was in the hands of the printer, Lenin was in the hands of the police. Without any flourish, with precision and a cool contempt for his jailers ("getting information out of Lenin was like milking Pharaoh's cows—he gave little"), he went about his methodical task of turning his cell into a library for revolutionary research, a workshop for launching a Party, and a school for strikers. His family and friends were drafted into the service of combing the libraries for reference works to feed the composition of *The Development of Capitalism in Russia,* a treatise begun in a jail cell and finished in exile in a Siberian hut. Secret messages were exchanged in ingenious codes and in invisible ink, Lenin decoding his notes in hot tea and writing his communications in milk, whose innocent inkwells—hollowed pellets of bread—could be swallowed in an instant. "Today I swallowed six inkpots," he wrote. When a wave of industrial disturbances swept St. Petersburg in 1896, Lenin was ready with his pamphlet *On Strikes.* Another manifesto, written most inappropriately in milk, was to rouse Social Democrats to *The Workers' Holiday: The First of May.* When the authorities attacked his revolutionary party, Lenin, from a jail cell which the police had provided, replied with a proclamation, *To the Czar's Government,* being very much amused by the odd circumstances which put him in

718

a position to compose the rejoinder with more safety than any comrade at large. "They can't catch me," he laughed in his cell. It was while serving his jail sentence that Lenin made the first draft program for what was to be the Bolshevik Party. He would keep to a diet and to physical exercises, doing fifty prostrations at a stretch, "without bending the knees" as he wrote to his mother, and "not in the least perturbed that the warder, in peeping through the little window, would wonder in amazement why this man had suddenly grown so pious when he had not once asked to visit the prison church." At the end of fourteen months, in this comfortable under-cover routine of sleight-of-hand magic serving a revolution, Lenin regretted being released from captivity into the comparative freedom of Siberian exile. "A pity they are letting me out so soon," he remarked. "I would have liked to do a little more work on the book. It will be difficult to obtain books in Siberia." Between prison and exile he was granted a farewell interlude of three days' freedom; he used them in secret conference among political comrades who were debating the issues between the older Russian populism and the rising tougher Marxist force. He continued the bitter debate in the furthest corners of the Siberian taiga, pouring out a stream of correspondence, articles, and works, culminating in the *Protest* with which in 1899 he greeted the *Credo* of the "legal Marxists," inspired by the new and growing revisionism of Edouard Bernstein. There was a wholesome quality about life in Siberian exile, and Lenin the scholar learned to shoot duck, snipe, grouse, and partridge. He lived on the government's eight roubles a month and what he earned by writing. He subscribed to the magazines and read philosophy. He bathed in the river and played chess. With the help of the political exile, Krupskaya, whom he married in Siberia, he set up a home in which he translated Sidney Webb's *Theory and Practice of English Trade Unionism* and finished his book on *The Development of Capitalism in Russia*. He fished and talked with the peasants and acted as a sort of confidant and judge among them. He read Kant, Pushkin, Lermontov, Nekrassov, Turgenev, Tolstoy, Zola, and Herzen. On festive occasions he met with other political exiles in what were virtually little congresses, garnished with songs. He sent abroad, to Plekhanov, his program for a political party. He was turning thirty years of age, coming to the end of his exile and the beginning of his mature work. Ulianov was beginning to sign his work with a new name: Ulianov was becoming Lenin.

BOOKS, BOOKS, AND THE WRONG UNDERWEAR

Petersburg. The house of preliminary detention
2nd/14th January, 1896 [1]

I HAVE a plan which has been interesting me intensely ever since my arrest and the interest is increasing. For a long time I have been studying a question in economics (the sale of goods produced by industry within the country).

I have collected some books on the subject, formed a scheme of work and I have even written something about it with a view to issuing a book, if the material exceeds the length of an article for a periodical. I do not want to give up this work, but I am faced with the alternative either of writing it here or of giving up the idea altogether.

I realize that the idea of writing it here will be faced with many obstacles. However, I think I ought to make an attempt. Some of the obstacles, the so to speak independent obstacles, are being set aside. Those who have been detained are allowed to do literary work. I made a point of asking the Public Prosecutor about this, although I knew about it before (even those in prison are allowed this). He also confirmed that there was no limit set on the number of books permitted. Also, books can be returned; consequently one can make use of libraries, which means that in this particular matters are satisfactory. Other obstacles are more serious—procuring the books. Many books are necessary and I append a list of those which I need at once, and it will require a good deal of trouble to get them. I do not know whether it will be possible to get them all. The Library of the Free Economic Society can probably be relied upon. If you leave a deposit, books can be borrowed for a period of two months, but this library is very incomplete. If through some writer or professor [2] one could make use of the University Library or

---

[1] To A. K. Chebotareva, the wife of a close friend of the Lenin family where Lenin used to board. Actually, the letter was meant for his comrades, Krupskaya among them. The book list contained the names of a number of works Lenin really needed for writing his work on *The Development of Capitalism in Russia*. The titles marked with a question mark were either real or fictitious, but they concealed the names or nicknames of those comrades about whose fate he was anxious. E.g., Mayne-Read "The Mynoga," Russian for lamprey, a fish, was an inquiry about Krupskaya, whose nickname was Minoga. A reply to this list, which unfortunately is lost, was sent in the same conspiratorial way.

[2] Lenin is hinting at P. B. Struve and A. N. Potresov. P. B. Struve, a Social Democrat in the '90's. The most outstanding representative of "legal Marxism" in the '90's, an economist and publicist. Became a Menshevik. A. N. Potresov, a Social Democrat, contributor to Marxist journals. At II Congress of the Russian Social-Democratic Labor Party joined the Mensheviks.

the Library of the Scholars' Committee of the Ministry of Finance, then the problem of obtaining books would be solved. Some of the books will have to be bought and I think I can allot a certain sum of money for this.

The last and most difficult obstacle is the delivery of the books. It is not like bringing a couple of books now and again; it will be essential to have them brought regularly over a long period, to have them fetched from the libraries, brought here and then returned. I do not know how this can be arranged. It might be done this way: some porter, messenger or lad could be chosen and I would pay him to fetch the books. Of course there would need to be an accurate and regular exchange of books both because of the conditions of my work and because of the library regulations. All this must be properly arranged.

"The tale is soon told. . . ."

I feel that the scheme will not be so easy to carry out and that it may turn out to be a chimera. Perhaps you will not think it useless to hand this letter over to someone else to seek advice—while I will wait for an answer.

The list of books is divided into two parts, just as my work is divided into two parts: (a) the general theoretical part, which requires fewer books, so that I hope to write it whatever happens, but it will require more preparatory work; (b) the application of theoretical situations to Russian facts. This part needs very many books. The main difficulties will be: (1) provincial editions: however, I have some of them and others can be ordered (minor monographs), while others can be obtained from friends who are statisticians, (2) Government editions—works of Commissions, reports, protocols and Minutes of Congresses, Meetings, etc. These are important and are more difficult to procure. Some are in the Library of the Free Economic Society—perhaps all of them.

I append a long list because I intend to cover a wide field. Of course, if I can keep to the plan, the list may become longer as the work progresses. It may not be possible to get certain books and then I shall have to narrow the theme correspondingly. This is quite possible, especially in regard to the second part.

I have omitted books from the list which are in the library here and those which I have marked with a cross.

As I am working from memory, I think I may have muddled some of the titles and where I am not certain, I have used a question mark.

721

THE POLITICAL MAN : *Vladimir Ilyich Lenin*

Petersburg. The house of preliminary detention
12th/24th January, 1896 [3]

I received some provisions from you yesterday and just before that someone brought me a number of different things to eat, so I am accumulating
quite a store: for instance, I could almost begin trading in tea, but I don't
think I should be allowed to do so, because, if I were to compete with the
little shop here, the victory would undoubtedly be mine. I eat very little
bread. I try to keep to a certain diet—but you have brought such an enormous quantity of bread, I think it will last a week and will probably become
as hard as the Sunday cake in Oblomovka.[4]

I have everything I need and even more than I need. For instance, someone has brought me a suit, waistcoat and shawl, all of which being superfluous have been sent at once to the Military Depot. My health is satisfactory.
I can have mineral water here; it is brought to me from the chemist on the
day I order it. I sleep about nine hours a day and dream about the various
chapters in my next book. Is Mother well and the rest of our people at home?
Give them my love.

From,

V. ULIANOV

P.S. If you happen to come again, please bring me a pencil which has the
lead inserted in a holder. The ordinary wooden pencils are inconvenient:
penknives are not allowed. The warder has to sharpen the pencils and he
does this unwillingly and takes his time over it.

It would also be good to receive the oval box containing an enema: it is
in the drawer of my clothes cupboard. You may be able to do this without a
certificate. Give the housekeeper a tip and tell her to take a cab, bring the
box here and hand it over in exchange for a receipt. Unfortunately she is as
obstinate as Korobochka.[5] There is no immediate need for this so it is not
worth buying one.

Petersburg. The house of preliminary detention
14th/26th February, 1896 [6]

Yesterday I received your letter of the 12th/24th and I am sending you
a second letter of authorization, which may actually be superfluous, but I

---

[3] To A. I. Elizarova, Lenin's sister.
[4] A reference to Goncharov's novel *Oblomov*.
[5] A character in Gogol's *Dead Souls*.
[6] To A. I. Elizarova, Lenin's sister.

722

am not sure. I also received some of my things yesterday and it made me think my first letter had probably been received. In any case I am sending you the authorization according to your letter and the one from Alexandra Kirillovna.[7] I have enough underclothes and everything; do not send any more underclothes, because I have nowhere to put them. However, I could pass it over to the Depot, so as to finish with the matter once and for all.

I am very grateful to Alexandra Kirillovna for the trouble she took over the dentist: I am quite ashamed to have caused so much bother. No special pass is required for the dentist, for I have the Public Prosecutor's permission to see him and I wrote to him only after I had received the permission. The day and time when he comes does not matter. Obviously I cannot guarantee not to be absent if, for instance, I am up for interrogation, but I think the sooner he comes the more chance there will be of avoiding such a happening. I am not writing to Mr. Dobkovich (dentist, Vazhinsky's assistant): He lives next door to my former flat—(Gorokhovaya 59) and perhaps you will call and explain the position to him.

With regard to my books, I have already sent a short list of those I should like to receive. I am very grateful for the books by Golovin and Schippel received yesterday.[8] From my own books I must add *dictionaries* to the list. I am now translating from the German and would ask you to send me Pavlovsky's dictionary.

Some underclothes have been sent to me evidently belonging to someone else. They are not mine and ought to be returned; when you come, please ask for them and I will hand them over to you.

I am quite well,

V. ULIANOV

P.S. I am very glad to hear that Mother and Mark have recovered.

Petersburg. The house of preliminary detention
16th/28th January, 1896

Yesterday I received your letter of the 14th/26th and I hasten to answer it, although I have little hope of your receiving my reply before Thursday.

---

[7] A. K. Chebotareva.

[8] K. Golovin: *The Peasant Without Progress, or Progress Without the Peasant.* M. Schippel: *Technical Progress in Modern Industry* or *The Circulation of Money and Its Social Significance.*

I have already written to you about returning the other person's under-clothing. I have gathered it together and you must ask for it when you come, or else tell whoever comes here to ask for it in my name. I am not returning all of it, because some of it is in the wash (perhaps you will ask somebody to collect the rest of it later on). For the time being I am taking the liberty of keeping the travelling rug which is very useful here.

Next, I have been making inquiries about books: a small box may be left in the Depot here. Some clothes may also be put in it: an overcoat, a pair of trousers and a hat. The waistcoat, jacket and shawl which were brought here can be taken back. Of course it is no use having all my books brought here. In the list which you sent me there are some books which are not mine: for instance *Factory Industry* and *Kobelyatsky* [*A reference book for factory inspectors and manufacturers*, 1895] belong to Alexandra Kirillovna and I borrowed some other book from her. Also the *Sborniki of the Saratov Zemstvo* and the *Zemsko Statistical Sborniki of the Province of Voronezh* were lent, I believe, for a short time by some statistician. Perhaps you will find out if I may keep them for a time: it is no use bringing them here now. Also, I do not think Pogozhev [*Factory Life in Germany and Russia*, 1882] or the *Collected Edition of Compulsory Decrees for St. Petersburg* are mine either (aren't they library books?). The codes of law and law textbooks are obviously not necessary here. I would ask you to bring Ricardo [*On the Principles of Political Economy and Taxation*, 1895], Beltov [*On the Question of the Development of the Monistic View on History*, 1895], N.—on [*Outlines of Our Post Reform Social Economy*, 1893], Ingram [*History of Political Economy*, 1891], Foville [*La France Economique, Statistique raisonnée et comparative*, 1887–89], Zemstvo official publications (of the Tver, Nizhegorod, Saratov Provinces). Tie them into one bundle, count them; it is no use making a list: I think the bundle could be left in the Depot. In this way the question of books would be settled and there would be no need to bother any more. I shall be able to take books from the Depot (after inspection).

I am so afraid I am causing you too much trouble. Please do not worry too much about it, especially about sending the books on the list; there will be time for this later, for I have enough books for the present.

Your,

V. ULIANOV

P.S. About linen: I would ask you to add some pillow cases and towels. I am re-reading Shelgunov with interest and I am studying Tugan-Baranovsky [*Industrial Crises in Contemporary England, their Causes and Influence on National Life,* 1894]. His research is solid but his plan is vague (for instance, at the end) and I confess I don't understand him. I shall have to get the second volume of *Capital.*

RED ROSA:

Rosa Luxemburg

LETTERS TO SONIA LIEBKNECHT

LETTERS TO HANS

~~~~~~

IN HER private life Red Rosa nursed an almost painful sensibility. She is betrayed by those prison letters which are so agitated—of all things—by birds, beasts and flowers, and which speak of biology much more eloquently than of revolution. Although as a leading radical of her time her life was expended on dogmas; in the words of Bertram D. Wolfe "Rosa was not the kind to make a good church member, nor to tolerate an attempt to build a new church around her." Rosa Luxemburg was a nonconformist among nonconformists. Beginning her career as a young feminine intruder into a man's world of international politics, she won her seat among the bearded Fathers of the Party, and rapidly developed a personal friendship with Karl Kautsky, August Bebel, Franz Mehring, Clara Zetkin, as well as Karl and Sonia Liebknecht. She led the fight against the democratic socialist reform party of Edouard Bernstein. Reform and revolution, she said, are not "like hot and cold dishes at the buffet of history to be chosen according to taste." She also extended her polemics with the reformists against comrades on the left. She declared that Lenin's ultra-centralism was calculated "to dragoon the movement rather than to educate it" and suggested that "mistakes made by a really revolutionary working class movement are historically incomparably more fruitful and valuable than the infallibility of the best Central Committee that ever existed." For her opposition to the World War, she sat in a German prison, there putting into her *Spartakus Letters* her judgment of the Russian Revolution and her concept of revolutionary democracy and freedom. "Freedom only for the supporters of the government," she wrote, "only for the members of one party—however numerous they may be—is no freedom at all. Freedom is always and exclusively freedom for the one who thinks differently. Not because of any fanatical concept of 'justice' but because all that is instructive, wholesome and purifying in political freedom depends on this essential characteristic, and its effectiveness vanishes when 'freedom' becomes a special privilege." With a note that is reminiscent of her private letters so lyrical about birds, wasps, and beasts of burden, she

concluded that "socialism by its very nature cannot be introduced by ukase. ... Only unobstructed, effervescing life falls into a thousand new forms and improvisations, brings to light creative force, itself corrects all mistaken attempts." She was curiously different from the intellectual giants with whom she engaged in combat, putting her trust into spontaneity before discipline, and into people before party. She was denounced as a Bakuninist, a Blanquist, a blood-wader; some branded her with "mysticism," with a "theory of spontaneity." If Amazons are capable of mysticism, they must find it somewhere in the joy of battle, which is what elated the Amazon of marxist dialectics, Rosa Luxemburg. Physically slight, handicapped by an ailment of the hip and leg, she once tried to convey her formula for revolutionary virility in one of her prison letters to Karl Kautsky. "You must do it with a will," she exhorted her comrade-in-arms, "and with heart and soul, not merely as a troublesome intermezzo. The general public becomes infected with the spirit of the combatants, and the joy of battle lends all arguments a higher tone and a greater moral pitch."

Her initiation into prison came in 1904 for "insulting" Wilhelm II by the indiscreet remark that "any man who talks about the secure and good living of the German workers has no idea of the real facts." She was freed, in a manner much against her will, by a coronation amnesty in Saxony. The historical events of 1905 stirred her to exaltation: "We are living in the glorious days of the Russian Revolution." She was smuggled across the frontier into her native Poland. Warsaw was under martial law, its workers on.strike, but the revolutionary insurrection in Moscow was already crushed. Among all the complexity of the nationalist question as between Russian and Polish workers, she maneuvered the affiliation of the Polish and Russian social-democratic parties. The Warsaw police jailed her, but could not stem the tide of pamphlets and articles which poured out as contraband from her cell until the day she was released. The World War brought tragic crisis and cleavage into the ranks of the Second International. With Leo Jogiches, Clara Zetkin, Franz Mehring, and Karl Liebknecht she founded the *Spartakusbund* in Germany to stop the war and start the proletarian revolution. From 1915 to 1918 she languished in various jails writing the *Junius Pamphlet* on the crisis of social democracy, and her criticism of the Russian Revolution under Lenin and Trotzky. She was busy on many fronts, public and private. From her prison she directed the formation of the left-wing elements into a Spartakus movement. With her long and nostalgic letters she was mothering Sonia Liebknecht whose husband had been jailed, and nursing her friendship with

the man at the front (Dr. Hans Dieffenbach), who was destined not to return to her. When the war ended in revolution; when the Spartakus program agitated for Workers' and Soldiers' Councils; when the German communist party was born; when the Berlin workers were crushed in the *Spartakuswoche;* and when Ebert became president of the republic, Rosa Luxemburg and Karl Liebknecht were arrested by an order of the government. Both were rapidly and brutally murdered in 1919 by the soldiers who had them in custody. The frail and mutilated body of Rosa Luxemburg was thrown into the Landwehr Canal, fulfilling her hope to die at her post on the street or in prison. But she had always kept another and a paradoxical estimate of herself. Writing from prison to Louise Kautsky she had once confided: "But don't you see, I just must have *somebody* who will believe that it is only by mistake that I am gallivanting about in the whirlpool of history and that I am in reality born to mind geese." When she died in that "whirlpool of history"—the filthy waters of a canal—it was said "the old sow is already afloat." In one of her letters to Sonia Liebknecht she had explained:

I feel sometimes as if I were not a real human being at all, but a bird, some kind of animal that has taken on a human face. Inside, I feel much more at home in a little scrap of garden ... than in a party congress. To you I can say all this, you won't suspect me immediately of being a traitor to socialism. You know of course that in spite of this I want to die at my post: in a street battle or a penitentiary. But in my inner conscience I belong more to the titmice than to my 'comrades.' And it is not that in nature, like so many politicians who have gone inwardly bankrupt, I find peace, a refuge. Quite the contrary, I find in nature, as among men, so much cruelty everywhere that it causes me a great deal of suffering.

LETTERS TO SONIA LIEBKNECHT

Corsica

Wronke, January 15, 1917

... TODAY I had a moment of bitterness. The whistle of the locomotive, at 3:19, told me of Mathilda's departure. For a few minutes I ran along the wall like a caged beast, doing the usual "walk" ten times in a row. My heart ached with grief that I too couldn't go away from here, far away. But it doesn't matter; my heart was given a rap directly and had to be still; it is

already used to obeying like a well-trained dog. But enough about myself. Sonitschka, do you still know what we had planned to do when the war was over? We were going to take a trip together to the South. And we will. I know you dream of going with me to Italy, for you the most beautiful country in the world. And I, I've planned to drag you to Corsica. That is even better than Italy. It makes one forget Europe, at least modern Europe. Imagine a heroic landscape, drawn in large strokes, with mountains and valleys sternly outlined. Above, masses of bare rocks, dark grey, below rich olive groves, cherry laurels and century-old chestnut trees. And over all this, a calm such as might have preceded the creation of the world—no human voice, no bird's cry, only the noise of a little river winding somewhere between the stones, and up among the crevices of the rocks, the murmur of the wind—the same that swelled the sails of Ulysses' ship. And the people you meet are in complete harmony with the landscape. Suddenly, at the bend of a path, appears a caravan—the Corsicans still walk in line one behind the other, not in groups like our peasants. The caravan is usually preceded by a dog; then very slowly comes a goat, or a little donkey carrying bags full of chestnuts. This little donkey is followed by a big mule: on its back, astraddle, legs hanging straight down, a woman with a child in her arms. She holds herself straight, slim as a cypress, motionless; beside her, his carriage firm and peaceful, walks a man with a large beard. Both are silent. You would swear it was the Holy Family. And you meet scenes like this everywhere. It affected me each time, until I would gladly have knelt down as I always feel a desire to do before perfect beauty. In those countries the Bible and the life of ancient time are still real. Every night we would sleep in a different place, and would already be on the road when the sun rose. Does this mean anything to you? I would be so happy to be able to show you that world. . . .

Yours,

ROSA

Double Cage

Wronke, February 18, 1917

. . . For a long time nothing had shaken me as much as Martha's report of your visit to Karl and the impression it made on you to see him behind a grille. Why didn't you tell me about it? I have a special right to take part in your suffering, and would never belittle it. Moreover, what I read reminded me acutely of the moment when I saw my brothers and sisters again

729

for the first time, ten years ago, in the fortress of Varsovia. There, they take you into a sort of double cage, with sides made of wire grille, that is into a little cage locked up in the middle of a larger one, and it is across the glint of two superimposed grilles that you have to talk. On top of this, the visit came on the day following a hunger strike that had lasted six days, and I was so weakened that the captain (commander of the fortress) was almost obliged to carry me into the parlor. I had to cling to the wire of the cage with both hands to keep from falling, which probably gave me even more the look of a wild beast in a zoo. The cage was in a rather dark corner of the room and my brother pressed his face against the wire. "Where are you?" he kept asking. And at the same time he was wiping from his glasses the tears that prevented his seeing. How happy I would be if I could be in the cage at Luckau now, and so spare Karl this trial! . . .

Yours,

ROSA

Life is indivisible . . .

Wronke, April 19, 1917

I was very pleased by the greeting in your card of yesterday, though it was sad. How I wish I could be near you now, to make you laugh as I used to—you remember—after Karl's arrest, when we both rather shocked the people in the Cafe Fürstenhof with our untimely outbursts of laughter.

What good times those were in spite of everything! Our daily automobile ride, every morning, Potsdamerplatz, then the trip to the prison across the Tiergarten all in flower, down Lehrter Street with its tall trees, so peaceful; then on the way back the inevitable stop at the Fürstenhof and your equally inevitable visit to my house, at Sudende, where the splendor of May was over everything; the intimate hours that we passed in my kitchen, where you and Mimi[1] waited patiently at the little white-covered table for the results of my culinary art. (Do you remember the string beans *à la Parisienne?* . . .) And added to all this I remember a long series of warm and brilliant days; it is really only in such weather that one feels the true joy of Spring. Afterwards in the evening, my regular visits in your little room—I do so love to see you housekeeping; it suits you to perfection, standing beside the table, with your young girl's figure, and pouring tea. Finally toward midnight we took

---

[1] The cat.

one another home, through the dark sweet-smelling streets. Do you remember that magnificent moonlit night at Sudende when I was walking home with you, and the gables of the houses, standing out in sharp angles against the infinitely soft blue background of the sky, reminded us of fortresses?

Sonitschka, I would like always to be like that when I am near you, to distract you, chatter or be silent with you, so that you wouldn't fall back into your dark and desperate thoughts. In your card you ask: "Why is everything like this?" Child that you are, it is life that is "like this," and always has been, and it is all indivisible: the suffering, the separations, the nostalgia. We must know how to take it as a whole, leaving out nothing, and to find order and beauty in all that it offers. At least, that is what I do. And not because of any wisdom that I might have acquired by reflection, but simply by virtue of my nature itself. I feel instinctively that this is the only way of taking life, and that is why I am truly happy, in any circumstances. I would not wish for anything to be wiped out of my life, and would want nothing of what is, or has been to be changed. If I could only bring you too to this conception of life! . . .

Yours,

ROSA

"I belong more to the titmice than to my 'comrades' . . ."

Wronke, May 2, 1917

. . . Do you remember how one morning last April, at ten o'clock, I called you both on the telephone and asked you to come with me to the Botanical Gardens and hear the nightingale, that was giving a concert there? We crouched on rocks in a dense thicket, near a ravine where water was trickling slowly; after the nightingale's song we heard a monotonous and plaintive cry, that might be given something like this "Glee-glee-glee-gleec." I claimed it was some kind of marsh bird, and Karl thought I was right, but we couldn't find out what it was. Well! suddenly near here, a few days ago, I heard that same plaintive cry, early in the morning, so that my heart began to throb with impatience at the idea of knowing at last who it was that cried so. I couldn't rest until today, when I finally found it: it is not a marsh bird, it is the "wry-neck," a kind of magpie. It is hardly bigger than a sparrow, and the reason for its name is that when it is in danger it tries to appal its enemies with funny gestures and contortions of the head. It lives on nothing but ants, which it gathers on its sticky tongue like the ant-eating bear,

731

and this is why the Spaniards call it "hormiguero"—the ant-eating bird. Moerike even wrote a nice little humorous poem on it, that Hugo Wolf set to music. I feel as if I had been given a present, now that I've found who the bird is with the plaintive voice. You might write Karl about it, it would please him.

What am I reading? Mostly books on natural sciences: geography, botany and zoology. Yesterday I read a book on the cause of the disappearance of song birds in Germany. The cultivation of forests, gardens, and land, becoming more and more widespread and systematic, takes away all their natural means of making their nests and looking for their food. Cultivation actually does do away little by little with hollow trees, fallow lands, brushwood, and withered leaves that have fallen on the ground. I felt quite gloomy reading about it. Not that I am worried about the singing of birds because of the pleasure it gives me, but it is the very idea of a silent and inevitable disappearance of those little defenseless beings that distresses me so that tears come to my eyes. It reminds me of a Russian book by Professor Siebert on the disappearance of the Red-Skins in North America, that I read when I was still in Zurich. The Red-Skins, just like the birds, are driven little by little from their domain by civilized man, and doomed to a cruel and silent death.

But perhaps it is a disease in me, to have such ardent emotions about everything. I feel sometimes as if I were not a real human being at all, but a bird, some kind of animal that has taken on a human face. Inside, I feel much more at home in a little scrap of garden, like here, or in a field, stretched out on the grass and surrounded by bumble-bees, than in a party congress. To you I can say all this, you won't suspect me immediately of being a traitor to socialism. You know of course that in spite of this I want to die at my post: in a street battle or a penitentiary. But in my inner conscience I belong more to the titmice than to my "comrades." And it is not that in nature, like so many politicians who have gone inwardly bankrupt, I find peace, a refuge. Quite the contrary, I find in nature, as among men, so much cruelty everywhere that it causes me a great deal of suffering. For example, the little episode that I am going to tell you refuses to leave my mind. It was last spring, I was coming back from a walk in the fields, on a quiet and abandoned road, when suddenly I noticed a little dark spot on the ground. I bent down and was a witness to this mute tragedy: a beetle was lying on his back, and, disabled, was defending himself with his legs while a whole heap of ants swarmed over him and were eating him alive. I shuddered, got out my handkerchief, and began chasing the little brutes away. They were rude and

tenacious, so that I had to carry on a long struggle with them, and when I had finally succeeded in freeing the poor martyr and had laid him far away on the grass, two of his legs had already been eaten off. I rushed away, obsessed by the painful feeling that after all I had only done the beetle a rather doubtful kindness.

The long evenings are already here. How I used to love this time of day. At Sudende there were a great many blackbirds. Here, I see and hear none. All through the winter I fed a pair of them and now they have vanished. At Sudende at this hour of the evening I used to stroll in the streets; it was so beautiful when suddenly, in the last violet glimmer of day, the rose-coloured gas flames were lit, jumping timidly as if they felt ill at ease in the dusk. In the street, the vague silhouette of a housewife would rise up, bustling, or a servant would dash to the grocery or the bakery to get something. The shoemaker's children, friends of mine, used to go on playing outside in the dark, until a brisk voice called them back into the house. At that hour there was always a stray blackbird that couldn't find a resting-place, and that suddenly, like an ill-bred child, would let out a little cry or fly abruptly from one branch to another. And there I was, in the middle of the street, counting the first stars, and I had no desire to leave the soft air and the dusk, where day and night were melting softly into one another, and shut myself up in the house.

Sonitschka, I will write to you soon. Be calm and cheerful. Everything will be all right, for Karl too. Goodbye until the next letter.

I kiss you.

Yours,

ROSA

"*This huge lunatic asylum*"

Mid-November, 1917

My dearest Sonitschka,

I hope soon to have a way of getting this letter to you. It has grieved me not to be able to write you sooner, and I have missed the beloved habit of talking with you, at least by letter, more than I can say. But the few letters I had permission to write I owed to Hans D.[2] who was waiting for them. And now, it is all over. The last two letters I wrote to him were addressed

---

[2] Doctor Hans Dieffenbach, one of Rosa Luxemburg's intimate friends, who fell in the World War. A selection from her letters to him follows this group to Sonia Liebknecht.

RED ROSA : *Rosa Luxemburg*

to a dead man, and one has already been sent back to me. I can still not believe that this has happened. But it is better not to speak of it. I prefer to settle such things within myself, and when people beat all around the bush to break the bad news and "console" one with their moaning, as N. did, it only irritates me. Why do those who are my nearest friends still know me so little, and hold me in such poor esteem? Don't they understand that the best and most delicate thing one can do in such a situation is to say simply and straightforwardly: he is dead. . . . That wounded me. But let's not say any more about it.

. . . How I regret the months and years that I pass here. How many lovely hours we could have lived together, in spite of all the frightful events that are going on now in the world! You know, Sonitschka, the longer it lasts and the more the infamy and atrociousness of things surpass all bounds and all dimensions, the quieter and more unshaken I become. I tell myself that we cannot apply moral standards to an element, a hurricane, a flood, an eclipse of the sun, but must accept them as something given and use them as objects of investigation and knowledge.

Certainly, from an objective point of view, these are the only possible courses of History, and we must follow History without losing sight of the main line. I have a feeling that all this mud that we are wading through, this huge lunatic asylum in which we live, could be transformed overnight, as by a magic wand, into their opposite, into something great and heroic, and that if the war lasts a few years more this change must take place . . . inexorably. Read *The Gods are Athirst* by Anatole France. It is a piece of work that I admire, above all because the author, with the intuition of a genius into all that is universally human, seems to be telling us. "Look, it is out of personalities like these, out of such daily pettiness, that at a given moment in History are born the most sublime deeds and the most gigantic events." One must accept everything that happens in society, just as in private life, calmly, one must see things in their larger meanings and take them with a smile. I firmly believe that at the end of the war everything will turn for the better, but it seems to me obvious that we must pass first through a period of the most dreadful human suffering.

By the way, what I have just written reminds me of something I want to tell you, because it seems to me touching and full of poetry. I read recently in a scientific work on the migrations of birds—a phenomenon that up to now has been rather enigmatic—that the following observation has been made on the subject: at the time of the great voyage toward the seas in the

South, a hundred different kinds of birds, that are usually in a state of rabid war and devour each other reciprocally, cross the seas side by side in the most perfect understanding. Thus, in the great flocks of birds on the way to Egypt, blackening the sky as they rise into the air, you can see flying in absolute trust in the midst of birds of prey that ordinarily pursue them—hawks, eagles, falcons, owls—thousands of little song birds, such as swallows, wrens, nightingales. So it would seem that during the voyage there reigns a sort of tacit "God's truce." They are all straining toward a common goal and fall to the ground half dead with exhaustion, near the Nile, separating later according to their kinds and countries. And even better: it appears that on the long stretches of the voyage the big birds carry the little ones on their backs; thus great flocks of cranes have been seen carrying on their backs a lot of tiny birds that were chirping happily. Isn't it charming?

. . . The other day, as I was thumbing through an anthology of poems, gotten together without taste and as if by accident, I came across a poem by Hugo von Hoffmannsthal. As a rule I am not fond of his poetry. It seems too artificial, precious, and rather muddy; it's impossible for me to understand it. But I liked this poem very much, it made a great impression on me. I copied it. Perhaps you would like to read it.

I am plunged at the moment in geology. Perhaps you think of it as a dry science, but it is far from that. I am studying it feverishly and with real satisfaction, it broadens considerably one's intellectual horizon and does more than any other science to give a whole and harmonious view of nature; I would like to tell you a lot of things about it, but for that we would have to be able to talk, strolling together some morning in the fields at Sudende, or taking one another home several times in the evening, by moonlight. What are you reading? How far have you gotten in the *Lessing-Legende?* I want to know everything you are doing. Write to me right away, in the same way if possible, or otherwise in the official way without mentioning this letter. I am already counting the weeks until I will be able to see you here again. It will be soon after the new year, won't it? What does Karl say in his letters? When will you see him again? Give him my best greetings. I kiss you and press your hand, my dear, dear Sonitschka. Write soon and at length.

Yours,

ROSA

RED ROSA : *Rosa Luxemburg*

State of joy . . . and pity

Breslau, mid-December, 1917

. . . It is a year now that Karl has been imprisoned at Luckau. I have thought of it often during this month. And it is exactly a year since you came to see me at Wronke and brought me the nice little Christmas tree. . . . This time I had one bought, but it was hurt in handling and some of its branches are off,—no comparison with last year's.—I wonder how I am going to fasten on the eight little candles I have just gotten for it. This is my third Christmas in uniform. But don't take it tragically. I am calmer and happier than ever. Last night I stayed awake a long time—I can't go to sleep any more before one o'clock in the morning—and as we have to go to bed at ten, I have time to dream about a good many things in the dark. This is what I was thinking: how strange it is, I said to myself, that I am in a constant state of joy, a kind of drunkenness, and for no reason at all. I am stretched out in a dark cell, on a mattress hard as rock. Around me, a deathly silence reigns in the house, I might believe I was in my tomb. The lantern that burns all night in front of the prison casts a glittering reflection on the ceiling. From time to time you hear, from very far away, a train passing, or very near, under the window, the sentry coughing or taking a few slow, heavy steps to stretch his legs. The gravel crunches so desperately beneath his boots, it seems the breath, there in the damp, somber night, of everything desolate, everything hopeless in the world. I am stretched out there alone, wrapped in the dark folds of night, of weariness, of captivity, and nevertheless my heart beats with an incomprehensible inner joy, a joy new to me, as if I were walking in a field of flowers under a radiant sun. And in the shadow of my dungeon I smile at life, as if I possessed a magic secret by which everything wicked and sad could be transformed into light and happiness. I search in vain a reason for such joy, but find nothing and can only rest amazed. I think the secret is nothing else than life itself; the deep darkness of night is beautiful and soft as velvet if one knows how to see into it. And in the crunching of the wet gravel, under the slow, heavy steps of the sentry, life sings for those who know how to hear. At these moments I think of you, and wish that I could pass on to you that enchanted key, so that you too might feel at all times the beauty and joy in life, so that you too might live enchanted and walk through life as in a flowering field. Far be it from me to offer you imaginary joys and preach asceticism. What I wish for you is real and palpable joys. I would like to communicate to you

736

too my own inexhaustible inner joy, so that I can be at peace thinking of you, and that you may pass through life in a mantle embroidered with stars, that will protect you from all that is mean, trivial and agonizing in existence.

. . . Sonitschka, do you know "The Bewitched Fork" by Platen? Could you send it or bring it to me? Karl once mentioned it, saying that he had read it at home. The poems of George are very beautiful, I remember now where the lines come from: "And in the rattling of russet ears! . . ." that you used to like to recite as we walked in the fields. Could you, when you have time, make me a copy of the "New Amadis," I am so fond of that poem—which I know like so many others through the music of Hugo Wolf—but I haven't it here. Are you still reading the *Lessing-Legende?* I have gone back to Lange's *History of Materialism,* which stimulates me and always refreshes my spirit. I wish you would read it some day.

Ah! Sonia dear, I have just had an acutely painful experience. In the courtyard where I take my walks there arrive every day wagons chock full of fodder-bags, worn-out soldiers' coats and shirts that are often blood-stained. . . . They unload them here, distribute them among the cells, where the prisoners mend them, then come and take them away. It was a few days ago, one of these wagons had just come into the court. But this time it was being hauled by water buffaloes instead of horses. It was the first time I had seen these animals close to. They have a broader and more powerful build than our oxen, their heads are flat and their horns exceedingly curved, which makes their skull resemble that of our sheep. They have an entirely black face and big soft eyes. The soldiers who drive the team say that these animals come from Roumania, and are trophies of war. . . . It seems that it was very hard to catch them—they were still running wild—and even harder, after the freedom they had enjoyed, to turn them into beasts of burden. They managed to break them in only by beating them, until they had learned down to the very depths of their flesh the full meaning of: *Vae victis!* . . . There are now more than a hundred and fifty of them in Breslau, and after the abundant pastures of Roumania, they have been reduced to the most scanty fodder, wholly inadequate rations. They are worked unsparingly, and dragging as they do all kinds of loads they will soon die off.—Well, a few days ago one of these wagons loaded with bags had just come into the courtyard. The load was so heavy and piled so high that the buffaloes couldn't get over the threshold of the entrance. The soldier that was with them began to hit them so violently with the thick end of his whip that the prison matron, shocked, asked him if he had no pity for animals. "Just like

people have pity for us men!" he answered, a nasty smile on his lips, and he began beating harder than ever. . . . Finally the animals managed to get over the obstacle, but one of them was bleeding. Sonitschka, the toughness of buffalo hide is proverbial, yet it had been torn.

While they were unloading the wagon the animals stood impassive and exhausted, and one of them, the one that was bleeding, kept looking sadly straight ahead. Its whole face and its big black eyes, so soft, had the expression of a child that has cried for a long time, a child that has been severely punished without knowing why, and that doesn't know what to do any more to escape from torment and brutality. I was in front of the team, and the wounded animal looked at me; the tears sprang to my eyes—they were "its" tears. One could not tremble more painfully before the suffering of one's dearest brother than I did in my impotence before that silent pain. Lost forever, the vast delicious green meadows of Roumánia. There, the way the sun shone, the breath of the wind, the singing of birds was all different, and the herdsman's call echoed far and melodious. Here, the horrible street, the stifling stable, the hay mixed with rotten straw, and above all these terrible unknown men and the blows, the blood flowing from the new wound . . . oh, my poor buffalo, my poor beloved brother, here we are both of us powerless and silent, both united in sorrow, weakness and nostalgia.

Meanwhile the women prisoners were jostling each other and bustling around the wagon. They unloaded the heavy sacks and dragged them into the house. As for the soldier, he had both hands thrust in his pockets and was striding around the court, whistling a vulgar tune. And all the splendor of the war passed before my eyes. . . .

Write to me quickly, I kiss you, Sonitschka.

Yours,

ROSA

Birds

Breslau, May 12, 1918

. . . The profound affinity that binds me to all living nature "en dépit de l'humanité" takes forms that are almost unhealthy, a result, I suppose, of my nervous condition. Down below, in the courtyard, a pair of tufted larks have just had a little one, the three others probably died. And the little one has already learned to run very well. Perhaps you've noticed the way tufted

738

larks run. They take tiny hurried steps, not at all like sparrows, which jump with both legs at once. The little one is beginning to fly too, but he still can't find enough food by himself, insects and little caterpillars, especially as it is cold these days. Every evening he appears in the courtyard in front of my window and lets out little sharp, plaintive cries. The two old ones answer immediately in a choked and worried voice: "Houeet, houeet," and they start running all over, looking desperately for food, in the dusk and the cold, and hurrying to cram it down his beak as soon as they find it. This goes on now every evening, around eight-thirty. And when I hear the little plaintive cries under the window, and see the worry and the anxious look of the two little parents, my heart aches. And yet I can do nothing for them, because tufted larks are very timid and fly away when you throw them crumbs of bread, behaving in this quite differently from pigeons and sparrows, which run after me like dogs. There is no use telling myself that all this is ridiculous and that I am not responsible for all the hungry tufted larks, just as I can't weep over the fate of all the buffaloes that are beaten—as they are here. For all my talk, it makes me really ill to see such things. For instance, if the starling that wears me out with his prattling from one day's end to the other, stops for a few days, I can't rest for fear something has happened to him, and I wait in torment for him to begin his insipid chattering again and reassure me that he is well. In this way, from the depth of my cell, I am bound by a thousand little imperceptible ties to thousands of creatures, big and small, taking to my heart all that concerns them, worrying and suffering for them, even reproaching myself about them. . . . You too are one of these birds, one of these creatures with which I live, from afar, in constant sympathy. I grieve with you that the years are passing irretrievably and we are not able truly to "live." But be brave and patient! We will live, and our lives will be filled with great events. At the moment, we still see only the disappearance of the old world, of which every day tears off another piece, and that is sweeping on at every instant toward new catastrophes. . . . And what is even stranger is that most people are not aware of it, and go on believing that there is firm ground under their feet. . . .

Yours,

ROSA

Free Soon

Breslau, October 18, 1918

Darling Sonitschka,

I wrote to you the day before yesterday. I have still received no answer to the telegram that I sent to the Chancellor. It may take a few days longer. But one thing certain is that my mind is at such a pitch that it is impossible for me now to receive my friends under supervision. I have put up with it patiently all these years, and under different circumstances could have gone on being patient much longer, but now that everything has changed from top to bottom I no longer have the strength to take that on myself. To be watched during my conversations, and to be unable to speak about what interests me so acutely, has become such a torment for me that I prefer to give up all visits until we can meet once more as free men.

In any case this can't last much longer. Since they have freed Dittmann and Kurt Eisner, they can't keep me in prison much longer, and Karl will be free soon too. So let's wait to see each other until we can do it in Berlin.

In the meanwhile, all my greetings.

Yours always,

ROSA

[*Translated by Eleanor Clark*]

LETTERS TO HANS[3]

"Kindness and pride"

Fortress of Wronke in Posen
January 7, 1917

HÄNSCHEN: today is Sunday, a day that has always been fatal for me, and for the first time since I've been here I feel "as poor and forsaken as that God from Nazareth." But just today, to make up for it, I had the feeling: I must write to Hänschen. You aren't angry with me for being silent so long? In spite of my silence, I've been so happy whenever there was a letter from you. I've laughed like a fool over them and thought of you a good deal. Hänschen, when will we have our lovely evenings in Sudende again,—you

---

[3] Addressed to a friend serving in the German army, Dr. Hans Dieffenbach, who fell in the World War.

reading Goethe to me in between countless cups of tea, and I lying on the sofa, happy and lazy, with Mimi; or else arguing about God and the world, until midnight when Hänschen takes a desperate look at the clock, throws on his hat and dashes off to the station at a wild gallop, whistling Figaro back to me from the corner? After the war I'm afraid, there will be no more quiet and genial comfort. And, God, I have so little inclination for the tussle that's coming. For ever and ever to be surrounded by those same charming figures, the same Ad. Hoffm. with his "native" Berlin wit and his inexpressibles (begging your pardon) that look like two collapsing Doric columns, and forever to be looking at father Pfannkuch and his same old brown velour hat with the broad brim. It makes me shudder to think that till the end of my life I shall have these things around me. "Thrones crash, empires burst asunder," the world stands on its head, and when it's all over I'm still stuck in the same "vicious circle," the same few dozen people—*et plus ça change plus ça reste tout à fait la même chose.* So be prepared for anything: I still have no idea what's going to become of me, but as you know, I'm a land of unlimited possibilities. But for you at last I have found a suitable occupation. That is—*entendons-nous*—an avocation. Your vocation remains as before, casting light and radiance into my earthly existence, or as you gallantly call it in your last (received) letter: being my court jester. Aside from that, you should create a genre not yet represented in German literature: the literary and historical essay. For this form is not, as a Franz Blei imagines, a refuge for intellectual impotence in all other fields, but an art form as strict and justified as the song in music. Why is the essay, so brilliantly represented in England and France, totally lacking in Germany? I think it is because the Germans possess too much pedantic thoroughness and too little intellectual grace. After the war, sir, we'll have to put an end to your sipping around in every flower bed like a butterfly. Please send for Macaulay in the Tauchnitz edition (*Historical and Critical Essays*) and read him carefully.

The drama in S. was a harder blow to me than you imagine. A blow to my peace and my friendship. You will speak to me of pity. You know that I feel and suffer with every creature; when a wasp slips into my ink-well, I wash it three times in luke-warm water and dry it in the sun on my balcony, to give back its bit of life. But tell me, why shouldn't I, in this case, feel pity for the *other* side, that is being roasted alive and passed through the seven circles of the German hell on every God-given day? And besides, my pity as my friendship have definite limits: they end exactly where vileness begins.

My friends must have their accounts in clean order, and not only in their public, but in their private and intimate lives as well. But to thunder big words in public about the "freedom of the individual," and in private to enslave a human soul out of mad passion,—that I neither understand nor forgive. In all this, I miss the two basic elements of the feminine nature: kindness and pride. Good God, if even from a distance I suspect that someone doesn't like me, my very thoughts shun his company like frightened birds; even to let my eyes rest on him seems to me presumptuous. How can one let oneself go in such a way? You will speak to me of terrible suffering. Well, let me tell you, Hänschen, if my best friend were to say: I have the choice between doing something vile or dying of grief, I would answer with icy calm: then die. With *you* I have a calm, comforting conviction that you are incapable, even in thoughts, of doing anything vile, and even though your temperament, as blond as a Vienna roll, and your eternally cool hands often irritate me. I say: blessed be lack of temperament if it is guaranty that you will never storm like a panther over the happiness and peace of other people. But as a matter of fact, that has nothing to do with temperament, you know I have enough of that to set a prairie on fire, yet the peace and the simple wish of every other person is to me a sacred thing; I would rather let it kill me than defile it. Enough of this, I won't say a word to anyone but you about the dreary business.

I haven't thanked you yet for the Santa Claus. Of course, I should have been happier to get it, not *"in nuce"* but all packed up with articles of your choosing; but from that one-horse town, I know, the most you could have sent me would have been your piano or your orderly, and for them I haven't room. When are you going to get the war over, so we can go to hear Figaro again? Ah, I have my suspicions about you. You leave victory over the French to others and content yourself with quieter victories over the French girls, *petit vaurien*. And that's why the war isn't getting anywhere. But I will stand for no "annexations," do you hear? And above all I request a detailed report and a "complete, penitent confession." Write me direct to Wronke in Posen, Fortress, Dr. P. Lübeck. Write soon. Yes, I forgot: I am doing well here, don't worry about me. Send me more pictures of yourself and your nag.

Affectionately,

Your R.

RED ROSA : *Rosa Luxemburg*

Of economics and lake nostalgia

Wronke in Posen, Fortress
March 8, 1917

Hänschen, of the thousand things I have to tell you, one more handful. Now I am back in a calmer frame of mind, and so I will write you. That letter I tore up, I didn't send it for fear of making you sad; in black and white a passing depression seems much more tragic than it really is. Now I am writing you mainly for the following reason. Fräulein Mathilde J., who is here, is going to Posen and hopes to see you; I put her up to it, feeling that it would be all right with you. She will give you a detailed account of me and bring you my boiling hot greetings—but something else too. And this something is—my manuscript of the *Antikritik,* my reply to Eckstein, Bauer and Co., in defense of my book on accumulation.[4] You, unhappy man, are elected to be the second reader of this opus (the first of course was Mehring who read the manuscript several times and the first time called it "simply brilliant, a really magnificent, stirring achievement," without its equal since the death of Marx; later—meanwhile we had a passing "growl," as he calls it—he expressed himself with greater moderation. . . .). Actually I am rather proud of the work and feel sure it will survive me. It is far more mature than the *Accumulation* itself: I have brought the form to the greatest simplicity, it is without incidentals, without coquetry and flim-flam, simple, reduced to essential lines; you might say it was "naked" as a block of marble. In general, that is how my taste runs today, to esteem only what is simple, quiet and broad, in scientific work as in art. That is why the famous first volume of Marx's *Capital,* overloaded as it is with rococo ornaments in Hegelian style, is now a horror to me (from the party standpoint the penalty for this is five years in the workhouse and ten years' loss of civil rights. . . .). Of course the reader, to have a scientific appreciation of my *Antikritik,* must have economics in general and Marxist economics in particular at his fingertips. And how many such mortals are there today? Not half a dozen. From this standpoint my words are a luxury article and ought to be printed on handmade paper. But the *Antikritik* at least is entirely free from the algebraic formulae which create such a panic in the "simple reader." On the whole, I think you will understand the thing. What Mehring most praised was "the crystal clarity and transparency of presenta-

---

[4] *Die Akkumulation des Kapitals.*

743

tion." So you must read it and give me your opinion "as a simple man of the people." With regard to the artistic side of it, your opinion is of the greatest value to me. But at the same time I want to see how much of it you will understand. So rub your eyes and get to work. *Surge puer,* or if you can't do that, read it lying down, but do get started and write me how it impresses you. After all, one more little taste of economics won't hurt you.

Ah, Hänschen, if only the winter were over. This weather crushes me, at present I can bear no hardness, either in men or in nature. Each year at this time I used to begin my travel preparations, for by the 7th or 10th of April I was always by the Lake of Geneva. Now I haven't seen it for three years. Oh how blue and beautiful it is. Do you remember what a surprise it is, when after the barren stretch from Bern to Lausanne and one last dreadfully long tunnel, you suddenly hover over the broad blue surface of the lake. Every time my heart opens like a butterfly. And then the magnificent ride from Lausanne to Clarens with the tiny little stations every twenty minutes; far below by the water a cluster of little houses grouped around a white church, the calm, singing cry of the conductor, and then the station bell begins to ring, three times, and again three times, and again—the train begins slowly to move, but the bell goes on tinkling, so bright and gay. And as you ride on, the blue mirror of the lake keeps shifting its surface, sometimes it slants upward, sometimes downward, and below, the little steamers crawl along like beetles fallen in the water, dragging a long train of white foam after them. And across the lake you see the abrupt white mountain wall, usually veiled in blue mist at the bottom, so that the upper, snowy parts hover unreal in the sky. And over it all, the great dazzling Dent du Midi. Good Lord, when shall I spend April there again? Each time, the air and calm and gaiety are like balm pouring into my soul. In my Chailly sur Clarens the vineyards are still overgrown with last year's weeds. They are just beginning to hoe them. I can still saunter through the vineyards, and pick the red dead-nettles and the fragrant sapphire-blue mascaris that grow wild there in unlimited quantities. At eleven o'clock, lunch is brought up for the peasants, the father in shirt-sleeves puts down his spade and sits on the ground, and his wife and children squat around him; the basket is opened and the family consumes the meal in silence. The father wipes the sweat from his forehead with his sleeve, for here in the vineyard the April sun is good and hot. And I lie silent nearby. I let the sun warm me all through, blink at the vintner and his family, and gnaw on a blade of grass, not a single thought in my head, but in my whole body the single feeling:

744

oh Lord, how beautiful the world is, and life. And up on the Col de Jamen a little train climbs up from the Glion like a dark caterpillar, above it in the air a little veil of smoke, fluttering in the air like a departing friend waving in the distance . . .

Hänschen, adieu,

R.

Botany

Dear Hänschen:

In the midst of my fine, painfully built-up equilibrium, yesterday before going to sleep I was again seized by a despair much blacker than the night. And today is another gray day, instead of sun a cold east wind . . . I feel like a frozen bumble-bee: did you ever find such a bumble-bee in the garden, in the first frosty autumn mornings, lying on its back in the grass, as still as death, with its little legs pulled in and its fuzz covered with frost? Only when the sun warms it through, do the legs slowly begin to stir and stretch, then the little body rolls over and finally starts to buzz and lifts itself heavily into the air. It was always my business to kneel down over these frozen bumble-bees and rouse them to life with the warm breath of my mouth. If only the sun would awaken poor me from my deathly chill. Sometimes I struggle against the devil within me, like Luther—with my inkwell. You are my victim and will have to stand up under a barrage of letters. By the time you have loaded your big gun, I'll have given you such a shower with my small calibers that you'll be scared out of your wits. Incidentally—if you load your cannon with the same rapidity at the front, our present retreat on the Somme and Ancre really doesn't surprise me, and *you* will have it on your conscience if we have to make peace without annexing fair Flanders . . .

I never experienced a spring so consciously and in such deep draughts as last year just at this time. Perhaps because it was after a year in a cell, or because I now know every shrub and every weed in detail, so that I can follow their growth exactly. Do you remember how only a few years ago we tried to guess what a certain yellow-flowering shrub in Sudende was? You "suggested" calling it "laburnum." Of course it was nothing of the sort. How happy I am that three years ago I suddenly flung myself into botanizing, as in everything with all my fire, my whole being, so that I forgot the world, the party, my work, and day and night only the one passion filled me: to wander around in the springtime fields, to gather armfuls of plants, to come

745

home and arrange them, identify them and enter them in my notebooks. I lived that whole spring as if in a fever, how I suffered when I had some new plant before me and for a long time couldn't identify and classify it; in such cases I almost fell in a faint, and Gertrude got so angry she threatened to "take away" the plants. But now, to make up for it, I am at home in the green realm, I have stormed it with passion, and everything that seizes you with such fire has firm roots within you.

Last spring I had a partner in these wanderings: Karl L. Liebknecht. You doubtless know how he had been living for years: nothing but parliament, sessions, commissions, conferences, always rushing, always on the jump from the city railway to the streetcar, from the streetcar to a cab, all his pockets stuffed full of notebooks, both arms full of newspapers which he had just bought and he couldn't possibly find time to read, body and soul covered with the dust of the streets, yet always with the amiable young laugh on his face. Last spring I made him pause a little and remember that there is a world apart from the Reichstag and the Landtag, and several times he strolled with me and Sonya through the fields and the Botanical Gardens. He could take as much pleasure as a child at the sight of a birch tree with young catkins. Once we hiked through the fields to Marienfelde. You know the way too—do you remember—the two of us once went there in the fall, we had to walk through the stubble. But last April with Karl it was in the morning and the fields were covered with the fresh green of the winter plantings. A balmy fitful wind chased gray clouds back and forth across the sky, and the fields now gleamed in bright sunshine, now turned emerald green in the shadow,—it was glorious, and we tramped along in silence. Suddenly Karl stopped and began to take strange leaps, but his face remained serious. I watched him in amazement, I was even a little frightened. "What's the matter?" I asked him. "I'm so blissfully happy," he answered, and of course both of us couldn't help laughing like mad.

Affectionately,

R.

You call me the "fairest jewel" in the necklace of Hindenburg's apes from Africa and Asia. No, you are mistaken. By official statement I am *no* "prisoner of war." Proof: I have to stamp my letters.

RED ROSA : *Rosa Luxemburg*

A Wasp

Wronke i. P. April 5, 1917

Dear Hänschen. Good morning. May my little arrow nail you right at your threshold, bring you heartiest Easter greeting from Wronke and many thanks for three letters and six splendid volumes of Grillparzer. First, to set your mind at rest: I have punctually received everything you sent, except for the one mysterious letter of the 20th, which strayed off somewhere, which after all can happen "in the best of families." So you can keep on writing without concern; as a check, let us *number* the letters (not post-cards) from now on; but you yourself must make a note of the numbers, so as to create no confusion . . .

Hänschen, a wasp. Really, the first slender young wasp, apparently born this morning, is buzzing here in my room. She flew in through the open window and flung herself at once on the closed upper pane. An inch lower the window is open wide, but she stubbornly clings to the upper pane and keeps sliding up and down with an angry buzzing, as though someone were to blame for her being so stupid. Oh how lovely this dull stubborn buzzing is, how homelike it sounds. It reminds one so of summer, heat, my open balcony in Sudende with the broad view of rolling fields and clumps of trees, of Mimi lying lazy in the sun, wrapped up like a soft little bundle, blinking up at the buzzing wasp. And now I have the same work as every other summer: I must climb up on the chair—even so, I hardly reach the uppermost pane—and carefully catch the wasp and send her out into the open, otherwise she'll torture herself half to death on the glass. They never do anything to me; out of doors they even sit down on my lips, and it tickles; but I am afraid to hurt *her* when I take hold of her. But finally I succeed and suddenly it is still in the room. Only in my ears and heart a sunny echo still sounds. Hänschen, you must be happy, life is so beautiful. The wasp has said so again, and she knows.

Best greetings to your old gentleman and your aunt.

R.

The Prism

Wronke, May 12, 1917

Dear Hans:

Received No. 5, many thanks; I am waiting for your stylistic corrections (in part, as I see, they refer to oversights on the part of the typist). Your

747

remark that some places in the *Antikritik* are so mangled as to be unintelligible, is making me revise the thing myself after all. Otherwise I am never able to re-read anything once it is written. The stronger I experience a thing while writing, the more it is over and done with afterward. I know, Hänschen, that I write on economic things for six persons, but actually I write them only for one person: myself. The time when I was writing the *Accumulation of Capital* was one of the happiest of my life. I really lived as though intoxicated, day and night I saw and heard nothing beside this problem unfolding so beautifully before me, and I don't know which gave me greater pleasure: the process of thinking, when I strolled slowly up and down, dragging a complex question with me through the room, attentively observed by Mimi who lay on the red plush table cover, her paws drawn up under her, following my wanderings with her intelligent face,—or the creation, the literary forming with pen in hand. Do you know that I wrote the whole thirty galleys in four months without stopping—an unheard of speed —and sent it directly to the printer's without once reading through the rough draft. It was pretty much the same in the Barnim Strasse with the *Antikritik*. And then, after a work so strongly experienced, I lose all interest in it, so much so that I hardly bothered about a publisher for it. Of course, in view of my "circumstances" in the last year and a half, this was rather difficult. You definitely overestimate Eckstein. His "criticism" was nothing but revenge for long and vain attempts at friendship, sharply rebuffed by me, and it was this transference of the "all too human" to the Alpine regions of pure science that filled me with such contempt for him. As a matter of fact, he could also be very charming and witty. Once at the Kautskys, when I was making desperate efforts in the vestibule to get my jacket down from the clothes tree, cursing my Lilliputian dimensions, he gallantly held out the jacket and smilingly muttered Wolf's song: *"Auch kleine Dinge können uns entzücken. . . ."* [5] (You know that Hugo Wolf was allied to the Eckstein household in Vienna and is the family god.) Your idea of my writing a book about Tolstoy doesn't appeal to me in the least. For whom? What for, Hänschen? Everyone can read Tolstoy's books, and anyone to whom they do not impart the strong breath of life will not get it by commentaries. Can you "explain" to anyone what Mozart's music is? Can you "explain" to anyone wherein the magic of life consists, if he himself does not sense it in the smallest and most everyday things, or rather: if he does not bear it in him-

---

[5] Little things can delight us too.

self: And for that reason I regard the whole gigantic Goethe literature, for instance (i.e., the literature about Goethe), as a waste of paper, and it is my opinion that far too many books have been written; from sheer literature people forget to look at the beautiful world.

Since the first we have been having a series of sunny days; as I wake up, the first ray of sunlight greets me, for my windows face the east. In Sudende, where my place, as you know, is like a lantern, open to the sun from all sides, these morning hours are very lovely. After breakfast I would usually take my paper-weight, a crystal prism with the countless edges and corners, and set it in the sun. The light broke up into a hundred little splashes of rainbow on the walls and ceiling. Mimi looked on with enthusiasm, especially when I moved the prism and made the spots of color race along the wall and dance about. At first she ran and jumped and tried to catch them, but soon she found out that they were "nothing," just an optical illusion, and after that she sat motionless, following the dance with merry eyes. We got delightful effects when one of the little rainbows fell on a white hyacinth or on the marble head over the desk, or on the big bronze clock in front of the mirror. The neat, sun-filled room with the bright carpet breathed peace and well-being, through the open balcony door you heard only the twittering of the sparrows, the hum of the streetcar gliding by from time to time, or the bright metallic tapping of the workers mending the rails somewhere. Then I took my hat and went out into the fields to see what had grown during the night, and to gather fresh juicy grass for Mimi. Here, too, I go out in the little garden right after breakfast and have a wonderful occupation: watering my "plantation" outside the window. I sent for a pretty little watering can, and I have to run back and forth to the trough a dozen times before the border is moist enough. The spray sparkles in the morning sun, and the drops tremble for a long while on the pink and blue hyacinths which are already half open. Why am I sad in spite of all this? I almost think I have overestimated the power of the sun in the sky, it can shine like this and sometimes it doesn't warm me at all, if my own heart lends it no warmth.

R.

Lonely

Wronke, June 23, 1917

Hänschen, good morning, here I am again. Today I feel so lonely, I must refresh myself a little by chatting with you. Today I spent the siesta pre-

scribed by the doctor lying on the sofa, I read newspapers and decided at half past two that it was time to get up. A moment later I fell asleep and had a wonderful dream, very lively but of uncertain content. I remember only that someone nice was with me, that I touched his lips with my finger and asked him: "Whose mouth is that?" He answered: "Mine." "Oh, no," I cried laughing, "that mouth belongs to me." I awoke from laughing at this nonsense and looked at the clock: it was still half past two, so apparently my long dream had lasted only a second, but it left me with the feeling of a precious experience, and I went back to the garden comforted. Soon another lovely thing happened to me: a robin sat down on the wall right behind me and sang to me a little. Most of the birds now are taken up entirely with family cares, it's only here and there that one sings for a moment. This robin had visited me several times at the beginning of May. I don't know if you are really familiar with this bird and his song. Like so many other things, it was only here that I really came to know him, and I love him far more than the famous nightingale. The nightingale with his brilliant note is too much of a prima donna for me, he calls to mind an audience, loud triumphs, hymns of praise. The robin has a small delicate voice and sings a strange intimate melody that sounds like an up-beat, a little piece of reveille; do you remember the trumpet note in the distance in Fidelio, that breaks the tension and seems to split the darkness of night? The robin's song sounds something like that, only it is sung in a gentle tremolo of infinite sweetness, giving an effect of vagueness, like a memory lost in dream. My heart is convulsed with joy and pain when I hear this song, and at once I see my life and the world in a new light, as if the clouds were breaking and a bright sunbeam were falling on the earth.

Today I felt so soft, so mild from this little song on the wall that couldn't have lasted longer than a minute. At once I regretted all the harm I had ever done to anyone and all my harsh thoughts, and I decided to be good again, simply good at any price: that is better than "being right" and booking every little injury. And then I decided to write you this very day, though since yesterday I have a little pad on my desk with seven precepts by which I expect to live from now on, and the first is: "Write no letters." So you see, that is how I keep my iron precepts, that is how weak I am. If, as you write in your last letter, the stronger sex like women best when they show themselves weak, you must be delighted with me: ah, I am so weak here, weaker than I would like to be. I must say, though, that your childish lips spoke truer than you suspected. In this connection I had a funny experience. You

must have seen Camille Huysmans at the Copenhagen Congress, the tall young fellow with the dark curls and the typical Flemish face? He is now one of the leading lights at the Stockholm Conference. For ten years the two of us belonged to the International Bureau and for ten years we hated one another, in so far as my "pigeon heart" (the expression comes from—Heinrich Schultz) is capable of such a feeling. Why, it is hard to say. I think he can't bear women who are active in politics, and I guess his impertinent face got on my nerves. It so happened that at the last session in Brussels, which .in view of the imminence of war took place at the end of July 1914, we were together for a few hours. We were sitting in a fashionable restaurant and there was a vase of gladioli on the table; I was immersed in the flowers and took no part in the political discussion. Then the conversation turned to my departure, and my helplessness in "earthly things" came to light, my eternal need of a protector to buy my ticket, put me on the right train, collect my lost suitcases—in short my whole reprehensible weakness which has given you so many merry moments. Huysmans watched me in silence the whole time, and in an hour the hatred of ten years was transformed into glowing friendship. It was laughable. At last he had seen me weak and was in his element. At once he took my destiny in hand, dragged me to his place for a midnight supper with Anseele, the charming little Walloon, brought me a cat, played and sang Mozart and Schubert. He has a good piano and a pleasant tenor voice, it was a revelation to him that music is the breath of life to me. He sang Schubert's *Grenzen der Menscheit.* *"Und mit uns spielen Wolken und Winde."* [6] He sang a few times with his funny Flemish pronunciation. Then of course he brought me to the train, carrying my bag himself; he sat down in the compartment with me and suddenly decided: *"Mais il est impossible de vois laisser voyager seule."* As though I were really a babe in arms. I barely managed to persuade him not to accompany me at least to the German border; he jumped out only when the train was beginning to move and called after me: *"Au revoir à Paris."* For we were supposed to hold a congress in Paris in two weeks. That was on July 31. But when my train arrived in Berlin, the mobilization was in full swing and two days later poor Huysmans' beloved Belgium was occupied. I couldn't help repeating: *"Und mit uns spielen Wolken und Wind."*

In two weeks a full year of my imprisonment will be over, or—except for the little interruption,—two full years. Oh how good an hour or two of sim-

---

[6] "And the clouds and winds play with me."

ple conversation would feel. In the visiting hours, of course, we just run hastily through the business matters, and most of the time I'm on pins and needles. And aside from that, I neither see nor hear a human soul.

Now it is nine at night, but of course as light as day. It is so still here around me, only the ticking of the clock and in the distance the muffled barking of a dog. How strangely homelike this distant barking of dogs at evening in the country. At once I see a comfortable peasant's hut, a man in shirtsleeves standing in the doorway, with a pipe in his mouth, chatting with an old woman from the neighborhood; from inside bright children's voices and the clatter of dishes, and outside the smell of ripe wheat and the first hesitant croaking of the frogs . . .

Adieu, Hänschen

R.

[Translated from the German by Ralph Manheim]

THE BATTLE AND THE BOOK:

Adolf Hitler

YEARS OF STUDY AND SUFFERING IN VIENNA

~~~~~~

... I believe it is with libraries as with other cemeteries, where some philosophers affirm, that a certain spirit, which they call *brutum hominis*, hovers over the monument, till the body is corrupted and turns to dust or to worms, but then vanishes or dissolves: So, we may say, a restless spirit haunts over every book, till dust or worms have seized upon it, which to some may happen in a few days, but to others later....

JONATHAN SWIFT, *The Battle of the Books*

MORE than two decades ago, *Mein Kampf* was put down on paper in a prison fortress. For Europe, the place was prophetic. *Mein Kampf* fattened on mockery and lived to become the epitaph of the old order. This "masterpiece of an illiterate" is politically the silliest as well as the most important book written in our century. It is not just a book. It is an autobiography, a confession, a success story, a history, a tale of Vienna, a lesson in propaganda, an oration on race, a pamphlet on partisanship, a guide to foreign policy, an essay on culture, and a bible for daily conduct. For the shrewdest exposition of this work, go to the revelation made by its encyclopaedic index. A great deal is said about the hero Hitler, about Germany, marxism, parliamentarianism, war, national socialism, foreign countries; but nearly as much is said about nature, propaganda, marriage, opera, diseases, women, prostitution, painting, and how to read a book. *Mein Kampf's* readers are urged on to discipline, faith, force, hardness, sacrifice and will power; and are being saved from cowardice, half-measures, humaneness, liberty, and eroticism. In *Mein Kampf*, as its best English translator, Ralph Manheim, puts it, "the logic is purely psychological."

The primary experience which galvanized Adolf Hitler came to him in Vienna, in abject poverty and intellectual humiliation. By the time he was sentenced to five years' confinement in the Bavarian fortress of Landsberg, following the abortive *putsch* of 1923, he had theoretically rounded out his theology, his politics, and his creed of leadership. The Leader who fled in an automobile from the corpses of the *putsch* (while Ludendorff was still risking his neck on the battlefield) arrived in jail with a guilty conscience —and an Iron Cross pinned on his chest. As everybody knows, the trial was a farce, and the Landsberg fortress was more like a sanatorium for con-

valescence from political defeat than a jail for a dangerous insurrectionist. Hitler was not released in nine short months because he ceased to be a danger to the state; he was freed because he had proven himself a greater danger to the state than some observers had hoped or realized. They were not disappointed.

In his prison, Hitler had a nearly perfect setting for the composition of *Mein Kampf:* his disciples, a spare room for guests, devoted secretaries, awed jailers, and a typewriter. On his birthday his chambers were like a flower shop. His less ascetic companions, of whom there were about forty, drank beer and played at knucklebones. Otto Strasser relates that a council of war was called by the prisoners to discuss ways and means of protecting themselves from the Leader's incessant eloquence, and they came to the sly conclusion that Hitler must be kept busy writing a book. Several party members had already delivered a number of tracts, but Hitler had never set down the *Eine Abrechnung* with which he planned to "settle accounts" with certain right-wing rivals. Undoubtedly *Mein Kampf* evolved as a collaboration of many hands and minds. In the jail's spare room for guests, Karl Haushofer, a friend of Rudolf Hess, spent many hours with Hitler on geopolitics. From the typing of the disciples, *Mein Kampf* emerged in its original form "a hotchpotch of commonplaces, schoolboy reminiscences, personal opinions, expressions of personal animosities . . . in the style of a fifth-form schoolboy"—and, according to Strasser, all this crudity was drastically edited by a Father Staempfle, whose memory of the literary blemishes Hitler wiped out in the purge of 1934. According to Konrad Heiden, *Mein Kampf's* royalties bought the eagle's nest at Berchtesgaden.

The book was not a success until it became nearly an obligation to display it. By the time the Nazis undertook to give *Mein Kampf* to newlyweds presenting themselves to the registrar, to students who had earned prizes, to employees who had served their masters for a lifetime, and to women who had satisfied the quota for breeding offspring, it had achieved a circulation exceeding five million. This was the book which *Simplizissimus* had carelessly caricatured in the hands of a weary peddling Hitler, to whom a stout burgher was saying over his foaming tankard of beer: "The book's a bit dear, neighbor. Haven't you got any matches?" In 1936 a biographer of Hitler could still laugh at the structure of one of his sentences: "Whoever has not himself been in the tentacles of this throttling viper will never know its fangs." A viper, it seems, has no tentacles; a natural snake which coils

itself around a man has no fangs. Though shocking to good zoologists, Hitler's vipers developed both tentacles and fangs.

YEARS OF STUDY AND SUFFERING IN VIENNA

[In the second chapter of *Mein Kampf*, Adolf Hitler recounts how amidst the frustrations of his unhappy youth he came to look upon Austrian Social Democracy as the "infamous spiritual terror . . . [exerted] particularly on the bourgeoisie." Having arrived in Vienna from the provinces "to become 'something,'" he found out that he was unfit for a career in painting and unprepared to enter a school of architecture. He credits this period, when "the Goddess of Suffering took me in her arms," with having made him hard. Vienna, the gay, represents "merely the living memory of the saddest period of my life." Tormented and surrounded by economic insecurity, by what the son of a government official who wanted to become something judged as lower-class "moral and ethical coarseness," he began to pay increasing attention to the "loathsome humanitarian morality" of the Social Democratic labor press. "For me," he says, "immersion in the literature and press of this doctrine and organization meant finding my way back to my own people." At this time he made a convenient and soul-healing discovery: he "learned to understand the connection" between Jews and Social Democracy. Having acquired a principle which had virtually wholesale propor tions, and which could account without charge for everything and anything, including nature, race, culture, nationality, marxism, hunger, insecurity, humiliation, and the failure to win dialectical arguments, Hitler found himself compensated, manfully forceful, and transformed: "In this period there took shape within me a world picture and a philosophy which became the granite foundation of all my acts. In addition to what I then created, I have had to learn little; and I have had to alter nothing."]

WHAT I knew of Social Democracy in my youth was exceedingly little and very inaccurate.

I was profoundly pleased that it should carry on the struggle for universal suffrage and the secret ballot. For even then my intelligence told me that this must help to weaken the Habsburg régime which I so hated. In the conviction that the Austrian Empire could never be preserved except by victimizing

its Germans, but that even the price of a gradual Slavization of the German element by no means provided a guaranty of an empire really capable of survival, since the power of the Slavs to uphold the state must be estimated as exceedingly dubious, I welcomed every development which in my opinion would inevitably lead to the collapse of this impossible state which condemned ten million Germans to death. The more the linguistic Babel corroded and disorganized parliament, the closer drew the inevitable hour of the disintegration of this Babylonian Empire, and with it the hour of freedom for my German-Austrian people. Only in this way could the *Anschluss* with the old mother country be restored.

Consequently, this activity of the Social Democracy was not displeasing to me. And the fact that it strove to improve the living conditions of the worker, as, in my innocence, I was still stupid enough to believe, likewise seemed to speak rather for it than against it. What most repelled me was its hostile attitude toward the struggle for the preservation of Germanism, its disgraceful courting of the Slavic 'comrade,' who accepted this declaration of love in so far as it was bound up with practical concessions, but otherwise maintained a lofty and arrogant reserve, thus giving the obtrusive beggars their deserved reward.

Thus, at the age of seventeen the word 'Marxism' was as yet little known to me, while 'Social Democracy' and socialism seemed to me identical concepts. Here again it required the fist of Fate to open my eyes to this unprecedented betrayal of the peoples.

Up to that time I had known the Social Democratic Party only as an onlooker at a few mass demonstrations, without possessing even the slightest insight into the mentality of its adherents or the nature of its doctrine; but now, at one stroke, I came into contact with the products of its education and 'philosophy.' And in a few months I obtained what might otherwise have required decades: an understanding of a pestilential whore, cloaking herself as social virtue and brotherly love, from which I hope humanity will rid this earth with the greatest dispatch, since otherwise the earth might well become rid of humanity.

My first encounter with the Social Democrats occurred during my employment as a building worker.

From the very beginning it was none too pleasant. My clothing was still more or less in order, my speech cultivated, and my manner reserved. I was still so busy with my own destiny that I could not concern myself much with the people around me. I looked for work only to avoid starvation, only

756

to obtain an opportunity of continuing my education, though ever so slowly. Perhaps I would not have concerned myself at all with my new environment if on the third or fourth day an event had not taken place which forced me at once to take a position. I was asked to join the organization.

My knowledge of trade-union organization was at that time practically non-existent. I could not have proved that its existence was either beneficial or harmful. When I was told that I had to join, I refused. The reason I gave was that I did not understand the matter, but that I would not let myself be forced into anything. Perhaps my first reason accounts for my not being thrown out at once. They may perhaps have hoped to convert me or break down my resistance in a few days. In any event, they had made a big mistake. At the end of two weeks I could no longer have joined, even if I had wanted to. In these two weeks I came to know the men around me more closely, and no power in the world could have moved me to join an organization whose members had meanwhile come to appear to me in so unfavorable a light.

During the first days I was irritable.

At noon some of the workers went to the near-by taverns while others remained at the building site and ate a lunch which, as a rule, was quite wretched. These were the married men whose wives brought them their noonday soup in pathetic bowls. Toward the end of the week their number always increased, why I did not understand until later. On these occasions politics was discussed.

I drank my bottle of milk and ate my piece of bread somewhere off to one side, and cautiously studied my new associates or reflected on my miserable lot. Nevertheless, I heard more than enough; and often it seemed to me that they purposely moved closer to me, perhaps in order to make me take a position. In any case, what I heard was of such a nature as to infuriate me in the extreme. These men rejected everything: the nation as an invention of the 'capitalistic' (how often was I forced to hear this single word!) classes; the fatherland as an instrument of the bourgeoisie for the exploitation of the working class; the authority of law as a means for oppressing the proletariat; the school as an institution for breeding slaves and slaveholders; religion as a means for stultifying the people and making them easier to exploit; morality as a symptom of stupid, sheeplike patience, etc. There was absolutely nothing which was not drawn through the mud of a terrifying depth.

At first I tried to keep silent. But at length it became impossible. I began to take a position and to oppose them. But I was forced to recognize that

this was utterly hopeless until I possessed certain definite knowledge of the controversial points. And so I began to examine the sources from which they drew this supposed wisdom. I studied book after book, pamphlet after pamphlet.

From then on our discussions at work were often very heated. I argued back, from day to day better informed than my antagonists concerning their own knowledge, until one day they made use of the weapon which most readily conquers reason: terror and violence. A few of the spokesmen on the opposing side forced me either to leave the building at once or be thrown off the scaffolding. Since I was alone and resistance seemed hopeless, I preferred, richer by one experience, to follow the former counsel.

I went away filled with disgust, but at the same time so agitated that it would have been utterly impossible for me to turn my back on the whole business. No, after the first surge of indignation, my stubbornness regained the upper hand. I was determined to go to work on another building in spite of my experience. In this decision I was reinforced by Poverty which, a few weeks later, after I had spent what little I had saved from my wages, enfolded me in her heartless arms. I had to go back whether I wanted to or not. The same old story began anew and ended very much the same as the first time.

I wrestled with my innermost soul: are these people human, worthy to belong to a great nation?

A painful question; for if it is answered in the affirmative, the struggle for my nationality really ceases to be worth the hardships and sacrifices which the best of us have to make for the sake of such scum; and if it is answered in the negative, our nation is pitifully poor in *human beings*.

On such days of reflection and cogitation, I pondered with anxious concern on the masses of those no longer belonging to their people and saw them swelling to the proportions of a menacing army.

With what changed feeling I now gazed at the endless columns of a mass demonstration of Viennese workers that took place one day as they marched past four abreast! For nearly two hours I stood there watching with bated breath the gigantic human dragon slowly winding by. In oppressed anxiety, I finally left the place and sauntered homeward. In a tobacco shop on the way I saw the *Arbeiter-Zeitung,* the central organ of the old Austrian Social Democracy. It was available in a cheap people's café, to which I often went to read newspapers; but up to that time I had not been able to bring myself to spend more than two minutes on the miserable sheet, whose whole tone

affected me like moral vitriol. Depressed by the demonstration, I was driven on by an inner voice to buy the sheet and read it carefully. That evening I did so, fighting down the fury that rose up in me from time to time at this concentrated solution of lies.

More than any theoretical literature, my daily reading of the Social Democratic press enabled me to study the inner nature of these thought-processes.

For what a difference between the glittering phrases about freedom, beauty, and dignity in the theoretical literature, the delusive welter of words seemingly expressing the most profound and laborious wisdom, the loathsome humanitarian morality—all this written with the incredible gall that comes with prophetic certainty—and the brutal daily press, shunning no villainy, employing every means of slander, lying with a virtuosity that would bend iron beams, all in the name of this gospel of a new humanity. The one is addressed to the simpletons of the middle, not to mention the upper, educated, 'classes,' the other to the masses.

For me immersion in the literature and press of this doctrine and organization meant finding my way back to my own people.

What had seemed to me an unbridgable gulf became the source of a greater love than ever before.

Only a fool can behold the work of this villainous poisoner and still condemn the victim. The more independent I made myself in the next few years, the clearer grew my perspective, hence my insight into the inner causes of the Social Democratic successes. I now understood the significance of the brutal demand that I read only Red papers, attend only Red meetings, read only Red books, etc. With plastic clarity I saw before my eyes the inevitable result of this doctrine of intolerance.

The psyche of the great masses is not receptive to anything that is half-hearted and weak.

Like the woman, whose psychic state is determined less by grounds of abstract reason than by an indefinable emotional longing for a force which will complement her nature, and who, consequently, would rather bow to a strong man than dominate a weakling, likewise the masses love a commander more than a petitioner and feel inwardly more satisfied by a doctrine, tolerating no other beside itself, than by the granting of liberalistic freedom with which, as a rule, they can do little, and are prone to feel that they have been abandoned. They are equally unaware of their shameless spiritual terrorization and the hideous abuse of their human freedom, for they absolutely fail to suspect the inner insanity of the whole doctrine. All they see is the

759

ruthless force and brutality of its calculated manifestations, to which they always submit in the end.

If Social Democracy is opposed by a doctrine of greater truth, but equal brutality of methods, the latter will conquer, though this may require the bitterest struggle.

I WAS A GERMAN:

Ernst Toller

LETTERS TO: *Fritz von Unruh*

Tessa

Mrs. L.

The Governor of the Fortress

Theodore Lessing

Romain Rolland

Stefan Zweig

"WHAT does the dramatic poet experience when his vision is realized on the stage?" a German critic wrote in his column with experimental curiosity after seeing one of Toller's productions. To which the playwright, who, for excellent reasons, had not yet seen a single one of his pieces performed, replied: *"Dear Sir:* Will you send your request to the Bavarian Ministry of Justice? Will you tell him that you will be dreadfully hurt if you do not get an answer from me? Perhaps he will grant me two weeks' leave after three years of imprisonment . . . and I would tell you with scrupulous care what I experienced at the realization of my 'vision.' "

However much Ernst Toller suffered from his socialist "vision" in a Bavarian prison between 1919 and 1924, he suffered more later in freedom. The child found his enemies in the world of grownups, and the poet was to find them in men who seemed to blunder into their worst deeds from sheer lack of imagination. A doubting Thomas, a non-conformist among the masses and revolutionary leaders, Toller tormented himself with the question: "Must a man of action always be dogged by guilt? . . . Can a man be an individualist and a mass-man at one and the same time? . . . The problem seemed to be insoluble."

The anguish which finished off Toller in exile was not what destroyed his friend Stefan Zweig, to whom the end of Europe was the collapse of everything; nor Walter Hasenclever, who took poison in a French internment camp to escape the sadism of the approaching Nazis. Ernst Toller had a wider, or perhaps a narrower love than the culture of Europe; his conflict was never better resolved, personally or artistically, than when he labored as a

761

political martyr. He tells us that when the prison doors clanged behind him on the bitterness, the confusion, and the bloodshed of the Bavarian revolution, in which he was thrust into leadership, "I felt strangely care-free and cheerful." He faced the dilemma, "Should I escape or should I write my play?" He stayed in prison and read Marx, Bakunin, Luxemburg, the Webbs —as he had previously read Weber, Dehmel, and Mann. He wrote his most passionate plays. They came to him swiftly and inevitably out of the prison air, *Masses and Men* in a torrent of inspiration for two nights, and *Hinkemann* from seeing on the wall of his cell two oval patches of sunlight, driving him on to the solution of the problem of how the world would seem to a man who had been emasculated in the war. He stayed in jail to eat warbread mixed with clay and turnip soup. When at thirty he was "free" and his hair had turned gray, he felt at once that he had never been alone all those five years: "The sun and moon had consoled me, the wind that flurried the puddles in the yard, the grass that sprang up in the spring in the cracks of the stones. All these were my friends, telling of greetings from the world outside, of comradeship among the prisoners, of belief in a world of justice, of freedom, of humanity, in a world without fear and without hunger." He wrote his plays, *The Machine-Wreckers, Transfiguration, Masses and Man, Hinkemann, The Unfettered Wotan, The Revenge of the Derided Lovers, War and Peace,* and the poetry of *The Swallow Book.* Only a few miles away Adolf Hitler was writing *Mein Kampf* in a more comfortable Bavarian jail.

In "freedom" and exile, Toller had to face a shrinking of faith and creative will, the expanding world of Hitler, and the bitter disaster of the Spanish Republic. Like his own rebellious youth, the German revolution was retreating into oblivion. He remembered the bureaucratic Philistines who had botched that revolution; the masses who had shouted for socialism and had no conception of what socialism should be; that Kurt Eisner and Karl Liebknecht were dead voices. Thousands were speculating on war and other thousands were celebrating the death of freedom in Germany. The people, the masses, were silent. Toller, who hated bloodshed and caused blood to be shed, had never been a Party man, even as the leader of the Bavarian Soviets. To Theodore Lessing he had written: "The individual can *will* death. The masses must will life. And as we are at once individual man and masses, we choose life and death." This key to his play *Masses and Man* opens a door on his greater drama, that of his own turbulent life. At least for himself as an individual, he found salvation in death. Richard Dehmel admired

the stoicism of the youthful Toller who wrote, "I was myself Mother to myself." In 1939, in exile, in the New York hotel where he committed suicide, stoicism had deserted Toller, the most passionate young spirit of Europe after the First World War. In the poem *To All Prisoners*,[1] he sought an affirmation which, one hopes, cannot be strangled by a hanging:

> Twilight, Sister of all in prison,
> Your silence turns to melody.
> On my narrow plank I lie, I listen. . . .
> I hear your heart beating.
> The heart of those locked in the prisons of the world,
> Yonder . . . yonder . . . yonder . . .
> Brothers of mine: fighters, rebels, I salute you
> It is a world they would deny you,
> It is your world that lives in your wills.
> And I salute you, brothers in the gaols of Africa and Asia,
> And you, brothers, in the convict prisons of the world,
> Thieves and burglars, homicides, murderers,
> Brothers now of one doom, I salute you.
>
> What man can say to himself, that he is not a prisoner?
>
> I hear your heart beating
> Yonder . . . yonder . . . yonder . . .
> Oh that it were given to me to listen
> With the homeless love of the God of men's dreams,
> I should hear
> The one heartbeat
> Of all races of men
> Of all beasts
> Of all woods
> Of all flowers
> Of all stones.
> I should hear
> The one heartbeat
> Of all
> That has life.

---

[1] *Look Through the Bars*, Ernst Toller, Farrar & Rinehart, 1937.

LETTERS

To Fritz von Unruh [2]

Stadelheim 1919

DEAR FRITZ VON UNRUH,

I shall never get used to "prisoner's humility"; and, though I am frequently sad and embittered, I am glad of that,—that I can't get "used."

There's one of the most horrible weaknesses of the German character: that "getting used" to all institutions that deny the spirit—the surrender to inhuman rules, the being comfortable in servitude, the shirking of responsibility, the deafness to the call of one's own conscience. (Worship of power is the reverse of the worship of slavery!) You are right; the ghosts of rottenness are more impudent than ever. Every day as I read the newspapers, I can smell the stench of decay.

We stood lonely in the war; lonely once more we stand to-day. I don't deceive myself—forgotten, forgotten what the heart spake on the threshold of life and death; forgotten, forgotten the knowledge that seemed branded on the spirit, like the scars of wounds. Ours was the sacred duty to preach, and, in spite of the darkness, again and again to preach the simple truths of humanity and of the life of brotherhood.

You know that my skill, my art belong to the workers; but in living with them and for them I am also living for mankind which includes *all that has being.*

I hate nobody. How could we hate men who believe that they control that which drives them, that driving fate which will hold us as long as this earth has breath.

Believe me, it is hard not to hate—only the realization of the compulsion behind compulsion in men's lives gives us knowledge and makes us wise and understanding.

To Tessa

Niederschönenfeld 1920

MY DEAR,

When, on a wan evening in February, I took the field-path to the prison, the distant landscape filled my eyes, eyes freed from month after month of

---

[2] Fritz von Unruh, a German author.

tormenting prison walls; when there came to me the smell of mother earth I was at first terrified, I looked round in such profound shyness that my three warders came closer and were more watchful.

But then I breathed deeply in a happy silence.

In those remote fields stood a lonely birch-tree, with tender, frail branches. Memory touched me. The landscape was familiar to me: this was like the landscape of my home. What do they know of your beauties, those who scorn you, because the east wind is yours, because your name sounds unlovely in the ears that are stopped with the bitter cry of hate? [3]

When we walk in the prison yard our eyes rise to the plank fence, five metres high, rise to the iron spikes which the fence wears for its diadem, rise and fall in sudden dizziness down the precipices of our dark longing. But when we look through the cracks in the fence and see the barbed wire outside and the posts for the warders who spy on us through little holes, then we laugh scornfully and sing a song of defiance and of freedom.

The grass grows stunted in the yard.

Spring is coming. Do you hear? Spring! Here this word is shouted; it is sung to ourselves, it is caressed like a vase of price. How many years it is since I saw the Spring! Last year, I was in hiding, in the flat of friends who were ready to take risks for me, from a mob of unleashed soldiers; two years ago I was in a military prison and before that in the war that lasted for a hundred years or more—one doesn't count.

I have found in the grass the first daisies, white daisies with a rosy flush. A golden buttercup winked at the fence. The trees have tiny buds; every day I watch them grow. And yesterday, when I looked through my iron-barred window I saw the birch-tree, clad in a veil of green.

The willows, too, by the pond, gleamed in a velvety green.

O green of fields and meadows! O coloured dance of green in sunshine! O delicate marvel of these days!

Since this morning I am not allowed any longer to look out. For two weeks the prisoners are "deprived of the walk in the yard" (and for six weeks of the right to send letters) because they could not hold their tongues, because they protested against this type of confinement in a fortress. The Government of the Free State of Bavaria has changed the character of this punishment: it is not what it was when it was inflicted on officers and

---

[3] The landscape of the Eastern Provinces, of Posen especially, which was the author's home, was regarded by the rest of Germany as being without beauty. In reality the landscape has the melancholy beauty of the Russian plains.

students whose affairs of honour brought them an honourable imprisonment. Revolutionary Socialists are sentenced to confinement in a fortress. Actually they are thrown into old prisons; and their imprisonment is intensified by tortures and all kinds of torments in order to break their spirit. Of course we live in a Free State.

Do you believe your punishments make us bow our heads or that thus you can paralyse our firm will?

One man has been shot "while attempting to escape," shot for the sake of "order and discipline"; another enjoys the benefit of the black-and-gold Republic.

But you cannot forbid our songs.

Do you hear when we are singing?

To Mrs. L.[4]

Stadelheim 1919

Dear ——,

Do you remember Charlotte Stieglitz, the poet's wife—the woman who killed herself because she believed the great shock would save her husband from his state of lethargy and sterility, and arouse his buried creative power? In everyday life there are innumerable small sacrifices round which there is no romantic glory, which have not death for consequence, but which are infinitely lovely and, in their anonymity, infinitely brave.

Perhaps it is really not so hard to die for a man one loves; perhaps it is harder to live for the beloved one.

We are a hundred men here in prison, separated from our wives for months. Every conversation between any two men always ends in the same way—women.

The high walls prevent any view. Within the walls is a small hut. It was, we heard, some sort of wash-house, which was not used. One day one of us saw that the shutters of the hut were opened. He saw two women at work. One stayed in the wash-house, the other went away and locked the door. Soon we knew all. The two women were a wardress and a prisoner, who was to be released in a short time. She had been sentenced to eight years' imprisonment for child-murder. She had already served five years; in a few weeks' time she was to be pardoned.

---

[4] Confiscated letter.

It would be too complicated to tell you how we contrived to exchange notes with the girl. First playful and harmless ones, then feverish, passionate and confused ones. Everything which, in that closed-in existence, had come in dreams, wishes and fantasies went out to that woman. One morning she gave us a signal. We were to stand near the window at a certain hour.

Impossible to describe what happened. The woman opened her dress and stood naked at the window. She was surprised and taken away. We never saw her again. But we learned that the pardon had been annulled.

Never has a woman moved me so much as that little prisoner, who, in order to make men happy for a few seconds (in a very questionable way) suffered with unsophisticated wisdom three more years in prison.

I often wanted to describe this experience in a short story. But I felt shy. You, dear friend, will understand. You once said to me that the finest things in life have a touch of something which only by the merest *nuance* separates them from trash.

To Tessa

27.5.23

DEAR,

I am summoned by the Head Governor. In his hand I see a telegram. "You have had no news from your mother for a long time?" I stare at him, "My mother is . . . ?" "No, don't be alarmed, the worst has not happened." "Tell me!"—"Your brother-in-law has telegraphed that your mother's condition is very serious. He asks leave for you. I am not entitled to give you leave; but I advise you to make immediate application to the ministry; I promise it shall be forwarded by the next post."

I go upstairs. The old woman dying. Perhaps in that very hour. . . . Perhaps already dead. And if she is still alive how much is she longing to see me once more; once more to talk to me, to embrace me. Feverishly I send telegrams to the ministry, to Dr. H., to Parliament. I cannot write the petition. A comrade makes a rough draft, I copy it, send it down.

From my home, too, there was a petition on its way to the ministry; accompanied by a telegram with the official doctor's certificate. Perhaps it is already in the Ministry of Justice; perhaps the answer is already on its way while my thoughts are chasing one another; perhaps at this very moment the Governor is starting for our cells to tell me . . . that I may travel at once . . . that I may reach my mother while she is still alive. That I shall never again

see her alive has been kept from me to spare me; that I am to be let accompany her on her last journey . . . that . . . that . . . my head's bursting. . . . With the help of my friend I put a few clothes together, borrow a suit-case, shove my things in; get my clothes ready, my linen—at the latest the answer of the Ministry of Justice will come this evening. . . .

Waiting begins.

Waiting: in emotion, worn out, smitten by a thousand perchances which are balanced by other perchances—the waiting of weakness.

The waiting of the prisoner.

Evening comes. No news.

A night creeps slowly near, wraps me in the black folds of a silent embrace. Soft folds, in which all tension melts. But then become stiff, ever stiffer, change into a coffin that is too narrow, not deep enough, that crushes the breast-bone, breaks the limbs. . . .

Night of unending torments.

The next morning. Heavy with purposeless fatigue.

No news.

Again a night, again a day.

If only the news came! It matters not—what? It matters not—what.

It is I who am dying. Too late. Or not. Now comes lethargy.

Now agony.

There I lie in bed at my last gasp and there I stand by the bed and look at myself. No! It is not I who looks on; it is my father. He stands there in his shirt, with motes dancing, really dancing! before his breast; a lock dances, really dances! before his mouth. But my father has been dead these thirteen years.

On the fourth day a telegram comes from my brother-in-law: "Condition unchanged." I scarcely pay any attention to it. How many hours have gone by like this! . . . Ninety? Ninety-one? 92, 93, 94, 95, 96, 97. . . .

"You are to come to the office."

The Chief Governor: Answer of the Ministry. My petition: application cannot be considered. The decision is matter of fact, laconic. I do not wince. From that moment, what has shattered me these last days is blown away. A definite peacefulness comes over my mind; it would never have abandoned me had I had detailed news of my mother's dying—you can understand that. Luckily there was different news. My mother gathered new strength; the hope of seeing me again may have given her power. To-day she is getting up again. Of course she does not know that my application was refused.

Still hopes.

On one of these nights a cow in the near stable gave birth to a calf. Through the whole night I heard her moaning. A deep groan, shattering, aching, as if a man was groaning. Then again her groan sounded dull, broken like a cry of a hungry child that cries himself to sleep.

In some farmhouse a dog started barking. A second answers yelpingly. A third begins sleepingly, then louder, more crossly. A fourth, a fifth, a sixth. And then the dogs of the whole village bark. I can almost feel how they tug at their chains, how they want to get together and can't, how their anger becomes rage, how they rave, rebel, howl—until they get tired and stop. Now and then a howling sound like a cry of a man who cannot understand at all . . . then silence.

By the pond outside a bird is singing . . . incessantly, at quite short intervals, he utters a high complaining trill, a sound of such abysmal complaint as I have never heard a bird sing.

This bird, too,—he sang.

To Tessa

Niederschönenfeld 1.9.1920

DEAR,

While I write to you they are giving the first performance of *Transfiguration* in Hamburg. And I can't even see my own work on the stage! I laugh at my own sentimentality—but, in spite of all, it is rather painful.

I've got out of bed to-day for the first time. The wound in my foot is healing well; but the doctor thinks that I may always have a stiff toe as a keepsake; but as I can move the lower joint fairly well, there's evidently no serious damage. I daresay the stiffness wouldn't have occurred could I have had treatment from a specialist; but, said the doctor, "You're in prison, not at liberty."

The post brought your letter. You are in the South now. For a long time I lay on my plank-bed and dreamed—dreamed with you of Venice, Milan, Rome, Naples.—You lucky ones! I am so happy that you can travel in the lands of my longing. Lands of Life—Colours—Abundance—Warmth—Sun —Blue skies—The songs of the women.

I throw myself on the bed sometimes and have to bite the pillow in my wild and impetuous craving for life.

Don't be afraid! I won't be beaten, I will not break down. Of that I am certain; prison walls shall not break my spirit!

Outside: Blood—Murder—Anguish—Hunger—Millions in need. That, that weighs on me far more. And the foreboding of the fate of Europe in the next decades.

The power that we cannot grasp, the power that leads on to the one horrible road.

Oh, if only I could believe as once I did, in a new birth, in a purer creation!

When I see written up: the day of Righteousness is at hand! The triumph of Humanity comes in holiness! Then some voice within me cries, You lie!

Humanity—always helpless—always crucified.

Righteousness—there is a bitter taste on my tongue.

I have believed in the redemptive power of Socialism; that, perhaps, was my "Life-lie," perhaps. . . .

Socialism? The new and necessary economic order—is not that enough? A gigantic task. And man? And man?

I chafe. My very roots are torn up.

I was bound to confront this crisis. Here is no "weakness," no "results of prison"——

In the grey stone-building it is very cold.

Heaven is not kind to us: for days it has rained. I greet you and I am close to you, yes, yes, I am close to you. And when, at times, I am not—it is not into an abyss that loneliness leads me; in loneliness new paths are revealed, as to men who have fallen asleep in a meadow and wake up and look round them with a beautiful smile.

To the Governor of the Fortress

Niederschönenfeld 23.4.20

SIR,

As I am told, you have confiscated my sketch *Execution* because of its propagandist content. *Execution* is a little picture of the Revolution. Perhaps it is the scene "Revolution" which makes it "propagandist"? Then all the histories of revolution in the literature of the world would have to be confiscated; (and there is a long row of volumes written on that subject).

What is the subject of my little sketch? A woman gives refuge in her house to a rebel and, in order to save him, hides in her bosom the hand-

grenade which was in his possession. The room is invaded by soldiers and one of them finds the hand-grenade on the woman. Everyone who carries weapons is to be shot and so the woman suffers this sentence from the court-martial.

It is the nature of a court-martial to judge quickly without thorough examination. It is known that innocent people are often sentenced; and it is also known that young, inexperienced officers are often the judges.

When the woman comes to the place of execution she is greeted by rude insults from the soldiers. The war has made them brutal.

I remind you of those war-poems which were full of blood and hatred; of the trains with the often unspeakably beastly scribblings on them; and, finally, of the gate of Stadelheim where, in the early days of May 1919 one could read, "Here Spartacists are given a quick and painless death. . . ." "Here blood-and-liver sausage is made from Spartacists' blood."

Do you find incitement in this, that I let the soldiers speak as soldiers do speak at such times? (And to whom will what I write be anything new?)

The very soldier who has treated the woman most brutally undergoes a spiritual transfiguration. After the volley the woman seems to be still alive; he gives her the *coup-de-grâce,* and he looks into her eyes which gaze at him with boundless kindness, which know nothing of fury and hatred, which rather speak of compassion for the murderer.

The soldier, confounded, shaken to the soul, leaps up, breaks his rifle on the wall, shouts and raves. Wherever he looks, he sees the eyes of the woman. At last he flings himself on the dead, kisses her lips, her face, her eyes . . . and, out of his mind, moans to her a love song.

Where is the propaganda in this?

That the soldier has recognized in those seconds that the woman, so kind, so full of spiritual majesty, is not worthy of death? That in sudden recognition he learns the truth—no man has the right to sentence another human being to death?

That he, overwhelmed by the times of which this incident is a parable, rebels and, unable to bear the anguish, loses his mind?

The poet does not write for expediency. He either *must* write—or does not write at all.

And every work written by a poet is "propagandist" in so far as one regards as "propaganda" a human appeal.

To Professor Theodor Lessing[5]

Niederschönenfeld 1920

DEAR PROFESSOR,

Masses and Man presents an experience, the burden of which man can bear only once, perhaps, without breaking—freedom of the needs of his soul. Freedom, which should not deny, by an external formula essentially deceptive, the fact of discord, but would accept the discord as destined.

The individual can *will* death. The masses must will life. And as we are at once individual man and masses, we choose life and death.

To Romain Rolland

Niederschönenfeld 1921

DEAR MONSIEUR ROLLAND,

It was only to-day that I received your letter, which is precious to me. As it was in a foreign language it was not given to me by the authorities and had to be forwarded to my mother who has translated it for me and sent the German version.

If you could only know how happy I am at what you write! When I showed your letter to my comrade he said, smiling: "A man would go to prison for this." Of course that is not to be taken literally. Prison profanes humanity.

The songs from prison—I'm posting them to you to-day—try to be more than songs: an Epistle, a summons, a proclamation to men who feel their responsibility and yet who, in their towns, go by the houses with the iron bars and never divine, never comprehend that by their indifference they shoulder a heavy load of guilt. I stop: is not the earth, in our time, a witches' cauldron of murder and crime, of torture and of starvation for the body and the soul of man? Oh, who in this chaos will listen to my voice? Whom can my voice rouse to greater insight, to human brotherhood? The great ones of our day? Those who lead their peoples from precipice to precipice, is it likely they will have ears for the questions from the lower orders? No.

To the men of the future, the young, to those who believe in the healing

---

[5] Theodor Lessing, a famous German scientist; an ardent fighter for justice and the freedom of mankind. A courageous pacifist. He was persecuted by the reactionaries, who frequently made it impossible for him to deliver his University lectures. He lived in exile after Hitler came into power and was murdered at his hotel in Czechoslovakia by German Nazis.

power of humanity, to whom humanity is a reality, greater than all the realities of the politicians of to-day, to those who feel they are oppressed and who desire that all oppression shall cease—to these my songs will speak.

And if, as from a grain of wheat, future deeds spring from them, they will have accomplished what art can.

Whitman's words that "who touches a book touches a man" apply to every book. In many writers one touches a word machine.

The root of every poem is personal experience.

What we call form is love.

To Stefan Zweig

Niederschönenfeld 1921

DEAR ZWEIG,

No, a man is not foolhardy who, himself at liberty and free from care, praises his fate to a prisoner—so long as he desires the inner perfection of the prisoner. Because one would speak so only to a man who one believes has spiritual strength enough to mature during his imprisonment. And I believe this strength has grown in me. Only the other day I wrote to Herr Tal, who, he tells me, is anxious to secure my release by the assistance of the German intellectuals, that, greatly touched as I was by his sympathy, I must ask him to abandon his plan. Tal fears that my creative powers will be damaged for life. I can't help smiling a little. We are living at a time when so many "would-be's" and "might-be's" are running around, men who lack any profound sense of compulsion, who can say either "Yea" or "Nay." It is about time that men voluntarily, from inescapable devotion, find the courage to live the ideas which they profess. That they see how essential such a life is. That they should give up thinking that life's meaning lies in making pictures of life.

My fate seldom oppresses me, because I will it, have always willed it—and I believe that I am secure against the danger of leaving the prison-house full of bitterness and resentment.

(That I belong to those who fight ruthlessly against the defilement of the image of humanity—no one outside can have an idea of how dreadful is that defiling—you will understand. Too few feel their responsibility, and that is why such things are possible. But I cannot discuss that problem now.)

You say of Romain Rolland that he "loves humanity because he pities it rather than believes in it." That is, perhaps, the only constant and unembittered love.

773

If belief be often disappointed, as it must be, it changes into enmity and bitterness and hatred of humanity. I can imagine fighters for whom it would not be a matter of crucial importance whether they had that belief or no; they fight under the power of an idea—the idea of co-operation for conscious self-development in a society. To go on in this task (economically the most important aspect of Socialism) means the overcoming of social disorder by building up a community life. By that the mysterious, the irrational element in life is not, as even some dogmatic Socialists believe, wholly rationalized; but it is limited, it goes back to its place and stays there in all its incomprehensibility.

Is it not the destiny of European man to be this kind of fighter, this heroic kind?

THEY CAUGHT A TARTAR:

Georgi Dimitrov

NOTES FOR A SPEECH

THE Reichstag Fire lit the whole German landscape exactly twenty-seven days after Adolf Hitler came into power. The rape of the polls and the Nazi terror followed. For a moment, the last comfortable laughter at Goering, Goebbels, and Hitler rose like a phoenix from the Reichstag's parliamentary ashes. That uneasy laughter was heard around the world on the occasion of the Leipzig trial of four suspected communists (three of them Bulgarians and one a German) and a Dutch idiot. The idiot, Marinus van der Lubbe, went to his death more like a lamb than an incendiary of parliaments, but one of the Bulgarians proved to be a boomerang. As the correspondent of the London *Times* reported, "they caught a Tartar when they took Georgi Dimitrov." Hitler called the Reichstag Fire a "sign from heaven" and the next day Goering obeyed the will of heaven by putting all the communist and socialist deputies into jail. Before a solemn but uncomfortable German supreme court, the Bulgarian scapegoat, Dimitrov, showed neither fear nor humility. He would not behave "as a disreputable Bulgarian communist should who is under grave suspicion of tampering with the edifice of the Reich." He overcame the enormous handicap of his comic obscurity as a Bulgarian, and unpopularity as a communist, by calling a spade a spade. The high court was scandalized by the things Dimitrov said, but the foreign newspapers were delighted and soon reported that it was the prisoner, Dimitrov, who was really conducting the trial. It was said of him that "he means to force the tribunal into becoming a stage. . . . The whole courtroom is suddenly charged with political energy. . . . It is all one whatever role he played in the burning of the Reichstag. At any rate it has been proved already that Dimitrov is a moral incendiary of the most monstrous dimensions. . . . The civilized world must wipe out this programme of the Third International become flesh, if it does not want to be swallowed up in a bloody night without end." There were calculated references in the press to "a savage Bulgaria" and "an uncivilized Balkan type," but the amazing Dimitrov said in that Leipzig court: "The only savages and barbarians in Bulgaria are the fascists. But I ask you, Mr. Chairman—in what country are the fascists not barbarians and savages?" He turned on the

pathetic idiot, van der Lubbe, who in a state of semi-stupor had admitted to firing the Reichstag. "This miserable Faust," said the Bulgarian with a German phrase, "will not say who was his Mephistopheles." Mephistopheles in the shape of Goering himself obliged the ends of justice by appearing in court. As a photographer's souvenir of 1934, there is a vivid print of the fat and powerful frame of Goering planted on the floor of the august German Supreme Court, with his arrogant back, the leather boots, the fat parted feet. Goering, between whose official residence and the Reichstag building stretched an underground passage whose story was never revealed, led the judges along another path of speculation. "I knew, as by intuition," he said, "that the communists fired the Reichstag. It was a political crime," and turning to Dimitrov, "the criminals were in your party." "Does the witness know," asked Dimitrov with pride, "that this criminal party rules the sixth part of the earth? . . . Are you afraid of the question, Herr Minister Goering?" Dimitrov prodded. Goering, Premier of Prussia, Reich Air Minister, Speaker of the Reichstag, General of the Reichswehr and Police, stamped the floor of the decorous Supreme Court with anger: "I'm not afraid of you at all, you crook. I'm not here to be questioned by you. You'll be sorry yet if I catch you when you come out of prison." While the poor idiot, van der Lubbe, was relieved of his misery by the learned judges, the Tartar, Dimitrov, was acquitted for lack of evidence to the echoes of international laughter.

NOTES FOR A SPEECH[1]

Born on 18th June 1882 at Radomir, near Sofia.
Left High School in the 4th class, worked as a compositor up to 1904.
Son of the Bulgarian working class.
Born and brought up in the ranks of the revolutionary workers' movement (I have been active in this movement from the age of 15).
For thirty years member of the Bulgarian Communist Party—(formerly the Party of the so-called "Narrow-Minded" Left Social-Democrats).
For twenty-one years member of the Central Committee of the Communist Party of Bulgaria.
From 1904 to 1923 Secretary of the Trade Union Federation.
From 1913 to 1923 Party Deputy for Sofia in the Bulgarian Parliament—

---

[1] Prepared by Dimitrov in his prison for the first address in court.

also representative of the Party in the Municipal Council of Sofia and in the Regional Council of Sofia (Diet).

At the same time I was active as a Party speaker and writer.

9th June 1923—Military putsch—overthrow of Stambuliski's Government —by officers and Macedonian terrorists under the patronage of the King himself, aided by Social-Democrats and from abroad.

Thousands and thousands of peasants, workers, intellectuals murdered, Stambuliski murdered.

Largest parties—Peasants' League and Communist Party—dissolved.

All rights and liberties of the mass of the people abolished. Introduction of a military-Fascist régime. Boundless indignation—rising of the mass of the people inevitable.

23rd September—*Insurrection* of the workers and peasants under the leadership of the Communist Party against the oppressors of the people and the usurpers of power, *for* a workers' and peasants' government.

In this insurrection I was delegated by my Party to take an active and leading part.

After a week of armed struggle the insurrection was defeated. Fighting every step of the way, with about a thousand of my comrades in arms I crossed over into Yugo-Slavian territory.

There we were treated at first as political prisoners and later as political refugees.

From that time onwards—exactly ten years—I have been living abroad as a political refugee and a political writer—unregistered and under a false name, because abroad as well I was threatened with death by my enemies.

Some months after the September insurrection I was sentenced to death in my absence—as the press announced at the time. I never had the opportunity of seeing the judgment passed upon me.

I am proud of the heroic insurrection!

I only regret that I and my Party were not yet *real Bolsheviks* at that time. For this reason we were unable successfully to organise and lead this historic people's insurrection with the proletariat at its head. Our un-Bolshevik organisation, policy and tactics, the lack of revolutionary experience, and especially our opportunist and so-called neutral attitude on the occasion of the military-Fascist coup on 9th June—did much to help the murderers and executioners of the Bulgarian people, the usurpers of State power, to suppress the insurrection of the masses.

But the Party has learned and appreciated the bloody lessons of this experi-

ence, and the struggle for the emancipation of the Bulgarian workers and peasants, under the leadership of the Communist Party, enlightened by the great experience of the September insurrection, is going unfalteringly forward to the final victory.

In order to root out communism, immediately after the insurrection and in the two following years, the government's Fascist gangs murdered more than 20,000 workers, peasants and intellectuals in a bestial manner. My brother, too, was murdered, in the police prison. But, notwithstanding this, communism has incomparably deeper and stronger roots in Bulgaria now than in the year 1923—undoubtedly a useful warning for all the eager extirpators of communism in other countries—for all the many varieties of modern Cervantes heroes!

1st October 1923 I journeyed to Vienna.

Support for my suffering fellow-fighters in Yugo-Slavia. Campaign for the defence of persecuted and bestially slaughtered class comrades in Bulgaria.

Here, for three months, I edited and published the Party organ, *Arbeiterzeitung*. Published two pamphlets against the bloody White Terror in Bulgaria, in Bulgarian, German and English.

In the spring of 1924 went to Moscow as a political refugee and political writer and stayed until the end of 1926.

In 1927 I was again in Vienna, in connection with the projected amnesty, up to the autumn of 1929. I was not amnestied. Publication of the Party paper, *Kommunistische Fahne,* connection with certain Party papers.

From the autumn of 1929 I was settled in Berlin—far fewer Bulgarian refugees were there, and therefore safer incognito.

Two fairly long interruptions—from November 1929 to May 1930, and from December 1931 to June 1932, in Soviet Russia.

I returned specially to Berlin in the summer of 1932 in connection with the last draft Amnesty Law, in order personally to organise the amnesty campaign.

Journeys to Vienna, Amsterdam, Paris.

I have never taken part in German politics—have no contacts with the Communist Party of Germany. This was not necessary for my work.

But I openly state that if I had needed these contacts for my work I certainly should have been associated with the Communist Party of Germany.

I was in touch with *International Press Correspondence* only because of my articles.

It is true that I am a Bolshevik, a proletarian revolutionary. I must em-

phasize *proletarian* revolutionary because this is a period of confusion in which even the German Crown Prince is accustomed to proclaim himself a revolutionary, and in which there are also such crazy revolutionaries as, for instance, van der Lubbe! It is also true that as a Member of the Central Committee of the Bulgarian Party, and a Member of the Executive of the Communist International, I am a responsible and a leading Communist.

And I am very ready to accept full responsibility for all the decisions, documents, and actions of my Bulgarian Party and of the Communist International. But precisely for this reason I am not a terrorist adventurer, an instigator of putsches or an incendiary!

Further, it is perfectly true that I am in favour of the proletarian revolution and the dictatorship of the proletariat. I am firmly convinced that this is the only way out of, the only salvation from, the economic crisis and the catastrophe of war under capitalism.

And the fight for the dictatorship of the proletariat and for the victory of communism is, without any doubt, *the whole substance of my life*. I should like to live at least another twenty years for communism and then quietly die. But precisely for this reason I am a convinced opponent of the methods of individual terror and the instigation of putsches.

And this not from any sentimental or humanitarian considerations. In agreement with our Leninist theory, and with the decisions and discipline of the Communist International, which for me and for every true Communist are the supreme law, I am opposed to individual terror and to putschist activities from the standpoint of revolutionary usefulness, in the interests of the proletarian revolution and of communism itself.

I am, in fact, an enthusiastic follower and admirer of the Communist Party of the Soviet Union, because this Party rules the largest country in the world —a sixth part of the earth—and with our great leader Stalin at its head is building up socialism with such heroism and with such success. But I have never been an emissary in Germany of the Communist Party of the Soviet Union, as the indictment tries to indicate.

The only breach of the law which I have committed in Germany consists in the fact that I have lived there unregistered and under a false name. But unfortunately it was impossible for me to live in any other way!

With the burning of the Reichstag I had absolutely nothing to do, whether directly or indirectly. The Reichstag incendiary, van der Lubbe, I now see for the first time in this hall. When, early in the morning of the 28th February, in the train from Munich to Berlin, I read in the papers about the

burning of the Reichstag, I immediately took the view that the instigators of this action were either despicable provocateurs or mentally and politically demented people, and in any case criminals in relation to the German working class and to communism.

I am now more inclined to assume that the burning of the Reichstag—this anti-Communist undertaking—must have taken place as a result of an alliance between provocation and madness.

It would hardly be possible to make a graver attack upon my revolutionary, political and personal honour than to cast upon me the suspicion and the accusation that I had a share in this crime against the people and against communism.

My consolation was, and is to this day, that my Bulgarian comrades-in-arms, the class comrades abroad, the revolutionary proletarians in Germany, and all who are acquainted with me in some degree, cannot doubt for a single instant that I am innocent.

I can say with every confidence that I have had just as much to do with the burning of the Reichstag as, for instance, any foreign correspondent in this hall or the judges themselves could have had.

At the same time I wish to state most emphatically that I have had absolutely no connection, not even a chance connection or the most remote connection, with this crime.

During the preliminary examination I submitted two written statements—on the 20th March and the 30th May—where practically everything essential in my defence has already been said.

On the other hand I did not sign the depositions at the preliminary examinations because they were incomplete and tendentious. My whole preliminary examination was based on the express intention of turning me into an incendiary of the Reichstag for the benefit of the Supreme Court—at any price, and in spite of the facts which disproved this; and even after the preliminary investigation, which had lasted for months, had still failed—as I now see clearly—to discover the real criminals.

A GOOD SHOEMAKER AND A POOR FISH PEDDLER:

Nicola Sacco
Bartolomeo Vanzetti

THE LETTERS OF NICOLA SACCO:

"the good red rose"
"this spontaneous affection"
"terrible I said yes, but beauty at same time"
"You don't know Ines"
"Remember this, Dante"

THE LETTERS OF BARTOLOMEO VANZETTI:

"a meditation perhaps"
"little of abdom and much of heart"
"if tragedy is compelled to us"
"Please let me speak of Italy"
"the right of love"
"the reasons why I tell you, young Comrade"

~~~~~~

If it had not been for these thing, I might have live out my life talking at street corners to scorning men. I might have die, unmarked, unknown, a failure. Now we are not a failure. This is our career and our triumph. Never in our full life could we hope to do such work for tolerance, for joostice, for man's onderstanding of man as now we do by accident. Our words—our lives—our pains—nothing! The taking of our lives—lives of a good shoemaker and a poor fish-peddler—all! That last moment belongs to us—that agony is our triumph.

BARTOLOMEO VANZETTI

MORE was involved in the Sacco-Vanzetti case than the lives of two obscure immigrant Italians, more than the paradox of two pacifist anarchists tried for common robbery and murder. In 1920, a year of hysterical red scare, the ancient demonology of colonial Salem rose from the grave and all the neo-Cotton Mathers, inside and outside Massachusetts, were sure again that "An Army of Devils is horribly broke in upon the place which is

781

the *Centre,* and after a sort, the First-born of our *English Settlements."* Nicola Sacco and Bartolomeo Vanzetti, the shoemaker and the fish peddler, active radicals among the foreign-born workers in New England factories, stepped into their roles as martyrs without much surprise. They were as well equipped to acknowledge their sudden martyrdom, as respectable New Englanders were to accept, as natural and almost self-evident, a kinship between philosophical anarchism and murder. Writing an account of his own life (during his imprisonment) Vanzetti easily found a theory of justice in his theme, *The Story of a Proletarian Life.* Across the barricades of public opinion Judge Webster Thayer projected the indelible image of a judge who had asked, during the festivities of a football game, the immoral and triumphant question, "Did you see what I did to those anarchistic bastards the other day?" It was this cleavage of class, morality, even dignity, which, between 1920 and 1927, the seven long years between the arrest and the electrocution, translated a case of robbery and murder into an issue of outraged justice. The world-wide indignation, the protest in every language, the feeling of frustration and horror among millions, the epidemic of an almost personal grief in the farthest corners of the earth, today seem almost fantastic. The reaction came with mass meetings, parades, general strikes, and even riots and bombs. In nearly all the capitals of the world ordinary men and women were moved out of the routine of their daily lives by an anger against the thought of judicial error and prejudice. They made a contribution to the defense of Sacco and Vanzetti which amounted to more than $350,000—a pious tithe from thousands of wage envelopes. Newspapers accused Massachusetts of having turned the law into an instrument of torture; and intellectuals of the middle class—scientists, professors, writers, and savants—concentrated on Dedham Jail the greatest barrage of pity and anger since the Dreyfus affair at the turn of the century. With the smell of burned flesh still in the air, John Dos Passos was to write down the emotion of the hour:

all right you have won   you will kill the brave men our friends tonight
America our nation has been beaten by strangers who have turned our language
inside out who have taken the clean words our fathers spoke and made them slimy
and foul
*   their hired men sit on the judge's bench they sit back with their feet on the*
tables under the dome of the State House they are ignorant of our beliefs they
have the dollars the guns the armed forces the powerplants
*   they have built the electricchairs and hired the executioners to throw the switch*
all right we are two nations

Yet, miraculously, the most adequate statement of protest came from the prisoners themselves. Asked whether he had "anything to say why sentence of death should not be passed" on him, Vanzetti replied in his broken English: "You see it is seven years that we are in jail. What we have suffered during these seven years no human tongue can say, and yet you see before you, not trembling, you see me looking you in your eyes straight, not blushing not changing color, not ashamed or in fear."

On native grounds, in Massachusetts, the trial certainly involved a test of the machinery of Americanization. That Sacco was a conscientious objector and a draft evader, and that Vanzetti was a philosophical anarchist, was not sufficient to demonstrate, as the prosecutor wanted to show, a predisposition to robbery and murder. Obligated to answer either with *yes* or *no* the cross-examiner's question, "Did you love this country in the month of May 1917?" Sacco said "Yes"; and asked, "Is your love of the United States of America commensurate with the amount of money you can get in this country per week?" he said, "I never loved money." The prosecuting attorney for Massachusetts, who was confusing two issues with legal adroitness, had not read one of Sacco's prison letters in which he wrote, "You will excuse my poor Shakespear English: poor, yes, because I have not get yet all the song and harmony of this beautiful language." Much as the draft evader, Sacco, apologized to the children of Harvard University for his "poor Shakespear English"—so Vanzetti, who had dug ditches, quarried in stone pits, roasted in brickyards, and consoled himself with Proudhon for his trials as an immigrant proletariat American, also offered a justification. In one of his prison letters, Vanzetti wrote: "Oh, friend, the anarchism is as beauty as a woman for me, perhaps even more since it include all the rest and me and her. Calm, serene, honest, natural, viril, muddy and celestial at once, austere, heroic, fearless, fatal, generous and implacable—all these and more it is." It is a curious fact that Vanzetti, during the days before his execution, was reading *The Rise of American Civilization.* He was greatly excited by differences of opinion with the historian of that epic story of the hard, economic facts of the American dream. Vanzetti joked when it became evident that his reading and Americanization would be interrupted: "the only great trouble is that Massachusetts' hanger may not give me time to finish the lecture, all the rest is O.K."

A GOOD SHOEMAKER : *Nicola Sacco*

THE LETTERS OF NICOLA SACCO

"the good red rose"

February 26, 1924. Dedham Jail

MY DEAR FRIEND MRS. JACK: [1]

. . . Every night when the light goes out I take a long walk and really I do not know how long I walk, because the most of the time I forget myself to go to sleep, and so I continue to walk and I count, one, two, three, four steps and turn backward and continue to count, one, two, three four and so on. But between all this time my mind it is always so full of ideas that one gos and one comes. . . . I find one of my mostly beautiful remembrance while I am thinking and walking, frequently I stop to my window cell and through those sad bars I stop and look at the nature into crepuscular of night, and the stars in the beauti blue sky. So last night the stars they was moor bright and the sky it was moor blue than I did ever seen; while I was looking it appear in my mind the idea to think of something of my youth and write the idea to my good friend Mrs. Jack first thing in morning. So here where I am right with you, and always I will try to be, yes, because I am study to understand your beautiful language and I know I will love it. And I will hope that one day I could surprise the feel of my gratitude towards all this fierce legion of friends and comrades.

The flowers you send to me last week it renew in my mind the remembrance of my youth. It complete sixteen years ago this past autumn that I left my father vineyards. Every year in autumn right after the collection I usd take care my father vineyard and sometime I usd keep watch, because near our vineyard they was a few big farmer and surronder our vineyard they was vast extension of prairie and hundreds animal they used pasturage day and night on those vast prairie. So the most of night I remane there to sleep to watch the animal to not let coming near our vineyard. The little town of Torremaggiore it is not very far from our vineyard, only twenty minete of walk and I used go back and forth in morning an night and I usd bring to my dear an poor mother two big basket full of vegetables and fruits and big bounch flowers. The place where I used to sleep it was a big large hayrick that my good father and my brothers and I build. The hayrick

---

[1] Mrs. Cerise Jack attended the trial and visited the prisoners as a member of the New England Civil Liberties Committee. During the winter of 1923–4 she gave Sacco lessons in English.

it was set in one corner near the well in the middle of our vineyard, and surronde this sweet hayrick they was many plants and flowers except the red rose, because they was pretty hard to find the good red rose and I did love them so much that I was always hunting for find one plant of those good—red rose!

About sixty step from our vineyard we have a large piece of land full of any quantity of vegetables that my brothers and I we used cultivate them. So every morning before the sun shining used comes up and at night after the sun goes out I used put one quart of water on every plant of flowers and vegetables and the smal fruit trees. While I was finishing my work the sun shining was just coming up and I used always jump upon well wall and look at the beauty sun shining and I do not know how long I usd remane there look at that enchanted scene of beautiful. If I was a poet probably I could discribe the red rays of the loving sun shining and the bright blue sky and the perfume of my garden and flowers, the smell of the violet that was comes from the vast verdant prairie, and the singing of the birds, that was almost the joy of deliriany. So after all this enjoyment I used come back to my work singing one of my favourite song an on way singing I used full the bascket of fruit and vegetables and bunch of flowers that I used make a lovely bouquet. And in the middle the longuest flowers I used always put one of lovely red rose and I used walk one mile a way from our place to get one of them good red rose that I always hunting and love to find, the good red rose. . . .

"this spontaneous affection"

April 9, 1924. Dedham Jail

MY DEAR FRIEND MRS. JACK:

Yesterday I said to you that when a man remains all day long back of these sad bars you feel your mind sometime very tired and exhausted of ideas, but when we see a friend and especially a friend that we feel to be bound together in one faith and in one fraternal affection many ideas coming back again. It is sweet to see a friend after a little period of time. I remember another day that I had past like yesterday it was right after when I came back from Mexico sometime into the middle of September nineteen seventeen, and at that time I was unoccupied.

So in one lovely morning of September when the rays of sunshine are still warm in the soul of oppressed humanity, I was looking for a job around

the city of Boston and away I was going towards South Boston, I met one of my most dear comrades, and just as soon as we saw each other we ran one into the embrace of the other and we kissed each other on both sides of the cheeks. And yet it was not a very long time since we had seen each other, because a few weeks before we were in Mexcio together; but this spontaneous affection it shows at all times in the heart of one who has reciprocal love and sublime faith and such a remembrance it will never disappear in the heart of the proletarian.

So your surprise visit Mrs. Jack it was a great relieve for the reclus, and I was enjoy to see you back again in good health and always in that good old spirit. . . .

"terrible I said yes, but beauty at same time"

March 15, 1924. *Dedham Jail*

MY DEAR FRIEND MRS. JACK:

It has been past a few day now that I had in my mind to write you a letter and I always try to find some good idea, but it was hard because the sky it has been covered for several day now with full of cloud; and you know that my most beauty idea I find by looking at the clear and blue sky. . . .

So Wednesday night I went to sleep with idea to write you at first thing in morning but when I was into bed I begen to turn this way an the other way and I was try my best to sleep. So after while I fall sleep, enddid I do not know how long I been sleep when I was up again with a terrible dream . . . terrible I said yes, but beauty at same time, and here way it is. The dream it was develope in one place in mine camp of Pennsylvania state, and here it was a big large number of laborers in strike for better wages and the masses of workers they was impatient tired of long waiting, because the bos who own the col mine there threw out of the house a big number people, of poor mother and child and for the moment they were living under the tent in one concentration camp. But here the poor mother they was not pacific yet, because they know that they would soon send the soldiers to chase the mother out of the camp.

And so the big masse of the workers they was in complete revolt from the cruelty the bos of the mine. In this camp they were two or three speakers and every one of them they was used a kind and warm word for the freedom

of the people. While the immensity of the work masses they were applauding the speakers, the soldiers comes with bayonet gun for chase the crowd, but after word they find out they was wrong because every one of the strikers they stand still like one man. And so the fight it was beginning, and while the fight was begin I jump upon a little hill in meddle of the crowd and I begin to say, Friend and comrade and brotherhood, not one of us is going to move a step, and who will try to move it will be vile and coward, here the fight is to go to finish. So I turn over towards the soldiers and I said, Brothers you will not fire on your own brothers just because they tell you to fire, no brothers, remember that everyone of us we have mother and child, and you know that we fight for freedom which is your freedom. We want one fatherland, one sole, one house, and better bread. So while I was finish to say that last word one of the soldiers fire towards me and the ball past through my heart, and while I was fall on ground with my right hand close to my heart I awake up with sweet dream! So when I was awake I had my right hand still tightly upon my heart like if it was hold back the speed of the beating of my heart. I turn over towards my window cell and through the shade of night I was looking at sky, and while look the stars it bright my face and the shadow soon disapear. Soon the idea it comes in my mind to write my dream to my dear teacher and for moment I thought that Fairhope, Alabama was to far away but the spirit, the voice the lesson of my dear and good friend and teacher Mrs. Jack it is remained in my heart and blessed my soul. . . .

"You don't know Ines"[2]

July 19, 1927. Charlestown State Prison

MY DEAR INES:

I would like that you should understand what I am going to say to you, and I wish I could write you so plain, for I long so much to have you hear all the heart-beat eagerness of your father, for I love you so much as you are the dearest little beloved one.

It is quite hard indeed to make you understand in your young age but I am going to try from the bottom of my heart to make you understand how dear you are to your father's soul. If I cannot succeed in doing that, I know

---

[2] Ines, Sacco's daughter, was born after his arrest, and was seven years old at this date. His son, Dante, was about thirteen years old.

that you will save this letter and read it over in future years to come and you will see and feel the same heart-beat affection as your father feels in writing it to you.

I will bring with me your little and so dearest letter and carry it right under my heart to the last day of my life. When I die, it will be buried with your father who loves you so much, as I do also your brother Dante and holy dear mother.

You don't know Ines, how dear and great your letter was to your father. It is the most golden present that you could have given to me or that I could have wished for in these sad days.

It was the greatest treasure and sweetness in my struggling life that I could have lived with you and your brother Dante and your mother in a neat little farm, and learn all your sincere words and tender affection. Then in the summertime to be sitting with you in the home nest under the oak tree shade—beginning to teach you of life and how to read and write, to see you running, laughing, crying and singing through the verdent fields picking the wild flowers here and there from one tree to another, and from the clear, vivid stream to your mother's embrace.

The same I have wished to see for other poor girls, and their brothers, happy with their mother and father as I dreamed for us—but it was not so and the nightmare of the lower classes saddened very badly your father's soul.

For the things of beauty and of good in this life, mother nature gave to us all, for the conquest and the joy of liberty. The men of this dying old society, they brutally have pulled me away from the embrace of your brother and your poor mother. But, in spite of all, the free spirit of your father's faith still survives, and I have lived for it and for the dream that some day I would have come back to life, to the embrace of your dear mother, among our friends and comrades again, but woe is me!

I know that you are good and surely you love your mother, Dante and all the beloved ones—and I am sure that you love me also a little, for I love you much and then so much. You do not know Ines, how often I think of you every day. You are in my heart, in my vision, in every single of this sad walled cell, in the sky and everywhere my gaze rests.

Meantime, give my best paternal greetings to all the friends and comrades, and doubly so to our beloved ones. Love and kisses to your brother and mother.

With the most affectionate kiss and ineffable caress from him who loves

you so much that he constantly thinks of you. Best warm greetings from Bartolo to you all.

Your Father

"Remember this, Dante"

August 18, 1927. Charlestown State Prison

MY DEAR SON AND COMPANION:

Since the day I saw you last I had always the idea to write you this letter, but the length of my hunger strike and the thought I might not be able to explain myself, made me put it off all this time.

The other day, I ended my hunger strike and just as soon as I did that I thought of you to write to you, but I find that I did not have enough strength and I cannot finish it at one time. However, I want to get it down in any way before they take us again to the death-house, because it is my conviction that just as soon as the court refuses a new trial to us they will take us there. And between Friday and Monday, if nothing happens, they will electrocute us right after midnight, on August 22nd. Therefore, here I am, right with you with love and with open heart as ever I was yesterday.

I never thought that our inseparable life could be separated, but the thought of seven dolorous years makes it seem it did come, but then it has not changed really the unrest and the heart-beat of affection. That has remained as it was. More. I say that our ineffable affection reciprocal, is today more than any other time, of course. That is not only a great deal but it is grand because you can see the real brotherly love, not only in joy but also and more in the struggle of suffering. Remember this, Dante. We have demonstrated this, and modesty apart, we are proud of it.

Much we have suffered during this long Calvary. We protest today as we protested yesterday. We protest always for our freedom.

If I stopped hunger strike the other day, it was because there was no more sign of life in me. Because I protested with my hunger strike yesterday as today I protest for life and not for death.

I sacrificed because I wanted to come back to the embrace of your dear little sister Ines and your mother and all the beloved friends and comrades of life and not death. So Son, today life begins to revive slow and calm, but yet without horizon and always with sadness and visions of death.

Well, my dear boy, after your mother had talked to me so much and I had

dreamed of you day and night, how joyful it was to see you at last. To have talked with you like we used to in the days—in those days. Much I told you on that visit and more I wanted to say, but I saw that you will remain the same affectionate boy, faithful to your mother who loves you so much, and I did not want to hurt your sensibilities any longer, because I am sure that you will continue to be the same boy and remember what I have told you. I knew that and what here I am going to tell you will touch your sensibilities, but don't cry Dante, because many tears have been wasted, as your mother's have been wasted for seven years, and never did any good. So, Son, instead of crying, be strong, so as to be able to comfort your mother, and when you want to distract your mother from the discouraging soulness, I will tell you what I used to do. To take her for a long walk in the quiet country, gathering wild flowers here and there, resting under the shade of trees, between the harmony of the vivid stream and the gentle tranquility of the mothernature, and I am sure that she will enjoy this very much, as you surely would be happy for it. But remember always, Dante, in the play of happiness, don't you use all for yourself only, but down yourself just one step, at your side and help the weak ones that cry for help, help the prosecuted and the victim, because that are your better friends; they are the comrades that fight and fall as your father and Bartolo fought and fell yesterday for the conquest of the joy of freedom for all and the poor workers. In this struggle of life you will find more love and you will be loved.

I am sure that from what your mother told me about what you said during these last terrible days when I was lying in the iniquitous death-house—that description gave me happiness because it showed you will be the beloved boy I had always dreamed.

Therefore whatever should happen tomorrow, nobody knows, but if they should kill us, you must not forget to look at your friends and comrades with the smiling gaze of gratitude as you look at your beloved ones, because they love you as they love every one of the fallen persecuted comrades. I tell you, your father that is all the life to you, your father that loved you and saw them, and knows their noble faith (that is mine) their supreme sacrifice that they are still doing for our freedom, for I have fought with them, and they are the ones that still hold the last of our hope that today they can still save us from electrocution, it is the struggle and fight between the rich and the poor for safety and freedom, Son, which you will understand in the future of your years to come, of this unrest and struggle of life's death.

Much I thought of you when I was lying in the death-house—the singing,

the kind tender voices of the children from the playground, where there was all the life and the joy of liberty—just one step from the wall which contains the buried agony of three buried souls. It would remind me so often of you and your sister Ines, and I wish I could see you every moment. But I feel better that you did not come to the death-house so that you could not see the horrible picture of three lying in agony waiting to be electrocuted, because I do not know what effect it would have on your young age. But then, in another way if you were not so sensitive it would be very useful to you tomorrow when you could use this horrible memory to hold up to the world the shame of the country in this cruel persecution and unjust death. Yes, Dante, they can crucify our bodies today as they are doing, but they cannot destroy our ideas, that will remain for the youth of the future to come.

Dante, when I said three human lives buried, I meant to say that with us there is another a young man by the name of Celestino Maderios that is to be electrocuted at the same time with us. He has been twice before in that horrible death-house, that should be destroyed with the hammers of real progress—that horrible house that will shame forever the future of the citizens of Massachusetts. They should destroy that house and put up a factory or school, to teach many of the hundreds of the poor orphan boys of the world.

Dante, I say once more to love and be nearest to your mother and the beloved ones in these sad days, and I am sure that with your brave heart and kind goodness they will feel less discomfort. And you will also not forget to love me a little for I do—O, Sonny! thinking so much and so often of you.

Best fraternal greetings to all the beloved ones, love and kisses to your little Ines and mother. Most hearty affectionate embrace.

Your Father and Companion

P.S. Bartolo send you the most affectionate greetings. I hope that your mother will help you to understand this letter because I could have written much better and more simple, if I was feeling good. But I am so weak.

THE LETTERS OF BARTOLOMEO VANZETTI

"a meditation perhaps"

July 22, 1921. Charlestown Prison

My dear Mrs. Glendower Evans:[3]

I was just thinking what I would to do for past the long days jail: I was saying to myself: Do some work. But what? Write. A gentle motherly figure came to my mind and I rehear the voice: Why don't you write something now? It will be useful to you when you will be free. Just at that time I received your letter.

Thanks to you from the bottom of my heart for your confidence in my innocence; I am so. I did not spittel a drop of blood, or steal a cent in all my life. A little knowledge of the past; a sorrowful experience of the life itself had gave to me some ideas very different from those of many other umane beings. But I wish to convince my fellowmen that only with virtue and honesty is possible for us to find a little happiness in the world. I preached: I worked. I worked with all my faculties that the social wealth would belong to every umane creatures, so well as it was the fruit of the work of all. But this do not mean robbery for a insurrection.

The insurrection, the great movements of the soul, do not need dollars. It need love, light, spirit of sacrifice, ideas, conscience, instincts. It need more conscience, more hope and more goodness. And all this blessed things can be seeded, awoked, growed up in the heart of man in many ways, but not by robbery and murder for robbery.

I like you to know that I think of Italy, so speaking. From the universal family, turning to this humble son, I will say that, as far as my needs, wish and aspirations call, I do not need to become a bandit. I like the teaching of Tolstoi, Saint Francesco and Dante. I like the example of Cincinati and Garibaldi. The epicurean joi do not like to me. A little roof, a field, a few books and food is all what I need. I do not care for money, for leisure, for mondane ambition. And honest, even in this world of lambs and wolves I can have those things. My father has many field, houses, garden. He deal in wine and fruits and granaries. He wrote to me many times to come back

---

[3] Mrs. Ely Glendower Evans became interested in the prisoners during their trial.

home, and be a business man. Well, this supposed murderer had answered to him that my conscience do not permit to me to be a business man and I will gain my bread by work his field.

And more: The clearness of mind, the peace of the conscience, the determination and force of will, the intelligence, all, all what make the man feeling to be a part of the life, force and intelligence of the universe, will be brake by a crime. I know that, I see that, I tell that to everybody: Do not violate the law of nature, if you do not want to be a miserable. I remember: it was a night without moon, but starry. I sit alone in the darkness, I was sorry, very sorry. With the face in my hands I began to look at the stars. I feel that my soul want goes away from my body, and I have had to make an effort to keep it in my chest. So, I am the son of Nature, and I am so rich that I do not need any money. And for this they say I am a murderer and condemned me to death. Death? It is nothing. Abbominium is cruel thing.

Now you advise me to study. Yes, it would be a good thing. But I do not know enough this language to be able to make any study through it. I will like to read Longfellow's, Paine's, Franklin's and Jefferson's works, but I cannot. I would like to study mathematics, physics, history and science, but I have not a sufficient elementary school to begin such studies, especially the two first and I cannot study without work, hard physical work, sunshine and winds; free, blessing wind. There is no flame without the atmospheric gasses; and no light of genius in any soul without they communion with Mother Nature.

I hope to see you very soon; I will tell you more in the matter. I will write something, a meditation perhaps and name it: Waiting for the Hanger. I have lost the confidence in the justice of man. I mean in what is called so; not of course, of that sentiment which lay in the heart of man, and that no infernal force will be strong enough to soffocate it. Your assistance and the assistance of so many good men and women, had made my cross much more light. I will not forget it.

I beg your pardon for such a long letter, but I feel so reminiscent to you that hundred pages would not be sufficient to extern my sentiments and feelings. I am sure you will excuse me. Salve.

AND A POOR FISH PEDDLER : *Bartolomeo Vanzetti*

"little of abdom and much of heart"

1921. *Charlestown State Prison*

DEAR MRS. EVANS:

The "wake up" rings here in Charlestown at 7 A. M. but yesterday morning, the officer call me at six o'clock. "Go to put on your own clothes," he tell me with hurried way. I went and I found my old clothing horribly wrinkled. There were nobody at the work, at such hour, so, after a useless protest I was compelled to put them on as they were. Well, I was saying to myself, returning to the cell: There is, after all, something worse than this. Sure it was: On the table I found my breakfast, a cup of coffee, three slices of bread, two frankforts and mashed potatoes, all so cold as ice cream can be.

After such a breakfast, an official took me in the "Guard Room." The little chauffeur, an old officer, and the bravest one were waiting for me. I was chained with the last one, and all four left the room and went down to the street where the automobile was ready. Six or seven officers stood at the door, with their right hand near the back pocket, ready to protect me from any attack. One must be most ungrateful man of the world for not feeling quite reconoscent.

As the machine start I asked for tobacco. They stop at the nearest corner and the old officer went to buy some of it. A young policeman begin to speak with the remaining officers, he leaning himself in such a manner to put his head in the automobile. His eyes, dark and clear, look at me with an ill-concealed curiosity, and I perceive his wonder at my common harmless presence. Surely he had expected something different. Meanwhile I was looking at the people going up and down of the streets. I can tell which of them are employed and which are not by their way of walking.

The former went straight ahead as men who know where he want to go and when he must arrive. The second look around, above, and below, as a man who lost himself, and do not know what he has to do. Little farther I meet a little compatriot. He is a little fellow of the South, with yellow pale face dry by a copious dayly sweat, but his mustachs are well curled up. He is very petty, and it look like if he were the centre of the world. I cannot help but smile. I never see him before but I know where he go, what he thinks; his hopes. I knew him, as I know myself; probably better than myself. "Take that way; avoid civilization," the brave officer is now crying to the driver who obey silently. Surely enough this man hope that such high language is incomprehensible to me.

794

AND A POOR FISH PEDDLER : *Bartolomeo Vanzetti*

So we enter now into a Park the name of which I already forget, but the beauty of it, I will never forget anymore. If I were poet and know the metre, I would write a song of it in third rhyme. I am not a poet, but neither so profane to disturb such splendor with my poor ink. The concerned officer point to me a big brick building, saying, "It is the Fine Arts Museum." He point many other buildings saying that they are almost all a private schools. I was then regretting to have only a pair of eyes, able to look in one direction alone. I observe everything, the trees, the bushes, the grass, the rocks, and the brook along the way, on which I was raptured. The drops of dew look like pearls; the sky reflects himself in the waters of the brook, and let one think that it is bottomless. But beauty over all tell to me a wonderful history of one day, far away, a day when the waters in a gigantic and confounded waves, left this place suddenly.

I look now to those which pass at my side in automobiles. But what a difference between these men that I meet now, and those I met a little while ago, a little far away going to work, or walking round about; what a difference! The big buildings had now give the place to a more modest ones, which become more and more rare, until only a little, humble, odd, funny houses, rise here and there from the accidentated soil. O, funny, humble, old, little houses that I love; little house always big enough for the greatest loves, and most saint affections. Here I see two girls of the people going to work. They look like to be sisters. Their shoulders are more large than those of the girls I meet a little before, but little curved. On their pale faces are lines of sorrow and distress. There is sobberness and suffering in their big, deep, full eyes. Poor plebian girls, where are the roses of your springtime?

I found myself in front of Dedham Jail. We enter. A little ugly Napolitan barber has such a care and zeal of my looking, as if I am the Mayor of Naple.

They locked me at No. 61. Now the news of my arrival is known by all the human canaries of the place. The poor boys do their best to give me a glance, a word, a cheer up. Little after I was brought to the Court, protected by a numerous American Cossack, as if I and Nick were a Russian Czars.

At last we come back to Charlestown, and I have had the opportunity to look at the sky and see the stars, as in the old days at home. The workers were then coming back home. Still in their confused forms I can see the "little of abdom and much of heart" as Gori sang. One of them appear to be a Latin, strong and noble. This is one of those who will win the battle that the citizens had lost, I say to myself.

AND A POOR FISH PEDDLER : *Bartolomeo Vanzetti*

Few minutes after we stop in front of the Prison, and little after I found myself carefully closed in my room, where a supper, something like tea and coffee, boiled beef and mashed potatoes with few slices of bread, wait for me, all as cold as ice cream can be.

"if tragedy is compelled to us"

February 27, 1924. Charlestown Prison

DEAR COMRADE BLACKWELL: [4]

Yours of the 23rd has reached me. You are right. Neither do I expect any good from that letter to the judge. I have never expected, nor do I expect anything from him, other than some ten thousand volts divided in few times; some meters of cheap board and 4x7x8 feet hole in the ground.

No matter how much sympathy I try to bestow upon him, or with how much understanding I try to judge his actions; I only and alone can see him a self-conceited narrow-minded little tyrant, believing himself to be just, and believing his utterly unjust and unnecessary social office to be a necessity and a good. He is a bigot, and therefore, cruel. At the time of our arrest and trials, his peers were seeing red all around, and he saw red more than his peers.

He was ready to kill us even before the trials, for he deadly hates the subversive, and he believed to have become judge of the State Supreme Court by eliminating us via Law. For he knows that the servants of Capital were always remunerated by the Bosses for a crusifixion of some rebel or lover.

I do not know if his conduct during the trial was determined by his preconceptions, hate and ignorance, or if he consciously murdered us by details of bad faith, double playing, simulation, etc. I know that he did it. I know that even now he does not want to give us another trial though he could not deny it. And this is why he delays so much to give the answer. . . .

And if I am wrong, if according to his own standard, he is fair; if he wishes to be just, ('til now he is very unjust) then he could be hurt by my letter, but also enlightened. And if he would not forgive the crude defence of a man extremely wronged, then, not even a sparrow would I submit to him as arbiter.

An almost centenial struggle against every form of exploitation, oppression and fraud, taught us that "the wolf eats him who makes himself a sheep."

---

[4] Miss Alice Stone Blackwell.

I am not sure, but I believe, that there are no pamphlets in Italian language, which treat with detail the case. This is the second reason of my letter and the 3rd reason is, my wish to say what no one else can say—silence would be cowardness—and treat the case accordingly to my own criterions. This may hurt me, but will help the Cause. Otherwise, if it means a life sentence, I prefer to be burnt away once and for all, and I also know that those in height, upon the back and the heads of the slaves, are against me. . . .

There is no spirit of sacrifice in this deed. I simply realize to be in merciless hands, and do my utmost to say to my enemy that he is wrong. In a way that helps the cause. The great one, not the small. My only hope remains in the solidariety of friends and comrades and of the workers. After having spent $200,000, we are still at the beginning. The work of the lawyers are useless before the law.

It has helped only because they brought the fact to the conscience and consciousness of the People. That is why Nick and I were not yet roasted. Authority, Power, and Privilege would not last a day upon the face of the earth, were it not because those who possess them, and those who prostitute their arms to their defence do suppress, repress, mercilessly and inescapable every efforts of liberations of each and all the rebels.

I abhor useless violence. I would my blood to prevent the sheading of blood, but neither the abyss nor the earth, nor the heavens, have a law which condemns the self-defense. Not every woman has sacrificed to bring forth one more rufian, idiot, or coward to the world. There are yet some men. And if tragedy is compelled to us, who knows; who knows if to speak now is not my duty?

The champion of life and of the liberty should not yield before the death. The struggle for the liberty, between the oppressor and the oppressed, shall continue beyond the life, beyond the graves. I know what they have done and are doing to me and to thousands of others, rebels and lovers. And I know that they are and will always be ready to do against us. I know the millions of youth that they slandered, the virgins that they have torn in the breast; the millions of wives that they have widowed; the millions of bastards that they let to miasma of the gutter, or grown to the fratricide. I know the old fathers and mothers whom they killed by breaking their hearts; and all the children that they starved and are starving to death; and the hospitals and the crazy-houses filled of their victims, and the little criminals, victims, irresponsible and semi-compelled to crime that they mercilessly

executed or entombed alive. They have never had pity for our children, our women, our dear, poor old fathers and mothers—and they never will have it.

The sorrow of their victims torture me in blood and spirit. As for me, I would forgive them, but I could not, for I would be a traitor of the race. Until not a man will be exploited or oppressed by another man, we will never bend the banner of freedom.

Are they not ready to do with other comrades what they are doing to us? Are they not more willing than ever to squeeze out the worker's blood for more gold? Are they not preparing a greater war?˙

I will ask for revenge—I will tell that I will die gladly by the hands of the. hanger after having known to have been vindicated. I mean "eye for an eye, ear for an ear," and even more, since to win it is necessary that 100 enemies fall to each of us.

The only vengence which could placate me is the realization of freedom, the great deliverance which would beneficiate all my friends as well as all my enemies: All. But till that, the struggle goes on, til we are breath to breath with the enemy fighting with short arms, till then, to fight is our duty, our right, our necessity. For, one of the two. Either we must go on and win, or we must ask for an armistice. And who will grant it to us? Since the enemy has no scruples nor pity, to ask pity of him is to encourage him to slander our fellows, to try to grant to him the immunity for his crimes against us; it would be as a matricide.

The more I live, the more I suffer, the more I learn, the more I am inclined to forgive, to be generous, and that the violence as such does not resolve the problem of life. And the more I love and learn that "the right of all to violence does not go together with the liberty, but that it begins when the liberty ends." The slave has the right and duty to arise against his master. My supreme aim, that of the Anarchist is, "the complete elimination of violence from the rapports (relations)."

To be possible, we must have freedom and justice. Now we have the opposite of them, because through errors and consequent aberations, men have risen as tyrants, deceiters and exploiters of other men, believing to gain their personal, familiar and cast welfare by such deed. Through both tyranny and servitude, we have lost our capacity of liberty and we are making life evermore miserable, operating our own antedistruction.

Since "only the liberty, or the struggle for liberty, may be school of liberty" and since mine is but self and racial defence, why should not I use the truth to defend myself? It is supremely sweet to me—my consciousness of

superiority, of righteousness, to know that I can judge and that the future shall bow to me, the doomed, and curse my judges.

Well, I have said many things which I sincerely believe to be so. But there are surely some mistake! Who possesses the absolute, or even the absolute-relative truth? So your point of view may be right, and I also realized that you spoke exclusively for my own good.

Wisdom is not only comprehension, but also many other faculties together; among which discrimination and sense of measure are prominent. I will try to be wise ! ! ! ! ! ! I will think it over and over again. . . .

Altogether, sometime, in my solitude, I think that the world is gradually forgetting this son of it, entombed alive. But, I will bear my cross. There are those who will never forget me. . . .

P.S. I began to study arithmetic, and I find that my mind works in the same way. A Mathematic mind then? I asked it since I wonder that during 36 years no one else had perceived it, and the one who did it, fear to [do] me wrong.

"Please let me speak of Italy"

September 15, 1924. Charlestown Prison

Dear Comrade Blackwell:

. . . I am tired, tired, tired: I ask if to live like now, for love of life, is not, rather than wisdom or heroism, mere cowardness. And in my conscience, has riped the moral sanction to die and to kill for freedom. I am ready, and I may be mistaken, but most probably I will not die as a rabbit or a worm.

My heart is the tabernacle in which my mother, and she was brave, lives. If a good hour will strike me, I will tell you of her. Not now, it is impossible now.

Italy is weeping tears of blood, bleeding her best blood. The fascista's crimes, especially their crime against Matteotti alive and Matteotti dead, have precipitated the events—the historical Nemesis. . . .

Please let me speak of Italy of which destiny I may be more interested than my own. . . . Grossly speaking, Italy is split in two parts: fascismo and anti-fascismo. But the situation, the reality is far more complicated than it appears.

The "opposition" is composed of the Liberals, Democratic, Demo-socialist, the three differing Socialist Parties, the Republican, the Communist and the Anarchist, and the Popular (Catholic party).

799

AND A POOR FISH PEDDLER : *Bartolomeo Vanzetti*

The Fascismo has on his side the Pope, the King, the financier, industrial and Rural Capitalism.

Now, the liberals who have helped the formation of the fascism are swinging. The Democrats are steadily against the fascismo; the republicans are also swinging, and the Anarchist are firm; but the reformist are ready to betray again if Mussolini would be so gentlemanly to cut with them the power-pie.

But there is more and worse: the socialist are feared by the liberals, the democrats and the republican, while they fear the communist who fear them and the liberal, the democrat, and the anarchist. And the Anarchist distrust all the others.

Let us look at the other side: The king dislikes the pope, and the pope, the king. But a common danger makes them allied. The king who has the army and officialdom faithful to him, dislikes the fascismo and Mussolini, but he must stick with them or end in the Rome's main sewer. Mussolini and the most intelligent head bandits would like to get peace, and ask the venal adversary to partake of the Power's pie—but the dreadful condition of the people, the daily violence of the fascisti-thugs do not consent any normalization, and Mussolini is practically black-mailed and slave of the Capitalists who he has black-mailed and enslaved, and of the scum of his own band, to which he must obey or be stabbed. That Mussolini shall be killed is fatal, but most probably killed by his friends than by his enemy. Historical nemesis cynical as he deserves.

What about the Italian People; the great masses in the fields, the navy, the shops and the studios?

The lower are the best. The unpolitical masses who make life possible, are naturally well gifted, relatively good, purely good in all that survives in them of primordial. But they are dwarfed, brutalized, corrupted, cowardized by thousands of years of slavery, servilism, bestial toiling, sordity, poverty, unspeakable suffering, ignorance, and worse of all, by honors. But in spite of all this shame, horror and disgrace, they are the only ones who look to the stars and not the mud. Nor are they guilty. Guilty is the church, the monarchy, the capitalism, the militarism, the Burocrasy, and the yellow, pink, red, scarlet bad shepherds, demagogues and politician.

The political proletariat is very heterogeneous: Mazzinian, demo-social, socialist, communist and anarchist.

Mazzinian and anarchist are the best blood, and they are surely superior to the gray masses—unconscious and idealess—but they are few. The others

have been too domesticated by their leaders—"plenty of eat, little of work," belly of mine become a hub; safety first, gradual conquest, historical fatalism, and fascista blackjack over all.

Besides that they look for power, are much servilized and *"imborghesiti."* Yet, they have fought heroical battles, and would be capable of great acts, were the worms so good to eat the leaders alive. Gigi Damiani has raffaelistically painted these truths in his *The Problem of Liberty*.

Thus Italy's condition is equivocal, comic, but over all, tragic. And no worthy son of a good mother can look at it without sorrow, aggravation and anguish. There is death and even worse than death, all round. The task is titanic, the mean men are gnomes and dwarfed.

How will be the future? It will be tears of blood, crimes, degeneration, diseases, insanity and death—or the life and its liberation reached through a terrific lavacrus of blood, through aspiration, heroic sacrifice, and fire. This is the truth. Hard even to look upon.

Republicans, democrats and socialists have a program. The re-establishment of the constitutional grants: freedom of press, speech, and association; annultation of the past election and new election; the abolition of the fascista Militia.

The communists are for "the power to themselves," the name don't matter. And they are playing Don Quixottes.

You will surely admit that we, poor, hated, dispised, wronged, exacrated anarchist have a hard job to get a straight way (straight to our criterion) among such an entanglement.

People in general are not yet capable of liberty, others are contrary to it, so that it would be impossible to establish general anarchist order after the fascismo vanquishment. On the other hand there are places whose population is almost totally anarchist. Also the first necessity is to crush the fascismo now, and it is a work that requires the cooperation of all the parties contrary to the fascismo.

[Unfinished]

"the right of love"

December, 1924. Charlestown Prison

DEAR MRS. EVANS:

For the water in liquid state, freedom is, to flow from a relative up to a relative down; or vice versa when the water is in vapor state. For the fire,

freedom is, to expand and to arise. In short, freedom is, for each and all the things of the universe, *to follows their natural tendencies*—and to fulfill their own virtues, qualities and capacities.

This,—and not at all an abstraction, nor an abstract right which enable someone to say of a man, dead for want of food, that he has not die of starvation, but for not having exercised his right and his freedom to eat—is my idea of liberty.

Please, permit me to prove you the trueness of this true conception of freedom by applying it to Nick and myself. Am I without a lover? Yes, but I would like to have a lover. Have I not, by nature, the instinct, the faculties and, therefore, the right of love? Of course yes, but it would be better if not, for having them but not the freedom to realize them, it all become an excruciable laughing stock.

Has Nick a wife? Yes, and a good one; but not being free, he must either thinks that she is consoling herself with somebody else, or that she is suffering the unspeakable agony of a loving woman compelled to mourn a living lover.

Have I no children? Well—I would like to have or to generate some children. Have Nick some children—yes, and what his heart experiences when he thinks of them—is a thing known by him alone.

O the blessing green of the wilderness and of the open land—O the blue vastness of the oceans—the fragrances of the flowers and the sweetness of the fruits—The sky reflecting lakes—the singing torrents—the telling brooks—O the valleys, the hills—the awful Alps! O the mistic dawn—the roses of the aurora, the glory of the moon—O the sunset—the twilight—O the supreme extasies and mystery of the starry night, heavenly creature of the eternity.

Yes, Yes, all this is real actuallity but not to us, not to us chained—and just and simply because we, being chained, have not the freedom to use our natural faculty of locomotion to carry us from our cells to the open horizons —under the sun at daytime—under the visible stars at night.

AND A POOR FISH PEDDLER : *Bartolomeo Vanzetti*

"the reasons why I tell you, young Comrade"

July 23, 1927. Charlestown Prison

DEAR LITTLE COMRADE [LI PEI KAN]: [5]

Your letter dated July 11th was given to me a few days ago, and it gives me joy each time I read it. I will not try to find words with which to thank you for your little picture you sent me. Youth is the hope of mankind, and my heart exults when I look at your photograph and say to myself "Lo! one of those who will pluck and uphold, highly, the flag of freedom, the flag of our supremely beautiful anarchy, which is now slowly falling down from our weakening hands,"—and a good one, as for that. You need to live for many others years, and hard ones, before to realize and understand what comfort and joy such a thought is to your old and dying Bartolo.

I have read of that—say, incident, and I thought it happened to you. It is less bad if it happened to an elderly one, because the elders are more worried and hardened by the vicissitude and adversities of life, so that they can bear better the hard blows of fate, while the young ones are more tender, and could be bent and split by black adversities. You will surely resist to all, and separate all, I am sure of it.

In regards to what you said of our Ideal in your letter, I fundamentally agree with all of it. My words on this subject, of my antecedent letter, were principally intended to fortify your spirit to better face the tremendous struggle for freedom and prevent future delusions by weakening fatalism and fortify voluntarism in you, as I do with all our young ones and neophites.

Perhaps you know Proudhon better than I, but if not, I advise you to study him. Read his *Peace and War*. I think he approached truth in many subjects nearer than other more recent great ones.

To my understanding, we are actually certainly dragged, with the rest of mankind, toward tyranny and darkness. Where will we land?

The relatively known history testifies, it is true, that mankind has continuously progressed, slowly, insteadily, with advances and retrocessions, yet, steadily progressed.

But the dead civilizations tell their tale as well and what came and passed before the dawn of our historical knowledge, we cannot know. History, like

---

[5] Li Pei Kan of Shanghai, China, a student at the Collège de Château-Thierry, Aisne, France, during the last years of the Sacco-Vanzetti case. He wrote several pamphlets on the case in Chinese

evolution, as we know of it now, fails far from explaining the request of a deep thinker. Then, what will follow to this age of reversion and tyranny? A false democracy again, which in its turn would inevitably yield to another tide of tyranny? As it is happening from thousands of years?

Anarchy, the anarchists alone, we only can break these deadly circles and set life in such a way that by a natural synchronism, produced by the very nature of the things which create the new order, more exactly, which constitute the new order, history will be streamed toward the infinite sea of freedom, instead to turn in the above said dead, close circle, as, it seems, it did 'til now.

It is a titanic task—but humanly possible, and if we know, we will create the happy kingdom of Freedom when the traviated, misled tralignated working class, and people of all classes will, most instinctively, join us for the greatest emancipation of the history. But even then we will have to be at the brightness of our task, or else, only a new tyranny will be substitute to the present one as corollary of the immense holocaust.

These are the reasons why I tell you, young Comrade, heavy and hard words, just as your juvenile ardor, enthusiasm and faith bliss me, I hope my old experience will complete and fortify you. . . .

And now, dear Li, I embrace you with brotherly and glad heart.

GIVE US THIS DAY OUR DAILY BREAD:

Odell Waller

FROM SUNUP UNTIL SUNDOWN

IN 1940 an obscure Negro sharecropper was sentenced to death by a white jury for killing his landlord in a quarrel over fifty sacks of wheat. The sharecropper pleaded self-defense. The conviction was based on the testimony of one eyewitness, a Negro youth of eighteen who lived in the landlord's household. Himself a tenant and mortgage-ridden farmer, the landlord had evicted the sharecropper's family from their land shortly before the fatal shooting. He had also confiscated their share of the wheat crop at threshing time. A curious sequel to the shooting was that the sons of the landlord voluntarily returned the fifty sacks of wheat to the sharecropper's wife. The jurors in the trial were citizens of Virginia who, unlike the accused, paid poll taxes—a circumstance to which the defense pointed as a violation of the constitutional right of trial by a "jury of peers." For killing a Negro, such a poll tax paying jury, serving under the same judge, had previously acquitted another Virginian, whose skin was white, in deliberations which took exactly fifteen minutes.

This provincial country shooting came to symbolize on a national scale the issues of the sharecropper system and of Negro rights. "Though Waller himself was a slayer," wrote Thomas Sancton, "in many a Negro consciousness he became the symbol of Negro toil in the white man's fields, of Negro fate in the white man's courts, of every black body which has swung at the end of a rope from barn or bridge."

The life story of the obscure sharecropper was published by the defense. With his mother and wife he had worked for his landlord under a system of shares. For every four sacks of wheat which the family harvested, three went into the landlord's barn. Receiving half the tobacco crop on his own small patch, the sharecropper paid back with the labor of his family on the landlord's own tobacco crop, "but whenever it came to my crop, wouldn't be nobody helping but jes' me and mine." The wheat went into their daily bread, and the tobacco brought so little money that the hog would be killed in the first cold weather of the year. The tobacco depression cut down the sharecropper's land to two acres and soon eliminated the cash crop. The sharecropper proposed to his landlord a more equitable scheme of "sharing,"

but "he wanted to get me taxed into working the whole crop for him, I was jes' getting into debt everywhere. I had to quit because I diten has crop enough to make a living." He hired himself out to another employer after he had planted the wheat. Worried by his own act of independence, he left to his landlord the substitute labor of a cousin, his mother's service as domestic, and the use of his binder for the coming wheat harvest. In his absence the landlord came to owe the sharecropper's mother a wage debt of $7.50. She demanded the accumulated sum as a condition for working in the tobacco fields. Provoked by this further self-assertion, the landlord had this family evicted from their home and land. But he continued to use their labor and binder on the wheat crop, from which they still hoped to save their share. These circumstances the sharecropper discovered on returning from his other employment to the scene of the fatal conflict. "I was not trying to kill I was aiming to keep him from killing me," he said. The man whom the sharecropper killed had taught Sunday School in his church and was regarded in the white community as one who all his life had never spared himself from farm labor. In the tobacco depression he had sunk into tenancy, bitterness, and violence. "It does not seem to me strange," wrote Jonathan Daniels, "to suppose that the white man was trying to cheat the Negro. It does not seem to me difficult to believe that the young Negro went to demand his rights more in terror than in murderousness. My observation is that more scared men kill than brutal ones."

On the fate that made him a murderer, the sharecropper added his own opinion to that of his judges, his jury, and his friends. An illiterate man, he struggled to find the words and the principle that could explain why "I worked hard from sunup until sundown trying to make a living for my family and it ended in death for me."

FROM SUNUP UNTIL SUNDOWN[1]

I REALIZE I haven't lived so upright in the past with the laws of the Good Lord and with the laws of the land. As my time comes near each second means I am one nearer my grave. I have asked God to forgive me and I feel that he has. One thing you can't make a young person out of an old one and you can't make an old person out of a young one. It takes time and exprnce

---

[1] *Odell Waller's Dying Statement,* written the day before his execution and handed to Edmund M. Preston, Richmond, Virginia, associate of John F. Finerty as volunteer counsel for the Workers Defense League in the Odell Waller case.

[experience]. All you people take this under consideration. Have you ever thought about some people are allowed a chance over and over again then there are others are allowed little chance [—] some no chance at all. When a fellow accident [accidentally] falls dont get one [on] him with both feet [—] help him up, and when he is see another ditch he will walk around it an advise others of the place so they can seen it. If you mash him down he cant advise others of the danger. This is Odell Waller speaking & axident [accident] fell an some good people tried to help me.

Others did everything they could against me so the governor & the coats [courts] dont no [know] the true facts. First I will say dont work for a man two [too] poor to pay you. He will steel [steal] and take from you. In my case I worked hard from sunup until sundown trying to make a living for my family an it ended up to mean death for me. When the wheat was threshed I was in Maryland working 7 days a week 10 to 12 hours per day sending money home to pay for harvesting & thrashing the wheat and had told mother to have Robert to bring my share from the machine when it was threshed. Robert hope [helped] measure the wheat an my share was 52 bushels. His wagon was there to move my share. Mr. Davis was too poor to see me have the wheat and wouldn't let Robert cary [carry] to mothers house [—] took it and locked it in his store house. I diten [did not] owe him one penny. I should have gave him the wheat if I had to beg for bread and eat out of other people garbage cans. Now going after the wheat I wasn't thinking of shoting [shooting] Mr. Davis. When I left home I put the gun in the truck and the pistol in my parket [pocket] planing [planning] on gitting out of the truck up at the road coming around the edge of the woods seeing a rabbit or some thing. I told that in cort [court].

Here is how Thomas was at Davis. His father an law [father-in-law] had cut Curtis Williams and was in jail. Curtis lived on the next farm working with a farmer. Thomas said he was going to go over an see Curtis about going to the trial that morning and I will be back an help load the wheat. He got off and went down cross the field to Curtis. I spoke to Mr. Davis & Henry a Negro staying with Davis. They spoke. I told Mr. Davis I come after my share of the wheat. Henry said you cant carry that wheat all on that truck. I said I can make two trips then. Davis spoke you ant [ain't] going to carry that wheat away from here. I told him I diten [did not] see why. I diten owe him any thing. When I said that Davis flue hot [got mad] and began to cursh [curse] about the wheat. Naturly [naturally] I got angry and from one word to another. Davis thrut [thrust] his hand in his pocket in an expct [expect] to draw a gun. If he diten have one he was bluffing. He

frightened me. I pulled a gun an begin shoting [shooting] not intending to kill him. I was frightened. I dont noe [know] what become of Henry. I dont no how many times I shot. I thue [threw] the pistol away. I no Davis had a pistol for I have seen it in his parket [pocket]. He carried it for his son Edgar. They always had trouble and Davis tried to make Edgar leave so he could take his tobacco crop in 39 [1939]. Edgar wouldnt leave. He said I fight dady [daddy] every day before he take my crop. Edgar said after this year he can have the farm so Edgar and Frank Davis both left in 40 [1940]. Now here it is a Negro have shot a white man. Thomas Younger was with me. Got off the truck going over to Curtis Williams. Naturly the law got them. They scared like I would have been or any other Negro is liable to say any thing. Also Henry staying there with Davis so they lied like a dog. Thomas Young & Curtis told I said I was going to kill Mr. Davis. I never told nether one that. Henry eating from Mr. Davis table he had better tell a lie on me for Mr. Davis if he new [knew] what was best. Even the law questioned Archard Waller Birk Fitzearlds the boy driving the truck. They diten lie. The law come an got my mother and wife an carried them to Chatham. Kept them up there in the night it wouldnt have surprised me if they hadnt told a lie on me threw [through] fear of the law. Thank God they diten tell a lie.

The Good Book says a lie is the worst thing a person can tell so I no lies was told on me. They no they lied and God no they lied so in the great day God will say you fellows lied on Odell Waller so I appreciate every effert [effort] the people put forth to try to save me. It is a none [known] fact man is the ruler over earth but God is the ruler of all. Man can say Odell you must die at a certen [certain] time then God can call man an say you must die.

Refering to my carictor [character] when I started to violate the laws of the land I was farming working part time day an night trying to make something. During the year I bought a car. One time the end of the year I diten have any thing to pay for it with the man was going to take it back. I wanted to keep the can I diten believe in robin [robbing] and steeling so I bought 2 gallons of whiskey from a fellow & gave him $5.00 for it. I sold that at 50 or 60¢ per pint took that money and bought some more. When I sold that I made a little payment on the car. I kept on bying an selling paying on cars. That got me that rep [reputation]. As the avage [average] boy do I wanted to ride fast. I was pulled my permit took. I waited the time out and went to the motor vehicle man for another permit. He told me I would

have to put up a $10,000 bond before I could get another permit. Where were I going to git the money Rob a Bank. I wasnt thinking of nothing like that so I drove some without a permit. I was caught for that. One Sunday I put a razor in my parket [pocket] to carry it to a friends house to have it sharpened. I got on a car with some more boys and we went by to see a boy had been in a fight that Saturday night. Me an some more boys was out there in the yard cutting some fire wood for the sick man during the time Mr. Hubard Bailey & another officer drove up to the house with the boy who cut the sick boy. When Mr. Baley got out of the car I thought about the razor I had in my parket. It was an old car sitting at the wood pile. I droped [dropped] the razor in it. The other officer saw me. He said get that gun that fellow put in the car. I rached over an grabed the razor out of the car an out run Mr. Baley. Several weeks after that I was at Chatham to a tent shoe [show]. Mr. Baley had told the town law when they caught me up there to lock me up so they did. When I was runing across the field I passed a briar patch and thrue the razor in it. Mr. Baley couldn't catch me an he went back an got the razor. My father was at the trial and told them it was his razor an why I had it. They gave it back to father all right. When I was tried Mr. Joseph Whitehead commonwealth attorney called Mr. Bailey county officer to testifie against me. This is the last man should lie. Here is what he said Odell Waller was a bootlegger that was true. Odell been caught reckless driving an after his permit had been taken caught carry a razor he is a dangous boy. The judge said what about him dangerous. With the best respects to Mr. Baley here is where he lied. Odell threten him with gravels from my feet running. All of that to make it hard on me all I could do was set there an take it. You take big people as the president governors judge their children will never have to suffer. They has plenty money. Born in a mention (mansion) nothing to never wory about. I am glad some people ar that luck.

The penitentiary all over the United States are full of people ho [who] was pore tried to work and have something couldnt dos [do] that maid them steel an rob. Look at that fellow here he wanted a bicycle his people was to pore to buy him one. To get a bicycle he kills a man wife an dauter to get the money. Look at the Lees bug [Leesburg] case those fellows killed that lawyer an took his car. They were looking for money they were. While they are in prison for life thats what happens to the poor people. I wont say any more.

[signed] ODELL WALLER

THE TERRIBLE MEEK:

Mohandas K. Gandhi

M*AHA* means great, and *atma* soul. Mahatma is The Great Soul and, according to Tagore, the liberated ego which rediscovers itself in all other souls. Long before Mahatma Gandhi had liberated his ego, he landed in England in a white flannel suit, under a self-imposed oath to live as a celibate and never touch wine or meat. But he came to the realization that he had "wasted a lot of time and money trying to become an Englishman." He grew into the proportions of a saint and troubled the imagination and conscience of Christians between two world wars. He never learned the art of rendering unto Caesar the things which are Caesar's. He has drawn his physical nourishment from goat's milk; his political weapons from Tolstoy and Thoreau; his creed from the *Gita* and the *Sermon on the Mount*—and from the works of an Englishman, John Ruskin.

When Gandhi assumed leadership of the Indian nationalist movement in 1918 he revolutionized the conventions of rebellion with a handful of bootleg salt, a spinning wheel, and a loin cloth. His public weapon was *satyagraha,* non-violent civil disobedience; his private weapon, fasting. The Amritsar massacre, which resulted from his launching the first all-national demonstration of non-violence, ended with his own penitential fast because he was convinced that he had committed a "Himalayan Blunder." Sitting *dharna* across the threshold of a reluctant opponent is an antique ritual in India. Whether he fasted to punish himself, or to purify the conscience of Imperial Government, or only to force an Indian Prince to abide by his word, Gandhi has doggedly sat *dharna* on the threshold of international politics through the Second World War.

This little saint who laughs like a child and believes in "cow protection" (a cow is "a poem of pity") has managed to praise everything which our West has concluded is an evil and worthy of social reform: Poverty and Suffering and Chastity. The spiritual dictator of the Hindus is a stern moralist who has dispossessed the lovely old turbans of his followers with the ugly Gandhi cap. He can transform a rude political jail, or even the palace of the Agha Khan at Poona, into a monastery of piety. "The religious value of jail discipline," he wrote to his disciple C. F. Andrews, "is enhanced by renounc-

ing privileges. . . . While I read the *Gita* my thoughts fly far away. But when I turn to the spinning wheel . . . my attention is directed on a single point." This attention directed on a single point is the secret of the saint and politician.

In public confession, Gandhi has not spared himself less than St. Augustine or Rousseau or Tolstoy; during a long imprisonment between 1922 and 1924 he dictated all his sins with startling frankness in *The Story of My Experiments with Truth*. The lashes of Gandhi the saint are laid hard on the back of Gandhi the sinner. In his translations for English friends from Sanskrit scriptures, during his later imprisonment in Yeravda Jail, Gandhi asks of God: "Who is there on earth amongst men/ So crooked-hearted/ So evil, gross and treacherous as I?" And in another verse: "Forgive all secret sins of thought/ All sins worked forth in deed, by hands or feet/ All sins of speech/ All sins of eyes, or ears:/ And in my flesh this day/ Thy will be done." But always the sinner in Gandhi contributes to the saint the pride of conviction that "in experiments of faith there are no failures."

SCHOOL DAYS

AMONGST my few friends at the high school I had, at different times, two who might be called intimate. One of these friendships did not last long, though I never forsook my friend. He gave me up, because I made friends with the other. This latter friendship I regard as a tragedy in my life. It lasted a long time and I began it in the spirit of a reformer. This companion was originally my elder brother's friend. They were classmates together. I knew his weaknesses, but I regarded him as a faithful friend. My mother, my eldest brother, and my wife warned me that I was in bad company. I was too proud a husband to heed my wife's warning. But I did not dare at first to go against the opinion of my mother and my eldest brother. Nevertheless I pleaded with them, saying, "I know he has the weaknesses you attribute to him, but you do not know his virtues. He cannot lead me astray, because my association with him is meant to lead him right. For I am sure if he mends his ways, he will be a splendid man. I beg you not to be anxious on my account."

I do not think this satisfied them, but they accepted my explanation and let me go my way. Since then, I have seen that I had calculated wrongly. One who tries to reform another cannot afford to have close intimacy with

him during the process. True friendship is an identity of souls rarely to be found in this world. Only between like natures can friendship be altogether worthy and enduring. Friends react on one another. Hence, in friendship, there is very little scope for the reformation of a friend. I am of opinion that all exclusive intimacies are to be avoided; for man far more readily takes in vice than virtue. And he who would be friends with God must remain alone, or make the whole world his friend. I may be wrong, but my effort to cultivate an intimate friendship proved a failure.

A wave of "reform" in other directions was sweeping over Rajkot at the time when I first came across this friend. He told me that many of our teachers were secretly taking meat and wine. He also named many well known people of Rajkot as belonging to the same company. There were also some high school boys among them. When I heard this, I was painfully surprised and asked my friend the reason. He explained it to me in this way. "We are a weak people," he said, "because we do not eat meat. The English are able to rule over us, because they are meat-eaters. You know how hardy I am, and a great runner, too. It is because I am a meat-eater. Meat-eaters do not have boils or tumours; and even if they sometimes happen to have any, they heal quickly. Our teachers and other distinguished people who eat meat are no fools. They know its virtues. You should do likewise. There is nothing like trying. Try and see what strength it gives."

All these pleas on behalf of meat-eating were not advanced at a single sitting. They were the substance of a long and elaborate argument which my friend was trying to impress upon me from time to time. My elder brother had already fallen. He therefore supported him. I certainly looked feeble-bodied by the side of my brother and this friend. Both of them were hardier, stronger, and more daring than I was. This friend's exploits cast a spell over me. He could run long distances with extraordinary speed and excelled in high and long jumping. He could put up with any amount of corporal punishment. He would often display his exploits to me; and as one is always dazzled when he sees in others the qualities that he lacks himself, I was also dazzled by my friend's exploits. This was accompanied by a strong desire to be like him. I could hardly jump or run. Why should not I also be as strong as he?

Again I was a coward. I used to be haunted by the fear of thieves, ghosts, and serpents. I did not dare to stir out of doors at night. Darkness was a terror to me. It was almost impossible for me to sleep in the dark, since I would imagine ghosts coming from one direction, thieves from another, and

serpents from a third. I could not therefore bear to sleep without a light in the room. How could I disclose my fears to my wife sleeping by my side, now at the threshold of youth? I knew that she had more courage than I, and this made me ashamed of myself. She knew no fear of serpents and ghosts. She could go out anywhere in the dark. My friend knew all these weaknesses of mine. He would tell me that he could hold in his hand live serpents, could defy thieves and did not believe in ghosts. And all this was, of course, the result of eating meat.

A doggerel of Narmad's was in vogue amongst us schoolboys as follows:

> Behold the mighty Englishman;
> He rules the Indian small,
> Because being a meat-eater
> He is five cubits tall.

All this had its due effect upon me, and I was at last defeated. It began to grow on me that meat-eating was good; that it would make me strong and daring; that if the whole country took to it the English could be overcome.

A day was thereupon fixed for beginning the experiment. It had to be conducted in secret. The Gandhis were Vaishnavas. My parents were particularly staunch in their faith. The family had even its own temples. Jainism [1] was strong in Gujarat, and its influence was felt everywhere and on all occasions. The opposition to and abhorrence of meat-eating that existed in Gujarat among the Jains and Vaishnavas was to be seen nowhere else either in India or outside India in such strength. These were the religious traditions in which I was born, and I was extremely devoted to my parents. The moment that they would come to know of my having eaten meat they would be shocked to death. Moreover, my love of truth made me especially reluctant. It is not possible for me to say that I did not know that I should have to deceive my parents if I began eating meat. But my mind was bent on "reform." It was not a question of pleasing the palate. There was no thought in my mind that meat had a particularly good relish. It was simply that I wished to be strong and daring and desired my countrymen also to be the same, so that we might be able to defeat the English and make India

---

[1] The Jain religion was established in India during the same epoch as the Buddhist religion. One of its chief tenets is the strict abstention from taking the life of any living creature. It was owing partly to the influence of the Jain faith that the doctrine of Ahimsa obtained such a hold of the religious consciousness of India. In western India Vaishnavas sometimes retain, along with their own faith, the Jain philosophy of life. This was the practice in the Gandhi family.

813

free. The word "Swaraj" (self-government) I had not yet heard. But I knew what freedom meant. The frenzy of "reform" blinded me. And having ensured secrecy, I persuaded myself that mere hiding the deed from my parents was no departure from truth.

So the day came. It is difficult fully to describe my condition. There was, on the one hand, the zeal for "reform" together with the novelty of making a momentous departure in life. There was on the other hand the shame of hiding like a thief in order to do this very thing. Which of the two swayed me most it would be impossible to say. We went in search of a lonely spot by the river, and there I saw meat for the first time in my life. We had also bread baked in English fashion. Neither gave me any relish. The goat's meat was as tough as leather and I simply could not eat it. Indeed, I became so sick that I had to leave off in disgust.

Afterwards I passed a very bad night. A horrible nightmare haunted me. Every time I dropped off to sleep, it would seem as though a live goat were bleating inside me; and I would jump up full of remorse. But then I would remind myself that what I had done was a duty, and so I would become more cheerful. My friend was not one to give in easily. He now began to cook various delicacies along with the meat and dress them neatly. And for our place of dining, no longer the secluded spot on the river was chosen, but a State house, with its dining hall and tables and chairs, about which my friend had made arrangements in collusion with the chief cook there. This bait had its effect. I got over my dislike for English bread; forswore my compassion for the goats, and became a relisher of meat dishes, if not of meat itself. This went on for about a year. But not more than half a dozen of such dinners were enjoyed in all; because the State house was not available every day, and there was the difficulty about preparing frequently expensive savoury meat dishes. I had no money to pay for this "reform." My friend had therefore always to find the wherewithal and I had no knowledge from whence he found it. But find it he did, because he was bent on turning me into a meat-eater. But even his means must have been limited, and hence these dinners had necessarily to be few and far between.

Whenever I had occasion to indulge in these surreptitious meals, dinner at home was out of the question. My mother would naturally ask me to come and take my food and want to know the reason why I did not wish to eat. "I have no appetite to-day," I would say, "there is something wrong with my digestion." It was not without compunction that I devised these pretexts. I knew I was lying, and lying to my mother. Also I was aware that if

my mother and father came to hear of my having become a meat-eater, they would be shocked beyond words. This knowledge was gnawing at my heart. Therefore I said to myself: "Though it is essential to eat meat, and also to take up food 'reform,' yet deceiving and lying to one's father and mother are worse than abstinence from meat. In my parents' lifetime, therefore, such things must be out of the question. When my parents have passed away and I have found my freedom, then I will eat meat openly. But until that moment arrives I will abstain from it."

This decision I communicated to my friend, and I have never since gone back upon it. My parents never knew what an offence two of their sons had committed. Thus meat was abjured by me at last out of the purity of my desire not to lie to my parents; but I did not abjure the company of my friend. My zeal for setting him right had proved disastrous for me, and all the time I was completely unconscious of the fact.

The same company would have led me into faithlessness to my wife. But I was saved by a narrow margin. My friend once took me to a brothel. He sent me in with the necessary instructions. It was all prearranged. The bill had already been paid. I went into the jaws of sin, but God in his infinite mercy protected me against myself. I was almost struck blind and dumb in this den of vice and came away without committing the deed for which my friend had taken me. I felt as though my manhood had been injured, and wished to sink into the ground for shame. But I have ever since given thanks to God for having saved me. I can recall four more similar incidents in my life; and in most of them my good fortune rather than any effort on my part saved me. From a strictly ethical point of view, all these occasions must be regarded as moral lapses; for the carnal passion was there, and this was as bad as the act. But from the ordinary point of view, a man who is preserved from physically committing sin is regarded as saved. And I was kept from sin only in that sense. There are some actions from which an escape is a godsend both for the man who escapes and for those about him. Man, as soon as he gets back his consciousness of right, is thankful to the divine mercy for the escape. As we know that a human being often succumbs to temptation, however much he may resist it, we also know that divine providence often intercedes and saves him in spite of himself. How all this happens; how far man's will is free; to what extent he is a creature of circumstances; how far fate enters on the scene—all this is a mystery and will remain a mystery.

But to go on with the story. Even this was far from opening my eyes to

the viciousness of my friend's company. Therefore I had many more bitter draughts in store until my eyes were actually opened by an ocular demonstration of some of his lapses quite unexpected by me. These will come later. One thing, however, I must mention now, as it pertains to the same period. One of the reasons of my differences with my wife was undoubtedly the company of this friend. I was both a devoted and jealous husband, and this friend fanned the flame of my suspicions about my wife. I never could doubt his veracity. And I have never forgiven myself the violence of which I have been guilty in often having pained my wife by acting on his information. Only a Hindu wife tolerates these hardships, and that is why I have always regarded woman as an incarnation of tolerance. A servant wrongly suspected may throw up his job; a son in the same case may leave his father's roof; a friend may put an end to the friendship. A wife, even if she suspects her husband, will keep quiet. But if the husband suspects her, she is ruined. Where can she go? A Hindu wife may not seek divorce in a law court. Law has no redress for her. And I can never forget or forgive myself for having driven my wife to that desperation.

The canker of suspicion was rooted out only when I understood Ahimsa [2] in all its bearings. I saw then the glory of Brahmacharya [3] and realised that the wife is not the husband's bondslave but his companion and his helpmate, and an equal partner in all his joys and sorrows—as free as the husband to choose her own path. Whenever I think of those dark days of doubt and suspicion, I am filled with loathing at my folly and my lustful cruelty, and I deplore my blind devotion to my friend.

I have still to relate some of my failings during this period and also previous to it, which date from before my marriage or soon after. A relative and I became fond of smoking. Not that we saw any good in smoking, or were enamoured of the smell of a cigarette. We simply imagined a sort of pleasure in emitting clouds of smoke from our mouths. My uncle had the habit; and when we saw him smoking, we thought we should copy his example. But we had no money. So we began pilfering stumps of cigarettes which had been thrown away by my uncle.

The stumps, however, were not always available, and could not give much smoke either. So we began to steal coppers from the servant's pocket money

---

[2] Ahimsa means, literally, innocence, non-violence. In its positive aspect, it has the equivalence of love.

[3] Brahmacharya means, literally, conduct that leads one to God. Its technical meaning is self-restraint, particularly continence.

in order to purchase Indian cigarettes. But the question was where to keep them. We could not, of course, smoke in the presence of our elders. Somehow we managed for a few weeks with these stolen coppers to get Indian cigarettes. In the meantime, we heard that the stalks of a certain plant were porous and could be smoked. So we got them and began this kind of smoking. But we were far from being satisfied with such things as these. Our want of independence began to hurt us. It was unbearable that we should be unable to do anything without the permission of our elders. At last, in sheer disgust, we decided to commit suicide!

But how were we to do it? From what place were we to get the poison? We heard that Datura seeds were an effective poison. Off we went to the jungle in search of these seeds, and obtained them. Evening was thought to be the auspicious hour. We went to Kedarji Mandir,[4] put melted butter in the temple-lamp, paid a visit to the shrine and then looked for a lonely corner. But our courage failed us. Supposing we were not instantly killed? And what was the good of killing ourselves after all? Why not rather put up with the lack of independence? Nevertheless, we swallowed two or three seeds. We did not dare to take more. Both of us now fought shy of death. We decided to go to Ramji Mandir to compose ourselves and to dismiss the thought of suicide. Thus I realised that it was not as easy to commit suicide as to contemplate it. Since that evening, whenever I have heard of someone threatening to commit suicide, it has had little effect on me.

The thought of suicide ultimately resulted in both of us abandoning the habit of smoking stumps of cigarettes and of stealing the servant's coppers for the purpose of smoking. From that time onward, ever since I have reached manhood. I have never desired to smoke. The habit of smoking has come to appear to me barbarous, dirty and harmful. I have never understood why there is such a rage for smoking throughout the world. It is almost unbearable to me to travel in a compartment full of tobacco smoke and I become choked for want of fresh air.

But much more serious than this theft was the one I was guilty of a little later. This other theft was committed when I was fifteen. In this case, I stole a bit of gold out of my meat-eating brother's armlet. This brother had run into a debt of about twenty-five rupees. He had on his arm an armlet of solid gold. It was not difficult to clip a bit out of it.

Well, it was done, and the debt cleared. But this became more than I could

---

[4] Temple.

bear. I resolved never to steal again. I also made up my mind to confess it to my father. But I did not dare to speak. Not that I was afraid of my father beating me; for I do not recall his ever having beaten any of us. No, I was afraid of the pain I should cause him. But I felt that the risk must be taken; that there could not be a cleansing without a clean confession. At last I decided to write out the confession and then submit it to my father and ask his forgiveness. So I wrote it on a slip of paper and handed it to him myself. In this note, not only was my guilt confessed but I also asked adequate punishment for it. The note was ended with a request to him not to punish himself for my offence, and also a pledge that I would never steal again.

I was trembling all over as I handed the confession to my father. He was then suffering from fistula and was confined to bed. His bed was a bare plank of wood. I handed him the note and sat opposite. As he read it through, tears like pearl drops trickled down his cheeks, wetting the paper. For a moment he closed his eyes in thought and then tore up the note. He had sat up to read it. He again lay down. I also shed tears when I saw my father's agony. If I were a painter I could draw a picture of the whole scene to-day. It is still so vivid in my mind. Those pearl drops of love cleansed my heart, and washed my sin away. Only he who has experienced such love can know what it is. As the hymn says:

> Only he
> Who is smitten with the arrows of love,
> Knows its power.

This was, for me, an object lesson in Ahimsa. Then I could read in it nothing more than a father's affection. But to-day I know that it was pure Ahimsa. When such Ahimsa becomes all-embracing, it transforms everything it touches. There is no limit to its powers. This sort of sublime forgiveness was not natural to my father. I had thought that he would be angry, say hard things, and strike his forehead. But he was wonderfully quiet; and I believe this was due to my clean confession. A clean confession, combined with a promise never to commit the sin again, when offered before one who has the right to receive it, is the purest type of repentance. I know that my confession made my father feel absolutely safe about me, and increased his affection for me beyond measure.

The time about which I am now writing was my sixteenth year. My father was bedridden, suffering from fistula. My mother along with an old servant of the house and myself were his principal attendants. The duties of

a nurse devolved upon me. These mainly consisted in dressing the wound, giving my father his medicine, and compounding drugs whenever they had to be made up at home. Every night I massaged his legs and retired only when he asked me to do so or after he had fallen asleep. Such service was dear to me. I do not remember ever having neglected it. All the time at my disposal, after the performance of the daily toilet, was divided between school and attending on my father. I would only go out for an evening walk when he permitted me or when he was feeling better.

This was also the time when my wife was expecting a baby. Such a circumstance, as I can see to-day, meant a double shame for me. First of all, I did not restrain myself, as I should have done, whilst I was yet a student. And secondly, this carnal desire had got the better of what I regarded as my duty as a student, and of what was even a greater duty, my devotion to my parents. Every night, while my hands were busy massaging my father's legs, my mind was hovering about the bedroom, and that too at a time when religion, medical science, and common sense alike forbade sexual intercourse. I was always glad to be relieved from my duty, and went straight to the bedroom after doing obeisance to my father.

At the same time my father was getting worse every day. Ayurvedic physicians had tried all their ointments, Hakims [5] their plasters, and local quacks their remedies. An English surgeon had also used his skill. As the last and only resort he had recommended a surgical operation. But the family physician came in the way. He disapproved of an operation being performed at such an advanced age. This family physician was competent and well-known, and his advice prevailed. The operation was abandoned, and various medicines purchased for the purpose went to no account. I have an impression that if the family physician had allowed the operation to be performed the wound would have been easily healed. The operation also was to have been undertaken by a surgeon who was then of high repute in Bombay. But God had willed otherwise. When death is imminent, who can think of the right remedy? My father returned from Bombay with all the paraphernalia for the operation which were now useless. He despaired of living any longer. He was getting weaker and weaker, until at last he had to be asked to perform the necessary functions in bed. But up to the last he refused to do any-

---

[5] Ayurvedic medicine represents the Hindu form of medical treatment according to the Vedas. The Muhammadan treatment is called Yunani (Greek). Its practising doctors are called Hakims.

thing of the kind, always insisting on going through the strain of leaving his bed—the Vaishnava rules about external cleanliness are so inexorable.

Such cleanliness is quite essential no doubt, but Western medical science has taught that all the toilet functions, including a bath, can be done in bed with the strictest regard to cleanliness, and without any discomfort to the patient, the bed always remaining spotlessly clean. I should regard such cleanliness as quite consistent with the tenets of the Vaishnava religion. But my father's insistence on leaving the bed only struck me with wonder at that time, and I had nothing but admiration for him.

The dreadful night came at last. My uncle was then in Rajkot. I have a faint recollection that he had arrived after having received news that my father was getting worse. The brothers were deeply attached to each other. My uncle would sit near my father's bed the whole day, and would insist on sleeping by his bedside after sending us all to sleep. No one had dreamt that this was to be the fateful night. The danger of course was there all the while.

It was about 10:30 or 11 p.m. I was giving the massage. My uncle offered to relieve me. I was glad and went straight to the bedroom. My wife, poor thing, was fast asleep. But how could she sleep when I was there? I woke her up. In five or six minutes, however, the servant knocked at the door. I started with alarm. "Get up," he said, "Father is very ill." I knew of course that he was ill, and so I guessed what "very ill" meant at that moment. I sprang out of bed.

"What is the matter? Do tell me!"

"Father is no more."

So all was over! I had but to wring my hands. I felt deeply ashamed and miserable and ran to my father's room. If animal passion had not blinded me, I should have been spared the torture of separation from my father during his last moments and should have been massaging him. He would have died in my arms. But now it was my uncle who had been given this honour. He was so deeply devoted to his elder brother that he had earned the reward of doing him these last services. My father had forebodings of the coming event. He had made a sign for pen and paper, and written: "Prepare for the last rites." He had then snapped the amulet off his arm, and also his gold necklace of Tulasi-beads [6] and flung them aside. A moment after this he was no more.

The shame, to which I have referred above, was this shame of my carnal

---

[6] The Tulasi plant is sacred in India. The beads would be used as a kind of rosary.

desire even at the critical hour of my father's death, which had demanded wakeful service. It is a blot I have never been able either to efface or to forget; and I have always thought, that although my devotion to my parents knew no bounds, so that I would have given up anything for it, yet it was weighed in the balance that hour and found unpardonably wanting, because my mind was in the grip of lust. I have therefore always regarded myself as a lustful, though a faithful husband. It took me long to get free from these shackles, and I had to pass through many ordeals before I could find release.

Before I close this chapter of my double shame, I may mention that the poor mite of a baby that was born to my wife scarcely breathed for more than three or four days. Nothing else could be expected. Let all those who are married be warned by my example.

THE PANDIT SOCIALIST:

Jawaharlal Nehru

~~~~~~

"GANDHI is the female spirit, while Nehru is the male spirit," interprets Anup Singh. "The people listen to Nehru, Nehru listens to Gandhi, and Gandhi listens only to God." But from the mysteries of Gandhi, most western minds turn with relief to the internationally minded Nehru. He is a disciple of Gandhi, but not Gandhism. Nehru of Harrow and Cambridge is spiritually an Englishman, notwithstanding a great many postgraduate years in English jails. Nehru links our kind of logic to the understanding of India, whereas Gandhi mystifies us with symbols of salt, spinning wheel, and masochism. Nehru, the adorer of Lenin as of Gandhi, wants not only freedom for India but a social revolution. In the rise against fascism, in India's boycott against Japanese goods, in the tragedies of Ethiopia and Spain, Nehru has been the keeper of nationalist India's international conscience. This son of Brahmins who, as president, read the Declaration of Independence to the Indian National Congress, has seen the massacre of Amritsar, has tasted on his own flesh the policeman's bamboo stick tipped with brass, and has led father and mother and wife in his twelve-year journeys into English jails: "We try to tie up the loose ends of our lives and work, to pack up our toothbrushes, and generally to prepare ourselves mentally for whatever may come."

Nehru gives us one of those still rare opportunities of seeing our western world as others see it—in his autobiography *Toward Freedom,* and in *Glimpses of World History,* a batch of informal letters to his daughter Almira written in prison between 1931 and 1934. That historical correspondence begins with Akbar, the father of Indian nationalism, and ends with the days of Lenin. Written in jail without benefit of any aids in research except the famous history by H. G. Wells, this curious work tells us more about Nehru than about history. But the autobiography (written in 1934-5) is a subtle work of introspective analysis. Living and working in jail, Nehru, for comic relief, developed the habit of drawing an outline of Professor McDougall's cube for the measurement of introversion and extraversion to dis-

cover how often he changed in captivity from one state to another. Frequently standing on his head on the prison floor, Nehru expected no more from that exercise than the certainty of retaining his sense of humor. His native subtlety and irony mushroomed in confinement. Nehru once inserted anonymously into an Indian newspaper the following self-addressed attack: "Jawaharlal cannot become a fascist. He is too much of an aristocrat for the crudity and vulgarity of fascism. His very face and voice tell us that. His face and voice are definitely private . . . and yet he has all the makings of a dictator in him—vast popularity, a strong will, energy, pride. . . . His conceit is already formidable. It must be checked. We want no Caesars. . . . It is not through Caesarism that India will attain freedom."

More intelligible to us than Gandhi, Nehru is nevertheless not an open book. But we can understand something of the intellectual side of his autobiography in terms of *The Education of Henry Adams,* which it perhaps somewhat resembles. While Henry Adams turned from coal and the dynamo to Mont-Saint Michel and Thomas Aquinas, Nehru passed by the medievalism of India, the lessons of Cambridge, and even the religion of Gandhi, for a mixture of the faith of Lenin and the logic of science. The journeys of both Henry Adams and Jawaharlal Nehru ended in skepticism. For his part, Nehru has confessed: "I am a stranger and alien, and alien to the West. I cannot be of it. But in my own country also, sometimes, I have an exile's feeling."

NEHRU KI JAI![1]

THE Lahore Congress remains fresh in my memory—a vivid patch. That is natural, for I played a leading role there and, for a moment, occupied the center of the stage; and I like to think sometimes of the emotions that filled me during those crowded days. I can never forget the magnificent welcome that the people of Lahore gave me, tremendous in its volume and its intensity. I knew well that this overflowing enthusiasm was for a symbol and an idea, not for me personally; yet it was no little thing for a person to become that symbol, even for a while, in the eyes and hearts of great numbers of people, and I felt exhilarated and lifted out of myself. But my personal reactions were of little account, and there were big issues at stake. The whole atmosphere was electric and surcharged with the gravity of the occasion. Our

---

[1] Hail Nehru!

decisions were not going to be mere criticisms or protests or expressions of opinion, but a call to action which was bound to convulse the country and affect the lives of millions.

What the distant future held for us and our country, none dared prophesy; the immediate future was clear enough, and it held the promise of strife and suffering for us and those who were dear to us. This thought sobered our enthusiasms and made us very conscious of our responsibility. Every vote that we gave became a message of farewell to ease, comfort, domestic happiness, and the intercourse of friends, and an invitation to lonely days and nights and physical and mental distress.

The main resolution on independence, and the action to be taken in furtherance of our freedom struggle, was passed almost unanimously, barely a score of persons, out of many thousands, voting against it. The All-India Congress Committee had been authorized to plan and carry out our campaign, but all knew that the real decision lay with Gandhiji.

The Lahore Congress was attended by large numbers of people from the Frontier Province near by. Individual delegates from this province had always come to the Congress sessions, and for some years past Khan Abdul Ghaffar Khan had been attending and taking part in our deliberations. In Lahore for the first time a large batch of earnest young men from the Frontier came into touch with all-India political currents. Their fresh minds were impressed, and they returned with a sense of unity with the rest of India in the struggle for freedom and full of enthusiasm for it. They were simple but effective men of action, less given to talk and quibbling than the people of any other province in India, and they started organizing their people and spreading the new ideas. They met with success, and the men and women of the Frontier, the latest to join in India's struggle, played an outstanding and remarkable part from 1930 onward.

Immediately after the Lahore Congress, and in obedience to its mandate, my father called upon the Congress members of the Legislative Assembly and the provincial councils to resign from their seats. Nearly all of them came out in a body, a very few refusing to do so, although this involved a breach of their election promises.

Still we were vague about the future. In spite of the enthusiasm shown at the Congress session, no one knew what the response of the country would be to a program of action. We had burned our boats and could not go back, but the country ahead of us was an almost strange and uncharted land. To give a start to our campaign, and partly also to judge the temper of the coun-

try, January 26 was fixed as Independence Day, when a pledge of independence was to be taken all over the country.[2]

And so, full of doubt about our program, but pushed on by enthusiasm and the desire to do something effective, we waited for the march of events. I was in Allahabad during the early part of January; my father was mostly away. It was the time of the great annual fair, the *Magh Mela;* probably it was the special *Kumbh* year, and hundreds of thousands of men and women were continually streaming into Allahabad, or holy Prayag, as it was to the pilgrims. They were all kinds of people, chiefly peasants, also laborers, shopkeepers, artisans, merchants, businessmen, professional people—indeed, it was a cross section of Hindu India. As I watched these great crowds and the unending streams of people going to and from the river, I wondered how they would react to the call for civil resistance and peaceful direct action. How many of them knew or cared for the Lahore decisions? How amazingly powerful was that faith which had for thousands of years brought them and their forbears from every corner of India to bathe in the holy Ganga! Could they not divert some of this tremendous energy to political and economic action to better their own lot? Or were their minds too full of the trappings and traditions of their religion to leave room for other thoughts? I knew, of course, that these other thoughts were already there, stirring the placid stillness of ages. It was the movement of these vague ideas and desires among the masses that had caused the upheavals of the past dozen years and had changed the face of India. There was no doubt about their existence and of the dynamic energy behind them. But still doubt came and questions arose to which there was no immediate answer. How far had these ideas spread? What strength lay behind them, what capacity for organized action, for long endurance?

Our house attracted crowds of pilgrims. It lay conveniently situated near one of the places of pilgrimage, Bharadwaj, where in olden times there was a university, and on the days of the *mela* an endless stream of visitors would come to us from dawn to dusk. Curiosity, I suppose, brought most of them, and the desire to see well-known persons they had heard of, especially my father. But a large proportion of those who came were politically inclined and asked questions about the Congress and what it had decided and what

---

[2] The Lahore Congress convened in December 1929 and formally adopted *Purna Swaraj,* or complete independence, as its creed. The flag of Indian independence was unfurled at the Congress on the stroke of midnight on December 31, 1929 and Independence Day was celebrated for the first time on January 26, 1930.

was going to happen; also they were full of their own economic troubles and wanted to know what they should do about them. Our political slogans they knew well, and all day the house resounded with them. I started the day by saying a few words to each group of twenty or fifty or a hundred as it came, one after the other; but soon this proved an impossible undertaking, and I silently saluted them when they came. There was a limit to this, too, and then I tried to hide myself. It was all in vain. The slogans became louder and louder, the verandas of the house were full of these visitors of ours, each door and window had a collection of prying eyes. It was impossible to work or talk or feed or, indeed, do anything. This was not only embarrassing, it was annoying and irritating. Yet there they were, these people looking up with shining eyes full of affection, with generations of poverty and suffering behind them, and still pouring out their gratitude and love and asking for little in return, except fellow feeling and sympathy. It was impossible not to feel humbled and awed by this abundance of affection and devotion.

A dear friend of ours was staying with us at the time, and often it became impossible to carry on any conversation with her, for every five minutes or less I had to go out to say a word or two to a crowd that had assembled, and in between we listened to the slogans and shouting outside. She was amused at my plight and a little impressed, I think, by what she considered my great popularity with the masses. (As a matter of fact the principal attraction was my father, but, as he was away, I had to face the music.) She turned to me suddenly and asked me how I liked this hero worship. Did I not feel proud of it? I hesitated a little before answering, and this led her to think that she had, perhaps, embarrassed me by too personal a question. She apologized. She had not embarrassed me in the least, but I found the question difficult to answer. My mind wandered away, and I began to analyze my own feelings and reactions. They were very mixed.

It was true that I had achieved, almost accidentally as it were, an unusual degree of popularity with the masses; I was appreciated by the intelligentsia; to young men and women I was a bit of a hero, and a halo of romance seemed to surround me in their eyes. Songs had been written about me, and the most impossible and ridiculous legends had grown up. Even my opponents had often put in a good word for me and patronizingly admitted that I was not lacking in competence or in good faith.

Only a saint, perhaps, or an inhuman monster could survive all this, unscathed and unaffected, and I can place myself in neither of these categories. It went to my head, intoxicated me a little, and gave me confidence and

strength. I became (I imagine so, for it is a difficult task to look at oneself from outside) just a little bit autocratic in my ways, just a shade dictatorial. And yet I do not think that my conceit increased markedly. I had a fair measure of my abilities, I thought, and I was by no means humble about them. But I knew well enough that, there was nothing at all remarkable about them, and I was very conscious of my failings. A habit of introspection probably helped me to retain my balance and view many happenings connected with myself in a detached manner. Experience of public life showed me that popularity was often the handmaiden of undesirable persons; it was certainly not an invariable sign of virtue or intelligence. Was I popular, then, because of my failings or my accomplishments? Why, indeed, was I popular?

Not because of intellectual attainments, for they were not extraordinary, and, in any event, they do not make for popularity. Not because of so-called sacrifices, for it is patent that hundreds and thousands in our own day in India have suffered infinitely more, even to the point of the last sacrifice. My reputation as a hero is entirely a bogus one; I do not feel at all heroic, and generally the heroic attitude or the dramatic pose in life strikes me as silly. As for romance, I should say that I am the least romantic of individuals. It is true that I have some physical and mental courage, but the background of that is probably pride—personal, group, and national—and a reluctance to be coerced into anything.

I had no satisfactory answer to my question. Then I proceeded along a different line of inquiry. I found that one of the most persistent legends about my father and myself was to the effect that we used to send our linen weekly from India to a Paris laundry. We have repeatedly contradicted this, but the legend persists. Anything more fantastic and absurd it is difficult for me to imagine, and, if anyone is foolish enough to indulge in this wasteful snobbery, I should have thought he would get a special mention for being a prize fool.

Another equally persistent legend, often repeated in spite of denial, is that I was at school with the Prince of Wales. The story goes on to say that when the Prince came to India in 1921 he asked for me; I was then in jail. As a matter of fact, I was not only not at school with him, but I have never had the advantage of meeting him or speaking to him.

I do not mean to imply that my reputation or popularity, such as they are, depend on these or similar legends. They may have a more secure foundation, but there is no doubt that the superstructure has a thick covering of snobbery, as is evidenced by these stories. At any rate, there is the idea of

mixing in high society and living a life of luxury and then renouncing it all; renunciation has always appealed to the Indian mind. As a basis for a reputation this does not at all appeal to me. I prefer the active virtues to the passive ones, and renunciation and sacrifice for their own sakes have little appeal for me. I do value them from another point of view—that of mental and spiritual training—just as a simple and regular life is necessary for the athlete to keep in good physical condition. And the capacity for endurance and perseverance in spite of hard knocks is essential for those who wish to dabble in great undertakings. But I have no liking or attraction for the ascetic view of life, the negation of life, the terrified abstention from its joys and sensations. I have not consciously renounced anything that I really valued; but then, values change.

The question that my friend had asked me still remained unanswered: did I not feel proud of this hero worship of the crowd? I disliked it and wanted to run away from it, yet I had got used to it; when it was wholly absent, I rather missed it. Neither way brought satisfaction, but, on the whole, the crowd had filled some inner need of mine. The notion that I could influence them and move them to action gave me a sense of authority over their minds and hearts; this satisfied, to some extent, my will to power. On their part, they exercised a subtle tyranny over me, for their confidence and affection moved inner depths within me and evoked emotional responses. Individualist as I was, sometimes the barriers of individuality seemed to melt away, and I felt that it would be better to be accursed with these unhappy people than to be saved alone. But the barriers were too solid to disappear, and I peeped over them with wondering eyes at this phenomenon which I failed to understand.

Conceit, like fat on the human body, grows imperceptibly, layer upon layer, and the person whom it affects is unconscious of the daily accretion. Fortunately the hard knocks of a mad world tone it down or even squash it completely, and there has been no lack of these hard knocks for us in India during recent years. The school of life has been a difficult one for us, and suffering is a hard taskmaster.

I have been fortunate in another respect also—the possession of family members and friends and comrades, who have helped me to retain a proper perspective and not to lose my mental equilibrium. Public functions, addresses by municipalities, local boards, and other public bodies, processions, and the like, used to be a great strain on my nerves and my sense of humor

and reality. The most extravagant and pompous language would be used, and everybody would look so solemn and pious that I felt an almost uncontrollable desire to laugh, or to stick out my tongue, or stand on my head, just for the pleasure of shocking and watching the reactions on the faces at that august assembly! Fortunately for my reputation and for the sober respectability of public life in India, I have suppressed this mad desire and usually behaved with due propriety. But not always. Sometimes there has been an exhibition on my part in a crowded meeting, or more often in processions, which I find extraordinarily trying. I have suddenly left a procession, arranged in our honor, and disappeared in the crowd, leaving my wife or some other person to carry on, perched up in a car or carriage, with that procession.

This continuous effort to suppress one's feelings and behave in public is a bit of a strain, and the usual result is that one puts on a glum and solid look on public occasions. Perhaps because of this I was once described in an article in a Hindu magazine as resembling a Hindu widow! I must say that, much as I admire Hindu widows of the old type, this gave me a shock. The author evidently meant to praise me for some qualities he thought I possessed—a spirit of gentle resignation and renunciation and a smileless devotion to work. I had hoped that I possessed—and, indeed, I wish that Hindu widows would possess—more active and aggressive qualities and the capacity for humor and laughter. Gandhiji once told an interviewer that if he had not had the gift of humor he might have committed suicide, or something to this effect. I would not presume to go so far, yet life certainly would have been almost intolerable for me but for the humor and light touches that some people gave to it.

My very popularity and the brave addresses that came my way, full (as is, indeed, the custom of all such addresses in India) of choice and flowery language and extravagant conceits, became subjects for raillery in the circle of my family and intimate friends. The high-sounding and pompous words and titles that were often used for all those prominent in the national movement, were picked out by my wife and sisters and others and bandied about irreverently. I was addressed as *Bharat Bhushan*—"Jewel of India," *Tyaga-murti*—"O Embodiment of Sacrifice"; this light-hearted treatment soothed me, and the tension of those solemn public gatherings, where I had to remain on my best behavior, gradually relaxed. Even my little daughter joined in the game. Only my mother insisted on taking me seriously, and she never

wholly approved of any sarcasm or raillery at the expense of her darling boy. Father was amused; he had a way of quietly expressing his deep understanding and sympathy.

But all these shouting crowds, the dull and wearying public functions, the interminable arguments, and the dust and tumble of politics touched me on the surface only, though sometimes the touch was sharp and pointed. My real conflict lay within me, a conflict of ideas, desires, and loyalties, of subconscious depths struggling with outer circumstances, of an inner hunger unsatisfied. I became a battleground, where various forces struggled for mastery. I sought an escape from this; I tried to find harmony and equilibrium, and in this attempt I rushed into action. That gave me some peace; outer conflict relieved the strain of the inner struggle.

Why am I writing all this sitting here in prison? The quest is still the same, in prison or outside, and I write down my past feelings and experiences in the hope that this may bring me some peace and psychic satisfaction.

GANDHI FASTS

Our peaceful and monotonous routine in jail was suddenly upset in the middle of September 1932 by a bombshell. News came that Gandhiji had decided to "fast unto death" in disapproval of the separate electorates given by Mr. Ramsay MacDonald's communal award to the depressed classes.[3] What a capacity he had to give shocks to people! Suddenly all manner of ideas rushed into my head; all kinds of possibilities and contingencies rose up before me and upset my equilibrium completely. For two days I was in darkness with no light to show the way out, my heart sinking when I thought of some results of Gandhiji's action. The personal aspect was powerful enough, and I thought with anguish that I might not see him again. It was over a year ago that I had seen him last on board ship on the way to England. Was that going to be my last sight of him?

And then I felt annoyed with him for choosing a side issue for his final sacrifice. What would be the result on our freedom movement? Would not

---

[3] A provisional decree determining the degree of representation to be held by various Indian groups in the provincial assemblies. It was opposed for many reasons by Indian nationalists, and by Gandhi particularly, because it established a separate electorate for the depressed classes and thus, in his view, widened the cleavage between these classes and other Hindus.

the larger issues fade into the background, for the time being at least? And, if he attained his immediate object and got a joint electorate for the depressed classes, would not that result in a reaction and a feeling that something had been achieved and nothing more need be done for a while? And was not his action a recognition, and in part an acceptance, of the communal award and the general scheme of things as sponsored by the Government? Was this consistent with non-cooperation and civil disobedience? After so much sacrifice and brave endeavor, was our movement to tail off into something insignificant?

I felt angry with him at his religious and sentimental approach to a political question, and his frequent references to God in connection with it. He even seemed to suggest that God had indicated the very date of the fast. What a terrible example to set!

If Bapu died! What would India be like then? And how would her politics run? There seemed to be a dreary and dismal future ahead, and despair seized my heart when I thought of it.

So I thought and thought, while confusion reigned in my head, with anger and hopelessness, and love for him who was the cause of this upheaval. I hardly knew what to do, and I was irritable and short-tempered with everybody, most of all with myself.

And then a strange thing happened to me. I had quite an emotional crisis, and at the end of it I felt calmer, and the future seemed not so dark. Bapu had a curious knack of doing the right thing at the psychological moment, and it might be that his action—impossible to justify as it was from my point of view—would lead to great results, not only in the narrow field in which it was confined, but in the wider aspects of our national struggle. And, even if Bapu died, our struggle for freedom would go on. So whatever happened, one had to keep ready and fit for it. Having made up my mind to face even Gandhiji's death without flinching. I felt calm and collected and ready to face the world and all it might offer.

Then came news of the tremendous upheaval all over the country, a magic wave of enthusiasm running through Hindu society, and untouchability appeared to be doomed. What a magician, I thought, was this little man sitting in Yeravda Prison, and how well he knew how to pull the strings that move people's hearts!

A telegram from him reached me. It was the first message I had received from him since my conviction, and it did me good to hear from him after that long interval. In this telegram he said:

During all these days of agony you have been before mind's eye. I am most anxious to know your opinion. You know how I value your opinion. Saw Indu [and] Sarup's children. Indu looked happy and in possession of more flesh. Doing very well. Wire reply. Love.

It was extraordinary, and yet it was characteristic of him, that in the agony of his fast and in the midst of his many preoccupations, he should refer to the visit of my daughter and my sister's children to him, and even mention that Indira had put on flesh! (My sister was also in prison then and all these children were at school in Poona.) He never forgets the seemingly little things in life which really mean so much.

News also came to me just then that some settlement had been reached over the electorate issue. The superintendent of the jail was good enough to allow me to send an answer to Gandhiji, and I sent him the following telegram:

Your telegram and brief news that some settlement reached filled me with relief and joy. First news of your decision to fast caused mental agony and confusion, but ultimately optimism triumphed and I regained peace of mind. No sacrifice too great for suppressed downtrodden classes. Freedom must be judged by freedom of lowest but feel danger of other issues obscuring only goal. Am unable to judge from religious viewpoint. Danger your methods being exploited by others but how can I presume to advise a magician. Love.

A "pact" was signed by various people gathered in Poona; with unusual speed the British Prime Minister accepted it and varied his previous award accordingly, and the fast was broken. I disliked such pacts and agreements greatly, but I welcomed the Poona Pact apart from its contents.

The excitement was over, and we reverted to our jail routine. News of the Harijan movement and of Gandhiji's activities from prison came to us, and I was not very happy about it. There was no doubt that a tremendous push had been given to the movement to end untouchability and raise the unhappy depressed classes, not so much by the pact as by the crusading enthusiasm created all over the country. That was to be welcomed. But it was equally obvious that civil disobedience had suffered. The country's attention had been diverted to other issues, and many Congress workers had turned to the Harijan cause. Probably most of these people wanted an excuse to revert to safer activities which did not involve the risk of jail-going or, worse still, lathee

blows and confiscations of property. That was natural, and it was not fair to expect all the thousands of our workers to keep always ready for intense suffering and the break-up and destruction of their homes. But still it was painful to watch this slow decay of our great movement. Civil disobedience was, however, still going on, and occasionally there were mass demonstrations like the Calcutta Congress in March-April 1933. Gandhiji was in Yeravda Prison, but he had been given certain privileges to meet people and issue directions for the Harijan movements. Somehow this took away from the sting of his being in prison. All this depressed me.

Many months later, early in May 1933, Gandhiji began his twenty-one-day fast. The first news of this had again come as a shock to me, but I accepted it as an inevitable occurrence and schooled myself to it. Indeed I was irritated that people should urge him to give it up, after he had made up his mind and declared it to the public. For me the fast was an incomprehensible thing, and, if I had been asked before the decision had been taken, I would certainly have spoken strongly against it. But I attached great value to Gandhiji's word, and it seemed to me wrong for anyone to try to make him break it, in a personal matter which, to him, was of supreme importance. So, unhappy as I was, I put up with it.

A few days before beginning his fast he wrote to me, a typical letter which moved me very much. As he asked for a reply I sent him the following telegram:

Your letter. What can I say about matters I do not understand? I feel lost in strange country where you are the only familiar landmark and I try to grope my way in dark but I stumble. Whatever happens my love and thoughts will be with you.

I had struggled against my utter disapproval of his act and my desire not to hurt him. I felt, however, that I had not sent him a cheerful message, and now that he was bent on undergoing his terrible ordeal, which might even end in his death, I ought to cheer him up as much as I could. Little things make a difference psychologically, and he would have to strain every nerve to survive. I felt also that we should accept whatever happened, even his death, if unhappily it should occur, with a stout heart. So I sent him another telegram:

Now that you are launched on your great enterprise may I send you again love and greetings and assure you that I feel more clearly now that whatever happens it is well and whatever happens you win.

833

He survived the fast. On the first day of it he was discharged from prison, and on his advice civil disobedience was suspended for six weeks.

Again I watched the emotional upheaval of the country during the fast, and I wondered more and more if this was the right method in politics. It seemed to be sheer revivalism, and clear thinking had not a ghost of a chance against it. All India, or most of it, stared reverently at the Mahatma and expected him to perform miracle after miracle and put an end to untouchability and get *Swaraj* and so on—and did precious little itself! And Gandhiji did not encourage others to think; his insistence was only on purity and sacrifice. I felt that I was drifting further and further away from him mentally, in spite of my strong emotional attachment to him. Often enough he was guided in his political activities by an unerring instinct. He had the flair for action, but was the way of faith the right way to train a nation? It might pay for a short while, but in the long run?

And I could not understand how he could accept, as he seemed to do, the present social order, which was based on violence and conflict. Within me also conflict raged, and I was torn between rival loyalties. I knew that there was trouble ahead for me, when the enforced protection of jail was removed. I felt lonely and homeless; and India, to whom I had given my love and for whom I had labored, seemed a strange and bewildering land to me. Was it my fault that I could not enter into the spirit and ways of thinking of my countrymen? Even with my closest associates I felt that an invisible barrier came between us, and, unhappy at being unable to overcome it, I shrank back into my shell. The old world seemed to envelop them, the old world of past ideologies, hopes, and desires. The new world was yet far distant.

> *Wandering between two worlds, one dead,*
> *The other powerless to be born,*
> *With nowhere yet to rest his head.*

QUEEN REVENGE AT RIOM:

Léon Blum

"YOU INVITE A MAN ALREADY CONDEMNED TO ANSWER THE INDICT-
MENT OF YOUR TRIBUNAL"   "THE PRESENT TRIAL IS NO LONGER
THE TRIAL OF FRANCE. . . . IT WILL BECOME FATALLY THE TRIAL
OF THE REPUBLIC"

~~~~~~

. . . our fathers had the Dreyfus and Boulanger affairs; their fathers had the Commune and Marshal MacMahon's attempted coup d'état; and their grandfathers had
the Revolution of 1848 and the coup d'état of Napoleon III. The previous generation had fought the Restoration or supported its inglorious disciplines, and those
who preceded them had been the men of the Revolution or the Empire. Riom is
merely the last link in the chain.

PIERRE COT, *Triumph of Treason*

TO EXPLAIN the early climate of Hitlerism by means of a French
parallel, Léon Blum used this sentence by Maurras: "Between 1871 and
1890 France was governed by Queen Revenge." It was this ancient lady who
presided in 1942 at the Riom trial of Léon Blum, Edouard Daladier, Maurice
Gamelin, and their "accomplices." Riom was an act of vengeance against the
Popular Front by those who had said "better Hitler than Blum." Charged
with responsibility for the French defeat, the accused were arrested in the
summer of 1940 and sentenced by Marshal Pétain to life imprisonment. As in
the trial scene which puzzled Alice in Wonderland, the sentence came first
and the verdict afterwards. But the verdict, like the process of justice, was
unusual. Blum, a man of seventy, after eighteen months in prison, found the
moral reserves to become the accuser. After Blum and Daladier had spoken,
the debate at Riom—very loudly—ended in silence.

Léon Blum, who admired Disraeli, learned from Stendhal, and followed
Jaures, has contributed something unique, even for France, in the personality of a politician. At the convention of Tours when the French socialist
party was split in the early twenties, a communist speaker paid Blum a very
careful compliment: "You were born in the bourgeoisie and you might have
remained there, highly considered for your social situation and your culture.
You are an intellectual. Like Jaures you found your way to socialism. You
have brought to that proletariat to which I and all that I love (father,
mother, brothers, sisters) belong, the help of your knowledge and devotion.

835

Well! I say that when a man sacrifices, as Jaures did, all his relations to fight for the proletariat, that a man has a right to be respected. . . ." But, as it happens, Blum had sacrificed no relations for the proletariat. The convention of Tours took away from Blum's socialist faction its majority, its party machinery, its funds, and even its newspaper *L'Humanité*. Blum, the cultivated bourgeois, the clever lawyer, and the intellectual critic, who had turned to socialism with the Dreyfus affair and to leadership after the assassination of Jaures, succeeded in rebuilding the socialist party from the ruins of its cleavage and the mocking compliments of the left wing.

Blum's nonconformist excursions from politics have annoyed those who, like André Simone, thought that "there always remained a gulf between his private tastes and his public responsibilities." Before Blum had applied himself seriously to reading Saint Simon, Fourier, Proudhon, and Karl Marx under the influence of the Dreyfusards and Jaures, Clemenceau dubbed him "the modern Alcibiades." There was a period in Blum's life when he fulfilled that role with pleasure. He wrote with charm on Renan, Bourget, Kipling, and Anatole France—and with a catholic taste which did not exclude the editing of a racing column. He was capable of saying that "socialism is born of the revolt of all our feelings that have been wounded by life" without becoming doctrinaire in his own comfortable living. He dined well and danced well in the company of those who were not wounded and had not revolted. He managed to review the plays both for *Le Matin* and *L'Humanité*. It was a period in Blum's life when he rendered unto Disraeli what belonged to Jaures and unto Jaures what belonged to Disraeli. To Stendhal he was very faithful; he wrote a book on marriage of which a London reviewer remarked that no Briton could have published it and remained in public office. This treatise on marriage, deriving from a sentiment of Stendhal that to love and be loved is not enough, and that there must be the same kind of love, contends that organized monogamy is generally a lopsided affair between unequals in experience. He appealed to young people to get rid of "the principle, or as I should say, the prejudice of virginity." He dedicated the book to his wife: "My excuse for making such a dedication public property is this: it implies that no feeling of dissatisfaction entered into the idea of the book. On the contrary, what entered into the plan of it was a sense of gratitude, and it has been written by a happy man." Confessing at once to happiness *and* socialism, Blum exposed himself to the potshots of all who wanted either to prevent or to postpone this attractive combination.

In 1914 Blum became a deputy. From 1919 to 1928 he represented the

Seine and after 1929 Narbonne. As chairman of the socialist party and editor of *Le Populaire* he opposed socialist participation in the government until the crisis of 1936 which brought on the Popular Front. In foreign politics he had aimed to bring together the Weimar Republic and France and preached general disarmament. In the early thirties Blum saw that neither the victory of 1918 nor the creation of new states around Germany had driven fear out of French hearts—just as after Napoleon was dead and buried, Europe was still afraid of a Napoleonic France. A Frenchman, he thought that he recognized in Hitlerism an envious and aggressive patriotism, the patriotism of a vanquished nation. He shared with social democrats in Germany the belief that Hitler was miles away from power, but that if power came to him—and it came in two or three years—he would feel a "heavy mantle of wisdom and circumspection fall on his shoulders." Events forcibly re-educated this optimism, just as the fortunes of war and the treason trial at Riom were to descend with such brutality and tragic irony on this singularly brilliant and refined Frenchman. Of the Popular Front period, Blum said at Riom: "I recall with a certain pride the words which an English statesman uttered at the close of his Parliamentary career, when, having repealed the Corn Laws and then been thrown from office after that victory, he said: 'I leave a name which shall be pronounced with hatred or with anger by monopolists and speculators, but one which will perhaps be remembered with thankfulness in the homes of those whose lot in this world is to toil.' For my part, I, too, have experienced a feeling and a pride of this kind, and I think I have the right to express it here before my judges." Reaction on the right regarded Léon Blum as a dangerous politician, radicals on the left as a weak man of compromises. But those friends who urged him to escape out of occupied France, from a fate that was certain, were sure of his fundamental trait, courage. "I shall not leave unless the Government leaves France," he said. "If they do not go then I stay. I am the leader of the socialist party. I am a Jew. It is my duty to stay." The first prison chosen for this dangerous man of seventy years was a cold and damp fortress five thousand feet high in a remote corner of the Pyrenees at the summit of five hundred and six steps.[1]

---

[1] *As proofs of this book were read (Mussolini's physical and political corpse having been exhibited in Milan and Hitler's hunted in German basements) a host of political prisoners were streaming westward: Paul Reynaud, Edouard Daladier, Albert Sarraut, Yvan Delbos Maurice-Gustave Gamelin, Léon Jouhaux, Edouard Herriot, Maxime Weygand, Léon Blum, and others. Marshal Henri-Philippe Pétain was returning to the Paris of the Fourth Republic a prisoner, installed in furnished rooms of the Montrouge fort, not far from the place where men condemned to death by the purge were shot. A "Goering Art Exhibition"*

LEON BLUM TO HIS JUDGES AT RIOM

"You invite a man already condemned to answer the indictment of your tribunal"

October 20, 1941

Gentlemen:

You have given me a five day period of grace to present my defense against the indictment signed by the Prosecutor-General of the court.

I had been informed of the indictment on October 15, at 6:45 P.M., a few minutes before Marshal Pétain announced on the radio the sentence already delivered by him against me. On the morning of the seventeenth, the reasons for this sentence were already made public through the press in the form of propositions issued by the Council of Political Justice. The Council declared, and Marshal Pétain sanctioned that declaration by application of punishment, that I had betrayed the duties of my office.

Thus you invite a man already condemned, and condemned on the basis of the same charges, to answer the indictment of your tribunal. Is not this a cruel mockery? What meaning will my answer have? Has not the case already been settled before the world? There has been talk of separation of powers, that is of the special nature of judiciary authority and of its independence from executive power. Homage has been paid to this beautiful principle. But in fact you have been forestalled: the case has been prejudged against you as well as against me. Citing the same facts, and by virtue of the same charges, will you really be free to affect or to weaken by your future verdict the character and the motivation of the sentence already given by the supreme authority of the state? I should be embarrassed to stress this point further before French magistrates.

---

was being held under the auspices of an ironical American army; Niemoeller, the martyr, and Thyssen, the industrialist, were being equally liberated from concentration camps; Pierre Laval was waiting in the Montjuich fortress of Barcelona; the intellectual remains of an American poet, Ezra Pound, were being taken into custody by Americans near Genoa; and George Bernard Shaw was writing to the London Times *that Eamon de Valera, who visited the German Minister in Dublin to extend condolences when Hitler's death was reported, "comes out of it as a champion of the Christian chivalry we are all pretending to admire." At this time, on his 73rd birthday, after four and a half years of captivity and just before his liberation, the friends of Léon Blum were publishing his book,* On a Human Scale, *which he wrote while confined at Bourrassol, near Vichy—a book dedicated to "all adolescents who are growing up far from their imprisoned fathers" and all those who "seek a guiding star in darkened skies."*

My answer will be limited to three observations or, to be more precise, to three points of procedure.

Here is the first. I do not know to what extent the Council of Political Justice was informed of your investigation. I wish to recall, however, the attitude which I constantly and deliberately preserved throughout the procedure conducted in accordance with the Council's secret practice, a practice long condemned by French law.

In the course of the three examinations by the investigating magistrate (I do not include the first examination of identity), I systematically limited myself to purely general explanations. I did not call upon a single witness or produce a single document. Nor did I discuss any of the testimony or documents gathered by the prosecution. I did not point out, as it would have been easy to do, the errors of partiality or the contradictions contained in many of them. Explicitly and formally, I reserved such discussion, as well as other means of my defense, for the day that was to come, for the day of public debate and trial. Hence I wish to register a protest, a complete and absolute protest against the contradictory character of the investigation conducted in my case.

The Council of Political Justice, assuming the none-too-probable hypothesis that they had knowledge of the record of your proceedings against me, delivered judgment in my case without having given me any opportunity whatsoever to exercise my rights of defense, whether by me or for me.

An office-holder accused publicly of having compromised by governmental action the interests and security of my country, I had a right to public presentation of my case, to self-defense and public reparation. I repeat with regret that I can hope for no protection of my rights from your justice. But I preserve and affirm my right to justify myself before my country, before international opinion, and if I may be permitted to say so, before history.

Second observation. My counsel, M. Le Trocquer and M. Spanien, presented the court with a note which was submitted on January 18. From that time on and throughout the early period of the investigation, it became evident that the defeat of French arms could not be reasonably explained by the shortage of means and machines placed at the disposal of the army. We therefore asked the court to extend its investigation into the conduct of military operations. We pointed out that an inquiry into events such as our army's entrance into Belgium, the rupture of the front on the Meuse, and the lack of a proper offensive after those events—that such an inquiry was obligatory for the court, and in our opinion even imperative.

Since last January, and with the gradual prolongation of the investigation, the opinion expressed in my counsel's note has become a certainty. It is now established that the general armament program for land forces introduced for the first time by the government of which I was the head, and the execution of that program, were at the time of our entrance into the conflict ahead of the original schedule.

It has been established that for the greater part of the mechanical equipment which played a determining part in the battle there did not exist a decisive numerical disproportion between ourselves and the enemy. Hence, since January, the problems of the manner in which these arms were employed, and the strategic conduct of operations, called for your investigation with even greater urgency than before that date.

The court has paid no attention to the note presented by my counsel. The result is that the indictment was arrived at without any inquiry into two groups of facts. These facts, on the morning of our defeat, were irresistibly pointed out by unanimous public opinion—the opinion of soldiers and citizens alike.

One group of facts: the mistakes of our command. The other group of facts: that suspicious combination of conscious or unconscious complicity which unmanned the French forces confronting the enemy, and which are called in general parlance "fifth column" and "treason." By this I understand not mere "dereliction in discharge of duties of office" but outright treason.

And now the third observation. It obviously follows from the charges and pronouncement of the Council of Political Justice that the accusations against me are aimed primarily at the laws voted and applied, as well as at the social policies practised by the government of which I was the head, and are not at all aimed at any positive act of my own.

I affirm once more with even greater force the declaration made by me in the course of my interrogation:

"By the republican constitution of 1875 the sovereignty belongs to the French people and is expressed through general suffrage. This sovereignty is delegated to Parliament. When criminal responsibility is imputed to a man, to the head of government, without first establishing or even alleging anything that touches him personally, without adducing a single fact contrary to honesty, to honor, to official application to duty, labor and conscience; when such a man is incriminated exclusively because he carried out policies commanded by sovereign general suffrage, policies controlled and approved by the Parliament to which the sovereignty had been delegated, then it is not

the man, nor the head of government, but the republican system and regime itself that is being put on trial. On my convictions of a lifetime I shall be proud to face that trial."

I am, gentlemen, etc.,

LÉON BLUM

"The present trial is no longer the trial of France. . . . It will become fatally the trial of the Republic"

I

[General Gamelin refused to testify before the court at Riom and Blum began with a reference to Gamelin's silence: "The decision which General Gamelin has taken does not concern only him alone. Its meaning and its consequences affect us all. For my part, I cannot remain silent on the reflections with which it inspires me. I will not pretend to be surprised. General Gamelin's attitude has been reported for some time. Now that it is an accomplished fact, a fact which has just been concluded before us all, I do not believe that anyone here is able to resist a heartrending emotion. By his gesture, General Gamelin voluntarily identifies himself with our unhappy army. But the first consequence which stands revealed in your minds as in mine is that even before this trial begins there exists within it a gaping void."]

YOUR mission is to establish and sanction responsibilities. Responsibilities for what? For a military defeat. However, by your decree, everything that concerns the conduct of the military operations has already been thrown out of the trial. For greater safety you have condemned in advance to the shadow and silence of the secret session, all the dispositions, accusations, discussions which this military category of problems could have evoked even accessorily. But there still remained General Gamelin, commander in chief of the land forces from the beginning of the campaign until May 19. His presence would have irresistibly drawn the trial toward the military aspects of the problems which you wished to exclude. His contact with the executives of every degree cited as witnesses would have forced the military discussion and brought to light, for good or ill, the truth. But he will no longer be present at the trial. It is not to be considered that he is present if he does not participate except as a silent spectator. You have already withdrawn the material; General Gamelin has merely withdrawn his person. The result is that in a debate on the responsibilities for the defeat of the war the war itself will be absent.

It is difficult to conceive of a more revolting paradox for the spirit. Why

was your jurisdiction created, why was your session called? Because the French people wished to understand how its army had been conquered in this war. Nobody can misunderstand that the instinct of the people attributed, above all, military causes to this military defeat. And you, charged with the investigation of these causes, you have brought so many extraneous things into this trial, you will have thrown out the war from it.

For it is indeed you, gentlemen, who will have reduced General Gamelin to silence, to absence. He has given you his reasons. He wishes neither to stand up against the sentence already pronounced against him by a chief, who was at the same time the highest source of our doctrine of war technique, nor to make himself at your bar the accuser of his subordinates. His silence is therefore dictated to him on the one hand by the decision of Marshal Pétain, but on the other hand by your indictment and decree. The only military man accused, further inquiry is incumbent upon him to determine complete and mysterious responsibility for the military defeat. He cannot dismiss this responsibility without throwing it upon others; he cannot weaken his responsibility except in reporting the part of others. However, this determination of the respective responsibilities, and this airing, this was your mission, your duty. You have refused to fulfill it and General Gamelin refuses today to fulfill it in your place. In declining your mission as judges you have forced him either to keep quiet or to make of himself a public accuser of men who were under your jurisdiction to accuse and who remained for him his companions in arms. He has chosen to keep silent. This silence and the respect which it draws are in reality a judgment against yourselves.

For my part, I share this respect but I do not intend that we should share the silence. When I say we, I mean the friends who are helping me and I mean myself.

It is not that I do not feel myself restricted exactly as General Gamelin both by the sentence of Marshal Pétain and by the indictment. When the General states that he is already condemned before even appearing before his judges, he is right, but he is not the only one to find himself in this unparalleled situation. This fundamental judicial iniquity and baseness applies to him in the same degree as to all the accused present at your bar. These men whom your duty as judges obliges you to presume innocent until the hour of your verdict are presenting themselves to you already condemned. The highest authority of the state has declared them guilty by the same means, under the same penal qualification, and the condemnation by this authority has already been executed. There is in this something which

confounds the reason as well as the written law, which particularly breaks with the most authentic traditions of the French spirit, which affronts all free conscience in the world. Marshal Pétain's sentence is not based in any degree upon his position in any hierarchy of jurisdiction, although he is the chief of the army, but is based on himself as the chief of the state, as the man who holds complete political power. His sentence is not a disciplinary condemnation, but a political condemnation dependent on the public proposition of a political Council of Justice. I could even affirm that this political condemnation strikes political men still more directly than a soldier.

As for your indictment, if it does not place us before the same moral scruple, it carries a restraint just as serious and just as insupportable for our defense.

You throw out from the discussion everything which could involve the military commandment during the war: that is to say, all which touches upon the doctrines of war, on the conceptions of strategy, on military operations, on the effective use of modern arms. You intend to concentrate the accusation on the preparation of materials, I will even say on the quantitative preparation of armament. But the best prepared army in the world, the army most richly endowed in matériel, will succumb if the faults of the command have placed it in a strategic position without issue or if the weakness of the command did not inspire in it the will to fight. On the other hand, the matériel, however great in quantity, cannot be everywhere at once. If the theories for employing this matériel are defective, if the plans are faulty, if the foresight is lacking or mistaken, an army no matter how well equipped in matériel can find itself in an irremediable state of inferiority at the place and at the hour where the enemy's attack will have surprised it. These remarks are clear to the point of banality, but they are strangely confirmed by your instruction of military silence, for France and the world will learn with amazement what were really the numerical balances between French matériel and enemy matériel at the moment of the entrance into the war and at the time of the German attack. The question of knowing whether the mistakes of the command had not been the determining cause of the defeat, became then without possible contradiction prejudicial in character. It is in this sense that to fulfill your mission you should have pushed the inquiry, and this is what we were demanding with insistence, my lawyers and I, in a note placed in your hands over a year ago. Not only did you not push this essential investigation, but by your indictment and decree you forbid us to undertake it before the bar.

I could say then in my turn: "You have spoiled my defense to the point of rendering it powerless. Judge me, condemn me for the second time, I will keep still." However, we will speak. We will not refrain from drawing the logical consequences of the situation in which we are imprisoned. From the very beginning of the discussion, we are going to devote ourselves to the loyal and persistent effort which will be attempted to modify this situation, or rather to break it. I know well that there is one thing about which we can do nothing, about which you yourselves can do nothing, that is the sen-tence which Marshal Pétain pronounced against us, against you. At the moment that it was given you yourselves felt the attack, the restraint. You have tried to disengage and to keep free your independence as judges; you know better than I that you have not succeeded in this. Has the indictment against us convinced you? Do you really feel yourselves free to render a verdict of acquittal against the men who have already been declared guilty by a chief of state to whom you have pledged your personal loyalty? You know well that he has not left you any other choice but to strike us more strongly than he has already done. But in this respect you are actually with-out power. You have been judged against as we have been judged against; an indelible stamp has been set in advance on your future verdict. But if we cannot attempt anything effectively as concerns the sentence of Marshal Pétain or its consequences, this is not quite the same situation as concerns your legal indictment.

Upon this ground we can and we shall struggle. We can and we shall attempt to re-establish the trial within the bounds of legality, integrity and loyalty, and that is what we shall undertake with the ardent desire to draw from a frank discussion all the content, all that possibly remains of truth. We will do this less for ourselves, who are already condemned, than for the country, for world opinion, and, may I say, for history.

We do not despair of this effort before undertaking it. In his message Marshal Pétain said, placing you before the accomplished fact of his con-demnation: "The discussion is to take place in full clarity . . . I have weighed the advantages and the inconveniences. . . ." We will arm ourselves with these words as if their real intention had been truly to allow freedom of judgment to your consciences. Allow me to tell you, gentlemen, I have been a magistrate, as have most of you. I have been a magistrate for almost a quarter of a century. My career as magistrate was already well filled when I was called in spite of myself into public life. I have always been a member of higher courts, the Council of State, the Tribunal of Conflicts. I know what

it is to have the conscience of a magistrate and I believe I know what is the state of the conscience of a higher court. This sovereignty is not for the judge a privilege, a convenience, but is a charge upon him. The realization that there is no court of appeal above him nor a power of annulment, far from freeing the judge, only increases his sense of responsibility. What is to be decided will be definitive, irreparable. At the same time that we invoke your professional conscience we will appeal to your love of country. Once already your patriotic sense has changed the face of this trial. When it had been undertaken, it was undertaken as the trial of the Responsibility for the War, that is to say France was on trial. You have refused this interpretation. The apparent sign of your refusal is the absence on these benches of Paul Reynaud and Georges Mandel, necessary personages in any discussion on the responsibility for causing the war—who were aimed at directly by one of the formulas of the text which empowered you—and against whom, however, no instructions have been even begun—and who have not been keeping us company in the Prison of Portalet.

Take notice: the present trial is no longer the trial of France, but if it remains what it is, it will become fatally the trial of the Republic. A discussion on the responsibilities of the defeat, from which all the military responsibilities have been excluded by prejudice, becomes by the force of circumstances at the same time a willful attempt against the truth, a prejudice against the Republican regime. The Marshal's message leads us to fear that this is the real attitude that is expected of you. Do you believe that this serves the interests of your country, answers the will of the country which is demanding the truth and which has not denied nor renounced the Republic?

We will then try (the word always has the same sense) to substitute for this partisan prejudice the calm and courageous inquiry for which the country is waiting. We shall propose to you the means. We wish to do this with your help, but if we were deprived of your support we should not grow discouraged, we would still fight on. Our duty toward the country, which we still expect to serve even after this, will not have been modified by your refusal; on the contrary, it will have been rendered the more pressing. Because this refusal on your part would clearly signify that the discussion in the court is maintained by you in full knowledge of the cause, within the limits and in the character which belongs to the court today, that is: the Trial of the Republic which still remains the legal form of government in the country, trial of the system, of the customs, of the democratic methods, a trial of the policy of justice, and of social conciliation which the govern-

ment over which I presided practised. And then it will be incumbent upon us to prove to France that it is not the degenerate people who, for having believed in liberty and in progress, must expiate its ideal and bow to punishment. If the Republic remains the accused, we will remain at our post of combat as her defenders and her witnesses.

II

I desire to strengthen by several remarks of a slightly different order the decisive observations already submitted to the court.

The text of the first article, first paragraph, of the indictment of August 1, 1940, is so clear that it seems it ought to escape all contradiction.

It fixes a landmark in time, September 4, 1939. It embraces two categories of acts relative to this fixed point.

On the one hand, acts committed prior to this date: those acts which led from a state of peace to a state of war.

On the other hand, posterior acts: those which have aggravated the situation thus created.

For the first category of acts, the text fixes the fourth of September as its end and limit. For the second category, the text fixes this date as its point of departure.

This poses the question: what should be the date which we can fix as the point of origin for the acts of the first category, those actions before war was declared. The text does not say explicitly but it does point out.

The acts of the first category, these pre-war actions, are those which led from a state of peace to a state of war. The infractions which the text of the indictment aims at must then necessarily have come after the state of peace such as it existed for the last time with certainty; the peace existing at a given moment of time under incontestable conditions, the question is in knowing how and by the course of which acts France passed from this state of peace to the state of war. From this point, if you had followed through your information in this direction, what date should you fix upon as a beginning? When did a state of absolute peace exist for the last time before the war between France and Germany? I do not believe that any hesitation can arise in this respect. The date indicated by the text was that of the Munich Pacts. Munich was not only a special arrangement for a given difficulty by an agreement for general and solemn peace, an agreement contracted for a long number of years with the bilateral obligation of consultations and

friendly investigations on all European difficulties. The texts are formal, the commentaries of Chancellor Hitler coincide with those of Mr. Chamberlain and those of Edouard Daladier. This memory may seem strange today, but the fact is so. It was affirmed, promised at Munich, that the agreement was for peace. Your inquiry on the passage from peace to war could not have been fixed on any other point.

Here is the point of eventual departure, of origin, fixed by the acts of the first category, those acts which preceded the state of war. For the origin of the acts of the second there can be no discussion possible, since it is explicitly fixed by the text itself. I do not review the incontrovertible demonstration which has been given to you. To inform you of the facts considered by you as acts of aggravation, but occurring after September 4, 1939, it has been necessary: that the Public Prosecutor's speech suppress from his interpretation the essential word, the final word, and that you extract it from the same text.

It is the alteration of the text, and this alone, which has permitted you to fix the point of time on this side of September 4. But the legal point of departure being thus eliminated by us, which then were you going to choose?

One date only was admissible, only one date entered into the logic of your error. In default of the date explicitly fixed by the text, in default of an implicit indication of it which would be looked for in vain, there was this time only one point of departure possible, the one which corresponds to the delay of the limitation.

However, the Public Prosecutor in express terms, and the Court, as it appears from its instruction, have arbitrarily chosen *the beginning of the legislature of 1936*.

Why, I allow myself to ask? Was the rearmament of France not imposed as a duty upon the ministerial charge except from June 1936? Or was this duty thoroughly fulfilled up to June 1936?

I indicate in my turn certain references.

The Nazi Party takes power on March 1933. The Third Reich leaves the League of Nations at the end of 1933, and from this point on it arms openly.

On the 16th of March 1935 obligatory military service is re-established in Germany.

I know well that the year 1933 marks in France a certain effort to attempt a peaceful co-existence with the totalitarian dictatorships. It is the year of the Four Power Pact. But from the beginning of 1934 the offer of quantita-

tive limitation of armaments is discarded by the French government. The famous note of April 17 is sent—against the advice of M. Barthou, Minister of Foreign Affairs.

"France will only rely on itself for the care of its own security"—which means that the Conference for Disarmament is practically closed and that Chancellor Hitler demands his complete liberty to rearm. From this moment it would become necessary for us to rearm if we wished to maintain "the margin of superiority" which we do not wish to renounce. There was then a *strong* government with full powers: Gaston Doumergue was President of the Council, Andre Tardieu was Minister of State, Marshal Pétain was Minister of War. There did not then exist the first trace of a modern war machine. What was done, however? What was the importance of credits? What was the sum of effective commands? What works were engaged in? Only General Denain, Air Minister, pleaded without stopping the immediate execution of a vast program, but the dossier shows with what hastiness and what incoherence. The duties of the ministerial charge were evident, imperious. Were those duties fulfilled?

To judge this it is sufficient to recall the affair of March 7, 1936, two years later. Gentlemen, stir up your memories. Remember the accent of the first words publicly pronounced by the representatives of our government, then the backing down of the French position. Complete information would have shown you what account had been rendered by the technical ministers of the state of our military forces, and what weight their report had upon the decision or absence of decision of the government. This incident, whose consequences were so serious, suffices to show in what state of *material preparation* the Ministry of June 1936 found the army. Your instruction should have taken account of this balance. But for the three years of 1933 to 1936, what has been done? And as for that which *was* done, was it in accordance with the needs and the dangers?

The *use* of war materials is of greater importance than its quantity. During the campaign the obsolescence, the inadequacy of our war theories, of our tactical conceptions, appeared with tragic evidence. But these outworn doctrines and these conceptions did not come to the world with the legislature of the Popular Front. Long before June 1936, and indeed since the last war, the doctrine of invulnerable fronts was professed, inculcated, and practised, the absolute faith in fortification and in the defensive, the distrust of armor-plated tanks, and above all the distrust of the role of aviation in warfare. Documents abound and under what signatures!

Then why did the indictment not go higher? Your decree is silent upon this. The Prosecution puts forth several explanations which are strangely embarrassing. They may be summed as follows: "Even supposing that the predecessors of the accused were blameworthy, this would not discharge their responsibility." What a surprising conception of equality, of justice! Thus among those guilty of the same crime, some are exempted and some are attacked. On what is this discrimination based if not upon standards of political order? Is it not evident to the contrary that if our predecessors were recognized as guilty, our fault would be more or less mitigated, for we would have been carrying the weight of the situation which was handed down to us? The government over which I presided put into operation a united program which by its size and importance had no comparison with those which preceded it. And this program was not a program on paper; it was carried out; military credits never were lacking; and *at the moment of entrance into war it was in advance of the foreseen delays of execution.* If it did not succeed, if it did not undertake a more methodical industrial plan in launching bases of production, it is because it was put into operation too late, and this tardy embarkation is precisely what places the responsibilities before June 1936.

It cannot be alleged that this date of June 1936 corresponds to a dangerous period in the relations between France and Germany. I will not enter into any detail on this point, but the proof would be and will be easy. Well then, what does it represent? This date can only represent the arrival to power after the general elections which upset the majority of a government known as the Popular Front. To set this date by decree as June 1936 in default of any other conceivable and intelligent reason is to recognize that a political prejudice, perhaps political reprisal, has dictated the choice. The intention is clear. They are trying to fasten upon the Popular Front, on the working class and the social policy that it practised, and upon democratic institutions, the responsibility of the military defeat.

I ask you only to think about this, gentlemen: a political phenomenon like the Popular Front does not rise like a mushroom in one or two Sundays of voting. It is tied up with what precedes it and in a large measure is the result of what precedes it. It is not an absolute beginning and one cannot isolate it. I will re-establish, when it is necessary, the misunderstood and maligned truth regarding the government of the Popular Front. I will show what its work was in the establishment of interior peace, in the order of international peace, in the order of the material, moral, political preparation

849

for the defense of the country. But if you believe that its work was evil, if you believe that, then it was necessary to extend your instruction to those who brought it about either by direct action or through inevitable reaction. Seek out the principal authors of whom we could only have been the accomplices.

For the Popular Front was nothing else but the reflection of a distinctive defense! On the one hand against the dangers which were menacing the Republic, and of which the agitation of the semi-military leagues and the riot of February 6 had been the striking signs. On the other hand, against the prolongation of the economic crisis which hindered the working class masses, the peasant population, the middle class of the country, and which was translated into the atrophy of business, the continuous fall of agricultural prices and wages, unemployment, misery.

Perhaps you will be surprised to hear that the promoters of the Popular Front were M. Doriot and M. Gaston Bergery. But its true authors are those who attempted the reversal of Republican institutions, those who by their reactionary remedies had prolonged and aggravated the world crisis in France.

Embrace then, in your indictments, the conspirators of February 6 and those of the fascist Cagoule and the men who closed their eyes on their assaults or who protected them with secret complicity. It is they who provoked the spontaneous coalition of the popular masses always passionately attached to liberty. The direct repercussion upon the defeat is here evident, for these disrupting, underhanded tricks aggravated the divisions of the country, attacked its confidence in itself, in its institutions, in its ideal, and compromised its capacity for resistance to danger. On the other hand, give your attention to the champions of the gold standard at any price and of deflation. They are guilty of this misery, of this suffering, of this revolt of the working class, of which the elections of May 1936 were the expression. Here again, direct repercussion in the country at the moment when massive rearmament was going on. Here is the cause of a great part of the technical difficulties which were so hard to surmount for the execution of the programs as well as the working class difficulties which we went to so much trouble to ameliorate. Face the balance sheet! Take account of the factories closed or darkened, the tools not kept up or renewed, because the margin of profit did not allow for amortization or investment, and of the specialists dispersed by unemployment.

They were able to choose and did freely choose their policy. Our policy

was dictated by theirs, or rather we were not able to choose except between the policy that we practised and civil war. Civil war was certainly not the means of accelerating industry and certainly not the best means of avoiding a foreign war.

Our duty, the duty of our charge, was to prevent this flood. It was to revive the confidence of the country in free institutions and in consequence to show ourselves scrupulously faithful to the program which the will of universal suffrage had imposed upon us. It was to revive a tired and spoiled economy by methods contrary to those which had already thrown the country into so terrible a condition. This duty we fulfilled. If you believe that its accomplishments were harmful to the interests of the country, begin by inquiring of those who placed the necessity for these policies on our shoulders.

In reviewing the history of the last ten years you have not the right, therefore, to stop at the date which you have chosen. The judicial delay of the prescriptions alone can furnish you with a point of departure. You will have a hard time to find another date which the reasons of historical order could justify. Your point of departure, the Popular Front government, does not justify itself by anything, by any viewpoint either historical or judicial. My demonstration of this brooks no refusal. It seems to me, and I believe, that I can defy the accusation, whatever be its dialectics, and answer with supportable contradiction. It can be explained by only one reason which I do not wish to repeat and against which you would assuredly defend yourself:

If you were to persevere in the system of the prosecution's instruction and indictment you would proclaim that the trial is a political enterprise, that you are political judges—and we should only have to register its avowal.

A NOTE OF THANKS

ACKNOWLEDGMENTS AND SOURCES

BIBLIOGRAPHY

INDEX OF AUTHORS AND WORKS

A NOTE OF THANKS

> Begin at the beginning, and go on till
> you come to the end: then stop.
>
> *Alice in Wonderland*

THIS anthology owes infinitely less to me as commentator or even inno-
vator than to the great masters on whose estates I have poached and to
the scholarly brains which I picked on my long journey of exploration. I
don't know how a wholly just acknowledgment is possible. Shall I express
gratitude to my great prisoners for their misfortunes—or thank their inquisitors? Shall I salute the jail wardens who allowed them pen and ink and
paper? In a sense the theme of this book is justice, yet I cannot myself distribute it accurately now and render it fully. Certainly my thanks are due to
countless historians, biographers, translators, critics, and wits. I have turned
over many, many hundreds of volumes and journals and entered territories
where angels might fear to tread. But I traveled the whole journey through
the world's jails alone and all errors of omission and commission are mine
alone.

Without precedent and signposts, my searches were necessarily wide and
wholesale. As I have recounted in my preface to the book, they frequently led
into many a blind alley and retreat. After all the forced marches, discoveries
and failures, I present, by way of a working bibliography, only a selected
body of books—those in English more or less accessible in any good library.
These books will disclose to the reader the sources of my omnis-
cience, the paternity of my facts, and the stimuli of my judgments. I hope
my bibliography will tempt him to read for himself far afield under expert
guidance. In each of some sixty-five introductions, before each body of
selections, I made it my duty to telescope a complex phenomenon or a
subtle mind into a handful of preparatory paragraphs. I do not have to be
told that I have not succeeded sixty-five times. Let disgruntled readers—and
may there be many of them—appease an appetite which I have only hoped to
whet by reading some of our most memorable pages of criticism and biography and general literature. As for myself, I remain, faithfully theirs, a
catalytic agent.

My wife, Mina Brownstone, read the manuscript from the beginning to
the bitter end, with greater charity than even marital conventions have a

right to prescribe in such matters; she knows I am thanking her for a great deal more than ridding these pages of the bigger weeds. I am grateful to Mr. Fred T. Marsh of the editorial staff of E. P. Dutton & Company for his constant encouragement while the work was in progress, and to Mr. Elliott B. Macrae, president of E. P. Dutton & Company, for his personal understanding of the problems and needs involved in the creation of this book.

To the New York Public Library I feel apologetic for my constant invasions of its rich stacks and altogether thankful that I found there nearly every reference which this work demanded. But will I be considered an ungrateful guest for having longed, in every weather silently and unlawfully— in an institution which devotes a whole room to the literature of tobacco—for a corner in which to smoke? I mean, of course, a smokers' retreat other than the traffic-walk between two petrified lions on Fifth Avenue.

Isidore Abramowitz

ACKNOWLEDGMENTS AND SOURCES

PART I

For permission to use the selections in this anthology acknowledgments and thanks are due to the following authors, publishers, translators, editors, agents, or holders of copyright:

Selection from:	*The source:*
SOCRATES	*The Apology,* Translated by F. M. Stawell, In *Socratic Discourses by Plato and Xenophon,* Everyman's Library, E. P. Dutton & Co., Inc., 1937.
BOETHIUS	*The Consolation of Philosophy,* Translated by W. V. Cooper, The Temple Classics, J. M. Dent & Sons Ltd., London, 1901.
MARCO POLO	*The Travels of Marco Polo the Venetian,* With an Introduction by John Masefield, E. P. Dutton & Co., Inc., 1926.
JEANNE D'ARC	*The Trial of Jeanne D'Arc,* A Complete Translation of the Text of the Original Documents, With an Introduction by W. P. Barrett, etc., 1932. Reprinted in the United States with the permission of Gotham House Inc. and in Canada with the permission of George Routledge & Sons Ltd.
FRANÇOIS VILLON	*The Poems of François Villon,* Translated by Lewis Wharton, With an Introduction by D. B. Wyndham Lewis, J. M. Dent & Sons Ltd., London, 1935.
CHRISTOPHER COLUMBUS	*Select Documents Illustrating the Four Voyages of Columbus,* Including Those Contained in R. H. Major's Select Letters of Christopher Columbus, Translated and Edited by Cecil Jane; Volume One: The First and Second Voyages; Volume Two: The Third and Fourth Voyages; With a Supplementary Introduction by E. G. R. Taylor; Printed for the Hakluyt Society, London, 1930–1933. Reprinted by permission of the Council of the Hakluyt Society.
HUGO GROTIUS	From *The Jurisprudence of Holland* by Hugo Grotius, Translated by R. W. Lee, 1926–1936. By permission of The Clarendon Press, Oxford.

THE GREAT PRISONERS : *Acknowledgments and Sources*

Selection from:	*The source:*
TOMMASO CAMPANELLA	*City of the Sun,* In *Ideal Commonwealths,* Edited by Henry Morley, E. P. Dutton & Co., Inc.
ANNE HUTCHINSON	Reprinted by permission of the President and Fellows of Harvard College from Thomas Hutchinson's *The History of the Colony and Province of Massachusetts-Bay,* Edited by Lawrence Shaw Mayo, Harvard University Press, Cambridge, Massachusetts, 1936.
CHARLES I OF ENGLAND	*The Letters, Speeches, and Proclamations of King Charles I,* Edited by Charles A. Petrie, Cassell & Co. Ltd., London, 1935. Reprinted by permission of Sir Charles A. Petrie.
NAPOLEON BONAPARTE	*Napoleon Self-Revealed in Three Hundred Letters,* Translated and Edited by J. M. Thompson, Houghton Mifflin Co., 1934.
	The Corsican: A Diary of Napoleon's Life in His Own Words, Compiled by R. M. Johnston, Houghton Mifflin Co., 1930.
ROBERT EMMET	From *Dear Robert Emmet* by R. W. Postgate. Copyright, 1932, by Vanguard Press, Inc. Reprinted by permission of The Vanguard Press.
WILFRID SCAWEN BLUNT	*In Vinculis: Sonnets Written in an Irish Prison, 1888,* Wilfrid Scawen Blunt, London, 1889, Kegan Paul, Trench & Trubner & Co. Ltd.
PADRAIC H. PEARSE	"The Wayfarer," in *Collected Works of Padraic H. Pearse: Plays/Stories/Poems; Political Writings and Speeches, 1917 & 1922,* Maunsel & Roberts Ltd., Dublin & London. By permission of The Talbot Press, Dublin.
CONSTANCE MARKIEVICZ	*Prison Letters of Countess Markievicz* (Constance Gore-Booth), Also Poems and Articles Relating to Easter Week by Eva Gore-Booth, And a Biographical Sketch by Esther Roper, With a Preface by Eamon De Valera, 1934, Longmans, Green & Co., Inc., New York & Longmans, Green & Co. Ltd., London. By permission of the author's Literary Executor.
FYODOR DOSTOEVSKY	*Letters of Fyodor Michailovitch Dostoevsky to His Family and Friends,* Translated by Ethel Colburn Mayne, Chatto & Windus, 1914.

856

Selection from:	*The source:*
FYODOR DOSTOEVSKY	*Dostoevsky: Letters and Reminiscences,* Translated from the Russian by S. S. Koteliansky and J. Middleton Murry, London, Chatto & Windus, 1923. Reprinted by permission of Mr. S. S. Koteliansky.
OSCAR WILDE	From *De Profundis,* Oscar Wilde, Methuen & Co. Ltd., Authorised Edition of 1938. With the permission of Mr. Vyvyan Holland, the owner of the copyright.
O. HENRY	*O. Henry Biography,* C. Alphonso Smith, Doubleday, Page & Co., 1916. By permission of C. Alphonso Smith, Lieutenant Commander, USNR.
ALFRED DREYFUS	*The Dreyfus Case by the Man Alfred Dreyfus and His Son Pierre Dreyfus,* Translated and Edited by Donald C. McKay, Yale University Press, 1937.
FRANCISCO FERRER	*The Life, Trial, and Death of Francisco Ferrer,* William Archer, London, Chapman & Hall Ltd., 1911.
EUGENE V. DEBS	*Debs* by David Karsner, published by Liveright Publishing Corporation.
VLADIMIR ILYICH LENIN	*The Letters of Lenin,* Translated and Edited by Elizabeth Hill and Doris Mudie, Harcourt, Brace & Co., 1937.
ROSA LUXEMBURG	*Letters of Rosa Luxemburg,* Translated in the June 1938 issue of *Partisan Review* by Eleanor Clark and in the July-August 1943 issue of *Partisan Review* by Ralph Manheim. By permission of *Partisan Review.*
ADOLF HITLER	*Mein Kampf,* Adolf Hitler, Translated by Ralph Manheim, Houghton Mifflin Co., 1943.
ERNST TOLLER	From *Look Through the Bars,* copyright, 1937, by Ernst Toller, and reprinted by permission of Farrar & Rinehart, Inc.
GEORGI DIMITROV	*Dimitroff's Letters from Prison,* Compiled by Alfred Kurella, Translated by Dona Torr and Michael Davidson, International Publishers, 1935.

Selection from:	*The source:*
NICOLA SACCO and BARTOLOMEO VANZETTI	From *The Letters of Sacco and Vanzetti,* Edited by Marion Denman Frankfurter and Gardner Jackson. Copyright 1928 by The Viking Press, Inc. By permission of The Viking Press, Inc., New York.
ODELL WALLER	*Odell Waller's Dying Statement,* Written the day before his execution and handed to Edmund M. Preston, Richmond, Virginia, associate of John F. Finerty as volunteer counsel of the Workers Defense League, at 112 East 19th Street in New York City, in the Odell Waller case.
MOHANDAS K. GANDHI	*Mahatma Gandhi: His Own Story,* Edited by C. F. Andrews, Allen & Unwin Ltd., London, 1930-1931.
JAWAHARLAL NEHRU	*Toward Freedom: The Autobiography of Jawaharlal Nehru,* John Day Co., 1941.
LÉON BLUM	*France Speaks: A Weekly Correspondence on Democratic France,* Edited by Jean Rollin and Albert Grand in New York. Reprinted with the permission of M. Jean Rollin.

PART II

The sources of other materials in this anthology are as follows:

JOHN HUSS	*Letters of John Huss Written During His Exile and Imprisonment,* With Martin Luther's Preface, Emile De Bonnechose, Translated by C. Mackenzie, Edinburgh, William Whyte & Co., 1846.
THOMAS MORE	*The Wisdom and Wit of Blessed Thomas More,* Edited by T. E. Bridgett, London, Burns & Oates, 1892.
	Utopia and a Dialogue of Comfort Against Tribulation, Sir Thomas More, Everyman's Library, E. P. Dutton & Co., Inc., 1941.
GIORDANO BRUNO	*Life of Giordano Bruno the Nolan,* I. Frith, Boston, Ticknor & Co., 1887.
JOHN DONNE	*The Life and Letters of John Donne,* Edmund Gosse, William Heinemann, London, 1899.
GEORGE WITHER	*Miscellaneous Works of George Wither,* Spenser Society Publications, 1878.

Selection from:	*The source:*
JAMES HOWELL	*Familiar Letters or Epistolae Ho-Elianae*, James Howell, The Temple Classics, J. M. Dent & Sons Ltd.
JOHN BUNYAN	*Grace Abounding to the Chief of Sinners; A Relation of Bunyan's Imprisonment; The Life and Death of Mr. Badman; The Pilgrim's Progress*, Everyman's Library, E. P. Dutton & Co., Inc., 1928.
GEORGE FOX	*The Journal of George Fox*, A Revised Text Prepared and Edited by Norman Penney, With an Introduction by Rufus M. Jones, E. P. Dutton & Co., Inc., 1924.
	The Journal of George Fox, Edited from the Manuscript by Norman Penney, With an Introduction by T. Edmund Harvey, Cambridge, 1925.
WILLIAM PENN	*Select Works of William Penn*, London, 1825.
MADAME ROLAND	*An Appeal to Impartial Posterity by Citizeness Roland*, etc., London, 1795.
	The Private Memoirs of Madame Roland, Edited by Edward Gilpin Johnson, A. C. McClurg, Chicago, 1900.
ANDRÉ CHÉNIER	*Ouevres Poétiques de André Chénier*, Paris, 1925.
	Chanticleer: A Study of the French Muse, J. C. Legge, E. P. Dutton & Co., Inc., 1935.
GRACCHUS BABEUF	*The Last Episode of the French Revolution, Being a History of Gracchus Babeuf and the Conspiracy of the Equals*, Ernest Belfort Bax, London, Grant Richards Ltd., 1911.
MORDECAI SHEFTALL	*Historical Collections of Georgia*, George White, 1855.
TOUSSAINT L'OUVERTURE	*Toussaint L'Ouverture: A Biography and Autobiography*, John R. Beard, Boston, James Redpath Publisher, 1863.
JOHN MITCHEL	*Jail Journal*, John Mitchel, N. Y., The Citizen, 1854.
CHARLES STEWART PARNELL	*Charles Stewart Parnell: His Love Story and Political Life*, Katherine O'Shea, 1914. G. H. Doran & Co., New York; Cassell & Co. Ltd., London.

THE GREAT PRISONERS : *Acknowledgments and Sources*

Selection from:	*The source:*
MICHAEL DAVITT	*Leaves from a Prison Diary,* Michael Davitt, N. Y., Ford's National Library, 1886.
LEIGH HUNT	*The Examiner,* London, 1812–1815.
WILLIAM LLOYD GARRISON	*Liberator,* January 12, 1830; *Boston Courier,* May 24, 1830.
JOHN BROWN	*New York Herald,* 1859.
HONORÉ DE BALZAC	*The Letters of Honoré de Balzac to Madame Hanska,* Translated by Katherine Prescott Wormsley, Little, Brown & Co., 1911 ("Copyright 1900, Hardy, Pratt & Co., Boston").
MICHAEL BAKUNIN	*The Confession,* M. A. Bakunin, With an Introduction by V. Polonsky, 1921, Gosizdat (The State Press), Moscow, U.S.S.R.
PAUL VERLAINE	*Ouevres Completes de Paul Verlaine,* Paris, 1930, A. Messeine.
	The Symbolist Movement in Literature, Arthur Symons, E. P. Dutton & Co., Inc., 1919.
ALFRED DREYFUS	*Five Years of My Life, 1894–1899,* Alfred Dreyfus, McClure, Philips & Co., 1901.

The works of ST. PAUL, JAMES I OF SCOTLAND, HENRY HOWARD, EARL OF SURREY, SIR WALTER RALEIGH, RICHARD LOVELACE, DANIEL DEFOE, CAMILLE DESMOULINS, THOMAS PAINE, JOHN ANDRÉ, SIR ROGER CASEMENT, and others—as well as many of the titles already listed—can be found, of course, in any number of editions. At least one source for each selection in this volume is cited in the Bibliography that follows. The Bibliography also lists gratefully the works from which quotations have been used in the Introductions. The editor has diligently attempted to track down the copyright owners of each selection. Under conditions of war the task has not been an easy one. The editor apologizes beforehand to any rightful owner of copyright not properly credited in this edition. In the event of another edition, both editor and publishers will be glad and eager to make amends publicly should any error or neglect be brought to their attention.

I. A.

BIBLIOGRAPHY

SOCRATES. 470 B.C. (?)-399 B.C. *The Euthyphro, The Apology, Crito* in *Socratic Discourses by Plato and Xenophon,* Everyman's Library, E. P. Dutton & Co., 1937. *Socrates,* A. E. Taylor, D. Appleton & Co., 1935. *The Composition of Plato's Apology,* R. Hackforth, Cambridge, 1933. *The Trial of Socrates,* Coleman Phillipson, London, Stevens & Sons Ltd., 1928.

PAUL. *The New Testament,* Everyman's Library, E. P. Dutton & Co. *Paul, A Study in Social and Religious History,* Adolf Deissman, London, Hodder & Stoughton Ltd., 1926. *Judaism and St. Paul: Two Essays,* C. G. Montefiore, E. P. Dutton & Co., 1915. *The Life of St. Paul, The Man and the Apostle,* F. J. Foakes-Jackson, Boni & Liveright, 1926. *St. Paul,* A. H. McNeile, Cambridge, 1920. *The Living Thoughts of St. Paul,* Presented by Jacques Maritain, Longmans, Green & Co., 1941. *Saint Paul,* Ernest Renan, 1869. *The Mind of St. Paul,* Irwin Edman, Henry Holt & Co., 1935. *Pliny's Letters,* William Heinemann, London, Loeb Classics Series, 1915.

BOETHIUS. 480-524 A.D. *The Consolation of Philosophy,* Translated by W. V. Cooper, The Temple Classics, J. M. Dent & Sons, London, 1901. *Boethius,* H. M. Barrett, Cambridge, 1940. *The Tradition of Boethius,* H. R. Patch, Oxford University Press, 1935. *Founders of the Middle Ages,* E. K. Rand, Harvard University Press, 1928. *King Alfred's Books,* G. F. Browne, Macmillan Co., 1920. *Boethius and Dante,* The Bibliophile Society, Boston, 1930. *History and Literature of Christianity from Tertullian to Boethius,* Pierre de Labriolle, Alfred A. Knopf, 1925. *Theological Tractates and Consolation of Philosophy,* Latin Text and English Translation by Stewart and Rand, Loeb Classical Library, G. P. Putnam, 1918. *Consolation of Philosophy,* English Translation by H. R. James, New Universal Library, London, Routledge & Sons.

MARCO POLO. 1254-1324. *The Travels of Marco Polo the Venetian,* With an Introduction by John Masefield, E. P. Dutton & Co. & J. M. Dent, 1926. *The Book of Ser Marco Polo,* Translated and Edited with Notes by Sir Henry Yule, John Murray, London, 1921. *Venetian Adventurer,* By Henry H. Hart, Stanford University Press and Oxford University Press, 1942. *The Quest for Cathay,* Sir Percy Sykes, A. & C. Black, London, 1936.

JAMES I OF SCOTLAND. 1394-1437. *The Kingis Quair,* Edited from the Manuscript by W. M. Mackenzie, Faber & Faber, London, 1939. *The Kingis Quair,* Edited by Walter W. Skeat, William Blackwood & Sons, 1911. *The Kingis Quair and the Quare of Jelusy,* Edited by A. Lawson, London, A. & C. Black, 1910. *James I, King of Scots,* E. W. M. Balfour-Melville, London, Methuen & Co., 1936. *Scottish Poetry from Barbour to James VI,* Edited by M. M. Gray, London, J. M. Dent & Sons, 1935. *The Language of the Kingis Quair,* By W. A. Craigie in *Essays and Studies by Members of the English Association,* Volume 25, 1939, Collected by Percy Simpson, 1940.

JOHN HUSS. 1369–1415. *Letters of John Huss Written During His Exile and Imprisonment, With Martin Luther's Preface,* Emile De Bonnechose, Translated by C. Mackenzie, Edinburgh, William Whyte & Co., 1846. *De Ecclesia: The Church,* John Huss, Translated by D. S. Schaff, Charles Scribner's Sons, 1915. *The Life and Times of Master John Hus* (1909) and *The Hussite Wars* (1915), The Count Lutzow, E. P. Dutton & Co. *John Huss,* D. S. Schaff, Charles Scribner's, 1915. *The Dawn of the Reformation:* Volume I, The Age of Wycliffe; Volume II, The Age of Hus, H. B. Workman, London, 1901. *John Hus and the Czech Reform,* M. Spinka, University of Chicago Press, 1941. *Hus and his Followers,* Jan Herben, London, 1926. *Jan Hus,* R. R. Betts, in *History: The Quarterly Journal of the Historical Association,* London, September, 1939. *English and Czech Influences on the Husite Movement,* R. R. Betts, Transactions of the Royal Historical Society, Fourth Series, Volume 21, London, 1939.

JEANNE D'ARC. 1412–1431. *The Trial of Jeanne D'Arc.* A Complete Translation of the Text of the Original Documents, With an Introduction by W. P. Barrett, With an Essay on the Trial of Jeanne D'Arc, Etc., By Pierre Champion, Translated from the French by C. Taylor and R. H. Kerr, Gotham House, 1932. *Joan of Arc: Self-Portrait,* Compiled and translated into English from the original Latin and French Sources by Willard Trask, Stackpole Sons, 1936. *Jeanne D'Arc,* Edited by T. D. Murray, 1902. *The Life of Joan of Arc,* Anatole France, John Lane, London, 1909. *Saint Joan: A Chronicle Play,* Bernard Shaw, Brentano's, 1924. *Joan of Arc,* Milton Waldman, Little, Brown & Co., 1935. *Saint Joan of Arc,* V. Sackville-West. Doubleday, Doran, 1936. *Inquisition and Liberty,* C. G. Coulton, William Heinemann, London, 1938.

FRANÇOIS VILLON. 1431–?. *The Poems of François Villon,* Translated by Lewis Wharton, With an Introduction by D. B. Wyndham Lewis, J. M. Dent & Sons Ltd., London, 1935. *François Villon: A Documented Survey,* D. B. Wyndham Lewis, Coward McCann, 1928. *The Testament of François Villon,* Translated by John Heron Lepper, Including the Texts of John Payne and others, Liveright Publishing Corporation, 1924. *François Villon,* H. DeVere Stacpoole, London, Hutchinson & Co., 1916.

THOMAS MORE. 1478–1535. *The Wisdom and Wit of Blessed Thomas More,* Edited by T. E. Bridgett, London, Burns & Oates, 1892. *Utopia and a Dialogue of Comfort Against Tribulation,* Sir Thomas More, Everyman's Library, E. P. Dutton & Co., 1941. *Thomas More,* R. W. Chambers, Harcourt Brace & Co., 1936. *The Place of Saint Thomas More in English Literature and History,* R. W. Chambers, Longmans, Green & Co., 1937. *Sir Thomas More and His Friends,* E. M. G. Routh, Oxford University Press, 1934. *A Portrait of Thomas More,* Algernon Cecil, Eyre & Spottiswoode, London, 1937.

HENRY HOWARD, EARL OF SURREY. 1517–1547. *The Poems of Henry Howard, Earl of Surrey,* Edited by F. M. Padelford, University of Washington Press, Seattle, 1920, Revised edition 1928. *Henry Howard, Earl of Surrey,* Edwin Cassady, The Modern Language Association of America, 1938. *Henry VIII,* A. F. Pollard, Longmans, Green & Co., 1934.

CHRISTOPHER COLUMBUS. 1451–1506. *Select Documents Illustrating the Four Voyages of Columbus Including Those Contained in R. H. Major's Select Letters of Christopher Columbus,* Translated and Edited by Cecil Jane, Volume 1: The First and Second Voyages; Volume 2: The Third and Fourth Voyages, With a Supplementary Introduction by E. G. R. Taylor, Printed for the Hakluyt Society, London, 1930–1933. *Christopher Columbus,* Salvador De Madariaga, Macmillan, 1940. *In the American Grain,* William Carlos Williams, Albert & Charles Boni, 1925. *Admiral of the Ocean Sea: A Life of Christopher Columbus,* Samuel Eliot Morison, Little, Brown & Co., 1942. *Christopher Columbus,* Jakob Wassermann, Martin Secker, London, 1930. *The Truth About Columbus and the Discovery of America,* Charles Duff, Grayson & Grayson, London, 1936. *The Voyages of Christopher Columbus,* Translated and edited by Cecil Jane, The Argonaut Press, London, 1930.

GALILEO GALILEI. 1564–1642. *Memorials of Galileo Galilei,* J. J. Fahie, London, 1929. *The Private Life of Galileo,* London, Macmillan, 1870. *Galileo and Freedom of Thought,* F. S. Taylor, C. A. Watts & Co., London, 1938. *Galileo,* E. Namer, Robert M. McBride, 1931. *Milton and the Telescope,* Marjorie Nicolson, in *E. L. H.: A Journal of English Literary History,* April 1935.

GIORDANO BRUNO. 1548–1600. *Life of Giordano Bruno the Nolan,* I. Frith, Boston, Ticknor & Co., 1887. *Giordano Bruno,* J. L. McIntyre, Macmillan, 1903. *Giordano Bruno,* W. Boulting, Kegan Paul, Trench, Trubner & Co., London, 1914. *History of Italian Literature,* Francesco De Sanctis, Harcourt, Brace & Co., 1931. *Giordano Bruno Before the Venetian Inquisition* and *The Ultimate Fate of Giordano Bruno,* in *Essays on Foreign Subjects,* by John Third Marquess of Bute, Alex Gardner, London, 1901. *Giordano Bruno and Oxford,* A. M. Pellegrini, April 1942, *Huntington Library Quarterly. Giordano Bruno's Conflict with Oxford* (January 1939) and *The Religious Policy of Giordano Bruno* (April–July 1939–1940), by F. A. Yates in *Journal of the Warburg Institute.*

TOMMASO CAMPANELLA. 1568–1639. *City of the Sun* in *Ideal Commonwealths,* Edited by Henry Morley, E. P. Dutton & Co. *The Defence of Galileo of Thomas Campanella,* Translated by Grant McColley, April–July 1937, *Smith College Studies in History. The Sonnets of Michael Angelo and Tommaso Campanella,* Translated into Rhymed English by J. A. Symonds, London, Smith, Elder & Co., 1878. *Tommaso Campanella and His Poetry,* Edmund G. Gardner, Oxford, 1923.

JOHN DONNE. 1573–1631. *John Donne: Complete Poetry and Selected Prose,* edited by John Hayward, The Nonesuch Press, 1929. *The Lives of Doctor John Donne, Sir Henry Wotton, Etc.,* by Isaak Walton, Methuen & Co., London, 1895. *The Life and Letters of John Donne,* Edmund Gosse, William Heinemann, London, 1899. *John Donne,* Hugh I'Anson Fausset, Jonathan Cape, 1924. *John Donne and the New Philosophy,* Charles Monroe Coffin, Columbia University Press, 1937.

HUGO GROTIUS. 1583–1645. *The Jurisprudence of Holland,* Hugo Grotius, Text and Translation with Brief Notes and a Commentary by R. W. Lee, Oxford:

At The Clarendon Press, 1926–1936. *Hugo Grotius,* R. W. Lee, from *The Proceedings of the British Academy,* Volume XVI, London, Humphrey Milford, 1930. *The Life and Works of Hugo Grotius,* W. S. M. Knight, *The Grotius Society Publications No. 4,* London, Sweet & Maxwell Ltd., 1925. *Grotius: The Law of War and Peace, 1625,* Translated with an Introduction by W. S. M. Knight, Peace Classics, Volume 3, Peace Book Co., London.

WALTER RALEIGH. 1552–1618. *The Poems of Sir Walter Ralegh,* Edited by Agnes M. C. Latham, London, Constable & Co. Ltd., 1929. *The School of Night,* M. C. Bradbrook, Cambridge, 1936. *The Works of Sir Walter Ralegh, Kt., Now First Collected: To Which are Prefixed the Lives of the Author by Oldys and Birch,* 8 volumes, Oxford, 1829. *The Life of Sir Walter Ralegh,* Edward Edwards, Macmillan & Co., 1868. *Sir Walter Ralegh: Last of the Elizabethans,* Edward Thompson, Yale University Press, 1936. *Sir Walter Raleigh,* Milton Waldman, Harper & Bros., 1928. *Sir Walter Ralegh,* Eric Ecclestone, Penguin Books, 1941. *The History of the World and Ralegh's Skepticism,* Ernest A. Stratham, in *The Huntington Library Quarterly,* April 1940, Huntington Library, San Marino, California. *Sir Walter Ralegh's History of the World,* Charles Firth, in *Essays Historical and Literary,* Oxford, 1938. *Shakespeare and the Stoicism of Seneca,* T. S. Eliot, in *Elizabethan Essays,* 1934. *Sir Walter Ralegh,* Edited by W. Roy Macklin, E. P. Dutton & Co.

CHARLES I OF ENGLAND. 1600–1649. *A Compleat History of the Life and Raigne of King Charles from his Cradle to his Grave,* Collected and Written by William Sanderson, Esq., London, 1658. *The Letters, Speeches, and Proclamations of King Charles I,* Edited by Charles A. Petrie, Cassell & Co., Ltd., London, 1935. *Charles I in Captivity,* Edited by G. S. Stevenson, D. Appleton & Co., 1927. *Trial of King Charles I,* J. G. Muddiman, William Hodge & Co., Ltd., Edinburgh & London, 1928. *Charles I as Patron of Poetry and Drama,* M. B. Pickel, London, Frederick Muller Ltd., 1936. *Gossip in the Seventeenth and Eighteenth Centuries,* John Beresford, London, Richard Cobden-Sanderson, 1923.

GEORGE WITHER. 1588–1667. *Miscellaneous Works of George Wither,* Spenser Society Publications, 1878, Manchester, England. *Dictionary of National Biography. George Wither in Prison,* J. Milton French, in *Publications of the Modern Language Association of America,* December 1930. *On the Poetical Works of George Wither,* Charles Lamb, in *The Complete Works in Prose and Verse of Charles Lamb,* Chatto & Windus, 1876. *George Wither,* William C. Hall, *The Manchester Quarterly,* Volume 26, 1907, Pages 285-311. Charles Lamb and George Wither, in *Miscellanies* by Algernon Charles Swinburne, Chatto & Windus, London, 1896.

RICHARD LOVELACE. 1618–1658. *The Poems of Richard Lovelace,* Edited by C. H. Wilkinson, Oxford, 1930. *The Cavalier Spirit and its Influence on the Life and Work of Richard Lovelace,* Cyril Hughes Hartman, E. P. Dutton & Co., 1925.

ANNE HUTCHINSON. 1591–1643. *The History of the Colony and Province of*

Massachusetts Bay, By Thomas Hutchinson, Edited by Lawrence Shaw Mayo, Harvard University Press, Cambridge, Massachusetts, Two Volumes, 1936. *A Woman Misunderstood, Anne, Wife of William Hutchinson*, Reginald Pelham Bolton, New York, 1931. *An American Jezebel, The Life of Anne Hutchinson*, Helen Augur, Brentano's, 1930. *Unafraid, A Life of Anne Hutchinson*, Winifred Key Rugg, Houghton Mifflin Co., 1930. *Anne Hutchinson*, Edith Curtis, Washburn & Thomas, Cambridge, 1930. *The Colonial Mind*, Vernon Louis Parrington, Harcourt, Brace & Co., 1927. *The New England Mind: The 17th Century*, Macmillan, 1939. *The Puritan*, Perry Miller & Thomas H. Johnson, American Book Co., 1938. *The Case Against Anne Hutchinson*, E. S. Morgan, in *The New England Quarterly*, December 1937.

JAMES HOWELL. 1594–1666. *Familiar Letters or Epistolae Ho-Elianae*, by James Howell, The Temple Classics, J. M. Dent & Sons, Ltd. *James Howell*, A. C. Harwood, in *London Mercury*, 1924, Volume 10, Pages 167-178. *Notes on the Writings of James Howell*, William Harvey Vann, Baylor College, 1924.

JOHN BUNYAN. 1628–1688. *Grace Abounding to the Chief of Sinners; A Relation of Bunyan's Imprisonment; The Life and Death of Mr. Badman; The Pilgrim's Progress*, No. 815 & 204, Everyman's Lib. *The Works of John Bunyan*, Edited by George Offor, Blackie, Glasgow, 1853. *John Bunyan*, John Brown, Revised by F. M. Harrison, Hulbert Publishing Co., London, 1928. *John Bunyan, Mechanick Preacher*, William York Tindall, Columbia University Press, 1934. *John Bunyan*, G. B. Harrison, Doubleday, Doran & Co., 1928. *John Bunyan*, Jack Lindsay, Methuen & Co., 1937. *John Bunyan in Relation to his Times*, E. A. Knox, Longmans, Green & Co., 1928. *The Life and Writings of John Bunyan*, H. E. B. Speight, Harper & Bros., 1928.

GEORGE FOX. 1624–1691. *The Journal of George Fox*, A Revised Text Prepared and Edited by Norman Penney, With an Introduction by Rufus M. Jones, E. P. Dutton & Co., 1924. *The Journal of George Fox*, Edited from the Manuscript by Norman Penney, With an Introduction by T. Edmund Harvey, Cambridge, 1925. *George Fox*, Thomas Hodgkin, Houghton Mifflin Co., 1896. *George Fox*, Rufus M. Jones, Harper & Bros., 1930. *The Personality of George Fox*, A. N. Brayshaw, London, Allenson & Co., 1933. *The Founder of Quakerism*, Rachel Knight, London, Swarthmore Press, 1922. *The Man of Fire and Steel*, Edited by John S. Hoyland, London, James Clarke & Co., 1932. *The Beginnings of Quakerism*, William C. Braithwaite, Macmillan, 1912. *History of Quakerism*, Elbert Russell, Macmillan, 1942.

WILLIAM PENN. 1644–1718. *The Select Works Of William Penn*, London, 1825. *The Life Of William Penn*, London, 1825. *The Life Of William Penn*, M. Janney, 1851. *William Penn*, J. W. Graham, Headley Bros., London, 1916. *William Penn*, C. E. Vulliamy, Geoffrey Bles Ltd., London, 1933. *William Penn*, W. J. Hull, Oxford University Press, 1937. *William Penn As Social Philosopher*, E. C. O. Beatty, Columbia University Press, 1939.

DANIEL DEFOE. 1659–1731. *The Shortest Way with the Dissenters*, by Daniel Defoe, in *Famous Pamphlets*, Edited by Henry Morley, George Routledge & Sons, 1886. *Defoe's Review*, Columbia University Press, 1938. *The Life and*

Strange Adventures of Daniel De Foe, Paul Dottin, Macaulay Co., 1929. *Defoe,* James Sutherland, Methuen & Co., London, 1937. *The Life of Daniel Defoe,* Thomas Wright, London, C. J. Farncombe & Sons, 1931. *Daniel Defoe,* by A. E. Levett in *The Social and Political Ideas of Some English Thinkers of the Augustan Age,* Edited by F. J. C. Hearnshaw, George G. Harrap & Co., 1928. *Defoe,* by W. P. Trent, Volume 9, *Cambridge History of English Literature,* 1920. *Kings and Desperate Men,* Louis Kronenberger, Alfred A. Knopf, 1942.

MANON JEANNE PHLIPON ROLAND. 1754–1793. *An Appeal to Impartial Posterity by Citizeness Roland, Etc.,* London, 1795. *The Private Memoirs of Madame Roland,* Edited by Edward Gilpin Johnson, A. C. McClurg, Chicago, 1900. *The Life of Madame Roland,* Madeline Clemenceau-Jacquemaire, Longmans, Green & Co., 1930. *Madame Roland,* M. P. Wilcocks, Hutchinson & Co., London, 1936. *A Lady Who Loved Herself,* Catherine Young, Alfred A. Knopf, 1930. *The Memoirs and the Letters of Madame Roland,* by Carl Becker, in *American Historical Review,* July 1928.

CAMILLE DESMOULINS. 1760–1794. *Camille Desmoulins,* Piers Compton, Eric Partridge Ltd. At the Scholartis Press, London, 1933. *Twelve Portraits of the French Revolution,* Henri Beraud, Translated by Madeleine Boyd, Little, Brown & Co., 1928. *Camille Desmoulins,* Violet Methley, E. P. Dutton & Co., 1915. *Camille Desmoulins and his Wife,* Jules Claretie, Smith, Elder & Co., 1876.

ANDRÉ MARIE CHÉNIER. 1762–1794. *Oeuvres poétiques de André Chénier,* Paris, 1925. *Andre Chenier,* J. B. Morton, in *For Hillaire Belloc,* Sheed & Ward, 1942. *Andre Chenier,* Helen Clergue, in *The Edinburgh Review,* January 1923; *The Nineteenth Century,* February 1926. *Chanticleer: A Study of the French Muse,* J. G. Legge, E. P. Dutton & Co., 1935.

FRANÇOIS NOEL (GRACCHUS) BABEUF. 1760–1797. *The Last Episode of the French Revolution, Being A History of Gracchus Babeuf and the Conspiracy of the Equals,* Ernest Belfort Bax, London, Grant Richards Ltd., 1911. *After Robespierre* (Alfred A. Knopf, 1931) and *The Fall of Robespierre* (London, Williams & Norgate Ltd. 1927) by Albert Mathiez. *Buonarroti's History of Babeuf's Conspiracy for Equality, Etc.,* London, 1836. *Babeuf and the Equals,* Max Nomad, in *The Modern Quarterly,* Summer 1939. *Babeuf and Babouvism,* Samuel Bernstein, in *Science and Society,* Winter 1937 and Spring 1938.

THOMAS PAINE. 1737–1809. *The Life and Works of Thomas Paine,* Patriots' Edition, Edited by William M. Van der Weyde, Ten Volumes, Thomas Paine National Historical Association, New Rochelle, New York, 1925. *The Living Thoughts of Thomas Paine,* Presented by John Dos Passos, Longmans, Green & Co., 1940. *The Life of Thomas Paine,* M. D. Conway, G. P. Putnam's Sons, 1892. *Shelley, Godwin, and Their Circle,* H. N. Brailsford, Henry Holt & Co., 1913. *Thomas Paine,* Kingsley Martin, Fabian Society, London, 1925. *Thomas Paine,* Frank Smith, Frederick A. Stokes Co., 1938. *Thomas Paine,* M. A. Best, Harcourt, Brace & Co., 1927. *Thomas Paine,* Hesketh Pearson, Harper & Bros., 1937. *Thomas Paine,* F. J. Gould, Small, Maynard & Co., 1925.

THE GREAT PRISONERS : *Bibliography*

JOHN ANDRÉ. 1751–1780. *Secret History of the American Revolution,* Carl Van Doren, Viking Press, 1941. *The Life and Career of Major John Andre,* Winthrop Sargent, Edited by William Abbatt, N. Y., William Abbatt, 1902. *The Crisis of the Revolution,* William Abbatt, Empire State Society, Sons of the American Revolution, N. Y., William Abbatt, 1899. *Narrative and Critical History of America,* Edited by Justin Winsor, Volume 6, Part 2, Houghton Mifflin Co., 1887. *Major Andre's Journal,* Tarreytown, N. Y., William Abbatt, 1930. *The Two Spies: Nathan Hale & John Andre,* B. J. Lossing, D. Appleton & Co., 1907.

MORDECAI SHEFTALL. 1735–1797. *Historical Collections of Georgia, Etc.,* George White, 1855. *Publications of the American Jewish Historical Society:* 1893, No. 1, *The Settlement of the Jews of Georgia,* Charles C. Jones; 1902, No. 10, *The Jews of Georgia in Colonial Times,* Leon Huhner; 1909, No. 17, *The Jews of Georgia from the Outbreak of the Revolution to the Close of the 18th Century,* Leon Huhner. *The Jewish Encyclopaedia.*

FRANÇOIS DOMINIQUE TOUSSAINT (L'OUVERTURE). 1743–1803. *Toussaint L'Ouverture: A Biography and Autobiography,* John R. Beard, Boston, James Redpath, Publisher, 1863 edition. *Histoire de Toussaint-Louverture,* H. Pauleus Sannon, Imprimerie Aug. Heraux, Port-au-Prince, Haiti, 1933. *The Black Jacobins,* C. L. R. James, Dial Press, 1938. *The Black Napoleon,* Percy Waxman, Harcourt, Brace & Co.

NAPOLEON BONAPARTE. 1769–1821. *Napoleon Self-Revealed in Three Hundred Letters,* Translated and Edited by J. M. Thompson, Houghton Mifflin Co., 1934. *The Corsican: A Diary of Napoleon's Life in His Own Words,* Compiled by R. M. Johnston, Houghton Mifflin Co., 1930. *Memoirs of Napoleon I Compiled from his own Writings,* F. M. Kircheisen, Duffield & Co., 1929. *Napoleon in Exile,* Norwood Young, John C. Winston Co., Philadelphia, 1914–1915. *The Return of Napoleon,* Henry Houssaye, Longmans, Green & Co., 1934. *A Selection from the Letters and Despatches of the First Napoleon,* D. A. Bingham, London, Chapman & Hall, 1884. *Napoleon Speaks,* Albert Carr, Viking Press, 1941. *Napoleon in Review,* G. G. Andrews, Alfred A. Knopf, 1939. *St. Helena,* Octave Aubry, J. B. Lippincott Co., 1936. *Napoleon,* Jacques Bainville, London, Jonathan Cape, 1932.

LEIGH HUNT. 1784–1859. *The Examiner,* 1812–1815. *The Poetical Works of Leigh Hunt,* Edited by H. S. Milford, Oxford University Press, 1923. Edmund Blunden's *Leigh Hunt: A Biography,* 1930, and *Leigh Hunt's "Examiner" Examined,* 1928, London, Cobden-Sanderson. *Shelley-Leigh Hunt,* R. Brimley Johnson, London, Ingpen & Grant, 1929. *The Correspondence of Leigh Hunt,* Edited by his eldest son, London, Smith, Elder & Co., 1862. *My Leigh Hunt Library,* Luther A. Brewer, University of Iowa Press, Iowa City, Iowa, 1938.

WILLIAM LLOYD GARRISON. 1805–1879. *William Lloyd Garrison, The Story of his Life Told by his Children,* Houghton Mifflin Co., 1894. *William Lloyd Garrison,* John Jay Chapman, Moffat Yard & Co., 1913, Atlantic Monthly Press,

1921. *William Lloyd Garrison,* Lindsay Swift, Philadelphia, George W. Jacobs, 1911. *Let My People Go,* Henrietta Buckmaster, Harper & Bros., 1941.
JOHN BROWN. 1800–1859. *John Brown,* Oswald Garrison Villard, Houghton Mifflin Co. 1911 and Alfred A. Knopf 1943. *John Brown,* Robert Penn Warren, Payson & Clarke Ltd. 1929. *The Life of John Brown,* F. S. Sanborn, Boston, Roberts Bros., 1891. *John Brown,* David Karsner, Dodd, Mead & Co., 1934. *The Life of Henry David Thoreau,* F. B. Sanborn, Boston, 1891. *Familiar Letters of Henry David Thoreau,* Edited by F. B. Sanborn, Houghton Mifflin Co., 1894. *The Journals of Bronson Alcott,* Edited by Odell Shepard, Little, Brown & Co., 1938. *Letters and Journals of Thomas Wentworth Higginson,* Edited by M. T. Higginson, Houghton Mifflin Co., 1921.
HONORÉ DE BALZAC. 1799–1850. *The Letters of Honoré de Balzac to Madame Hanska, Etc.,* Translated by Katherine Prescott Wormsley, Little, Brown & Co., 1911. *Women in the Life of Balzac,* Juanita Helen Floyd, Henry Holt, 1921.
FYODOR DOSTOEVSKY. 1821–1881. *Dostoevsky: Letters and Reminiscences,* Translated from the Russian by S. S. Koteliansky and J. Middleton Murry, Alfred A. Knopf, 1923. *Letters of Fyodor Michailovitch Dostoevsky to his Family and Friends,* Translated by Ethel Colburn Mayne, Macmillan Co., 1914. *Dostoevsky,* Edward Hallet Carr, Houghton Mifflin Co., 1931. *Dostoevsky,* Avrahm Yarmolinsky, Harcourt, Brace & Co., 1934, *House of the Dead,* Fyodor Dostoevsky, Everyman's Library, E. P. Dutton & Co.
MICHAEL BAKUNIN. 1814–1876. *The Confession, and Letter to Alexander II,* M. A. Bakunin, Edited by Viateslav Polonsky, Gosizdat (State Publications). 1921, Moscow, U.S.S.R. (in Russian). *Michael Bakunin,* Edward Hallet Carr, Macmillan & Co., London, 1937. *Apostles of Revolution,* Max Nomad, Little, Brown & Co., 1939.
ROBERT EMMET. 1778–1803. *Dear Robert Emmet: A Biography,* R. W. Postgate, Vanguard Press, 1932. *Robert Emmet,* Catriona MacLeod, London: Gerald Duckworth & Co., Dublin: The Talbot Press, 1935. *The Life and Times of Robert Emmet* and *The United Irishmen* by R. R. Madden.
JOHN MITCHEL. 1815–1875. *Jail Journal,* John Mitchel, Dublin: M. H. Gill & Sons Ltd., London: T. Fisher Unwin, 1913 & 1918 editions. *Life of John Mitchel,* William Dillon, Kegan Paul, Trench, London, 1888. *John Mitchel,* Louis J. Walsh, Gerald Duckworth & Co., London, and The Talbot Press, Dublin, 1934. *John Mitchel,* P. S. O'Hegarty, Maunsel & Co., Dublin & London, 1917. *The Life of John Mitchel,* P. A. Sillard, James Duffy & Co., Dublin, 1901. *John Mitchel,* Emile Montegat, Maunsel & Co., Dublin, 1915. *Irish Literature and Drama in the English Language,* Stephen Gwynn, Thomas Nelson & Sons, 1936. *Bibliography of the Writings of John Mitchel,* M. J. MacManus, in *The Dublin Magazine,* April–June 1941.
CHARLES STEWART PARNELL. 1846–1891. *Charles Stewart Parnell: His Love Story and Political Life,* Katherine O'Shea, G. H. Doran & Co., 1914. *Parnell,* John Haslip, F. A. Stokes & Co., 1937. *Parnell,* St. John Ervine, London, Ernest Benn Ltd., 1935. *Chief ·and Tribune: Parnell and Davitt,* M. M. O'Hara, Maunsel & Co. Ltd., Dublin & London, 1919. *Studies in Sublime Failures,*

Shane Leslie, London, Ernest Benn Ltd., 1932. *Parnell Vindicated,* Henry Harrison, Richard R. Smith, 1931. *The Life of Charles Stewart Parnell,* R. Barry O'Brien, London, Smith, Elder & Co., 1898.

MICHAEL DAVITT. 1846–1906. *Michael Davitt,* F. Sheehy-Skeffington, T. Fisher Unwin, London, 1908. *Chief and Tribune: Davitt and Parnell,* M. M. O'Hara, Maunsell & Co., Dublin & London, 1919. *The Fall of Feudalism in Ireland,* Michael Davitt, Harper & Bros., 1904. *Michael Davitt,* J. Keir Hardie & T. M. Kettle, in *The Socialist Review,* Volume 1, 1908, Pages 410-422. *Michael Davitt in Penal Servitude,* T. W. Moody, in *Studies: An Irish Quarterly Review,* December 1941 and March 1942. *Leaves from a Prison Diary, Etc.,* Michael Davitt, New York, Ford's National Library, 1886.

WILFRID SCAWEN BLUNT. 1840–1922. *Wilfrid Scawen Blunt,* Edith Finch, Jonathan Cape, London, 1938. *Wilfrid Blunt* in *Men Were Different* by Shane Leslie, Michael Joseph Ltd., London, 1937. *The Land War in Ireland,* Wilfrid Scawen Blunt, Stephen Swift & Co. Ltd., London, 1912. *In Vinculis: Sonnets Written in an Irish Prison, 1888,* Kegan Paul, Trench & Co., London, 1889. *The Poetical Works of Wilfrid Scawen Blunt,* Macmillan & Co., London, 1914. *Poems,* Wilfrid Scawen Blunt, Alfred A. Knopf, 1923.

PADRAIC H. PEARSE. 1879–1916. *Collected Works of Padraic H. Pearse:* Plays/Stories/Poems; Political Writings and Speeches, 1917 & 1922, Maunsel & Roberts Ltd., Dublin & London. *Patrick H. Pearse,* Louis N. Le Roux, Dublin, The Talbot Press Ltd., 1932. *The Man Called Pearse,* Desmond Ryan, Maunsel & Co. Ltd., Dublin & London, 1919. *Leaders of the Irish Revolutionary Brotherhood: Thomas MacDonagh, P. H. Pearse, Joseph Mary Plunkett, Sir Roger Casement,* Edited by Padraic Colum and E. J. O'Brien, Boston, Small, Maynard & Co., 1916. *Padraic Pearse,* Denis Gwynn in *The Dublin Review,* January–March 1923.

ROGER CASEMENT. 1864–1916. *Trial of Sir Roger Casement,* Edited by George H. Knott, William Hodge & Co., London, & Cromarty Law Book Co., Philadelphia, 1917. *Roger Casement,* Geoffrey de C. Parmiter, London, Arthur Barker Ltd., 1936. *Traitor or Patriot: The Life and Death of Roger Casement,* Denis Gwynn, Jonathan Cape & Harrison Smith, 1931. *Sir Roger Casement's Diaries: His Mission to Germany and the Findlay Affair,* Edited by Dr. Charles E. Curry, 1922, Arche Pub. Co., Munich. *The Career of Roger Casement,* by Padraic Colum, in October–December *The Dublin Review. Last Changes, Last Chances,* Henry W. Nevinson, Nisbet & Co., London, 1928. *The Irish Republic,* Dorothy Macardle, Victor Gollancz, London, 1937.

CONSTANCE GORE-BOOTH (COUNTESS MARKIEVICZ). 1868–1927. *Prison Letters of Countess Markievicz* (Constance Gore-Booth), Also Poems and Articles Relating to Easter Week by Eva Gore-Booth, And a Biographical Sketch by Esther Roper, With a Preface by President De Valera, Longmans, Green & Co., 1934. *Constance Markievicz, Or the Average Revolutionary: A Biography,* By Sean O'Faolain, Jonathan Cape, London, 1934.

PAUL VERLAINE. 1844–1896. *The Symbolist Movement in Literature,* Arthur Symons, E. P. Dutton & Co., 1919. *Ouevres Completes de Paul Verlaine,*

A. Messeine, Paris, 1930. *Paul Verlaine,* Harold Nicolson, Houghton Mifflin Co., 1921. *Paul Verlaine,* Bechofer Roberts, Jarrolds, London, 1937. *Poet Under Saturn,* Marcel Coulon, Humphrey Toulmin, London, 1932.

OSCAR WILDE. 1854–1900. *De Profundis,* Oscar Wilde, Methuen & Co. Ltd., London, & G. P. Putnam's Sons, New York, 1905 and later editions. *The Complete Works of Oscar Wilde,* Doubleday, Page & Co., 1923. *Oscar Wilde,* Frank Harris, Garden City Pub. Co., 1930 (other editions). *Oscar Wilde,* Boris Brasol, Charles Scribner's Sons, 1938. *Oscar Wilde and the Yellow Nineties,* Frances Winwar, Harper & Bros., 1940. *The Life of Oscar Wilde,* R. H. Sherard, Dodd, Mead & Co., 1928. *Bernard Shaw, Frank Harris, Oscar Wilde,* R. H. Sherard, T. Werner Laurie Ltd., London, 1937. *Aspects of Wilde,* Vincent O'Sullivan, Henry Holt & Co., 1936. *Oscar Wilde,* G. J. Renier, Peter Davies Ltd., London, 1923.

O. HENRY (WILLIAM SYDNEY PORTER). 1862–1910. *O. Henry Biography,* C. Alphonso Smith, Doubleday, Page & Co., 1916. *The Caliph of Bagdad,* Robert H. Davis & Arthur B. Maurice, D. Appleton & Co., 1931. *Through the Shadows with O. Henry,* Al Jennings, A. L. Burt & Co. *The Complete Works of O. Henry,* Edited by William Lyon Phelps, Garden Pub. Co., 1937. *Dictionary of American Biography. O. Henry's Linguistic Unconventionalities,* Margaret Cannell, in *American Speech,* December 1937. *The New American Literature, 1890–1930,* Fred Lewis Pattee, D. Appleton-Century Co., 1937. *Bill Porter: A Drama of O. Henry in Prison,* Upton Sinclair, Published by the author, Pasadena, California, 1925. *A Bibliography of William Sydney Porter (O. Henry),* Paul S. Clarkson, The Caxton Printers Ltd., Caldwell, Idaho, 1938.

ALFRED DREYFUS. 1859–1935. *The Dreyfus Case by the Man Alfred Dreyfus and His Son Pierre Dreyfus,* Translated and Edited by Donald C. McKay, Yale University Press, 1937. *Five Years of My Life, 1894–1899,* Alfred Dreyfus, McClure, Philips & Co., 1901. *The Dreyfus Case,* Armand Charpentier, London, Geoffrey Bles, 1935. *From the Dreyfus Affair to France Today,* by Hannah Arendt in *Jewish Social Studies,* July 1942. *Dreyfus: His Life and Letters,* by Pierre Dreyfus, Hutchinson & Co., London, 1937. *Traitor! Traitor!* by J. D. Kerkhoff, Greenberg Publishers, 1930. *Dreyfus,* Walther Steinthal, George Allen & Unwin Ltd., London, 1930. *The Letters of Captain Dreyfus to his Wife,* Harper & Bros., 1899. *Zola and His Time,* Matthew Josephson, Macaulay Co., 1928. *Jean Jaures,* J. H. Jackson, London, George Allen & Unwin Ltd., 1943. *Theodore Herzl,* Alex Bein, Translated by Maurice Samuel, Jewish Publication Society of America, Philadelphia, 1940.

FRANCISCO FERRER Y GUARDIA. 1859–1909. *The Life, Trial, and Death of Francisco Ferrer,* William Archer, London, Chapman & Hall Ltd., 1911. *Francisco Ferrer,* Edited by Leonard D. Abbott, Francisco Ferrer Association. *The Origin and Ideals of the Modern School,* Francisco Ferrer, London, Watts & Co., 1913. *The "Trial" of Ferrer,* James De Angulo, N. Y., Labor News Co., 1911. *The Martyrdom of Ferrer,* Joseph McCabe, Watts & Co., London, 1909. Publication of the Modern School, Stelton, N. J., 1940. *Francisco Ferrer: Criminal*

Conspirator: A Reply to the Articles by William Archer in McClure's Magazine, November–December 1910, John A. Ryan, B. Herder, 1911.

EUGENE VICTOR DEBS. 1855–1926. *Debs,* David Karsner, Boni & Liveright, 1919. *Eugene V. Debs,* McAlister Coleman, Greenberg Publishers, 1930. *Talks with Debs in Terre Haute,* David Karsner, *The New York Call,* 1922. *Heroes I Have Known,* Max Eastman, Simon & Schuster, 1942. *The Debs White Book,* Appeal to Reason, Girard, Kansas.

VLADIMIR ILYICH LENIN. 1870–1924. *The Letters of Lenin,* Translated and Edited by Elizabeth Hill and Doris Mudie, Harcourt, Brace & Co., 1937. *Memories of Lenin,* Nadezhda D. Krupskaya, Translated by E. Verney, London, Martin Lawrence, 1930. *Lenin,* James Maxton, Peter Davies, 1932. *Lenin,* Ralph Fox, Victor Gollancz, 1933. *Lenin,* D. Mirsky, Little, Brown & Co., 1931. *To the Finland Station,* Edmund Wilson, Harcourt, Brace & Co., 1940.

ROSA LUXEMBURG. 1870–1919. *Letters from Prison,* by Rosa Luxemburg, June 1938 and July–August 1943, *Partisan Review,* New York. *Rosa Luxemburg,* Paul Frolich, London, V. Gollancz, 1940. *Rosa Luxemburg: Letters to Karl and Luise Kautsky from 1896 to 1918,* Edited by Luise Kautsky, Robert M. McBride, 1925. *The Russian Revolution,* Rosa Luxemburg, Translation and Introduction by Bertram D. Wolfe, Workers Age Publishers, N. Y., May 1940. *Reform or Revolution,* Rosa Luxemburg, The Three Arrows Press, 1937. *The Crisis in the German Social Democracy (The Junius Pamphlet),* Rosa Luxemburg, N. Y., The Socialist Pub. Co., 1919.

ADOLF HITLER. 1889–1945(?). *Mein Kampf,* Adolf Hitler, Translated by Ralph Manheim, Boston, Houghton Mifflin Co., 1943 (other editions). *Hitler,* Konrad Heiden, Alfred A. Knopf, 1936. *Der Fuehrer,* Konrad Heiden, Houghton Mifflin Co., 1944. *Hitler,* Rudolf Olden, Covici, Friede, 1936. *What Mein Kampf Means to America,* Francis Hackett, Reynal & Hitchcock, 1941. *Hitler and I,* Otto Strasser, Houghton Mifflin & Co., 1940.

ERNST TOLLER. 1893–1939. *Look Through the Bars: Letters from Prison, Poems, and a New Version of the Swallow Book,* Ernst Toller, Translated from the German by R. Ellis Roberts, Farrar & Rinehart, 1937. *I Was a German,* Ernst Toller, William Morrow. *Seven Plays,* Ernst Toller, John Lane & Bodley Head, London, 1935. *Ernst Toller: The Swallow Book,* Translated by Selden Rodman, *Twice-a-Year,* Fall-Winter 1939.

GEORGI DIMITROV. 1882–   . *Dimitroff's Letters from Prison,* Compiled by Alfred Kurella, Translated by Dona Torr & Michael Davidson, International Publishers, 1935. *Dimitrov,* Stella D. Blagoyeva, International Publishers, 1934. *The Burning of the Reichstag,* Douglas Reed, London, Victor Gollancz, 1934. *The Reichstag Fire Trial, etc.,* London, John Lane, 1934.

NICOLA SACCO. 1891–1927. BARTOLOMEO VANZETTI. 1888–1927. *The Letters of Sacco & Vanzetti,* Edited by Marion Denman Frankfurter & Gardner Jackson, Viking Press, 1928. *The Sacco-Vanzetti Case,* Osmond K. Fraenkel, Alfred A. Knopf, 1931. *The Sacco-Vanzetti Case: Transcript of the Record of the Trial of Nicola Sacco and Bartolomeo Vanzetti in the Courts of Massachusetts and Subsequent Proceedings, 1920-1927,* 5 Volumes, Henry Holt &

Co., 1928–1929. *After Twelve Years,* Michael A. Musmanno, Alfred A. Knopf, 1939. *The Untried Case,* H. B. Ehrmann, Vanguard Press, 1933. *The Story of a Proletarian Life,* Bartolomeo Vanzetti, Translated from the Italian by Eugene Lyons, Sacco-Vanzetti Defense Committee, 1923. *The Life and Death of Sacco & Vanzetti,* Eugene Lyons, International Publishers, 1927. *Facing the Chair: Story of the Americanization of Two Foreign-Born Workmen,* John Dos Passos, Sacco-Vanzetti Defense Committee, 1927.

ODELL WALLER. 1917–1942. *Odell Waller's Dying Statement,* Written the day before his execution and handed to Edmund M. Preston, Richmond, Virginia, associate of John F. Finerty as volunteer counsel for the Workers Defense League (112 East 19th Street, New York City) in the Odell Waller case. *"All For Mr. Davis": The Story of Sharecropper Odell Waller,* Pauli Murray & Murray Kempton, Workers Defense League. *The Waller Case,* Thomas Sancton, *The New Republic,* July 13, 1942.

MOHANDAS KARAMSCHAND GANDHI. 1869–   . *Mahatma Gandhi: His Own Story* and *Mahatma Gandhi At Work: His Own Story Continued,* Edited by C. F. Andrews, Macmillan & Co., 1930–1931. *Songs from Prison: Translation of Indian Lyrics Made in Jail by M. K. Gandhi,* Adapted for the Press by John S. Hoyland, London, George Allen & Unwin Ltd., 1934. Krishnalal J. Shridharani's *War Without Violence: The Sociology of Gandhi's Satyagraha,* Harcourt, Brace & Co. 1939, and *My India, My America,* Duell, Sloan & Pearce. *The Tragedy of Gandhi,* Glorney Bolton, London, George Allen & Unwin Ltd., 1934. *What Does Gandhi Want?* T. A. Raman, Oxford University Press, 1942. *Gandhi-Wavell Correspondence* in *Common Sense,* August 1944.

JAWAHARLAL NEHRU. 1889–   . *Toward Freedom: The Autobiography of Jawaharlal Nehru,* John Day Co., 1941. *Glimpses of World History,* Jawaharlal Nehru, John Day Co., 1942. *Nehru,* Anup Singh, John Day Co., 1939. *My India, My America,* Krishnalal Shridharani, Duell, Sloan & Pearce, 1941.

LÉON BLUM, 1872–   . *Léon Blum,* Geoffrey Fraser & Thadee Natanson, V. Gollancz Ltd., London, 1937. *Léon Blum,* Richard L. Stokes, Coward, McCann, 1937. *France Speaks,* A Weekly Correspondence on Democratic France, Based on Reports Received from Confidential Sources in Occupied and Unoccupied France, Edited by Jean Rollin and Albert Grand, New York City. *Triumph of Treason,* Pierre Cot, Ziff-Davis Publishing Co., 1944. *The Gravediggers of France,* by Pertinax, Doubleday, Doran & Co., 1944.

INDEX OF AUTHORS AND WORKS [1]

ANDRÉ, John (1751–1780):
A Gibbet and a Gentleman, 392
letters to George Washington, 394
 "The person in your possession is
 Major André," 394
 "not to die on a gibbet," 395

BABEUF, Gracchus (1760–1797):
The Conspiracy of the Equals, 370
letter to Felix Lepelletier, 372
 "A sacrifice that friendship can
 make": Babeuf's Request, 372
BAKUNIN, Michael (1814–1876):
Little Father and the Penitent, 622
memorandum to Nicholas I of Rus-
 sia, 625
 Confession to the Czar, 625
 Bakunin as "Imploring Criminal,"
 643
BALZAC, Honoré de (1799–1850):
Droll Story, 592
letter to Madame Hanska, 592
 "This is one of the thousand acci-
 dents of our Parisian life," 592
BLUM, Léon (1872–   ):
Queen Revenge at Riom, 835
defense speeches in the Riom trial,
 838
 "You invite a man already con-
 demned, etc.," 838
 "The present trial is no longer the
 trial of France, etc.," 841

BLUNT, Wilfrid Scawen (1840–1922):
Balfour's Criminal, 506
sonnets from *In Vinculis*, 507
 In Vinculis, 507
BOETHIUS, Anicius Manlius Severinus
 (480–524):
The Eighth Spirit, 37
from *The Consolation of Philosophy*,
 38
 The Consolation of Philosophy, 38
BROWN, John (1800–1859):
Of December 2, 1859, 578
documents from his trial and impris-
 onment, 581
 The Cross-Examination of John
 Brown, 581
 The Last Speech, 589
 John Brown's Will, 590
 One More Sentence, 591
BRUNO, Giordano (1548–1600):
First Saint of the Modern World, 127
confession before the Inquisition, 128
 Bruno to the Inquisitors, 128
BUNYAN, John (1628–1688):
The Chief of Sinners, 237
from *Grace Abounding*, *The Pil-
 grim's Progress*, 239
 The Devil and John Bunyan, 239
 The Temptation of the Bells,
 239
 Of the Poor Women Sitting at a
 Door in the Sun, 240

---

[1] Many of the titles for selections listed in this index, especially in the case of fragments
from large works, are my own adaptations to the function and architecture of this book.
For the full original titles from which selections were taken and excerpts quoted, see
Acknowledgments & Sources, Part I & Part II, pages 855-860, and the Bibliography, pages
861-872. This index—in the order of their appearance—offers the name of a contributor;
his dates; my title for his introduction to the reader; a characterization of the type of
matter selected from his works; and my titles for his selections devised for use in this
context.

Thou art my love, Thou art my love, 242
Sell him, Sell him, Sell him, 243
The Hound of Heaven, 245
City of the Living God, 246
Vanity Fair, 246

CAMPANELLA, Tommaso (1568–1639):
I Will Not Be Silent, 136
from his utopia, *The City of the Sun*, 137
The City of the Sun, 137
CASEMENT, Roger (1864–1916):
The Shirt of Nessus, 518
speech in defense at the trial, 520
"If it be treason," 520
CHARLES I of England (1600–1649):
The Axe's Edge, 204
document of his imprisonment, 206
    Charles I to the Prince of Wales, 206
CHÉNIER, André Marie (1762–1794):
The Blood of a Poet, 363
poem written at Saint-Lazare, 364
    Saint-Lazare (in French), 364
    Saint-Lazare (in English), 365
COLUMBUS, Christopher (1451–1506):
God's Ambassador, 107
prison letter after his third voyage, 109
Letter to the Nurse Juana de la Torres, 109

DAVITT, Michael (1846–1906):
Of the Irish Earth, 489
from *Leaves from a Prison Diary*, 490
    Lectures to a Pet Blackbird, 490
    Preface to a Blackbird, 490
    First Lecture to a Blackbird, 491
    Second Lecture to a Blackbird, 495
    Third Lecture to a Blackbird, 498
    Epilogue to a Blackbird, 505

DEBS, Eugene Victor (1855–1926):
Convict # 9653, 707
message for Labor Day; address to the Court, 709
    "Dear Sir and Brother," 709
    "Your Honor," 713
DEFOE, Daniel (1659–1731):
Pillory with Flowers, 289
poem composed in Newgate, 292
    A Hymn to the Pillory, 292
DESMOULINS, Camille (1760–1794):
Pity and the Guillotine, 356
letters to his wife Lucile, 357
    "a 'C' and a 'D,' our two names," 357
    "I die the victim of those jests," 358
DIMITROV, Georgi (1882–   ):
They Caught a Tartar, 775
defense outline during Reichstag Fire trial, 776
    Notes for a Speech, 776
DONNE, John (1573–1631):
John Donne-Anne Donne-Undone, 174
letters to his father-in-law, Sir George More, 176
    "my submission, my repentance," 176
    "it hath much profited me that I am dejected," 177
    "as the devil in the article," 178
DOSTOEVSKY, Fyodor (1821–1881):
The Crime and the Punishment, 601
letters to his brother Michael, 603
    From the Peter-and-Paul Fortress, 603
    A Letter from Siberia, 611
DREYFUS, Alfred (1859–1935):
My Honor! My Honor!, 681
letters to his wife· from the diary on Devil's Island 684
    Letters to Lucie, 684
    From the Diary on Devil's Island, 689

EMMET, Robert (1778–1803):
The Patriot, 449
speech in his defense at the trial, 451
Speech in the Dock, 451

FERRER y Guardia, Francisco (1859–1909):
A Spanish Dreyfus, 694
documents of his imprisonment, 696
"I beg every editor," 696
"I will try to tell you about my case," 698
An Interrupted Letter, 704
Testament of a Rationalist, 705
Education: for Soledad, 706
Fox, George (1624–1691):
The Man in Leather, 255
from the *Great* and *Short* journals, 258
From the Journals of George Fox: 258
The Interview with Oliver Cromwell, 258
A nasty, stinking place, 260
Why don't ye imprison the Book?, 263

GALILEO, Galilei (1564–1642):
For Thinking in Astronomy, 123
declaration before the Inquisition, 125
Galileo's Recantation, 125
GANDHI, Mohandas Karamschand (1869–):
The Terrible Meek, 810
from his autobiography, 811
School Days, 811
GARRISON, William Lloyd (1805–1879):
Yankee Perfectionist, 572
writings in his Baltimore jail, 575
To the Editor of the Boston Courier, 575
To Mr. Francis Todd, Merchant, 575
Freedom of the Mind, 576

GROTIUS, Hugo (1583–1645):
A Jurist in Jail, 119
from *The Jurisprudence of Holland,* 120
Of the Legal Condition of Persons, 120

HENRY, O.: *see* O. Henry
HITLER, Adolf (1889-1945?):
The Book and the Battle, 753
from *Mein Kampf,* 755
Years of Study and Suffering in Vienna, 755
HOWARD, Henry, Earl of Surrey: *see* Surrey
HOWELL, James (1594–1666):
A Priggish Little Clerk, 223
from *Epistolae Ho-Elianae,* 224
"I was committed to the Fleet," 224
"You write to me of wiving," 225
"And so I fell a-thinking how, etc.," 227
"A parcel of Indian perfume, etc.," 229
A Perfect Description of the People and Country of Scotland, 231
HUNT, Leigh (1784–1859):
The Wit in the Dungeon, 549
essays in *The Examiner,* 552
The Fable of the Fish, 552
On the Unphilosophical Conduct of Sir Humphrey Davy, 554
Bonaparte Fallen and London in April, 560
Elba's One Hundred and One Rounds of Canon, 563
HUSS, John (1369–1415):
The Protestant Pioneer, 70
letters to his friends, 71.
The Dream of John Huss, 71
The Council, 71
The Obstinate Heretic, 72

HUTCHINSON, Anne (1591–1643):
Forty Theocrats and a Woman, 307
her trial by the General Court at
Newtown in Massachusetts, 309
The Trial of Mrs. Anne Hutchin-
son, 309

JAMES I of Scotland (1394–1437):
Prince and Poet, 65
from *The Kingis Quair,* 66
The Coming of Love, 66
JEANNE d'Arc (1412–1431):
The Private Voice, 75
from the original documents of her
trial, 77
The Trial of Jeanne d'Arc, 77

LENIN, Vladimir Ilyich (1870–1924):
The Political Man, 718
letters to his family and friends, 720
Books, Books, and the Wrong Un-
derwear, 720
LOVELACE, Richard (1618–1658):
Prison as a Gentleman's Art, 216
poems composed in the Gatehouse
and Peterhouse prisons, 217
To Althea. From Prison, 217
The Vintage to the Dungeon, 218
A Mock-Song, 219
To Lucasta. From Prison, 220
LUXEMBURG, Rosa (1870–1919):
Red Rosa, 726
letters to her friends Sonia Lieb-
knecht and Dr. Hans Dieffen-
bach, 728
Letters to Sonia Liebknecht:
Corsica, 728
Double Cage, 729
Life is indivisible . . ., 730
"I belong more to the titmice
than to my 'comrades,'" 731
"this huge lunatic asylum," 733
State of Joy . . . and Pity, 736
Birds, 738
Free Soon, 740

Letters to Hans:
"kindness and pride," 740
Of economics and lake nostal-
gia, 743
Botany, 745
A Wasp, 747
The Prism, 747
Lonely, 749

MARKIEVICZ (Gore-Booth), Countess
Constance (1868–1927):
The Countess and the People, 531
letters to her sister, Eva Gore-Booth,
533
Of Bills, Wigs, and Naphtha Balls,
533
Of Poems, Wild Geese, and Blake,
536
"The brown wind of Connaught,"
540
"President of so many things," 543
MEAD, William: *see* William Penn
MITCHEL, John (1815–1875):
A Prisoner with a Diary, 458
from *Jail Journal,* 459
A Blast Against Macaulay and
Bacon, 459
Doppelganger and the Ego, 470
MORE, Sir Thomas (1478–1535):
A Witty Saint in a Hair Shirt, 155
from *A Dialogue of Comfort* and
other writings in the Tower, 156
A Provoking Wife, 156
The Wolf, the Ass, and the Fox,
158
Talkative Nun and Talkative
Wife, 162
Love of Flattery, 163
Godly Meditation, 166
Letter to his Daughter Margaret,
168

NAPOLEON Bonaparte (1769–1821):
The Prisoner of Europe, 426
from the records of Elba and St.
Helena, 429

Elba: A Correspondence, 429
As Themistocles Did, 437
St. Helena: A Diary, 438
NEHRU, Jawaharlal (1889–):
The Pandit Socialist, 822
from his autobiography *Toward Freedom,* 823
Nehru Ki Jai!, 823
Gandhi Fasts, 830

O. HENRY (William Sydney Porter) (1862–1910):
Grandee of the Gas-Light Era, 669
letters to his little daughter, 671
Jabberwocky for Margaret, 671
ORATION (Anonymous, 1814):
Eight Millions of Free People: An American Oration, 568
An oration delivered by permission on board the Nassau prison-ship at Chatham, England, on the 4th of July, 1814, by an American seaman, prisoner of war, 568
"I recite these things my countrymen, etc.," 568

PAINE, Thomas (1737–1809):
Founding Fathers' Poor Relation, 377
appeal to the French Convention and memorial to James Monroe, 380
Appeal to the Convention, 380
Memorial to James Monroe, 382
PARNELL, Charles Stewart (1846–1891):
Ireland or Isolde, 483
correspondence from Kilmainham Jail, 485
Parnell to Katherine O'Shea, 485
PAUL, Saint (born Saul of Tarsus, dates uncertain):
I Paul the Prisoner of Jesus Christ, 28
The Letters of Paul to the Philippians and Philemon, 31
"Whom I have begotten in my bonds," 31

"I know both how to be abased, etc.," 32
PEARSE, Padraic H. (1879–1916):
Easter Rising 1916, 516
poem composed in Kilmainham Jail, 517
The Wayfarer, 517
PENN, William (1644–1718):
The People's Ancient and Just Liberties Asserted in the Trial of William Penn and William Mead, 271
Penn's own record of the sessions held at Old Bailey in London: William Penn to the English Reader, 271
The Trial, 273
POLO, Marco (1254–1324):
Bookkeeper of Wonderland, 50
from *The Travels of Marco Polo,* 52
Of the Noble and Magnificent City of King-Sai, 52
PORTER, William Sydney:
see O. Henry

RALEIGH, Sir Walter (1552–1618):
Most Loftie, Insolent and Passionate, 188
from his prose, poetry, and correspondence in the Tower, 191
The Lie, 191
Preface to the History of the World, 194
The Conclusion, 198
The Passionate Man's Pilgrimage, 199
A Letter to his Wife, 201
Even Such Is Time, 203
ROLAND, de la Platière, Madame Manon Jeanne Phlipon (1754–1793):
Queen of the Girondists, 343
from her writings in the Abbey and St. Pelagie, 344
Self-Portrait, 344

The Commune of Paris: May 31, 1793, 349

For Whom I Desired Liberty, 353

SACCO, Nicola (1891–1927):

A Good Shoemaker and a Poor Fish Peddler, 781

from his prison correspondence, 784

The Letters of Nicola Sacco:

"the good red rose," 784

"this spontaneous affection," 785

"terrible I said yes, but beauty at same time," 786

"you don't know Ines," 787

"remember this, Dante," 789

SHEFTALL, Mordecai (1735–1797):

A Prisoner of War, 396

memorandum in British captivity, 397

Capture of Mordecai Sheftall, & Etc., 397

SOCRATES (470–399 B.C.):

The Examined Life, 3

Plato's account of the trial and imprisonment, 5

The Apology:

Before the Verdict, 5

After the Verdict and before the Sentence, 22

After the Sentence of Death, 25

SURREY, Henry Howard, Earl of (1517–1547):

Hamlet Without the Prince, 169

poems composed during his imprisonment in Windsor Castle and the Fleet, 170

Lament for his Lost Boyhood, 170

A Satire on London, the Modern Babylon, 172

TOLLER, Ernst (1893–1939):

I Was a German, 761

correspondence ɪrom a Bavarian prison, 764

Letters to:

Fritz von Unruh, 764

Tessa, 764, 767, 769

Mrs. L., 766

The Governor of the Fortress, 770

Theodore Lessing, 772

Romain Rolland, 772

Stefan Zweig, 773

TOUSSAINT L'OUVERTURE, François Dominique (1743–1803):

The First of the Blacks, 400

his memorandum to Napoleon, 402

Memoir of General Toussaint L'Ouverture, Written by Himself, 402

VANZETTI, Bartolomeo (1888–1927):

A Good Shoemaker and a Poor Fish Peddler, 781

from his prison correspondence, 792

The Letters of Bartolomeo Vanzetti:

"a meditation perhaps," 792

"little of abdom and much of heart," 794

"if tragedy is compelled to us," 796

"please let me speak of Italy," 799

"the right of love," 801

"the reasons why I tell you, young Comrade," 803

VERLAINE, Paul (1844–1896):

The Bohemian and the Crucifix, 648

poems from *Sagesse* composed in a jail in Mons, 649

Le Ciel (in French), 649

Autre (in French), 650

O mon Dieu (in English translation), 651

VILLON, François (1431–?):

Alas, Poor Yorick!, 99

poems composed in the dungeon of Meun-sur-Loire and the Châtelet, 100

The Debate between the Heart and the Body, 100

Quatrain, 103

The Epitaph in the Form of a Ballade, 103

Ballade of the Appeal of Villon, 104

The Request of Villon, 105

WALLER, Odell (1917–1942):

Give Us This Day Our Daily Bread, 805

statement written the day before his execution, 806

From Sunup Until Sundown, 806

WILDE, Oscar Fingal O'Flahertie Wills (1854–1900);

Mrs. Grundy and the Fat Boy, 654

correspondence and from *De Profundis,* 656

"I sit between Gilles de Retz and the Marquis de Sade," 656

"I don't defend my conduct, I explain it," 658

From *De Profundis,* 660

WITHER, George (1588–1667):

Virtue in a Naughty World, 179

from *The Shepherd's Hunting* and other verse written in the Marshalsea, 181

In Praise of Poetry, 181

Satire to King James, 186

Copyright 1946 by
E. P. Dutton & Co., Inc.
Reprinted 1972 by arrangement.

Library of Congress Cataloging in Publication Data

Abramowitz, Isidore, 1901-   ed.
   The great prisoners.

   (Essay index reprint series)
   Bibliography: p.
   1. Literature--Collections. 2. Prisoners.
I. Title.
[PN6069.P7A2 1972]   808.8   74-38782
ISBN 0-8369-2563-7

PRINTED IN THE UNITED STATES OF AMERICA
BY
NEW WORLD BOOK MANUFACTURING CO., INC.
HALLANDALE, FLORIDA 33009

PRISONERS

The First
Anthology of Literature
Written in Prison

Selected and Edited by

ISIDORE ABRAMOWITZ

With Analytical Introductions
to the Time and Place and Circumstances
of Each Prisoner and Imprisonment,
A General Preface to the Whole,
And a Selected Bibliography.

Essay Index Reprint Series

BOOKS FOR LIBRARIES PRESS
FREEPORT, NEW YORK

THE GREAT

SOCRATES
ST. PAUL
BOETHIUS
MARCO POLO
JAMES I OF SCOTLAND
JOHN HUSS
JEANNE D'ARC
FRANÇOIS VILLON
CHRISTOPHER COLUMBUS
HUGO GROTIUS
GALILEO GALILEI
GIORDANO BRUNO
TOMMASO CAMPANELLA
THOMAS MORE
SURREY
JOHN DONNE
GEORGE WITHER
WALTER RALEIGH
CHARLES I OF ENGLAND
RICHARD LOVELACE
JAMES HOWELL
JOHN BUNYAN
GEORGE FOX
WILLIAM PENN
DANIEL DEFOE
ANNE HUTCHINSON
MADAME ROLAND
CAMILLE DESMOULINS
ANDRÉ CHÉNIER
GRACCHUS BABEUF
THOMAS PAINE
JOHN ANDRÉ
MORDECAI SHEFTALL

TOUSSAINT L'OUVERTURE
NAPOLEON
ROBERT EMMET
JOHN MITCHEL
CHARLES STEWART PARNELL
MICHAEL DAVITT
WILFRID SCAWEN BLUNT
PADRAIC PEARSE
ROGER CASEMENT
CONSTANCE MARKIEVICZ
LEIGH HUNT
WILLIAM LLOYD GARRISON
JOHN BROWN
HONORÉ DE BALZAC
FYODOR DOSTOEVSKY
MICHAEL BAKUNIN
PAUL VERLAINE
OSCAR WILDE
O. HENRY
ALFRED DREYFUS
FRANCISCO FERRER
EUGENE V. DEBS
VLADIMIR ILYICH LENIN
ROSA LUXEMBURG
ADOLF HITLER
ERNST TOLLER
GEORGI DIMITROV
NICOLA SACCO
BARTOLOMEO VANZETTI
ODELL WALLER
MOHANDAS K. GANDHI
JAWAHARLAL NEHRU
LÉON BLUM

The Great Prisoners